Children's Books in Children's Hands

An Introduction to Their Literature

Second Edition

Charles Temple
Hobart and William Smith Colleges

Miriam Martinez
University of Texas at San Antonio

Junko Yokota
National-Louis University

Alice Naylor
Appalachian State University

With Contributions by
Evelyn B. Freeman
The Ohio State University

Allyn and Bacon
Boston   London   Toronto   Sydney   Tokyo   Singapore

Editor-in-Chief, Education: Paul Smith
Executive Editor: Virginia Lanigan
Series Editor: Aurora Martinez
Sr. Developmental Editor: Linda Bieze
Editorial Assistant: Beth Slater
Executive Marketing Manager: Amy Cronin
Production Administrator: Paula Carroll
Editorial Production Service: Sally Lifland/Lifland et al., Bookmakers
Composition and Prepress Buyer: Linda Cox
Manufacturing Manager: Megan Cochran
Cover Administrator: Linda Knowles
Composition: Publishers' Design and Production Services, Inc.

Copyright © 2002, 1998 by Allyn & Bacon
A Pearson Education Company
75 Arlington St.
Boston, MA 02116

Internet: www.ablongman.com

Library of Congress Cataloging-in-Publication Data

Children's books in children's hands : an introduction to their literature / Charles Temple
... [et al.] ; with contribution by Evelyn B. Freeman.—2nd ed.
    p. cm.
  Includes bibliographical references and index.
  ISBN 0-205-31846-0
  1. Children's literature—History and criticism. 2. Children—Books and reading. I.
Temple, Charles A., [date] II. Freeman, Evelyn B. (Evelyn Blossom), [date]
PN1009.A1 C5118 2001
809'.89282—dc21

2001033671

Printed in the United States of America

10 9 8 7 6 5 4 3 2   RRD-OH   06 05 04 03 02

Brief Contents

Contents

2 Literary Elements of Children's Literature   30

Part Two   Exploring the Genres of Children's
Literature   135

5   Traditional Literature   136

7 Poetry for Children   235

10 Modern Fantasy and Science Fiction 349

11 Informational Books and Biography
by Evelyn Freeman   393

Part Three   Creating the Literature-Based Classroom   429

12   Inviting Children into Literature   430

13 Encouraging Response to Literature: Literary Discussion   469

Preface

Suppose there were a long-lived squadron of extraterrestrials that checked in on Earth once every century over many thousands of years. Surely they would recognize, from their previous visits, what some of us Earthlings are doing now, in the opening days of the twenty-first century, as we read a book to a classroom of students. "Typical," they might say. "Those Earthlings are always sharing what they think is important with their children through stories."

The circumstances in which humans have shared stories have changed over time, true enough. The earliest stories were told as people huddled around the campfires wrapped in animal skins. Later, stories were shared in a temple with camel skins spread on the floor or in a drafty cathedral packed with wide-eyed and bedraggled pilgrims. Sometimes people told stories in front of a fireplace, as the wind howled around a cottage way out on the prairie. Sometimes the stories were shared in the cold, heaving berth of a grimy steamer bound for Ellis Island. Sometimes grandparents or parents told children stories in order to pass on family history. But, whatever the circumstances, the habit of delighting, enchanting, instructing, and challenging through the medium of story—through *literature*— has always been at the center of the way humans brought up their young. There are many reasons why.

Some say stories educate the imagination—fire the spirit with a sense of possibility. Though this is no doubt true, contemporary children's books also help children understand the pressing issues of their lives—from sibling rivalry to the pull of the peer group to the limiting viciousness of racism.

Some say sharing literature virtually makes childhood possible, by giving children a separate world of images and ideas that insulates them from everyday reality. Though this may be true, children's books also fascinate youngsters by explaining the workings of the real world—from desert ecosystems to the origins of napkins and forks to the structure of DNA.

Some say children's books pass on the truths and values that adults hold to be most important. Though this is often the case, many children's books and many teachers challenge children to think for themselves, to find their own truths.

And some say children's books pass on a cultural heritage and tell children who they are. Though this is often true, contemporary children's literature also acquaints children with many cultures other than their own and may thus help increase tolerance and cooperation in today's diverse society.

In the second edition of this book, we seek to explain the vital importance of sharing ideas with the young through children's literature and nurturing a richer appreciation of the books themselves. We had several goals in writing this book:

- To help the adult reader recognize the many ways children benefit from literature at different times in their lives and appreciate what happens when a child is engaged by a book

■ To acquaint the adult reader with the wealth of children's books that are available today and to enable that reader to make critical judgments about them

■ To equip the reader with a range of proven strategies to bring children together with books productively and pleasurably

HOW THIS BOOK IS ORGANIZED

Part One of this book, "Understanding Literature and the Child Reader," orients the reader to the study of children's literature. Chapter 1, "Children's Books in Children's Hands," introduces the child reader and the reading process, focusing on children's intellectual and personality development and on the nature of children's responses to literature. Chapter 2, "Literacy Elements of Children's Literature," introduces a set of literary concepts with which to approach children's books, describing how plots are organized, how characters are drawn, and how themes are developed. Chapter 3, "The Child Reader Responds to Literature," discusses reader response theory and its implications for the study and sharing of children's literature. Chapter 4, "Literature Representing Diverse Perspectives," reflects this book's strong emphasis on multicultural and international literature. It investigates the ways various cultural groups are depicted in children's literature, highlights the progress that has been made in publishing children's books that represent various cultural groups more extensively and fairly, surveys the multicultural and international books that are available, and sets out guidelines for selecting high-quality multicultural books for children.

Part Two, "Exploring the Genres of Children's Literature," surveys children's books by genre. Each of the chapters in this part outlines the historical development of a particular genre, examines the literary qualities that distinguish the genre and the reading demands those qualities place on the child, reviews outstanding examples of works from the genre, and sets out criteria for selecting good works in the genre. Each chapter closes with an extensive annotated list of recommended books in the genre.

Chapter 5, "Traditional Literature," looks at folk literature from many times and cultures. Chapter 6, "Picture Books," focuses on how art and text combine to form unique works. Chapter 7, "Poetry for Children," surveys the genre from nursery rhymes to contemporary multicultural poetry for children. Chapter 8, "Realistic Fiction," looks at ways authors create believable books that are set in the "here and now" and that address the wide-ranging problems and delights of today's children. Books set in times that may be many generations removed from our own are discussed in Chapter 9, "Historical Fiction," which explains the origins of the current emphasis on meticulous accuracy in this genre. Many highly imaginative works are explored in Chapter 10, "Modern Fantasy and Science Fiction," which considers the artistry that enables readers to enter hypothetical worlds. Chapter 11, "Informational Books and Biography," surveys a growing area of children's literature, in which talented writers present the real world and its people to young readers in skillfully focused works that can be as riveting as fiction.

Part Three, "Creating the Literature-Based Classroom," was written for current and future teachers and librarians and anyone else who wants to share literature with children in ways that ensure that they will get the most from the encounters. Chapter 12, "Inviting Children into Literature," explains how to entice children into literature through the creation of classroom libraries and through activities such as reading aloud, storytelling, readers theater, and journal writing. Conducting book discussions with children so that they are empowered to say what they feel and are encouraged to grow through the discussions is the topic of Chapter 13, "Encouraging Response to Literature: Literary Discussion." Constructing literature units and literature-based content-area units and guiding children through them is the focus of the new Chapter 14, "Literary and Content Units." This chapter, like the others in this part, provides extensive lists of recommended books for use in the literature-based classroom.

The appendixes offer two lists of useful information: the recipients of major children's book awards and the publishers of children's magazines. In addition, you can find the following updated appendixes on the book's website (www.ablongman.com/temple2e): Professional Organizations, Children's Book Publishers' Addresses, Book Selection Aids, and Children's Literature Web Sites.

NEW FEATURES OF THE SECOND EDITION

Among the new features and enhancements that distinguish this edition are the following:

- **A new Chapter 14, "Literary and Content Units,"** built around a distinction between literary units and literature-based content units, exploring the development of both types of units and including lists of books that can be used in a variety of different units
- **Increased quality and quantity of illustrations** in Chapter 6, "Picture Books," to help readers understand how to develop children's visual literacy
- **Increased discussion of the censorship issue** in Chapter 1, "Children's Books in Children's Hands," to guide readers in thinking about this ongoing controversy in the schools
- **A new table, "Kinds of Traditional Tales,"** in Chapter 5, "Traditional Literature," and many additional annotated references to traditional literature from a number of cultures, to help readers understand the vast variety found in this genre
- **A revised and updated section on reader response** in Chapter 3, "The Child Reader Responds to Literature," including the most current research findings on children's responses to literature
- **A new section on preparing to be a discussion leader** added to Chapter 13, "Encouraging Response to Literature," to help teachers guide literary discussions in the classroom
- **A revised and updated section on literature discussion** in Chapter 13, including the most current findings on children's participation in literature discussions

PEDAGOGICAL ENRICHMENT AND FEATURES OF THIS BOOK

Each chapter includes an **"Ask the Author"** (or Illustrator, Editor, or Educator) box, in which a prominent children's author, illustrator, editor, or educator responds to a question related to the chapter content. Each chapter also features an **"Issue to Consider"** box, which presents a highly debated issue in children's literature related to that chapter's content. Many of both these types of boxes are new in this edition.

Several useful features appear at the end of every chapter. **"Teaching Ideas"** provide valuable, practical lessons and activities for sharing literature with children in the classroom. **"Experiences for Your Learning"** are activities readers of this book can do to increase and deepen their own understanding of the chapter content. Finally, extensive lists of **"Recommended Books"** offer publication data, a brief annotation, and interest level by age for every book listed.

SUPPLEMENTS TO AID STUDENTS

Students and instructors will find these supplements invaluable in extending their learning from the book:

■ Children's Literature and Learning CD-ROM, Version 2.0, allows users to quickly perform key word searches to browse through information about all the books discussed in the text and its appendixes, and, if desired, print out a convenient "shopping list" to take along to the bookstore or library.

■ A new "Professionals in Action: Children's Literature: Meet the Authors" video, available to instructors who adopt the text, offers interviews with and readings by several of the children's book authors and illustrators featured in the text.

■ A Companion Website with Online Practice Tests at www.ablongman.com/temple2e helps students test their understanding of the text material and go deeper into text topics, by reviewing learning objectives for each chapter, taking practice tests, exploring related websites, and enjoying other interactive features. In addition, the following updated appendixes are included on the website: Professional Organizations, Children's Book Publishers' Addresses, Book Selection Aids, and Children's Literature Web Sites.

■ An Instructor's Manual with Test Items.

■ A Computerized Testbank for IBM and Macintosh.

ACKNOWLEDGMENTS

Frances Temple and Nancy Roser helped shape our thinking early in the project; we are grateful to both. We also wish to thank Nancy for suggesting the title of the book, which so aptly captures our mission as the authors. Bird Stasz and her students at Wells College used the first edition in manuscript form and tried out many of the exercises with the children at Peachtown School in Aurora, New York, where Bill Schara is head teacher. We thank all these people for their encouragement and valuable feedback.

Joy Moss, teacher educator at the University of Rochester (New York) and an elementary school literature teacher, brought to bear her considerable experiences in sharing literature with children as she read and commented on the first edition of the book in its formative stages.

Thanks are due to Evelyn B. Freeman, who contributed and extensively revised Chapter 11, "Informational Books and Biography." Evie's delightful energy, enthusiasm for her field of specialty, and impressive bibliographic knowledge in that area resulted in what many reviewers deemed the most complete and authoritative discussion of informational books for children they've encountered in any survey text.

We have long admired the colorful and vibrant art of Frané Lessac, whose illustrations graced the first edition of the book; so we were honored when she agreed to create three new illustrations for this edition. And we are once again delighted with the results.

Thanks also go to the talented children's books authors, illustrators, editors, and educators who so generously shared their thoughts and experiences for "Ask the Author" features. In addition, several writer and illustrator friends gave us a look inside their craft: thanks to the Rochester Writers Group, especially Cynthia DeFelice, Ellen Stoll Walsh, M. J. Auch, Vivian Vande Velde, and Robin Pulver; also to Barbara Seuling and Bill Hooks. Several children's book editors did much the same thing; we wish to thank Matilda Welter, Refna Wilkin, Kent Brown, and Richard Jackson.

For their expert knowledge of children's books, our thanks go to Pat Farthing and Susan Golden, children's literature specialists of the Belk Library at Appalachian State University; to Lisa Neale of Watauga County (North Carolina) Public Library; and to Sara McLaughlin and Lucy Goldberg of Baker Demonstration School Library. For editorial help and invaluable insights, thanks to Bill Teale, Celia Whitlock, Sarah Borders, Cheri Triplett, Dottie Black, and Jeanne Chaney. A special thank you goes to Kathleen Emdad and Maureen Doyle Endres for their unwavering support.

We gratefully acknowledge the thoughtful and expert suggestions of those who responded to questionnaires and reviewed the manuscript for both editions:

Alma Flor Ada, *University of San Francisco*

Paulette Babner, *Cape Cod Community College*

John Beach, *University of Nebraska at Omaha*

Linda DeGroff, *University of Georgia*

Peter Fisher, *National-Louis University*

Connie Golden, *Marietta College*

M. Jean Greenlaw, *University of North Texas*

Dan Hade, *Penn State University*

Darwin L. Henderson, *University of Cincinnati*

Janet Hill, *Kent State University*

Judith Hillman, *St. Michael's College*

Miriam J. Johnson, *Bridgewater State College*

Nancy J. Johnson, *Western Washington University*

Linda Leonard Lamme, *University of Florida*

Barbara A. Lehman, *The Ohio State University*

Susan Lehr, *Skidmore College*

Amy A. McClure, *Ohio Wesleyan University*

Dianne L. Monson, *University of Minnesota*

Richard Osterburg, *California State University, Fresno*

T. Gail Pritchard, *University of Alabama*

Sam Sebesta, *University of Washington*

Lesley Shapiro, *National-Louis University*

Charlotte Skinner, *Arkansas State University*

Elizabeth A. Smith, *Otterbein College*

Jeff Smith, *Roosevelt High School, Kent, Ohio*

Karen J. Sweeney, *Wayne State College*

The staff at Allyn and Bacon deserves much credit for helping us pull this off: Linda Bieze, our development editor through all stages of the project; Beth Slater, editorial assistant; and especially our editors, Aurora Martinez and Virginia Lanigan, who provided good cheer and good sense along the way.

Charles Temple
Miriam Martinez
Junko Yokota
Alice Naylor

About the Authors

The authors of this text were drawn together by a love of children's books and a fascination with the people who make them and by the hope that another generation of students, teachers, librarians, and parents could be inspired to take up the challenge of getting those works into the hands of children.

Charles Temple is a banjo-picking storyteller and teacher educator at Hobart and William Smith Colleges in Geneva, New York. He has written many books in the field of reading and language arts and several books for children. As codirector of the International Reading Association and the Open Society Institute's Reading & Writing for Critical Thinking Project, Dr. Temple works with a network of 30,000 teachers in Europe, Asia, Africa, and Central America who are using literature to encourage students to explore their own and others' responses and develop their critical thinking. He also helps teachers of Roma (gypsy) children in Central Europe produce multicultural children's books for their students.

Miriam Martinez is a teacher educator and department chair at the University of Texas at San Antonio who loves nothing more than getting lost in good books, including children's books, of course! She is currently a member of the International Reading Association's Commission on Excellence in Elementary Teacher Preparation for Reading Instruction. She served for seven years as the coeditor of "Bookalogues," a children's book review column in the journal *Language Arts*; she also served as a reviewer for the eleventh edition of *Adventuring with Books* (1998), published by the National Council of Teachers of English. Dr. Martinez coedited *Book Talk and Beyond: Children and Teachers Respond to Literature* (1995), published by the International Reading Association. The focus of her research and writing is on ways of bringing children and books together to foster students' literary and literacy development.

Junko Yokota is a teacher educator at National-Louis University in Evanston, Illinois. She was a classroom teacher and a school librarian during the first ten years of her career. She edited the third edition of *Kaleidoscope*, a publication of the National Council of Teachers of English that presents reviews of multicultural children's books. Dr. Yokota is a recipient of the Virginia Hamilton Award for Contribution to Multicultural Literature. She was a member of the 1997 Caldecott Award Committee, the 2001 Batchelder Award Committee, and the 2002 Newbery Award Committee. She currently coedits the children's book review column in *Language Arts* with Mingshui Cai.

Alice Naylor is a teacher educator at Appalachian State University in Boone, North Carolina. She began her career as a librarian and storyteller and fell naturally into being a teacher of children's literature and storytelling. For five years, she hosted a weekly children's television program for the Milwaukee Public Library. She has served on many children's book award committees for the Association of Library Service to Children and the National Council of Teachers of English; she served twice on the John Newbery Medal Committee, once as chair, and was chair of the Batchelder Committee. She coauthored *Children Talking about Books* (Oryx, 1993) with a former student, Sarah Borders. Her passion is teaching teachers to value and love literature—and her efforts have been acknowledged by several outstanding teacher awards from her university.

Part One

Understanding Literature and the Child Reader

1 Children's Books in Children's Hands

Wish I *could* let him make a little noise. It's not natural, I know, to keep an animal so quiet. But he's *happy*-quiet, not *scared*-quiet. I know that much.

I move my arms off my face after a while and let him rest his paws on my chest, and I'm lying there petting his head and he's got this happy dog-smile on his face. The breeze is blowing cool air in from the west, and I figure I'm about as happy right then as you can get in your whole life.

And then I hear someone say, "Marty." I look up, and there's Ma.

In an upstate New York classroom, Midge Burns is reading to her third-graders. The book is Phyllis Reynolds Naylor's **Shiloh,** which tells what happens when Marty, an Appalachian mountain boy, shelters a runaway beagle named Shiloh from its cruel and abusive owner, Judd Travers. Marty's action threatens the equilibrium of the close-knit rural community and brings stress to his family. The tension is reflected in the students' body language. They groan when Marty's secret is discovered by his mother—and cheer when she agrees to let Marty keep the dog a while longer.

"Who do you think was to blame for what happened in this story?" asks Mrs. Burns when the book is finally closed. The ensuing conversation lasts an hour.

. . . and they tucked him in bed
all soft and warm
and they held his paw
and they sang him a song.

A four-year-old child in her mother's lap hears Margaret Wise Brown's **Little Fur Family** and is filled with a secure feeling of being a special child, very much loved. In the coming months, the child picks up the book every now and then, and that same feeling of warmth and security comes over her each time she does.

A teacher reads aloud from George Ancona's picture book **Pablo Remembers: The Fiesta of the Day of the Dead.** Miguel—quiet Miguel—suddenly comes to life: *"El día de los muertos!"* he exclaims. The other children listen with fascination as he gives the proper pronunciation to the Spanish words in the book. Miguel then carefully finds the English words to describe this old Mexican celebration, when the spirits of loved ones are felt to come near the living.

Brown Bear, Brown Bear, What Do You See? by Bill Martin, Jr., with illustrations by Eric Carle, has helped countless young children get off to a confident start as readers.

Brown bear, brown bear, what do you see?
I see a yellow duck looking at me.

In a first-grade classroom on the South Pacific island of Fiji, the teacher has created a hand-lettered enlarged version of Bill Martin, Jr.'s **Brown Bear, Brown Bear, What Do You See?** She reads it to her assembled children, pointing with a ruler to each word. Even before she has finished the first reading, children are anticipating what she is going to say next. The second time through, the children, supported by the patterned text and the illustrations, are reading along with her. There are no bears on Fiji, though, and soon the children are writing their own book based on Bill Martin's pattern but featuring a mongoose, a cockatiel, a python, and other local animals. Martin's book has helped these children of Fiji learn to read and write.

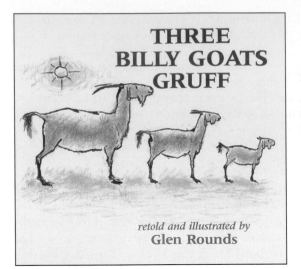

THREE BILLY GOATS GRUFF

retold and illustrated by
Glen Rounds

Illustration 1.1
Children enjoy acting out stories with strong story lines such as *The Three Billy Goats Gruff.* (*Three Billy Goats Gruff* retold and illustrated by Glen Rounds. Copyright © 1993 by Glen Rounds. Reprinted by permission of Holiday House.)

Trip-trap, trip-trap, trip-trap, trip-trap.
"WHO'S THAT WALKING ON MY BRIDGE?" roared
the Troll.
"It is I, Little Billy Goat Gruff."

In a South Texas classroom, Jackie murmurs, "Oh, good," when Ms. Sloan sends her group to the library center, a favorite in the classroom. Some of her fellow students browse through the collection looking for particular books. Jackie says, "Let's do *Three Billy Goats Gruff.*" Four other children agree and cut short their search. Now the five children—three goats, one troll, and a narrator—are acting out this folktale that is so well known to them from their teacher's reading it aloud. And of course one performance will not do. Everyone wants a chance to be the troll!

Good books—like good paintings, plays, movies, sculptures, and other creative works—merit appreciation in their own right. But good books serve children in some specific ways. Good children's books can evoke strong feelings and come to stand for childhood emotions, much in the way a security blanket does. Good books can give children reference points for understanding their own experiences, lessons that may last a lifetime. Good books may validate for children their own culture and open windows onto other cultures. Good books may help children understand how they and their neighbors think through moral issues and give them important experiences in clarifying differences and building consensus. Good books, and the sharing of them, cultivate children's capacity for empathy and compassion. Good books educate the imagination, as children stretch to visualize what it would be like to walk in the shoes of a character in a book. Good books may give children much of the motivation and even the concepts they need to learn to read and the models that show them how to write. Good books offer children delight, mystery, charm, an experience of awe, and companionship. Good books may invite children to play with language. Good picture books cultivate children's visual literacy and their aesthetic sense. Good books of all kinds nurture children's appreciation of the author's craft.

WHAT ARE GOOD BOOKS FOR CHILDREN?

For the student of children's literature, there is a lot to understand. What are good books for each child? That is something all of us want to know, whether we are or are going to be parents, teachers, librarians, booksellers, book editors, authors, or just well-read citizens. The answers to this question will be complex, because books aren't simply good in the abstract. A book may lead to a satisfying experience for a particular child or group of children with particular interests, concerns, and backgrounds in certain situations.

The answers will depend partly on an understanding of the ways in which readers respond to literature and how they differ in their responses at different ages. The answers will be made still richer by an understanding of how reading books from different cultures affects children—whether a child from a particular cultural group is reading books about others in that culture or another child is discovering through a book the particular ways people in varied cultures strive to get along.

To know what good books are for different children requires some intelligent way of talking about goodness and mediocrity in books—that, is, we will need an accepted set of terms for looking at the literary features of children's books. Identifying good books—especially in terms of an author or an illustrator's achievement—also requires a sense of where children's books have come from. Children's books have a history, and that history is intertwined with the history of the life stage called childhood.

Having considered these background issues, you will be ready to look more closely at the books themselves: the kinds of books available, the evolution of books over the years, and exemplary writers and illustrators of children's books.

Finally, many of you will want answers to other questions: What can I do to create a love of reading in every child, and how can I use books to expand children's knowledge? Answers to those questions will range from ways of putting books into children's hands to ways of engaging children in books, to ways of constructing instructional units that use children's literature. All of these topics are what this book is about.

WHAT IS CHILDREN'S LITERATURE?

Children's literature is the collection of books that are read to and by children. That collection is enormous: There are more than 50,000 English-language children's titles in print. It is still growing: Five thousand new titles are published every year in the United States alone. And it is old: The tradition of publishing literature for English-speaking children dates back 250 years, predating the founding of the American republic.

Children's literature spans the range from alphabet books and nursery rhyme collections for the very young through novels and informational books for adolescents (or young adults, as they are called in the book trade)—in other words, from birth to about age fifteen.

Today, most children's books are written expressly for children. But there are books written originally for adults that have become popular with children—from an earlier period, John Bunyan's *Pilgrim's Progress* and Daniel Defoe's *Robinson Crusoe* and, more recently, *Platero and I (Platero y yo)* by Juan Ramon Jimenez. Other works, such as Charles Perrault's "Sleeping Beauty in the Woods" and Miguel de Cervantes' *Don Quixote*—were written for adults but have been adapted for children. And the oral tradition—myths, ballads, epics, and folktales—comprises a large body of material that was told to adults and children alike, including the well-known stories "Jack and the Beanstalk," "Rapunzel," "Brer Rabbit and the Briar Patch," "Cucarachita Martina and Ratoncito Perez," and "Anansi the Spider."

Today, children's books are published by the juvenile books branches of large publishing houses such as Random House and Houghton Mifflin, as well as by publishers that serve the children's market exclusively, such as Orchard Books and Candlewick Press. Many publishers offer books published under imprints, which might, like Atheneum, be the name of an originally independent publisher that has been taken over by a larger house or, like Richard Jackson Books, Margaret K. McElderry Books, and Walter Lorraine Books, reflect arrangements by which publishers allow their most successful editors to publish books under their own names.

Sales of children's books have increased tremendously in recent years, to the point at which publishing children's books is currently the most robust of many publishers' activities. Classroom teachers are using more children's literature than ever. And as more families have gotten the message about the importance of having children's books in the home, sales of these books to individuals have at last surpassed sales to schools and libraries. Major newspapers review books for children just as they review adult fare. Since the success of the *Harry Potter* series, some papers now have a separate children's best-seller list.

Qualities of Children's Literature

As teachers of college courses on children's literature, we sometimes catch ourselves smiling to see an adult student smuggling **Frog and Toad Are Friends** to class between a copy of *War and Peace* and a thick tome on organic chemistry. That image sometimes makes us stop to ask: What is the study of children's literature doing in a college curriculum? Just how serious is the quality of children's books? There are several ways to answer these questions.

First, it must be said that although children's books might seem deceptively simple, their simplicity is achieved through hard work by talented writers. Many people try to produce books for children, but the percentage of manuscripts that are actually published is unbelievably small. In a recent year, one major publishing house received five thousand unsolicited manuscripts and published two of them.

Award-winning author Katherine Paterson compares writing a children's book to composing music. She suggests that a good children's book is like a score for a chamber quartet, rather than a work for a full symphony. The work for the chamber quartet is less elaborate; but if its melodies are pleasing and its harmonies are apt, it will have no less quality than a full orchestral work. In the same way, a good children's book will have fewer layers of complexity than a good book for adults, but if it is created with great care, it can also have excellence.

Second, because children's literature grew out of the folktales from oral traditions, children's books contain many timeless stories that know no age boundaries. In *The Anatomy of Criticism*, Northrop Frye wrote that all literature is one fabric, woven of many strands of plot, image, and theme that have been told over and over in stories around the world, throughout all time. The most basic stories—those that tell of virtue rewarded, of straying into danger and struggling to get back out, of learning to distinguish the things of lasting value, of finding one's true qualities and putting them to the service of others—are the materials out of which all literature is made. They are found in their purest form in myths and folktales from around the world and in books for children.

Third, children's books are worthy of serious study because the education of children warrants society's best energies. Good books will help children by making them literate, giving them knowledge of the world and empathy for those with whom they share it, offering them stories and images to furnish their minds and nurture their imaginations, and kindling their appreciation for language well used. Given its worthy goals, such literature deserves attention and respect.

What makes a book a children's book? A children's book usually has these qualities:

■ *A child protagonist and an issue that concerns children.* A children's book usually has a central character who is the age of the intended audience. Children identify more easily with one of their own. Even when the central character is not a child—as in

"Cinderella," for example—children need to feel that the central issues of a story concern them in some way.

- *A straightforward story line, with a linear and limited time sequence in a confined setting.* Books for younger children usually focus on one or two main characters, cover short time sequences (they are usually—but not always—told straight through from problem to solution, without flashbacks), and most often are set in one place. When writing for older children, authors gradually take more license with time sequences and may interweave more than one plot strand, as Sharon Creech does in **Walk Two Moons.**

- *Language that is concrete and vivid and not overly complex.* The words in children's books—especially in picture books—primarily name actors and actions. Books without pictures need to have more verbal description to help children visualize characters and settings. They use dialogue to move the story along. And they give glimpses of the characters' motives. In all these cases, readers see more of what characters do than of what they say, and certainly than of what they think.

Qualities of Outstanding Children's Literature

What makes a good children's book? Qualities that make outstanding children's books apply to excellent literature for any age. If a book satisfies the following criteria, it is a good children's book:

- *Good books expand awareness.* Good books give children names for things in the world and for their own experiences. Good books take children inside other people's perspectives and let children "walk two moons" in their shoes. They broaden children's understanding of the world and capacity for empathy.

- *Good books provide an enjoyable read that doesn't overtly teach or moralize.* Many children's books turn out to be about something—to have themes, in fact—and it is often possible to derive a lesson from them. But if a book seems too obviously contrived to teach a lesson, children (and critics) will not tolerate it.

- *Good books tell the truth.* Outstanding children's books usually deal with significant truths about the human experience. Moreover, the characters in them are true to life, and the insights the books imply are accurate, perhaps even wise.

- *Good books embody quality.* The words are precisely chosen and often poetic in their sound and imagery; the plot is convincing, the characters believable, and the description telling.

- *Good books have integrity.* The genre, plot, language, characters, style, theme, and illustrations, if any, all come together to make a satisfying whole.

- *Good books show originality.* Excellent children's books introduce readers to unique characters or situations or show them the world from a unique viewpoint; they stretch the minds of readers, giving them new ways to think about the world and new possibilities to think about.

Ask the Critic . . . *Betsy Hearne*

Betsy Hearne

Some critics, such as Northrop Frye and E. D. Hirsch, Jr., maintain that there are some stories that all Western children could benefit from being exposed to. Do you agree? Do you believe there are some core stories or works that all children should know, or do you see the issue another way?

The idea of canonizing stories that all Western children should know is understandably controversial. On the one hand, this would solve problems in defining curriculum, testing educational achievement, and establishing cultural frames of reference in a multicultural environment. Yet realizing such an idea raises as many questions as it answers. Literature is not a science with objective, quantifiable standards of measurement. Who will decide which stories belong in the canon? How do we incorporate individual differences (both adults' and children's) into the subjective task of assessing a story's importance? Is it possible to reconcile myriad conflicting values in a small selection or, conversely, reflect representative values in a large selection? In terms of use, a core of "approved" stories is bound to take precedence over other texts. What are the implications for publishing new texts? And how long do we wait before inducting a story? Some books and stories that are now considered classics met with a negative reaction when they were first published. This includes traditional fairy tales, picture books such as *Where the Wild Things Are*, and many examples of fiction across two centuries.

On the practical front, what are the effects of mandating stories to creative teachers, who may find such a prescription stifling? Sometimes it is more effective to study one story in depth, establishing a process and a set of principles that can then be applied broadly, than to cover a predetermined core, which can easily become an exercise in superficial exposure. Certainly, the identification of a canon of stories, those that have appealed to both critics

> ### Favorite Books as a Child
>
> My favorite story growing up was "East of the Sun and West of the Moon," which may explain why my favorite children's books now are *Tuck Everlasting* by Natalie Babbitt and *Holes* by Louis Sachar—both novels with strong folktale and fantasy elements.

and children over a long period of time, would require a balanced emphasis on the often warring factors of high quality and general appeal.

Proponents of a clearly defined—and, by implication, required—body of stories common to all children either believe that these questions are answerable or believe that the disadvantages of compromise are worth the advantages of commonality. My own experience of reviewing, teaching, and storytelling over several decades has persuaded me that adult consensus on these issues is rare, if not impossible, and that children and stories are a quirky, unpredictable match depending on personality, peer group, family environment, and many other factors. Of course every child needs *some* stories. But selecting the *same* stories for "all Western children" involves the kind of generalized social and aesthetic assumptions that have plagued efforts to establish a literary canon in higher education. I would suggest that a buffet of stories, from which children and adults can choose together, is preferable to a set menu.

Betsy Hearne is a professor in the Graduate School of Library and Information Science at the University of Illinois at Urbana-Champaign, where she teaches children's literature and storytelling. She is the author of numerous articles and books, including Choosing Books for Children: A Commonsense Guide; *the folktale anthology* Beauties and Beasts; *several novels for children (most recently* Listening for Leroy *and* Wishes, Kisses, and Pigs); *and a picture book,* Seven Brave Women, *which won the 1998 Jane Addams Children's Book Award. The former children's book editor of* Booklist *and of* The Bulletin of the Center for Children's Books, *she has reviewed books for thirty years and contributes regularly to the* New York Times Book Review.

CHILDREN'S BOOKS AND CHILDHOOD

The criteria for excellence just outlined have not always held true. That is because the life stage of childhood has changed throughout history as adults changed their definition of it and their views of young people. Literature for children has changed, too, following the fortunes of childhood as a life stage.

In the past six centuries, children in the West have, in turn, been treated in the following ways:

- They have been ignored.
- They have been suspected of harboring great evil.
- They have been felt to be in need of moral instruction and idealistic example.
- Sometimes, they have been understood as they were and given a good read.
- They have *all* been treated with respect.

Let's look at these phases in more detail.

Children Were Ignored

It has been said that until roughly five hundred years ago, childhood as we know it did not exist in the West (Aries, 1962). That is because, up to the Renaissance, children's activities—the games they played and the stories they heard—were not separated from those of adults. Children drank alcoholic beverages, smoked tobacco, and used coarse language. After the age of seven, most children were made to work in the kitchen, in the fields, or in shops. When the village storyteller could be persuaded to tell a tale, children and adults alike gathered around to hear it. In medieval England, games such as Red Rover could involve people of all ages in a village.

It is not surprising, then, that books were not written expressly for children in those times. The few children who could read had no choice but to turn to adult fare. The ballad "Robin Hood," for example, was known as far back as 1360 A.D., and three printed versions of the legend existed before 1534. Child readers, then as now, enjoyed and accepted the romantic concept of robbing the rich to help the poor. Other romantic stories circulating at the time were those about King Arthur and the Knights of the Round Table and about Bevis, a thirteenth-century hero who hacked his way out of dungeons and slew dragons.

In 1476, William Caxton established the first printing press in England, and in 1477, he published one of the earliest books expressly for children. Called *A Booke of Curteseye,* it was filled with do's and don'ts for an audience of aristocratic boys preparing for social engagements and military careers.

Children Were Suspected of Harboring Great Evil

By the seventeenth century, more works were being written for children, but most did not make for enjoyable reading. The Puritans, the stern religious exiles who established the English colonies in America, infused early American children's works with their certainty that the devil could enter young bodies. They even wrote poems exalting death at an early age—better to die innocent than grow corrupted. Given the didactic and fiery messages of Puritan authors, it is not surprising that most of their works are no longer read. Here is an example of Puritan prose written in 1702 by one Thomas Parkhurst:

> My dear Children, consider what comfort it will be unto you when you have come to dye, that when other children have been playing, you have been praying. The time will come, for ought you know very shortly, . . . when thou shalt be sick upon thy bed, and thou shalt be struggling for life, thy poor little body will be trembling, so that the very bed will shake under thee, thine eyestrings will break, and then thy heartstrings will break; . . . then, O then, the remembrance of thy holy life will give thee reassurance of the love of God.

Despite this bleak view, nonetheless, there were some bright moments. Books were generally instructional and religious in nature, but many writers did sugarcoat their instruction with rhymes, riddles, and good stories. Also, children continued to find adult fare to their liking. John Bunyan's *Pilgrim's Progress* was read for generations. What made it palatable to children was its portrayal of a sense of family. Children are presumed to have skipped over the lengthy religious commentary to savor the happy family life. Indeed, the story of Christian can still hold the imagination of children who read the adapted, abridged, and illustrated versions.

Children of the fifteenth to eighteenth centuries also turned to hornbooks and chapbooks for their reading fare. In both England and America, peddlers traveled from town to town selling items such as pots, pans, needles, medicine, and hornbooks—which looked like paddles, averaged two and a half by five inches, were usually made of wood, and often were attached to a leather thong so that children could hang them around the neck or wrist. The lesson sheet or story was pasted onto the flat surface, then covered with horn, a film of protective material similar to animal horn. Hornbooks were filled with lessons in religion, manners, the alphabet, and reading.

The same traveling salesmen who peddled hornbooks inspired the invention of chapbooks ("chap" is derived from the word "cheap"). Chapbooks were made of folded sheets of paper and so were inexpensive to produce and light to carry. They contained popular stories of the day, such as "Jack, the Giant Killer," "The History of Sir Richard Whittington," and "Saint George and the Dragon," and also large numbers of cautionary tales, illustrating the do's and don'ts of childhood. Contemporary author Gail E. Haley has written and illustrated *Dream Peddler,* about a fictitious chapbook peddler who was proud of his profession because he gave children fairy tales and adventures to cultivate their dreams.

Children Were Felt to Be in Need of Moral Instruction and Idealistic Example

In 1693, John Locke published *Some Thoughts Concerning Education,* which influenced child-rearing practices on both sides of the Atlantic. The book's exhortation that "some easy pleasant book" be given to children was good for the circulation of children's books. Nonetheless, the books still promoted strict moralistic teachings, if in narrative form.

At the dawn of the eighteenth century, more playful and pleasurable literature began to emerge. The verses of Isaac Watts were popular, and although to a contemporary ear they sound overly moralistic and didactic, for their time they were less so than those of his predecessors. In 1743, Mary Cooper published *The*

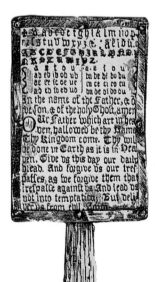

Illustration 1.2
Hornbooks, the reading fare of many early American children, usually contained an alphabet and a prayer or psalm.

Child's New Plaything, Being a Spelling Book Intended to Make the Learning to Read a Diversion. An American edition of the book came out in 1750 with even more "diversions," reflecting a change in how stories for children were perceived. The *New England Primer,* which combined alphabet and catechism, was the most widely read book of the period, another indication of the instructive mindset of the eighteenth century.

During this period, children also continued to read books written for adults. Many of Daniel Defoe's works were popular with children. In fact, *The Life and Surprising Adventures of Robinson Crusoe of York, Marine,* with its fearless optimism and high adventure, proved popular with children for the better part of two centuries. Jonathan Swift's *Gulliver's Travels* was another book that was published for adults but adopted by children. Although the book is filled with heavy satire, reflecting Swift's strong objections to the imperfections of humankind in general and Englishmen in particular, its language and plot are irresistible.

An innovative entrepreneur named John Newbery prepared the way for the blossoming of children's literature in the nineteenth and twentieth centuries. Newbery moved to London in 1744 and launched the first commercially successful company dedicated almost exclusively to publishing beautiful and pleasurable children's books. In his thirty-year career, Newbery published twenty titles for children in attractive, playful formats, including the accordion book, made of one long strip folded accordion-style to form "pages." He was the first to introduce illustrations by first-rate artists, and he published books in more permanent, attractive bindings than the popular, less expensive chapbooks. His books have been described as homey and were clearly intended to appeal to children.

Newbery is believed also to have written some of the books he published, including *A Little Pretty Pocket-Book* and *The History of Little Goody Two-Shoes.* Read for the better part of a century in England and the United States, *Little Goody Two-Shoes* was the first best-seller written for children (and one of the longest lasting). The book might not be familiar to you, but the phrase "goody two shoes" is still used to mean a person with overly perfect behavior.

More than a century after Newbery's death, Daniel Melcher of the Wilson Publishing Company made a donation to the American Library Association to establish an annual award for the most distinguished contribution to literature for children. Fittingly, the award was named after John Newbery. (A list of the award winners and the honor books over the past eight decades appears in Appendix A.)

Children Were (and Are) Sometimes Understood as They Were and Given a Good Read

Darton (1966) defines books for children as "printed words produced ostensibly to give children spontaneous pleasure." It was in the nineteenth and twentieth centuries that books truly fitting Darton's definition emerged. Nineteenth-century books for children have become today's classics. Books written in that century that still circulate briskly include Hans Christian Andersen's *The Ugly Duckling* and *The Little Mermaid,* Carlo Collodi's *The Adventures of Pinocchio,* Lewis Carroll's *Alice's Adventures in Wonderland,* Louisa May Alcott's *Little Women,* and Mark Twain's *The Adventures of Tom Sawyer* and *The Adventures of Huckleberry Finn.* Nonetheless, though wonderful classics came out of the nineteenth century, there is simply nothing to compare with the rich diversity of children's literature in the twentieth century. The exciting

changes in children's literature that have occurred over the past two centuries will be explored in depth in the genre chapters of this text (Chapters 6–11).

Children Are All *Treated with Respect*

Up until the 1960s, in the United States, children's literature featured white children almost exclusively. Then, with the Civil Rights movement waking mainstream Americans to the realization that their conception of "us" was largely limited to white, English-speaking children, Nancy Larrick (1965) wrote a path-breaking article for the *Saturday Review* in which she pointed out the paucity of nonwhite characters in books for children. Shortly afterward, the Council on Interracial Books for Children was established, with the goal of persuading writers and artists of color to produce works for children. The American Library Association added to its Newbery and Caldecott Awards the Coretta Scott King Award, to celebrate books that honorably and accurately depict African American children (see Chapter 4).

These efforts opened the door to a wealth of talent. Not only has the representation of minority children in English-language children's literature increased substantially in the last twenty-five years, but the writers and artists of color who have broken into print are among the best we have. Children's books are written by, and feature, African Americans, Latinos, Asian Americans, and Native Americans, as well as children from families of limited means and those who otherwise depart from the older stereotype of white, middle-class, two-parent homes. Far more international literature is available for the American child reader—especially books from Latin America and Asia—and these book are written with greater sensitivity than in the past. Gone are the stereotypical depictions of people from other continents; the norm is to have people from other cultures write their own books or be presented as they would present themselves. Indeed, a whole subfield of multicultural children's literature has emerged to help librarians, teachers, and parents take advantage of the multicultural works that are available. (Chapter 3 of this book is devoted to that subject.)

Illustration 1.4
Harlem, a Caldecott Honor Book, introduces young readers to the poet's own African American neighborhood. (*Harlem,* a poem by Walter Dean Myers, pictures by Christopher Myers. Published by Scholastic Press, a division of Scholastic Inc. Copyright © 1997. Reprinted by permission.)

If the above paragraphs seem to take an American perspective almost exclusively, that is because multicultural children's literature is largely a North American phenomenon. Outside of the United States, Canada, and Great Britain, other countries have not much embraced the concept of giving balanced representation to the varieties of children who inhabit their schools. This is a movement of which we should be proud.

The history of children's literature does not really fit such a neat pattern as the foregoing presentation might suggest, of course. For one thing, the tendency to moralize and to socialize children through books is not entirely gone. Although more books than ever before are created with pure enjoyment as their goal, many adults still associate children's books with moral teaching, as the recent popularity of William Bennett's *The Children's Book of Virtues* clearly demonstrates. Indeed, any children's librarian can tell you of the tensions between those who want to restrict children's reading to the works they consider to be wholesome and others who struggle against what they see as the censorship of children's literature.

We should also acknowledge that even within North America, children's books are not experienced by all children, at least not in their homes. While children's literature was enjoying its golden age throughout the 1800s and children's books were becoming part of life among better-off families, many children in Europe and America were struggling their lives away in mines and factories without hope of an education, much less of finding diversion in books written for young people. Similarly, in our own day, when children's literature in America has exploded with color and diversity, many American children never see or hear a children's book read aloud at home (Heath, 1984).

CHILDREN'S DEVELOPMENT AND RESPONSE TO LITERATURE

There is no doubt that books give children edification and delight. There is also no doubt that what children take from books changes as they pass from age to age and have experiences with books and with supportive adults who share books with them. In the sections that follow, to gain an understanding of children's book preferences at different levels of development, we look at the interplay of children's intellectual, social, and personality development as well as their developing ability to read. We begin with the period of early childhood.

Experiencing Books in Early Childhood

Children's books serve many purposes in early childhood, some of them emotional, some social, some intellectual, some linguistic, and some literary. Let's consider the contributions of children's books to young children's lives.

There is no doubt that reading aloud a favorite book occasions a closeness between a parent and a child. Good books for preschoolers may do this in two ways. Books for reading at bedtime, such as Margaret Wise Brown's *Goodnight Moon* and P. D. Eastman's *Are You My Mother?,* often express a theme of security and closeness. But these books build closeness in another way: They so often invite reading and rereading at bedtime that they may become family rituals. The importance of these rituals cannot be overstressed. Psychologists since Freud have noted the importance of an intimate bond between parent and child to the child's later emotional well-being. Mary Ainsworth and her associates (1982) noted that starting in the first few weeks of life and culminating by age 2, a child may form a strong and positive *attachment* to one or both parents and to caregivers, and this attachment can provide a bedrock of well-being that prepares a child to form friendships with other children and to explore and learn from the world. Daniel Stern (1982) observed that parents and children learn each other through patterned interactions such as turn taking in face-to-face play. One important patterned interaction occurs when parents and preschool teachers share a book with a child: showing a picture, having the child name the picture, turning the page, and showing another picture.

More than intimacy is involved in early encounters with books, however. For one thing, the child is also learning language from such exchanges. When a child sees a picture of an object at the same time as hearing his or her parent read the word for it, the child learns a concept. The parent reinforces the learning by pointing to the picture and asking, "What's that?" The child answers, and the parent affirms the child's answer or corrects it. Such a procedure becomes a kind of informal teaching routine, a form of *scaffolding*, an enjoyable moment of shared focus through which a parent helps a child learn language (Ninio and Bruner, 1978). Of course, not just bedtime stories but also nursery rhymes and concept books lend themselves to these beneficial early reading transactions.

It is also true that the child is learning things *about* language from these early being-read-to experiences. Years ago, linguists (Ervin-Tripp and Miller, 1977) found that some children become oriented early in life to think of language primarily as something that expresses emotions and that may accompany actions: We laugh and tease as we slap a friend on the back. Other children may become oriented to think of language mainly as something that refers to things: We use words to say what happened to us today, and the words make pictures appear in our friend's mind. Of course, language does both things and much more. But the child who is read to comes to expect language to refer to things, to make it possible for the listener to visualize things that may not be present in the here and now. That child's orientation to language may predispose him to become a reader—because books use language to refer to things.

Moreover, as Gordon Wells (1985) has pointed out, as a child hears the same words intoned every time his or her parent reads a book aloud, the child comes to think of language as something that is real. To understand this point, note that years before she can read, language for a child is just sound, sensations that vanish as soon as they are heard. But if language can be retrieved, can be called forth each time a parent opens a book, it must be real. And it must also be representable; in fact, a child learns that a key function of a book is to help a reader produce just the language that the book calls forth.

A child in a parent's lap learns other important lessons about the ways books work. The child learns that books have fronts, backs, and pages. Pages have tops and bottoms, print and pictures. Eventually, the child will learn that even though pictures might seem more fun to look at, it is the print that "talks." A child may learn favorite authors, too: Dr. Seuss's books have the funny rhythms and rhymes; Rosemary Wells's books have the bunnies that have feelings; Eric Carle makes books with holes in the pictures.

In summary, during early childhood, children find a special closeness in being read to, and these reading-aloud episodes figure importantly in forming relationships that are necessary to children's emotional and cognitive well-being.

The reading-aloud episode is also an enjoyable and important opportunity for learning language. Moreover, it is a time to learn about language: Language is real, it can be represented, it comes in certain patterns, it calls pictures to mind. Early experiences with books show a child what books are for, how they are put together, how they work, and even who wrote and illustrated them. It is a fortunate child who learns these lessons early in life; she or he will be richer for them intellectually and linguistically and will find it natural to learn to read when she or he goes to school.

Experiencing Books in the Preschool and Early Primary School Years

As they approach kindergarten age, children are more actively following not only rhymes, but also books with plots. Children are imbibing story plots at this age. Stein and Glenn's research (Stein and Glenn, 1979) showed that, just as children learn the grammar of their native language by speaking with adults, children learn the "grammar" of stories from their exposure to them. By grammar, they meant elements such as a *character* in a *setting* who has a *problem*, makes *attempts* to solve it, and finally reaches some *resolution* that has a *consequence*: a new state of affairs. When Stein and Glenn told kindergarten children a story that had these elements rearranged out of order, the children spontaneously arranged them properly when they retold the story. Knowing the grammar of stories will go a long way toward preparing a child to understand them.

Children are clearly enthralled with the content of stories, too. Kieran Egan (1992) observed that strongly plotted stories—especially fairy tales and folktales—have a powerful appeal to children of this age, perhaps because they are concerned with the most basic dimensions of life. Stories, as Frank Kermode (2000) observed, give children frameworks for understanding what life means. After all, it is in stories that people and events are clearly good or bad, heroic or not, whereas in real life, it might be hard to tell. Real people act out of a complex of motives, and their actions may have both good and bad consequences.

Folktales, fairy tales, and other clearly plotted fiction for younger children show characters who are unambiguously good and bad, or if they stray from what is the "right" path, the characters learn clear lessons from what happens. The young girls in both **The Talking Eggs** and **Mufaro's Beautiful Daughters** are kind and generous, and they are rewarded. The vain sisters are not. In both **Sylvester and the Magic Pebble** and **Strega Nona,** the characters use their new powers—in both these cases, magic—carelessly and suffer the consequences.

In later years, children might question whether life's choices are really so simple or virtue so easy to come by, but in the years from 4 to 7, children seem to want some general reassurance that actions matter; that there is some connection between the ways we behave and the ways things turn out for us and that we can tell what is good to do and what is not. The basic story plots that children like to hear at this age give them pointers for making sense of the actions and consequences they experience in their lives.

Children in the 4–7 age range are not given to long, interpretive discussions. Because they cannot easily tell fiction from nonfiction (Applebee, 1975), children are likely to accept stories as accounts of what really happened to someone somewhere. Susan Lehr's research (1988) did show that kindergarteners could recognize that two stories have the same theme, especially if the children had rich experiences with literature. It is still not likely to dawn on young children that a story can be an elaborate metaphor for a truth on a different plane.

Piaget demonstrated this point by asking children the meaning of statements such as "When the cat's away, the mice will play." Children in this age group thought the expression referred only to cats and mice; they didn't seem to get the connection to children's behavior when the teacher is out of the room (Piaget, 1955). From her observations of kindergarten-age children responding to a story without any special prompt from the teacher, Janet Hickman (1992) found that they tended to respond with their bodies—clapping, moving, and shouting refrains.

Given encouragement from a teacher, however, kindergarten and first-grade children can become quite involved in the moral dimensions of stories. Their thinking, though deeply felt, is sometimes one-sided. For example, a group of first-graders heard Norma Green's *The Hole in the Dike,* about a Dutch boy who saved Holland from a flood when he stuck his finger in a hole in the dike. Several were puzzled when, at the end of the book, the boy was called the Hero of Holland. "But he was naughty! He stayed out all night at the dike and he should have gone straight home!" said one. "He should be punished for breaking the rules . . . and making his mom worry!" said another. These children focused narrowly on one side of the problem—the rule infraction—rather than on the greater good the boy did.

Similarly, five-year-old Mirel was indignant when the vulnerable pig played tricks on the wolf in Susan Meddaugh's hilarious picture book *Hog-Eye,* even though the wolf had kidnapped the pig and intended to eat it. Mirel's thinking seems to have centered on the pig's playing tricks on the wolf, and she lost sight of the fact that the wolf had something far worse in mind for the pig.

Nonetheless, children at this age sometimes think and act in ways that most of us would consider highly moral. For example, a real six-year-old, Ruby Bridges, had to walk, accompanied by federal marshals, though a double row of white parents who shouted racist threats at her when she, a small black girl, integrated an all-white school. Robert Coles writes, in *The Story of Ruby Bridges:*

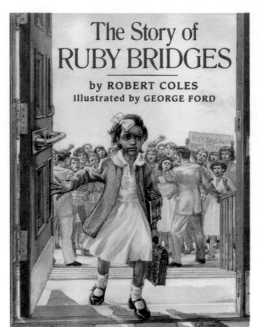

Illustration 1.5
The real-life of story of the six-year-old girl who helped integrate schools in New Orleans is a plot that engages young readers in *The Story of Ruby Bridges.* (*The Story of Ruby Bridges* by Robert Coles. Illustrated by George Ford. Published by Scholastic Press, a division of Scholastic Inc. Copyright © 1995. Reprinted by permission.)

Suddenly, Ruby stopped—right in front of the mob of howling and screaming people. She stood there facing all of those men and women. She seemed to be talking to them. Mrs. Henry [Ruby's teacher] saw Ruby's lips moving and wondered what Ruby could be saying.

The crowd seemed ready to kill her. The marshals were frightened. They tried to persuade Ruby to move along. They tried to hurry her into the school, but Ruby wouldn't budge.

Then Ruby stopped talking and walked into the school.

When she went into the classroom, Mrs. Henry . . . told Ruby that she'd been watching and that she was surprised when Ruby stopped and talked with the people in the mob.

. . . "I didn't stop to talk to them," she said. . . . "I wasn't talking. I was praying. I was praying for them." (n. pag.)

Learning to Read

The period from ages 4 to 7 straddles what reading specialists call the periods of *emergent literacy* and *beginning reading.* Emergent literacy refers to the acquisition of a host of concepts about print, about language, and about the activities of reading and writing that provide the foundation for learning the skills of literacy. We have already mentioned some of these concepts: the fact that print, and not pictures, "talks" and the fact that books are read from front to back and from top to bottom. We described the insight that language is real, that it not only expresses emotions but refers to things—it makes pictures in our minds. Children must also discover that language comes to us in units of words (not always an obvious concept, since in speech, we run our words together) and that words are represented in print by groups of letters bound by spaces. Furthermore, spoken words can be divided into syllables and syllables into phonemes (for example, the three sounds that correspond to the C, A, and T in "cat"). In English, writing is based on the *alphabetic principle,* which (roughly) relates letters or groups of letters to phonemes in words.

Learning to read requires, among other things, that children understand the alphabetic principle and learn to negotiate the relationships between letters and sounds. A valuable source for learning the alphabetic principle and letter-sound relationships is rhymes: A child who learns to read the line "Cat in the Hat" is a step away from realizing that the rhyming words "cat" and "hat" share a collection of sounds, "-at" (some call these shared sounds a *phonogram pattern*), and are distinguished only by their beginnings, the "kuh" and "huh" sounds. That child is ready to perceive the phonemes "kuh" and "huh" and will soon come to recognize that the letter C spells one of the sounds and H spells the other.

Of course, another source of knowledge of the alphabetic principle is alphabet books: books that call attention to one letter at a time and show children a group of objects that begin with the sound that is spelled by that letter. Together with some judicious teaching, rhyming books (such as **The Cat in the Hat** and **Sheep in a Jeep**) and alphabet books provide children with an enjoyable source of the information they will need to crack the code of English spelling.

Along with discovering the alphabetic principle, children learn to recognize words and store in memory a growing body of words they can recognize immediately. Building this *sight vocabulary* is helped along if children think of words in families, such as *bank, tank, sank, spank, thank*. Again, rhyming books such as **Sheep in a Jeep** and **The Cat in the Hat** provide sources of word families. Resourceful teachers will make *word walls* (Cunningham, 1999) of these word families—that is, make displays of them on the wall, grouped together. They may also invite children to use *word sort* activities with the words (Bear et al., 1999)—that is, play grouping games with the word patterns.

Children are learning to make meaning from books, too, at this age. As we noted, they are learning the patterns that structure the plots of stories and to use those patterns to recognize main characters, their goals, and their attempts to reach those goals. Resourceful teachers will structure their story talk with children around these story elements, ask children what the character's problem is and what she or he wants to do, and ask them to predict how the character will do it.

Kindergarten and first-grade children face a special dilemma when it comes to their own reading. Children at this age may have been listening to increasingly sophisticated fare, which may even include chapter books for some. Yet their own reading skills limit them to materials with only a few words per line and only a few syllables per word. Fortunately, a solution to this problem has been provided by many ingenious writers, from Dr. Seuss to Bill Martin, Jr., to many others who write *easy readers*. These books with short words and highly patterned language allow children to practice their fledgling reading skills. Some easy readers also offer meanings worth pondering. For instance, Arnold Lobel's many *Frog and Toad* books and James Marshall's *George and Martha* books have stories that are worth talking about.

Experiencing Books in the Primary Grades

As they advance from second grade toward the upper primary grades, children's thinking changes, allowing them to notice more, to think of several aspects of a problem at once, and to distinguish confidently between fact and fiction. Most children begin to read with real fluency, and now they develop preferences for authors and styles of books. Although the prolific readers might prefer to "keep reading, keep reading," rather than to stop and ponder the meaning of what they have read, thoughtful teachers and parents who are able to engage these children in conversations about books are invariably rewarded with surprising insights expressed by these children (Matthews, 1982; Temple, 1992).

The topics these children prefer to read about are widely varied. The children are enthralled by magic (note the phenomenal appeal of the *Harry Potter* books for third- and fourth-grade children and beyond), but the magic must be carefully developed and must conform to a consistent logic. The same goes for fantasy: Children are no longer so satisfied by the easy magic of fairy tales; they are concerned with the details of how things work (Egan, 1992).

Children in the 7–10 age range like to read books that show possibilities for individual achievement. The personality theorist Erik Erikson (1968) noted that at this age, children are developing a sense of *initiative* and later of *industry.* A story like Rosemary Wells's ***Hazel's Amazing Mother,*** in which a heroic parent saves a child from many improbable situations, appeals to a younger child more than to this age group. Now the child wants to read about children who solve their problems themselves. For example, after hearing Jane Yolen's ***The Emperor and the Kite,*** Elizabeth Hillman's ***Min-Yo and the Moon Dragon,*** and Robert D. San Souci's ***The Samurai's Daughter: A Japanese Legend,*** a group of second-graders discussed the heroines in these tales: "I like stories about girls who go on adventures!" "Min-Yo and the emperor's daughter were so small . . . but they saved their kingdoms!" "Even though they were little . . . they did big things!" "And they didn't use magic . . . but they were very brave and smart." "The Samurai's daughter was a pearl diver . . . that's how she knew how to kill the sea monster. . . . She didn't need magic. . . . I bet her father was really surprised that she could do all that . . . even though she's a girl!"

Children's thinking becomes more flexible after age 7, and this makes possible deeper insights into literature. In their preschool years, children might have preferred books with clear moral orientations—stories that, like "Cinderella," unambiguously contrast good and bad—but now they enjoy books with more complexity. For example, children in an advanced second-grade class were asked to respond to Aesop's fable "The Grasshopper and the Ant" and Leo Lionni's modern version, ***Frederick.*** After listening to Aesop's fable, most of the children agreed that the ant was right to let the grasshopper starve because the grasshopper didn't do the work to get food for the winter. However, after listening to ***Frederick,*** most of the children developed a new perspective. Frederick did not collect grain with the other, hard-working mice, but they tolerated his uniqueness and recognized his contribution as an artist. His poetry provided food for the mind and the imagination during the long, dark days of winter. The children contrasted the acceptance of individual differences in Lionni's story with the harsh justice of the ant in

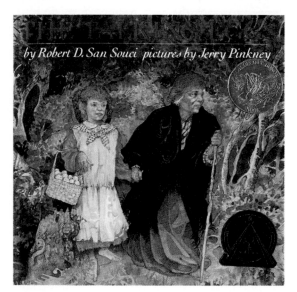

Illustration 1.6
Young readers feel a kinship with the kind younger sister in *The Talking Eggs,* a Creole variant of "Cinderella." (*The Talking Eggs* by Robert D. San Souci, pictures by Jerry Pinkney. Copyright © 1989. Used by permission of Dial Books for Young Readers, a division of Penguin Putnam Inc.)

Illustration 1.7
Though *Frederick* appears to be a simple picture book, this story offers children the opportunity to reflect on the unique contributions that individuals can make to their communities. (*Frederick* by Leo Lionni, copyright © 1967 by Leo Lionni. Copyright renewed 1995 by Leo Lionni. Used by permission of Random House Children's Books, a division of Random House, Inc.)

Aesop's fable: "I liked *Frederick* better. Everybody's different, and you shouldn't punish someone just because they're different." "I think the Ant should have read *Frederick*. . . . I bet Grasshopper's music could have made the Ant happier during the winter."

As children consider the moral dimensions of a story, they also may take the motives of a character into account, although this kind of sophistication doesn't happen all at once. For example, when William Steig's **The Real Thief** was read aloud to third- and fourth-graders, most of them empathized with the mouse, Derek, who stole a number of items from the royal treasury: "He's not a real villain . . . he's not really bad . . . he just wanted to make his place nicer so he could feel more special . . . and important." "He didn't mean to get Gawain in trouble." "And anyway, he put it back later when Gawain got accused. I feel sorry for Derek. I'm glad the author let him get a second chance." A few still held to their earlier way of seeing moral issues: "He stole, and that's wrong, and he should be punished!" "I didn't like the ending because he didn't really get punished."

Becoming Prolific Readers

By late second grade, children have reached the possibility of becoming readers. If they can find books and authors they enjoy, many will become prolific readers. It is important to guide children to the right books. Research shows that some of the best suggestions for books to read come from other children, but all children will need exposure to many, many interesting books, in many genres, by many authors. Ideas for sharing books with children are found in the third section of this book.

Children are developing their capacity to comprehend what they read, too. Research by Pearson and Johnson (1978) suggests that comprehension consists of several aspects:

- *The ability to relate what they already know to what they are reading.* For example, in making sense of a story, a comprehending reader will summon up what she knows about a particular setting, of a particular historical period, or of people who follow certain trades.

- *The ability to follow the pattern set up by the genre.* For example, a child who is reading a *pourquoi* tale will know that he or she is following a fanciful account of how something came to be. The child will expect some magic but will look for a connection between the premise of the story and some phenomenon in the real world that the story seeks to explain.

- *The ability to visualize or form images of what is read about.* As a child reads Natalie Babbitt's description of the hot day in August in the beginning of **Tuck Everlasting,** she should be able to feel the stagnant stickiness and picture the hazy humidity of the air.

- *The ability to recognize main ideas and supporting details.* As he or she reads a story, the child should recognize important events that set up main problems and follow the successions of attempts and outcomes as the main character seeks to reach his or her goal.

- *The ability to summarize.* A child who can fill out a story map of a plot can be said to have this ability. The same can be said about a child who can compose a *cinquain,* a five-line descriptive poem, about a character or about the topic of an informational book.

In the primary school years, although they might not always initiate them, children flourish on discussions of what they read. The depths of children's insights about literature, as well as the critical tools they bring to discussion, grow rapidly, especially with the guidance of a teacher who is skilled at managing discussions. (The chapters in the last section of this book will help you to become such a teacher!) The exchanges transcribed in the sections above demonstrate the value of having open discussions of literature. As children who still think in less mature ways hear their more advanced classmates state their positions and their reasons for them, the less mature children are challenged to question their own thinking; eventually, they will advance to more sophisticated levels of reasoning.

Experiencing Books in the Upper Elementary and Middle Grades

As children pass through the later primary and middle school years, developments in their ability to reason go hand in hand with their greater sense of seriousness about their life roles. Intellectually, children are more flexible in their reasoning and are accordingly able to enjoy stories with more complex plot structures. In the social realm, children can give consideration to more than one point of view at a time and hence develop a better developed sense of fairness. In their personal development, as Erikson put it, children are driven to gain a sense of *industry*: On the one hand, they enjoy books about children who are or become good at doing things; on the other hand, they soak up books that will give them the information they need to become good at things.

As children advance into middle school, further cognitive and emotional changes take place that influence their responses to literature. Chroniclers of cognitive development note that young people's minds can more readily think about abstractions. They now enjoy ideas almost for their own sake. Hence, it is not surprising that Janet Hickman (1992) found many children in fifth grade who enjoyed analyzing the motives of characters and the themes and implications of stories. Older students do too.

With a growing ability to entertain abstractions comes a new focus on "-isms." Younger children can certainly understand issues of social justice and environmental protection, especially as they affect characters or places they care about, but early adolescent students engage these issues more easily and may care about issues themselves, such as racism, feminism, and environmentalism, as passionately as younger children care about the people and places that are affected by those issues.

Early adolescents are also more conscious of themselves than younger children. (The difference between younger and older children's awareness of themselves is a source of comedy in Beverly Cleary's books about Ramona Quimby.) Erikson suggests that adolescents are becoming preoccupied with developing a sense of *identity*: They are beginning to wonder who they are.

According to Erikson, the question "Who am I?" is answered by asking two more questions. The first is "Who am I part of?" or "Who are my people?" The second is "What can I do?" or "What is my role?" As Erikson noted, the question "Who are my people?" is often rephrased as "Are *these* really my people?," and adolescents can become critical of the shortcomings and hypocrisies of the adults in the society in which they must soon take their own place as adults. Therefore, a sense of idealism may be a theme of this age group. A couple of generations ago, "What can I do?" was a question that was asked more often by boys than by girls. Girls more often asked "Who are my people?," according to James Marcia's research (see Damon, 1992). One effect of the feminist movement may be that both sexes now ask both questions more often.

The interplay of the issues raised above is reflected in the literature that children enjoy in late childhood and early adolescence. It is not surprising that stories such as *Stone Fox, Hatchet,* and *Julie of the Wolves* appeal to children in the late elementary grades. They concern young people who, almost against their will, develop talents that help them to win in adult competition or to survive in the wilderness against heavy odds. All three books, in addition to their other qualities, appeal to young people who are concerned with being good at things, at developing a sense of industry. Jerry Spinelli's *Maniac Magee,* a modern day pseudo-legend about a boy who breaks the color barrier with acts of skill and kindness, and Bruce Brooks's earlier *The Moves Make the Man,* which treated similar problems in a more realistic vein, add to the theme of developing a sense of industry and a concern with racism. Thus, both books also engage young people's growing ability to think about social justice issues, and appeal to their idealism.

Louis Sachar's *Holes,* a surrealistic story about a boy who is falsely sentenced to a labor camp for early adolescents, satirizes any preoccupation with being good at tasks that adults set out for children and instead lays a stress on themes of social justice while encouraging the critical side of young people's idealism: skepticism about the motives of adults in authority.

A great many books about finding an identity are written for early adolescents. The problems of adolescence are legion. Young people may lose themselves in the group. They may feel that they die many deaths as they are rejected by this or that companion or by this or that cohort. They may yield to the ever-present temptation to sell themselves short by falling into crime, drugs, or materialism. Self-definition can mean identifying with a nationality different from that of one's parents or coming to grips once and for all with one's racial identity. It certainly means defining one's sexual orientation. Books can help. Books reflect identities back to people. Whether biographies, essays, realistic fiction, or poetry, many books are about young people's struggle for self-definition, their struggle against the problems of adolescence, and their suddenly awakened recognition of justice and hypocrisy.

Reading at This Age

With their greater mental flexibility, late elementary and early adolescent readers are able to follow more complex plot structures and devices. They can make a narrative emerge from the fictionalized medieval diary entries of Karen Cushman's *Catherine Called Birdy* or from the weavings of memoranda, letters, and court records in Avi's *Nothing but the Truth.* They can savor the irony in Mildred Taylor's *Roll of Thunder, Hear My Cry* when Cassie Logan, the often unreliable narrator, expresses anger at her mother when the reader knows, but Cassie doesn't, that her mother is protecting her from dangers (posed by murderous racists) that Cassie can't yet visualize. They can begin to sense, in Frances Temple's *Grab Hands and Run,* the injustice of treating war refugees like criminals, even though the book's protagonists never complain about injustice. It might even occur to them to wonder—after reading and being moved by so many books about the Holocaust, from *Anne Frank: The Diary of a Young Girl* to Lois Lowry's *Number the Stars*—why Jews are so often portrayed as victims but rarely actors in their own defense.

At the middle school level, children begin reading more critically and often choose books that focus on issues of identity, mirroring their own struggle for a newly emerging identity.

Reading at this age can, to a greater extent than before, involve deep and complex discussions. Young people can explore characters' motives, themes of works, authors' artistry, and even the treatment of the same theme in different books.

They can also read critically. As Temple (1992) suggests, they can "read against the grain," bringing to light implicit assumptions about the sexes and people of different social groups. As Alan Luke suggests (1997), they can begin to ask questions such as, "What other readings can be made of this text?," "Whose voice is at play in this text?," and "Whose voice is silenced?"

Before leaving the topic of children's development and children's literature, we should note that children's development is not like shifting through the gears of an automobile. When it comes to reading and responding to literature, development is not strictly a stage-by-stage process. Younger children often behave in ways that were ascribed here to older children and vice versa. Moreover, exposure to literature and the experience of discussing books can make an enormous difference in the sophistication of children's literary understanding, and these differences are detectable as early as kindergarten (Lehr, 1988). Data collected by Wilson, Fielding, and Anderson (see Stanovich, 1992) suggest that in the typical fifth-grade class, the top group of students may read more than 200 times as many book pages in a year as the lowest group of students. The quantity of reading and the quality of the discussions children experience make significant differences in the sophistication with which they are able to read.

GENRES OF CHILDREN'S LITERATURE

Authors rely on conventions of plot, characterization, and theme to shape readers' responses. They also work within an awareness of genre. "Genre" is a French word meaning "kind" or "type." Once readers know what genre they're reading, they know what to expect from a text, whether magic, realism, humor, or facts.

What are the recognized genres of children's books? These are traditional literature (including folktales and fairy tales, myths, epics, and ballads), poetry of all kinds, fantasy and science fiction, realistic fiction, historical fiction, informational books and biographies, and picture books (a curious category, because picture books can fit into any of the other genres). We will devote the whole middle portion of this book to exploring children's books by genre. Traditional literature is covered in Chapter 5. Picture books are the subject of Chapter 6. Poetry is considered in Chapter 7. In Chapter 8, we consider realistic fiction. In Chapter 9, the topic is historical fiction. Fantasy and science fiction are covered in Chapter 10. And in Chapter 11, we look at informational books and biographies.

The idea of genre means that both author and reader are working within a set of expectations. Informational books describe things in the real world. Realistic fiction usually does not describe things in the real world, yet it does describe things that could happen there. If a book describes things that couldn't happen, it's probably a fairy tale, a fantasy, or a work of science fiction. In each of the chapters devoted to a genre, we include a section that explores what it means to write and read within the genre. We also trace the evolution of books in that genre and describe outstanding writers, past and present, who work within it.

CENSORSHIP AND CHILDREN'S LITERATURE

All teachers make decisions about what books to put into children's hands. Of course teachers choose books that they think will interest children and that will appeal to the children's level of understanding. Of course they choose books that they think have some sort of merit. But at the same time teachers make some books available, they deny children access to others. When teachers deny children access to books because they think those books are too risqué or controversial or when other adults put pressure on teachers to deny access to certain books, then we are dealing with the issue of censorship.

Simply put, censorship means to deny someone access to books or ideas (Naylor, 1991). The First Amendment of the Constitution of the United States reads, "Congress shall make no law respecting an establishment of religion, or prohibiting the free exercise thereof; or abridging the freedom of speech, or of the press. . . ." This language suggests that individual freedom is at issue whenever teachers or other school officials deny children's access to written materials. But many parents claim the right to expect teachers not to expose children to material on topics that the parents would rather handle more delicately at home or keep away from their children altogether. Teachers, for their part, may choose to introduce children to a book they know will stretch their minds and not to share books they consider trashy. Whose rights should prevail? And how should the issue of rights be squared with the requirements of responsible education?

Some topics seem to raise more pressures for censorship than others, and the controversial topics are not always the ones we might expect. In society at large, the areas in which the media feel the most pressure for censorship are sex and violence, especially in our entertainment. These topics seem to cause less controversy in schools, though (Traw, 1996), perhaps because there is something closer to a consensus among parents and teachers that books with more than trace amounts of sex and violence should not be circulated at school. It is true that there is the occasional book such as Judy Blume's *Forever* that describes sexual

Illustration 1.8
Books like the popular Captain Underpants series that deal with bodily functions are, surprisingly, seldom censored in schools. (*Captain Underpants and the Perilous Plot of Professor Poopypants* by Dav Pilkey. Published by Scholastic Press, a division of Scholastic Inc. Copyright © 2000. Reprinted by permission.)

acts (and, sure enough, this book has suffered campaigns to get it off the shelves). But for the most part, in children's literature, sex is off limits, and few people want to argue about it. Other bodily functions seem to escape censorship, however. Taro Gomi's *Everyone Poops* and Shinto Cho's *The Gas We Pass* are sometimes found in school, and Dav Pilkey's *Captain Underpants* series, with titles such as *Captain Underpants and the Perilous Plot of Professor Poopypants*, is freely distributed during "Drop Everything and Read" time, even in third grade.

The surprisingly difficult issue is religion. Religion seems to come up in two ways. We are familiar with the direct way, as exemplified by the state school board of Kansas's recent decision (later overturned) to require biology teachers to teach Creationism—the biblically based doctrine that God really did create man and woman in his own image—and not evolution—the theory that human beings descended from prehuman primates. Usually, religious censorship comes up in less direct ways, as groups of parents and other citizens campaign against books that they believe spread antireligious ideas. Especially vulnerable to censorship are books about magic and witches.

The *Harry Potter* books and even Tomie dePaola's *Strega Nona* books have evoked campaigns for removal from people who believe the descriptions of magic that permeate them are not harmless fun but suggestive of Satanism. Sometimes the criticisms miss the target entirely. For instance, the storyteller Joseph Bruchac described visiting a school district in South Dakota where a citizens' group had demanded that the school remove all books from the library having to do with Transcendentalism. (The parents apparently confused the nineteenth-century literary movement led by Ralph Waldo Emerson with a popular method of meditation.) But whether the groups bringing complaints about books have done their homework or not, schools and teachers need to be prepared to defend their choice of books.

Arguments over religion and alleged Satanism may deflect attention from another kind of passive censorship that is also serious: What are we leaving out? James Loewen filled a book with teachings that were either distorted in or missing altogether from the typical American school curriculum. He entitled his book *Lies My Teacher Taught Me: Everything Your American History Book Got Wrong* (Loewen, 1996). If our children are going to sharpen their minds and forge better ways of living in the future, they will need access to materials that challenge the status quo. But teachers who have been beleaguered by parents upset about Strega Nona or Harry Potter might not be very daring when it comes to looking at the true story of Christopher Columbus, the struggle to improve working conditions in America, or even the constructive role religion has played in U.S. life. Because censorship removes from consideration materials that might stretch children's minds, the American Library Association (ALA) has issued statements opposing it. Here is why:

Why is censorship harmful?

Censorship is harmful because it results in the opposite of true education and learning. In the process of acquiring knowledge and searching for truth, students can learn to discriminate—to make decisions rationally and logically in light of the evidence. By suppressing all materials containing ideas or themes with which they do not agree, censors produce a sterile conformity and a lack of intellectual and emotional growth in students. (ALA web page, November 2, 2000)

What seems clear is that in some districts, at least, there is less consensus about what schools should teach and less trust on the part of the parents than there was before the drumbeat of critiques of U.S. schools that began in the 1980s. How should teachers conduct themselves in the face of the occasional demands for censorship of children's reading fare in the schools?

We recommend the following steps:

1. *Stay aware of what is in your classroom library and the groups of books you assign, and know why they are there.* You should be confident that the books you are making available have literary merit, are enjoyable, raise interesting and important themes, and broaden children's awareness of people and places and events. You should be confident that they are not mean-spirited, racist, or prurient.

2. *Make sure that your school has responsible guidelines for choosing books.* One source of such guidelines is the National Council of Teachers of English (NCTE), 111 Kenyon Road, Urbana, Illinois 61801. NCTE has a special section on their website devoted to the topic of censorship, including suggested guidelines for choosing materials for students to read. The address is <www.ncte.org/censorship>.

3. *Be prepared to speak up for the contribution that good books make to children's education.* Also be prepared to explain the benefit to individual children and to society as a whole when students learn to distinguish what is worthwhile from what is not worthwhile and to entertain ideas and points of view that are different from their own.

4. *Realize that others may disagree with your choice of a certain book, for reasons they believe are right.* Be prepared to recognize their concern for their child and to respect that concern.

5. *Be aware that, should the choice of books in your classroom or school be criticized in ways that you believe are unfair or misguided, and should calm conversation not resolve the problem, there are resources that can help.* One is the American Library Association, which has an Office for Intellectual Freedom. The website of the American Library Association is at <www.ala.org>, and the website for the Office for Intellectual Freedom is found at <ww.ala.org/alaorg/oif>. Their toll-free telephone number is 800-545-2433. Another source of help is the National Council of Teachers of English, whose website is found at <www.ncte.org>.

RESOURCES FOR CHILDREN'S BOOKS

Studying children's literature in college differs in many ways from studying other literature, especially in this way: The focus is turned as much or more toward contemporary books for children as it is toward great works of the past. That is because—with the explosion in the number of books published for children, improvements in the technology of color reproduction, and a growing diversity in the range of people children need to know and care about—many of the very best books for contemporary children have appeared in the past twenty years. And they continue to be published every year. Therefore, to be well read in children's books, you must read backwards and forwards: Read the best of the books already published, and read the best of those coming out. For the best books already published, you can count on the Recommended Books section at the end of each chapter (especially those in Chapters 5–11). The most important books in the development of each genre are discussed in each chapter in the section on historical development. If you want a historical perspective on children's literature, you should read those books as well. But what of the new books? How can you find your way to those that are best?

Several journals have emerged to review children's books and to promote the best ones. These journals, which include *The Horn Book Magazine, School Library Journal, Booklist, Bookbird,* and *The New Advocate* as well as the book review sections of several professional magazines such as *The Reading Teacher* and *Language Arts,* have slightly different emphases and target audiences, so you should consider the information on this textbook's web page carefully.

Many organizations promote children's literature. Subscribing to their publications and attending their regional and national conferences are excellent ways to keep abreast of new children's books. Publishers display new books at the larger professional gatherings. Names and addresses of professional groups concerned with children's literature are listed on this textbook's web page.

BRINGING CHILDREN AND BOOKS TOGETHER

This text is mostly about children's books—their types and notable titles, their features, and their effects on readers. Nonetheless, teachers throughout North America are using children's books as never before in every part of the school day. Therefore, the chapters that make up the last third of this book are devoted to ways of sharing books with children.

Negotiating the symbol system is a barrier to reading literature. So the first priority is to involve children in literature without having them struggle to read it. That means refining your skill at reading aloud, working on your storytelling (and involving children in storytelling too), and engaging children in drama. Such activities engage children in the meaning and the beauty and the fascination of literature without making an obstacle out of reading the words. Reading will come in due time—and even when it does, by reading aloud, storytelling, and engaging in drama, you can engage children in texts that are more elaborate and rewarding than the simple ones they can read themselves. Chapter 12 ("Inviting Children into Literature") lays out techniques for all these activities.

Encouraging children's voluntary reading is enormously important, too. We want children to love reading right from the first. If they have had more television than bedtime stories in their early lives, this is all the more reason to entice them with free access to colorful books. Ways of setting up classroom libraries to invite exploring and free reading are also described in Chapter 12. As solitary and cozy as reading can be, it is also a rewarding social activity. People who read enjoy talking to others about books. A good book chat deepens a reader's insights into a text and even provides a window into the ways in which other people think. Book talks that are open and informal have been shown to invite more thoughtful and satisfying participation from children than sessions that are dominated by the teacher's pedagogical purposes. That is why the emphasis in Chapter 13 ("Encouraging Response to Literature: Literary Discussion") is on book clubs. More and more teachers use this name for discussions that are flexible and maximally open to children's ideas and feelings about books. That chapter describes several ways to arrange for such discussions.

As teachers discover the power of literature to teach about the world, children's books are being used across the curriculum. There is a logic that leads from this story to that nonfiction book to that interview to this art project. That logic is woven into the web of literature units. Chapter 14 ("Literature Units in the Curriculum") discusses in detail several approaches to thematic teaching using literature.

TEACHING IDEAS

Learning about the Books Children Like. Interview four children of different ages about their favorite books. Note carefully what they say. Is there a difference in what children of different ages admire in books? How do their criteria for good children's books compare with those set out in this chapter?

Finding Different Ways to Use Books with Children. Interview three teachers of the elementary grades. Ask them how many different ways they use children's books with their students. Compare their answers with the vignettes found on pages 3–4.

Investigating Ways in Which Children's Books Have Changed over the Years. Find a school librarian or a children's librarian who has worked in the field for thirty years or more. Ask her or him to talk about the ways in which the books for children have changed, children's interests have changed, and parents' concerns about their children's reading have changed—and how these have remained the same. Prepare a two-column list of ways in which children's books have remained the same and ways in which they have changed. Share your list with your peers.

EXPERIENCES FOR YOUR LEARNING

1. Reread the vignettes on pages 3–4. Can you think of books that served you in each of those ways when you were a child? Are there other ways in which books appealed to you? Compare your answers with those of your classmates.

2. Pick a children's book. Evaluate it according to the criteria of a good children's book set out on pages 6–7. How does it fare? Are there other criteria of excellence that you would propose?

3. This chapter stated that many or most of the best books for children have been published in the past twenty years. Do you agree? Why do you think that claim is true—or false? What exceptions to that claim can you think of?

4. This chapter stated that children's books have changed throughout history, roughly as views of childhood changed. What trends do you see at work in society that may change children's literature in the next twenty years? What qualities or values would you expect to see remain the same in children's literature?

REFERENCES

Ainsworth, Mary D. S. "Attachment: Retrospect and Prospect." *The Place of Attachment in Human Behavior.* Ed. C. M. Parkes and J. Stevenson-Hinde. Basic Books, 1982.

Alcott, Louisa May. *Little Women.* Questar, 1868/1991.
Ancona, George. *Pablo Remembers: The Fiesta of the Day of the Dead.* Lothrop, Lee & Shepard, 1993.

Andersen, Hans Christian. *The Little Mermaid*. Random House, 1892/1993.

———. *The Ugly Duckling*. Dover, 1914/1992.

Applebee, Arthur. *The Child's Concept of Story*. University of Chicago Press, 1975.

Aries, Phillippe. *Centuries of Childhood: A Social History of Family Life*. Knopf, 1962.

Asbjornsen, Peter, and J. E. Moe. *The Three Billy Goats Gruff*. Illustrated by Glen Rounds. Holiday House, 1993.

Avi. *Nothing but the Truth*. Orchard Books, 1991.

Babbit, Natalie. *Tuck Everlasting*. Farrar, 1975.

Bear, Donald, Marcia Invernizzi, Shane Templeton, and Francine Johnston. *Words Their Way: Word Study for Phonics, Vocabulary, and Spelling Instruction*. Prentice Hall, 1999.

Bennett, William J. *The Children's Book of Virtues*. Illustrated by Michael Hague. Simon & Schuster, 1995.

Blume, Judy. *Forever*. Pocket Books, 1996.

Brooks, Bruce. *The Moves Make the Man*. Harper Collins Children's Books, 1984.

Brown, Margaret Wise. *Goodnight, Moon*. HarperCollins, 1991.

———. *Little Fur Family*. Illustrated by Garth Williams. HarperCollins, 1991.

Bunyan, John. *Pilgrim's Progress*. Dent, 1678/1911.

Carroll, Lewis. *Alice's Adventures in Wonderland*. Castle Books, 1865/1978.

Caxton, William. *A Booke of Curteseye*, 1477.

Cervantes, Miguel de. *Don Quixote*. Oxford University Press, 1605/1992.

Cho, Shinta. *The Gas We Pass*. Kane/Miller Book Publishers, 1994.

Coles, Robert. *The Story of Ruby Bridges*. Illustrated by George Ford. Scholastic, Inc. 1995.

Collodi, Carlo. *The Adventures of Pinocchio*. Knopf, 1883/1988.

Cooper, Mary. *The Child's New Plaything, Being a Spelling Book Intended to Make the Learning to Read a Diversion*, 1743.

Creech, Sharon. *Walk Two Moons*. HarperCollins, 1994.

Cunningham, Patricia. *Phonics They Use*. Addison Wesley, 1999.

Cushman, Karen. *Catherine Called Birdy*. Houghton Mifflin Company, 1984.

Damon, William. *The Social World of the Child*. Jossey-Bass, 1977.

Darton, F. J. Harvey. *Children's Books in England: Five Centuries of Social Life*. 2nd ed. Cambridge University Press, 1966.

Defoe, Daniel. *Robinson Crusoe*. Running Press, 1719/1991.

dePaola, Tomie. *Strega Nona*. Simon & Schuster, 1979.

Dr. Seuss. *Cat in a Hat*. Random House, 1957.

Eastman, P. D. *Are You My Mother?* Random House, 1988.

Egan, Kieran. "Individual Development in Literacy." *Stories and Readers*. Ed. Charles Temple and Patrick Collins. Christopher-Gordon, 1992.

Erikson, Erik. *Identity: Youth and Crisis*. Norton, 1968.

Ervin-Tripp, Susan, and W. Miller. "Early Discourse: Some Questions about Questions." *Interaction, Questions, and the Development of Language*. Ed. M. Lewis and L. A. Rosenbaum. Academic Press, 1977.

Frank, Anne. *Anne Frank: The Diary of a Young Girl*. Amereon, Limited, 1967.

Frye, Northrop. *The Anatomy of Criticism*. Princeton University Press, 1957.

Gardiner, John Reynolds. *Stone Fox*. Illustrated by Marcia Sewall. Crowell, 1980.

George, Jean Craighead. *Julie of the Wolves*. Illustrated by John Schoenherr. Harper Collins Publisher, 1972.

Gomi, Taro. *Everyone Poops*. Kane/Miller Book Publishers, 1993.

Green, Norma. *Hole in the Dike*. Scholastic, 1993.

Haley, Gail E. *Dream Peddler*. Dutton, 1993.

Heath, Shirley Brice. "What No Bedtime Story Means: Narrative Skills at Home and School." *Language in Society* 11.1 (April 1982): 49–76.

Hickman, Janet. "What Comes Naturally: Growth and Change in Children's Free Response to Literature." *Stories and Readers*. Ed. Charles Temple and Patrick Collins. Christopher-Gordon, 1992.

Hillman, Elizabeth. *Min Yo and the Moon Dragon*. Illustrated by John Wallner. Harcourt Brace, 1992.

Holman, Felice. *The Wild Children*. New York: Scribner's, 1983.

http://www.ala.org/alaorg/oif/intellectualfreedomandcensorship.html "Intellectual Freedom and Censorship Q and A."

Jimenez, Juan Ramon. *Platero and I*. Translated by Antonio de Nicolas. Universe.com, 2000.

Kermode, Frank. *The Sense of an Ending*. Oxford University Press, 2000.

Konner, Robert. *Becoming Attached*. Warner, 1994.

Larrick, Nancy. "The All-White World of Children's Books." *Saturday Review* (1965, September 11): 63–65.

Lehr, Susan. "The Child's Developing Sense of Theme as a Response to Literature." *Reading Research Quarterly* 23.3 (1988): 337–357.

Lionni, Leo. *Frederick*. Pantheon, 1967.

Locke, John. *Some Thoughts Concerning Education*, 1693.

Loewen, James. *Lies My Teacher Told Me: Everything Your American History Textbook Got Wrong*. Touchstone, 1996.

Lowry, Lois. *Number the Stars*. Houghton Mifflin Company, 1990.

Luke, Alan. "Getting Over Method: Literacy Teaching as Work in 'New Times.'" *Language Arts* 75.4 (April 1998): 305–13.

Martin, Bill, Jr. *Brown Bear, Brown Bear, What Do You See?* Illustrated by Eric Carle. Henry Holt, 1983.

Matthews, Gareth. *Dialogues with Children*. Harvard University Press, 1984.

———. *Philosophy and the Young Child*. Harvard University Press, 1980.

Meddaugh, Susan. *Hog-Eye*. Houghton Mifflin, 1995.

Myers, Walter Dean. *Harlem, A Poem*. Scholastic, 1997.

Naylor, Alice. "Censorship." *Children and Books*. 8th ed. Ed. Zena Sutherland and May Hill Arbuthnot. HarperCollins, 1991.

Naylor, Phyllis Reynolds. *Shiloh*. Atheneum, 1990.

New England Primer. Compiled by Benjamin Harris. c. 1686.

Newbery, John. *The History of Little Goody Two-Shoes.* Singing Tree Press. 1766/1970.

———. *A Little Pretty Pocket-Book.* Harcourt, Brace & World, 1744/1967.

Ninio, Annette, and Jerome Bruner. "The Achievement and Antecedents of Labeling." *Journal of Child Language* (1978): 5 5–15.

O'Dell, Scott. *Island of the Blue Dolphins.* Houghton Mifflin, 1960.

Paulsen, Gary. *Hatchet.* Macmillan Publishing Company, 1986.

Pearson, P. David, and Dale Johnson. *Teaching Reading Comprehension.* Holt, Rinehart and Winston, 1978.

Perrault, Charles. "Sleeping Beauty in the Woods" (La belle au bois dormant). *Mercure gallant,* February 1696.

Piaget, Jean. *The Language and Thought of the Child.* World, 1955.

Pilkey, Dav. *Captain Underpants and the Perilous Plot of Professor Poopypants: The Fourth Epic Novel.* Scholastic, 2000.

Sachar, Louis. *Holes.* Farrar, Straus & Giroux, Inc, 1998.

San Souci, Robert D. *The Samurai's Daughter: A Japanese Legend.* Dial, 1992.

———. *The Talking Eggs: A Folktale from the American South.* Illustrated by Jerry Pinkney. Dutton, 1989.

Shaw, Nancy. *Sheep in a Jeep.* Illustrated by Margot Apple. Houghton Mifflin, 1997.

Spinelli, Jerry. *Maniac Magee.* Little, Brown & Company, 1991.

Stanovich, Keith. "Are We Overselling Literacy?" *Stories and Readers.* Ed. Charles Temple and Patrick Collins. Christopher-Gordon, 1992.

Steig, William. *The Real Thief.* Farrar, Straus, & Giroux. 1985.

———. *Sylvester and the Magic Pebble.* Simon and Schuster, 1969.

Stein, N. L., and C. G. Glenn. "An Analysis of Story Comprehension in Elementary School Children." *New Directions in Discourse Processing.* Ed. R. O. Freedle. Vol. 2. Ablex, 1979.

Steptoe, John. *Mufaro's Beautiful Daughters: An African Tale.* Lothrop, Lee, and Shepard, 1997.

Stern, Daniel. *The First Relationship.* Harvard University Press, 1977.

Swift, Jonathan. *Gulliver's Travels.* William Morrow, 1726/1983.

Taylor, Mildred D. *Roll of Thunder, Hear My Cry.* Dial, 1976.

Temple, Charles. "What If 'Beauty' Had Been Ugly? Reading against the Grain of Gender Bias in Children's Books." *Language Arts* 70.2 (February 1993). 89–93.

Temple, Frances. *Grab Hands and Run.* Orchard Books, 1993.

Traw, Rick. "Beware! Here There Be Beasties: Responding to Fundamentalist Censors." *The New Advocate,* 9.1 (Winter 1996): 35–56.

Twain, Mark. *The Adventures of Huckleberry Finn.* Webster, 1885.

———. *The Adventures of Tom Sawyer.* American Publishing, 1876.

Walsh, Daniel, Gary Price, and Mark Gillingham. "The Critical but Transitory Importance of Letter Naming." *Reading Research Quarterly* 23 (1988): 108–22.

Wells, Gordon. "Oral and Literate Competencies in the Early School Years." *Literacy, Language, and Learning.* Ed. David Olsen, Nancy Torrance, and A. Hilyard. Cambridge Univ. Press, 1985.

Wells, Rosemary. *Hazel's Amazing Mother.* Dial, 1985.

Yolen, Jane. *The Emperor and the Kite.* Illustrated by Ed Young. Putnam, 1988.

2 Literary Elements of Children's Literature

Once upon a time, far away in Japan, a poor young artist sat alone in his little house, waiting for his dinner. His housekeeper had gone to market, and he sat sighing to think of all the things he wished she would bring home. He expected her to hurry in at any minute, bowing and opening her little basket to show him how wisely she had spent their few pennies. He heard her step, and jumped up. He was very hungry!

But the housekeeper lingered by the door, and the basket stayed shut.

"Come," he cried. "What is in that basket?"

The housekeeper trembled, and held the basket tight in two hands. "It has seemed to me, sir," she said, "that we are very lonely here." Her wrinkled face looked humble and obstinate.

from The Cat Who Went to Heaven
by Elizabeth Coatsworth

THE ARTISTRY OF LITERARY ELEMENTS

Literature is a miracle. With words on a page, a writer can take readers to a place that never was, let them know people who never lived, and help them share adventures that never happened—and, in spite of the artifice, create something truer than life itself.

Is it possible to look closely at the magic of literature without destroying its ability to amaze us? We think so. It may actually enhance our appreciation of a work to have a vocabulary and a set of concepts to help us admire its wonders or note the shortcomings of a less-than-satisfactory work.

In this chapter, we describe the aspects of literary quality that critics and teachers most often refer to when they talk about texts. Knowing these will give us a vocabulary for evaluating texts and also for exploring the elements of them that move readers.

We will ground our discussion with numerous examples taken from a few key books: Phyllis Naylor's *Shiloh,* Mildred Taylor's *Roll of Thunder, Hear My Cry,* Natalie Babbitt's *Tuck Everlasting,* and Alma Flor Ada's *The Gold Coin.* Although it is not necessary for you to have read these books before you read this chapter, you will definitely get more out of the chapter if you do so.

The main elements of a literary work are the *setting*, the *characterization*, the *plot*, the *themes*, the *stance of the implied reader*, the *point of view*, and the *author's style*. Let's first take a closer look at each of these literary elements and then consider some special literary features of informational books and poetry.

SETTINGS: HOW DO AUTHORS CREATE TIMES AND PLACES?

The setting is the time and place in which the events of a story are imagined to have occurred. An important part of any author's task is to help the reader visualize the events being narrated and the people who are living them. Because whatever is visualized must be seen in time and space, the setting of the story is an important part of the reader's invitation into an imaginary experience.

Ask the Editor . . .

Richard W. Jackson

What was the best manuscript you ever received, and what qualities do you look for in an author?

The best manuscript I've received? *Ever?* You might have asked me to choose between my children! There are several bests. Paula Fox's *Maurice's Room*—she'd written only three chapters at the time I first saw it but I remember reading them aloud to my wife and saying, "This woman will win the Newbery medal someday." And she did. Such vividness in the people, such kindness in the humor. And such a voice. Also a favorite—the text for *The Relatives Came* by Cynthia Rylant, for somewhat the same reasons. I believe we didn't change a word, though "best" for me doesn't mean word perfect. More important than immediate perfection is the breath of life in a piece. Frances Temple's *Taste of Salt* was another revelation—a "breathing" book about modern Haiti, about brave young people whose lives were, at the time, largely unimaginable by Americans (of any age). The book is written in two first-person teenage voices, and there is urgency in every word. For "I" stories, urgency is crucial.

Even "light" books, such as Avi's *S.O.R. Losers* or Judy Blume's *Are You There God? It's Me, Margaret,* depend on urgency for their success. In funny stories as well as serious, you need to sense the narrator's urge to bend your ear. *Toning the Sweep* by Angela Johnson is another unique example of urgent voice. It began as a collection of quick scenes, poetic impressions, snippets of conversation about a girl witnessing her grandmother's struggle with cancer; it grew into a novel over several years. Thrilling years.

I look for long-term associations with writers or illustrators and rarely take on anyone published by many houses—for snobbish reasons, I suppose. I look for loyalty and for brains. For devotion to hard work and a certain delicacy of touch. I listen for voice. Just this minute the phone rang and—speaking of voice—a cheery one said, "I've figured out how to do it, the whole book. It was our conversation yesterday that helped." The caller was Theresa Nelson, a superb novelist whose first book, *The 25-cent Miracle,* is another best. She's written four beauties since. My response to such calls has remained unchanging since 1962: gratitude and joy.

> ### Favorite Books as a Child
>
> *The 500 Hats of Bartholomew Cubbins* by Dr. Seuss (which appealed to my theatrical instincts)
>
> *Alice's Adventures in Wonderland* by Lewis Carroll (because it is the only book I recall being read aloud to me)

Richard W. Jackson is editor of Richard Jackson Books, an imprint of Orchard Books, which publishes some thirty new titles a year. His articles have appeared in The Horn Book Magazine, School Library Journal, *and* The New Advocate.

How explicitly the setting is described varies with the genre. In a folktale, the setting may get scant mention, yet it can still have symbolic significance. In realistic fiction, the setting can be used to add *verisimilitude*, or lifelikeness, to the story and make it easier for readers to believe in the events. In a survival story, the setting plays the role of antagonist—almost as if it were a character. In historical fiction or in stories from other cultures, the setting may share center stage with the characters and events, since readers may be as curious about what life is or was like in that setting as they are about what happens in the story. The same can be said of science fiction or fantasy—genres in which the author is free to make up whole new worlds. Let's look, then, at how settings vary with some of these genres.

Settings in Folktales and Fairy Tales

The Grimms' story "The Frog Prince" (Grimm and Grimm, 1972) has this setting:

> In olden times when wishing still helped one, there lived a king whose daughters were all beautiful, but the youngest was so beautiful that the sun itself, which had seen so much, was astonished whenever it shone in her face. Close by the king's castle lay a dark forest, and under an old lime-tree in the forest was a well, and when the day was very warm, the King's child went out into the forest and sat down beside the cool fountain. (p. 17)

The first sentence introduces this "no-particular-time" when magical things happened. Japanese folktales often begin just as simply: "Once long ago in the middle of the mountains . . . ." Native American tales often say, "Many lifetimes ago, in the days of the Ancient Ones . . . ." Arabic folktales sometimes begin "There was, and there was not, in the fullness of time . . . ." Young children's first question about these tales, of course, is "Did this really happen?" The storyteller doesn't want to deny the ultimate truth of the story, so she or he finds a way of saying that these events were cast in a setting that is beyond the everyday, where things can be morally true, if not factually so.

Settings in folktales are briefly described. They represent everywhere and nowhere, but they often have particular associations. In European tales, *home* is where normal life is lived, securely. The *forest* is where one may be tested by sinister forces. The *country* is where simple but honest folk live, whereas the *city* is the place of sophisticated but possibly treacherous people. A *hovel* is a place one usually wants to rise above (but may have to learn to settle for), and a *palace* is the residence of those who were born privileged or who have had triumphant success. Because the genre of folk stories tends to use these same settings with the same connotations again and again, the mere mention of them usually suffices to cue the reader's imagination to generate his or her own associations for them.

Settings in Realistic Fiction

Settings in realistic fiction are usually described with greater detail. Because the settings in realistic faction are almost infinitely various, authors must describe in detail the settings they have in mind. Here are the opening lines of *Shiloh:*

> The day Shiloh come, we're having us a big Sunday dinner. Dara Lynn's dipping bread in her glass of cold tea, the way she likes, and Becky pushes her beans up over the edge of her plate in her rush to get 'em down. (p. 11)

These lines reveal the "country ways" of Marty's family, through their way of speech and their table manners. Knowing how people act and talk can provide one sort of clue to the setting. Two pages further into the book, Marty takes the reader for a walk around the physical setting:

> We live high up in the hills above Friendly, but hardly anybody knows where that is. Friendly's near Sistersville, which is halfway between

Illustration 2.1
Newbery medal-winner *Shiloh* poses a thought-provoking ethical dilemma that pits animal rights—and a boy's love for a dog—against property rights. (*Shiloh* by Phyllis R. Naylor, copyright © 1991 by Phyllis Reynolds Naylor. Cover illustration by Jacqueline Rogers. Used by permission of Dell Publishing, a division of Random House, Inc.)

Wheeling and Parkersburg. Used to be, Daddy told me, Sistersville was one of the best places you could live in the whole state. You ask me the best place to live, I'd say right where we are, a little four-room house with hills on three sides.

Afternoon is my second-best time to go up in the hills, though; morning's the best, especially in summer. Early, early morning. One morning I saw three kinds of animals, not counting cats, dogs, frogs, cows, and horses. Saw a groundhog, saw a doe with two fawns, and saw a gray fox with a reddish head. Bet his daddy was a gray fox and his ma was a red one. (pp. 12–13)

Here are more clues to the setting: Whatever happens in the story will have to be consistent with a Southern rural mountain environment. Good writers don't waste details, so the reader can expect the ways of nature and animals to figure in this story.

Settings as Important Features in Themselves

In some genres, settings can figure so strongly as to share attention with the characters in the story. The setting may produce challenges that characters must strive against. The grinding and desolate urban setting of Jerry Spinelli's *Maniac Magee* seems to have permeated people's attitudes with harshness, and Maniac must struggle against both in his quest for humanity.

The racist society of Mississippi during the depression of the 1930s, portrayed in Mildred Taylor's *Roll of Thunder, Hear My Cry,* shows readers what the Logan children must endure. The implications of racial antagonism affect everything that happens in the book.

In multicultural literature, details of the setting may seem commonplace to one group but be striking to another. For example, Alma Flor Ada's *My Name Is Maria Isabel* begins:

Maria Isabel looked at the cup of coffee with milk and the buttered toast in front of her. But she couldn't bring herself to eat.

Her mother said, "Maribel, cariño, hurry up."

Her father added, "You don't want to be late on your first day, do you?" (p. 1)

Children who trace their origins to the Spanish-speaking Caribbean or to Central America will find that scene reassuringly familiar. But other readers might be surprised that a young girl would drink coffee for breakfast, moved at the mother's affectionate shortening of the girl's name, and impressed that the mother speaks to her daughter in two languages. In effect, the setting is functioning almost as a character in the story.

In a historical novel, the details of the setting may also go a long way to satisfy young readers' curiosity about a place that is far removed in time. The earthiness of English village life early in the fourteenth century is brought home in the first paragraph of Karen Cushman's *The Midwife's Apprentice:*

When animal droppings and garbage and spoiled straw are piled up in a great heap, the rotting and moiling give forth heat. Usually no one gets close enough to notice because of the stench. But the girl noticed and, on that frosty night, burrowed deep into the warm, rotting muck, heedless of the smell. (p. 1)

Here again, although the characters also do much to impress themselves on readers, the setting of this historical novel continually surprises and informs them.

CHARACTERIZATION: HOW DO PEOPLE EMERGE FROM THE PAGE?

Characterization is the art of creating people out of words on the page. When a writer has done a good job of characterization, readers feel as if they have gotten to know another person. How does a writer achieve that?

Erik Erikson (1968) suggested that we know people by three things: by what they do and how they do it, by the others they affiliate with and how they feel about each other, and by the way they feel about themselves. These same dynamics work in literature. In coming to know a character in a work of literature, though, readers are affected by one more variable: the role the character plays in the story. Let's look at each of these dimensions.

Characters Are Developed through Their Actions

In a guidebook for fiction writers, Anne Bernays and Pamela Painter (1995) remind us of a character in F. Scott Fitzgerald's *The Great Gatsby* who wore cufflinks made of human molars. Rather than saying "He was insensitive, domineering, and gross," Fitzgerald simply gave us that one detail—and that detail made readers see the character more clearly than descriptive words ever could have.

When readers meet Marty on the first page of *Shiloh,* they hear this exchange:

> "I looked that rabbit over good, Marty, and you won't find any buckshot in that thigh," Dad says, buttering his bread. "I shot him in the neck."
>
> Somehow I wish he hadn't said that. I push the meat from one side of my plate to the other, through the sweet potatoes and back again.
> "Did it die right off?" I ask, knowing I can't eat at all unless it had.
> "Soon enough."
> "You shoot its head clean off?" Darlene asks. She's like that.
> Dad chews real slow before he answers. "Not quite," he says, and goes on eating.
> Which is when I leave the table. (pp. 11–12)

Here, too, readers get to know Marty by what he does and says rather than by what the author says about him. Marty is the most sensitive member of a family that is used to earthy living, but he is trying to hang in there. Readers absorb that impression better because they infer it from the above exchange, rather than being told it directly.

Characters Are Developed through Their Relations with Others

Characters are also brought to life when readers see who "their people" are—and how they relate to them. Cassie in **Roll of Thunder, Hear My Cry** is an African American child, a member of a black community in segregationist Mississippi during the Depression. Marty in **Shiloh** is a member of a hard-working

THE GOLD COIN
by Alma Flor Ada
illustrated by Neil Waldman

Illustration 2.2
An original book with the simplicity and moral clarity of a folktale, *The Gold Coin* has a linear story line that culminates in a surprise ending. (*The Gold Coin* written by Alma Flor Ada, illustrated by Neil Waldman. Text copyright © 1991 by Alma Flor Ada. Illustrations copyright © 1991 by Neil Waldman. Used by permission of Atheneum Books for Young Readers, an imprint of Simon & Schuster Children's Publishing.)

and frugal family in rural Appalachia. Jason in *The Giver* lives in a deliberately wholesome family in a bland, engineered society.

Often, book characters are portrayed as being out of harmony with their group. In *Shiloh,* Marty is at home in the woods with a rifle in his hands; but unlike the rest of his family, he is sensitive to the suffering of animals. Jesse, in Katherine Paterson's *Bridge to Terabithia,* is more sensitive than the rest of his farm family; his friend Lesley is more down-to-earth than her idealistic professional family. They are more like each other than like their own kin. Cassie, in *Roll of Thunder, Hear My Cry,* belongs to a family that refuses to accept second-class citizenship in a society harshly governed by whites. Cassie doesn't understand, however, as her parents do, the care and skill it takes for a black family to avoid disaster in that situation. Juan, the thief in Alma Flor Ada's *The Gold Coin,* doesn't belong to anybody. Yet as he pursues Doña Josefa through the countryside to rob her, his series of contacts with other working people eventually draws him into the human family.

In all of these cases, the characters come to life through a sort of comparison and contrast: A character is like the group in some ways but strikingly different from it in some particular way.

Characters can also be drawn in opposition to other, contrasting characters. In *Shiloh,* Marty's ethics are starkly contrasted with those of the brutish Judd Travers, who lies, cheats, and abuses his animals. Marty also differs from his best friend, David Howard, who comes from better-off professional people living in town and who is not nearly as robust as Marty. In *The Gold Coin,* Juan the thief is starkly contrasted with Doña Josefa the healer: He wants nothing but to take; she wants nothing but to give.

In sum, it is often possible to find two characters in a story who are drawn as opposites, making the attributes of both clearer.

Characters Are Developed through Their Sense of Themselves

In *Roll of Thunder, Hear My Cry,* Cassie Logan can't imagine why she should step off the sidewalk when a white girl tells her to. She experiences horror and outrage when her grandmother, Big Ma, forces her to apologize to her offender. Readers know Cassie by her unquestioned sense of her own worth.

The central conflict in *Shiloh* comes about because Marty is keeping a dog away from its owner, in violation of the law and common behavior and against the wishes of his parents. The author shows how Marty experiences this conflict by having him utter this prayer:

> "Jesus," I whisper finally, "which you want me to do? Be one hundred percent honest and carry that dog back to Judd so that one of your creatures can be kicked and starved all over again, or keep him here and fatten him up to glorify your creation?"
>
> The question seemed to answer itself, and I'm pretty proud of that prayer. (p. 57)

Readers get to know Marty all the better through this expression of his thoughts. As characters get to know themselves, readers get to know them. By comparing their own experiences to those of the characters, readers get to know themselves a little better, too.

Characters Are Developed through the Roles They Play in the Plot

If a character in a story is cast in the role of the protagonist, or the hero, readers are inclined to be sympathetic toward him or her. If the character is cast as the antagonist, the villain or the hero's rival, readers are disposed to "fill in the blanks" with bad qualities. This happens in real life, too: Just listen to what emotional sports fans say about players on the opposing team!

If the character is cast as the helper, readers might expect her or him to be loyal and generous, possibly amusing—but not more beautiful, brave, or admirable than the hero. If the character plays the role of receiver, the person whom the hero wants to rescue or otherwise help, readers expect that person to be deserving of that help (Souriau, 1955).

How much the plot influences the way we think of characters, though, depends on the genre of the story. In a folktale, readers can be told almost nothing about a character and yet be sympathetic or unsympathetic depending on whether the character plays a hero or a villain. Readers pull for Jack—even though he has been presented as lazy and stupid—because he is cast as the hero of "Jack and the Beanstalk." Readers are not sorry when the giant meets a bad end, even though he has been robbed and then killed—because he opposes the hero, Jack. Readers rarely notice that the giant's wife is left widowed and abandoned up in the sky; her function in the story is to play the role of helper to Jack, and our attention leaves her once her role is done.

In realistic fiction, however, the writer is obliged to go further and spell out the characters' motives and personal qualities. Even an antagonistic character's motives must be explained. In *Shiloh,* for example, the author leads readers to understand Judd Travers's insensitive manners by planting hints about his own harsh upbringing.

Illustration 2.3

As we allow ourselves to assume the role of the implied reader of *Roll of Thunder, Hear My Cry,* we may take on the emotional and intellectual perspective of those who have suffered painful racial oppression. (*Roll of Thunder, Hear My Cry* by Mildred D. Taylor. Illustration copyright © 1991 by Max Ginsburg. Used by permission of Puffin Books, a division of Penguin Putnam Inc.)

When a writer creates well-developed characters—those whose thoughts, feelings, and attitudes are evident through what they think, say, and do in the story—readers feel they are getting to know other people.

Taking us inside the motives of characters—whether they are sympathetic or not—is one of the great contributions literature makes to our understanding of other people. For centuries before the discipline of psychology was invented, people counted on literature for insights into what makes other people do what they do.

PLOTS: HOW DO STORIES HAPPEN?

A plot is a meaningful ordering of events with their consequences, a "what happened to whom and why." A plot is the conveyor belt that pulls a reader through the text, getting to know characters and scenes along the way, before arriving at a cumulative insight.

Plots fascinate people. When you add up not just the literature people read, but also the films and videos they watch and the TV shows (don't forget the soap operas) they view during so many hours each day, it is clear that most people consider plots a staple of life.

Ask a person to recount his or her day, and likely as not the person will weave a plot, starring himself or herself as the main character—hero or victim. Critics have noted that we all depend on plots to give meaning to our lives. As critic Frank Kermode (1975) pointed out, our daily lives have no clear meaning without an answer to the question "What is it all adding up to?" We never really know what our lives are adding up to until they're over, so we crave a sense of an ending, which we find in the plots of stories, because only stories—and dead people's lives—have endings.

Stories are frameworks that give meaning to events. Much as words and concepts give people the means to name and think about the phenomena that surround them, stories—plots—give them ways of finding meaning in the dynamic events and the ongoing processes of their lives. It's no wonder people are hungry for plots.

In this section, we look at the plots in several ways. We look first at the conflicts that give rise to plots, then we look at the structure of plots. Common plot types will be the next topic, followed by a consideration of some of the twists and turns of plots that authors have at their disposal: techniques such as episodes within plots, surface and underlying plots, and the interplay of genre with plots.

Plots and Conflicts

Plots unfold when a character is drawn toward a significant goal and faces some kind of conflict in reaching it. Conflicts in fiction usually take one of four different forms: there may be conflict between the character and some rival person, between the character and himself or herself, between the character and the environment, or between the character and society.

Conflict between Characters. In J. K. Rowling's *Harry Potter and the Sorcerer's Stone,* the ultimate conflict is between Harry Potter and Voldemort, the wicked sorcerer who killed Harry's parents and who is intent on doing further evil in the world. Along the way, there are other conflicts: between Harry

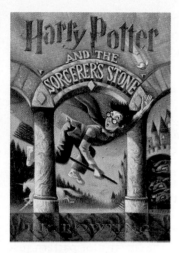

Illustration 2.4
Readers are propelled through the pages of *Harry Potter and the Sorcerer's Stone* by the imminent threat of conflict between Harry Potter and the evil sorcerer Voldemort. (*Harry Potter and the Sorcerer's Stone*, written by J. K. Rowling, illustrated by Mary Grandpre. HARRY POTTER, characters, names, and all related indicia are trademarks of Warner Bros. 2001. Reprinted by permission.)

and his step-family, the Dursleys, and between Harry and his friends and the residents of Slytherin Hall, a rival dormitory within Hogwarts School.

Roald Dahl's books often introduce conflicts between characters: between Danny and his father and Victor Hazlett, the wealthy landowner, in *Danny the Champion of the World* or between Matilda and her ghastly parents in *Matilda.*

Posing conflict between characters is a surefire way for authors to engage readers. It is not surprising that so many action shows on television and escape fiction use conflict between "good guys" and "bad guys." Sophisticated literature usually employs some other kinds of conflicts, often in combination with each other.

Conflict within a Character. In William Steig's *Spinky Sulks,* problems arise because Spinky gets his feelings hurt too easily: Rather than rolling with punches that come from relationships, he withdraws and sulks. Thus, the conflict in the book is located within Spinky himself: It is a tension between his need to have friends and the fragile emotions that keep him from interacting. In Mildred Pitts Walker's *Justin and the Best Biscuits in the World,* Justin's internal struggle has to do with overcoming his confused identity after the death of his father. He solves his problem by coming to rely on the example of his grandfather, a cowboy, to discover that a man is not just macho, but also able to cook, make his own bed, and wash his own dishes.

Conflicts between characters and themselves, or internal conflicts, are often combined with other kinds of conflicts. Willy, the protagonist in John Reynolds Gardiner's *Stone Fox,* must first overcome self-doubts before throwing himself into the challenge a dogsled race. The heroine in Scott O'Dell's *Island of the Blue Dolphins* must overcome her belief that women are helpless before she can succeed against the hardships of living alone on a small island off the coast of California.

Conflict between a Character and the Environment. Books with survival themes pit their protagonists against the environment. Gary Paulsen's books do this brilliantly, as in *Hatchet,* in which a boy learns to survive in the woods after an airplane crash, and *The Voyage of the Frog,* in which a boy survives an ocean crossing on a sailboat. In Jean Craighead George's *Julie of the Wolves,* the heroine survives in the Arctic tundra by adopting the ways of the wolves.

Conflict between a Character and Society. Characters in books are often at odds with society. Sometimes society embraces some evil or some prejudice against which the character must struggle. Such is the case in the racist Depression-era society in the South against which the Logans struggle in *Roll of Thunder, Hear My Cry* or the violent and racially divided community in which Jerry Spinelli's Maniac Magee struggles to be friends to all. Such is also the case in Elizabeth George Speare's *The Witch of Blackbird Pond,* in which we find Kit, the protagonist, being tried for witchcraft by her narrow-minded neighbors in colonial America. In other books, the struggle with society comes about not because society is particularly evil, but just because it is what it is. For example, in Gary Soto's sophisticated stories in *Baseball in April,* we meet well-drawn Mexican American characters struggling to get along in Fresno, California.

Poverty and ethnic segregation shape the characters' actions and limit their possibilities; yet the point of the stories is not to complain about social evils, but rather to show how typical young people deal with the small and large issues of their lives in such a setting.

Plot Structures

The events in a typical plot are set in motion by a *complication*, in which the main character experiences a *problem* and explicitly or implicitly sets a *goal*. The plot continues with *rising action*, in which the character strives to reach the goal and solve the problem. Toward the end, the plot arrives at a *climax*, in which tension is at its height as the matter of the character's success or failure is about to be decided. And the plot culminates in the *resolution*, in which the problem is decided, for good or ill. Some plots close with a *denouement*, which is a brief display of the characters' state of affairs after the resolution.

Most folktales and other simple stories follow the linear plot pattern just described. In Alma Flor Ada's **The Gold Coin,** the adventure begins when Juan approaches a hut he plans to rob and spies an old woman inside holding a gold coin and saying, "I must be the richest person in the world." The *complication* arises when Juan breaks into the hut after the woman leaves and finds no gold coin: Now he must follow her. Of course, his *goal* is to have the coin. Tensions mount (the *rising action*) throughout the story as Juan follows the old woman, Doña Josefa, to one farm after another—where he is told of a generous and helpful act she has just performed and is given work to do to pass the time before the farmers can take him to his next destination. The *climax* is the surprising events that befall Juan when he catches up with Doña Josefa alone on the road. And the *resolution* follows when Juan realizes that he has been transformed. The *denouement* in this story is tactfully left for the reader to imagine. How will Juan lead his life, now that he has learned the value of being trusted by others, of being generous?

Recurring Plots

Some plot forms are used again and again in stories. To lump them together by their common forms is to take nothing away from them; on the contrary, it may point out their larger psychic meaning and their contribution to our understanding of the human drama.

The Initiation Story. In traditional societies in which initiation rituals are still required of young people, a high price is exacted for reaching adulthood. In one anthropologist's account (Turnbull, 1982), initiates are commonly taken out of the tribe and into the woods, where they are exposed to extreme pain or danger. Their childhood is stripped from them as their old clothes and other possessions are confiscated and burned. They are taught weighty secrets and given new responsibilities, before finally being reintroduced to the tribe, where the community pays homage to them and recognizes their new state.

Children's literature is full of initiation stories, in which a young character is given some challenge to get through; having successfully met the challenge, she or he is recognized as being more mature or more worthy. "Jack and the Beanstalk" and "Hansel and Gretel" are initiation stories. *Nessa's Fish,* written by Nancy Luenn and illustrated by Neil Waldman, is an initiation story that tells of a young Inuit girl's thoughtful and heroic efforts to save her incapacitated grandmother, who is stranded out on the ice with a cache of fish. Gary Paulsen's **Hatchet** is an initiation story of a boy's survival in the woods; Katherine

Illustration 2.5
A sophisticated children's initiation story like *Amazing Grace* can make a first grader's struggle for success seem heroic and satisfying. (*Amazing Grace* by Mary Hoffman. Illustrations by Caroline Binch. Copyright © 1991 by Mary Hoffmann, text. Copyright © 1991 by Caroline Binch, illustrations. Used by permission of Dial Books for Young Readers, a division of Penguin Putnam Inc.)

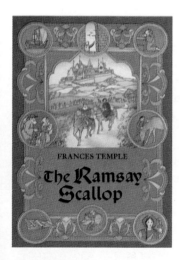

Illustration 2.6
In *The Ramsay Scallop,* a young couple's pilgrimage from England to Spain transforms their views of the world and of one another. (*The Ramsay Scallop* by Frances Temple, cover illustration by Wendy Anderson Halperin. Published by Orchard Books, an imprint of Scholastic Inc. Illustration copyright © 1994 by Wendy Anderson Halperin. Reprinted by permission.)

Paterson's *Lyddie* is an initiation story about a girl's learning to stand up for herself in the harsh environment of early industrial Lowell, Massachusetts. Mary Hoffman's *Amazing Grace,* illustrated by Caroline Binch, is an initiation story about an African American girl's efforts to transcend the limits of race and sex and play the part of Peter Pan in a first-grade play.

Becoming initiated sometimes implies trade-offs: The protagonist must trade innocence for experience. Hansel and Gretel lost their childhood and experienced horror before they could be reunited with their father, in what must have been an uneasy relationship. In Roald Dahl's *Danny the Champion of the World,* Danny learns a terrible secret about his father and his father's family. The knowledge destroys his cozy domesticity with his father, but it also enables Danny to save his father from danger and eventually to become a family and community hero.

Growing up requires pain and struggle, embracing some things and giving up others—scary steps for a child. Initiation stories point the way, not by revealing the particular path a child will take, because that is necessarily unique to each person, but by offering the hope and assurance that there is sunlight up above the clouds.

The Journey. Another metaphor for arduous progress and change is the journey. People all over the world have been motivated by deep urges to uproot themselves and travel long distances. As hunter-gatherers, humans ranged widely over the landscape, following animals or seeking greener habitats. Since ancient times, different cultures have had the custom of making pilgrimages to religious places—to Rome, Canterbury, Mecca, Santiago de Compostela, Lourdes—a practice that survives today. Voyages of discovery, for trade, to make war or bring comfort to the suffering—all seem to follow some deep-seated human urge to go, to see, and to be changed along the way.

Cynthia Voigt's *The Homecoming* is an unforgettable example of the journey, as the children of the Tillerman family go in search of someone to raise them. Sharon Creech's *Walk Two Moons,* another story of a child's journey in search of family, won the Newbery Medal in 1995. Frances Temple's *The Ramsay Scallop* goes to the roots of the tradition, as it recounts a young betrothed couple's pilgrimage from England to Spain in the year 1299. In all of these stories, the characters grow in their awareness of other people and of themselves with every challenge they meet along the way, and thus the journey itself ultimately means more than the destination. Surely there is a lesson in this for young readers.

Episodes: Stories within Stories

Many books, especially those for older children, give us patterns of episodes within a larger plots. Beverly Cleary's *Ramona and Her Father* is a good example. The story begins with Mr. Quimby's losing his job. His unemployment is the main conflict of the story, and it will not be resolved until the last few pages. This main problem spawns several smaller problems—each with a story of its own (and each providing provisional closure when read in a single sitting). Some of the problems last through several chapters. For example, because Ramona and Beezus see more of their father, they grow concerned about his smoking, and they start a guerrilla campaign to make him stop. Some problems last only through a single chapter—such as the antics that occur when Ramona imagines she might become a highly paid child actor in a TV advertisement, able to support her besieged family in lavish style.

Illustration 2.7
Louis Sachar won a Newbery Award for this tale about a boy sentenced to dig holes in the dry lake bottom of a work camp where he has an unforeseen opportunity to break the family curse. (Jacket design by Vladimir Radunsky from *Holes* by Louis Sachar. Copyright © 1998 by Louis Sachar. Jacket design copyright © 1998 by Vladimir Radunsky. Reprinted by permission of Farrar, Straus and Giroux, LLC.)

Ramona and Her Father has an intricate pattern of plot and episodes: one main problem leading logically to several smaller problems that pull the child reader through one, two, or three chapters, each with its own closure, until the main conflict of the book is resolved.

The "Real" Story versus the Story as Revealed

In the first pages of Louis Sachar's Newbery Award–winning book *Holes,* we meet the ne'er-do-well great-great-grandson of a ne'er-do-well prospector who, though innocent, is being sent to a juvenile detention camp. During the early chapters of the book, we follow the inmates at the camp as they are forced to dig holes on a dry lake bed, presumably as an exercise in penitence, under the heartless supervision of stern guards and a surrealistically sadistic warden. Only in the last chapters does it become clear what is really going on: The great-great-grandfather had, indeed, found a treasure many years before, and the daily hole digging is not a penitential exercise after all but an attempt by the warden to use the inmates at the camp to help her recover that treasure. It is as if *Holes* were really two stories, one on top of the other: the underlying "real" story (the great-great-grandfather's treasure and the warden's manipulation of the boys to find it) and the story-as-narrated (the boys' experiences at the detention camp), through which the "real" story is gradually revealed.

In *Holes* and in most other mystery stories, then, there are really two stories: the incomplete narrative that is fed to the reader page by page and the underlying or "real" story that the narrative points to (Barthes, 1974). Mystery and suspense are created as readers ask themselves what is really going on—that is, as the author uses his or her narrative to give hints about the underlying story, and the readers try to figure out what that story is.

Variations in Time

A simple story is told straight through, with events following one after another. But in some stories, the action is liberated from a straight time sequence. These stories use flashbacks, in which events that happened before are recalled into the time of the narration, like Dicey Tillerman's memories of going to see her mother, recalled during her travels in Cynthia Voigt's *The Homecoming.*

Tuck Everlasting employs time shifts, too. Near the beginning of the book, Winnie Foster observes Jesse Tuck uncovering and drinking from the spring that magically stops one from aging. A short while later, readers learn that the Tuck family had drunk from the spring eighty-seven years before. Finally, in the epilogue to the book, set seventy years after the main action, the Tucks come on Winnie's grave—and thus answer the lingering question of whether Winnie will drink from the spring and remain young forever.

Illustration 2.8
Natalie Babbitt uses the image of a wheel in the text of *Tuck Everlasting* to remind the reader how important it is to accept that one is part of the life cycle. (Jacket design from *Tuck Everlasting* by Natalie Babbitt. Copyright © 1975 by Natalie Babbitt. Reprinted by permission of Farrar, Straus and Giroux, LLC.)

Plot and Genre

The genre of a story determines the range of possible actions that can happen in it. In a folktale, it is acceptable if a cockroach marries a mouse, which is what happens in "Cucarchita Martina and Ratoncito Perez," or if a spider spins greedy plots, as Anansi does in "Anansi the Spider." On the other hand, it would be quite surprising if Brian Robeson, the reluctant survivor in *Hatchet,* were rescued from his wilderness isolation by a spaceship or if Lesley and Jesse encountered a talking animal on their island retreat in Katherine Paterson's Newbery Medal winner *The Bridge to Terabithia.*

Some stories, especially mysteries, create tension and suspense by keeping readers guessing not only about what will happen, but also about what genre of story they are reading—and thus about what kinds of events, and what kinds of causes of those events, to expect (Todorov, 1973). In *The House of Dies Drear,* which hovers between realistic fiction and fantasy, readers don't know until the very end whether the story is dealing with natural or supernatural events, because Virginia Hamilton plants ambiguous clues that could point either way. Only in the last few pages is it clear which realm of possibility readers have been given and which genre of book—realistic fiction or fantasy—they have just read.

In Cynthia Rylant's Newbery Medal–winning novel *Missing May,* readers are left wondering until the very end whether a spiritualist can really help a bereft widower to contact his dead wife. When that solution doesn't work out, the reader, like the characters in Rylant's touching book, is brought back to the conviction that people must make the best they can of life within the limits of their mortality—seeking small epiphanies in their relationships with others, perhaps, but not counting on breakthroughs to another world.

Jerry Spinelli played with genre in an interesting way in crafting *Maniac Magee.* By passing on the oral histories about Maniac before letting readers in on the story, he gave his book the cast of a legend. The story wavers between realistic fiction and legend, which has the effect of underscoring the legendary importance of someone's breaching the racial barrier in contemporary urban America while showing the real-life innocence and vulnerability of the heroic kid who does the breaching.

THEMES: HOW DO STORIES CONVEY MEANING?

A theme is an issue or a lesson that a story brings to a readers' consciousness. Beyond the question "What happened to whom and why?" readers sometimes ask, "What is this work really about?," "What does it mean?," or even "Why did the author write this work?" Answers to those questions are usually statements of theme.

Explicit and Implicit Themes

Themes may be stated explicitly or suggested implicitly by the text. A good example of an explicit theme is found in the Zuñi story *The Dragonfly's Tale,* retold and illustrated by Kristina Rodanas. A community that has long been blessed by bounteous crops suddenly experiences famine when the people squander their food and callously offend the two goddesses who have been responsible for their bounty. When the village goes off in search of something to eat, a thoughtful and generous boy and girl again win the favor of the goddesses. The theme of the story, the virtues of conservation and kindness, is made explicit in the closing lines of the book:

> From then on, the people were careful not to take the Corn Maidens' gifts for granted. They respected the boy and his sister, and learned their ways of kindness. The cornfields thrived, and all the Ashiwi prospered. (n. pag.)

An implicit theme is an idea that is strongly suggested but not explicitly stated. In Alma Flor Ada's *The Gold Coin,* there is no explicit mention of the lesson that giving is better than taking or that the esteem of one's fellows is

Are themes really there?

As we've mentioned, the theme of a contemporary literary work is more often implied than explicitly stated. Not surprisingly, the identification and interpretation of themes that are not explicitly stated give rise to lively debates. Critics argue not only about what the theme of a specific work really is, but also about whether the inherent difficulty in identifying implied themes makes it impossible to state *any* book's theme definitively. While some critics claim that skilled readers are adept at discovering themes that less skilled readers will miss, others (known as "deconstructionists" or "transactionalists" in the field of literary theory) insist that what a book means—its theme—lies entirely in the experience, background, and personality of each reader who encounters it.

These differing opinions certainly do not prevent literary critics, authors, and book lovers from discussing themes. Readers often have different ideas about the theme of a particular book. And authors sometimes even disagree with what the critics identify as the themes of their books!

What do you think? If you have read Natalie Babbitt's *Tuck Everlasting,* for example, what would you say the theme is? Do you agree with what the author says it is? With what your teacher or classmates think it is? How will you decide what the theme is?

more valuable than gold. Readers have to infer those ideas from what happens in the story.

Especially in contemporary literature, stating themes is not always an easy or foolproof matter. Good writers rarely start with explicit themes in mind. Author Frances Temple (1994a) explained her approach to themes this way: "At first, I'm just getting out the story. Once it's written down, I can go through and see what the story is adding up to—and then as I rewrite I can make sure that what stays in the book pulls more or less in the same direction."

Many authors express surprise, however, at the themes others find in their works. For instance, Charles Temple was surprised to read in a review of his ***Shanty Boat*** (illustrated by Melanie Hall) that the work was about the importance of respecting differences. Temple had thought it was just a rhyme about a quirky old guy who lived on a boat; he had created it as an exaggerated portrait of his own brother.

Themes and Images

Often, writers plant images in their works that come to stand for a central idea or theme. For example, Natalie Babbitt's ***Tuck Everlasting*** begins:

> The first week of August hangs at the very top of summer, the top of the live-long year, like the highest seat of a Ferris wheel when it pauses in its turning. (p. 3)

Later in the book, Tuck seems to state the theme of the book explicitly, again using the image of the wheel:

> Not now. Your time's not now. But dying's part of the wheel, right there next to being born. You can't pick out the pieces you like and leave the rest. Being part of the whole thing, that's the blessing. (p. 63)

Thus, Natalie Babbitt uses the image of the wheel to stand for the inevitability of the life cycle: birth, growth, decline, and death.

Reading against the Grain

The explicit and implicit themes described above were the sort many authors might have agreed were present in the work. But if we define a theme, as the critic Rebecca Lukens does, as a source of "insight into people and how they think and feel" (Lukens, 1990), then there are other layers of themes that we must take into account. These are layers of themes that the authors may not have intended.

Almost every work of literature takes some stance toward the social order: toward the relative roles and attributes of males and females, old and young, rich and poor, and so on. Of course, those stances are not always explicit. A work of literature may overtly argue for the status quo, may implicitly take the status quo for granted, or may argue for a different social order.

Reading against the grain is a way to examine the unexamined, question the unquestioned, and hold up to scrutiny the unspoken assertions the text is making about the way lives are lived in society. Reading against the grain means asking, "Is this book a true portrait of how people behave? Is it a portrait of how they ought to behave?"

One fruitful way to read against the grain is to ask questions about differences in a text's portrayals of various characters:

- Males and females
- Old people and young people
- People of different social classes
- People of different races
- Americans and Third World residents
- People who are differently abled

Another way to read against the grain is to list the characteristic actions taken by different people in the story and then to match those actions with the rewards the people receive. An examination of the story "Beauty and the Beast" to determine the ways in which males and females acted and the rewards or punishments they received revealed that males were rewarded for going after what they wanted—although they had to learn the hard way to be respectful of all sorts of people. Women, though, were rewarded for not going after what they wanted—for focusing on serving others and being pure (Temple, 1993).

Another way to examine the unexamined is to ask: What would have been different if these events had happened to another character? For example, in Phyllis Reynolds Naylor's *Shiloh,* what if Marty's little sister, Dara Lynn, had found the dog instead of Marty? Would her parents have taken her devotion to the dog as seriously? Would she have had the freedom to keep it secretly and arrange to give it food? What does this tell the reader about the range of activity boys and girls are permitted? What if Marty's well-to-do friend David Howard had found Shiloh? Would he have gone to so much trouble not to confront Judd with his mistreatment of animals—or would he simply have called the authorities? Would he and his family have been so careful not to make an enemy of Judd? What does this tell us about the range of options open to people from different social classes?

A text is a piece of virtual experience that can be held up and examined from many angles. As the questions above make clear, readers can find interesting meanings to talk about in almost any text, whether an author intended those meanings or not.

THE STANCE OF THE IMPLIED READER

Besides the plot, the setting, the characters, and the theme, one more device is written into a work: the stance of the implied reader (Booth, 1961; Iser, 1974). The implied reader is the ideal interpreter of a work, as imagined by the author. The implied reader is not directly mentioned in the text, but his or her activity is essential to making the text "work." To say that events or characters in a text are exciting, funny, sad, suspenseful, heroic, blameworthy, or even understandable really means that the events or characters are perceived in those ways by some reader. Those qualities do not exist except as responses of a reader to a work. Therefore, in constructing a piece of literature, the writer must consciously or unconsciously keep an ideal reader in mind and arrange the details of the work in such a way as to evoke the desired responses from that reader.

As they begin to read a work, actual readers implicitly take the perspective of the implied reader and begin to have emotional and intellectual reactions to the work in ways the author has scripted for them. Or else they don't: If a book is too silly, too "hard," or too far outside their usual way of seeing things, the actual readers might not be willing or able to take the stance of the implied reader, and the book will not work for them.

There are at least three ways in which an actual reader can take the stance of the implied reader. The first is by identifying with characters. The second is by taking a moral perspective on the story. The third is by filling in gaps to make the story "work."

Identifying with Characters

When the reader discovers in **Shiloh** that Marty is eating only part of his supper and spiriting away the rest for his dog, the reader begins to feel—as Phyllis Naylor surely intended the reader to feel—Marty's uneasiness and regret over having to disappoint his mother. When the reader reads that Marty has sneaked up the hill after dinner one evening to feed Shiloh the smuggled food—and when suddenly his mother walks up and confronts him—the reader feels Marty's shock, his embarrassment, and finally his relief at having his secret shared. The reader has identified with Marty; the reader has participated in Marty's actions and reactions so that what happens to Marty happens vicariously to the reader.

Identification is a powerful way of learning from a text. It puts the reader into the shoes of a character, makes the reader suffer what the character suffers, face the dilemmas that character faces, and feel the consequences of the choices they (the character and, vicariously, the reader) have made.

Another striking example of the way an author fosters identification is found in Mildred Taylor's **Roll of Thunder, Hear My Cry.** In the very first scene of the book, readers are walking along in Depression-era Mississippi with the Logan children, following an unpaved road with steep banks on either side and skirting deep-red muddy pools. A school bus careens along behind them. But it doesn't stop to pick them up. Instead, the driver veers into a puddle and raises a wave of thick red ooze that douses their clothes, hair, and bodies. The driver grins wildly, and the young passengers laugh and jeer as the bus roars on. The children wring out their clothes and keep walking. The bus driver and the passengers are white. The Logan children—and, through identifying with them, the readers—are black.

For white students, the effect of reading that scene can be as transforming as Mildred Taylor intended it to be—but only if they accept the stance of the implied reader.

Taking the Intended Moral Stance

Another way in which the text influences readers is by inviting them to take a moral stance on the story—a stance the author has staked out as part of the construction of the work. As we noted above, for a story to work, the author has to be able to count on readers to believe that some goals are worthwhile, that some events are exciting, that some things people say are funny or sad or shocking. If readers adopt these views—if only for the duration of the reading—the book will come together for them. If they don't, it won't. So far, so good.

But no readers hold precisely the orientations asked of them by all books. They occasionally have to stretch to accept a certain point of view for the time during which they participate in a certain book. This stretching has consequences. We have all had the experience of being told a joke that was so sexist, racist, or otherwise mean-spirited that we had to decide whether to keep listening, scold the teller, or walk away. It's the times we didn't quite muster the energy to do either of the latter two that are most bothersome. If, for the sake of the humor, we temporarily agree to take the stance the joke requires of us, we may give a polite laugh, but feel compromised. That is because we have just agreed to live the life of a bigot, if only for two minutes.

Author Mildred Taylor challenges readers to take a moral stance early in *Roll of Thunder, Hear My Cry.* Following the muddy road incident, the Logan children dig the bottom out of one of the puddles, so that when the driver again tries to douse the children with mud, he breaks the axle of the bus. Will readers go along with that? If they do, they will close ranks with the Logans for the duration of the book. If they don't, they have an uneasy reading experience ahead of them.

Many of the late Roald Dahl's very popular books, such as *Danny the Champion of the World, Matilda, George's Marvelous Medicine,* and *Charlie and the Chocolate Factory* presented unlikeable characters with no redeeming features. Sometimes they were other children, sometimes teachers, sometimes relatives, sometimes parents. Each of these characters harmed the protagonist in some way, and each of them received a bad outcome of one sort or another. In the meantime, we readers seem to be invited to harbor ill feelings toward these characters and to delight in the bad things that befall them. For many readers, though—especially those who try to respond to objectionable people not with hatred but with understanding—Dahl's books raise moral challenges. The challenge is not in what Dahl says explicitly, but in the emotional stance he sets out for readers to take. Some readers are unwilling to take it.

Filling in the Gaps

The implied reader functions in one last way. A writer friend of ours says, "You have to trust your readers to figure some things out for themselves. They'll feel more like they're with you if you let them have the fun of figuring things out. Telling them too much spoils the fun."

Writers leave gaps in their work to be filled in by the reader's realizations. In Maurice Sendak's **Where the Wild Things Are,** for example, a visual clue is given early in the book as to where the Wild Things came from. (Can you find it?)

In Harry Allard and James Marshall's **Miss Nelson Is Missing!,** readers are never told where Miss Viola Swamp, the no-nonsense substitute teacher, came from—or, for that matter, where she went. But at the end of the story the reader sees Miss Nelson reading in bed, next to a closet with an ugly black dress hanging in it—just like the one Viola Swamp wore. And there's a box on the shelf marked in upside-down letters that spell "wig."

In **Shiloh,** Marty's mother tells him she's afraid that if she doesn't tell his father that Marty has been hiding the dog, his father might wonder what other secrets she has been keeping from him. She doesn't come right out and say that she's afraid of creating suspicions of marital infidelity in her husband's mind. But that Marty's mother is thinking about sexual fidelity is strongly suggested by the very next scene. As she's washing dishes, she sings along as a singer on the country music station croons:

> It's you I wanna come home to,
> It's you to bake my bread,
> It's you to light my fire,
> It's you to share my bed. (p. 85)

She blushes slightly when Marty enters the kitchen and hears her singing.

POINT OF VIEW

Point of view is the perspective from which the events in a story are perceived and narrated. The choices of point of view are first person (in which one of the characters in the work narrates the story, using the first-person pronoun "I") and third person (in which a narrator outside the story relates events that happened to those in it, using the third-person pronouns "she," "he" and "they"). When the author's knowledge of events shifts freely between different characters' points of view and the author describes events no one character could have known, he or she is writing from the point of view known as third-person omniscient ("all-knowing").

Stories in the First Person

Stories in the first person, such as **Shiloh,** tell the tale through a character's voice. Narration in the first person lends an immediacy to the action and lets readers know what the character is feeling. But it also limits readers to that character's perspective.

Stories in the Third Person

Most of the time, authors describe the action as happening to someone else—him, her, or them. This point of view is called third-person narration.

Writing in the third person gives the author a broader range of choices of what to show the reader. Writing in the third person doesn't excuse an author from keeping a unified point of view, though. Skilled writers narrate events as if from one character's point of view at a time. For example, in **Tuck Everlasting,** when Winnie and Tuck paddle out in a rowboat, Babbitt uses her narrator's voice to begin describing the scene, but soon she anchors the reader's perspective in Winnie's eyes:

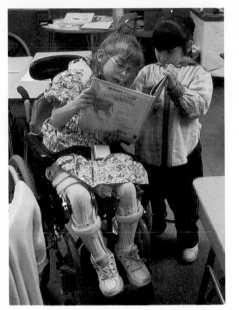

When a book makes you hear a distinctive voice in your head or when you find a passage so compelling you have to share it with a friend, chances are you're responding to an author's style.

The rowboat had drifted at last to the end of the pond, but now its bow bumped into the rotting branches of a fallen tree that thrust its thick fingers into the water. . . . The water slipped past . . . and farther down Winnie could see that it hurried into a curve, around a leaning willow, and disappeared. (pp. 62–63)

Then Tuck speaks and explains their predicament of being stuck:

That's what us Tucks are, Winnie. Stuck so's we can't move on. We ain't part of the wheel no more. Dropped off, Winnie. (p. 63)

And the reader gets an internal reaction from Winnie:

Winnie blinked, and all at once her mind was flooded with the realization of what he was saying. (p. 63)

Even though the story is narrated in the third person, there is only one perspective at a time. When Winnie is around, the perspective is hers. Readers see things through her eyes and experience her emotions. The fact that Winnie is the age of the likely readers of this book is no accident. Even though she is not the narrator, she is the readers' guide to the strange events of the story.

STYLE

Style is not what is said, but how it is said. When a book makes you hear a distinct voice in your head or when you find a passage so good you want to read it to a friend, chances are you're responding to style. Style is not the same thing as talent. A talented writer may write in different styles and may have a gift for matching a style with the content of each book she or he writes.

Some of the elements of style are words, images, metaphors, sounds, and voice. Let's look at each.

Words

The poet William Carlos Williams wrote, "Each object in nature and each idea has an exact name." Good writers behave as if that were true, and they strive to name experiences exactly. Mark Twain wrote, "The difference between the right word, and almost the right word, is the difference between the lightning bug and the lightning."

But what makes a word "right"? Good word choices are concrete and vivid—they show, rather than sum up and judge. Or if they sum up and judge, they do so exactly. Good words create fresh images. Good writing crackles with insight.

Writing can be sparse or rich, as writers use few words or many to create impressions. Rich writing was more common in the nineteenth century and early in the twentieth. Note this passage from Kenneth Grahame's immortal *The Wind in the Willows:*

Never in his life had he seen a river before—this sleek, sinuous, full-bodied animal, chasing and chuckling, gripping things with a gurgle and leaving them with a laugh, to fling itself on fresh playmates that shook themselves free, and were caught and held again. All was

Illustration 2.9
Narrated in the voice of a twelve-year-old refugee, *Grab Hands and Run* uses simple syntax and vocabulary that nonetheless describe moving scenes and powerful events. (A cover from *Grab Hands and Run* by Frances Temple. Illustration copyright © 1993 by Frances Nolting Temple. Published by Orchard Books, an imprint of Scholastic Inc. Reprinted by permission.)

a-shake and a-shiver—glints and gleams and sparkles, rustle and swirl, chatter and bubble. (pp. 3–4)

Grahame's language consists of long sentences awash with colorful adjectives, images, and metaphors.

Spare writing can also be powerful. Frances Temple told *Grab Hands and Run* in the voice of twelve-year-old Felipe, and so the words she chose are simple and direct. Here is a scene from a parsonage in Guatemala, where refugees from the civil war in El Salvador find momentary protection:

Another little girl comes in, a child with big dark eyes, younger than Romy. Father Ramon opens his arms to her and speaks gently, but at the sight of him she begins to scream and fastens herself around the leg of a table. Her screams are terrible, and no one can stop them.

Father Ramon looks so upset that I follow him into the courtyard. "Why does she scream, Padre?" I ask him. "Can I help?"

"Ask the soldiers why she screams, son," says Father Ramon. I have never heard anyone sound so sad. (p. 62)

Word choice doesn't depend on a fancy vocabulary—just on exact descriptions.

Images

Imagery is the art of making readers experience details as if through their five senses. Alexander Carmichael had a good phrase for it: "bringing the different characters before the mind as clearly as the sculptor brings the figure before the eye" (quoted in Briggs, 1977, p. 10). That's the art of imagery—whether it is characters, settings, or actions that are illuminated for the mind's eye. The trick might be no more than mentioning sensory details: The writer mentions, however offhandedly, how things smelled, felt, tasted, sounded, and looked. But the effect is of living the moments described, rather than hearing a summary of them. Here is a moment from *Tuck Everlasting*:

Shifting his position, he turned his attention to a little pile of pebbles next to him. As Winnie watched, scarcely breathing, he moved the pile carefully to one side, pebble by pebble. Beneath the pile, the ground was shiny wet. The boy lifted a final stone and Winnie saw a low spurt of water, arching up and returning, like a fountain, into the ground. He bent and put his lips to the spurt, drinking noiselessly, and then he sat up again and drew his shirt sleeve across his mouth. As he did this, he turned his face in her direction—and their eyes met. (p. 26)

Read that passage again, and see how many senses it appeals to. You feel the shifts of posture in your body and the quiet breathing in your chest. You relish the many visual images—the shiny wet ground, the spurt of water arching and returning. You hear the silence of the stealthy motions. You almost taste the water and feel the rough swipe of the shirt sleeve across your lips. With her skillful use of imagery, Babbitt has not so much described this scene as enacted it.

Metaphors

To use a metaphor is to describe one thing in terms of something else. Technically, there is a distinction between a simile, which is an overt comparison that says "X is like Y"; a true metaphor, which talks about X as if it were Y; and personification, which ascribes human features, actions, or motives to something that isn't human.

Here is *Tuck Everlasting* again:

> The road that led to Treegap had been trod out long before by a herd of cows who were, to say the least, relaxed. It wandered along in curves and easy angles, swayed off and up in a pleasant tangent to the top of a small hill, ambled down again between fringes of bee-hung clover, and then cut sidewise across a meadow. (p. 5)

This isn't quite personification: The road is described as if it were not a person, but a cow—wandering, swaying, and ambling. To describe the road this way is to enliven the writing with unobtrusive magic.

Sounds

Aristotle advised writers to get the sounds of language and the sense would take care of itself. In the voice of a good prose writer, the sounds of language speak almost as beautifully as they do in poetry.

You might think of poetry as rhyme and rhythm, but to catch the poetry of prose, you must widen your scope. Prose doesn't often rhyme, but its sounds speak to each other through consonance (a run of similar consonant sounds) and assonance (a run of similar vowel sounds). Prose doesn't scan into this meter or that, but there is a rhythm to the flow of the words: a sing-song cadence, a pell-mell dash, or a chant and refrain.

Listen to the sounds from a page of Patricia MacLachlan's prose text from her picture book *What You Know First:*

> We'll sleep in the hay with our eyes open
> Until they drop shut.
> Listening
>   to the rain on the tin roof
>   the wind rattling the windows
> Waking when the rooster crows
> In sunlight. (n. pag.)

Do you hear the r's and the w's echoing each other? That is consonance. Do you hear the words that begin with vowels, too ("eyes open"), as well as the similar vowel sounds ("windows" and "crows") speaking to each other? Both are examples of assonance. Read the passage aloud and listen for the rhythm. Hear the flow of the words until the abrupt "drop shut." See how those choppy words break the flow, just as closed eyes signal that the flow of consciousness has been interrupted by sleep.

For more on rhythm, here is an excerpt from Bruce Brooks's *The Moves Make the Man:*

> . . . cradling the ball and at the last minute pulling my left hand away like Oscar Robertson and snapping that lubricated right wrist and knowing, feeling it right straight through from the tips of the fingers that had let fly the ball and touched it all the way to the last, straight down the front edge of my body to my toes just before they hit the ground again, that the shot was true, feeling the swish and tickle of the net cords rushing quick down my nerves, and landing square and jaunty in time to watch, along with everybody else, as the ball popped

through the net without a single bit of deceit, so clean it kicked the bottom of the cords back up and looped them over the rim, which is called a bottoms up and means you shot it perfect and some people even count them three points in street games. (p. 70)

That is one long sentence! The rhythm is the breathless tumble of an athlete's thoughts, which find expression in the equally breathless patter of sportscasters.

Another sound device in Brooks's passage is onomatopoeia—using the sound of words themselves to convey a sound impression. Brooks does this in the phrase "feeling the swish and tickle of the net cords rushing quick down my nerves."

Voice

Voice in literature has to do with the way the author comes across—from folksy to impersonal, from bold to timid, from expert to unreliable. Especially if the author writes in the first person, the voice of the piece may involve the narrator's dialect, personality, and slant on the world. Listen to Lucille Clifton's narrator in *Three Wishes:*

My name is Zenobia, after somebody in the Bible. My name is Zenobia and everybody call me Nobie. Everybody but Victor. He call me Lena, after Lena Horne, and when I get grown I'm goin' to Hollywood and sing in the movies and Victorius is gonna go with me 'cause he's my best friend. That's his real name. (p. 1)

But even if a book is written in the third person, the narrator can come across as someone to be reckoned with. Natalie Babbitt begins *Tuck Everlasting* with these words:

The first week of August hangs at the very top of summer, the top of the live-long year, like the highest seat of a Ferris wheel when it pauses in its turning. The weeks that come before only climb from balmy spring, and those that follow drop to the chill of autumn, but the first week of August is motionless, and hot. It is curiously silent, too, with blank white dawns and glaring noons, and sunsets smeared with too much color. Often at night there is lightning, but it quivers all alone. There is no thunder, no relieving rain. These are strange and breathless days, the dog days when people are led to do things they are sure to feel sorry for after. (p. 3)

Listen to the tone she takes. Authoritative, knowledgeable, impersonal—maybe even a little bossy. (The weather's not like that where *we* live.) This is the voice of a storyteller who is fully in charge.

Now listen to Roald Dahl's first words in *Matilda:*

It's a funny thing about mothers and fathers. Even when their own child is the most disgusting little blister you could ever imagine, they still think that he or she is wonderful.

Some parents go further. They become so blinded by adoration they manage to convince themselves their child has qualities of genius.

Well, there is nothing very wrong with all this. It's the way of the world. It is only when the parents begin telling us about the brilliance of their own revolting offspring, that we start shouting, "Bring us a basin! We're going to be sick!" (p. 7)

A good informational book—like good literature of any genre—has the capacity to engage young readers through humor, vivid imagery, and engaging style, while making accurate information readily accessible to them.

Dahl's voice is outrageous, spicy, opinionated—but likely to be a lot of fun. Dahl seems to be out to undermine his own narrator's authority. Likely as not, children will feel compelled to talk back to him.

TEACHING IDEAS

Exploring Folktale Settings. How many folktales do children know with forests in them? Make a chart in which children describe things that happen in forests, the kinds of creatures the characters encounter, and the kinds of challenges they face. Later, during a writing workshop, children might want to write stories in which transforming things happen to characters in a forest.

Using Plot Structure to Guide Predictions. Choose a story to read aloud to a group of students. Write the parts of the story that conform to the plot structure described on page 40 (complication, rising action, climax, resolution, and denouement) on separate pieces of tagboard. Before reading the story, ask the students to arrange the parts of the story in the order in which they think events might unfold. Then read the story. Finally, ask the students to go back and check the accuracy of their predictions.

Plotting the Story Journey. Students can make a kind of graph to plot a story journey. Drawing a line from left to right across a chart, they can make the line go up for events when morale is high and down for events when morale is low. Above the line, they can write in what happened. Below the line, they can write in how a character felt or what she or he learned.

Discussing the Implied Reader. Introduce the idea of the implied reader (though not necessarily the term). After students have read or heard a simple story, such as "Jack and the Beanstalk," ask them, "Did you feel closer to one character out of all the characters in this story? If so, which character and why? Did you get the feeling the author wanted you to feel closer to and want to be more like one character? What was it about the way the story was written that made you feel closer to that character?"

More on the Implied Reader. To pursue children's growing awareness of the dynamics of the implied reader, ask them, "Were there times in the story when you felt that you really liked what was going on? When? What did you especially like about these times? Were there times in the story when you didn't especially like what was going on? Were there things in the story that you thought maybe the author felt were okay, but you didn't?"

EXPERIENCES FOR YOUR LEARNING

1. Think of two different characters in a book you've recently read—say, *The Gold Coin.* Prepare a Venn diagram, writing the features of personality and temperament the characters have in common in the overlapping area and those that separate them in the other parts of each circle. Compare your diagram with those of your classmates.

2. Make three columns on a piece of paper. In the left-hand column, list three male and three female characters in *Shiloh.* In the middle column, write two or three major actions these people took in the book. In the right-hand column, list the rewards or punishments they received at the end. Discuss these results. Can you formulate a statement that explains the pattern of who is rewarded and who is not in the story?

3. Choose a short but poignant scene from *Tuck Everlasting.* (Chapter 12 will work nicely.) Think through the scene from a different character's point of view—visualize the scene, for example, from Tuck's point of view rather than Winnie's. Which of Tuck's concerns come to the surface that do not in the scene as written? How does Winnie appear?

RECOMMENDED BOOKS

* indicates a picture book; *I* indicates interest level (P = preschool, YA = young adult)

Books with Striking Settings

Avi. *The True Confessions of Charlotte Doyle.* Orchard, 1990. Life on an eighteenth-century merchant ship, with Charlotte living "before the mast." (**I:** 11–YA)

Cameron, Ann. *The Most Beautiful Place in the World.* Knopf, 1988. What it's like to live as a peasant child in a Guatemalan village. (**I:** 8–10)

Cushman, Karen. *Catherine Called Birdy.* Clarion, 1994. The diary of a fourteen-year-old re-creates thirteenth-century English life. (**I:** 11–YA)

Naylor, Phyllis Reynolds. *Shiloh.* Atheneum, 1990. Marty, an Appalachian mountain boy, shelters a runaway beagle named Shiloh from its cruel and abusive owner. (**I:** 8–11)

Paulsen, Gary. *Hatchet.* Bradbury, 1987. The Canadian wilderness is the setting in which Paulsen's character struggles to survive. (**I:** 11–YA)

Rowling, J. K. *Harry Potter and the Sorcerer's Stone.* Scholastic, 1997. Hogwarts School, where Harry goes to study wizardry, is full of unending surprises, from the doors that must be tickled to be opened to the portraits that walk off the job, to the ghosts who drift through at odd times. (**I:** 9–14)

Soto, Gary. *Baseball in April and Other Stories.* Harcourt, 1990. Young life among mostly poor Mexican Americans in contemporary Fresno, California. (**I:** 11–YA)

Taylor, Mildred D. *Roll of Thunder, Hear My Cry.* Dial, 1976. The Logan family endures racism in Mississippi in the 1930s. (**I:** 11–YA)

*Williams, Sherley A. *Working Cotton.* Illustrated by Carole Byard. Harcourt, 1992. Spreads of cotton rows and the blank eyes of the young narrator reveal the dawn-to-dusk life of pickers in a California cotton field. (**I:** 5–9)

Books with Interesting Characterization

*Ada, Alma Flor. *The Gold Coin.* Macmillan, 1991. In this original story with folktale elements, the young thief Juan pursues Doña Josepha through the countryside to rob her of her gold coin but learns trust and generosity along the way. (**I:** 9–11)

Cleary, Beverly. *Dear Mr. Henshaw.* Morrow, 1983. Leigh Botts, the son of divorced parents, is portrayed through his correspondence with a children's author. (I: 9–11)

———. *Ramona Quimby, Age 8*. Morrow, 1981. Any of Cleary's Ramona books are examples of excellent characterization. (I: 8–10)

*Cooney, Barbara. *Miss Rumphius*. Viking, 1982. A remarkable turn-of-the-century New England lady comes to life through the eyes of a young friend. (I: 5–9)

Cushman, Karen. *The Midwife's Apprentice*. Clarion, 1995. Alyce, a homeless waif taken in by a midwife, is given an opportunity to find an identity and make a place for herself in medieval England. (I: 11–YA)

Dahl, Roald. *The BFG*. Farrar, 1982. The Big Friendly Giant comes across as a real person in this imaginative story. (I: 9–12)

———. *Danny the Champion of the World*. Farrar, 1982. Danny's is perhaps the most remarkable of fathers. (I: 9–12)

Gardiner, John Reynolds. *Stone Fox*. Illustrated by Marcia Sewall. Crowell, 1980. When his grandfather is disabled, Willy tries to win money by competing in a dogsled race against a legendary trail driver named Stone Fox. (I: 9–12)

Hamilton, Virginia. *M. C. Higgins the Great*. Simon & Schuster, 1974. A dreamy rural African American hero emerges from the pages of this Newbery Medal–winning novel. (I: 11–YA)

*Houston, Gloria. *My Great-Aunt Arizona*. Illustrated by Susan Condie Lamb. Harper, 1992. A portrait of a remarkable Appalachian schoolteacher at the turn of the century. (I: 6–10)

MacLachlan, Patricia. *Sarah, Plain and Tall*. Harper, 1985. The story of the wooing of a mail-order bride from Maine by a lonely prairie family. (I: 8–12)

Myers, Walter Dean. *The Mouse Rap*. HarperCollins, 1990. The life and times of a thirteen-year-old resident of Harlem. (I: 9–12)

Paterson, Katherine. *The Great Gilly Hopkins*. HarperCollins, 1978. A veteran of many foster homes comes to life in this novel. (I: 9–12)

*Say, Allen. *Grandfather's Journey*. Houghton Mifflin, 1993. The story of a young man's immigration to the United States from Japan, how he fared, and why he went back. (I: 5–10)

Woodson, Jacqueline. *Last Summer with Maizon*. Delacorte, 1992. Inside the thoughts of a contemporary African American girl from the city. (I: 12–YA)

Books with Interesting Plots

Babbitt, Natalie. *Tuck Everlasting*. Farrar, 1975. Young Winnie encounters and befriends members of the Tuck family, who have been endowed with the burdensome gift of everlasting life. (I: 10–YA)

*Barrett, Judi. *Cloudy with a Chance of Meatballs*. Illustrated by Ron Barrett. Atheneum, 1978. Life is easy in the town of Chew and Swallow, where food comes from the sky—until the weather takes a turn for the worse. (I: 7–10)

Bunting, Eve. *The Hideout*. Harcourt, 1991. Andy runs away from home and finds the key to a luxurious suite in a grand hotel. What he thinks is a lucky break turns out to be a terrifying experience. (I: 8–12)

Cleary, Beverly. *Ramona and Her Father*. Morrow, 1978. The problem of the father's unemployment gives rise to smaller problems, whetting the reader's curiosity for the long term and the short term. (I: 7–10)

Coatsworth, Elizabeth. *The Cat Who Went to Heaven*. Illustrated by Lynd Ward. Collier/Macmillan, 1958. A magical cat teaches an impoverished painter to be generous and patient. (I: 10–12)

Cole, Brock. *The Goats*. Farrar, 1990. When they are left naked on a deserted island by their fellow campers, two preadolescents learn to stand up for themselves. (I: 11–YA)

*dePaola, Tomie. *Strega Nona*. Simon & Schuster, 1979. The story of the witch Strega Nona and the fool Big Anthony has a straightforward plot, with an interesting contrast of characters. (I: 5–8)

Hahn, Mary Downing. *Stepping on the Cracks*. Clarion, 1991. In the midst of World War II, Elizabeth and her best friend discover a conscientious objector living in the woods near their home. (I: 11–12)

Hamilton, Virginia. *The House of Dies Drear*. Simon & Schuster, 1968. As we noted in this chapter, this African American historical mystery novel is a good example of a surface story slowly revealing an underlying story. (I: 11–13)

Hite, Sid. *An Even Break*. Holt, 1995. When twelve-year-old Frisk gets a summer job managing a pool for kids age 15 and up, he has to work hard to prove he's the right person for the job. (I: 10–13)

Kellogg, Steven. *Much Bigger than Martin*. Dial, 1976. More than anything a boy wants to be as big as his older brother so he won't be left out of activities. (I: 5–8)

Paulsen, Gary. *The Voyage of the Frog*. Orchard, 1989. A survival story of a perilous ocean crossing, in which a young boy proves what he's made of. (I: 11–YA)

Rowling, J. K. *Harry Potter and the Chamber of Secrets*. Scholastic, 1998. Harry and his friends Ron and Hermione must unearth the secret of the dangerous force that threatens "mudbloods," wizards who are descended from pure wizard lineage. (I: 9–adult)

Sachar, Louis. *Holes*. Farrar, Straus, and Giroux, 1998. Newbery Award–winning tale of young Stanley Yelnats's arduous days digging holes in the dry lake bottom at a reformatory where the digging is said to be for penitence, but there may be another purpose, connected to a treasure. (I: 9–12)

*Steig, William. *The Amazing Bone*. Farrar, 1976. This book, like Steig's *Sylvester and the Magic Pebble*, *Caleb and Kate,* and *Roland, the Minstrel Pig,* has a straightforward plot that follows the pattern described in this chapter: conflict, rising action, climax, resolution, denouement. (I: 5–10)

Temple, Frances. *Grab Hands and Run*. Orchard, 1993. A journey story about the flight of a Salvadoran refugee family from their homeland through the United States to Canada. (I: 10–13)

Turner, Megan Whelan. *The Thief*. Greenwillow, 1996. A Newberry Honor Book, in which Gen, a thief and a prisoner for life, is promised his freedom if he will steal a precious jewel for the king's magus. (I: 9–12)

Voigt, Cynthia. *The Homecoming*. Atheneum, 1983. Determined to keep her family together after her mother disappears, Dicey leads her siblings on a secret journey to find a grandmother they have never known. (I: 12–YA)

Yarbrough, Camille. *The Shimmershine Queens*. Putnam, 1989. Angie and her best friend struggle to maintain pride and self-respect in the midst of negative peer pressure. (I: 11–12)

Books with Interesting Themes

Ada, Alma Flor. *My Name Is Maria Isabel*. Atheneum, 1993. What it's like to come into an urban American school from another place, where people speak another language. (I: 8–11)

*Barrett, Joyce Durham. *Willy's Not the Hugging Kind*. Illustrated by Pat Cummings. HarperCollins, 1989. Willie decides he's too big for hugs, but he soon discovers how much he misses them. (I: 5–7)

*Bunting, Eve. *A Day's Work*. Illustrated by Ron Himler. Clarion, 1994. Francisco learns a lesson about honesty and pride from his grandfather. (I: 6–8)

*Clifton, Lucille. *Everett Anderson's Goodbye*. Illustrated by Ann Grifalconi. Holt, 1983. A boy goes through the grieving process after his father dies. (I: 4–7)

*———. *Everett Anderson's Nine Month Long*. Illustrated by Ann Grifalconi. Holt, 1978. While Everett Anderson waits for a new baby to be born, he works out the wrinkles in his relationship with his new stepfather. (I: 4–7)

Demi. *The Empty Pot*. Holt, 1990. A little boy is rewarded for his honesty. (I: 5–8)

*dePaola, Tomie. *The Legend of the Bluebonnet*. Putnam, 1983. A young girl sacrifices her most precious possession to save her people from drought. (I: 5–8)

*de Regniers, Beatrice Schenk. *May I Bring a Friend?* Illustrated by Beni Montresor. Atheneum, 1980. When the king and queen invite a little boy to tea, he brings a host of animal friends and then reciprocates by inviting the king and queen to the zoo for tea. (I: 4–6)

*Hesse, Karen. *Lester's Dog*. Illustrated by Nancy Carpenter. Crown, 1993. More than anything, a boy fears Lester's vicious dog, but his loyalty to his deaf friends helps him triumph over his fear. (I: 4–7)

*Hoffman, Mary. *Amazing Grace*. Illustrated by Caroline Binch. Dial, 1991. Grace's grandmother helps her realize she can do anything she wants to. (I: 5–9)

MacLachlan, Patricia. *Journey*. Delacorte, 1991. Having been deserted by his mother and father, Journey sets out to discover his past and learns that things can be good enough without being perfect. (I: 10–12)

*Ness, Evaline. *Sam, Bangs and Moonshine*. Holt, 1966. In an important step in growing up, Sam discovers that imagination cannot be allowed to get in the way of responsibility. (I: 6–10)

*Rodanas, Kristina. *The Dragonfly's Tale*. Clarion, 1992. A Zuñi legend with a conservationist theme. Most folktales and legends strongly emphasize themes. (I: 6–10)

Talbert, Marc. *A Sunburned Prayer*. Simon & Schuster, 1995. Eloy determines to go alone on a pilgrimage to save his grandmother, who is dying of cancer. (I: 10–12)

Thesman, Jean. *Rachel Chance*. Houghton Mifflin, 1990. When Rachel's baby brother is kidnapped by a charismatic preacher, Rachel sets out to find him. (I: 11–YA)

*Williams, Vera B. *A Chair for My Mother*. Mulberry, 1982. A little girl and her family pull together to make a new home when theirs is destroyed by fire. (I: 6–10)

RESOURCES

Egoff, Sheila, G. T. Stubbs, and L. F. Ashley. *Only Connect: Readings on Children's Literature.* 2nd ed. Oxford University Press, 1980.

Frye, Northrop. *The Educated Imagination.* Indiana University Press, 1964.

Hearne, Betsy, and Marilyn Kaye. *Celebrating Children's Literature.* Lothrop, Lee, & Shepard, 1981.

Hunt, Peter. *Children's Literature: The Development of Criticism.* Routledge, 1990.

Lukens, Rebecca. *A Critical Handbook of Children's Literature.* 4th ed. HarperCollins, 1990.

May, Jill. *Children's Literature and Critical Theory.* Oxford University Press, 1995.

Nodleman, Perry, ed. *Touchstones: Reflections on the Best in Children's Literature.* Children's Literature Association, 1985.

Sale, Roger. *Fairy Tales and After: Snow White to E. B. White.* Harvard University Press, 1978.

Scholes, Robert. *Structuralism in Literature.* Yale University Press, 1974.

Temple, Charles, and Patrick Collins, eds. *Stories and Readers.* Christopher-Gordon, 1992.

REFERENCES

Allard, Harry. *Miss Nelson Is Missing!* Illustrated by James Marshall. Houghton Mifflin, 1977.

Barthes, Roland. *S/Z.* Trans. Richard Miller. Hill & Wang, 1974.

Bernays, Anne, and Pamela Painter. *Guide for Fiction Writers.* HarperCollins, 1995.

Booth, Wayne. *The Rhetoric of Fiction.* University of Chicago Press, 1961.

Briggs, Katherine. *British Folktales.* Pantheon, 1977.

Brooks, Bruce. *The Moves Make the Man.* HarperCollins, 1984.

Clifton, Lucille. *The Three Wishes.* Yearling, 1994.

Creech, Sharon. *Walk Two Moons.* HarperCollins, 1994.

Dahl, Roald. *Charlie and the Chocolate Factory.* Knopf, 1985.

———. *George's Marvelous Medicine.* Knopf, 1982.

———. *Matilda.* Viking, 1988.

Erikson, Erik H. *Identity: Youth and Crisis.* Norton, 1968.

George, Jean Craighead. *Julie of the Wolves.* HarperCollins, 1974.

Grahame, Kenneth. *The Wind in the Willows.* Scribner's, 1908/1953.

Grimm, Jacob, and Wilhelm Grimm. *The Complete Grimms' Fairy Tales.* Pantheon, 1972.

Iser, Wolfgang. *The Implied Reader: Patterns of Communication in Prose Fiction from Bunyan to Beckett.* Johns Hopkins University Press, 1974.

Kermode, Frank. *The Sense of an Ending.* University of Chicago Press, 1975.

Lowry, Lois. *The Giver.* Houghton Mifflin, 1993.

Luenn, Nancy. *Nessa's Fish.* Illustrated by Neil Waldman. Atheneum, 1990.

Lukens, Rebecca. *A Critical Handbook to Children's Literature.* 4th ed. HarperCollins, 1990.

MacLachlan, Patricia. *What You Know First.* Illustrated by Barry Moser. HarperCollins, 1995.

O'Dell, Scott. *Island of the Blue Dolphins.* Houghton Mifflin, 1960.

Paterson, Katherine. *The Bridge to Terabithia.* HarperCollins, 1978.

———. *Lyddie.* Lodestar, 1991.

Rylant, Cynthia. *Missing May.* Orchard, 1992.

Sendak, Maurice. *Where the Wild Things Are.* Harper & Row, 1963.

Souriau, Etienne. *Les Deux Cent Milles Situations Dramatiques.* Flammarion, 1955.

Speare, Elizabeth George. *The Witch of Blackbird Pond.* Houghton Mifflin, 1958.

Spinelli, Jerry. *Maniac Magee.* Little, Brown, 1990.

Steig, William. *Spinky Sulks.* Sunburst, 1991.

Temple, Charles. *Shanty Boat.* Illustrated by Melanie Hall. Houghton Mifflin, 1993a.

———. "'What If Beauty Had Been Ugly?' Reading against the Grain of Gender Bias in Children's Books." *Language Arts* 70 (February 1993b): 89–93.

Temple, Frances. Personal communication. 1994a.

———. *The Ramsey Scallop.* Orchard, 1994b.

Todorov, Tzvetan. *The Fantastic: A Structural Approach to a Literary Genre.* Translated by Richard Howard. Case Western Reserve, 1973.

Turnbull, Colin. *The Human Cycle.* HarperCollins, 1982.

Walker, Mildred Pitts. *Justin and the Best Biscuits in the World.* Lothrop, Lee, and Shepard, 1988.

3 The Child Reader Responds to Literature

In literature class Mr. Joseph was reading a book to us, a chapter at a time. It was called *The Year in San Fernando*, and it was the only thing that could make Marlon Peters and his gang pay attention. In fact, whenever it was time for *The Year in San Fernando*, Marlon Peters and Naushad Ali would pick up their chairs and move to the front of the class. There they sat, as still as statues, listening. If anyone made the slightest noise, the two of them would turn and glare at that person. But nobody would willfully disturb Mr. Joseph when he was reading this story. The whole class was captivated. It was a story about us, and our world! We were surprised, and thrilled, that the ordinary, everyday things we took part in could find their way into a story! It meant that we were real, and had weight, like the people in stories.

from **For the Life of Laetitia**
by Merle Hodge

Teachers long to see the kind of reader involvement in books that author Merle Hodge describes in **For the Life of Laetitia.** Reading is commonly described as a reader/text interaction, and teachers who understand both the readers (the children who will be enthusiastically reading and listening to literature) and the texts (children's literature) are likely to be in a good position to nurture this type of engagement. Although the major thrust of this book is learning about the literature you'll be channeling into the hands of children, this chapter ventures into different territory. Here we consider what happens when readers read literature, how reading literature may differ from other types of reading, and what research reveals about how children in particular respond to literature.

READER RESPONSE THEORY

When readers read literature, their personal memories, feelings, and thought associations may be evoked by the text—whether or not the author anticipated those reactions (and how would you know?). When we look at readers' personal responses during an encounter with a piece of literature, we are viewing reading as a transaction. This perspective on reading is also known as reader response theory.

In recent years, reader response theory, which was first articulated by Louise Rosenblatt in 1938, has been having a huge impact in elementary classrooms. To understand reader response theory, you might find it helpful to reflect on your own reading experiences. Think of a story you have really gotten into and try to describe what that experience was like. Perhaps you became so wrapped up in the book that you flew from page to page to discover how the twists and turns of the story line would unfold, and even though it was 2:00 A.M., you simply could not stop reading. Maybe it was a different sort of book, one in which you found so much to ponder that you spent as much time reflecting and wondering as reading. Or perhaps it was a book in which a character's plight moved you to tears. Or was it a book whose language was so evocative that you read it aloud just to savor the author's words? When a person becomes immersed in reading a piece of literature, she or he is engaged in what Louise

Rosenblatt (1993) calls *aesthetic reading*. Rosenblatt describes the experience this way:

> In aesthetic reading . . . we draw on our reservoir of past experience with people and the world, our past inner linkage of words and things, our past encounters with spoken or written text. We listen to the sound of the words in the inner ear; we lend our sensations, our emotions, our sense of being alive, to the new experiences which, we feel, correspond to the text. We participate in the story, we identify with the characters, we share their conflicts and their feeling. (p. 9)

According to Rosenblatt, aesthetic reading lies at one end of a reading continuum, while what she has called *efferent reading* lies at the other end. When reading efferently, readers are intent on gaining information through their reading—on finding out when to take their medicine, how to put the bookshelves together, or what position a candidate takes on immigration. Readers who pick up particular texts move more toward one end or the other of the reading continuum, depending on their purposes for reading. The reader's role is of great importance in aesthetic reading, and because readers bring their own experiences, feelings, and perspectives to a text, the literary experience can be very personal. This is not to say, however, that the text is unimportant. Though it is readers who construct literary meaning, drawing on both their own experiences and the text itself, Rosenblatt has described the text as a blueprint that guides the reader.

Snuggled up in a favorite reading spot, a child can easily become lost in a good book.

Children can become totally caught up in the world of a story. However, in school settings, this won't happen if children are asked to read literature only for information—to answer comprehension questions or to find five new words in the story. So if teachers are to succeed in nurturing committed, lifelong readers, it is essential that children discover the joys of reading literature. As you prepare to help students read literature aesthetically, we think you will find it helpful to understand more about the reader/text transaction and how children respond to literature.

Richard Beach (1993) identifies five different perspectives on the reader/text transaction: experiential, developmental, social, cultural, and textual. Each represents a different window onto the same response process. See Table 3.1 for a definition of each perspective.

EXPERIENTIAL PERSPECTIVE ON READER RESPONSE

People who look at literary reading from an experiential perspective emphasize the reader in the reader/text transaction. Judith Langer (1990), a reading response theorist, has described aesthetic reading from such a perspective. "Envisionment building" is the term that Langer uses to describe literary meaning making. An envisionment is what a reader understands about a story, and as readers move through stories, their understanding grows and sometimes even changes dramatically. For example, one preservice teacher reported that she initially envisioned Jerry Spinelli's **Maniac Magee** as a book about homelessness, but as she read on, she began to envision it as being about racial divisiveness and conflict.

Table 3.1 Five Perspectives on Reader Response

Perspective	Definition
Experiential	A perspective that emphasizes the role of the reader's personal experiences and feelings in shaping response
Developmental	A perspective that recognizes that children in different stages of cognitive, moral, and social development respond to literature differently
Social	A perspective that recognizes that a reader's literary transaction can be shaped by the responses of other readers
Cultural	A perspective that recognizes that reader's cultural values, attitudes, and assumptions shape their transactions with texts
Textual	A perspective that recognizes that readers' responses are influenced by their knowledge of narrative conventions, literary elements, genre conventions, and other aspects of a text

Langer's Model of Literary Meaning Making

According to Langer, in creating their envisionments, readers may assume any one of four different stances (or different relationships with a text) as they read:

- *Being out and stepping in:* Readers make their initial contact with a book.

- *Being in and moving through:* Readers build a personal envisionment.

- *Being in and stepping out:* Readers reflect on the way(s) in which a book relates to their own life or the lives of others.

- *Stepping out and objectifying the experience:* Readers reflect on the story as a crafted object.

Being Out and Stepping In. Readers assume the stance of being out and stepping in as they make their initial contact with a book. They try to get enough information about the genre, setting, characters, and story line to begin to build an envisionment. They might even start this process before reading the first page as they look at the dust jacket or book cover; and the process continues as they begin reading the story and make the acquaintance of characters and discover the basic story situation. For example, a reader picking up Louis Sachar's **Holes** might first note that the dust jacket shows a scene of what appears to be a crater-pocked surface of a distant planet. Then, in the first chapter, the reader makes a number of surprising discoveries: The story is set not in space but at Camp Green Lake, a place described as a wasteland in Texas. Camp Green Lake is run not by a camp director but by a warden, and the campers at Camp Green Lake spend their time digging holes, not playing tennis or riding horses. At this point, readers are likely to have more questions than answers and consequently may still feel very much outside the story. In fact, at the beginning of Chapter 2, the narrator

Young children begin to learn how to engage in "envision building" by participating in storybook reading with mature readers.

poses the very question readers are likely to be asking at this point:

Why would anyone go to Camp Green Lake?

The reader soon discovers the answer: Camp Green Lake isn't a summer camp at all. It is a juvenile detention center. And with that information revealed, readers are likely to make their entry into *Holes.*

Being In and Moving Through. When readers are in and moving through, they become absorbed in the story world, using text information and their own store of information to build their envisionment. Readers who are in and moving through try to understand why characters behave as they do, why events are unfolding as they are, and what is likely to happen. Readers who are caught up in *Holes* are likely to find themselves turning pages to try to discover why the warden requires each boy to dig a five-foot hole every day. As the story unfolds and the protagonist, Stanley Yelnats, escapes into the dry lake bed, readers read on to discover how—or if—Stanley will survive his ordeal.

Being In and Stepping Out. When they are in and stepping out, readers use the text as a basis for reflecting on their own lives, on the lives of others, or even on the human experience. When readers of *Holes* discuss issues related to the juvenile justice system, they are stepping out of the story world. Even young children can step out of story worlds to reflect on how a story relates to their own experiences or to those of others. This is how a second-grader, Daniel, responded when his teacher read Cynthia Rylant's *This Year's Garden:* "I liked this story because it was very good. I felt like I was doing the work in my garden. Every year I help my granddad garden."

Stepping Out and Objectifying the Experience. Langer's final stance, stepping out and objectifying the experience, is one in which readers distance themselves from the text world and talk about the work as a crafted object,

Illustration 3.1
This Year's Garden relates the joys of planting and caring for a garden. (*This Year's Garden* by Cynthia Rylant, pictures by Mary Szilagyi. Text copyright © 1987 by Cynthia Rylant. Illustrations copyright © 1987 by Mary Szilagyi. Used with permission of Aladdin Paperbacks for Young Readers, an imprint of Simon & Schuster Children's Publishing.)

Illustration 3.2

Liza Lou and the Yeller Belly Swamp features a spunky heroine who uses her wits to survive the dangers that await her in the swamp. (*Liza Lou and the Yeller Belly Swamp* by Mercer Mayer. Copyright © 1976 by Mercer Mayer. Used with permission of Aladdin Paperbacks for Young Readers, an imprint of Simon & Schuster Children's Publishing.)

about other texts the story reminds them of, or about their own responses to the story. The reader who remarked on the clever way Louis Sachar intertwined three story lines was stepping out of *Holes* to reflect on the way in which the author structured his work. So was the second-grader who interrupted her teacher's reading of Mercer Mayer's *Liza Lou and the Yeller Belly Swamp* to observe, "This story has three stories in it!"

Research on Children's Responses to Literature

The above examples suggest that children engage in the envisionment building Judith Langer described. Although researchers have not directly applied Langer's model to young children's literary meaning making, existing research reveals that children do assume the stances Langer identified in her model. Children clearly become engaged in story worlds (Martinez and Roser, 1994), and this engagement is active and dynamic. For example, Marjorie Hancock (1993) found that the sixth-graders in her study wrote journal entries that showed they were attempting "to make sense of the emerging plot and characters" (p. 343) by questioning, predicting, and interpreting. Lawrence Sipe (1998) found that the first- and second-graders in his study engaged in much the same kinds of processes.

Although early researchers concluded that children's text-centered responses occurred at literal levels (Applebee, 1978), more recent research findings have shown that even young children can generate thematic statements for stories (Lehr, 1988), make interpretations about other facets of stories as well (Many, 1991; McGee, 1992), and analyze text and illustrations (Sipe, 1998).

Children also respond to the ways in which an author has crafted a work of literature. This is just what Marcia, a fifth-grader, did when discussing Sharon Creech's *Chasing Redbird* with her classmates: "Sharon Creech made this book interesting because it has a lot of mysteries and you want to read more to find out." Though response to craft appears to be less frequent than other types of response (Hancock, 1993; McGee, 1992; Sipe, 1998), children seem especially likely to step out of the story world to make observations about craft when teachers direct attention toward the artistry of literature (Bloem & Manna, 1999; Kiefer, 1983; Roser, Martinez, Mrosla, & Ingold, 1999).

Children respond to literature in reader-centered ways as well. They build bridges between their personal experiences and the literature they read, making what Marilyn Cochran-Smith (1984) has termed "life to text connections." For example, children might talk about their own pets when listening to a story about a child and his pet. Hickman (1981) described the personal associations children make when reading literature, as have numerous other researchers (e.g., Farest & Miller, 1993; Raphael, McMahon, Goatley, Bentley, Boyd, Pardo, & Woodman, 1992; Short, 1992; Sipe, 1998; Wollman-Bonilla, 1989). The personal experiences children bring with them to literature study also include experiences with other texts, and various researchers have found that children make intertextual connections when responding to literature (Farest & Miller, 1993; Short, 1992; Sipe, 1998). Children also become personally involved with characters as they vicariously step into character roles and make judgments about how they would feel in a character's situation (Hancock, 1993; McGee, 1992; Wollman-Bonilla & Werchadlo, 1995).

Children also do what Langer termed stepping out of stories to reflect on how the stories relate to their own lives or the lives of others. McGinley and Kamberelis (1996) found that third- and fourth-graders attempted to understand

and negotiate social relationships and significant social problems through literature. In effect, the children used literature as a lens through which they could better understand their own personal experiences and their world. Cochran-Smith even found that preschoolers engaged in text-to-life transactions in which they extended or related story situations or information to their own life experiences. Sometimes they made these text-to-life connections long after hearing a story, as they played or worked in situations that were well removed from storybook reading. In *Wally's Stories: Conversations in the Kindergarten* (1981), author and kindergarten teacher Vivian Paley includes many examples of text-to-life connections. In one instance, one of her kindergartners told about going to another child's house only to find that the child would not let him in. A classmate proposed a literature-inspired solution: going down the chimney of the house. A second classmate provided a caution (also inspired by "The Three Little Pigs"): Going down the chimney just might result in getting boiled. It is evident the story experience does not always end for young children when the reading is finished; a story can become a lens through which children attempt to understand their world.

DEVELOPMENTAL PERSPECTIVE ON READER RESPONSE

Educators who assume a developmental perspective on reader response realize that children in different stages of cognitive, moral, and social development think about the world in very different ways and that these differences are reflected in the ways they respond to stories. Arthur Applebee (1978) and Janet Hickman (1981) conducted extensive studies of how children's responses to literature change across age levels. Applebee interviewed six-year-olds and nine-year-olds and asked thirteen-year-olds and seventeen-year-olds to write about literature. Hickman obtained her data by spending a full semester observing and recording children's spontaneous responses to literature in three combined-grade classrooms: kindergarten-first, second-third, and fourth-fifth. Both researchers found distinctive differences in the ways children of different ages respond to literature.

Applebee found that when young children (the six-year-olds in his study) were invited to talk about a favorite story, they did so by retelling the plot in great detail. (If you have ever made the mistake of asking a young child to tell you about a movie, you could probably have anticipated this finding!) However, nine-year-olds responded to the same invitation ("Tell about a favorite story") by briefly summarizing a story line. Applebee also included thirteen- and seventeen-year-olds in his study. None of the six- and nine-year-olds whom he interviewed analyzed or made generalizations about stories; in contrast, the thirteen- and seventeen-year-olds, with their more sophisticated cognitive abilities, typically analyzed the structures of stories and made generalizations about their meanings.

Hickman found that children spontaneously expressed their ideas, feelings, and understanding about stories in many different forms, not just by talking and writing. The children responded to literature through movement—by clapping, smiling, kissing book covers. Their literature-based artwork, writing, and dramatic presentations were also vehicles for expressing responses. The younger children in Hickman's study were especially likely to rely on nonverbal ways of expressing their responses. Hickman found other differences in the responses from the younger (kindergarten–first grade) and older (fourth–fifth grade) children in her study. These differences are summarized in Table 3.2. However, the

Table 3.2   Characteristic Responses of Children in Hickman's Study

Responses of Kindergartners and First-Graders	Responses of Fourth- and Fifth-Graders
Relied on their bodies to express responses as they imitated movements in stories, acted out story elements to explain them, and incorporated story elements in their dramatic play	Expressed strong feelings for and against particular selections
Collected story elements in pictures rather than trying to present a cohesive story line through their artwork	Demonstrated extensive knowledge of story conventions and story structure in their literature-based writing, artwork, and skits
Spent time browsing in their independent contacts with books—that is, picked up a book, briefly flipped through its pages, and then moved on to the next book	Sustained their attention for long periods of time in their independent contacts with books
Were concerned with sorting out what was happening in stories and frequently used a retelling strategy when answering questions about stories	Had less need to focus on literal meanings in their verbal responses
Made personal statements that were loosely tied to the story	Often revealed connections between their own experiences and an interpreted story meaning
Expressed a concern with the reality of stories by talking about whether stories were "true" or "possible"	Relied on literary terminology in discussing the reality of stories
Could reduce stories to "lessons" when invited to interpret their meaning	Expressed understanding of meaning using disembedded thematic statements
Expressed more interest in stories than in the authors of stories	Clearly recognized the role of author as the creator of a story

responses of the second- and third-graders in her study were much harder to characterize. At times, they responded much as the kindergartners and first-graders did; at other times, their responses were more sophisticated, like those of the fourth- and fifth-graders. What set the second- and third-graders apart was their concern with becoming independent readers. They spent long periods of time reading and had much to say about the conventions of print.

Hickman, like Applebee, found that younger children were likely to become caught up in the action of stories. However, Hickman found the kindergartners and first-graders could also reduce stories to "lessons" when invited to interpret the meaning of a story. For example, in response to "The Little Red Hen," one child said, "When someone already baked a cake and you haven't helped, they're probably just gonna say no." This child expressed the story's lesson in the context of the story situation. The young children in Hickman's study clearly learned from stories, just as they learn from events in real life. By contrast, Hickman found that the fourth- and fifth-graders expressed their understanding of meaning using more abstract thematic statements that were not tied directly to the content of a story.

Although the work of both Applebee and Hickman helps to explain the developmental differences in children's responses, Hickman's work, which was done in a naturalistic classroom setting, also demonstrates how important it is to watch children closely if you want to understand how they interact with literature. Just asking children questions about stories doesn't give a complete picture; it might tell you about their story comprehension but not necessarily about what they are thinking, feeling, and wondering. To learn about those things, it is important to observe students throughout the day—watching their body movements; seeing how they express their ideas about stories through art, writing, and drama; and listening to their spontaneously expressed ideas during storybook reading and literature discussion and at times when stories are not the focus of activity.

As the research described in this section suggests, children of different ages respond to literature in different (though equally interesting) ways. Therefore, it is important for teachers to become attuned to how children of different ages think about literature. Yet it is also important to realize children of the same age may exhibit individual styles of response (Galda, 1982; Hancock, 1993). For example, Lawrence Sipe (1998) characterized one of the first-graders in his study as a child whose specialties in responding were logical reasoning and close analysis. By contrast, second-grader Charles typically expressed his response through performance, while first-grader Krissy frequently invented alternatives to the plots of stories. So age alone doesn't prepare children to get the most out of books. Factors such as exposure to and experience with literature—factors that teachers can certainly influence—are equally important (Lehr, 1988).

SOCIAL PERSPECTIVE ON READER RESPONSE

Social factors also affect reader response, as do the context and temporal factors that are so integrally bound up with social factors in the classroom. Research in this area is especially important for educators because of the insights it yields into the creation of classrooms that nurture children's growth as responders to texts. Just as teachers can't simply wait for children to become better readers or to master increasingly complex math concepts, they shouldn't wait for children to respond more deeply to the literature they encounter. Instead, teachers need to take the necessary steps to see that such growth occurs. To do this, they must understand the social, contextual, and temporal factors that influence children's thinking about literature.

The Literature-Rich Classroom

Janet Hickman was the first person in the United States to study children's spontaneous responses to literature in a naturalistic setting, and she was also the first to notice the way in which context shapes children's responses. Because the classrooms in which she conducted her study were literature-rich, Hickman knew that it was important to describe what the teachers did that nurtured their students' growth as responders. She found that these teachers invited responses to literature through the physical context they created, the ways they used time, and the ways they encouraged response. In particular, Hickman (1981) recommended that teachers do the following:

- Build extensive book collections and fill the classroom with attractive displays of books.
- Select high-quality books and present them in related sets (for example, books about Halloween, African folktales, or friendship stories).
- Build in ample time for all children to interact with books daily.

- Share literature with children daily by reading aloud and by introducing new books before putting them on display in the classroom.

- Encourage students to share their thinking about literature.

- Support children's understanding of literary craft by providing them with critical terminology when they have an idea but need the words to talk about it more easily.

- Encourage children to explore books through art, writing, and drama and support their efforts by providing time, space, materials, and ideas for projects and by ensuring that they have opportunities to share their work with peers.

- Provide children with opportunities to revisit some books repeatedly.

Evolution of Response

Children's responses to stories can evolve over time, becoming deeper and more insightful. Reading stories repeatedly to children seems to be an effective vehicle for fostering such growth. Janet Hickman identified repeated readings of stories as one of the classroom factors that encourage rich responses. A number of other investigators have looked specifically at what happens when children hear stories repeatedly. Miriam Martinez and Nancy Roser (1985) found that the story talk of preschoolers changed when parents and teachers read stories to them repeatedly. The children talked more about familiar stories than about unfamiliar ones. Also, on a first reading of a story, the children tended to share fewer observations about the story and instead asked more questions as they worked to sort out characters and story events. On subsequent readings, the children chose to explore different facets of the stories, a finding that suggests that as they gained control over particular facets, they became able to shift their attention to others. However, if they did return to discuss a portion of a story they had previously talked about, the children showed more insightful thinking than they had initially. Lesley Morrow (1988) compared the responses of four-year-olds who heard stories read repeatedly to those of other four-year-olds who listened to different stories read only one time. The children who heard repeated readings of a story made more comments than did the children who listened to different books, and they also shared a wider variety of responses and more complex interpretive responses.

Children enjoy expressing their responses to literature through their artwork.

The above studies focused on very young children. Researcher Amy McClure (1985) investigated responses to poetry in a combined fifth- and sixth-grade classroom. The teacher in this classroom frequently reread the same poems, and these rereadings enabled her students to move beyond hearing the words of the poem to really reflecting on meaning.

Other strategies, in addition to repeated readings of literature, also encourage the deepening of children's responses over time. Janet Hickman (1981) found that when children worked on response activities (art projects, writing, and the like), they seemed to think more deeply about stories. Similarly, Joanne Golden and her colleagues (1992) and Lynda Weston (1993) found children's responses to stories continued to grow as they engaged in drama, art, and writing activities based on literature. These activities are discussed in Chapters 12 and 13.

Literature Discussion

The actual reading of a text is a solitary experience, but Susan Hepler and Janet Hickman (1982) once observed that "the literary transaction, the one-to-one conversation between author and the audience, is frequently surrounded by other voices" (p. 279). In the elementary classroom, these other voices are those of the teacher and classmates. Ralph Peterson and Maryann Eeds (1995) believe that when readers come together to share their varied interpretations of a piece of literature, the "meaning potential of the text is expanded" (p. 21). For example, some fourth-graders worked collaboratively to create meaning after listening to a chapter in Elizabeth Winthrop's *Castle in the Attic,* a time-travel fantasy set primarily in medieval times. Just after William, the young protagonist of the story, confronts Alastor, the wicked wizard who turned much of the kingdom's populace into lead, Alastor disappears. The discussion begins in response to an entry Gavin wrote in his response journal:

GAVIN: I wonder what is going to happen to the lead people.

MRS. FRY: You're worried about all those lead people that are in there. What is your thought—what do you think might happen to the lead people?

GAVIN: I think maybe there's some kind of spell that can reverse it that they have to find.

MRS. FRY: Somehow or other they're going to have to find a spell that will reverse it. Okay—any guess, any ideas?

GINA: He could go into Alastor's room now that the wizard's gone.

CHRIS: I think he should, well, when William turned Alastor into lead, well, he has to find a way to turn him back because the token was on his neck, the one that restores you to normal size was on his neck.

MONICA: He grabbed it. He grabbed both.

CHRIS: Oh, I thought he just grabbed the lead.

MELISSA: I don't think they should go in Alastor's room because it didn't say where Alastor ended up. He's probably just like the Silver Knight. He went back in time probably.

MRS. FRY: So what you're worried about is if they go into the room, they might find him there.

TASHA: They turned him to lead. And last time when Alastor turned the Silver Knight to lead, he went back in time.

LAURA: I disagree with Melissa because remember, he said they grabbed the necklace when he was tumbling inside the gallery. And then he started doing something, and then Mrs. Calendar turned around and said something, and he turned to a lead person. So he's still in the gallery, and he can't move his hands.

ALLISON: It said that he vanished.

This is a wonderful example of the way in which children can better understand a story by talking and working together.

Chapter 13 examines literature discussion at length, with particular emphasis on how teachers can ensure that their students have the opportunity to share their insights into literature. To prepare you for that chapter, let's look at what research has to say about literature discussions in elementary school.

Literature Discussions in Elementary Classrooms. How does participation in literature discussions enrich elementary students' literary experiences? Maryann Eeds and Deborah Wells (1989) studied fifth- and sixth-grade literature discussion groups facilitated by preservice teachers who participated as group members with the students. Eeds and Wells found four ways in which participation in these groups enriched the students' literature experiences. First, when students were confused about characters or story events, their peers helped them sort out their confusions. A second way in which these fifth- and sixth-graders worked together to build meaning was by sharing personal stories related to the books they read. A personal story is a window onto a reader's interpreted meaning, and sharing personal stories gave the students insights into the interpretations of their peers. The students also worked collaboratively to build meaning by extending and enriching one another's predictions and hypotheses. Finally, the students critiqued stories together, commenting on the author's purpose and on issues related to the crafting of books.

Children gain new insights into a story by listening to what their peers and teachers say about it.

Young Children and Literature Discussion. Eeds and Wells's study shows that children can engage in collaborative meaning making, but the participants in that study were fifth- and sixth-graders. Can younger children do the same? Lea McGee (1992) used Eeds's term "grand conversations" to describe the conversations the first-grade students in her study participated in after listening to stories read aloud. They responded in rich and diverse ways—sharing personal reactions, interpretations, and evaluations as well as more text-focused responses related to textual structure and the techniques used by the author. Similarly, Jennifer Battle (1995) found that the bilingual kindergartners in her study engaged enthusiastically in literature discussion and grappled with and negotiated ideas collaboratively.

Teacher Roles in Literature Discussion Groups. Janice Almasi (1995) studied teacher-led and peer-led discussion groups in fourth-grade classrooms. In the teacher-led groups, the teachers assumed a traditional role in which they directed discussion by asking questions and evaluating students' answers. In the peer-led groups, teachers played minimal roles: scaffolding (or supporting) interaction and discussion only as necessary. Their ultimate goal was for students to be able to conduct literature discussions without any teacher support. The differences between the two types of groups were remarkable. The students in the peer-led groups were far more reflective. When they had difficulty understanding or interpreting texts, they sought the group's help in working through the confusion. In the teacher-led groups, this type of student-initiated reflective thinking rarely occurred, because the teacher was typically in charge of initiating topics of discussion. In addition, students in peer-led groups talked almost twice as much as those in teacher-led groups. Students in peer-led groups heard more alternative story interpretations than did students in teacher-led groups, and they were more likely to establish the discussion agenda than were the students in teacher-led groups. Finally, in the peer-led groups, the students asked the questions instead of the teacher.

The teachers in the peer-led groups that Almasi studied played minimal roles in literature discussion, but other researchers have found that teachers can contribute to rich literature discussion when they assume somewhat more involved roles. Eeds and Wells (1989) found that the preservice teachers who were most successful in leading conversations about literature were highly encouraging, asked few questions, and responded to many opportunities to talk about literary elements. By watching for opportunities to discuss and label literary elements, the teachers added depth to discussions and helped the students acquire literary insights (and the language of literature).

CULTURAL PERSPECTIVE ON READER RESPONSE

We are all cultural beings who belong to particular ethnic, class, and gender groups and, as members of these groups, share values, attitudes, assumptions, and knowledge with other group members. Patricia Enciso (1994) says that our cultural understandings are "everywhere and always a part of how we interpret the world and our place in it" (p. 532). So, of course, cultural understandings shape readers' transactions with texts, either supporting or constraining them. A teacher's response to Sherley Anne Williams's **Working Cotton** reflected a cultural perspective. In this book, Williams documents a day that an African

Illustration 3.3
The use of a first-person narrator in *Working Cotton* immerses the reader in the myriad emotions of a young migrant worker. (Cover illustration from *Working Cotton* by Sherley Anne Williams. Illustration copyright © 1992 by Carole Byard, reprinted by permission of Harcourt, Inc.)

Ask the Author . . . *Pat Mora*

Do you find that children from different cultural backgrounds respond differently to your work? If so, in what ways?

The question goes to the heart of the complex experience of being human. We all breathe and sleep, eat, and fear. I sometimes joke that we're all united by being post-birth and pre-death. These shared human experiences allow us at our best to be empathetic and also to savor international art, including literature. Picasso and O'Keeffe, like Tolstoy or Neruda or Dickinson, move us because of our human similarities. They too lived in skin. Neither country of origin, color, class, religion, gender, nor language changes the fact that we humans itch and dream. And yet, and yet, we do arrive into this world to particular parents in particular places. The family staple can be beans, rice, potatoes, *yuca*. "Aunt" and "tía" technically mean the same thing, but the words are different in the mouth. Each of us belongs to many communities—some by birth, circumstance, choice.

Children are no different, of course. They enter my books, my words bringing with them all they are—their language as well as their curiosity. Do children who are bilingual and/or Latino respond to my work in a particular way? At this time in history, *yes,* because they haven't seen enough families like theirs in books. I like to think they find comfort and validation, a home in books. Though it has been years, I still feel the quiet little girl in New Jersey who rubbed up against me as she left my author presentation and whispered, "I'm Spanish, too." I knew what she meant.

But children, praise the heavens, don't always see or feel the barriers to connections that we adults do. They're not intimidated by Spanish: They want to try it. And all students know how it feels to be different the way Stella feels in *The Rainbow Tulip.* They feel with her and for their wounded selves. On a lighter note, most children like to make animal sounds. They're ready to howl like coyotes whether in English or Spanish, preferably both. Best not forget the poets of many colors. Some children enjoy the rhyming sounds in my books, the quiet spaces between the words, the smooth and prickly words, their music; the taste of the words in the mouth, some in English, some in Spanish, green and lavender flavors.

Pat Mora, born in El Paso, Texas, has written many award-winning books for children and adults, including Tomás and the Library Lady *and* My Own True Name. *She's the proud mother of three grown children, who are delighted that Mom now has a house in Santa Fe. Her husband Vern thinks it's not a bad idea either.*

Favorite Books as a Child

The poetry volume of the *Childcraft* series. I remember looking at the row of orange books, pulling out this volume when I was home sick (maybe not that sick) and leisurely savoring the music.

Little House on the Prairie by Laura Ingalls Wilder. What delight to discover this whole series in the El Paso Public Library long before the TV adaptations. I loved the coziness of the books, the family closeness, the triumphs over adversity.

Secret of the Old Clock by Carolyn Keene. Yes, though it's not fashionable to admit it, I liked the *Nancy Drew* books. Part of the pleasure was sharing them with my younger sister, Cissy, and also having my aunt, whom we called Lobo, read them to us, a niece on each side.

American child spends working in the cotton fields with her family, who are migrant workers. On first reading this book, the teacher observed how impressed she was by the beauty of the illustrations and the straightforward manner in which the story is narrated; nonetheless, she put the book aside, finding this story about a child working in the fields from sunup to sundown too painful to share with children. Her initial response was constrained by cultural experiences. Only later, when she realized that *Working Cotton* is a book with which migrant students can readily connect, did it come down off her shelf.

Although we are becoming increasingly aware of the likely impact of culture on children's responses to literature, little research has been done in this area. One early study, done by Rudine Sims (1983), investigated the responses of a ten-year-old African American girl to books about African Americans. Sims interviewed the girl about the books she had read and discovered that she preferred books related to her own African American experiences and having characters with whom she could identify. In particular, she liked strong, active, female, black characters. Elizabeth Smith (1995) also found that fifth-grade African American students in her class who were struggling and reluctant readers avidly sought out books about African Americans and responded to these books differently than they did to other books. The research of Sims and Smith underscores the importance of bringing into the classroom literature that authentically represents students' cultures. Finding the right books is likely to require an investment of time and energy, but the effort is worth making.

Coming together to talk about literature allows people with different perspectives (sometimes vastly different ones) to exchange ideas, to step into the shoes of others and thereby to calibrate their own judgments. For example, Mexican American students from rural backgrounds could help their peers better understand and appreciate Carmen Lomas Garza's *Family Pictures*. In effect, participants in literature discussion can share cultural insights that make the literary experience a richer one for other participants. This happened in a university class when a group of preservice teachers discussed *Maniac Magee*. The students, most of whom were white middle-class females, did not believe the book was realistic—especially the scenes set in the McNab home. In particular, they questioned the authenticity of the scene in which Maniac mistakes the roaches covering the floor for raisins and the scene in which the McNab twins jump through a hole in the ceiling from the second floor to the first. At this point, a student who had sat quietly on the sidelines for most of the semester spoke up, explaining that she lived in a housing project and had firsthand experience with the kinds of living conditions Spinelli described. Her classmates listened intently and thereafter viewed both the book and their classmate's contributions to discussion in a different light. Cultural differences often have a positive effect when students are encouraged to help their fellow students interpret a book by sharing their related cultural experiences. However, it is also important to be aware that children's conversations about a book are sometimes constrained by their cultural perspectives—just as cross-cultural conversations about social issues are too often constrained. Researcher Patricia Enciso (1994) found this to be the case when she discussed *Maniac Magee* with fourth- and fifth-graders. She found that the white students and the African American students at times made different connections to the book, which stymied their discussions. When the students discussed the scene in which Maniac takes a bite of Mars Bar's candy bar, cultural miscommunication occurred. The white children were appalled that Maniac took a bite of the candy. However, they insisted that their reaction stemmed from a concern about germs. Yet when an African American student expressed sympathy toward Mars Bar, the other students were not willing to even discuss the boy's response to an African American character whom they viewed as an antagonist.

Teachers must be ever alert to cultural roadblocks that may arise and put a damper on literature discussion and must attempt to help students get around those roadblocks. Constructivist theory maintains that one's interpretation of an event, influenced as it is by one's unique culture-based experience, is the event. In light of this theory, it is important for teachers to encourage students to come together in literature study as diverse members of society and to consider actively the issues and experiences found in literature. The very act of considering literature will reveal how differently students think about things and will provide opportunities to understand others' points of view.

Like students, teachers bring cultural perspectives to texts. These perspectives can have an effect on the kinds of literature a teacher selects. More important, how the teacher responds to and perceives the literature will influence how she or he guides the literature discussion. Teachers need to monitor their own culturally based responses to texts to ensure that they do not constrain students' responses.

Should teachers encourage students to focus on author's craft during literature discussion?

Reader response theorists maintain that during the reader/text interaction, readers' personal memories, feelings, and thought associations are evoked by the stories they read. So when readers—including children—get together to talk about books, they often share some of those personal stories. We also know that when reading children are especially likely to become caught up in the story world. They are interested in the characters they meet in stories and in the events in which characters are caught up—much as they are interested in the lives of people they meet. So children very naturally explore these story worlds in their literature discussions. Given children's natural propensity to talk about story characters and events and their personal responses to the story, many educators argue that teachers should make these the topics of literature discussion groups.

Other educators take a different stance. They argue that for response to reach its richest potential, readers must move beyond the story world and personal responses to that story world to focus on issues related to the author's craft. In other words, children should be encouraged to step outside the story world and do what Langer calls objictifying their experience with the text. If they are encouraged to attend to the literary elements and the ways in which authors manipulate those elements, children will come to more fully appreciate the richness of literature and learn more about literature. Further, children who gain insights into the author's craft will be more likely to grow as writers themselves.

This position is countered by those who argue that a focus on craft is likely to result in an overanalysis of literature that is inappropriate for children. Instead, teachers should follow children's leads in discussion and build on their interests, even if this means that discussion never touches on what the author did that makes readers respond as they do.

How should teachers conduct literature discussions with children? Should they let discussions center on the topics children introduce, even if this means children only explore the story world and their personal responses to that story world? Or should the teacher at times nudge children beyond what might be their first interests to talk about the author's craft? What do you think?

TEXTUAL PERSPECTIVE ON READER RESPONSE

Earlier, we said that aesthetic reading is a reader/text transaction in which the reader brings to bear on the text his or her experience, knowledge, beliefs, and feelings. Knowledge about texts is one type of knowledge readers bring to the transaction, and textual theorists place special emphasis on such knowledge. The more experience readers (or listeners) have had with literature, the greater their store of knowledge about how literature works. This store may include knowledge of narrative and expository conventions, genre conventions, literary elements, literary language, visual elements, and design.

Preschoolers who have been read to have already begun to build a store of literary knowledge, as evidenced by their use of "once upon a time" to begin their own stories or by the concern they express when a wolf enters the scene as they are listening to a story—they know full well that this stock character is not to be trusted. You can sometimes even anticipate how textual knowledge is likely to influence children's transactions with particular books. Children's delight in Jon Scieszka's *The Stinky Cheese Man and Other Fairly Stupid Tales* can be understood (at least in part) in light of a textual perspective on response. Scieszka's wonderfully mixed-up fantasy violates every imaginable book convention: The book begins with text, which is followed by the title page. Readers are invited to put their own name into the dedication (which happens to be written upside down). The table of contents is shown falling onto the characters in "Chicken Licken." One of the characters (the Little Red Hen) insists on narrating her story at the most inopportune times. Children love this story—if they have already acquired an understanding of how stories work.

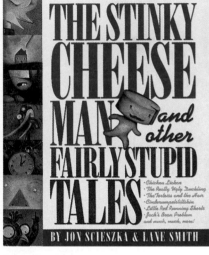

Illustration 3.4
Both the story lines of traditional tales and the features of typical book formats are humorously manipulated in *The Stinky Cheese Man and Other Fairly Stupid Tales* (a Caldecott Honor Book). (*The Stinky Cheese Man and Other Fairly Stupid Tales* by Jon Scieszka. Text copyright © 1992 by Jon Scieszka. Illustration copyright © 1992 by Lane Smith. Used by permission of Viking Penguin, a division of Penguin Putnam Inc.)

Readers also bring knowledge of other texts to the reading of particular books, and reading a story in light of other stories can enrich readers' responses (Cairney, 1992; Short, 1992). This was true in the case of the preservice teacher who connected Florence Parry Heide and Judith Heide Gilliland's *The Day of Ahmed's Secret* to Eve Bunting's *The Wednesday Surprise*: "The story reminds me of *The Wednesday Surprise*. In that book, it's the grandmother who learns to read, but it's the grandmother and the little girl who share the secret. And just like Ahmed, they can hardly wait to share the secret with their family."

Creating intertextuality, the process of bringing knowledge of one text to make meaning of another, is something mature readers do, and children can also be encouraged to read one story in light of another. In fact, part of the delight children find in *The Stinky Cheese Man and Other Fairly Stupid Tales* can be explained with reference to intertextuality. The book is a collection of folktale spin-offs; for example, the title story, "The Stinky Cheese Man," is a spin-off of "The Gingerbread Man"; "The Princess and the Bowling Ball" is a spin-off of "The Princess and the Pea"; and "Jack's Bean Problem" is clearly related to "Jack and the Beanstalk." Children who know the original tales are the ones who most delight in Scieszka's work.

There are indications that children are sensitive to and knowledgeable about text features—whether they choose to talk about them or not. For example, when children have been exposed to literature, they often use literary language and literary conventions in their dramatizations and their writing, and this is true of even very young children. However, actual research on children's knowledge about how texts work is limited. Georgia Green and Margaret Laff (1980) found that many five-year-olds, without any reference to illustrations, were

Illustration 3.5
In Eve Bunting's sensitive exploration of adult literacy, a child teaches her grandmother to read. (Cover from *The Wednesday Surprise* by Eve Bunting, illustrated by Donald Carrick. Jacket art copyright © 1989 by Donald Carrick. Reprinted by permission of Clarion Books/Houghton Mifflin Company. All rights reserved.)

able to discriminate among the diverse writing styles of Bill Peet, Virginia Kahl, Beatrix Potter, Dr. Seuss, and Margaret Wise Brown. They did so by matching stories written by the same author. Some of these young children were even able to explain the basis on which they matched stories. In Chapter 14, we discuss ways of helping children build their store of knowledge about how texts work.

In this chapter, we have looked at literary meaning making from various perspectives—experiential, developmental, social, cultural, and textual. These five windows onto literary meaning making complement one another. By understanding each perspective, you will be able to make better decisions as a teacher. In addition, by knowing mature readers understand a text in light of others they have read, you will be more likely to encourage your students to make connections among stories; and by realizing readers understand stories in light of their own cultural experiences, you will recognize the importance of selecting multicultural titles for your students.

TEACHING IDEAS

Helping Children Step into Stories. Langer (1990) admits that sometimes it is difficult to step into a story. To help your students step into new stories, you can encourage them to adopt the habit of reading dust jackets and book covers. Also, to help with initial envisionment building, you might sometimes read the first chapter of a book aloud and then let students continue to read on their own.

Helping Children Talk about Literary Crafting. Langer says that readers sometimes step out and objectify a literary experience. In doing so, readers think about or talk about how a story is crafted. However, we have found that children do not always choose to talk about the ways authors and illustrators craft their works. One way of encouraging children to think about issues of crafting is to share distinctly crafted stories with them. For example, in *Two Bad Ants,* Chris Van Allsburg repeatedly draws attention to perspective in his illustrations. Bill Martin, Jr., and John Archambault's spooky story *The Ghost-Eye Tree* offers the perfect opportunity to talk about a story's mood. Author/illustrator Jan Brett creates distinctive borders for the illustrations in her picture books. Illustrator Julie Vivas uses space in a dramatic fashion in her illustrations. Author Eric Carle frequently relies on repetition in his work. You are likely to find that as you share such distinctive works with children, they become more sensitive to how authors and illustrators craft their stories.

Illustration 3.6
Chris Van Allsburg achieves dramatic effects through his manipulation of perspective in *Two Bad Ants*. (Cover from *Two Bad Ants* by Chris Van Allsburg. Copyright © 1988 by Chris Van Allsburg. Reprinted by permission of Houghton Mifflin Company. All rights reserved.)

Helping Children Connect Life and Literature. Children come from families with very different literature traditions. Not all children are in a habit of making what Cochran-Smith (1984) called "text-to-life transactions." That is, not all children use stories as lenses through which to view the world. Teachers can encourage this type of response by modeling. Develop the habit of connecting children's literature to life experiences. For example, you might describe bad days as "Alexander days"—a reference to Judith Viorst's *Alexander and the Terrible, Horrible, No Good, Very Bad Day.* And there is no better description for a mischievous child than David from David Shannon's *No, David!*

Reading a Story Repeatedly. One way of deciding which book to read repeatedly to younger students is to invite them to select a book they want to hear again. More likely than not, children will select a book they find both interesting and challenging. If you work with younger children, you want repeated readings to become routine in your classroom. One way of doing this is to designate a particular day of the week as the day on which you'll revisit an "old friend."

EXPERIENCES FOR YOUR LEARNING

1. Langer (1990) says readers assume different stances (or different relationships to a text) as they read. Review the discussion on pages 61–63 of the four stances Langer describes: being out and stepping in, being in and moving through, being in and stepping out, and stepping out and objectifying the experience. Then select a book to read, perhaps *Holes*, and as you read, keep a journal in which you record your responses to the book. After completing the book, go back and identify the different stances you assumed as you responded to the book.

2. Discuss a piece of multicultural literature such as Camille Yarbrough's *The Shimmershine Queens* with a group of peers from different cultural backgrounds. How, if at all, do your different cultural perspectives come into play in the discussion?

3. As children acquire experience with literature, their knowledge of how texts work increases. Read Jon Scieszka's *The Stinky Cheese Man and Other Fairly Stupid Tales* to children of different ages. Describe how differences in the children's responses to the story might be understood in light of their textual knowledge.

4. Hickman (1981) identified physical features of classrooms that support rich literary responses. Visit two classrooms, and note which of the features listed on pages 66–67 are present. What differences do you find in the two classrooms? Can you discern any differences in the richness of the children's responses to literature? To what extent might differences in the physical features of the classrooms account for the differences in children's responses?

5. Children enjoy sharing personal memories and feelings that stories evoke. However, some people argue very young children go off on tangents when sharing personal associations. Read a story to a group of first- or second-graders and invite them to join in an open-ended discussion by asking, "What did you notice or what were you reminded of as you listened to the story?" Share the children's responses with a group of peers and address the following question: "Are children more likely to benefit from an open-ended discussion or a discussion guided by teacher questions?"

RECOMMENDED BOOKS

* indicates a picture book; I indicates interest level (P = preschool, YA = young adult)

*Bunting, Eve. *The Wednesday Surprise*. Illustrated by Donald Carrick. Clarion, 1989. A little girl teaches her grandmother to read. (**I:** 6–9)

Creech, Sharon. *Chasing Redbird*. Joanna Cotler/HarperCollins, 1997. A young girl is determined to prove herself by clearing the long lost trail which she discovers. (**I:** 10–14)

*Garza, Carmen Lomas. *Family Pictures*. As told to Harriet Rohmer. Spanish version by Rosalma Zubizarreta. Children's Book Press, 1990. Artist

Carmen Garza portrays scenes from her childhood in a Mexican American community in South Texas. (**I:** 6–10)

*Heide, Florence Parry, and Judith Heide Gilliland. *The Day of Ahmed's Secret*. Illustrated by Ted Lewin. Lothrop, Lee & Shepard, 1990. As a boy moves through the streets of Cairo doing his work, he looks forward to the evening, when he can share his secret with his family: He has learned to write his name. (**I:** 6–10)

Hodge, Merle. *For the Life of Laetitia*. Farrar, 1993. A girl leaves behind her life with her extended family in a rural community to attend school in the city and live with her father's second family. (I: 11–YA)

*Martin, Bill, Jr., and John Archambault. *The Ghost-Eye Tree*. Illustrated by Ted Rand. Holt, 1985/1995. This story about a brother and sister's scary experience with a haunted tree can easily be adapted for readers theater. (I: P–9)

*Mayer, Mercer. *Liza Lou and the Yeller Belly Swamp*. Aladdin, 1976/1997. Liza Lou proves to be too clever for the witches, haunts, and gobblygooks of the Yeller Belly Swamp. (I: P–8)

Mora, Pat. *My Own True Name: New and Selected Poems for Young Adults, 1984–1999*. Arte Publico, 2000. Mora's poems focus on life and family in bicultural settings. (I: YA)

*———. *The Rainbow Tulip*. Viking, 1999. A Mexican American immigrant girl feels caught between the Spanish- and English-speaking worlds. (I: P–8)

*———. *Tomás and the Library Lady*. Knopf, 1997. The true story of Tomás Rivera, a migrant worker whose interest in books, sparked by a librarian, led him to become a university chancellor. (I: P–8)

*Rylant, Cynthia. *This Year's Garden*. Illustrated by Mary Szilagy. Aladdin, 1987. This is a celebration of a family's garden. (I: P–8)

Sachar, Louis. *Holes*. Farrar, 1998. When Stanley Yelnats is sent to a juvenile detention center for a crime he didn't commit, he is sure it is just another instance of the family curse, but his stay at Camp Green Lake presents him with the opportunity to finally break that curse. (I: 10 and up)

*Scieszka, Jon. *The Stinky Cheese Man and Other Fairly Stupid Tales*. Illustrated by Lane Smith. Viking, 1992. A novel format is used in presenting humorous spin-offs of familiar European folktales and fairy tales. (I: 6 and up)

*Shannon, David. *No, David!* Scholastic, 1998. A little boy creates mischief throughout the day as his exasperated mother tries to rein him in. (I: P–7)

Spinelli, Jerry. *Maniac Magee*. Little, Brown, 1990. On his way to becoming a legend, a homeless boy brings together the two sides of a racially divided town. (I: 9–12)

*Van Allsburg, Chris. *Two Bad Ants*. Houghton Mifflin, 1988. A visit to a house spells near disaster for two ants. (I: P–9)

*Viorst, Judith. *Alexander and the Terrible, Horrible, No Good, Very Bad Day*. Illustrated by Ray Cruz. Atheneum, 1972. Alexander tells about all the things that have gone wrong in a single day. (I: P–8)

*Williams, Sherley Anne. *Working Cotton*. Illustrated by Carole Byard. Harcourt, 1992. A young girl describes a day spent in the fields with her migrant worker family. (I: P–8)

Winthrop, Elizabeth. *Castle in the Attic*. Holiday House, 1985. A boy travels back in time to confront a wicked wizard and save a kingdom. (I: 6–10)

Yarbrough, Camille. *The Shimmershine Queens*. Penguin Putnam, 1996. Angie loves to dream about her future, but her dreams begin to fade in the face of peer pressure. (I: 10–YA)

RESOURCES

Applebee, Arthur. *The Child's Concept of Story*. University of Chicago Press, 1978.

Beach, Richard. *A Teacher's Introduction to Reader-Response Theories*. National Council of Teachers of English, 1993.

Langer, Judith A. *Literature Instruction: A Focus on Student Response*. National Council of Teachers of English, 1992.

Lehr, Susan. *The Child's Developing Sense of Theme: Responses to Literature*. Columbia University Teachers College Press, 1990.

Roser, Nancy, and Miriam Martinez, eds. *Book Talk and Beyond: Children and Teachers Respond to Literature*. International Reading Association, 1995.

Short, Kathy Gnagey, and Kathryn Mitchell, eds. *Talking about Books: Literature Discussion Groups in K–8 Classrooms*. Heinemann, 1998.

REFERENCES

Almasi, Janice. "The Nature of Fourth Graders' Sociocognitive Conflicts in Peer-Led and Teacher-Led Discussions of Literature." *Reading Research Quarterly 30* (1995): 314–51.

Applebee, Arthur. *The Child's Concept of Story*. University of Chicago Press, 1978.

Battle, Jennifer. "Collaborative Story Talk in a Bilingual Kindergarten." *Book Talk and Beyond: Children and Teachers Respond to Literature*. Ed. Nancy Roser and Miriam Martinez. International Reading Association, 1995, pp. 157–67.

Beach, Richard. *A Teacher's Introduction to Reader-Response Theories.* National Council of Teachers of English, 1993.

Bloem, Patricia L., and Anthony L. Manna. "A Chorus of Questions: Readers Respond to Patricia Polacco." *The Reading Teacher* 52 (1999): 802–808.

Cairney, Trevor H. "Fostering and Building Students' Intertextual Histories." *Language Arts* 69 (1992): 502–7.

Cochran-Smith, Marilyn. (1984). *The Making of a Reader.* Ablex.

Eeds, Maryann, and Deborah Wells. "Grand Conversations: An Exploration of Meaning Construction in Literature Study Groups." *Research in the Teaching of English* 23 (1989): 4–29.

Enciso, Patricia E. "Cultural Identity and Response to Literature: Running Lessons from *Maniac Magee.*" *Language Arts* 71 (1994): 524–33.

Farest, Cindy, and Carolyn Miller. "Children's Insights into Literature: Using Dialogue Journals to Invite Literary Response." *Examining Central Issues in Literacy Research, Theory, and Practice: Forty-second Yearbook of the National Reading Conference.* Ed. Donald J. Leu and Charles K. Kinzer. National Reading Conference, 1993, pp. 271–8.

Galda, L. "Assuming the Spectator Stance: An Examination of the Responses of Three Young Readers." *Research in the Teaching of English* 16 (1982): 1–20.

Golden, Joanne M., Annyce Meiners, and Stanley Lewis. "The Growth of Story Meaning." *Language Arts* 69 (1992): 36–43.

Green, Georgia M., and Margaret O. Laff. "Five-Year-Olds' Recognition of Authorship by Literary Style." Technical Report No. 181. University of Illinois Center for the Study of Reading, 1980.

Hancock, Marjorie R. "Exploring the Meaning-making Process through the Content of Literature Response Journals: A Case Study Investigation." *Research in the Teaching of English* 27 (1993): 335–68.

Hepler, Susan, and Janet Hickman. "'The Book Was Okay. I Love You'—Social Aspects of Response to Literature." *Theory into Practice* 21 (1982): 278–83.

Hickman, Janet. "A New Perspective on Response to Literature: Research in an Elementary School Setting." *Research in the Teaching of English* 15 (1981): 343–54.

Kiefer, Barbara. "The Responses of Children in a Combination First/Second Grade Classroom to Picture Books in a Variety of Artistic Styles." *Journal of Research and Development in Education* 16 (1983): 14–20.

Langer, Judith. "Understanding Literature." *Language Arts* 67 (1990): 812–16.

Lehr, Susan. "The Child's Developing Sense of Theme as a Response to Literature." *Reading Research Quarterly* 23 (1988): 337–57.

McClure, Amy A. "Children's Responses to Poetry in a Supportive Context." Diss. The Ohio State University, 1985.

McGee, Lea M. "An Exploration of Meaning Construction in First Graders' Grand Conversations." *Literacy Research, Theory, and Practice: Views from Many Perspectives.* Ed. Charles K. Kinzer and Donald J. Leu. National Reading Conference, 1992, pp. 177–86.

McGinley, William, and George Kamberelis. "*Maniac Magee* and *Ragtime Tumpie:* Children Negotiating Self and World through Reading and Writing." *Research in the Teaching of English* 30 (1996): 75–113.

Many, Joyce E. "The Effects of Stance and Age Level on Children's Literary Responses." *Journal of Reading Behavior* 23 (1991): 61–85.

Martinez, Miriam, and Nancy Roser. "Read It Again: The Value of Repeated Readings during Storytime." *The Reading Teacher* 38 (1985): 782–86.

———. "Children's Responses to a Chapter Book across Grade Levels: Implications for Sustained Text." *Multidimensional Aspects of Literacy Research, Theory, and Practice: Forty-third Yearbook of the National Reading Conference.* Ed. Charles K. Kinzer and Donald J. Leu. National Reading Conference, 1994, pp. 317–24.

Morrow, Lesley M. "Young Children's Responses to One-to-One Story Readings in School Settings." *Reading Research Quarterly* 23 (1988): 89–107.

Paley, Vivian. *Wally's Stories: Conversations in the Kindergarten.* Harvard University Press, 1981.

Peterson, Ralph, and Maryann Eeds. "More Compelling Questions in Reading Education." *Reading Today* (1995, June/July): 21.

Raphael, Taffy E., Susan I. McMahon, Virginia J. Goatley, Jessica L. Bentley, Fenice B. Boyd, Laura S. Pardo, and Deborah A. Woodman. "Research Directions: Literature and Discussion in the Reading Program." *Language Arts* 69 (1992): 54–61.

Rosenblatt, Louise M. *Literature as Exploration.* 4th ed. MLA, 1938.

———. "The Literary Transaction: Evocation and Response." *Journeying: Children Responding to Literature.* Ed. Kathleen E. Holland, Rachael A. Hungerford, and Shirley B. Ernst. Heinemann, 1993, pp. 6–23.

Roser, Nancy, Miriam Martinez, Heather Mrosla, and Jeannette Ingold. "What Happens to Book Talk When the Author Joins the Literature Circle?" National Reading Conference, Wyndham Palace, Orlando, 4 Dec. 1999.

Short, Kathy G. "Intertextuality: Searching for Patterns That Connect." *Literacy Research, Theory, and Practice: Views from Many Perspectives: Forty-first Yearbook of the National Reading Conference.* Ed. Charles K. Kinzer and Donald J. Leu. National Reading Conference, 1992, pp. 187–97.

Sims, Rudine. "Strong Black Girls: A Ten-Year-Old Responds to Fiction about Afro-Americans." *Journal of Research and Development in Education* 16 (1983): 21–8.

Sipe, Lawrence R. "Individual Literary Response Styles of First and Second Graders." *Forty-seventh Yearbook of the National Reading Conference.* Ed. Timothy Shanahan and Flora V. Rodriguez-Brown. National Reading Conference, 1998, pp. 76–89.

Smith, Elizabeth B. "Anchored in Our Literature: Students Responding to African American Literature." *Language Arts* 72 (1995): 571–74.

Weston, Lynda Hobson. "The Evolution of Response through Discussion, Drama, Writing, and Art in a Fourth Grade." *Journeying: Children Responding to Literature*. Ed. Kathleen E. Holland, Rachael A. Hungerford, and Shirley B. Ernst. Heinemann, 1993, pp. 137–50.

Wollman-Bonilla, Julie E. (1989). "Reading Journals: Invitations to Participate in Literature." *The Reading Teacher*, 42, 112–120.
———, and Barbara Werchadlo. "Literature Response Journals in a First-Grade Classroom." *Language Arts* 72 (1995): 562–70.

4 Literature Representing Diverse Perspectives

"I'm a sophomore," Sheila said. "Three more years in this place."

"And you just got here, Maizon," Charli said, bouncing down next to me. She had more energy than Li'l Jay.

"Buckle your seat belt, girlfriend, 'cause you in for one heck of a ride."

"Charli. You're slipping," Marie said, frowning.

"Oh, chill out, Marie." Charli waved her hand and lay back on the bed. "We're among our own."

from **Maizon at Blue Hill**
by Jacqueline Woodson

In **Maizon at Blue Hill,** a girl enters a private academy and discovers that she is one of only five African American students there. Incidents throughout the book reveal how she feels in this situation, how she sees her place in this setting, and how she interacts with others. The passage above implies that people feel and act differently when they are able to say, "We're among our own." How does being among people whose perspectives are different from your own make you feel? Reading and discussing books such as **Maizon at Blue Hill** allows children to reflect on what it means to live in a diverse world and how issues of diversity affect them.

Why should we have multicultural literature, really? That is a fair question. Some critics worry that the rise of multicultural education in the United

States may fragment our loyalties and loosen our civic ties to each other. For example, a noted historian wrote a book entitled *The Disuniting of America* (Schlesinger, 1991) that offers this premise. But James Banks (2000), an energetic proponent of multicultural education, argues that multicultural education is fully American, because the United States is a society that was founded on the premise of providing justice and the pursuit of happiness for its citizens and recognizing the culture and potential of different groups is necessary to their pursuit of happiness and justice.

Multicultural children's books can make a contribution here. Beverlee Tatum, a psychologist who has studied racism, explains why. Most of us live in racially segregated neighborhoods (Tatum, 1999). Tatum suggests that our earliest experiences take place among people of the same race as ourselves. We count on secondhand sources—books, movies, and television—for our ideas about people from other races and ethnic and religious backgrounds. If those sources give caricatured impressions of other races or leave them out all together, we are likely as children to form deep-seated concepts that people of other races are silly, unimportant, or, at the very least, much different than we. If we belong to a race that is caricatured or excluded, we might internalize the idea that *we* are unimportant in the eyes of the world.

The best defense against allowing racist views to take hold of our children is to surround them with rich, realistic information about children from many other races. If they have that information, then the concepts or preconceptions they form about people from other races will show people as they are, with their differences, similarities, and individuality.

This is the role that multicultural literature needs to fill.

DIVERSE PERSPECTIVES IN THE UNITED STATES

Schools in the United States are seeing a tremendous increase in the cultural and ethnic diversity of the children they serve. According to the 1990 census, "people of color" make up 25 percent of the U.S. population. It is believed that by 2020, nearly half of the students in U.S. schools will be "of color" (Pallas, Natriello, and McDill, 1989). That reality, along with our expanding relationships with countries around the world, increases the need for children to see themselves as members of a multicultural global community. Because good literature reaches the minds and hearts of its readers, reading and discussing multicultural literature will broaden children's perspectives and increase their understanding in a way that affects—for the better, we hope—how people live in this pluralistic society.

Multicultural education theorists define pluralism as diversity in "ethnic, racial, linguistic, religious, economic, and gender [characteristics], among others" (Nieto, 1996). Nieto argues "that all students of all backgrounds, languages, and experiences need to be acknowledged, valued, and used as important sources of their education" (p. 8). This inclusive definition of pluralism correlates with beliefs about the need for diverse perspectives in education. Banks (1999) asks that multicultural education include voices that have been marginalized in the past but not ignore the achievements of Western civilization in doing so. The goal of multicultural education is freedom—helping students develop the knowledge, attitudes, and skills that will allow them to participate in a democratic and free society. Banks acknowledges that students should know their own culture before they can successfully participate in other cultures.

The United States is a diverse society, and this diversity has many sources. The obvious ways in which both the general and school populations are diverse are gender, culture, ethnic and racial background, language, and physical and mental abilities. Less often acknowledged are differences in social class. All of these differences can affect the ways people see themselves and others. And all must be taken into account in forging a working democracy or a harmonious classroom.

THE ROLE OF SCHOOLS IN PRESENTING MULTIPLE PERSPECTIVES

Schools face many demands in shaping the curriculum. Some of these demands are made by people who want the curriculum to be presented from one perspective: their own. Multiple viewpoints serve students best. If students are shown only male, white, able-bodied characters, then female students, children of ethnic diversity, students with disabilities, and children with learning exceptionalities are likely to feel that the school day is not planned with them in mind. They may even feel that their place in society in general is questionable. Although strides have been made in addressing issues of antibias curriculum that works toward social justice, more work is needed. Schools can be instrumental in providing opportunities for students to read and discuss material from multiple viewpoints. Such discussions are important in developing attitudes of open-mindedness about diversity. This chapter (and this book) recommends books that offer multiple perspectives.

LITERATURE'S ROLE IN INFLUENCING THE READER'S PERSPECTIVE

What role does literature have in influencing children's understanding of diverse perspectives? Depending on their experiences, some children feel uncomfortable when presented with an opportunity to interact with someone who is different from themselves. How can children resolve their misunderstanding, lack of understanding, or fear? Developing a hypersensitivity that leads to avoidance is a serious mistake. "Many people have an inhibition about talking with someone in a wheelchair. They don't know quite what to say, so they don't say anything at all and ignore both the person and the chair" (Haldane, 1991, n.pag.). People may respond to any kind of diversity in this way. Although it is a vicarious experience, interacting with diverse people through literature can help. Literature that portrays diversity in natural ways can provide realistic images as well as spark discussion.

Fiction and informational books are powerful vehicles for helping students understand other cultures, because they offer cultural insights in natural ways. Such books should not be narrowly viewed as replacements for social studies textbooks; too often, students miss the richness of the writing if they read merely to locate cultural information. However, fiction and informational books can enhance children's understanding of cultures by involving them emotionally. The narrower focus of such books allows for deeper exploration of the thoughts, feelings, and experiences of people from diverse groups. Thus, through story, readers take an emotional stake in understanding how and why people live as they do.

Milton Meltzer (1989) believes that the writer has a social responsibility and that "writing about social issues need not depress and dispirit readers; it should provide them with courage. If they learn to confront life as it is, it may give them the heart to strive to make it better" (p. 157). Meltzer is saying that literature is a powerful vehicle when it treats issues honestly. But, as Jean Little (1990) points out, literature that is designed to present object lessons, in which teachers point out the "good messages," appears self-righteous and rarely changes people's opinions. Well-written books that speak from the writer's vision pull readers into the characters' experiences and emotions and build compassion, thereby having a lasting effect on readers' understandings of the world in which they live.

Books depicting diverse perspectives are found in all genres of children's literature. In this chapter, we will examine the criteria for viewing multicultural and international issues, as well as issues of gender, social diversity, and exceptionality, in children's books. These criteria form a foundation for evaluating the literature you encounter in all the genre chapters that follow.

MULTICULTURAL LITERATURE DEFINED

Although there is general agreement that multicultural literature is about people who are not in the mainstream, there is no consensus as to what constitutes nonmainstream populations (Cai and Bishop, 1994). Some contend that multicultural literature is that by or about people of color in the United States. Many include literature about religious minorities (such as the Amish and Jews) or about people who live in specific regions of the United States (such as Appalachia). Some include literature about diverse lifestyles (such as families headed by same-sex parents or people with disabilities). Some include books about people in countries outside the United States. There is value in having an inclusive definition when considering issues of diversity; however, too broad a definition dilutes the focus.

We will define multicultural literature as literature that reflects the multitude of cultural groups within the United States. To address the issues of multiculturalism that are most salient to our study of children's literature, we will focus on literature that reflects ethnic and regional groups whose cultures historically have been less represented than European cultures. A related body of literature is international literature—literature that is about countries outside the United States or that was originally written and published in countries outside the United States. Literature that addresses many other kinds of diversities— social diversity, diversity in gender preference, and differences in ways of learning, to name a few—should also be included under the larger umbrella of "literature reflecting diverse perspectives."

One reason we focus on books about ethnic groups within the United States is that these books reflect experiences of the children in U.S. schools today, since most were either born or raised in this country. Often, books of this type are classified as African American, Asian American, Latin American, or Native American. *Through My Eyes* is a personal account written by Ruby Bridges, telling her story of how she integrated a New Orleans school at the age of six, accompanied by federal marshals who enforced the integration order despite the screaming and angry segregationists who tried to block it. Through photographs, poignant text narrated by Bridges herself, accounts recorded by her teacher Mrs. Henry, and accompanying news clippings and other documentation, this uniquely American story provides an example of an ethnic American experience.

We use the term "multicultural" rather than "minority," with its implied reference to groups that have been historically "minor" in number compared to the "majority." Some groups that historically have been considered "minorities" are no longer numerically in the minority. Unfortunately, however, underrepresentation and misrepresentation of these groups continue. Virginia Hamilton's (1993) term "parallel cultures" has gained wide acceptance because it defines various cultures as parallel to the mainstream, rather than in a minority status. However, the ideal is not simply existence on parallel planes but an interaction between cultures that leads to interdependence.

THE VALUE OF MULTICULTURAL LITERATURE

Why should children's books deliberately include the perspectives of people from many backgrounds? This is a legitimate question. Some people believe that the "melting pot" is the target that literature should strive for—it shouldn't accentuate ethnic and cultural differences, because that emphasizes the stresses tearing apart the fabric of society.

There are two compelling reasons for making sure children's literature includes the perspectives of people from many groups. First, students feel welcome in school to the extent to which they find themselves and their experiences represented in the books and materials they find there. Second, students need to understand and empathize with people who are different from themselves. If books do not portray differences, students cannot learn to transcend them.

Rudine Sims Bishop (1990) uses the metaphor of mirrors and windows to emphasize these two values of multicultural literature. Mirrors let readers see reflections of their own lives; windows let them see others' lives. Multicultural literature provides both types of experience. What value is there in seeing oneself represented in literature? Quite simply, it engenders a sense of pride. When readers encounter images of people they consider like themselves in a book, they take more interest in the book and feel a sense of involvement in the literary discussion that follows their reading. What value is there in seeing others represented in literature? Books that act as windows into experiences that are different from our own stretch the range of experiences we have had. Lee Galda (2000) makes an interesting analogy connecting windows with mirrors; in certain types of light, windows show reflections of self in varying degrees of clarity. Likewise, books that are windows to outside experiences should offer the possibility that readers will see some type of reflection of themselves.

IDENTIFYING MULTICULTURAL BOOKS

All multicultural books depict people of diverse cultures, but the degree to which such books focus on cultural or social issues varies significantly. It is not enough to count the diverse faces in a book; the important thing is how the members of various cultures are portrayed. There is a range of degrees of cultural specificity in books, from merely visual inclusion that shows diverse faces to books that are entirely based on specific cultural aspects. The full range of depicting diversity is needed, but they differ in the degree and the specificity of their emphasis and, accordingly, in the cultural understandings that they offer to the reader. In some books, people of different cultures are deliberately included so that the illustrations appear visually diverse, but the text does not require that characters be of a particular culture. Diversity is incidentally depicted. In others, the culture is more than highlighted; it is central to the book. All details in the book focus on the culture. At the two ends of the continuum of specificity in depicting diversity are "Culturally Generic Books" and "Culturally Specific Books."

Culturally Generic Books

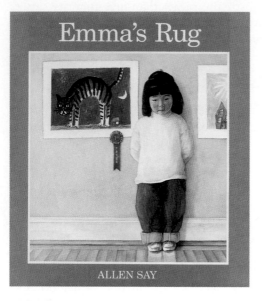

Culturally generic books are "generically American" in theme and plot (Sims Bishop, 1992). Sometimes the inclusion appears to be merely incidental, and at other times it is purposefully and prominently featuring multicultural characters, but in all cases the theme remains generic to any culture. An example of culturally generic books is *Emma's Rug* by Allen Say. In the story, Emma is an artistic child who finds inspiration by gazing into a small white rug she has always had in her room. One day, her mother washes the rug, and Emma is sure that her inspiration can no longer be found in the very clean rug. Visually, Emma is portrayed as an Asian American child, but no details in the text identify Emma by a particular ethnicity. Emma's struggle is universal—one that children could experience regardless of their culture. Still, books that depict multicultural inclusiveness even when the focus is not on any aspect of diversity are important because they increase readers' exposure and awareness. In addition, books that show the universality of themes allow students to find connections across cultures.

Illustration 4.1
Emma learns that inspiration for art is in the world all around her and that she does not have to rely on the images she "sees" in her special rug. (Cover from *Emma's Rug* by Allen Say. Copyright © 1996 by Allen Say. Reprinted by permission of Houghton Mifflin Company. All rights reserved.)

Culturally Specific Books

Culturally specific books illuminate the experience of members of a particular cultural group (Sims Bishop, 1992). The nuances of daily life are captured accurately, reflecting language use, attitudes, values, and beliefs of members of the group portrayed. Such details add texture to the writing, making the stories more real and more believable and therefore making it more likely that readers will see the stories as authentic. An example of a culturally specific book is Mildred Taylor's *Roll of Thunder, Hear My Cry*. Not only are the descriptions of situations and events historically accurate, but the character names, the forms of address, the dialogue, and the interactions are true to the culture of the people whose lives are reflected.

Although they differ in the depth of the cultural experiences they provide to readers, the full range of inclusiveness in multicultural books contributes to readers' understandings of their own and others' cultures. Sometimes, readers see themselves and others as sharing universal experiences, and therefore cultural group membership need not be explicitly discussed. But it is culturally specific books that offer the insights necessary to truly further readers' understanding of different cultures.

EVOLUTION OF MULTICULTURAL LITERATURE

From the time children's books were first published in this country until well after World War II, most reflected mainstream characters, settings, values, and lifestyles. Children usually learned to read from books that presented primarily European American lifestyles and values. People who did not resemble the so-called American ideal—people of African, Asian, Latino/a, and Southern European origins, as well as Native Americans—were regularly singled out for discrimination. Likewise, early portrayals of nonmainstream characters tended to be highly stereotypical. Such characters were portrayed as cute, savage, primitive, uncouth, untrustworthy, or underdeveloped. Since the late 1960s, increasing efforts have been made to include honest depictions of people from all cultural groups in children's books—not simply to talk about them, but to narrate their perspectives and experiences through their eyes and in their voices.

Although several individuals (for example, Augusta Baker, Virginia Lacy, and Charlamae Rollins) campaigned for inclusion of people of diversity in children's books before 1965, the wake-up call that made the U.S. public aware of the situation is usually considered to be Nancy Larrick's 1965 article in the *Saturday Review,* "The All-White World of Children's Books." In her study, Larrick found that only 6.7 percent of children's books published between 1962 and 1964 included any African Americans in illustrations or text, and just 0.9 percent depicted them in contemporary settings. Other cultural groups were represented even less. The decade that followed saw an increase in the number of books that included people of diversity. The Council for Interracial Books for Children was founded in 1966 to heighten public awareness of diversity issues related to children's books. The Coretta Scott King Award was established in 1969 to give recognition annually to an African American author and an African American illustrator who contributed the most distinguished work of the previous year.

Larrick's study was replicated a decade later in order to examine how things had changed (Chall, Radwin, French, and Hall, 1985). The percentages had more than doubled: 14.4 percent of all children's books published from 1973 to 1975 included African Americans in text or illustrations, and 4 percent showed them in contemporary settings. This increase was attributed in part to the civil rights movement, along with long overdue recognition of the inequities highlighted by Larrick and others. However, Rollock (1984) found that these increases were only temporary and that in the five years after the Chall study, between 1979 and 1984, only 1.5 percent of newly published children's books included African Americans.

Limited data are available on representation in children's books of groups other than African Americans. But sources such as the Council on Interracial Books for Children (1975), Nieto (1983), Schon (1988), and Sims (1985) indicate that there has been even less representation of groups such as Asian Americans, Native Americans, and Latino/as.

The beginning of the 1990s saw the largest surge to date in multicultural publishing in the children's book field. Sims Bishop's (1991) note of optimism reflected a general increase in the level of awareness and understanding of the importance of multicultural literature. But despite the increase in numbers of multicultural publications, a study by Reimer (1992) revealed a lack of multicultural representation in popular booklists such as the International Reading Association's annual "Children's Choices" (the 1989 list was used in her study), Jim Trelease's *The New Read-Aloud Handbook* (1989), and former U.S. Secretary of Education William Bennett's list of recommended reading for elementary students (Bennett, 1988).

Other problems were highlighted in the early 1990s. Because of the predominance of European American writers and illustrators, multicultural literature was presented primarily from an "outside" perspective. Related to this problem was the fact that some Native Americans believed that mainstream authors had stolen stories without considering the specific rules regarding who had access to those stories. Another problem was the grouping of related but distinctly separate cultures under one label (for example, labeling Mexican

Americans, Puerto Rican Americans, and Cuban Americans as "Hispanic"). In addition, there was a lack of teacher awareness of the importance of including multiple cultural perspectives in the classroom (Harris, 1997; Reimer, 1992; Sims Bishop, 1992). Unfortunately, inaccuracies, stereotypes, tokenism, bias, language flaws, and narrowness of representation continued to plague some books (Barrera, Thompson, and Dressman, 1997).

Currently, authors, illustrators, publishers, and educators are paying more attention to the issues of "authenticity" that were raised in the early 1990s and before. Authors and illustrators from diverse cultures are accepting the call to create culturally authentic work. (Ironically, many had tried unsuccessfully to have their work published in earlier years. In many cases, it was the annual contest sponsored by the Council on Interracial Books for Children that led to the publication of books written by people from diverse cultures.) Today, publishers are seeking ways to ensure authenticity in the books they produce. Librarians and reviewers are recognizing authenticity as a critical criterion in evaluating multicultural books. And teachers are working to include authentic multicultural books as featured reading materials in their classrooms. However, they should also look critically at the books from years past that are still found in many school libraries and classrooms. Although such books have value in specialized collections that allow people to see historic trends in the publication of multicultural books, teachers should be careful that young readers are not exposed to these books without some discussion of the damaging racist or stereotypical images they contain.

ISSUES RELATED TO MULTICULTURAL LITERATURE

To evaluate the influence of multicultural literature on children's understanding of the world around them and to establish criteria for good multicultural literature, we need to consider several issues: (1) whether a work presents cultural details authentically, (2) whether the author writes from an inside or an outside perspective, (3) whether a work promotes stereotypes, and (4) which cultural group is being described in the work. Consideration of these issues can guide teachers in selecting multicultural literature and facilitating discussions of such literature among their students.

Cultural Authenticity

When a book presents a theme that is true to a culture and is filled with specific details that are authentic, members of that culture who read it feel that their experiences have been reflected and illuminated for others to share. Culturally authentic books are written by authors who have developed a "culturally conscious" way to "provide exceptional aesthetic experiences: [to] entertain, educate, and inform; and . . . engender racial pride" (Harris, 1990, p. 551). However, when a book distorts or misrepresents information about a culture, such misinformation leads to misunderstandings of that culture by those in other cultures and creates feelings of betrayal in members of that culture.

Examples of culturally authentic books are Carmen Lomas Garza's *In My Family/En mi familia* and her earlier book *Family Pictures/Cuadros de familia.* Based on the author's life in South Texas, these books include various paintings that illustrate events in her childhood, accompanied by bilingual text. In *Family Pictures/Cuadros de familia,* the page entitled "Birthday Party/Cumpleaños" begins with "That's me hitting the piñata at my sixth birthday party." Following the English sentence is the Spanish translation: "Ésa soy yo, pegándole a la piñata en la fiesta que me dieron cuando cumplí seis años." Readers can identify specific details, such as the framed picture of the Last Supper, the flamenco dancers on the calendar, and the assembling of the tamales, all of which are culturally authentic. Through illustrations and text, *In My Family/En mi familia* tells about the making of empañadas, birthday barbecue parties, and summer dance time. Mexican American readers can feel a sense of kinship with the creator of such books—a sense of shared experiences and understandings. Readers outside the culture can gain new insights from these authentic depictions of the culture.

When a book lacks authenticity, it is likely to convey misleading images of a culture. Sometimes, the text gives readers a stereotyped or dated image of a culture; other times, confused illustrations depict a culture in inappropriate ways. Readers outside the portrayed culture might not be able to discern what is authentic and what is not.

Perspective: Insider or Outsider

The perspective of the writer has become a major issue in multicultural literature: Does the author have an "inside" or an "outside" perspective on the culture being portrayed? An author with an inside perspective writes as a member of the culture and therefore is more likely to portray the cultural group authentically. An author with an outside perspective writes from a point of view of a nonmember of the group being portrayed. But even among those inside a culture, the range of cultural experiences and opinions regarding the depictions of the culture vary, showing the multidimensionality of any culture (Noll, 1995).

Members of the dominant culture have had multiple opportunities to see their world interpreted through eyes like their own. But they may not have had the experience of being wrongly portrayed, and therefore they may not know the feeling of betrayal at having their culture misrepresented. An outsider might miss the rhythm, accent, and flavor that make the ethnic experience live for the insider audience. An outsider's interpretation of an ethnic experience may be filled with details that are factually accurate, but the presentation may be bland and dry, lacking the cultural nuances that would make it come alive. A simple missed or misrepresented detail may be enough to negate authenticity for members of the culture being portrayed (Kaplan, 1995).

In his article "Can We Fly across Cultural Gaps on the Wings of Imagination? Ethnicity, Experience, and Cultural Authenticity," Cai (1995) compares a novel by Laurence Yep, an insider of the Chinese culture, to one by Vanya Oakes, an outsider. Through detailed comparisons, Cai clearly outlines the differences between the inside and outside perspectives. Can those born outside a culture produce authentic material about that culture? Some say no. Others, such as scholar Henry Louis Gates, Jr., W. E. B. Du Bois Professor of Literature at Harvard, believe that inside perspective can be gained by cultural outsiders. Gates believes that "no human culture is inaccessible to someone who makes the effort to understand, to learn, to inhabit another world" (cited in Sims Bishop, 1992, p. 42). Certainly, not all books by mainstream writers and illustrators depicting diversity contain stereotypes. Good depictions can be found in the works of Ezra Jack Keats, Verna Aardema, and Ann Grifalconi. Some, through their own life experiences and extensive research, have been able to create culturally authentic portrayals of a group different from that into which they were

Illustration 4.2
The illusion of an insider's point of view is generated by the author's and illustrator's in-depth research for *Little Oh*. (*Little Oh* by Laura Krauss Melmed, illustrated by Jim LaMarche. Copyright © 1997. Used by permission of Lothrop Lee & Shepard, a division of HarperCollins Publishers.)

born. Many African Americans view Arnold Adoff's writing as having an inside perspective, yet he is not African American. Many of his books, such as *Black is brown is tan,* speak from his biracial family's experiences. Similarly, Demi's picture books, such as *The Empty Pot* and *Chingis Khan,* are set in China. Although Demi was not born Chinese, her thoroughness of research is evident, and readers who are Chinese find that her work reflects the perspective of insiders. Author Laura Krauss Melmed (1999) documents the thoroughness of research that she and illustrator Jim LaMarche completed in creating a picturebook set in Japan, *Little Oh.*

Clearly, the issue of insider versus outsider authorship is complex. However, books that present authentic voices and images—no matter who created them—offer a uniquely valuable contribution to literature about a culture. They allow readers within the culture to enjoy the sense of kinship and pride that come from having one's own experience accurately portrayed. They also broaden the perspective of readers from other cultures and offer them fresh insights about the cultural group depicted.

Stereotyping and Other Unacceptable Depictions of Cultural Groups

When a single set of attributes is assigned to an entire cultural group, diversity and individuality are overlooked, and stereotyping results. A stereotyped impression of a cultural group may be created by how characters are portrayed, how characters interact with one another, how a book's setting is described, how a theme is treated, or simply how information is conveyed. It is important to remember, though, that stereotypes often originate in some kernel of behavior that is true to a culture. How do we distinguish between details that make up cultural specificity and globalized stereotypes? Usually negative (but sometimes positive) attributes that are assumed always to be true simply because of one's membership in a cultural group are typically stereotypes. It is sometimes indeed difficult to distinguish between cultural details and stereotypes. One way to distinguish is by finding out whether or not members of the cultural group embrace the attribute as defining themselves.

In years past, literature often depicted nonmainstream cultures in patronizing and condescending ways. Stereotypes abounded in images created by mainstream writers and illustrators. Books such as the 1899 book by Bannerman, *The Story of Little Black Sambo,* and Bishop's 1938 *The Five Chinese Brothers* presented negative and stereotyped images of blacks and Asians, respectively. Although *The Story of Little Black Sambo* is set in India, the illustrations in the original edition depict stereotyped images of blacks. The story line of *The Five Chinese Brothers* requires that the brothers look alike; however, the book depicts all the Chinese people of the village as identical and with yellow skin. Some more recent books are also controversial because of their stereotyped images. Despite the explanations at the end of the book that document distinctions among ten of the tribes, some Native Americans believe that Virginia Grossman and Sylvia Long's 1991 book, *Ten Little Rabbits,* is problematic. Too often, Native American characters are portrayed as animals or depicted as something to be "counted," perpetuating the myth that all Native American people are alike—in this case, "they just wear different blankets" (McCarty, 1995). Stereotyped images of Latinos include "Mexican men wearing wide-brimmed hats snoozing under a giant cactus" and images of "sarapes, piñatas, burros, bare feet, and broken English" (Council on Interracial Books for Children, 1974).

Many books that present stereotypical images of a cultural group are still in print and may be on the shelf of your local bookstore, school library, or public library. Sometimes, these books are purchased by adults who remember them from their childhood and want to share them with young children. However, having loved a book as a child is not in itself an adequate selection criterion, unless you are prepared to take advantage of this teachable moment to discuss stereotypes in older books that represent dominant cultural mores of those times. Ginny Moore Kruse, Director of the Cooperative Children's Book Center at the University of Wisconsin, Madison, cautions against the use of materials that contain "hurtful images" or perpetuate erroneous information about cultures (1991).

In recent years, efforts have been made to replace stereotyped images in old stories by publishing new versions. Sometimes, the original author/illustrator team creates the revised version, as in the case of a story set in Alaska and titled **On Mother's Lap,** written by Ann Herbert Scott and illustrated by Glo Coalson. Margaret Mahy provided new text for **The Seven Chinese Brothers,** which was illustrated by Jean and Mou-sien Tseng. Julius Lester and Jerry Pinkney collaborated in the creation of **Sam and the Tigers,** a retelling of the Sambo story in the African American tradition. In **The Story of Little Babaji,** Fred Marcellino reillustrated Helen Bannerman's original text for the Sambo story, renaming the characters with Indian names and depicting the setting in India, as the text indicates.

Identification of Cultural Groups

For some time, there has been ongoing discussion as to which groups should be included under the "multicultural literature" umbrella. African Americans, Asian Americans, Latino/as, and Native Americans are always included. However, other groups outside the mainstream have some of the same problems of being underrepresented and misrepresented in children's literature and deserve attention as teachers and librarians evaluate and select multicultural literature.

Jewish Americans. Until recent years, there were not many books that reflected Jewish history, religion, and culture. Books such as Lois Lowry's **Number the Stars** share an important part of Jewish history with readers who may or may not be familiar with the Holocaust. The story is about a strong friendship and about people who help others who are facing unjust treatment. The specific circumstances focus on the Danish resistance to the Holocaust, but the themes are universal.

Some contemporary works are important in that they offer possibilities for understanding the lives of Jewish Americans today. In Sonia Levitin's **The Golem and the Dragon Girl,** a Chinese American girl and a Jewish American boy find that their two cultures have parallels that make them feel less different from each other.

Patricia Polacco tells of her own family's heritage and traditions in **The Keeping Quilt.** Passing on the traditions of her heritage is the important theme of this book, which is filled with such cultural markers as a babushka and a wedding huppa. By some definitions, this book would be identified as multicultural because it is about a Jewish family that emigrated from Russia; by other definitions, it would not be considered a multicultural book.

Illustration 4.3
In *The Keeping Quilt,* which won an award from the Association of Jewish Libraries, varied uses of an old quilt symbolize the passing on of family traditions and heritage. (*The Keeping Quilt* written and illustrated by Patricia Polacco. Copyright © 1988 by Patricia Polacco. Used by permission of Simon & Schuster Books for Young Readers, an imprint of Simon & Schuster Children's Publishing.)

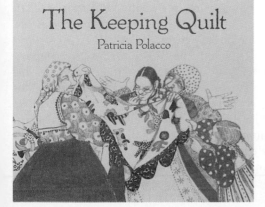

However, books such as these help readers to gain insights into a culture and a history that reading only "mainstream" literature cannot provide.

Appalachian Americans. Another group that has historically been underrepresented in children's literature is the people of the Appalachian region of the United States, who have a distinct culture and way of life. Books such as those by Cynthia Rylant, George Ella Lyon, and Gloria Houston authentically reflect this group's experiences. In Gloria Houston's *My Great-Aunt Arizona,* for example, details of the schoolhouse are accurately depicted. Also, the fact that five generations of the family in the book attended the same school and had Aunt Arizona as their teacher is typical of real-life Appalachian families of the era. *The Relatives Came* by Cynthia Rylant reflects the universal experience of family members coming together for a reunion. However, that experience takes on a special meaning from the fact that Appalachian people are separated from their neighbors by mountains and therefore often live in relative isolation. Both text and illustrations support the sense of distance traveled along small mountain roads. But it is the activities of the family—"hugging and eating and breathing together"—that give readers vivid insight into the experience.

European Americans. European American cultures are usually excluded from the multicultural umbrella because they make up the mainstream population in the United States and have generally been well represented in the literature of the past. However, Swedish Americans, Italian Americans, and the other European American groups have rich and distinct cultural heritages. Because the literature of the past most frequently depicted a generic American experience, not much attention was given to any of these European American cultures separately. Therefore, although European American cultural groups do not need the corrective attention that other groups might need, teachers and librarians should not overlook books that give insight into experiences of specific European American cultures.

MAJOR AUTHORS AND ILLUSTRATORS OF MULTICULTURAL LITERATURE

A few authors and illustrators are profiled in this section. Others are included in the genre sections of Part Two of this book.

Alma Flor Ada

Alma Flor Ada was born in Cuba, was educated in Spain and Peru, and now lives in San Francisco, where she is a professor at the University of San Francisco. She is active in the promotion of bilingualism, writing books in both Spanish and English as well as translating books written by others.

As a child, Alma Flor Ada was fortunate to be surrounded by storytellers. Her grandmother and her uncle told many stories, and her father passed on his knowledge of the world by making up stories. Ada's books include retellings of traditional tales and a contemporary story set in a Latin American country, as well as a story about the cultural conflict experienced by a child who grows up in an ethnic community in the United States.

The Rooster Who Went to His Uncle's Wedding is a retelling of a traditional Latin American folktale. In cumulative style, it recounts a rooster's efforts to solicit help in cleaning his dirty beak before he goes to his uncle's wedding.

Ask the Author... *Alma Flor Ada*

How do you feel about the argument that one has to be a member of a culture to write about it?

The more intimately connected an author is with the reality she explores, the greater the possibility to portray it authentically and to make a positive impression on the reader. Does this require that the author be a member of a specific culture? Not necessarily. If an author possesses ample knowledge about a culture and can develop the understanding of its intricacies, she will be able to write with a responsible degree of authenticity.

Otherwise, authors would be tremendously restricted about what they can write: Men could not write about women, nor women about men, and historical novels would not be possible.

It is not only a matter of cultural background, but of the responsibility one takes in learning, observing, reflecting, experiencing, suffering, struggling to understand that makes the vision of an author sincere.

But let's be aware that authors frequently write about another culture opportunistically, because there is an interest or a demand, because the culture seems colorful or appealing.

It is very difficult to become intimately familiar with another culture, even after living many years in its midst. Therefore, there is a great risk that, in spite of the best intentions, the author who writes from outside a culture may not do justice to its essence. Even while knowing many things factually about a culture, an author can miss the intrinsic expression of the cultural values that make all the difference.

> ### Favorite Books as a Child
>
> I learned to read at a very young age, and read voraciously. Since there never were enough new books, I read them over and over again, until I almost knew them by heart. Poetry was always a delight, and I memorized very many poems, which I still remember today. My very first book was *Heidi* by Johanna Spyri, in a copy inherited from my mother, and it continued being a favorite throughout childhood, because I also was blessed with the opportunity to spend long hours alone in nature. *Little Women* by Louisa May Alcott came next and perhaps gave me the secret aspiration to write. I also loved long, well-told adventure stories like Dumas's *The Three Musketeers*, Emilio Salgari's *Sandokan*, and all of Dickens.

What must not be forgotten is that children always deserve the truth at its best.

Children who belong to minority cultures and see themselves and their people constantly stereotyped, ignored, or misrepresented deserve to hear authentic voices showing the complexity and richness of their experience. Children who may have limited or dubious understanding of other cultures deserve to get to know them from those who can best represent them.

In the multicultural society of the United States, many times the books we have are visions from specific cultures, but we still are short on books that portray the cultures interacting with each other: the friendships, rivalry, love, sharing, losses, experienced by characters of diverse backgrounds as they come together. Perhaps better than reclaiming the right to write about the other, we would do well in writing about us in relationship to the other, or about us as someone else's other, until such glorious day in which there will be no other, but us, each in our radiant uniqueness, enriched by our past and our culture, but equally central, equally respected, equally valued and embraced in brotherly, in sisterly, love.

Alma Flor Ada is the author of many award-winning books for children and adolescents including childhood memories Under the Royal Palms *and* Where the Flame Trees Bloom; *whimsical letter collections* Dear Peter Rabbit *and* Yours Truly, Goldilocks; *and beloved stories such as* The Gold Coin *and* My Name Is Maria Isabel. *Alma Flor, a professor at the University of San Francisco, attributes her productivity to the support of her four children and now rejoices in sharing her books with her eight grandchildren.*

The dilemma is solved with the help of the sun, which has always enjoyed the rooster's morning song. *The Gold Coin* tells the story of how a thief is transformed. A young thief follows Doña Josefa with the intent of taking her gold coin but changes his mind as he meets the people whom Doña Josefa has helped. *My Name Is María Isabel/Me llamo María Isabel* is about a little girl who must find a way to express pride in her heritage amidst people who misunderstand her culture. Ada's autobiographical book, *Under the Royal Palms: A Childhood in Cuba,* was awarded the Pura Belpré Award in 2000.

Arnold Adoff

Arnold Adoff was born in the Bronx and began his teaching career in Harlem. He was disturbed to find that the textbooks his students were using included very little literature that reflected their lives. After collecting poetry written by African Americans so that his students would hear the voices of people such as Langston Hughes and Gwendolyn Brooks, Adoff edited and published his first book in 1970, *I Am the Darker Brother: An Anthology of Modern Poems by Negro Americans.* During the next decade, Adoff continued to anthologize poems that focused on the experiences of African Americans.

Adoff's own poetry often expresses ethnic pride and addresses issues of race relations. Adoff, of Jewish heritage, is married to African American writer Virginia Hamilton, and together they have two children. Adoff has written two books that focus on what it means to be of biracial heritage: *Black is brown is tan* and *All the Colors of the Race.* His poetry has a rhythmic, unrhymed quality that is meant to be shared aloud and a visual playfulness that is meant to be seen on the page. His works are frequently on lists of notable books. In 1988, Adoff was honored with the National Council of Teachers of English Award for Excellence in Poetry for Children for his lifetime contribution.

Joseph Bruchac

Joseph Bruchac's rich cultural heritage includes Abenaki ancestry, and his writing is lauded for its authentic images of Native Americans. He has written novels, compiled poetry and folktales, and coauthored volumes of stories and activities. *Keepers of the Earth: Native American Stories and Environmental Activities for Children* is part of a series of books coauthored with Michael J. Caduto that present stories about animals and other aspects of nature, followed by various activities for children, to be guided by teachers or other adults.

Bruchac has written poems and retold folktales that have been published as picture books. He and Jonathan London coauthored *Thirteen Moons on Turtle's Back: A Native American Year of Moons.* The thirteen poems are based on the belief of many Native American groups that each of the thirteen moons in a year holds a story; each poem reflects a different Native American group. *The First Strawberries: A Cherokee Story* is a retelling of the legend of a couple whose quarrel was resolved when the sun sent gifts of raspberries, blueberries, blackberries, and finally strawberries. In *A Boy Called Slow,* Bruchac offers a portrayal of the childhood life of Sitting Bull, a Lakota hero.

Ashley Bryan

Ashley Bryan says that he cannot remember a time when he wasn't a creator of books. Even as early as kindergarten, he created hundreds of handmade books with the encouragement of his family. Bryan later pursued the formal study of art and has taught art to children and adults. He developed his own style based on the influences of the art of his African ancestors. Bryan has done block printing, painting that is reminiscent of woodcuts, and painting in other styles.

Bryan is known for both writing and illustrating. *Beat the Story-Drum, Pum-Pum; What a Morning! The Christmas Story in Black Spirituals;* and *Ashley Bryan's ABC of African American Poetry* were honored with the Coretta Scott King Award for illustration. *Lion and the Ostrich Chicks and Other African Folk Tales* was awarded the Coretta Scott King Award for writing. Another of the books for which he is well known is *The Dancing Granny,* which was inspired by Bryan's grandmother's visit from the West Indies when she was in her seventies. She learned the latest dance steps and outdanced her great-grandchildren.

Bryan's interest in text, music, and art is evident in his books, as he combines these elements to create an overall effect. Bryan's text is influenced by his study of African American poets and his belief that poetry and stories are meant to be shared aloud. His dramatic storytelling style can be "heard" in his texts, which make readers feel as though they were listening to a storyteller. To research folktales, Bryan begins with the scholarly collections made in the nineteenth century by missionaries and anthropologists. He then relies on his own background knowledge and his storytelling ability to create an original version. In addition, he has published several collections of African American spirituals. Bryan's desire in sharing them is to bring the musical genius of these works to a wider audience.

Today, Bryan lives on a small island off the coast of Maine, where he has spent summers painting for fifty years. He continues to produce books for children; entertain others with his storytelling; and collect beach glass, shells, and driftwood for creating puppets.

Eloise Greenfield

Eloise Greenfield has published many award-winning picture books, collections of poetry, and biographies during the last two decades. Among her most noted books is *Honey, I Love and Other Love Poems,* illustrated by Leo and Diane Dillon. These poems speak to the goals that Greenfield hopes to achieve in her work: to provide young children with words to love and grow on and to portray African American children who have a good self-concept. Most of Greenfield's work depicts relationships among families and friends. In *Grandpa's Face,* illustrated by Floyd Cooper, a girl's relationship with her grandfather is central to the story. Although most of the themes are universal, details such as language use give authenticity to the African American experiences portrayed. Greenfield's desire to give children information about their black heritage led her to produce a number of biographies of African Americans, such as *Rosa Parks* and *Mary McLeod Bethune.*

Greenfield's numerous awards include the Coretta Scott King Award for *Africa Dreams; Nathaniel Talking* and *Night on Neighborhood Street* were Coretta Scott King Honor Books. *Africa Dreams* tells the story of a young girl who dreams of someday visiting her granddaddy's village in Africa. Both *Nathaniel Talking* and *Night on Neighborhood Street* are poetry books featuring a young boy who narrates his experiences growing up in his neighborhood. They were illustrated by Jan Spivey Gilchrist, with whom Greenfield has also collaborated on a series of board books for the very young.

Virginia Hamilton

For thirty years, Virginia Hamilton has been publishing a wide variety of work that includes folktales, biographies, and stories about families. All are tied together in their focus on African American experiences. Hamilton says that she regards herself as a storyteller and believes that people tell stories to "keep their cultural heritage safe, to save the very language in which heritage is made symbolic through story" (Hamilton, 1995):

> I see my books and the language I use in them as empowering me to give utterance to my dreams and wishes and those of other African Americans like myself. I see the imaginative use of language and ideas as a way to illuminate a human condition, lest we forget where we came from. All of us came from somewhere else.
>
> My work, as a novelist, a biographer, and a creator and compiler of stories, has been to portray the essence of a people who are a parallel culture community in America. (p. 440)

Among Hamilton's many awards are the 1975 Newbery Medal for *M. C. Higgins, the Great;* the Newbery Honor Book awards for *The Planet of Junior Brown* in 1972, *Sweet Whispers, Brother Rush* in 1983, and *In the Beginning: Creation Stories from around the World* in 1989; Coretta Scott King awards for *The People Could Fly: American Black Folktales* in 1986, *Anthony Burns: The Defeat and Triumph of a Fugitive Slave* in 1989, and *Her Stories* in 1996. The 1992 Hans Christian Andersen Award was presented by the International Board on Books for Young People for the body of her work and the influence it has had on young readers around the world. Her books are widely translated.

Walter Dean Myers

Walter Dean Myers's writing career was launched in 1968 when he won the Council on Interracial Books for Children's picture book competition. A multitalented writer, Myers began his writing career with picture books and informational books. However, he is best known for his notable contribution to young adult literature reflecting the lives of contemporary African Americans. Many of his novels draw on his childhood experiences growing up in New York City's Harlem. *Fast Sam, Cool Clyde, and Stuff* and *Scorpions* are both stories of gang rivalry in an urban setting. *The Mouse Rap* tells the story of an urban youth called Mouse, who opens each chapter with rap verse.

Myers's more recent publications reveal a shift in his creative focus. He won the 1991 Coretta Scott King Award for the informational book *Now Is Your Time! The African American Struggle for Freedom,* and the biography *Malcolm X: By Any Means Necessary* was a 1994 Honor Book. He paired with his artistic son, Christopher, to create *Harlem,* which won both the 1998 Caldecott Honor Award and a Coretta Scott King Honor Award. For two volumes of poetry, *Brown Angels: An Album of Pictures and Verse* and *Glorious Angels,* he collected old photographs and imagined the lives behind them. *Glory Field* is historical fiction that traces 250 years of a family's history. *Shadow of the Red Moon* is a futuristic fantasy. He turns to writing biography in *At Her Majesty's Request: An African Princess in Victorian England.*

Myers's awards are numerous and varied. He has won the Coretta Scott King Award five times: in 1980 for *The Young Landlords,* in 1985 for *Motown and Didi: A Love Story,* in 1989 for *Fallen Angels,* in 1991 for *Now Is Your Time! The African American Struggle for Freedom,* and in 1997 for *Slam!* In

Ask the Author . . . *Minfong Ho*

How do you feel about the argument that one has to be a member of a culture to write about it?

Minfong Ho

To me, writing fiction set in the Asia of my childhood is rather like building a suspension bridge over to another world. A good writer, like any responsible engineer, must make sure that her bridge will bear the weight of those who venture across it, especially if they are trusting young children. And yes, strong plot lines and good characterization are crucial to keep these young readers suspended above the chasm of disbelief. But what happens when they have crossed over to the other side? Don't they deserve to plant their feet on ground as solid as the land they had just left?

For fiction to be solidly grounded in reality, it must be authentic. Especially if the reality introduced "on the other side" is unfamiliar territory, I feel that it is the writer's responsibility to present it accurately and feelingly.

I was born in Myanmar and grew up in Thailand, where I lived until I was sixteen. My basic childhood experiences, the smells and sights and sounds of everyday life, are embedded in the texture of Thailand. I later taught at a Thai university and got to know many of the students there, as well as the farmers that they worked with. And yet I am not Thai. As the daughter of overseas Chinese parents, I was raised with traditional Chinese values and schooling. Does that mean that I have no right to write about the

---

Favorite Books as a Child

I Can Fly by Ruth Krauss. I loved the book to tatters before I learned to speak English (much less read it), so it was with great delight that I saw a copy of it last year and read it for the first time. It was every bit as wonderful as I had remembered it forty years ago.

Chinese comic books, especially about *The Three Kingdoms*.

Not really books—but they were my first exposure to illustrated storytelling: the elaborate murals painted on Wat Prakeow and the Emerald Temple in Bangkok, which featured the story of Hanuman in the Ramayana.

Thai students and Thai farmers that were the subject of my novel *Rice without Rain*?

Similarly, although I was a relief worker at the Thai-Cambodian border, I was neither Khmer nor a refugee. Does that mean *The Clay Marble,* which grew out of that experience, was not really authentic?

Who's to say who should speak for whom? Must writers be exact mirror-images of the people they choose to write novels about for their stories to be ruled authentic? That would be like claiming that all bridges be built over flat land so they could be guaranteed safe.

All things being equal, if the writer is of the same skin color and speaks the same language as the people she writes about, then of course she's more likely to portray them with more sensitivity than someone who is completely different. Yet I feel that none of those factors—race, sex, class, even language—matters as much as experience and empathy. If someone has lived and worked so closely within another community that she has assimilated their experiences, then I think she can come to feel what they feel. After all, empathy, like that leap of imagination, can bring someone over to "the other side." And if the someone is a writer, then building a suspension bridge back is the only natural thing to do, to help bring others across.

Born in Myanmar of Chinese parents, Minfong Ho grew up in Thailand, where she learned to speak Chinese, Thai, and English more or less interchangeably. Reflecting her multifaceted heritage, her books—which include Rice without Rain, The Clay Marble, *and* Hush! A Thai Lullabye—*have received numerous awards both in the United States and abroad.*

1989 *Scorpions* and in 1993 *Somewhere in the Darkness* were named Newbery Honor Books. In 1992, Walter Dean Myers was named the winner of the Margaret A. Edwards Award for Outstanding Contribution to Literature for Young Adults. *Monster* was named the first winner of the Michael Printz Award for excellence in young adult literature in 2000.

Allen Say

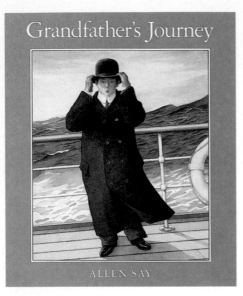

Born and raised in Japan, Allen Say emigrated to the United States when he was sixteen and is now a U.S. citizen. Say's books often have themes showing his love of both countries. His talent and interest in drawing led him, by age twelve, to be apprenticed to a renowned cartoonist. In his 1979 autobiography, *The Ink-Keeper's Apprentice,* Say recounts his early life and the start of his career as an artist. Some of his picture books, including *Grandfather's Journey* and *Tea with Milk,* are autobiographical.

Say's illustrations are extremely effective in capturing the overall ambience of his settings and are painstakingly accurate in detail. For example, whereas the scissors used by the woman sewing in *The Boy of the Three-Year Nap* are Japanese sewing scissors, the scissors used by the mother in *Tree of Cranes* are the kind used in Japan for flower arranging and gardening. Although such details will not be noticeable to all, his attention to them confirms the overall impression of authenticity in Say's work.

Allen Say has received wide recognition for his work. *The Boy of the Three-Year Nap* was a 1989 Caldecott Honor Book. Say won the 1994 Caldecott Medal for *Grandfather's Journey.*

Illustration 4.4
Grandfather's Journey is an autobiographical account that reflects the emotions of many immigrants whose strong love of "home" is aroused by two very different countries. (Cover from *Grandfather's Journey* by Allen Say. Copyright © 1993 by Allen Say. Reprinted by permission of Houghton Mifflin Company. All rights reserved.)

Gary Soto

It was not until 1990 that Gary Soto, author of books and poetry for adults, published his first juvenile work, *Baseball in April and Other Stories.* Since then, he has published other widely acclaimed collections of short stories and poetry, novels, and picture books. The details of Soto's writing reflect his Mexican American ancestry, as he recounts various experiences growing up in the industrial part of Fresno, California. Soto's childhood memories are revealed in his poems in *Neighborhood Odes.* In "Ode to a Sprinkler," Soto reminisces about the sprinkler that provided many hours of water play in the summer. He recalls his love of competition and playground games, as well as hours of play with the discarded things in his neighborhood.

In *Taking Sides,* Lincoln Mendoza moves from the barrio of his childhood to a suburban neighborhood where being Latino sets him apart from his basketball teammates. Readers can follow Lincoln's continuing search for his cultural identity as he goes abroad as a foreign exchange student in *Pacific Crossing.* Soto has published a number of picture books, including *Too Many Tamales* and *Chato's Kitchen. Too Many Tamales* tells the story of a little girl who secretly tries on her mother's ring while making tamales, then must talk her cousins into eating a mound of tamales to try and find the lost ring. In *Chato's Kitchen,* Chato the cat's plan to "welcome" the mice family into the barrio humorously ends differently than he anticipated. In addition to receiving other awards, Soto's *Baseball in April* was recognized as an honor book in the first year of the Pura Belpré Children's Book Award.

John Steptoe

During his high school years, John Steptoe recognized a need for children's books containing authentic dialogue that black children could relate to, so he decided to write them himself. The 1969 publication of *Stevie* received much attention. To tell this story of a little boy who initially resents having to share his mother and his possessions with a younger boy who eventually becomes like a little brother, the nineteen-year-old author and illustrator used black dialect and depicted an urban setting. The numerous awards bestowed on this book were just precursors to the many others Steptoe would earn in his short life.

His two children influenced some of his work; they are featured in *Daddy Is a Monster . . . Sometimes,* in which two boys discuss their father and realize that he's not mean all the time. Steptoe also illustrated the work of others, such as Arnold Adoff's *All the Colors of the Race.*

Steptoe's last few books were particularly noteworthy. *The Story of Jumping Mouse: A Native American Legend* was a 1985 Caldecott Honor Book. Generosity is the virtue that is rewarded in this story, as Jumping Mouse sets off to see the far-off land. In 1988, *Mufaro's Beautiful Daughters: An African Tale* earned the Coretta Scott King Award for illustration and was named a Caldecott Honor Book. In this Cinderella-themed story, Mufaro has two beautiful daughters with very different personalities. Both vie to become the wife of the king, but it is the good-natured daughter who is rewarded for her kindness toward others. John Steptoe's final book, *Baby Says,* was one of the first board books for babies that depicted an African American baby. Steptoe died in 1989 at the age of 38. His son, Javaka Steptoe, is now publishing such noteworthy books as *In Daddy's Arms I Am Tall,* the winner of the 1998 Coretta Scott King Honor Book for Illustration.

Mildred Taylor

Mildred Taylor's books allow readers to get a glimpse into the tragic history of injustice and violence against African Americans. Taylor relies on experiences she had growing up to provide the events in her books. Born in Mississippi and raised in Ohio, she experienced many of the circumstances of the Logan family featured in her books. Taylor brings to life the injustices endured by African Americans living in the strictly segregated society of the South. Many members of the Logan family are based on her own family members, and the feelings of the main character, Cassie, resemble the author's.

As a child, Taylor realized that her people's stories were not found in the textbooks she encountered. Having had the good fortune to come from a family of storytellers, Taylor had heard many stories of African Americans and their heritage; she, in turn, put these stories on paper. Taylor wrote *Song of the Trees* in four days, for a contest sponsored by the Council on Interracial Books for Children. This story won the contest in the African American category and introduced the Logan family.

Mildred Taylor's books have won many awards. *Roll of Thunder, Hear My Cry,* her second book, won the 1977 Newbery Medal. The Logan family's story was continued in *Let the Circle Be Unbroken,* the winner of the 1982 Coretta Scott King Award. Several other books about the Logan family followed: *The Friendship, The Gold Cadillac, The Road to Memphis, Mississippi Bridge,* and *The Well.* Both *The Friendship* and *The Road to Memphis* won the Coretta Scott King Award.

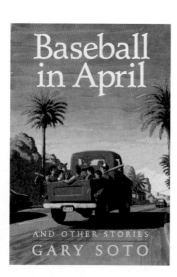

Illustration 4.5
Baseball in April and Other Stories features both humorous and poignant stories about growing up Mexican American in Fresno, California. The book was named an honor book in the first year of the Pura Belpré Children's Book Award. (*Baseball in April and Other Stories* by Gary Soto, illustrated by Mauricio Gomez Morin, translated by Ted Lopez Mills, cover illustration by Barry Root. Jacket copyright © 1990 by Barry Root. Used by permission of Harcourt, Inc. and Barry Root.)

Mildred Pitts Walter

Mildred Pitts Walter was an elementary school teacher in Los Angeles for nearly twenty years. As an activist during the years of the civil rights movement, Walter sought to improve the future for African Americans. During the 1960s, lamenting the scarcity of African Americans in books for children, a publisher encouraged her to fill that void. With the 1971 publication of two picture books about an African American girl in an urban setting, Walter began her career as a writer of books for children. But by then the sociopolitical climate had changed, and it was not easy to get books about African American experiences published. More than a decade later, however, the climate changed again; Walter's writing had developed, and her publishing career resumed. In 1980, she published *Ty's One-Man Band,* a story of a boy who meets a mysterious man who can make music with ordinary household things—a washboard, a wooden spoon, a tin pail, and a comb.

Family, nuclear and extended, and community are important to Walter's personal life and work. Although her childhood in rural Louisiana was filled with the hardships of poverty and racial prejudice, her family passed on the work ethic and gave her support as she developed her sense of self. Later, Walter realized that the community that had supported her in her early years was based on the traditions of the African village, her heritage. Those years were critical in establishing Walter's understanding of racial tensions in social settings as well as the strength-building bonds of family life, two themes commonly found in her writing. In *Justin and the Best Biscuits in the World,* ten-year-old Justin, whose father died earlier, finds himself in search of a male role model. During a visit to his grandfather's ranch, Justin learns that cowboys must become self-sufficient by learning to do the jobs that Justin earlier deemed "women's work." This book won the 1987 Coretta Scott King Award.

Mildred Pitts Walter has also written an original folktale, *Brother to the Wind,* and an informational book taking a historical look at voting rights in Mississippi, *Mississippi Challenge.* Other books such as *My Mama Needs Me, Mariah Keeps Cool,* and *Mariah Loves Rock* focus on contemporary African American family life.

Laurence Yep

Laurence Yep grew up in a black neighborhood, felt like an outsider at his school in Chinatown because he didn't speak Chinese, and attended a high school with mostly white students. He identifies writing as the activity that helped him clarify his own cultural identity. Six years of researching Chinese American history led to the writing of *Dragonwings,* one of his most highly acclaimed books. Yep found extensive factual documentation of the work experiences of the Chinese men who immigrated to the United States during the nineteenth century, yet it required much imagination to portray the human emotions arising from the daily life experiences and the hardships these men suffered. *Dragonwings* was named a 1976 Newbery Honor Book, in addition to receiving numerous other prestigious awards. The inspiration for this story began when Yep read about a Chinese American, Fung Joe Guey, who built and flew "dragonwings" at about the same time the Wright brothers made their first flights. Another work of historical fiction reflecting the experiences of early Chinese immigrants is Yep's 1994 Newbery Honor Book *Dragon's Gate.* This book recounts the involvement of the Chinese in building the transcontinental railroad.

Illustration 4.6
Despite the hardships he and his son must endure, a Chinese immigrant to California will not give up his dream of building a flying machine. *Dragonwings* was named a Newbery Honor Book in 1976. (*Dragonwings* by Laurence Yep. Jacket copyright © 1987. Used by permission of HarperCollins Children's Books, a division of HarperCollins Publishers.)

Yep has written science fiction, fantasy, historical fiction, realistic fiction, and an autobiography and has retold folktales. He has edited Asian American short stories and poetry and published picture books and a number of shorter, realistic stories that reflect contemporary experiences of young Chinese Americans. In *Later, Gator,* two brothers who usually do not get along at all collaborate on a scheme to hide a pet alligator. The story continues in *Cockroach Cooties.*

CRITERIA FOR EVALUATING AND SELECTING MULTICULTURAL LITERATURE

With the growth in the number of multicultural books, it is important to select those of quality. Naturally, when judging the quality of multicultural books, a teacher should apply the criteria for evaluating the various genres of children's literature that are discussed throughout this text. In addition, there are specific questions to consider regarding multicultural books:

- Do the author and illustrator present insider perspectives?
- Is the culture portrayed multidimensionally?
- Are cultural details naturally integrated?
- Are details accurate and is the interpretation current?
- Is language used authentically?
- Is the collection balanced?

Do the Author and Illustrator Present Insider Perspectives?

The author should maintain an insider's mind-set and point of view when writing about a cultural group in order to portray it authentically. Voices such as Patricia Polacco's and Pat Mora's are inside voices because these authors write of experiences based on their own heritage. Polacco's *The Keeping Quilt* and Mora's *A Birthday Basket for Tía* both tell of the authors' personal lives. However, as we discussed earlier in this chapter, the crucial issue is not heritage by fact of birth, but whether the author thinks as a member of the group or as an outsider looking in. Careful research and experience living within the culture contribute to Demi's inside voice in a book such as *Liang and the Magic Paintbrush.*

Illustrations should be accurate, true to the time period portrayed, and culturally authentic. They must not stereotype, homogenize, or ridicule any cultural group. Racial groups should be depicted with a variety of physical features that are not overemphasized. Illustrations play a major role in transmitting cultural images, especially in picture books. Often, a book's cover illustration sends an immediate message about the book's perspective.

Is the Culture Portrayed Multidimensionally?

Cultural groups should be presented multidimensionally to help readers realize the depth and breadth of experiences within cultures. For example, *El Chino,* a biography of Billy Wong, tells the story of a son of Chinese immigrants who became a bullfighter despite what was expected of him by others. To pursue

How much artistic license should be given to illustrators as they create images of a culture?

Some illustrators argue that demands for absolute accuracy of every detail rob the illustrator of the right to use imagination and individual style in portraying an image. They contend that unless the illustrations are photographs, the style of illustration will influence the degree of attention to detail.

Others argue that accurate details in illustrations create the overall sense of cultural authenticity. They point out that misconceptions may develop from incorrect images. In some cases, highly regarded illustrators whose work is exceptional from an artistic viewpoint have been criticized for creating images that "mix" cultures. Critics say that this mixing of cultures robs each culture of its distinction. Yet the illustrators express their desire to create unified images of cultures that sometimes share a common voice. One example is *Brother Eagle, Sister Sky: A Message from Chief Seattle* (1991) by Susan Jeffers. Controversy arose over the text because the words were based on a script for a 1971 television commercial decrying pollution. Controversy arose over the illustrations because they mixed images of Native American cultures and contained inaccuracies of both history and culture. Jeffers defended her position by stating that the important point is that the book reflects a Native American philosophy (Noll, 1995).

How do you view this issue of authenticity versus artistic license in children's book illustrations? How will the type of illustrations affect child readers who do not intimately know the culture portrayed? How will the illustrations affect child readers whose own cultures are portrayed? What do you think?

his dream, he had to fight those expectations. Others said, "Who's ever heard of a Chinese athlete?" and "Only the Spaniards can become true matadors." But he remembered what his father had said: "In America, you can be anything you want to be." Presenting a culture's multidimensionality means presenting the members of that culture in a range of ways. A book should especially be free of any tokenism, in which cultures might be represented to give a head count of politically correct inclusion, without much purpose.

Cultural groups should not be presented through images that could lead to stereotyping. There is no particular experience that is so universal as to be defined as "The _____ Experience." Rather, multiple dimensions of all cultures should be presented objectively, without bias. Roles of cultural members should also be varied, as in *Justin and the Best Biscuits in the World,* in which the African American grandfather, a rancher, serves as an important role model for his grandson.

Are Cultural Details Naturally Integrated?

The flow of the story should be maintained while the cultural details necessary to make it come alive are related. These details should be presented in context so that cumbersome explanations are not necessary. If longer explanations are needed, footnotes or endnotes can serve to clarify. Laurence Yep's

Dragon's Gate is filled with cultural details. The hardships endured, the power relationships and the actions they lead to, the dialogues among the Chinese workers, and the dialogues between the Chinese workers and their white bosses are all described with a completeness that gives readers insight into the lives of the men who left their families behind in hopes of getting rich in a foreign land. These details are necessary for readers to develop deepened understanding and empathy.

Are Details Accurate and Is the Interpretation Current?

Details must be accurate and true to the situation in which they are presented. Factual errors, omissions, and changes are sometimes indicative of sloppy research and presentation. Other times, these problems may actually reflect an attempt on the author's part to meet the expectations of a mainstream readership with preconceived notions of cultures. Series books that focus on children in various countries are sometimes guilty of such intentional errors. One book featuring a child in the Netherlands included all the preconceived images that mainstream readers might expect to find: a blonde girl wakes up, puts on her wooden shoes, and passes a windmill and a field of tulips on her way to school!

There are also series books that are written according to a formula, such as books about other countries in which authors fill in the blanks of standardized formats. In many cases, these authors have no firsthand experience with the country they write about.

Currency of interpretation can sometimes be evaluated by considering recency of copyright and thoroughness of revision. Books that claim to cite current statistics should be carefully analyzed to determine whether the statistic reported is still appropriate, years after the book is published. Sometimes, the interpretation of factual information is more influential than the facts themselves. The author's understanding of the culture determines his or her choice of words, which in turn influences the readers' perceptions. For example, reference to a Japanese father as "honorable father" is a literal translation of the word *otoosan.* The "o" at the beginning of the word for father denotes the honoring of the person addressed. However, constantly referring to each adult as "honorable" may lead readers to an exaggerated, stereotypical view that is not in keeping with the actual personal interactions described in the story.

Is Language Used Authentically?

The language and dialect spoken by characters should authentically portray the kinds of interactions that are typical of those characters, and terminology that refers to aspects of culture should be acceptable by contemporary standards. For example, Gary Soto writes from the perspective of a Mexican American who grew up in California. Readers who have a background similar to his sense a true voice of their experiences. In his book *Pacific Crossing,* Soto portrays two teenage Mexican American boys as foreign exchange students in Japan. Soto uses terminology and phrases that Mexican Americans might use to communicate with each another. He also follows the Japanese language's very strict rules of verbal exchange, which take into consideration the gender, the age, and the familiarity of the speakers. Katherine Paterson's translations of Japanese folktales such as Momoko Ishii's *The Tongue-Cut Sparrow* and Sumiko Yagawa's *The Crane Wife* retain onomatopoeic words that echo the sounds of the Japanese language within the storytelling format.

Is the Collection Balanced?

A special consideration is the need to present children with a balanced collection of multicultural books. The term "collection" refers to the books that are available in a school, classroom, or public library and also to the books selected to serve as teaching units within a classroom. Budget constraints, space limitations, and the need to present readers with the best possible choices make careful decisions regarding book collections a necessity. Readers need to be able to find recommended books readily, not buried under an avalanche of mediocre books. It is generally accepted that purchasing multiple copies of excellent books is better than including mediocre books simply to increase the size of the collection. Because a great number of high-quality multicultural books are available today, there is no need to include books simply to fulfill a quota.

To compile a balanced multicultural collection, a teacher or librarian should assess needs and match available quality books with those identified needs. In assessing needs, consideration should be given to (1) readers' preferences, (2) existing multicultural books in the collection, (3) curricular needs, (4) the availability of quality multicultural books, and (5) provision of a strong selection across genres. In addition, the compiler should ensure that adequate numbers of books are available for recreational reading, for teacher read-alouds, and for placement in the classroom library.

Consider Readers' Preferences. Both teachers and librarians need to acquire an understanding of the general background knowledge and the preferences of the readers for whom the particular collection is being developed, including the range of materials they enjoy and the types of books they choose. Often, children will be interested in reading books about their own cultural group, but that is not always the case. Some readers will voluntarily read books about other cultural groups; others might need to be introduced to and encouraged to select such books.

Survey Multicultural Books Already in the Collection. Multicultural books that are already in the collection form the core of the collection and help to determine what is needed. Overselecting or underselecting certain types of books can be avoided by conducting a careful inventory of existing books in the collection. Is there an overabundance of folktales from various cultures? Are there enough contemporary stories about people of diversity? Are there books that show multiple perspectives? Familiarity with the existing collection also allows a teacher or librarian to weed out and discard books that are not culturally appropriate.

Assess Curricular Needs. It is important to assess curricular needs to determine what is needed to supplement units of study. Because of the current emphasis on literature-based curriculum, more and more high-quality books are being used in all curricular areas. As teachers and librarians work together to obtain books that fit the needs of the curriculum, they should attempt to include books that extend beyond the basic information and enhance multicultural understanding.

Determine the Availability of High-Quality Multicultural Books. Determine the availability of quality multicultural books because no matter what the needs are, only high-quality books should be considered. Obtaining lower-quality books simply to fill a shelf is not recommended.

Provide a Strong Selection across Genres. Another goal in establishing a balanced collection of multicultural books is to provide a variety of different genres. For example, when creating a collection of books about Mexico, the teacher or librarian should make a point to include folklore, history, informational books, picture books, historical fiction, biography, poetry, and modern realistic fiction. There should be books set in Mexico as well as books about Mexican Americans. The books must represent a broad range of experiences and voices if readers are to understand the diverse nature of Mexico and its people.

INTERNATIONAL LITERATURE DEFINED

Another category of literature that can provide readers with diverse perspectives is international literature. Traditionally, the term "international literature" applied to books originally written and published outside the United States (Tomlinson, 1998). If these books were originally written in a language other than English, they were translated for the U.S. audience. In recent years, an increasing number of books set entirely in foreign countries have been written and published in the United States (Freeman and Lehman, 2001). Both types of international books are discussed here.

Literature That Originates Outside of the United States

The first category of international literature is books written and published in countries outside the United States and translated into English if originally written in another language. Mem Fox's *Possum Magic* is an English-language book originally published in Australia. In this fantasy of a possum made invisible by magic, the possum's grandmother tries to remember how to make him visible once again. Along the way, readers hear the names of the Australian cities to which Hush and Grandmother journey and the various Australian foods they eat at each stop. Christina Bjork's series about Linnea is another example of quality international literature. *Linnea in Monet's Garden* was originally written in Swedish and then was translated into English and made available to the U.S. audience. Importing books from abroad makes the works of the best authors and illustrators in the world available to children in the United States.

Literature about Other Countries, Written and Published in the United States

The second category of international literature is books set in a country other than the United States but written and published in the United States. These books are set in a "root country"—that is, a country from which some American children's ancestors originally came. Although most children will not have lived long, if ever, in the country of their family's origin, they may feel a connection to it. Beverley Naidoo's *Journey to Jo'burg: A South African Story* tells of how Naledi travels to Jo'burg to deliver the news of her baby sister's near-death from an illness to her mother, who works and lives in the home of white people. The circumstances described in the story accurately reflect a recent period in South African history that is likely somewhat removed in immediacy from the lives of American children of South African ancestry.

The primary purpose for all international books is the same: to tell a compelling story. However, because international books that originate in the country portrayed and international books that are written and published in the United

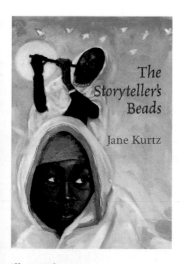

Illustration 4.7
Fleeing their drought- and violence-stricken land, two young Ethiopian refugees overcome their prejudices and find solace in the old stories passed down by one of their grandmothers. (Cover illustration from *The Storyteller's Beads* by Jane Kurtz, copyright © 1998 by James Ransome, reproduced by permission of Harcourt, Inc.)

States have different intended audiences, they contribute to children's understanding of world cultures in different ways. Books originating in a foreign country allow U.S. readers to experience native perceptions of that country. International books written in the United States include information that may enlighten nonnative readers about a foreign country.

CRITERIA FOR EVALUATING AND SELECTING INTERNATIONAL LITERATURE

With the exception of authenticity, the evaluation and selection issues previously discussed in connection with multicultural literature are also important for international literature originating outside the United States. Although many countries publish material that is about cultures outside their own, the books that get exported to other countries tend to be about native experiences. When one's own country is the setting, cultural authenticity is expected, as both author and illustrator have an inside perspective. Two crucial issues specific to international literature are the intended audience and the quality of the translation.

Intended Audience

An international book is originally written from the perspective of an author within the country, with readers in that country as the intended audience. Only later is the book taken abroad to other countries. When a book travels away from its intended audience, sometimes the new audience needs support to help them understand it. Teachers should consider these questions: Is the book geared specifically toward readers in the book's country of origin, or does it make the transition to a broader audience outside of that country? Who will be able to empathize and identify with the story? Books written in the United States and intended for American children tend to include explanations of things that readers native to the country portrayed take for granted. Similarly, books originally written for readers in another country often assume understandings that only the original intended audience would have. Sometimes, misinterpretations may occur when details are not understood; other times, inability to pick up details doesn't detract from the reader's understanding of the story as a whole.

As an example, let's examine Akiko Hayashi's illustrations of the series of books about Anna. The pictures are laden with cultural details—mailboxes attached on the inside of the front door, slippers in the entryway, artificial flowers on the street light, a place where children wash their hands at the park. Even the way Anna steps on the back of her shoes shows she is rushing as she tries to discover the identity of her new friend in *Anna's Secret Friend.* Japanese children would pick up these details because they are very natural to their understanding of home and community. American children might not take particular note of these details or might find them interesting but not different enough to interfere with an understanding of the story.

Sometimes, details in the original edition of a book, which would be innately understood by the original audience, are explained when the book is prepared in an international edition. Uri Orlev's Batchelder Award book *The Lady with the Hat* has two characters stopping for a meal while on a trip in a remote area of Palestine. Foods such as hummus, tahini, shashlik, kebab, baklava, and Turkish coffee are described for readers who are unfamiliar with them—for example, "small cakes filled with pistachio nuts and honey that were called baklava."

Translation

An issue of critical concern with international books is translation. When a book was originally published in a language other than English, the translator who makes it available to English-language readers plays an important role in how the material is received by the new audience. The translator is as important as the author and illustrator in presenting the story. A skilled translator does not merely present the author's words in another language, but instead interprets the words, selecting ways to evoke images and emotions that reflect the author's original intent. The translator must consider several things:

■ Creating a flow in the translated language, despite differences in the sentence structures of the two languages

■ Balancing the amount of "foreign" information to maintain readability and reader attention yet retain the unique details that make the work authentic

■ Explaining foreign situations that are unknown to readers while maintaining the pace of the original text

Even when a book is from another English-language country, some differences in language use are noticeable to U.S. readers. Should these differences be changed? When comprehension may suffer, the answer is yes. But maintaining as much of the original language as possible is part of maintaining the authenticity of the book. In Mem Fox's book *Shoes from Grandpa,* originally published in Australia, the family was enjoying a "barbie." A U.S. audience, unexposed to this name for a barbecue, might imagine the doll known as Barbie. The word was changed in this case. Yet in another of Mem Fox's books, *Possum Magic,* references to Australian foods such as "mornay, vegemite and pavlova" were maintained in the U.S. version. These words, though unknown to most American children, do not interfere with their understanding of the story. With the words left in, the story remains true to the original context of the Australian culture. A benefit of this approach is that U.S. children are introduced to vocabulary that expands their knowledge of another country.

It does require extra effort to make international books accessible to U.S. audiences. But the benefits gained from including international books in children's repertoire make the extra effort worthwhile. One notable example of an international book is Mitsumasa Anno's *All in a Day.* A young child is on a deserted island, somewhere near the international date line. Each double-page spread shows this child in the center section, with text to one side. Across the top and the bottom of the spread are depictions of what New Year's Day might be like for children in eight different countries; each picture is by an illustrator from that country. Each time the reader turns a page, three hours have passed. In the preface to the book, Anno asks readers to consider the fact that while some children sleep, others play, and while some swim, others build snowmen. He points out that differences exist around the world in homes, clothes, languages, and so on, but he also notes that there are some things that remain the same around the world, such as facial

Illustration 4.8
Mitsumasa Anno created *All in a Day* because he believes that world understanding begins with children imagining the lives of other children around the world. (*All in a Day* by Mitsumasa Anno. Copyright © 1986 by Kuso-Kubo, Raymond Briggs, Ron Brooks, Gian Calvi, Eric Carle, Leo & Diane Dillon, Akiko Hayashi, Nicolai Ye, Popov & Zhu Chengliang. Used by permission of Philomel Books, a division of Penguin Putnam Inc.)

expressions, the sounds of laughing or crying, and the moon and the sun in the sky. Anno and his team of illustrators offer a note of optimism. Their hope—and ours as well—is that by the time the children of today grow up, the world will have become a better place. This book exemplifies a sense of world community from a child's point of view. Although the book was originally published in Japanese, the composition of the illustration team and the theme make this book truly international.

AWARDS FOR MULTICULTURAL AND INTERNATIONAL LITERATURE

Illustration 4.9
Children can share in other countries' heritages by reading folktales from those cultures, such as *Lon Po Po*, the Chinese "Little Red Riding Hood." (*Lon Po Po* by Ed Young. Copyright © 1989 by Ed Young. Used by permission of Philomel Books, a division of Penguin Putnam Inc.)

Multicultural books qualify for all of the general awards that are given to children's literature, such as the Caldecott Medal and the Newbery Medal. Several multicultural books have been recipients of such awards. For example, Ed Young was presented the Caldecott Medal for *Lon Po Po: A Red-Riding Hood Story from China.* However, some awards are designated specifically for multicultural and international literature. Some are given for a single book, and others for the author's or illustrator's entire body of work. The awards are intended to bring attention to various aspects of multicultural book publishing. The most prestigious of these awards are the Coretta Scott King Award, the Pura Belpré Award, the Hans Christian Andersen Award, and the Mildred Batchelder Award. In addition, awards are sometimes given to previously unpublished authors and illustrators to encourage the writing and illustrating of books on multicultural subjects. Sometimes, these awards have played important roles in launching the careers of authors and illustrators. Awards provide public recognition for a book, author, or illustrator and serve as selection and evaluation tools.

The Coretta Scott King Award

At an American Library Association conference in 1969, after lamenting the fact that a "minority" author or illustrator had never been awarded the Newbery or Caldecott Medal, school librarians Mabel McKissick and Glyndon Greer were encouraged by publisher John Carroll to launch a new award highlighting the accomplishments of African American authors and illustrators. The award was named in honor of Coretta Scott King to "commemorate the life and work of Martin Luther King, Jr." as well as to honor his wife for "courage and determination in continuing to work for peace and brotherhood" (Smith, 1994). The Coretta Scott King Award has been presented at the annual meeting of the American Library Association since 1972 and has been recognized as an official ALA award since 1982. Selection criteria for the award have evolved with the increase in the number of books from which to choose. At the beginning, any book that reflected some aspect of the black experience or embraced concepts of brotherhood was considered. In recent years, however, the criteria have become more stringent and now specify that "recipients are African American authors and illustrators whose distinguished books promote an understanding and appreciation of the culture and contribution of all people to the realization of the 'American dream.'" Refer to Appendix A for a list of past winners and honor books.

Since 1993, the Genesis Award certificate of recognition has been given to African American authors and illustrators who show significant promise in their

Illustration 4.10
The story of *Tar Beach* (both a winner of the Coretta Scott King Award and a Caldecott Honor Book in 1992) originally appeared in the form of a "story quilt," with the text surrounding a central picture on a quilt. [*Tar Beach (Woman on a Beach Series #1)* by Faith Ringgold. Faith Ringgold © 1988. Reproduced with permission of Faith Ringgold Studio. Photograph by David Heald © The Solomon R. Guggenheim Foundation, New York. Book published by Random House, Inc.]

work. Basic criteria for this award are the same as for the Coretta Scott King Award, but winners can have no more than three published works.

The Pura Belpré Award

The Pura Belpré Award, established in 1996, is sponsored jointly by Reforma (a national association to promote library services to Spanish speakers) and the American Library Association's Association of Library Services to Children. It is awarded biannually to a Latino/a writer and illustrator whose work best depicts and celebrates Latino heritage. A complete list of past winners can be found in Appendix A.

The Asian Pacific American Award for Literature

The Asian Pacific American Award for Literature was presented for the first time in 2001 by the National Conference on Asian Pacific American Librarians. It is given every other year to Asian Pacific American writers in three categories, one of which is literature for children and young adults. Authors of fiction and nonfiction books are eligible, and both the author and the illustrator of picture books are jointly eligible. The first book to be honored was **The Trip Back Home,** written by Janet Wong and illustrated by Bo Jia. **Cool Melons Turn to Frogs!,** written by Matthew Gollub and illustrated by Kazuko Stone, was named the honor book.

The Hans Christian Andersen Award

The International Board on Books for Young People (IBBY) established the Hans Christian Andersen Award in 1956. The purpose of this international award is to honor an author who has made a significant contribution to children's literature; an award for illustrators has been offered since 1966. The entire body of work by an author or an illustrator is considered, and national IBBY chapters nominate an author and an illustrator from their country. This award is given every two years at the IBBY World Congress, which is held in various locations throughout the world. Past U.S. winners include author Meindert DeJong in 1962, illustrator Maurice Sendak in 1970, author Scott O'Dell in 1972, author Paula Fox in 1978, author Virginia Hamilton in 1992, and author

Katherine Paterson in 1998. Some winners from other countries have books published in the United States, among them Astrid Lindgren from Sweden, Svend Otto S. from Denmark, Suekichi Akaba and Mitsumasa Anno from Japan, Lygia Bojunga Nunes from Brazil, Patricia Wrightson and Robert Ingpen from Australia, Lisbeth Zwerger from Austria, and Anthony Browne from England. A complete list of past winners can be found in Appendix A.

The Mildred Batchelder Award

The Mildred Batchelder Award was established in 1966 by the American Library Association's Association of Library Services to Children (ALSC) to promote international exchange of books for young people; it has been given to a U.S. publisher annually since 1968, unless no book is deemed worthy in a particular year. The award is named in honor of a former executive director of the ALSC. Books originally published in a foreign language in a foreign country and translated and published in the United States in the year preceding the award are considered. The citation is given to publishers to recognize their commitment to bringing books from abroad and making them available to young people in this country. With the exception of a few picture books, including the 1983 winner *Hiroshima No Pika* and the 1987 winner *Rose Blanche,* most books are novels for older children. A complete list of past winners can be found in Appendix A.

Other International Book Awards

Many countries have book awards equivalent to the Caldecott and Newbery Medals. Great Britain has the Kate Greenaway Medal and the Carnegie Medal. Canada has the Amelia Frances Howard-Gibbon Medal and the Canadian Children's Book of the Year award. Australia has the Picture Book of the Year award and the Australian Children's Book of the Year for Young Readers award. The major book awards given by other English-language countries are included in Appendix A.

More multicultural books are being published today than in any previous decade, and an increasing number of international books are continuing to find their way onto bookstore and library shelves. Thus, teachers and parents have the opportunity and the responsibility to select high-quality multicultural and international books. In her book *Against Borders,* Hazel Rochman (1993) suggests that teachers and parents look for books that fight against the idea of borders that separate people and seek out books that help readers tear down those borders by beginning to understand people around the world.

LITERATURE PORTRAYING OTHER DIVERSE PERSPECTIVES

Literature plays a vital role in providing vicarious experience in interacting with others, whether those others are like ourselves or very different. In some cases, literature confirms a reader's firsthand experiences in interacting with people of differing perspectives; in other cases, literature substitutes for experiences the reader might not have had firsthand.

Literature Portraying Gender Equity and Gender Roles

Father leaves for the office carrying a briefcase and wearing a topcoat and hat. Mother stays home and does housework, wearing a dress. Boys have adventures and are brave. Girls need protection and are passive. Images such as these abounded in children's books of the past and can still be found in some books today. The danger is that children who experience only books with these messages will come away with the idea that these images represent the norm of gender roles. Well-written gender-sensitive literature fights stereotypes by depicting the diversity and multidimensionality of men and women, girls and boys.

The following criteria should be used to evaluate the content of messages that are sent to readers regarding gender issues: Occupations should be gender-free, achievements should be judged without gender bias, both parents should share family responsibilities, and gender stereotyping based on physical description and behaviors should be avoided (Rudman, 1995). It is important to evaluate character portrayal, interactions among characters, and societal expectations of character roles. Sexist language is a sign of the writer's perspective on gender roles and therefore should be avoided at all times.

Gender Equity. Gender equity has different facets. A book reflecting gender equity shows equal opportunities for both genders in the workplace and depicts multiple and diverse personal roles for individuals of both genders. Children begin receiving messages about their gender's places and roles in society from the time they are infants. These messages come from family, friends, books, media, and society in general. What are the messages found in books?

Let's examine a message from a book published in 1957. Gene Zion's **Dear Garbage Man** is still in print and available to children through book club order forms distributed in schools. In it, Stan the garbage man tries to "recycle" people's unwanted trash by redistributing it to others. The accompanying text reads, "After everyone had helped themselves, fathers went to work and mothers went back to the dishes." The next day, the new owners realize that these items are indeed trash and return them to the garbage man. At first, he is disappointed, but then a "big smile brighten[s] his face" as he says, "All this stuff will fill in lots and lots of swamps!" The driver responds, "Stan, you're a real garbage man now!" This books presents several gender stereotypes: Jobs involving physical labor are reserved for men; all garbage collectors are men; men go to work and women do dishes. And, of course, the ecological message of this book is troubling. Because books often reflect societal values and prejudices that prevail at the time of writing, some older books contain themes and messages that are not considered appropriate for children today.

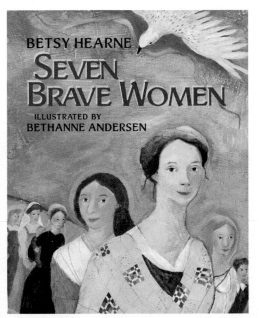

Illustration 4.11
In *Seven Brave Women,* courage is revealed in the everyday lives and actions of diverse women. (*Seven Brave Women* by Betsy Hearne, illustrated by Bethanne Andersen. Copyright © 1997. Used by permission of Greenwillow, a division of HarperCollins Publishers.)

Some books do a good job of portraying nontraditional gender roles in believable ways that are natural to the story. For example, Katherine Paterson's **The King's Equal** depicts a prince who is searching for a princess who is "his equal," only to find that he must prove to be "her equal." Rachel Isadora's **Max** is about a boy who finds that taking dance class with his sister is a great way to warm up for his baseball games on Saturdays. Betsy Hearne's **Seven Brave Women** describes the strength and contributions of women from her own life. These women's lives are not marked by the wars they fought in history, but tell "herstory" of courage and leadership nevertheless. Readers find a female not just having an adventure but leading many outrageous adventures when they read about Ms. Frizzle, a teacher who takes her class on field trips on the *Magic School Bus* in the series by Joanna Cole.

It is a problem, though, when books try too hard—when they depict the opposites of the stereotyped gender roles in hard-to-believe ways or are didactic in presentation. Anthony Browne's **Piggybook** addresses the problem of women who are enslaved to their families. The front cover shows the mother carrying her husband and two sons "piggyback." As the story unfolds, the illustrations show the males of the family (and their surroundings) turning more and more piglike until finally the mother leaves them with a note stating "You are pigs." When they plead for her return, this mother—who has previously been depicted washing dishes, vacuuming carpets, making beds, ironing, cooking, and washing clothes, in shadowy pictures without her face showing—now fixes the car! The story is humorous in many ways. But such a dramatic change in roles, especially one that requires the sudden acquisition of specific knowledge, is hardly believable and perhaps trivializes the importance of representing equal gender opportunities and roles.

Homosexuality and Alternative Family Structures. The school curriculum at the primary level is most often developed around the concept of a nuclear family composed of a mother, father, and their children. However, over the past decades, schools have become increasingly populated with children whose home life does not fit that model. Although people typically think of a nontraditional family as a single-parent family or one in which grandparents raise the children, many variant households are headed by lesbian or gay parents. When the New York State Board of Education required that first-grade curricula include the reading of **Daddy's Roommate,** much controversy surrounded the issue of alternative lifestyles. This picture book depicts a divorced father who lives with his homosexual partner. In a book for older children, Jacqueline Woodson's **From the Notebooks of Melanin Sun,** the central character is a boy whose mother is in love with a woman. Books such as these portray what it means for the children when their parents have a partner of the same gender.

Literature Portraying Social Diversity

American society also shows its diversity in many ways besides the cultural identities of ethnicity, race, physical/mental ability, and gender. Poverty, low social class, homelessness, illiteracy, and a migrant lifestyle, among other factors, just as significantly create an identifying culture. Living and working under those circumstances affects the way people experience the world and the way the world views them. It is important to note that poverty, the most common of social diversities, is often found in conjunction with other types of social diversity, so children's books dealing with any form of social diversity may touch on poverty as well.

In choosing children's books depicting social diversity, of utmost importance is finding authentic, nonstereotyped portrayals that are believable. Eve Bunting has written several books that deal with sensitive issues of social diversity. **The Wednesday Surprise** begins with seven-year-old Anna and her grandmother spending Wednesday nights together while Mom works late at the office and Dad is away on his truck. Every week, Grandma brings a bag of picture books to Anna's house and they "read the story together, out loud," book after book. The surprise is for Dad's birthday. When Grandma stands up and begins reading aloud, "Mom and Dad and Sam are all astonished." When did she learn to read? Grandma reveals that Anna taught her on Wednesday nights and then she took the books home and practiced. This family had urged Grandma to go to classes to learn to read; instead, she found that reading picture books with her granddaughter was a good incentive.

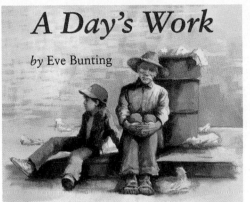

A Day's Work

by Eve Bunting

Illustrated by Ronald Himler

Illustration 4.12

A Day's Work looks at the plight of new immigrants when a boy and his non-English-speaking grandfather misunderstand the directions for a job they are hired to do. (Cover from *A Day's Work* by Eve Bunting, illustrated by Ronald Himler. Jacket art copyright © 1994 by Ronald Himler. Reprinted by permission of Clarion Books/Houghton Mifflin Company. All rights reserved.)

Eve Bunting's *A Day's Work* looks at the plight of new immigrants. A little boy and his non-English-speaking grandfather are hired off a street corner to pull weeds. Inadvertently, they pull up all the plants and leave all the weeds. The grandfather insists on redoing the job, and in an unexpected act of patience and understanding, the employer rehires the boy and his grandfather.

Readers of Frances Temple's *Grab Hands and Run* find themselves drawn into the story of a family escaping a threat on their lives in El Salvador. Through the eyes of the young narrator, Felipe, the story of the dangerous journey north to Canada is told. In Fran Leeper Buss's *Journey of the Sparrows,* three siblings are smuggled into the United States nailed into crates. Once in the United States, they must hide from immigration officials, find work so that they can get food and shelter, and save enough money to send for the rest of the family they have left behind. The rich details throughout both books fill in gaps in the experiences of most readers. Most of us can't imagine a life filled with constant hunger and fear of being found and returned to a land of certain death. Because of the array of human emotions that ring true, readers come to believe in the reality of the situations portrayed in these books.

Literature about People with Exceptionalities

Literature about people with exceptionalities or special needs portrays those with physical, mental, emotional, or learning disabilities, as well as gifted and talented children. Sometimes, an exceptionality is a life-threatening or debilitating illness that alters a person's ability to lead life in the same way a healthy child can.

There are many stereotyped views that distort children's understanding of exceptional learners and give rise to fear, pity, and misunderstandings of intellectual and social abilities. Exceptional children should be portrayed in books as individuals with many facets to their lives. They should not be considered heroic for learning to live with disabilities and differing abilities. Also important is how people with exceptionalities are treated by others. When a book portrays exceptional learners in unconventional ways, readers might feel betrayed or may be led to accept a mistaken image.

A number of informational books use photographs and narration to provide contemporary images of people with disabilities. *Helping Hands: How Monkeys Assist People Who Are Disabled* is the story of a teenager with quadriplegia and his helper monkey, a capuchin named Willie. The text and accompanying photographs show how Willie is trained to assist: He can fetch a sandwich from the refrigerator, warm it in the microwave, and serve it on a tray. Such information can help children to get a sense of one aspect of daily life for someone who is quadriplegic. In *Handtalk School,* readers follow a day at a residential school for the deaf and see children communicating through American Sign Language (ASL) as well as with a telephone device for the deaf (TDD). The book shows signed messages with accompanying text so that readers can follow along.

Biographies of both famous and ordinary people provide glimpses into the lives of exceptional learners. Author Jean Little's autobiography, *Little by Little: A Writer's Education,* describes how her "bad eyes" led to a childhood full of ridicule and rejection until she found that her retreat into her imagination paved the way for her career as a writer.

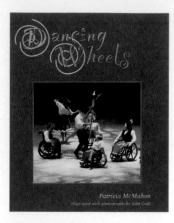

Illustration 4.13
The Dancing Wheels dance company includes both "standing" dancers and "sitting" dancers, who travel across the country, performing with energy and commitment.
(Cover from *Dancing Wheels* by Patricia McMahon, photographs by John Goodt. Jacket photograph copyright © 2000 by John Goodt. Reprinted by permission of Houghton Mifflin Company. All rights reserved.)

Fantasy books can provide an interesting vehicle by which to consider the perspective of people with disabilities. In Franny Billingsley's **Well Wished,** Nura wishes at the magic well that her friend Catty, who is wheelchair bound, could have a body like hers. What happens instead is that the two girls enter each other's body. The notion of "don't judge until you've experienced someone else's life" is illustrated in a way that is not possible in real life. Nevertheless, this fantasy offers readers an opportunity to take another point of view.

Fictional books can depict exceptional children in ways that provide insight for readers. In Alfred Slote's **Hang Tough, Paul Mather,** the protagonist is twelve-year-old Paul, who has leukemia. Paul's enthusiasm for baseball and his relationship with his teammates give readers a realistic glimpse of what it means to live with the illness and the accompanying treatments. In Terry Trueman's **Stuck in Neutral,** fourteen-year-old Shawn is believed to have the mental age of three or four months. But Shawn narrates the story, showing that he has amazing memory and perceptive thinking; it's just that his total inability to control his muscles, because of cerebral palsy, makes him unable to communicate. This is speculation fiction; we do not truly know what goes on in the minds of those who appear to be incapable of communicating. But reading a book such as this will certainly cause readers to pause and reflect on our reactions and responses to people with disabilities.

TEACHERS' ROLES IN PRESENTING MULTIPLE AND DIVERSE PERSPECTIVES

It is important for teachers to read a wide variety of books. Personal reading of high-quality adult books depicting diverse perspectives enhances the teacher's understanding of the world. Professional reading offers teachers theories on why reading a broad range of books is helpful. Reading children's books allows teachers to identify books appropriate in content and level for the children with whom they will be shared.

Understanding Diverse Perspectives through Adult Literature

Reading is important both to enhance current understandings and to add new perspectives on the world. Teachers frequently seek out books that provide such reading experiences for their students. But it is also important for teachers to read adult books so that they can better understand diverse perspectives. A children's book offers a certain level of insight into diversity. A young adult book allows more space and time to reflect on issues. An adult book allows readers to think about these issues in even greater depth.

Research indicates that students frequently relate best to a teacher's messages when the students' cultural background is similar to the teacher's (Au, 1993; Delpit, 1988). Teachers understand the world from their own cultural perspectives, and it is impossible to share the background of each of their students. One way in which teachers can try to build their background is by joining a discussion group that discusses adult books depicting diverse viewpoints; such discussions take the understandings gained from reading to a deeper level. By building their own background, teachers can enhance their ability to facilitate discussions of literature with their students.

Understanding Diverse Perspectives through Professional Literature

Teachers can choose from a variety of professional materials dealing with literature that reflects diversity. Such professional materials discuss the importance of reading multicultural literature, recommend criteria for evaluation and selection, and present methods for discussing and eliciting responses to the literature. Often, there are annotated bibliographies to help teachers to identify books that may interest students. Reading professional materials improves understanding of the critical role teachers play in making multicultural literature accessible to children.

Helping Children Gain Diverse Perspectives

It is generally accepted that children's reading choices are often based on recommendations of peers and influential adults. Therefore, teachers, library media specialists, and other influential adults have a responsibility to be knowledgeable about books that offer a wide variety of perspectives.

Teachers can help to ensure that their students gain a variety of perspectives by keeping diversity in mind when they are selecting reading material for the whole class and when they are deciding what choices are offered to students in book clubs and are available to students for individual free choice. The importance of the school librarian or media specialist in acting as a consultant to the teacher and to individual students in choosing reading materials cannot be overlooked.

Even more important than the role teachers and librarians play in the selection of reading materials is their role in facilitating discussions and in providing opportunities for responding to literature. Chapter 13 details the critical role of the teacher in leading discussion. Chapter 14 describes the many ways in which teachers can provide opportunities for students to respond to literature.

TEACHING IDEAS

Assess Gender Roles in Books Published in the Past. Begin discussion by having children list gender characteristics they believe to be true. Find some books (for example, *Dear Garbage Man*) that show outdated images of gender roles. Challenge the children to identify ways the books no longer reflect society. Lead a discussion that focuses on issues of gender equality. Compare comments made during the discussion with the gender characteristics identified earlier.

Identify Cultural Markers. Cultural markers are found in culturally authentic books. They are the details that are true to a culture—artifacts, character behavior, language use, physical descriptions. Select a picture book that includes cultural markers and have children list all those they encounter in either the text or the illustrations.

Connect Books with Similar Themes, across Differing Cultures. Present a set of books that have similar themes but represent different cultures. Examples of themes are the search for freedom, immigrating to the United States, coming of age, friendships and peer relationships, and intergenerational relationships. Have children realize the universality of many themes but also how the details of the stories differ if they are culturally bound.

Research Family History and Stories. Have children ask their families about their heritage and what stories the adults remember from their childhood. Families could orally tell the stories into a tape recorder or videocamera or write them down to be shared with the class. This might serve as the beginning of a book, created by the child.

Connect to International Books. If possible, collect some books that are translations of books the children might know in their original English editions. Show how children in other countries are reading books that they may also have read. Then present some books that are international books published in the United States and emphasize the country of origin so that children may understand how children in other countries have also enjoyed the same book.

EXPERIENCES FOR YOUR LEARNING

1. Divide children into separate groups by gender, and have each of them create a list of books that they find especially meaningful. What similarities exist in their preferences? What differences are there? What might this mean for you, as to the kinds of books you read and recommend to children? Does your reading reflect a gender bias?

2. Research the personal background of an author or illustrator whose work in total appears to be culturally authentic. In what ways does the background offer explanations for how the author or illustrator connects to the culture she or he represents?

3. Collect a sampling of books that portray the lives of people with exceptionalities and analyze the ways the people are presented to readers. Are they portrayed as individuals with many facets to their lives? Do other characters treat them with fear or pity? Are they considered heroic because they can live with disabilities?

4. Carl Tomlinson suggests the pairing of a familiar book with an international book so that readers may compare and contrast the two. For example, *Chibi: A True Story from Japan* could be paired with *Make Way for Ducklings.* A setting like Boston Public Garden may well be familiar to many children, but they might find a parallel in a similar story of ducklings in search of a safe home at the Imperial Palace moat in Japan.

5. Select a social issue and find several children's books about it. Compare and contrast the treatments of the issue. Do the books treat the issue in a believable way? Do they deal with the issue honestly? What messages are communicated to children?

6. Survey the multicultural books that are available in your public or school library and collect a representative sample. Look at the books in light of the issues discussed in this chapter. Are they written and illustrated from an inside or an outside perspective? Is there evidence of stereotyping or other unacceptable depictions of cultural groups? Are cultural details presented authentically? As a collection, what messages do these books send to readers regarding different cultures?

7. Storytelling is popular throughout the world, and many cultures have unique ways of telling stories. Select a story to tell, study the culture's storytelling style, and practice presenting the story to others. Resources that may be of help include Anne Pellowski's *Hidden Stories in Plants* (1990), *Family Story-Telling Handbook* (1987), and *The Story Vine* (1984).

RECOMMENDED BOOKS

* indicates a picture book; I indicates interest level (P = preschool, YA = young adult)

Multicultural literature and literature portraying various types of diversity can be found throughout this textbook. These lists represent a sampling of recommended books. In particular, Chapter 8, "Realistic Fiction," includes titles that depict realistic portrayals of people of diversity. A list of recommended books can be found at the end of that chapter.

African and African American

*Aardema, Verna. *Rabbit Makes a Monkey of Lion: A Swahili Tale*. Illustrated by Jerry Pinkney. Dial, 1989. To "make a monkey" of someone is to make the person appear to be a fool, and this Swahili tale is about a little rabbit that outwits the big lion. (I: P–7)

*———. *Who's in Rabbit's House? A Masai Tale*. Illustrated by Leo Dillon and Diane Dillon. Dial, 1977. Rabbit's friends try to get rid of a mysterious Long One that is occupying Rabbit's House—and the solution is a surprising one. The illustrations portray this story as a play, acted out by Masai wearing masks. (I: P–8)

*———. *Why Mosquitoes Buzz in People's Ears: A West African Tale*. Illustrated by Leo Dillon and Diane Dillon. Dial, 1978. A chain of events is started when a mosquito tells a big lie. (I: P–8)

*Adoff, Arnold. *All the Colors of the Race*. Illustrated by John Steptoe. Lothrop, Lee & Shepard, 1982. The poems in this book deal with issues of race. (I: 8–11)

———, ed. *My Black Me: A Beginning Book of Black Poetry*. Dutton, 1974/1994. This anthology opens with Adoff's words "This book of Black is for you." Poets such as Langston Hughes, Lucille Clifton, Nikki Giovanni, and Imamu Amiri Baraka contributed to the anthology. (I: 9–YA)

Bridges, Ruby. *Through My Eyes*. Scholastic, 1999. Ruby Bridges is known for her role in integrating a New Orleans school at the age of six. She narrates her story, which also includes passages written by her teacher, Mrs. Henry; newspaper quotes and other citations; and photographs. (I: 6–12)

*Bryan, Ashley. *Ashley Bryan's ABC of African American Poetry*. Atheneum, 1998. Poetry of African American poets (arranged in alphabetical order) is accompanied by Bryan's colorful illustrations. (I: 6–9)

———. *Beat the Story-Drum, Pum-Pum*. Atheneum, 1980. This collection of retellings includes five Nigerian folktales. (I: 7–10)

———. *Sing to the Sun*. Harper/Collins, 1992. This collection of original poetry and art by Ashley Bryan celebrates life and the emotions aroused by everyday occurrences. (I: 6–10)

*Caines, Jeannette. *I Need a Lunch Box*. Illustrated by Pat Cummings. HarperCollins, 1988. A preschool boy longs for a lunch box like the ones his school-age siblings have, so that he can store his treasures in it. (I: P–7).

*———. *Just Us Women*. Illustrated by Pat Cummings. Harper & Row, 1982. A young girl and her Aunt Martha take a car trip that allows "just us women" to do whatever they like along the way. (I: 6–9)

Cameron, Ann. *Gloria's Way*. Illustrated by Lil Toft. Foster/Farrar, 2000. Six warm-hearted short stories are about Gloria and her parents and friends Julian, Huey, and Latisha from Cameron's earlier books. See also *The Stories Julian Tells* (1981), *The Stories Huey Tells* (1995), etc. (I: 6–8)

*Clifton, Lucille. *Some of the Days of Everett Anderson*. Illustrated by Evaline Ness. Holt, 1970/1987. Everett Anderson, a black six-year-old who lives in Apt. 14A, tells how he spends his time. Related titles are *Everett Anderson's Friend* (1976), *Everett Anderson's Christmas Coming* (1971/1991), and *Everett Anderson's Goodbye* (1983/1988). (I: P–7)

*Cooper, Floyd. *Coming Home: From the Life of Langston Hughes*. Philomel, 1994. This picture book biography of the African American poet describes his childhood and his search for "home." (I: 7–10)

*Crews, Donald. *Bigmama's*. Greenwillow, 1991. This is an autobiographical story of visiting "Bigmama's" house and visiting with relatives in the summertimes during Donald Crews's youth. Also by Crews is *Shortcut* (1992). (I: P–8)

Curtis, Christopher Paul. *The Watsons Go to Birmingham—1963*. Delacorte, 1995. The Watsons are an African American family from Flint, Michigan. Their 1963 summer visit to Grandmother in Alabama changes their lives dramatically. (I: 10–YA)

———. *Bud, Not Buddy*. Delacorte, 1999. In 1930s Michigan, Bud leaves the orphanage to seek the jazz musician he believes is his father. (I: 10–YA)

English, Karen. *Francie*. Farrar, Straus Giroux, 1999. Twelve-year-old Francie longs to leave behind the racism in 1930s Alabama to join her Pullman porter father in Chicago. (I: 10–and up)

Feelings, Tom. *The Middle Passage: White Ships Black Cargo*. Dial, 1995. This wordless book dramatically depicts the hardships of the journey across the Atlantic Ocean made by Africans bound for slavery in America. (I: 10–YA)

*———. *Soul Looks Back in Wonder*. Dial, 1993. Feelings created the stunning art, which is accompanied by the voices of noted poets, including Maya Angelou, Langston Hughes, and Lucille Clifton, who write of their African American heritage. (I: 9–YA)

*Flournoy, Valerie. *The Patchwork Quilt*. Illustrated by Jerry Pinkney. Dial, 1985. As Tanya helps her mother and grandmother create a quilt from the scraps of their family's clothes, she comes to realize the stories and memories the quilt holds. A sequel is *Tanya's Reunion* (1995). (I: 6–9)

*Fox, Mem. *Sophie*. Illustrated by Aminah Brenda Lynn Robinson. Harcourt Brace, 1989. Sophie holds onto her grandfather's hand as she grows up. He holds onto hers as he gets smaller and older. (I: P–6)

*Giovanni, Nikki. *Spin a Soft Black Song*. Illustrated by George Martins. HarperCollins, 1971/1985. This is a collection of poems reflecting African American children's everyday thoughts in their own voices. (I: 6–10)

Govenar, Alan (collector and editor). *Osceola: Memories of a Sharecropper's Daughter*. Illustrated by Shane W. Evans. Jump at the Sun/Hyperion, 2000. In her straightforward and personal voice, Osceola Mays recalls a childhood in the early 1900s as a sharecropper's daughter. (I: 8–12)

*Greenfield, Eloise. *Africa Dreams*. Illustrated by Carole Byard. Harper, 1977/1989. A young African American girl dreams about what it would be like to visit her granddaddy's village. (I: P–8)

*———. *Grandpa's Face*. Illustrated by Floyd Cooper. Philomel, 1988. Tamika is afraid of losing her Grandpa's love when she notices him making mean faces as he practices his role as an actor. (I: 6–9)

*———. *Honey, I Love and Other Love Poems*. Illustrated by Diane Dillon and Leo Dillon. Harper, 1978. These poems, narrated by a young African American girl, tell of love and friendship. (I: 7–9)

*———. *Nathaniel Talking*. Illustrated by Jan Spivey Gilchrist. Black Butterfly, 1988. Through various forms of poetry, Nathaniel talks about the happenings in his neighborhood from his eight-year-old perspective. A related title is *Night on Neighborhood Street* (Dial, 1991). (I: 7–9)

———. *Rosa Parks*. Illustrated by Eric Marlow. Harper, 1973. This biography about Rosa Parks tells how her stance set off the Montgomery bus strike and the civil rights struggle that followed. (I: 7–9)

*Grimes, Nikki. *Meet Danitra Brown*. Illustrated by Floyd Cooper. Lothrop, Lee & Shepard, 1994. Through poetry, Zuri Jackson relates her feelings about her special friendship with a "splendiferous" girl, Danitra Brown. (I: 6–9)

Hamilton, Virginia. *Her Stories: African American Folktales, Fairy Tales, and True Tales*. Illustrated by Leo and Diane Dillon. Scholastic, 1995. This collection of stories is about women in African American folktales, fairy tales, animal stories, supernatural tales, legends, and biographical accounts. (I: 9–YA)

———. *The House of Dies Drear*. Illustrated by Eros Keith. Simon & Schuster, 1968. When a history professor and his son move into a rented house, they find the spirits of the past—those who passed through the house when it was a station on the Underground Railroad. The sequel is *The Mystery of Drear House* (1987). (I: 10–YA)

———. *Many Thousand Gone: African Americans from Slavery to Freedom*. Illustrated by Leo and Diane Dillon. Knopf, 1993. This book tells the stories of many slaves who made it to freedom through the Underground Railroad. (I: 10–YA)

———. *M. C. Higgins, the Great*. Macmillan, 1974. M.C. has to reconcile his love for his mountain home with its pending destruction by a slag heap. (I: 10–12)

———. *The People Could Fly: American Black Folktales*. Illustrated by Leo Dillon and Diane Dillon. Knopf, 1985/ 1999. This collection of 24 American black folktales includes a range from familiar to lesser known. (I: 9–13)

———. *Zeely*. Illustrated by Symeon Shimin. Macmillan, 1967. Eleven-year-old Geeder learns to move from her dreams to reality as she acquires better self-understanding with the help of Zeely, a queenlike figure who is extraordinarily tall, beautiful, and kind. (I: 11–YA)

Haskins, Jim. *Get on Board: The Story of the Underground Railroad*. Scholastic, 1993. This book explores the ways slaves escaped north to freedom, including the Underground Railroad, and the ways in which slave owners tried to keep the slaves from escaping. (I: 10–12)

*Havill, Juanita. *Jamaica's Find*. Illustrated by Anne Sibley O'Brien. Houghton Mifflin, 1986. Jamaica finds a stuffed dog at the playground and must cope with her desire to keep the toy. Sequels are *Jamaica Tag-Along* (1989) and *Jamaica and Brianna* (1993). (I: P–8)

*Hooks, William H. *Freedom's Fruit*. Illustrated by James Ransome. Knopf, 1996. To gain freedom for Sheba and her beloved, Mama, a slave and a conjurer, casts a spell on her master's grapes. (I: 8–11)

*Hopkinson, Deborah. *Sweet Clara and the Freedom Quilt*. Illustrated by James Ransome. Knopf, 1993. Clara is determined to be reunited with her mother and to find their way north to freedom. She uses her skills as a seamstress, listens to the conversations around her, and creates a quilt that maps the way to freedom. (I: 7–10)

*Howard, Elizabeth Fitzgerald. *Aunt Flossie's Hats (and Crab Cakes Later)*. Illustrated by James Ransome. Clarion, 1991. For Sarah and Susan, visiting their great-great-aunt Flossie means sipping tea and eating cookies while trying on her many hats and listening to the stories associated with them. (I: 6–9)

*Hudson, Wade, comp. *Pass It On: African-American Poetry for Children*. Illustrated by Floyd Cooper. Scholastic, 1993. This book of poetry about African American experiences has contributions by poets such as Langston Hughes, Nikki Giovanni, Eloise Greenfield, and Lucille Clifton. See also *How Sweet the Sound: African-American Songs for Children*, 1995. (I: 8–10)

Hurmence, Belinda. *Slavery Time When I Was Chillun*. Putnam, 1997. This is a selection of twelve oral histories from former slaves, taken from the over 2,000 that were collected by the Library of Congress in 1936. (I: 10 and up)

*Johnson, Angela. *Do Like Kyla*. Illustrated by James E. Ransome. Orchard, 1990. All day long, a little girl follows her big sister Kyla around, "doing like Kyla," but at the end of the day, "Kyla does just like me." (I: P–7)

*———. *One of Three*. Illustrated by David Soman. Orchard, 1991. The youngest of three sisters describes what it is like to be "one of three." (I: P–7)

*———. *Tell Me a Story, Mama*. Illustrated by David Soman. Orchard, 1989. At bedtime, a little girl asks, "Tell me a story, Mama, about when you were little." But then, she tells a story herself, with Mama only adding comments. (I: P–8)

*Lawrence, Jacob. *Harriet and the Promised Land*. Simon & Schuster, 1968. The life of Harriet Tubman is described in verse, and the story of her commitment to helping fellow slaves to freedom is told. (I: 9–11)

Lester, Julius. *Long Journey Home: Stories from Black History*. Dial, 1972/1993. Six stories, based on the lives of real people, tell about the impact of escaping from slavery on the lives of individuals and families. (I: 11–YA)

*———. *Sam and the Tigers*. Illustrated by Jerry Pinkney. Dial, 1996. Based on the story "Little Black Sambo," this new version is told in Lester's "Southern black storytelling voice," with Pinkney's illustrations setting the story in the mythical land of Sam-sam-sa-mara. (I: 6–9)

*Little, Lessie Jones. *Children of Long Ago*. Illustrated by Jan Spivey Gilchrist. Lee & Low, 1988/2000. This collection of poems reflects on the author's peaceful childhood experience of growing up in the early 1900s. (I: 7–9)

*Marzollo, Jean. *Happy Birthday, Martin Luther King*. Illustrated by J. Brian Pinkney. Scholastic, 1993. Simple text explains why we celebrate the birthday of famous civil rights leader Dr. Martin Luther King, Jr. (I: 6–9)

Mathis, Sharon Bell. *The Hundred Penny Box*. Illustrated by Leo and Diane Dillon. Puffin, 1975. Great-great-aunt Dew is a hundred years old and has a box with a penny in it for each of her birthdays. Michael loves to listen to the stories each penny holds and intercedes on her behalf when his mother wants to throw out the old "hundred penny box" and buy a new one. (I: 8–10)

Mattox, Cheryl Warren. *Shake It to the One That You Love the Best: Play Songs and Lullabies from Black Musical Traditions*. Illustrated by Varnette P. Honeywood and Brenda Joysmith. Sobrante, CA: Warren-Mattox, 1989. African American songs that accompany jump rope, hopscotch, and other games are featured in this collection. (I: P–9)

*McKissack, Patricia. *Flossie and the Fox*. Illustrated by Rachel Isadora. Dial, 1986. A little girl meets a creature in the woods and insists on his proof of identity as a fox before she will give up her eggs. (I: 7–9)

*Mollel, Tololwa M. *The King and the Tortoise*. Illustrated by Kathy Blankley. Clarion, 1993. When the king challenges the animals of his kingdom to make him a robe of smoke to prove they are more clever than he is, only the tortoise is able to outsmart the king. (I: 7–10)

*———. *My Rows and Piles of Coins*. Illustrated by E. B. Lewis. Clarion, 1999. Saruni saves his piles of coins, arranged in rows, in hopes of buying a bicycle to help his mother carry heavy goods to market in Tanzania. (I: 6–9)

Myers, Walter Dean. *At Her Majesty's Request: An African Princess in Victorian England*. Scholastic, 1999. In the 1840s, an orphaned African princess is rescued from becoming a live sacrifice and taken to England, where her upbringing is overseen by Queen Victoria. (I: 10–YA)

*———. *Brown Angels*. HarperCollins, 1993. Photographs of African American children from the turn of the century provide inspiration for the poems written by Myers. A related title is *Glorious Angels* (1995). (I: 7–9)

*———. *Harlem*. Illustrated by Christopher Myers. Scholastic, 1997. Poetic text and vibrant collage illustrations offer vivid images of everyday life, as well as the art, music, and literature that define Harlem. (I: 12 and up)

———. *Malcolm X: By Any Means Necessary*. Scholastic, 1993. This is the story of the famous civil rights leader Malcolm X. (I: 9–11)

Naidoo, Beverley. *Journey to Jo'burg: A South African Story*. Harper, 1986. Naledi travels from her South African village to Johannesburg to deliver news of her baby sister's near-death from an illness to her mother, who works and lives in the home of some white people. (I: 9–11)

*Pinkney, Andrea Davis. *Dear Benjamin Banneker*. Illustrated by Brian Pinkney. Harcourt, 1994. Benjamin Banneker was an accomplished mathematician and astronomer and was the first black creator of an almanac. When he realized the injustice of the words in the Declaration of Independence proclaiming that "all men are created equal," he wrote to Secretary of State Thomas Jefferson. (I: 7–9)

*———. *Seven Candles for Kwanzaa*. Illustrated by Brian Pinkney. Dial, 1993. This book describes the seven-day festival of Kwanzaa, a holiday during which Americans of African descent celebrate their ancestral values. (I: 6–9)

*Pinkney, Brian. *JoJo's Flying Side Kick*. Simon & Schuster, 1995. When JoJo is to be tested to earn her yellow belt in tae kwon do class, she gets a lot of advice from others. At the moment of the test, though, she realizes for herself how to perform the flying side kick and break the board. (I: P–8)

*Pinkney, Gloria. *Back Home*. Illustrated by Jerry Pinkney. Dial, 1992. Eight-year-old Ernestine takes a train trip to visit relatives at the North Carolina farm where she was born. The prequel is *The Sunday Outing* (1994). (I: 6–9)

*Raschka, Chris. *Charlie Parker Played Be Bop*. Orchard, 1992. Lively words in rhythmic text seem like the bebop music of the famous jazz saxophonist. (I: P–8)

*Ringgold, Faith. *Tar Beach*. Crown, 1991. A young girl remembers spending summer evenings on the "tar beach" on the roof of their apartment building, imagining that she could fly over Manhattan and claim all she saw for herself and her family. (I: 6–9)

*Schroeder, Alan. *Minty: A Story of Young Harriet Tubman*. Illustrated by Jerry Pinkney. Dial, 1996. Harriet Tubman's "cradle" name was Araminta, and therefore she was nicknamed Minty. She was a slave on the Brodas plantation in the 1820s, and not only did she always long to escape, she prepared for it. (I: 7–9)

*———. *Satchmo's Blues*. Illustrated by Floyd Cooper. Doubleday, 1996. This fictionalized account of Louis Armstrong's childhood in New Orleans describes how he worked and earned his first trumpet. (I: 6–10)

Schwartz, Virginia Frances. *Send One Angel Down*. Holiday House, 2000. Raised in the hardship of slavery, Eliza, fathered by her master, finds unexpected freedom when a northern abolitionist buys her. (I: 12–YA)

*Siegelson, Kim L. *In the Time of the Drums*. Illustrated by Brian Pinkney. Jump at the Sun/Hyperion, 1999. A conjure woman leads a group of slaves off of the boat and back into the water toward Africa. (I: 10 and up)

*Sisulu, Elinor Batezat. *The Day Gogo Went to Vote: South Africa*. Illustrated by Sharon Wilson. Little, Brown, 1996. Thembi and her great-grandmother participate in the election on the historic day on which black South Africans were allowed to vote for the first time. (I: 7–10)

*Steptoe, Javaka, illustrator. *In Daddy's Arms I Am Tall: African Americans Celebrating Fathers*. Lee & Low, 1997. A collection of poetry focusing on the important role of fathers in the lives of their children. (I: P–10)

*Steptoe, John. *Baby Says*. Lothrop, Lee & Shepard, 1988. In this nearly wordless book, a baby and his big brother learn to play together. (I: P)

*———. *Mufaro's Beautiful Daughters: An African Tale*. Lothrop, Lee & Shepard, 1987. Mufaro's daughters are both beautiful, and both vie to be chosen as the new wife of the king. Nyasha's gentle and kind temperament contrasts with Manyara's greed and mean-spiritedness as they encounter various creatures along their separate journeys to the city. (I: P–7)

Taylor, Mildred. *The Friendship*. Illustrated by Max Ginsburg. Dial, 1987. In 1930s rural Mississippi, the four Logan children witness a confrontation when Mr. Tom Bee, an elderly black man, calls a white storekeeper by his first name. Other titles about the Logans include *Road to Memphis* (1990) and *The Well* (1995). (I: 8–11)

———. *The Gold Cadillac*. Illustrated by Michael Hays. Dial, 1987. Father brings home a new gold

Cadillac, and 'Lois and Wilmato are proud to be riding in it. But driving south from Ohio to Mississippi to visit relatives, the family faces prejudice and racism and must temporarily trade the Cadillac for a less conspicuous car. (I: 8–11)

————. *Mississippi Bridge.* Illustrated by Max Ginsburg. Dial, 1990. In the 1930s, amidst racial tension, black passengers are ordered off a bus to accommodate white passengers. Crossing the flooded river on a weak bridge, the bus is swept off and the passengers die. (I: 10–12)

————. *Roll of Thunder, Hear My Cry.* Illustrated by Jerry Pinkney. Dial, 1976. The Logan family faces many problems associated with being black in the rural South during the Depression. The sequel is *Let the Circle Be Unbroken* (1981). See also *Song of the Trees* (1975). (I: 11–13)

Walter, Mildred Pitts. *Justin and the Best Biscuits in the World.* Illustrated by Catherine Stock. Lothrop, Lee & Shepard, 1986. Justin lives in a house full of women and considers cooking and cleaning to be "women's work." Spending time on his grandfather's ranch shows Justin a different view of work. (I: 9–11)

————. *Mariah Keeps Cool.* Macmillan, 1990. Mariah's concerns center on swimming meets, but she finds that her world changes when a half-sister moves into her home. See also *Mariah Loves Rock* (1989). (I: 8–11)

*————. *My Mama Needs Me.* Illustrated by Pat Cummings. Lothrop, Lee & Shepard, 1983. Jason is so anxious to help his mother care for his new baby sister that he refuses to play with his friends or to leave the house. (I: P–7)

*————. *Ty's One-Man Band.* 1980. Illustrated by Margot Tomes. Macmillan, 1987. Ty's one-legged friend Andro can produce music with a washboard, wooden spoons, a comb, and a tin pail. (I: 6–8)

*Williams, Sherley Anne. *Working Cotton.* Illustrated by Carole Byard. Harcourt, 1992. A little girl tells how her migrant family spends the day, from dawn to dusk, picking cotton in the fields of central California. (I: P–8)

Woodson, Jacqueline. *Last Summer with Maizon.* Delacorte, 1992. Margaret knows that after the summer ends, her best friend, Maizon, will be leaving their neighborhood in Brooklyn to attend a boarding school where she has won a scholarship. See also *Maizon at Blue Hill* (1992) and *Between Madison and Palmetto* (1995). (I: 11–YA)

*Young, Ruth. *Golden Bear.* Illustrated by Rachel Isadora. Viking, 1992. A little boy and his "golden bear" are constant companions throughout the day. (I: P–6)

Asian and Asian American

*Chinn, Karen. *Sam and the Lucky Money.* Illustrated by Cornelius Van Wright and Ying-Hwa Hu. Lee & Low, 1995. Chinese New Year means gifts of money in red envelopes for children. When he sees a homeless man, Sam struggles with the knowledge that he is free to spend his "lucky money" in any way he wishes. (I: 6–9)

*Choi, Sook Nyul. *Halmoni and the Picnic.* Illustrated by Karen M. Dugan. Houghton Mifflin, 1993. When the class plans a field trip, a classmate invites Yunmi's halmoni (grandmother) to serve as a chaperone. Yunmi worries about what her classmates will think of her grandmother's Korean ways and foods. (I: 6–9)

————. *Year of Impossible Goodbyes.* Houghton Mifflin, 1991. Ten-year-old Sookan and her family live under the cruelties of Japanese occupation of their homeland of Korea during the 1940s. When the Communists defeat the Japanese, Sookan and her family make a dangerous escape south. Sequels are *Echoes of the White Giraffe* (1993) and *My Brother My Sister and I* (1994). (I: 11–YA)

*Coerr, Eleanor. *Sadako.* Illustrated by Ed Young. Putnam, 1993. Believing in the Japanese tradition that folding a thousand origami cranes will restore her health, a little girl named Sadako tries to survive the leukemia that resulted from the bombing of Hiroshima. See also the longer novel *Sadako and the Thousand Paper Cranes.* (I: 9–12)

*Demi. *Chingis Khan.* Holt, 1991. This picture book presents a biography of the famous king of the Mongols. (I: 9-11)

*————. *The Dragon's Tale and Other Animal Fables of the Chinese Zodiac.* Holt, 1996. Twelve fables tell the stories of the animals of the Chinese zodiac. (I: 7–11)

*————. *The Empty Pot.* Holt, 1990. The Emperor distributes seeds to children across China, and the one who grows the best flower will inherit the kingdom. Ping finds that he must face the emperor honestly with his empty pot when springtime comes, as nothing has grown from the seed he was given. (I: 6–9)

*————. *Liang and the Magic Paintbrush.* Holt, 1980. A small boy in China is given a paintbrush, and everything he paints magically comes to life. (I: 6–9)

*Hamanaka, Sheila. *The Journey.* Orchard, 1990. A historical look at Japanese Americans is provided through closeup details of an actual mural, accompanied by text explaining the significance of each section. (I: 10–YA)

*Han, Suzanne Crowder. *The Rabbit's Escape.* Illustrated by Yumi Heo. Holt, 1995. The Dragon King of the East Sea's illness can be cured only by eating raw liver of a rabbit. Faithful Turtle returns from land with a rabbit, but Rabbit cleverly finds a way to be taken back there. Bilingual Korean/English text. (I: P–8)

Ho, Minfong. *The Clay Marble.* Farrar, 1991. Rebuilding homes and lives in a camp near the Thai border, families struggle to survive the destruction of war. A marble made from clay serves as a toy and a gesture of friendship between children in this camp. (I: 12–YA)

*Hong, Lily Toy. *Two of Everything.* Whitman, 1993. While digging in his field, Mr. Haktak finds a big pot, and everything he puts in it comes out doubled. He faces a dilemma when his wife falls into the pot! (I: 6–9)

*Hoyt-Goldsmith, Diane. *Hoang Anh: A Vietnamese-American Boy.* Photographs by Lawrence Migdale. Holiday House, 1992. Through colorful photographs and text narrated by Hoang Anh, this Vietnamese American boy describes his daily life with his family in California and how the traditional culture and customs exist alongside his life as a contemporary American boy. (I: 7–10)

*Ishii, Momoko. *The Tongue-Cut Sparrow.* Illustrated by Suekichi Akaba. Translated by Katherine Paterson. Dutton, 1987. When an old man and his wife care for a sparrow, each of them is rewarded according to his or her kindness or greediness. (I: 6–9)

Jiang, Ji Li. *Red Scarf Girl: A Memoir of the Cultural Revolution.* HarperCollins, 1997. Ji Li wore her red scarf as the emblem of her devoted membership in the Young Pioneers, committed to the future of Communist China, when the course of her entire world changed with the beginning of the Chinese Cultural Revolution in 1966. (I: 10–YA)

Lee, Marie G. *If It Hadn't Been for Yoon Jun.* Houghton Mifflin, 1993. Alice Larson was adopted as an infant and is now a seventh-grade cheerleader who runs with a popular crowd. She is reluctant when asked to help the new Korean boy, Yoon Jun, adjust to the American school. However, she develops an interest in her own Korean heritage. (I: 12–YA)

*Mahy, Margaret. *The Seven Chinese Brothers.* Illustrated by Jean and Mou-sien Tseng. Scholastic, 1990. When one brother is ordered executed, the seven brothers take turns escaping death by virtue of their extraordinary abilities. (I: 6–9)

*Melmed, Laura Krauss. *Little Oh.* Illustrated by Jim LaMarche. Lothrop, 1997. An origami doll is separated from the woman who made her, but the ensu-

ing adventure and reunion turn her into a live daughter. (I: 7–9)

*Mochizuki, Ken. *Baseball Saved Us.* Illustrated by Dom Lee. Lee & Low, 1993. While forced to live in an internment camp for Japanese Americans during World War II, a young boy learns to play baseball. (I: 6–9)

*Morimoto, Junko. *My Hiroshima.* Viking, 1987. The author recalls her childhood in Hiroshima and what happened on the day of the atomic bomb. (I: 9–12)

*Namioka, Lensey. *The Loyal Cat.* Illustrated by Aki Sogabe. Harcourt, 1995. Huku is a loyal cat with magical power. He helps the priest Tetsuzan just far enough out of poverty to make repairs to the modest temple and to eat again. (I: 7–9)

*Rappaport, Doreen. *The Journey of Meng.* Illustrated by Yang Ming-Yi. Dial, 1991. In this well-known Chinese tale, Meng travels far to deliver warm clothes to her husband, a scholar, who has been forced into manual labor at the Great Wall. (I: 7–9)

*Rhee, Nami. *Magic Spring.* Putnam, 1993. An elderly couple return to their youth after taking a sip of water from a magic spring, but their greedy neighbor ends up with unexpected results. (I: 6–9)

*Say, Allen. *El Chino.* Houghton Mifflin, 1990. This picture book biography of Bong Way "Bill" Wong tells how he became a famous Chinese American bullfighter in Spain. (I: 6–9)

*———. *Emma's Rug.* Houghton Mifflin, 1996. Emma finds artistic inspiration in her small white rug, but when her mother washes it clean, Emma is sure that she can no longer draw or paint. (I: 6–9)

*———. *Grandfather's Journey.* Houghton Mifflin, 1993. A Japanese man emigrates to the United States and learns to love his new home but misses his homeland. When visiting Japan, he finds that the war will keep him from returning to the United States. A related title is *Tree of Cranes* (1991). (I: 6–9)

*———. *Tea with Milk.* Houghton Mifflin, 1999. A Japanese American woman returns with her parents to Japan in the 1950s and resolves conflicts between her American ways and the ways of a woman in Japan. (I: 9–12)

*Shea, Pegi Deitz. *The Whispering Cloth: A Refugee's Story.* Illustrated by Anita Riggio. Stitched by You Yang. Boyds Mills, 1995. Mai practices stitching borders in embroidered story cloths while in a Thai refugee camp with her grandmother. She finds a story within herself so that she, too, can stitch her own pa'ndau. (I: 7–10)

*Snyder, Dianne. *The Boy of the Three-Year Nap.* Illustrated by Allen Say. Houghton Mifflin, 1988.

Taro is a lazy boy who sleeps so much that people say he would nap for three years if left alone. He schemes to get rich without doing any work, but his plan backfires when it proceeds farther than he had hoped. (I: 6–9)

*Turner, Ann. *Through Moon and Stars and Night Skies*. Illustrated by James Graham Hale. Harper & Row, 1990. A little boy reminisces about how he came from far away and was adopted by his new family. (I: P–6)

*Uchida, Yoshiko. *The Bracelet*. Illustrated by Joanna Yardley. Philomel, 1976/1993. Emi and her family are sent to an internment camp during World War II. Emi loses the bracelet that was a gift from her best friend, but she comes to realize that she does not need the physical reminder of her friendship to remember. (I: 6–9)

———. *A Jar of Dreams*. Macmillan, 1981. Faced with the prejudice against Japanese in the 1930s in California, Rinko wants to be as American as possible. When Aunt Waka visits from Japan, Rinko begins to understand the strength of her family and the Japanese American community. Related titles are *The Best Bad Thing* (1983) and *The Happiest Ending* (1985). (I: 9–11)

———. *Journey to Topaz: A Story of the Japanese-American Evacuation*. 1971. Illustrated by Donald Carick. Berkeley, CA: Creative Arts, 1984. Eleven-year-old Yuki and her family are sent to an internment camp in the desert, following the bombing of Pearl Harbor. A sequel is *Journey Home* (Macmillan, 1978). (I: 9–12)

Vuong, Lynette Dyer. *The Golden Carp and Other Tales from Vietnam*. Illustrated by Manabu Saito. Lothrop, Lee & Shepard, 1993. This collection of six tales of ancient Vietnam describes such virtues as courage, bravery, and honesty. See also *The Brocaded Slipper and Other Vietnamese Tales* (1982). (I: 8–11)

Watkins, Yoko Kawashima. *So Far from the Bamboo Grove*. Lothrop, Lee & Shepard, 1986. The story of escaping Korea to return to Japan at the end of World War II is a fictionalized version of the author's life. (I: 10–12)

———. *Tales from the Bamboo Grove*. Illustrations by Jean and Mou-Sien Tseng. Bradbury, 1992. Six retellings of traditional Japanese tales are included in this collection: "Dragon Princess, Tatsuko," "The Fox Wife," "Why Is Seawater Salty?," "Yayoi and the Spirit Tree," "Monkey and Crab," and "The Grandmother Who Became an Island." (I: 7–11)

Wong, Janet. *The Trip Back Home*. Illustrated by Bo Jia. Harcourt, 2000. A Korean American child visits her mother's homeland with her. (I: 6–9)

*Xiong, Blia. *Nine-in-One, Grr! Grr! A Folktale from the Hmong People of Laos*. Adapted by Cathy Spagnoli. Illustrated by Nancy Hom. Children's Book Press, 1989. Tiger is promised nine cubs a year by the god, Shao. Bird fears that tigers will overtake the land and tries to think of a way to prevent that from happening. (I: 6–10)

*Yacowitz, Caryn. *The Jade Stone*. Illustrated by Ju-Hong Chen. Holiday House, 1992. Although Chan Lo has been directed by the Great Emperor of All China to carve a dragon of wind and fire out of the perfect piece of jade, he discovers he must listen to the stone's spirit crying out to be something else. (I: 7–9)

*Yagawa, Sumiko. *The Crane Wife*. Illustrated by Suekichi Akaba. Translated by Katherine Paterson. Morrow, 1987. A lonely man's kindness is rewarded with the mysterious arrival of a wife. When his curiosity goes too far, he is punished by her departure. (I: 6–9)

*Yee, Paul. *Ghost Train*. Illustrated by Harvey Chan. Groundwood, 1996. Choon-Yi finally arrives in North America to join her father, but he has been killed while building the railroad. Summoned to put her talent in painting to create a "fire-train," she dreams a fantasy that brings all who have died on board her painted train so that their souls may return home to China with her. (I: 9–12)

Yep, Laurence. *Dragon's Gate*. HarperCollins, 1993. In 1867, Chinese men came to the United States and found work digging and dynamiting tunnels through the rocks of the Sierra Mountains so that the railroad could cross the nation. (I: 11–YA)

———. *Dragonwings*. Harper, 1975/1987. Moon Shadow leaves his remote Chinese village in 1903 to join his father, Windrider, in California. Together, they survive the 1906 earthquake and the hardships of life in the "Golden Mountain" as they work to realize their dream of building a dragon-like flying machine. (I: 10–12)

———. *Later, Gator*. HarperCollins, 1995. Two brothers who usually do not get along find that they must cooperate with each other when they wind up with a pet alligator they know their parents will not approve of. See also *Cockroach Cooties* (2000). (I: 8–10)

———. *The Star Fisher*. Morrow, 1991. This fictionalized biography of Laurence Yep's grandmother tells of fifteen-year-old Joan Lee and her family's move from Ohio to West Virginia in the 1920s. Being the only Asians in the community, they face the problem of being "different" from their neighbors. (I: 11–YA)

*Young, Ed. *Cat and Rat: The Legend of the Chinese Zodiac*. Holt, 1995. This is the story of how the twelve animals became part of the Chinese zodiac. (I: 7–10)

*———. *Lon Po Po: A Red-Riding Hood Story from China*. Philomel, 1989. When mother leaves the children at home, a wolf enters their house. The children must think quickly and come up with a plan to outsmart the wolf. (I: 7–10)

Latino/Latina

*Ada, Alma Flor. *The Gold Coin*. Atheneum, 1991. When a thief follows a healer woman in an attempt to steal her gold coin, he finds himself transformed by witnessing her acts of kindness. (I: 7–10)

———. *My Name Is María Isabel/Me llamo María Isabel*. Atheneum, 1993. When María Isabel Salazar Lopez enters a new classroom, the teacher decides to call her "Mary Lopez" because there are already two girls named Maria in the class. (I: 7–10)

*———. *The Rooster Who Went to His Uncle's Wedding*. Illustrated by Kathleen Kuchera. Putnam, 1993. Told in cumulative form, this folktale from Latin America is about how Rooster needs his beak cleaned in time to attend his uncle's wedding. It is the sun, who has long enjoyed the rooster's morning call, who sets off the chain of events that makes it possible. (I: 6–9)

———. *Under the Royal Palms: A Childhood in Cuba*. Atheneum, 1998. Author Ada offers a memoir of her childhood, with vivid descriptions of island life with her family. This is a companion book to *Where the Flame Trees Bloom* (1994). (I: 9–12)

*Ancona, George. *Pablo Remembers: The Fiesta of the Day of the Dead*. Lothrop, Lee & Shepard, 1993. Pablo and his family prepare for the three-day fiesta of El Día de Los Muertos, a festival to honor the spirits of the dead. (I: 6–9)

*———. *The Piñata Maker/El piñatero*. Harcourt, 1994. Don Ricardo is a craftsman in Ejutla de Crespo in southern Mexico. He makes piñatas for birthday parties and other fiestas. Bilingual text. (I: 6–9)

*Cowley, Joy. *Gracias, the Thanksgiving Turkey*. Illustrated by Joe Cepeda. Scholastic, 1996. Papa sends Miguel a turkey with instructions to fatten the bird for Thanksgiving dinner, but Miguel becomes attached to his new pet. (I: 6–9)

*Czernecki, Stefan, and Timothy Rhodes. *The Hummingbirds' Gift*. Illustrated by Stefan Czernecki with straw weavings by Julianna Reyes de Silva and Juan Hilario Silva. Hyperion, 1994. This story tells how the village of Tzintzuntzan, Mexico, was given

the Tarascan Indian name for "the place of the hummingbirds." The illustrations combine woven straw figures called panicuas with gouache paintings. (I: 6–9)

*Delacre, Lulu. *Arroz con leche: Popular Songs and Rhymes from Latin America*. Scholastic, 1989. The songs and rhymes in this bilingual collection are known throughout the Spanish-speaking countries. A related title is *Las Navidades: Popular Christmas Songs from Latin America* (1990). (I: P–8)

———. *Golden Tales: Myths, Legends and Folktales from Latin America*. Scholastic, 1996. The twelve classic tales in this collection come from four cultures of Latin America—Taino, Zapotec, Muisca, and Inca—and from many different countries. (I: 9–12)

*Dorros, Arthur. *Abuela*. Illustrated by Elisa Kleven. Dutton, 1991. Rosalba imagines that she goes flying over New York City with her adventurous grandma, Abuela. Also by Dorros is *Isla* (1995). (I: P–8)

*Emberley, Rebecca. *My House/Mi casa: A Book in Two Languages*. Little, Brown, 1990. Things commonly found in a house are labeled throughout the illustrations in both English and Spanish. A related title is *Taking a Walk/Caminando: A Book in Two Languages* (1990). (I: P–7)

*Garza, Carmen Lomas. *Family Pictures/Cuadros de familia*. Children's Book Press, 1990. Bilingual text accompanies folk art illustrations depicting the author's experiences of growing up Mexican American in South Texas. Another book by Garza is *In My Family/En mi familia* (1996). (I: 6–10)

González, Lucía M. *Señor Cat's Romance and Other Favorite Stories from Latin America*. Illustrated by Lulu Delacre. Scholastic, 1997. Each of the six tales about outrageous Señor Cat, silly Juan Bobo, and others is followed by a note about the culture it comes from. (I: 6–9)

*Madrigal, Antonio Hernández. *Erandi's Braids*. Illustrated by Tomie dePaola. Putnam, 1999. Set in 1940s Mexico, this story tells how Erandi sells her braids so that her mother can get a new fishing net. (I: 6–9)

*Markun, Patricia Maloney. *The Little Painter of Sabana Grande*. Illustrated by Robert Casilla. Bradbury, 1993. Fernando makes his paints the way the country people of Panama make theirs—out of charcoal from burned tree stumps, berries, dried grasses, and clay. His father realizes how hard it must be for Fernando not to have paints and allows him to paint on the exterior walls of the house. (I: 6–9)

*Martinez, Alejandro Cruz. *The Woman Who Outshone the Sun/La mujer que brillaba aún más que el sol*. Illustrated by Fernando Olivera. Story by Rosalma Zubizarreta, Harriet Rohmer, and David Schecter from a poem by Alejandro Cruz Martinez. Children's Book Press, 1991. This retelling of a Zapotec Indian legend from Mexico is the story of Llucia Zenteno, a beautiful woman who possesses magical powers. When she is sent away from a mountain village, she takes its water away in punishment. (I: 7–10)

Mohr, Nicholasa. *Felita*. 1979. Bantam, 1990. Moving is always hard, but when Felita's family moves to an area where there aren't other Puerto Rican families speaking Spanish, the adjustment feels even more lonely. Also by Mohr is *Going Home* (1986). (I: 9–12)

*Mora, Pat. *A Birthday Basket for Tía*. Illustrated by Cecily Lan. Macmillan, 1992. Cecila wants to find the perfect present for her great-aunt's ninetieth birthday. (I: P–6)

*———. *Tómas and the Library Lady*. Illustrated by Raúl Colón. Knopf, 1997. A librarian helps Tómas connect his life with books while living in Iowa as a migrant farm worker. (I: 6–9)

*Roe, Eileen. *Con mi hermano/With My Brother*. Illustrated by Robert Casilla. Bradbury, 1991. In bilingual text, a little boy describes his big brother with admiration and looks forward to the day when he will be like his big brother. (I: P–6)

Ryan, Pam Muñoz. *Esperanza Rising*. Scholastic, 2000. Esperanza lives a privileged and wealthy life in Mexico when circumstances force her to flee to California with her mother, and work in a farm labor camp. (I: 12–YA)

Soto, Gary. *Baseball in April and Other Stories*. Harcourt, 1990. The eleven short stories in this collection tell of experiences growing up Mexican American in Fresno, California. (I: 9–12)

*———. *Chato's Kitchen*. Putnam, 1995. Illustrated by Susan Guevara. Cool cat Chato is thrilled to see who has moved into the barrio—a family of tasty-looking mice. When they accept a dinner invitation, Chato is filled with anticipation as he prepares the frijoles, guacamole, arroz, tortillas, and more, but things go differently than he expects when the mice's friend shows up. See also *Chato and the Party Animals* (2000). (I: 7–9)

———. *Neighborhood Odes*. Illustrated by David Diaz. Harcourt, 1992. These twenty-one poems describe various everyday joys of growing up in a Mexican American neighborhood. (I: 9–YA)

*———. *The Old Man and His Door*. Illustrated by Joe Cepeda. Putnam, 1996. The story is based on a Mexican song that goes "La puerta. El puerco. There's no difference to el viejo." Misunderstanding his wife's instructions on what to take to a party, an old man takes a door instead of a pig. But the door proves useful along the way, and the old man has many surprises for his wife. (I: P–8)

———. *Taking Sides*. Harcourt, 1991. Lincoln Mendoza moves from his familiar neighborhood to the suburbs when his mother gets a better-paying job. When the basketball team of his new school plays against his former team, he realizes he needs to sort out his self-identity. (I: 10–12)

*———. *Too Many Tamales*. Illustrated by Ed Martinez. Putnam, 1993. While helping to make tamales, Maria slips her mother's diamond ring on her hand to admire it. When she realizes that the ring is missing, she enlists the help of her cousins in eating the tamales until the ring is found. (I: 6–9)

*Torres, Leyla. *Saturday Sancocho*. Mirasol/Farrar, 1995. María Líli's mother decides to make sancocho but needs a chicken; the two go to the marketplace to trade eggs for a series of items. (I: 6–9)

Native American

*Begay, Shonto. *Navajo: Visions and Voices across the Mesa*. Scholastic, 1995. Twenty paintings and original poems are paired to present a personal voice of what it means to live as a Navajo in today's world. (I: 10 and up)

Bierhorst, John. *The Deetkatoo: Native American Stories about Little People*. Illustrated by Ron Hilbert Coy. Morrow, 1998. This book compiles twenty-two stories of little people from fourteen different native cultures and is well documented with notes, a guide to cultures, and a bibliography. (I: 10 and up)

*Bruchac, Joseph. *Between Earth and Sky: Legends of Native American Sacred Places*. Illustrated by Thomas Locker. Harcourt, 1996. A man teaches his nephew about the sacredness of living things. Various Native American legends tell of sacred places. (I: 10–13)

*———. *A Boy Called Slow*. Illustrated by Rocco Baviera. Philomel, 1994. A Lakota boy's childhood name "Slow" is changed to "Sitting Bull" as he matures through his deeds. (I: 9–12)

*———. *The First Strawberries: A Cherokee Story*. Illustrated by Anna Vojtech. Dial, 1993. This folktale tells how the first man's arrogance causes the first woman to leave when he becomes angry at her for spending time on flowers rather than on preparing dinner. (I: P–8)

*————, and Gayle Ross. *The Story of the Milky Way: A Cherokee Tale.* Illustrated by Virginia A. Stroud. Dial, 1995. The People chase away a spirit dog who is stealing their cornmeal, and their bravery is forever commemorated by the grains of cornmeal that turned into stars. (I: 6–9)

*————, and Jonathan London. *Thirteen Moons on Turtle's Back: A Native American Year of Moons.* Illustrated by Thomas Locker. Philomel, 1992. Many Native American tribes relate the thirteen moons of the year to the pattern of thirteen large scales on the turtle's back. Poems—each based on a story from a different Native American nation, such as the Cherokee, Cree, or Sioux—make up the text for this book. (I: 8–10)

*Bunting, Eve. *Cheyenne Again.* Illustrated by Irving Toddy. Clarion, 1995. Set in the late 1880s, this story is of a ten-year-old Cheyenne boy named Young Bull, who was taken away from his family and home and sent to a boarding school to learn the white people's ways. The illustrator experienced a similar situation in his own life. (I: 6–9)

Caduto, Michael J., and Joseph Bruchac. *Keepers of the Earth: Native American Stories and Environmental Activities for Children.* Illustrated by John Kahionhes Fadden and Carol Wood. Golden, CO: Fulcrum, 1988. This book's purpose is to teach children about Native American cultures and the link between humans and nature through an interdisciplinary approach. Twenty-three sets of lessons each feature a story followed by suggested activities to enhance learning. See also *Keepers of the Animals: Native American Stories and Wildlife Activities for Children* (1991); *Keepers of Life: Discovering Plants through Native American Stories and Earth Activities for Children* (1994). (I: 6–12)

*Cohen, Caron Lee. *The Mud Pony.* Illustrated by Shonto Begay. Scholastic, 1988. A poor boy creates a mud pony and cares for it as if it were real. He dreams that the pony comes alive, and he awakens to find that it will guide him through many ordeals. (I: 6–9)

*de Paola, Tomie. *The Legend of the Bluebonnet.* Putnam, 1983. She-Who-Is-Alone gives up her most valued possession—her doll from her deceased parents—to stop the drought and save her people from a famine. The scattered ashes of her doll come up as the bluebonnet, the state flower of Texas. A related title is *The Legend of the Indian Paintbrush* (1983). (I: 6–9)

Dorris, Michael. *Morning Girl.* Hyperion, 1992. Morning Girl and her younger brother Star Boy describe their island life in alternating chapters. The story closes with the arrival of the first Europeans to her world. (I: 9–12)

*Ekoomiak, Normee. *Arctic Memories.* Holt, 1988. Appliquéd, stitched, and painted illustrations show everyday and special events in the lives of Inuits of the past. Through bilingual Inuktitut and English text, the author/illustrator describes his memories of his childhood in an Inuit community in northern Quebec. (I: 7–10)

Erdrich, Louise. *The Birchbark House.* Hyperion, 1999. Seven-year-old Omakayas is an Ojibwa girl whose daily life on an island in Lake Superior is depicted during the U.S. westward movement. (I: 7–10)

*Esbensen, Barbara Juster. *The Star Maiden: An Ojibway Tale.* Illustrated by Helen K. Davie. Little, Brown, 1988. A star that wants to come to Earth considers what kind of flower to come as—a wild rose, a bluebonnet, or a water lily. (I: 8–10)

*Goble, Paul. *Death of the Iron Horse.* Bradbury, 1987. Fearful of what will happen as the white men approach their territory, a group of Cheyenne braves derail a freight train in 1867, believing it to be an Iron Horse whose rails are binding Mother Earth. (I: 8–10)

*————. *The Girl Who Loved Wild Horses.* Macmillan, 1978. A girl's love of horses leads her to be among them, where her family finds her. She finds that she feels a sense of belonging when she is with the horses. (I: 6–8)

*Hoyt-Goldsmith, Diane. *Cherokee Summer.* Photographs by Lawrence Migdale. Holiday House, 1993. A young Cherokee girl describes contemporary life, telling of day-to-day experiences as well as a little about the Cherokee language, traditions, a legend, and a stomp dance. A related title is *Pueblo Storyteller* (1991), about a young Cochiti Indian girl. (I: 8–10)

Left Hand Bull, Jacqueline and Suzanne Haldane. *Lakota Hoop Dancer.* Photographs by Suzanne Haldane. Dutton, 1999. A Lakota man performs the hoop dance to a variety of audiences in order to share with others the culture he works to keep alive. (I: 7–10)

Lelooska. *Echoes of the Elders: The Stories and Paintings of Chief Lelooska.* Edited by Christine Normandin. DK Ink, 1997. Chief Lelooska dedicated his life as a storyteller and artist to preserve the culture of the Northwest Coast Indians. The stories and art are brought to life with the inclusion of a CD. See also *Spirit of the Cedar People: More Stories and Paintings of Chief Lelooska* (1998). (I: 7–10)

*Martin, Rafe. *The Boy Who Lived with the Seals.* Illustrated by David Shannon. Putnam, 1993. This story of a lost boy who grows up with seals is from Chinook Indian legend. Years later, his parents find him and reclaim him as their son, but the boy hears the seals calling and longs to rejoin them. (I: 6–9)

Ortiz, Simon. *The People Shall Continue*. Children's Book Press, 1988. This book briefly traces the history of the North American Indians from Creation to the present. (I: 9–12)

*Osofsky, Audrey. *Dreamcatcher*. Illustrated by Ed Young. Orchard, 1992. While an Ojibway baby sleeps, the dream catcher snags bad dreams and lets only the good dreams through the center hole in the web. (I: 6–9)

*Ross, Gayle. *How Turtle's Back Was Cracked*. Illustrated by Murv Jacob. Dial, 1995. Turtle is always boasting, and the wolves decide they've heard enough. This story tells how Turtle's shell ended up breaking into twelve pieces and why, even today, you can see the lines where it was put back together. (I: 6–9)

*Scott, Ann Herbert. *On Mother's Lap*. Illustrated by Glo Coalson. Clarion, 1972/1992. Michael enjoys rocking in Mother's lap—along with Dolly, Boat, reindeer blanket, and puppy—until Mother hears the baby crying. The illustrator created the original sketches while living in an Inuit village. (I: P–6)

*Sneve, Virginia Driving Hawk. *The Hopis*. Illustrated by Ronald Himler. Holiday House, 1995. This book is part of the series *The First Americans* (which includes *The Sioux, The Navajos, The Seminoles, The Nez Perce, The Iroquois*). The creation story of the Hopis, their history, arts and crafts, lifestyle, religion, and how they live today are discussed. (I: 7–10)

*Steptoe, John. *The Story of Jumping Mouse: A Native American Legend*. Lothrop, Lee & Shepard, 1984. Jumping Mouse sets out to find the "far-off land." He finds that his generosity pays off as each of the animals he encounters bestows a gift to ensure his safe passage to his "far-off land." (I: 9–13)

Wood, Nancy, ed. *The Serpent's Tongue: Prose, Poetry, and Art of the New Mexico Pueblos*. Dutton, 1997. This 230-page anthology brings together poetry, prose, photographs, and paintings that pay homage to the Pueblos of New Mexico. (I: 12–YA)

*Yolen, Jane. *Encounter*. Illustrated by David Shannon. Harcourt, 1992. This story is narrated by a young Taino boy, who tells of the arrival of Columbus and his ships in 1492. (I: 7–11)

Other Cultures

*Best, Cari. *Three Cheers for Catherine the Great!* Illustrated by Giselle Potter. Kroupa/DK Ink, 1999. Sara's beloved Russian grandmother asks for "no presents" but Sara finds a special present: She and her grandmother exchange language lessons. (I: 6–9)

*Burgie, Irving. *Caribbean Carnival: Songs of the West Indies*. Illustrated by Frané Lessac. Morrow/Tambourine, 1992. This collection of Calypso classics and Caribbean folksongs includes the lyrics and musical notations for piano and guitar accompaniment. Lessac's primitive paintings depict the colorful island setting. (I: all ages)

*Houston, Gloria. *My Great-Aunt Arizona*. Illustrated by Susan Condie Lamb. Harper, 1992. Arizona Houston Hughes was born in a log cabin in the Blue Ridge Mountains, and she grew up to become a teacher in the one-room school she had attended as a child. Arizona inspires generations of children to imagine the faraway places they will someday visit. (I: 6–9)

Joseph, Lynn. *A Wave in Her Pocket: Stories from Trinidad*. Illustrated by Brian Pinkney. Clarion, 1991. Tantie, the family storyteller, shares six stories that originated in Trinidad, West Africa, and in her imagination. A sequel is *The Mermaid's Twin Sister: More Stories from Trinidad* (1994). (I: 8–12)

Lowry, Lois. *Number the Stars*. Houghton Mifflin, 1989. When the Nazis come to find the Jews, ten-year-old Annemarie's family shelters a Jewish girl and participates as part of the Danish resistance in helping Jews escape to Sweden. (I: 10–13)

*Nye, Naomi Shihab. *Sitti's Secrets*. Illustrated by Nancy Carpenter. Four Winds, 1994. An American girl can't speak Arabic, the language of her grandmother—her sitti—but she remembers that they learned to communicate during time they spent together in Palestine. (I: 6–9)

———. *Habibi*. Simon & Schuster, 1998. Liyana and her family move from St. Louis to Jerusalem because her father wants his children to know the other half of their heritage. (I: 12–YA)

*Polacco, Patricia. *The Keeping Quilt*. Simon & Schuster, 1988. A quilt made of scraps from clothes of family members left behind in Russia is passed down through the generations. The quilt serves a multitude of purposes: to welcome babies into the world, as a tent during play time, as a picnic cloth for a romantic date, and as a wedding huppa. (I: 7–10)

———. *Mrs. Katz and Tush*. Bantam, 1992. A lonely Jewish widow gains companionship when an African American boy gives her a kitten. (I: 6–9)

*Rylant, Cynthia. *The Relatives Came*. Illustrated by Stephen Gammell. Bradbury, 1985. This book celebrates a family reunion in the Appalachian mountains, where relatives must travel over winding mountain roads for a visit. (I: P–8)

*San Souci, Robert D. *The Faithful Friend*. Illustrated by Brian Pinkney. Simon & Schuster, 1995. In this traditional tale from the French West Indies island of Martinique, Clemente and Hippolyte are friends who find love, strange zombies, and danger. (I: 7–10)

*———. *Sukey and the Mermaid*. Illustrated by Brian Pinkney. Four Winds, 1992. Sukey is unhappy with her life at home until she meets Mama Jo, a mermaid. (I: 7–10)

International Books

*Bjork, Christina. *Linnea in Monet's Garden*. Illustrated by Lena Anderson. Farrar Straus Giroux, 1987. Linnea visits impressionist painter Claude Monet's home and garden in Giverny, France, and readers learn about his art. (I: 9–12)

*Brenner, Barbara, and Julia Takaya. *Chibi: A True Story from Japan*. Illustrated by June Otani. Clarion, 1996. In a story reminiscent of McCloskey's *Make Way for Ducklings,* a wild duck family seeks a safe home in the Imperial Palace moat in downtown Toyko. (I: P–8)

*Fox, Mem. *Possum Magic*. Illustrated by Julie Vivas. Harcourt, 1991. Hush is an invisible possum whose request to Grandma Poss to make her visible again leads them on a quest throughout Australia, searching for the solution. (I: P–8)

*———. *Shoes from Grandpa*. Illustrated by Patricia Mullins. Orchard, 1992. Grandpa buys Jesse a pair of shoes, and the cumulative story takes off with family members all buying something "to go with the shoes from Grandpa." (I: 6–9)

*Gallaz, Christophe, and Innocenti, Roberto. *Rose Blanche*. Illustrated by Roberto Innocenti. Creative Education, 1985. In a story set in World War II Germany, Rose's curiosity leads her to follow a truck and discover a concentration camp, where she is compelled to try to help by sharing her food. (I: 10 and up)

*Maruki, Toshi. *Hiroshima No Pika*. Illustrated by Toshi Maruki. Lothrop/Morrow, 1982. The effect of the atomic bombing of Hiroshima is described, including what happens to seven-year-old Mii and her parents. (I: 10 and up)

Orlev, Uri. *The Lady with the Hat*. Translated by Hillel Halkin. Houghton Mifflin, 1995. Seventeen-year-old Yulek is a concentration camp survivor who resolves to begin a new life in a Palestinian kibbutz, despite the British blockade. See also *The Man from the Other Side* (1991). (I: 12 and up)

Multiple Cultures

*Adoff, Arnold. *Black is brown is tan*. Illustrated by Emily Arnold McCully. Harper, 1973. Two children with a "chocolate momma," a "white" daddy, and "granny white and grandma black" share the joys of being a family. (I: 6–9)

*Dooley, Norah. *Everybody Cooks Rice*. Illustrated by Peter J. Thornton. Carolrhoda, 1991. It is dinner time and Carrie sets out to find her little brother. At each home, she finds that rice is part of the family's evening meal, but that it is prepared differently because of the various cultural backgrounds of the families. A related title is *Everybody Bakes Bread* (1996). (I: 6–9)

Jenness, Aylette. *Families: A Celebration of Diversity, Commitment, and Love*. Houghton Mifflin, 1990. Photographs and brief text introduce seventeen families of varying composition, including divorced parents, stepfamilies, gay parents, foster siblings, and extended families. (I: 7–10)

Kurtz, Jane. *The Storyteller's Beads*. Gulliver/Harcourt, 1998. Sahay realizes that she must flee to Sudan for her survival when her family is violently killed during a time of famine in Ethiopia. Rahel, who is blind and Jewish, is fleeing also, but with hopes of getting to Israel to escape prejudice as well as hunger. The story is set in the 1980s during the Israeli airlifts. (I: 12 and up)

Levitin, Sonia. *The Golem and the Dragon Girl*. Illustrated by Ellen Thompson. Dial, 1993. A Jewish American boy and a Chinese American girl find that their cultures have interesting parallels. (I: 10–14)

Nelson, Vaunda Micheaux. *Mayfield Crossing*. Illustrated by Leonard Jenkins. Putnam, 1993. When the school in Mayfield Crossing closes and its black students are sent to another school, they face racial and socioeconomic prejudices for the first time. See also *Beyond Mayfield* (1999). (I: 8–12)

*Nikola-Lisa, W. *Bein' with You This Way*. Illustrated by Michael Bryant. Lee & Low, 1994. Through upbeat rhythm, the text points out and celebrates people's physical similarities and differences. (I: P–8)

*Rosen, Michael. *Elijah's Angel: A Story for Chanukah and Christmas*. Illustrated by Aminah Brenda Lynn Robinson. Harcourt, 1992. This story is based on an actual friendship between a young Jewish boy and an elderly African American barber who is a Christian. A gift exchange of a carved angel and a menorah is symbolic of their friendship. (I: 9–12)

Rosenberg, Maxine. *Living in Two Worlds*. Lothrop, Lee & Shepard, 1986. Five children, each of whom has parents of different ethnicities, describe their experiences growing up biracial. (I: 9–12)

Soto, Gary. *Pacific Crossing*. Harcourt, 1992. When two Mexican American boys go to Japan as foreign exchange students to study martial arts, they realize that the bonds of friendship with people in their host country outweigh their cultural differences. (I: 10–14)

Spinelli, Jerry. *Maniac Magee*. Little, Brown, 1990. Twelve-year-old Jeffrey Lionel Magee earns the nickname "Maniac" in this tall tale because of the incredible feats he supposedly performs. Maniac crosses racial boundaries separating the East End and the West End. (I: 10–12)

Woodson, Jacqueline. *Maizon at Blue Hill*. Delacorte, 1992. Maizon enters a private boarding school and learns to deal with being one of only five African American students. She spends much time reflecting on what it feels like to be different from most. (I: 11–YA)

World Cultures Compared

*Anno, Mitsumasa. *All in a Day*. Philomel, 1986. The narrator, on a deserted island near the international date line, describes how children in eight countries celebrate New Year's Day. (I: 6–9)

*Lankford, Mary. *Hopscotch around the World*. Illustrated by Karen Milone. Morrow, 1992. This book gives general descriptions, historical significance, cultural notes, geographical notes, and language notes on nineteen versions of hopscotch played around the world. (I: 6–10)

*Lewin, Ted. *Market!* Lothrop, Lee & Shepard, 1996. A look at marketplaces in Ecuador, Nepal, Ireland, Uganda, Morocco, and the United States, showing the various things people bring to sell or trade. (I: 6–9)

*Morris, Ann. *Houses and Homes*. Photography by Ken Heyman. Lothrop, Lee & Shepard, 1992. Through photographs and simple text, readers are introduced to the varieties of homes in which people around the world live, ranging from Buckingham Palace to houses on stilts, houses on boats, and straw huts. Morris and Heyman have created several other books in the same format. (I: 5–9)

Nye, Naomi Shihab, ed. *This Same Sky: A Collection of Poems from around the World*. Four Winds, 1992. The many forms of life under "this same sky"—human, animal, and nature—are reflected in poems written by 129 poets from 68 different countries. (I: 10–YA)

Social Diversity

*Bunting, Eve. *A Day's Work*. Clarion, 1994. A boy and his grandfather find work by the day, and when they misunderstand the directions and mistakenly perform the roadside job of pulling weeds all wrong, they make arrangements to correct their mistake the next day. (I: 6–8)

*———. *Fly Away Home*. Illustrated by Ronald Himler. Clarion, 1991. A homeless father and son pass the time in the airport. A trapped bird that is freed gives the little boy hope about his future. (I: 6–9)

*———. *Smoky Night*. Illustrated by David Diaz. Harcourt, 1994. The Los Angeles riots are seen from the perspective of a little boy and his mother as they seek shelter from danger. (I: 9–11)

*———. *The Wednesday Surprise*. Illustrated by Donald Carrick. Clarion, 1989. Anna and her grandmother spend every Wednesday together, reading. The surprise comes on Anna's father's birthday when Grandma gets up and reads for the first time, having learned from her "smart" grandchild. (I: 6–9)

Buss, Fran Leeper. *Journey of the Sparrows*. Penguin/Lodestar, 1991. Three siblings escape the war in El Salvador and head for the hope of new life, nailed into a crate on the back of a truck. (I: 12–YA)

*Dugan, Barbara. *Loop the Loop*. Illustrated by James Stevenson. Greenwillow, 1992. While playing outside, Anne encounters Mrs. Simpson, a woman who rides in a wheelchair, claims to be 969 years old, and performs fabulous tricks with a yo-yo. When Mrs. Simpson breaks her hip, Anne takes Mrs. Simpson's cat and a yo-yo to the hospital. (I: 6–9)

Hamilton, Virginia. *Plain City*. Scholastic, 1993. Buhlaire, a child of mixed racial heritage, is ostracized by peers for her family's unusual habits. Her mother sings in clubs, and she thinks her father is Missing in Action—until one day, a homeless man appears. (I: 11–YA)

*Hausherr, Rosemarie. *Celebrating Families*. Scholastic, 1997. Color photos and accompanying text introduce children from single-parent families, adoptive families, extended families, and other types of families. (I: 6–9)

Holt, Kimberly Willis. *When Zachary Beaver Came to Town*. Holt, 1999. In west Texas in 1971, Toby deals with his mother's departure and befriends 600-pound Zachary Beaver. (I: 9–12)

Jenness, Aylette. *Families: A Celebration of Diversity, Commitment, and Love*. Houghton Mifflin, 1990. Definitions of families today are diverse, as is family membership. Personal voices describe what it is like to be part of various family compositions. (I: 7–10)

Paterson, Katherine. *The Flip Flop Girl*. Viking, 1994. Father's death is hard enough to cope with, but moving to a new place, living with grandmother, and dealing with poverty make life even more difficult. (I: 9–12)

———. *The Great Gilly Hopkins*. Crowell, 1978. Gilly's attempts to be difficult and unlikable lead to her being moved from one foster home to another. Trotter, a foster mother, helps Gilly accept the love and security she craves. (I: 9–12)

*Pearson, Susan. *Happy Birthday, Grampie*. Illustrated by Ronald Himler. Dial, 1987. Age has taken away Grampie's vision, and he has forgotten English and reverted to his mother tongue, Swedish. Martha makes Grampie a card he can feel and hopes that it will communicate her birthday wishes. (I: 6–9)

*Sun, Chyng Feng. *Mama Bear*. Illustrated by Lolly Robinson. Houghton Mifflin, 1994. Mei-Mei wants a big toy bear she sees in a store window, but her mother needs money to fix the furnace so that they can keep warm this winter. (I: P–8)

Temple, Frances. *Grab Hands and Run*. Orchard, 1993. Felipe and his family face threats to their lives at their home in El Salvador. He tells the story of their escape and the dangerous journey to Canada. (I: 12–YA)

———. *Tonight, by Sea*. Orchard, 1995. Poverty and government brutality make life in Haiti unbearable, so Paulie and other villagers help her uncle build a boat so that they can secretly attempt to escape to the United States. (I: 12–YA)

Gender Issues

*Cole, Joanna. *The Magic School Bus at the Waterworks*. Illustrated by Bruce Degen. Scholastic, 1986. In the *Magic School Bus* series, Ms. Frizzle is the adventuresome teacher who leads the class on an unusual variety of field trips. (I: 6–9)

*Hearne, Betsy. *Seven Brave Women*. Illustrated by Bethanne Andersen. Greenwillow, 1997. This book tells of seven women whose lives are not marked by their contributions to wars in history but showed courage and strength in "herstory." (I: 7–10)

*Hoffman, Mary. *Amazing Grace*. Illustrated by Caroline Binch. Dial, 1991. When Grace is told by classmates that she can't be Peter Pan in the class play because she's black and a girl, she proves otherwise. See also *Boundless Grace* (1995); and *Starring Grace* (2000). (I: 6–8)

*Isadora, Rachel. *Max*. Macmillan, 1976. Max finds that taking dance lessons with his sister is a nice warm-up to his afternoon baseball games. (I: 5–8)

*Merrill, Jean. *The Girl Who Loved Caterpillars*. Illustrated by Floyd Cooper. Philomel, 1992. This is a retelling of a twelfth-century Japanese story of Izumi, a free-spirited girl who preferred studying caterpillars to learning the arts of the ancient court. (I: 7–10)

*Paterson, Katherine. *The King's Equal*. Illustrated by Vladimir Vagin. HarperCollins, 1992. A prince in search of a princess to be his equal finds that he must prove to be her equal as well. (I: 7–10)

———. *Lyddie*. Penguin/Lodestar, 1991. In the mid-1800s, Lyddie becomes a factory girl in the mill town of Lowell, Massachusetts, to earn wages in an attempt to save the family farm. (I: 11–YA)

*Willhoite, Michael. *Daddy's Roommate*. Alyson Wonderland, 1990. Following a divorce, Daddy lives with another man. (I: P–8)

Woodson, Jacqueline. *From the Notebooks of Melanin Sun*. Scholastic/Blue Sky, 1995. Melanin Sun faces the everyday challenges of a thirteen-year-old growing up, but life is complicated when he hears rumors about his mother's love for a woman of a different race. (I: 12–YA)

*Zolotow, Charlotte. *William's Doll*. Illustrated by William P. du Bois. Harper, 1972. William participates in traditional activities for boys but also wants a doll. Despite objections from male characters, Grandmother gets William a doll so that he can prepare for when he will be a father. (I: P–8)

Exceptional Learners

*Barrett, Mary Brigid. *Sing to the Stars*. Illustrated by Sandra Speidel. Little, Brown, 1994. When an accident takes his daughter's life and leaves him blind, Mr. Washington stops playing the piano. Ephram plays his violin and convinces Mr. Washington to join him on the stage so that they can make music together. (I: 8–10)

Billingsley, Franny. *Well Wished*. Atheneum, 1997. When Nuria wishes at a magical well that wheelchair-bound Catty could have a body like hers, the two girls surprisingly end up in each other's body. (I: 9–12)

*Booth, B. D. *Mandy*. Illustrated by Jim Lamarche. Lothrop, Lee & Shepard, 1991. Mandy's musings about why she fears the dark and wonderings about the sounds of the world allow readers to get inside the thinking of a child with hearing loss. (I: 6–8)

*Brown, Tricia. *Someone Special Just Like You*. Photographs by Fran Ortiz. Holt, 1982. Photographs and simple text addressed to the reader show children with various disabilities engaged in activities in which all children participate. (I: P–6)

Byars, Betsy. *Summer of the Swans.* Illustrated by Ted CoConis. Viking, 1970. Sara learns to cope with her feelings of resentment toward her younger brother, who is developmentally delayed. (I: 10–13)

*Cohen, Miriam. *See You Tomorrow, Charles.* Illustrated by Lillian Hoban. Greenwillow, 1983. In this book (part of a series), Charles is a child with vision loss in a class of first-graders who learn with and from each other. (I: 5–7)

Fleischman, Paul. *Mind's Eye.* Holt, 1999. Courtney is paralyzed at sixteen, and her eighty-eight-year-old roommate teaches her to rely on her mind in order to survive. (I: YA)

*Fleming, Virginia. *Be Good to Eddie Lee.* Illustrated by Floyd Cooper. Philomel, 1993. Christy learns to appreciate the sensitive heart of Eddie Lee, a child with Down syndrome, when he noisily tags along on a visit to the woods in search of frog eggs. (I: 7–9)

*Haldane, Suzanne. *Helping Hands: How Monkeys Assist People Who Are Disabled.* Dutton, 1991. A teen boy with quadriplegia performs daily routines with the aid of a monkey. (I: 6–12)

*Krull, Kathleen. *Wilma Unlimited.* Illustrated by David Diaz. Harcourt Brace, 1997. Wilma overcomes wearing braces on her legs to become a winning Olympic runner. (I: 6–10)

McMahon, Patricia. *Dancing Wheels.* Illustrated with photographs by John Godt. Houghton Mifflin, 2000. The Dancing Wheels dance company includes both "standing" dancers and "sitting" dancers, who travel across the country, performing with energy and commitment. (I: 8–12)

*Miller, Mary Beth, and George Ancona. *Handtalk School.* Four Winds, 1991. A guide to a day in a boarding school for children with hearing loss shows, through color photographs, the use of American Sign Language to communicate. (I: all ages)

*Millman, Isaac. *Moses Goes to School.* Foster/Farrar, 2000. Moses and other deaf children in his school are shown communicating in ASL and learning to read and write in standard English. American Sign Language accompanies the text and illustrations. See also *Moses Goes to a Concert* (1998). (I: P–8)

Philbrick, Rodman. *Freak the Mighty.* Blue Sky Press/Scholastic, 1993. A boy with physical size and might and a boy with intellectual brilliance are the book's main characters. Separately, each lacks what the other has, but together they become "Freak the Mighty." (I: 10–14)

Rosenberg, Maxine B. *Finding a Way: Living with Exceptional Brothers and Sisters.* Lothrop, Lee & Shepard, 1988. Three children describe what it is like to have siblings with physical disorders: diabetes, severe asthma, and spina bifida. (I: 7–9)

Slote, Alfred. *Hang Tough, Paul Mather.* Lippincott, 1973. Twelve-year-old Paul's enthusiasm for baseball helps him through the difficulty of living with treatments for leukemia. (I: 9–11)

Trueman, Terry. *Stuck in Neutral.* HarperCollins, 2000. Narrator fourteen-year-old Shawn describes his exceptional ability to remember all he hears, but the world believes that he is retarded because cerebral palsy has left him with total inability to control his muscles in any communicable way. (I: 12–YA)

RESOURCES

Cai, Mingshui, and Rudine Sims Bishop. "Multicultural Literature for Children: Towards a Clarification of the Concept." *The Need for Story: Cultural Diversity in Classroom and Community.* Ed. A. H. Dyson and C. Genishi. National Council of Teachers of English, 1994.

Collier, Laurie, and Joyce Nakamura. *Major Authors and Illustrators for Children and Young Adults: A Selection of Sketches from Something about the Author.* Gale Research, 1993.

Cooperative Children's Book Center. *The Multicolored Mirror: Cultural Substance in Literature for Children and Young Adults.* Ed. Merri V. Lindgren. Highsmith, 1991.

Friedberg, Joan Brest, June B. Mullins, and Adelaide Weir Sukiennik. *Portraying Persons with Disabilities: An Annotated Bibliography of Nonfiction for Children and Teenagers.* Bowker, 1992.

Grossman, Herbert, and Suzanne H. Grossman. *Gender Issues in Education.* Allyn & Bacon, 1994.

Harris, Violet J., Junko Yokota, Georgia Johnson, and Oralia Garza de Cortes. "Bookalogues: Multicultural Literature." *Language Arts 70* (1993): 215–44.

Henkin, Roxanne, and Junko Yokota. "Inclusive Reading: Literature Portraying Families with Gay and Lesbian Parents." *Democracy & Education, 13* (3) (1999): 60–61.

Kruse, Ginny Moore, Kathleen T. Horning, and Megan Schliesman, with Tana Elias. *Multicultural Literature for Children and Young Adults: A Selected Listing of Books by and about People of Color, Volume 2.* Cooperative Children's Book Center, 1997.

Miller-Lachmann, Lyn. *Our Family, Our Friends, Our World.* Bowker, 1992.

Robertson, Debra. *Portraying Persons with Disabilities: An Annotated Bibliography of Fiction for Children and Teenagers.* Bowker, 1992.

Rochman, Hazel. *Against Borders: Promoting Books for a Multicultural World*. American Library Association, 1993.

Rudman, Masha Kabakow. *Children's Literature: An Issues Approach*. 3rd ed. Longman, 1995.

Schon, Isabel. *The Best of the Latino Heritage: A Guide to the Best Juvenile Books about Latino People and Cultures*. Scarecrow Press, 1997.

Silvey, Anita. *Children's Books and Their Creators*. Houghton Mifflin, 1995.

Sims, Rudine. *Shadow and Substance: Afro-American Experience in Contemporary Children's Fiction*. 2nd ed. National Council of Teachers of English/American Library Association, 1982.

Sims Bishop, Rudine, and the Multicultural Booklist Committee, eds. *Kaleidoscope*. National Council of Teachers of English, 1995.

Slapin, Beverly, and Doris Seale. *Through Indian Eyes: The Native Experience in Books for Children*.

American Indian Studies Center, University of California, 1998.

Smith, Henrietta M., ed. *The Coretta Scott King Awards Book: From Vision to Reality*. American Library Association, 1994.

Yokota, Junko. "Asian and Asian American Literature for Children: Implications for Classroom Teachers and Librarians." *Multicultural Literature and Literacies: Making Space for Difference*. Ed. Suzanne Miller and Barbara McCaskill. State University of New York Press, 1993. 229–46.

———. "Issues in Selecting Multicultural Children's Literature." *Language Arts* 70 (1993): 156–67.

———, ed. *Kaleidoscope: A Multicultural Booklist for Grades K–8*. 3rd ed. National Council of Teachers of English, 2000.

———. "Ten International Books for Children." *Journal of Children's Literature*, 25 (1) (1999): 48–54.

REFERENCES

Adoff, Arnold. *I Am the Darker Brother: An Anthology of Modern Poems by Negro Americans*. Macmillan, 1970.

Au, Kathryn H. *Literacy Instruction in Multicultural Settings*. Harcourt, 1993.

Banks, James. *Cultural Diversity and Education: Foundations, Curriculum, and Teaching*. Allyn & Bacon, 2000.

———. *An Introduction to Multicultural Education*. 2nd ed. Allyn & Bacon, 1999.

Bannerman, Helen. *The Story of Little Babaji*. Illustrated by Fred Marcellino. HarperCollins, 1996.

———. *The Story of Little Black Sambo*. HarperCollins, 1899.

Barrera, Rosalinda B., Verlinda D. Thompson, and Mark Dressman, eds. *Kaleidoscope: A Multicultural Booklist for Grades K–8*. 2nd ed. National Council of Teachers of English, 1997.

Bennett, William. "Education Secretary Bennett's Suggested List for Elementary-School Pupils." *Chronicle of Higher Education* (1988, September 14): B3.

Bishop, Claire Huchet. *The Five Chinese Brothers*. Illustrated by Kurt Wiese. Coward, 1938.

Browne, Anthony. *Piggybook*. Knopf, 1986.

Bryan, Ashley. *The Dancing Granny*. Aladdin, 1987.

———. *Lion and the Ostrich Chicks and Other African Folk Tales*. Aladdin, 1986/1996.

———. *What a Morning! The Christmas Story in Black Spirituals*. Little Simon, 1987/1996.

Cai, Mingshui. "Can We Fly across Cultural Gaps on the Wings of Imagination? Ethnicity, Experience, and Cultural Authenticity." *The New Advocate* 8.1 (1995): 1–16.

———. "Multiple Definitions of Multicultural Literacy: Is the Debate Really Just 'Ivory Tower' Bickering?" *The New Advocate* 11 (1998): 311–324.

Cai, Mingshui, and Rudine Sims Bishop. "Multicultural Literature for Children: Towards a Clarification of the Concept." *The Need for Story: Cultural Diversity in Classroom and Community*. Ed. Anne Haas Dyson and Celia Genishi. National Council of Teachers of English, 1994.

Chall, J. S., E. Radwin, V. W. French, and C. R. Hall. "Blacks in the World of Children's Books." *The Black American in Books for Children*. 2nd ed. Ed. Donnarae MacCann and G. Woodard. Scarecrow, 1985, pp. 211–21.

Council on Interracial Books for Children. Special issue on Puerto Rican materials. *Bulletin of the Council on Interracial Books for Children* 4 (1974).

———. Special issue on Chicano materials. *Bulletin of the Council on Interracial Books for Children* 5 (1975).

Delpit, Lisa D. "The Silenced Dialogue: Power and Pedagogy in Educating Other People's Children." *Harvard Educational Review* 58 (1988): 280–98.

Freeman, Evelyn, and Barbara Lehman. *Global Perspectives in Children's Literature*. Allyn & Bacon, 2001.

Galda, Lee. Personal communication, November 2000.

Gollub, Matthew. *Cool Melons Turn to Frogs! The Life and Poems of Issa*. Illustrated by Kazuko G. Stone. Lee & Low, 1998.

Greenfield, Eloise. *Mary McLeod Bethune*. Illustrated by Jerry Pinkney. HarperTrophy, 1977/1994.

Grossman, Virginia, and Sylvia Long. *Ten Little Rabbits*. New York: Chronicle, 1991.

Hamilton, Virginia. *Anthony Burns: The Defeat and Triumph of a Fugitive Slave*. Laureleaf, 1988/1993.

———. "Everything of Value: Moral Realism in Literature for Children" (May Hill Arbuthnot Lecture). *Journal of Youth Services in Libraries* 6 (Summer 1993): 363–77.

———. *In the Beginning: Creation Stories from around the World*. Illustrated by Barry Moser. Harcourt, 1988.

———. "Laura Ingalls Wilder Medal Acceptance." *Horn Book* 71.4 (July/August 1995): 436–41.

———. *The Planet of Junior Brown*. Macmillan, 1971.

———. *Sweet Whispers, Brother Rush*. Putnam, 1982.

Harris, Violet J. "African American Children's Literature: The First One Hundred Years." *Journal of Negro Education* 59 (1990): 540–55.

———, ed. *Using Multiethnic Literature in the K–8 Classroom.* Christopher-Gordon Publishers, 1997.

Jeffers, Susan. *Brother Eagle, Sister Sky: A Message from Chief Seattle.* Dial, 1991.

Kaplan, Esther. Personal communication, December 1995.

Kruse, G. M., and K. T. Horning, with M. V. Lindgren, and K. Odahowski. *Multicultural Literature for Children and Young Adults: A Selected Listing of Books 1980–1990 by and about People of Color.* Cooperative Children's Book Center, 1991.

Larrick, Nancy. "The All-White World of Children's Books." *Saturday Review* (1965, September 11): 63–65.

Little, Jean. *Little by Little: A Writer's Education.* Penguin, 1987.

———. "A Writer's Social Responsibility." *The New Advocate* 3.2 (1990): 79–88.

McCarty, Teresa L. "What's Wrong with Ten Little Rabbits?" *The New Advocate* 8.2 (1995): 97–98.

McCloskey, Robert. *Make Way for Ducklings.* Viking, 1941.

Melmed, Laura Krauss. "Little Oh: A Story Unfolds." *Book Links* (1999): 4–44.

Meltzer, Milton. "The Social Responsibility of the Writer." *The New Advocate* 2.3 (1989): 155–57.

Myers, Walter Dean. *Fallen Angels.* Scholastic, 1988.

———. *Fast Sam, Cool Clyde, and Stuff.* Viking, 1975/1988.

———. *Glory Field.* Scholastic, 1994; Point, 1996.

———. *Monster.* HarperCollins, 2000.

———. *Motown and Didi: A Love Story.* Viking, 1984.

———. *The Mouse Rap.* HarperTrophy, 1990/1992.

———. *Now Is Your Time! The African American Struggle for Freedom.* HarperCollins, 1991.

———. *Scorpions.* HarperCollins, 1988/1990.

———. *Shadow of the Red Moon.* Point, 1997.

———. *Slam!* Scholastic, 1998.

———. *Somewhere in the Darkness.* Scholastic, 1992.

———. *The Young Landlords.* Viking, 1989.

Nieto, Sonia. "Puerto Ricans in Children's Literature and History Texts: A Ten-Year Update." *Bulletin of the Council on Interracial Books for Children* 14 (1983).

———. Affirming Diversity. 2nd ed. Longman, 1996.

Noll, Elizabeth. "Accuracy and Authenticity in American Indian Children's Literature: The Social Responsibility of Authors and Illustrators." *The New Advocate* 8.1 (1995): 29–43.

Pallas, A. M., G. Natriello, and E. L. McDill. "The Changing Nature of the Disadvantaged Population: Current Dimensions and Future Trends." *Educational Researcher* 18.5 (1989): 16–22.

Pellowski, Anne. *The Family Story-Telling Handbook: How to Use Stories, Anecdotes, Rhymes, Handkerchiefs, Paper, and Other Objects to Enrich Your Family Traditions.* Illustrated by Lynn Sweat. Macmillan, 1987.

———. *Hidden Stories in Plants: Unusual and Easy-to-Tell Stories from around the World Together with Creative Things to Do While Telling Them.* Macmillan, 1990.

———. *The Story Vine: A Source Book of Unusual and Easy-to-Tell Stories from around the World.* Illustrated by Lynn Sweat. Macmillan, 1984.

Reimer, K. M. "Multiethnic Literature: Holding Fast to Dreams." *Language Arts* 69 (1992): 14–21.

Rochman, Hazel. *Against Borders: Promoting Books for a Multicultural World.* American Library Association, 1993.

Rollock, Barbara. *The Black Experience in Children's Books.* 2nd ed. New York Public Library, 1984.

Rudman, Masha Kabakow. *Children's Literature: An Issues Approach.* 3rd ed. Longman, 1995.

Say, Allen. *The Ink-Keeper's Apprentice.* Houghton Mifflin, 1979.

Schlesinger, Arthur M. *The Disuniting of America.* The Larger Agenda Publishers, 1991.

Schon, Isabel. *A Hispanic Heritage: A Guide to Juvenile Books about Hispanic People and Culture.* 3rd ed. Scarecrow, 1988.

Sims, Rudine. "Children's Books about Blacks: A Mid-Eighties Status Report." *Children's Literature Review 8* (1985): 9–13.

Sims Bishop, Rudine. "African American Literature for Children: Anchor, Compass, and Sail." *Perspectives 7* (1991): ix–xii.

———. "Mirrors, Windows, and Sliding Glass Doors." *Perspectives 6* (1990): ix–xi.

———. "Multicultural Literature for Children: Making Informed Choices." *Teaching Multicultural Literature in Grades K–8.* Ed. Violet Harris. Christopher-Gordon, 1992, pp. 37–54.

Smith, Henrietta M., ed. *The Coretta Scott King Awards Book: From Vision to Reality.* American Library Association, 1994.

Steptoe, John. *Daddy Is a Monster . . . Sometimes.* Harper, 1980.

———. *Stevie.* HarperTrophy, 1969/1986.

Tatum, Beverlee. *Why Are All the Black Kids Sitting Together in the Cafeteria?* St. Martins, 1999.

Tomlinson, Carl M., ed. *Children's Books from Other Countries.* Scarecrow Press, 1998.

Trelease, Jim. *The New Read-Aloud Handbook.* Viking Penguin, 1989.

Tsutsui, Yoriko. *Anna's Secret Friend.* Illustrated by Akiko Hayashi. Viking, 1987.

Walter, Mildred Pitts. *Brother to the Wind.* Morrow, 1985.

Zion, Gene. *Dear Garbage Man.* Illustrations by Margaret Bloy Graham. Harper & Row, 1957.

Part Two

Exploring the Genres of Children's Literature

5 Traditional Literature

Beloved friend, my boon companion . . .
start now to sing with me, begin to recite together . . .
Let us clasp hand in hand, fingers in fingers,
so that we may sing fine things, give voice to the best things
for those dear ones to hear, for those desiring to know them
among the rising younger generation . . .

from The Kalevala
compiled by Elias Lonnrot

These words introduce the long collection of ancient Finnish poems called *The Kalevala,* twenty thousand lines of wisdom and magic that recount the exploits of heroes and common folk from Viking times. For well over a thousand years before they were written down, the verses that make up *The Kalevala* were memorized by illiterate poets, who, huddled with their listeners around peat fires, could recite them for a whole week of evenings.

TRADITIONAL LITERATURE DEFINED

Traditional literature is the body of stories and poems that came to us by oral transmission and whose authors are unknown. "Literature" is something of a misnomer, since these works were told and heard long before they were written and read. Thus, the works that make up the body of traditional literature have met a standard that most other children's literature has not: Traditional works are so appealing and so memorable that they passed from generation to generation without the aid of writing. Even after having been written down, traditional works, because they are not considered the property of any one author, continue to inspire storytellers, writers, and artists (as well as choreographers, filmmakers, and musicians) to produce new versions.

Besides having demonstrated a timeless popularity, traditional literature makes up a very important part of children's literature for three other reasons:

1. Traditional stories and poems had to have clear structures, plots, rhymes, or rhythms to be remembered. These features appeal to children.

2. Traditional literature invites participation: Listeners had to learn these stories and poems, or else they would have died out. Traditional literature still makes an active and exciting entry point into verbal texts.

3. When it comes to children's fare, oral traditions are still stronger than written ones in many cultures. Therefore, traditional literature is a vital part of multicultural literature.

THE EVOLUTION OF TRADITIONAL LITERATURE

Where did the literature in the oral tradition come from? And how did it develop into written material? Of course, we cannot know what the first stories were, but those opening words of *The Kalevala* offer a clue about their nature:

> Let us . . . give voice to the best things
> for those dear ones to hear, for those desiring to know them
> among the rising younger generation . . .

Stories surely arose because people wanted to remember the best things (and sometimes the worst) and pass them on. For young Iron Age Finns, the stories that make up *The Kalevala* answered certain questions: "Who are we?" "What should we believe?" "How should we behave?" Most of the oldest stories offered answers to the important questions about the human experience and passed on a people's accumulated wisdom as to what the young should know, aspire to, and believe, forging a cultural identity in the process.

Whether we are speaking of *The Kalevala, The Odyssey* (the epic of the ancient Greek hero Odysseus), or *The Popol Vuh* (the legend of the Toltec emperor Quetzalcoatl), traditional works relied on strong plots, legendary characters, fantastic events, and the clear polarization of qualities such as good and evil. They employed chants, refrains, and poetic language, for these devices aid memory. They also relied on the economy of symbolism; though often short, the old stories could be understood on many levels and invited pondering for their truths and their applications to real life, long after the telling was done.

Where writing and formal education advanced, however, the oral tradition was pushed to the periphery. (Even by the fourth century B.C., Plato wrote of his distrust for storytellers and myth mongers.) In Europe, formal schools such as those inspired by the German theologian Martin Luther (1483–1546) were established to teach people to read religious texts and then other works. Science slowly matured, with theories to rival mythical accounts of the world. With the spread of education, culture slowly divided between knowledge that was written down and folk beliefs. Among the educated, the terms "myth" and "old wives' tale" took on the connotations they still have in popular parlance: the unreliable lore of unsophisticated people.

But traditional lore still flourished, especially outside church and school. Folktales and legends drew their truths from the old myths and religious stories and continued to mix these with the people's own fantasies and fears. Folktales and legends came to constitute the unofficial lore of a culture. In church, the priest said, "Thou shalt not steal" and urged the congregation to practice mercy and forgiveness; in the words of the storyteller, however, Jack still robbed fabulous riches from the giant, and Snow White still honeymooned while her wicked stepmother danced to hell in hot iron shoes. Teachers stressed book learning and the virtues of hard work, but in folktales, a simpleton such as Juan Bobo was always more likely to succeed than someone more diligent.

In contemporary times, myths, folktales, and legends have gained a new appreciation by anthropologists, psychologists, literary critics, and, of course, teachers and children. Some anthropologists claim that the stories told in a society constitute the people's way of understanding themselves. Roy Rapaport, for example, argues that the stories told and read in a society are "loosely joined into a more or less coherent *mythos,* which, in its entirety, expresses or represents that society's *logos* (its conception of the world's moral and natural order) and how it came to be" (Rapaport, 1986, p. 319). We need to know our stories to know who we are.

The psychologist Carl Jung (1961, 1989) observed that folktales serve a society the way dreams serve an individual, symbolizing our deepest fears and wishes and pointing the way to order and happiness. To Jung, knowing our folk stories was a way of gaining wisdom and reassurance for meeting the challenges of life.

Northrop Frye (1971), a noted literary critic, finds a different value in myths and folktales. Frye believes that literature is cumulative—that virtually everything written draws on and builds on what was written before. Myths and folktales are our oldest stories, and they form the foundation for everything that has been written since. Frye maintains that we need to know those old stories so we can better understand and appreciate the new ones.

Joseph Campbell, a literary scholar and student of mythology, went one step further: We use myths and story patterns not only to understand literature, but also to understand the patterns of our lives. Bruno Bettelheim (1975), a child psychologist, argued in a similar vein that fairy tales and folktales point to the very meaning of life. Like Jung, Bettelheim argued that fairy tales could be therapeutic and reassuring: They inform the heart and nurture the spirit.

The modern appreciation of folktales can be traced to a definite source: two brothers from Germany.

Traditional Literature in Many Forms

Traditional Literature	Traditional literature consists of stories, songs, poems, and riddles from anonymous sources. Works of traditional literature were usually passed on by word of mouth before being written down. Most of these works were commonly told for the instruction or the delight of adults as well as children. The association of folktales and fairy tales with predominantly child audiences began only about 200 years ago, with the brothers Grimm. There is considerable overlap in the categories set out below. Readers might reasonably disagree on whether a particular story is a fairy tale or a hero tale, a tall tale or a pourquoi tale, and so on. The categories are intended to call attention to the variety of forms we find to appreciate in traditional literature, rather than to make fine distinctions.
Myths	Myths are very old stories that tell of a people's origins and contain the basis for their beliefs in a moral, spiritual, and temporal order. Our best-known myths tell of the exploits of the Greek, Roman, and Norse gods.
Fables	Fables are short, didactic stories, often accompanied by a moral, or an explicit statement of a lesson to guide the hearers' behavior. The most famous fables were written by the Greek storyteller Aesop.
Epics	Epics are long stories, usually in verse form, that tell the exploits of a hero. The old English story of Beowulf and the ancient Greek story of Ulysses told in *The Odyssey* are both epics. Epics usually have a more formal tone than ballads and often include invocations to the gods.
Ballads	Ballads are stories in song form, consisting of many verses and usually dealing with sad deaths (such as the English

	ballad *Lord Randall*) but sometimes with heroic deeds, such as the *Ballad of Robin Hood*. They tend to use less formal language than epics do.
Legends	Stories about saints or other possibly historic heroes or major events that are important to a people are called legends, especially if they have an air of truth to them, as if they were at some time told to be believed. We speak of the *legend* of King Arthur, which is a series of episodes linked to a hero we are not certain ever existed. We also speak of *legends* about George Washington, stories—such as the cutting down of the cherry tree—whose veracity is questionable but that are told about a historical figure.
Folk Rhymes	Folk rhymes are verses from anonymous sources that are passed on from generation to generation. They often can be categorized as those that were taught to children by their parents, such as nursery rhymes or Mother Goose rhymes, and those that are passed from children to children, such as skipping rhymes and chants.
Folktales	Folktales are stories of cleverness, adventure, or trickery, told sparely with active plots but little development of setting or characters. There are many varieties of folktales, including fairy tales, pourquoi tales, and tall tales.
Fairy Tales	Folktales with a stress on magical elements, especially with fairy godmothers, are known as fairy tales. The best known come from French sources, especially Charles Perrault (e.g., "Cinderella," "Sleeping Beauty"), and from Russian sources (e.g., "Vasilisa the Beautiful," "Ivan, the Grey Wolf, and the Firebird").
Apprenticeship Tales and Hero Tales	Tales in which a young person learns lessons on the way to growing up are called apprenticeship tales. "Hansel and Gretel" is an apprenticeship tale because the two children learn to be crafty and independent to survive. If the character rises to a much better estate or wins great riches or prestige, as Jack does in "Jack and the Beanstalk," we call the story a hero tale.
Numskull Tales	Numskull tales feature unlikely heroes who triumph precisely because they do not do the smart thing. Typically, they commit a deed so outrageous that they make a royal person laugh and are awarded with success as a result, as in "Hans Clodhopper."
Pourquoi Tales	"Pourquoi" means "why" in French, and pourquoi tales explain why or how things came into existence. *Why Mosquitoes Buzz in People's Ears,* retold by Verna Aardema, is a popular pourquoi tale.
Trickster Tales	Stories about characters who fool other characters are called trickster tales. Trickster tales are popular in West African folklore, where we meet characters such as Turtle and Anansi the Spider. They are also popular in Native American stories, with characters such as Coyote and Glooscap.

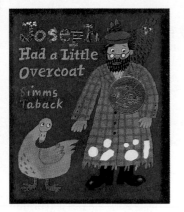

Illustration 5.1
Simms Taback won a Caldecott Medal for this lively retelling in story form of a Yiddish folk song.
(*Joseph Had a Little Overcoat* by Simms Taback. Copyright © 2000. Used by permission of Viking Children's Books, a division of Penguin Putnam Inc.)

Tall Tales	Tall tales, greatly exaggerated exploits of larger-than-life heroes, have been particularly popular in the United States, where regions of the country or occupational groups have had their own outsized champions such as Pecos Bill, the cowboy; Paul Bunyan, the lumberjack; or Stormalong, the sailor.
Cumulative Tales	A special kind of story pattern in which one thing builds on another is called a cumulative tale. The best-known cumulative tale in English is probably "The House That Jack Built." The Yiddish story *Joseph Had a Little Overcoat* (adapted by SImms Taback from a folk song) is also a cumulative tale.

The Brothers Grimm and the Elevation of Folktales

In the early nineteenth century, two scholars of language built a bridge between the oral tradition and the written one. Jacob and Wilhelm Grimm, born in 1785 and 1786, respectively, in Hanau, Germany, were well known in their time as scholars of language. While studying law at Marburg, the Grimm brothers became fired with the conviction, promoted by the poet and dramatist Clemens Brentano and the legal scholar Friedrich Karl von Savigny, that the spirit and culture of the German people resided in the old tales and legends. Soon after, the Grimms began their quest for German folktales. The two hundred tales they gathered have been translated into seventy languages and have made a contribution to world literature that has been likened to that of the Bible.

Germany in the early nineteenth century was a loose federation of principalities, where landowners held most of the wealth and the peasants' lives were kept primitive. Roads were bad, communication was limited, and education was largely unavailable to the poor—conditions that made for hard lives but created fertile ground for storytelling. The Grimm brothers collected stories from many people, but their greatest source was a peasant woman named Frau Viehmannin who lived near Kassell.

As linguists, the Grimms wanted to keep the tales faithful to the original telling, and Frau Viehmannin, or "Gammer Grethel," as she was later called, learned to tell her tales slowly enough that the brothers could write them down almost verbatim. Still, some editing was inevitable as they heard competing versions of the same tales. For example, some tellers had a wolf, not a witch, occupying the house of sweets where Hansel and Gretel's misadventures took place.

The Grimms published the first volume of their ***Kinder und Hausmärchen*** (***Nursery and Household Tales***) in 1812 and the second in 1815. The books received a cool critical reception, but they sold briskly and were soon translated and read throughout Europe and the United States.

The Grimms introduced "Hansel and Gretel," "Snow White," "Little Red Riding Hood," and a host of other stories to a wide audience. Furthermore, the commercial success of their books aroused new interest in the few existing collections of oral tales and inspired other people to collect tales in their own countries.

Folktales from Everywhere

Inspired by the Grimms, Joseph Jacobs (1854–1916) and Andrew Lang (1844–1912) collected and published folktales from the British Isles. Jacobs published *English Fairy Tales* in 1890 and *Celtic Fairy Tales* in 1892. Lang's *Blue Fairy Book,* published in 1889, is still widely enjoyed. Collections of folktales from Russia, Italy, Spain, and Scandinavia soon followed.

Whereas the Grimms modified some of the tales they collected, the Dane Hans Christian Andersen (1805–1875) made up several of the most famous tales in the world's collection of stories, while he also collected traditional stories. Andersen gave us "The Emperor's New Clothes," "The Princess and the Pea," "The Little Mermaid," and "The Little Match Girl," among many others.

In the United States, Joel Chandler Harris (1848–1908) collected stories he had learned as a boy from slaves in Georgia and later narrated in the voice of a fictional character named Uncle Remus. The tales of "The Tar Baby" and "Brer Rabbit and Brer Fox," among many others, were first written down by Harris, who took pains to transcribe the African American dialect as he heard it (though versions that are more pleasing to the contemporary ear have become available since—especially those retold by Julius Lester). Native American stories were collected early in the twentieth century by anthropologists and linguists (although many stories that have never been "collected" are still being told by Native Americans today). Many tall tales—especially of lumberjacks, cowboys, riverboat characters, and canal boat drivers—arose from the American experience and became famous all over the world (creating interesting stereotypes of what American life was like).

The 1930s saw a great harvest of American folktales. A New Deal program under the Works Progress Administration sent writers and anthropologists into the cabins of the rural South, ahead of power lines and telephones, collecting tales such as "Wiley and the Hairy Man," "Taily Po," and "Little Eight John." Richard Chase visited storytellers in Appalachia in the 1940s to collect *The Jack Tales,* American variants of European folktales reworked in a mountain setting. Farther west, stories of ranch life and cattle drives were collected from men and

Illustration 5.2
Julius Lester, a specialist in African American studies, has recently created lively retellings of the stories of Uncle Remus. (*The Last Tales of Uncle Remus* by Julius Lester. Illustrations copyright © 1994 by Jerry Pinkney. Used by permission of Dial Books for Young Readers, a division of Penguin Putnam Inc.)

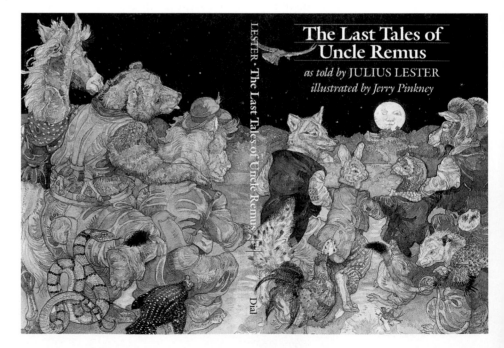

women who experienced them and were written up in many fine books by a Texan, J. Frank Dobie (1888–1964), and others. In New York State, stories of the Erie Canal were collected by Walter D. Edmonds, and they inspired his original works, including *The Matchlock Gun,* which won the Newbery Medal in 1942.

Throughout the first decades of the twentieth century, folksong collector John Lomax gathered cowboy songs throughout the Southwest. Later, his son Alan Lomax, with the support of the Smithsonian Institute, continued collecting songs among African American workers and prisoners in the Southeast and from people in the mountain cabins of the Appalachians. The result of their work, *The Folksongs of North America,* complements the collections by poet Carl Sandburg and balladeer John Jacob Nyles and offers amazing riches of song from the common folk of this country.

Folklore as a Field of Study

Folklore became the focus of serious academic study in the middle of the nineteenth century. (The word "folklore" was coined in 1846 by W. J. Thoms.) By the early twentieth century, so much folk material had been collected from all around the world that some way was needed to organize and make sense of it.

Even a quick comparison of folktale collections shows intriguing similarities among tales from widely separate places. Grouping similar folktales, however, is not a simple matter. The story that we know as "Cinderella," for example, has many variants. It originated long ago in China, where it was called "Yeh-hsien." In France, the tale was known as "Cendrillon"; in Germany, "Aschenputtel;" and in England, "Cap-O-Rushes." In North America, the tale was known among the Algonquin people as "The Rough-Faced Girl" and among the Pueblo as "Turkey Girl." There are some 650 variations in all, most having different names. How could you look up different versions of the same story if each has a different name? And suppose it was not the whole story you want to compare but a single detail— say, the prince's recognizing the true princess by fitting her with a shoe or a pumpkin that turns into a carriage?

It was to solve these problems that Antti Aarne and Stith Thompson compiled their six-volume work *The Types of the Folktale,* published in Helsinki in 1961. In it, they distinguished between a *motif,* which is a strand of events or a telling detail that makes up a story, and a *tale type,* which is a weaving together of many motifs to make a recognizable story pattern. Careful storytellers often refer to the tale type number. For example, in her useful collection of Cinderella stories, Judith Sierra reminds us that these stories are given the number 510 by Aarne and Thompson (1992).

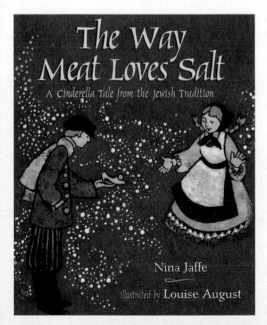

Illustration 5.3
The Cinderella tale has variants in many different cultures, including this version from the Jewish tradition. (*The Way Meat Loves Salt* by Nina Jaffe, illustrated by Louise August. Illustrations copyright © 1998 by Louise August. Reprinted by permission of Henry Holt and Company, LLC.)

Fortunately for teachers and librarians, the gifted storyteller and folklore scholar Margaret Read MacDonald produced a one-volume simplification of the Aarne-Thompson index, called *The StoryTeller's Sourcebook: A Subject, Title, and Motif-Index to Folklore Collections for Children* (1982). After a few minutes' orientation, you can easily find your way around this work. Because MacDonald cites children's books among other materials, you can pull together, from those in your own library, books that constitute variations of the same tale or that use the same motifs.

CATEGORIES OF TRADITIONAL LITERATURE

The traditional literature that is available to children today consists of many sorts of narratives, including folktales, myths, fables, pourquoi tales, and tall tales. There is poetry, too—from epics and ballads to folksongs to Mother Goose and skipping rhymes. Some also include riddles, jokes, and games. As we look more closely at these types of traditional literature, please bear in mind that some texts fit into more than one of the categories.

Myths and Religious Stories

Myths and religious stories are texts that try to explain the mysteries of the universe in terms that are understandable to the average person. As Carl Jung observed, because people's certainty stops with the world they have at hand, myths use familiar images as symbols to point beyond what people can know directly (Jung, 1961).

Myths and religious stories offer answers to questions such as "How did the world come to be?," "Why are we here?," "What is a good person, and why does it matter if I am a good person?," and "What happens to us after we die?"

Sometimes mythical answers clash with scientific explanations. For example, both the account of the creation offered by the Biblical story of Adam and Eve and the Native American tales of the world forming on Turtle's back clash with the scientific explanations of the Big Bang theory and the origins of life on earth as arising from certain amino acids. Just as often, though, myths offer a different kind of truth from scientific explanations. The Greek myth of Dionysus, for example, warns us with gruesome examples that great unhappiness may result when men and women are too far polarized, with one gender supposed to be unfeeling, rigid, and punishing and the other limited to qualities of physical beauty, sensuality, and intuition. In a similar way, the Zuñi myth that Kristina Rodanas retold and illustrated as *Dragonfly's Tale* warned that famine and unhappiness would surely come if the people took nature's bounty for granted. The truths of both these myths are arguably still relevant today.

Illustration 5.4
Religious stories from the Bible offer answers to some of humanity's basic questions about origins. (*Be Not Far From Me: The Oldest Love Story* by Eric A. Kimmel, illustrated by David Diaz. Text copyright © 1998 by Eric A. Kimmel. Illustrations copyright © 1998 by David Diaz. Used by permission of Simon & Schuster Books for Young Readers, an imprint of Simon & Schuster Children's Publishing.)

Fables

Fables are short dramatic tales, often with animal characters, that point to a clear lesson. The lesson is often stated explicitly at the end, where it takes the form of a proverb: a short memorable statement of advice or an observation about human nature. For example, the fable "The Dog and His Shadow" tells of a greedy dog, carrying a piece of meat over a bridge across a brook, who sees its reflection in the water and snaps at the illusory meat, only to lose the meat it already had. "A bird in the hand is worth two in the bush" is the moral we are given at the end. "He who tries to please everybody pleases nobody" concludes the fable of "The Farmer, His Son, and the Ass," about a pair who try, ridiculously, to follow strangers' advice as they take their donkey to market.

The fables attributed to the Greek storyteller Aesop, who was said to have been a slave living around 600 B.C., have instructed children and their parents for thousands of years, though different generations have changed the morals to suit the mores of the day. Aesop's fables include such well-known tales as "The Town Mouse and the Country Mouse," "The Fox and the Grapes," and "The Lion and

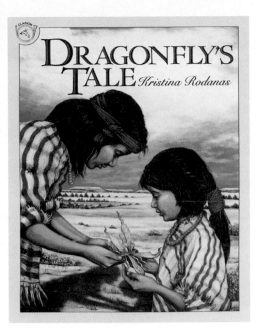

the Mouse." The seventeenth-century French poet Jean de La Fontaine published several of Aesop's fables in verse form. A modern collection of fables written and illustrated by Arnold Lobel is fittingly entitled *Fables*.

Folktales of Many Kinds

Folktales are stories that have been passed on by word of mouth and have unknown originators. They come in many forms.

Trickster Tales. Tricksters are characters who try to get the better of others through cunning and guile. Brer Rabbit is a trickster. Many trickster stories that were told among African American slaves used animals as codes for power relationships: Brer Bear has far more power than Brer Rabbit, but sometimes the latter outsmarts the former with his cunning—just as slaves could sometimes outwit their more powerful masters. Another trickster of African origin is Anansi the Spider, hero of many tales told in the Caribbean and West Africa. In Native American tales, Coyote is a trickster. Trickster tales are popular with children, who like the idea of weak characters using their wits to get the better of more powerful characters.

Pourquoi Tales. Pourquoi tales—stories that explain why—came about to feed, in often delightful ways, children's insatiable thirst for explanations. Pourquoi tales range from the serious to the playful: from the seven days of creation in the book of Genesis to the Greek explanation for the seasons in the story of Demeter; to the beautiful Masai story *The Orphan Boy*, retold by Tololwa Mollel and illustrated by Paul Morin, which explains why the planet Venus appears as the morning star in the east but as the evening star in the west; to the Cuban story of *Medio pollito/Half-Chicken*, a tongue-in-cheek account of the origin of the ornamental rooster that sits atop many a weathervane, retold in Spanish and English by Alma Flor Ada with illustrations by Kim Howard.

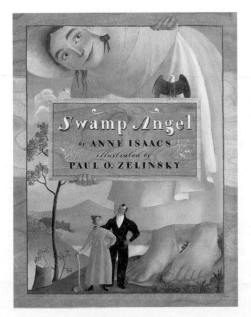

Tall Tales. Tall tales are greatly exaggerated accounts of the exploits of local heroes. Often these heroes are members of a vocational group. For example, New England sailors told the tale of Stormalong. Cowboys in the Old West told the exaggerated adventures of Pecos Bill. African American laborers had the story of John Henry, the steel-driving man. Even Japanese women had the wonderful tale of the "Three Strong Women." After all, bragging is a way for members of a group to express who they are; when the bragging takes the form of a story, we have a tall tale. More recently, perhaps to add some balance to the gender ratio of these exaggerated heroes, Anne Isaacs has given us an original tall tale, *Swamp Angel*.

Are tales of stereotyped strong men and wilting women still worth sharing with today's children?

You cannot read far in traditional folk stories without forming the unsettling impression that males are the active heroes and females are the passive prizes the heroes win in the end. Cinderella, Rapunzel, Sleeping Beauty—all of them act virtuously, look stunning, and wait (sometimes for excessive periods of time) for a prince to give them a future. As one third-grader put it, "Boys get to do exciting things outside. All girls get to do is sit around and look beautiful."

Should we, as adults, simply avoid sharing with children traditional tales like "Cinderella" and "The Sleeping Beauty" that have limited roles for females? Should we share them anyway? Or should we invite children to question the roles males and females play? What do you think?

Cumulative Tales. Cumulative tales are built up by repeating lines and adding to them. A Cuban folktale called *The Bossy Gallito,* in a version retold by Lucia M. Gonzalez and illustrated by Lulu Delacre, is a good example: A rooster is dressed up and making his way to his uncle's wedding when he spies a kernel of corn lying in a mud puddle. Pecking it, he muddies his beak, so he commands the grass to clean his beak. The grass refuses, so he commands a lamb to frighten the grass; but the lamb refuses, so he commands a dog to frighten the lamb; and so on. Finally, some creature agrees and sets a whole sequence of coercion in motion until the rooster's beak is cleaned and he can proceed to the wedding. The structure of *The Bossy Gallito* closely parallels the English story of "The Old Lady and the Pig," collected by Joseph Jacobs, in which an old woman calls on a series of helpers to goad a pig who is stuck in a stile (a passageway through a fence). The Vietnamese story *Toad Is the Uncle of Heaven,* retold and illustrated by Jeanne M. Lee, tells of an honorable toad who recruits other thirsty helpers as he makes his way to the palace of the King of Heaven to plead for rain. Each helper adds just the needed touch to achieve a solution, exactly as they do in the German tale "The Brementown Musicians." Songs such as "The Twelve Days of Christmas," "There Was an Old Woman Who Swallowed a Fly," and the Spanish song "Estaba la Rana Sentada Cantando Debajo del Agua" follow cumulative patterns. The form of the cumulative tale was well suited to the oral tradition, since the repetition of lines gave the listeners plenty of chances to learn them. These tales are agreeable to children for the same reason.

Fairy Tales. Fairy tales are folktales that involve magical possibilities. "Cinderella," "Snow White and the Seven Dwarfs," and "Rumpelstiltskin" fit the definition. So does the African tale retold by John Steptoe as *Mufaro's Beautiful Daughters* and the African American tale *The Talking Eggs* by Sans Souci. The plots of these stories stem from common drives and aspirations of ordinary people, and the magic often functions to lavish great rewards on the heroes for their goodness or steadfastness.

Apprenticeship Tales and Hero Tales. Apprenticeship tales and hero tales explain how a character rises from a lowly estate to a high one or from being ignored or threatened to being recognized and rewarded for her or his qualities. Apprenticeship tales such as the English tale "Jack and the Beanstalk," the Iroquois "Bending Willow," and the French "Beauty and the Beast" are exciting, but they are also partly didactic: All teach lessons about qualities of character that are likely to be rewarded in the end.

Numskull Tales. Numskull tales are stories of fools and idiots. We said earlier that in folktales, the simpleton is more likely to succeed than the sage. When he or she does, the story is of the type called the numskull tale. Numskull tales are popular around the world, from China to the Appalachian Mountains. Hans Christian Andersen's "Hans Clodhopper" tells of the numskull brother who wins the hand of the princess when he speaks up stupidly but confidently in her presence. The success of the movie *Forrest Gump* shows that we still like to believe that a numskull might just win the day.

Epics and Ballads

Epics and ballads are long narrative poems that tell of the heroic or tragic doings of a hero. In the many centuries before writing was widespread, long accounts that had to be remembered intact were highly structured and usually rhymed. Long rhymed accounts in traditional literature come to us in two main forms: epics and ballads.

Epics. Epics are extended accounts of the exploits of national heroes, often intended to provide the young with models to emulate and ideals to embrace. In former times, their telling could carry over several days; in written form, they fill whole books. The ancient story of Odysseus is an epic; so are the early English tale of Beowulf and the Spanish *Poema de mio Cid,* about a medieval Christian hero in the Reconquest of Spain from the Moors.

Ballads. Narratives in song, ballads, were especially popular in England from the fourteenth century on. English and Scottish ballads are mostly built of four-line stanzas and can run from a half-dozen stanzas (the length of a modern popular song) to more than four hundred (a whole evening's entertainment, and then some). The ballad form was carried from the British Isles to North America, where, in the nineteenth and early twentieth centuries, it had an even more robust following than in Europe. The Appalachian Mountains have a strong tradition of narrative songs, such as "Tom Dooley" and "Little Omie Wise." In the western United States, many cowboy ballads, such as "The Streets of Laredo" and "The Colorado Trail," followed this tradition.

Folk Songs and Poems

Songs and poems shorter than ballads but aimed at more mature listeners than nursery rhymes make up another category of traditional literature. "I Been Working on the Railroad," "Cielito Lindo," and "I Wish I Was a Mole in the Ground" are folk songs that have been sung for generations. They were made up by unknown singers, and verses were added by other singers. Folk songs appeal to children because their lyrics are often colorful and their melodies are catchy but accessible. Most folk songs can be sung easily a capella (without instrumental accompaniment) or with the aid of an autoharp or guitar. Many folk songs have been made into children's books. An American folk song built on a cumulative pattern was made into a picture book by Simms Taback, ***There Was an Old Lady Who Swallowed a Fly,*** and won a Caldecott Honor.

Mother Goose Rhymes

Babies love to be bounced on grownups' knees, and the bouncers need rhythms and poems to sustain those rhythms. Perhaps that is how the nursery rhymes known as the Mother Goose rhymes were born. A popular version of Mother Goose rhymes, brought out by John Newbery's publishing house in the eighteenth century, was one of the first children's books published in English. The Frenchman Charles Perrault first used the name "Mother Goose" in the title of a collection of eight tales (not rhymes). His *Contes de ma Mere l'Oye (Tales of My Mother Goose),* published around 1697, contained favorite tales such as "Sleeping Beauty in the Woods" and "Little Red Riding Hood." In 1781, John Newbery's firm published the first English edition of *Mother Goose's Melody* as a collection of rhymes and jingles, which began the association of the name "Mother Goose" with highly rhythmic nursery rhymes.

Since then, many of the very best illustrators of children's books have published editions of these familiar rhymes. Randolph Caldecott's picture book *Hey Diddle Diddle* was probably published in the 1870s. In 1882, Kate Greenaway produced a beautiful version of *Mother Goose or the Old Nursery Rhymes.* Arthur Rackham's *Mother Goose: The Old Nursery Rhymes* was originally published around the end of the nineteenth century. Other classic versions were created by Tasha Tudor, Blanche Fisher Wright, and Feodor Rojankovsky.

Mother Goose equivalents and nursery rhymes are found in cultures around the world. They developed separately from the ones known in the Western world. Among books of Mother Goose and nursery rhymes from other cultures that have been published for English-speaking children are Robert Wyndham's *Chinese Mother Goose Rhymes,* illustrated by Ed Young, and Lulu Delacre's *Arroz con leche: Popular Songs and Rhymes from Latin America.* A popular bilingual Spanish/English collection of rhymes in the Mother Tradition is *Tortillitas para Mama and Other Spanish Nursery Rhymes,* selected and translated by Margot C. Griego, Betsy L. Bucks, Sharon S. Gilbert, and Laurel H. Kimball and illustrated by Barbara Cooney. A more recent choice is Nelly Palacio Jaramillo's *Grandmother's Nursery Rhymes/Las Nanas de Abuelita: Lullabies, Tongue Twisters, and Riddles from South America,* illustrated by Elivia Savadler. Patricia Polacco's *Babushka's Mother Goose* includes Russian names and alludes to experiences from the Russian heritage.

Skipping Rhymes and Chants

Unlike Mother Goose rhymes, which were introduced to children by adults, skipping rhymes and other playground chants are recited by children themselves and passed on from child to child. Jump-rope and skipping rhymes are popular with children around the world. Here is one from Zambia:

> Ifula insa twnagale na
> Myiza ifula insa insa
> Twangala na mayiza.

> "Rain come, rain come.
> We want to play on the rain.
> Rain come, rain come.
> We want to play on the rain."

Skipping rhymes are highly rhythmic, and they often comment, however obliquely, on adult activities such as romancing. Consider this one from the United States:

Cinderella, dressed in yellow,
Went upstairs and kissed a fellow.

Riddles

Riddles are questions with clever, usually metaphorical, answers. Children in the United States have long amused each other with riddles. These classic ones have nearly fallen out of use:

A box without hinges, key, or lid
Yet golden treasure inside is hid. (An egg)

Round as an apple
Deep as a cup
All the king's horses
Can't pull it up. (A well)

But variations of the old riddles still survive among children:

What has a head and can't think,
Has legs and can't walk? (A bed)

What has four eyes and can't see? (Mississippi)

Still more common in children's oral tradition are jokes made in the pattern of riddles (Bronner, 1988):

What did the mother bullet say to the father bullet?
We're going to have a BB.

HOW TRADITIONAL LITERATURE WORKS

With no system of recording but the human memory, traditional literature had to be memorable, so it relied on catchy patterns of plot and language. Here we describe some of those devices, beginning with plots.

The Plot Structures of Folktales: Propp's Morphology

In the 1920s, a Russian critic named Vladimir Propp (1928) was struck by the similarity in the plots of the folktales told in his culture. He analyzed a collection of one hundred Russian folktales and found that all were built from a limited set of roles and actions.

Some of the stories fit the pattern of the *victim-hero:* Someone in the family leaves home, but before this happens, the hero is warned against doing something. The hero does it anyway. The villain comes spying and finds out that the hero, or others in his or her care, are defenseless. The villain tries to trick the hero out of his or her person or goods, and the hero falls for the trick. The villain hurts someone in the family, and so on. We recognize variations of this pattern in the English tales "Snow White and the Seven Dwarfs" and "The Three Little Pigs," in the Chinese tale "Lon Po Po," and in the African American tale "The Gunny Wolf." Children's author and storyteller George Shannon assembled a multicultural collection of tales that follow this pattern, called *A Knock at the Door.*

Other stories that Propp analyzed fit the pattern of the *seeker-hero:* Someone in the family needs something and makes that need known. The hero rises to the challenge to seek the desired thing and leaves home. Along the way, the hero meets a test or challenge, which prepares him or her to receive the help of a magical helper, which the hero later receives. The hero is magically transported to the place where the desired object can be found and enters direct combat with the villain. The hero might be branded (which leads to his or her recognition later). The villain is defeated, the threat is lifted, or the sought-for object is retrieved, and the hero leaves for home. The hero may be chased and rescued from pursuit. The hero may return home unrecognized to find that a false hero has presented claims in his or her absence. A further challenge is made to the hero, in which the hero triumphs and is recognized. The false hero is unmasked and punished. The hero is married and becomes the ruler of the realm.

The seeker-hero pattern fits the Scandinavian tale "East of the Sun, West of the Moon," the English tale "Jack and the Beanstalk," and many others.

Why do so many stories follow these patterns? There are two possible explanations. One is that they all derived from the same geographical source—a common story told in one place and time. But such a common starting point for all folktales has not been found and doesn't seem likely to be, since very similar stories (such as the 650 variants of the Cinderella story) have long been told in widely scattered parts of the globe. Another possibility is that the stories all come from the same psychological source; that is, they all stem from basic life experiences, hopes, and fears that are common to all people in all places and times. This is what Propp himself concluded at the end of his study.

Joseph Campbell's Hero Cycle

Noted scholar of mythology Joseph Campbell read the mythology, folktales, and religious literature of the world and concluded that one archetypal plot was repeated over and over. ("Archetype" means "old form," and an archetype is a device or a plot structure that is repeated in many stories.) Therefore, he named his 1968 book *The Hero with a Thousand Faces*. The hero cycle unfolds in several episodes (see Figure 5.1).

- *The hero at home.* In the beginning of the story, the hero is often the lowest of the low, unrecognized but perhaps having a questioning nature or a quiet ambition to find out who he or she really is.

- *The call to adventure.* Soon some problem arises that causes the hero to go on a quest. In traditional literature, the hero often has to compete for the chance to go, as he or she is naturally overlooked in favor of an older or more glamorous sibling.

- *The tests.* Before proceeding very far on the adventure, the hero is faced with challenges or tests. If these are met with cleverness, courage, or kindness, the hero often receives some magical help that enables him or her to proceed on the quest.

- *The helper.* The helper is a person or peculiar creature that provides the magical aid the hero needs to cross the threshold into the place where the object of the quest is usually found. Sometimes the helper provides other miraculous equipment that enables the hero to succeed.

- *The land of adventure.* The quest leads the hero into what Campbell calls "the Land of Adventure." Like Never-Never Land, Narnia, or the land beyond the "wrinkle in time," this is often a magical place, impossible to reach without the aid the hero received from the helper. Once the hero is there, the adventures begin in earnest, but the hero's true powers come into play, enabling the hero to rise to the challenges.

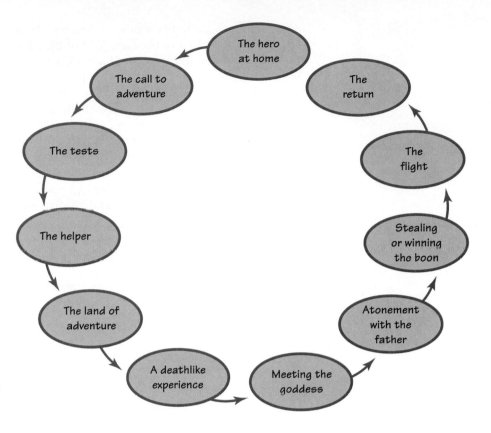

Figure 5.1
Campbell's hero cycle seems to tell many stories at once—a child's journey to adulthood, a rediscovery of meaning in midlife, a summary of a whole life's journey.

- *A deathlike experience.* Once the hero arrives in the Land of Adventure, he or she may have a death and rebirth experience: The hero's childish nature must die off, and his or her more mature, heroic nature must be born. Tomb imagery is very often used at this point.

- *Meeting the goddess.* If the hero is male, he may encounter a beautiful but formidable female figure who may challenge or love him but in any case confirms him as a worthy contender.

- *Atonement with the father.* The hero often comes up against a stern father figure who challenges him or her severely. Sometimes the hero overthrows the father figure. At the least, the hero forces the father figure to recognize his or her status as a hero.

- *Stealing or winning the boon.* The object of the quest is often some magical gift or some boon, elixir, or remedy that is needed back at home. The hero wins this object or steals it.

- *The flight.* If the hero steals the elixir or the object, the hero will run for his or her life, pursued by powerful forces. It will take more trickery and bravery to get away.

- *The return.* When the hero returns home, he or she brings what was needed to keep life going along comfortably. Sometimes the hero arrives in splendor and enters into royal marriage. Sometimes the hero slips into quiet reflection, a changed person, more whole, more integrated, proven.

The hero cycle fits a host of stories—from the story of Hercules to the Norwegian tale "East of the Sun, West of the Moon" (available in a picture book version retold and illustrated by Laszlo Gal), to the Russian tale "Ivan, the Grey Wolf, and the Firebird," to the Iroquois tale "The Boy Who Lived with the Bears." In story after story, from culture after culture, a person of humble origins who is somehow special receives a challenge, is tested and receives special aid, crosses into a land of adventure, suffers a death and rebirth experience, meets and bests an authority, wins something of value, escapes with that boon, and returns home as a fully developed person.

This plot has been repeated so often that many have wondered whether the plot itself might have symbolic meaning. Some say that it is the story of growing up—of adolescents being tested and confirmed and taking their place in adult society. Others have said that it applies to the psychic journey of middle-aged people seeking what the Swiss psychologist Carl Jung called individuation—a discovery and integration of the true powers they had unknowingly thrust aside in the strivings of adolescence and early adulthood (Jung, 1961). Indeed, it is part of the magic of stories that they can have powerful meanings for people in different stages of life, all at the same time.

Lévi-Strauss's Structured Opposites

Hero versus villain, home sweet home versus land of adventure—folk literature is known for its stark contrasts. The French anthropologist Claude Lévi-Strauss (1957) asserted that these contrasts are not accidental. People learn about the truths of this world by paying attention first to those things that are most starkly opposite to each other: hot and cold, up and down, light and dark, male and female, very good and very bad. Only after they establish the basic contrasts in experience do they look at the middle ground—the lukewarm, the shades of gray, the moderate.

In folk literature, stark contrasts are common. Characters are young or old, sympathetic or despicable, very modest or very vain. Lévi-Strauss noted that a set of contrasts in a story can stand for another set of contrasts in the real world, and often those contrasts deal with an issue that people find too painful or controversial to talk about directly. Thus, stories become a safe way of exploring and resolving issues that people can't or won't confront.

For example, what are the contrasts in "Jack and the Beanstalk"? There are many: Jack/the giant, the earth/the land in the sky, Jack's mother/the giant's wife, Jack at the beginning/Jack at the end, Jack as he seems to be/Jack as he really is.

When you contrast Jack and the giant, differences come tumbling out. Jack is young; the giant is old. Jack is small; the giant is huge. Jack has nothing but ambition; the giant has wealth and the fear of losing it. Jack seems insignificant but is really a hero; the giant is fierce, but his brutishness makes him vulnerable. Jack is on the way up; the giant is on the way down (pun intended!).

When Lévi-Strauss looks at opposing characters such as these, he treats them as interchangeable elements in fixed relation to each other—like subjects and objects in a sentence—and sees what other items would fit in their slots. For example, for the opposing characters in the story of "Jack and the Beanstalk," we have the following:

Jack	The Giant
young	old
small	huge

clever	stupid
seems weak	seems strong
needy	greedy
poor, questing	privileged

What other characters share those sets of features? Pairs that come to mind are David and Goliath, Juan Bobo and the devil, Taran and the Horned King, Gretel and the Witch, Hamlet and Claudius, and Harry Potter and Voldemort.

What do the stories about such pairs have in common? We might say that these stories stand for, among other things, the competition between young people on their way up, trying to win the freedom and recognition that come with maturity, and the older generation, struggling to hold onto those privileges.

Psychoanalytic Dynamics of Traditional Literature

Sigmund Freud (1923), the first great explorer of the human unconscious, made two large claims about human nature that shed light on the workings of folk literature. The first is that the most important preoccupations of people's lives—the most basic fears, secret lusts, and ambitions—follow patterns that were laid down in early childhood, in the drama of the relationships with parents and siblings. The second is that humans have an amazing capacity to symbolize and call on this capacity whenever they need a substitute for what they really want—especially if that is unattainable or inappropriate.

The first claim, about the power of the early drama of the family, suggests that since the preschool and early school years, every adult has craved nurturance, control, love, and recognition for his or her competence. The second claim, about the human capacity for symbolizing, led Freud to believe that humans produce dreams, art, and literature as symbolic (and therefore "safe") ways of exploring those basic urges and reducing some of the tension people feel because of them. Freud's followers, especially Carl Jung, decided that folktales and fairy tales served a community in the same way as dreams serve an individual—as symbolic and safe ways of working out deep-seated and powerful psychic material.

In 1975, the child therapist Bruno Bettelheim published the most ambitious application of psychoanalytic theory to children's reading of fairy tales. Entitled *The Uses of Enchantment* (1975), Bettelheim's book is an extensive exploration of the deeper meanings the most familiar fairy tales might have for people's lives.

Many of Bettelheim's interpretations seem plausible. For example, he finds that "Hansel and Gretel" explores children's fears of having to separate from the family and having to get along in the world by cultivating their own talents and relying on their own wits. Hansel and Gretel rise to the challenge of going into the world and facing dangers on their own, and when they do, they are able to be reunited with their father—but as peers, rather than as dependents. Hansel and Gretel point the way for children to do the same.

By explicating a certain set of hidden meanings in each story, Bettelheim implies that most children understand fairy tales in just the ways he describes. But even setting aside the limits on understanding symbols imposed by children's cognitive development (Winner, 1982), it seems unlikely that all children see the meanings in folk stories exactly as Bettelheim does. Another psychoanalytic critic, Norman Holland (1975), observed that readers saw in stories what they wanted to see or were concerned about—or, conversely, that they refused to see the elements of stories that reminded them of drives and urges they were afraid of. To Holland, a story is not so much a densely layered painting as a screen onto which readers project their own deepest concerns. Holland's observations are in line with the reader response theory described in Chapter 3.

TRADITIONAL LITERATURE FROM MANY CULTURES

There is an abundance of outstanding examples of literature from traditional sources. A good number of the illustrated books that have won the Caldecott Medal have been traditional tales. When it comes to traditional tales from parallel cultures, the offerings are rich indeed.

Classical Myths

Some well-known myths originated in Egypt and in Scandinavia; myths told among the South American Indians continue to be reworked in Latin American literature; and the myths of Native Americans survive in folktales and inspire large new audiences of ecology-minded young people. Greek and Roman myths gave us the names of the planets: Mercury, Venus, Mars, Jupiter, Saturn, Uranus, Neptune, and Pluto. They gave us the names of many of the months and one day of the week: January (named for the Roman god Janus, the god who looks forward and backward), March (named for the Roman god Mars, the god of war), June (named for Juno, in Roman mythology, the queen of the gods), and Saturday (for the Roman god Saturn, the god of agriculture). Norse mythology gave us the names for other days of the week: Tuesday (for Tiw, the Norse god of war), Wednesday (for Woden, also called Oden, the chief god of Norse mythology), Thursday (for Thor, the god of thunder and oldest son of Woden), and Friday (for Friga, Woden's wife, the goddess of love and the hearth).

The myths to which we most often hear allusions are the Greek and Roman myths. (The gods who figure in the Roman myths were essentially Greek gods by other names.) The ancient Roman writer Ovid is the earliest literary source for these myths. His collection of tales, called *The Metamorphoses,* chronicles many of the old myths, with the theme of transformation loosely joining the fifteen books of what is otherwise a collection of separate stories.

The ancient Greeks personified the forces of nature as gods: heroes created in human form, with superhuman powers but with human frailties, too. They could suffer anger, envy, pride, and lust.

Zeus, son of Chronos, was first among the twelve gods of the pantheon ("pantheon" is Greek for "all gods," or the fellowship of the gods) and ruler of the universe. With the other eleven gods, he lived on Mount Olympus; from there, they could observe the goings-on of humans and sometimes meddle in them. Hera was Zeus's wife, the goddess of marriage. Hera was a jealous wife, and Zeus's dalliances with mortal women gave her reason to be. Poseidon, the god of the sea, was the brother of Zeus, and storms at sea were considered his making. Hestia was their sister, the goddess of the household. Hades, brother of Zeus, was the lord of death and governed the underworld. A son of Zeus, Ares, was the god of war. Another son, Apollo, the god of light, drove the sun chariot across the sky. He was the favorite god of the poets, since he was the maker of music. His twin sister, Artemis, was the moon goddess, the goddess of growing things and of the hunt. Athena was Zeus's favorite daughter, born from his forehead; she was the goddess of wisdom. Another daughter, Aphrodite, was the goddess of love. Her brother Hermes was the messenger of the gods. Hephaestus, the god of fire, forged the armor of the gods and became the favorite of black-smiths and craftspersons.

There were lesser gods, too. Dionysus, child of a union between Zeus and the mortal woman Semele, was the god of wine and vegetation; he came to represent people's animalistic and intuitive side, as opposed to their order and reason. Demeter was the goddess of grain. It was her daughter Persephone who was carried away by Hades to the underworld. The seasons of the year—six months of summer and six months of winter—resulted from a bargain Demeter struck with Hades.

The Romans adopted the Greek gods but gave most of them new names:

Greek Name	Roman Name
Zeus (god of the universe)	Jupiter
Hera (goddess of marriage)	Juno
Poseidon (god of the sea)	Neptune
Hermes (messenger god)	Mercury
Aphrodite (goddess of love)	Venus
Hades (god of the underworld)	Pluto
Ares (god of war)	Mars
Apollo (sun god)	Apollo
Artemis (goddess of vegetation and the hunt)	Diana
Athena (goddess of wisdom)	Minerva
Hestia (goddess of the household)	Vesta
Hephaestus (god of fire)	Vulcan
Dionysus (god of wine)	Bacchus
Demeter (goddess of grain)	Ceres

Traditional Literature from the British Isles

England, Scotland, Wales, and Ireland are different nations within the British Isles. England is home to peoples who are descendants of the Angles and Saxons—Germanic stock—as well as of Vikings from Denmark and French from Normandy. Scotland, Ireland, and Wales are peopled by Celts, an ancient race from Central Europe, whose shaping influence on language and culture continues, especially with the various Celtic revival movements, to this day.

In Ireland and Wales, the oral tradition was highly organized, owing to the institution of the bards, professional poet/historians who were commissioned by the kings to learn and recite epic poems and genealogies. Bards were expected to know as many as four hundred epic poems, and they often studied for twenty years to learn them. Indeed, a bardic college was established in Tara, the ancient capital of Ireland, to pass on the old stories. In England, literacy was more widespread. Because literacy and the oral tradition are somewhat incompatible, the oral tradition was much more scattered in England than in Ireland.

Irish Folklore. In Ireland, everyone knows everyone, or so it seems—and even the folktales are likely to mention people with real names. Irish folklore tells of legendary Irish heroes: CuCulhain, Finn McCool, Cormac MacArt, and Saint Patrick. There are stories of courageous and honorable acts, and there are stories

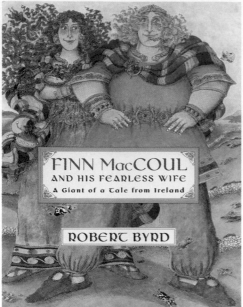

Illustration 5.7
The legendary Irish giant in this tale gets help from his clever wife in defeating his opponent. (*Finn MacCoul and His Fearless Wife* by Robert Byrd. Copyright © 1999. Used by permission of Dutton Signet, a division of Penguin Putnam Inc.)

of the struggle of Christianity to assert itself over the older Celtic religion of the Druid priests—stories that may go back sixteen hundred years. There is often magic in the tales, usually centering on giants or the little people called fairies or leprechauns. The little people keep to themselves, though once in a lifetime some human might happen on a group of them. Then there is a chance of hearing "the fulparenee and the folparnee and the rap-lay hoota, and the roolya-boolya" (Jacobs, 1958) as the little people make merry. Fairies and leprechauns possess magical powers that humans can sometimes use, but the fairies and leprechauns rarely cooperate willingly. From time to time, fairies are said to steal a human baby and take it below ground to strengthen their stock; such a baby is called a *strayaway child*. If fairies steal a human child, they replace her or him with one of their own. These fairy babies—called *changelings*—look like the children they replace, but they have awful tempers and can never be taught good manners. So if your baby is especially difficult, the tradition advises, chances are it's a changeling.

Scottish Folklore. Scottish folklore has given us tales of Rob Roy, Robert Bruce, and other Scottish chiefs. These tales and many others were compiled in an extensive collection called *The Scottish Tradition: A Collection of Scottish Folk Literature* by David Buchan. The storytelling tradition has been kept alive to this day, especially by the tinkers, itinerant traders who live on the fringes of society, much as gypsies do. Duncan Williamson, author of a fine collection of Scottish folktales (*Tales of the Seal People: Scottish Folk Tales*), was a tinker in his younger days. His tales of the *selchies,* or seal people, tap an especially interesting vein of Scottish folklore.

Welsh Folklore. In Wales, much of the folklore recalls exploits of real or fictional heroes, just as it does in Ireland. A fourteenth-century epic called *The Mabinogion* compiled the outstanding hero stories of Wales. The prolific children's author Lloyd Alexander traces his ancestry from Wales and credits the Welsh epics with the romantic adventurism of his own tales.

English Folklore. In England, the oral tradition included the epic of *Beowulf*, a stirring tale of the hero's struggle against Grendel, the water monster. Probably composed in the eighth century, *Beowulf* was drawn from both the old Viking tradition and early Christian beliefs.

At the heart of the English oral tradition is the story of King Arthur and the Knights of the Round Table. The story has been traced back to the seventh century and seems to have derived from old Celtic hero tales. Arthur, illegitimate son of Uther Pendragon, shows his heroic qualities by pulling the sword, Excalibur, from the stone. Merlin, the court magician, reveals Arthur's royal lineage. Arthur marries Guinevere, arms himself with the great sword Excalibur, and is joined at the Round Table by the famous knights Sir Lancelot, Sir Gawain, Sir Galahad, and others.

Almost as central to the English oral tradition is the ballad of Robin Hood and his Merry Men. Robin Hood has an uncertain historical basis, but the background to the ballad of the poacher-hero was real enough: the landowners' exluding people from hunting or fishing in vast expanses of countryside. (To this day in England, landowners own the fish in their streams and the deer in their woods.)

Other shaping events of the later Middle Ages were the Crusades, idealistic campaigns by English and other European Christians to drive the Moslems out of the Holy Land, which was considered to be the eastern Mediterranean city of Jerusalem and its surroundings. At the same time, Christian heroes sought the Holy Grail, the chalice with which Jesus Christ was said to have celebrated the Last Supper. Even after centuries of striving, neither effort was successful, but both provided the grist for many tales.

English folklore, as its accomplished contemporary chronicler Katherine Briggs notes, is short on fairy tales; English folk characters are more likely to succeed on cunning and pluck than by magical aid. On the other hand, there may be other-worldly villains—giants, particularly, as in stories like "Jack the Giant-Killer" and "Jack and the Beanstalk." There are stories that make fun of both pretensions and silliness—especially the tale "The Three Sillies," in which a groom, on a bet, goes in search of three people sillier than his fiancée's family.

"The Little Red Hen" and "The Three Little Pigs" both stress the virtue of industry. "The Old Woman Who Lived in a Vinegar Bottle" is a variation of "The Fisherman and His Wife"; both show the folly of wishing for more than you have. On the other hand, the hero of "The Pedlar of Swaffham" succeeds by following a dream.

Illustration 5.8
Zelinsky's elaborate retelling of this tale from the brothers Grimm is accompanied by illustrations done in oil in the Italian Renaissance tradition. The book won the Caldecott Medal for 1997. (*Rapunzel* by Paul O. Zelinsky. Copyright © 1997. Used by permission of Dutton Signet, a division of Penguin Putnam Inc.)

German Traditional Literature

German traditional literature was ably collected and distributed, as we noted earlier in this chapter, by Jacob and Wilhelm Grimm. "Hansel and Gretel," "Rapunzel," "Rumplestiltskin," "The Brementown Musicians," "Snow White and the Seven Dwarfs"—a great number of favorite tales came from German sources. One German tale, "Iron John," is not often told to children but has become the basis for a men's movement led by the prominent American poet Robert Bly (1992). The story tells of an ancient man who has lain for centuries beneath the moss at the bottom of a pond. The boy in the story drains the pond, resurrects Iron John, and learns the lessons of manhood from him. Bly believes that the story stands for the importance of having manly things communicated from man to man; without this, he claims, the male spirit sickens.

Scandinavian Traditional Literature

The northernmost countries of Europe were home to seafaring folk who for centuries passed the time during the long, dark winters by telling stories. Those stories are so forceful and eloquent that they are known around the world. The Norse mythology told tales of Balder, the god of light; of Tiw, the god of war; of Woden, the giver of order and creator of man and woman; of Thor, the god of thunder and might; and of Friga, Woden's wife and the goddess of love and domesticity—deities who gave us the names of days of the week.

The best-known collection of Scandinavian folktales is ***Norwegian Folk Tales,*** published in 1845 by Peter Christen Asbjorsen (1812–1885) and Jorgen Moe (1813–1882) and translated by the Englishman Sir George Webbe Dasent (1817–1896). The most famous of these tales is "East of the Sun and West of the

Moon," a lively story that begins much like the French story "Beauty and the Beast" but goes on to become a quest story that includes the mix of trolls, giants, witches, and hags that is typical of Norwegian folktales.

The Dane Hans Christian Andersen (1805–1875) ranks with the Grimms as a giant of world literature, especially of literature for children. His work is difficult to categorize. Like the Frenchman Charles Perrault (whose work is discussed below), Andersen retold traditional tales to give them his particular twist; he also wrote scores of original tales in traditional form. His story "The Emperor's New Clothes" (retold from an old Spanish tale with Moorish origins) has become a worldwide metaphor for the dangers of believing in other people's pretensions. His original stories "The Ugly Duckling," "The Little Mermaid," and "The Steadfast Tin Soldier" are crystalline tales with gentle lessons for the young.

French Traditional Literature

"Little Red Riding Hood," "Cinderella," "Beauty and the Beast," "Puss in Boots," "Sleeping Beauty"—a startling number of the best-known fairytales came to us from French versions. That is not to say they originated in France; variations of most of them were told in other parts of the world, too. As we noted earlier in this chapter, the basic story in "Cinderella" was told from China to Persia to England to the sweat lodges of the Algonquin people. The British could have chosen the German tale "Aschenputtel" or one in which the heroine had a black sheep for a fairy godmother. But it was the particular set of features in the French version that appealed to them, and they passed it on to North Americans.

Charles Perrault (1628–1703), a lawyer who worked for King Louis XIV, assembled the most popular collection of French fairytales, called *Histoires ou Contes du temps passé (Stories or Tales of Times Past)*. The collection included "Cinderella," "The Sleeping Beauty in the Woods," "Little Red Riding Hood," "Puss in Boots," "The Foolish Wishes," and "Blue Beard."

If some of these tales wax excessively enthusiastic about glittering ballrooms, and if the heroines sometimes seem drawn like moths to candles by the gaiety of palace life, it helps to remember that the tales took their form during the long reign of the Sun King, Louis XIV. His sumptuous courtly life has never been equaled, and he controlled the nobility by enmeshing them in countless social functions and keeping them guessing about who was in favor and who was out.

Russian Folktales

Russian folktales are a treasure trove of adventure stories, wonder tales, and anecdotes. Often playful, the tales abound in impossible quests, mysterious helpers, magical transformations, and dazzling rewards. Many of the structural features of other European tales are there: The old Tsar is dying, and he needs something. Three brothers are called on a quest, but the youngest and least significant—he may be a peasant or of noble birth—is the one who triumphs.

But Russian folktales are played out on a wider canvas than most. Heroes on their quests are propelled "through the thrice-ninth land to the thrice-ninth kingdom"—images that reflect the vastness of the Russian motherland. Russian folktales also have one of the great fixtures of world folklore: Baba Yaga ("Baba" means "Granny"). Baba Yaga lives in a hut perched on chicken feet that spins around three times and stops with the door facing you—provided you say the right words. Her nose grows down to her chin, and she flies around in a mortar, spurring it with a pestle, sweeping the way in front of her with a broom, and crying "Foo! foo! foo! foo!" She is too weird to be really frightening—and besides, although the young heroes are sometimes sorely tested by her, they always triumph.

The champion of Russian fairytales was Aleksandr Afanasyev (1826–1871), an ethnographer who collected and published six hundred tales between 1855 and 1864. Unlike the Grimms, whom he sought to emulate, Afanasyev got all but a dozen of his tales from other collectors.

Folklore from North America

Though folklore exists wherever people have established traditions, a few strands of North American folklore are especially well known: the Native American, African American, Appalachian, pioneer, and Western. There are also the tall tales and historical legends. The oldest—by twenty thousand years—and perhaps the only American folklore that can truly claim to be original is that in the Native American tradition.

Native American Tales. Of course, Native American tales are as diverse as the hundreds of tribes in North America. Nonetheless, there are themes that are common to most Native American tribes as egalitarian tribal societies, just as there are themes that are common to most European nations as hierarchically arranged, power-and-ownership societies.

For example, many Native American tales speak of animals. But unlike European animal tales, in which animals are so often stand-ins for human characters, Native American tales more often have as their point helping listeners better understand the animals' characteristics. Curiosity about the real powers of animals stems from the totemic tradition, in which traditional peoples identify with an animal in order to share its wisdom and prowess. Identifying with, rather than having control over, is a powerful dynamic in Native American folklore, and it has led to this folklore's being tied naturally to environmental education, as the warm reception of Joseph Bruchac's *Keepers of the Earth* and *Keepers of the Animals* has demonstrated.

Native American folklore also has many trickster stories, often featuring Coyote. There are creation stories, too, which are important because stories about beginnings explain a people's understanding of how things are ordered.

African American Folklore. The experiences of slavery, faith, resistance, and solidarity have given a unique character to African American folklore. African Americans have a rich oral tradition that encompasses folk and gospel music as well as verbal games and stories.

The West African regions from which slaves were brought to the United States had trading settlements that were originally established by Europeans—primarily by the Portuguese, but also by the English and French. So pidgin or patois—mixtures of African languages and one of those three European languages—became the language of slaves in the New World. Pidgin English survived well into this century in rural Jamaica and the Bahamas and in the Gullah dialect of the Sea Islands of South Carolina and Georgia. In Haiti, Creole stands with French as one of the two official languages.

Along with their languages, Africans brought stories and proverbs (indeed, most West African languages are riddled with stories and proverbs). Many stories told of tricksters—usually a spider (sometimes called Anansi, a name given this character by the Ashanti people of Ghana), a turtle, or a hare.

Slaves were taught the Christian religion, and their religious songs, known as spirituals, such as "Twelve Gates to the City," "Rock My Soul in the Bosom of

Ask the Author...

Patricia C. McKissack

Patricia C. McKissack [signature]

Are you struck more by the universal qualities of African American folktales or by the particular insights they provide about the experiences of African Americans?

"Children growing up without stories are adrift without an anchor," said Joseph Campbell. From fairytales, myths, and legends, children learn about their world and how to live with others in it. When I was growing up, however, my classroom literature anthologies didn't contain any folktales from the African American culture. I wasn't encouraged to read them either. And sadly, "plantation stories" recorded from our oral tradition were written in such an unfamiliar dialect that I felt ashamed and embarrassed when they were presented. Had it not been for my family, all of whom were master storytellers, I would have, indeed, been "adrift without an anchor."

Now, as a writer and storyteller, I am particularly proud of the way my slave ancestors salvaged West African story remnants, reshaped old folk heroes, and cast them in new tales. These stories were sometimes humorous, sometimes sad, and sometimes very scary, but each one recorded the unique experiences of African Americans—who used their lore to teach,

> ### Favorite Books as a Child
>
> Worldwide fairytales, myths, and legends are the kinds of reading materials I'd want with me on a desert island, but Hans Christian Andersen's "The Ugly Duckling" was my childhood favorite. The story helped me cope with the day-to-day humiliation I encountered growing up in the segregated South.
>
> *A Complete Collection of Poems* by Paul Laurence Dunbar was one of my favorite books, because I enjoyed Dunbar's ability to write using several language patterns.
>
> I loved scary stories, especially Edgar Allan Poe's "The Fall of the House of Usher."

to entertain, and to cope in a cruel and hostile environment. African American folktales have survived the horrors of slavery and have even transcended the adverse effects of racism and discrimination. I am pleased that today they are rightfully placed among the larger body of respected American folktales with universal appeal.

I guess that's why I am an advocate of *multicultural literacy*, because I believe it is important to expose children to a variety of story experiences. It broadens the pool of ideas from which to expand their problem-solving and decision-making skills. Actually, it takes nothing from one culture to appreciate another culture's stories. The results might be as exciting as a meeting between Br'er Rabbit and Peter Rabbit or between my Flossie and Little Red Riding Hood.

---

*Patricia C. McKissack and her husband, Fredrick L. McKissack, have coauthored many award-winning nonfiction titles. However, Pat's solo picture books—*Mirandy and Brother Wind, Flossie and the Fox, A Million Fish . . . More or Less, *and* Nettie Jo's Friends—*have won the hearts of young readers all over the world. When Pat isn't writing, she enjoys traveling in search of new stories.*

Abraham," "Michael, Row the Boat Ashore," and "I Am a Poor Wayfaring Stranger," are some of the most stirring folk music we have. To the chagrin of the whites, slaves seized on the liberation message of Christianity—the story of the Hebrew children in bondage and their miraculous flight out of Egypt, led by Moses. Themes of liberation were reflected in many black spirituals, including "Go Down, Moses":

When Israel was in Egypt land,
Let my people go!
Oppressed so hard, they could not stand,
Let my people go!
Go down, Moses, way down in Egypt land.
Tell old Pharaoh,
Let my people go!

Some songs also contained coded encouragements for slaves to escape along the Underground Railroad. The best known is "Follow the Drinking Gourd," referring to the Big Dipper, a beacon in the northern sky for slaves escaping from Southern plantations.

Appalachian Folklore. Settlers of Scottish, Irish, and English descent settled the mountains of the southeastern United States. Proudly self-reliant and somewhat isolated from the outside by their terrain, people of the Appalachian mountains nurtured a culture rich in stories, riddles, and folk songs. Much of the folklore is traceable to the British Isles; in fact, entire ballads from the seventeenth and eighteenth centuries were sung in the mountains well into the twentieth century. Stories of Jack abound, as do various stories of the wiles of the devil and the ways in which clever people can trick him.

Tall Tales and Labor Stories. Wherever people worked hard and formed close-knit communities, folklore abounded. Lumberjacks lived long weeks and months in the woods, cutting trees to make lumber and harvesting logs to fire the steel mills that supported the early Industrial Revolution in North America. Felling the huge trees with axes and cutting them to length with handsaws were jobs so hard and thankless that they are almost unimaginable now. When dark crept through the silent woods, lumberjacks retired to rude and drafty shanties, where they took turns sitting in the "deacon's chair" and telling whoppers. The greatest whoppers of them all were those told about Paul Bunyan, with his two-headed axe that could cut trees "coming and going."

Cowboys lived almost the whole year out in the open, in every kind of weather. They had a wide repertoire of delightful songs, such as "Git Along, Little Dogies," "Red River Valley," "The Colorado Trail," and "Root, Hog, or Die," as well as a number of tall tales—the best-known of which tells of the larger-than-life cowboy, Pecos Bill. Other folk stories have preserved the life and times of Mississippi riverboat people, of pioneers and settlers, of people along the Erie Canal, of railroad workers, and of farmers from all regions.

Legends and tales abound from every period of U.S. history. Revolutionary times, the Civil War, World War I, the Great Depression, the migration off the farm to the cities, the labor movement, World War II, the civil rights struggle, the women's movement—all of these and more have evoked tales that run the gamut from true accounts to far-fetched legends.

Hispanic Folklore

Americans with Hispanic backgrounds share a culture that was brought from Spain but mixed with the cultures of the peoples the Spaniards encountered in the New World or imported as slaves: Indians from North, Central, and South America, as well as Africans. (A word or two on terms is in order. "Hispanic" refers to people of partly Spanish descent living in North or South America. "Latin American" refers to people of partly Spanish, Portuguese, or French descent from Central or South America or the Caribbean. People of partly

Spanish descent who are living in the United States often refer to themselves as "Latinos" or "Latinas.")

Mexican and Mexican American folklore mixes stories of Christian saints with traditional beliefs that go back to the Aztecs and the Mayans. The folk medical practice known as *curanderismo*, still practiced among Hispanic peoples of Mexico and the Southwest, exemplifies this same mix. Spanish priests brought the belief that prayers to specific saints, as well as the use of plants and herbs, were effective against troubles of the body and spirit. Indigenous peoples grafted these beliefs onto local practices and expanded on them by applying their greater knowledge of local medicinal herbs. Spiritual medicine hasn't been taught by the Catholic Church in Spain for centuries, but the practice of *curanderismo* continues in the New World to this day.

In Mexico, folk stories chronicle the magically curative exploits of Señor San Antonio, and San Miguel figures in local legends having to do with rain and drought. Among Mexican Americans in the Southwest, stories are still told of people's attempts to outwit the devil; many of these feature Pedro de Ordinales, a rough-and-ready lucky bumbler who was apparently imported from Spain. A character who plays a similar role in Mexican and Mexican American folklore is Juan Bobo.

Cuban, Puerto Rican, and Dominican folklore reflects influences from Africa as well as Spain; it also preserves some stories from the original peoples of those islands, who were driven to extinction within fifty years of the arrival of the Europeans in 1492. This folklore includes many animal stories. One of the oddest involves Ratoncito ("Mousy") Perez (also a Spanish import) and Cucarachita ("Little Cockroach") Martina. Cucarachita Martina is serious about marriage, but Ratoncito Perez is apparently in it only for the wedding feast. In any case, his gluttony brings him to a bad end. Curiously, in Spain, Ratoncito Perez is the tooth fairy.

African Folklore

In the thousand years before Europeans colonized Africa, the continent saw several great empires: Zimbabwe in the east and Mali, Ghana, and Songhai in the west. Moslem traders and missionaries linked much of Africa to Arabia and to Islamic culture. In the fifteenth century, when the Portuguese came to Benin (now in Nigeria), they were so impressed with the level of civilization that they opened diplomatic relations with that country.

Africa's long history was kept alive in poem and song. In West Africa, the griots, like the bards of Ireland, kept official histories. Some of their recitations could take twelve days. Poets, too, composed lays (ballads or verses) to praise kings or mourn them.

Africans who were not converted to Islam or Christianity (and these conversions began over a thousand years ago) shared beliefs that are collectively called *animism*. Many objects in nature are thought by animists to be endowed with spirits—so many that there is no real separation between religion and secular life. The tasks of daily living are carried out with the spirits in mind.

Storytelling was always popular in many parts of Africa, and stories deal with many themes. There are creation myths, stories of the gods, animal stories (especially the trickster tales featuring a turtle, hare, or spider), stories of arguments between neighbors or between men and women, and many proverbs that point out the proper way to live. Some stories are left for the hearers to finish. And some storytellers have the custom of inviting hearers to help tell their sto-

Illustration 5.9
This retelling of a Chinese folktale revolves around a hunter who receives a magical gift to help his village in a time of drought. (*The Hunter* by Mary Casanova, illustrations by Ed Young. Text copyright © 2000 by Mary Casanova. Illustrations copyright © 2000 by Ed Young. Used by permission of Atheneum Books for Young Readers, an imprint of Simon & Schuster Children's Publishing.)

ries. (Typically, a person interrupts the teller and says, "I was there, and I saw _____"; whereupon the teller weaves this detail into the story.)

African stories, especially those from the lands in the west from which the slaves came, have greatly contributed to the African American folk tradition.

Asian Folklore

Asia is a big and diverse place; one fifth of humanity lives in China alone. It is hard to make generalizations about Asian folklore that would not also seem true for many other parts of the world. Nonetheless, China and Japan—to speak of two countries—had ancient cultures and written literature before the Europeans did. Japan has a highly developed contemporary literature for children.

Many Asian folktales seem almost parablelike. There is the Burmese story of the man who was so impatient that he pulled his rice plants up a little every day to make them as tall as his neighbors'. Of course, the plants withered and died. There is the Chinese story of a woman who is threatened by a monster and who receives offers of help from a number of different strangers; together, they defeat the monster for good. "Cultivate virtues, especially those of prudence, modesty, and a collaborative spirit" seems to be the message of many of these tales.

Folklore across Cultures

We have endeavored to show what distinguishes the folklore of many different cultural groups. Nonetheless, if you read widely in the folklore of the world, you are far more likely to be struck by the similarities than by the differences.

In the earliest written story known to humankind, the Mesopotamian hero Gilgamesh is bereft when a close friend dies. Gilgamesh tries to the limits of his being to understand where his friend has gone and maybe even to bring him back. Many of us have been there. Gilgamesh is our brother.

A father in a folktale from Burma—a place about as far from the United States as you can get—sends his son into the world. He wishes more than anything for his son to have a good life, but his son thinks that good life means enjoying many material things. Will the son learn real values in time? Do you know any parents who haven't fretted over that question as their child approached maturity?

Parents must leave home, and they warn their children not to let strangers in. A malicious stranger comes. The children are on their own to face the danger. Have you ever seen a child not shiver with anticipation at such a prospect?

As storytellers the world over know, the most important things are the most basic. The Greeks even made gods out of those basic qualities and concerns: power, wisdom, insight, reverie, love, mirth, skill, art, science, the earth, the sea, home, marriage, fate, war, and death. For many of the same basic qualities and concerns, the Celts had runes—symbols carved on bones and carried in a pouch—to be read at crucial points in people's lives. The Chinese considered roughly the same factors in the *I Ching: The Book of Changes*. As Vladimir Propp concluded many decades ago, all folktales have a common source: the human spirit.

DERIVATIVE LITERATURE

A host of books have been written in the form of, as embellishment on, or as a direct spoof of some traditional story. Alma Flor Ada's *The Gold Coin,* illustrated by Neil Waldman, is an original story with a folktale's simplicity, crafted by a reteller of Latin American folktales. Jane Yolen's *Greyling* is an original version of a selchie story; this noted U.S. author lives much of the time in Scotland, where such tales are part of the folklore.

Robin McKinley has rewritten the story "Beauty and the Beast" as a fantasy novel, called *Beauty.* Nearly every nuance of the Arthurian legend is explored in a retelling by T. H. White in *The Once and Future King.*

Jon Scieszka is a master at spoofs on folktales, and his hilarious books delight children who know the originals. *The True Story of the 3 Little Pigs!,* illustrated by Lane Smith, tells the other side of the story, as narrated by A. Wolf from behind bars. (As Jerome Bruner has written, narrative was born with the first excuse!) Scieszka's *The Frog Prince, Continued* takes up the question "What happens after the 'happily ever after'?" And his *The Stinky Cheese Man and Other Fairly Stupid Tales* violates every imaginable convention of fairytale books.

Robert Munsch's *The Paper Bag Princess* is a popular modernist rejoinder to the active prince/passive princess syndrome. Jane Yolen's *Sleeping Ugly,* another spoof on the traditional formula of "handsome prince wins beautiful heroine," explores what really counts in a relationship.

All of these books are interesting in their own right, and especially for the comparisons to traditional literature that they invite.

CRITERIA FOR SELECTING TRADITIONAL LITERATURE

Traditional tales have been favorite fare for children's literature as long as there has been children's literature. In choosing suitable traditional literature for children, several issues are brought into relief. Especially important to consider are stereotypical or even prejudicial treatment of characters of different sexes, races, and national groups and questions of fidelity to the source or the genre, including issues of violence and disagreeableness.

Avoiding Stereotypes and Prejudice

Traditional literature, as we said at the outset, is often strongly didactic: It exists to tell hearers who they are and how they should behave. The trouble is, these stories are usually based on the realities of many generations ago, and they may contain either overt teachings or covert attitudes that have no place in contemporary society.

Western society tolerated public expressions of racism and sexism until quite recently; so we don't have to go back very far in literature to find unwholesome stereotypes openly displayed. We discussed multicultural issues in Chapter 4. But what about gender stereotypes? Should adults still read "Cinderella," "Sleeping Beauty," "Beauty and the Beast," and the like to children? These stories show females as domestic prizes for charming princes to come and win. Some teachers and parents avoid these stories altogether; others read them with children but hold up their gender stereotypes for critical appraisal. Children have lively things to say about these issues if the discussion is truly open. We recommend that teachers who share these tales also offer stories that show strong female characters. Even in traditional literature these stories exist, as the collections *Tatterhood and Other Tales, The Maid of the North,* and the Greek story *Mr. Semolina Semolinus,* retold by Anthony Manna and Christoudula Mitakidou, have ably demonstrated. These books feature stories drawn from the folklore of the whole world and give girls and women strong roles.

Respecting Original Sources

Because folk literature conveys the values and beliefs of a people, teachers often use it to acquaint children with other cultures. Because even a small detail or a single saying can reveal something worth knowing about the people who originated a story, it is desirable that folk material be true to the source from which it came. On the other hand, much folk material must be translated from other languages, and since most of these materials were shared by adults and speak of things unfamiliar to children living in North America, some degree of adaptation is unavoidable. Teachers will want to know, then, where the folk material came from; a responsible work will state its sources. Teachers also will want assurance that the adaptation was carefully done, so as to communicate the truth and spirit of the original material. One way of gaining this assurance is to seek stories from authors with reputations for careful treatment of the source material—authors such as Harold Courlander, Joseph Bruchac, Paul Goble, John Bierhorst, Rafe Martin, and Verna Aardema. Another way is to rely on expert reviews, such as those found in *The School Library Journal* and *The Horn Book.*

TEACHING IDEAS

Discovering the Hero Cycle in Stories. After explaining the steps of the hero cycle, read "Jack and the Beanstalk" to children (in third grade or higher) and ask them to see how many matches they can find between that story and the hero cycle. Read them the stories of Hercules and Orpheus (from the d'Aulaires' *Book of Greek Myths*), and ask them to do the same. Later, see whether they can find parallels to the hero cycle in folktales such as "Hansel and Gretel," "The Orphan Boy and the Elk Dogs," and "Bending Willow."

Finding Lessons in Traditional Tales. Ask students in grades 4 through 6 to choose two or three main characters in a traditional tale. Have them jot down notes about the way these characters behave and the rewards or punishments they meet in the end. What do their findings tell about the ways the stories suggest boys and girls—or older people and younger people—should behave?

Contrasting Traditional Tales. Ask children in second grade or higher to examine two very different traditional tales and contrast the characters and the settings. What other characters do these characters remind them of? What settings in other stories remind them of the settings in these stories? What do these differences remind them of in real life?

Describing Conflict in Fables. Rosemary Deen and Ann Marie Ponsot (1980) suggest an activity for writing fables that can work with children from second grade on. Give the children these instructions: Think of two very different characters (they can be people or animals). Make them argue. Keeping description to a minimum, write down their conversation, alternating between the two voices. Then, introduce an unexpected calamity (e.g., a tree falls on them, a wolf tries to gobble them up). Finally, resolve the argument. (The resolution could be a "last word" from one or both of them that "just goes to show you.")

Comparing and Contrasting Traditional Characters. Ask students in grades 1 and beyond to examine three trickster tales from African sources (stories about Anansi would be a good bet), three from European sources (stories about Jack would be appropriate), and three from Native American sources (stories about Coyote would be ideal). Ask them to note the ways in which the trickster characters are the same and different. Write their answers on a chart, for comparison. (See the suggestions for the language chart in Chapter 13.)

EXPERIENCES FOR YOUR LEARNING

1. Find as many variations as you can of the familiar European fairy tales "Cinderella," "Hansel and Gretel," and "The Three Little Pigs." What do they have in common? What makes each one unique to its cultural setting?

2. Read four tales from the Grimms' collection and six from Mexico, Japan, or Africa. For each tale, describe the characteristics of the heroes, the situations they find themselves in, the kinds of solutions they try, and the message the story suggests. On the basis of these tales, try to make statements about the sorts of issues that are important to each culture.

3. Analyze a familiar fairy tale, such as "Sleeping Beauty," "Snow White and the Seven Dwarfs," or "Cinderella." Describe as explicitly as you can what the story seems to be saying to readers about their lives. What are the story's symbols, and what do they mean? Compare your analysis with the ones offered by Bruno Bettelheim in *The Uses of Enchantment* (1975).

RECOMMENDED BOOKS

* indicates a picture book; **I** indicates interest level (P = preschool, YA = young adult)

Greek and Roman Myths

*Aliki. *The Gods and Goddesses of Olympus*. Harper-Collins, 1994. This book tells the story of how the gods and goddesses came to live at Olympus and provides a sketch of each of the twelve major gods and goddesses. (**I:** 6–10)

*———. *The Olympians: Great Gods and Goddesses of Ancient Greece*. Holiday House, 1984. Sketches of the key figures in the Pantheon. (**I:** 8–10)

D'Aulaire, Ingri, and Edgar Parin D'Aulaire. *Book of Greek Myths*. Doubleday, 1962. The stories of the major Greek gods and goddesses are intelligently told and beautifully illustrated. (**I:** 8–12)

*Hutton, Warwick. *Persephone*. McElderry, 1994. A beautiful retelling of the myth of the goddess who was spirited away to the underworld by Pluto. (**I:** 7–12)

*Orgel, Doris. *Ariadne, Awake!* Illustrated by Barry Moser. Viking, 1994. The story focuses on Ariadne, who helped Theseus find his way through the labyrinth to kill the Minotaur. It does a nice job of refocusing what is usually told as a male hero story. (**I:** 11–13)

*Wells, Rosemary. *Max and Ruby's First Greek Myth: Pandora's Box*. Dial, 1993. The characters of Max and Ruby tell the story of Pandora's box as an object lesson. You probably won't find mythology made any more accessible to younger children than it is here. (**I:** 5–7)

North American Tales

Chase, Richard. *Grandfather Tales*. Houghton Mifflin, 1948. Twenty-five tales from the Appalachians are interspersed with the banter of the teller and his family. (**I:** 8–YA)

———. *The Jack Tales: Folk Tales from the Southern Appalachians*. Houghton Mifflin, 1943. Recently reissued in paperback, this is a collection of hair-raising stories featuring the plucky folk hero. (I: 8–YA)

*Haley, Gail E. *Jack and the Bean Tree*. Crown, 1986. An Appalachian variant of the beanstalk tale. (I: 6–10)

———. *Mountain Jack Tales*. Dutton, 1992. More tales of the Appalachian tricksters Jack and Mutsmag (Jack's female counterpart) by a storyteller and folklorist who is also a consummate illustrator. (I: 8–12)

*Hooks, William. *Moss Gown*. Illustrated by Donald Carrick. Clarion, 1987. A Cinderella story from the author's native eastern North Carolina. (I: 7–10)

*Isaacs, Anne. *Swamp Angel*. Illustrated by Paul Zelinsky. Dutton, 1994. An original tall tale with a female character. Zelinsky painted the illustrations for the book on wood veneers for an antique look. (I: 6–9)

*Kellogg, Steven. *Johnny Appleseed*. Morrow, 1988. Active and expressive drawings illustrate this entry in Kellogg's tall tales series. (I: 6–10)

*———. *Mike Fink: A Tall Tale*. Morrow, 1992. Another colorful entry in Kellogg's American tall tales series. (I: 6–10)

*———. *Paul Bunyan*. Morrow, 1988. Kellogg's art brings this tall tale of a lumberjack to life. (I: 6–10)

*———. *Pecos Bill*. Mulberry, 1986. Lively and expressive drawings and clever details highlight this retelling of the Western tall tale of Pecos Bill and Slewfoot Sue. (I: 6–10)

Folktales from Great Britain

Briggs, Katherine, ed. *British Folktales*. Pantheon, 1977. An adult collection of traditional tales as they were collected from folk storytellers, in interesting dialects. (I: YA)

Buchan, David. *Scottish Tradition: A Collection of Scottish Folk Literature*. Routledge, 1984. An adult collection but suitable for read-alouds. (I: YA)

*Chaucer, Geoffrey. *The Canterbury Tales*. Adapted by Barbara Cohen. Illustrated by Trina Schart Hyman. Lothrop, Lee, & Shepard, 1988. A collection of four beautifully illustrated tales from Chaucer's story of a medieval English pilgrimage to Canterbury. (I: 11–YA)

*Galdone, Paul. *The Little Red Hen*. Seabury, 1973. An old tale of industry and rewards that is good for acting out. (I: 5–7)

*———. *What's in Fox's Sack?* Clarion, 1982. A kidnap-minded fox is outsmarted by a clever old woman. (I: 5–8)

*Hodges, Margaret. *St. George and the Dragon*. Illustrated by Trina Schart Hyman. Little, Brown, 1984. A Caldecott Honor Book with stunning illustrations. (I: 8–10)

*———, and Margery Evernden. *Of Swords and Sorcerers: The Adventures of King Arthur and His Knights*. Illustrated by David Frampton. Scribner's, 1993. The legend of Arthur's life is told, along with stories of Merlin, Guinevere, Percival, and Galahad. (I: 12–13)

Jacobs, Joseph. *Celtic Fairy Tales*. Frederick Muller, 1958. Jacobs, a noted collector who was born in Australia, pursued a writing career in England, and died in New York, retold these tales for children in 1890. (I: 9–12)

———. *English Fairy Tales*. Illustrated by John D. Batten. Dover, 1967. (Originally published in 1898.) Well-told versions of stories familiar to Anglo-Saxon children. (I: 9–12)

Jones, Gwyn. *Welsh Legends and Folktales*. Puffin, 1982. A collection of more than thirty active tales from Wales. (I: 11–13)

*Leeson, Robert. *The Story of Robin Hood*. Illustrated by Barbara Lofthouse. Larousse Kingfisher, 1994. A retelling of the story from the ballads, well illustrated and with source notes. (I: 8–10)

*Marshall, James. *Goldilocks and the Three Bears*. Dial, 1988. A humorous adaptation by the creator of George and Martha. (I: 5–8)

*Shannon, Mark. *Gawain and the Green Knight*. Illustrated by David Shannon. Putnam, 1994. A favorite story from the Arthurian legends is retold with powerful illustrations. (I: 8–YA)

Williams, Marcia. *The Adventures of Robin Hood*. Candlewick Press, 1997. Eleven adventures of the man who robbed the rich and gave to the poor are retold in lively comic strip format. (I: 8–10)

German Folktales

*Galdone, Paul. *Hansel and Gretel*. Illustrated by Paul Galdone. McGraw-Hill, 1982. A version that will not horrify young children. (I: 7–9)

*Hyman, Trina Schart. *Little Red Riding Hood*. Illustrated by Trina Schart Hyman. Holiday House, 1983. A beautiful adaptation by an award-winning artist. (I: 7–9)

*Kimmel, Eric. *Iron John*. Illustrated by Trina Schart Hyman. Holiday House, 1994. The story of a prince who is trained in manly things by the wild man who lives in the woods. (I: 8–12)

*Rogasky, Barbara. *Rapunzel: From the Brothers Grimm*. Illustrated by Trina Schart Hyman. Holiday

House, 1982. A runaway ponytail leads to love. (**I: 7–9**)

*Zelinsky, Paul O. *Rapunzel.* Dutton, 1997. Zelinsky's elaborate retelling of this tale from the Grimms draws on elements from early French and Italian sources, and the illustrations are oil paintings from the Italian Renaissance tradition. The book won the Caldecott Medal for 1997. (**I: 6–11**)

*————. *Rumplestiltskin.* Dutton, 1986. A guess-my-name story. The English version is "Tom Tit Tot." (**I: 7–9**)

French Fairytales

*Mayer, Marianna. *Beauty and the Beast.* Illustrated by Mercer Mayer. Macmillan, 1978. The ink and watercolor drawings are very expressive in this tale of love's redeeming powers. (**I: 8–11**)

Perrault, Charles. *Favorite Fairy Tales.* Ed. Jennifer Mulherin. Grosset & Dunlap, 1983. This version has the original illustrations as they were published in England in the eighteenth century. (**I: 10–12**)

*————. *The Glass Slipper: Charles Perrault's Tales of Times Past.* Translated by John Bierhorst. Illustrated by Mitchell Miller. Four Winds, 1981. A translation of Perrault's tales by a careful reteller of world folk literature. (**I: 8–10**)

*————. *Puss in Boots.* Illustrated by Marcia Brown. Scribner's, 1952. A resourceful cat makes his master a rich man. As Joseph Campbell would say, this story stars the "magic helper." (**I: 5–9**)

*San Jose, Christine. *Cinderella.* Illustrated by Debra Santini. Boyds Mills Press, 1994. This version is set in New York City at the turn of the century, another period of elegant balls. (**I: 8–11**)

Greek Folktales

*Aliki, *The Eggs.* Harper, 1994. An honest but forgetful sea captain is saved by a clever lawyer from having to pay an unreasonable debt. (**I: 6–9**)

*Manna, Anthony, and Christoudula Mitakidou. *Mr. Semolina Semolinus: A Greek Folktale.* Illustrated by Giselle Potter. Atheneum, 1997. In a quest tale with a feminist twist, Areti, a young princess, fashions a perfect suitor for herself out of cookie ingredients but has to retrieve him when an evil queen snatches him away. (**I: 6–9**)

Jewish Folktales

*Jaffe, Nina. *In the Month of Kislev: A Story for Hanukkah.* Illustrated by Louise August. Viking, 1992. Storyteller Nina Jaffe here recounts a version of a traditional tale, "The Stolen Smells," in which a clever rabbi keeps a jealous baker from doing harm to an impoverished family. (**I: 6–9**)

*————. *The Way Meat Loves Salt: A Cinderella Tale from the Jewish Tradition.* Illustrated by Louise August. Henry Holt, 1998. This Yiddish tale from Eastern Europe is part Cinderella and part King Lear. When a father asks his children how much they love him, Mireleh, the youngest and most honest, replies, "The way meat loves salt." The father takes offense and banishes her until one day she is able to teach him the true meaning of her words. (**I: 7–11**)

*Kimmel, Eric. *The Adventures of Hershel of Ostropol.* Illustrated by Trina Schart Hyman. Holiday House, 1995. Yiddish trickster tales from a Jewish community in Ukraine. (**I: 7–11**)

*————. *Asher and the Capmakers: A Hanukkah Story.* Illustrated by Will Hillenbrand. Holiday House, 1993. Not exactly a folk tale, Kimmel's offering for Hanukkah shows off the wonders of Jerusalem through the eyes of a young boy who is taken there by fairies. (**I: 6–9**)

*Singer, Isaac Bashevis. *Mazel and Shlimazel: Or the Milk of a Lioness.* Translated by Elizabeth Shub, with photographs by Margot Zemach. Farrar Straus & Giroux, 1995. Mazel is the spirit of good luck, and Schlimazel is the spirit of bad luck. Guess which one wins out and gets to marry the princess? Isaac Bashevis Singer won the Nobel Prize for Literature in 1978. (**I: 6–9**)

*Taback, Simms. *Joseph Had a Little Overcoat.* Viking, 2000. Taback won a Caldecott Medal for this lively retelling in story form of a Yiddish folk song. The die-cut illustrations add to the amusement. Song lyrics and music are included. (**I: all ages**)

*Wisniewski, David. *Golem.* Houghton Mifflin, 1996. Wisniewski won the Caldecott Medal for this retelling of a Jewish legend from the ghetto of Prague, in which a giant is brought to life out of clay for the protection of a community of Jews in danger of persecution. (**I: 7–10**)

Scandinavian Tales

Andersen, Hans Christian. *The Complete Hans Christian Andersen Fairy Tales.* Edited by Lily Owens. Grammercy, 1993. Hans Christian Andersen, from Denmark, is a special case in folklore. He was more a creator than a collector, but his tales shine with the brilliance and insight of the best folktales, and stories like "The Emperor's New Clothes," "The Ugly Duckling," "The Little Mermaid," and "The Princess and the Pea" are well known the world over. (**I: all ages**)

*——. *The Emperor's New Clothes.* Translated by Naomi Lewis and illustrated Angela Barrett. Candlewick Press, 1997. A famous tale about gullibility, peer pressure, and truth. (I: 5–10)

*——. *The Little Mermaid: The Original Story.* Illustrated by Charles Santore. Random House, 1997. This story was adapted by Disney, so Random House reissued a version that sticks close to Andersen's original tale about a mermaid who seeks independence and love. (I: 6–10)

*——. *The Princess and the Pea.* Illustrated by Janet Stevens. Holiday House, 1989. A classic story about a lumpy bed and a real princess. (I: 5–10)

*——. *The Ugly Duckling.* Illustrated by Jerry Pinkney. Morrow, 1999. Pinkney has won the Coretta Scott King Award and the Caldecott Medal, and here he does a fine job of illustrating a tale about a little waterfowl who was different. (I: 4–9)

*Asbjornsen, Peter Christen. *The Man Who Kept House.* Illustrated by Svend Otto Sorensen. Margaret McElderry, 1992. In this traditional Norse tale, a man finds that keeping house is not as easy as he had claimed. (I: 6–9)

*——. *The Three Billy Goats Gruff.* Illustrated by Glen Rounds. Holiday House, 1993. Glen Rounds's pen-and-ink and watercolor illustrations add character to the popular story of goats, a bridge, and a troll. (I: 5–9)

*d'Aulaire, Ingri, and Parin d'Aulaire. *D'Aulaires' Trolls.* Dell, 1972/1993. The d'Aulaires provide a wealth of lore about trolls as they recount a few of the Norse legends from which they came. (I: 6–10)

*Lynch, P. J. *East O' the Sun and West O' the Moon.* Candlewick Press, 1991. Lynch's illustrations capture the wonder and mystery of this Norwegian quest tale. (I: 6–10)

Russian Folktales

Afanasyev, Aleksandr. *Russian Folk Tales.* Translated by Robert Chandler. Illustrated by Ivan Bilibin. Random House, 1984. These seven tales are perfectly illustrated by Bilibin. Children will want to hear them again and again. (I: 7–12)

——. *Russian Folktales.* Translated by Norbert Guterman. Pantheon, 1945. This is a collection of over two hundred tales, with commentary by Roman Jacokson. (I: 7–14)

*Gilchrist, Cherry. *Prince Ivan and the Firebird.* Illustrated by Andrei Troshkov. Barefoot, 1994. One of the most exciting of Afanasyev's tales, richly illustrated. (I: 6–10)

MacAughrean, Geraldine. *Grandma Chickenlegs.* Carolrhoda Picture Books, 1999. A retelling of a Baba Yaga story in lively contemporary language. A young girl survives a trip to the witch's house. (I: 5–9)

*Mayer, Marianna. *Baba Yaga and Vasilisa the Brave.* Illustrated by K. Y. Craft. Morrow, 1994. Two of children's favorite Russian characters in one story. Vasilisa succeeds with the help of the doll her dead mother gave her. (I: 6–10)

*Sherman, Josepha. *Vasilisa the Wise.* Illustrated by Robert D. San Souci. Harcourt, 1988. "Mornings are wiser than evenings," says Vasilisa the Wise, and she saves her husband from peril. (I: 5–8)

African American Stories

*Bang, Molly Garrett. *Wiley and the Hairy Man.* Macmillan, 1976. A spooky African American tale from Alabama, taken from Botkin's *Treasury of American Folklore.* (I: 6–9)

*DeFelice, Cynthia. *Willy's Silly Grandma.* Illustrated by Shelley Jackson. Orchard, 1997. DeFelice reworks the story "Little Eight John," a traditional African American story, into a new story that is a larger exploration of superstition. (I: 6–9)

Hamilton, Virginia. *Her Stories: African American Folktales, Fairy Tales, and True Tales.* Illustrated by Leo and Diane Dillon. Scholastic, 1995. Sixteen folktales and three true accounts from American black women. (I: 9–YA)

——. *The People Could Fly: American Black Folktales.* Illustrated by Leo and Diane Dillon. Knopf, 1985. Twenty-four tales plus a bibliography; includes "Wiley, His Mother, and the Hairy Man" and "Little Eight John." Some of the stories are full of emotional power. (I: 9–YA)

Harris, Joel Chandler. *The Tales of Uncle Remus.* Adapted by Julius Lester and illustrated by Jerry Pinkney. Dial, 1987. Lester's voice makes these tales a joy to read aloud, and Pinkney's illustrations bring the characters to life. A Coretta Scott King Award Honor Book. (I: all ages)

——. *More Tales of Uncle Remus.* Adapted by Julius Lester and illustrated by Jerry Pinkney. Dial, 1988. More tales in this series, retold in a more accessible voice by a scholar of African American literature and Hebrew studies and illustrated in scratchboard by a talented artist. A Coretta Scott King Award Honor Book. (I: all ages)

——. *Further Tales of Uncle Remus.* Adapted by Julius Lester and illustrated by Jerry Pinkney. Dial, 1989. Further tales in the same series. (I: all ages)

———. *The Last Tales of Uncle Remus.* Adapted by Julius Lester and illustrated by Jerry Pinkney. Dial, 1994. Lester and Pinkney have given us a fine gift by rescuing these stories from the aura of an earlier generation of white people's romanticizing of slavery. (I: all ages)

*Jacquith, Priscilla. *Bo Rabbit Smart for True: Tall Tales from the Gullah.* Illustrated by Ed Young. Philomel, 1981. These tales were collected from African Americans living in the Sea Islands of South Carolina and Georgia. (I: 9–12)

*Lester, Julius. *John Henry.* Illustrated by Jerry Pinkney. Dial, 1994. A lively and careful retelling of this tall tale that pits human against machine. (I: 8–10)

*Temple, Frances. *Tiger Soup: An Anansi Story from Jamaica.* Orchard, 1994. Anansi tricks Tiger, then teaches the monkeys a song that suggests that they did it. (I: 5–8)

Turenne de Pres, Francois. *Children of Yayoute: Folktales of Haiti.* Universe, 1994. Twelve tales originally published in Haiti in 1949, with colorful illustrations. (I: 7–10)

*Winter, Jeanette. *Follow the Drinking Gourd.* Knopf, 1992. The song was said to have been a sort of oral roadmap for the Underground Railroad during slave times. The somber illustrations bring some of the drama to life. (I: 5–8)

Native American Stories

Bruchac, Joseph. *Dog People: Native Dog Stories.* Illustrated by Murv Jacob. Fulcrum Kids, 1995. Six stories told for thousands of years among the Abenaki people about dogs as companions of humans; complete with a glossary of terms. (I: 7–10)

*———. *The First Strawberries: A Cherokee Story.* Illustrated by Anna Vojtech. Dial, 1993. A touching and lyrical story about the first man and the first woman, the overcoming of anger, and the origin of strawberries. (I: 7–10)

*———. *The Great Ball Game: A Muskogee Story.* Illustrated by Susan L. Roth. Dial, 1994. In this pourquoi tale, the birds and the animals square off in a game of stickball to decide who will have dominion over the land; the bat sides with the animals and wins the game. (I: 7–10)

*———, and Gayle Ross. *The Girl Who Married the Moon.* Troll/BridgeWater, 1994. Tales with girl protagonists from sixteen Indian nations, with commentary. (I: 10–13)

*Cohen, Caron Lee. *The Mud Pony.* Illustrated by Shonto Begay. Scholastic, 1988. A boy rises from his lowly origin to the position of chief with the aid of a magical pony in this Pawnee tale. The first children's book illustrated by Begay, a Navajo. (I: 7–10)

*Goble, Paul. *Dream Wolf.* Bradbury, 1990. A brother and sister wander off from their family and spend the night on the mountainside. A wolf rescues them and leads them to safety. With illustrations inspired by traditional paintings of Plains tribes. (I: 7–10)

*———. *Her Seven Brothers.* Bradbury, 1988. In this Cheyenne pourquoi tale about the origin of the Big Dipper, an only child goes in search of brothers after making beautiful clothing for them in the certainty that she will one day find them. (I: 8–11)

*———. *Iktomi and the Buzzard: A Plains Indian Story.* Orchard, 1994. Another in a series about Iktomi, the trickster of the Plains Indians. (I: 7–10)

*Luenn, Nancy. *Nessa's Fish.* Illustrated by Neil Waldman. Atheneum, 1990. A brave Inuit girl defends her ailing grandmother and a cache of fish from marauding animals on the desolate ice. (I: 7–10)

*McDermott, Gerald. *Coyote: A Trickster Tale from the American Southwest.* Harcourt, 1994. A Native American trickster tale from the Zuñi people, presented by a master illustrator. (I: 6–9)

*Pollock, Penny. *The Turkey Girl: A Zuni Cinderella Story.* Illustrated by Ed Young. Little, Brown, 1996. This rich pourquoi tale with a moral about keeping one's word is also a valuable take on the Cinderella story, with breathtaking illustrations. (I: 7–9)

*Rodanas, Kristina. *Dragonfly's Tale.* Clarion Books, 1992. This Zuñi tale with young protagonists promotes conservation and generosity and has a pourquoi twist, too. (I: 6–9)

*Ross, Gayle. *How Rabbit Tricked Otter and Other Cherokee Stories.* Illustrated by Murv Jacob. HarperCollins, 1994. Fifteen tales about the trickster Rabbit, by a master storyteller of Cherokee descent. (I: 8–12)

*———. *How Turtle's Back Was Cracked: A Traditional Cherokee Tale.* Illustrated by Murv Jacob. Dial, 1995. A pourquoi tale reminiscent of "Brer Rabbit and the Briar Patch," retold in a lively voice by a master storyteller. Students might want to compare this version with Tololwa Mollel's *The Flying Tortoise: An Igbo Tale,* which is based on a story from Southern Nigeria. (I: 6–9)

*San Souci, Robert. *Sootface: An Ojibwa Cinderella Story.* Illustrated by Daniel San Souci. Bantam, 1997. In a story that closely parallels the Algonquin tale "The Rough-Faced Girl," an invisible warrior chooses as his bride the young woman with the truest qualities, and this turns out to be the

Sootface, she who cooks and washes for her more outwardly beautiful and vainer sisters. (I: 6–9)

*Young, Ed. *Moon Mother: A Native American Creation Tale.* HarperCollins, 1993. A beautiful creation story, with subtle pastel illustrations by an award-winning artist. (I: 7–10)

Tales from Africa

*Aardema, Verna. *Bringing the Rain to Kapiti Plain: A Nandi Tale.* Illustrated by Beatrice Vidal. Dial, 1981. Can there be more rhythmic language than in this tale from Kenya? This poem is written in a cumulative format. (I: 6–10)

*———. *Misoso: Once upon a Time Tales from Africa.* Illustrated by Reynold Ruffins. Apple Soup, 1994. Twelve tales from many parts of Africa for young readers. (I: 6–10)

*———. *Why Mosquitoes Buzz in People's Ears.* Illustrated by Leo and Diane Dillon. Dial, 1978. A cumulative pourquoi tale. (I: 5–10)

*Bryan, Ashley. *Beat the Story-Drum, Pum-Pum.* Atheneum, 1987. A collection of African tales to be read aloud—or, if you've ever heard Bryan read, you might say roared aloud. (I: 6–10)

*———. *Turtle Knows Your Name.* Atheneum, 1989. West Indian tales, good for oral reading and acting out. (I: 6–10)

*Courlander, Harold. *The Crest and the Hide.* Illustrated by Monica Vachula. Coward, McCann, 1982. One of our best folktale collectors presents twenty tales from across Africa, identified by society and region. (I: 10–YA)

*Diakité, Baba Wagué. *The Hunterman and the Crocodile.* Scholastic, 1997. A nicely patterned tale with a moral about people's responsibility to nature, illustrated with bold ceramic prints. (I: 6–11)

*Gerson, Mary-Joan. *Why the Sky Is Far Away: A Nigerian Folktale.* Illustrated by Carla Golembe. Little, Brown, 1992. A lively pourquoi tale whose theme is the importance of preventing waste. This pairs nicely with *The Dragonfly's Tale,* a Native American story. (I: 6–10)

*Haley, Gail E. *A Story, a Story.* Atheneum, 1970. A traditional African tale about how Anansi won stories from the Sky God; a Caldecott winner. (I: 5–10)

*Kimmel, Eric. *Anansi and the Moss-Covered Rock.* Illustrated by Janet Stevens. Holiday House, 1988. Kimmel and Stevens teamed up to produce lively renditions of the Anansi tales, which are popular in West Africa and the Caribbean. In this tale, Anansi tricks the animals in the forest with a moss-covered rock until little deer gives him his come-uppance. The repetition makes this story good for reading aloud and for storytelling. (I: 6–9)

*———. *Anansi Goes Fishing.* Illustrated by Janet Stevens. Holiday House, 1993. Stevens's lively drawings give this West African folktale a contemporary flair. In a rare turn of events, Anansi the trickster is roundly tricked by turtle. (I: 6–9)

*———. *Anansi and the Talking Melon.* Illustrated by Janet Stevens. Holiday House, 1995. Anansi the trickster bores his way into one of elephant's melons and insults the animals one by one in this very funny tale. (I: 6–9)

*Knutson, Barbara. *Why the Crab Has No Head.* Carolrhoda, 1987. A pourquoi tale from Zaire. (I: 5–9)

*Lester, Julius. *How Many Spots Does a Leopard Have?* Illustrated by David Shannon. Scholastic, 1989. Folktales from Africa and from the Jewish tradition. (I: 9–12)

*McDermott, Gerald. *Anansi the Spider.* Holt, 1972. A Caldecott-winning tale of the trickster from West Africa. (I: 7–10)

*Mollel, Tololwa. *The Flying Tortoise: An Igbo Tale.* Illustrated by Barbara Spurll. Clarion, 1994. Greedy Tortoise persuades the birds to lend him feathers so that he can fly up to feast with the Skylanders. When he eats all the food himself, they repay him harshly and his shell is shattered. (I: 6–10)

*———. *The Orphan Boy.* Illustrated by Paul Morin. Clarion, 1990. A touching pourquoi tale from the Masai people of East Africa, about the tragic power of overweening curiosity and the reason for the transit of Venus. (I: 6–10)

*Steptoe, John. *Mufaro's Beautiful Daughters.* Lothrop, Lee & Shepard, 1987. The humblest and kindest daughter gets the reward in this Caldecott winner. (I: 6–10)

Latin American Stories

*Ada, Alma Flor. *The Gold Coin.* Illustrated by Neil Waldman. Aladdin, 1991. In this original folktale, a thief is made into an honest man in spite of himself, as he pursues a woman whose wealth turns out to be her generous spirit. (I: 5–11)

*———. *The Great-Great-Granddaughter of Cucarachita Martina.* Illustrated by Ana Lopez Escriva. Scholastic, 1993. A modern retelling of a Caribbean folktale. (I: 6–10)

*———. *Medio pollito/Half-Chicken.* Illustrated by Kim Howard. Doubleday, 1995. In Spanish and in

English, this tongue-in-cheek pourquoi tale from Cuba explains the origin of the weather vane. (I: 6–10)

*———. *The Rooster Who Went to His Uncle's Wedding*. Illustrated by Kathleen Kuchera. Putnam, 1993. A cumulative tale from Cuba (same as the bilingual story *The Bossy Gallito/El gallo de bodas*). (I: 6–10)

Aldana, Patricia, ed. *Jade and Iron: Latin American Tales from Two Cultures*. Translated by Hugh Hazleton. Illustrated by Luis Garay. Douglas & McIntyre, 1996. The first group of seven stories comes from indigenous peoples of Central and South America; the second group of seven came to Central and South America from Spain. (I: 8–13)

*Arnold, Sandra. *Child of the Sun*. Illustrated by Dave Albers. Troll Associates, 1995. A Cuban creation story from the Ciboney people, a pre-Columbian tribe, which tells of the first man and woman and explains the origin of solar eclipses. (I: 7–11)

Campos, Anthony John. *Mexican Folktales*. Univ. of Arizona Press, 1977. The author learned these twenty-seven short tales from his family, who came to California from Jalisco, Mexico. (I: 8–12)

*de Paola, Tomie. *The Legend of the Poinsettia*. Putnam, 1994. A Mexican legend of Christmas. (I: 7–10)

*Ehlert, Lois. *Moon Rope: A Peruvian Folktale/Un lazo a la luna: Una leyenda Peruana*. Harcourt, 1992. A pourquoi tale in English and Spanish that explains why Mole lives in the ground and why we see Fox's likeness in the moon. (I: 6–8)

*Gonzalez, Lucia M. *The Bossy Gallito/El gallo de bodas*. Illustrated by Lulu Delacre. Harcourt, 1994. A Spanish/English version of the cumulative tale of a rooster who wanted his beak cleaned (the same story as *The Rooster Who Went to His Uncle's Wedding*). (I: 7–10)

*Johnston, Tony. *The Tale of Rabbit and Coyote*. Illustrated by Tomie de Paola. Putnam, 1994. A Zapotec pourquoi tale from the Oaxaca region of Mexico, told with some Spanish terms, explaining why Coyote howls at the moon. (I: 6–9)

*Martinez, Alejandro Cruz. *The Woman Who Outshone the Sun/La mujer que brillaba aún más que el sol*. Illustrated by Fernando Olivera. Children's Book Press, 1991. With a touch of magical realism, this ancient Zapotec myth from Southern Mexico shares a message of the importance of accepting differences. (I: 6–10)

*Ober, Hal. *How Music Came to the World: An Ancient Mexican Myth*. Illustrated by Carol Ober. Houghton Mifflin, 1994. The sky god and the wind god cooperate to bring music to the earth in this ancient story. (I: 8–11)

*Reasoner, Charles. *Night Owl and the Rooster: A Haitian Legend*. Troll Associates, 1995. A touching tale of an owl who is helped to accept his odd looks by his true love. (I: 7–10)

*Rohmer, Harriet. *Uncle Nacho's Hat/El sombrero de Tio Nacho*. Illustrated by Mira Reisberg. Children's Book Press, 1989. Originally a play performed by the Puppet Workshop of Nicaraguan National Television, the story explores the difficulty of getting rid of an old hat (or an old habit) when given a new one. (I: 7–11)

Asian Folktales

*Casanova, Mary. *The Hunter*. Illustrated by Ed Young. Atheneum, 2000. A retelling of a Chinese tale in which a generous hunter is given a magical gift that allows him to provide for his village in a time of drought—but only if he does not reveal the source of the magic. (I: 7–11)

*Climo, Shirley. *The Korean Cinderella*. Illustrated by Ruth Heller. HarperTrophy, 1996. Pear Blossom plays the Cinderella role in this Asian story, and the magical aid comes to her by means of *tokgabis*, magical creatures in the forms of frogs, sparrows, and an ox. (I: 4–8)

*Ishii, Momoko. *The Tongue-Cut Sparrow*. Translated by Katherine Paterson. Illustrated by Suekichi Akaba. Dutton/Lodestar, 1987. A kind old man and his greedy wife get their just deserts from a little sparrow. Comparable to "The Fisherman's Wife," "The Talking Eggs," "Mufaro's Beautiful Daughters," and "Three Perfect Peaches." (I: 7–10)

*Lee, Jeanne M. *Toad Is the Uncle of Heaven*. Holt, 1985. Something of a cumulative tale, about a toad that asks the king of heaven to end a drought. The many helpers whom he recruits lend their aid at propitious moments, just as they do in the Grimms' "The Brementown Musicians" or in the Chinese tale "The Terrible Nung Gwama." (I: 7–10)

*McDermott, Gerald. *The Stonecutter*. Puffin, 1975. Tasaku, a lowly stonecutter, wishes for increasing power. (I: 7–12)

*Morimoto, Junko. *The Inch Boy*. Puffin, 1986. A Japanese Tom Thumb story. (I: 6–10)

Sakade, Florence, ed. *Japanese Children's Favorite Stories*. Illustrated by Yoshisuke Kurosaki. Tuttle, 1958. Here are twenty classic folktales of Japan, with authentic illustrations. (I: 10–12)

———. *Kintaro's Adventures and Other Japanese Children's Stories*. Illustrated by Yoshio Hayashi. Tuttle, 1958. These are stories well known among

Japanese children, retold in traditional settings. (I: 10–12)

*San Souci, Robert. *Fa Mulan: The Story of Woman Warrior*. Illustrated by Jean Tseng and Mou-sien Tseng. Hyperion, 1998. The story of Fa Mulan dates back to fifth or sixth century A.D. and tells of a girl who cuts her hair and joins the Chinese army to battle against the Tartars because her aged father has been conscripted. (I: 7–11)

*———. *The Samurai's Daughter*. Illustrated by Stephen Johnson. Dial, 1992. Tokoyo follows her father into exile and fights many natural and supernatural threats along the way in this exciting Japanese tale with a strong female hero. (I: 6–10)

*Uchida, Yoshiko. *The Two Foolish Cats*. McElderry, 1987. Two cats quarrel foolishly over rice cakes until the wise old monkey unexpectedly stops their argument. (I: 5–9)

*———. *The Wise Old Woman*. Illustrated by Martin Springett. McElderry, 1994. A Japanese tale about a village that discriminates against old people. An old woman's wisdom saves the village from a marauding conqueror. (I: 6–10)

*Xiong, Blia. *Nine-in-One, Grr! Grr!* Adapted by Cathy Spagnoli. Illustrated by Nancy Hom. Children's Book Press, 1989. When the great god Shao tells First Tiger how many cubs she will have, Bird confuses her into believing she will have fewer—and so she does. A story from the Hmong people of Laos. (I: 6–10)

*Yacowitz, Caryn. *The Jade Stone: A Chinese Folktale*. Illustrated by Ju-Hong Chen. Holiday House, 1992. In this thoughtful tale, a master stonecutter listens to the rock and carves what it wants to be—a decision that causes him to defy the emperor and nearly costs his life. (I: 6–11)

*Yagawa, Sumiko. *The Crane Wife*. Translated by Katherine Peterson. Illustrated by Suekichi Akaba. Morrow, 1987. In repayment for a kind deed, a crane changes a peasant into a beautiful woman who becomes his wife and weaves exquisite cloth to support them. (I: 8–10)

*Yep, Laurence. *The Boy Who Swallowed Snakes*. Illustrated by Jean and Mou-Sien Tseng. Scholastic, 1994. In this original folktale in a Chinese setting, a boy swallows a poisonous snake as an act of heroism and flourishes in the end. (I: 8–10)

———. *The Ghost Fox*. Illustrated by Jean Tseng and Mou-Sien Tseng. Scholastic, 1994. For intermediate readers, a moving and ancient tale about a boy who rescues his mother's soul from a ghost fox. (I: 8–11)

*———. *The Junior Thunder Lord*. Illustrated by Robert Van Nutt. Troll/BridgeWater, 1994. A

seventeenth-century Chinese tale about a merchant's act of kindness, which is unexpectedly and magnificently rewarded. (I: 8–10)

Middle Eastern Folktales

*Ben Ezer, Ehud. *Hosni the Dreamer: An Arabian Tale*. Illustrated by Uri Shulevitz. Farrar Straus & Giroux, 1997. Hosni is a shepherd who talks to his sheep by day and listens to the tales of the old ones by night. He is laughed at when he spends his last dinars on a poem, but all turns out for the best. (I: 7–11)

*Climo, Shirley. *The Persian Cinderella*. Illustrated by Robert Florczak. HarperCollins, 1999. Climo has retold other Cinderella tales. In this one, from ancient Persia by way of *The Arabian Nights*, Settareh, whose name means "star," is helped by a magical blue jar to rise above her rags and attract the favor of the prince at the New Year's celebration. (I: 7–11)

*Kimmel, Eric. *The Tale of Ali Baba and the Forty Thieves: A Story from the Arabian Nights*. Illustrated by Will Hillenbrand. Holiday House, 1996. In this, the most familiar of the tales in the Arabian Nights, the one that gave us "open sesame," Ali Baba finds a treasure cave, sees his brother succumb to greed, and wins the aid of a kind slave girl. (I: 4–8).

*———. *The Three Princes: A Tale from the East*. Illustrated by Leonard Everett Fisher. Holiday House, 1994. An unnamed princess has three princes for suitors, and though she loves the youngest, he has nothing to give her, so she sends the three of them on a quest to find the most wonderful things. The rivals end up saving her life, and the story becomes a model of cooperation as well as competition. (I: 7–11)

*Hickox, Rebecca. *The Golden Sandal: A Middle Eastern Cinderella Story*. Illustrated by Will Hillenbrand. Holiday House, 1999. In this retelling of an Iraqi folktale "The Little Red Fish and the Clog of Gold," the Cinderella figure is named Maha, her magical helper is a fish, and the glass slipper is—can you guess? (I: 4–8)

*Shepard, Aaron. *Forty Fortunes: A Tale of Iran*. Illustrated by Alisher Dianov. Clarion Books, 1999. Shepard has been honored by the American Library Association and the National Council for the Social Studies for his retellings of world folktales. This story might be paired with the Grimms' "Brementown Musicians" because the unlikely hero, hounded by his wife into working as a storyteller, accidentally recovers stolen fortunes from a band of thieves. (I: 5–10)

Derivative Folktales and Spoofs

*Minters, Frances. *Cinder-Elly*. Illustrated by G. Brian Karas. Viking, 1994. In this story, told in a fast moving rhyme, an urban Cinderella longs to go to the basketball game, gets there with the magical aid of a bag lady, and wins the attention of Prince Charming, the star shooter. (I: 7–11)

*Munsch, Robert. *The Paper Bag Princess*. Illustrated by Michael Martchenko. Annick Press, 1988. Canadian author Munsch created a popular tale in which a female hero, Princess Elizabeth, rescues Prince Ronald from captivity by a dragon who has burned all Elizabeth's clothes and left her draped in a paper bag. Vain Prince Ronald doesn't approve of women who dress in paper bags, even if they do save his life. Read on. (I: 7–9)

*Scieszka, Jon. *The Frog Prince, Continued*. Illustrated by Steve Johnson. Puffin, 1994. Jon Scieszka has carved out a niche for himself with his clever retellings of classic fairy tales. This one explores what might have happened if the prince really *had* tried to give up his froggy ways and live happily ever after with a human beauty. (I: 6–11)

*———. *Squids Will Be Squids*. Illustrated by Lane Smith. Puffin, 1998. Starting with the premise "If you can't say something nice about someone, change the guy's name to Donkey or Squid," Scieszka goes on to coin a host of fables about the moral challenges of modern life, such as believing what you see on TV or taking pride in having a lot of possessions. (I: 6–11)

*———. *The Stinky Cheese Man and Other Fairly Stupid Tales*. Illustrated by Lane Smith. Viking, 1992. This book not only turns half a dozen classic fairy tales on their ears, but trashes the conventions of book layout too. Scieszka is aided in this inspired assault on tradition by the artist Lane Smith and an ingenious book designer. (I: 6–11)

*———. *The True Story of the 3 Little Pigs*. Illustrated by Lane Smith. Puffin, 1996. Everyone has a story to tell, it seems; this one, narrated from behind bars, is an attempt by A. Wolf to put a positive spin on those unfortunate events concerning three pigs. (I: 6–11)

*Williams, Jay. *Petronella*. Illustrated by Margaret Organ-Kean. Moon Mountain Publishing, 2000. The original of this reworking of the stereotyped active-male/passive-female hero story was published in 1973 and is out of print, but the story is well worth having and this new version is welcome. *Petronella,* about a nontraditional hero by that name, makes an interesting story to look at through the lens of Joseph Campbell's hero cycle. (I: 7–11)

*Yolen, Jane. *Sleeping Ugly*. Illustrated by Diane Stanley. Paper Star, 1997. Jane Yolen's nearly classic spoof on the beautiful princess paradigm has depth. The handsome prince bypasses Princess Miserella and takes up with Plain Jane, a nicer, lower-maintenance companion. (I: 7–11)

Multicultural Collections

Cole, Joanna, ed. *Best Loved Folktales of the World*. Anchor, 1983. This is a particularly good collection to have for a quick read-aloud in school. There are 200 tales here, organized by their region of origin. (I: 5–10)

De Spain, Pleasant, ed. *Thirty-Three Multicultural Tales to Tell*. Illustrated by Joe Schlichta. August House, 1993. As the title suggests, the emphasis is on storytelling. De Spain is a popular storyteller, and his publisher caters to storytellers. (I: 7–11)

Hearne, Betsy, ed. *Beauties and Beasts*. Illustrated by Joanne Caroselli. Oryx Press, 1993. Hearne has researched the Beauty and the Beast tale type and has here reproduced two dozen versions of it from nearly every part of the world. (I: 5–10)

MacDonald, Margaret Read. *Peace Tales: World Folktales to Talk About*. Linnet Books, 1992. MacDonald, a folklore scholar, storyteller, and children's librarian, is a highly reliable source of stories and tips on telling them. These tales from many countries focus on conflict and its resolution and are very useful as discussion starters. (I: 5–11)

Shannon, George. *A Knock at the Door*. Oryx Press, 1992. "The Three Little Pigs" and thirty-four variations of it from all over the world are presented. This multicultural series from Oryx Press also includes *Cinderella Tales* by Judith Sierra and *Beauties and Beasts* by Betsy Hearne. (I: 5–10)

Sierra, Judith, ed. *Cinderella*. Illustrated by Joanne Caroselli. Oryx Press, 1992. Cinderella tales from many parts of the world are written out here for reading aloud or storytelling, with scholarly notes on sources added as an appendix. (I: 5–10)

———, and Robert Kaminski, eds. *Multicultural Folktales: Stories to Tell to Young Children*. Oryx Press, 1991. Dozens of tales from most parts of the world, prefaced by instructions on telling stories and using the flannel board and accompanied by flannel board cutouts. (I: 4–7)

Walker, Richard, ed. *The Barefoot Book of Trickster Tales*. Illustrated by Claudio Munoz. Barefoot Books, 1998. Tricksters are nearly universal character types, found in tales told around the world. Focusing on trickster tales is a useful way to highlight common themes in tales from diverse places. The tales retold here come from Native American, Ghanaian, Russian, Kampuchean, Bengali, Swiss, Turkish, and American sources. (**I:** all ages)

Yolen, Jane. *Favorite Folktales from around the World.* Pantheon, 1988. Hundreds of tales have been collected by Yolen and grouped internationally by categories such as "True Loves and False," "Tricksters, Rogues, and Cheats," "The Fool: Numbskulls and Noodleheads," and "Heroes: Likely and Unlikely." A few are well known, but many will be new to most readers. (**I:** all ages)

RESOURCES

Bettelheim, Bruno. *The Uses of Enchantment.* Vintage, 1975.

Bronner, Simon, ed. *American Children's Folklore.* August House, 1988.

Luthi, Max. *The European Folktale: Form and Future.* ISHI, 1981.

McCarthy, William Bernard, ed. *Jack in Two Worlds.* Univ. of North Carolina Press, 1994.

McGlathery, James, ed. *The Brothers Grimm and Folktale.* Univ. of Illinois Press, 1991.

Miller, Jay. Introduction. *Coyote Stories,* by Mourning Dove. Univ. of Nebraska Press, 1990.

Ong, Walter. *Orality and Literacy: The Technologizing of the Word.* Methuen, 1985.

Von Franz, Marie Louise. *Interpretation of Fairy Tales.* Spring Publications, 1970.

REFERENCES

Aarne, Antti. *The Types of the Folktale.* Translated and revised by Stith Thompson. Folklore Fellows Communication No. 184. Academia Scientiarum Fennica, 1961.

Bettelheim, Bruno. *The Uses of Enchantment.* Vintage, 1975.

Bly, Robert. *Iron John: A Book about Men.* Vintage, 1992.

Bronner, Simon, ed. *American Children's Folklore.* August House, 1988.

Bruchac, Joseph. *Keepers of the Animals.* Fulcrum, 1991.

———. *Keepers of the Earth.* Fulcrum, 1988.

Campbell, Joseph. *The Hero with a Thousand Faces.* Bollingen, 1968.

Deen, Rosemary, and Ann Marie Ponsot. *Beat Not the Poor Desk.* Boynton-Cook, 1980.

Delacre, Lulu. *Arroz con leche: Popular Songs and Rhymes from Latin America.* Scholastic, 1989.

Edmonds, Walter D. *The Matchlock Gun.* Dodd Mead, 1941.

Freud, Sigmund. *New Introductory Lectures on Psychoanalysis.* Norton, 1923.

Frye, Northrop. *Anatomy of Criticism.* Princeton Univ. Press, 1971.

Griego, Margot C., Bucks, Betsy L., Gilbert, Sharon S., and Kimball, Laurel H. *Tortillitas para Mama and Other Spanish Nursery Rhymes.* Illustrated by Barbara Cooney. Holt, 1981.

Holland, Norman. *Five Readers Reading.* Yale Univ. Press, 1975.

Jacobs, Joseph. *Celtic Fairy Tales.* Frederick Muller, 1958.

Jaramillo, Nelly Palacio. *Grandmother's Nursery Rhymes/Las Nanas de Abuelita: Lullabies, Tongue Twisters, and Riddles from South America.* Illustrated by Elivia Savadler. Holt, 1996.

Jung, Carl, ed. *Man and His Symbols.* Dell, 1961.

———. *Memories, Dream, and Reflections.* Vintage, 1989.

Lévi-Strauss, Claude. "The Structural Study of Myth." *Structural Anthropology.* Basic Books, 1957.

Lobel, Arnold. *Fables.* HarperCollins, 1980.

Lomax, Alan. *The Folksongs of North America.* Dolphin, 1975.

Lonnrot, Elias, comp. *The Kalevala.* Translated by Francis Peabody Magoun, Jr. Harvard Univ. Press, 1963.

MacDonald, Margaret Read. *The StoryTeller's Sourcebook: A Subject, Title, and Motif-Index to Folklore Collections for Children.* Neal-Schuman/Gale Research, 1982.

McKinley, Robin. *Beauty.* 1978

Phelps, Ethel Johnston. *The Maid of the North: Feminist Folktales from around the World.* Holt, 1981.

———. *Tatterhood and Other Tales.* Illustrated by Pamela Baldwin-Ford. Feminist Press at the City University of New York, 1978.

Polacco, Patricia. *Babushka's Mother Goose.* Putnam, 1995.

Propp, Vladimir. *The Morphology of the Folktale.* 1928. Univ. of Texas Press, 1968.

Rapaport, Roy. "Desecrating the Holy Woman: Derek Freeman's Attack on Margaret Mead." *American Scholar* 55(3) (Summer 1986): 313-347.

San Souci, Robert. *The Talking Eggs.* Dial, 1989.

Taback, Simms. *There Was an Old Lady Who Swallowed a Fly.* Viking, 1997.

White, T. H. *The Once and Future King.* Putnam, 1939.

Williamson, Duncan. *Tales of the Seal People: Scottish Folk Tales.* Interlink, 1992.

Winner, Ellen. *Invented Worlds: A Psychology of the Arts.* Harvard Univ. Press, 1982.

Wyndham, Robert. *Chinese Mother Goose Rhymes.* Illustrated by Ed Young. Putnam, 1968.

Yolen, Jane. *Greyling.* Illustrated by David Ray. Putnam, 1991.

6 Picture Books

The gratifying thing about good art is the longer one looks at it the more one sees, the more one sees, the deeper one feels, and the deeper one feels the more profoundly one thinks. Looking at art is everything!

from Picture Books for Children, *4th ed.*
by Patricia J. Cianciolo

PICTURE BOOKS DEFINED

Today's picture books are filled with good art—art that invites repeated lingering, elicits a depth of feeling, and promotes profound thinking. A picture book in the purest sense refers to a book that relies solely on illustrations to convey its message, but a broader definition includes books in which the illustrations combine with text to create a message. A picture book can take many forms. It can be a wordless book, which tells a story solely through illustrations. It can be an illustrated book, in which the words carry most of the message, but illustrations either depict what is stated in the text or decorate the page. It can be a picture storybook, in which a tale is told through a combination of illustrations and text, each amplifying the other to create a unified whole. Much of the discussion in this chapter focuses on the picture storybook.

THE EVOLUTION OF PICTURE BOOKS

Since the publication in 1658 of the first picture book, many factors have influenced the evolution of these books for children. Picture books have changed as their creators have explored the interplay of text and illustrations and refined their concepts of picture books. Developments in printing technology have influenced the technical as well as the artistic aspects of creating picture books.

The Development of the Concept of the Picture Book

What is generally considered the first picture book is **Orbis Sensualium Pictus (The Visible World in Pictures),** published in 1658 by Johannes Amos Comenius (1592–1670), a visionary educator from what is now the Republic of Slovakia. Comenius believed that children should be taught about practical matters in the language they used daily, in addition to being taught the "dead" languages, history, and catechisms, as was popular at the time. He added illustrations to informational text to increase children's understanding and pleasure. Following the lead of Comenius, most picture books of the seventeenth and eighteenth centuries were created to educate children and guide their moral behavior.

Children's book publishing advanced dramatically under the leadership of John Newbery (1713–1767). In 1744, Newbery established a company in London dedicated almost exclusively to publishing beautiful children's books. He created books for children in attractive, playful formats, including the accordion book, which was a long strip folded accordionlike to form "pages." He was the first to introduce illustrations by accomplished artists, and his books had permanent, attractive bindings.

Picture books flourished in England during the nineteenth century. Much of the credit for changes in picture books is given to Edmund Evans, an artist, publisher, and printer. Evans advanced the development of picture books by recognizing the importance of the relationship between illustration and book design. In addition, using photographic techniques, he created copies that closely resembled the original illustrations to improve the color printing process. Evans persuaded artists such as Randolph Caldecott (1846–1886), Walter Crane (1845–1915), and Kate Greenaway (1846–1901) to create books for children (Kiefer, 1995).

Walter Crane is known for his careful attention to his books' designs and for synchronizing text and illustrations. He was among the first to attend to the overall effect of double-page spreads and to the use of color and beautifully designed pages. Some of the books Crane illustrated in the 1860s are still being reproduced, including his *Sing a Song of Sixpence* and *The House That Jack Built.*

Another notable creator of picture books from the late nineteenth century was Kate Greenaway, whose portrayal of an idealized childhood can be seen in *A—Apple Pie.* Greenaway's enchantment with the Victorian world is evident in her illustrations, which are filled with flowers, gardens, and happy, prettily dressed children.

The picture book form made the greatest leap toward its modern manifestation in the hands of English illustrator Randolph Caldecott, of whom Maurice Sendak (1990) wrote:

> He devised an ingenious juxtaposition of picture and word, a counterpoint that never happened before. Words are left out—but the picture says it. Pictures are left out—but the word says it. In short, it is the invention of the picture book. (p. 21)

Caldecott built on Crane's ideas about book design, perfecting the unification of text and illustration and allowing illustrations to interpret and extend the text beyond what the words implied. Also, Caldecott created illustrations that were not contained within borders, so characters virtually bounced off the pages.

Later, another English illustrator, Beatrix Potter (1866–1943), recognized the need to consider the audience when creating children's books. She insisted that her books be appropriately sized for little hands. Potter's stories of woodland animals are endearing not only because of the well-written text, but also because of the meticulously drawn illustrations.

By the 1930s, the concept of the modern picture book had basically taken shape. The illustrations extended the text, the text and illustrations were interdependent, and the importance of the book's entire design was recognized (Schwartz, 1982).

Changes in Printing Technology

Improvements in printing technology over the years account for great changes in the appearance of picture books. Paper, the use of color, printing quality, and art styles have contributed to the evolution of the picture book.

Illustrations in early picture books were created using a relief method such as wood-block printing. Artists carved illustrations on wood blocks by cutting away the background. The resulting images, which stood above the rest of the block, were inked and impressed on paper by printing machines. Comenius created *Orbis Sensualium Pictus* on wood blocks and included elaborate illustrations and designs in the page borders, a carryover from the hand-decorated manuscripts that were created before the advent of the printing press. Each illus-

Illustration 6.1
Lithography was commonly used to create illustrations for children's picture books of the past. (*Puss in Boots* by Charles Perrault, illustrated by Hans Fischer. Copyright © 1996 by Nord-Sud Verlag AG, Gossau Zurich, Switzerland. Used by permission of North-South Books, Inc., New York.)

tration had to be painstakingly carved on a separate block. John Newbery, who was the first to produce books whose primary purpose was to amuse children, used wood engravings for most of his publications. Thomas Bewick perfected wood engraving in the late eighteenth century and is best known for being the first to add color to illustrations. Every book was colored by hand; ironically, some of those hands belonged to children who worked under sweatshop conditions.

In the late nineteenth century, metal plates and metal engravings were used. William Blake used etchings on metal plates to illustrate his *Songs of Innocence.* Walter Crane's illustrations in *Absurd ABC* were hand-colored, and the typography in that book was considered to be as excellent as the pictures. John Tenniel's illustrations of *Alice's Adventures in Wonderland* were printed by letterpress from metal engravings.

Lithography, a process invented in the late eighteenth century, allowed artists to work on flat stones that had a very hard, smoothly polished surface. Images were drawn on the stone with wax crayons or touche, a crayonlike liquid material. The ink adhered to the waxed portions of the stone; images were then printed on dampened paper using enormous pressure. One example of fine lithography can be seen in Hans Fischer's 1958 illustrations for Charles Perrault's *Puss in Boots.*

The use of photography and letterpress printing revolutionized the printing of picture books in the early twentieth century. At first, colors had to be separated by hand, and the process was both tedious and expensive. It was not until illustrators could turn color separation over to machines that the number of full-color illustrations in picture books increased. Photography and later the laser scanner made the greatest impact on the quality of art reproduction.

In the twentieth century, printing technology has improved tremendously, and art can be reproduced so that it closely resembles its original form. Picture books have become objects of great beauty. The use of computer technology to create picture books may lead to a new era of book illustration. Since the advent of the laser scanner, the printing process imposes few limitations on the artist. It is amazing what illustrators have been able to use: Imaginative picture books have been made with collages of cardboard, cereal, and plastic, as David Diaz did in illustrating Eve Bunting's *Smoky Night,* the 1995 Caldecott-winning book, or even wood veneers, which is what Paul O. Zelinsky used to illustrate Anne Isaacs's *Swamp Angel,* a 1995 Caldecott Honor Book.

Computer technology itself offers illustrators a new medium. Artists have different reactions to the use of computers to create art. Some suggest that technology separates the artist from the reader and that children will always prefer illustrations in which "the hand of the artist" is recognizable. On the other hand, Don and Audrey Wood, two highly regarded illustrators, have made such a complete transition to computer-generated art that they have given up paintbrushes entirely. Also, a new generation of digital art illustrators is now emerging.

Authors and Illustrators Who Have Defined the Field

The work of many early authors and illustrators has contributed to the shaping and defining of the field of picture books. Many are mentioned in the previous sections, on the development of the concept of the picture book and changes in printing technology. Some early works continue to be enjoyed by children today, evidence of the timeless appeal of these creations.

Beatrix Potter's 1902 publication of *The Tale of Peter Rabbit* is celebrated as her debut as a creator of children's books, although her first book was published earlier. This story originally appeared in a series of letters in 1893 to Noel, the son of her former governess, intended to cheer him up when he was ill with scarlet fever. Potter included black-and-white drawings to accompany the story. Years later, after several publication rejections, she used her own funds to have the book published. Frederick Warne & Co. agreed to publish this "little book for little hands" on the condition that Potter provide color illustrations. More than twenty other books followed. The tales of such animal characters as Pigling Bland, Squirrel Nutkin, Jemima Puddleduck, Benjamin Bunny, Hunca Munca, and Jeremy Fisher are known by children all around the world.

Before the 1930s, the picture books that were available to children in the United States were typically imported from England and other European countries. However, between 1930 and 1960, many authors and illustrators came from Europe and joined those working in the United States to establish a solid foundation of American picture books. Ludwig Bemelmans, Roger Duvoisin, Feodor Rojankovsky, and Tomi Ungerer were among those who emigrated from Europe. American picture book creators of that time were Robert McCloskey, Wanda Gág, Robert Lawson, Virginia Lee Burton, Marie Hall Ets, and Margaret Wise Brown. Many of the books created during that era continue to be popular with children.

Wanda Gág's 1929 book *Millions of Cats* still delights readers with the repeated phrases "Hundreds of cats, Thousands of cats, Millions and billions and trillions of cats." The lonely man who sets out to find a cat to keep him and his wife company simply cannot choose from among the millions of cats, each with unique qualities. The lines of the hills and roads in the black-and-white illustrations show the long distance the man travels in search of a cat and echo the long line of cats that follow him home.

Many adults today remember reading Virginia Lee Burton's 1939 story of *Mike Mulligan and His Steam Shovel* as they grew up. When new electric and diesel shovels take jobs away from steam shovels, Mike takes his steam shovel, Mary Anne, to Popperville and proves that she can dig "as much in one day as a hundred men could dig in a week." The house in Burton's 1942 *The Little House* was said to be so well built that the "great-great-grandchildren's great-great-grandchildren" would live there. Although both of these works are more than a half-century old, they meet contemporary criteria for good picture books.

Of the many books written by Margaret Wise Brown, the one most cherished by millions of readers over the years is *Goodnight Moon.* In this bedtime story, published in 1947, a little rabbit is in bed, saying goodnight to each item in the bedroom and outside the window. Gradually, the lights dim until it is dark in the room, and the rabbit falls asleep.

Robert McCloskey's 1942 Caldecott-winning *Make Way for Ducklings* made Boston Public Garden famous all over the world to children who read and reread the endearing story of a duck family in search of a place to live. Among McCloskey's other books from the 1940s and 1950s that continue to enjoy wide popularity are *Blueberries for Sal* and *Time of Wonder,* both depicting life in rural Maine.

Marcia Brown's first book was published in 1946, and only one year later she produced her first Caldecott Honor Book, *Stone Soup: An Old Tale.* Her interest in folktales and fairy tales continued in the many books that followed. She values the passing of stories down through generations and enjoys helping to preserve traditional tales. In fact, all three of Brown's Caldecott Medal books are folktales or fairy tales: *Cinderella* in 1955, *Once a Mouse* in 1962, and *Shadow* in 1983. Each is illustrated with a different medium: *Cinderella* (written by Charles Perrault) was created with watercolors; *Once a Mouse* has woodcut-style illustrations; *Shadow* mixes collage, paint, and print.

Ezra Jack Keats is known for his distinctive collages and his depictions of the daily life of inner-city children. Although his books were published in the 1960s and 1970s, they are still enjoyed by children today. In the 1963 Caldecott winner, *The Snowy Day,* Keats used a variety of papers—gift wrap, wallpaper, and other printed papers—to add color and texture to his illustrations. Peter wakes up to a snowy scene outside his window and spends the day playing in the snow. Keats continued to depict Peter's experiences in subsequent books. Although the experiences depicted are often universal—getting a new baby sister in *Peter's Chair* and playing in the neighborhood in *Apt. 3*—the details of the setting clearly place these stories in city neighborhoods. Keats's picture books are enjoyed in translations by children in many countries.

John Steptoe knew from the time he was in high school that he wanted to write and illustrate books for African American children because of the great need for books these children could relate to. Immediately after high school, Steptoe published his first book, *Stevie.* Although the theme—a boy's jealousy at having to share his mother's attention with a younger boy—is universal and can be appreciated by all children, regardless of race, the book uses language to which African American children can relate directly. Steptoe continued to write and illustrate books that met his goal of providing for the literary needs of African American children, winning wide acclaim and numerous book awards, including the Coretta Scott King Award for illustrations. In addition to illustrating his own books, Steptoe also illustrated works of other noted African American writers, including Lucille Clifton's *All Us Come Cross the Water,* Eloise Greenfield's *She Come Bringing Me That Little Baby Girl,* and Adoff's *All the Colors of the Race: Poems.* Later in his career, John Steptoe created two books of ethnic folktales that became Caldecott Honor Books: *The Story of Jumping Mouse: A Native American Legend* in 1985 and *Mufaro's Beautiful Daughters: An African Tale* in 1988.

CATEGORIES OF PICTURE BOOKS

Picture books have a range of purposes, from introducing rhymes and serving as manipulative toys to helping children learn concepts. In this section, we organize picture books into five groups: early childhood books, wordless books, picture books with minimal text, beginning readers' books, and picture storybooks. Early childhood books are those primarily intended for the youngest children and include board books, books of Mother Goose and nursery rhymes, concept books, alphabet books, counting books, and toy books. (Mother Goose and nursery rhyme books are discussed in Chapter 5, "Traditional Literature.") Wordless books vary more in intended age. Their primary purpose is to allow readers to create the text mentally while looking at the pictures. Picture books with minimal text are closely related to wordless books. Beginning readers' books give children a start at reading independently. Picture storybooks comprise the largest subgroup of picture books. The stories are written specifically to be embellished by illustrations and are told through the marriage of text and illustrations.

Early Childhood Books

Many children enjoy books from the moment they are held in an adult's lap and have a book shared with them or are able to hold them on their own. Some books are particularly appropriate for young children, because of both their form and their content. The novelty of toy books sustains children's curiosity, and the durable format of board books stands up to rough treatment from little hands (and teeth). The rhythmic rhymes of Mother Goose make it easy for little ones to chant along. Concept books introduce young children to informational books, alphabet books help them to explore the language in its written form, and counting books provide opportunities to practice math concepts.

Toy Books. Preschoolers can become acquainted with books very early, thanks to cloth, vinyl, and board books. What these books usually have in common is a sturdy or washable construction and simple pictures, showing one object per page. They are typically eight to ten pages long. If there are any words, they may simply label objects on the page. For slightly older children, pop-ups, pull-tabs, flaps to lift, half-pages, and other gadgets invite playful manipulation. Classic toy books include Dorothy Kunhardt's *Pat the Bunny,* a tactile and participatory book that is still in print sixty years after its first edition, and *The Nutshell Library,* a boxed set of miniature books by Maurice Sendak that children have read for forty years.

Among books for the very youngest are board books by noted author/illustrators such as Nancy Tafuri, Lucy Cousins, and Helen Oxenbury. Board books often come in series of three to four titles centered on topics of immediate interest to very young children, such as animals, things babies do, or family members. Tana Hoban created two books for newborns: *Black on White* and *White on Black.* Both books show shadows of objects on solid backgrounds, creating high contrast between black and white. John Steptoe's *Baby Says* features African American babies, as do books by Eloise Greenfield with Jan Spivey Gilchrist, Angela Shelf Medearis, and Andrea Pinkney with Brian Pinkney. In another board book series, Rosemary Wells humorously chronicles the antics of Max. Other board books are reproductions of picture books originally published in hardback for older children, such as the board book version of Eric Carle's *The Very Busy Spider* or Peggy Rathmann's *Good Night, Gorilla.*

Some books are not quite board books but books with pages that are thicker and glossier than usual book pages. Cut-out shapes layer and unlayer on sixteen boldly colored pages to create various animal faces in *Color Zoo,* by Lois Ehlert, which was a Caldecott Honor Book. She used the same method to create her *Color Farm.* In addition to the heavy card stock paper versions of the original, these books are now available as board books.

Some pop-up books are fairly straightforward, with single-fold pop-ups; other paper-engineered pop-ups are more elaborate, often with moving parts. One particularly popular series is the lift-the-flap series by Eric Hill about a dog named Spot. In *Where's Spot?,* children lift flaps to help mother dog Sally open the door, look inside a wardrobe, and peek under the bed to search for her pup Spot. In Mark Inkpen's *Where, Oh Where, Is Kipper's Bear?,* Kipper the dog searches for his bear. Young readers delight in finding the bear under the covers, reading a book by flashlight—which turns on when they lift up the quilt.

Children shiver with anticipation and delight as they turn each page of Jan Pienkowski's *Dinner Time* and a different creature's mouth pops out at the reader, declaring, "I'm going to eat you for my dinner." Particularly fine examples of paper-engineeered books are created by Robert Sabuda. For the most part, they are intended for an older audience than toddlers—in fact, the elaborate and complex designs appeal to all ages. *Cookie Count* is a counting book that features all types of cookies—from fortune cookies with mice pulling the for-

Illustration 6.2
This book presents delicious-looking and intricately crafted pop-up cookies from one to ten. (*Cookie Count: A Tasty Pop-Up* by Robert Sabuda. Copyright © 1997 by Robert Sabuda. Used by permission of Simon & Schuster Books for Young Readers, an imprint of Simon & Schuster Children's Publishing.)

tunes out to the cookies that form the gingerbread house at the end. Some books combine pop-ups with pull-tabs, flaps, and other parts to be manipulated. One example is Paul Zelinsky's *The Wheels on the Bus*. In addition to wheels that turn, the book has a bus door that swings open, passengers who board, wipers that swish, babies who cry open-mouthed, and mothers who shake their fingers.

Eric Carle's picture books have toy components that are integral to the story line. In *The Very Hungry Caterpillar,* actual holes in a series of illustrations of food indicate where the caterpillar dined. *The Very Quiet Cricket* searches for a friend until he finally meets another cricket; at that point, readers hear the sound of a cricket (produced by a computer chip embedded in the book). The raised surface of the spider's web in *The Very Busy Spider* becomes increasingly larger as the spider continues to spin. When the firefly meets friends in *The Very Lonely Firefly,* they light up.

Dan Harper's *Telling Time with Mama Cat* is an example of a toy book in which the toy, a clock, allows the reader to manipulate the hands of the clock while reading the story. Some books are toys themselves. *Maisy's Pop-Up Playhouse,* by Lucy Cousins, looks like a book but opens up to create a doll house for Maisy the mouse. The house has a bedroom, a kitchen, and a bathroom and includes cutouts of dishes, pots and pans, and toys for the tub. Can David Pelham's *Sam's Sandwich* be called a book? Sam smirks as he creates an unusual sandwich for his sister—filled with the usual sandwich fillings as well as surprise creatures from the garden. Each page folds out in the shape of the filling, and the covers are the bread. These toy books are artistic creations that stimulate children to create their own stories as they play with them.

Concept Books. Concept books convey knowledge, answering the question "What's that?" They cover a wide range of topics—the alphabet, numbers, colors, shapes, and opposites, to name a few. To appreciate the contribution of these picture books, you need only think about how difficult it sometimes is to describe and convey the meaning of concepts in words alone. Because of their significance and abundance, alphabet and counting books are discussed separately in this section. The important thing to remember when evaluating concept books is how clearly the information is presented and how appropriate it is to the reader's conceptual development.

Tana Hoban is perhaps the most prolific creator of concept books, and hers rely on photographs to relay information. One book, *26 Letters and 99 Cents,* introduces the alphabet when it is read from one end and the concept of money when it is turned over and read from the other end. Bruce McMillan also creates photographic concept and information books. *One, Two, One Pair* shows objects that come in pairs: hands, feet, socks, mittens, boots, and skates. We see a child prepare to go skating and follow as pairs are introduced—but surprise! The child is also part of a pair, and a twin is introduced at the skating pond.

Two concept books that explore the primary colors and how colors mix are Ann Jonas's *Color Dance* and Ellen Stoll Walsh's *Mouse Paint*. Both concepts are explored in the context of a story. In *Color Dance,* three girls dance with red, yellow, and blue sheets of sheer fabric. As they dance and their sheets cross, new colors are made. In *Mouse Paint,* three mice splash around in red, yellow, and blue paint. When they dance around in each other's puddles, new colors are made.

Sometimes, concepts are introduced within the context of a simple story. In Donald Crews's Caldecott Honor Book *Freight Train,* children are introduced to colors and the names of types of cars in a freight train. The book does much more than merely label objects, however. It shows the movement of the train in darkness and daylight by blurring the colors of the cars and introduces children to words such as "tunnel" and "trestle." Lois Ehlert's books also introduce concepts within a storyline. In **Planting a Rainbow,** the story begins, "Every year, Mom and I plant a rainbow." It goes on to describe how bulbs are planted in the fall and seedlings and seeds in the spring, and then they watch the rainbow grow. The next six pages are cut so that a strip of color shows in staggered form along the end of each page. As you flip each colored strip in rainbow order, the flowers in the featured color are shown in full bloom. For example, a tulip, a zinnia, a tiger lily, and a poppy are shown as orange flowers. The concept of color is made clear through this straightforward storyline that ends with the child and mother picking all colors of flowers throughout the summer.

Alphabet Books. Alphabet books are one of the oldest and most popular varieties of concept books. Preschoolers are often first exposed to the alphabet through picture books, and such books are available in large numbers. A traditional alphabet book shows a one-to-one correspondence between a letter and an object whose name begins with that letter. Typically, there is one letter and one object per page. One example is Bert Kitchen's **Animal Alphabet.** Each page of this book has a clearly printed letter and a picture of an animal, familiar or less familiar. More complex alphabet books show more objects per page to illustrate the featured letter; the "B" may be represented by a bicycle as a central picture, but birds, bells, and beans may be found in the border. **Anno's Alphabet** is subtitled "An Adventure in Imagination." For each letter, an intricate, unusual object beginning with that letter is pictured. For the beginner, these pictures are often too sophisticated for simple letter-sound associations. This kind of book is for children who know the alphabet and are willing to extend their knowledge of its application. Finally, some alphabet books challenge readers to discover as many objects as they can find hidden throughout a very busy illustration that includes numerous objects with names that begin with the featured letter. **Animalia** by Graeme Base is an example of such a book. The text on one page says, "Beautiful Blue Butterflies Basking by a Babbling Brook," and objects that begin with the letter B—baboon, bassoon, bee, beetle, book, bear, bonnet—are hidden on the page.

Many books play with the sounds of language while introducing the alphabet. A popular one is Bill Martin, Jr., and John Archambault's **Chicka Chicka Boom Boom.** Children especially enjoy the rhythmic, rhyming text that tells the story of alphabet letters vying to see which can climb to the top of the coconut tree first. A similar rhyming book featuring the letters of the alphabet is Jane Bayer's **A, My Name Is Alice,** whose alphabet rhymes are illustrated by Steven Kellogg. The rhymes are traditional accompaniments to playground games such as jump rope or ball games: "A, my name is Alice and my husband's name is Alex. We come from Alaska and we sell ants. Alice is an Ape. Alex is an Anteater." A different way of playing with the sounds of language is through alliteration. Maurice Sendak's **Alligators All Around** has "Alligators all around / bursting balloons / catching colds / doing dishes." Crescent Dragonwagon's **Alligator Arrived with Apples,** illustrated by José Aruego and Ariane Dewey, has various animals arriving for a Thanksgiving feast, each bringing foods beginning with the same letter as its name: "Bear Brought Banana Bread, Biscuits, and Butter."

A large variety of themed alphabet books are also available. One book with a food theme is **Eating the Alphabet: Fruits and Vegetables from A to Z,** by Lois Ehlert, which shows a variety of fruits and vegetables in alphabetical order. Another alphabet book with a food theme is Arnold Lobel's **On Market Street,** illustrated by Anita Lobel, in which each page depicts a letter composed of fruits, vegetables, and other market items that begin with that letter. *The Handmade Alphabet,* by Laura Rankin, introduces the hand and finger positions used by the American Sign Language Association for the letters of the alphabet. Each page also shows an object that begins with the featured letter.

The alphabet is used to organize all kinds of information at many conceptual levels; there is a rich array of alphabet books for all ages. *The Z Was Zapped,* by Chris Van Allsburg, is an alphabet book that is suitable for intermediate-grade students. Each letter establishes a rather dark theatrical scene within a larger drama of what happens to each letter from A to Z. Leo and Diane Dillon won the Caldecott Medal for their illustrations for Margaret Musgrove's *Ashanti to Zulu: African Traditions,* in which each letter introduces a paragraph of text about a tribe on the African continent. In George Shannon's *Tomorrow's Alphabet,* the alphabet is the organizing sequence to help children predict what things will become in the future. For example, "A is for seed—tomorrow's APPLE/ B is for eggs—tomorrow's BIRDS."

It is clear that some alphabet books are meant for children who are old enough to understand complex ideas. David Pelletier's Caldecott Honor Book *The Graphic Alphabet* takes alphabet letters and artistically places them in graphic art that depicts the word: The "i" of iceberg is nearly submerged beneath the water level, but a shadow of the lower portion of the letter can be seen below the surface, and the "h" is seen "hovering" in midair. Another alphabet book that is more artistic than practical in its rendition of the concept is Suse MacDonald's *Alphabatics.* Each letter of the alphabet transforms from its block letter presentation by twisting, turning, and changing its shape to become part of the featured object that represents the letter. The "A" turns upside down with the tip submerged in water, and the bottom half of the letter becomes the boat represented by "Ark."

Counting Books. Counting books introduce children to a mathematical concept. The most basic counting books clearly show a number and easily identifiable objects to count, without much background clutter to confuse children. Eric Carle's *1, 2, 3 to the Zoo* is about animals on their way to the zoo aboard a train. Each double-page spread shows a number on the upper left and a boxcar with the correct number of a particular animal on board. The eleventh page is a foldout in which children can see all the animals in their zoo home and the empty train.

Denise Fleming's *Count!* encourages children to count from one to ten vibrantly colored, action-oriented creatures. Then the book continues counting by tens to fifty. Diana Pomeroy's *One Potato: A Counting Book of Potato Prints* features fruits and vegetables from one to ten, then by tens to fifty, and ends with 100 sunflower seeds. All of the art in this book is created with potato prints, and potato-printing instructions for adult readers are included at the end of the book.

Lois Ehlert's *Fish Eyes: A Book You Can Count On* encourages children to count the fish on a page, then add one more by counting the narrator fish. The illustrations have cut-out eyes for children to count. *Ten Black Dots,* by Donald Crews, shows dots placed in a child's world—"2/Two dots can make the eyes of a fox" or "5/Five dots can make buttons on a coat." The solid black dots are easy to find and count on all the backgrounds.

Books like Eric Carle's *The Very Hungry Caterpillar* offer a child an opportunity to count numbers within a story line. Children can count the fruit the caterpillar eats, while listening to the story being read. Inspired by a hole in the road that caused a traffic back up during its repair, Nikola-Lisa tells the story in

One Hole in the Road. Dan Yaccarino illustrates the numbers of flagmen, barricades, stoplights, engineers, and hammers needed to fix that hole.

Wordless Books

The pictures tell all in wordless books, and it is an artistic feat to make the stories intriguing, understandable, and satisfying. The text resides in the mind of the reader, who must interpret the pictures to understand the story. Wordless books give children the opportunity to be flexible in their interpretation of a story: They can discuss possibilities for the text, look for clues in the illustrations, and practice storytelling. Wordless books have been popular for years; Pat Hutchins's *Changes, Changes* remains, after more than thirty years, one of the best wordless picture books. The characters and setting are established with images made from wood blocks. The story line of two wooden figures resourcefully creating objects to fit varying dilemmas is action packed, and the theme is easily grasped yet thought-provoking.

Peter Spier created numerous wordless books. In *Rain,* the story opens on the endpapers as a brother and sister play outside in the sun. An approaching dark cloud brings a sudden rainstorm, and the children don rain gear so that they can delight in the changes that rain brings. He alters the pace—from a single picture taking up the entire double spread to a series of ten smaller pictures—to create a sequence that moves the story along. Emily Arnold McCully's *Picnic* tells the story of a mouse family whose picnic is interrupted when they realize that one child is missing. They drive back along the bumpy road and then continue their picnic once they have been reunited with the mouse who had gotten bumped out of the truck.

David Wiesner's *Tuesday* won the Caldecott Medal in 1992. The only text is the notation about time of day on Tuesday. The hilarious exploits of a community of frogs who fly hither and yon on lily pads linger in the reader's visual memory as the many shades of green immerse the reader in the frog world. Another book by Wiesner, *Sector 7,* is seemingly a story told in illustration rather than through words. However, a closer look at the book reveals that much of what is to be interpreted from this presentation is found in the words embedded within the illustrations. Readers discover what happens at Sector 7—creating and dispatching clouds according to schedule, waiting for other clouds to return to the station—through a double spread in which words on the departures and arrivals board as well as signs for "Waiting Room" and "Assignment Station" clue the readers in.

Sisters Jacqueline Preiss Weitzman and Robin Preiss Glassner teamed up to create *You Can't Take a Balloon into The Metropolitan Museum.* Careful observers will note that there are parallel stories within this book: the one that depicts the little girl and her grandmother observing the art in the museum and the one that depicts the city life outside the museum as the balloon passes scenes that parallel what is being seen in the museum. The question for readers to ponder is "Does art reflect life, or does life reflect art?"

Wordless storybooks such as these offer children many opportunities to imagine what the text could be. Note, however, that not all wordless books contain stories. Some wordless books are simply a themed set of pictures.

Picture Books with Minimal Text

Books with minimal text are a related category to wordless books. The story is told predominantly through the illustrations, as in wordless books, but a

Illustration 6.3
When Sophie is made to share a toy with her sister, the changes in Sophie's feelings are reflected in the changes in the colors used in the story's illustrations. (A cover from *When Sophie Gets Angry—Really, Really Angry . . .* by Molly Bang, cover illustration by Molly Bang. Published by Scholastic Press, a division of Scholastic Inc. Copyright © 1999 by Molly Bang. Reprinted by permission.)

few words are strategically included. In some cases, those few words are critical to the story; in other cases, they amplify the story but are not critical to its success. In Peggy Rathmann's *Good Night, Gorilla,* the zookeeper walks from cage to cage wishing the animals goodnight, oblivious to the fact that the gorilla has taken his keys and is letting each animal out. The animals follow the zookeeper home and into the bedroom, where his wife discovers the animals. She then leads them back to the zoo. The only text is the repeated refrain, "Good night _____." This story would work even without the text, because the humor is obvious in the illustrations alone. Chris Raschka's *Yo! Yes?* shows two boys encountering each other and using minimal dialogue to communicate: "Yo!" exclaims the first, and the second responds, "Yes?" With continued one- and two-word exclamations, utterances, and questions, one tries to strike up a friendship and the other considers the possibility. Although the text is minimal, it is critical to the story. In addition to the words used, the text size, color, and use of punctuation marks add to the fullness of the story. In David Shannon's *No, David!,* mother is always having to tell her rambunctious son, "No, David, no!" "No! No! No!" "I said no, David!" The other lines in the book are all cautionary commands—that is, all except the last line of the story.

Molly Bang's story of Sophie's anger at being required to share her toy with her sister is expressed precisely in the minimal text that accompanies the expressive illustrations in *When Sophie Gets Angry—Really, Really, Angry.* Her explosive anger is vividly portrayed in the illustrations, and the accompanying text endorses the emotion.

In Jane Simmons's *Come Along, Daisy,* Mama Duck urges her duckling to keep up, but Daisy is distracted playing and gets separated from her mother. Although there is more than minimal text, the text is quite simple and the story can be understood just by viewing the illustrations, which show Daisy happily in the midst of the pond while playing and then starkly alone when she realizes that her mother is no longer in sight.

Beginning Readers' Books

Children need books they can read independently as they practice their emerging reading abilities. Some books are more likely to be a success with beginning readers because of their predictable format. Other books are more likely to be accessible to beginning readers because of their controlled vocabulary.

Predictable Books. Predictable books have highly structured or repetitive texts that are easy for fledgling readers to read independently. For children, being able to predict what will happen serves as a motivation to read and provides great satisfaction. Predictable books often use rhythms and rhymes or simple story structures to make it easy for the young reader to perceive the pattern of the text and use it to guess upcoming words. Such factors encourage emerging readers to take risks—the reward is being in on what is happening.

As you recall from Chapter 5 ("Traditional Literature"), rhythms and rhymes and story structure are what helped people recite songs, poems, and folktales from memory before literacy was widespread. Predictable books also use these devices from oral language to support beginning readers. Predictable books have been available for many years. Some, like Marjorie Flack's *Ask Mr. Bear* and Charles Shaw's *It Looked Like Spilt Milk,* have become classics. However, since the 1980s, there has been a tremendous increase in the availability of predictable books. This increase can be attributed in large part to the role these books play in beginning reading instruction in schools.

A pioneer writer in this format is children's author and educator Bill Martin, Jr. Over three decades ago, Martin set out to write a series of books that would be easy for beginners to read. Of these Instant Readers, perhaps the best known is *Brown Bear, Brown Bear, What Do You See?* On one page, the text says, "Brown Bear, Brown Bear, what do you see?" The next page reads, "I see a yellow duck looking at me," and on that page readers find a yellow duck created by illustrator Eric Carle. The language pattern and illustrations work together so nicely that countless beginning readers have been able to recite/read the book after a brief introduction.

Uri Shulevitz's *One Monday Morning* uses a cumulative pattern and supportive illustrations to enumerate the important people who come to visit the young narrator in his urban apartment. *The Napping House,* by Audrey and Don Wood, repeats the phrase "In a napping house, where everyone is sleeping" and builds a story by adding a new sleepy character on each page—along with an array of interesting words about sleeping, such as "dozing," "napping," and "snoring."

Though not all books that are enlarged are predictable books, many of the "big books" used for beginning reading instruction are three-foot-high versions of predictable books. Children can watch as the teacher points to the words as they are read. The numerous instructional possibilities that arise from allowing children to see the text make big books especially popular in primary classrooms (Holdaway, 1979). Teachers of young children often use big books in front of a class or small group as students read in unison. Big books that are not predictable books are used in library storytimes or classroom read-aloud sessions. The advantage of big books in these situations is that the illustrations are large enough for all the children to see.

Easy Readers. Easy readers are often among the first books that children read independently. Although they are not strictly picture storybooks as described later in this chapter, they have a formula that includes a generous amount of illustration throughout the book. They typically have some kind of controlled vocabulary—that is, the number of words, the types of words, and the sentence structure and length are determined by a formula that estimates the relative reading level of a book. The controlled vocabulary can result in poor writing, and some easy reader books are reminiscent of basal readers of the past. However, many easy readers combine literary merit with an opportunity for beginning readers to read on their own successfully.

One of the most innovative and famous writers of easy reader books was Dr. Seuss (a pseudonym for Theodor Seuss Geisel). In the 1930s, Dr. Seuss wrote such children's books as *The Five Hundred Hats of Bartholomew Cubbins* and *And to Think That I Saw It on Mulberry Street.* In 1957, convinced that beginning readers were being given uninteresting stories stifled by controlled vocabulary in basal readers of the time, Dr. Seuss changed the outlook on easy reader books when he published *The Cat in the Hat.* With a limited number of words, he tells the story of a cat whose outlandish behavior stuns two well-behaved children who have been left alone in their house for a short while. Dr. Seuss went on to delight generations of beginning readers with more outrageous characters and out-of-the-ordinary events told in easy-reading verse in *Hop on Pop* and *Green Eggs and Ham,* among others.

Since then, many easy readers have been written. *Henry and Mudge: The First Book of Their Adventures,* by Cynthia Rylant, is the first of a series of easy readers by this award-winning author. The text uses limited vocabulary yet has the qualities of poetry, as this excerpt about Mudge the dog shows:

He couldn't smell Henry.
He couldn't smell
his front porch.
He couldn't smell
the street he lived on.
Mudge looked all around
and didn't see anything
or anyone
he knew.

The friendly crayon line drawings by Sucie Stevenson enliven the text and encourage fledgling readers by giving visual clues to what the words must be.

Arnold Lobel is another writer who has written brilliantly within the constraints of limited numbers of words and simple sentence structures. In 1971, his *Frog and Toad Are Friends* was named a Caldecott Honor Book for its illustrations. And *Frog and Toad Together* was a 1973 Newbery Honor Book.

James Marshall's wit and creativity are evident in his many humorous easy-reading books. His text and illustrations are seemingly simple, yet the character and plot development is rich and complete. In *Three by the Sea* (written under the pseudonym Edward Marshall), readers meet Lolly, Spider, and Sam, who are having a picnic at the beach. Children are propelled to continue reading as they anticipate what will happen when a rat buys a cat to be his friend or when a monster comes out of the sea and finds three children on a beach. Young readers are equally motivated to read about Fox attempting to make money at various jobs so that he can buy a new bike in *Fox on the Job.*

Denys Cazet's *Minnie and Moo Go Dancing* and *Minnie and Moo Go to the Moon* are both humorous short stories that describe the antics of two cows. When they go dancing, they are horrified at the thought that the hamburgers served as refreshments are made from cows—Could they be former friends? Watercolor illustrations maintain the lighthearted appeal of these humorous stories.

Betsy Byars's *My Brother Ant* offers beginning readers a chance to practice reading text that is humorous in the way it portrays two brothers and their relationship. Likewise, Laura Kvasnosky's *Zelda and Ivy* offers stories of two sisters (portrayed as foxes). Both series are likely to appeal to child readers in that they portray family relationships at the age level of the readers.

Some easy readers are more advanced, to meet the needs of children's developing reading ability. Although they are longer and include more complex words, the qualities that make easy readers readable are still present. Tomie dePaola's Newbery Honor Book *26 Fairmount Avenue* is the beginning of a series of easy reader chapter books that are based on his life. DePaola maintains a child's voice as he describes the events of his childhood. The stories continue in *Here We All Are* and *On My Own.* The engaging text is likely to make readers feel that they are hearing a friend relate the events of his daily life. Other more complex easy readers include the *Mr. Putter and Tabby* series by Cynthia Rylant and the *Pinky and Rex* series by James Howe.

Books like these fill a vital need. Many preschoolers have grown accustomed to having their parents and teachers read fascinating and eloquent books

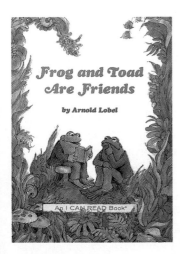

Illustration 6.4
Good stories, simple text, well-matched illustrations, and the effective use of line breaks and white space all combine to give beginning readers successful reading experiences. Arnold Lobel's *Frog and Toad Are Friends* is a good example of an inviting book for beginning readers. (*Frog and Toad Are Friends* by Arnold Lobel. Copyright © 1979. Used by permission of HarperCollins Juvenile Books, a division of HarperCollins Publishers.)

to them, and when children reach school age, although parents and teachers may continue to read to them, it will take much time and hard practice before they will be able to read such books for themselves. Easy readers, though, can be interesting and pithy books in highly readable language. Maintaining quality in a format in which simplicity is paramount can be difficult, but the efforts of such authors as Joanna Cole, Tomie dePaola, Jean Fritz, Arnold Lobel, James Marshall, and Dr. Seuss are rewarded when young readers can enjoy interesting content in well-crafted language.

Picture Storybooks

There are more picture storybooks than any other type of picture book. As defined earlier, a picture storybook is one in which the text and the illustrations work together to amplify each other—in other words, part of the story is told through the illustrations and part is told through the text. Text and illustrations do not merely reflect each other; combined, they tell a story that goes beyond what one tells alone. The next section explains how picture storybooks work.

HOW PICTURE STORYBOOKS WORK

When we read a story that moves us deeply, we often speak of the setting, characters, plot, and other elements of the book that contributed to its effect. But if a picture moves us, most of us do not have a set of terms readily available for describing what caused the picture's effect. Picture books afford readers the opportunity to deepen their understanding of visual communication—their visual literacy. Knowing some terms can help teachers and parents talk as knowledgeably about pictures as about texts and better appreciate the principles that govern how picture book illustrations communicate meaning. The following elements of visual communication will concern us here:

■ Layout, including page turns, borders, and the number and placement of frames on a page

■ Characterization, which refers to the consistent visual identity of the characters

Illustration 6.5
Because her family cannot afford a train ticket, a young girl is mailed (by train) to visit her grandmother. This story is based on an event that occurred in 1914. (*Mailing May* by Michael O. Tunnell, illustrated by Ted Rand. Copyright © 1997. Used by permission of Greenwillow, a division of HarperCollins Publishers.)

- Perspective, settings, and other repeated phenomena
- Backgrounds
- Color, especially as it relates to mood
- Picture/text relationships—that is, which aspects of the communication are carried by the text and which are conveyed by the pictures and how the pictures and text interact

Clearly, much goes into the creating of picture books. Many people besides the author and illustrator are involved in creating the final product. Editors, art directors, and printers all have professional roles. Decisions about the book size, paper type, endpapers, and book jacket all contribute to the finished book.

The Layout of Picture Books

Children's books are printed in multiples of eight pages, and picture books are typically thirty-two pages long. One page is taken up by the title page, a second by the copyright information, and often another by the dedication—leaving the illustrator of most picture books a little less than thirty pages to work with. Within these few pages, the illustrator creates a visual world. By laying out the illustrations in a particular way, the illustrator controls the readers' journey through that world, much as a tour guide leads a group through a city or a landscape. Like a tour guide, the illustrator can move readers quickly from place to place and happening to happening or cause readers to pause in one spot and let impressions settle in.

Single Pages and Double-Page Spreads. As a rule, putting a picture on each page propels readers through the story at an even pace, whereas putting more than one picture on a page is a way to depict a series of actions or the rapid occurrence of actions. Spreading a single picture across two facing pages (a double-page spread) can signal a pause, a moment to ponder the events.

In *The Amazing Bone,* written and illustrated by William Steig, a succession of one-page illustrations shows Pearl's quick progress through the bustle of town life. A double-page spread showing Pearl sitting on the ground in the woods under trees raining wild cherry blossoms conveys a sense of her being overwhelmed by the beauty (and the seeming innocence) of nature.

In Sherley Anne Williams's *Working Cotton,* illustrator Carole Byard created a series of double-page spreads. These spreads communicate the boundless flatness of the migrant workers' world, where the child works from dark to dark in a field that appears to go on forever. This landscape is emphasized by the horizontally wide shape of the book.

Philipe Dupasquier's book *Dear Daddy* has an unusual layout: Pictures covering the lower halves of the pages show the events in the girl's life, while pictures across the top halves show her father's activities as a merchant seaman aboard a ship steaming around the world. Toward the end of the story, the pictures converge; finally, with Daddy's return, father and daughter occupy the visual space together.

Borders. Borders around pictures offer a means for the illustrator to control how intimately readers feel involved with the pictures. Some illustrators put decorative borders around four sides. These may put the action at some distance, sentimentalize it, or make it clear that the time period or place depicted is remote.

Trina Schart Hyman uses borders in an interesting way in Margaret Hodges's *St. George and the Dragon.* Each border suggests a stained glass window, and

Illustration 6.6
Trina Schart Hyman's borders in *St. George and the Dragon* remind viewers of stained glass images on church windows. [*St. George and the Dragon* by Margaret Hodges & Trina Schart Hyman. Copyright © 1984 by Margaret Hodges (text); copyright © 1984 by Trina Schart Hyman. Used by permission of Little, Brown and Company (Inc.).]

she reinforces this impression by sometimes drawing smaller images in the border panels in a way that embellishes the images in the center panel but that also makes it seem as if the images were painted on the glass, rather than seen through a window. On other pages, though, the images in the center intrude into the borders, and then we get the impression that we are looking not at static images in a stained glass window but through clear leaded glass at real figures just on the other side.

In *Where the Wild Things Are,* author and illustrator Maurice Sendak uses borders in a striking way. The sizes of the borders wax and wane with the crescendo and decrescendo of Max's wild adventures. In the opening pages, plain white borders contain relatively small pictures of Max. As his fantasy grows, though, so do the pictures—first filling a page, then spilling onto the opposite page, until the "wild rumpus" in the middle of the book pushes margins and words off the double-page spreads. As order returns, so do the borders—until on the last page, the pictures are gone, leaving nothing but text.

In other books, the lack of borders gives an informality and a sense of the picture going beyond the pages of the book. Jerry Pinkney's illustrations for Hans Christian Andersen's **The Ugly Duckling** bleed off the edges of the paper, and readers suppose that they were cut off from the world beyond the pages, restricted by the page size. This format seems especially fitting for a glimpse of the natural world.

Page Turns. Page turns allow an illustrator to create and relieve suspense. William Moebius (1986) called this phenomenon "the drama of the turning page." Many illustrators make use of this technique to add dramatic interest. When Nancy Winslow Parker illustrated John Langstaff's text **Oh, A-Hunting We Will Go,** she broke up the verse of the folk song as follows:

> Oh, a-hunting we will go.
> A-hunting we will go.
> We'll catch a fox
> [page turn]
> And put him in a box,
> And then we'll let him go.

With each successive verse, children are implicitly challenged to guess where each animal will be put before they turn the page and read the completed rhyme.

Sometimes, an illustrator will include clues that lead readers to the next page. In **I Went Walking** by Mem Fox, Julie Vivas gives readers a glimpse of a portion of the animal on the following page in the background of the previous page.

The Last Page. The last page of a picture book is often used for something of an afterword. Many illustrators reserve this last page for an epilogue, a comment on what has gone before. Maurice Sendak used the last page of **Where the Wild Things Are** to tell the reader that Max's supper was still hot after he returned from his antics with the Wild Things. Dav Pilkey used the last page of **The Paperboy** to show readers that after finishing his route, the paperboy went back to bed and entered a dream world. At times, authors and illustrators create an explicit epilogue. Kevin Henkes creates such a statement in **Chrysanthemum,**

so readers know "what happened" beyond the denouement concluding Chrysanthemum's name dilemma.

Characterization

Characterization refers to the way in which an illustrator makes readers identify a particular character and continue to recognize that character throughout the changes of scene or status in the whole book. This is not easy. Leonardo da Vinci painted only one Mona Lisa, but would we always recognize the Mona Lisa if da Vinci had had to depict her fifteen or twenty times, in different perspectives and in different circumstances? That is the challenge faced by the illustrator of virtually every picture book. To meet that challenge, some artists, such as Ted Lewin, hire models to pose for their drawings in different settings. Others, such as Jerry Pinkney, rely on family members to serve as models. When artists work purely from the imagination, though, they must decide on identifying features by which readers will immediately know their characters. When reading Arnold Lobel's books, for instance, we can keep Frog and Toad straight in our minds because Frog is always green and Toad is always brown.

It was Grandma's birthday.

Max made her an earthworm birthday cake.

"No, Max," said Max's sister, Ruby. "We are going to make Grandma an angel surprise cake with raspberry-fluff icing."

Illustration 6.7
In an effort to decorate his earthworm cake for Grandma's birthday, Max repeatedly attempts to write "Red-Hot Marshmallow Squirters" on the grocery list. (*Bunny Cakes* by Rosemary Wells. Copyright © 1997. Used by permission of Dial Books for Young Readers, a division of Penguin Putnam Inc.)

Features of a character may become so recognizable that even a part of a character may serve to identify the whole. In James Marshall's ***Fox and His Friends,*** for example, readers can recognize little sister Louise just from the tip of her tail hanging down into the frame from her perch atop a telephone pole. Similarly, in Mem Fox's ***Hattie and the Fox,*** just the presence of a nose in the bushes signals that a fox is stalking the barnyard animals.

Rosemary Wells's rabbits are wonderfully endearing. She draws them with large faces, big eyes, and small mouths. Max seems to be passively suffering his plight, and Ruby is manipulating things to her liking; either way, they evoke sympathy. A researcher of animal behavior, Iraneus Eibl-Eibesfeldt (1975), observed that among the higher animal species (including humans), adults are hereditarily conditioned to accept a certain array of features as "cute"—and when they see this array, their nurturant behavior is triggered. The array includes a head that is large in proportion to the body, a large forehead, big eyes, and a small mouth. The pictures of Max and Ruby in ***Bunny Cakes,*** by Rosemary Wells, show many of these features.

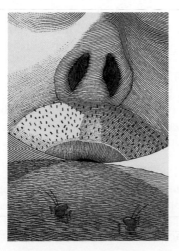

Illustration 6.8
Illustrations in *Two Bad Ants* show the world as seen from an ant's-eye view. (*Two Bad Ants* by Chris Van Allsburg. Copyright © 1988 by Chris Van Allsburg. Reprinted by permission of Houghton Mifflin Company. All rights reserved.)

Perspective

Illustrators use a variety of perspectives to give readers different vantage points from which to view the situation. In Chris Van Allsburg's ***Two Bad Ants,*** two ants decide to stay behind in a kitchen when their fellow ants return to the colony with crystals requested by the queen. The two ants find themselves being scooped out of the bed of crystals into a boiling lake of brown bitter water. Thus begins their dangerous adventure, which moves from coffee cup to toaster to garbage disposal to electrical outlet. Readers watch the ants' adventure from various perspectives—looking down to see the ants on the ground and up to see them on the kitchen counter. When the ants are in the coffee cup being rushed toward the mouth of the coffee drinker, the perspective is from directly behind the ants, and readers see the mouth just as the ants see it. Then the view is from inside the toaster, and the ants are seen sitting on top of the bread crust. The close-up view of the water faucet makes it easy to see why the ants might mistake it for a waterfall.

In Istvan Banyai's *Zoom,* readers first see an up-close picture; with each page turn, the lens is pulled back so that more of the object shows until, finally, the earth is but a speck on the page. The pattern is repeated in *Rezoom.* Readers are challenged to look closely and consider the perspective of the illustration compared to that of the previous page and the page that follows.

Backgrounds

Characters are often identified by the objects that surround them. In William Steig's *The Amazing Bone,* Pearl seems most at home in the spring forest, gently showered by cherry blossoms. In spite of his dapper appearance, the loathsome wolf that accosts her lives in a ramshackle cottage with the screen door hanging from one hinge and trash scattered about the overgrown front yard. His slovenly surroundings indicate an uncaring heart. In *Where the Wild Things Are,* Max's room becomes overgrown with trees and bushes, a signal that wildness is taking hold of him.

In *A New Coat for Anna,* written by Harriet Ziefert and illustrated by Anita Lobel, piles of urban wreckage, peopled by maimed veterans with palms outstretched, dramatize the state of want, sadness, and shock in which Anna and her mother are living. The wilderness that surrounds Sylvester-turned-rock, in William Steig's *Sylvester and the Magic Pebble,* conveys his terrible state of loneliness and isolation—a state that will surely last forever unless he finds some spectacular solution to his problem.

Color

Color is often used to reflect emotions and communicate moods. Both particular colors and their intensity are used to convey a mood to readers. Janice Del Negro's spooky storytelling in *Lucy Dove* is perfectly partnered with Leonid Gore's acrylic paintings. The colors are appropriately dark and somber, reflecting the mood in the eerie graveyard and the scary monster. Even the light in the illustrations casts an unnatural aura.

Arnold Lobel portrays Frog and Toad in greens and browns and uses the same colors for his backgrounds. This reminds readers of the natural camouflage of frogs and toads, whose skins blend into the landscape. The muted colors also prepare readers for plots that are more inwardly directed and thoughtful than overt and active.

James Marshall uses color symbolically even in the seemingly light cartoon-style illustrations of his *Hansel and Gretel.* The sky looming beyond the trees that are disorienting the lost children and behind the witch's gingerbread house is pure black. The illustrations are completely free of this ominous color only when Hansel and Gretel cross the lake on a duck's back and arrive at home, where their father waits.

An especially skillful use of color is found in Anita Lobel's illustrations for *A New Coat for Anna.* Set in a European city after World War II, the book tells of Anna's mother, apparently widowed, who barters family heirlooms to a shepherd, a weaver, a dye maker, and a tailor—each of whom contributes something to making Anna a new coat. The story opens with the drab colors of a city in

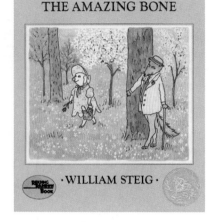

Illustration 6.9
William Steig's *The Amazing Bone* is an example of a book whose characters are firmly defined by place. (Jacket design from *The Amazing Bone* by William Steig. Copyright © 1976 by William Steig. Reprinted by permission of Farrar, Straus and Giroux, LLC.)

ruins, and the drabness is echoed by the bleak expression on the face of Anna's sad, exhausted mother. As each new character enters the story, a bit more color enters, too, until the story culminates in a festive Christmas celebration with greenery and yellow candles and Anna at the center of things in her brand-new bright red coat. By giving up bits of her past and reaching out to others, Anna's mother has created a community, and she and her new friends have brought color and joy back into each other's lives.

Even though the most obvious difference between children's books of the early twentieth century and those of the present is the quality and quantity of color used, black and white still remains a viable, and at times preferred, alternative for book illustrations. Black-and-white illustrations communicate mood primarily through the intensity of black tones used in shading, the boldness of lines, and the placement of the illustration against the amount of white space. Cross-hatching, or crisscrossing of lines, can add texture and depth. Wanda Gág used black-and-white pen-and-ink drawings in her first book, *Millions of Cats.* In some of his books, Chris Van Allsburg used a soft Conté pencil and pencil dust to create books that are entirely black and white; *The Garden of Abdul Gasazi, The Mysteries of Harris Burdick,* and *Jumanji* all won awards. John Steptoe used black-and-white pencil drawings in *The Story of Jumping Mouse: A Native American Legend,* which was named a 1985 Caldecott Honor Book.

Picture/Text Relationships

If the relationship between the illustrations and the text is handled skillfully, the illustrations support the text, but not in a completely predictable way. Children will be more actively engaged if part of the meaning of the story is left for them to infer from the illustrations.

In *Where the Wild Things Are,* the hand drawing of a Wild Thing "by Max" on the wall is a clue to the observant reader that the wild things Max

Illustration 6.11
Readers of *Officer Buckle and Gloria* must observe the illustrations to catch the humor in the story, which is not told through text alone.
(Officer Buckle and Gloria by Peggy Rathmann. Text and illustration copyright © 1995 by Peggy Rathmann. Used by permission of G. P. Putnam's Sons, a division of Penguin Putnam Inc.)

encounters have been created out of his imagination. In the same vein, in Harry Allard's *Miss Nelson Is Missing!,* artist James Marshall drew a box marked "wig" in upside-down letters next to an ugly black dress in the open closet next to Miss Nelson's bed. Observant readers will pick up this clue to the mystery of the disappearance of Miss Viola Swamp, Miss Nelson's harsh alter ego.

Author and illustrator Susan Meddaugh blurs the line between her two roles to produce interesting picture-text relationships in her recent works. In **Martha Speaks,** Meddaugh tells the story of a family dog that gains the gift of speech after eating alphabet soup. Martha, the suddenly loquacious dog, spews language all over the page. The reader soon tires of reading it all, just as the family tires of hearing it. Meanwhile, the text of the story proceeds in the print at the bottom of the page. In **Hog-Eye,** a story about a little pig that outwits a mean but illiterate wolf, the pig pretends to read from a book of magic spells. Those who can read can see what the hapless wolf cannot: The pig is reading from a tome entitled *Getting to Know Your Carburetor.*

The 1996 Caldecott Medal winner, **Officer Buckle and Gloria** by Peggy Rathmann, tells of a police officer who makes tiresome speeches about home and school safety. Interest in his presentations suddenly increases a hundredfold when he begins to take a police dog, Gloria, with him. Because Gloria stands just behind him, Officer Buckle doesn't see that the dog is pantomiming and generally cutting up while he gives his otherwise boring speech. The text doesn't mention Gloria's antics, either. We readers are in on a secret that Officer Buckle doesn't know, because we are informed by the pictures as well as the text. The most telling picture of all is the one in which Officer Buckle discovers, by way of television, what Gloria has been up to. In addition to depicting Officer Buckle's reaction and Gloria's response, the picture includes the large mirror that hangs on the wall behind the couch, which allows the reader to see what is showing on the television screen.

Illustration 6.12
In this picture, Officer Buckle discovers (via his television screen) what the reader already knew—that Gloria has been cutting up through all his safety presentations.
(Officer Buckle and Gloria by Peggy Rathmann. Text and illustration copyright © 1995 by Peggy Rathmann. Used by permission of G. P. Putnam's Sons, a division of Penguin Putnam Inc.)

That night, Officer Buckle watched himself on the 10 o'clock news.

APPRECIATING THE ARTISTIC CRAFT OF THE PICTURE BOOK

The illustrations in picture books for children have become increasingly sophisticated over the years as the picture book has developed. In addition, changes in printing technology have made it possible to reproduce a much greater range of artwork. This section focuses on two aspects of art in picture books: elements of design and artistic media.

Elements of Design

Artists rely on various elements of design to communicate with their audience. When artwork is done well, the reader can enjoy the aesthetics of the illustrations and appreciate the emotions conveyed through the manipulation of artistic elements. The elements of design are line, color, light, shape, and texture. The combination of line, color, light, shape, and texture is called composition.

Let's examine one book in some depth and look at the use of these elements. In *The Paperboy,* Dav Pilkey presents the story of a paperboy's morning. As the story begins, the paperboy is asleep in his bed; readers see him rising, eating breakfast, folding papers, delivering on his route, returning home, and getting back into bed for some "time for dreaming." Throughout all of this, he is accompanied by his dog.

Line. Lines can be thin and light or heavy and bold; they can be straight, jagged, or curved. Line is used effectively in *The Paperboy* to create the rolling shapes of the hills in the background, which give a sense of long distances. Line also conveys the sense of fast movement when the paperboy and his dog are returning home: The dog's tail is horizontal, and the paperboy's empty bag is flying behind him.

Color. Color can range over the full spectrum, or it can be limited to a defined range—for example, black and white and the various shades of gray in between. One instance of dramatic use of color in *The Paperboy* is the single beam of the yellow headlight from the paperboy's bicycle, seen against the dark colors of the neighborhood before dawn.

Illustration 6.13
The author used line effectively in *The Paperboy* to convey the impression of depth and movement. (*The Paperboy* by Dav Pilkey. Published by Orchard Books, an imprint of Scholastic Inc. Copyright © 1996 by Dav Pilkey. Reprinted by permission.)

And when the paperboy has delivered his last newspaper, he and his dog race home.

And his empty red bag flaps behind him in the cold morning air.

Illustration 6.14
In this illustration, Pilkey has a nightlight create the small amount of light in the hallway, signifying the darkness of the early morning hour. (*The Paperboy* by Dav Pilkey. Published by Orchard Books, an imprint of Scholastic Inc. Copyright © 1996 by Dav Pilkey. Reprinted by permission.)

Light. Pilkey uses light to show the time of day in *The Paperboy*. When the lamp beside the boy's bed is turned on, his room lights up, but it is dark outside. Only a nightlight gives light in the hallway when the paperboy is getting up in the morning. By the time he returns from his route, though, light is peeking from underneath his parents' door, and the light in his sister's room can be seen beyond the doorway.

Shape. Shape is created when spaces are contained by a combination of lines. The triangular roof, the side-by-side arrangement of the rectangular doors in the hallway, the two square windows in the kitchen, and the big rectangular work table in the garage all combine with the center gutter of the book to give the house in *The Paperboy* a symmetrical feel—one that creates a sense of solid security in the paperboy's home. In the opening double-page spread, the predictable shapes of the houses give a sense of a solid community life. The rolling

Illustration 6.15
Through lines and shading, Pilkey gives texture to the wood boards of the ceiling and floor. (*The Paperboy* by Dav Pilkey. Published by Orchard Books, an imprint of Scholastic Inc. Copyright © 1996 by Dav Pilkey. Reprinted by permission.)

shapes of the land separate the houses and give a sense of distance between them, even though they are painted close together on the page. The sense of distance and spaciousness leads the reader to think that this is more a rural area than an urban one.

Texture. Texture is the illusion of a tactile surface created in an illustration. In *The Paperboy,* texture in the wood boards of the ceiling and floor is created through the use of lines and shading. The shading of the trees also contributes texture.

Artistic Media

The artists who create picture books rely on a number of media to express their visions of the stories. Some illustrators use a "signature" medium almost exclusively; others select different media depending on how they want to express their view of the particular story. The examples in this section vary from informational books to various genres of fiction and are not necessarily picture storybooks.

Painting: Watercolor, Gouache, Oil, and Other Paints. More children's books are illustrated with watercolor than with any other medium. Watercolors allow illustrators to convey many emotions. Watercolor paintings can be solidly intense or watery and fluid-looking, depending on the amount of water used. Gouache is a type of watercolor paint that contains an added white powder to create a more opaque finished product. Artists who desire an opaque look may also use acrylic paints or oil paints.

Allen Say is a noted illustrator who works in watercolor. In his Caldecott-winning book *Grandfather's Journey,* Say tells the story of how his grandfather left Japan and made the United States his home. When the grandfather visited Japan years later, World War II prohibited him from returning to the United States. Now his grandson has followed in his path and says, "The funny thing is, the moment I am in one country, I am homesick for the other." The natural beauty of each country is depicted in watercolor views of ocean, mountains, and greenery. The prequel to this story is Say's *Tree of Cranes.*

Frané Lessac uses gouache to create vividly colorful images of the Caribbean Islands in many books, such as *The Chalk Doll* by Charlotte Pomerantz, in which a mother reminisces about a childhood in Jamaica. In *Caribbean Alphabet,* she uses the alphabet to list unique qualities of the islands—for example, breadfruit, hibiscus, reggae, and steel bands. In Susan Guevara's illustrations in acrylic paint on scratchboard for Gary Soto's *Chato and the Party Animals,* readers see the lines that mark the movement of the paint brush. These marks, and the heavy use of color, add to the vibrancy and energy of the book.

Thomas Locker characteristically uses oil paintings that give viewers a sense of wide landscapes, such as those in Lenny Hort's *The Boy Who Held Back the Sea.* Paul Zelinsky's *Rumpelstiltskin* is also rendered in oil paint, an appropriate medium to complement the medieval setting. Floyd Cooper employs a variation on

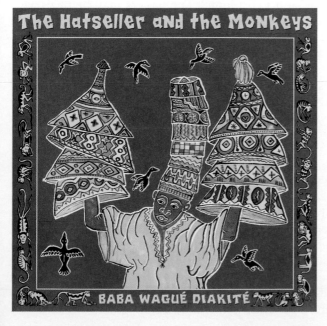

Illustration 6.16
The illustrations for this delightful West African story are painted on ceramic tiles. (*The Hatseller and the Monkeys* by Baba Wagué Diakité. Published by Scholastic Press, a division of Scholastic Inc. Copyright © 1998. Reprinted by permission.)

Illustration 6.17
The pastel hues of Gammell's colored pencils add to the sense of family intimacy as a grandfather re-creates for his grandchildren his days in vaudeville. (*Song and Dance Man* by Karen Ackerman. Cover illustration copyright © 1988 by Stephen Gammell. Used by permission of Alfred A. Knopf Children's Books, a division of Random House, Inc.)

Illustration 6.18
In illustrating *Scary Stories to Tell in the Dark*, Stephen Gammell used black-and-white pencil drawings to create a mood of impending peril. (*Scary Stories to Tell in the Dark* by Alvin Schwartz, illustrated by Stephen Gammell. Copyright © 1987. Used by permission of HarperCollins Children's Books, a division of HarperCollins Publishers.)

oil painting in which he applies a very thin layer of paint to a surface and, when it dries, creates areas of light by using an eraser; he then adds color at the end. He used this technique to create the illustrations in *I Have Heard of a Land* by Joyce Carol Thomas, as well as in all of his other works.

Some illustrators paint on surfaces other than paper. Baba Wagué Diakité's *The Hatseller and the Monkeys*, a West African story about monkeys who steal hats from a hatseller while he naps, is painted on ceramic tiles. Paul Zelinsky's illustrations in the Caldecott Honor Book *Swamp Angel* by Anne Isaacs were painted on wood veneers.

Pencil Drawing. Stephen Gammell uses pencils to convey a range of emotions, from the happy, nostalgic feel of Karen Ackerman's *Song and Dance Man* to the sinister, gory tone of Alvin Schwartz's *Scary Stories* series. Pencils can be used to create strong lines, shaded areas, smudged shadows, and fine details. Readers sense the warmth of relationships in various books depicting family events, illustrated by Gammell with colored pencils. For instance, in *Song and Dance Man,* pastel hues against the white background give a soft glow to the attic in which the grandfather and his grandchildren share a moment from the past, as the grandfather dances and reminisces about the time when he was a song and dance man. Few areas are solidly shaded; rather, visible lines help guide the reader's eyes to areas of focus and give dimension to objects. Gammell's work in *Scary Stories to Tell in the Dark,* by Alvin Schwartz, seems a far cry from that in *Song and Dance Man,* even though both are pencil illustrations. In the *Scary Stories* book, the black-and-white images have unfinished lines, supporting the sense of the haunted as being unpredictably present and only partially visible. Even without color, we can clearly visualize the blood dripping. The jagged lines create feelings of horror. Gammell shows the range of artistic expression possible with one medium.

Paper Crafts: Collage, Papermaking, Cut Paper. Various forms of paper crafts are used by illustrators of children's books. The most commonly used form is collage, in which, traditionally, various types of paper are cut or torn and pieced together onto a background to create a picture, as in the art of Ezra Jack Keats, Eric Carle, and Leo Lionni. The papers may be of varying weights and colors—anything from gift wrap to wallpaper to handmade paper. To create the art for *Saint Valentine,* Robert Sabuda cut marbleized and hand-made paper into tiny squares and created a mosaic for each illustration, using over a thousand paper bits for each full-page illustration. To create the art for *Wings,* Christopher Myers used magazine pictures, paper of varying types, and even paper that presumably comes from an envelope on which the U.S. Post Office had printed the coding for mail. Holly Meade was inspired by Thai art forms to create the collage work in *Hush!,* by Minfong Ho, a lullaby story set in Thailand.

Illustrator Denise Fleming creates vibrant illustrations by making a sheet of handmade paper for each illustration. She makes a pulp out of cotton rag fiber and water, adds color, and spreads the pulp out on a framed wire screen to create a background. The framed screen allows the excess water to drip out. Using plastic squeeze bottles filled with colored pulp, she pours shapes on the background or fills in her hand-cut stencils. For *Barnyard Banter,* she added various items such as hair from her horse's mane to create interesting dimensions and textures; pieces of burlap potato sacks became part of a wire pen for peacocks, and coffee grounds helped to create the image of soil. The completed piece is dried through a special process. Fleming's book *In the Small, Small Pond* was named a

Illustration 6.19
Illustrator Robert Sabuda created Chinese-style paper-cut art to give each triple spread in this book a scroll-like effect. (*The Paper Dragon* by Marguerite W. Davol, illustrated by Robert Sabuda. Text copyright © 1997 by Margaret W. Davol. Illustrations copyright © 1997 by Robert Sabuda. Used by permission of Atheneum Books for Young Readers, an imprint of Simon & Schuster Children's Publishing.)

Caldecott Honor Book. The illustrations show the creatures of a small pond in their daily environment. Fleming captures their movements and activities with alliterative and rhyming phrases—for example, "lash, lunge, herons plunge" and "sweep, swoop, swallows scoop."

David Wisniewski used cut paper to create the illustrations for his 1997 Caldecott Medal winner, **The Golem,** as well as for his other books. He uses an X-Acto knife to cut intricate designs and layers pieces to achieve a three-dimensional effect. Robert Sabuda created the art for **The Paper Dragon,** by Marguerite W. Davol, in the style of Chinese paper-cut art by making precise and detailed cuts in tissue paper he painted. Each illustration is three pages long; the double spreads have a page that folds out, thereby creating a scroll-like effect.

Three-Dimensional Art. As book production technology advanced, the possibilities of artistic media became much less limited. In recent times, there has been an increase in the use of three-dimensional art.

Many illustrators do not limit themselves to paper when creating collages but employ a wide range of materials, including three-dimensional objects. For his 1995 Caldecott-winning book **Smoky Night,** written by Eve Bunting, David Diaz used matches, plastic bags, hangers, cereal, bubble wrap, and shoe soles, in addition to a variety of papers, to create collage backgrounds to frame his acrylic paintings and the text in this book depicting the 1992 Los Angeles riots. Lois Ehlert's *Snowballs* shows a family of snowpeople—complete with dog and cat—created with birdseed, a knit hat, seashells, a compass, a cinnamon stick, a pinecone, luggage claim checks, plastic forks, and toy fish, among other things. In another collage book, **Red Leaf, Yellow Leaf,** about a sugar maple tree, Ehlert used a kite, twine, ribbon, birdseed, burlap, twigs, and roots to create the illustrations.

In Joan Steiner's **Look-Alikes,** the double spreads look, at first glance, like scenes such as a train station, a playground, or a street. Closer inspection reveals that the picture is made entirely by using real objects to create a world of miniature scale; cinnamon sticks serve as logs, and a razor blade is converted into a vacuum cleaner. Her second book is entitled **Look-Alikes Jr.: Find More Than 700 Hidden Everyday Objects.**

Illustration 6.20
Using three-dimensional art for the illustrations in *Look Alikes,* Joan Steiner creates a world of miniature scale from real objects. [*Look Alikes* by Joan Steiner. Copyright © 1998 by Joan Steiner. By permission of Little, Brown and Company (Inc.).]

Illustration 6.21
Woodcut is the medium Keizaburo Tejima uses to create the images of nature in all of his books. (*Swan Sky* by Keizaburo Tejima. New York: Philomel Books, 1983.)

Scratchboard. Brian Pinkney is known for using scratchboard as his signature medium. Scratchboard pictures are created by using sharp instruments to scratch away the top surface of a board, leaving precise lines on the surface. Pinkney believes that his passion for carving and painting come together in scratchboard: He both carves the pictures and paints them when creating his book illustrations. For Robert D. San Souci's *Sukey and the Mermaid,* the story of how Sukey's luck changes when she meets a black mermaid, Pinkney created a black-and-white scratchboard. A photographic technique made it possible for him to add color to a print of the original scratchboard piece to produce the finished product. He used a similar technique to illustrate *Duke Ellington: The Piano Prince and His Orchestra,* by Andrea Davis Pinkney, but with a vivid use of colors to give a more painted effect.

Woodcut. Woodcut illustrations were particularly common in books of the past but are still used today. Marcia Brown's *Once a Mouse,* rendered in woodcut, was awarded the 1962 Caldecott Medal. Ed Emberley used woodcuts to illustrate Barbara Emberley's *Drummer Hoff,* which won a Caldecott Medal in 1968. Gail E. Haley's *A Story, a Story,* the 1971 Caldecott winner, has illustrations carved on wood blocks. Keizaburo Tejima gives readers a sense of connection to the natural world through his woodcuts in *Swan Sky,* which tells the story of the migration of swans. One year, a swan, ill and unable to go to the summer home, is left behind by her family. The woodcut illustrations fully use the natural effect of the wood grain to illustrate the ripples in the lake, the reflections of the mountains, and the feathers of the swans. More recently, Barry Moser used a synthetic wood engraving medium to create the illustrations for Madeline Moser's *Ever Heard of an Aardwolf?* The images were printed in black and white, laser-scanned and enlarged, then hand-colored with watercolors.

Photography. Several children's book illustrators use photography to create visual images. Tana Hoban and Bruce McMillan have created many books with photographs that communicate basic concepts to young children. In *Shapes, Shapes, Shapes,* Hoban's photographs of scenes and objects that children see in their environment exemplify the concepts of various shapes. In McMillan's *Counting Wildflowers,* readers are presented with a numeral, the number word, and a photograph of the corresponding number of wildflowers. George Ancona relies on photographs in books such as *Carnaval* to lend an air of immediacy to stories focused on particular groups of people and their celebration. Walter Dean Myers collected old photographs for *Brown Angels: An Album of Pictures and Verse* and for *Glorious Angels: A Celebration of Children.* The photographs provided the impetus for poetry; he created the poetry while imagining the lives of the people the photographs portrayed. In all of the books just described, the illustrator is the photographer, and photography itself is the art form. Photography has also been used to capture images of original three-dimensional art; in such cases, photography serves as the vehicle for exhibiting the original art. One example is the cut-paper art that David Wiesnewski creates for his books and then has photographed by a professional. The photographer gets name credit for his role in bringing the original images to the book form, but it is Wiesnewski who is considered the illustrator.

Computer-Generated Art. Among those generating art on the computer are many newcomers to the field of book illustrating, along with veteran illustrators who are trying a new medium. J. Otto Siebold illustrated the *Mr. Lunch* books entirely with computer-generated art. Nina Crews created *You Are Here* by taking original photographs and manipulating them digitally on the computer to create a collage. In the book, two sisters embark on a magical journey, shrinking small enough to ride a toy airplane throughout their dining room. The computer allowed Crews to adjust the proportions of the objects she had photographed so that readers could see how the sisters could ride a toy airplane and call a cat a "monster." Veteran illustrators Don Wood and Audrey Wood gave up their paintbrushes and turned completely to their computers to create drawings for their books *Bright and Early Thursday Evening: A Tangled Tale* and *The Red Racer.* Janet Stevens relies on a computer to embellish her art in *Cook-a-Doodle-Doo,* a humorous twist on the "Little Red Hen" story. Along the

Illustration 6.22
The computer graphics for this tale were created using Adobe Photoshop software. (*Henny-Penny* by Jane Wattenberg. Published by Scholastic Press, a division of Scholastic Inc. Copyright © 2000 by Jane Wattenberg. Reprinted by permission.)

sidebars that border the main story, cooking tips are included. Her detailed explanation can be found at her website. Jane Wattenberg's *Henny-Penny* was created by using Adobe Photoshop. Wattenberg photographed her own fowls and then manipulated the images on the computer to create her photo-compositions. For *Rolie Polie Olie,* William Joyce imaginatively rendered the scene of this science fiction story using computer-generated images that have a three-dimensional effect.

Mixed Media. Illustrators often combine different media in creating their work. Many illustrators combine pen and ink with watercolor washes. Patricia Polacco uses pencil to create initial sketches and then finishes them with watercolors, but the original pencil markings are often visible as part of the final product. Eric Carle paints on his tissue papers and pencils in details on his collages. Ruth Heller combines a large number of media—magic markers, paints, colored pencils, and others. In his 2000 Caldecott-winning book, *Joseph Had a Little Overcoat,* Simms Taback used watercolor, gouache, pencil, ink, and collages—of photographs of people, handmade paper, and pictures of textured items like braided rugs and sweaters. For Arnold Adoff's *Love Letters,* Lisa Desimini used photographs, sculptured models, oil paint, collages of three-dimensional objects, and computer graphics.

CREATORS OF PICTURE BOOKS

Space limitations make it impossible to give a biographical sketch of every important picture book author or illustrator. We have chosen to highlight only a few; many others are mentioned in earlier discussions in this chapter, and still others are included as featured authors and illustrators in other chapters.

Mitsumasa Anno

Mitsumasa Anno, a Japanese author and illustrator, is a world-renowned contributor to the picture book field. He is best known for his wordless "journey" books, mathematical game books, and books with playful twists of visual perceptions. Anno's highly detailed and imaginative work appeals to all ages because his books offer multiple levels of humor and intrigue. His books combine technical sophistication with creative text, illustrations, and design. Many of his books also include detailed historic, scientific, or mathematical information for adult readers who share these books with children.

Anno delights in including mathematical and scientific details to make learning these ways of thinking enjoyable and interesting. In *Anno's Counting House,* the reader first sees all ten children living in the house on the left side of the double-page spread, and then watches them move into the house on the right one by one. Children can see who has moved and what belongings the child has taken, but they can also note that the total number of children shown in both houses is always ten.

Anno also manipulates visual perception in a way that makes the physically impossible seem probable. For example, *Upside-Downers: More Pictures to Stretch the Imagination* is a book that bends the "rules" for enjoying books. A pair of jokers and the four kings leave a deck of cards, but nobody can tell what's up and what's down. In the author's postscript, Anno suggests that a child can sit opposite a parent and they can read the book to each other at the same time—or a child can read alone, turn the book around, and then read it from the other direction, upside down.

Illustration 6.23
Knowledge of history and popular culture will enable readers to find many interesting details in this double-page picture of New York City by Anno. (*Anno's U.S.A.* by Mitsumasa Anno. Illustration by Mitsumasa Anno. Copyright © 1983 by Kuso-Kobo. Used by permission of Philomel Books, a division of Penguin Putnam Inc.)

Anno's Journey begins a series of books that are filled with images of the countries he visits. Historical events, literary figures, and cultural markers fill the pages of the wordless books simply titled *Anno's U.S.A., Anno's Italy,* and *Anno's Britain.* On the double-page spread depicting New York City in *Anno's U.S.A.,* readers will delight in discovering the surprises embedded in the art: the Macy's Thanksgiving Day Parade with floats representing characters from *Where the Wild Things Are,* Tarzan, and the New York Public Library lions; Marilyn Monroe standing on a street corner with the wind sweeping her skirt up; and Native Americans selling Manhattan island.

Anno was born and raised in a small town in western Japan. He taught art at an elementary school in Tokyo for ten years before becoming a full-time artist. In addition to his numerous picture books, Anno creates many other works of art such as paintings, calendars, and stationery. In 1985, he was awarded the Hans Christian Andersen Award for Illustration, given by the International Board on Books for Young People to honor an illustrator who has made a significant contribution to children's literature worldwide.

Eric Carle

Eric Carle spent his first six years in the United States and has happy memories of kindergarten, freely creating art on large sheets of paper with big brushes and bright colors. However, most of his childhood was spent in his parents'

Illustration 6.24

Eric Carle uses painted tissue-paper collages to tell the story of a hungry caterpillar that eats its way through a host of foods before spinning a cocoon and finally becoming a butterfly. (*The Very Hungry Caterpillar* by Eric Carle. Copyright © 1984. Reprinted by permission of Putnam Publishing Group Juvenile Books, a division of Penguin Putnam Inc.)

homeland, Germany, during World War II. Carle's introduction to the world of children's book illustration came when a pink lobster he had created for an advertising job caught the eye of author Bill Martin, Jr., who solicited Carle's work for a series of books he had written.

Eric Carle's many picture books are immediately recognizable because of his unique painted tissue-paper collages. Perhaps his best known book is *The Very Hungry Caterpillar,* in which a little egg hatches and the hungry caterpillar eats its way through various foods, spins a cocoon, and becomes a butterfly. This lesson on metamorphosis is accompanied by an introduction to numbers and the days of the week. Carle's many toy books, described earlier in this chapter, employ partial pages, holes, cutouts, pop-ups, electronic sound chips, lights, and more. Carle tries to create books that combine heartfelt stories with opportunities for learning and play, and without a doubt, he has succeeded frequently. Among his well-known titles are *The Grouchy Ladybug, The Very Busy Spider,* and *The Very Quiet Cricket.*

Carle has a mission to honor and preserve the creation of picture books and has recently established a museum as a place to examine and celebrate picture books. In addition, his videotape offers viewers an explanation of how he creates his art, and his book *The Art of Eric Carle* offers readers an opportunity to study his works.

Tomie dePaola

Tomie dePaola has illustrated over a hundred books for children. His work is characteristically done in watercolor in a folk art style. His contributions to picture books are appreciated by the many children who have read his wide range of books. Readers have the opportunity to learn much about dePaola's life through his books, for many of his books are autobiographical. DePaola's loving family relationships are the root of his books *Nana Upstairs & Nana Downstairs* and *Now One Foot, Now the Other* and *Tom,* all books that depict an intergenerational affection and bond, as well as a child dealing with the loss brought about by death. His Italian and Irish heritage are the

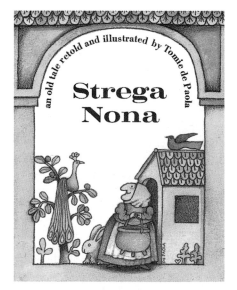

Illustration 6.25

The illustrations in this Caldecott Honor Book are excellent examples of Tomie de Paola's signature watercolor paintings. (*Strega Nona,* by Tomie de Paola. Copyright © 1975 by Tomie de Paola. Used by permission of Simon & Schuster Books for Young Readers, an imprint of Simon & Schuster Children's Publishing.)

source of his interest in those cultures, which several of his books reflect. Perhaps the best known is *Strega Nona,* which was named a Caldecott Honor Book. In it, an Italian "Grandma Witch" with a magical touch leaves her helper, Big Anthony, home alone. Big Anthony seizes this opportunity to prove to the townspeople that Strega Nona's magic pot can cook pasta by itself. He doesn't remember, however, how to get it to stop cooking. The punishment fits the crime: Big Anthony must eat all the pasta!

In *The Art Lesson,* readers learn of Tomie's early interest in art; in fact, by age 4, he knew that he wanted to be an artist, and he soon knew that he would create picture books. After his years at

Pratt Institute of Art, dePaola entered a Benedictine monastery. This period of his life influenced the eventual creation of a number of books with religious stories or themes.

Books published in the early 1970s, such as *The Cloud Book, Charlie Needs a Cloak,* and *The Popcorn Book,* made Tomie dePaola a leader in writing informational books—books with the intent of offering information to children—that were set to a story. After years of creating picture books, dePaola has now turned to writing chapter books. The first in his autobiographical series, *26 Fairmount Avenue,* was named a 2000 Newbery Honor Book. Published in the same year, Barbara Elleman's comprehensive biography, *Tomie dePaola: His Art & His Stories,* offers readers an in-depth look at the life and work of this popular author and illustrator. The series continues with *Here We All Are* and *On My Own.*

Leo and Diane Dillon

The artwork created by Leo and Diane Dillon is unique in that each piece is truly a work of collaboration, so much so that neither artist can identify who contributed which part to a finished product. They speak of a "third artist" who is a combination of both of them yet different from each as individuals. The Dillons attribute their collaborative ability to their control of artistic techniques: They maintain that one of them could begin a line and the other could continue it without detectable interruption.

The first and second children's books the Dillons illustrated earned them the distinction of being the first (and only, so far) to receive the Caldecott Medal in two consecutive years. Verna Aardema's *Why Mosquitoes Buzz in People's Ears: A West African Tale,* told in cumulative verse format, has various animals passing along different versions of a rumor. For this book, the Dillons interpreted the text with stylized watercolor paintings that were influenced by batik art. Margaret Musgrove's *Ashanti to Zulu: African Traditions* uses an alphabet book format to describe aspects of daily life among the diverse cultures of Africa. For this book, the Dillons created art that was factually accurate as well as elegant and that captured both the commonality and diversity of human experiences.

The Dillons have collaborated on some books with their son, Lee Dillon, a painter and sculptor. Lee and his parents created the artwork for *Pish, Posh, Said Hieronymus Bosch,* a poem by Nancy Willard that describes the influence of the famous painter's imaginative creatures on his housekeeper. Lee carved a frame, incorporating some of these unusual creatures. Leo and Diane's paintings are centered in this frame, giving it the look of a "window" through which readers view the story. *Aida,* by Leontyne Price, is another book on which the three Dillons collaborated. Lee created a metal frame that was used as the border of each page. Leo and Diane's attention to detail is reflected in the design of this book. Of particular interest is their incorporation of marbelized paper and their creation of highly decorative endpapers.

In addition to illustrating picture books, the Dillons have created the art for many book jackets and for longer works of fiction. For the body of their work

Illustration 6.26
Leo and Diane Dillon used stylized watercolor paintings patterned after batik art to illustrate this winner of the Caldecott Medal. (*Why Mosquitoes Buzz in People's Ears* by Verna Aardema, pictures by Leo and Diane Dillon. Copyright © 1987. Used by permission of Dial Books for Young Readers, a division of Penguin Putnam Inc.)

and the lasting contribution they have made to children's books, the U.S. Board of Books for Young People (USBBY) selected Leo and Diane Dillon as the 1996 U.S. nominees for the Hans Christian Andersen Award.

Kevin Henkes

Best known for his books portraying mice in real-life, childlike situations, Kevin Henkes enjoys wide popularity as a picture book author and illustrator. His cartoon-style drawings of mice, done in pen and ink with watercolors, take on personalities of typical children (and adults). Henkes depicts the personalities through facial expressions, the movements of the mice, and the poses they take. The predicaments the mice face—arrival of a new sibling, being teased by classmates, having an imaginary friend—are situations that are familiar to almost everyone.

Illustration 6.27
Using watercolor and pen, Kevin Henkes creates memorable mice characters such as lively Lilly, who loves school—and her teacher.
(*Lilly's Purple Plastic Purse* by Kevin Henkes. Copyright © 1996. Used by permission of Greenwillow, a division of HarperCollins Publishers.)

Henkes's mice characters are memorable: Chrysanthemum, with whom we empathize over the agonies of being teased for her name; Sheila Rae, the bravest girl imaginable, who discovers that she needs her quiet little sister, who has an inner strength that shines in times of distress; Chester and Wilson, who live predictable lives filled with routines and precautions until they encounter Lilly, the self-proclaimed queen, who lives for thrilling moments of adventure. Henkes has both written and illustrated most of his books. Among his many popular titles are *Chrysanthemum; Julius, the Baby of the World; Sheila Rae, the Brave; A Weekend with Wendell;* and *Lilly's Purple Plastic Purse.* In 1994, Henkes's *Owen* was named a Caldecott Honor Book. This book shows how one mouse family deals with a soon-to-be-kindergartener who refuses to give up a security blanket. In *Wemberly Worried,* Henkes portrays the emotions of a child who worries about absolutely everything, real and imagined.

Kevin Henkes is also the author of a number of realistic novels that sensitively deal with serious issues faced by preteens and teens. These titles are discussed in Chapter 8.

Leo Lionni

Leo Lionni started his career as a commercial artist. His career as a children's book author and illustrator began when he told a story to his grandchildren to pass the time while they were traveling together by train. Later published as a book, the story was about two children depicted as colors—blue and yellow—who hug and become green. *Little Blue and Little Yellow* was illustrated with torn-paper collage, which portrayed human emotions abstractly. Lionni continued to write and illustrate many books whose characters embodied concepts important in human relationships.

Inch by Inch, Lionni's second book, was named a Caldecott Honor Book (one of three of his books to win that award). In this story, an inchworm outwits predators and survives by measuring them "inch by inch." For this book, Lionni mixed crayon with collage. In another story of survival, *Swimmy,* a school of fish gathers into a formation resembling a large fish to fend off predators who have eaten Swimmy's family. The combination of sponge printing and watercolor in this book effectively depicts the underwater world.

Leo Lionni has created several books with mice as characters, all done in torn-paper collage style. *Frederick* is particularly well known, both for the artwork and for the story. As a family of mice gathers supplies to prepare for the coming winter, Frederick "stores up" stories and poetry as his contribution.

Jerry Pinkney

Encouraged by support for his early interest in drawing, Jerry Pinkney began his art career with a greeting card company; he later established his own studio to do advertising and textbook illustrating. His wide array of creations includes calendars and postage stamps. Pinkney's entry into picture book illustration in the 1960s and 1970s was timely in that publishers were seeking black artists. Jerry Pinkney's watercolor illustrations are widely recognized for their natural reflection of people, animals, and the world in which they live. As he paints, he relies on models for inspiration and reference, often using family members. Along with other family members, he even dressed up and posed as an animal when illustrating Julius Lester's book *The Tales of Uncle Remus.* He takes particular pride in his devotion to illustrating African Americans, which has been recognized through his three Coretta Scott King Awards: in 1986 for Valerie Flournoy's *The Patchwork Quilt,* in 1987 for Crescent Dragonwagon's *Half a Moon and One Whole Star,* and again in 1988 for Patricia McKissack's *Mirandy and Brother Wind.* He also has four Caldecott Honor Books: *The Talking Eggs: A Folktale from the American South* by Robert San Souci, *Mirandy and Brother Wind, John Henry* by Julius Lester, and *The Ugly Duckling.*

Pinkney's goal of serving as an inspiration to his own family and to other African Americans has clearly been realized. Jerry's wife, Gloria Jean Pinkney, has authored picture books such as *The Sunday Outing;* Jerry's son Brian Pinkney is a highly acclaimed illustrator, who has worked in collaboration with his wife, Andrea Davis Pinkney, on such works as *Duke Ellington: The Piano Prince;* and Jerry's son Myles has used his talent in photography to illustrate books of poetry such as Nikki Grimes's *It's Raining Laughter* and Sandra Pinkney's *Shades of Black.*

Maurice Sendak

Maurice Sendak spent many of his childhood years sick in bed, reading comics, drawing, writing stories, and imagining the lives of the people in the houses in his neighborhood. From this beginning came a career devoted to the arts. Sendak is known for creating characters who are imaginative, strong-willed, and clever. In 1962, Sendak created *The Nutshell Library,* a set of four two-by-four-inch books: *Chicken Soup with Rice: A Book of Months, One Was Johnny: A Counting Book, Alligators All Around: An Alphabet,* and *Pierre: A Cautionary Tale.* These stories remain popular today.

The publication of *Where the Wild Things Are* in 1963 brought much attention. Many adults feared that the Wild Things were too frightening for young children, but others applauded the central character's ability to deal with the strong emotions children face. The book was honored with the 1964 Caldecott Medal and remains one of the most popular and best known picture books for children.

Other Sendak books have also been the subject of controversy. When *In the Night Kitchen* was published in 1970, it was criticized for the nudity of the central character and for the use of cartoon-style illustration. Some found the portrayal of babies' experiences in *Outside Over There* disturbing. Both books arose out of Sendak's own experiences, and he believes that they are personally significant. More recently, *We Are All in the Dumps with Jack and Guy* has disturbed some readers with its portrayal of homelessness.

In 1966, Maurice Sendak was the first American to be a recipient of the International Board on Books for Young People's Hans Christian Andersen

Ask the Author and Illustrator...

Jon Scieszka and Lane Smith

How do you come up with such imaginative and unique books?

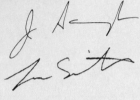

I would love to describe how I get up before dawn every day, light my special candle of inspiration, and sit down to write for twelve hours. But I never do that. Then I could say I sit in a little shed and write on an old board I put across my lap, but Roald Dahl already said that. Maybe I used to work at an ad agency and someone challenged me to write a book for kids using only 100 different words. Nah. That was Dr. Seuss.

I don't know. Lane, how do we come up with such imaginative and unique books?

"I get up before dawn every day, light my special candle of inspiration, and sit down to paint and draw for twelve hours."

You do not.

"I go out to my little shed and draw on an old board I put across my lap?"

No.

"I used to work in an ad agency . . ."

Thanks for your help, Dr. Seuss.

I've never really given much thought to how we put our books together. I do the writing thing just like most other authors—writing, rewriting, reading the stuff to kids and teachers, then rewriting some more. And Lane does the sketching, painting, and repainting thing like most other illustrators.

Favorite Books as a Child

(Scieszka)	(Smith)
Green Eggs and Ham by Dr. Seuss	*The Carrot Seed* by Crockett Johnson
Grimms' Fairy Tales	*Treehorn × 3* by Florence Parry Heide, illustrated by E. Gorey
The Carrot Seed by Crockett Johnson	*How the Grinch Stole Christmas* by Dr. Seuss

---

Award. Since then, Sendak has stretched his artistic contributions beyond picture books. In addition to illustrating books, Sendak creates sets and costumes for children's theater, often based on his own books.

William Steig

William Steig is an illustrator and author whose accomplishments in both areas are laudable. Steig began his first career as a freelance artist, most notably as a cartoonist for *The New Yorker*. Steig's entry into the children's book field came at the age of sixty, at the instigation of a colleague at *The New Yorker*, children's book author Robert Kraus. His first book was *C D B!*, a book of word games. Only a year later, **Sylvester and the Magic Pebble** brought him recognition as a highly talented creator of children's books, as it won numerous awards,

But, now that I think of it, we do have two secret ingredients that set us apart from those other Brand X books.

One, Lane and I are friends and work together. After I get a story to where I like it, I give it to Lane. He thinks about it, fools around with different ways to illustrate it; then we talk and goof around with changes in both the writing and the illustration to fit the new ideas. A lot of authors and illustrators never get this chance to work together.

Two, we have a secret weapon—our designer Molly Leach (who also happens to be Lane's wife and my wife's best friend and part of the reason Lane and I met and started working together and . . . that's a whole other story). As the designer, Molly is the one who takes the text and the illustrations and decides how to weave them together and present them on the page so everything works together.

So in *The Stinky Cheese Man,* it was Molly who came up with the idea to have the type grow and shrink to fit the page. And when Jack was telling his story endlessly over and over and over, I thought it would be funny if the text just ran off the page. Molly showed us how it would look better if the type got smaller and smaller.

For a book like *Math Curse,* the story stayed pretty close to the early finished draft. Lane came up with the idea to show the narrator under the spell of the curse. And we left it up to Molly to figure out how to cram all of the words, problems, and paintings into a picture book that looked kind of like a math book but not so ugly or so much like a math book that it would scare all of our readers away.

Our books look unique because we get to work in a unique way. Three people collaborate on getting the text, the illustration, and the design working to tell one story.

So, in conclusion, Lane and I make our imaginative and unique books by getting up before dawn every day, sitting in a little shed, working for an ad agency, and thanking our lucky stars that we get to work together and with Ace Designer, Molly Leach.

Illustration 6.28
Jon Scieszka's humorous text in *Math Curse* is amplified through Lane Smith's illustrations and through the book's design. (*Math Curse* by Jon Scieszka, illustrated by Lane Smith. Copyright © 1995. Used by permission of Viking Children's Books, a division of Penguin Putnam Inc.)

Jon Scieszka is the author of The True Story of the 3 Little Pigs!; The Frog Prince, Continued; The Stinky Cheese Man and Other Fairly Stupid Tales; The Book That Jack Wrote; Math Curse; *and the* Time Warp Trio *series. He's a lumberjack in his spare time. He once climbed Mount Everest in his bare feet. And he enjoys potato chips and making up lies. Lane Smith's bio is exactly the same as Jon's, except a couple of the book titles are different.*

including the 1970 Caldecott Medal. It is the story of a donkey whose parents miss him after he is turned into a rock. *The Amazing Bone* was a 1977 Caldecott Honor Book. The magical powers of the amazing bone save Pearl the Pig from being gobbled up by the wolf. Steig's Newbery Honor Books are *Abel's Island,* in 1977, and a picture book, *Doctor De Soto,* in 1983. In *Doctor De Soto,* a mouse dentist is asked to remove a bothersome tooth from a fox patient, leading readers to ponder who the clever one is in this story. Steig's signature cartoon style uses anthropomorphized animals to tell humorous tales of moral behavior. Magical happenings are taken in stride as wondrous but believable events in daily life. *Pete's a Pizza* features a human child who is saddened to see the rain alter his outdoor plans; his parents good-naturedly play with him indoors, pretending to make him into a pizza.

Ask the Illustrator... *Robert Sabuda*

Robert Sabuda

What challenges do you face in changing the artistic medium with every book you create?

One of the greatest thrills that comes with being a grownup children's book artist is that you can do whatever you want (without having your mother yelling in the background for you to "clean up that mess RIGHT *NOW!*"). I can choose to draw, paint, cut, paste, or create batik from boiling vats of hot wax. (Don't let anyone tell you that working in children's books isn't, at times, thrillingly dangerous.)

But having all of these possibilities open to an artist can at times seem daunting. Which technique is the right one? How can it complement the story without overwhelming it? Can I learn a new technique if I don't already know it? Why did I say I could do this? How did I fake my way into this field? Shouldn't I clean up this mess RIGHT *NOW*?!

As you can see, working in a variety of techniques is fraught with questions, usually extremely painful ones that deal with insecurity and a desire for your publisher to remain interested in your work.

It does, however, have its rewards. Working with differ-ent techniques allows one to grow and evolve artistically. Just as a plant gets tired of sitting in the same old soil (you have to add things, like manure, to keep the plant interested, I think), the artist must examine his creative setting and spice it up a bit. When you grow up during the frighteningly diverse period of video games and music television, the thought of doing the same exact thing over and over is a recipe for death by boredom.

So I always strive to create something new to keep me eager and interested in my own work. (Boy, it's all about me, me, me, isn't it?) As scary as it sometimes is to face a blank piece of paper or canvas or cloth or carefully pulled bark from the rare, endangered and highly toxic Michigan Albino tree, I wouldn't give it up for the world.

Just as long as I still don't have to clean up the mess.

> ### Favorite Books as a Child
>
> The *Frog and Toad* Series by Arnold Lobel
>
> The *Nancy Drew Mystery* Series by Carolyn Keene

Robert Sabuda, a current resident of New York City, grew up in Pinckney, Michigan. He attended Pratt Art Institute in New York and is the author, illustrator, and paper engineer of many award-winning books for young readers. His titles include Tutankhamen's Gift, *a New York Times Best Book of the Year, and* The Paper Dragon, *an ALA Notable Book. He is also a four-time medalist of the Dimensional Illustrators Awards Show for such pop-up titles as* Christmas Alphabet *and* Cookie Count!

Steig's illustrations have a doodling quality to them; they show movement and spontaneity in their lines. For the totality of his contribution to children's literature worldwide, William Steig was designated a U.S. nominee for the Hans Christian Andersen Award in both the illustration category and the writing category.

Chris Van Allsburg

Chris Van Allsburg's first book, *The Garden of Abdul Gasazi,* was published in 1979 and was a 1980 Caldecott Honor Book. Within a few years, he had achieved notoriety as a remarkable creator of picture books and won two Caldecott Medals. The first was in 1982 for his second book, *Jumanji.* This jungle adventure story is about two children playing a board game in which landing on particular squares has real consequences: Lions roar, monkeys create havoc, rhinos stampede, and a volcano erupts. The second Caldecott Medal was awarded in 1986 for *The Polar Express,* in which children board a late-night "polar express" train and visit Santa at the North Pole. The book quickly became established as a Christmas classic, especially popular among adult readers reminiscing on their childhoods.

Van Allsburg's early work was done in black pencil, but his later works are full-color paintings. Stories like *The Wreck of the Zephyr* cross between reality and fantasy in ways that make fantasy believable and reality questionable; the illustrations have similar effects. One of his books that requires readers to let their imaginations fill in the unknown is *The Mysteries of Harris Burdick.* It takes the form of a portfolio of paintings, each with only a title and a caption. Readers are to imagine the story behind each painting. Perhaps the appeal of Van Allsburg's books for children and adults alike lies in this lack of distinction between reality and fantasy—and in the subtlety of the interpretations allowed by his highly imaginative work.

More recently, Van Allsburg has created picture books with a social message. *Just a Dream* raises the issue of what happens when people don't take care of their environment. Walter abuses the environment until a nightmare reveals what his future will be like. Walter's attitude and behavior toward the environment make a complete turnaround when he awakes. Readers find a cautionary tale in *The Sweetest Fig,* in which Monsieur Bibot is given two figs in payment for extracting a tooth—figs that can make his dream come true. An unexpected turn of events leaves readers pondering after they close the book, "How will Monsieur Bibot's treatment of his dog and of others repay him in the future?"

Rosemary Wells

Rosemary Wells creates humorous stories about animals who are caught in situations and relationships much like those in which children find themselves with their friends and siblings. She cites events in her own and her children's lives as the models for many of her situations. Wells believes that her animal characters are able to convey deeply felt emotions that are familiar to children and adults alike. In many of her books, the succinct dialogue is supplemented by a narrator's voice that offers humorous explanations of what thoughts are going through the characters' heads and what the characters are doing.

Perhaps the best known of Wells's works are her stories about Max and Ruby, rabbit siblings. The interactions between little brother Max and big sister Ruby reflect ways in which human siblings often interact. In a board book series about this brother-sister pair, readers find Ruby giving instructions that Max pretends not to understand; the humor comes from Ruby's exasperation as Max revels in his responses to her edicts. In *Max's Breakfast,* Ruby tries repeatedly to convince Max to eat his egg. The joke is on Ruby when Max announces, "All Gone," as Ruby finishes the egg in her attempt to show Max how yummy it is. In *Bunny Cakes,* Max is making Grandma an earthworm birthday cake, but Ruby thinks that an angel surprise cake with raspberry-fluff icing is more appropriate. As Ruby sends Max to the store for flour and eggs, he repeatedly attempts to write on the grocery list the Red-Hot Marshmallow Squirters he needs for his earthworm cake. Wells perceptively captures Max's initial but determined attempts at written communication, while all throughout the production of the cakes, the big sister Ruby/little brother Max relationship continues as expected.

Illustration 6.29
The precision of paper-cut collage and the dramatic use of color are combined in this Caldecott Honor Book. (*Seven Blind Mice* by Ed Young. Illustration copyright © 1992 by Ed Young. Used by permission of Philomel Books, a division of Penguin Putnam Inc.)

Ed Young

Born and raised in China, Ed Young emigrated to the United States when he was twenty years old. His childhood years in China influence much of his work as an artist. Early in his career, he primarily illustrated the writing of others. The most noted among his early illustrated books is Jane Yolen's *The Emperor and the Kite,* which was a 1969 Caldecott Honor Book. Young illustrated several other texts with Chinese origins, including *Chinese Mother Goose Rhymes* by Robert Wyndham, *Yeh-Shen: A Cinderella Story from China* by Ai-Ling Louie, *White Wave: A Chinese Tale* by Diane Wolkstein, and *The Hunter: A Chinese Folktale* by Mary Casanova.

Ed Young has both written and illustrated a number of books. For his 1989 book *Lon Po Po: A Red Riding Hood Story from China,* Young was awarded the Caldecott Medal. In this version, the children make good decisions and outwit the wolf. A 1994 Caldecott Honor Book, *Seven Blind Mice* is the story of six blind mice who separately explore a mysterious "thing" and report different interpretations to the others. The seventh mouse examines the whole "thing" more thoroughly and combines the other six interpretations to reveal what the "thing" is. The origin of the Chinese zodiac, a twelve-year cycle of years named for animals, is explained in *Cat and Rat.* One of the most interesting aspects of Young's work is the diverse range of media he works with, from chalk, watercolor, and collage to mixed media.

CRITERIA FOR SELECTING PICTURE BOOKS

The plethora of picture books currently available makes the task of evaluation and selection complex. These days, picture books are enjoyed by readers of all ages—from infants to adults. Finding high-quality picture books to meet individual needs is quite possible. But two important questions must be answered first: How do teachers and librarians evaluate quality in picture books? What are the criteria for selecting particular picture books?

Evaluating Quality in Picture Books

In evaluating the quality of a picture book, it is important to consider the following:

▪ Text (literary elements)

▪ Illustrations (artistic elements)

▪ Integration of text and illustrations

Text. Is the story line strong enough to be interesting without the pictures? Will the text alone hold children's attention? When a book is read to a group, some children may not be able to see the pictures. Some teachers prefer to read the story the first time through without showing the pictures. Under these circumstances, interesting text is essential.

Is the language of the text skillfully crafted? Children will want to hear and see a favorite picture book again and again. Skillfully crafted text can enhance

Are picture books being designed more for adult buyers than for child readers?

Picture books are the biggest selling type of children's book. In the past, picture books were designed for preschoolers and young children. Decades ago, books such as those produced by Marie Hall Ets and Virginia Lee Burton were created for that audience. Today, picture books such as those by Eric Hill, Denise Fleming, and Mem Fox are still appropriate for young children. However, many picture books have reached a level of sophistication in both art and text that raises a question as to whom the books were created for.

Certainly, there are picture books today that appeal to all ages. Sally Lodge (1992) calls these sophisticated books "crossovers," books that are successful in both juvenile and adult markets. She believes that publishers cannot always predict which books will become crossover books. Celebrities such as Whoopie Goldberg, Carly Simon, and Dolly Parton have recently published picture books that publishers hope will appeal to adult buyers who recognize such names. There are also picture books that have reprints of fine art from museums around the world or illustrations that reflect an adult sensibility in art appreciation. The text of some books seems to address issues that many children are not yet prepared to understand.

> What do you think? Are picture books purchased for their appeal to the adult buyers or for their appeal to child readers? Are the exquisite art and sophisticated humor of many picture books more appealing to parents than to children? Who, then, is the audience for these picture books?

children's understanding of language and expose them to the rich possibilities of language use.

Illustrations. Is the art accessible and interesting to the intended audience? Does the art help children to see things in a new way? Does it leave room for the child's imagination? Will children want to turn to it again and again? A book that children want to return to repeatedly is a better investment than one whose charms are quickly depleted. Do the illustrations communicate not just literally but symbolically through the use of colors, framing, shading, and the like?

Integration of Text and Illustrations. Do the pictures fit the text? Given that the text and the pictures may have been created independently, how well do they work together? Do the text and the pictures seem to clarify, enhance, and extend each other?

Does the interplay between picture and text exercise the reader's imagination? Children do not need to be shown everything the text has said or told everything the pictures have shown. Children's imaginations are stretched when their senses fill in the gaps between pictures and text.

Are the illustrations well spaced and closely synchronized with the text? Earlier in this chapter, we noted how illustrators can employ the drama of the turning page, speeding or slowing readers' progress through a text. Are these devices used in pleasing ways?

Will the pictures hold interest long enough for the text to be read? When children are being read to, they must focus their attention on the pictures while the text is read. The balance between pictures and text is ideal when children have not lost interest in a picture long before the text is read or lost track of the story line while still engrossed in the details of a picture.

Picture Book Selection Criteria

In addition to determining the quality of a picture book, it is important to know whether a book is appropriate for particular children in particular situations. We can determine a book's appropriateness by considering the following:

- Intended audience
- Intended purpose
- Makeup of the collection

Intended Audience. Who is the intended audience? What are the interests and needs of the children who will be reading the book? What level of sophistication is appropriate for the intended audience? What backgrounds do the children have, both experientially and as readers?

Intended Purpose. How will this book be used? Is the format of the book appropriate for the intended purpose? How does it fit the children's interests and needs? How does it match curricular or other purposes?

Makeup of the Collection. What other books are available to the children? How does this book fit in with other books to which the children have access? Is there a good balance in the variety of books available for the purpose expressed?

Awards for Picture Books

Many awards honor high-quality picture books and their creators. Here, we highlight two of the most widely recognized awards given to illustrators: the Caldecott Medal and the Coretta Scott King Award for illustrations. In addition, we describe an award for the text of picture books: the Charlotte Zolotow Award.

Caldecott Medal. The American Library Association's Association of Library Service to Children honored Randolph Caldecott in 1938 by giving his name to an annual award for the most distinguished picture book published in the previous year. Funds to establish the Caldecott Medal were donated to the ALA by Frederick Melcher, president of the Wilson Publishing Company. Books that have won the medal for their illustrations have a gold seal on the jackets, and honor books have a silver seal. A list of Caldecott winners and honor books appears in Appendix A.

Coretta Scott King Award. Each year, the American Library Association gives one Coretta Scott King Award for writing and one for illustrations, as well as honor book citations. The ALA's guidelines for the award state that "recipients are African American authors and illustrators whose distinguished books promote an understanding and appreciation of the culture and contribution of all people to the realization of the 'American dream.'" Appendix A lists all previous winners and honor books.

Charlotte Zolotow Award. The Charlotte Zolotow Award is presented to the author who is honored for having written the best picture book text published in the United States in the preceding year. The award was established in 1998 to honor editor and author Charlotte Zolotow, and it is administered by the Cooperative Children's Book Center at the University of Wisconsin–Madison. Appendix A lists all previous winners and honor books.

TEACHING IDEAS

Observing Details in Wordless Books. The pictures in wordless books are often full of detailed information, presented in a holistic, intricately woven artistic style. To hone children's visual observation skills, have them find as much pictorial information as they can in a variety of wordless books. In *Animalia,* children can look for items beginning with the featured alphabet letter; in *Anno's U.S.A.,* older children can look for pictures of cultural artifacts, historical events, famous people, and the like. In wordless books that tell a story, children can look for ways in which the details of the illustration add to the main story line.

Comparing Illustrations in Different Versions of the Same Story. Have children examine three or more illustrated versions of a common story. For example, compare Simms Taback's *Joseph Had a Little Overcoat* to Phoebe Gilman's *Something from Nothing* and Steve Sanfield's *Bit by Bit,* illustrated by Susan Gaber. Have children note differences that inform viewers of the illustrator's perspective and interpretation of the story. Are there details that clearly set the story in a particular culture or time period?

Interpreting the Story as Told through Illustration. Select some books that have a strong story line that can be interpreted through the illustrations. Have children examine the illustrations without reading the text and try to tell the story as they see it. Then read the text, and discuss how the story is similar to or different from the story they interpreted through illustration alone. Go back through the illustrations and check whether they see things differently or see additional ways of interpreting the story after hearing the text.

EXPERIENCES FOR YOUR LEARNING

1. Study some books that are considered predictable books in terms of supporting emerging readers, and determine what qualities make each book likely to offer successful reading experiences for beginning readers. Does the book have rhythm, rhyme, or repetition? Does it include sequences that are predictable? Is there a strong match between the text and clear illustrations? Is the text based on concepts that are well known to young children?

2. Study some picture books that you would be most likely to select for your own pleasure. What qualities appeal to you as an adult? What qualities do you think appeal to children? Are the same qualities likely to appeal to adults and to children? What makes picture books appeal to a wide age range of readers?

3. Select a book from an earlier era, such as the ones discussed in the section of this chapter entitled "Authors and Illustrators Who Have Defined

the Field." What qualities still appeal to readers today? What qualities appear dated? What qualities in recently published books are likely to remain popular in future years? What qualities are likely to be time sensitive?

4. Select some alphabet books for different audiences, such as preschoolers and elementary school children, and some that appeal to all ages. What makes each alphabet book appropriate for its intended audience?

RECOMMENDED BOOKS

I indicates interest level by age (P = preschool, YA = young adult)

Toy Books

Ahlberg, Janet, and Allan Ahlberg. *The Jolly Postman or Other People's Letters.* Little, Brown, 1986. A postman delivers letters to and from various fairy tale characters. Miniature letters, cards and postcards are included. (**I:** P–8)

Carle, Eric. *The Honeybee and the Robber.* Paper engineering by James Diaz, Tor Lokvig, and John Strejan. Philomel, 1981. A little bee prevents a bear from stealing the honey. Children can make the book move by pulling tabs, lifting a flap, and opening a pop-up page. There are detailed facts for older readers at the end of the book. (**I:** 6–8)

Cousins, Lucy. *Maisy's Pop-Up Playhouse.* Candlewick, 1995. Pages of this book fold down to create rooms in a playhouse. (**I:** P)

Ehlert, Lois. *Color Zoo.* HarperCollins, 1989. As they turn the pages, children see various shapes that unlayer to reveal different animal faces. Shape names and animal names are included. A related title is *Color Farm* (1990). (**I:** P)

Harper, Dan. *Telling Time with Mama Cat.* Illustrated by Barry Moser and Cara Moser. Harcourt, 1998. A fold-out clock allows children to manipulate the movable hands as they follow Mama Cat throughout her busy day. (**I:** P–8)

Hill, Eric. *Where's Spot?* Putnam, 1980. Sally looks for Spot, who has not eaten his dinner. Children lift flaps to help search for the missing puppy. Over twenty other books about Spot (with Spanish versions of some titles) are available. (**I:** P)

Hoban, Tana. *Black on White.* Greenwillow, 1993. This board book shows black shapes of familiar objects such as an elephant, a butterfly, and a leaf on a white background. Its companion book is *White on Black* (1993). (**I:** P)

———. *Look! Look! Look!* Greenwillow, 1988. Children view part of an object through a hole on alternating pages and try to guess what the whole object may be. (**I:** P–7)

Inkpen, Mick. *Where, Oh Where, Is Kipper's Bear?* Red Wagon Books/Harcourt, 1995. Kipper, the dog's teddy bear, is missing; flaps, pop-ups, and pull tabs help readers search for the missing bear. (**I:** P)

Kunhardt, Dorothy. *Pat the Bunny.* Western, 1940/1968. This interactive book invites children to touch, smell, look, and feel as they play with Paul and Judy. (**I:** P)

Pelham, David. *Sam's Sandwich.* Illustrated by David Pelham and Harry Willock. Dutton, 1990. Sam sneaks in creatures from the garden as his sister Samantha assembles her sandwich. The covers of the book are the bread, and readers unfold pages that serve as the sandwich fillings. A related title is *Sam's Pizza* (1996). (**I:** P–7)

Pienkowski, Jan. *Dinner Time.* Text by Anne Carter. Paper engineering by Marcin Stajewski and James Roger Diaz. Gallery Five, 1981. Pop-up mouths show how animals prey on one another for dinner. (**I:** P)

Sabuda, Robert. *Cookie Count: A Tasty Pop-up.* Little Simon, 1997. This book presents delicious-looking and intricately crafted pop-up cookies from one to ten. (**I:** P–8)

Sendak, Maurice. *The Nutshell Library.* Harper & Row, 1962. This set of four miniature books includes *Alligators All Around, Chicken Soup with Rice: A Book of Months, One Was Johnny: A Counting Book,* and *Pierre: A Cautionary Tale.* The first book is an alphabet book; the second is a series of poems about enjoying chicken soup all the months of the year; the third is a counting book; and the fourth is a cautionary tale. (**I:** P–7)

Steptoe, John. *Baby Says.* Lothrop, Lee & Shepard, 1988. This nearly wordless picture book shows a young African American child learning to play with his baby brother. (**I:** P)

Wells, Rosemary. *Max's First Word.* Dial, 1979. Ruby works hard to expand Max's vocabulary from his one word—"bang." Other humorous stories in board book format about Max and Ruby are *Max's Bedtime* (1985), *Max's Birthday* (1985), and *Max's Breakfast* (1985). (**I:** P)

Zelinsky, Paul O. *The Wheels on the Bus*. Dutton, 1990. This pop-up rendition of a popular action song shows movements for each verse as readers push, pull, or lift tabs on the pages. (**I:** P–6)

Alphabet Books

Anno, Mitsumasa. *Anno's Alphabet: An Adventure in Imagination*. Harper, 1975. An individual letter is shown on one page, and a single object beginning with that letter is shown on the facing page. The imaginative drawings depict wood letter shapes that could not possibly be cut as shown, and the items matching the letters are often unusual. (**I:** P–7)

Aylesworth, Jim. *The Folks in the Valley: A Pennsylvania Dutch ABC*. Illustrated by Stefano Vitale. HarperCollins, 1992. Dutch motifs are used to present the alphabet. (**I:** P–7)

Base, Graeme. *Animalia*. Abrams, 1987. For each letter of the alphabet, an alliterative phrase describes what various animals are doing. Illustrations are filled with items beginning with the featured letter. (**I:** all ages)

Bayer, Jane. *A, My Name Is Alice*. Illustrated by Steven Kellogg. Dial, 1984. This familiar jump-rope and ball-bouncing chant has a verse for every letter of the alphabet. The animals and their names, the places they come from, and the things they sell all begin with the featured letter. (**I:** P–7)

Dragonwagon, Crescent. *Alligator Arrived with Apples: A Potluck Alphabet Feast*. Illustrated by José Aruego and Ariane Dewey. Macmillan, 1987. Alliterative text describes various animals bringing food for a Thanksgiving feast. (**I:** P–7)

Ehlert, Lois. *Eating the Alphabet: Fruits and Vegetables from A to Z*. Harcourt, 1989. Fruits and vegetables are displayed in alphabetical order. (**I:** P–7)

Feelings, Muriel. *Jambo Means Hello: A Swahili Alphabet Book*. Dial, 1974. Readers are introduced, via the alphabet, to the Swahili culture. (**I:** P–9)

Greenaway, Kate. *A—Apple Pie*. Warne, 1886. A is an apple pie, and the words that tell what happens follow the alphabet letter by letter: "bit it," "cut it," "dealt it," etc. (**I:** P–6)

Kitchen, Bert. *Animal Alphabet*. Dial, 1984. Each letter of the alphabet is shown with an unusual animal whose name begins with the letter. (**I:** P–6)

Lessac, Frané. *Caribbean Alphabet*. Tambourine, 1989. The alphabet is used to organize images of the Caribbean islands, from food and animals to popular culture. (**I:** P–8)

Lobel, Anita. *Alison's Zinnia*. Greenwillow, 1990. This alphabet book has a gamelike format, using girls' names and flower names. (**I:** 6–8)

Lobel, Arnold. *On Market Street*. Illustrated by Anita Lobel. Greenwillow, 1981. Alphabet letters are depicted as people whose bodies are made up of objects beginning with that letter. (**I:** P–7)

MacDonald, Suse. *Alphabatics*. Bradbury, 1986. Each letter spins and changes into an object whose name begins with that letter. (**I:** P–7)

Martin, Bill, Jr., and John Archambault. *Chicka Chicka Boom Boom*. Simon & Schuster, 1989. The alphabet letters race up a coconut tree in this rhythmic, rhyming verse. (**I:** P–7)

Musgrove, Margaret. *Ashanti to Zulu: African Traditions*. Illustrated by Leo and Diane Dillon. Dial, 1976. Twenty-six African tribes are shown in alphabetical order, and their cultural traditions are described. (**I:** 7–11)

Pelletier, David. *The Graphic Alphabet*. Orchard, 1996. Alphabet letters are presented in such a way that a word beginning with that letter is visually represented. (**I:** 7–10)

Provensen, Alice, and Martin Provensen. *A Peaceable Kingdom: The Shaker Abecedarius*. Viking, 1978. The alphabet animal rhymes first published in the Shaker manifesto of July 1882 are newly illustrated in this edition. (**I:** P–7)

Rankin, Laura. *The Handmade Alphabet*. Dial, 1991. The hand sign for each letter of the alphabet is shown, along with an item whose name begins with the letter. (**I:** P–9)

Sendak, Maurice. *Alligators All Around*. Harper, 1962. Part of the Nutshell Library. Alligators are described in many ways in alliterative phrases. (**I:** P–8)

Shannon, George. *Tomorrow's Alphabet*. Illustrated by Donald Crews. Greenwillow, 1996. The concept of things changing over time is explored in this alphabet book—for example, "A is for seed—tomorrow's apple." (**I:** P–6)

Van Allsburg, Chris. *The Z Was Zapped*. Houghton Mifflin, 1987. Twenty-six one-act plays show what happens to each letter of the alphabet. (**I:** 8–10)

Counting Books

Anno, Mitsumasa. *Anno's Counting Book*. Crowell, 1977. Illustrations of landscapes include objects that can be counted. (**I:** P)

———. *Anno's Counting House*. Philomel, 1982. Cutout windows of two houses show ten people who move from one house to the other. Readers will enjoy finding out who has moved and what items they have taken with them, adding to one house and subtracting from the other to count the ten people. (**I:** P–7)

Bang, Molly. *Ten, Nine, Eight*. Greenwillow, 1983. Objects are counted backwards in this bedtime story. (I: P)

Carle, Eric. *1, 2, 3 to the Zoo*. Putnam, 1968. Beginning with one elephant and ending with ten birds, each car in the train has one more zoo animal than the one before it. At the end, readers unfold a page to see all the animals at their destination and an empty train along the bottom of the page. (I: P)

Christelow, Eileen. *Five Little Monkeys Jumping on the Bed*. Clarion, 1989. Humorous illustrations accompany this familiar chant of what happens when, one by one, the monkeys fall off and hit their heads. (I: P–7)

Crews, Donald. *Ten Black Dots*. Greenwillow, 1986. Big black dots are counted from one to ten and shown as parts of familiar objects. For example, "Three dots can make a snowman's face." (I: P–5)

Ehlert, Lois. *Fish Eyes: A Book You Can Count On*. Harcourt, 1990. The text is narrated in the voice of a young child who imagines touring the underwater world and seeing brightly colored fish. This counting book includes the concept of "one more" as the guide fish is added to the count on each page. (I: P–6)

Feelings, Muriel. *Moja Means One: A Swahili Counting Book*. Illustrated by Tom Feelings. Dial, 1971. Scenes of Africa are shown in this counting book. (I: P and up)

Fleming, Denise. *Count!* Holt, 1992. This vibrantly colored counting book shows one through ten animals to be counted. There are also small creatures to be counted by tens. (I: P)

Giganti, Paul, Jr. *Each Orange Had Eight Slices: A Counting Book*. Illustrated by Donald Crews. Greenwillow, 1992. Mathematical concepts are shown in the illustrations. (I: P–8)

Haskins, Jim. *Count Your Way through Italy*. Illustrated by Beth Wright. Carolrhoda, 1990. This is one of a series of books that combine an introduction to counting in various languages with information about the countries. (I: 6–9)

Nikola-Lisa, W. *One Hole in the Road*. Illustrated by Dan Yaccarino. Holt, 1996. The numbers 1 through 10 are introduced while workers fix a hole in the road. (I: P–6)

Pomeroy, Diana. *One Potato: A Counting Book of Potato Prints*. Harcourt, 1996. Potato print illustrations are used to count fruits and vegetables from one to ten, then by tens to fifty; the book ends with an illustration of 100 sunflower seeds. (I: P–7)

Walsh, Ellen Stoll. *Mouse Count*. Harcourt, 1991. A hungry snake counts mice. After they trick the snake into looking for more mice to fill up his jar, the mice tumble out as they "uncount" themselves. (I: P–7)

Wise, William. *Ten Sly Piranhas: A Counting Story in Reverse (A Tale of Wickedness—and Worse!)*. Illustrated by Victoria Chess. Dial, 1993. As the ten fish disappear, they are counted down. (I: P–6)

Concept Books

Crews, Donald. *Freight Train*. Greenwillow, 1978. As a freight train passes by, readers are introduced to colors, names of train cars, and the concepts of darkness and light. (I: P–7)

Ehlert, Lois. *Planting a Rainbow*. Harcourt, 1988. As the colored strips—in rainbow order—are flipped, flowers in the featured color appear. (I: P–5)

Hoban, Tana. *All About Where*. Greenwillow, 1991. Words that describe "where" are listed on either side of an across-a-spread photograph. Readers use those words to tell where objects are found in the illustration. (I: P)

———. *Over, Under, and Through and Other Spatial Concepts*. Macmillan, 1973. Photographs show relationships of spatial concepts. (I: P)

———. *Shapes, Shapes, Shapes*. Greenwillow, 1986. Shapes in the environment are shown in photographs. (I: P)

———. *26 Letters and 99 Cents*. Greenwillow, 1987. Open the book one way, and find letters of the alphabet matched with objects whose names begin with each letter. Turn the book over and open it from the opposite end, and count money up to 99 cents. (I: P–8)

Jonas, Ann. *Color Dance*. Greenwillow, 1989. Dancers with colored scarves introduce the primary colors. When their scarves overlap, the secondary colors are visible. (I: P–5)

McMillan, Bruce. *The Baby Zoo*. Scholastic, 1992. A few lines of description accompany each photograph of baby animals. (I: P)

———. *Counting Wildflowers*. Lothrop, Lee & Shepard, 1986. Colored photographs of wildflowers provide children with opportunities to count. (I: P)

———. *One, Two, One Pair*. Scholastic, 1991. This counting book shows one item and a matching item to illustrate how the two together make one pair. (I: P)

Walsh, Ellen Stoll. *Mouse Paint*. Harcourt, 1989. Three white mice splash around in primary colored paint. When they dance in each other's colors, they make new colors. But when the cat comes around, they must find a way to keep from being seen. (I: P–5)

Wordless Books

Anno, Mitsumasa. *Anno's Journey.* Philomel, 1978. The small towns and cities of Europe are shown, with cultural and historic details hidden throughout each page. Also by this author/illustrator are *Anno's Britain* (1982), *Anno's Italy* (1980), and *Anno's U.S.A.* (Putnam, 1983/1992). (I: 7 and up)

Baker, Jeannie. *Window.* Greenwillow, 1991. Collage illustrations show environmental changes as seen through a window of a house, as the boy who lives there grows from babyhood to adulthood. See also *Where the Forest Meets the Sea* (1988). (I: 6–9)

Bang, Molly. *The Grey Lady and the Strawberry Snatcher.* Four Winds, 1980. The strawberry snatcher follows the Grey Lady through town and forest in hopes of snatching her strawberries but instead comes across blackberries along the way. (I: P–6)

Banyai, Istvan. *Zoom.* Viking, 1995. Like a camera's zoom lens, each page backs up to show more and more of the big picture so that readers are challenged to think about what they see as part of a larger scene. See also *Rezoom* (1995). (I: 7 and up)

Briggs, Raymond. *The Snowman.* Random House, 1978. A boy enjoys an adventurous night with a snowman that comes to life. (I: P–9)

dePaola, Tomie. *Pancakes for Breakfast.* Harcourt, 1978. This wordless book tells a story of how pancakes are made. (I: P–6)

Hutchins, Pat. *Changes, Changes.* Macmillan, 1971. A story unfolds as two wooden dolls continuously change the things they create out of wooden blocks. (I: P–7)

McCully, Emily Arnold. *Picnic.* Harper & Row, 1984. When the family goes on a picnic, one mouse is bumped out of the car and left behind. The mice are also featured in *School* (1987). (I: P–8)

Spier, Peter. *Rain.* Doubleday, 1982. A brother and sister don their raingear and enjoy playing outside during a rainstorm. (I: P–8)

Van Allsburg, Chris. *The Mysteries of Harris Burdick.* Houghton Mifflin, 1984. The book begins with an explanation of how Harris Burdick delivered a stack of pictures with titles and captions but mysteriously disappeared without delivering the accompanying stories. (I: 8–12)

Wiesner, David. *Tuesday.* Clarion, 1991. On a mysterious Tuesday night, frogs float through the air on their lily pads. The mystery of this strange occurrence is complicated when the book closes with shadows of flying pigs. (I: P–9)

———. *Sector 7.* Clarion, 1999. A boy is whisked into the clouds while on a school field trip and discovers a use for his artistic talent and imagination when he goes to Sector 7, where clouds are given assignments. (I: P–9)

Wietzman, Jacqueline Preiss, and Robin Preiss Glasser. *You Can't Take a Balloon into The Metropolitan Museum.* Dial, 1998. When a little girl's balloon that she has left for safekeeping with a museum guard flies out over the city, viewers are treated to city scenes that parallel the art seen in the museum by the little girl and her grandmother. See also *You Can't Take a Balloon into The National Gallery* (2000). (I: P–8)

Books with Minimal Text

Bang, Molly. *When Sophie Gets Angry—Really, Really Angry.* Scholastic, 1999. The power of a young child's emotional outpouring when required to share a toy is realistically presented. (I: P–7)

Raschka, Chris. *Yo! Yes?* Orchard, 1993. Two boys use expressive body language and one- and two-word utterances to communicate. One is lonely; the other offers to be his friend. (I: P–7)

Rathmann, Peggy. *Good Night, Gorilla.* Putnam, 1994. In this nearly wordless story, as a zookeeper says good night to the animals in the zoo, the gorilla follows, unlocking their cages so that the animals can follow the zookeeper home. (I: P)

Shannon, David. *No, David!* Blue Sky/Scholastic, 1998. Mother must repeatedly tell her preschool son "No" in an attempt to stop his inappropriate behavior. (I: P–6)

Tafuri, Nancy. *Have You Seen My Duckling?* Greenwillow, 1984. A mother duck leads her ducklings around the lake as they search for a missing duckling. (I: P)

Easy Readers

Byars, Betsy. *My Brother, Ant.* Illustrated by Marc Simont. Viking, 1996. Ant's big brother narrates a series of stories that depict a delightfully realistic sibling relationship. The sequel is *Ant Plays Bear* (1997). (I: P–7)

Cazet, Denys. *Minnie and Moo Go Dancing.* DK Ink, 1998. Humorous short stories describe the antics of two cows; they wonder with horror if the hamburgers being served as refreshments at the dance are former friends. Also in the series are *Minnie and Moo Go to the Moon* (1998), *Minnie and Moo Go to Paris* (1999), *Minnie and Moo Save the Earth* (1999), *Minnie and Moo and the Mask of Zorro* (2000), and *Minnie and Moo and the Thanksgiving Tree* (2000). (I: P–7)

Cole, Joanna, and Stephanie Calmenson. *Ready . . . Set . . . Read!* Doubleday, 1990. This is an anthology of short stories that are easy to read. **(I: P–7)**

dePaola, Tomie. *26 Fairmount Avenue.* Putnam, 1999. Short chapters relay the incidents of Tomie's own childhood as his family built and moved to their new home. The sequels are *Here We All Are* (2000) and *On My Way* (2001). **(I: P–7)**

Ehrlich, Amy. *Leo, Zack and Emmie.* Dial, 1981. Stories of friendship among three children are told in easy-to-read format. See also *Leo, Zack and Emmie Together Again* (1987). **(I: P–7)**

Hopkins, Lee Bennett, ed. *Surprises.* Illustrated by Megan Lloyd. Harper & Row, 1984. Lee Bennett Hopkins has compiled many poems that beginning readers can read easily. **(I: P–8)**

Kvasnosky, Laura McGee. *Zelda and Ivy.* Candlewick, 1998. Three short stories focus on the day-to-day events that show the bond as well as sibling rivalry between two fox sisters, Zelda and Ivy. Sequels are *Zelda and Ivy and the Boy Next Door* (1999) and *Zelda and Ivy One Christmas* (2000). **(I: P–7)**

Lobel, Arnold. *Frog and Toad Are Friends.* Harper & Row, 1970/1979. Five short stories tell of the friendship between Frog and Toad. Sequels are *Frog and Toad Together* (1972) and *Frog and Toad All Year* (1976). **(I: P–8)**

Marshall, (James) Edward. *Fox and His Friends.* Illustrated by James Marshall. Dial, 1982. In this humorous story, Fox wishes his tag-along sister would not be with him when he plays with his friends. Other stories about Fox are *Fox in Love* (1982), *Fox at School* (1983), *Fox on Wheels* (1983), *Fox All Week* (1984), and *Fox on the Job* (1988). **(I: 6–8)**

————. *Three by the Sea.* Illustrated by James Marshall. Dial, 1981. Lolly, Spider, and Sam go to the seashore and try to outdo each other in telling the most interesting story. See also *Four on the Shore* (1985). **(I: 6–8)**

Rylant, Cynthia. *Henry and Mudge: The First Book of Their Adventures.* Illustrated by Sucie Stevenson. Simon & Schuster/Aladdin, 1987. A lonely boy named Henry finds companionship with a big dog named Mudge. Other stories about Henry and Mudge include *Henry and Mudge and the Happy Cat* (1990), *Henry and Mudge and the Bedtime Thump* (1991), and *Henry and Mudge and the Long Weekend* (1992). **(I: 6–8)**

————. *Mr. Putter and Tabby Pour the Tea.* Illustrated by Arthur Howard. Harcourt, 1994. An elderly man goes to the animal shelter to get a pet cat. A related title is *Mr. Putter and Tabby Walk the Dog* (1994). **(I: 6–8)**

Seuss, Dr. *The Cat in the Hat.* Random House, 1957. One rainy day, when two children are home alone, an entertaining cat comes and creates chaos and wild fun. The sequel is *The Cat in the Hat Comes Back* (1958). **(I: P–8)**

————. *Green Eggs and Ham.* Random House, 1960. Sam-I-Am insists on a favorable response from the dog to his offering of green eggs and ham, but the dog remains persistent in refusing. **(I: P–8)**

————. *Hop on Pop.* Random House, 1963. Words with short "o" sounds tell a humorous story of creatures hopping on Pop. Other Seuss titles are *One Fish, Two Fish, Red Fish, Blue Fish* (1960) and *Fox in Socks* (1965). **(I: P–7)**

Van Leeuwen, Jean. *Tales of Oliver Pig.* Illustrated by Arnold Lobel. Dial, 1979. This is a collection of five short stories about a pig named Oliver. Related titles are *More Tales of Oliver Pig* (1981), *Oliver Pig at School* (1990), and *Oliver and Amanda's Halloween* (1992). **(I: P–8)**

Wiseman, Bernard. *Morris Goes to School.* Harper & Row, 1970. Morris the moose decides to go to school to learn to count. A sequel is *Morris Has a Cold* (1978). **(I: P–8)**

Predictable Books

Flack, Marjorie. *Ask Mr. Bear.* Macmillan, 1960. A little boy asks various animals what he should give his mother for her birthday. **(I: P–7)**

Fox, Mem. *Hattie and the Fox.* Illustrated by Patricia Mullins. Bradbury, 1987. As Hattie the hen tries to warn the barnyard animals of danger, more and more of a fox is revealed in the bushes. **(I: P–7)**

————. *I Went Walking.* Illustrated by Julie Vivas. Harcourt, 1990. A child goes walking and encounters a series of animals, with their tails showing on the previous page to offer clues of what animal is next. **(I: P–7)**

Langstaff, John. *Oh, A-Hunting We Will Go.* Illustrated by Nancy Winslow Parker. Macmillan, 1974. Rhyming couplets in this folk song tell of a group of children who go hunting and find various animals they place somewhere temporarily—for example, "We'll catch a goat, and put him in a boat, and then we'll let him go." **(I: P–8)**

Martin, Bill, Jr. *Brown Bear, Brown Bear, What Do You See?* Illustrated by Eric Carle. Holt, 1967/1983. Patterned, repetitive language is used to introduce colors and animal names. See also *Polar Bear, Polar Bear* (1991). **(I: P–7)**

Numeroff, Laura Joffe. *If You Give a Mouse a Cookie.* Illustrated by Felicia Bond. Harper, 1985. A circular story of cause and effect, beginning and ending with a mouse and a cookie. Related titles include *If You Give a Moose a Muffin* (1991) and *If You Give a Pig a Pancake* (1998). (I: P–8)

Shaw, Charles G. *It Looked Like Spilt Milk.* Harper, 1947. Patterned language describes various objects that can be seen in clouds. (I: P–7)

Shulevitz, Uri. *One Monday Morning.* Macmillan, 1967. Repetitive text depicts visitors on one Monday morning. (I: P–6)

Wood, Audrey. *The Napping House.* Illustrated by Don Wood. Harcourt, 1984. It is naptime, and the little boy, his granny, and various animals are piled on the bed. One wakeful flea causes everyone to spring up from naptime. (I: P–7)

Picture Storybooks

Aardema, Verna. *Who's in Rabbit's House?* Illustrated by Leo and Diane Dillon. Dial, 1969/1977. Someone is inside Rabbit's house and won't let her in. (I: P–9)

———. *Why Mosquitoes Buzz in People's Ears: A West African Tale.* Illustrated by Leo and Diane Dillon. Dial, 1987. A mosquito tells a lie to an iguana and sets off a chain of events. (I: 6–9)

Ackerman, Karen. *Song and Dance Man.* Illustrated by Stephen Gammell. Knopf, 1992. Grandpa reminisces about the bygone days when he danced in vaudeville. (I: 6–8)

Aliki. *A Medieval Feast.* Harper & Row, 1983. Preparations for a medieval feast at an English manor house are described with accompanying lavish illustrations. (I: 7–10)

Allard, Harry. *Miss Nelson Is Missing!* Illustrated by James Marshall. Houghton Mifflin, 1977. The children behave badly, and their sweet teacher, Miss Nelson, disappears. She is replaced by Miss Viola Swamp, who is out to set the children straight. Sequels are *Miss Nelson Is Back* (1982) and *Miss Nelson Has a Field Day* (1985). (I: 6–9)

Babbitt, Natalie. *BUB: Or the Very Best Thing.* HarperCollins, 1994. A King and Queen search for the very best thing they can do for their son, who tells them it is "bub"—love. (I: 7–10)

Baer, Gene. *Thump, Thump, Rat-a-Tat-Tat.* Illustrated by Lois Ehlert. Harper & Row, 1989. Bold illustrations show a marching band getting louder and larger as it approaches and then becoming softer and smaller as it continues down the street. Also in board book format. (I: P–7)

Baker, Jeannie. *Where the Forest Meets the Sea.* Greenwillow, 1988. Exquisitely detailed and textured collage illustrations show an Australian forest. (I: 6–9)

Baker, Keith. *Who Is the Beast?* Harcourt, 1990. A tiger points out similarities between him and the other jungle animals to show why he is not to be feared. (I: P–7)

Bang, Molly. *Goose.* Blue Sky/Scholastic, 1996. A goose egg rolls out of its nest, and the baby goose is adopted by a woodchuck family. (I: P–7)

Birdseye, Tom. *Air Mail to the Moon.* Illustrated by Stephen Gammell. Holiday House, 1992. Ora Mae Cotton dreams of what she'll do with the money from the tooth fairy, but before the tooth fairy can come, Ora Mae discovers that her tooth is missing. She vows to send the thief "airmail" to the moon—when she shoves her hand into her pants pocket and feels something hard. (I: 6–9)

———. *Soap! Soap! Don't Forget the Soap!: An Appalachian Folktale.* Illustrated by Andrew Glass. Holiday House, 1993. A boy has trouble remembering his errand when he repeats what the people he meets along the way say to him. (I: 6–9)

Blos, Joan W. *Old Henry.* Illustrated by Stephen Gammell. Morrow/Mulberry, 1987. Henry is misunderstood by his neighbors and sent away. (I: 6–9)

Brett, Jan. *Annie and the Wild Animals.* Houghton Mifflin, 1985. Annie's cat is missing, and Annie tries to befriend various wild animals. (I: P–8)

———. *The Mitten.* Putnam, 1989. Nicki's lost mitten provides snug shelter for various animals until a bear sneezes. See also *The Hat* (1997). (I: P–8)

Brown, Marc. *Arthur's Eyes.* Little, Brown, 1979. Arthur needs glasses and must learn to cope with the teasing of others and adjust to wearing glasses. Eventually, he is pleased to have new glasses. There are many other books about Arthur, his friends, and his sister, D.W. (I: 6–8)

Brown, Marcia. *Once a Mouse.* Scribner's, 1961. This fable from India is illustrated with woodcuts. (I: 6–9)

———, translator and illustrator. *Shadow.* Macmillan, 1982. Brown's translation of a poem by French poet Blaise Cendrars is about a dancing image, Shadow, that rises from ashes, brought to life by African storytellers. (I: 7–9)

Brown, Margaret Wise. *Goodnight Moon.* Illustrated by Clement Hurd. Harper, 1947. A young rabbit says good night to various objects in the room and outside the window. (I: P)

Browne, Anthony. *Voices in the Park.* Knopf, 1998. A mother and her daughter take their dog to the park, and a father and his son take their dog to the park.

This book depicts four points of view on this singular event. (I: 6–9)

Bunting, Eve. *Smoky Night*. Illustrated by David Diaz. Harcourt, 1994. The Los Angeles riots provided the impetus for the creation of this book. Families learn about acceptance and being good neighbors in order to survive difficult times. (I: 9–11)

Burleigh, Robert. *Flight*. Illustrated by Mike Wimmer. Philomel, 1991. Charles Lindbergh's 1927 nonstop solo flight from New York to Paris is described in this book. (I: 6–9)

Burningham, John. *Come Away from the Water, Shirley*. Crowell, 1977. There are two stories in this family's trip to the beach. One is Shirley's daydreaming about pirate ships and gangplanks; the other is about the actual events and the parental warnings about how to behave at the beach. (I: P–8)

———. *Mr. Gumpy's Outing*. Harper, 1976. Mr. Gumpy meets many animals that ask to go along on his boat outing. A related title is *Mr. Gumpy's Motor Car* (1976). (I: P–6)

Burton, Virginia Lee. *The Little House*. Houghton Mifflin, 1942/1978. A house that was built in the countryside finds that, as the years go by, it is becoming run down and is being surrounded by a city. (I: P–7)

———. *Mike Mulligan and His Steam Shovel*. Houghton Mifflin, 1939. Mike Mulligan and his steam shovel, Mary Anne, prove that they can dig more in one day than one hundred men can dig in a week. (I: P–7)

Carle, Eric. *The Grouchy Ladybug*. Scholastic, 1977. Each hour of the day, a grouchy ladybug asks increasingly larger creatures if they want to fight. Ultimately, the ladybug learns a lesson. (I: P–7)

———. *A House for Hermit Crab*. Picture Book Studio, 1987. A hermit crab outgrows its shell and seeks a larger home. (I: P–7)

———. *Rooster's Off to See the World*. Picture Book Studio, 1972. A rooster sets off to see the world. In this book featuring mathematical concepts of addition and subtraction, Rooster is joined by others who return home when it gets dark. (I: P–7)

———. *The Secret Birthday Message*. Harper & Row, 1986. A little boy receives a letter with a coded set of directions on how to find his birthday present. (I: P–7)

———. *The Tiny Seed*. Picture Book Studio, 1991. In autumn, many seeds blow high in the wind and encounter various perils, but a surviving tiny seed grows into a flower. (I: P–7)

———. *Today Is Monday*. Putnam, 1992. The illustrations for this familiar song about eating different kinds of food on each day of the week depict animals bringing foods to hungry children. (I: P–6)

———. *The Very Hungry Caterpillar*. Philomel, 1984. A little caterpillar eats "holes" through the food on the pages, and the cycle of metamorphosis is explained when it emerges from a cocoon as a butterfly. See also *The Very Busy Spider* (1985), *The Very Quiet Cricket* (1990), *The Very Lonely Firefly* (1995), and *The Very Clumsy Click Beetle* (1999). (I: P–7)

Cherry, Lynne. *The Great Kapok Tree: A Tale of the Amazon Rain Forest*. Harcourt, 1990. When a man takes a nap before cutting down the great kapok tree in the rain forest, the animals that depend on the tree for their survival appear in a dream and convince him not to chop it down. (I: 6–9)

———. *A River Ran Wild: An Environmental History*. Harcourt Brace, 1992. This book traces the history of the Nashua River from 7,000 years ago until recent times, with double-spread pages featuring significant influences to the river. (I: 9–12)

Cole, Joanna. *The Magic School Bus on the Ocean Floor*. Illustrated by Bruce Degen. Scholastic, 1992. In the *Magic School Bus* series, Ms. Frizzle takes her class on many field trips on the magic school bus. This time, they go to the ocean floor and explore ocean life there. (I: 6–8)

Cooney, Barbara. *Miss Rumphius*. Viking, 1982. Miss Rumphius travels the world, making it more beautiful as she plants lupines. (I: 6–9)

Cowley, Joy. *Gracias the Thanksgiving Turkey*. Illustrated by Joe Cepeda. Scholastic, 1996. Miguel becomes attached to the turkey that his father has sent home to be fattened up for Thanksgiving. (I: 6–9)

Crews, Nina. *You Are Here*. Greenwillow, 1998. Two sisters shrink and embark on a magical journey. (I: P–8)

Cuyler, Margery. *That's Good! That's Bad!* Illustrated by David Catrow. Holt, 1991. In alternating courses of good luck and bad luck, a little boy's balloon starts him on an adventure. (I: P–7)

de Brunhoff, Jean. *The Story of Babar*. 1933. Random House, 1961. Babar becomes the king of the elephants. (I: P–7)

dePaola, Tomie. *The Art Lesson*. Putnam, 1997. In this autobiographical story, Tomie recalls his childhood passion for drawing and how it was met by adults with frustration as well as support. (I: P–7)

———. *The Cloud Book*. Holiday House, 1975. This book describes the ten most common types of clouds and tells how weather predictions can be made by examining clouds. Also included are myths about cloud types. (**I:** 6–9)

————. *Nana Upstairs and Nana Downstairs.* Autobiographical stories of Tomie's relationship with his grandmothers. Putnam, 1973. See also *Now One Foot, Now the Other* (1981), *Tom* (1993), and *Watch Out for the Chicken Feet in Your Soup* (1974). (**I:** 6–8)

————. *Strega Nona.* Simon & Schuster, 1979. "Grandma Witch" hires a helper, Big Anthony, who thinks that he has found the secret of how to make the magic pot cook pasta. What he doesn't know is how to make it stop. Sequels are *Big Anthony and the Magic Ring* (1979), *Strega Nona's Magic Lessons* (1982), *Merry Christmas, Strega Nona* (1986), *Strega Nona Meets Her Match* (1993), and *Strega Nona: Her Story* (1996). (**I:** P–7)

Dupasquier, Philippe. *Dear Daddy.* Puffin, 1988. A little girl's daily activities are depicted alongside the daily activities of her father, who is away at sea. (**I:** 6–8)

Duvoisin, Roger. *Petunia.* Knopf, 1950. Petunia is a silly goose who thinks that all she has to do to gain wisdom is carry a book. (**I:** P–7)

Ehlert, Lois. *Feathers for Lunch.* Harcourt, 1990. A housecat hopes to catch one of the birds in the backyard for lunch, but all get away safely, and the cat ends up with only feathers. Bird descriptions are included. (**I:** P–7)

————. *Growing Vegetable Soup.* Harcourt, 1987. Father and child plant seeds and sprouts and grow the vegetables that make a soup. (**I:** P–5)

————. *Moon Rope/Un lazo a la luna.* Translated into Spanish by Amy Prince. Harcourt, 1992. This adaptation of a Peruvian folktale tells how Fox and Mole try to climb to the moon on a rope made of woven grass. (**I:** 6–9)

————. *Market Day.* Harcourt, 2000. Collages of folk art show the trip to town square and the events of market day. (**I:** P–7)

————. *Red Leaf, Yellow Leaf.* Harcourt, 1991. The life cycle of a maple tree is shown through collage illustrations. (**I:** P–7)

————. *Snowballs.* Harcourt, 1995. Children create a snow family, using a large variety of items they had saved: a luggage tag, a toy fish, popcorn, etc. (**I:** P–6)

Emberley, Barbara. *Drummer Hoff.* Illustrated by Ed Emberley. Simon & Schuster, 1967. The story of how a cannon is fired is told through rhyming couplets in cumulative text. (**I:** 5–8)

Ernst, Lisa Campbell. *When Bluebell Sang.* Macmillan, 1989. Bluebell is a cow that leads a peaceful life in the meadows until one day fame takes her on the road and under the spotlights. (**I:** 5–8)

————. *Zinnia and Dot.* Viking Penguin, 1992. Zinnia and Dot are two hens that are full of pride. When a weasel steals their eggs, they must learn to cooperate to save the one egg that is left behind. (**I:** 6–9)

Falconer, Ian. *Olivia.* Atheneum, 2000. Through text and illustration, readers see Olivia as a little pig whose daily life is lived fully and expressively. (**I:** P–8)

Fleming, Denise. *Barnyard Banter.* Holt, 1994. Barnyard animals noisily occupy their places on the farm, but the goose is missing. (**I:** P–6)

————. *In the Small, Small Pond.* Holt, 1993. Pond life is depicted with vividly colored illustrations. (**I:** P–6)

————. *In the Tall, Tall Grass.* Holt, 1991. A young child finds a variety of creatures in the tall, tall grass and describes their movements with rhyming, poetic text. (**I:** P–6)

————. *Where Once There Was a Wood.* Holt, 1996. Many kinds of wildlife lose their homes when housing developments are constructed. Endnotes invite readers to take action in creating wildlife habitats in their backyards and communities. (**I:** P–8)

Flournoy, Valerie. *The Patchwork Quilt.* Illustrated by Jerry Pinkney. Dial, 1985. Creating a quilt leads to collecting many family memories. (**I:** 6–9)

Fox, Mem. *Koala Lou.* Illustrated by Pamela Lofts. Harcourt, 1988. Koala Lou longs for the days before the other children came along, when her mother used to tell Koala Lou how much she loved her. Koala Lou enters a race in her attempt to win her mother's affections again. (**I:** P–7)

————. *Night Noises.* Illustrated by Terry Denton. Harcourt, 1989. Lily Laceby, rumored to be ninety, dozes in her chair and dreams of years gone by. Her dog, Butch Aggie, hears strange noises outside—lots of relatives arriving for a surprise party! (**I:** P–7)

————. *Possum Magic.* Illustrated by Julie Vivas. Harcourt, 1990. Grandma Poss turns Hush invisible and Hush enjoys many adventures because she can't be seen. But later, Grandma Poss and Hush must travel throughout Australian cities, eating Australian foods, in an attempt to remember the magic to make Hush visible again. (**I:** P–7)

————. *Wilfrid Gordon McDonald Partridge.* Illustrated by Julie Vivas. Kane/Miller, 1985. Wilfrid Gordon McDonald Partridge is worried because everyone is talking about Miss Nancy's lost memory. In his attempt to find out what "memory" is, he restores Miss Nancy's memory in an unusual way. (**I:** 6–9)

Gág, Wanda. *Millions of Cats*. Coward, McCann, 1929. When a lonely old man cannot choose among hundreds of cats, thousands of cats, millions and billions and trillions of cats, the cats fight it out as each claims to be the prettiest. (I: P–7)

Gauch, Patricia Lee. *Dance, Tanya*. Illustrated by Satomi Ichikawa. Philomel, 1989. Tanya longs to be able to dance ballet on stage when she grows up. (I: P–7)

Ginsburg, Mirra. *Across the Stream*. Illustrated by Nancy Tafuri. Greenwillow, 1982. A bad dream threatens a hen and her chicks, and they are saved by a duck and her ducklings. (I: P–7)

Goble, Paul. *The Girl Who Loved Wild Horses*. Macmillan, 1978. A girl finds that she communes with horses more easily than she does with her people and goes to join the wild horses. (I: P–7)

Griffith, Helen V. *Georgia Music*. Illustrated by James Stevenson. Greenwillow, 1986. A grandfather and his granddaughter enjoy different types of music: his mouth organ and the birds and insects around his cabin. (I: 6–9)

Haley, Gail E. *A Story, a Story*. Atheneum, 1970. This is an African tale in which Anansi the Spider makes a bargain with the Sky God. (I: P–8)

Hall, Donald. *Ox-Cart Man*. Illustrated by Barbara Cooney. Viking, 1979. In nineteenth-century New England, a family fills an ox cart with the extra things they have grown or made during the previous year. After everything in the cart is sold, the family purchases supplies and goes through another year of growing things and making things to sell. (I: 6–8)

Heide, Florence Parry, and Judith Heide Gilliland. *The Day of Ahmed's Secret*. Illustrated by Ted Lewin. Lothrop, 1990. Young Ahmed works in his city of Cairo, anticipating the end of his day when he can share his proud secret with his family. (I: P–8)

Henkes, Kevin. *Chester's Way*. Greenwillow, 1988. Chester and Wilson, two inseparable friends, find room in their friendship for another when Lilly moves into the neighborhood and proves herself a true friend. (I: P–7)

———. *Chrysanthemum*. Greenwillow, 1991. Chrysanthemum is pleased with her name until classmates tease her about it. With the help of the music teacher's affirmation, Chrysanthemum "blooms" as she regains pride in her name. (I: P–6)

———. *Julius, the Baby of the World*. Greenwillow, 1990. Lilly cannot stand the attention showered on her new baby brother, Julius. She suddenly develops pride in him when a cousin makes unpleasant remarks about him. (I: P–8)

———. *Lilly's Purple Plastic Purse*. Greenwillow, 1996. Lilly disrupts class to show off her new purple plastic purse and is devastated when Mr. Slinger, the teacher whom she idolizes, confiscates the purse until the end of the day. (I: P–8)

———. *Owen*. Greenwillow, 1993. Owen is about to start school, and his nosy next-door neighbor is sure that there must be a way to get Owen to give up his security blanket. (I: P–7)

———. *Sheila Rae, the Brave*. Greenwillow, 1987. Sheila Rae isn't afraid of anything, or so it seems, until she takes a wrong turn on the way home one day. It is little sister Louise—whom Sheila Rae refers to as the "scaredy cat"—who comes to the rescue. (I: P–6)

———. *A Weekend with Wendell*. Greenwillow, 1987. Wendell is a weekend guest at Sophie's house, and he makes all the rules and demands they play by them. Sophie decides to stand up to Wendell's tyranny and makes him be the burning building while she plays the role of fire chief. (I: P–6)

———. *Wemberly Worried*. Greenwillow, 2000. Wemberly worries obsessively about everything, from big things to little things, and needs much assurance. (I: P–7)

Hesse, Karen. *Come On, Rain*. Illustrated by Jon Muth. Scholastic, 1999. The arrival of rain at last cools off the heat of summer as mothers join their daughters outside. (I: P–8)

Hest, Amy. *Baby Duck and the Bad Eyeglasses*. Illustrated by Jill Barton. Candlewick, 1996. Baby Duck is unhappy about her new eyeglasses until her Grandpa helps her overcome her feelings. (I: P–7)

Ho, Minfong. *Hush!* Illustrated by Holly Meade. Orchard, 1996. In this lullaby set in Thailand, a mother tries to quiet the animals so that her baby can sleep. (I: P–8)

Hoban, Russell. *A Baby Sister for Frances*. Illustrated by Lillian Hoban. Harper & Row, 1964. Frances the badger tries to adjust to having a new baby sister around. A few of the other stories about Frances are *Bread and Jam for Frances* (1964), *Best Friends for Frances* (1969), and *A Bargain for Frances* (1970). (I: 6–8)

Hodges, Margaret. *St. George and the Dragon*. Illustrated by Trina Schart Hyman. Little, Brown, 1984. This adaptation of Edmund Spenser's *Faerie Queene* tells how the Red Cross Knight slays the dragon and ends its terrorizing of the English countryside. (I: 8–12)

Hogrogian, Nonny. *One Fine Day*. Macmillan, 1971. A thirsty fox drinks milk from an old woman's pail, and she cuts off its tail. The woman will not return the tail until the fox returns her milk. Thus begins the circular tale in which the fox must ask for the help of many to retrieve its tail. Based on an Armenian folktale. (I: P–8)

Hort, Lenny. *The Boy Who Held Back the Sea.* Illustrated by Thomas Locker. Dial, 1987. This is the story of a young, mischievous boy who saves his town from flooding by plugging a hole in the dike. (I: 7–9)

Houston, Gloria. *My Great-Aunt Arizona.* Illustrated by Susan Condie Lamb. HarperCollins, 1992. A girl reflects on her great-aunt's teaching career in the Appalachian mountains. (I: 6–8)

Hughes, Shirley. *Dogger.* 1977. Lothrop, 1988. A favorite stuffed dog is missing, and the loss creates agony for the owner. (I: P–8)

Hutchins, Pat. *The Doorbell Rang.* Greenwillow, 1986. Ma has baked cookies for Victoria and Sam, but every time the doorbell rings, more friends join them and there are fewer cookies to go around. (I: P–7)

Hyman, Trina Schart. *Little Red Riding Hood.* Holiday House, 1983. Beautiful paintings illustrate this Caldecott-winning version of the familiar tale of a little girl who is sent to visit her sick grandmother. (I: 6–9)

Innocenti, Roberto. *Rose Blanche.* Stewart, Tabori & Chang, 1985. A young girl visits a German concentration camp with small gifts of food. (I: 9 and up)

Isaacs, Anne. *Swamp Angel.* Dutton, 1994. Illustrated by Paul O. Zelinsky. A tall tale about a bear-wrestling heroine who helps settlers in Tennessee. (I: 6–9)

Isadora, Rachel. *Ben's Trumpet.* Greenwillow, 1979. Ben wants to learn to play a trumpet, and a nightclub owner helps him realize his dream. (I: 6–9)

Johnson, Crockett. *Harold and the Purple Crayon.* Harper & Row, 1958. Harold goes on a walk, using his purple crayon to draw pictures that create an adventure. Three sequels are *Harold's Trip to the Sky* (1957), *Harold's Circus* (1959), and *A Picture for Harold's Room* (1960). (I: P–7)

Johnson, D. B. *Henry Hikes to Fitchburg.* Houghton Mifflin, 2000. Inspired by the life of Thoreau, this story tells how two bears get to Fitchburg: one by working and earning fare on a train, the other by walking and enjoying the journey. (I: 6–10)

Johnston, Tony. *The Wagon.* Illustrated by James E. Ransome. Tambourine/Morrow, 1996. A boy born into slavery builds a wagon for his master, imagining that it is the glorious chariot of freedom in the song "Swing Low, Sweet Chariot." (I: 6–9)

Jonas, Ann. *Round Trip.* Greenwillow, 1983. The journey begins at dawn in a quiet neighborhood and passes through the countryside on the way to the city. Then readers turn the book upside down and see what the illustrations depict when viewed from the opposite direction, completing a round trip back to the neighborhood. (I: P–9)

Jorgensen, Gail. *Crocodile Beat.* Illustrated by Patricia Mullins. Bradbury, 1989. Rhythmic, rhyming text tells of animals playing by the riverbank. When Crocodile awakens intending to have the animals for lunch, Lion puts an end to the crocodile's plan. (I: P–6)

Joyce, William. *George Shrinks.* HarperCollins, 1991. George is suddenly a "Tom Thumb" in his normal-sized world, and he encounters the delights and fears of being small. (I: 6–9)

———. *Rolie Polie Olie.* HarperCollins, 1999. The round Rolie Polie Olie's day is described in rhythmic text, with three-dimensional computer-generated illustrations that create an ambience appropriate for science fiction. (I: P–7)

Kasza, Keiko. *A Mother for Choco.* Putnam, 1992. Choco goes in search of mother, only to find that nobody looks like him. Instead, he meets a mother who asks what a mother would do. (I: P–7)

———. *The Rat and the Tiger.* Putnam, 1993. Tiger always bullies his small friend Rat, until one day Rat decides to turn the tables. (I: P–7)

———. *Wolf's Chicken Stew.* Putnam, 1987. Wolf is very hungry for chicken stew and finds the perfect chicken. His attempts to fatten her up backfire. (I: P–7)

Keats, Ezra Jack. *Goggles!* Macmillan, 1969. Archie and Willie are met by bullies and must think quickly to return home safely. (I: P–7)

———. *Maggie and the Pirate.* 1979. Macmillan, 1987. A "pirate" steals Maggie's pet cricket, Niki, and the cricket cage Maggie's father made. (I: 6–8)

———. *Peter's Chair.* Harper, 1967. Peter is jealous of his new baby sister and refuses to give her his chair until he discovers that he has outgrown it. (I: P–7)

———. *The Snowy Day.* Viking, 1962. Peter plays outside following a big snowfall. (I: P–7)

Keller, Holly. *Harry and Tuck.* Greenwillow, 1993. Harrison and Tucker are twins and do everything alike and together. When they are placed in different kindergarten classes, they begin to gain a sense of independence. (I: P–6)

Kellogg, Steven. *A Rose for Pinkerton.* Dial, 1981. A family's Great Dane and a kitten are intended to be friends. See also *Pinkerton, Behave!* (1979) and *Prehistoric Pinkerton* (1987). (I: 6–9)

Kraus, Robert. *Leo the Late Bloomer.* Illustrated by José Aruego. Windmill, 1971/2000. Father tiger is anxious as his young son, Leo, seems unable to do anything yet. But in time, Leo finds that he has developed at his own rate. (I: P–6)

Leaf, Munro. *The Story of Ferdinand*. Illustrated by Robert Lawson. Viking, 1936. Ferdinand grows to be a big strong bull, but he is interested only in sitting and smelling flowers. When he accidentally sits on a bumblebee, his resulting behavior causes him to be chosen for the bullfights in Madrid. (I: P–9)

Lionni, Leo. *Frederick*. Knopf, 1967. The field mice work hard to prepare for winter, and it appears that Frederick is shirking his responsibilities. However, when winter comes, he is able to entertain the other mice with his poems describing the warmth of the sun and the colors of the flowers. A sequel is *Frederick and His Friends* (1981). (I: P–7)

————. *Inch by Inch*. Astor-Honor, 1962. To avoid being eaten by the birds who hold him captive, an inchworm cleverly sets off to measure the length of a nightingale's song. (I: P–7)

————. *Little Blue and Little Yellow*. Astor-Honor, 1959. Abstract shapes depict members of the blue family and the yellow family. When their children play and hug, they turn green. (I: P–6)

————. *Swimmy*. Pantheon, 1963. A little fish comes up with a clever plan to protect the small fish in the school from being eaten by larger fish: They swim together in the formation of a giant fish. (I: P–7)

Lobel, Arnold. *Fables*. Harper & Row, 1980. This collection has many fables told in the style of Aesop. (I: 7–9)

————. *The Rose in My Garden*. Greenwillow, 1984. Illustrated by Anita Lobel. Cumulative text tells the story of a bee asleep on a rose in the garden—until a cat chases a mouse through the garden. (I: P–8)

Lyon, George Ella. *Come a Tide*. Illustrated by Stephen Gammell. Orchard, 1990. High flood waters cause problems for a family. (I: P–8)

Macaulay, David. *Black and White*. Houghton Mifflin, 1990. This Caldecott winner presents four separate stories—or one intertwined story—about children, parents, trains, and cows. (I: 8–12)

————. *Why the Chicken Crossed the Road*. Houghton Mifflin, 1987. This is a cause-and-effect story that starts and ends with a chicken crossing the road. (I: P–9)

Marshall, James. *George and Martha*. Houghton Mifflin, 1972. George and Martha are two hippos who share a fun-filled day. Other titles are *George and Martha Encore* (1973), *George and Martha Rise and Shine* (1976), *George and Martha One Fine Day* (1978), *George and Martha Back in Town* (1984), and *George and Martha 'Round and 'Round* (1988). (I: P–8)

————. *Hansel and Gretel*. Dial, 1990. The well-known story of two children who are abandoned in the forest and who outsmart and escape from an evil witch is depicted with illustrations that are more light-hearted and humorous than those in many other versions. (I: 6–8)

Martin, Bill, Jr., and John Archambault. *The Ghost-Eye Tree*. Illustrated by Ted Rand. Holt, 1985. When a brother and sister are sent to fetch a pail of milk one dark and spooky night, their imaginations run wild as they hurry past the Ghost-Eye Tree. (I: P–8)

————. *Up and Down on the Merry-Go-Round*. Illustrated by Ted Rand. Holt, 1985. Rhythmic, rhyming text describes a delightful ride on a merry-go-round and all that can be seen from it. (I: P–6)

Martin, Rafe. *Will's Mammoth*. Illustrated by Stephen Gammell. Putnam, 1989. While playing in the snow one day, a little boy lets his imagination take off. (I: P–8)

Maruki, Toshi. *Hiroshima No Pika*. Lothrop, 1982. Expressionistic illustrations accompany the story, which describes what happens to a family after the atomic bombing of Hiroshima in August 1945. (I: 10 and up)

Mayer, Mercer. *There's a Nightmare in My Closet*. Dial, 1969. A boy is sure there is a nightmare living in his closet, but decides that he must confront the monster. (I: P–7)

McCloskey, Robert. *Blueberries for Sal*. Viking, 1948. A little girl goes blueberry picking with her mother and a little bear follows its mother, but the two children get their mothers mixed up! (I: P–7)

————. *Make Way for Ducklings*. Viking, 1941. Mr. and Mrs. Mallard set off in search of a perfect place to raise their family. They find that Boston Public Garden provides just the right home. (I: P–8)

————. *Time of Wonder*. Viking, 1957. A family living on an island in Maine deals with a summer hurricane. (I: P–9)

McCully, Emily Arnold. *Mirette on the High Wire*. Putnam, 1992. When a formerly great tightrope artist becomes fearful of walking the rope, it is a little girl, Mirette, who must help him overcome his fears. (I: 6–9)

McKissack, Patricia. *Mirandy and Brother Wind*. Knopf, 1988. Illustrated by Jerry Pinkney. Mirandy seeks Brother Wind as a partner to win the cake walk. (I: 6–9)

McLerran, Alice. *Roxaboxen*. Illustrated by Barbara Cooney. Lothrop, 1991. Marian and her sisters enjoy imaginary play with their friends as they create a community out of rocks on a hill. (**I**: 6–9)

McPhail, David. *Fix-It*. Dutton, 1984. Emma Bear is distressed to find that the television won't turn on, until Mother Bear reads her a good book. (**I**: P–6)

————. *Pigs Aplenty, Pigs Galore!* Dutton, 1993. Late one night, a man is reading when he discovers "pigs aplenty, pigs galore" in his house. More and more pigs arrive, wearing outrageous costumes and creating havoc. (**I**: P–8)

Meddaugh, Susan. *Hog Eye*. Houghton Mifflin, 1995. When the family demands an explanation for why a little pig missed school one day, she launches into a wild story of how she got on the wrong bus, took a shortcut through the forest, and met a wolf who tied her up and made her teach him how to make soup. The pig tells how she outwitted the wolf through the magic of "Hog-Eye." (**I**: 6–9)

————. *Martha Speaks*. Houghton Mifflin, 1992. Martha the dog is able to speak after eating alphabet soup. Her family is thrilled to be able to communicate with her verbally and hear her thoughts on various subjects. Sequels are *Martha Calling* (1994), *Martha Blah Blah* (1996), *Martha Walks the Dog* (1998), and *Martha and Skits* (2000). (**I**: 6–9)

Melmed, Laura Krauss. *The First Song Ever Sung*. Illustrated by Ed Young. Lothrop, 1993. When a Japanese boy repeatedly asks a question about the first song ever sung, different people and animals give their responses. (**I**: 6–8)

Moser, Madeline. *Ever Heard of an Aardwolf? A Miscellany of Uncommon Animals*. Illustrated by Barry Moser. Harcourt, 1996. Twenty unusual animals such as the aardwolf, the loris, the pangolin, the viscacha, and the solenodon are introduced with a brief paragraph about each animal; an appendix gives more detailed information. Illustrations are synthetic wood engravings. (**I**: 6–9)

Moss, Lloyd. *Zin! Zin! Zin! a Violin*. Illustrated by Marjorie Priceman. Simon & Schuster, 1995. A trombone begins playing solo and is joined by the trumpet, french horn, cello, violin, flute, clarinet, oboe, bassoon, and harp. (**I**: P–8)

Myers, Christopher. *Wings*. Scholastic, 2000. Ikarus Jackson is mocked for being different from others: He has wings. When the narrator learns to stand up for Ikarus, they both understand the power of embracing differences and celebrating individuality. (**I**: 6–10)

Narahashi, Keiko. *I Have a Friend*. Macmillan, 1987. A little boy talks about his friend who goes everywhere with him: his shadow. (**I**: P–7)

Ness, Evaline. *Sam, Bangs and Moonshine*. Holt, 1966. Sam always tells stories that her father calls "moonshine." One day, Sam's moonshine almost takes her friend Thomas's life. (**I**: 6–9)

Noble, Trinka Hakes. *The Day Jimmy's Boa Ate the Wash*. Illustrated by Steven Kellogg. Dial, 1980. A little girl tells her mother an outrageous story of her class field trip to the farm in reverse cause-and-effect order. A sequel is *Jimmy's Boa Bounces Back* (1984). (**I**: 6–9)

Peet, Bill. *Big Bad Bruce*. Houghton Mifflin, 1977. Bruce has fun rolling boulders down the hill and scaring the small creatures of Forevergreen Forest. When he almost hits Roxy, a little fox who is a witch, Bruce is in for a surprise. (**I**: P–8)

Perrault, Charles. *Cinderella*. Illustrated by Marcia Brown. Scribner's, 1954. This familiar French fairy tale has Caldecott-winning watercolor illustrations. (**I**: 6–9)

————. *Puss in Boots*. Illustrated by Hans Fischer. Translated by Anthea Bell. North-South Books, 1958/1996. This is the familiar tale of a clever cat that arranges for his poor master to marry into a royal family. The illustrations are lithographs. (**I**: 6–9)

————. *Puss in Boots*. Illustrated by Fred Marcellino. Translated by Malcolm Arthur. Farrar, 1990. This is another version of the famous story in which a miller's youngest son's inheritance is only a cat, but the cat proves to be clever and orchestrates a plan for his master to become the groom of the princess. (**I**: 6–9)

Pilkey, Dav. *The Paperboy*. Orchard, 1996. Readers get a sense of ritual as a boy gets out of bed and begins his daily routine of delivering the newspaper. (**I**: P–8)

Polacco, Patricia. *Appelemando's Dreams*. Philomel, 1991. Appelemando's dreams are vivid and entertaining, but only the children appreciate them at first. (**I**: 6–9)

————. *Babushka Baba Yaga*. Philomel, 1990. Baba Yaga loves children but disguises herself as a babushka so that the villagers won't be afraid of her. (**I**: 6–10)

————. *The Bee Tree*. Philomel, 1993. As a grandfather leads his daughter on a search for a bee tree, he compares it to the value of reading books. (**I**: 6–9)

————. *Thunder Cake*. Philomel, 1993. Grandmother helps her granddaughter overcome her fear of thunder. (**I**: 6–9)

Pomerantz, Charlotte. *The Chalk Doll*. Illustrated by Frané Lessac. Lippincott, 1989. Rose asks her mother to talk about her childhood in Jamaica. (**I**: 6–8)

Potter, Beatrix. *The Tale of Peter Rabbit*. Warne, 1902/1986. This is the story of Peter, a naughty rabbit who disobeys his mother and ends up caught in Mr. McGregor's garden. (I: P–8)

Price, Leontyne. *Aida*. Illustrated by Leo Dillon and Diane Dillon. Harcourt, 1990. This book tells the opera's famous love story in which a couple is united but the price is death. (I: 9–14)

Ransome, Arthur. *The Fool of the World and the Flying Ship*. Illustrated by Uri Shulevitz. Farrar, 1968. A Russian boy of poor background marries the czar's daughter. (I: 7–10)

Rathmann, Peggy. *Officer Buckle and Gloria*. Putnam, 1995. Officer Buckle makes school rounds, giving safety tips to children. His dog, Gloria, pantomimes the safety tips and is the one who actually keeps the children amused. (I: 6–9)

Rey, H. A. *Curious George*. Houghton Mifflin, 1941. George is a monkey who leaves the jungle with the man with a yellow hat. His mischievousness and curiosity get him into trouble. Other books about George—*Curious George Takes a Job* (1947), *Curious George Rides a Bike* (1952), *Curious George Gets a Medal* (1957), *Curious George Flies a Kite* (1973), and *Curious George Goes to the Hospital* (1973)—were written by H. A. Rey's wife, Margaret Rey. (I: P–8)

Rosen, Michael. *We're Going on a Bear Hunt*. Illustrated by Helen Oxenbury. Macmillan, 1989. A father takes his children on an imaginary bear hunt. They bravely go through various obstacles until they encounter the bear and make a mad dash home. Alternating full-color and black-and-white illustrations depict what part of the story actually happens and what part is imagination. (I: P–6)

Rylant, Cynthia. *Mr. Griggs' Work*. Illustrated by Julie Downing. Orchard, 1989. Mr. Griggs is a postal worker who loves his work so much that he cannot stop thinking about it. When he becomes ill, he cannot imagine that someone else is working at the post office in his place. (I: 6–8)

———. *When I Was Young in the Mountains*. Illustrated by Diane Goode. Dutton, 1982. Through poetic text that repeatedly begins "When I was young in the mountains," the narrator reminisces about her childhood in the Appalachian mountains. (I: 6–9)

San Souci, Robert D. *The Faithful Friend*. Illustrated by Brian Pinkney. Simon & Schuster, 1995. This is a retelling of a folktale from the Caribbean island of Martinique. The close bonds of friendship between Clement and Hippolyte break the spell cast by Monsieur Zabocat, a wizard, who opposes the marriage of his niece, Pauline, to Clement. (I: 7–10)

———. *Sukey and the Mermaid*. Illustrated by Brian Pinkney. Four Winds, 1992. Sukey lives on an island off the coast of South Carolina. When she runs to her secret hiding place by the sea to escape from the hard work imposed by her new stepfather, she meets a black mermaid named Mama Jo, who changes her life forever. (I: 6–9)

Say, Allen. *Emma's Rug*. Houghton Mifflin, 1996. Emma learns that inspiration for art is in the world all around her and that she does not have to rely on the images she "sees" in her special rug. (I: 6–9)

———. *Grandfather's Journey*. Houghton Mifflin, 1993. Say tells his own grandfather's story and expresses their mutual love for both Japan and America. (I: 8–10)

———. *Tree of Cranes*. Houghton Mifflin, 1991. A Japanese woman brings a small pine tree indoors, folds origami cranes to decorate it, and shares memories with her son of spending her childhood Christmases in America. (I: P–8)

Schaefer, Carole Lexa. *The Squiggle*. Illustrated by Pierr Morgan. Crown, 1996. On an outing with her class, a little girl finds a rope that she imagines to be part of a dragon, the Great Wall of China, and various other things. (I: P–7)

Schroeder, Alan. *Minty: A Story of Young Harriet Tubman*. Illustrated by Jerry Pinkney. Dial, 1996. Throughout Harriet Tubman's childhood, she dreamed and planned of escaping from slavery. (I: 6–9)

Schwartz, Amy. *Annabelle Swift, Kindergartner*. Orchard, 1988. Before the beginning of kindergarten, Annabelle's older sister gives tips on what to do at school. (I: P–6)

Sendak, Maurice. *Where the Wild Things Are*. Harper & Row, 1963/1989. When he is punished and sent to bed without supper, Max sails off to an imaginary world where he is the king of the Wild Things. (I: P–8)

Seuss, Dr. *And to Think That I Saw It on Mulberry Street*. Vanguard, 1937. A little boy imagines what would happen if the horse and cart he sees on his street were transformed into a circus bandwagon. (I: P–8)

———. *The Five Hundred Hats of Bartholomew Cubbins*. Random House, 1938. When Bartholomew tries to remove his hat to show respect to the king, another hat appears in its place. (I: P–8)

———. *Horton Hatches the Egg*. 1940. Random House, 1968. Mayzie the bird leaves for a vacation and leaves Horton the elephant to sit on her nest and tend her egg. (I: P–8)

Shulevitz, Uri. *Snow*. Farrar Straus Giroux, 1998. A little boy discovers a snowflake falling, but the adults do not pay attention. Soon, the boy is delightedly playing in snow with Mother Goose characters from a sign who come and join him. (**I**: P–7)

Simmons, Jane. *Come Along, Daisy!* Little, Brown, 1997. Mama Duck calls out, "Come along, Daisy!" But her duckling is too busy playing, until she suddenly discovers that she is all alone. (**I**: P)

Soto, Gary. *Chato and the Party Animals.* Illustrated by Susan Guevara. Putnam, 2000. Chato, the coolest cat in el barrio, throws a surprise party for his friend, Novio Boy. See also *Chato's Kitchen* (1995). (**I**: 6–10)

Steig, William. *The Amazing Bone.* Farrar, 1983. Pearl, a pig, finds a talking bone in the forest and picks it up to take home. When she encounters danger in the forest, the bone does amazing things to keep them safe. (**I**: 6–9)

———. *Doctor De Soto.* Farrar, 1982. A fox with a toothache tries to get a mouse dentist to work on the tooth—but the fox also has other plans for the mouse. A related title is *Doctor De Soto Goes to Africa* (1992). (**I**: 6–9)

———. *Pete's a Pizza.* HarperCollins, 1998. Pete is upset that rain has ruined his outdoor plans, but his parents cheer him up by pretending to make him into a pizza. (**I**: P–8)

———. *Spinky Sulks.* Farrar, 1988. Spinky sulks about everything, but circumstances change his attitude and behavior. (**I**: 6–9)

———. *Sylvester and the Magic Pebble.* Simon & Schuster, 1969. When Sylvester, a donkey, makes a wish while holding an extraordinary rock and turns himself into a rock, he finds that he is unable to turn himself back into a donkey. (**I**: 6–9)

Steiner, Joan. *Look-Alikes.* Little, Brown, 1998. A closer look at what appears to be a hotel lobby, an amusement park, or a general store reveals that everyday objects were used to create a miniature world. See also *Look-Alikes, Jr.* (1999). (**I**: P–10)

Steptoe, John. *Stevie.* Harper, 1969. A small boy resents having to share his mother with a little boy who is temporarily staying with them, until he realizes that the little boy is "kinda like a brother." (**I**: P–7)

———. *The Story of Jumping Mouse: A Native American Legend.* Lothrop, 1984. An unselfish mouse gives away what other animals need. Ultimately, the mouse is transformed into an eagle as a reward for its generosity. (**I**: 6–9)

Stevens, Janet. *Tops & Bottoms.* Harcourt, 1995. Clever and hard-working Hare outsmarts the land-rich but lazy Bear in order to "cash in" on the crops he grows. (**I**: 6–9)

———, and Susan Stevens Crummel. *Cook-a-Doodle-Doo!* Illustrated by Janet Stevens. Harcourt Brace, 1999. A hungry rooster seeks help in cooking up Great Granny's recipe for strawberry shortcake in this twist on the story of "The Little Red Hen." (**I**: 6–9)

Stevenson, James. *Could Be Worse!* Greenwillow, 1977. Grandpa tells his grandchildren a wild story. (**I**: 6–8)

Stewart, Sarah. *The Gardener.* Illustrated by David Small. Farrar, 1997. When Lydia is sent to live in an unfamiliar city and work, she brightens her life and her surroundings with her garden. (**I**: 6–9)

Stuve-Bodeen, Stephanie. *Elizabeti's Doll.* Illustrated by Christy Hale. Lee & Low, 1998. In this story set in Tanzania, Mother has a new baby and Elizabeti adopts a rock to serve as her doll. See also *Mama Elizabeti* (2000). (**I**: P–7)

Taback, Simms. *Joseph Had a Little Overcoat.* Viking, 1999. In this traditional tale, an old overcoat is recycled into a jacket, vest, scarf, necktie, handkerchief, button, and finally story. (**I**: P–8)

Tejima, Keizaburo. *Swan Sky.* Putnam, 1988. A young swan is unable to fly with the family when it is the season for migration. (**I**: P–8)

Thomas, Joyce Carol. *I Have Heard of a Land.* Illustrated by Floyd Cooper. HarperCollins, 1998. In the 1880s, an African American woman stakes a claim for free land in Oklahoma. (**I**: 6–10)

Tunnell, Michael O. *Mailing May.* Illustrated by Ted Rand. Tambourine/Greenwillow, 1997. Based on a true story, this book tells of a little girl sent on a train by parcel post mail in 1914 so that she can visit her grandmother. (**I**: 6–9)

Van Allsburg, Chris. *The Garden of Abdul Gasazi.* Houghton Mifflin, 1979. Alan chases Fritz the dog through the magician's garden and imagines that Fritz has been turned into a duck. (**I**: P–8)

———. *Jumanji.* Houghton Mifflin, 1981. Peter and Judy find an unusual board game that comes alive and turns the house into a jungle. (**I**: 7–10)

———. *Just a Dream.* Houghton Mifflin, 1990. Walter is careless about how he treats his environment. In a dream one night, he sees what the future will be like if everyone abuses the earth. He wakes up with a new determination. (**I**: P–8)

———. *The Polar Express.* Houghton Mifflin, 1985. Children board a night train headed for the North Pole. Santa grants the first wish of Christmas to a boy who asks for a bell from Santa's sleigh. (**I**: 6–9)

———. *The Sweetest Fig.* Houghton Mifflin, 1993. A woman leaves two figs as payment for work on her teeth, telling Monsieur Bibot that the figs make dreams come true. (I: 7–10)

————. *Two Bad Ants*. Houghton Mifflin, 1988. Two ants in search of sugar crystals for their queen divert from the path to seek adventure in the house. Their experiences prove terrifying. (I: 7–10)

Waber, Bernard. *Ira Sleeps Over*. Houghton Mifflin, 1972. Two boys have a sleepover and each is relieved to find that the other still sleeps with a stuffed animal. (I: P–7)

Waddell, Martin. *Can't You Sleep, Little Bear?* Illustrated by Barbara Firth. Candlewick, 1992. Little Bear's fear of the dark keeps him from falling asleep until Big Bear takes him outside to see the moon and the stars. (I: P–6)

————. *Farmer Duck*. Illustrated by Helen Oxenbury. Candlewick, 1992. A duck is overworked by a lazy farmer, and the barnyard animals rescue the duck and keep his family intact. (I: P–7)

Ward, Lynd. *The Biggest Bear*. Houghton Mifflin, 1952. When Johnny decides that he would like a bearskin on his wall, he goes out seeking the biggest bear. (I: 6–8).

Wattenberg, Jane. *Henny-Penny*. Scholastic, 2000. Henny-Penny outfoxes the fox in this retelling of the familiar tale, illustrated with digitized photo compositions. (I: 6–9)

Wells, Rosemary. *Max and Ruby's First Greek Myth: Pandora's Box*. Dial, 1993. Ruby tells the story of Pandora's box to her little brother Max. A sequel is *Max and Ruby's Midas: Another Greek Myth* (1995). (I: P–7)

————. *Bunny Cakes*. Dial, 1997. In an effort to decorate his earthworm cake for Grandma's birthday, Max repeatedly attempts to write "Red-Hot Marshmallow Squirters" on the grocery list. See also *Bunny Money* (1997). (I: P–8)

Wiesner, David. *June 29, 1999*. Clarion, 1992. Holly sends her science experiment vegetable seedlings high into the air. On June 29, 1999, a little over a month later, enormous vegetables appear all over earth, but when vegetables Holly did not send up begin to appear, everyone wonders where they came from. (I: 6–9)

Williams, Sherley Anne. *Working Cotton*. Illustrated by Carole Byard. Harcourt, 1992. A migrant family works in the cotton fields. (I: P–8)

Williams, Vera B. *A Chair for My Mother*. Greenwillow, 1982. When a fire destroys everything they own, a little girl saves money to buy Mother a comfortable chair in which to sit when she returns

home from work. A sequel is *Something Special for Me* (1983). (I: P–8)

————. *"More More More," Said the Baby: Three Love Stories*. Greenwillow, 1990. Three love stories show the loving relationships between each child and his or her parent. (I: P)

Wisniewski, David. *The Golem*. Clarion, 1996. A rabbi creates a clay giant, the golem, and brings it to life to help protect the Jews in Prague during the sixteenth century. (I: 9–12)

Wolkstein, Diane. *White Wave: A Chinese Tale*. Illustrated by Ed Young. Philomel, 1979. A Chinese farmer who finds a snail and cares for it discovers that the snail is nurturing him by providing him with food. The snail turns into White Wave, a moon goddess, and returns to the sky. (I: 6–9)

Wood, Audrey. *King Bidgood's in the Bathtub*. Illustrated by Don Wood. Harcourt, 1985. Throughout the day and into the night, King Bidgood won't leave his tub, to the great distress of his court. (I: P–8)

Yagawa, Sumiko. *The Crane Wife*. Illustrated by Suekichi Akaba. Translated by Katherine Paterson. Morrow, 1981. This traditional Japanese tale tells of a lonely man whose curiosity over the identity of his lovely wife leads to her departure. (I: 6–10)

Yolen, Jane. *The Emperor and the Kite*. Illustrated by Ed Young. Putnam, 1967/1988. The diligence and loyalty of the emperor's smallest daughter allow him to rule the land again after being overthrown by evil plotters. The watercolor paintings are reminiscent of Chinese cut-paper art. (I: 6–9)

————. *Owl Moon*. Illustrated by John Schoenherr. Philomel, 1987. A young boy goes "owling" with his father. (I: 7–9)

Yorinks, Arthur. *Hey, Al!* Illustrated by Richard Egielski. Farrar, 1986. Al is a janitor who lives in an apartment with his dog, Eddie. A large bird, calling "Hey, Al," offers them a new life in a place where they can be free of worries and cares. But Eddie and Al find their paradise back home. (I: 7–10)

Young, Ed. *Cat and Rat: The Legend of the Chinese Zodiac*. Holt, 1995. The Jade Emperor invites all the animals to participate in a race. This story tells how the twelve animals became part of the zodiac and why cat and rat will always remain enemies. (I: 6–9)

————. *Lon Po Po: A Red Riding Hood Story from China*. Philomel, 1989. This Chinese variation of the Red Riding Hood story depicts three children left home alone when their mother goes to visit their grandmother. When the wolf enters the house, the children outsmart the wolf and get rid of it. (**I:** 6–10)

————. *Seven Blind Mice*. Philomel, 1992. One by one, the blind mice feel the "thing" and describe various body parts they each feel. (**I:** P–9)

Zelinsky, Paul. *Rumpelstiltskin*. Dutton, 1986. Zelinsky's oil paintings richly depict this familiar tale of a young woman who must either discover the name of the little man or give him her first-born child in exchange for assistance in weaving straw into gold. (**I:** 7–9)

Ziefert, Harriet. *A New Coat for Anna*. Illustrated by Anita Lobel. Knopf, 1986. In Europe at the end of World War II, there is no money for a new coat. Anna's mother gives away her precious belongings to have a coat made for Anna. (**I:** P–8)

Zolotow, Charlotte. *Do You Know What I'll Do?* Illustrated by Javaka Steptoe. HarperCollins, 2000. This 1958 text of a loving brother and sister relationship has been reillustrated with collage images of African American siblings. (**I:** P–7)

————. *William's Doll*. Illustrated by William Pene du Bois. Harper & Row, 1972. William wants a doll, and various family members give differing responses to his request. (**I:** P–8)

RESOURCES

Aliki. *How a Book Is Made*. Harper & Row, 1986.

Bader, Barbara. *American Picturebooks from Noah's Ark to the Beast Within*. Macmillan, 1976.

Bang, Molly. *Picture This: Perception and Composition*. Little, Brown, 1991.

Carle, Eric. *The Art of Eric Carle*. Philomel, 1996.

Christelow, Eileen. *What Do Authors Do?* Clarion, 1995.

————. *What Do Illustrators Do?* Clarion, 1999.

Cianciolo, Patricia J. *The Illustrations in Children's Books*. William C. Brown, 1976.

————. *Picture Books for Children*. 4th ed. American Library Association, 1997.

Collier, Laurie, and Joyce Nakamura. *Major Authors and Illustrators for Children and Young Adults: A Selection of Sketches from Something about the Author*. Gale Research, 1993.

Cummings, Pat, comp. and ed. *Talking with Artists* (3 vols.). Bradbury, 1992, 1995, 1999.

Cummins, Julie. *Children's Book Illustration and Design*. PBC International, 1997.

Elleman, Barbara. *Tomie dePaola: His Art & His Stories*. Putnam, 1999.

Lacy, Lynn. *Art and Design in Children's Picture Books*. American Library Association, 1986.

Marcus, Leonard S. *Author Talk: Conversations with Judy Blume, Bruce Brooks, Karen Cushman, Russell Freedman, Lee Bennett Hopkins, James Howe, Johanna Hurwitz, E.L. Konigsburg, Lois Lowry, Ann M. Martin, Nicholasa Mohr, Gary Paulsen, Jon Scieszka, Seymour Simon, and Laurence Yep*. Simon & Schuster, 2000.

Nodleman, Perry. *Words about Pictures: The Narrative Art of Children's Picture Books*. Univ. of Georgia Press, 1988.

Pitz, Henry C. *Illustrating Children's Books*. Watson-Guptill, 1963.

Schwarcz, Joseph H., and Chava Schwarcz. *The Picture Book Comes of Age*. American Library Association, 1991.

Shulevitz, Uri. *Writing with Pictures: How to Write and Illustrate Children's Books*. Watson-Guptill, 1985/1997.

Silvey, Anita. *Children's Books and Their Creators*. Houghton Mifflin, 1995.

Spitz, Ellen Handler. *Inside Picture Books*. Yale Univ. Press, 1999.

Stevens, Janet. *From Pictures to Words: A Book about Making a Book*. Holiday House, 1995.

Stewig, John Warren. *Looking at Picture Books*. Highsmith, 1995.

REFERENCES

Adoff, Arnold. *Love Letters*. Illustrated by Lisa Desimini. Blue Sky Press/Scholastic, 1997.

————. *All the Colors of the Race: Poems*. Illustrated by John Steptoe. Morrow, 1987.

Ancona, George. *Carnaval*. Harcourt, 1999.

Andersen, Hans Christian. *The Ugly Duckling*. Adapted and illustrated by Jerry Pinkney. Morrow, 1999.

Anno, Mitsumasa. *Upside-Downers: More Pictures to Stretch the Imagination*. Weatherhill, 1971.

Blake, William. *Songs of Innocence and Songs of Experience*. Dover, 1789/1992.

Brown, Marcia. *Stone Soup: An Old Tale*. Aladdin, 1947/1987.

Carroll, Lewis. *Alice's Adventures in Wonderland*. Illustrated by John Tenniel. Macmillan, 1865.

Casanova, Mary. *The Hunter: A Chinese Folktale*. Illustrated by Ed Young. Atheneum/Simon & Schuster, 2000.

Clifton, Lucille. *All Us Come 'Cross the Water.* Illustrated by John Steptoe. Holt, 1973.

Crane, Walter. *Absurd ABC.* George Routledge & Sons, c. 1865.

———. *The House That Jack Built.* George Routledge & Sons, c. 1865.

———. *Sing a Song of Sixpence.* George Routledge & Sons, c. 1865.

Davol, Marguerite W. *The Paper Dragon.* Illustrated by Robert Sabuda. Atheneum, 1997.

Del Negro, Janice. *Lucy Dove.* Illustrated by Leonid Gore. DK Ink, 1998.

dePaola, Tomie. *Charlie Needs a Cloak.* Prentice-Hall, 1973.

———. *The Cloud Book.* Holiday House, 1975.

———. *The Popcorn Book.* Holiday House, 1988.

Diakité, Baba Wagué. *The Hatseller and the Monkeys.* Scholastic, 1999.

———. *The Hunterman and the Crocodile.* Scholastic, 1997.

Dragonwagon, Crescent. *Half a Moon and One Whole Star.* Illustrated by Jerry Pinkney. Aladdin, 1990.

Eibl-Eibesfeldt, Iraneus. *Ethology: The Biology of Behavior,* 2nd ed. Holt, 1975.

Gilman, Phoebe. *Something from Nothing.* Scholastic, 1993.

Greenfield, Eloise. *She Come Bringing Me That Little Baby Girl.* Illustrated by John Steptoe. Lippincott, 1974.

Grimes, Nikki. *It's Raining Laughter.* Photographs by Myles C. Pinkney. Dial, 1997.

Holdaway, Don. *The Foundations of Literacy.* Ashton Scholastic, 1979.

Keats, Ezra Jack. *Apt. 3.* Viking, 1974/1999.

Kiefer, Barbara Z. *The Potential of Picturebooks: From Visual Literacy to Aesthetic Understanding.* Merrill/Prentice-Hall, 1995.

Lester, Julius. *John Henry.* Illustrated by Jerry Pinkney. Dial, 1994.

———. *The Tales of Uncle Remus: The Adventures of Brer Rabbit.* Illustrated by Jerry Pinkney. Dutton, 1987.

Lodge, Sally. "The Making of a Crossover: One Book, Two Markets." *Publisher's Weekly* 239 (23 Nov. 1992): 39–42.

Louie, Ai-Ling. *Yeh-Shen: A Cinderella Story from China.* Illustrated by Ed Young. Putnam, 1982.

Moebius, William. "Introduction to Picturebook Codes." *Word & Image* 2.2 (1986): 141–52.

Myers, Walter Dean. *Brown Angels: An Album of Pictures and Verse.* HarperCollins, 1993.

———. *Glorious Angels: A Celebration of Children.* HarperCollins, 1996.

Pinkney, Andrea Davis. *Duke Ellington: The Piano Prince and His Orchestra.* Illustrated by Brian Pinkney. Hyperion, 1998.

Pinkney, Gloria. *The Sunday Outing.* Illustrated by Jerry Pinkney. Dial, 1994.

Pinkney, Sandra. *Shades of Black: A Celebration of Our Children.* Illustrated by Myles C. Pinkney. Scholastic, 2000.

Sabuda, Robert. *Saint Valentine.* Aladdin, 1992.

Sanfield, Steve. *Bit by Bit.* Philomel, 1995.

San Souci, Robert D. *The Talking Eggs: A Folktale from the American South.* Illustrated by Jerry Pinkney. Dial, 1989.

Schwartz, Alvin. *Scary Stories to Tell in the Dark.* Illustrated by Stephen Gammell. HarperCollins, 1985.

Schwartz, Joseph H. *Ways of the Illustrator: Visual Communication in Children's Literature.* American Library Association, 1982.

Sendak, Maurice. *Caldecott and Co.* Farrar, Straus & Giroux, 1990.

———. *In the Night Kitchen.* Harper, 1970.

———. *Outside Over There.* HarperCollins, 1981.

———. *We Are All in the Dumps with Jack and Guy: Two Nursery Rhymes with Pictures.* HarperCollins, 1993.

Steig, William. *Abel's Island.* Farrar, 1976.

———. *C D B!,* 2nd ed. Simon & Schuster, 2000.

Steiner, Joan. *Look Alikes.* Little, Brown, 1998.

———. *Look Alikes, Jr.: Find More Than 700 Hidden Everyday Objects.* Little, Brown, 1998.

Steptoe, John. *Mufaro's Beautiful Daughters: An African Tale.* Lothrop, 1987.

Van Allsburg, Chris. *The Wreck of the Zephyr.* Houghton Mifflin, 1983.

Willard, Nancy. *Pish, Posh, Said Hieronymus Bosch.* Illustrated by Lee Dillon. Harcourt, 1991.

Wood, Audrey. *Bright and Early Thursday Evening: A Tangled Tale.* Illustrated by Don Wood. Harcourt, 1996.

———. *The Red Racer.* Simon & Schuster, 1996.

Wyndham, Robert. *Chinese Mother Goose Rhymes.* Illustrated by Ed Young. PaperStar, 1968/1998.

7 Poetry for Children

What is poetry? Who knows?
Not a rose, but the scent of a rose;
Not the sky, but the light in the sky;
Not the fly, but the gleam of the fly;
Not the sea, but the sound of the sea;
Not myself, but what makes me
See, hear, and feel something that prose
Cannot: and what it is, who knows?

"Poetry"
by Eleanor Farjeon

WHAT IS POETRY?

It is impossible to coin a definition of poetry that some poem or other won't slither around. We might say that poems are made of rhymed and rhythmic language—but poems like this one by Byrd Baylor are not:

Desert Tortoise

I am the old one here.

Mice
and snakes
and deer
and butterflies
and badgers
come and go.
Centipedes
and eagles
come and go.

But tortoises
grow old
and stay . . .

We might say that poems are words arranged in a visually striking fashion that is different from the arrangement of prose—but some poems aren't. One example is "Football" by Walt Mason:

Football

The game was ended, and the noise at last had died away, and now they gathered up the boys where they in pieces lay. And one was hammered in the ground by many a jolt and jar; some fragments never have been found, they flew away so far. They found a stack of tawny hair, some fourteen cubits high; it was the halfback, lying there, where he had crawled to die. They placed the pieces on a door, and from the crimson field, that hero then they gently bore, like soldier on his shield. The surgeon toiled the livelong night above the gory wreck; he got the ribs adjusted right, the wishbone, and the neck. He soldered on the ears and toes, and got the spine in place, and fixed a gutta-percha nose upon the mangled face. And then he washed his hands and said: "I'm glad that task is done!" The halfback raised his fractured head, and cried: "I call this fun!"

Should we distinguish between "poems" and "rhymes"?

When Emily Dickinson spoke of poetry as writing that made her so cold no fire could ever warm her, presumably she didn't mean the likes of "Jack Sprat could eat no fat/His wife could eat no lean." Some authorities would say that this is not real poetry but rather should be called "verse" or "rhyme" (Lukens, 1992). According to that way of thinking, "poetry" is written expression that strikes readers in many ways at once—with sound, image, and meaning—and that repays careful rereading to savor the artistry and ponder the associations. Works that fall short—although perhaps very enjoyable—should be called "verse" or "rhymes."

The "Emily Dickinson test" might work with most nursery rhymes, but how would the Belle of Amherst's body temperature have responded to the poems of Shel Silverstein or Jack Prelutsky or David McCord or Eve Merriam? And if it could be proved—as some claim to have done—that many nursery rhymes contain cleverly encoded social and political messages, would we still be content to call these works mere rhymes?

The poem-versus-rhyme distinction is useful if it keeps us from expecting too much from every bit of verse we read. But the distinction is bound to lead to some unhappiness, as someone sniffs that one of your favorite poems is not a poem at all, but only a rhyme.

> What do you think? Should we make a distinction between poems and rhymes?

We might say poems wed image and sound in especially pleasing ways—but good prose often does this, too. For example, consider this excerpt from *Charlotte's Web,* by E. B. White:

> The barn was very large. It was very old. It smelled of hay and it smelled of manure. It smelled of perspiration of tired horses and the wonderful sweet breath of patient cows. It often had a sort of peaceful smell—as though nothing bad could happen ever again in the world. (p. 13)

Still, we usually know poetry when we see it. Poetry is a concise and memorable cast of language, with intense feeling, imagery, and qualities of sound that bounce pleasingly off the tongue, tickle the ear, and leave the mind something to ponder. Poetry, being the most memorable structure for language, has a particularly affecting honing of sound and meaning, giving it a special appeal to children—yet also inspiring the great American poet Emily Dickinson to exclaim, "If [writing] makes me so cold no fire can ever warm me, I know that it is poetry."

CATEGORIES OF POETRY FOR CHILDREN

Children enjoy several widely acknowledged kinds of poetry: nursery rhymes, jump-rope rhymes, folk poems, lyric poems, nonsense verse, and narrative poems. Poems can also be classified by their forms: sonnets, limericks, haiku, concrete poems, and others. Some poems, of course, resist easy categorization.

Nursery Rhymes

Nursery rhymes are verses by anonymous poets that are highly rhythmic, tightly rhymed, and popular with small children. Nursery rhymes have been recited to and by children since medieval times. Indeed, the associations in many nursery rhymes can be traced back several centuries.

> Baa, baa, black sheep, have you any wool?
> Yes, sir, yes, sir—three bags full.
> One for my master and one for my dame,
> And one for the little boy who lives down the lane.

This traditional rhyme dates from feudal times, when vassals paid shares of their produce to the powerful lords and ladies (masters and dames) who owned the lands of England.

> Ring around the roses,
> Pocket full of posies,
> Ashes, ashes,
> We all fall down.

This rhyme is said to refer to the Black Death, the bubonic plague, which killed a fourth of the population of England in the fourteenth century. The ring around the roses was a telltale rash of an infected person; the pocket full of posies was for protection against the "bad airs" that were believed to spread the sickness; and the ashes and falling down refer to the people who were stricken and died with dramatic suddenness (the disease ran its course in four days) and whose bodies were piled up and burned.

Nursery rhymes have pleasing sounds. This one sends the tongue tapping around all parts of the mouth—perhaps that is why small children love to recite it:

> Polly put the kettle on,
> Polly put the kettle on,
> Polly put the kettle on,
> We'll all have tea.
>
> Sukey take it off again,
> Sukey take it off again,

Sukey take it off again,
They've all gone away.

Many traditional rhymes also have accompanying motions. This one is a favorite when bouncing small children on one's knees:

This is the way the ladies ride,
Tri, tre, tre, tree!
Tri, tre, tre, tree!
This is the way the ladies ride,
Tri, tre, tre, tree!

And small children delight in having their toes wiggled to "This Little Piggie":

This little piggy went to market.
This little piggy stayed home.
This little piggy ate roast beef.
This little piggy ate none.
This little piggy cried "Wee! wee! wee!"
All the way home.

Jump-Rope and Counting-Out Rhymes

Unlike nursery rhymes, which are usually introduced to children by their parents or sitters, children's folk rhymes are anonymous verses passed on from child to child. Thus, they constitute—as *The Lore and Language of School Children* (2001), the title of the well-known book by British experts Iona and Peter Opie, suggests—an actual folklore that is the province of children themselves.

Hand-clapping rhymes such as this one often accompany children's play:

My boyfriend's name is Davy
He's in the U.S. Navy
With a pickle for his nose, cherries on his toes
That's the way my story goes.

Counting-out rhymes are perennially popular, too:

Bubble gum, bubble gum in a dish
How many pieces do you wish?
1, 2, 3 . . .

Children also enjoy rhythmic alphabet games such as this one:

A, my name is Annie,
And my husband's name is Al.
We come from Arkansas,
And we sell apples.

B, my name is Barbara,
And my husband's name is Bill . . .

And here's a popular jump-rope rhyme:

Cinderella
Dressed in yellow
Went upstairs
And kissed a fellow
Made a mistake and kissed a snake.

Came back down with a belly ache.
How many doctors does it take?
One . . . Two . . . Three . . . Four . . .

Francelia Butler's *Skipping around the World* has 350 skipping rhymes collected over forty years from seventy countries, and many of them turn out to have reworked adult themes, including historic military campaigns, politics, death, love, and sex.

Several collections of children's folk rhymes are currently in print (see the Recommended Books list at the end of this chapter). That these rhymes have to be written down at all shows adults' recognition that children's oral traditions need some bolstering against the inroads of canned commercial media.

Folk Songs Popular among Children

Another source of folk rhymes is folk songs that are popular with children. Some children's folk songs go back hundreds of years. "Oats, Peas, Beans, and Barley Grow" was sung in medieval times in England. Perhaps it's no coincidence that the plants in the song are mentioned in the order of proper crop rotation practiced by farmers for centuries.

Other folk songs that are popular with children are from more recent times. The song about the legendary John Henry, a mythical turn-of-the-century African American railroad worker, was recently made into a picture book by Julius Lester. Here is a verse:

When John Henry was a little baby
Sittin' on his mama's knee,
He picked up a hammer and a little piece of steel
And said, "Hammerin's gonna be the death of me, Lord, Lord,
Hammerin's gonna be the death of me."

John Langstaff, as a promoter of traditional folk music, dance, and rituals in his position as director of *Revels,* has made a number of excellent picture books of English folk songs over the years. His *Oh, A-Hunting We Will Go,* first published in 1974, is still a favorite. Ashley Bryan and John Langstaff have collaborated on books of African American spirituals, such as *What a Morning!* An interesting collection of Appalachian riddles, rhymes, and folk songs for children is *Granny Will Your Dog Bite? and Other Mountain Rhymes,* collected by

Illustration 7.2
Simms Taback's version of an old American folk song won a Caldecott Honor Medal. The die-cut illustrations add to the story's humor. (*There Was an Old Lady Who Swallowed a Fly* by Simms Taback. Copyright © 1997. Used by permission of Viking Children's Books, a division of Penguin Putnam Inc.)

Gerald Milnes and illustrated by Kimberly Bulcken Root (the book is available with a cassette recording). The delightfully absurd folk song "There Was an Old Lady Who Swallowed a Fly" has been developed into a picture book with hilarious illustrations by Caldecott Award–winning illustrator Simms Taback.

Woody Guthrie was the most famous American folk singer, and his "This Land Is Your Land" comes close to being an alternative national anthem. In 1998, folk artist Kathy Jakobsen brought out a picture book version of the song, with a tribute to Guthrie by Pete Seeger and illustrations of the places Guthrie traveled. The book includes verses, not usually sung, that show Guthrie's commitment to poor people:

> In the squares of a city, in the shadow of a steeple,
> By the relief office I seen my people
> As they stood there hungry, I stood there asking,
> Is this land made for you and me?*

Guthrie's song and the illustrations in this provocative book might inspire an inquiry into the social history of the United States during the Depression and the Dust Bowl era.

Lyric or Expressive Poems

The original lyrics were Greek poems that were accompanied by the lyre, a small harp. Today's lyric or expressive poems are works of emotion, observation, or insight. The category includes a huge number of poems.

Good examples of the genre are the poems in Nikki Grimes's collection *Hopscotch Love,* all observations about love from a young person's point of view. Here is an example:

> Sugar
> Honey
> Sweetie pie
> Shortcake
> Cupcake
> Sweet Dumplin'
> Chocolate Drop—
> Seems to me
> That love
> Might lead
> To cavities.

This anonymous reflection on the frog is a wonderful spoof of a lyric poem:

> What a wonderful bird the frog are—
> When he stand, he sit almost;
> When he hop, he fly almost.
> He ain't got no sense hardly;
> He ain't got no tail hardly either.
> When he sit, he sit on what he ain't got almost.

Naomi Shihab Nye, a poet and anthologist frequently seen in the schools, collected this lyric poem from an elementary-aged poet named Peter Acosta who

---

This Land Is Your Land Words and Music by Woody Guthrie. TRO-©-Copyright 1956 (Renewed) 1958 (Renewed) 1970 (Renewed) Ludlow Music., Inc., New York, New York. Used by permission.

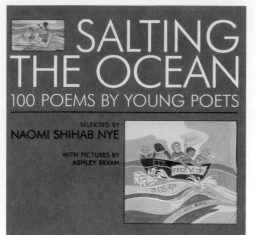

Illustration 7.3

In this volume, poet Naomi Shihab Nye has collected works of young poets who have taken part in her school workshops. (*Salting the Ocean* by Naomi Shihab Nye, with pictures by Ashley Bryan. Copyright © 2000. Used by permission of Greenwillow, a division of HarperCollins Publishers.)

participated in one of her writing workshops; it was published in *Salting the Ocean: 100 Poems by Young Poets:*

Ode to My Size

I sing to the size I am,
small and black-haired person.
There are two boys and two girls
that are taller than me.
And when they pass by I wish,
I wish I was tall myself.
I sing the size of me and my
companion that sits beside me. We
are both small but he is a little bigger
than me but I don't care about that.
I am just glad that I am a person.

Narrative Poems

Poems that tell stories are among the oldest of all poems, for at one time all stories that had wide currency were told in verse form. As you saw in Chapter 5, *The Odyssey, The Iliad, Beowulf,* and the *Poema de mio Cid* were all originally told in verse. In the Middle Ages, ballads—long narrative poems—told the stories of Robin Hood, Lord Randall, and other heroes.

Narrative poetry written expressly for children began in the nineteenth century. Clement Clarke Moore's "A Visit from St. Nicholas, or 'Twas the Night before Christmas," published in 1822, not only helped to establish the genre of narrative poetry for children but also contributed to the Santa Claus lore that is still widely circulated in North America. Robert Service's poems have long been popular for their exciting plots involving tough men in wilderness settings: the Yukon and the old West. The most famous of his poems, *The Cremation of Sam McGee,* was brought out in 1986 as a picture book with inspired illustrations by Ted Harrison. Here is a sample of the poem:

There are strange things done
in the midnight sun
By the men who moil for gold;
The arctic trails have their secret tales
   That would make your blood run cold;
The Northern Lights
      have seen queer sights,
   But the queerest they ever did see
Was that night on the marge of Lake Lebarge
I cremated Sam McGee.

One of the great American narrative poems is Ernest Lawrence Thayer's *Casey at the Bat,* a favorite of generations of young people:

The outlook wasn't brilliant for the Mudville nine that day;
The score stood four to two with but one inning left to play . . .

Ludwig Bemelmans popularized rhyming narratives for modern children with his many books about Madeline, the feisty young resident of the convent

Illustration 7.4

Janet S. Wong's narrative poem "Good Luck Gold," featured in the title of this anthology, displays courage in the face of racism. (*Good Luck Gold and Other Poems* by Janet S. Wong. Copyright © 1994 by Janet S. Wong. Used by permission of Margaret K. McElderry books, an imprint of Simon & Schuster Children's Publishing.)

school in Paris. And Roy Gerrard continues to turn out imaginative contributions to the narrative poem genre: *Rosy and the Rustlers, Sir Frances Drake,* and others.

Janet S. Wong, a West Coast poet of Korean and Chinese ancestry, gives us the following narrative of courage in the face of racism, from her *Good Luck Gold and Other Poems.* (Note how the rhymes within each verse are mirrored.)

> All the white kids are eating.
> "Let's go, Dad," I say.
> "Let's get out of this place."
> But Dad doesn't move.
> He's going to prove
> the Asian race
> is equal. We stay
> and take our silent beating.
> He folds his arms
> across his chest
> glaring at the waitresses who
> pass by like cattle
> ready for a western battle.
> They will not look, they refuse to
> surrender even to my best
> wishing on bracelet charms.
>
> "Consider this part of your education,"
> Dad says. I wonder how long
> we'll be ignored, like hungry ghosts
> of Chinese men who laid this track,
> never making their journeys back
> but leaving milestones and signposts
> to follow. "Why do they treat us so wrong?"
> I wonder. "Don't they know we're on vacation?"
>
> A drunk shouts at us and
> gets louder and redder
> in the face
> when we pay
> him no mind. I say
> "Let's get out of this place.
> We're not equal. We're better,"
> as I pull Dad by the hand.

Nonsense Verse

In the middle of the last century, the English poet Edward Lear was the first to publish nonsense verse. Lear's "The Jumblies" is also known as "They Went to Sea in a Sieve":

> They went to sea in a sieve, they did;
>   In a sieve they went to sea;
> In spite of all their friends would say,
> On a winter's morn, on a stormy day,
>   In a sieve they went to sea.

Illustration 7.5
"Alligator Pie" is a classic nonsense poem that delights young readers.
(*Alligator Pie,* Poems by Dennis Lee, Pictures by Frank Newfeld.)

Nonsense poetry is alive and well among modern writers. Canadian poet Dennis Lee is a master of the art:

Alligator Pie

Alligator pie, alligator pie,
If I don't get some I think I'm gonna die.
Give away the green grass, give away the sky,
But don't give away my alligator pie . . .

Shel Silverstein's nonsense poetry is among the most popular these days. Here's a sample from *Where the Sidewalk Ends:*

Chester

Chester come to school and said,
"Durn! I've growed another head!"
The teacher said, "It's time you knowed
The word is 'grew' instead of 'growed.'"

Form Poems: Limericks

Up until the beginning of this century, most poems in English had identifiable rhyme schemes and rhythmic patterns. Today, most poetry is more varied in its structure and use of sounds. A few common forms of poetry persist, however. The limerick is one of the most popular of the forms still current. Why? X. J. and Dorothy Kennedy offer a poem by way of explanation:

Well, it's partly the shape of the thing
That makes the old limerick swing—
    Its accordion pleats
    Full of light, airy beats
Take it up like a kite on the wing!

Limericks came into being in the early nineteenth century and found an early champion at midcentury in the nonsense poet Edward Lear. Lear so popularized the form that it is closely identified with him. Here is one of his limericks:

There was an Old Man who said, "Hush!
I perceive a young bird in this bush!"
    When they said, "Is it small?"
    He replied, "Not at all;
It is four times as big as the bush!"

Form Poems: Haiku

Another common form of poetry is the haiku, a three-line nonrhyming poem developed in Japan. Haiku traditionally contain seventeen syllables, five in the first line, seven in the middle, and five in the last (although English-language haiku don't always follow that requirement). Most haiku make an observation about nature in a particular moment and a particular place:

Now at the black pond
    twilight slowly abandons
the lone blue heron.

Dialogue Poems

Poems for two or more voices are enjoyable to read aloud. Dialogue poems are as old as Mother Goose rhymes:

"Old woman, old woman,
Shall we go a'shearing?"

"Speak a little louder sir,
I'm very hard of hearing."

"Old woman, old woman,
Shall I kiss you dearly?"

"Yes, sir, yes, sir,
I hear you very clearly."

Paul Fleischman won a Newbery Award in 1988 for *Joyful Noise: Poems for Two Voices*, illustrated by Eric Beddows. These poems have delighted many school children, who read them aloud in pairs.

Grasshoppers

Sap's rising	
	Ground's warming
Grasshoppers are	Grasshoppers are
hatching out	hatching out
Autumn-laid eggs	
	splitting
Young stepping	
into spring	
Grasshoppers	Grasshoppers
hopping	hopping
high	
Grassjumpers	Grassjumpers
jumping	jumping
	far
Vaulting from	
leaf to leaf	
stem to stem	leaf to leaf
plant to plant	stem to stem
	Grass-
leapers	leapers
Grass-	
bounders	bounders
	Grass-
springers	springers
Grass-	
soarers	Soarers
Leapfrogging	Leapfrogging
longjumping	longjumping
grasshoppers.	grasshoppers.

Janet Wong uses the dialogue form to dramatic effect in "Speak Up," from *Good Luck Gold:*

Speak Up

You're Korean, aren't you?	
	Yes.
Why don't you speak	
Korean?	
	Just don't, I guess.

Say something Korean.

I don't speak it.
I can't.

C'mon. Say something.

Halmoni. Grandmother.
Haraboji. Grandfather.
Imo. Aunt.

Say some other stuff.
Sounds funny.
Sounds strange.

Hey, let's listen to you
For a change.

Listen to me?

Say some foreign words.

But I'm American,
can't you see?

Your family came from
somewhere else.
Sometime.

But I was born here.

So was I.

Free Verse

Poetry that has no discernible form at all is free verse. Free verse has no rhyme or particular rhythm but makes its impressions with an intensity of insight or feeling, a clarity of vision, and sounds and rhythms that ebb and flow with the intensity of the poet's feelings about the subject matter. Here is an example of free verse by Valerie Worth from *All the Small Poems:*

Dog

Under a maple tree
The dog lies down,
Lolls his limp
Tongue, yawns,
Rests his long chin carefully between
Front paws:
Looks up, alert;
Chops, with heavy
Jaws, at a slow fly,
Blinks, rolls
On his side,
Sighs, closes
His eyes: sleeps
All afternoon
In his loose skin.

Here, with no meter or rhyme scheme to worry about, the poet can let the poem take its own shape. She sets out a series of images. She makes cadences in patterns and then suddenly breaks them, reflecting the erratic behavior of the poem's subject. She uses a series of sounds that echo each other (the dog lies down . . . Lolls his limp . . .), and then she shifts to other sounds.

THE EVOLUTION OF CHILDREN'S POETRY

Early Poetry for Children

Donald Hall, an American, and Iona and Peter Opie, both British, have put together historical collections of poems written in English for children. The early parts of both chronologically arranged collections make rather grim reading. Up until William Blake's *Songs of Innocence,* published in the late eighteenth century, the poems were cheerless, moralistic, didactic, and often downright mean-spirited. Here, for instance, is the beginning of an English alphabet poem from around 1700:

A was an Archer, and shot at a frog,
B was a Blindman, and led by a dog,
C was a Cutpurse, and lived in disgrace,
D was a Drunkard, and had a red face.
E was an Eater, a glutton was he,
F was a Fighter, and fought with a flea,
G was a Giant, and pulled down a house . . .

Early American poems for children were every bit as dour. Some poems exalted early death as the greatest aspiration of a young child; for by dying young, children reduced their chances of falling into sin. Other poems impressed on children the horrors of eternal damnation for their "original sin."

More Sympathetic Voices

The poems of the English poet William Blake (1757–1827) were something new. They appealed to children without preaching or sentimentalizing. In fact, in his *Songs of Innocence,* Blake was the first to write with sympathy of the plight of child laborers:

The Chimney Sweeper

When my mother died I was very young,
And my father sold me while yet my tongue
Could scarcely cry "'weep! 'weep! 'weep! 'weep!"
So your chimneys I sweep, and in soot I sleep.

The better poets from Blake's time on left off the moralizing and wrote for children's enjoyment. The long narrative poems of Robert Browning (1812–1889) are imaginative and entertaining. Here is the beginning of *The Pied Piper of Hamelin:*

Hamelin Town's in Brunswick,
    By famous Hanover city;
The river Weser, deep and wide,
Washes its wall by the southern side;
A pleasanter spot you never spied;
    But, when begins my ditty,
Almost five hundred years ago,
To see the townsfolk suffer so
    From vermin, was a pity.

    Rats!
They fought the dogs and killed the cats,

And bit the babies in their cradles,
And ate the cheeses out of vats,
    And licked the soup from cooks' own ladles,
Split open kegs of salted sprats,
Made nests inside men's Sunday hats,
And even spoiled the women's chats
    By drowning their speaking
    With shrieking and squeaking
In fifty different sharps and flats . . .

From the mid-nineteenth century on, the poetry gets more and more delightful. We've already mentioned Edward Lear's nonsense verse, which plays with language and enlivens the imagination. In *Alice's Adventures in Wonderland* (1865), Lewis Carroll confidently spoofed the moralistic doggerel that was so prominent in poetry for children just a short time before:

Speak roughly to your little boy,
And beat him when he sneezes:
He only does it to annoy,
Because he knows it teases.

Christina Rossetti (1830–1894) could be thoughtful and accessible at the same time, as in "The Wind" (from *Complete Poems of Christina Rossetti*):

Who has seen the wind?
    Neither you nor I;
But when the leaves hang trembling
    The wind is passing through.

Who has seen the wind?
    Neither you nor I;
But when the trees bow down their heads
    The wind is passing by.

Robert Louis Stevenson (1850–1894) gave us the great adventure novels *Treasure Island* and *Kidnapped.* His *A Child's Garden of Verses,* written at the end of the nineteenth century, is still much admired; through the middle of the twentieth century, it was among the most widely read of poetry collections. Stevenson could be gentle, yet savvy to a child's point of view:

Looking Forward

When I am grown to man's estate
I shall be very proud and great,
And tell the other girls and boys
Not to meddle with my toys.

At the turn of the century and after, Rudyard Kipling, A. A. Milne, T. S. Eliot, and others appealed to children with exciting and delightful poems, with words and rhythms well suited to their themes.

Kipling's poems reflected the high adventure of a life lived in exotic places, as this fragment of "The Smuggler's Song" (from *Puck of Pook's Hill*) shows:

If you wake at midnight and hear horses' feet,
Don't go drawing back the blind, or looking in the street,
Them that asks no questions isn't told a lie.
Watch the wall, my darling, while the Gentlemen go by!
   Five and twenty ponies,
   Trotting through the dark—
   Brandy for the parson,
   'Baccy for the Clerk
   Laces for a lady; letters for a spy;
   And watch the wall, my darling, while the Gentlemen go by!

Contemporary Poetry for Children

During the twentieth century, poetry for children continued to evolve. One noticeable change was freedom from formality: Nonrhyming poems became more common, and the language of poetry more folksy. Another change was a greater inclusion of the minority experience in poetry for children, beginning with the poetry of Langston Hughes in the 1920s. Still another change was a more honest and direct voice in the poetry. As we have seen, in earlier centuries, the attitude of the poet could be aloof and punishing. Later, it became sentimental and reassuring. In the contemporary era, the voice of the poet has become more honest and confiding—both poet and child live in a troubled world, in which even adults often feel little power. Modern poets do not offer a naive reassurance they do not feel.

The voice of Langston Hughes's narrator in "Mother to Son" (from *The Dream Keeper and Other Poems*) reflects the shift. The narrator is teaching a message of optimism, but the optimism is based on perseverance in grim circumstances. This world is a far cry from the cozy, sheltered world of the imagination constructed by poets in the nineteenth century. Note how Hughes uses a staircase in a slum dwelling as a metaphor for a hard life:

Mother to Son

Well, son, I'll tell you:
Life for me ain't been no crystal stair.
It's had tacks in it,
And splinters,
And boards torn up,
And places with no carpet on the floor—
Bare.
But all the time
I'se been a-climbin' on,
And reachin' landin's,
And turnin' corners,
And sometimes goin' in the dark
Where there ain't been no light.
So, boy, don't you turn back.
Don't you set down on the steps
'Cause you finds it kinder hard.
Don't you fall now—
For I'se still goin', honey,
I'se still climbin',
And life for me ain't been no crystal stair.

The honest and not superior voice is evident in the work of many modern poets who write for children, such as Eve Merriam, Myra Cohn Livingston, Nikki Giovanni, and Gary Soto. It is evident in Nikki Giovanni's "dance poem" (from *Spin a Soft Black Song*), in which the mother sounds almost desperate as she tries to cheer her children—or have them cheer her:

come nataki dance with me
bring your pablum dance with me
pull your plait and whirl around
come nataki dance with me

won't you tony dance with me
stop your crying dance with me
feel the rhythm of my arms
don't let's cry now dance with me

tommy stop your tearing up
don't you hear the music
don't you feel the happy beat
don't bite tony dance with me
mommy needs a partner . . .

Contemporary children's poets still write with insight and humor about the joys and scrapes of childhood, as Nikki Grimes does in "True Love Blues" (from *Hopscotch Blues*):

True Love Blues

Love means putting others first—
That's what love's about.
Lord says you gotta put me first
'Cause that's what love's about.
But the way you hog that apple pie
Proves you still ain't figured that out.

But they also write about urban issues, about poverty and racism, about the dangers of environmental pollution, about the overmechanization and erosion of human values in our lives—as in this poem by Eve Merriam (from *Chortles*):

Sing a Song of Subways

Sing a song of subways
Never see the sun;
Four-and-twenty people
In room for one.

When the doors are opened—
Everybody run.

The Many Voices of Children's Poetry

Many contemporary poets write to foster racial pride, as oppression has made pride hard to come by. Lucille Clifton writes eloquently to this end in "Listen Children" (in Arnold Adoff's *My Black Me*):

Illustration 7.6
Arnold Adoff's powerful collection of poems brings well-known black poets, as well as commanding but lesser-known ones, into classrooms. (*My Black Me* by Arnold Adoff, editor. Illustration copyright © 1974 by Tyrone Geter. Used by permission of Dutton Signet, a division of Penguin Putnam Inc.)

listen children
keep this in the place
you have for keeping
always
keep it all ways

we have never hated black

listen
we have been ashamed
hopeless   tired   mad

but always
all ways
we loved us

we have always loved each other
children   all ways

pass it on

A breakthrough in contemporary literature for children was the publication of poetry from all quarters of American culture and from around the world as well. Poetry from the Caribbean is earthy and colorful, as this poem by Monica Gunning (from *Not a Copper Penny in Me House*) demonstrates:

The Corner Shop

"Chil', me stone broke," Grandma sighs.
"Not a copper penny in me house.
Go tell Maas Charles at the corner shop
I want to trust a pound of codfish
and two pounds of rice.
I'll pay him when the produce dealer
buys me dried pimento crop in season."

Maas Charles never says no.
He knows everyone in the village
by their first names.
He scoops from his bin, weighs and wraps,
adds to his credit sheet on the wall
a new amount under Grandma's name.
Grandma always says,
"Thank God for Maas Charles."

Poetry from Latin American communities can be worldly and upbeat or wise and deep. Many collections are available in Spanish and English translations, like this poem from Mexico by Raul Banuelos (in *The Tree Is Older Than You Are*, edited by Naomi Shihab Nye):

Agua y tierra

El agua
es la luz
con raiz en la tierra.

Water and Earth

Water
is the light
with roots in the earth.

Beberla	To drink it
es echarse a caminar	is to journey
como un rio.	like a river.

A clear and lively new voice in poetry for children is Janet Wong, an American poet of Korean and Chinese descent. Wong writes for young people of many ages. She writes about racism. She writes about driving automobiles. For young children, she writes about sounds around the house, in *Buzz,* illustrated by Margaret Chodos-Irvine:

Illustration 7.7
Janet Wong's celebration of household sounds is filled with noises—all sounding like "buzzzz." (Cover illustration from *Buzz* by Janet Wong, illustrations copyright © 2000 by Margaret Chodos-Irvine, reprinted by permission of Harcourt, Inc.)

> Mommy grinds coffee
> BUZZZZZZZZZZ
>
> While I fly my airplane
> BUZZZZZZZZZZ
>
> over the oatmeal
> BUZZZZZZZZZZ
>
> and past the apple juice
> BUZZZZZZZZZZ—
>
> OH NO!
> Splash
>   Landing!

Finally, though we mentioned that poetry for children continues to evolve, we should note that evolution in poetry for children is not the same thing as evolution in the design of automobiles. A Saturn is obviously a more sophisticated car than a Model T Ford, but a poem by Jack Prelutsky is not more sophisticated than a poem by A. A. Milne or one by Langston Hughes. As new poems are written, they add to the body of poetry available to children, without necessarily replacing it. Children today have access to exciting new poems that speak to contemporary realities; they can also read the best poems of the past.

ELEMENTS OF POETRY

Ask yourself this question: What do you like about a favorite poem? If you can't quite put your finger on it, consider the main features that critics agree make up a good poem: sounds, images, and forms.

Sounds

Most poetry for children is crafted with a keen ear for sound. That's why it is often best read aloud. Sounds are the musical aspect of poetry. Just as music is said to speak the language of the emotions, so the sounds of poetry—rhythm, rhyme, alliteration, and onomatopoeia—choreograph much of the listener's emotional experience.

Rhythm. Rhythm is the beat of a poem. Rhythm can be a direct route to the emotions. The rhythm of a slow heartbeat has a calming effect, even on a newborn, whereas the sound of a fast heartbeat causes anxiety. The pulse of a graduation march sweeps us along with dignity and pride; the pounding of a military drum keeps soldiers advancing in step with one another. The rhythm of a marching band makes us want to run to get a better look. Wallace Stevens captured the martial rhythm of a marching band in his poem "John Smith and His Son, John Smith" (from *The Collected Poems of Wallace Stevens*):

John Smith and his son, John Smith,
   And his son's son John, and-a-one
   And-a-two and-a-three
And a rum-tum-tum, and-a
Lean John, and his son, lean John,
   And his lean son's John, and-a-one
   And-a-two and-a-three
And a drum-rum-rum, and-a
Rich John, and his son, rich John,
   And his rich son's John, and-a-one
   And-a-two and-a-three . . .

The rhythm of this poem implicitly compares a proud parade of marchers to the passing of generations within a family.

Rhythm is prominent in many children's poems—and perhaps nowhere more so than in the work of NCTE award–winner David McCord. In his poem "The Pickety Fence" (from *One at a Time*), you can hear the rhythm of a stick dragging staccato across the pickets:

The pickety fence
The pickety fence
Give it a lick it's
The pickety fence
Give it a lick it's
A clickety fence
Give it a lick it's
A lickety fence
Give it a lick
Give it a lick
Give it a lick
With a rickety stick
Pickety
Pickety
Pickety
Pick

Children delight in clapping along to the rhythm of such poetry.

Rhyme. Along with rhythm, rhyme lends a musical quality to poetry by building patterns of repetition. Rhymes delight us—but they do more. Rhymes function in a poem to link words, to play them against each other, to build on their emotional content, as we see in this poem by Walter de la Mare (1923):

The Horseman

I heard a horseman
   Ride over the hill;
The moon shone clear,
The night was still;
His helm was silver,
   And pale was he;
And the horse he rode
   Was of ivory.

Illustration 7.8

This rhymed picture book evokes the sights, sounds, and sensations of a day-long train ride. (Cover from *Train* by Charles Temple, illustrated by Larry Johnson. Jacket illustration copyright © 1996 by Larry Johnson. Reprinted by permission of Houghton Mifflin Company. All rights reserved.)

Rhymes are most pleasing when they surprise us. And poets can build up suspense by delaying rhymes when they are expected, as in this excerpt from Charles Temple's ***Train:***

> The train stands trembling on the C&O track,
> As the whistle puffs a warning, long and low.
> Now the smoke starts chuffing from the short
>   smokestack
> And the lights go sweeping
> And the engine goes rumbling
> And the wheels go squeaking kind of slow . . .

Of course, the rhyming words should suit the meaning of the poem, and not be included merely for the sake of sound. The rhymes in Christina Rossetti's "Caterpillar" (from ***Complete Poems of Christina Rossetti***) are skillfully done:

> Brown and furry
> Caterpillar in a hurry,
> Take your walk
> To the shady leaf, or stalk,
> Or what not,
> Which may be the chosen spot.
> No toad spy you,
> Hovering bird of prey pass by you;
> Spin and die,
> To live again a butterfly.

Alliteration. Poems also may have repeated sounds that are more subtle than rhymes. These repeated sounds come in two common forms: *consonance,* the stringing together of similar consonant sounds, and *assonance,* the making of a series of similar vowel sounds. Together, consonance and assonance are known as *alliteration.*

Listen to this line from a poem by Rowena Bennett: "There once was a witch of Willowby Wood. . . ." A series of similar consonant sounds ties her words together; this is an example of consonance. No matter that "once" begins with o; the initial w sounds knit Bennett's words into a sonorous fabric.

Consonance doesn't have to be smooth, though. A succession of percussive consonants can sound like feet walking on dry sticks, as in this anonymous Welsh poem translated by Gwyn Williams (in ***The Rattle Bag,*** edited by Heaney and Hughes):

> Dinogad's speckled petticoat
> was made of skins and speckled stoat:
> whip whip whipalong
> eight times we'll sing the song.

The succession of consonant clusters in Alfred, Lord Tennyson's "The Eagle" (1851) helps us to see and feel the bird's harsh, desolate perch; when the consonants give way to smoother sounds, they suggest the expansive beauty of the landscape below:

> He clasps the crag with crooked hands;
> Close to the sun in lonely lands,
> Ringed with the azure world, he stands . . .

Assonance, the use of a series of similar vowel sounds, also ties the words in a line together. Note the repeated short vowel sounds in "clasps," "crag," and "hands" in Tennyson's poem. Carl Sandburg also used assonance skillfully in "Splinter" (from *The Complete Poems of Carl Sandburg*):

> The voice of the last cricket
> across the first frost
> is one kind of goodbye.
> It is so thin a splinter of singing.

Note the high thin "ih" sounds in the last line, holding out against the more ponderous "ah" sounds in the second.

Onomatopoeia. When words in a poem imitate actual sounds of things (such as "moo," "oink," "bam"), the poet is using onomatopoeia. Hilaire Belloc gave us some fine examples of onomatopoeia as he described Spanish dancers in these lines from "Tarantella" (in *The Rattle Bag*):

> . . . And the Hip! Hop! Hap!
> Of the clap
> Of the hands . . .
> . . . And the Ting, Tong, Tang of the Guitar . . .

In sum, poets use sounds deliberately to approximate the emotional qualities of their subjects and to weave words together into tight compositions. Good poets blend sounds so skillfully that we feel the effects without being aware of the devices they have used. Note how Rodney Bennet employs rhythm, rhyme, alliteration, and onomatopoeia in this poem (in *Knock at a Star,* edited by Kennedy and Kennedy):

Windy Nights

> Rumbling in the chimneys,
>   Rattling at the doors,
> Round the roofs and round the roads
>   The rude wind roars;
> Raging through the darkness,
>   Raving through the trees
> Racing off again across
>   The great grey seas.

Images

When a poem seems to "put us in the picture," chances are the poet has used *imagery,* an appeal to the senses, using details that enable us to imagine how things look, sound, feel, smell, or taste.

In "The Child on Top of a Greenhouse," Theodore Roethke first anchors our impressions in the narrator's point of view by reporting what the narrator sees, hears, and feels:

> The wind billowing out the seat of my britches,
> My feet crackling splinters of glass and dried putty,
> The half-grown chrysanthemums staring up like accusers,
> Up through the streaked glass, flashing with sunlight,
> A few white clouds all rushing eastward,
> A line of elms plunging and tossing like horses,
> And everyone, everyone pointing up and shouting!

By the end of the poem, the danger of the narrator's situation sinks in. We realize that the child's absorption in sensory details, in which we have shared, has made him oblivious to the perils of climbing on top of a greenhouse.

Mary O'Neill's poem "My Fingers" about the sense of touch is full of tactile imagery:

> My fingers are antennae.
> Whatever they touch:
> Bud, rose, apple,
> Cellophane, crutch—
> They race the feel
> Into my brain,
> Plant it there and
> Begin again.
> This is how I knew
> Hot from cold
> Before I was even
> Two years old.

Imagery is one of poetry's great contributions to human awareness. With imagery, poems name sensations and expand people's consciousness of their minute-to-minute experiences.

Toddlers have the wonderful power to put words together in new ways: A naked child spread his arms and proclaimed, "I'm barefoot all over!" Making words do new work is one of the poet's greatest talents, too. Poets often use language in fresh ways by making comparisons: similes and metaphors and personifications.

The definitions of these terms never do justice to their power. A *simile* is defined as an explicit comparison, using the word "like" or "as." A *metaphor* lacks those two words and is a direct comparison in which one thing is described as if it were another. *Personification* is a sort of metaphor in which an inanimate thing is described as if it were human (or, at least, had sensations and will). But look what writers do with these literary devices. Practically all mythology is built on personification. The ancient Norse myths, for example, personified the reckless forces of nature in the character of Thor. Most religious writing is built around metaphor and simile: Having no direct experience of any world but this one, religious writers use familiar terms to speak of things beyond.

The Mexican poet Alberto Forcada compares a belly button to the knot in a balloon in this translated poem (in **The Tree Is Older Than You,** edited by Nye), making a simile:

Ombligo	Belly Button
Como los globos	Like the balloons
que flotan en las fiestas,	that float at parties,
tengo, para no desinflarme,	I have a knot on my belly
un nudo en el estómago.	so I won't go flat.

In "Mirrorment" (in **Sing a Song of Popcorn,** edited by de Regniers et al.), A. R. Ammons equates flowers and birds, making a metaphor:

> Birds are flowers flying
> and flowers perched birds.

Dorothy Aldis slips an almost unnoticed metaphor into her poem "When I Was Lost" (from *All Together*):

Underneath my belt
My stomach was a stone.
Sinking was the way I felt.
And hollow.
And alone.

Roethke's young narrator in "The Child on Top of a Greenhouse" said that the half-grown chrysanthemums were "staring up at him like accusers." This comparison gave the flowers human senses and motives—it personified them. Langston Hughes personified rain in his "April Rain Song" (from *The Dream Keeper and Other Poems*):

Let the rain kiss you.
Let the rain beat upon your head with silver liquid drops.
Let the rain sing you a lullaby.
The rain makes running pools in the gutter.
The rain plays a little sleep-song on our roof at night.
And I love the rain.

In summary, all of these ways of making likenesses—similes, metaphors, and personification—expand the power of language. In so doing, they expand our perceptions, too: They make us, the readers and hearers, experience the world in new ways.

Forms

The arrangement of words on the page affects their look, readers' progress through them, and the emphasis given to some of the words.

Shel Silverstein uses a columnar arrangement in his poem "Valentine" (from *Where the Sidewalk Ends*):

I got a valentine from Timmy
                        Jimmy
                        Tillie
                        Billy
                        Nicky
                        Micky
                        Ricky
                        Dicky
                        Laura
                        Nora
                        Cora
                        Flora
                        Donnie
                        Ronnie
                        Lonnie
                        Connie
                        Eva even sent me two
                        But I didn't get *none* from you.

This poem, of course, is a list. Its arrangement invites reading one name at a time, as if a child were keeping track of who her friends are.

Sometimes poets arrange their words to look like their topic. Consider Bobbi Katz's "Spring Is" (in *The Random House Book of Poetry for Children,* edited by Jack Prelutsky):

Spring is when
    the morning sputters like
bacon
    and
        your
            sneakers
                run
                    down
                        the
                            stairs
so fast you can hardly keep up with them
and
spring is when
    your scrambled eggs
        jump
            off
                the
                    plate
and turn into a million daffodils
trembling in the sunshine.

In this poem, the progressively indented lines resemble the staircase that the sneakers run down.

Insight

Above and beyond the effects of particular literary devices, poems often startle us with insight—a noticing of things that makes us say, "Yes—that's it! But I never found a way of saying it before." Some insights are simple but still surprising, like this one in Philip Whalen's poem "Early Spring" (in Paul Janeczko's *This Delicious Day*):

The dog writes on the window with his nose.

Some insights are more complicated, such as those in this poem by Naomi Shihab Nye (from *Words under the Words*):

Famous

The river is famous to the fish.

The loud voice is famous to silence,
which knew it would inherit the earth
before anybody said so.

The cat sleeping on the fence is famous to the birds
watching him from the birdhouse.

The tear is famous, briefly, to the cheek.

The idea you carry close to your bosom
is famous to your bosom.

The boot is famous to the earth,

more famous than the dress shoe,
which is famous only to floors.

The bent photograph is famous to the one who carries it
and not at all famous to the one who is pictured.

I want to be famous to shuffling men
who smile while crossing streets,
sticky children in grocery lines,
famous as the one who smiled back.

I want to be famous the way a pulley is famous,
or a buttonhole, not because it did anything spectacular,
but because it never forgot what it could do.

Imagery is one of poetry's great values, but insight is even greater. Good poems are often noteworthy for their concentrated clarity of understanding. The insight expressed in Naomi Shihab Nye's poem might well have been elaborated by another writer into a book-length manuscript.

CRITERIA FOR SELECTING POETRY

When we are choosing good poetry for children, we face two issues right off: What are the criteria that define good poetry? What kinds of poetry do children like? Although there are many fine poems that children like, the answers to these two questions, as we shall see, are not always in easy balance.

Choosing Good Poetry for Children

Good poems for children must satisfy the same criteria for quality as any other form of children's literature—except that their shorter form puts a special emphasis on qualities such as skilled use of language, imagery, and insight.

Sounds. Poems don't have to rhyme. Among those that do, though, the better ones have exact rhymes (they don't try to pass off near misses, like "alone" and "home"). Better poems also have fresh rhymes: Readers cannot predict with boring certainty what the words at the ends of the lines will be. Above all, the rhymes don't get in the way of the poem's images and meanings.

Poems do not have to have fixed rhythms. But if they do, the rhythms should be consistent enough for children to discern them, yet not so consistent as to become monotonous. It is a very tall order to mix rhymes with exact word choices and to use clear rhythms that aren't cloying. No wonder so many modern poets avoid rhymes and fixed rhythms altogether. If a poet opts for blank verse, though, we still expect a careful handling of sound and meter. If their poems don't rhyme, poets must match the sounds of their words to the emotional tone of their topics. If their poems don't have a fixed rhythm throughout, poets must write in syllables that match the pace of the reading to the meaning of the poem.

Images. Good poems bring clear images to the mind's eye. Whether they use language denotatively with precise word choices or connotatively with metaphors, similes, and symbols—good poems serve as models of the ways in which language can name experiences and even as vehicles that take readers beyond experience.

Insight. Finally, good poems surprise us with fresh or wise observations. In so doing, they expand our awareness and raise our spirits.

How can we keep children's liking for poetry alive?

Jack Prelutsky, a very popular poet among North American children, explains the problem this way (1983, p. 18):

> For very young children, poetry is as natural as breathing. . . . But then something happens to this early love affair with poetry. At some point during their school careers, many children seem to lose their interest and enthusiasm for poetry and their easygoing pleasure in its sounds and images.

What is to be done? What kinds of poems will keep children's interest alive? Here is Prelutsky's answer (1983, p. 18):

> . . . poems that evoke laughter and delight, poems that cause a palpable ripple of surprise by the unexpected comparisons they make, poems that paint pictures with words that are as vivid as brushstrokes, poems that reawaken pleasure in the sounds and meanings of language.

A contrasting opinion was expressed by Myra Cohn Livingston (1992, p. 9):

> [Poetry] is now pouring from the publishers, but much of it is little more than prose arranged as poetry, overblown metaphors, tired clichés, and light verse that caters to many of the baser emotions, calculated to give children a quick laugh. It has, in many instances, no sign of helping children evolve, but on the contrary [allows them to] remain in the same old place.

Prelutsky and Livingston have written very different poetry. Prelutsky creates rhymed and rhythmic poems that are noted for their humor and surprising twists. Livingston's poems take more varied forms, including blank verse, and most of them explore serious themes. One has the feeling, reading their comments, that each might consider the other's poetry part of the problem.

> What do you think? In order to keep children's interest in poetry alive, should we offer them mostly poems that are enjoyable? Or should we offer them mostly poems that take their inner complexities seriously? Should the poems be immediately rewarding? Or should they challenge children to ponder their meanings and associations? Or is there some middle ground?

These features summarize what adult readers look for in good poetry. But are these the features children like?

Children's Preferences in Poetry

Young children have an affinity for poetry. Unfortunately, children's pleasure in poetry does not always survive middle childhood, when poetry for the young moves beyond the merely playful, to more ambitious uses of language.

What sorts of poetry do elementary school children like? Studies of children's poetry preferences over the past quarter-century have yielded fairly consistent answers. A study by Kutiper and Wilson (1993) reached findings very similar to those of a landmark study done by Terry (1974) twenty years earlier. Kutiper and Wilson summarized their findings as follows (pp. 28–35):

1. The narrative form of poetry is popular with readers of all ages, while free verse and haiku are the most disliked forms.

2. Students prefer poems that contain rhyme, rhythm, and sound.

3. Children most enjoy poetry that contains humor, familiar experiences—and animals.

4. Younger students (elementary and middle school and junior high age) prefer contemporary poems.

5. Students dislike poems that contain (extensive) visual imagery or figurative language.

In terms of particular poets, according to the same study, elementary-grade students prefer the light and funny poetry of Jack Prelutsky and Shel Silverstein far above any other. Poetry that critics deem to have greater literary merit has nowhere near the circulation of the works of these two poets.

How Can We Expand Children's Taste in Poetry?

Of course, findings like those above don't settle anything. If worth were reducible to popularity, all children's fiction would come from *The Babysitter's Club* series, and all their food would be chosen from McDonald's menu. Since what children enjoy is largely synonymous with whatever is most familiar to them, our task as advocates of literature is to expand the range of poetry children know and, eventually, the range that they consider enjoyable.

There are three main ways to enhance children's appreciation of poetry. One way is to share poetry informally with children every chance you get. Children will appreciate poems if you offer them for their content—for the insights and feelings they communicate—rather than as complex objects to be analyzed. A second way to promote poetry is to have children practice choral speaking and performance. Most poetry is best read aloud, and the variations possible with a voice choir can make poems sound magnificent. A third way to encourage appreciation of poetry is to encourage children to write it. Writing poetry gives children a connection to what poets are trying to do. Ways of engaging children in poetry are described at length in Chapter 12, "Inviting Children into Literature."

MAJOR CHILDREN'S POETS AND THEIR WORKS

Hundreds of poets have written for children, but we will look closely at only a handful who are especially noteworthy, both for their insight and literary skill and for their acceptance by children over the years. We will begin with contemporary poets and work backwards. The first ten poets have won the National Council of Teachers of English (NCTE) Award for Excellence in Poetry for Children, which goes to a living poet for exceptional quality in a body of work (not just one book or poem) for children ages 3 to 13.

David McCord

David McCord was the first recipient of the NCTE poetry award, in 1977. His books of poems include *All Small: Poems by David McCord, Away and Ago: Rhymes of the Never Was and Always Is, Every Time I Climb a Tree, One at a Time,* and *The Star in the Pail.*

Ask the Poet . . . *Naomi Shihab Nye*

Naomi Shihab Nye

What advice do you have for teachers who want to help children appreciate poetry that isn't necessarily playful?

Poems have as many moods as people do. Often, when we're little, we learn nursery rhymes and funny, bouncy poems. We like repeating rhythms, even nonsense words—poems that make us laugh and stretch the boundaries of language. Some of us continue to like these poems no matter what age we are.

But there is much more to poetry. As we grow, hopefully we have a chance to read poems of many styles which echo all the varieties of human experience. Poems may help us understand universal human moods such as sadness, loneliness, alienation, anger, confusion better and more quickly than any other kind of writing, since poetry is such an intimate, immediate kind of writing. Surprisingly, poems about silence and emptiness can be some of the most moving poems! Many teenagers say they write best when they are depressed because a "negative emotion" often causes them to focus intensely. After writing, people often feel better, too,

because that "serious emotion" found a shape for itself, a simple, comforting outlet, in words.

As readers, we bring our own experiences to every poem that we read. Quickly we understand that not all people will respond to every poem or understand every poem in the same way. Some poems may not "touch us" at all. A lot depends on what we have experienced ourselves, our individuality, our personal taste. Sometimes a single image will invite us into a poem. A metaphor or simile may awaken a fresh understanding of something we thought we knew. Reading poems makes us larger people—It extends our empathy, helping us understand how others feel and giving us insight into the many worlds within and around all of us, whether the subjects and moods are things we too have experienced or things we learn about mostly through reading.

Favorite Books as a Child

Favorite Poems Old & New
edited by Helen Ferris

The Important Book
by Margaret Wise Brown

Mister Dog
by Margaret Wise Brown

Naomi Shihab Nye has written poems since she was 6 years old. Her most recent collections of poems are Fuel *and* Red Suitcase. *She has also edited anthologies of poetry for young readers, including* This Same Sky, The Tree Is Older Than You Are, *and* What Have You Lost? *She also writes children's books, essays, and novels for teens. She lives in San Antonio with her husband and son.*

One of McCord's poems that delights most preschoolers is "I Want You to Meet . . .":

> . . . Meet Ladybug
> her little sister Sadiebug,
> her mother, Mrs. Gradybug,
> her aunt, that nice oldmaidybug,
> and Baby—she's a fraidybug.

Another of his poems, "The Pickety Fence," was highlighted earlier in this chapter for its brilliant use of rhythm.

Aileen Fisher

Aileen Fisher won the NCTE poetry award in 1978. She has written more than a half-dozen books of poems for children, including *Out in the Dark and Daylight,* illustrated by Gail Owens, and *Always Wondering: Some Favorite Poems of Aileen Fisher,* illustrated by Joan Sandin. Her poems bounce with rhythm and rhyme, but they always offer children a glimmer of insight. Here's an example:

Noises

We play we are soldiers:
Tramp! Tramp! Tramp!
We play we are horses:
Stamp! Stamp! Stamp!
We play we have boots on:
Scuff! Scuff! Scuff!
Till Mother tells us, "Quiet!
　　Enough's enough."

We play we know secrets:
Sh! Sh! Sh!
We play that we are whispers:
Sp! Sp! Sp!
We play that we are sleepy:
Yawn! Yawn! Yawn!
Till Mother says, "I wonder
　　where everybody's gone?"

Karla Kuskin

Of her poem "I Have a Friend," Karla Kuskin wrote, "The smallest observation can be the start of a poem. I thought of [this one] as I tried to talk to my daughter Julia (then about seven years old) while she endlessly practiced standing on her hands":

I have a friend who keeps standing on her hands.
That's fine,
Except I find it very difficult to talk to her
Unless I stand on mine.

Kuskin's poems are delightfully absurd, and she punches her ideas home with a splendid variety of rhythms and rhyme schemes. Her books of poetry include *Any Me I Want to Be* and *Dogs & Dragons, Trees & Dreams.* She won the NCTE poetry award in 1979. Ironically, Kuskin, who is also an illustrator, had designed the medallion for the award three years earlier!

Myra Cohn Livingston

Myra Cohn Livingston published more than a dozen books of her own poems and edited nearly a dozen collections of other people's poetry for children before her death in 1996. Her poems show her empathy with all children in their joys and private hurts—for example, "Circles" alludes sensitively to how it feels to come from a broken home:

I am speaking of circles.

The circle we made around the table,

our hands brushing as we passed the potatoes.
The circle we made in our potatoes
to pour in gravy, whirling in its round bowl.
The circle we made every evening
finding our own place at the table
with its own napkin in its own ring.

I am speaking of circles broken.

Livingston often used blank verse; when she used rhymes, the bitterness of her themes could clash with the prettiness of the forms, as in this poem:

His Girlfriend

She smiles a lot.
She's pretty, I guess.
She tries to be nice,

but it's really a mess
to go out and have fun,
pretending you care,
laughing at jokes,
when your real mom's not there.

Myra Cohn Livingston's collections of poems include **Birthday Poems,** illustrated by Margot Tomes; **Earth Songs,** illustrated by Leonard Everett Fisher; and **There Was a Place and Other Poems.** She won the NCTE poetry award in 1980.

Arnold Adoff

Children are often inspired by Arnold Adoff's poems to play with the arrangement of words on the page. Consider this poem:

My Mouth

stays shut
     but
food just
finds
     a way
         my tongue says
we are
     full today
     but
         teeth just
         grin
     and
     say
         come in
i am always hungry.

Adoff taught in the city schools of New York for many years. Though he is white, he has been a champion of the poetry of the African American community—see, for example, his edited collection **My Black Me: A Beginning Book of Black Poetry.** His book **All the Colors of the Race** celebrates the experiences of biracial children. Adoff won the NCTE poetry award in 1988. (See Chapter 4 for more information about Arnold Adoff.)

Eve Merriam

Few writers for children have been more adventurous with language than Eve Merriam, who died in 1992. She could rhyme, but she could also imitate the sound of her topic almost perfectly, as in this poem:

Windshield Wiper

fog smear	fog smear
tissue paper	tissue paper
clear the blear	clear the smear
fog more	fog more
splat splat	downpour
rubber scraper	rubber scraper
overshoes	macintosh
bumbershoot	muddle on
slosh through	slosh through
drying up	drying up
sky lighter	sky lighter
nearly clear	nearly clear

clearing clearing veer
clear here clear

Merriam published more than a half-dozen books of poems. Some of her titles are **Blackberry Ink, Chortles: New and Selected Wordplay Poems,** and **You Be Good and I'll Be Night: Jump on the Bed Poems.** Her poems have also been included in most contemporary anthologies of poetry for children. She won the NCTE poetry award in 1981.

John Ciardi

John Ciardi (pronounced "chardee") could be wonderfully subversive in his poems. Just look at this verse from "The Happy Family":

Before the children say goodnight,
    Mother, Father, stop and think:
Have you screwed their heads on tight?
    Have you washed their ears with ink?

Or these two couplets from "What Did You Learn at the Zoo?":

Gorillas are good, gorillas are bad,
But all of them look a lot like Dad.

Some do one thing, some another,
But all of them scream a lot like Mother.

Ciardi won the NCTE poetry award in 1982 and died in 1986. A popular book of his poems is **You Read to Me, I'll Read to You.** Several of his works from the 1960s have been reissued, including **The Monster Den; Or, Look What Happened at My House—and to It,** illustrated by Edward Gorey, and **The Reason for the Pelican,** illustrated by Dominic Catalano.

Lilian Moore

The poems of Lilian Moore can be cheerful, but all of them make children notice things. Her poem "Construction," for instance, puts a human being back into the superhuman undertaking of skyscraper construction:

The giant mouth
chews
rocks
spews them
and is back for
more.

The giant arm
swings up
with a girder
for
the fourteenth floor.

Down there,
a tiny man
is
telling them
where
to put a skyscraper.

Moore's books of poetry include *I Feel the Same Way,* illustrated by Robert Quackenbush; *Something New Begins,* illustrated by Mary J. Dunton; and *Think of Shadows,* illustrated by Deborah Robison. She won the NCTE poetry award in 1985.

Valerie Worth

Known for her "small poems," five volumes of which were illustrated by Natalie Babbitt, Valerie Worth found things to celebrate in everyday objects, large and small. Consider "safety pin":

Closed, it sleeps
On its side
Quietly,
The silver
image
Of some
Small fish;

Opened, it snaps
Its tail out
Like a thin
Shrimp, and looks
At the sharp
Point with a
Surprised eye.

Worth won the NCTE poetry award in 1991. She died in 1994. Her books of poems include *All the Small Poems* and *Small Poems Again,* both illustrated by Natalie Babbitt.

Barbara Juster Esbensen

Barbara Juster Esbensen's poems flash with insight. Many of them are rhymed and rhythmical. "Snake" moves playfully from one level of reality to another:

The word begins to
hiss as soon as the first
letter
goes on   S
s-s-s-s-s-s   forked tongue flickers
Hard eyes stare
Already the rest of the poem
shrinks back from
his narrow speed   The paper
draws in its breath   SNAKE
loops around the pencil
slides
among the typewriter keys   slips
like a silk shoelace
away

Esbensen's books of poems include *Echoes for the Eye: Poems to Celebrate Patterns in Nature,* illustrated by Helen K. Davie; *Dance with Me,* illustrated by Megan Lloyd; and *Who Shrank My Grandmother's House? Poems of Discovery,* illustrated by Eric Beddows. Esbensen won the NCTE poetry award in 1994. She died in 1996.

Naomi Shihab Nye

Naomi Shihab Nye began writing poetry when she was 6 years old and published her first poem the next year. The daughter of a Palestinian father and an American mother, Nye has traveled back to the Middle East to explore her roots. Her own poems, collected in *Fuel, The Red Suitcase,* and *Words under the Words,* are simply worded works of insight and wisdom, and they hold a special appeal to middle-grade and older students. She has edited a collection of poems from many countries (*This Same Sky*), a book of bilingual (English and Spanish) poems (*The Tree Is Older Than You Are*), and a collection of poems written by young poets in the many workshops she has conducted in the schools (*Salting the Ocean*).

Nye's commitment to the human race, one person at a time, comes through in "Shoulders":

Shoulders

A man crosses the street in rain,
stepping gently, looking two times north and south,
because his son is asleep on his shoulder.
No car must splash him.
No car drive too near to his shadow.

This man carries the world's most sensitive cargo
but he's not marked.
Nowhere does his jacket say FRAGILE,
HANDLE WITH CARE.

His ear fills up with breathing.
He hears the hum of a boy's dream
deep inside him.

We're not going to be able
to live in this world

Illustration 7.9
This collection contains English translations of more than one hundred poems from around the world. (*This Same Sky* by Naomi Shihab Nye. Copyright © 1992 by Naomi Shihab Nye. Used by permission of Simon & Schuster Books for Young Readers, an imprint of Simon & Schuster Children's Publishing.)

if we're not willing to do what he's doing
with one another.

The road will only be wide.
The rain will never stop falling.

Paul Janeczko

Anyone wishing to infect students from upper elementary grades through high school with a love for poetry wants to be familiar with poet and anthologist Paul Janeczko's work. Janeczko was a high school teacher himself before the poet's life took over, and since then he has crisscrossed the United States doing readings and giving workshops on poetry for young people and their teachers. At the same time, he has published more than twenty anthologies of poems for young people, including *Stone Bench in an Empty Park, Don't Forget to Fly: A Cycle of Modern Poems, This Delicious Day: 65 Poems,* and *The Music of What Happens: Poems That Tell Stories.* Many of Janeczko's collections teach readers about poetry, with commentaries by Janeczko the editor and by the poets themselves, as in *The Place My Words Are Looking For: What Poets Say about and through Their Work, Poetspeak: In Their Work, About Their Work,* and *Poetry from A to Z: A Guide for Young Writers.* His own poems have been collected in *Brickyard Summer* (illustrated by K. Rush) and *That Sweet Diamond: Baseball Poems.*

Here are two of Janeczko's haiku:

Screeching and clawing
A trash truck drowns out the protests
from the alley cat

Stickball players shout
as moonlight floods their field
from curb to curb

Jack Prelutsky

A popular poet, Jack Prelutsky has produced a prodigious amount of poetry for the young over the past two decades. His poems are funny, ironic, and lively, and they address the challenges and joys of modern childhood. An example is "No Girls Allowed":

. . . We play hide-and-go-seek
and the girls wander near.
They say, "Please let us hide."
We pretend not to hear.

We don't care for girls
so we don't let them in,
we think that they're dumb—
and besides, they might win.

Prelutsky has produced many books of poems, including *The Baby Uggs Are Hatching,* illustrated by James Stevenson; *Beneath a Blue Umbrella,* illustrated by Garth Williams; *The New Kid on the Block,* illustrated by James Stevenson; and *The Dragons Are Singing Tonight,* illustrated by Peter Sis. He has also edited many popular anthologies, including *For Laughing Out Loud* and the *Random House Book of Poetry for Children,* illustrated by Arnold Lobel.

Shel Silverstein

In the 1970s, Shel Silverstein was to children's poetry what Judy Blume was to children's novels—a fresh and irreverent voice that projected a mischievous take on life and utterly resisted the sentimentality that had long been associated with children's literature. Silverstein's books of poetry, which include *Where the Sidewalk Ends* and *A Light in the Attic,* are eminently popular with children, if not always with critics. Silverstein died in 1999.

Oh Have You Heard?

Oh have you heard it's time for vaccinations?
I think someone put salt into your tea.
They're giving us eleven-month vacations.
And Florida has sunk into the sea.

Oh have you heard the President has measles?
The principal has just burned down the school.
Your hair is full of ants and purple weasels—
APRIL FOOL!

Nikki Grimes

Nikki Grimes describes herself as a poet who thrives on challenges. She has written poems to match the happy moods of photographs (*It's Raining Laughter,* with photographs by Myles Pinkney), poems about family relationships (*A Dime a Dozen,* illustrated by Angelo), and poems that say new things about love (*Hopscotch Love: A Family Treasury of Love Poems,* illustrated by Melodye Benson Rosales). A collection of her poems that explore a friendship between two girls (*Meet Dinitra Brown,* illustrated by Floyd Cooper) won the Coretta Scott King Award.

Grimes can touch important and difficult themes with a sense of hope and confidence that opens the way for children to talk about the same themes. Consider "Sister Love," for instance:

My sister and I dream of adoption–someday.
In the dream, we're never apart.
Then this nice lady comes to the group home
With a girl-shaped hole in her heart.

The nice lady seemed to like Kari and me
But she only had spare room for one.
Her home was fairly small, she said,
And she already had a son.

My age was closest to her boy's
So she asked if I wanted to go.
I squeezed my sister's trembling hand
And whispered, "Thanks, but no."

Nikki Giovanni

Nikki Giovanni's "tell it like it is" poems speak in the voices of African American children and their parents. Without rhyme, other obvious formalities, or sentimentalism, her poems magically evoke the anxieties, joys, and frustrations of real people in real situations. Reading her poems reminds all her listeners, no matter how small or downtrodden they feel, that their point of view is important, too. Consider this lyric poem:

Winter Poem

once a snowflake fell
on my brow and i loved
it so much and i kissed
it and it was happy and called its cousins
and brothers and a web
of snow engulfed me then
i reached to love them all
and i squeezed them and they became
a spring rain and i stood perfectly
still and was a flower

Ego-Tripping and Other Poems for Young is one collection of lively poems; *Spin a Soft Black Song* is another.

Langston Hughes

Langston Hughes (1902–1967) was the first African American poet to be widely read by children. Born in Joplin, Missouri, Hughes became a prominent member of the literary and artistic movement known as the Harlem Renaissance. Hughes's poems explore the sounds and rhythms of the urban black experience before midcentury, as well as describing an idealized vision of Africa. Although he wrote most of his poetry before the Civil Rights movement of the 1960s, poems such as "Dream Deferred" (1951) speak eloquently and powerfully of the injustices African Americans have endured in this country:

What happens to a dream deferred?

Does it dry up
like a raisin in the sun?
Or fester like a sore—
And then run?
Does it stink like rotten meat?
Or crust and sugar over—
like a syrupy sweet?

Maybe it just sags
like a heavy load.

Or does it explode?

With its experimental style and its solid grounding in the voice and realities of the city, Hughes's poetry has lost none of its freshness or urgency over the decades. The poems in *The Dream Keeper and Other Poems,* originally published in 1932, are still relevant today.

A. A. Milne

Alan Alexander Milne (1882–1956) created the famous Winnie the Pooh stories using his son, Christopher Robin, as the model for the human child in the stories. Milne's volumes of poetry for children, *When We Were Very Young* and *Now We Are Six,* perfectly portray the importance of the young child to the young child. Long before people understood what the psychologist Jean Piaget meant by "egocentrism," they had seen the concept demonstrated eloquently in verses such as "Buckingham Palace" (1924):

> They're changing the guard at Buckingham Palace—
> Christopher Robin went down with Alice.
> A face looked out, but it wasn't the King's.
> "He's much too busy a-signing things,"
> > Says Alice.
>
> They're changing the guard at Buckingham Palace—
> Christopher Robin went down with Alice.
> "Do you think the King knows all about me?"
> "Sure to, dear, but it's time for tea,"
> > Says Alice.

Milne's poems use sounds and rhythms perfectly (here, his rhythm catches the cadence of a regimental drumbeat). Because young children like to respond to poetry with movement, Milne's poems are good choices for reading aloud and moving to.

Robert Louis Stevenson

Robert Louis Stevenson (1850–1894) was born in Scotland but did much of his best known writing in the United States before he settled in Samoa toward the end of his life. Stevenson's lyrics from *A Child's Garden of Verses* have been household staples for over a century—and with good reason. The poet had a keen insight into the wonders and frustrations experienced by young children, and he skillfully matched those ideas with direct and sonorous language. Some of Stevenson's poems seem overly flowery for today's young readers, but many poems in his repertoire still speak to the issues of young life and offer strong examples of language beautifully used. Consider "At the Seaside":

> When I was down beside the sea,
> A wooden spade they gave to me
> To dig the sandy shore.
>
> My holes were hollow like a cup,
> In every hole the sea came up,
> Till it could hold no more.

TEACHING IDEAS

Choral Reading. After reading the section entitled "Engaging Children in Poetry" in Chapter 12, read a dozen poems aloud. Choose three that would sound good if read chorally. Script them to be read by a chorus of five or six voices, allowing for different solo and choral parts, as well as for the dynamics of loud and soft, fast and slow, staccato and glissando. Try these arrangements out with children. After the children have rehearsed several times, tape-record them.

Creating Metaphors. Mary O'Neill's poem "My Fingers" on page 256 is really a list of tactile sensations. Using her poem as a model, ask a group of children to write a list of tastes, or sounds, or shapes, or colors. Remind them to think metaphorically; for example, "round" can refer to a wheel or to the consequences of a bad deed.

Creating a Poem Collage. Have children make a poem collage. Pass out copies of a lyric or expressive poem. Have the children read it aloud, with each child taking a line. Then go around the room, having each child chant out a line or phrase he or she found especially striking. Finally, invite them to cut the poems apart and reassemble the lines or phrases as they see fit. If they want, they may repeat a line or phrase, for special emphasis.

EXPERIENCES FOR YOUR LEARNING

1. Compile your own anthology of poems for children. Organize it around a theme or an issue—for example, poems for choral reading, poems from many cultures, or poems to celebrate holidays. So that you can become acquainted with contemporary poetry, use ten different sources, choose no more than two poems per source, and make sure they were published within the last fifteen years. (Thanks to Linnea Henderson for this suggestion.)

2. A good poem may sound natural, but on examination it is likely to turn out to have been very carefully crafted. Take a poem such as A. A. Milne's "Happiness." Try substituting other words for any of Milne's. Does the poem sound as good?

3. Put together a collection of rhymes that accompany activities—jump-rope rhymes and the like. Ask for examples from friends and fellow students. Be especially attuned to rhymes from different cultures: Mexican American, Asian American, African American, and Appalachian.

4. Since singing folk songs is an excellent way to participate in poetry and rhyme, learn to play a musical instrument—one that lets you play and sing at the same time. The easiest is the autoharp; all you do is press the button marked with the letter of the chord (most song books include guitar chords). A guitar is not too hard, once your fingers get adjusted, and there are four-string versions, to make the chording simpler to learn.

RECOMMENDED BOOKS

* indicates a picture book; I indicates interest level (P = preschool, YA = young adult)

*Adoff, Arnold. *All the Colors of the Race.* Illustrated by John Steptoe. Lothrop, Lee, & Shepard, 1982. Drawing on the experience of the poet's own family, these poems are about the experiences of mixed-race children. (**I:** 5–9)

———. *In for Winter, Out for Spring.* Harcourt, 1991. Collected poems by the NCTE award–winning urban poet. (**I:** 5–8)

———, ed. *My Black Me: A Beginning Book of Black Poetry.* Rev. ed. Dutton, 1994. Adoff includes poems by Imamu Amiri Baraka, Lucille Clifton, Nikki Giovanni, Langston Hughes, and a dozen others who are better known to adults than to children but who all celebrate the black experience. (**I:** 9–12)

Aldis, Dorothy. *All Together.* 1928. Putnam, 1952. Insightful poems from a child's-eye view, in casual rhyme. (**I:** 7–11)

Axelrod, Alan, and Dan Fox, eds. *Songs of the Wild West.* Metropolitan Museum of Art/Simon & Schuster, 1991. Some favorite songs from the Old West, illustrated with fine Western art. (**I:** all ages)

Baylor, Byrd. *Desert Voices.* Scribner's, 1981. Unrhymed poems on desert topics by the author of "I'm in Charge of Celebrations." (**I:** 8–11)

Berry, James, ed. *Classic Poems to Read Aloud.* Larousse Kingfisher, 1995. An excellent collection of poems from many cultures. (**I:** 10–YA)

Brooks, Gwendolyn. *Bronzeville Boys and Girls.* HarperCollins, 1967. Poems for children by the first African American woman to win a Pulitzer Prize. (**I:** 8–11)

*Browning, Robert. *The Pied Piper of Hamelin.* Illustrated by Kate Greenaway. Dover Publications, 1997. This is a reprint of a version first published in England in 1887. (**I:** 4–8)

*Bruchac, Joseph. *The Earth under Sky Bear's Feet: Native American Poems of the Land.* Illustrated by

Thomas Locker. Putnam, 1995. Most of these poems are reflections on the Sky Bear constellation, also known as the Big Dipper. Some of Locker's rich oil paintings are magnificent. (I: 7–11)

*Bryan, Ashley. *Sing to the Sun.* HarperCollins, 1992. Bryan's Caribbean background comes through in his lively poems—some with choruses—and his bright palette. (I: 7–10)

*Burgie, Irving. *Caribbean Carnival: Songs of the West Indies.* Illustrated by Frané Lessac. Morrow/Tambourine, 1992. Thirteen songs include the familiar "Day-O," "Yellow Bird," "Michael Row the Boat Ashore," and "Jamaica Farewell." Also includes one song in Spanish, "Que Bonita Bandera!" from Puerto Rico. (I: 6–12)

*Ciardi, John. *Doodle Soup.* Illustrated by Merle Nacht. Houghton Mifflin, 1985. Funny poems by a master of the genre. (I: 6–8)

———. *You Read to Me, I'll Read to You.* Harper Trophy, 1987. Favorite poems for children by a much-loved poet. (I: 7–11)

*Cole, Joanna, and Stephanie Calmenson. *Miss Mary Mack and Other Children's Street Rhymes.* Illustrated by Alan Tiegreen. Morrow/Beech Tree, 1990. Jump-rope rhymes and more from city streets. (I: 4–8)

Cole, William, ed. *Poem Stew.* Illustrated by Karen Ann Weinhaus. Harper Trophy, 1981. This Reading Rainbow book contains fifty-seven humorous poems by the likes of Shel Silverstein, Dennis Lee, John Ciardi, X. J. Kennedy, and William Cole. (I: 6–10)

*———. *A Zooful of Animals.* Illustrated by Lynn Munsinger. Houghton Mifflin, 1992. Forty-five poems about animals by John Ciardi, Theodore Roethke, Jack Prelutsky, and others. (I: 5–7)

Cullinan, Bernice, ed. *A Jar of Tiny Stars: Poems from NCTE Award–Winning Poets.* Wordsong/Boyds Mills Press, 1996. Thirty-five hundred children chose their five favorite poems from the works of each of the poets who won the NCTE poetry award through 1994. (I: 6–13)

Dahl, Roald. *Revolting Rhymes.* Bantam, 1983. If you like Roald Dahl, you'll like this hilarious collection of poems—some of which are in dubious taste. (I: 9–12)

Delacre, Lulu. *Arroz con leche: Popular Songs and Rhythms from Latin America.* Scholastic, 1989. Twelve poems from Puerto Rico, Mexico, and Argentina are first presented as verses in English and Spanish; the musical scores, with simple guitar chords, are provided in the back. (I: 6–11)

Demi. *In the Eyes of the Cat: Japanese Poetry for All Seasons.* Illustrated by Tze-Si Huang. Holt, 1992. Some of these short poems are four hundred years old, and some are recent. All crackle with keen observation and insight. (I: 7–12)

*dePaola, Tomie. *The Friendly Beasts.* Putnam, 1981. This lovely old English carol of the Christmas story is a favorite of many children. With music for piano. (I: 5–6)

———. *Tomie dePaola's Book of Poems.* Putnam, 1988. These eighty-six poems, many well known, range from works by contemporary poets such as Aileen Fisher, Valerie Worth, and Jack Prelutsky to poems by Emily Dickinson, Robert Louis Stevenson, and William Blake. (I: 5–12)

de Regniers, Beatrice Schenk, Eva Moore, Mary Michaels White, and Jan Carr, eds. *Sing a Song of Popcorn: Every Child's Book of Poems.* Scholastic, 1988. A beautifully illustrated large-format collection (all of the illustrators are Caldecott winners). (I: 7–12)

Dunn, Sonja. *Butterscotch Dreams.* Heinemann, 1987. Lively chants and games by a popular Canadian performer and educator. (I: 6–10)

*Esbensen, Barbara Juster. *Dance with Me.* Illustrated by Megan Lloyd. HarperCollins, 1995. Fifteen poems by an award-winning poet. (I: 5–12)

———. *Echoes for the Eyes: Poems to Celebrate Patterns in Nature.* Illustrated by Helen K. Davie. HarperCollins, 1996. These poems celebrate visual patterns in nature: spirals, branches, polygons, meanders, and circles. (I: 7–11)

———. *Words with Wrinkled Knees.* HarperCollins, 1987. More poems by the NCTE award–winning poet. (I: 6–12)

Farjeon, Eleanor. *Eleanor Farjeon's Poems for Children.* Lippincott, 1951. Farjeon won the first Hans Christian Andersen Award for her contribution to children's literature of the world. The poems are touching, funny, and insightful. (I: 7–11)

Farrell, Kate, and Kenneth Koch, eds. *Talking to the Sun: An Illustrated Anthology of Poems for Young People.* Holt, 1985. A beautifully illustrated collection of poems old and new from international sources. Many won't strike you as "children's poems" on a first reading, but there is much to ponder in them. (I: 11–YA)

*Fleischman, Paul. *I Am Phoenix: Poems for Two Voices.* Illustrated by Ken Nutt. Harper Trophy, 1989. Poems about birds, set for two voices. (I: 9–12)

*———. *Joyful Noise: Poems for Two Voices*. Harper, 1988. This book of poems about insects won a Newbery Medal. (I: 9–12)

Fox, Dan. *Go in and out the Window: An Illustrated Songbook for Young People*. Holt, 1987. Whether sung or read chorally, these are fine poems, illustrated with classic art. (I: 10–12)

*Gerrard, Roy. *Rosie and the Rustlers*. Sunburst, 1991. A narrative poem about cowboys and girls, drawn with short bodies and tall hats. (I: 5–9)

*———. *Sir Francis Drake: His Daring Deeds*. Farrar, Strauss, and Giroux, 1988. A narrative poem about the English privateer. (I: 6–10)

*Giovanni, Nikki. *Ego-Tripping and Other Poems for Young*. Illustrated by George Ford. Lawrence Hill, 1993. Thirty-three poems in the lively and direct voice of a gifted urban poet. (I: 10–YA)

*———. *Spin a Soft Black Song*. Illustrated by George Martins. Farrar, 1985. Fine poems for children by a noted African American poet. (I: 8–12)

*Greenfield, Eloise. *Honey, I Love and Other Poems*. Illustrated by Leo and Diane Dillon. Harper Trophy, 1978. Poems for young people by a highly esteemed African American poet. (I: 6–10)

*———. *Nathaniel Talking*. Illustrated by Jan Spivey Gilchrist. Writers & Readers/Black Butterfly, 1988. Fifteen poems from the point of view of Nathaniel, an urban African American boy. (I: 7–11)

*———. *Night on Neighborhood Street*. Illustrated by Jan Spivey Gilchrist. Puffin, 1991. Seventeen poems depicting lives of urban African American children. (I: 6–10)

*Grimes, Nikki. *Come Sunday*. Illustrated by Michael Bryant. Eerdman, 1996. A colorful series of poems brings to life Latasha's Sunday in an African American church. (I: 7–10)

*———. *A Dime a Dozen*. Illustrated by Angelo. Dial, 1998. A series of poems about family relationships, told with honesty and insight. (I: 7–10)

———. *Hopscotch Love: A Family Treasury of Love Poems*. Illustrated by Melodye Benson Rosales. Lothrop, Lee, & Shepard, 1999. Sometimes funny, sometimes touching, always insightful, this is a surprisingly fresh series of poetic comments on our most written-about emotion. (I: 9–12)

*———. *It's Raining Laughter*. Photographs by Myles Pinkney. Dial, 1997. Exuberant poems about the many dimensions of happiness. (I: 8–10).

*———. *Meet Danitra Brown*. Illustrated by Floyd Cooper. Mulberry, 1997. Danitra Brown is described in a series of poems in the voice of Danitra's best friend, with details that reveal much about what character means in a young person. (I: 7–9).

*Gunning, Monica. *Not a Copper Penny in Me House*. Illustrated by Frané Lessac. Wordsong/Boyds Mills, 1993. A dozen poems and naive illustrations celebrate rural life in Jamaica. (I: 6–10)

*Guthrie, Woody. *This Land Is Your Land*. Illustrated by Kathy Jakobsen. Little, Brown, 1998. A fascinating tribute to America's most prolific folk singer and the times that shaped him: the Depression Era and the Dust Bowl. (I: all ages)

Harrison, Michael, and Christopher Stuart-Clark, eds. *The Oxford Treasury of Children's Poems*. Oxford Univ. Press, 1988. A lively collection, mostly by English poets, with classics from such authors as Robert Louis Stevenson and Edward Lear. (I: 6–11)

Heaney, Seamus, and Ted Hughes, eds. *The Rattle Bag*. Faber & Faber, 1982. Available in paperback in Canada (and elsewhere), an extensive collection of poems from the oral tradition and from poets writing in English. (I: all ages)

Hoban, Russell. *Egg Thoughts and Other Frances Songs*. Harper, 1972. Children who like Hoban's Frances books will love these poems, which are Frances's musings on everything from fickle friends to Lorna Doone cookies ("You are plain and you are square/And your flavor's only fair"). (I: 6–9)

Hopkins, Lee Bennett, ed. *Best Friends*. Illustrated by James Watts. Harper, 1986. Poems about friends by Gwendolyn Brooks, Judith Viorst, Langston Hughes, and others. (I: 10–12)

———. *Good Books, Good Times*. Trumpet Club, 1990. Poems about books by a favorite children's poet and anthologist. (I: 8–10)

———. *Side by Side: Poems to Read Together*. Simon & Schuster, 1988. Another fine collection by a noted children's poet and anthologist. (I: 7–10)

Hudson, Wade, ed. *Pass It On: African American Poetry for Children*. Illustrated by Floyd Cooper. Scholastic, 1993. Poems by Eloise Greenfield, Lucille Clifton, Gwendolyn Brooks, Langston Hughes, and others. (I: 8–12)

Hughes, Langston. *The Book of Rhythms*. Introduction by Wynton Marsalis. Oxford Univ. Press, 1995. Hughes wrote this lively illustrated text to make children aware of rhythm in all things—not just in poetry, but in music, art, and life. (I: 7–11)

———. *The Dream Keeper and Other Poems*. Illustrated by Jerry Pinkney. Knopf, 1996. Poems suitable for young people by one of America's greatest poets, who was a leader of the Harlem Renaissance. (I: 8–YA)

Janeczko, Paul B. *That Sweet Diamond: Baseball Poems*. Illustrated by Carole Katchen. Atheneum, 1998. Janeczko catches the tension and the grace and the joys of the sport, from the players to the plays to the fans. (I: 9–12).

———. *The Place My Words Are Looking For: What Poets Say about and through Their Work*. Bradbury, 1990. Poems by Cynthia Rylant, Gary Soto, Gwendolyn Brooks, Myra Cohn Livingston, Naomi Shihab Nye, and others, with comments by the poets. (I: 12–YA)

———. *Poetry from A to Z: A Guide for Young Writers*. Bradbury, 1994. Poems by Naomi Shihab Nye, Lilian Moore, Patricia Hubbell, and Myra Cohn Livingston are given, along with comments by the poets and suggestions for writing poems. (I: 11–YA)

*———, ed. *Stone Bench in an Empty Park*. Illustrated by Henri Silberman. Orchard, 2000. Janeczko has directed the insight-bearing light of the haiku form to urban scenes and matched poems from Nikki Grimes, Issa, and others to black-and-white photographs by Henri Silberman. (I: 12–YA)

———. *This Delicious Day: 65 Poems*. Orchard, 1987. Sixty-five thoughtful poems, presented with a minimum of editorial comment to invite meditation. (I: 12–YA)

*Jaramillo, Nelly Palacio, ed. *Grandmother's Nursery Rhymes/Las Nanas de Abuelita: Lullabies, Tongue Twisters, and Riddles from South America*. Illustrated by Elivia Savadler. Holt, 1996. A bilingual book of poems from Latin America with lively illustrations. (I: 4–8).

*Johnson, James Weldon. *The Creation*. Illustrated by James E. Ransome. Holiday House, 1994. Johnson composed "Lift Every Voice and Sing," considered by many to be the African American national anthem. His long poem "The Creation" recalls the oratory of Southern black preachers of the last century. (I: 7–13)

Kennedy, X. J., and Dorothy Kennedy, eds. *Knock at a Star,* 2nd edition. Little, Brown, 1999. This welcome second edition is a fine collection of poems organized by categories with helpful commentary by the authors, themselves established poets. Nearly half of the poems have been changed from the first edition, which appeared in 1982, and the editors have included several more accessible poems. (I: 9–YA)

———, eds. *Talking Like the Rain*. Illustrated by Jane Dyer. Little, Brown, 1992. A large-format, illustrated collection of poems for children, drawn from many sources by these noted poets. (I: 7–12)

Krull, Kathleen. *Gonna Sing My Head Off! American Folk Songs for Children*. Illustrated by Allen Garns. Knopf, 1992. With piano arrangements and guitar chords, these sixty-three songs are the best of the old and not-so-old songs that "folkies" in the United States have been singing for years. (I: P–12)

*Langstaff, John. *Oh, A'Hunting We Will Go*. Illustrated by Nancy Winslow Parker. Alladin, 1974/1991. An English folk song in picture book form. The couplets are spread across page turns, inviting the children to guess the endings. (I: 4–9)

*———. *What a Morning! The Christmas Story in Black Spirituals*. Illustrated by Ashley Bryan. Simon & Schuster/McElderry, 1987. Five spirituals with glorious illustrations, background notes, and stirring musical arrangements. (I: all ages)

Larrick, Nancy, ed. *Piping Down the Valleys Wild*. Illustrated by Ellen Raskin. Dell, 1968. A most useful collection of pleasing poems suitable for children, drawn from a range of contemporary and classic poets. (I: 9–YA)

Lear, Edward. *The Complete Book of Nonsense*. Dodd, Mead, 1846/1946. A complete collection of poems by the world's most influential nonsense poet. Includes "The Jumblies," or "They Went to Sea in a Sieve," and "The Owl and the Pussycat." (I: 5–9)

Lee, Dennis. *Alligator Pie*. Illustrated by Frank Newfield. Houghton Mifflin, 1974. These memorable poems on nonsensical subjects are as tightly rhymed and rhythmical as jump-rope rhymes. (I: 7–10)

———. *Garbage Delight*. Illustrated by Frank Newfield. Houghton Mifflin, 1977. A good source for the nonsense poems of this award-winning Canadian poet. (I: 7–10)

Lester, Julius. *John Henry*. Illustrated by Jerry Pinkney. Dial, 1994. An African American folk song that pits the "steel-driving man" against a steam drill. (I: 8–10)

Livingston, Myra Cohn. *There Was a Place and Other Poems*. Simon & Schuster/McElderry, 1988. Poems about sadnesses children bear, particularly as families have been broken apart. (I: 10–YA)

———. *Valentine Poems*. Holiday House, 1987. This well-known poet manages to do fresh things with a well-worn topic in this collection of poems for Valentine's Day. (I: 8–12)

Lyne, Sanford. *Ten Second Rainshowers: Poems by Young People*. Illustrated by Virginia Halstead. Simon & Schuster, 1996. Lyne has worked for many years as a poet in the schools, and here he collects poems from 130 young poets aged 8 to 18. Full-color illustrations set off each section. (I: 6–11)

McCord, David. *One at a Time.* Illustrated by Henry B. Kane. Little, Brown, 1986. McCord's poems include "The Pickety Fence," a percussive and rhythmic poem. (I: 8–12)

Merriam, Eve. *Chortles: New and Selected Wordplay Poems.* Morrow, 1989. The late Eve Merriam was a master experimenter with words. (I: 9–YA)

———. *The Inner City Mother Goose.* Simon & Schuster, 1969. Poems on urban themes patterned on older forms and with an ironic flavor. (I: 9–YA)

Milne, A. A. *Now We Are Six.* Illustrated by Ernest H. Shepard. E. P. Dutton, 1988. Short rhythmic poems from a child's point of view, from the author of *The House at Pooh Corner.* (I: 4–7)

———. *When We Were Very Young.* Illustrated by Ernest H. Shepard. E. P. Dutton, 1988. Lively poems about lively children, these poems were originally published in 1924 and constitute some of the best selling children's poem collections of all time. (I: 4–7)

Milnes, Gerald. *Granny Will Your Dog Bite? and Other Mountain Rhymes.* Illustrated by Kimberly Bulcken Root. Knopf, 1990. Milnes learned these songs from his West Virginia neighbors. Root's illustrations evoke the mountain setting from which the songs came. (I: 6–12)

Moore, Lilian. *Go with the Poem.* McGraw-Hill, 1979. Ninety lively poems for children by modern poets. (I: 8–12)

*Mora, Pat. *Confetti: Poems for Children.* Illustrated by Enrique O. Sanchez. Lee and Low, 1996. A baker's dozen short poems celebrate life in English, with Spanish words and a glossary. (I: 5–8)

Nye, Naomi Shihab. *Fuel: Poems.* Boa Editions, 1998. A Spanish literary critic warned us that "familiarity consumes everything around us." In these small poems, Nye gives us a model for celebrating the meaning in everyday things: fuel for living meaningful lives, as it were. (I: 8–adult)

———. *Red Suitcase: Poems.* Boa Editions, 1994. Nye is a Palestinian American, married to a New Englander, living in Texas. These poems shed light on her many landscapes, one at a time, with her characteristic plain-spoken wisdom and humility. (I: 8–adult)

———, ed. *Salting the Ocean: 100 Poems by Young Poets.* Illustrated by Ashley Bryan. Greenwillow, 2000. Nye presents poems collected from her extensive work as a poet in the schools. The poems are lively celebrations of insight into sound, and hearing them is an invitation to other young people to take leaps with language. (I: 6–10)

———, ed. *This Same Sky: A Collection of Poems from around the World.* Macmillan, 1992. English translations of more than one hundred poems from all of the continents except North America. (I: 8–YA)

———, ed. *The Tree Is Older than You: Bilingual Poems from Mexico.* Simon & Schuster, 1995. A wonderfully illustrated collection of poems from Mexico, in Spanish with side-by-side translation. (I: 8–YA)

———. *Words under the Words.* Eighth Mountain Press, 1995. This is not really a children's collection, but Nye is so insightful, so generous of spirit, and so clear that many of these poems will appeal to middle-grade students. (I: 12–YA)

———, and Paul Janeczko, eds. *I Feel a Little Jumpy around You: A Book of Her Poems & His Poems Collected in Pairs.* Simon & Schuster, 1996. A fascinating collection of ninety-six paired poems, one from a young woman's perspective and the other from a young man's, on a range of topics, including relationships. (I: 12–YA)

O'Neill, Mary. *My Fingers Are Always Bringing Me News.* Doubleday, 1969. Poems celebrating the sense of touch, by the author of *Hailstones and Halibut Bones.* (I: 6–10)

Patterson, Annie, and Peter Blood. *Rise Up Singing.* Sing Out!, 1990. Hundreds of folk songs, some with music and all with guitar chords. Tape recordings of the songs are available. (I: all ages)

Phillip, Neil. *Singing America: Poems That Define a Nation.* Illustrated by Michael McCurdy. Viking, 1995. Containing famous and should-be-famous poems from every period of U.S. history, the book is a wonderful source book of basic American poetry. (I: 8–YA)

*Prelutsky, Jack. *The New Kid on the Block.* Illustrated by James Stevenson. Greenwillow, 1984. The new kid in this collection who is intimidating the boys in the neighborhood is a girl, of course. (I: 5–12)

———, ed. *The Random House Book of Poetry for Children.* Illustrated by Arnold Lobel. Random House, 1983. An extensive anthology collected by one of America's favorite children's poets. (I: 7–12)

———. *Something Big Has Been Here.* Illustrated by James Stevenson. Greenwillow, 1990. These lively poems range from the hilarious to the serious. (I: 5–12)

Roethke, Theodore. *The Collected Poems of Theodore Roethke.* Doubleday, 1946. Not all of these poems were written for children; nonetheless, they are full of rich imagery and sometimes startling insights. (I: 10–YA)

Rosen, Michael, ed. *The Kingfisher Book of Children's Poetry*. Larousse Kingfisher, 1993. This thick collection comes from England. Not illustrated, but a good classroom resource. (I: 7–YA)

Rylant, Cynthia. *But I'll Be Back Again: An Album*. Orchard, 1989. Poems describing the difficult Appalachian childhood of a Newbery award–winning author and poet. (I: 12–YA)

Sanchez, Trinidad, Jr. *Why Am I So Brown?* MARCH/Abrazo, 1991. Poems describing the Latino experience, for middle school and high school students. (I: 12–YA)

Sandburg, Carl. *Good Morning, America*. Harcourt, 1928. Poems for young and old by one of America's outstanding poets. (I: 10–YA)

———. *Rainbows Are Made: Poems*. Harcourt, 1982. A good source of poems for children by one of America's great poets. (I: 9–12)

Schwartz, Alvin. *And the Green Grass Grew All Around: Folk Poetry for Children*. Illustrated by Sue Truesdell. HarperCollins, 1992. You'll probably remember many of these poems from your childhood. All are suitable for children and make lively choral reading. Nice illustrations, too. (I: 6–YA)

Seeger, Ruth Crawford. *American Folksongs for Children*. Doubleday, 1976. A fine collection of folk songs with accompanying games. Music and guitar chords are included. (I: all ages)

*Service, Robert W. *The Cremation of Sam McGee*. Illustrated by Ted Harrison. Greenwillow, 1986. Originally published in 1907, this narrative poem turns out to be a tall tale with a surprise ending. The illustrations are abstract but colorful. (I: all ages)

Silverstein, Shel. *Where the Sidewalk Ends*. HarperCollins, 1974. Funny and irreverent poems by one of the most popular of children's poets. (I: 5–12)

*Sneve, Virginia Driving Hawk. *Dancing Teepee*. Illustrated by Stephen Gammell. Holiday House, 1989. Traditional poems still popular among Native American young people, these are mostly brief, lyrical observations on various topics. (I: 8–12)

*Stevenson, Robert Louis. *A Child's Garden of Verses*. Illustrated by Tasha Tudor. Simon & Schuster, 1999. Probably the most enduringly popular book of poems for children in the English language. Though over a hundred years old, most of the poems are still enjoyable. (I: 4–adult)

Strickland, Dorothy, and Michael Strickland. *Families: Poems Celebrating the African American Experience*.

Wordsong/Boyds Mills, 1994. An upbeat collection by outstanding African American poets, including Gwendolyn Brooks, Nikki Giovanni, Lucille Clifton, Langston Hughes—and also Arnold Adoff. (I: 7–12)

*Temple, Charles. *Train*. Illustrated by Larry Johnson. Houghton Mifflin, 1996. A rhymed picture book evokes a train ride that lasts from early morning to late at night. (I: 6–9)

*Thayer, Ernest L. *Casey at the Bat*. 1888. Illustrated by Patricia Polacco. Putnam, 1992. A classic American baseball story set to verse. (I: 8–YA)

*Viorst, Judith. *If I Were in Charge of the World and Other Worries*. Illustrated by Lynn Cherry. Atheneum, 1981. Viorst penetrates to the heart of the foibles of children and their parents. (I: 12–YA)

*Watson, Clyde. *Father Fox's Pennyrhymes*. Illustrated by Wendy Watson. HarperCollins, 1987. Watson has an uncanny ability to create poems that sound fresh off the playground. His sister's illustrations are full of fascinating details and conversations in balloons. (I: P–9)

*Wong, Janet S. *Buzz*. Illustrated by Margaret Chodos-Irvine. Harcourt, 2000. A celebration of household sounds, most sounding like "buzzzz." A popular poet's first offering for young children. (I: 4–7).

———. *Good Luck Gold and Other Poems*. Margaret McElderry, 1994. Strong personalized poems from an Asian American point of view. (I: 9–YA)

*———. *The Rainbow Hand*. Illustrated by Jennifer Hewitson. McElderry, 1999. These poems are simple and unrhymed, but they shed light on many of the meanings mothers hold for us, from early childhood and through life. (I: 8–11)

*———. *A Suitcase of Seaweed and Other Poems*. Simon & Schuster, 1996. Wong offers poems that comment on all three of her heritages: Korean, Chinese, and American, with an autobiographical sketch introducing each section. (I: 8–11)

*Worth, Valerie. *All the Small Poems*. Illustrated by Natalie Babbitt. Farrar, 1987. Worth is a master at finding wonder in small and everyday things: a magnet, a cricket, a sleeping dog. (I: 8 and up)

Yolen, Jane. *Best Witches: Poems for Halloween*. Putnam, 1983. Yolen's assemblage of witches has a contemporary flair. (I: 6–10)

*———. *Dinosaur Dances*. Illustrated by Bruce Degen. Putnam, 1990. Yolen's poems invoke the unlikely spectacle of dinosaurs dancing the whole gamut of dances. (I: 7–9)

RESOURCES

Copeland, Jeffrey S., ed. *Speaking of Poets: Interviews with Poets Who Write for Children and Young Adults.* National Council of Teachers of English, 1993.

Esbensen, Barbara. *A Celebration of Bees.* HarperCollins, 1987.

Hopkins, Lee Bennett. *Pass the Poetry, Please!* HarperCollins, 1987.

Janeczko, Paul B., ed. *The Place My Words Are Looking For: What Poets Say about and through Their Work.* Bradbury, 1990.

———. *Poetspeak: In Their Work, about Their Work: A Special Kind of Poetry Anthology.* Simon & Schuster, 1991.

Larrick, Nancy. *Let's Do a Poem.* Delacorte, 1991.

Livingston, Myra Cohn. *Poem-Making: Ways to Begin Writing Poetry.* HarperCollins, 1991.

———. "Poetry and the Self." *Fanfare: The Christopher-Gordon Children's Literature Annual.* Ed. Joel Taxel. Christopher-Gordon, 1992.

Lukens, Rebecca J. *A Critical Handbook of Children's Literature,* 4th ed. HarperCollins, 1992.

McClure, Amy, et al. *Sunrises and Songs: Reading and Writing Poetry in an Elementary Classroom.* Heinemann, 1990.

Wolf, Alan. *It's Show Time! Poetry from Page to Stage.* Poetry Alive!, 1993.

REFERENCES

Blake, William. *Songs of Innocence and Songs of Experience.* Dover, 1789/1992.

Browning, Robert. *The Pied Piper of Hamelin.* Routledge, 1888.

Butler, Francelia. *Skipping around the World: The Ritual Nature of Folk Rhymes.* Ballantine, 1989.

Carroll, Lewis. *Alice's Adventures in Wonderland.* Illustrated by Sir John Tenniel. Dover, 1865/1993.

Ciardi, John. *The Monster Den; or, Look What Happened at My House—and to It.* Illustrated by Edward Gorey. Lippincott, 1966.

———. *The Reason for the Pelican.* Illustrated by Dominic Catalano. Wordsong/Boyds Mills, 1994.

de la Mare, Walter. *Peacock Pie.* Holt, 1923.

Esbensen, Barbara Juster. *Who Shrank My Grandmother's House?: Poems of Discovery.* Illustrated by Eric Beddows. HarperCollins, 1992.

Fisher, Aileen. *Always Wondering: Some Favorite Poems of Aileen Fisher.* Harper, 1991.

———. *Out in the Dark and Daylight.* Harper, 1980.

Hall, Donald, ed. *The Oxford Book of Children's Verse in America.* Oxford Univ. Press, 1985.

Janeczko, Paul. *Brickyard Summer.* Illustrated by Ken Rush. Orchard Books, 1989.

———. *Don't Forget to Fly: A Cycle of Modern Poems.* Bradbury, 1981.

———. *The Music of What Happens: Poems That Tell Stories.* Orchard Books, 1988.

Kipling, Rudyard. *Puck of Pook's Hill.* Doubleday, 1906.

Kuskin, Karla. *Any Me I Want to Be: Poems.* Harper, 1972.

———. *Dogs & Dragons, Trees & Dreams: A Collection of Poems.* Harper, 1980.

Kutiper, Karen, and Patricia Wilson. "Updating Poetry Preferences: A Look at the Poetry Children Like." *The Reading Teacher* 47.1 (September, 1993): 28–35.

Livingston, Myra Cohn. *Birthday Poems.* Illustrated by Margot Tomes. Holiday House, 1989.

———. *Earth Songs.* Illustrated by Leonard Everett Fisher. Holiday House, 1986.

Mason, Walt. "Football." *The Random House Book of Poetry for Children.* Ed. Jack Prelutsky. Illustrated by Arnold Lobel. Random House, 1983.

McCord, David. *All Small: Poems by David McCord.* Illustrated by Madelaine Gill Linden. Little, Brown, 1986.

———. *Away and Ago: Rhymes of the Never Was and Always Is.* Illustrated by Leslie Morrill. Little, Brown, 1975.

———. *Every Time I Climb a Tree.* Illustrated by Marc Simont. Little, Brown, 1967.

———. *The Star in the Pail.* Illustrated by Marc Simont. Little, Brown, 1975.

Merriam, Eve. *Blackberry Ink.* Illustrated by Hans Wilhelm. Morrow, 1985.

———. "The World outside My Skin." *Fanfare: The Christopher-Gordon Children's Literature Annual.* Ed. Joel Taxel. Christopher-Gordon, 1992.

———. *You Be Good and I'll Be Night: Jump on the Bed Poems.* Illustrated by Karen Lee Schmidt. Morrow, 1988.

Moore, Clement Clarke. "A Visit from St. Nicholas, or 'Twas the Night before Christmas." *The Oxford Book of Children's Verse in America.* Ed. Donald Hall. Oxford Univ. Press, 1985.

Moore, Lilian. *I Feel the Same Way.* Illustrated by Robert Quackenbush. Atheneum, 1967.

———. *I Thought I Heard the City.* Macmillan, 1967.

———. *Something New Begins.* Illustrated by Mary J. Dunton. Atheneum, 1982.

———. *Think of Shadows.* Illustrated by Deborah Robison. Atheneum, 1980.

Opie, Peter, and Iona Opie. *The Lore and Language of Schoolchildren.* New York Review of Books, 2001.

Prelutsky, Jack. *The Baby Uggs Are Hatching.* Illustrated by James Stevenson. Greenwillow, 1982.

———. *Beneath a Blue Umbrella.* Illustrated by Garth Williams. Greenwillow, 1990.

———. *The Dragons Are Singing Tonight.* Illustrated by Peter Sis. Greenwillow, 1993.

———, ed. *For Laughing Out Loud.* Illustrated by Marjorie Priceman. Knopf, 1991.

Rosetti, Christina. *Complete Poems of Christina Rossetti.* Edited by R. W. Crump. Louisiana State Univ. Press, 1979.

Sandburg, Carl. *The Complete Poems of Carl Sandburg.* Harcourt Brace Jovanovich, 1970.

Silverstein, Shel. *A Light in the Attic.* Harper, 1981.

Stevens, Wallace. *The Collected Poems of Wallace Stevens.* Vintage, 1990.

Tennyson, Alfred. "The Eagle." 1851. *Poems of Tennyson: 1830–1870.* Ed. T. Herbert Warren. Oxford Univ. Press, 1912.

Terry, Ann. *Children's Poetry Preferences: A National Survey of the Upper Elementary Grades.* National Council of Teachers of English, 1974.

White, E. B. *Charlotte's Web.* Harper Trophy, 1952.

Worth, Valerie. *Small Poems Again.* Illustrated by Natalie Babbitt. Farrar, Straus, 1985.

8 Realistic Fiction

"Your room's a firetrap. It will be as neat as a pin when we're done. You'll like it. You'll see." The tone of Henry's voice seemed to say, I know everything there is to know about anything that matters.

But Fanny did not like it. Her room looked empty, less comfortable, sad even.

from **Protecting Marie**
by Kevin Henkes

WHAT IS REALISTIC FICTION?

All fiction bears some relation to life as we know it. Kenneth Grahame's fanciful animal story **The Wind in the Willows** tells much about friendship. C. S. Lewis's allegorical fantasy **The Lion, the Witch and the Wardrobe** warns that youthful selfishness can lead to corruption. Nonetheless, the trappings of such books are fanciful: We wouldn't think of learning about the driving habits of toads from reading **The Wind in the Willows;** nor would we expect to find a trapdoor in the back of our closet after reading **The Lion, the Witch and the Wardrobe** (though some of us might check, just to be sure!). Realistic fiction, however, is a different story. Although the particular characters and plots are made up, the trappings of realistic novels are drawn from the world as it is.

In the above passage from **Protecting Marie,** the father tries to help clean Fanny's room, imposing his standards of neatness on his daughter; meanwhile, she struggles with her feelings on the matter. What is amazing about this passage, and many others like it, is that Henkes masterfully depicts emotions, thoughts, and behaviors that ring true to many preteen girls. This story raises many issues: a father trying to deal with his own aging and career direction, a daughter dealing with her own adolescence, relationships among family members. But the multifaceted, complex nature of this book allows it to rise above those "problem novels" that feel didactic or have a bibliotherapeutic intent. This is a book about relationships and self-identity, in which issues are explored within the context of the family.

Realistic fiction, then, brings the same moral challenges as any fiction does. But it presents these challenges in a here-and-now setting and in a way that says "Hey—this is happening. You or somebody near you could be going through these very experiences."

REALISTIC FICTION DEFINED

Realistic fiction is derived from actual circumstances, with realistic settings and characters who face problems and possibilities that are within the range of what is possible in real life. In addition, the events portrayed in realistic fiction raise moral questions that a reader might face in real life. Characters in realistic fiction for children usually have certain characteristics:

■ They resemble real people.
■ They live in a place that is or could be real.

- They participate in a plausible, if not probable, series of events.
- They are presented with a dilemma that is of interest to children.
- They discover a realistic solution.

Realistic fiction is not exaggeration or fantasy. There are no animals that talk; no anthropomorphized machines; no ghosts, giants, or supernatural happenings. Of course, works of realistic fiction do not literally recount real life, either. Works that do that are considered biographies or informational books.

THE VALUE OF REALISTIC FICTION

Of all the genres of children's literature, realistic fiction is the one that most closely approaches the reality of children's own lives. Reading realistic fiction can benefit children in several ways:

- They may come to feel that they are not alone.
- They may learn to reflect on the choices in their own lives.
- They may develop empathy for other people.
- They may see life experiences beyond their own.
- They may take a humorous, enjoyable look at life.

When child readers recognize in a story something similar to their own feelings or thoughts, they realize they are not alone. Realistic fiction helps readers to empathize with other people.

Realistic fiction helps readers to see beyond the limitations of their own experience. In Frances Temple's *Tonight, by Sea,* Paulie and her family become so harassed by government-backed thugs that they take their chances on the ocean in a small boat. That boat eventually brings Paulie to the United States. Though young readers are unlikely to get to know any of the many thousands of real "boat people" whom they have seen flicker across the television screen, they get to know Paulie's story. They know what happened to her and how she felt about it. They know why she sailed in that boat. They believe that in her place, they might have made the same choice. This book extends readers' knowledge of life experiences beyond their own.

Realistic fiction, then, offers readers the opportunity to see themselves reflected in the literature, as well as the opportunity to see the lives of people with very different lifestyles. It offers readers realistic views of the world in which they live.

THE EVOLUTION OF REALISTIC FICTION

Realistic fiction has been available for children for a surprisingly long time. The first title read by children that might be called realistic fiction was Daniel Defoe's *Robinson Crusoe,* published in 1719. Though written for the general reader, this book became associated with children in the mid-eighteenth century, when it was recommended for them by the philosopher Jean Jacques Rousseau. Rousseau's recommendation was timely, because publishers had begun to make the transition from publishing books for children about dying and repentance to publishing new forms of writing, including realistic fiction.

The Nineteenth Century

The first significant works of realistic fiction written expressly for children appeared in the mid-nineteenth century in England. Hannah More began writing fictionalized religious lessons that were more pleasing to children than the then-popular didactic tracts. At the same time, Anna Laetitia Barbauld was writing accessible and realistic nature stories.

Meanwhile, on the other side of the Atlantic, Americans developed strong nationalistic feelings after the War of 1812, and as a byproduct, they created their own distinctive literature for children. The break from the influence of British literature led to the publication of fewer instructional and sectarian books but more books that could be called entertaining realistic fiction.

The adventure story, a blending of the extraordinary with the possible, came into being with the works of James Fenimore Cooper. His *The Last of the Mohicans,* set on the frontier of New York State and published in 1826, is considered the first American novel. Louisa May Alcott's *Little Women* appeared in 1868. Alcott's work, based on her own family experiences, was the first to present the dilemma facing young women: how to balance interests inside and outside of the home. *Little Women* was enormously popular on both sides of the Atlantic with readers of all ages.

For boys, Horatio Alger's books such as *Ragged Dick* provided strong fictional images of the American dream of getting rich through determination, cleverness—and impressing powerful people. Alger's tales of lowly urban heroes going "from rags to riches" became lasting pieces of American culture.

Mark Twain's *The Adventures of Tom Sawyer* and *The Adventures of Huckleberry Finn,* published in the late nineteenth century, are considered by some to be two of the best American novels of any period. Both develop a strong sense of place—the Mississippi river towns of Mark Twain's childhood (Mark Twain was the pen name of Samuel Clemens). They are also quintessentially American novels, complete with issues of race and the conflict between overpious religion and the boisterous spirits of real people, all salted with the rich, gamy flavors of the frontier. Like other books of the period, Twain's works exalted "boys will be boys" naughtiness but restricted girls to straitlaced behavior. The double standard was alive and well in books for children.

The first of the great horse stories, Anna Sewell's *Black Beauty,* was published in 1877 and paved the way for the continuing popularity of realistic animal stories. Although Black Beauty is still read today, new editions have expurgated the elements of racism that were found in the original.

Also in the nineteenth century, when U.S. industry grew increasingly involved in international trade, the first realistic fiction about contemporary life in other countries became available. American author Mary Mapes Dodge based her book *Hans Brinker, or the Silver Skates* on careful research about Holland; Johanna Spyri's *Heidi* was written from the childhood reminiscences of a Swiss author and translated into English. Published in the late nineteenth century, both works informed American children about life in other lands, and both are still read today.

Toward the end of the nineteenth century, shortly after the Indian Wars drew to a close and the great cattle drives ended, many adventurers from the West, such as Buffalo Bill Cody, went East to glamorize the cowboy's and cowgirl's life in "Wild West Shows." The mass-produced dime novel appeared at the same time, and scores of these were written about the wild West.

The end of the nineteenth century saw a resurgence of sentimentalism toward the child. Frances Hodgson Burnett published *Little Lord Fauntleroy* in 1886; its somewhat saccharine plot involving a good and gentle boy who loves everyone and solves everyone's problems was a runaway success. After she moved to the United States, Burnett wrote *The Secret Garden,* a book with a more believable theme of children's redemptive effects on each other. This book is still popular with children.

The Twentieth Century

At the dawn of the twentieth century, writers continued to romanticize the innocence and beauty of children. The domestic novel flourished and was epitomized by *Pollyanna* by Eleanor Porter. Never having met her bitter and cross Aunt Polly before, Pollyanna exclaims, "Oh, I'm so glad, glad, glad to see you" (p. 16). Pollyanna gains power over difficulties by following her father's advice to face each hardship by finding something to be glad about. "Glad" clubs formed all over the United States, their members emulating Pollyanna's unquenchably optimistic view of the world.

A prolific writer and ingenious entrepreneur named Edward Stratemeyer began a "fiction factory" shortly after the turn of the century. Stratemeyer generated brief plot summaries and handed them to hack writers, who completed the books under fictitious names. Hundreds of series books about the Rover Boys, the Hardy Boys, Tom Swift, the Bobbsey Twins, and others were products of Stratemeyer's fertile imagination, if not his typewriter.

Edward Stratemeyer had produced thirteen hundred of his plot summaries by the time he died, a rich man, in 1930. His daughter Harriet Stratemeyer Adams began churning out the *Nancy Drew* series under the pen name Carolyn Keene. She is said to have written three hundred titles in the series, and two hundred million copies of them had been sold by the time she died in 1982, at age 89.

The *Hardy Boys* and *Nancy Drew* books are still being updated and marketed to new generations. But today, books from the Stratemeyer Syndicate compete with series such as the *Babysitters Club, Encyclopedia Brown,* and others, which crowd the shelves of bookstores and worry some teachers, parents, and librarians because of their sheer predictability and scant literary quality. (In fact, seventy years ago, adults' objections to the same shortcomings in the original Stratemeyer books were much more strident; teachers often spoke out against the books, and most libraries refused to stock them.)

Between the two world wars, a host of now-classic writers and illustrators began their work. Robert McCloskey wrote and illustrated nature stories for younger children and humorous ones for older children, the most famous of which are *Make Way for Ducklings* and *Homer Price.* A large crop of still-popular realistic fiction was published for the mid–elementary school reader, such as *The Box Car Children* by Gertrude Warner and *The Moffats* by Eleanor Estes, both of which were followed by more books about the same characters.

From New Realism to Diverse Perspectives

Until the eve of World War II, most of the protagonists in children's realistic fiction were white and middle class. Then Florence Crannell Means, herself white, wrote some books about children of color: *Shuttered Windows,* about an African American girl in an all-white school, and *The Moved Outers,* about the World War II internment of Japanese Americans. In 1945, Jesse Jasper Jackson published *Call Me Charley,* the first children's book by an African American to openly introduce the subject of racism. The character Charley was the only person of color in an all-white school.

Sexuality appeared in girls' books before the subject was addressed for boys. *Seventeenth Summer* by Maureen Daly introduced awakening sexuality and the teenage romance novel. The book was enormously popular up to the mid-1960s. In the 1970s, Judy Blume's *Are You There God? It's Me, Margaret* and *Forever* brought loud protests from censors because of their open discussion of sexuality. John Donovan's *I'll Get There, It Better Be Worth the Trip* tells of two thirteen-year-old boys, Davy and Altschuler, who suddenly find themselves facing the question of homosexuality when they exchange a kiss.

In the 1970s, Shelton Root (1977) described the unvarnished picture of children's life that was emerging in realistic fiction as "New Realism." Old realism depicted children's lives in more protected terms, glossing over circumstances that might lead children to feel helpless or hopeless. New Realism looked at the downside of life: children suffering from poverty, racism, sexism, war, economic upheavals, and parental irresponsibility. Characters often faced unsolvable problems or moral dilemmas. New Realism focused on adolescents as a distinct social group—not just extensions of their parents. Writing about problems became a way of describing life.

Since the 1970s, more writers of different races, nationalities, income groups, and sexual preferences have appeared on the children's book scene, writing about

ISSUE TO CONSIDER

Are contemporary books too realistic?

"New" or not, realism is still a dominant element in fiction for children. Truly disturbing social problems are depicted even in books that win critical acclaim. For example, of the four 1996 Newbery Honor Books, three are works of realistic fiction. Of these, one, *What Jamie Saw* (1995) by Carolyn Coman, is about child abuse; another, *Yolonda's Genius* (1995) by Carol Fenner, portrays drug abuse, racism, and obesity. The winner of the Newbery Medal, Karen Cushman's *The Midwife's Apprentice* (1995), is a work of historical fiction, but its protagonist is a homeless girl who sleeps in dung heaps and never experiences home or family. The winning books in the previous few years aren't much different. You might wonder whether such books are robbing children of the joy of reading about happy childhood. And is the continuing popularity of "gentler" books, such as Laura Ingalls Wilder's *Little House* series, or *The Boxcar Children,* or the many titles by E. Nesbit, an indication that many children, parents, and teachers do not appreciate the stronger contemporary fare?

On the other hand, Katherine Paterson was probably correct when she wrote, "Children who have never felt the sting of prejudice, who laugh freely and bring their parents joy are a tiny minority of all the children in the world" (1993, p. 67). Surely, as teachers and parents, we have some obligation to expose children to the realities of life as other people live it.

What do you think? Would you advocate choosing works of contemporary realism for reading in school?

life as they know it. Their themes go beyond New Realism, in that differences and hardships may be background factors in works that focus on the development of character or the pursuit of a worthwhile life. In her 1995 book *Like Sisters on the Homefront,* Rita Williams-Garcia does not dwell on teenage sexuality and abortion but uses these as background issues against which her characters grow from naiveté to knowledge. Contemporary authors of the young adult novel such as M. E. Kerr, Richard Peck, Norma Klein, Paula Danziger, Ron Koertge, Harry Mazer, Paul Zindel, Robert Cormier, Walter Dean Myers, and Norma Mazer sympathetically depict the culture of adolescents and their social and personal problems, as well as the new possibilities they face.

The broader range of topics in contemporary realistic fiction certainly expands young readers' awareness of the varieties of possible experience. But it also gives rise to disagreements between those who would shelter children from such material and those who believe that it is healthy for young people to explore difficult real-life issues in books.

CATEGORIES OF REALISTIC FICTION

Over the generations, when children have been asked what topics they enjoy in realistic fiction, their preferences have remained fairly constant. Barbara Elleman's (1986) retrospective bibliographies in *Booklist,* a publication of the American Library Association, are arranged by genres most requested by children. The most popular categories of realistic fiction are humor, mystery, and stories about survival. Hurley (1970) found in a summary of research that "there is an amazing consistency in patterns of reading interest, beginning in preschool" (p. 96).

It is surprising how many of these topics writers can get into one book. *Yolonda's Genius* by Carol Fenner, a 1996 Newbery Honor Book, works in the topics of school and friendship—as well as physical size and appearance, music, drugs, single-parent families, and life in the city versus life in the suburbs. In *Dancing Carl,* author Gary Paulsen includes sports (ice skating), school, and the meaning of love. Betsy Byars has humor, school, romance, writing, and moving away in her popular *The Burning Questions of Bingo Brown.*

It's clear that good books are not easily put into tidy categories. Rather, they cross multiple categories as they address the complexities of realistic portrayals of life. The following categories are broad ones, but they are the topics of the books that children, teachers, and parents regularly seek out.

Books about Self-Discovery and Growing Up

Many works of realistic fiction enable children to explore their own thoughts, feelings, and predispositions and to compare their inner experiences with those of others. Good books about self-discovery are even available for preschoolers. *"More More More" Said the Baby,* a 1991 Caldecott Honor Book by Vera Williams, promotes self-discovery with three stories in which a baby is the center of play and is given loving attention by a father, a grandmother, and a mother. Bernard Waber created the now-classic *Ira Sleeps Over,* in which he answered unasked questions of young children, such as "Am I the only person who sleeps with a teddy?" (Ira, of course, discovers that he is not.)

The complex plot of Bill and Vera Cleaver's novel *Where the Lilies Bloom* is underpinned by the issue of discovering one's self. Mary Call must make deci-

Illustration 8.1

Minna strives to develop her vibrato on the cello, as she also strives to develop family and peer relationships. (*The Facts and Fictions of Minna Pratt* by Patricia MacLachlan, illustrated by Ruth Sanderson. Copyright © 1988. Used by permission of HarperCollins Children's Books, a division of HarperCollins Publishers.)

sions for herself when she discovers that the advice her father gave her before he died doesn't work for her or for her sister.

Another way to discover one's self is to find one's own talents and passions. There are scores of titles about becoming good at sports (these will be treated in a later section), but *The Facts and Fictions of Minna Pratt,* by Patricia MacLachlan, is one of a few books that feature a child developing abilities in another area—in this case, playing the cello. Zilpha Keatley Snyder's main character in *Libby on Wednesday* wins a writing contest and ends up belonging to a writers' club, despite her aversion to being social. Libby learns to develop her writing—and her socialization and interpersonal relationships as well. In Beverly Cleary's *Dear Mr. Henshaw,* Leigh Botts is forced by teachers to write to an author, and soon he is writing for writing's sake. Nonetheless, given the importance of children's developing a sense of industry and competence during their early school years (an issue discussed in Chapter 1), it is lamentable that there are not more books celebrating children's development of their various talents.

Having navigated the sometimes arduous path to maturity, many adults have an impulse to share what they have learned with young people. So they write. For their part, children often say that they "can't wait" to grow up. So they enjoy reading about the processes of maturing and learning. No wonder growing up is a popular theme in children's literature. *Baseball in April and Other Stories,* by Gary Soto, shows Mexican American young people on both sides of the mysterious threshold of adolescence striving to get by in a California neighborhood where people make do with high hopes and limited means.

Overcoming self-doubt is one of the aspects of growing up. Written over fifty years ago, *The Hundred Dresses,* by Eleanor Estes, is a now-classic story about overcoming the cruelty of peer prejudice. Wanda Petronski is belittled by Peggy and Maddie for wearing the same dress every day, though she claims to have one hundred dresses at home. When Wanda's family moves away because of the prejudices they face, Wanda mails Peggy and Maddie drawings of themselves, each pictured in one of the hundred dresses she has designed. Maddie's and Peggy's consciences are pricked by Wanda's responding to malevolence with kindness. In Gina Willner-Pardo's *Daphne Eloise Slater, Who's Tall for Her Age,* Daphne Eloise bears the name-calling of classmate Leonard, who insists on calling her a giraffe. In the end, Daphne Eloise comes to the realization that she can't change Leonard, but she can control her reaction to his behavior and what she says to him. All in all, she realizes that she is a "pretty nice kid."

There are many series books about self-discovery and growing up. Perhaps this is because once an author has created a strong, memorable character, readers want to know how that character handles other issues of growing up. Characters such as Betsy Byars's Bingo Brown, Beverly Cleary's Ramona Quimby, Paula Danziger's Amber Brown, Lois Lowry's Anastasia Krupnik, and Phyllis Reynolds Naylor's Alice allow readers to enjoy growing up along with their "friends" in books. These books usually offer humorous yet serious looks at daily aspects of growing up.

Books about Families

Family stories abound in realistic fiction. They take as many twists and turns as do families in the real world. In *Shiloh,* Phyllis Reynolds Naylor has created a stable nuclear family in which each member cares about the others. Marty expresses that sense of belonging when he says, "You ask me the best place to live, I'd say right where we are, a little four-room house with hills on three sides."

In a different kind of family, a single mom and her daughter lose everything in a fire in Vera Williams's picture book *A Chair for My Mother.* The family works together to save enough money to buy a soft, comfortable chair—one in which mom and daughter can snuggle together. Getting acquainted with past generations of her African American family is important to Emily in *Toning the Sweep,* by Angela Johnson. Emily videotapes the storytelling that goes on while she helps her grandmother prepare for chemotherapy and eventual death.

Humorous accounts of growing up and dealing with family relationships are often found in books offered in series, such as Beverly Cleary's *Ramona Quimby, Age 8,* one of the books in the long-running series of Ramona, Beezus, and Henry books created by Beverly Cleary. Sibling relations are at the center of *Tales of a Fourth Grade Nothing,* by Judy Blume, which features Peter Hatcher and his exasperating but endearing little brother Fudge. Phyllis Reynolds Naylor's series chronicles Alice's experiences as she grows up; in *Alice in April,* Alice demands more appreciation from her father and brother.

Divorce, broken homes, alcoholism, child abuse, and same-sex relationships—all nearly absent from books written more than thirty years ago—are now widely treated in children's realistic fiction. Foster homes and wondering where and to whom one belongs are the themes of Betsy Byars's *The Pinballs* and Katherine Paterson's *The Great Gilly Hopkins.* The stress between family members of different generations disturbs the youngest member in Sharon Bell Mathis's novel *The Hundred Penny Box.* In *From the Notebooks of Melanin Sun,* Jacqueline Woodson treats very sensitively the issue of a young teenage boy's discovery that his mother is a lesbian.

Parents who are incapable of taking care of their children force us to reconsider the definition of family. In Janet Taylor Lisle's *Afternoon of the Elves,* Hillary is enchanted by Sara-Kate's imagination and talent for creating a tiny world for "elves" in her junky backyard. What Hillary begins to realize is that Sara-Kate does not have adults who take care of her. Is her father really in jail? What's wrong with the mother who is hidden from the public by Sara-Kate?

Books about Interpersonal Relations

Some useful works of realistic fiction revolve around the problems of getting along with others. In this area, a work of fiction can do what real life cannot do: allow us to experience the perspectives of more than one character. Charlotte Zolotow is a master at authoring picture books about relationships. *The Hating Book, The Quarreling Book,* and others of her works are about learning to get along with others.

The protagonist of *Harriet the Spy,* by Louise Fitzhugh, believes that she can become a writer by spying on her friends and neighbors and writing up her unflattering observations. However, after her friends see what she has written about them, she discovers that she needs friends more than she needs the aloofness she had associated with being a writer.

In *Crazy Lady!,* a Newbery Honor Book by Jane Leslie Conly, Vernon's mother has died, and his kindly but barely literate father is unable to assist Vernon in his troubled efforts to read. Vernon meets Maxine, the neighborhood alcoholic (commonly called the "Crazy Lady"), and her mentally challenged, mute son. As Vernon reaches out to help Maxine and her son Ronald, the relationship helps Vernon to come to terms with his learning disability as well as the loss of his mother.

In Chris Crutcher's *Ironman,* Beau's training for the triathlon is interrupted when he is mandated to attend anger management class in his high school. Beau had been using his sports training to take his mind off emotional and relationship issues; he must now take time from his training to deal with these serious issues. His relationship with his father has long been a troubled one, but upon hearing that his coach might be gay, Beau suddenly turns his back on the man who has always been a staunch supporter and confidant.

Books about School

The school day is a source of constant drama for young people. School is their stage, their proving ground, their source of social contacts. There are many good works of realistic fiction that explore the pushes and tugs of schooling.

Young children just entering school worry about what the experience will be like. Amy Schwartz's *Annabelle Swift, Kindergartner* helps to answer that question for children. Annabelle's sister informs her about what she needs to know to begin kindergarten. Annabelle, however, prefers to make her own way. Schwartz creates a believable kindergarten setting in this reassuring book.

No one has succeeded better at helping children see the teacher's point of view than Harry Allard in *Miss Nelson Is Missing!* and *Miss Nelson Is Back* (both illustrated by James Marshall). In the first, the children's bad behavior comes abruptly to an end when kind and gentle Miss Nelson appears to go on leave, to be replaced by a terrible disciplinarian, Miss Viola Swamp.

There are many books in series about school. Most are lighthearted and humorous looks at daily events and dilemmas faced at various grade levels. Among those just beginning to read chapter books, Suzy Kline's *Horrible Harry* series is popular. For example, in *Horrible Harry and the Dungeon,* students in Room 2B wonder whether Harry will be the new teacher Mr. Skooghammer's first "victim" of the dungeon—the suspension room in the basement. Likewise, Patricia Reilly Giff's Polk Street School kids provide book after book of school stories. In *Look Out, Washington, D.C.!,* they take a field trip to Washington, D.C.

The pitfalls of school for intermediate-grade children is the subject of Louis Sachar's thoughtful *There's a Boy in the Girls' Bathroom,* which provides telling details about an eleven-year-old bungler who learns to fit in. In Andrew Clements's *The Landry News,* fifth-grader Clara Landry decides to exercise freedom of speech and writes an editorial about a formerly creative teacher who has burned out to the point of merely passing out worksheets to students. Similarly, Avi's *Nothing but the Truth* explores issues of freedom of speech in the classroom.

Johanna Hurwitz addresses a common peer group problem in *Class Clown,* in which third-grader Lucas Cott decides to turn over a new leaf, only to discover that changing one's role in a group turns out to be more difficult than he thought. Among the other books by Hurwitz is *Class President,* in which Julio hides his ambitions in order to campaign for a classmate to win the nomination for class president.

School experience is problematic and even traumatic for some. In Susan Shreve's *The Flunking of Joshua T. Bates,* Joshua is devastated to learn that he must repeat the third grade. He faces taunting from former classmates, but a sympathetic teacher helps him find his strengths. In Elizabeth Levy's *Keep Ms. Sugarman in the Fourth Grade,* Jackie chains herself to a desk in protest when Ms.

Illustration 8.2
It was one thing for Lucas to be a clown when he felt like it, another when he was assigned the role of clown. (*Class Clown* by Johanna Hurwitz, illustrations by Sheila Hamanaka. Copyright © 1987. Used by permission of Morrow Junior Books, a division of HarperCollins Publishers.)

Sugarman is promoted to principal, because Ms. Sugarman was the first teacher to help her overcome self-doubt and reduce her visits to the principal's office. The teacher compares Jackie's efforts to great social protests in history, and Jackie learns to value her independence of thought rather than condemn herself for it.

At other times, school or a school assignment is merely the impetus for sounding an alarm that makes people aware of problems stemming from self and family. In Jack Gantos's *Joey Pigza Swallowed the Key,* school is seen from the perspective of a third-grade boy who is "out of control"—he has attention deficit/hyperactivity disorder. As adults, we may know what it's like to be around a child with ADHD, but how does it feel to be the child with ADHD or the classmates of the child? In the sequel, *Joey Pigza Out of Control,* Joey comes to know his previously absent father as he finds out the effects of being on and off his "meds," not just for school, but generally in day-to-day living. In two different books, a school assignment to keep a journal becomes a mechanism through which characters reveal some harsh truths about their home lives. In Margaret Peterson Haddix's *Don't You Dare Read This, Mrs. Dunphrey,* Tish finds her journal to be a safe place in which to spill her concerns about how to care for herself and her younger brother since her mother abandoned them. Likewise, in Joanne Rocklin's *For Your Eyes Only!* a journal reveals how two characters' home lives affect their school behavior.

Books about Sports

Sports enthusiasts enjoy reading play-by-play accounts of athletic contests. *Shoot for the Hoop,* by Matt Christopher, satisfies this craving. Beyond merely describing basketball action, however, the author creates a hero who not only is a good basketball player but also struggles with diabetes. In *Penalty Shot,* Jeff's skill on the ice is secondary to his struggles off the ice. Who is sabotaging his effort to improve his grades? And who is sending (in his name) threatening notes to his best friend? Christopher writes voluminously—he has published over fifty sports titles—and is the focus of a fan club. Better sports books such as Christopher's go beyond simply describing games and offer imaginative twists, well-developed characters, and a wide range of settings. Alfred Slote is another author who has written numerous popular sports stories for elementary school–age students. In *Hang Tough, Paul Mather,* Paul deals with his incurable blood disease by involving himself in baseball. In *Finding Buck McHenry,* a boy tries to enlist as the Little League team coach the school janitor he believes is a former famous baseball player from the Negro League.

There's a Girl in My Hammerlock, by Jerry Spinelli, describes a wrestling team that comes unglued when a girl joins the team. When Maisie doesn't make the cheerleading team, she decides to join the wrestling team to have an excuse to be closer to Eric, but eventually she develops a real interest in the sport itself and realizes that she truly enjoys wrestling. Avi's *S.O.R. Losers,* in which an unlikely soccer team strives for a winless season, is a hilarious antidote to the "winning is everything" ethos of too many school sports teams.

Robert Lipsyte has written over a dozen excellent sports books for older readers. *The Contender* tells of Alfred's desire to be a boxer; his coach teaches him the difference between being a contender (one who finds the effort its own reward) and being a champion (one who stands by truth and principles). Alfred becomes both. Chris Lynch has written excellent sports stories about teenage boys, in which sports serve as a metaphor for the development of the characters. Like his earlier book *Iceman,* which is about hockey, *Slot Machine* has plenty of play-by-play to

Illustration 8.3

The moves in basketball serve as metaphors for the moves in life, as friendships and family relationships are explored. (*The Moves Make the Man* by Bruce Brooks. Copyright © 1995. Used by permission of HarperTrophy, a division of HarperCollins Publishers.)

please the enthusiast, as well as an excellent thematic thread on friendship and wrestling with one's own identity—or finding one's "slot," as the story has it. Bruce Brooks's *The Moves Make the Man,* a story in which basketball provides metaphors for living in the world, was named a Newbery Honor Book.

Books about Nature and Animals

Authors who write animal and nature stories for children provide information about the natural world; they also help children build a commitment to the living things with which they share the world. Often, animals and nature serve to teach children important lessons about their own lives.

A good number of Gary Paulsen's books celebrate animal life and the wilderness, especially in the cold northern lands. His *Dogsong* takes readers on a dogsled ride with Inuit boy Russell Susskit, introducing them to the interactions of dogs and humans. Another book in which Paulsen explores sled dogs is *Woodsong,* which describes the Iditarod race.

Many realistic fiction picture books for younger children explore the multi-faceted wonders of nature. In Denise Fleming's *In the Small, Small Pond,* a child watches the variety of pond life in amazement. Lois Ehlert's *Red Leaf, Yellow Leaf* has a child planting and caring for a sugar maple tree. The informational aspect of the text adds much to the story. In the Caldecott-winning book *The Snowy Day,* by Ezra Jack Keats, Peter enjoys a snowy day in a variety of ways: making tracks, smacking snow off branches, making snow angels, throwing snowballs, and even taking one home. In *Owl Moon,* another story that takes place in the snow, John Schoenherr illustrates a night on which a father and a child go owling. Jane Yolen's text describes the setting vividly so that readers can vicariously experience the cold night and the awe of seeing the great owl. *Come a Tide,* written by George Ella Lyon and illustrated by Stephen Gammell, shows an Appalachian community undergoing a storm and flooding.

Many children, especially girls, go through a horse story phase. Why? Perhaps the association with horses gives girls a sense of freedom and power, as Poll (1961) suggests. Horse stories by Marguerite Henry and Walter Farley are perennial favorites. Both wrote about horses and other animals for over thirty years. Henry's *Misty of Chincoteague,* the 1948 Newbery Honor Book, and Farley's series of books about *The Black Stallion* remain justifiably popular. Jessie Haas continues to write horse stories for readers; her stories, such as *Beware the Mare,* are set in rural Vermont.

That animals provide companionship for humans is well accepted. But beyond that, animals offer life lessons for humans. That point is illuminated in a series of short stories found in *Every Living Thing* by Cynthia Rylant. In Kate DiCamillo's *Because of Winn-Dixie,* Opal adopts a stray dog from the local grocery store and names him after the store, Winn-Dixie. The friendly dog helps Opal adjust to her new community and also helps her to face the reality of who she is and to understand that the mother who abandoned her seven years ago isn't likely to ever return.

Books about Survival

There are many ways of considering what constitutes survival. It could be surviving tough experiences such as peer taunting and tormenting because a child does not fit in for some reason. It could also be surviving life circumstances. But most often when we think of survival, we think of surviving life-threatening situations.

In some books for children, nature is presented as a harsh adversary; in others, nature helps characters to survive. In many books, nature is portrayed as both harsh and helpful. In Gary Paulsen's Newbery Honor Book *Hatchet,* Brian finds himself alone in the wilderness after an airplane crash, and he must come to understand nature in order to find food and shelter to stay alive. In *Brian's Winter,* a companion book offering an alternative ending, the "what if" is explored: What if Brian had not been rescued before winter arrived and had had to survive in the Canadian wilderness? In Will Hobbs's *Far North,* Gabe and his Dene Indian roommate, Raymond, find themselves survivors of a plane crash. They make it through the winter in the Canadian wilderness with the guidance of a Dene elder who also survived the crash.

In *Julie of the Wolves,* a Newbery Medal winner by Jean Craighead George, Julie escapes from an arranged marriage in her Inuit village, surviving in the desolate Alaskan tundra by living with wolves. To be accepted by the wolves, she observes and mimics the intricacies of their behavior.

The sibling protagonists in *Toughboy and Sister,* by Kirkpatrick Hill, are eleven- and eight-year-old Athabascans who are stranded in a Yukon River camp after their father dies of alcoholism. The children struggle to find food and shelter until they are rescued by a neighbor, Natasha. In the sequel, *Winter Camp,* Natasha takes the children camping "like in the old days." A sled driver is injured, Natasha has to leave to get help, and the children must run the camp, all the time wishing for modern conveniences as nature threatens them with cruel cold, unsafe ice, and potentially dangerous fire.

Books about Romance and Sexuality

Works of realistic fiction that focus on romance cover topics that run the gamut from girl-boy friendships to explicit aspects of sexuality to the true meaning of love. It is often said that the experience of falling in love is indescribable, but several authors of realistic fiction have succeeded in finding apt words for intense feelings. Going to a movie with a boy and receiving a first kiss are explored in Sharon Creech's *Absolutely Normal Chaos. Anastasia at This Address,* one of a series of books by Lois Lowry about Anastasia's growing up, lets the reader share the heroine's experience of falling in love as she answers a personals ad. Robert Newton Peck's *Soup in Love* describes how Valentine's Day stirs Soup to try his first kiss.

In Louise Plummer's *The Unlikely Romance of Kate Bjorkman,* high schooler Kate explains that this is a story about her true romance with a great guy. As she tells her story, Kate includes "revision notes" that come to mind as she contemplates the writing of her romance novel. She refers to "The Romance Writer's Phrase Book" for suggestions, as well as making fun of some of the wording it suggests but she chooses not to use. Kate expresses typical feelings of attraction, joy, and jealousy in her relationship with Richard.

Beyond discussing growing interest in romance and sexuality, Young Adult novels deal more directly with issues of sexuality. These issues range from dealing with sexual behavior and its consequences, such as pregnancy, to the identity of sexual orientation.

Books about Mental, Physical, and Emotional Challenges

People in real life can flourish in spite of challenging mental, physical, and emotional conditions. The limiting factors they face are not just the challenging conditions, but also their own sense of the possible and the limited expectations of those around them. The trick for authors is to create characters who can achieve success without having the disability seem to give them special powers. Books that depict this diverse perspective are also discussed in Chapter 4.

In 1971, author Betsy Byars won a Newbery Medal for *The Summer of the Swans,* in which protagonist Sara's brother is mentally retarded. Sara feels awkward and self-conscious about her brother's condition and just about everything else in her life. When her brother is lost, Sara struggles to determine what really counts about herself and her relationships with others.

The Alfred Summer by Jan Slepian is distinguished for being one of the first books with a main character who is physically challenged. Cerebral palsy does not stop Lester from helping his friends build a boat in their basement, but overcoming his own and his mother's doubts about what he can accomplish takes some doing.

For younger children, *Be Good to Eddie Lee* by Violet Fleming and *Thumbs Up, Rico* by Maria Testa are two picture books that have characters with Down syndrome. Eddie Lee is able to see flowers and frog's eggs better than other children; Rico can't shoot a slam dunk, but he can draw an imaginative picture of one.

Emotional trauma can result in challenges that significantly alter life. In Konigsburg's *Silent to the Bone,* the story opens with thirteen-year-old Branwell dialing 911 to report that his baby sister is having difficulty breathing, but he is so traumatized that he cannot speak. He is sent to live in a juvenile behavioral center, and it is through his best friend's efforts that communication is restored. At first, it is merely blinking an eye in response to a question, then pointing a finger at cards when cued. Branwell must work through his emotional trauma before he can reestablish communication with the world.

Books about Moral Dilemmas and Moral Responsibility

Many works of realistic fiction for young people pose moral dilemmas that confront people in the real world. Some are personal dilemmas that characters cannot avoid; others have to do with social issues in which characters can choose to become involved. The word "dilemma" refers to the difficulty of making choices; often, there is no clear right or wrong—just a decision with consequences.

A good example of an unavoidable personal dilemma is found in Sharon Bell Mathis's Newbery Honor Book *The Hundred Penny Box,* in which Michael, the young protagonist, is caught in the middle of a conflict between his mother and a one-hundred-year-old aunt: Does he obey his mother's rules, or does he protect Aunt Dew's memories and dignity?

A story about a character caught up in a moral dilemma of his own making is Avi's *Nothing but the Truth: A Documentary Novel,* in which high school student Phillip Malloy falsely reports that his English teacher refused to let him sing the national anthem. The book has no narrator but rather uses diaries, newspaper clippings, memos, letters, dialogues, and radio talk-show scripts to recount the disastrous consequences of a distortion of the truth.

In *Shiloh,* Marty's desire for a dog begins the cycle of moral decision making. The dog he finds, Shiloh, belongs to someone but is abused. Which is morally worse: Marty's "stealing" a dog that he knows has an owner (by hiding it and lying to his parents) or returning the dog to Judd Travers, who will continue to physically abuse it? Moral questions are posed throughout the book, and readers have opportunities to discuss them as they explore their own beliefs.

Books about Social Diversity and Society

Getting along in different types of communities is the subject of many books written for young people. In *Scooter,* written and illustrated by Vera B. Williams, Elana Rose Rosen rides her scooter as she explores her new urban neighborhood, where she has just moved into a high-rise. A very different look at communities, *Smoky Night* by Eve Bunting, is based on the Los Angeles riots of 1993. The neighborhood conflicts raise questions of race and class, as the people consider basic human relations within their community.

Illustration 8.4
Yolonda plans various schemes to get her younger brother Andrew recognized for his musical genius. (*Yolonda's Genius* by Carol Fenner, illustrations by Stephen Marchesi. Text copyright © 1995 by Carol Fenner. Illustrations copyright © 1995 by Stephen Marchesi. Used by permission of Margaret K. McElderry books, an imprint of Simon & Schuster Children's Publishing.)

In *Junebug,* Alice Mead depicts the life of a boy who dreams of a big future but fears, as his tenth birthday approaches, that the local gangs and drug dealers will be pressuring him to join them. It is just this situation that worries Yolonda's mother in Carol Fenner's *Yolonda's Genius.* She moves from the inner city to the suburbs, looking for safety. However, Yolonda soon realizes that there are different types of danger to fear in different communities.

Homelessness is a subject in increasing numbers of children's books. Eve Bunting's picture book *Fly Away Home,* illustrated by Ronald Himler, depicts a boy and his father living at an airport, constantly moving around and trying not to get noticed by officials there. Paula Fox's *Monkey Island* is a haunting story of an eleven-year-old boy, Clay, who lives in a hotel room with his mother until she leaves and never comes back. He is befriended by two homeless men, who help him survive on the streets. Frances Temple's *Grab Hands and Run* was fictionalized from a true account of the flight of the surviving members of a Salvadoran family from their homeland and their search for a permanent home in the North after the father has been assassinated.

Books that depict diverse social perspectives are also addressed in Chapter 4.

Books about Death and Dying

Realistic fiction examines many aspects of death and dying: the natural process of aging, caring for the sick, grieving for lost loved ones, and the stages that lead from grief to acceptance. The death of an animal or pet is often a child's first experience with death, although books for children also describe the deaths of peers, siblings, parents, and grandparents.

In *The Accident,* by Carol Carrick with beautiful illustrations by Donald Carrick, Christopher is overcome by feelings of guilt and sadness when his dog is hit by a truck. In Judith Viorst's *The Tenth Good Thing about Barney,* the protagonist's mother suggests that he think of ten good things about the cat Barney, for the family to recite at its funeral.

A Taste of Blackberries is Doris Buchanan Smith's excellent contribution to understanding the stages of grief over the loss of a friend. When Jamie dies of an allergic reaction to a bee sting, his best friend must face the fact that Jamie will never return. The Newbery winner *Bridge to Terabithia,* by Katherine Paterson, gives the reader a rich character in Leslie, who will be remembered long after her accidental death.

The death of a grandparent is a theme that allows authors to write of death as a natural phenomenon associated with age. *Blackberries in the Dark,* by Mavis Jukes, shows a child and her grandmother going through rituals as a way of remembering the grandfather. In *Sun & Spoon* by Kevin Henkes, ten-year-old Spoon searches for a tangible object by which to remember his grandmother—perhaps one of the sun-themed objects she collected.

The death of parents is most difficult for children to endure. In Cynthia Rylant's *Missing May,* it is the aunt who has raised Summer who dies, but the loss is doubly hard because Summer has already lost her mother and father. For younger children, Lucille Clifton's *Everett Anderson's Goodbye* is a poetic account of the grief felt on the death of a father. In *The Eagle Kite,* Paula Fox describes Liam's anger, which arises not only because his father died of AIDS but also because he had not known of his father's homosexuality.

The treatment of death and dying varies across cultures, but there are obvious similarities. Three sixth-grade boys in Japan become curious about death in *The Friends,* by Kazumi Yumoto, and stake out an old man's house so that they may better understand what dying and death are about. However, it is their eventual friendship with the older man that enables the boys to understand death more fully.

Mystery Books

Mysteries have long been favorite recreational reading for adults, ever since Edgar Allan Poe published "The Murders in the Rue Morgue" in 1841. Although very few are considered serious literature, mystery stories enjoy wide appeal, especially among readers who enjoy the challenge of following the author's hints and diversions as they seek a solution to the mystery. Young people can enjoy mystery stories for the same reasons; many teachers prize the genre for the practice it provides young readers in looking for meaning.

Mystery books for young readers have as much variety as adult mysteries. In *The Westing Game,* a Newbery Honor Book by Ellen Raskin, the characters are involved in a battle of wits to inherit a million dollars. In her Newbery-winning adventure/mystery *From the Mixed-up Files of Mrs. Basil E. Frankweiler,* E. L. Konigsburg writes of a set of youthful protagonists who run away from home. Being knowledgeable New Yorkers, they figure out how to spend nights in the Metropolitan Museum of Art without being detected.

In *The Secret of Gumbo Grove,* author Eleanora Tate incorporates African American community history, into which the protagonist delves to solve a mystery. Virginia Hamilton does much the same thing in *The House of Dies Drear,* which uses the history of the Underground Railroad and a huge old house with secret passages as background for a mystery plot.

Many mysteries can be found in series. David Adler has penned a series of mysteries, one of which is *Cam Jansen and the Scary Snake Mystery.* Cam uses her photographic memory when a snake is mysteriously let loose on the library steps and her mother's bag with the video camera inside is missing. The books in the *Encyclopedia Brown* series by Donald Sobol call for readers to get involved in solving cases along with the son of a police chief. Each book contains several short mysteries, and the solutions are in the back of the book.

Humorous Books

In much realistic fiction, humorous incidents serve as a release from the more serious topical themes explored by the author. Many of the books previously discussed in this chapter fit into this category.

Authors who write chiefly humor for children are careful not to poke fun at the natural surprises children experience—and, often, their ineptness—as they learn about life. The challenge for authors of realistic fiction is to help children empathize with others and see the humor in the plight of characters whose first stabs at life's opportunities fail. Leigh Botts's letters in *Dear Mr. Henshaw,* by Beverly Cleary, are a good example. The letters begin when Leigh is in the second grade, so his growth up to sixth grade is clear, and it is okay to laugh about what he didn't know earlier.

Judy Blume's stories about sibling rivalry and parental approval are favorites among children—*Tales of a Fourth Grade Nothing* and *Superfudge,* especially. In the former, Peter Hatcher is annoyed at his little brother's antics, but to the reader they are funny. Peter's unnecessary concern about his own status in the family will ring true to many young readers. When Fudge swallows Peter's pet turtle, readers can feel Peter's pain and laugh at the same time.

Jamie Gilson is a popular writer of humorous stories. In *Hello, My Name Is Scrambled Eggs,* Tuan Nguyen's family moves in with the Trumbles. Harvey Trumble's attempt to teach Tuan the English language and American ways provides laughs for American readers. Gilson pokes enlightening fun at vegetarian cooking, the captivating influence of television, and horoscopes in *Can't Catch Me, I'm the Gingerbread Man.* Endangered Animal Month sets Richard and Ben in competition with Dawn Marie and troublesome Patrick over the real story about bats in *It Goes Eeeeeeeeeeeee!*

Adults often either function as the butt of the humor or buffer the pain of characters who are being laughed at. In Paula Danziger's *Make Like a Tree and Leave,* the humor includes puns, such as the title, and bathroom humor. For several pages, the characters argue about who is responsible for putting on a new toilet paper roll. Mrs. Martin tells her children about "making out" when she was young, and the children are horrified at the thought—and at the thought that Mr. and Mrs. Martin still make out—giving expression to the exact thoughts of many a child. Danziger has published a long list of amusing books for young and older children.

Beverly Cleary's characters, including Ramona and Henry Huggins, are strong, admirable children who can carry on in spite of mistakes and goofs. Readers laugh at the misunderstandings. Throughout *Ramona the Brave,* Ramona assumes that her teacher thinks she is a nuisance. The misconception motivates her to compensate and try to win approval, and all the time the reader is enjoying her mistake.

Betsy Byars's humor is often based on characters taking themselves more seriously than the reader thinks necessary. Byars wrote several books about Bingo Brown. This situation, from *The Burning Questions of Bingo Brown,* is typical:

> Bingo Brown fell in love three times during English classes. Bingo had never been in love before. He had never even worried about falling in love. He thought love couldn't start until a person had zits, so he had plenty of time. Bingo was worried about being called on. (p. 3)

Sheila Greenwald's heroine, Rosy Cole, provides amusing adventures for younger readers. In *Rosy Cole: She Walks in Beauty,* Rosy tries to become a model, giving the author the opportunity to point out some of the absurdities of the modeling profession. Many series books about growing up include much humor.

Series Books

Series books are popular with children because they take the guesswork out of choosing something to read. Their very sameness, however, means that these books do less to expand a child's awareness of and appreciation for literature than one-of-a-kind books. Nonetheless, parents and teachers, eager to foster the reading habit, often forgive the shortcomings of series books in the hope that once children are "hooked on books," they may move beyond series books to more substantial reading. Teachers are also aware that reading series books may be something of a status symbol in elementary school.

Series books have been available to children for most of this century, at least since the time of the fiction-writing syndicate of Edward Stratemeyer, the prolific producer of the books about Tom Swift, the Bobbsey Twins, the Hardy Boys, and Nancy Drew. Nowadays, series books are more popular than ever, and virtually all publishers welcome authors who can and will write engaging books in series.

Just as with any other books, the quality of series books varies. The worst are plagued by thin description, flat characters, and plots that pull readers from one suspenseful moment to another. The best—those by authors who have established themselves for their individual books—can be funny, upbeat, and full of delightful language play. Fourth-grader Amber Brown appears in a series of funny stories by Paula Danziger. Phyllis Reynolds Naylor writes a series about Alice, a thirteen-year-old whose mother's death means that she must become the "woman of the house" for her father and much older brother. Johanna Hurwitz's Aldo finds just about everything "interesting." In *Aldo Applesauce,* his becoming a vegetarian earns him various nicknames. In *Aldo Peanut Butter,* his puppies are named Peanut and Butter. All of these series books use good language, engaging themes, and well-rounded characters to give substance to the plots.

Books with Multicultural and International Themes

Books that portray the real-life experiences of people growing up in parallel cultures, outside the mainstream cultures of North America, are more plentiful now than they were in the past. In *Child of the Owl* and later in *Thief of Hearts,* Laurence Yep explores how Chinese American girls struggle to come to terms with their own identities. The title character in *Julie,* by Jean Craighead George, is an Alaskan Inuit who is faced with a difficult choice as she straddles two cultures; she learns to accommodate both old and new cultures. In *When the Nightingale Sings* by Joyce Carol Thomas, Marigold, who was born in a Southern swamp, finds her origins and a home in the African American community of which she is a part.

Books set outside North America cover the range of themes we have been discussing. Many highlight foreign settings, however, with the clear intention of expanding readers' awareness of life in other places.

Lyll Becerra de Jenkins wrote *The Honorable Prison* about her home country, Colombia. Her *Celebrating the Hero* tells of an American girl who goes back to Colombia to learn about her grandfather.

A moving book written by Pegi Deitz Shea (with illustrations by Anita Riggio and stitched in traditional Hmong pa'ndau by You Yang), *The Whispering Cloth* shows in pictures and text the pathos of having to leave one's native land. *A Boat to Nowhere,* by Maureen Crane Wartski, is one of two books about two war orphans who emigrate from Vietnam to a less-than-hospitable United States.

Frances Temple published her first book in 1992 and died in 1995, but in her brief career she broke new ground with her realistic works with political themes, set in other countries. Two of her books, set in Haiti, explore young

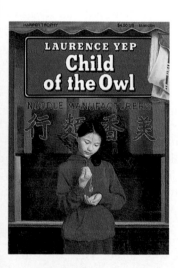

Illustration 8.5

For Casey, San Francisco's Chinatown was home, the earth that made her strong—and not the impediment to fulfillment she had once thought it was. (*Child of the Owl* by Laurence Yep, jacket art by Allen Say. Copyright © 1990. Used by permission of HarperTrophy, a division of HarperCollins Publishers.)

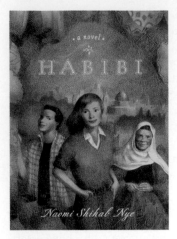

Illustration 8.6
Liyana negotiates adolescent and cultural identity when she moves from St. Louis to Jerusalem after her parents decide the children should get to know the "other half" of their heritage. (*Habibi* by Naomi Shihab Nye. Copyright © 1987 by Naomi Shihab Nye. Used by permission of Simon & Schuster Books for Young Readers, an imprint of Simon & Schuster Children's Publishing.)

people's struggles against political oppression: *Taste of Salt: A Story of Modern Haiti* won the Jane Addams Peace Award, and *Tonight, by Sea* won the Américas Award.

Overcoming prejudice is a major theme in multicultural books. The eight children in *Mayfield Crossing,* by Vaunda Micheaux Nelson, are excited about two things: baseball and going to a new, integrated school in the fall. The children at the new school, however, are unwilling to accept African American children on their ball team. The possibility of changing racist traditions opens up when blond and friendly Ivy accepts Meg's invitation to become the ninth player on the Mayfield Crossing team.

The hero of *Somewhere in the Darkness,* by Walter Dean Myers, is a very bright African American tenth-grader whose life seems to be falling apart. The school counselor doesn't help, his deceased mother's friend who cares for him can't help, and then his father returns unexpectedly (and illegally) from prison to convince Jimmy that he was not guilty of the crime for which he was convicted. In the end, the reader feels that Jimmy will be able to find the strength to put his own life together.

For more authors and titles of multicultural books and international books and a discussion of books from parallel cultures, see Chapter 4.

HOW REALISTIC FICTION WORKS

The term "realistic fiction" is something of a paradox. A work of fiction is contrived, yet readers are meant to believe that a work of realistic fiction is real, at least while they are engrossed in reading it. But this paradox contains some other seeming contradictions as well. Exploring two of them will clarify how realistic fiction "works."

An effective work of realistic fiction makes us believe that what it describes might really have happened. Yet because it is fiction, the work is organized into a plot—and that makes it quite different from real life, in which the lion's share of our days is made of meaningless details: minutes spent waiting for traffic lights to change, minutes spent searching for lost papers or misplaced keys, minutes spent half-listening to uninteresting conversations. In contrast, just about every detail in a work of fiction is meaningful. Why aren't we aware of the difference right off?

Although realistic fiction does not much resemble day-to-day reality, it does resemble the ways in which we represent that reality to ourselves and others. Fiction is not like life—but it is like our stories of our lives. By taking events from life and giving them meaning, fiction shows us how we find significance and purpose in our lives. Take, for example, the characters in Phyllis Reynolds Naylor's *Shiloh.* Judd Travers, a man without awareness who acts violently in the world, unthinkingly re-creates the violence with which he was raised. The boy Marty makes a commitment to protect the dog Shiloh and, in so doing, goes beyond blind obedience to his father and also beyond his mother's unexamined code of ethics. Marty is aware of what he is doing. He gradually comes to understand the reasons behind his father's demands, his mother's pure but insufficient morality, and Judd Travers's brutish nature—after which he reaches his own conclusions about what he should do. Then there is the reader. Thanks to Naylor's narrative, the reader is privileged to see these several ways of thinking through the moral issues in *Shiloh* and is allowed to make a personal judgment about them. It is not too great a step for readers to think of the issues in their lives in the complex ways Naylor reveals to them as they read *Shiloh.*

No wonder scholars who have studied the effects of literacy have claimed that reading expands awareness (Luria, 1976; Postman, 1994; Stanovich, 1992). Over time, the habit of reading allows children to see patterns in their lives, to look into their own motives and those of others, and to see possibilities for independent action.

A second contradiction of realistic fiction is the fact that it encourages one way of seeing events more than others, even as it presents a lifelike description of them. A story might seem to tell "what happened," but it almost invariably makes a point about what happened and causes readers to see the events in a certain way, with a slant. The slant of *Shiloh* vindicates Marty's opposition to the adults around him as he chooses to care for the dog. But the story might have been told differently: If Judd Travers had narrated the story, he might have stressed Marty's theft, disobedience of his parents, and violation of community norms. Because stories tend to emphasize one way of seeing events, it can be revealing to ask, in discussions about literature, "How would the events in this story have looked from a different character's point of view?"

MAJOR WRITERS OF REALISTIC FICTION AND THEIR WORKS

The writers discussed in the following sections are all from the United States. Of course, there are stellar writers who come from other English-speaking countries and others whose books have been translated into English. Some of those are discussed earlier in this chapter and in Chapter 4.

Avi

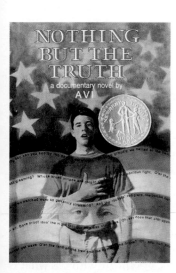

After a publisher accepted his first book, Avi Wortis was asked how he wanted his name to appear on the book. He answered "Avi," and his books have appeared without his last name ever since. As a child, Avi had problems with both reading and writing; now he likes to show his manuscripts covered with red pencil marks to special students in schools he visits. His book *The Man from the Sky* features a child who has difficulty reading books but has other abilities that initially are ignored by others. His desire to write novels followed attempts at playwriting and many years of working as a librarian and, he claims, grew out of a stubborn wish to prove something to those who had criticized his writing.

Avi writes historical as well as realistic fiction. In 1991, he won the Boston Globe–Horn Book Award for a historical novel, *The True Confessions of Charlotte Doyle,* which was also a Newbery Honor Book. The next year, he won the same awards for a work of realistic fiction, *Nothing but the Truth.* Among Avi's other popular and award-winning novels are *Romeo and Juliet, Together (and Alive) at Last* and *Who Was That Masked Man Anyway?* His strength as a writer lies mainly in his respect for children, but his books are also notable for gripping first chapters, terse action-filled writing, thematic richness, and imaginative variety in format.

Illustration 8.7
Ninth-grader Philip hums along to the national anthem and ends up suspended from school for two days. The story includes news clips, diary entries, school memos, and dialogue transcriptions. (*Nothing but the Truth* by Avi, cover illustration by Peter Catalanotto. Published by Orchard Books, an imprint of Scholastic Inc. Cover illustration copyright © 1991 by Peter Catalanotto. Reprinted by permission.)

Judy Blume

In 1996, Judy Blume received the Margaret Edwards Award for her lifetime contribution to literature for young adults. With millions of books sold, she is one of the most popular children's authors of all time—and also one of the most controversial. Blume took the world of children's books by storm during the

Ask the Author . . . *Sharon Creech*

How do you create and weave together the strands of your intricate plots?

Most of my stories begin with the image of a person and a place, and I write to discover the story. Very early on, the main character will mention other people, and I know that these people will have their own stories to tell. It is these stories that evolve into other strands of the plot.

Weaving them together is not as difficult as it might sound, because each day I merely pick up the previous strands and go wherever it feels right to go. If I feel the need to spend some time with the main character's grandparents, for example, I will do that, and then return to the central story. That central story will be affected by what I've learned from the grandparents, and so the different strands begin to intertwine.

Often I use the image of clearing a trail to describe the writing process. Like Zinny Taylor, who clears a long trail in *Chasing Redbird,* I am only clearing a little bit of the story trail at a time. Sometimes there are side paths that look interesting, and I'll follow those and then return to the main trail.

It is wonderful when you begin to see the patterns emerge—when you can see enough of the story to sense how one part relates to another. If I tried to predict the pattern—or the course of the story trail—in advance, I don't think I'd be so willing to allow it to change and evolve, and it is this changing and evolving that becomes most interesting to me. At the end, I can see how all the parts of the trail are connected, and then I revise, clearing patches that aren't yet smooth enough.

Sometimes students worry when they're writing their own stories that they have to know the whole story before they begin. I find it more exciting to know very little at the beginning, and to run down that trail wondering what I will find along the way.

> ### Favorite Books as a Child
>
> Unfortunately, I have a terrible memory for what books I read as a child.
>
> There is only one I clearly remember: *The Timbertoes* by Edna Aldredge and Jessie McKee illustrated by John Gee

Sharon Creech is the author of Walk Two Moons, *which received the Newbery Medal;* The Wanderer; Absolutely Normal Chaos; Bloomability; Pleasing the Ghost; *and* Chasing Redbird. *After spending eighteen years teaching and writing in Europe, Sharon Creech recently returned with her husband and grown children to the United States to live.*

1970s with stories on subjects—such as the viciousness of peer groups, sexuality, and hypocrisy—that were of intense concern to children but difficult for many adults to explore with them. That her works have struck a chord with children is obvious from their popularity, but their frankness—and perhaps the absence of any helpful or caring adult figures in many of them—has made them the most consistently controversial children's books ever. Judy Blume has stood up to her critics forthrightly and has long been active in the fight against those who would limit children's access to her books or those by other authors.

Blume's first book, ***The One in the Middle Is the Green Kangaroo,*** was published in 1969, and it remains a favorite for younger children. ***Tales of a Fourth Grade Nothing*** and its sequels are enormously popular with those in the middle elementary grades. Designed for young adolescents, ***Are You There God? It's Me, Margaret*** openly discusses menstruation and emerging female sexuality. Blume has said that she considers ***Blubber,*** a book about a group of children victimizing an overweight peer, her most important work because children must be told about their own cruelty if they are to raise their level of moral behavior. *Forever* is the target of the most censorship because it describes a sexual encounter explicitly, and *Starring Sally J. Freedman as Herself* is the most autobiographical, according to Blume.

Eve Bunting

Eve Bunting's early life in Northern Ireland, an area long beset by intergroup strife, nurtured her concern for the underdog and interest in social issues. Her storytelling abilities were honed during her childhood, entertaining the girls in her boarding school. She first considered writing for children when she took a writing for publication course at a junior college after immigrating to the United States. She has written more than 150 books in several genres for children of all ages. Her works of realistic fiction cover topics such as illness, drunken drivers, the environment, aging, the Holocaust, war, and literacy. Bunting's skill in addressing a wide range of social issues keeps her books from being didactic. She credits her ideas to the daily newspaper, weekly magazines, and generally observing life around her.

Bunting's characters represent a variety of class and ethnic groups. In 1994, the Caldecott Medal went to David Diaz for his illustration of Bunting's *Smoky Night,* which depicts people of different ethnic backgrounds coming together during the Los Angeles riots. *Fly Away Home* is a picture book about a homeless father and child who live in an airport. Bunting uses dialogue extensively in her books and centers issues on the everyday lives of her child characters. Bunting's lighthearted and fast-paced mystery *Coffin on a Case* tells how twelve-year-old Henry Coffin, son of a private investigator, helps a teenage girl pursue a missing mother.

Betsy Byars

Betsy Byars is one of the foremost writers of realistic fiction for children. Malcolm Usrey (1995) praises this prolific writer for creating books with an authentic Southern regional style, a sense of irony and humor, a charming and optimistic tone, and daring. One of Byars's strengths is her ability to create memorable adult characters. Byars tackles painful situations in children's lives for which solutions are not always at hand. For example, the foster children in *The Pinballs* feel like pinballs, being sent wherever the adults choose. Byars won the Newbery Medal in 1971 for *The Summer of the Swans,* which tells of a young girl who learns about herself as she searches for her lost brother, Charlie, who is mentally retarded.

Byars has created two series of books, both humorous and light in spirit but addressing serious day-to-day issues faced by children and their peers and families. She introduced an indomitable twelve-year-old, Bingo Brown, in *Bingo Brown and the Language of Love* and has followed his antics through several other books. The other series is about a not-too-ordinary family, the Blossoms. This vivacious and close-knit family is headed by Mother Blossom, who rides in a rodeo. Her children—Junior, Maggie, and Vern—are cared for by Pap, the grandfather, when she is absent.

Beverly Cleary

Beverly Cleary was a school librarian for a brief period, and she says in her autobiographies, *A Girl from Yamhill: A Memoir* and *My Own Two Feet:*

A Memoir, that she wrote books she sensed school children wanted and needed—books about other children who were like them, in ordinary settings and with ordinary lives. She certainly succeeded; the characters in Beverly Cleary's books—Henry Huggins, Beezus, the dog Ribsy, Otis Spofford, and above all Ramona—are as familiar to most middle elementary school children as their classmates. The seven books about Ramona span a twenty-nine-year writing period. Ramona starts as a four-year-old and progresses through the seven books to third grade. *Ramona Quimby, Age 8* and *Ramona and Her Father* were Newbery Honor Books. Her books are marked by their strong character delineation, humor, and joyfulness.

Cleary won the Newbery Medal for *Dear Mr. Henshaw,* a story related through the correspondence between an elementary school boy and a children's author. In 1975, Cleary won the Laura Ingalls Wilder Medal for lifetime achievement in children's literature.

Paula Fox

Paula Fox has written over two dozen books for children, all with unusual settings, engaging characters, and multilayered plots. Fox's strengths are the verisimilitude of her settings, her writing style, and her unforgettable characters. In 1978, Paula Fox was awarded the Hans Christian Andersen Medal for her worldwide contribution to children's literature.

Fox's first book, *Maurice's Room,* is about a boy who is fascinated with collecting "things" and their names—to the exasperation of his mother. *Monkey Island* is about a temporarily homeless child who takes refuge with others when his mother abandons him. *One-Eyed Cat,* a Newbery Honor Book, is a captivating story about a boy whose feelings of guilt over using a gun he has been told not to handle make him wonder whether he is responsible for having shot a cat. Fox won the Newbery Medal in 1974 for her only work of historical fiction, *The Slave Dancer,* about a young white boy's horrifying time playing the flute to provide music while African slaves are forced to exercise during the long ocean voyage to the United States.

E. L. Konigsburg

E. L. Konigsburg studied chemistry in college and began her adult life as a chemistry teacher. As a mother of three young children, she began writing in secret during the hours she spent waiting for children, doctors, and shoe salesmen. Her stories emerged out of these very experiences. Many of her books feature middle-class characters, inspired by her experiences with her own students and with her children. Often, her books feature children whose exceptional intelligence makes them outsiders to the mainstream of childhood experiences and who imaginatively create paths for themselves. Likewise, her own writing is imaginative, with intricate plot structures and character development.

Konigsburg published two books in 1967: *From the Mixed-up Files of Mrs. Basil E. Frankweiler* and *Jennifer, Hecate, Macbeth, William McKinley, and Me, Elizabeth.* The first won the Newbery Medal, and the second was a Newbery Honor Book. Thirty years later, in 1997, Konigsburg won the Newbery Medal again for *The View from Saturday,* a book about precocious sixth-graders.

Lois Lowry

Lois Lowry treats the large and small troubles of childhood gently but seriously in her realistic fiction. Her characters all manage to assume some responsi-

Illustration 8.8
When Branwell's baby sister goes into a coma from an injury, Bran calls 911 but is unable to speak. Connor must figure out a way to communicate with Bran in order to prove that Bran was not responsible for his sister's condition. (*Silent to the Bone* by E. L. Konigsburg. Copyright © 2000 by E. L. Konigsburg. Used by permission of Atheneum Books for Young Readers, an imprint of Simon & Schuster Children's Publishing.)

bility for solving their own problems. *A Summer to Die,* about sisters, life, and death, was her first novel. Lowry remains one of the most frequently read of children's authors. She has written a series of books about the character Anastasia, beginning with *Anastasia Krupnik* and continuing to depict the growing and maturing adolescent Anastasia in books such as *Anastasia at This Address.* The humor in the Anastasia books is in the language play and the hilarious descriptions of the best-laid plans going awry. In addition, Lowry portrays sympathetic adults who always come to the rescue of child characters.

Lois Lowry reflects on her own writing by comparing it to a past career as a photographer. She explains that, as a writer, she does much of what she did as a photographer—that is, she selects how to portray the world through the decisions she makes regarding focus, lens, and selection of images to portray. Lowry's two Newbery awards have been for works in genres other than realistic fiction: her historical fiction book *Number the Stars* and her science fiction book *The Giver.*

Phyllis Reynolds Naylor

Phyllis Naylor studied to be a clinical psychologist, but her interest in writing began in childhood. The author of over seventy books, Naylor is tuned in to the experiences of children and teens, and she writes on a wide range of topics. Her plots are designed to reveal interpersonal relationships but are laced with humor rather than didacticism. Her 1992 Newbery Medal winner, *Shiloh,* demonstrates her ability to suggest to young readers the larger moral issues that emerge from everyday, ordinary personal problems.

Naylor's series of books about Alice is set in the household of this upbeat, assertive middle-school girl. Alice's mother is dead, and she lives with her father and her much older brother. The stories are at once funny, wise, and convincing. *Alice in Rapture, Sort of* tells of Alice's first boyfriend. In *Reluctantly Alice,* Alice tries to advise her father and brother about their love lives. In *Alice in April,* she practices being the "woman of the house," and in *All But Alice,* she discovers the dangers of wanting to be a part of the "in" crowd.

Katherine Paterson

As the daughter of missionaries, Katherine Paterson grew up in China; she later lived in Japan as a missionary herself. Today, even when she is writing about an American setting, Paterson is able to show insight into the lives of an unusually broad range of characters. *The Great Gilly Hopkins* lets readers get to know a foster child who is learning about love; *Come Sing, Jimmy Jo* explores the music and the aspirations of Appalachian people; and Newbery Medal winner *Bridge to Terabithia* brings together children of different social classes.

Katherine Paterson's stories are notable for the richness of their philosophical and religious underpinnings. Her Newbery Medal–winning historical fiction *Jacob Have I Loved* is notable for its sense of place and the depth with which Paterson explores the rivalry between twin sisters. Paterson uses an afterword as a device to help the reader reflect on the themes. Paterson's writing weaves together multiple plot strands, each maintained through symbols and strong imagery. Her stories often reflect happenings or emotions in her own life. For example, her son's loss of a close friend is a tragedy that is portrayed in *Bridge to Terabithia.* It is Paterson's ability to place her own feelings into her writing and characters that gives her books their power. Katherine Paterson has been awarded the Hans Christian Andersen Award for recognition of her contribution to the world's children's literature.

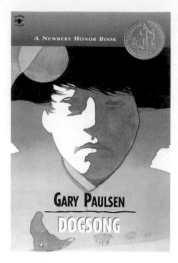

Illustration 8.9
Inuit culture teaches that every living thing has its own unique song, and through his dogsledding experiences Russell is able to learn his. (*Dogsong* written by Gary Paulsen, jacket painting by Neil Waldman. Text copyright © 1985 Bradbury Press. Used by permission of Atheneum Books for Young Readers, an imprint of Simon & Schuster's Children's Publishing.)

Gary Paulsen

Gary Paulsen had a rough childhood and an equally rough and varied adulthood before finding success as a children's author. He has more than fifty books to his credit, and many have won awards. His works are informed by his range of experiences—working as a truck driver, construction worker, and lumberjack and in other physically demanding jobs—and are permeated by the theme of survival. Paulsen has a passionate tie to nature and the wilderness, evident in his poetic, vivid writing about protagonists learning from nature as they set out on their own life journeys.

The brighter side of Paulsen's own childhood is reflected in the hilarious episodes of *Harris and Me: A Summer Remembered;* some of the less happy moments are recounted in *Eastern Sun, Western Moon: An Autobiographical Odyssey. Hatchet,* a Newbery Honor Book, is the story of a boy's survival in the Canadian wilderness. Paulsen wrote two sequels in response to popular demand: *The River,* in which his protagonist returns to collect data on survival for scientists, and *Brian's Winter,* in which the original story is extended. *The Winter Room,* another Newbery Honor Book, is a descriptive piece about a Minnesota logging cabin and the people in it. The Iditarod, a cross-Alaska dogsled race in which Paulsen has participated, plays a central role in two of his books, *Winterdance* and *Woodsong.* Paulsen's realistic fiction is intense and emotion-packed.

Cynthia Rylant

The works of versatile and prolific Appalachian writer Cynthia Rylant range from poetry to easy readers to young adult novels to picture books. Her books have been enhanced by a variety of illustrators; she has illustrated some herself. Rylant's topics range from aging to rural life, animal life, and nature. She won the Newbery Medal for *Missing May,* mentioned earlier. *A Fine White Dust,* about religious choice, was a Newbery Honor Book. Other memorable books for older readers include *Soda Jerk,* poetic reflections on small-town life from the perspective of a teenage boy, and *A Kindness,* which chronicles a young boy's adjustment to his mother's romantic involvement. Among Rylant's Appalachian stories is *A Blue-Eyed Daisy,* set in the coal mine country of West Virginia. Her own childhood experiences in West Virginia, living with her grandparents, led to such picture books as *The Relatives Came, When I Was Young in the Mountains,* and *Appalachia: The Voices of Sleeping Birds.*

Rylant also produced fourteen Henry and Mudge stories, all easy readers for younger children. First- and second-graders go from one emotional trauma to another with Henry and his dog Mudge in books such as *Henry and Mudge and the Careful Cousin.* Her easy reader books about Mr. Putter and Tabby are enjoyed by those who read beyond the Henry and Mudge books.

Cynthia Voigt

Although Cynthia Voigt knew since the ninth grade that she wanted to be a writer, it wasn't until she was a fifth-grade teacher that she began to seriously explore a career as a writer. She won a Newbery Medal for her first book, *Homecoming,* about a teenage girl who takes her brothers and sisters on a difficult journey to make a home with their estranged grandmother when their mother proves too incompetent to keep them. Voigt wrote five other books about the Tillerman family. *Dicey's Song* relates Dicey's hard work in making a family with her emotionally aloof grandmother on the Eastern Shore of Maryland.

Voigt provides rich and complex plots about siblings making their way in the world against great odds, often without strong adult guidance but with courage and family loyalty. Making a life after a car accident and an amputation is the subject of *Izzy, Willy-Nilly*. Voigt wrote about divorce in *A Solitary Blue,* a Newbery Honor Book. *When She Hollers* is a story about child abuse. Rich in imagery and undercurrents of emotion, and with a strong sense of place, Voigt's stories are unforgettable.

Vera Williams

The artist in Vera Williams preceded the writer, but since she began writing, Williams has written and illustrated lasting realistic fiction for young readers. Williams's stories are typically about strong, ethnically diverse girls and women. Her personal commitment to peace creates books with tranquil plots and characters who hold affectionate bonds with one another. Caldecott Honor book *A Chair for My Mother* and *Music, Music for Everyone* and *Something Special for Me* all revolve around one member of a family wanting to do something nice for another; the dilemmas usually involve financing the favor. Her characters often have a sincere enjoyment of the simpler sides of life. *Cherries and Cherry Pits* is a dreamy story about a child who draws pictures and tells tales to go with them. Her Caldecott Honor book *"More, More, More," Said the Baby: Three Love Stories* has three adults enjoying simple playtime activities with babies.

Adjusting to a move and her parents' divorce is the task facing *Scooter,* who accomplishes it with the help of her no-nonsense mother. Books that celebrate the power of ordinary people to help each other—a theme that is all too rare in American children's literature—are Williams's considerable contribution to children's literature.

Illustration 8.10
When fire destroys their belongings, a little girl saves coins to help buy a chair for the mother to rest on after working all day as a waitress.
(*A Chair For My Mother* by Vera B. Williams. Copyright © 1983. Used by permission of Greenwillow, a division of HarperCollins Publishers.)

Charlotte Zolotow

Charlotte Zolotow has said, "We are not different from the children we were, only more experienced, better able to disguise our feelings from others, if not from ourselves." From her books we know that Zolotow did not lose touch with childhood. Her books show unusual sensitivity in exploring children's relationships with family and other children. Several of her books are concerned with children's views of parents and grandparents. *A Father Like That* is a boy's description of what he would like in a father. *My Grandson Lew* is a tender book about remembering a grandfather's words after his death. *May I Visit?* expresses a child's fear that she won't be able to return home when she grows up. *Say It!* is a loving conversation between a mother and daughter as they take a walk. In *William's Doll,* a father becomes convinced that dolls help boys learn how to be fathers.

Other stories develop an understanding of communication among children. *The Unfriendly Book* is about jealousy; *The Hating Book* and *The Quarreling Book* are about what the titles suggest. *The Old Dog* is about grief. Zolotow's poetic prose and hopeful tone reveal the possibilities of the real world for young children.

CRITERIA FOR EVALUATING AND SELECTING REALISTIC FICTION

Adults write realistic fiction for children to provide a view of the world and to pass on some of the wisdom they have gained by living longer. Their hope is that their books leave children with something to reflect on about their own lives or those of others. It is not surprising that even the best of writers succumb once in a while to "teaching and preaching" in realistic fiction, especially when they feel that child readers might need a little help in getting at an important idea. In Phyllis Naylor's *Alice in April*, twelve-year-old Pamela says, "You know what? When you come right down to it, all we can do is just try to be the best friends to each other that we can and hope it's enough." Somehow that sounds more like an adult than the character Pamela. A little nudging toward an insight isn't objectionable, but if it's overdone, the writing may seem didactic.

In evaluating realistic fiction, we should remain wary of statements and attitudes that seem to condescend to children, implying that children wouldn't be capable of making their own moral judgments or of understanding the consequences of a character's actions. We adults can ask ourselves some questions in an effort to identify books with the "teaching and preaching" tendency—a tendency that doesn't contribute to the telling or reading of a good story. These questions help to identify the honesty of a book and an author's willingness to trust the reader to understand:

- Do the characters resemble real people you know?
- Are the events plausible? Will children believe that they could happen?
- Will children readily grasp the insights offered by the book? Are children led to those insights by the flow of the action rather than by the author's explicit instruction?

When selecting realistic fiction, teachers and librarians often focus on the topic of the book. Just because the book is said to address a topic, however, does not guarantee that it has a good story or even accurate or appropriate information on the topic. Therefore, teachers and librarians might want to consider the following questions before selecting a book:

- Are the descriptions of people accurate, given the historical and social setting?
- Does the plot avoid the manipulative devices of sentimentality and sensationalism?
- Is the style of writing (the vocabulary and sentence structure) pleasing, engaging, and suited to the time and place of the story?
- Is the plot resolution believable—not contrived to end in a certain way?
- Is the story imaginative or original so that it engages children's interest?

Authors express their attitudes toward children by the breadth of their inclusion of characters and perspectives.

- Do events, descriptions, or styles of speech demean classes of people or individuals?
- Does the author avoid condescending to children?

Finally, a book should add up to more than entertainment. Worthwhile realistic fiction leaves children with something to reflect on about their own lives or those of others.

TEACHING IDEAS

Real Life versus Fiction. Ask students in grades 3 through 6 to record in a diary all the events that happen to them in a single day—just the facts, without embellishment. Then have them exchange diaries with a friend and write up the friend's account as if it were a chapter in a work of realistic fiction. Afterwards, ask the students to compare the two versions. What was added to make the fictionalized version? What was left out? How did the dramatic contour (that is, the pattern of building suspense and its resolution) of the diary version compare with that of the fictionalized version? What was made clearer about the events of the day when they were fictionalized? What was distorted?

Anthropomorphic Animal Fantasies or Realistic Fiction? Provide students with a range of picture books in which animal characters take on human characteristics. Have students study them to find out why books that are characterized as fantasy have qualities that make them seem like realistic fiction. For example, what qualities in Kevin Henkes's picture books about anthropomorphic mice make the mice appear to resonate with human characteristics? What qualities in *Charlotte's Web* make the situations and solutions appear to be like those that humans face?

Censorship and Propriety. This chapter referred to the struggle between some adults who defend books that contain controversial material and others who want to put such books out of the reach of children. But what do children say? Ask a group of children in grades 2 through 6 what things they think should or should not be written about in the books they read. What disagreements emerge among them? How do the children think such disagreements should be resolved? Should the books be banned? Should they be made available only to those whose parents give permission for them to read them? Or should they be made available to all students, no matter what their parents think?

EXPERIENCES FOR YOUR LEARNING

1. As you read a book of contemporary realistic fiction, make note of references to the "real world" that assume an understanding simply through the name. For example, the reference to Winn-Dixie in the book *Because of Winn-Dixie* conjures the image of a supermarket for those who know it. Consider what a lack of knowledge of these references means to readers, particularly those who live outside the United States or who are newcomers to the country.

2. Read a work of contemporary realistic fiction that is set in an area of which you have intimate knowledge. Find details that let you know that the author also knows this setting and confirm for you the reality of the setting. How do these details influence the believability of the setting?

3. Read a work of contemporary realistic fiction that is set in an area that you do not know—perhaps a different region of the United States or

a different country. Find descriptive passages that paint a picture of the setting for you. How does the author make you feel as though you can imagine this place that you do not know?

4. With one or more partners, locate a sampling of picture books that are works of contemporary realistic fiction. Take turns reading them aloud without showing the pictures first, and write a quick response about the pictures painted in your mind as you listen. Then explore the pictures and discuss how the pictures contribute to the overall impression of the story. Look carefully at details that give you information about the characters' emotions and responses, in addition to a sense of the overall setting and actions.

RECOMMENDED BOOKS

* indicates a picture book; I indicates interest level (P = preschool, YA = young adult)

Books about Self-Discovery and Growing Up

Blume, Judy. *Are You There, God? It's Me, Margaret.* Dell, 1970. A preteen girl goes through puberty angst and openly discusses menstruation and emerging female sexuality. (**I:** 9–11)

*Caines, Jeannette. *Just Us Women.* Illustrated by Pat Cummings. Harper & Row, 1982. A young girl and her aunt go on an automobile trip to North Carolina and create their own adventures. (**I:** P–8)

Cleary, Beverly. *Beezus and Ramona.* Morrow, 1955. The first of a series about the indomitable and spirited Ramona and her older sister; here Ramona is a preschooler. (**I:** 8–10)

———. *Dear Mr. Henshaw.* Illustrated by Paul Zelinsky. Morrow, 1983. Lee first writes to an author as part of a school assignment. In the continued correspondence, Lee increasingly confides in Mr. Henshaw about various issues that concern him—his parents' divorce, relationships with peers, and so on. (**I:** 9–11)

Cleaver, Bill, and Vera Cleaver. *Where the Lilies Bloom.* HarperCollins, 1969. Mary Call acts on her father's advice until she discovers that it doesn't work for her or her sister. (**I:** 9–12)

Danziger, Paula. *Amber Brown Is Not a Crayon.* Illustrated by Tony Ross. Putnam, 1994. In this popular series about a spunky girl's dilemmas as she grows up, Amber's best friend Justin is moving away. Selected sequels are *Amber Brown Goes Fourth* (1995), *Amber Brown Sees Red* (1997), and *I, Amber Brown* (2000). (**I:** 8–11)

Estes, Eleanor. *The Hundred Dresses.* Harcourt, 1944. Wanda acts with kindness toward those who ridiculed her for wearing the same dress every day. (**I:** 7–10)

Fox, Paula. *Maurice's Room.* Macmillan, 1966. Maurice collects so many things that his parents decide to move to the country. (**I:** 8–10)

Gantos, Jack. *Joey Pigza Swallowed the Key.* Farrar Straus Giroux, 1998. Joey knows that he is "wired," and his behavior is out of control unless he is on his medication for ADHD. The sequel is *Joey Pigza Out of Control* (2000). (**I:** 9–12)

Haddix, Margaret Peterson. *Don't You Dare Read This, Mrs. Dunphrey.* Simon & Schuster, 1996. Tish confides in her school-assigned journal her fears about her mother's whereabouts and how Tish will cope with caring for herself and her younger brother in their mother's absence. (**I:** 12–YA)

*Hoffman, Mary. *Amazing Grace.* Dial, 1991. Illustrated by Caroline Binch. Grace has an amazing ability to act, but she is told by classmates that she cannot be Peter Pan in the class play because she is a girl and she is black. The sequel is *Boundless Grace* (1995), and the chapter book is *Starring Grace* (2000). (**I:** P–7)

Hurwitz, Johanna. *The Adventures of Ali Baba Bernstein.* Morrow, 1985. Eight-year-old David is convinced that his life will be more adventurous when he changes his name to Ali Baba. (**I:** 8–10)

Lowry, Lois. *Anastasia Krupnik.* Houghton Mifflin, 1979. In this first book in the series of many about Anastasia, the ten-year-old girl faces her first love and the news that she will soon have a baby brother. (**I:** 9–12)

MacLachlan, Patricia. *The Facts and Fictions of Minna Pratt.* HarperCollins, 1988. Minna plays the cello and learns about life and passions from her family, friends, and Mozart. (**I:** 10–YA)

———. *Journey.* Delacorte, 1991. When two children are left by their mother, the grandparents make a home for them. (**I:** 9–12)

Mori, Kyoko. *Shizuko's Daughter*. Holt, 1993. Following her mother's suicide, twelve-year-old Yuki must face her adolescent years amidst difficult relationships with her father and stepmother, as her creative spirit rebels against a culture that restricts her individuality. (I: 12 and up)

Myers, Walter Dean. *Darnell Rock Reporting*. Delacorte, 1994. A thirteen-year-old's family and friends doubt that Darnell will make it as a writer for the school newspaper. (I: 11–YA)

Paulsen, Gary. *Harris and Me: A Summer Remembered*. Harcourt, 1993. A city boy goes to live with his distant cousin on a farm, where he finds love and hilarious adventures. (I: 9–12)

Rocklin, Joanne. *For Your Eyes Only!* Scholastic, 1997. Through a school assignment to keep a journal, a girl expresses concern about another classmate's home abuse. (I: 10–13)

Snyder, Zilpha Keatley. *Libby on Wednesday*. Delacorte, 1990. Libby wins a writing contest and finds herself in a writing club where her writing flourishes but peer relationships are difficult. (I: 9–12)

Soto, Gary. *Baseball in April and Other Stories*. Harcourt, 1990. Tender stories of children fitting into families and of the Latino culture of California. (I: 10–YA)

*Waber, Bernard. *Ira Says Goodbye*. Houghton Mifflin, 1988. The story deals with the recognition of sadness that a child feels when a friend moves. The sequel is *Ira Sleeps Over* (1972). (I: P–7)

*Williams, Vera. *"More, More, More" Said the Baby: 3 Love Stories*. Greenwillow, 1990. A father, mother, and grandmother follow playful rituals with their babies. (I: P–K)

*Willner-Pardo, Gina. *Daphne Eloise Slater, Who's Tall for Her Age*. Illustrated by Glo Coalson. Clarion, 1997. Daphne Eloise resolves her reaction and attitude about being called a giraffe by a mean-spirited classmate. (I: 6–8)

*Zolotow, Charlotte. *The Old Dog*. HarperCollins, 1995. A boy remembers the fun he had with his dog. (I: P–K)

*———. *William's Doll*. Illustrated by William Pene du Bois. Harper & Row, 1972. A boy and his father disagree about playing with dolls. (I: P–7)

Books about Families

Blume, Judy. *The One in the Middle Is the Green Kangaroo*. Simon & Schuster, 1969/1981. A middle child gains self-confidence by being in a school play. (I: 7–9)

———. *Tales of a Fourth Grade Nothing*. Dutton, 1972. Readers will laugh and sympathize with Peter Hatcher's embarrassment over and envy of his pesky two-year-old brother, Fudge. Sequels are *Superfudge* (1980) and *Fudge-a-Mania* (1990). (I: 7–9)

Boyd, Candy Dawson. *Charlie Pippin*. Macmillan, 1987. Charlie earns money to help with her search for clues about her father's Vietnam War experience. (I: 10–12)

———. *Circle of Gold*. Scholastic, 1984. A young girl copes with her father's death and her mother's struggle to support the family. (I: 9–11)

Brooks, Bruce. *What Hearts*. HarperCollins, 1992. Four interrelated short stories show a boy learning about love and forgiveness at various stages of his life. (I: 11–YA)

Byars, Betsy. *The Pinballs*. Harper & Row, 1977. Three lonely foster children learn to care for each other and their foster parents. (I: 9–12)

Cleary, Beverly. *Ramona Quimby, Age 8*. Morrow, 1981. As a third-grader, Ramona finds that her life changes drastically when her father goes back to school. See also *Ramona and Her Father* (1977), in which Ramona campaigns to get her father to quit smoking. (I: 7–9)

Creech, Sharon. *Walk Two Moons*. HarperCollins, 1994. A thirteen-year-old girl and her grandparents follow the journey of her mother after she leaves them. (I: 10–YA)

*Gauch, Patricia Lee. *Christina Katerina and the Time She Quit the Family*. Illustrated by Elise Primavera. Putnam, 1987. Christina Katerina decides to "quit" her family so that she can do things her own way. She discovers that being part of a family isn't so bad after all. A sequel is *Christina Katerina and the Great Bear Train* (1990). (I: 6–9)

Henkes, Kevin. *Protecting Marie*. Greenwillow, 1995. Twelve-year-old Fanny, who is dealing with adolescence, and her temperamental artist father, who is trying to handle turning 60, have a tenuous relationship; a pet dog helps to establish trust. (I: 10–YA)

Johnson, Angela. *Toning the Sweep*. Orchard, 1993. Three generations of women come together and share memories of the past as the dying grandmother prepares to move in with her daughter and granddaughter. (I: 11–YA)

*Jukes, Mavis. *Like Jake and Me*. Illustrated by Lloyd Bloom. Knopf, 1984. A spider brings Alex and his stepfather closer together. (I: 8–10)

Lisle, Janet Taylor. *Afternoon of the Elves*. Orchard, 1989. Fascinated by her friend Sara-Kate's imagination and careful caring for her creation, a playground for "elves," Kate worries about who takes care of Sara-Kate. (I: 9–12)

Mathis, Sharon Bell. *The Hundred Penny Box*. Viking Press, 1975. Michael intercedes when his mother tries to toss out his beloved great great Aunt Dew's memorabilia. (I: 8–10)

Myers, Walter Dean. *Me, Mop, and the Moondance Kid*. Delacorte, 1988. Two adopted boys remain friends with an orphan girl who seeks to be adopted, too. (I: 9–12)

Naylor, Phyllis Reynolds. *Alice in April*. Atheneum, 1993. Thirteen-year-old Alice demands more appreciation from her father and older brother. Other books about Alice are *Alice in Rapture, Sort Of* (1989), *Reluctantly Alice* (1991), and *All But Alice* (1992). (I: 10–13)

Paterson, Katherine. *Flip-Flop Girl*. Dutton, 1994. A young girl finds it difficult to accept that her father has died. (I: 10–YA)

———. *The Great Gilly Hopkins*. Crowell, 1978. A foster child tries to avoid her own fears by plotting against those who are trying to help. (I: 10–12)

Thesman, Jean. *When the Road Ends*. Houghton Mifflin, 1992. When three foster children and an elderly invalid are abandoned by a cruel caretaker, they seek to define what it means to be a family of sorts. (I: 10–12)

Voigt, Cynthia. *Dicey's Song*. Atheneum, 1982. Dicey and her siblings, abandoned by their mother, try to adjust to life with grandmother. The preceding book in the series is *Homecoming* (1981); the following book is *A Solitary Blue* (1983). (I: 12–YA)

*Williams, Vera. *A Chair for My Mother*. Greenwillow, 1983. After all their furniture is lost in a fire, the family saves their spare change to buy a chair for mother. See also *Cherries and Cherry Pits* (1986), *Music, Music, for Everyone* (1984), and *Something Special for Me* (1983). (I: P–8)

Williams-Garcia, Rita. *Like Sisters on the Home Front*. Lodestar, 1995. A troubled teenager is sent South to live with relatives and experiences the healing power of family roots. (I: 12–YA)

Woodson, Jacqueline. *From the Notebooks of Melanin Sun*. Blue Sky/Scholastic, 1995. A teenage boy copes with the news that his mother is in love with another woman. (I: YA)

Books about Interpersonal Relationships

Blume, Judy. *Blubber*. Bradbury, 1974. Jill joins her fifth-grade classmates in tormenting an overweight peer until she becomes a victim and realizes the pain of such behavior. (I: 9–11)

Conly, Jane Leslie. *Crazy Lady!* HarperCollins, 1993. Vernon Dibbs is finding junior high a tough time in life, especially since the death of his mother. After he befriends an alcoholic neighbor, Maxine, and her special needs son, Ronald, Vernon learns many life lessons as he takes up the cause of raising enough money to send Ronald to the Special Olympics. (I: 10–12)

Crutcher, Chris. *Ironman*. Greenwillow, 1995. Beauregard Brewster, "Ironman," aspires to do well in the upcoming triathlon, but his training is interrupted when he is required to attend an anger management class in his high school to deal with personal relationships. (I: YA)

Danziger, Paula, and Ann M. Martin. *Snail Mail No More*. Harcourt, 2000. Tara and Elizabeth continue their correspondence begun in an earlier book, *P.S. Longer Letter Later*, and consult each other via email on various issues related to family and peer relationships. (I: 9–12)

Fitzhugh, Louise. *Harriet the Spy*. Harper & Row, 1964. Harriet learns that writing down everything you think can get you in trouble with your friends. The sequel is *The Long Secret* (1965). (I: 9–11)

Konigsburg, E. L. *Jennifer, Hecate, Macbeth, William McKinley, and Me, Elizabeth*. Atheneum, 1968. Elizabeth is the loneliest girl around until she meets Jennifer, a witch, and becomes her apprentice in this interracial friendship story. (I: 9–11)

Mohr, Nicholasa. *Felita*. Dial, 1979. Felita is an eight-year-old Puerto Rican girl growing up in a close-knit urban community; she is confronted with racism when her family moves to a new neighborhood. (I: 7–9)

———. *Going Home*. Puffin, 1986. When eleven-year-old Felita goes to Puerto Rico for the summer, she at first feels like an outsider but later learns to embrace her heritage. (I: 10–12)

Namioka, Lensey. *April and the Dragon Lady*. Browndeer, 1994. April is a Chinese American teenager, torn between her Americanized adolescence and caring for her grandmother, who adheres to Chinese customs and expectations about relationships. (I: 10–YA)

Paterson, Katherine. *Come Sing, Jimmie Jo*. Dutton, 1985. Eleven-year-old Jimmie Jo becomes famous as a country music singer, but fame brings complications, including a man who claims to be his real father. (I: 10–12)

Rylant, Cynthia. *Henry and Mudge and the Careful Cousin*. Simon & Schuster, 1994. Annie visits her cousin Henry and his constantly drooling big dog,

Mudge. Annie must adjust to Mudge's gregariousness and Henry to her timidity. (I: P–7)

Soto, Gary. *Boys at Work*. Delacorte, 1995. Rudy and Alex take on many jobs to pay for a broken disk player that belongs to a gang member. This is the sequel to *The Pool Party* (1993). (I: 9–12)

Woodson, Jacqueline. *I Hadn't Meant to Tell You This*. Delacorte, 1994. Racial and class barriers are overcome as two girls who have both lost their mothers bond in a friendship that allows them to confront the sexual abuse by one father. (I: 12–YA)

———. *Maizon at Blue Hill*. Delacorte, 1992. Winning a scholarship at a boarding school does not ensure Maizon's acceptance by the almost all-white student body. Companion books are *Last Summer with Maizon* (1992) and *Between Madison and Palmetto* (1995). (I: 12–YA)

*Zolotow, Charlotte. *The Hating Book*. Illustrated by Ben Schechter. HarperTrophy, 1969/1989. Two little girls think they hate each other until they talk about it. See also *The Quarreling Book* (illustrated by Arnold Lobel, 1963/1982). (I: P–7)

Books about School

*Allard, Harry. *Miss Nelson Is Missing!* Illustrated by James Marshall. Houghton Mifflin, 1985. Their beloved and kind teacher, Miss Nelson, is missing, and the strange substitute teacher, Viola Swamp, has the class worried. Sequels are *Miss Nelson Is Back* (1985) and *Miss Nelson Has a Field Day* (1985). (I: 7–10)

Clements, Andrew. *Frindle*. Simon & Schuster, 1996. Ten-year-old Nick likes to create distractions in school. As a challenge to his vocabulary-loving teacher, he attempts to introduce a new word into the English language. (I: 8–11)

———. *The Landry News*. Simon & Schuster, 1999. Clara Landry, aspiring journalist, publishes an editorial exposing the lack of teaching in her fifth-grade classroom, motivating Mr. Larson back into action as an inspired teacher. (I: 9–12)

*Cohen, Miriam. *Will I Have a Friend?* Illustrated by Lillian Hoban. Macmillan, 1967. Jim is entering kindergarten, and he worries about whether he will have a friend. This series includes *Starring First Grade* (Bantam, 1985) and *See You in Second Grade* (1990). (I: P–7)

Danziger, Paula. *The Cat Ate My Gymsuit*. Delacorte, 1974. Marcy, a junior high student who always tries to get out of gym class, leads the campaign to reinstate an unconventional teacher who was fired. The sequel is *There's a Bat in Bunk Five* (1980). (I: 11–YA)

DeClements, Barthe. *Sixth Grade Can Really Kill You*. Puffin, 1995. Acting up to compensate for reading problems is how Helen handles her learning disabilities. See also *Nothing's Fair in Fifth Grade* (1981). (I: 9–12)

Giff, Patricia Reilly. *Look Out, Washington, D.C.!* Dell, 1995. In this book from the *Polk Street School* series, the Polk Street School kids take a field trip to Washington, D.C. (I: 7–9)

Gilson, Jamie. *Thirteen Ways to Sink a Sub*. Illustrated by Linda Strauss Edwards. Lothrop, 1982. The fourth-grade girls and boys take up a challenge to see which side can make the substitute teacher cry first. The sequel is *4B Goes Wild* (1983). (I: 8–10)

Greene, Stephanie. *Owen Foote, Second Grade Strongman*. Illustrated by Dee De Rosa. Clarion, 1996. Owen does not like being called a "pipsqueak" by the school nurse on height-and-weight measuring day and becomes a class hero by defending his friend when the nurse calls him "too fat." The sequel is *Owen Foote, Frontiersman* (1999). (I: 6–9)

Hurwitz, Johanna. *Class President*. Illustrated by Sheila Hamanaka. Scholastic, 1990. Julio hides his ambitions in order to campaign for a classmate to win the nomination for class president. The sequel is *School Spirit* (1994). See also *Class Clown* (1987) and *Teacher's Pet* (1988). (I: 10–12)

Kline, Suzy. *Herbie Jones*. Putnam, 1985. In this book in the *Herbie Jones* series, third-grader Herbie and his friend Raymond work to be moved up from the lowest reading group. (I: 7–9)

———. *Horrible Harry and the Dungeon*. Illustrated by Frank Remkiewicz. Viking, 1996. Students in Room 2B wonder whether Harry will be the new teacher Mr. Skooghammer's first "victim" of the dungeon—the suspension room in the basement. There are many other books in this popular early chapter book series. (I: 6–9)

Konigsburg, E. L. *The View from Saturday*. Atheneum, 1996. Four "gifted" and eccentric sixth-graders form the school's winning Academic Bowl Team. Their lives and stories intersect in interesting ways. (I: 10–13)

Levy, Elizabeth. *Keep Ms. Sugarman in the Fourth Grade*. HarperCollins, 1992. Jackie needs the support of her teacher and doesn't think she can survive when Ms. Sugarman is promoted. (I: 8–10)

Park, Barbara. *Junie B. Jones and Her Big Fat Mouth*. Illustrated by Denise Brunkus. Random House, 1993. Junie B. Jones is a kindergartner whose challenges with daily tasks have humorous results. The sequel is *Junie B. Jones and the Yucky Blucky Fruitcake* (1995). (I: P–7)

Rocklin, Joanne. *For Your Eyes Only!* Scholastic, 1997. Sixth-grade substitute Mr. Moffat writes poetry on the board and distributes journals, encouraging the students to record their thoughts. The alternating entries profile Lucy, an aspiring poet, and Andy, an angry and abused child. (I: 10–12)

Sachar, Louis. *There's a Boy in the Girls' Bathroom.* Knopf, 1987. An inept, troublesome fifth-grader, Bradley Chalkers, finds a friend in the school counselor. (I: 10–12)

*Schwartz, Amy. *Annabelle Swift, Kindergartner.* Orchard, 1988. Annabelle's older sister Lucy teaches her what to expect in kindergarten, but when Annabelle gets there, her knowledge sparks laughter among the children. Ultimately, Annabelle wins the classmates' approval. (I: P–7)

Shreve, Susan. *The Flunking of Joshua T. Bates.* Illustrated by Diane DeGroat. Knopf, 1984. When Joshua finds out that he must repeat the third grade, he is devastated. He faces taunting from former classmates, but a sympathetic teacher helps him find his strengths. Sequels are *Joshua T. Bates Takes Charge* (1993) and *Joshua T. Bates in Trouble Again* (1997). (I: 7–10)

Books about Sports

Avi. *S.O.R. Losers.* Bradbury, 1984. The South Orange River soccer team is composed of unlikely seventh-grade athletes, who strive for an all-losing season. (I: 12–YA)

Bloor, Edward. *Tangerine.* Harcourt Brace, 1997. Despite the fact that Paul is legally blind, he convinces his parents to hide his disability so that he can use his amazing skill as a master soccer goalie. His ability to "see" life in ways of which others seem oblivious allows him to realize what's really wrong with his football hero older brother. (I: 12–YA)

Brooks, Bruce. *The Moves Make the Man.* HarperTrophy, 1995. An African American boy and a Caucasian boy, at first distrustful of each other, become friends through basketball. (I: 12–YA)

Christopher, Matt. *Penalty Shot.* Little, Brown, 1997. Jeff is a talented soccer player who gets suspended from the team for bad grades. His attempts to rejoin the team are sabotaged, and he must figure out a way to rectify the situation. There are many books in the series of sports stories by this author, including *Shoot for the Hoop* (1995). (I: 9–12)

Cohen, Barbara. *Thank You, Jackie Robinson.* Lothrop, 1974. The love of baseball helps a fatherless boy, Sam, cross boundaries of race, age, and religion to become close friends with a hotel cook named Davy. As Davy lies in a hospital bed dying, Sam brings him an autographed ball from Jackie Robinson. (I: 9–11)

Crutcher, Chris. *Staying Fat for Sarah Byrnes.* Greenwillow, 1993. Overweight Eric and burn-scarred Sarah are fast friends, bonded by their physical problems. When Eric trains for the swim team, their friendship is threatened, and Sarah must face the horrible truth of the accident that left her scarred. (I: YA)

Lipsyte, Robert. *The Brave.* HarperCollins, 1991. A seventeen-year-old Native American boy learns to control his anger by training with a retired boxer. See also *The Contender* (1967). (I: YA)

Lynch, Chris. *Iceman.* HarperCollins, 1994. Eric is a fourteen-year-old ice hockey player who transfers his anger and emotional vulnerability to violent behavior on the ice. See also *Slot Machine* (1995). (I: YA)

Slote, Alfred. *Finding Buck McHenry.* HarperCollins, 1991. As the Little League team coach, a boy tries to enlist the school janitor he believes is a former famous baseball player from the Negro League. (I: 9–12)

———. *Hang Tough, Paul Mather.* HarperTrophy, 1973/1993. Paul deals with his incurable blood disease by involving himself in baseball. (I: 9–12)

Soto, Gary. *Taking Sides.* Harcourt, 1991. Lincoln Mendoza moves to a white neighborhood and has to take sides on the basketball court. The sequel is *Pacific Crossing* (1992). (I: 9–12)

Spinelli, Jerry. *Crash.* Knopf, 1996. Crash earned his name by being a star athlete from babyhood to middle school, but he earned friendship through different behaviors. (I: 10–YA)

———. *There's a Girl in My Hammerlock.* Simon & Schuster, 1991. Maisie Potter doesn't make the cheerleading team, so she decides to be a wrestler in order to be close to Eric. Despite opposition from the coach, teammates, and girlfriends, Maisie discovers that she loves the sport. (I: 10–12)

Books about Nature and Animals

Byars, Betsy. *The Midnight Fox.* Viking, 1968. Ten-year-old Tom resents being sent to his uncle and aunt's farm while his parents travel but becomes interested in a black fox he follows to her den. (I: 9–12)

DiCamillo, Kate. *Because of Winn-Dixie.* Candlewick, 2000. Ten-year-old Opal encounters a friendly stray dog at the grocery store and, through him, learns to adapt to her new community in small-town Florida and come to peace with her mother's leaving. (I: 9–12)

Dickinson, Peter. *Chuck and Danielle*. Delacorte, 1996. This is a set of humorous episodic stories about Danielle and her high-strung and paranoid whippet, Chuck. Danielle is sure that her dog will one day save the world. (I: 9–12)

*Ehlert, Lois. *Red Leaf, Yellow Leaf*. Harcourt, 1991. A child describes how a sugar maple tree was planted and cared for, with informational text adding details. (I: P–8)

Farley, Walter. *The Black Stallion*. Random House, 1941/1991. When Alec is shipwrecked on a deserted island, he and a black stallion form a bond as he works to tame and then train him. This is the first of a series. (I: 9–12)

*Fleming, Denise. *In the Small, Small Pond*. Holt, 1993. A child observes pond life and activity in awe. (I: P–8)

Haas, Jessie. *Beware the Mare*. Greenwillow, 1993. Illustrated by Martha Haas. In a story set in rural Vermont, Lily and her horse-trading Gramp wonder why her new mare is named "Beware." Sequels are *A Blue for Beware* (1995), *Be Well, Beware* (1996), and *Beware and Stoogie* (1998). (I: 7–10)

Henry, Marguerite. *Misty of Chincoteague*. Illustrated by Wesley Dennis. Simon & Schuster, 1990. Paul and Maureen obtain a wild horse and her colt on the island of Chincoteague, off the eastern shore of Virginia. Sequels are *Sea Star* (1949/1991) and *Stormy, Misty's Foal* (1963/1991). (I: 9–11)

Hesse, Karen. *Sable*. Illustrated by Marcia Sewall. Holt, 1994. Sable, ten-year-old Tate's dog, is constantly stealing things and must be given away to a friend. Tate is determined to show responsibility and earn the right to keep her dog. (I: 7–9)

*Keats, Ezra Jack. *The Snowy Day*. Viking, 1962. Peter enjoys the variety of ways he can play in the snow. (I: P–7)

*Lyon, George Ella. *Come a Tide*. Illustrated by Stephen Gammell. Orchard, 1990. A girl provides an account of the spring floods at her rural homeplace. (I: P–8)

Mikaelsen, Ben. *Stranded*. Hyperion, 1995. Twelve-year-old Koby saves the lives of two injured pilot whales in the Florida Keys. In doing so, she confronts her feelings about her own injury that resulted in an artificial foot and the resulting tensions between her parents. (I: 10–YA)

Paulsen, Gary. *Dogsong*. Bradbury, 1985. The cold and mysteries of the wilderness are made real to readers of this story of a fourteen-year-old Eskimo boy who journeys 1400 miles on a dog sled. (I: 10–YA)

———. *Woodsong*. Bradbury, 1990. A family in the wilds of northern Minnesota recount their first dealings with sled dogs and the Iditarod race. (I: 12–YA)

Rylant, Cynthia. *Every Living Thing*. Macmillan, 1985. In a series of short stories, animals play an important role in helping people come to a better understanding of themselves and of others. (I: 9–12)

Tamar, Erika. *Junkyard Dog*. Knopf, 1995. Eleven-year-old Katie's heart goes out to save a junkyard dog, and through the dog she learns to develop self confidence and relationships with her stepfather and others. (I: 9–12)

*Yolen, Jane. *Owl Moon*. Illustrated by John Schoenherr. Putnam, 1987. A father and child go owling on a winter night. (I: P–8)

Books about Survival

Farmer, Nancy. *A Girl Named Disaster*. Orchard, 1996. Eleven-year-old Nhamo flees from her village in Mozambique to escape an arranged marriage to a cruel man. She travels alone to Zimbabwe in search of a father she does not know. (I: 10–YA)

George, Jean Craighead. *Julie of the Wolves*. Harper & Row, 1972. Running away from marriage at age 13 means learning to live with wolves to survive. Sequels are *Julie* (1996) and *Julie's Wolf Pack* (1997). (I: 9–12)

———. *My Side of the Mountain*. Penguin, 1959/1988. When Sam runs away to the Catskill Mountains, an old hollow tree becomes his home and a falcon and weasel his companions in the struggle for survival in the wilderness. The trilogy continues with *On the Far Side of the Mountain* (1990) and *Frightful's Mountain* (Dutton, 1999). (I: 10–12)

Hesse, Karen. *Phoenix Rising*. Holt, 1994. An accident at a nuclear power plant changes Nyle's life on a Vermont sheep farm, as she and others in her family and community attempt to survive the effects of fallout. She learns about relationships and death when Ezra, who was exposed to a radiation leak, comes to live at her grandmother's home. (I: 12–YA)

Hill, Kirkpatrick. *Toughboy and Sister*. McElderry, 1990. Siblings lose their parents and are stranded in a Yukon River camp. The sequel is *Winter Camp* (1993). (I: 9–11)

Hobbs, Will. *Far North*. Morrow, 1996. Fifteen-year-old Gabe, his Dene Indian roommate Raymond, and Dene elder Johnny Raven are stranded in the Canadian wilderness after a plane crash. The boys learn the skills they need to survive the harsh winter weather, the animals, and other dangers. See also *The Maze* (1998). (I: 12–YA)

Kehret, Peg. *Earthquake Terror.* Cobblehill, 1996. Following an earthquake, twelve-year-old Jonathon and his six-year-old sister Abby, whose walker is damaged, must figure out a way to survive on an island where they are camping. (I: 9–12)

Naylor, Phyllis Reynolds. *The Fear Place.* Atheneum, 1994. Twelve-year-old Doug must overcome his fear of heights and hatred for his older brother to rescue him from the dangerous ridge of a cliff. (I: 9–12)

Paulsen, Gary. *Hatchet.* Viking, 1987. Surviving fifty-three days in the wilderness helps Brian to cope with his parents' divorce. Companion books are *The River* (1991), *Brian's Winter* (1996), and *Brian's Return* (1996). (I: 9–12)

Books about Romance and Sexuality

Avi. *Romeo and Juliet, Together (and Alive) at Last.* Orchard, 1987. This funny story tells of Ed's intent to play matchmaker when two shy students are cast as the leads in the class production of Shakespeare's "Romeo and Juliet." (I: 10–12)

Bauer, Marion Dane, ed. *Am I Blue? Coming Out from the Silence.* HarperCollins, 1994. Sixteen short stories about homosexuality by such authors as Jane Yolen and M. E. Kerr deal with growing up gay or lesbian or having parents or friends who are gay or lesbian. (I: YA)

Creech, Sharon. *Absolutely Normal Chaos.* HarperCollins, 1995. Thirteen-year-old Mary Lou Finney is wrapped up in adolescence, as she chaotically deals with family, friends, and her feelings for Alex, with whom she exchanges her first kiss. (I: 10–12)

Greene, Bette. *Philip Hall Likes Me, I Reckon Maybe.* Dial, 1974. Eleven-year-old Beth thinks that Philip is the smartest of all, until she realizes that she is letting him beat her at everything. (I: 10–12)

Lowry, Lois. *Anastasia at This Address.* Houghton Mifflin, 1991. Thirteen-year-old Anastasia thinks that she is ready for romance and answers an ad in a singles column of the newspaper. (I: 9–12)

Naylor, Phyllis. *Alice in Rapture, Sort of.* Atheneum, 1989. The summer before entering seventh grade becomes one of turmoil, as Alice discovers that falling in love is not what she thought it would be. (I: 10–12)

Peck, Robert Newton. *Soup in Love.* Delacorte, 1992. Soup tries his first kiss on Valentine's Day. There are many other books in this series about Soup. (I: 8–11)

Plummer, Louise. *The Unlikely Romance of Kate Bjorkman.* Delacorte, 1995. High schooler Kate decides to write a romance novel based on her own life as she works out what it means to be in love and in a relationship with a college boy. (I: YA)

Rylant, Cynthia. *A Kindness.* Orchard, 1988. A fifteen-year-old faces the prospect of his unmarried mother having a baby. (I: YA)

Books about Mental, Physical, and Emotional Challenges

See also other titles in the Chapter 4 bibliography.

Avi. *The Man from the Sky.* Morrow, 1992. Eleven-year-old Jamie cannot read but can "read stories in clouds," and one day he witnesses a man jumping out of a plane with a company's payroll. (I: 9–12)

Byars, Betsy. *The Summer of the Swans.* Viking, 1970. Sara is self-conscious about her brother, who is mentally disabled, but reconsiders her feelings when he gets lost searching for the wild swans that return each year. (I: 10–YA)

Fleming, Violet. *Be Good to Eddie Lee.* Illustrated by Floyd Cooper. Philomel, 1993. Eddie Lee is able to see flowers and frog's eggs better than other children. (I: 7–9)

Konigsburg, E. L. *Silent to the Bone.* Jean Karl/Atheneum, 2000. Baby Nikki is in a coma, and thirteen-year-old Branwell is traumatized and has become mute. When the British au pair says that Branwell dropped the baby and shook her, best friend Connor must figure out a way to communicate with Branwell. (I: 11–13)

*Millman, Isaac. *Moses Goes to School.* Farrar Straus Giroux, 2000. Moses and his friends attend a special school for children who are deaf, where adaptations include typing a letter into a computer that translates into standard spoken English. The text is accompanied by American Sign Language. (I: P–8)

Slepian, Jan. *The Alfred Summer.* Philomel, 1980/2001. Cerebral palsy does not stop Lester from helping his friends, including Alfred, who is mentally retarded, to build a boat in their basement—but it takes some doing to overcome his own and his mother's doubts about what he can accomplish. (I: 12 and up).

*Testa, Maria. *Thumbs Up, Rico!* Illustrated by Diane Paterson. Albert Whitman, 1994. This easy chapter book follows Rico, a boy with Down syndrome, in three episodes as he makes a new friend, learns about sibling relationships, and creates a picture of which he is proud for a school assignment. (I: 6–9)

Books about Moral Dilemmas and Moral Responsibility

Avi. *Nothing but the Truth: A Documentary Novel.* Orchard, 1991. A ninth-grader's suspension for humming "The Star Spangled Banner" becomes the center of media attention as misinformation and misinterpretation create havoc. (I: 12–YA)

Bauer, Marion Dane. *On My Honor.* Clarion, 1986. After promising "on his honor" to his father that he will not go swimming, Joel feels responsible for Tony's drowning when the two friends break the promise. (I: 10–YA)

Fox, Paula. *One-Eyed Cat.* Dell, 1984. An eleven-year-old boy deals with his guilt feelings after shooting a gun he is not supposed to handle. Although the story is set in 1935, the dilemmas faced are true to contemporary times. (I: 10–YA)

Naylor, Phyllis Reynolds. *Shiloh.* Atheneum, 1991. Marty's desire to keep a mistreated beagle that he found in the hills surrounding his West Virginia home causes him to make many moral decisions about what's right and what's wrong. Sequels are *Shiloh Season* (1996) and *Saving Shiloh* (1997). (I: 9–12)

Rylant, Cynthia. *A Fine White Dust.* Bradbury, 1986. Thirteen-year-old Peter is captured in a hypnotic spell by a charismatic preacher and struggles to reconcile his own religious beliefs with those of family and community. (I: 10–YA)

Woodson, Jacqueline. *Miracle's Boys.* Putnam, 2000. When their father's drowning and their mother's death from diabetes leave three brothers orphans, Ty'ree gives up his college plans and focuses on trying to keep Charlie from a life of crime and Lafayette from inward withdrawal. (I: 12 and up)

Books about Social Diversity and Society

See also other titles in the Chapter 4 bibliography.

*Bunting, Eve. *Fly Away Home.* Illustrated by Ronald Himler. Clarion, 1991. A homeless boy and his father who live in an airport find hope in the freedom of a bird. (I: 7–9)

*———. *Smoky Night.* Illustrated by David Diaz. Harcourt Brace, 1994. The story depicts people of different ethnic backgrounds coming together during the Los Angeles riots of 1993. (I: 9 and up)

*———. *The Wednesday Surprise.* Clarion, 1989. Anna secretly teaches her grandmother to read. (I: 7–9)

Cole, Brock. *The Goats.* Farrar, 1990. Two summer campers are picked on by other campers and left naked on an island. As they swim to safety, steal clothes and food, and find a place to stay until help arrives, they develop a deep understanding of themselves and each other. (I: 12–YA)

Fenner, Carol. *Yolonda's Genius.* McElderry, 1995. When Yolonda's mother moves her children from the dangers of city life to a rural area, Yolonda's genius is in discovering not only her own but also her brother's talent. (I: 10–YA)

Fleischman, Paul. *Seedfolks.* Illustrated by Judy Pedersen. Harper, 1997. Suspicious neighbors become inspired by one another to transform a trash-filled city lot into a beautiful garden. (I: 10–YA)

Fox, Paula. *Monkey Island.* Orchard, 1991. Two men help a homeless boy after his mother abandons him. (I: 10–12)

Mead, Alice. *Junebug.* Farrar, 1995. Junebug has dreams of a better life and of becoming a boat captain someday but worries that his tenth birthday will bring pressures to join the gang of older boys in his housing project. The sequel is *Junebug and the Reverend* (1998). (I: 9–12)

*Tamar, Erika. *The Garden of Happiness.* Illustrated by Barbara Lambase. Harcourt, 1996. Marisol plants a seed in a crack in the sidewalk near her neglected neighborhood block. The sunflower that grows delights the neighborhood. (I: P–7)

Temple, Frances. *Grab Hands and Run.* Orchard, 1993. A Salvadoran family struggles to escape oppression and go to Canada. (I: 10–YA)

Williams, Vera. *Scooter.* Greenwillow, 1993. A child's scooter and her personality help her adjust to her new home in a high-rise. (I: 8–11)

Wolff, Virginia Euwer. *Make Lemonade.* Holt, 1993. Fourteen-year-old LaVaughn is determined to escape poverty but ends up babysitting for a single teen mom who has many problems to face. (I: 11–YA)

Books about Death and Dying

Bohlmeijer, Arno. *Something Very Sorry.* Translated by the author. Houghton Mifflin, 1996. (Originally published in the Netherlands as *Ik moetje iets heel jammers vertellen* by Vangorr Publishers, 1994.) Nine-year-old Rosemyn is in the hospital following a car accident in which all of her family members were seriously injured. What makes this book remarkable is the honesty of the narrator's voice as she anguishes over her mother's death. (I: 9–12)

*Carrick, Carol. *The Accident.* Illustrated by Donald Carrick. Seabury, 1976. A truck kills Christopher's dog, and he feels responsible. (I: 7–9)

*Clifton, Lucille. *Everett Anderson's Goodbye.* Illustrated by Ann Grifalconi. Holt, 1983. A story of

Everett's grief at losing his father, told in rhyme. (I: P–7)

Fox, Paula. *The Eagle Kite*. Orchard, 1995. Liam's father is dying of AIDS. His mother says that he got it from a blood transfusion, but Liam remembers the day he broke and buried his eagle kite—the day he saw his father embracing another man on the beach. (I: 10–YA)

Hamilton, Virginia. *Cousins*. Philomel, 1990. Cammy detests her nearly perfect cousin, Patty Ann, and wishes that she would disappear. When it happens, Cammy is not prepared for the accidental death. (I: 9–12)

Henkes, Kevin. *Sun & Spoon*. Greenwillow, 1997. When Spoon Gilmore's Gram dies, family members all search for ways to deal with their grief. Spoon searches for a concrete object by which he can remember her. (I: 10–YA).

Jukes, Mavis. *Blackberries in the Dark*. Knopf, 1985/1993. Following his grandfather's death, Austin goes to visit his grandmother, and they share their sadness as they work through their grief. (I: 8–11)

Lowry, Lois. *A Summer to Die*. Houghton Mifflin, 1977. Thirteen-year-old Meg gives up feelings of envy when she learns that her beautiful sister is fatally ill. (I: 10–YA)

MacLachlan, Patricia. *Baby*. Delacorte, 1993. Taking care of a baby left by a stranger helps a family come to terms with the death of an infant child. (I: 10–YA)

Park, Barbara. *Mick Harte Was Here*. Knopf, 1995. Thirteen-year-old Phoebe Hart narrates the story of losing her younger brother to a bike accident. (I: 9–12)

Paterson, Katherine. *Bridge to Terabithia*. Crowell, 1977. Despite their differences, Jess and Leslie forge an unexpected and special friendship, which ends in tragedy. (I: 9–12)

Pennebaker, Ruth. *Both Sides Now*. Holt, 2000. Liza must face a range of issues confronting teenagers, in addition to the fact that her mother is dying of breast cancer and the family is in denial. (I: 12 and up)

Rylant, Cynthia. *Missing May*. Dell, 1992. Orphaned, Summer feels fortunate to have an aunt and uncle who share their deep love for each other with her. But when Aunt May dies, Summer and Uncle Ob search for ways to overcome grief. (I: 10–YA)

Smith, Doris Buchanan. *A Taste of Blackberries*. Crowell, 1973. Jamie dies of an allergic reaction to a bee sting suffered while out to pick blackberries, and his best friend grieves. (I: 8–10)

*Viorst, Judith. *The Tenth Good Thing about Barney*. Illustrated by Erik Blegvad. Macmillan, 1971. At a funeral in his backyard, a little boy tries to think of ten good things to remember about his cat, Barney. (I: P–8)

Yumoto, Kazumi. *The Friends*. Translated by Cathy Hirano. Farrar Straus Giroux, 1996. (Originally published in Japan as *Natsu no niwa*, Fukutake Publishing, 1992.) Three boys are curious about death and spend their summer keeping surveillance on a man they are sure is old enough to die soon. Through the ensuing intergenerational friendship, the boys learn about life, living, and aging before they encounter death. (I: 10–YA)

Mystery and Suspense Books

Adler, David. *Cam Jansen and the Scary Snake Mystery*. Viking, 1997. A photographic memory helps Cam solve this mystery, in which a snake is let loose on the library steps and her mother's bag, with video camera inside, is stolen. There are many other Cam Jansen mysteries in this series. (I: 9–12)

Alcock, Vivien. *The Trial of Anna Cotman*. Delacorte, 1990. New to town, Anna seeks friends and joins a secret club that has strange rituals and frightening consequences for those who do not follow its rules. (I: 9–12)

Babbitt, Natalie. *Goody Hall*. Farrar, 1971/1986. In this gothic mystery of suspense and humor, a tutor likes his charges, but there is something strange about the Goody household. (I: 9–12)

*Base, Graeme. *The Eleventh Hour: A Curious Mystery*. Viking Kestrel, 1988. In a picture book mystery set to verse, readers must figure out who stole the feast for Horace the Elephant's eleventh birthday. Clues are cleverly embedded throughout the illustrations. (I: 9–YA)

Bunting, Eve. *Coffin on a Case*. Harper, 1992. Twelve-year-old Henry Coffin, son of a private investigator, pursues his own case by helping a teen search for her missing mother. (I: 10–12)

Byars, Betsy. *The Dark Stairs: A Herculeah Jones Mystery*. Viking, 1994. Thirteen-year-old Herculeah Jones, daughter of a police officer and a private investigator, and her partner Meat investigate the disappearance of the owner of Dead Oaks, an old house surrounded by stories of murder and insanity. Others in the *Herculeah Jones Mystery* series are *Tarot Says Beware* (1995), *Dead Letter* (1996), *Death's Door* (1997), and *Disappearing Acts* (1998). (I: 9–12)

Clifford, Eth. *Help! I'm a Prisoner in the Library*. Houghton Mifflin, 1979. Two sisters get trapped in a public library all night during a blizzard, and their fascination with the displays turns into fear as they hear strange noises in the dark. (I: 8–11)

Hamilton, Virginia. *The House of Dies Drear*. Silver Burdett Ginn, 1968. Members of an African American family find themselves dealing with a number of "ghosts" when they move into an old house where slaves used to be harbored in an Underground Railroad station. The sequel is *The Mystery of Drear House* (1987). (I: 10–YA)

Konigsburg, E. L. *From the Mixed-up Files of Mrs. Basil E. Frankweiler*. Atheneum, 1967. Siblings determine to remain hidden in the Metropolitan Museum of Art until they discover who created a mysterious sculpture. (I: 9–11)

Nixon, Joan Lowery. *The Other Side of Dark*. Delacorte, 1986. Lisa was thirteen when a gunshot put her into a four-year coma. When she wakes up, she realizes that she is the only witness to the identity of her mother's murderer. This book won the Edgar Allan Poe Mystery Writer's Award. (I: 12–YA)

Raskin, Ellen. *The Westing Game*. Dutton, 1978. When millionaire Sam Westing dies, he leaves words to the song "America the Beautiful" as clues for sixteen heirs to work out an intricate riddle and identify his murderer. (I: 9–12)

Sobol, Donald. *Encyclopedia Brown and the Case of the Slippery Salamander*. Delacorte, 1999. This is one in a series of detective stories starring ten-year-old Encyclopedia Brown and his partner Sally. Ten short cases are presented, challenging readers to figure out how they were solved, with answers at the back of the book. (I: 9–12)

Tate, Eleanora E. *The Secret of Gumbo Grove*. Watts, 1987. Raisin loves hearing stories of African Americans in the "old days," but while helping to clean up the church cemetery, she stumbles into a mystery. (I: 9–12)

Humorous Books

Bauer, Joan. *Squashed*. Delacorte, 1992. In a humorous story, sixteen-year-old Lisa competes in a pumpkin-growing contest, trying to get her pumpkin, Max, to put on 200 pounds while she herself loses 20 pounds. (I: 10–12)

Bunting, Eve. *Sixth Grade Sugar Babies*. Lippincott, 1990. Students learn to care for babies by taking care of bags of sugar. (I: 10–12)

Byars, Betsy. *The Burning Questions of Bingo Brown*. Viking, 1988. Bingo takes to heart the questions of love and right actions. See also *Bingo Brown and the Language of Love* (Viking 1989), *Bingo Brown* (1990), and *Bingo Brown's Guide to Romance* (1992). (I: 10–12)

Cameron, Ann. *The Stories Julian Tells*. Illustrated by Ann Strugnell. Knopf, 1981. Six short stories humorously describe events in Julian's life as he grows up. Other titles are *More Stories Julian Tells* (1986), *The Stories Huey Tells* (1995), and *More Stories Huey Tells* (1997). (I: 6–8)

Cleary, Beverly. *Ramona the Brave*. Morrow, 1975. This Ramona story has some of the funniest episodes in the series, including Ramona's breaking a raw egg on her head. (I: 12–YA)

Conford, Ellen. *Nibble, Nibble, Jenny Archer*. Illustrated by Diane Palmisciano. Little, Brown, 1993. Nine-year-old Jenny is excited about being chosen to appear in a TV commercial for a new "snack food"—until she realizes that it is meant for gerbils. There are many books in this series about Jenny Archer. (I: 7–9)

Danziger, Paula. *Make Like a Tree and Leave*. Delacorte, 1990. Martin has a knack for getting himself in trouble. For one, he wants to do a super job on his Egypt unit project, so he wraps a classmate in a plaster cast and then encounters trouble removing it. (I: 9–12)

Gilson, Jamie. *It Goes Eeeeeeeeeeee!* Illustrated by Diane DeGroat. Houghton Mifflin, 1994. Patrick, a new boy in school, is put in his place when Dawn Marie corrects his misinformation about bats. See also *Can't Catch Me, I'm the Gingerbread Man* (1981) and *Hello, My Name Is Scrambled Eggs* (1985). (I: 8–11)

Greenwald, Sheila. *Rosy Cole: She Grows and Graduates*. Orchard, 1997. Rosy is now an eighth-grader, and she and her friends are in the midst of making a decision about where to attend high school. Earlier titles include *Give Us a Great Big Smile, Rosy Cole* (1981), *Write on, Rosy!* (1988), and *Rosy Cole: She Walks in Beauty* (1994). (I: 10–12)

Hurwitz, Johanna. *Much Ado about Aldo*. Morrow, 1978. Aldo, who is interested in everything, takes a ribbing from his classmates. There are many titles in this series, including *Aldo Applesauce* (1979) and *Aldo Peanut Butter* (1990). (I: 8–10)

Kline, Suzy. *ORP*. Puffin, 1999. Orville Rudemeyer Pygenski, or ORP, is surprised when he decides to start an "I Hate My Name Club" and it draws many unlikely members with normal-sounding names. (I: 9–12)

Robinson, Barbara. *The Best Christmas Pageant Ever*. Tyndale House, 1972. The six rowdy Herdman siblings find themselves in the community Christmas pageant. The sequel is *The Best School Year Ever* (1994). (I: 8–12)

Rockwell, Thomas. *How to Eat Fried Worms*. Franklin Watts, 1973. Ten-year-old Billy decides on a bet to eat fifteen worms in fifteen days to earn $50 toward buying a new minibike. Luckily, his friends help by creating new concoctions each day. (I: 9–12)

Soto, Gary. *Summer on Wheels*. Scholastic, 1995. Hector and Mando go on a biking adventure in California, encountering a range of personalities along the way. This is the sequel to *Crazy Weekend* (1994). (I: 11–YA)

Books with Multicultural and International Themes

See also the titles in the Chapter 4 bibliography.

de Jenkins, Lyll Becerra. *Celebrating the Hero*. Lodestar, 1993. Camila learns there is more to her grandfather's life than legend had made her believe. (I: YA)

———. *The Honorable Prison*. Dutton, 1988. Marta's father, a newspaper editor in Colombia, is imprisoned with his family in their own house. (I: YA)

Guback, Georgia. *Luka's Quilt*. Greenwillow, 1994. The setting is Hawaii, where Luka is learning how to make a traditional two-color quilt. (I: 6–9)

Myers, Walter Dean. *Somewhere in the Darkness*. Scholastic, 1992. Jimmy learns that the truth isn't always what it seems on the surface. (I: 12–YA)

Nelson, Vaunda Micheaux. *Mayfield Crossing*. Putnam, 1993. The children in an all-white school gradually learn to accept their African American counterparts. See also *Beyond Mayfield* (1999). (I: 9–12)

Nye, Naomi Shihab. *Habibi*. Simon & Schuster, 1987. Liyana faces adjustment to a new culture when her parents move the family from St. Louis, Missouri, to Jerusalem so that she can become familiar with the "other half" of her heritage. (I: 10–13)

*Rylant, Cynthia. *The Relatives Came*. Bradbury, 1985. Family members come from various places to gather for a family reunion in this Appalachian setting (I: P–8). Other books that offer images of Appalachia include *When I Was Young in the Mountains* (illustrated by Diane Goode, Dutton, 1982), quiet reflections on a childhood of simple pleasures in the Appalachians (I: P–8); *A Blue-Eyed Daisy* (Dell, 1987), in which eleven-year-old Ellie's life in a coal mining town in West Virginia is portrayed (I: 9–12); and *Appalachia: The Voices of Sleeping Birds* (illustrated by Barry Moser, Harcourt, 1991), in which text and illustrations offer poetic images that establish a strong sense of the place and the people of the Appalachians. (I: P–8)

*Shea, Pegi Deitz. *The Whispering Cloth: A Refugee's Story*. Illustrated by Anita Riggio. Stitched by You Yang. Boyds Mill, 1994. Mai practices stitching borders in embroidered story cloths while in a Thai refugee camp with her grandmother. She finds a story within herself so that she, too, can stitch her own *pa'ndau*. (I: 6–9)

Temple, Frances. *Taste of Salt: A Story of Modern Haiti*. Orchard, 1992. Djo tells his story of suffering under the Haitian military dictatorship and the countermovement led by Aristide. (I: 12–YA)

———. *Tonight, by Sea*. Orchard, 1995. A Haitian family and friends finally complete the construction of a boat, which helps them escape the tyranny of the government before Aristide returns. (I: 11–YA)

Thomas, Joyce Carol. *When the Nightingale Sings*. HarperCollins, 1993. Born in a Florida swamp and raised by a foster family, Marigold discovers her origins when her talented voice is recognized at a Great Gospel Convention. (I: 12 and up)

Wartski, Maureen Crane. *A Boat to Nowhere*. Westminster, 1980. Two war orphans emigrate from Vietnam to a less-than-hospitable United States. (I: 9–12)

Yep, Laurence. *Child of the Owl*. HarperTrophy, 1990. A twelve-year-old girl living with her grandmother in San Francisco learns about her Chinese heritage. (I: 10–12)

———. *Thief of Hearts*. HarperCollins, 1995. Stacey has to decide whether to report a theft or to be loyal to another Chinese American girl. (I: 11–YA)

RESOURCES

Asher, Sandy, ed. *But That's Another Story*. Walker, 1996.

Baskin, Barbara H., and Karen H. Harris. *More Notes from a Different Drummer: A Guide to Juvenile Fiction Portraying the Disabled*. R. R. Bowker, 1984.

Blume, Judy. *Letters to Judy: What Your Kids Wish They Could Tell You*. Putnam, 1986.

Collier, Laurie, and Joyce Nakamura. *Major Authors and Illustrators for Children and Young Adults: A Selection of Sketches from Something about the Author*. Gale Research, 1993.

Dreyer, Sharon Spredemann. *The Bookfinder: A Guide to Children's Literature about Interests and Concerns of Youth Aged 2–18*, volumes 1–5. American Guidance Service, 1994.

Rudman, Masha K., Kathleen Dunne Gagne, and Joanne E. Bernstein. *Books to Help Children Cope with Separation and Loss*, 4th ed. Bowker, 1994.

Silvey, Anita. *Children's Books and Their Creators*. Houghton Mifflin, 1995.

Something about the Author. Gale Research, 1994.

REFERENCES

Alcott, Louisa May. *Little Women*. Macmillan, 1868/1962.

Alger, Horatio. *Ragged Dick, and Mark, the Match Boy*. Collier, 1897/1962.

Avi. *The True Confessions of Charlotte Doyle*. Orchard, 1990.

———. *Who Was That Masked Man Anyway?* Orchard, 1992.

Blume, Judy. *Forever*. Bradbury, 1975.

———. *Starring Sally J. Freedman as Herself*. Bradbury, 1977.

Burnett, Frances Hodgson. *Little Lord Fauntleroy*. Scribner, 1886.

———. *The Secret Garden*. Lippincott, 1910/1962.

Cleary, Beverly. *A Girl from Yamhill: A Memoir*. Morrow, 1988.

———. *My Own Two Feet: A Memoir*. Morrow, 1995.

Cooper, James Fenimore. *The Last of the Mohicans*. Scott, Foresman, 1826/1950.

Cushman, Karen. *The Midwife's Apprentice*. Clarion, 1995.

Daly, Maureen. *Seventeenth Summer*. Dodd, 1942.

Defoe, Daniel. *Robinson Crusoe*. Running Press, 1719/1991.

Dodge, Mary Mapes. *Hans Brinker, or the Silver Skates*. Doubleday, 1865/1932.

Donovan, John. *I'll Get There, It Better Be Worth the Trip*. Harper, 1969.

Elleman, Barbara. "Introduction." *Popular Reading for Children, II*. American Library Association, 1986, pp. v–vi.

Estes, Eleanor. *The Moffats*. Harcourt, 1941.

Fox, Paula. *The Slave Dancer*. Dell, 1973.

Grahame, Kenneth. *Wind in the Willows*. Scribner's, 1933.

Hurley, Richard J. "Reading Patterns of Children: What and Why They Read." *Reading Interests of Children and Young Adults*. Ed. Jean Kujoth. Scarecrow, 1970, pp. 96–97.

Jackson, Jesse Jasper. *Call Me Charley*. Harper, 1945.

Lewis, C. S. *The Lion, the Witch and the Wardrobe: A Story for Children*. Macmillan, 1950.

Lowry, Lois. *The Giver*. Houghton Mifflin, 1993.

———. *Number the Stars*. Houghton Mifflin, 1989.

Luria, A. R. *Cognitive Development: Its Cultural and Social Foundations*. Harvard Univ. Press, 1976.

McCloskey, Robert. *Homer Price*. Viking, 1943.

———. *Make Way for Ducklings*. Viking, 1941.

Means, Florence. *The Moved Outers*. Houghton Mifflin, 1945.

———. *Shuttered Windows*. Houghton Mifflin, 1938.

Naylor, Alice Phoebe, and Carol Wintercorn. "Judy Blume." *Dictionary of Literary Biography: American Writers for Children Since 1960: Fiction*, Vol. 52. Gale Research, 1986, pp. 30–38.

Paterson, Katherine. *Jacob Have I Loved*. Crowell, 1980.

———. *The Zena Sutherland Lectures: 1983–1992*. Edited by Betsy Hearne. Clarion, 1993.

Paulsen, Gary. *Dancing Carl*. Bradbury, 1983.

———. *Eastern Sun, Western Moon: An Autobiographical Odyssey*. Harcourt, 1993.

———. *The Winter Room*. Orchard, 1989.

———. *Winterdance: The Fine Madness of Running the Iditarod*. Harcourt, 1994.

Poll, Bernard. "Why Children Like Horse Stories." *Elementary Education* 38 (November, 1961): 473–74.

Porter, Eleanor. *Pollyanna*. L. C. Page, 1913.

Postman, Neil. *The Disappearance of Childhood*. Delacorte, 1994.

Root, Shelton. "The New Realism: Some Personal Reflections." *Language Arts* 54.1 (1977): 19–24.

Rylant, Cynthia. *Soda Jerk*. Orchard Books, 1990.

Sewell, Anna. *Black Beauty: The Autobiography of a Horse*. Dodd, Mead, 1877/1941.

Spyri, Joanna. *Heidi*. Scribner's, 1884/1946.

Stanovich, Keith. "Are We Overselling Literacy?" *Stories and Readers: New Perspectives on Literature in the Elementary Classroom*. Ed. Charles Temple and Patrick Collins. Christopher-Gordon, 1992, p. 217.

Twain, Mark. *The Adventures of Huckleberry Finn*. Chanticleer, 1885/1950.

———. *The Adventures of Tom Sawyer*. Scott, Foresman, 1876/1949.

Usrey, Malcolm. *Betsy Byars*. Twayne, 1995.

Voigt, Cynthia. *Izzy, Willy-Nilly*. Atheneum, 1986.

———. *When She Hollers*. Scholastic, 1994.

Warner, Gertrude Chandler. *The Boxcar Children*. Scott, Foresman, 1950.

Zolotow, Charlotte. *A Father Like That*. Illustrated by Joanne Scribner. HarperCollins, 1971/2001.

———. *May I Visit?* Illustrated by Erik Blegvad. HarperCollins, 1976.

———. *My Grandson Lew*. Illustrated by William Pene du Bois. HarperCollins, 1974/1986.

———. *Say It!* Greenwillow, 1980.

———. *The Unfriendly Book*. Illustrated by William Pene du Bois. HarperCollins, 1975.

9 Historical Fiction

"Pa," I said, "do you think—do you think it will all be over soon?"

"What will be over, Robbie?"

"The world. Do you think it's coming to an end?"

He didn't laugh. "We can't know that sort of thing for sure, son. But my hunch is that this old earth will be here a long time after we are." He was quiet for a minute. Then he added, "I think the world's at a sort of beginning, myself."

"A beginning?"

"Lots of things, things we can't even dream of today, will be happening in your lifetime. The world is changing so fast on us. Telephones, electricity, motorcars   who knows? You might live long enough to see flying machines."

I looked up at the stars and tried to imagine myself like a shooting star, flying up there in a motorcar with wings. Nothing seemed impossible anymore.

"I pray it will be a good century," he went on. "I want my children and my grandchildren to grow up in a world where people have learned to think with their minds and hearts and not with weapons of destruction."

from Preacher's Boy
by Katherine Paterson

Illustration 9.1
In *Preacher's Boy,* set at the dawn of the twentieth century, Katherine Paterson has created a strong storyline and engaging characters. (Cover from *Preacher's Boy* by Katherine Paterson. Copyright © 1999 by Minna Murra, Inc. Reprinted by permission of Clarion Books/Houghton Mifflin Company. All rights reserved.)

Having so recently welcomed the arrival of the twenty-first century, we know that our vision of the future is vastly different from that of Robbie and his father, who were welcoming an earlier new century—the twentieth. Perhaps we dream of space travel or a world transformed by an Internet economy. Yet it is still easy to feel connected to Robbie and his father, for who doesn't dream of a future where people will think with their minds and hearts? Writers of fine historical fiction are able to help readers feel connected to people and situations from the past, and this is what makes historical fiction an important tool in the classroom.

HISTORICAL FICTION DEFINED

Historical fiction is widely viewed as a work of fiction set in a time prior to when it was written. How far in the past must a story be set to qualify as historical fiction? Some say twenty-five years; others say fifty. The precise number of years doesn't matter. Perhaps what matters most is the child's perspective. To a child, a story set twenty years ago qualifies as being about "the good old days." So a book like Christopher Paul Curtis's **The Watsons Go to Birmingham—1963** falls in the realm of historical fiction, even though many adults view the civil rights movement of the 1960s as something that happened "just yesterday." The views of authors can also be considered in deciding whether a book is historical fiction. For example, author Kimberly Holt considers **When Zachary Beaver Came to Town,** a story set in a small Texas town in the 1970s, to be a "period piece" that is definitely historical because it is set in a past time period.

Yet even the general definition given above may sometimes be too limiting. Some books feature events that were contemporary at the time they were written, but with the passing of time the events have gained historical significance. One such book is Beverly Naidoo's *Journey to Jo'burg*, which details the journey of two black South African children who experience the harsh realities of apartheid as they travel from their homeland to Johannesburg. At the time of its publication, the book described contemporary conditions in South Africa. However, the apartheid system has since been dismantled, so the events in Naidoo's book are significant from an historical perspective. Books like this one can be considered historical fiction rather than contemporary realistic fiction.

Time Periods Emphasized in Historical Fiction

Authors in the United States who write historical fiction have typically chosen to write about the United States. This means that comparatively little historical fiction set in other parts of the world is readily available to American audiences. There is also an imbalance in the time periods about which American authors have chosen to write. Some periods in American history that have been written about most extensively include the American Revolutionary War, slavery and the Civil War, the westward movement, immigration, and World War II.

ISSUE TO CONSIDER

Does historical fiction have a place in the study of history?

Those who argue that historical fiction is an important tool in history instruction maintain that students must develop historical or social empathy to develop social studies understandings (Tomlinson, Tunnell, & Richgels, 1993). These advocates believe that children's literature is a tool that can help students develop such empathy. For example, in discussing history instruction, Levstik (1989) has observed that through literature students "encounter the complexities of historical events, where facts from the past become living, breathing drama, significant beyond their own time" (p. 136). Further, advocates argue that because writers of historical fiction do extensive research on the eras about which they write, literature is often a rich source of information.

On the opposing side are those who argue that literature must not be expected to bear the burden of social studies instruction. Literature is a fragile medium, they remind us, and it can readily be crushed if it is forced to bear too heavy an efferent load. When students are asked to read literature for the purpose of learning about the past, they may fail to enter the story world on aesthetic terms.

What do you think? Should historical fiction serve as a springboard for learning about the past? Or should readers primarily be encouraged to read historical fiction for an aesthetic experience? If you have read *The Midwife's Apprentice*, would you want students to read the book primarily as a means of learning about medieval times, or would you choose to have students explore the theme of living a fulfilling life through this book?

Value of Historical Fiction

Why should teachers introduce children to historical fiction? First, many works of historical fiction present wonderful stories that children can "step into" for a rich aesthetic experience. After all, who can read Patricia MacLachlan's *Sarah, Plain and Tall* and not be touched by Anna and Caleb's fervent hope that Sarah will choose to stay on the prairie and become their mother? Readers of Minfong Ho's *The Clay Marble* will be moved by young Dara's determination to reunite her family after it is separated by war along the border of Cambodia and Thailand. Who won't chuckle over Michael Tunnell's *Mailing May,* a picture book in which a young girl is mailed (by train) to see her grandmother because her family cannot afford a train ticket?

Teachers also want children to read historical fiction because children are naturally curious about the past, and historical fiction offers answers to some of their questions. Historical fiction has another special value: The genre may help readers to develop consciousness of how time and place influence who they are. That is, by better understanding the past, children better understand themselves, their community, their culture, and the world. In fact, the problems of today can often be understood only in light of times past.

You might wonder why we are recommending turning to historical fiction to help children learn about the past. Why not turn exclusively to textbooks and informational books written for children? Textbooks and informational books are important as sources of background for readers. However, historical fiction offers something that textbooks do not. Through historical fiction, children "encounter the complexities of historical events, where facts from the past become living, breathing drama, significant beyond their own time" (Levstik, 1989, p. 136). Although this dramatic element can be found in informational books by fine writers such as Milton Meltzer and Russell Freedman, it is too often missing from textbooks. According to Carl M. Tomlinson, Michael O. Tunnell, and Donald J. Richgels (1993), readers need "historical empathy" to develop historical understanding. That is, readers "must be able to perceive past events and issues as they were experienced by the people at the time" (p. 54). Helping readers to develop historical empathy is what historical fiction does best, by emphasizing human motives and ordinary people.

Tomlinson and his colleagues also note that historical coverage in textbooks and works of historical fiction differs dramatically. Writers of textbooks aim for broad coverage, whereas writers of historical fiction focus on a single subject and examine it in depth. Certainly, readers need the broad view to place the story situation in proper perspective, but the broad view alone is not sufficient.

THE EVOLUTION OF HISTORICAL FICTION

It is not possible to identify a single creator for most literary genres, but that is not the case with historical fiction. Sir Walter Scott is generally believed to be the first person to write a work of what we now call historical fiction (Blos, 1993). *Waverly,* Scott's first piece of historical fiction, was published in 1810 and was followed by others, including *Ivanhoe.* Though Scott didn't write specifically for children, his books were read by young and old.

Early historical fiction consisted primarily of adventure stories and contained lengthy descriptive passages and many inaccuracies. Early writers who wrote historical fiction specifically for children had their own agenda—teaching students historical information. By the 1930s, many of these works were romantic, highly idealized views of the past that contained an overwhelming amount of information (Tomlinson, Tunnell, and Richgels, 1993).

Fortunately, historical fiction has changed considerably in recent decades. By the 1940s and 1950s, serious works of historical fiction were being written for children, including Newbery Medal winners *Johnny Tremain* by Esther Forbes and *The Door in the Wall* by Marguerite de Angeli. The genre is no longer viewed simply as a vehicle for conveying historical information. Rather, writers strive to tell stories—stories that show how living in a particular time and place in the past shaped the lives of people, especially ordinary people. And though ordinary people sometimes become caught up in major historical events, historical fiction is not primarily about those events. For example, Laura Ingalls Wilder's books were inspired by her own experiences. These were among the early works of historical fiction for children that had stories to tell rather than information to convey. *The Little House in the Big Woods,* published in 1932, was the first of the *Little House* books. Like the others in the series, it is a warm story full of the everyday experiences of a close-knit frontier family. This shift to storytelling, however, does not mean that historical accuracy is unimportant. In fact, writers of historical fiction should be held accountable to standards of historical accuracy.

Style

The style of writing used in historical fiction has also changed. The ornate descriptions, the sometimes archaic language, and the lengthy factual passages are gone. The language of today's historical fiction is likely to be accessible to children. Consider the opening passage from Patricia MacLachlan's *Sarah Plain and Tall:*

> "Did Mama sing every day?" asked Caleb. "Every-single-day?" He sat close to the fire, his chin in his hand. It was dusk, and the dogs lay beside him on the warm hearthstones.
>
> "Every-single-day," I told him for the second time this week. For the twentieth time this month. The hundredth time this year? And the past few years? (p. 1)

It is the simplicity and immediacy of MacLachlan's language that pulls the reader into the story.

Historical Perspective

One of the most striking changes in historical fiction for children is in the perspective from which stories are told. Today's writers are less likely to assume idealized views of the past. Joel Taxel (1983) analyzed thirty-two pieces of historical fiction about the American Revolution written between 1899 and 1976; he discussed two of these books at length. The first, Esther Forbes's *Johnny Tremain,* which was published in 1943, encapsulates an idealized view of the American Revolution: The American patriots are viewed as a united people involved in a divinely inspired struggle for freedom and equality. The perspective in James and Christopher Collier's *My Brother Sam Is Dead,* written in 1974, stands in marked contrast: The colonists are a divided people; many of them remain loyal to the king of England. Tim Meeker, the book's protagonist, questions the values of the revolution, eventually choosing not to become part of the revolutionary fervor. Differing perspectives can be explained in large part by the times in which authors live and write. Esther Forbes wrote *Johnny Tremain* in the midst of the patriotic fervor of World War II, whereas *My Brother Sam Is Dead* was published in 1974, when the United States was waging an unpopular war in Vietnam.

Recent historical fiction for children has seen the emergence of many new perspectives. In *Encounter,* Jane Yolen used a picture book format to show Columbus through the eyes of a Taino child who tries to warn his people of the coming destruction he has seen in a dream. Perspectives on pioneer times have also changed in historical fiction for children. Until recently, the common perspective on pioneer life was of the sort seen in the *Little House* books: Though times were hard, a warm, united family was an ever-present, sustaining force. More recent books, such as Pam Conrad's *Prairie Songs* and Eve Bunting's *Dandelions,* explore the loneliness and isolation of pioneer life from a woman's perspective.

Subject Matter

The subject matter of historical fiction for children has changed as well. Authors of historical fiction set in the United States are writing about less well-known historical events and periods. Eve Bunting's *Train to Somewhere* is about the orphan trains that transported children to the West for adoption from the 1850s to the 1920s. In *Mine Eyes Have Seen,* Ann Rinaldi tells of the summer leading up to John Brown's raid on Harper's Ferry from the perspective of Brown's fifteen-year-old daughter. Gail Carson Levine's *Dave at Night* focuses on a young boy in a Jewish orphanage that is situated in Harlem in the midst of the Harlem Renaissance. And in *Greater than Angels,* Carol Matas writes about Jewish adolescents deported by the Nazis to the south of France and the courageous efforts of the French citizens to save these refugees.

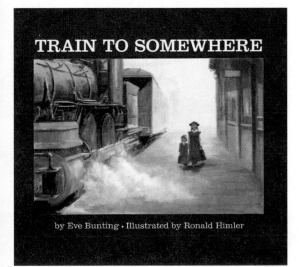

Illustration 9.2

In Eve Bunting's *Train to Somewhere,* a young orphan riding a train westward fears that no family will choose her. (Cover from *Train to Somewhere* by Eve Bunting, illustrated by Ronald Himler. Jacket illustration copyright © 1996 by Ronald Himler. Reprinted by permission of Clarion Books/Houghton Mifflin Company. All rights reserved.)

Writers of earlier times adhered to an unspoken code that children needed to be protected from the less savory aspects of the past (Tunnell, 1993). This is no longer true. Mildred Taylor and other writers have written about the senseless prejudice and violence that African Americans have faced. In *Journey to Topaz* and *The Bracelet,* Yoshiko Uchida wrote movingly about the experiences of Japanese Americans in internment camps during World War II. In *The Island on Bird Street,* Uri Orlev wrote about the suffering of Jews during World War II. Patricia Polacco's *The Butterfly,* a World War II story in picture book format, tells of a French woman who defied the occupying Nazis by giving refuge to a Jewish family.

Historical fiction about other parts of the world, especially Third World countries, is increasingly available to American audiences. In writing *The Year of Impossible Goodbyes,* Korean author Sook Nyul Choi drew on her family's experiences under Japanese occupation during World War II and their subsequent struggle to escape communist rule in what was to become North Korea. In Minfong Ho's *Rice without Rain,* Jinda and her family are caught up in the turbulence of the 1945 student movement in Thailand as they struggle to survive the drought that has hit their homeland. In *The Bomb,* Theodore Taylor tells a story about the Bikini Islanders who were forced to evacuate their homes to make way for nuclear testing by the United States. There is still too little historical fiction about other countries and cultures available to young American readers, but this situation is beginning to turn around.

Ask the Author . . . *Ann Rinaldi*

What sparks your interest in the different time periods about which you write?

I had done three contemporary novels about teens in the early 1980s, which were very successful. But since the mid-1970s I had been covering stories on the United States Bicentennial for the newspaper in Trenton, New Jersey, where I was a full-time columnist.

After taking part in the 200th anniversary celebration of the Crossing of the Delaware on Christmas Day in 1976, my fourteen-year-old son Ron became enthralled with the Revolutionary War, joined a local reenactment group, and his twelve-year-old sister Marcella followed. Through the 1980s, my husband and I took them all over the eastern seaboard for battles and encampments of the American Revolution. Eventually, we joined the group, and I had to make the clothing, cook the food,

learn the dances, songs, and lifestyle of the eighteenth century.

When I was at the reenactment of the surrender of the British to the Americans at Yorktown, Virginia, in 1981, I had a sense of *deja vu.* "What am I doing here?" I asked myself. "I've done this once before." It was so real, so enveloping, that I decided to write an historical novel so that years later, when the Bicentennial was over, young people could learn, almost firsthand, what our struggle for independence was like.

I wrote *Time Enough for Drums,* placing it in Trenton. Ten publishers turned it down, saying "We can't give young people history." I put it away in a drawer for years. Finally Holiday House, Inc., decided to give it a shot.

The book sold and was loved, went into paperback, and publishers have been asking me for history ever since. I knew, standing on the sidelines at Yorktown in 1981, watching the color and pageantry surrounding me, that kids would love a book like this. And indeed, today, almost every major publisher of Young Adult novels has a line of historicals out. History sells big.

Picture Books

The emergence in recent years of many works of historical fiction in picture book format is a noteworthy change. Some of these stories, such as Riki Levinson's *I Go with My Family to Grandma's,* are appropriate for children as young as ages 5 to 8, whereas stories such as Karen Ackerman's *The Tin Heart,* about the Civil War, are better suited for children in the upper elementary grades. Some picture books, such as Margaree Mitchell's *Uncle Jed's Barbershop,* a story about the segregated South during the Depression era, are even appropriate for students in middle school and beyond.

Many readers especially enjoy the picture book format because illustrations can bring hard-to-imagine settings to life. Illustrations often help readers to develop a feel for bygone eras that words alone may not convey. In Ken Mochizuki's *Baseball Saved Us,* Dom Lee's scenes depicting vast expanses of desert enclosed by barbed-wire fences and guard towers capture the desolation that Japanese Americans must surely have felt when imprisoned in their own country during World War II. Illustrations play another important role as well: They frequently convey information about the past that adds to, supports, or clarifies textual information. Through Thomas Locker's illustrations in Candace

I went on to explore other eras in our past. The Civil War, the Salem witch trials, the Ohio pioneers. I found that history is a gold mine of stories and that every era has something to teach us. I found Civil War stories that made me weep. The drawing of a battle-weary cavalryman on his patient horse, his coat and boots dusty, his sense of purpose imprinted on his face, turns me on to want to write about him, the same as the photograph of a pioneer woman holding a child in her arms with another tugging at her skirt, crossing the plains.

I firmly believe that our history in this country is the most underrated and reviled in the present-day scheme of things. When I was a child, I had no personal history. It was taken away from me, so I clung to the history about my country that I learned in school. How many children today have a personal history that is less than glowing, who could likewise take pride and dignity in the history of their country?

A footnote: The fourteen-year-old boy who took part in the Crossing of the Delaware in 1976 grew to become a responsible, contributing citizen, husband, and father. He never missed a Christmas crossing the

Delaware in the ensuing years and today, at age 38, plays General Nathaniel Greene.

Ann Rinaldi had only a high school education because her father, though he had the means, did not believe in college for girls. She has been writing since age 10. From 1970 to 1991, she was a columnist for The Trentonian Newspaper *in Trenton, New Jersey, writing three general-interest columns a week. The column was twice named best in the state by the New Jersey Press Association. She also wrote feature articles and editorials and credits her years in journalism for her ability to gather information, distill it, and create an interesting story. She left the paper in 1991 to pursue a full-time writing career. Her first seven books were written at night and on weekends.*

She lives in Branchburg, New Jersey, with her husband Ronald, a retired chief lineman for Public Service Gas and Electric. She has two grown children, Ronald II and Marcella. She also has five grandsons.

Her most recent publications include Amelia's War *(Scholastic, 1999),* The Coffin Quilt *(Harcourt Brace, 1999),* My Heart Is on the Ground *(Scholastic, 1999), and* The Journal of Jasper Jonathan Pierce *(Scholastic, 1999).*

Christiansen's **The Ice Horse,** readers discover how ice was harvested from rivers at the turn of the century.

Historical Fiction Series

Historical fiction series emerged as a strong trend in the 1990s. These series included *Dear America, Orphan Train Children, American Diaries,* and *Children of America.* Although the quality of series books varies, major children's authors have contributed to some of these series. For example, Kathryn Lasky, Jim Murphy, Patricia McKissack, and Karen Hesse are among the authors who have written books in the *Dear America* series. Many historical fiction series books have been pitched toward a younger audience and have featured female protagonists more often than male protagonists. Hence, many educators have welcomed the arrival of these series, claiming that they have awakened a new interest in history, especially among young girls.

All the changes in the genre in recent decades make for a bright future for children's historical fiction. Certainly, books in this genre have been awarded an impressive number of Newbery Medals and Honors in recent years: Patricia

Illustration 9.3
In Karen Cushman's *The Midwife's Apprentice,* a homeless waif seeks to do more than survive in the harsh world of medieval England; she seeks to become someone. (Cover from *The Midwife's Apprentice* by Karen Cushman. Jacket illustration copyright © 1995 by Trina Schart Hyman. Reprinted by permission of Clarion Books/Houghton Mifflin Company. All rights reserved.)

MacLachlan's *Sarah, Plain and Tall* (1985), Lois Lowry's *Number the Stars* (1989), Karen Cushman's *Catherine, Called Birdy* (1994), Christopher Curtis's *The Watsons Go to Birmingham, 1963* (1995), Karen Cushman's *The Midwife's Apprentice* (1995), Karen Hesse's *Out of the Dust* (1997), Patricia Reilly Giff's *Lily's Crossing* (1997), Christopher Curtis's *Bud, Not Buddy* (1999), and Jennifer Holm's *Our Only May Amelia* (1999). Given the special values of historical fiction, many teachers look forward to even more books of this caliber.

CATEGORIES OF HISTORICAL FICTION

Joan Blos (1993) identifies three types of historical fiction: (1) fictionalized memoirs, (2) fictionalized family history, and (3) fiction based on research. She notes that the author's relationship to the material is different for each type.

Fictionalized Memoirs

Because writers of fictionalized memoirs have lived through the bygone era about which they write, they are able to draw on their own experiences in crafting their stories. The result is often a story that is full of extraordinarily rich details about daily life and holds a special sense of immediacy for the reader. For example, it is easy to imagine how, in writing *Little House on the Prairie,* Laura Ingalls Wilder drew on personal memories to describe the family's first Christmas on the prairie:

> For Christmas dinner there was the tender, juicy, roasted turkey. There were the sweet potatoes, baked in the ashes and carefully wiped so that you could eat the good skins, too. There was a loaf of salt-rising bread made from the last of the white flour.
>
> And after all that there were stewed dried blackberries and little cakes. But these little cakes were made with brown sugar and they did not have white sugar sprinkled over their tops.
>
> Then Pa and Ma and Mr. Edwards sat by the fire and talked about Christmas times back in Tennessee and up north in the Big Woods. But Mary and Laura looked at their beautiful cakes and played with their pennies and drank their water out of their new cups. And little by little they licked and sucked their sticks of candy, till each stick was sharp-pointed on one end.
>
> That was a happy Christmas. (pp. 251–252)

If personal experiences serve as the inspiration for fictionalized memoirs, you may wonder why such books are not considered biography. The reason is, quite simply, that the writers fictionalize their personal experiences. For example, in the first paragraph of *Little House on the Prairie,* Ingalls says that Baby Carrie made the trip from the Big Woods, but her real sister Carrie had not yet been born when the family left their home in Wisconsin (Frey and Griffith, 1987).

Writers of fictionalized memoirs may draw on personal memories, but these memoirs are seen from an historical perspective—for the time about which the authors write may be vastly different from the time in which they are writing. Once again, Laura Ingalls Wilder is a good example. She was born in 1867 but did not publish *The Little House in the Big Woods,* the first of the *Little House* books, until 1932. Between 1867 (just two years after the Civil War ended) and 1932, the world changed enormously. People no longer crossed the country in covered wagons as Wilder's own family had done; instead, they relied on trains, cars, and sometimes even airplanes. Thus, the passage of time allows a writer to achieve historical perspective.

Fictionalized Family History

Many families treasure a tradition of passing family stories from one generation to the next, and family stories have fed the historical fiction of many writers. Sometimes historical fiction develops from only the barest snippet of a family story. Such was the case for writer Ann Turner. As Turner and her aunt looked at an old trunk together, her aunt remembered another old trunk (Turner, 1993):

> "You know, there used to be a very old trunk in Grandpa's house, in the basement. . . . It was an eighteenth-century trunk . . . a big, black domed thing covered with leather. . . . And there were two stories about it. One was that during the early period of settlement some of our ancestors escaped from an Indian attack in that trunk. The other story is that when the rebels came, some children were hidden in that trunk and escaped the rebels."
> "You mean we were Tories?" . . .
> "Oh, yes, some were . . . Anyway, I wonder what happened to that trunk." (p. 11)

Illustration 9.4
Katie's Trunk, a picture book about the American Revolution, is told from a Tory perspective. (*Katie's Trunk* by Ann Turner, illustrations by Ron Himler. Text copyright © 1993 by Ann Turner. Illustrations copyright © 1993 by Ron Himler. Used by permission of Simon & Schuster Books for Young Readers, an imprint of Simon & Schuster Children's Publishing.)

From this fleeting exchange grew *Katie's Trunk,* the story of a Tory child who hid in the family trunk when a band of patriots came to her home.

In other instances, relatively well developed stories are passed down, stories that writers can use with only a little fleshing out. According to Patricia Polacco, *Pink and Say,* her story of the friendship between two Union soldiers, was passed down through her family from her great-great-grandfather, who happened to be the white soldier in the story. In writing *Our Only May Amelia,* Jennifer Holm drew on the actual diary written by her grand-aunt to fashion this story about a young Finnish-American girl born on the Nasel River in Washington during the late nineteenth century.

Mildred Taylor's historical fiction is also fictionalized family history. Reviewers and critics have long marveled that someone who did not live through the Depression era could write about that period of American history with such authenticity. The answer lies, at least in part, in the family stories that Taylor listened to as a child. She was born in Mississippi, but her family moved to Toledo, Ohio, while she was still a baby. Though Taylor grew up in the North, she was connected to the South through the stories her father told about his own childhood in rural Mississippi. Also, each summer, the Taylors traveled to Mississippi to visit their extended family. Family stories were woven into the fabric of those summer visits with the Taylor clan, and many of the events narrated in those stories became events in the stories Taylor wrote.

Fiction Based on Research

Probably the bulk of historical fiction for children fits into the third type: fiction based on research. Writers who set their stories in eras about which they have no firsthand knowledge must perform research to ensure authenticity. Occasionally, a writer does the research after writing the story. This is how Pam Conrad worked when writing *Prairie Songs.* Conrad (1993) said that she had read so much historical fiction and so many journals written in pioneer times that she was confident she could write her story without doing research first—though she did research some details after the fact to verify their accuracy.

The amount of information available to writers can vary extensively. Writers who feature cultures with no writing systems frequently have only scant anthropological evidence to draw on. Michael Dorris faced this situation when writing *Morning Girl.* Set on a Bahamian island in 1492, the book centers on a sister and brother of the Taino tribe. The story ends as Morning Girl greets the white visitors who paddle to shore—men from Columbus's ship. Dorris (1992) noted that the Tainos had no writing system, and within a generation or two of Columbus's coming the tribe was wiped out by disease. The only written reference to these people was one Columbus included in his journal.

In contrast, writers who focus on literate societies often have a wealth of original sources as well as extensive reference material from which to draw their information. Frances Temple (1994) described the research she did in writing *The Ramsay Scallop,* a story about a couple's religious pilgrimage, set in Europe in 1300:

> More than seventy books turn up cited in my notes for *The Ramsay Scallop,* some in English, some in French or Spanish, some in medieval French. . . . One source led to another: art books; religious meditations; playscripts; a guidebook written in 1190 by a priest, with tips on where to find clean water and what to use to discourage fleas; histories, where I found a picture of Nana Sybille in her wheelbarrow; and song books. (p. 18)

Research can take other forms as well. In writing *The Apprenticeship of Lucas Whitaker,* a book about the devastation caused by consumption 150 years ago, author Cynthia DeFelice interviewed a pathologist and an archaeologist, examined old burial grounds using radar technology, and spent a day in an anthropologist's lab learning about folk medical practices (DeFelice, 1998).

HOW HISTORICAL FICTION WORKS

Historical fiction differs—at least in some ways—from other genres. Let's consider some of these critical aspects of historical fiction, which affect how it is written and read.

Setting

Because historical fiction takes place in a time removed from the reader, setting is an especially important element. The writer's obligation is to bring place and time to life for the reader by providing details that are neither romanticized nor distorted but as authentic as possible, given what is known about the era in which the story is set. Extensive research is the most likely means by which the writer obtains these rich details, especially if a story is about a literate culture that left extensive records. But when writers set stories in times about which little is known, they must rely on their imaginations to construct details of time and place that are consistent with what little is known about the period.

The importance of rich details of setting is evident in Gary Blackwood's *The Shakespeare Stealer.* As the young apprentice Widge views a new neighborhood of London, the first city he has ever visited, he is struck by all he sees:

> Here there were no gold-plated buildings or great cathedrals, only shabby rows of houses, cheek by jowl. With no space to spread side-

wise, they had arched over the street, like the trees on that desolate stretch of road where we had met the outlaws, nearly meeting above our heads, shutting out the sun.

There were no street vendors here, nor prosperous merchants, only sullen wives emptying their slop jars into the street, sometimes missing the scrawny, shoeless children playing there, sometimes not. Falconer strode heedlessly along, as if daring anyone to empty a chamber pot on his head. No one did. One house had been boarded up, and a crude wooden cross nailed to its front door. Beneath the cross were crawled the words LORD HAVE MERCY UPON US.

"Is that a church?" I said.

Falconer gave a derisive laugh. "That's a plague house, boy." (p. 12)

The details that Blackwood includes make it easy for the reader to envision how dramatically different the London of Shakespeare's day must have been from our own times. Details about setting are crucial, though it is equally crucial not to include so many as to overwhelm the story. Further, setting details must advance the story, as they do in *The Shakespeare Stealer.* Widge's attention to his new surroundings helps the reader to see just how inexperienced with city ways the young apprentice is.

Illustrated works of historical fiction provide additional details about setting through illustrations. In Gary Bowen's *Stranded at Plimoth Plantation 1626,* the main character is learning wood engraving, and his engravings, which are included as the book's illustrations, provide important information about Plimoth. Through Bowen's illustrations the reader/viewer discovers how small Plimoth was in 1626 and how basic the settlers' dwellings were.

The time and place in which a writer situates a story must be integral to the story. How can a reader judge whether this is the case? If the story could just as easily have been set in another era, then the setting is not essential to the story. The setting of *The Midwife's Apprentice* is central to the story. Cushman's story is set in medieval England, at a time when daily life was harsh and even cruel for those who were not members of the privileged classes. At the beginning of the book, the daily realities of survival so completely dominated the reality of the protagonist that, as she burrowed in a dung heap for warmth, "she dreamed of nothing, for she hoped for nothing and expected nothing. It was as cold and dark inside her as out in the frosty night" (p. 2).

Plot

According to Jean Fritz (1986), a writer of many works of historical fiction for children, the original sense of the word "history" is "to ask questions," and Fritz says that this is what she does as she delves into another time and place in order to craft a work of historical fiction. It is easy to imagine Karen Hesse, author of *Letters from Rifka,* doing just this. The book is about a young Jewish girl who sets out from Russia with her family but is not allowed by officials to cross the Atlantic because she has contracted ringworm. Left behind in the care of strangers, Rifka eventually makes the journey alone. In creating this dramatic emigration story, perhaps Hesse posed questions like these: What was it like to cross the ocean in search of a new life in a new land? Who were the people who made those journeys? Why did they do it? What uncertainties did they face? Such questions suggest possibilities for story conflict and the events that culminate in an eventual resolution of the conflict. Still other kinds of questions are posed in an attempt to ensure historical authenticity. In writing *Nowhere to Call*

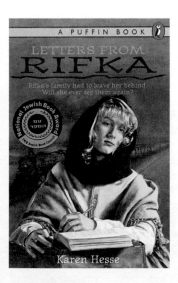

Illustration 9.5
Strong characterization marks *Letters from Rifka,* the story of a young immigrant girl who journeys to the United States on her own. (*Letters from Rifka* by Karen Hesse. Copyright © 1993. Reprinted by permission of Puffin Books, a division of Penguin Putnam Inc.)

Ask the Author . . .

Katherine Paterson

Katherine Paterson

What draws you to writing historical fiction?

I think the short answer to this question is I write about the past because I want to understand the present. Jill Paton Walsh once said, "If you want to understand a period in history, don't read the contemporary literature of that time, read the historical fiction." We're using the past, we who write historical fiction, to shed light on our own time.

I am blessed, as many of my contemporaries are, with a condition known as presbyopia. I always thought it very appropriate for a Presbyterian elder to have presbyopia, which coming from the Greek means "elderly eyes" and refers to the condition of not being able to focus on nearby objects, a condition that tends to afflict those of us who are aging. It is treated by prescribing spectacles. Now it seems to me as the torrent of events of the recent past has engulfed me, how difficult it has been to focus properly. Like every one of you, I suspect, I am asking for some coherent explanation of Kosovo, of Columbine. Even the newspapers are asking: What in the past has led us to this tragic day? So history becomes a pair of spectacles through which we try to focus our vision of the chaotic present.

We're not good at this. Since the 1960s, we've discounted history. We haven't thought it important for our young people to know the past. More recently, we have decided that the Internet will answer all their questions far better than any dusty book.

But history is story, and story doesn't fare well on the web. The web presupposes that one will wish to jump about and grab bits and pieces of information from a wide variety of sources. History is narrative in form; it deals with causes and effects, with acts and the consequences of those actions. History cares about space and linear time.

The web eschews narrative, ignores cause and effect, honors neither space or time. It is everywhere anytime, and thus no particular time or particular place is of real importance. I am not advocating closing down the Internet, but I am pleading that we pay attention to what we are doing when we allow it to reign unquestioned and supreme.

Still the history found in history books is the telling of events (usually wars) and the lives of the powerful. I love to embellish that record with the lives of ordinary people—young persons whose hopes and feelings and dreams a twenty-first-century young person might understand and care about. To me, the Industrial Revolution is only gears and machinery and statistics until I find in the midst of it a homesick farm girl working four looms in the lint-filled, ear-shattering weaving room of a nineteenth-century cotton mill.

Katherine Paterson in the author of thirteen novels for children and young people, including Bridge to Terabithia *and* Jacob Have I Loved, *Newbery winners in 1978 and 1981, and* The Great Gilly Hopkins, *a Newbery Honor Book.* The Great Gilly Hopkins *and* The Master Puppeteer *were National Book Award winners in 1979 and 1977. Other works of historical fiction that have won awards are* Of Nightingales That Weep *(Phoenix Award, 1994),* Lyddie *(IBBY Honor Book, 1996),* Jip, His Story *(Scott O'Dell Award, 1997), and* Preacher's Boy *(Jefferson Cup, 2000). In 1998, she was awarded the highest international prize for children's literature, the Hans Christian Andersen medal; and in 2000, the Library of Congress named her a Living Legend.*

Katherine Paterson was born in China. She is a graduate of King College, Bristol, Tennessee, and holds master's degrees from both the Presbyterian School of Christian Education, Richmond, Virginia, and Union Theological Seminary, New York City. She lived and worked for four years in Japan before her marriage. The Patersons live in Vermont and have four grown children and six grandchildren.

> ### *Favorite Books as a Child*
>
> *Winnie-the-Pooh* by A. A. Milne
>
> *The Secret Garden* by Frances Hodgson Burnett
>
> *The Yearling* by Marjorie Kinnan Rawlings

Illustration 9.6
Shakespeare's England is brought to life in *The Shakespeare Stealer,* the story of an orphan who stumbles into his role as an apprentice at the Globe Theatre. (*The Shakespeare Stealer* by Gary Blackwood. Copyright © 1998. Used by permission of Dutton Signet, a division of Penguin Putnam Inc.)

Home, a story about children who become hobos during the Great Depression, Cynthia DeFelice (1998) sought answers to a multitude of questions about train travel in 1930:

> How long would it have taken to ride from Pittsburgh to Cincinnati in a boxcar? What was the price of a passenger ticket from Philadelphia to Chicago? Did freight and passenger trains load and unload in different places? What did Broad Street station in Philadelphia look like then? Did trains have bathrooms and running water? Had refrigerator cars been invented yet? (p. 33)

Jean Fritz hopes that readers of historical fiction will also ask questions as they read a book—questions that may be quite similar to those asked by the writer. However, Violet Harris (1995) warns that young readers might not have sufficient historical knowledge of a period about which they are reading to ask questions, and she suggests that they be given opportunities to read informational books to gain the background that may be needed to read historical fiction.

In historical fiction, the writer creates a conflict that grows out of the time in which the story is set. Events must unfold plausibly, and the conflict must be resolved in a manner that is consistent with the historical context in which the story is situated. Gary Blackwood achieves all this in *The Shakespeare Stealer.* Widge, the book's protagonist, is an apprentice in the England of Shakespeare's day, a period in which England was a "paradise for women, a prison for servants, and a hell for horses. Prentices were too lowly to even deserve mention" (p. 7). Caught up in the often abusive apprenticeship system, Widge struggles to hide from the cruel master who has purchased him for the sole purpose of having him steal the script of *Hamlet* from the Globe's theatrical company. Widge is also an apprentice to friendship. When the Globe's troupe offers him the chance to become an apprentice at the Globe, Widge, who has spent most of his life serving uncaring masters, must struggle to accept the caring friendship extended by members of the troupe.

Characters

More often than not, the characters in historical fiction are ordinary people rather than figures of historical importance. Sometimes, they are swept up in great historical events of their time, as happens in Gloria Houston's ***Mountain Valor*** when a mountain family is almost destroyed by a renegade soldier during the Civil War. As often as not, though, the characters in historical fiction are living what can best be described as ordinary lives. For example, the children in Avi's frontier story ***The Barn*** must carry on with all the tasks of daily life when their father is crippled by a massive stroke.

At times, though, major historical figures do enter into works of historical fiction. Sometimes they play only a minor role. For example, in Donald Hall's ***When Willard Met Babe Ruth,*** a family is held together by a love of baseball and an interest in Babe Ruth, but the Babe himself plays only the briefest role in the story. In other books, historical figures play more prominent roles. In Ann Rinaldi's ***Finishing Becca,*** the protagonist is employed in the home of General Benedict Arnold and is able to observe the general's treason firsthand.

Whether their characters are ordinary people or important historical figures, writers of historical fiction strive to create authentic characters who behave in ways that are consistent with the period. Robbie, the protagonist in Katherine Paterson's ***Preacher's Boy,*** is caught up in the fear that the approaching end of the nineteenth century may also be the "End of the Age." Consequently, Robbie decides that he'll give up being a Christian and will instead live life to its fullest—which to Robbie means riding in a motorcar for the very first time.

Theme

We can discern a great deal about life by learning about our past, and writers of historical fiction frequently explore themes that are significant not only for the historical period of the story but also for the present. In a listing of the themes that she explored in her Newbery Medal winner *A Gathering of Days: A New England Girl's Journal, 1830–1832,* Joan Blos (1993) includes "parent loss, death, remarriage, teacher accountability, community control, civil rights, moral responsibility versus personal loyalty" (p. 14). All are still relevant today.

The themes found in historical fiction are diverse and significant: the senselessness of prejudice and violence, the importance of family and community, the destructiveness of oppression, the need for freedom and independence, the importance of loyalty, faith and honor, the need to reach out to others. Kathy Broderick (1994) observed that "we learn about the present from studying the past. Though some of the problems of the past have been solved, there are questions that the characters in . . . [books] ask that we are still asking today" (p. 19).

MAJOR WRITERS OF HISTORICAL FICTION AND THEIR WORKS

Many major writers of historical fiction have been mentioned earlier in this chapter. And some writers who have created truly notable works of historical fiction are not included as major writers of the genre because they do not write primarily historical fiction.

James Lincoln Collier and Christopher Collier

Brothers James and Christopher Collier come from a family of writers, but what makes their journey along the writing pathway unusual is that they have teamed up to write historical fiction for children. Each brother brings particular talents to the team. Before their collaboration, James was an established writer of fiction and nonfiction for children as well as adults. Christopher was a renowned historian, teacher, and scholarly writer. Their partnership began when Christopher, discouraged by dry history textbooks, approached his brother with a proposal: He would fashion the concept and provide the necessary historical information, and James would develop the characters and story line. Their first collaborative effort, *My Brother Sam Is Dead,* was named a Newbery Honor book.

The Colliers' treatment of issues related to the American Revolution was unlike that found in most other children's books about the war. Rather than presenting the war primarily as a conflict between the Americans and their British oppressors, the Colliers chose an alternative perspective: They presented it as an internal conflict that divided communities and even families.

Other pieces of historical fiction on which the Colliers have collaborated include *Jump Ship to Freedom,* the story of a runaway slave, and *War Comes to Willy Freeman,* about a young African American girl who must cope with the loss of her parents.

Karen Cushman

To date, Karen Cushman has published four books, all historical fiction, and she has established a remarkable record. Her first book, *Catherine, Called*

Birdy, was named a 1995 Newbery Honor Book, and the second, *The Midwife's Apprentice,* was awarded the 1996 Newbery Medal. These two books are set in the Middle Ages. *The Ballad of Lucy Whipple* is set in the California gold rush of 1848, and her most recent book, *Matilda Bone,* is set during medieval times.

Cushman says that she long ago turned from an interest in queens and kings and princesses and princes to an interest in ordinary people. That interest led her to do extensive research on the lives of ordinary people in medieval England, the setting of three of her four books. The protagonist of *Catherine, Called Birdy* is a strong-willed young lady who is determined not to marry the man her father has selected for her. In her journal, Birdy records with frequent humor her ongoing battle with her father, her changing perspectives on life, and many everyday occurrences. In *The Midwife's Apprentice,* a homeless and nameless girl is literally pulled from the dung heap where she is sleeping and given the opportunity to become a midwife's apprentice. Cushman chronicles the girl's transformation from a nameless waif to a person with a name, a place in the world, and a vision of whom she can become. In *Matilda Bone,* a young girl who has been raised and educated in the manor house is sent by the priest to live on Blood and Bone Alley. Matilda is at first dismayed by what she perceives to be the coarseness of life on Blood and Bone Alley and only slowly comes to appreciate the dependable, hardworking people she meets in her new life.

Paul Fleischman

Paul Fleischman's work extends across genres, and his historical fiction extends across eras. His novel *Bull Run,* about the first battle of the Civil War, is of note for its original format. Sixteen characters—each with a distinctive voice—step forward to tell their stories in one- and two-page segments. Whether Northerner or Southerner, each character quickly goes from naiveté to disillusionment with this first battle of the Civil War.

In *The Borning Room,* Fleischman wrote about changes in the Ohio frontier. In *Saturnalia,* he wrote about a Native American boy in colonial times who had been raised by white men but who longed to understand his true ancestry. *Saturnalia* was a Boston Globe/Horn Book Honor Book, and *The Borning Room* was named a Golden Kite Honor Book.

Scott O'Dell

Scott O'Dell, a prolific writer of historical fiction for children, is one of the few children's authors to have written about the period of the Spanish conquest and exploration of the New World. *The King's Fifth,* a Newbery Honor Book, is about a group of Spaniards who travel through Mexico and what is now the southwestern United States in search of gold—which brings only grief when they find it. *The Captive* is the first book in a trilogy about the conquests of the Mayan, Aztec, and Incan civilizations. In this book, Julian Escobar, a young seminarian, views his journey to the Americas as an opportunity to save the souls of the Indians, but the New World, filled with slavery and exploitation, is not what he had imagined. O'Dell continued the story of New World greed and corruption in *The Feathered Serpent* and *The Amethyst Ring.*

Scott O'Dell won the 1961 Newbery Medal for *Island of the Blue Dolphins,* a story about Karana, a young Native American girl who survived alone on an island off the coast of California for eighteen years. *Sing Down the Moon,* a Newbery Honor Book, is the story of the forced resettlement of the Navajos and of a young Navajo girl who determined to return to the home of her ancestors. O'Dell died in 1989 at the age of 91.

Uri Orlev

Uri Orlev, now an Israeli citizen, was born in Warsaw, Poland, in 1931. World War II broke out when he was 6 and lasted until he was 14. Orlev has said that the Holocaust was his childhood, and he has written about that tragic time for children. *The Island on Bird Street* tells the story of a Jewish boy who hides in a bombed-out building in the ghetto. In this "island," he struggles with terror, loneliness, and near starvation as he waits for his father to return. The story ends on a hopeful note as the boy and his father join the partisans who are resisting the Nazis. In *The Man from the Other Side,* a Polish boy and his father risk their lives to help the Jews who are confined to the Warsaw ghetto.

All of Orlev's books have been translated into English. He has been recognized internationally for his writing for children, and a number of his books have won the Mildred L. Batchelder Award, given annually by the American Library Association for the most outstanding book published originally in a foreign language. In recognition of his body of work, Orlev received the Hans Christian Andersen Award in 1996.

Elizabeth George Speare

Elizabeth George Speare always intended to be a writer; however, she was nearly fifty before she turned to professional writing. Born in 1908, Speare began her writing career in 1955 with magazine articles about family life. Not until 1957 did she publish her first historical fiction for children.

That first novel was *The Witch of Blackbird Pond,* the book for which Speare is best known. The story is set in colonial America. Kit, the protagonist, travels from her home in Barbados to live with her aunt's family in Puritan Connecticut. Kit's values and beliefs soon clash with those of members of the rigid Puritan community, and the clash culminates in Kit's being tried for witchcraft. *The Witch of Blackbird Pond* was awarded the Newbery Medal in 1959 by a unanimous vote—a very rare occurrence.

Speare has written other historical fiction as well: *Calico Captive,* set in the early nineteenth century; *The Bronze Bow,* set in Biblical Palestine; and *The Sign of the Beaver,* set on the Western frontier. Speare has received two Newbery Medals and the Laura Ingalls Wilder Award for her distinguished contribution to children's literature.

Rosemary Sutcliff

Rosemary Sutcliff has repeatedly demonstrated that historical fiction set in ancient times can appeal to children. She is most widely recognized for her works set in England, most especially for her trilogy about the days of the Roman occupation there. *The Eagle of the Ninth,* the first in the trilogy, is the story of a young Roman centurion who is beginning his military career in second-century England. *The Silver Branch* focuses on a junior surgeon caught up in the turbulent politics of third-century England. The third book in the trilogy, *The Lantern Bearers,* is set in the midst of the decline of Roman rule in England. Sutcliff explored the Saxon invasion of Britain in *Dawn Wind.*

Rosemary Sutcliff received numerous awards for her contributions to children's literature, including the Carnegie Medal and the Lewis Carroll Shelf Award. She died in 1992.

Mildred Taylor

Mildred Taylor has given a special gift to children's literature: the gift of the Logan family, an African American family living in rural Mississippi during the Depression. Readers met the Logan family in Taylor's first book, **Song of the Trees.** For **Roll of Thunder, Hear My Cry,** her second novel about the Logans, Taylor was awarded the Newbery Medal. The family's determination to keep their land and the necessity of surviving the racism directed at African Americans in rural Mississippi of the 1930s create the central tensions in **Roll of Thunder, Hear My Cry.** She continued to write about the themes and characters of her earlier books in later works, including **Let the Circle Be Unbroken, The Friendship, The Gold Cadillac, Mississippi Bridge,** and **The Well.**

Yoshiko Uchida

During her lifetime, Yoshiko Uchida was a prolific writer whose stories included folktales and contemporary realistic fiction. Yet she is best known for her historical novels, which give middle-grade readers a look into Japanese American heritage. Two of her books in particular are based on her own experiences during her teen and young adult years in U.S. internment camps for Japanese Americans in World War II. Uchida spent five months living in a horse stall at Tanforan Racetracks in California until her family was moved to Topaz, in the desert of Utah. **Journey to Topaz** and its sequel, **Journey Home,** tell the story of eleven-year-old Yuki Sakane and her family during the internment and the difficult years of readjustment that followed. **The Bracelet** is a picture book about a Japanese American girl who receives a bracelet from a non-Japanese friend as she leaves for internment in a horse stall at Tanforan Racetracks. It was Uchida's hope that sharing the pain of these experiences would prevent them from being repeated. Three novels, **A Jar of Dreams, The Best Bad Thing,** and **The Happiest Ending,** depict eleven-year-old Rinko's life during the Depression years of the 1930s. All of the novels address the sensitive issue of struggling with one's heritage amidst prejudice. For many young readers, Uchida's books are an introduction to issues faced by Japanese Americans as seen through the eyes of a main character close to their own age.

Uchida received a citation from the Contra Costa Chapter of the Japanese American Citizens League for her contribution to the cultural development of society. **Journey Home** was selected as a Children's Choices book by the International Reading Association and as a Notable Children's Trade Book in the Field of Social Studies by the National Council for Social Studies and the Children's Book Council.

Laura Ingalls Wilder

Since the publication of her first book in 1932, **The Little House in the Big Woods,** Laura Ingalls Wilder has been a favorite with children. Wilder was born in 1867 in Wisconsin and spent her early years there. During the rest of her childhood, she moved throughout the West with her family. These moves provided a wealth of material for the *Little House* books. The early stories feature the Ingalls family: Ma, Pa, Laura, older sister Mary, and younger sisters Carrie and Grace. In **These Happy Golden Years,** Laura becomes a teacher and meets her husband-to-be; **The First Four Years** is about the early years of their marriage. Narrated by Laura, the stories are told from a child's perspective, and the writing is noteworthy for its characterization, rich use of language, and descriptions of the joys and challenges of frontier life.

Though remembered as a writer, Wilder actually spent most of her adult life as a farm wife. Under the tutelage of her daughter Rose, she began to write later in life; she published *The Little House in the Big Woods* when she was 65. *On the Banks of Plum Creek* and *The Long Winter* were both Newbery Honor Books. She was the first recipient of the Laura Ingalls Wilder Award, an award that is now presented every five years in her honor by the American Library Association to an outstanding author or illustrator of children's books whose body of work has made a significant contribution to children's literature.

CRITERIA FOR SELECTING HISTORICAL FICTION

In evaluating historical fiction, teachers and librarians need to look for many of the same things they look for in other genres. Yet because historical fiction has distinct qualities, it is also necessary to use some genre-specific selection and evaluation criteria that have to do with authenticity. These criteria are discussed below:

■ Does the writer bring the setting to life through the inclusion of authentic details that do not overwhelm the story?

■ Do the characters behave in ways that are believable, given the time period in which they live?

■ Are the conflicts in the story plausible in light of the time period in which the story is set?

The writer (and the illustrator, if there is one) of historical fiction must make the work historically authentic. Writers must know the period about which they are writing so well that every detail is accurate.

Setting

It goes without saying that the setting of a work of historical fiction must be authentic. It is also important for the writer to include rich details that bring the setting to life for the reader. These details must be carefully integrated into the story. Serious writers of historical fiction do their homework. That is, they do the background research necessary to develop authentic settings. Sometimes, though, writers yield to the temptation to include more information about the time period than necessary—and in the process, they obscure their story with historical information.

Characters

Characters in historical fiction must think and behave in ways that are believable, given the time period in which they live. For example, Puritan New England, the setting of *The Witch of Blackbird Pond,* was an era in which women did not often assert themselves. Yet Kit, Elizabeth George Speare's protagonist, is a strong-willed young woman who leaves her grandfather's home in Barbados after he dies to live with her aunt and uncle in New England. Speare legitimizes Kit's behavior and makes her a believable character by allowing readers to discover, as the story unfolds, that the culture of Barbados was one in which young women were allowed far more independence than they were in Puritan New England.

The need to create characters who behave in believable ways for the time period can create a quandary for the author, who must also develop a character with whom today's readers can identify. Some critics argue that Karen Cushman's character Birdy, in *Catherine, Called Birdy,* was created with more attention to the present-day reader than to the ways in which young girls behaved in medieval times. Yet Birdy is an immensely popular character with young readers. If Cushman had opted for total historical accuracy about a period in which girls did very little, the story would have offered little to hold modern readers' interest—with the result that many readers might never have gotten a taste of medieval life.

Conflict

Authors of historical fiction strive to create conflicts that could arise in the time period of the story and to develop those conflicts in plausible ways. Mildred Taylor did this in *Roll of Thunder, Hear My Cry.* Mississippi in the 1930s was a place where racial tensions that had existed for decades were exacerbated by the grim economic realities of the Depression. The violence that erupts as a consequence of the boycott organized by the Logans is in keeping with the story's setting.

AWARDS FOR HISTORICAL FICTION

There is a lot of historical fiction for children available today, and teachers and librarians will want to choose the best to offer to young readers. Looking for award-winning books is one way to be assured of selecting high-quality books. As you've seen from earlier sections of this chapter, historical fiction is well represented among Newbery Medal winners and Honor Books. In addition, the Scott O'Dell Award for Historical Fiction was established in 1981 to encourage the writing and reading of historical fiction. The National Council for Social Studies annually identifies Notable Children's Trade Books in the Field of Social Studies, and historical fiction is frequently included among these books.

TEACHING IDEAS

Discovering How Authors Bring the Past to Life. Invite students to reread a work of historical fiction to find examples of writing that brings the past to life for them. Encourage students to pay particular attention to story events, what characters say and do, and the ways in which the author describes the story's setting. Have students start with a work of historical fiction in picture book format before moving on to chapter books.

Exploring Family Stories. Share with children works of historical fiction that are fictionalized family stories, such as *Pink and Say* or *Katie's Trunk.* Discuss with the children how the writers came up with ideas for their stories. Invite them to ask their grandparents, parents, or other older relatives and friends to talk about childhood memories. Ask children to share the stories they collect and decide which, if any, might make interesting material for a fictionalized family story.

Exploring Different Perspectives. Have children read two works of historical fiction set in the same period, such as Pam Conrad's *Prairie Songs* and Patricia MacLachlan's *Sarah, Plain and Tall,* both of which explore life on the western frontier. Discuss with the children how the authors' perspectives differ.

Getting Ready to Read Historical Fiction. Use Donna Ogle's (1986) K-W-L strategy when reading historical fiction with children. To use this comprehension strategy, ask students before they read a story what they know (K) about the time period in which the story is set and what they want (W) to know. Then, once they have read the story, ask them what they have learned (L) about the time period. Try this strategy with a story such as Laurence Yep's *Dragonwings,* about Chinese immigrants to the United States in the early twentieth century, or Eve Bunting's *Train to Somewhere,* about the orphan trains of the late nineteenth and early twentieth centuries.

EXPERIENCES FOR YOUR LEARNING

1. Read two books set in the same period and discuss with a classmate how the authors' perspectives on the period seem to differ. If you are interested in the medieval period, you might want to choose *The Ramsay Scallop* and *Catherine, Called Birdy.*

2. After reading Mildred Taylor's *Roll of Thunder, Hear My Cry,* read a fifth-grade social studies textbook to see what information it includes about race relations in the South during the 1930s and about the Depression. Discuss with a fellow student the differences in the way the textbook authors and Mildred Taylor handled these two topics.

3. Choose a piece of historical fiction to read aloud to a group of students. Consider a relatively short chapter book such as Mildred Taylor's *Mississippi Bridge* or Marguerite de Angeli's *The Door in the Wall* or a picture book such as Sherry Garland's *The Lotus Seed* or Margaree Mitchell's *Uncle Jed's*

Barbershop. Before reading the book to the group, talk with them to find out what they know about the time period in which the story is set. Once you have finished reading the story aloud, talk to the students again to find out what they have discovered about the time period. On the basis of your conversations with the students, discuss with a group of peers what you have learned about the values of historical fiction for children.

4. More and more historical fiction is being published in picture book format, and some of these picture books explore potentially disturbing subject matter. Teachers must make judgments about the appropriate audience for these books. Read a sampling of historical fiction picture books, and discuss with your classmates the most appropriate audience for these books. You might want to read Toshi Maruki's *Hiroshima no pika, The Whispering Cloth* by Pegi Shea, and *Baseball Saved Us* by Ken Mochizuki.

RECOMMENDED BOOKS

* indicates a picture book; I indicates interest level (P = preschool, YA = young adult)

Ancient Times through the Medieval Period

Cushman, Karen. *Catherine, Called Birdy.* Clarion, 1994. Through her journal, a young girl chronicles her daily life in medieval England. (**I:** 11–YA)

———. *Matilda Bone.* Clarion, 2000. Having grown up in a manor under the care of the local priest, Matilda is appalled at life on Blood and Bone Alley, where she has been sent to serve Peg the Bonesetter. (**I:** 10–14)

———. *The Midwife's Apprentice.* Clarion, 1995. A homeless waif in medieval England is given the opportunity to become a midwife's apprentice. (**I:** 10–14)

de Angeli, Marguerite. *The Door in the Wall.* Doubleday, 1949/1989. A young boy loses the use of his legs and is still able to save the town and serve the king. (**I:** 8–12)

Paterson, Katherine. *The Master Puppeteer*. Illustrated by Haru Wells. Harper, 1976. A youth describes life as a puppeteer in eighteenth-century Japan. (I: YA)

——. *The Sign of the Chrysanthemum*. Illustrated by Peter Landa. HarperCollins, 1973/1988. During troubled times in the Heian period in Japan, a boy searches for his father (I: 11–YA). See also *Of Nightingales That Weep* (1999) (I: 9–12).

Speare, Elizabeth George. *The Bronze Bow*. Houghton Mifflin, 1961/1997. Consumed by his hatred of the Roman occupiers of Palestine, a boy discovers the teachings of Jesus. (I: 11–YA)

Sutcliff, Rosemary. *Dawn Wind*. Illustrated by Charles Keeping. Oxford Univ. Press, 1961. A boy is sold into slavery by the Saxons, who have destroyed his people. (I: YA)

——. *The Eagle of the Ninth*. Illustrated by C. Walter Hodges. Farrar, 1954/1993. The story of a young Roman centurion in second-century England. Other books in the trilogy include *The Lantern Bearers* (1959) and *The Silver Branch* (1957). (I: YA)

Temple, Frances. *The Ramsay Scallop*. Orchard, 1994. A young couple's pilgrimage from England to Spain transforms their views of the world and each other. (I: 11–YA)

Williams, Laura E. *The Executioner's Daughter*. Holt, 2000. Born into the family of an executioner, Lily is faced with becoming her father's assistant when her mother dies. Yet Lily is determined to change her fate and instead become a healer. (I: 10–YA)

The European Renaissance

Blackwood, Gary. *The Shakespeare Stealer*. Dutton, 1998. Ordered by a cruel master to steal the script of *Hamlet* from the Globe Theatre, Widge confronts a new world when he is taken in and befriended by the Globe company. The sequel is *Shakespeare's Scribe* (2000). (I: 10 and up)

Konigsburg, E. L. *The Second Mrs. Giaconda*. Aladdin, 1975. Salai, apprentice to Leonardo da Vinci and loyal friend of Duchess Beatrice, is also a schemer. In this Renaissance story, Konigsburg creates a scenario in which young Salai schemes to ensure that his master will paint the portrait of the woman who would become known as the Mona Lisa. (I: 12 and up)

The Americas before 1600

Dorris, Michael. *Guests*. Hyperion, 1994/1999. This story of a young Native American boy's coming of age is entwined with the story of the first Thanksgiving. (I: 8–12)

——. *Morning Girl*. Hyperion, 1992. Life on an island is described by two Taino children prior to and on the day that Columbus lands. (I: 8–12)

O'Dell, Scott. *The Captive*. Houghton Mifflin, 1979. In the New World, a Jesuit priest journeys with a Spanish expedition and witnesses the enslavement and exploitation of the Mayans. Other titles in the trilogy include *The Amethyst Ring* (1983) and *The Feathered Serpent* (1981). (I: 11–YA)

——. *The King's Fifth*. Houghton Mifflin, 1966. Esteban de Sandoval is waiting to be tried for not turning over to the King of Spain a fifth of the treasure he found on his expedition through Mexico. (I: 11–YA)

*Yolen, Jane. *Encounter*. Illustrated by David Shannon. Harcourt, 1992. A Taino boy tries to warn his people of coming destruction when Columbus arrives on their island. (I: 8–12)

The American Colonies, 1600–1774

*Bowen, Gary. *Stranded at Plimoth Plantation 1626*. HarperCollins, 1994. An orphan stranded at Plimoth Plantation documents his life in the village. (I: 10–12)

*Bruchac, Joseph. *Squanto's Journey*. Illustrated by Greg Shed. Harcourt, 2000. This is the story of the Native American who befriended the settlers of Plymouth, despite his own suffering at the hands of the Europeans. (I: 8–11)

Clapp, Patricia. *Constance: A Story of Early Plymouth*. Peter Smith, 1968/1993. A girl details her life in the early days of the Plymouth settlement. (I: 11–YA)

Fleischman, Paul. *Saturnalia*. HarperCollins, 1992. A Narragansett boy, captured by whites at age 8, works as a printer's apprentice until he begins his search for his past. (I: 9–12)

Koller, Jackie French. *The Primrose Way*. Harcourt, 1992. A young girl in the New World becomes an interpreter between the Puritans and the Pawtuckets. (I: 9–12)

Rinaldi, Ann. *A Break with Charity: A Story about the Salem Witch Trials*. Harcourt, 1992. A young girl struggles to find the courage to tell the truth about the Salem witch hunt (I: YA). See also *The Journal of Jasper Jonathan Pierce* (Scholastic, 1999) (I: 9–12).

Speare, Elizabeth George. *The Witch of Blackbird Pond*. Houghton Mifflin, 1958. A girl is accused of witchcraft in colonial New England. (I: 10–YA)

The American Revolution

*Borden, Louise. *Sleds on Boston Common*. Illustrated by Robert Andrew Parker. Margaret K. McElderry/

Simon & Schuster, 2000. Henry didn't think times could get much worse in Boston in the winter of 1774, until the day he discovered British soldiers camped all over Boston Common, blocking the best sled runs in the city. (I: 6–9)

Bruchac, Joseph. *The Arrow Over the Door.* Illustrated by James Watling. Dial, 1998. Samuel and his Quaker community fear the approaching British and Indian raiders, while Stands Straight views all Americans as enemies. An encounter at a Quaker meeting brings new understandings to both boys and their communities. (I: 9–12)

Collier, James Lincoln, and Christopher Collier. *My Brother Sam Is Dead.* Simon & Schuster, 1974/1984. A family is torn apart as members take different sides during the American Revolution. (I: 10–YA)

————. *War Comes to Willy Freeman.* Delacorte, 1983. A free African American girl strives to maintain her freedom during the era of the American Revolution. (I: 10–12)

Forbes, Esther. *Johnny Tremain.* Houghton Mifflin, 1943. A silversmith's apprentice becomes part of the Sons of Liberty. (I: 10–YA)

Rinaldi, Ann. *The Fifth of March: A Story of the Boston Massacre.* Harcourt, 1993. A fourteen-year-old indentured servant is caught between the rebelling colonists and loyal Tories (I: YA). See also *Time Enough for Drums* (Holiday House, 1986). (I: YA)

————. *Finishing Becca.* Harcourt, 1994. Becca, sent to work for a wealthy family in Philadelphia, finds herself caught up in the intrigues of the American Revolution. (I: YA)

*Turner, Ann. *Katie's Trunk.* Illustrated by Ron Himler. Macmillan, 1992. A Tory child hides in a trunk when Patriots come to her home. (I: 5–9)

Life in the Early to Mid-Nineteenth Century

Auch, Mary Jane. *The Road to Home.* Holt, 2000. After her mother's death, Mem is faced with the nearly overwhelming task of caring for her siblings when her father is sidetracked by a job on the Erie Canal. This is the third book in a trilogy that includes *Journey to Nowhere* (1997) and *Frozen Summer* (1998). (I: 10–13)

Burgess, Melvin. *The Copper Treasure.* Illustrated by Richard Williams. Holt, 1998. Scavengers of coal on the muddy banks of the Thames, three boys undertake a deadly adventure to recover a treasure of copper they have discovered. (I: 9–12)

DeFelice, Cynthia. *The Apprenticeship of Lucas Whitaker.* Farrar, 1996. Having lost his family to

consumption, Lucas becomes a physician's apprentice and hopes to save his new community from consumption with a macabre folk remedy. (I: 10–13)

Giff, Patricia Reilly. *Nory Ryan's Song.* Delacorte, 2000. Faced with uncompromising English landlords and a blight that destroys the potato crop throughout Ireland, Nory must find a way to save herself and her family from starvation. (I: 10–13)

Hudson, Jan. *Sweetgrass.* Putnam, 1989/1999. Sweetgrass must help her people survive smallpox in the winter of 1838. (I: 9–12)

Slavery, the Civil War, and Reconstruction

*Ackerman, Karen. *The Tin Heart.* Illustrated by Michael Hays. Atheneum, 1990. Best friends Mahaley and Flora live on opposite sides of the Ohio River, but when the Civil War breaks out, the ferry stops running. (I: 8–12)

Collier, James, and Christopher Collier. *Jump Ship to Freedom.* Delacorte, 1981. A fourteen-year-old boy runs away to escape slavery. (I: 10–12)

Fleischman, Paul. *Bull Run.* HarperCollins, 1993. The first battle of the Civil War is described from sixteen different perspectives. (I: 10–YA)

*Hopkinson, Deborah. *Sweet Clara and the Freedom Quilt.* Illustrated by James Ransome. Knopf, 1993. Determined to escape from slavery, Clara sews a quilt that maps the way to freedom. (I: 8–12)

Houston, Gloria. *Mountain Valor.* Illustrated by Thomas B. Allen. Philomel, 1994. Valor's mountain family has already been divided by the Civil War. When a renegade soldier threatens to further destroy her family, Valor disguises herself as a boy and enters the war to save the ones she loves. (I: 10–13)

Hunt, Irene. *Across Five Aprils.* Scholastic, 1964/1999. Jethro grows up during the Civil War in the midst of a family and a community divided by that war. (I: 10–YA)

Paterson, Katherine. *Jip, His Story.* Puffin, 1998. Jip, an orphan who has grown up on a poor farm in Vermont, is caught up in the struggles between slave owners and abolitionists. (I: 10–13)

*Polacco, Patricia. *Pink and Say.* Philomel, 1994. During the Civil War, an African American Union soldier befriends a white one. (I: 8–12)

Rinaldi, Ann. *Mine Eyes Have Seen.* Scholastic, 1998. Annie Brown, the daughter of John Brown, bears witness to the events leading up to her father's attempt to foster a slave insurrection by raiding the federal armory at Harper's Ferry, West Virginia (I: 11 and up). See also *Amelia's War* (1999) (I: 9–12), *The Coffin Quilt* (Harcourt, 1999). (I: YA)

Rosen, Michael J. *A School for Pompey Walker*. Illustrated by Aminah Brenda Lynn Robinson. Harcourt, 1995. A former slave remembers how he raised money to build a school for all children. (I: 9–12)

Westward Movement in the United States

Avi. *The Barn*. Orchard, 1994. Set in the Oregon territory, this story tells of three children who build a barn in the vain attempt to keep a promise to their dying father. (I: 10–12)

Blos, Joan. *A Gathering of Days: A New England Girl's Journal, 1830–1832*. Scribner's, 1979. A thirteen-year-old girl chronicles her life on the family farm. (I: 10–12)

Bruchac, Joseph. *Sacajawea*. Harcourt, 2000. This fictional account of the Lewis and Clark expedition is told alternately from the viewpoints of William Clark and Sacajawea, the Indian translator and guide who accompanied the explorers. (I: 10–14)

*Bunting, Eve. *Dandelions*. Illustrated by Greg Shed. Harcourt, 1995. A family experiences mixed emotions as they travel across the prairie to settle in the Nebraska territory. (I: 8–12)

*———. *Train to Somewhere*. Illustrated by Ronald Himler. Clarion, 1996. The story of New York orphans taken out West to be placed with families. (I: 8–11)

Conrad, Pam. *Prairie Songs*. Harper, 1985. Louisa sees her neighbor driven mad by the loneliness she endures on the prairie. (I: 9–12)

Cushman, Karen. *The Ballad of Lucy Whipple*. Clarion, 1996. When Lucy, her mother, and her siblings arrive in California in the midst of the gold rush, Lucy directs every waking thought to how she will get back home to Massachusetts. (I: 10–12)

Fleischman, Paul. *The Borning Room*. Scholastic, 1991/1998. Georgina Lott, her life nearly over, reminisces about all that has happened to her. (I: 11–YA)

*Hall, Donald. *Ox-Cart Man*. Illustrated by Barbara Cooney. Viking, 1979. Life on a New England farm throughout a year. (I: P–9)

*Helldorfer, M. C. *Hog Music*. Illustrated by S. D. Schindler. Viking, 2000. When Aunt Liza sends her niece Lucy a birthday present from Baltimore, the box takes a delightfully circuitous route to Lucy's new home in Illinois. (I: 5–8)

Holm, Jennifer. *Our Only May Amelia*. HarperCollins, 1999. May Amelia, the only girl ever born on the Nasel River in Washington, finds adventure, joy, and tragedy in her Finnish-American frontier community. (I: 8–12)

*Karim, Roberta. *Kindle Me a Riddle: A Pioneer Story*. Illustrated by Bethanne Andersen. Greenwillow, 1999. As a pioneer family shares riddles throughout the day, young readers gain insights into the pioneer way of life. (I: 7–10)

Keehn, Sally M. *I Am Regina*. Philomel, 1991. A young girl is captured by Native Americans and must learn to live as they do to survive. (I: 10–YA)

*Kinsey-Warnock, Natalie. *Wilderness Cat*. Illustrated by Mark Graham. Dutton, 1992. A family fears that it won't survive the first winter in the Canadian wilderness. (I: 5–9)

Kurtz, Jane. *I'm Sorry, Almira Ann*. Illustrated by Susan Havicc. Holt, 1999. Sometimes unable to contain her "hasty spirit" as her family crosses the country by covered wagon, young Sarah must find a way to make amends when her exuberance accidentally results in harm to her best friend. (I: 7–10)

*Levitin, Sonia. *Boom Town*. Illustrated by Cat B. Smith. Orchard, 1998. After her family moves to California, where her father goes to work in the gold fields, Amanda decides to make her own fortune baking pies. (I: 6–10)

MacLachlan, Patricia. *Sarah, Plain and Tall*. Harper, 1985. A brother and sister hope that Sarah will choose to stay on the prairie and become their mother. (I: 9–12)

*McCully, Emily A. *An Outlaw Thanksgiving*. Dial, 1998. While traveling with her mother cross-country by train in 1896, a young girl unexpectedly shares Thanksgiving dinner with the notorious outlaw Butch Cassidy. (I: 7–11)

Meyer, Carolyn. *Where the Broken Heart Still Beats*. Harcourt, 1992. Cynthia is kidnapped by the Comanches, recaptured by the Rangers, and returned to her "home." (I: 10–YA)

O'Dell, Scott. *Island of the Blue Dolphins*. Houghton Mifflin, 1960/1990. When her people leave their island home, Karana is left to survive on her own. (I: 10–YA)

———. *Sing Down the Moon*. Houghton Mifflin, 1970. A Navajo girl recounts her journey to Fort Sumner as an Army prisoner. (I: 10–YA)

Rinaldi, Ann. *The Staircase*. Harcourt, 2000. After her father leaves her at a convent school in Santa Fe, Lizzy struggles to understand the ways of the Catholics who surround her and to deal with her own grief following the loss of her mother. (I: 10–13)

Speare, Elizabeth George. *Calico Captive*. Illustrated by W. T. Mars. Houghton Mifflin, 1957. Captured by Native Americans, a family is eventually sold as slaves in Montreal. (I: 10–12)

————. *The Sign of the Beaver.* Houghton Mifflin, 1983. A Native American boy teaches his white friend how to survive in his frontier cabin. (I: 9–12)

*Turner, Ann. *Dakota Dugout.* Illustrated by Ron Himler. Macmillan, 1985. A historical poem in which a grandmother tells her granddaughter about her earlier life in a sod house on the Dakota prairie. (I: 5–8)

*————. *Mississippi Mud.* Illustrated by Robert J. Blake. HarperCollins, 1997. Three members of a pioneer family share their dreams as they travel across the country to Oregon. (I: 7–11)

*Wilder, Laura Ingalls. *Christmas in the Big Woods.* Adapted from the *Little House* books. Illustrated by Renee Graef. HarperCollins, 1995. Christmas day is full of good times for the Ingalls family. Other adaptations in the series include *Dance at Grandpa's* (1994), *The Deer in the Woods* (1995), *Going to Town* (1995), and *Winter Days in the Big Woods* (1994). (I: P–8)

————. *The Little House in the Big Woods.* Illustrated by Garth Williams. Harper, 1932. This first book about the Ingalls family details their life in the Big Woods of Wisconsin. Other books in the series include *The First Four Years* (1971), *Little House on the Prairie* (1935), *The Long Winter* (1940), *On the Banks of Plum Creek* (1953), and *These Happy Golden Years* (1953). (I: 7–11)

Yep, Laurence. *Dragon's Gate.* HarperCollins, 1993. A Chinese boy joins his father in America, where he works under dire conditions to build the transcontinental railroad. (I: 10–YA)

Industrialization

Denenberg, Barry. *So Far from Home: The Diary of Mary Driscoll, an Irish Mill Girl.* Scholastic, 1997. Escaping the potato famine in Ireland, Mary Driscoll discovers that her new life in the textile mills of Lowell, Massachusetts, diverges dramatically from her dreams about America. The book is part of the *Dear America* series. (I: 10–14)

Howard, Ellen. *The Gate in the Wall.* Atheneum, 1999. Emma leaves the silk-spinning mills and finds a new life on the canals of Victorian England. (I: 9–12)

*McCully, Emily Arnold. *The Bobbin Girl.* Dial, 1996. This story about the injustices suffered by the women who worked in the cotton mills in Lowell, Massachusetts, is told from the perspective of a ten-year-old mill worker. (I: 8–12)

Paterson, Katherine. *Lyddie.* Dutton, 1991. After losing her parents and being separated from her brother and sister, Lyddie works in the textile mills to earn money to reunite her siblings. (I: 10–YA)

Immigration

Hesse, Karen. *Letters from Rifka.* Puffin, 1993. Rifka writes about fleeing Russia and having to stay behind in Belgium when her family goes on to the United States. (I: 9–12)

*Hest, Amy. *When Jessie Came Across the Sea.* Illustrated by P. J. Lynch. Candlewick, 1997. A thirteen-year-old Jewish orphan reluctantly leaves her grandmother and immigrates to New York City, where she works for three years sewing lace and earning money to bring her grandmother to the United States. (I: 8–12)

*Leighton, Maxinne R. *An Ellis Island Christmas.* Illustrated by Dennis Nolan. Viking, 1992. Having left Poland and braved ocean storms to join her father in America, Krysia arrives at Ellis Island on Christmas Eve. (I: 8–12)

Mayerson, Evelyn Wilde. *The Cat Who Escaped from Steerage.* Scribner's, 1990. A Polish girl smuggles a cat on board a ship headed for the United States. (I: 8–12)

*Rael, Elsa Okon. *What Zeesie Saw on Delancey Street.* Illustrated by Marjorie Priceman. Simon & Schuster, 1996. A young Jewish girl living in Manhattan attends her first "package party" and learns a lesson about generosity in her immigrant community. (I: 6–10)

Life in the Late Nineteenth Century and Early Twentieth Century

Armstrong, William H. *Sounder.* Harper, 1969. The story of an African American's life in the rural South. (I: 10–12)

*Christiansen, Candace. *The Ice Horse.* Illustrated by Thomas Locker. Dial, 1993. Before refrigerators, men harvested blocks of ice from the rivers to be used all year round. (I: 5–10)

Curtis, Christopher Paul. *Bud, Not Buddy.* Delacorte, 1999. Bud's mother has died, and the placements the orphanage finds for him never work out. So Bud sets out to find the man he is convinced must be his father. (I: 8–12)

DeFelice, Cynthia. *Nowhere to Call Home.* Farrar, 1999. Instead of going to live with her aunt in Chicago after her father commits suicide, Frankie decides to join the throngs of other children who have chosen the hobo life. (I: 9–12)

Haas, Jessie. *Unbroken.* Greenwillow, 1999. Harriet's mother had raised her daughter in town where she could get an education, but when Harriet is orphaned, she is sent to live with an aunt who has different ideas about raising children. (I: 11–14)

*Hall, Donald. *When Willard Met Babe Ruth*. Illustrated by Barry Moser. Harcourt, 1996. Babe Ruth touches the lives of three generations of the Babson family. (I: 6–10)

Hesse, Karen. *Out of the Dust*. Scholastic, 1997. In free-verse poetry, Billie Jo chronicles the seeming hopelessness of her Depression-era life in the Oklahoma panhandle. (I: YA)

*Houston, Gloria. *The Year of the Perfect Christmas Tree*. Illustrated by Barbara Cooney. Dial, 1988. Because her father is away at war, Ruthie and her mom deliver the Christmas tree to the church. (I: 5–9)

Ingold, Jeanette. *Airfield*. Harcourt, 1999. Spending the summer with her aunt and uncle in the midst of the Depression, Beatty becomes caught up in the drama of early aviation at the airfield where her uncle works. (I: 10–YA)

———. *Pictures, 1918*. Harcourt, 1998. In the midst of World War I, Asia becomes intrigued with exploring the possibilities of photography and with nurturing her relationship with Nick. (I: YA)

*Johnston, Tony. *Amber on the Mountain*. Illustrated by Robert Duncan. Dial, 1994. A mountain girl learns to read and write with the help of a friend. (I: 5–10)

*Lasky, Kathryn. *Marven of the Great North Woods*. Illustrated by Kevin Hawkes. Harcourt, 1997. Ten-year-old Marven finds a special friend when his Jewish parents send him to a Minnesota logging camp to escape the influenza epidemic of 1918. (I: 8–12)

Levine, Gail Carson. *Dave at Night*. HarperCollins, 1999. When Dave is placed in the Hebrew Home for Boys, an orphanage known also as the Hell Hole for Brats, he encounters cruelty, friendship, and (beyond the orphanage) the joys of the Harlem Renaissance. (I: 9–12)

*Levinson, Riki. *I Go with My Family to Grandma's*. Illustrated by Diane Goode. Dutton, 1986. An extended family living near New York City at the turn of the century uses many different modes of transportation to gather at the grandparents' home. (I: P–7)

*Miller, William. *The Piano*. Illustrated by Susan Keeter. Lee & Low, 2000. Tia loves music so much that she accepts a job as a maid in the home of a white woman so that she can hear more music. This is the story of how music bridges a racial divide in the deep South of the early 1900s. (I: 7–11)

*Mitchell, Margaree. *Uncle Jed's Barbershop*. Illustrated by James Ransome. Simon & Schuster, 1993. Even in the face of racial prejudice and eco-nomic hardship caused by the Depression, Uncle Jed pursues his dream of owning his own barbershop. (I: 9 and up)

Paterson, Katherine. *Preacher's Boy*. Clarion, 1999. Robbie's high-spirited ways often land him in the doghouse with his preacher father, but when one of his schemes endangers the life of someone else, Robbie finds the courage to face up to the consequences of his actions. (I: 9–12)

Recorvits, Helen. *Goodbye, Walter Malinski*. Farrar, 1999. An immigrant family struggles to survive and find happiness during the Depression. (I: 9–11)

Ritter, John H. *Choosing Up Sides*. Philomel, 1998. Luke is torn between becoming the baseball pitcher he longs to be and accepting the beliefs of his preacher father, who condemns all sports as evil. (I: 10–14)

Rostkowski, Margaret. *After the Dancing Days*. Harper, 1986. The story of a young girl's friendship with a wounded World War I veteran. (I: 10–YA)

*Rylant, Cynthia. *When I Was Young in the Mountains*. Illustrated by Diane Goode. Dutton, 1982. The memories of a young girl growing up in the Appalachian mountains. (I: 5–9)

*Stewart, Sarah. *The Gardener*. Illustrated by David Small. Farrar, 1997. The story is told in a series of letters. After Lydia Grace's father loses his job, she goes to live with her Uncle Jim in the city but takes her love for gardening with her. (I: 7–11)

Taylor, Mildred D. *The Friendship*. Dial, 1987. At the local store, children witness a confrontation between an elderly African American man and the white storekeeper. (I: 9–YA)

———. *Let the Circle Be Unbroken*. Dial, 1981. During the Great Depression, Cassie and her family must overcome racism in the South. (I: 10–12)

———. *Mississippi Bridge*. Illustrated by Max Ginsburg. Dial, 1990. Jeremy witnesses racism as a bus driver orders all African Americans off the bus to make room for white passengers. (I: 9–12)

———. *Roll of Thunder, Hear My Cry*. Dial, 1976. An African American family faces prejudice and discrimination in the South. (I: 10–12)

———. *Song of the Trees*. Dial, 1975. An African American family tries to save their forest from being logged during the Depression. (I: 9–12)

———. *The Well*. Dial, 1995. Racial tensions escalate between boys when the only water comes from the Logans' well. (I: 10–12)

Thesman, Jean. *Rachel Chance*. Houghton Mifflin, 1990. Baby Rider has disappeared, and it is up to Rachel and her grandfather to rescue him. (I: YA)

*Tunnell, Michael O. *Mailing May*. Illustrated by Ted Rand. Greenwillow, 1997. In 1914, a young girl is mailed (by train) to see her grandmother because her family cannot afford a train ticket. (I: 5–9)

Yep, Laurence. *Dragonwings*. Harper, 1975. The story of a Chinese boy immigrating to San Francisco to join his father. (I: YA)

World War II

Coerr, Eleanor. *Sadako and the Thousand Paper Cranes*. Putnam, 1977. The story of a survivor of the Hiroshima bombing who tries to make a thousand paper cranes to make her wish for health come true. (I: 10–12)

Giff, Patricia Reilly. *Lily's Crossing*. Delacorte, 1997. Feeling alone when her father enlists in the army, Lily befriends a refugee from the Nazis. (I: 9–12)

Hahn, Mary Downing. *As Ever, Gordy*. Avon, 1998. When Gordy moves back to his hometown, where everyone knows his family's troubled history, he must struggle to avoid slipping back into his trouble-making ways. This is a companion book to *Stepping on the Cracks* (1991). (I: 9–12)

———. *Stepping on the Cracks*. Clarion, 1991. While her brother is away at war, Elizabeth befriends an army deserter. (I: 10–12)

Lowry, Lois. *Number the Stars*. Houghton Mifflin, 1989. A story of how the Danes aided Jews in their flight to freedom. (I: 10–12)

*Maruki, Toshi. *Hiroshima No Pika*. Lothrop, 1980. The poignant story of one family's experiences on the day Hiroshima was bombed. (I: 8–12)

Matas, Carol. *Greater than Angels*. Simon & Schuster, 1998. A young Jewish girl is saved when she is sent to a French village whose citizens have banded together to save Jewish refugees. (I: 10 and up)

———. *In My Enemy's House*. Simon & Schuster, 1999. To save herself, a young Polish Jew disguises herself as a Christian and works for the Nazis. (I: YA)

*Mochizuki, Ken. *Baseball Saved Us*. Illustrated by Dom Lee. Lee & Low, 1993. A Japanese American boy's memories of life in an internment camp. (I: 8–12)

*Oppenheim, Shulamith Levey. *The Lily Cupboard*. Illustrated by Ronald Himler. HarperCollins, 1992/1995. A little girl hides from the Nazis on the farm of a sympathetic Dutch family. (I: 6–10)

Orlev, Uri. *The Island on Bird Street*. Translated by Hillel Halkin. Houghton Mifflin, 1984. A boy struggles to survive in the Warsaw ghetto as he waits for his father to return. (I: 11–YA)

———. *The Man from the Other Side*. Translated by Hillel Halkin. Houghton Mifflin, 1991. A man and his son risk their own lives to help the Jews in the Warsaw ghetto. (I: YA)

Polacco, Patricia. *The Butterfly*. Philomel, 2000. When Monique discovers the Jewish family her mother has hidden in their basement, she joins her mother in finding the courage to defy the Nazis who occupy their French village. (I: 10 and up)

Strickland, Brad. *When Mack Came Back*. Dial, 2000. Maury's brother is away at war when his brother's dog makes it back to the family farm. Maury is determined to keep the animal despite his father's objections. (I: 6–9)

Taylor, Theodore. *The Bomb*. Harcourt, 1995. Nuclear bombs are to be tested on Bikini Atoll, and Sorry and his people must move off the island. (I: YA)

*Uchida, Yoshiko. *The Bracelet*. Illustrated by Joanna Yardley. Philomel, 1993. Sent away to an internment camp during World War II, a young Japanese American girl discovers the power of memory. (I: 7–11)

———. *A Jar of Dreams*. Macmillan, 1981. Faced with prejudice against Japanese in the 1930s in California, Rinko wants to be as American as possible. When Aunt Waka visits from Japan, Rinko begins to understand the strength of her family and the Japanese American community. Related titles are *The Best Bad Thing* (1983) and *The Happiest Ending* (1985). (I: 9–11)

———. *Journey Home*. Atheneum, 1978. A Japanese American family returns from an internment camp to try and rebuild their lives in California. (I: 10–12)

———. *Journey to Topaz*. Creative Arts, 1988. A Japanese American family is sent away to an internment camp when World War II breaks out. (I: 10–12)

*Wild, Margaret. *Let the Celebrations Begin!* Illustrated by Julie Vivas. Orchard, 1991. A young girl in a Nazi concentration camp makes toys for the children in the camp. (I: 9–12)

Yep, Laurence. *Hiroshima*. Scholastic, 1995. The story of Sachi and the day the atomic bomb was dropped on her city of Hiroshima. (I: 10–12)

The Mid-Twentieth Century

Choi, Sook Nyul. *The Year of Impossible Goodbyes*. Dell, 1991/1993. When the war ends in Korea, the

Russians take over the northern half of the country, forcing Sookan and her family to flee to the south. Sequels are *Echoes of the White Giraffe* (1993) and *Gathering of Pearls* (1994). (I: 10–YA)

*Coleman, Evelyn. *White Socks Only.* Illustrated by Tyrone Geter. Albert Whitman, 1996. Grandma tells the story about her first trip alone into town during the days when segregation still existed in Mississippi. (I: 6–10)

Curtis, Christopher Paul. *The Watsons Go to Birmingham—1963.* Delacorte, 1995. An African American family from Detroit visits in Birmingham in 1963, the summer of the fateful church bombing that set the civil rights movement in motion. (I: 10–12)

English, Karen. *Francie.* Farrar, 1999. Francie longs for the time when she and her family can leave behind their life in Noble, Alabama, and all the prejudices and hardships it holds for African Americans. (I: 10 and up)

Ho, Minfong. *The Clay Marble.* Farrar, 1991. Dara's family is forced from their home in war-torn Cambodia only to be again embroiled in war in a refugee camp on the Thai border. (I: 10–12)

———. *Rice without Rain.* Lothrop, 1990. As Jinda and her family struggle to survive the drought that has hit Thailand, strangers from the city seem to offer a way to survive, but soon Jinda and her family are caught up in the turbulence of the 1945 student movement. (I: YA)

Holt, Kimberly Willis. *My Louisiana Sky.* Holt, 1998. After her Granny dies, Tiger Ann Parker wants to live with her aunt in Baton Rouge, leaving behind her mentally deficient parents in Saitter, Louisiana. Only when a hurricane strikes Saitter does Tiger Ann recognize the importance of family and home. (I: 10–14)

———. *When Zachary Beaver Came to Town.* Holt, 1999. Toby is having a hard summer, with his mother having left for Nashville and his best friend's brother in Vietnam. Then, when the "fattest boy in the world" comes to his small Texas town, Toby's summer becomes like no other he has ever known. (I: 10–13)

Laird, Elizabeth. *Kiss the Dust.* Penguin Putnam, 1991/1994. A Kurd family is driven from their home in Iraq to a harsh life in a refugee camp in Iran. (I: 10–YA)

Naidoo, Beverley. *Journey to Jo'burg: A South African Story.* Illustrated by Eric Velasquez. HarperCollins, 1987. A brother and sister are caught up in the cruelty of apartheid when they journey to Johannesburg to find their mother. (I: 10–12)

Nelson, Vaunda Micheaux. *Mayfield Crossing.* Putnam, 1993. When the school at Mayfield Crossing closes, Meg and her friends must learn to deal with the prejudice they encounter at their new school. (I: 8–12)

Robinet, Harriette Gillem. *Walking to the Bus-Rider Blues.* Atheneum, 2000. It is 1956, and Alfa finds that his life as an African American boy living in Montgomery, Alabama, is shaped both by forces of prejudice and by the philosophy of the bus boycott in which his people are caught up. (I: 9–12)

Sacks, Margaret. *Themba.* Illustrated by Wil Clay. Puffin, 1994. Themba goes to the city to find his father, who has failed to return from working in the South African gold mines. (I: 6–9)

*Shea, Pegi Deitz. *The Whispering Cloth: A Refugee's Story.* Illustrated by Anita Riggio. Stitched by You Yang. Boyds Mill Press, 1994. A young Hmong refugee stitches her own story on her first "story cloth." (I: 7–11)

Taylor, Mildred. *The Gold Cadillac.* Illustrated by Michael Hays. Dial, 1987. An African American family from the North experiences prejudice when they visit the South. (I: 9–12)

RESOURCES

Beck, Cathy, Nelson-Faulkner, Shari, and Pierce, Kathryn Mitchell. "Talking about Books: Historical Fiction: Teaching Tool or Literary Experience?" *Language Arts* 77 (2000): 546–555.

Chatton, Barbara. "The Civil War, Part I: Update." *Book Links* 5.1 (1995): 42–50.

———, and Judy Parks. "The Colonial Period." *Book Links* 4.3 (1995): 44–53.

———, and Shirley Tastad. "The Depression Years." *Book Links* 2.3 (1993): 31–37.

———. "1900–1919." *Book Links* 3.4 (1994): 50–56.

Elleman, Barbara. "The Columbus Encounter—Update." *Book Links* 2.1 (1992): 31–34.

Hopkins, Lee Bennett, ed. *More Books by More People.* Citation, 1974.

Steiner, Stanley, and Linda Marie Zaerr. "The Middle Ages." *Book Links* 4.2 (November, 1994): 11–15.

Tunnell, Michael O., and Richard Ammon, eds. *The Story of Ourselves: Teaching History through Children's Literature.* Heinemann, 1993.

REFERENCES

Blos, Joan W. "Perspectives on Historical Fiction." *The Story of Ourselves: Teaching History through Children's Literature*. Ed. Michael O. Tunnell and Richard Ammon. Heinemann, 1993, pp. 11–17.

Broderick, Kathy. "The Ramsay Scallop by Frances Temple." *Book Links* 4.2 (November 1994): 19.

Conrad, Pam. "Finding Ourselves in History." *The Story of Ourselves: Teaching History through Children's Literature*. Ed. Michael O. Tunnell and Richard Ammon. Heinemann, 1993, pp. 33–38.

DeFelice, Cynthia. "The Bones beneath the Flesh of Historical Fiction." *Book Links* 8.2 (November 1998): 30–34.

Dorris, Michael. "On Writing Morning Girl." *Book Links* 4.1 (September 1992): 32–33.

Frey, Charles, and John Griffith. *The Literary Heritage of Childhood: An Appraisal of Children's Classics in the Western Tradition*. Greenwood, 1987.

Fritz, Jean. "There Once Was." *The Horn Book Magazine* (July/August 1986): 432–35.

Harris, Violet. "Historical Fact and Fiction: Using Informational Books to Provide Background for Using Multicultural Literature." Teaching for Lifelong Learning, 85th Annual Convention of the National Council of Teachers of English, San Diego, November 1995.

Levstik, Linda. "A Gift of Time: Children's Historical Fiction." *Children's Literature in the Classroom: Weaving Charlotte's Web*. Ed. Janet Hickman and Bernice E. Cullinan. Christopher-Gordon, 1989, pp. 135–45.

Ogle, Donna. "K-W-L: A Teaching Model That Develops Active Reading of Expository Text." *The Reading Teacher* 39 (1986): 564–70.

Paterson, Katherine. *Bridge to Terabithia*. HarperCollins, 1978.

———. *Jacob Have I Loved*. Ty Crowell, 1980.

———. *The Great Gilly Hopkins*. HarperTrophy, 1987.

———. *Of Nightingales That Weep*. HarperTrophy, 1989.

Rinaldi, Ann. *My Heart Is on the Ground*. Scholastic, 1999.

Scott, Sir Walter. *Ivanhoe*. Edited by Graham Tulloch. Penguin, 2000.

———. *Waverly*. Edited by Andrew Hook. Viking, 1981.

Taxel, Joel. "The American Revolution in Children's Fiction." *Research in the Teaching of English* 17 (1983): 61–83.

Temple, Frances. "Researching The Ramsay Scallop." *Book Links* 4.2 (November 1994): 18.

Tomlinson, Carl M., Michael O. Tunnell, and Donald J. Richgels. "The Content and Writing of History in Textbooks and Trade Books." *The Story of Ourselves: Teaching History through Children's Literature*. Ed. Michael O. Tunnell and Richard Ammon. Heinemann, 1993, pp. 51–62.

Tunnell, Michael O. "Unmasking the Fiction of History: Children's Historical Literature Begins to Come of Age." *The Story of Ourselves: Teaching History through Children's Literature*. Ed. Michael O. Tunnell and Richard Ammon. Heinemann, 1993, pp. 79–90.

Turner, Ann. "On Writing Katie's Trunk." *Book Links* 2.5 (May 1993): 11.

10 Modern Fantasy and Science Fiction

She [Kate] said, "Watch," and she dipped the funnel into the dish and blew through it, and out of the funnel grew the most magnificent bubble I have ever seen, iridescent, gleaming.

"Look at it from here," said Kate, intent. "Just look at the light!" And in the sunlight, all the colors in the world were swimming over that glimmering sphere—swirling, glowing, achingly beautiful. Like a dancing rainbow the bubble hung there for a long moment; then it was gone.

I thought: That's fantasy.

I said: "I wish they didn't have to vanish so soon."

"But you can always blow another," Kate said.

from Dreams and Wishes: Essays on Writing for Children
by Susan Cooper

T his bubble metaphor comes from fantasy writer Susan Cooper, who was sitting in her study, contemplating a description of "fantasy," when her daughter Kate entered the room. It provides a visual image that shows how fantasy takes shape when a believer makes a new creation possible. Writers of fantasy do just that—they create magnificent bubbles so achingly beautiful that readers can only marvel and enjoy.

MODERN FANTASY AND SCIENCE FICTION DEFINED

Definition of Modern Fantasy

Fantasy literature has unexplainable magic, and it is this element that captures the minds and hearts of children. According to Lynn (1989),

Fantasy has been variously described as imaginative, fanciful, visionary, strange, otherworldly, supernatural, mysterious, frightening, magical, inexplicable, wondrous, dreamlike, and, paradoxically, realistic. It has been termed an awareness of the inexplicable existence of "magic" in the everyday world, a yearning for a sudden glimpse of something strange and wonderful, and a different and perhaps truer version of reality. (p. xxi)

Jean Greenlaw (1995a) adds that fantasy literature goes beyond the known world and imaginatively creates a new or transformed world. "Nonrational phenomena" have a significant role in fantasy, as do events, settings, and creatures that don't exist in the real world. The imaginative creation must be so well crafted that readers accept the fantasy through a "willing suspension of disbelief," though this happens only when story details are totally consistent with the fantastic elements.

Fantasy extends reality into the unknown. It gives readers a way of understanding the world they live in by going beyond it for a wider, imaginative vision. Sometimes people mistakenly think that fantasy is merely an escape from the complexity of reality to a simplistic world. Rather, the world created by fantasy can "refresh . . . delight . . . give a new vision," as it artfully presents rich charac-

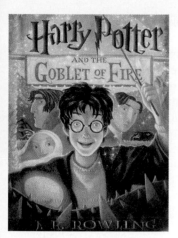

Illustration 10.1
The Triwizard Tournament pits contestants from three wizarding schools against each other in Book 4 of the *Harry Potter* series, *Harry Potter and the Goblet of Fire.* (*Harry Potter and the Goblet of Fire,* written by J. K. Rowling, illustrated by Mary Grandpre. HARRY POTTER, characters, names, and all related indicia are trademarks of Warner Bros. 2001. Reprinted by permission.)

ters and engaging and complex plots that are woven with fantastic elements (Alexander, 1971). For some readers, the strength and depth of emotion they experience as they triumph and despair along with characters go beyond what they could experience in a realistic world.

Modern fantasy falls into two major classifications: low fantasy and high fantasy. All authors who write fantasy draw on the here and now, what Lloyd Alexander calls the "primary world"—people's knowledge and experience of real life—for "raw material" (Alexander, 1971, p. 164). Low fantasy is actually set in the primary world, but the magical elements of fantasy make the story impossible. By contrast, writers of high fantasy take information and experiences from the primary world and project this information to create images and situations of a "secondary world." Authors of high fantasy create a secondary world whose concrete elements are impossible according to the logic of the primary world but consistent with its own laws. Some high fantasy stories remain totally in the created world, and some travel between that world and the primary world. Others involve a world within the primary world, marked by boundaries that keep the magic inside the created world (Tymn, Zahorski, and Boyer, 1979).

Definition of Science Fiction

Science fiction is a variety of fantasy in which an author, inspired by real developments in science, has conceived a version of reality different from the one we inhabit. Science fiction writers weave into stories and make plausible scientific concepts that are extrapolations of current scientific understandings (Greenlaw, 1995b). In short, they make readers believe the unbelievable because they convince them that it is possible.

Because works of science fiction make readers entertain possibilities that go well beyond the everyday, they have a useful role to play in educating the imagination, to borrow a phrase from the literary critic Northrop Frye (1957). The imagination, as Frye points out, is the source of all human invention. For example, people told stories about human flight for thousands of years before the Wright brothers' plane flew off a sand dune at Kitty Hawk. Humans would never have gotten off the ground if they hadn't long imagined the wonders of flight. Such imagining can be nourished by stories.

Distinction between Fantasy and Science Fiction

Greenlaw (1982) differentiates modern fantasy and science fiction this way: "Fantasy never could be. Science fiction has the possibility of being—maybe not in our time or on our planet, but the possibility of happening within some time and in some place" (p. 64). In other words, a story that is clearly impossible is called fantasy; a story with aspects of the improbable is called science fiction. The possibility that someday an invention or new knowledge could make the seemingly improbable possible distinguishes science fiction from other forms of fantasy. In 1869, Jules Verne wrote **Twenty Thousand Leagues under the Sea.** The idea of a submarine obviously existed in Verne's imagination, but no real submarine had yet been built. A submarine might have seemed improbable at the time, but as it turned out, it was very possible.

At times, it is difficult to make a clear distinction between science fiction and fantasy because certain books have characteristics of both genres. These hybrid books may present details purported to have scientific bases, yet also include elements that make the story clearly impossible. The result is a type of science fiction called "science fantasy." Science fantasy includes elements that were previously considered traditional in high fantasy (such as dragons, wizards, and fairies) as well as elements that are traditional in science fiction (space travel or interplanetary exploration). Science fantasy begins with an extrapolation based on scientific understanding, but the story is predominantly a fantasy.

We will discuss modern fantasy in the first half of this chapter and science fiction in the second half. This parallel structure will allow a more focused look at each genre.

THE EVOLUTION OF MODERN FANTASY

Myths, legends, and folktales are predecessors of the modern genres of fantasy and science fiction. For centuries, the oral tradition of storytelling passed along many tales of magical beings, fantastic occurrences, and imaginative places. The beginning of modern fantasy as a genre is traced to the nineteenth century, when stories that later became known as literary fairy tales were created in the style of stories from the oral tradition. These literary fairy tales included features of works from traditional folklore: generic settings in kingdoms far away in a distant time "long, long ago," one-dimensional stock characters, magical elements, and, quite often, happy endings. Unlike stories from the oral tradition, however, literary fairy tales have known authors. Notable examples are the works created by Hans Christian Andersen in the mid-nineteenth century. For example, in Andersen's "The Princess and the Pea," these elements of folklore are present: the setting in a time period described simply as "there once was . . . ," the stock characters of a prince and a princess, the magical way in which the princess felt the pea through layers and layers of mattresses, and the "lived happily ever after" ending.

Several nineteenth-century British writers turned their attention to creating fantasy for children. Many of these early works are now considered classics and are still enjoyed by today's children. *Alice's Adventures in Wonderland,* written by Charles Lutwidge Dodgson and published in 1865 under the pseudonym Lewis Carroll, was regarded as representing a turning point in writing for children because it was written with humor and imagination rather than with a didactic purpose. In the story, Alice falls into a rabbit hole and enters a fantastic world—a world that demands a sense of humor and an imaginative mind. Another early work of fantasy is George MacDonald's *At the Back of the North Wind,* published in 1871, about a boy who was swept off to an imaginary land where he has adventures with a cab-horse. Published in 1894, Rudyard Kipling's *The Jungle Book* is the story of Mowgli, a human child left in the jungle, raised by wolves, and nurtured by the wisdom of a bear, a python, and a panther.

J. M. Barrie's play *Peter and Wendy* had a large impact on fantasy for children when it was published in 1904; it was re-published in 1911 as *Peter Pan.* The story of how Peter teaches three children how to fly to Never Never Land so that they will never have to grow up is still well known and loved among children. Beatrix Potter is another early genius of the fantasy genre. Her childhood study of animals led to a thorough understanding of them and enabled her to draw and write imaginative stories that somehow seemed true to the animals' natures. Beginning in 1902 with the publication of *The Tale of Peter Rabbit,* Potter created a series of "little books," each featuring a different animal character. Another milestone book about personified animals, the *Wind in the Willows,* was created in 1908 by British writer Kenneth Grahame. In this series of stories depicting day-to-day events, woodland animals bond in complex friendships that reflect the trials and rewards human beings experience. In 1926, A. A. Milne created **Winnie-the-Pooh,** a classic story of personified toy animals. Milne gave a clear description of the personality of each character—Pooh, Eeyore, Tigger, Piglet, Owl, Kanga, and Roo—and young readers find the predictability of their words and actions in various circumstances reassuring.

Other lighthearted fantasies written in the first half of this century include Hugh Lofting's **The Story of Doctor Dolittle** in 1920 and P. L. Travers's **Mary Poppins** in 1934. Doctor Dolittle is an animal doctor who sets off with his dog, duck, pig, parrot, and owl to cure monkeys in Africa of a disease. In Travers's book, a seemingly prim and proper nanny named Mary Poppins enters the Banks household, and her arrival "on the East Wind" foreshadows the magical adventures ahead for the two children.

Fantasy literature was also being published in other European countries. Carlo Collodi's personified toy story **The Adventures of Pinocchio** was published in Italy in 1881. Children are still intrigued by this story of a lonely man who carves a marionette that comes to life and becomes his little boy. Young readers can relate to the choices that Pinocchio must learn to make: to do what is expected by parents, not to be enticed by strangers who offer tempting alternatives, and to tell the truth. The two-volume edition of **The Wonderful Adventures of Nils** (1906–1907), by Selma Lagerlöf, was originally published as a geography primer for Swedish children. The story became a classic when it was translated into other languages; children around the world were enchanted by the story of how Nils Holgersson became elf-sized and traveled all over Sweden on the back of a goose. In 1937, with **Babar,** France's Jean de Brunhoff began a series of stories recounting the adventures of an elephant named Babar and his family. Tove Jansson's **Finn Family Moomintroll** was the first in a series of humorous books published during the 1940s and 1950s in Finland about the Moomins, imaginary troll-like creatures living amidst magical powers. In Sweden in 1945, Astrid Lindgren published **Pippi Longstocking,** a fantasy featuring an eccentric protagonist: a little girl who lives her life in such an uncharacteristic way that children who read of her adventures are fascinated by the possibility that a child like that might exist. Pippi is a nine-year-old who does as she pleases whenever she wants to because she lives alone with no adults to supervise her activities. Mary Norton's **The Borrowers,** a story of a family of "little people" who live by "borrowing" everyday objects from humans, was published in England in 1953. This popular book was the start of a series about the Borrowers.

The first modern fantasy for children published in the United States was **The Wonderful Wizard of Oz,** created by Frank Baum in 1900. Baum created thirteen more volumes about Oz. They were so immensely popular that, after his death in 1919, his publisher hired Ruth Plumly Thompson to write nineteen more stories to satisfy the appetite of readers who loved the world of Oz.

Robert Lawson won the 1945 Newbery Medal for his personified animal story **Rabbit Hill.** The story centers around animals in the Connecticut countryside where Father and Mother Rabbit and Little Georgie live. The rumor is that new folks are coming to live in the big house, and all the animals who live in the surrounding area wonder what this will mean to them—how will they be treated?

A few years later, in 1952, E. B. White published a book that was to become a favorite of children in the United States and other countries. **Charlotte's Web** tells the story of Wilbur, a runt pig who is rescued from slaughter and then catapulted into fame by Charlotte, a kind spider who spins words of praise for Wilbur in her web.

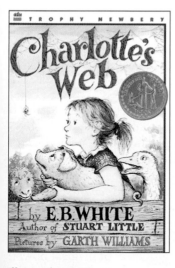

Illustration 10.2

The life of a shy runt pig is saved through the efforts of a clever, articulate spider named Charlotte in this extraordinarily popular animal fantasy by E. B. White. (*Charlotte's Web* by E. B. White, illustrated by Garth Williams. Copyright © 1999. Used by permission of HarperCollins Juvenile Books, a division of HarperCollins Publishers.)

Low fantasy stories are particularly prevalent in picture book format. Currently, authors such as Kevin Henkes, Rosemary Wells, Susan Meddaugh, and Lisa Campbell Ernst are producing high-quality picture book fantasies. Their work is discussed in more detail later in this chapter.

The mid-twentieth century marked the beginning of the publication of high fantasy series for children. J. R. R. Tolkien published *The Hobbit,* the first book in his popular series, in 1937. *The Chronicles of Narnia* is a seven-volume series published between 1950 and 1956 by C. S. Lewis, who wove Christian allegories throughout his stories set in the fantasy world of Narnia. *The Chronicles of Prydain,* a high fantasy series by Lloyd Alexander, began in 1964 with the publication of *The Book of Three.* Robin McKinley's quest fantasy *The Hero and the Crown* was published in 1984 and won the Newbery Medal in 1985. It was almost unique among high fantasy books because it featured a female protagonist. One of the newer high fantasy series is Brian Jacques's *Redwall* series, whose first volume was published in England in 1987. Philip Pullman's *Dark Materials* trilogy started with *The Golden Compass,* published in 1996, and ended with *The Amber Spylass,* published in 2000.

Fantasy reading at the beginning of the twenty-first century is marked by extraordinary levels of readership and fervor. The most popular series of the 1990s was R. L. Stine's *Goosebumps;* although the literary quality of most of the books does not match that of others listed in this section, the addictive reading behavior the series created in a large sector of the elementary school population cannot be overlooked. The publication of J. K. Rowling's *Harry Potter* books marks a phenomenon perhaps unequaled by any previously published books for children. With the first book, *Harry Potter and the Sorcerer's Stone,* readers—both children and adults—were hooked, and the promise of seven books in the series led to record-high levels of excitement and sales. All of this means that more people are reading and discussing fantasy than ever before.

CATEGORIES OF MODERN FANTASY

This section examines several categories of fantasy. However, as Egoff (1988) has pointed out, good literature "can never be fitted into one sterile slot." Some books fit into multiple genres. For example, Jane Yolen's *The Devil's Arithmetic* can be considered historical fiction because it is set mainly during the Holocaust; yet it might also be considered modern fantasy because the book's protagonist travels through time. Gail Carson Levine's *Ella Enchanted* is based on the fairy tale of Cinderella, yet it is a fully developed fantasy that goes far beyond the traditional tale. Even within the genre of fantasy, books can be placed in more than one category. For example, in Jon Scieszka's *Time Warp Trio* series, each story concerns a time slip, yet each begins with an object of magical power: a book. Further, authors are increasingly including elements of science fiction with fantasy. For example, works of T. A. Barron use elements of science fiction, mythology, and fantasy. Although it is hard to put books into neat categories, trying to do so allows for interesting comparisons.

Low Fantasy

Low fantasy features nonrational events that occur without explanation in the real world. Low fantasy is also known as light fantasy, for the tone is usually rather lighthearted, often humorous. Children typically read low fantasy at a younger age and tend to read more low fantasy than high fantasy overall. The forms of low fantasy include stories about personified animals, personified toys, outlandish characters and humorous situations, magical powers, extraordinary worlds, supernatural elements, and time slips. These forms are discussed here in the order in which children are likely to be introduced to them, which corresponds roughly to young readers' increasingly higher levels of engagement in the fantasy elements.

Personified Animals. Stories with animals talking and behaving as humans do are often called personified animal fantasies. Typically, this is the first type of fantasy book that young children encounter. Animal characters who behave like humans are said to be anthropomorphic. There are many picture books and even a number of novels about personified animals. In fact, many picture books for young children contain personified animals as characters, yet the situations they face are quite realistic to the children who read such books.

Lois Lowry's *Stay! Keeper's Story* begins, "I needed a child." Keeper, a dog, continues with an explanation of behaviors adults impose on their dogs (like insisting that dogs like to sleep in a cage or on a flea-retardant bed with cedar shavings) and how a child would better understand what a dog wants: "Dogs prefer to sleep snuggled right up beside a human, their heads on a feather pillow, with ears nicely spread out and the rest of the body curled on an innerspring mattress covered by percale sheets smelling of human breath and sweat." In stories like this, the dog's behavior is doglike, but his ability to have and to express thoughts in human language makes this book a fantasy.

Beatrix Potter's many personified animals may be among the first fantasy characters children are introduced to. In *The Tale of Peter Rabbit,* Potter mixes behaviors typical of rabbits with behaviors of humans. Peter and his family live in a sand bank underneath the roots of a tree, play in the fields, eat garden vegetables, and hop away from danger—all rabbitlike behaviors. But Mrs. Rabbit talks to her children using words, and the rabbits wear clothing and drink chamomile tea—all human behaviors. Kevin Henkes has written and illustrated many stories about personified mice. Sheila Rae, the brave older sister who suddenly panics and relies on the wits of her younger sister in *Sheila Rae, the Brave,* and Chester and Wilson, whose particular ways of doing things are disrupted by Lilly's move into the neighborhood in *Chester's Way,* are all mice. However, they not only behave like people but think like them, too. As children get older, they may encounter William Steig's personified animals. In *Doctor De Soto,* a fox gets a toothache and seeks the help of a dentist who is a mouse.

In Avi's book of personified animals *Poppy,* a deer mouse, tries to convince her family to move close to a large cornfield because it could provide food for them forever. This move is thwarted when the tyrannical great horned owl, Mr. Ocax, refuses to give his consent. An unlikely group of personified animals interacts in Cynthia Rylant's *Gooseberry Park.* A Labrador retriever named Kona befriends Stumpy, a squirrel in Gooseberry Park. When Stumpy is separated from her babies during an ice storm, a bat named Murray and a hermit crab named Gwendolyn team up with Kona to reunite the newborns with their mother.

Several popular stories about personified animals center around a community of animals. *Charlotte's Web* by E. B. White is one immensely popular example. When Wilbur is about to be slaughtered as the runt of the litter, he is rescued by a little girl, Fern. However, it is Charlotte, a spider, who calls the entire cast of barnyard animals into action to truly save Wilbur's life. British writer Dick King-Smith created the fantasy stories *Pigs Might Fly, Babe: The Gallant Pig,* and

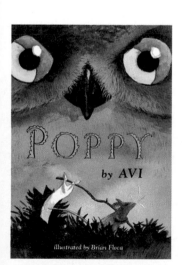

Illustration 10.3
The situations in which the characters in *Poppy* find themselves are set in the animal world, but the solutions arise out of thoughts and behaviors that are quite human. (A cover from *Poppy* by Avi, cover illustration by Brian Floca. Published by Orchard Books, an imprint of Scholastic Inc. Cover illustration copyright © 1995 by Peter Brian Floca. Reprinted by permission.)

Ace: The Very Important Pig. As in E. B. White's books, the barnyard animals in King-Smith's stories become the community within which the story takes place. *The Wind in the Willows,* by Kenneth Grahame, also features a community of animals. The four good friends—Ratty, Mole, Badger, and Toad—are animals with strong personal characteristics that define their roles. George Selden's *The Cricket in Times Square* is about a community of city-dwelling animals; other books in the series center on the same animals' visits to the country.

Personified Toys. Another type of fantasy that children enjoy features personified toys (as well as other inanimate objects) that come to life. In these books, toys are able to talk and behave like humans. The toys that come to life are typically stuffed animals or dolls. The reason may be that when children play, they frequently pretend that stuffed animals and dolls have human attributes.

Perhaps the best-known personified toy story is A. A. Milne's classic work *Winnie-the-Pooh.* The story was inspired by Milne's son, Christopher Robin, and his collection of stuffed animals.

The Castle in the Attic, by Elizabeth Winthrop, is a personified toy story in which a finger-high knight in a model castle comes alive when William, the young protagonist, picks him up. Lynne Reid Banks's *The Indian in the Cupboard* and its sequels are popular among children. A toy Indian and other toys come alive when Omri puts them in a magical cupboard. Having toys come alive, seeing the unfolding adventure as the toys engage in lifelike situations, and realizing what responsibility means are all part of the drama Omri and his friend Patrick experience. Although these popular books sensitively answer the question "What if toys came alive?," the toy people in them do not rise above stereotypes of Indians and cowboys, and the portrayal of the Indian is particularly problematic.

Pam Conrad's picture books about the escapades of a family of bathtub toys—consisting of Father, Mother, Grandmother, Grandfather, Child, and Dog—are quite believable. The events that the toy family experiences in *The Tub People* and *The Tub Grandfather*—Tub Child being lost down the drain when the bathwater is let out, Tub Grandfather being discovered under the radiator with layers of dust from having been lost a long time—are likely events in toys' "lives." The toys' thoughts, actions, and speech in these realistic situations are believable because they reflect how humans might think, act, and speak under similar circumstances. Richard Egielski's illustrations depict the tub people as realistic wooden dolls, extending the believability of the story. Although the dolls maintain stiff poses, they clearly express the emotions of the characters.

Illustration 10.4
A clash of generations occurs in the doll world when a hundred-year-old doll family meets a modern plastic doll family. (*The Doll People* by Laura Godwin. Copyright © 2000 Laura Godwin. Illustrations copyright © 2000 Brian Selznick. Reprinted by permission of Hyperion Books for Children.)

Ann Martin and Laura Godwin teamed up to create *The Doll People,* in which a hundred-year-old doll family is brought from England to America and passed down through the generations to the current owner, Kate. Eight-year-old Anabelle is a doll who reads her Aunt Sarah's journal and becomes obsessed with the need to solve the mystery of her aunt's disappearance in 1955. Humorous clashes of the ages come about with the arrival of a plastic family next door, with modern amenities such as a microwave oven. Illustrations by Brian Selznick throughout the book keep readers engagingly immersed in the doll world.

Outlandish Characters and Situations. Stories that appear to be realistic fiction but have characters who behave in outrageous, highly exaggerated ways are classified as fantasy with outlandish characters. These characters may possess abilities that are outside the range of normal human behavior or act in eccentric ways.

P. L. Travers created a series of stories about a character with magical abilities. The first of these was *Mary Poppins,* in which the unusual nanny arrives at the home of Jane and Michael Banks by way of an umbrella that carries her airborne on a gust of wind.

Swedish writer Astrid Lindgren is known around the world as the creator of *Pippi Longstocking* and two sequels, as well as more than a hundred other books. Pippi lives alone, without any adult supervision, and displays outrageous and eccentric behavior that keeps the neighborhood children constantly amused.

Magical Powers. The notion that magic might exist is an intriguing thought to children: Could there be sayings that make magical things happen, objects that hold magical powers, or other ways of bringing about magical events?

What could be more enticing than the dream that a better life than the one we live is owed to us and that we have magical powers? In J. K. Rowling's *Harry Potter and the Sorcerer's Stone,* Harry's existence is so lowly that readers could not recognize it as a "fair life." On the eve of his eleventh birthday, he receives an invitation to Hogwarts School of Witchcraft and Wizardry—and the news that he is the most famous wizard alive! Magical events abound throughout the *Harry Potter* books, and somehow all seem believable to the reader.

Natalie Babbitt's *Tuck Everlasting* has the ultimate magic in it: a spring that gives eternal life to those who drink from it. The source of this water is not explained, nor does the story offer an explanation of how it gives eternal life. All readers know is the consequences of drinking from the spring.

In *Lizard Music,* Daniel Pinkwater tells a humorous story of Victor, who discovers a mysterious band of lizards playing outrageous music on television late at night. A mysterious Chicken Man and his hen Claudia guide Victor to an invisible island—past the force field, under a deep-water barrier—to meet the music-playing lizards.

In William Steig's picture book *Sylvester and the Magic Pebble,* Sylvester is portrayed as a donkey who comes across a special pebble for his pebble collection—one that grants wishes. The problem arises when Sylvester wishes to turn into a rock temporarily to escape trouble but cannot revert back to being a donkey. This story of personified animals includes elements of magic.

Embellished Fairy Tales. In recent years, many fairy tales have been embellished with rich character development, detailed descriptions of setting, and finely developed plot, presenting a fuller story than the original traditional tales offered. In many cases, they answer questions provoked by the original tale: Why was Rumpelstiltskin interested in the miller's daughter's child? Why was Rapunzel's mother so loving yet cruel in locking her daughter up? Why did Jack trade a cow for a handful of magic beans? In almost all cases, the expanded versions remain true to the essential components of the original tales as we know them but put a new twist or offer a new perspective to readers.

In Gail Carson Levine's *Ella Enchanted,* a gift of "obedience" is bestowed on Ella by the fairy Lucinda, and it turns out to be a curse rather than a blessing. The story explores what happens when a child must be obedient, even against her own will. Robin McKinley offers readers two books based on Beauty and the Beast: *Beauty* and *Rose Daughter.* Published twenty years apart, the books have certain details that remain consistent, yet they offer two different stories based on the same essential framework.

The most prolific author in this category is Donna Jo Napoli, who began exploring the embellishment of fairy tales with the publication of *The Magic Circle,* in which she explores the witch's perspective on the Hansel and Gretel story. In *Zel,* she considers three perspectives on the Rapunzel story: those of the thirteen-year-old peasant daughter Zel, the nobleman who falls in love with her and wants to marry her, and the mother—who turns out to be a witch with a motive for locking up her daughter. Napoli continued her frog-turned-prince story, *Prince of the Pond,* in *Jimmy, the Pickpocket of the Palace.* When Jimmy, the frog son of a frog prince, shows up at the palace with a hurt leg, a princess kisses it. In keeping with the fairy tale story of the frog prince, Jimmy turns into a human. Searching for a magic ring that will convert him into a frog again so that he can save his pond from an evil hag, he leaves himself open to accusations of theft. Books like these offer readers opportunities to ponder what other known stories offer possibilities for embellishment.

Extraordinary Worlds. The first task of an author who creates a world that is very different from the one in which we live is to make it believable to readers. Sometimes a story begins with convincing characters in the known world who then move into an extraordinary world through various devices. For example, when Milo enters the mysterious tollbooth in Norton Juster's popular novel *The Phantom Tollbooth,* he finds an extraordinary world. In Roald Dahl's *Charlie and the Chocolate Factory,* the search for gold tickets hidden in chocolate bars takes place in the real world, but an invitation to enter a mysterious chocolate factory leads a selected few into an extraordinary world. In *Alice's Adventures in Wonderland,* Alice, a seemingly ordinary child, falls into a rabbit hole and finds an extraordinary world at the other end. In Eloise McGraw's *The Moorchild,* the human world and the "folk world" coexist side by side; the folk world is accessible only to folk, but folk can move in and out of the human world.

Other stories are set entirely in an extraordinary world. What makes the extraordinary world believable in Mary Norton's *The Borrowers* is the author's careful attention to the smallest of details when describing how the tiny Borrowers adapt various everyday human-size objects to their own uses.

Supernatural Elements. Scary stories with supernatural elements—ghosts, haunted houses, and the like—intrigue children. Margaret Mahy tells the story of a family with psychic powers in *The Haunting.* The family members struggle with what these powers do to their relationships with one another. Pam Conrad's *Stonewords* tells about Zoe, who is visited by the ghost of Zoe Louise. Zoe realizes that she must prevent Zoe Louise's untimely death, and to do so she must go back in time and change the course of events. In Mary Downing Hahn's *Wait till Helen Comes,* the ghost of Helen, who died years ago, waits by the pond to drown other children her age in hopes of getting a playmate. Molly must save her new stepsister from joining Helen.

Books with supernatural elements are not necessarily scary. Supernatural elements are taken in stride in stories such as Franny Billingsley's *The Folk Keeper.*

Among the most popular books with children today are stories that can be classified as fantasies with supernatural elements. Many children eagerly seek out these "horror stories" and "scary stories." The most popular series of the 1990s was R. L. Stine's *Goosebumps,* with over fifty titles. Though they vary, typically such books are of questionable literary quality.

Time Slips. In time-slip stories, characters move from one time period to another. This element of time travel allows the author to explore themes in ways

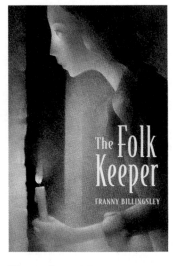

Illustration 10.5
In *The Folk Keeper,* Corinna assumes a male identity in order to take on the dangerous role of keeping the "folk" from wreaking havoc in the land. (*The Folk Keeper* by Franny Billingsley. Copyright © 1989 by Franny Billingsley. Used by permission of Atheneum Books for Young Readers, an imprint of Simon & Schuster Children's Publishing.)

not possible in stories that take place in a single time period. Typically, the time slips allow the characters to develop an understanding that enhances their development. Barbara Elleman (1985, p. 1407) notes that "time-slip plots often center on a particular historical period, a mystery that needs to be solved, or a common problem shared across generations." Going back in time allows characters to gain firsthand experience that deepens understanding of how historical events influence the present. Time slips in mysteries allow characters to find the clues to solve the mysteries. Sometimes, issues span generations, and in some time-slip stories, the protagonist finds ways to cope with issues by meeting others who have faced them in an earlier time. In *Tom's Midnight Garden,* Philippa Pearce tells the story of a boy who is bored with his summer until he discovers that when the grandfather clock strikes thirteen, he can enter the garden and play with a child from the past.

Jon Scieszka has written a series of books about three boys who make up the Time Warp Trio: *Knights of the Kitchen Table; The Not-So-Jolly Roger; The Good, the Bad, and the Goofy; Your Mother Was a Neanderthal; 2095; Tut, Tut;* and *Summer Reading Will Kill You.* The device that allows the boys to travel in time is a magical object, "The Book," which Joe receives as a birthday present from his uncle, a magician. When Joe and his two friends, Fred and Sam, open the book, they are whisked off to a different place and time—the medieval days of King Arthur, the days of pirates and buried treasure, the nineteenth century in the Old West, the Stone Age, the twenty-first century, or ancient Egypt.

Belinda Hurmence's *A Girl Called Boy* and Jane Yolen's *The Devil's Arithmetic* are time-slip stories as well as works of historical fiction. In both, the protagonists question what they believe to be excessive pride in heritage and an almost obsessive need to remember the past. In *A Girl Called Boy,* Blanche ("Boy") is transported back to the days of African American slavery. In *The Devil's Arithmetic,* Hannah is transported to the time of the Holocaust. Both return to the present with a deeper understanding of themselves as descendants of a particular heritage and a commitment not to forget the past. In another work of historical fiction and time slip, *King of Shadows,* Susan Cooper explores the days of Shakespeare. As Nat Fields acts out his role as Puck in "The Midsummer Night's Dream," both in the present day and with Will Shakespeare himself, Nat's present-day character comes to terms with his father's death through the relationship he has with Will Shakespeare in the past time period. The device of the time slip also allows readers to see the past through a present-day character's eyes, with explanations that clarify the differences.

Two other books have protagonists whose travel back in time allows them to explore their relationships with their parents. In Cynthia Voigt's *Building Blocks,* Brann is frustrated with his father and cannot understand him. When Brann creates a fortress with his father's childhood building blocks and enters it, he finds himself transported to the time of his father's childhood. In Canadian author Kit Pearson's *A Handful of Time,* a twelve-year-old girl finds an old watch under the floor while visiting her cousins. The watch takes her back to the time when her mother was the same age.

High Fantasy

As we mentioned earlier, high fantasy takes place in a created secondary world. Although much high fantasy is enjoyed by young adults, many middle school students and some elementary school readers are attracted to works of high fantasy. There are various categories of high fantasy: myth fantasy, gothic fantasy, epic/heroic fantasy, and sword and sorcery fantasy. Myth fantasy can be retellings of old myths, modern adaptations of old myths, or new inventions. Gothic fantasy includes elements such as fear of the unknown and the unnatural. Epic/heroic fantasy tries to re-create the world of the medieval epic and romance. Such fantasies are grand in their design and often have a strong emotional impact on readers. Heroic actions stem from the protagonist's commitment to serve "the common good." In many ways closely related to legends from the oral tradition, epic/hero fantasies often contain components of Arthurian, Welsh, Scandinavian, or other myths and legends. Sword and sorcery fantasy is similar to heroic fantasy. However, sword and sorcery fantasy is not to be confused with the "sword and sinew subgenre," which violates many of the characteristics of high fantasy. That subgenre includes a barbarian superhero, has much action, lacks thematic substance, uses a colloquial style of language, and sensationalizes violence (Egoff, 1988; Tymn, Zahorski, and Boyer, 1979).

Heroic romance is a form of high fantasy that draws from mythology and includes stories of heroes and worlds of great power. Alexander (1971) has called heroic romance a "cauldron of story" in which is found a "mythological mine-strone" that combines real history with imaginary history. Included is an array of characters, events, and situations—quests, tasks, swords, dragons, and other elements of heroic romance. Because fantasy is written on many levels, Alexander suggests that readers may "ladle up whatever suits (their) taste" and "digest it, assimilate it" as thoroughly as possible.

Tymn, Zahorski, and Boyer (1979) characterize high fantasy as having "noble characters, archetypes, and elevated style." The focus on morality in high fantasy requires a hero who is compassionate, courageous, and humane and who accomplishes many good deeds. The hero is often a representative human being, "Everyman," who may be a commoner-hero or a morally ambivalent hero. The commoner-hero is at first reluctant to become involved in the events that are unfolding but proves courageous, loyal, and generous. The morally ambivalent hero is basically good but is more concerned with maintaining independence and individuality. The imagery for the created world is often supported by the elevated speaking style of noble characters. The themes that are explored in high fantasies usually appear unrelated to personal concerns. They are generally universal and focus on an all-out struggle between good and evil in which entire worlds are at stake. These other worlds tend to be reminiscent of medieval worlds; Tolkien's Middle-Earth, Alexander's Prydain, and Lewis's Narnia are just a few. Authors of high fantasy often provide readers with a detailed map of the lands in the secondary world.

Lloyd Alexander (1978, p. 442) classifies the plots in high fantasy into five categories:

- Tests of identity, endurance, and character
- Tasks, imposed or undertaken voluntarily
- Quests for marvelous objects or animals
- Escapes from death, through disguise or substitution or with help
- Journeys to other lands or worlds

Sometimes authors combine two or more of the five plot categories, either in one book or in a series of books. Although a work of high fantasy presents an impossible world, the "undercurrent of rationality" makes the story believable. The universal vitality of fantasy is timeless and eternal (Alexander, 1971).

HOW FANTASY WORKS

Asked why anyone reads or writes fantasy, author Susan Cooper (1981) explained that fantasy goes one stage beyond realism in requiring complete intellectual surrender. Fantasy asks more of readers, and the best works of fantasy may offer readers more. She argues that the escape so often attributed to fantasy is indeed offered, but it is an inward rather than an outward escape, as readers learn to discover themselves. Cooper suggests that by going beyond the time and space of the known world, readers allow themselves to enter a dreamlike world that contains accumulated images and emotions of the human race.

Although different authors have their own thoughts on what makes a work fantasy, a number of generalizations can be made. First, fantasy includes literary elements that are characteristic of good literature, but one or more of these elements are transformed by the author into something magical or not possible in the known world. Fantasy is made believable by the consistent use of logic or laws of the created world and descriptive detail. The fantasy element cannot be brought out suddenly to magically solve problems. Whatever element makes the story a fantasy must be an integral part of the story, and all details must be consistent with that element. Fantasy is not an escape from reality, but a mirror in which reality is reflected and extended in the imagination. Finally, fantasy occurs in a secondary world created by the author, in the real world (the primary world) but with changed rules of logic, or in both worlds.

When reading fantasy, we accept the impossible by suspending disbelief. We know that donkeys cannot turn into rocks, little people do not live under the floor, and inquisitive girls do not go down rabbit holes. Those things simply don't happen. But if the author has done a good job, the power of the story is such that we suspend disbelief to find out what happens next. If at any time the author misses a detail and leaves the reader wondering about the inconsistency, the reader is apt to drop out, losing interest in what happens because he or she hasn't been convinced that the story could happen. Authors engage readers in fantasy by anchoring stories in plausibility.

Authors use a combination of devices in making the fantasy elements of a story believable to readers (Shapiro, 1996):

1. Many authors firmly ground a story in reality before gradually moving into fantasy. In other words, they begin the story in the primary world and move into the secondary world.

2. Authors have one of the characters mirror the disbelief of the reader. The narrator or protagonist reassures readers that the fantastic events are normal or real. When a believable character who initially doubted the fantasy is convinced, readers are likewise convinced.

3. Details of setting are an integral part of the story. Good authors make details so vivid that readers can see, hear, and feel the setting as they read the description.

4. Authors use consistent and distinct language for each character or group.

5. In some stories, something from the fantastic world is brought back to the real world to make a connection between the two worlds.

6. The plot has internal consistency and logic.

ISSUE TO CONSIDER

Can reading fantasy be inappropriate for children?

Fantasy literature has often been the subject of controversy. Some adults do not consider children capable of distinguishing between reality and fantasy, even though school curricula often state (and psychological studies hold) that children in the primary grades should be able to make that distinction. Others worry that fantasy is a genre that allows an escape from reality and that reading works of fantasy takes time away from more important kinds of reading that children need to be doing. Still others complain that fantasy literature is inappropriate for children because it refers to the supernatural.

In recent years, parents and others in some communities have opposed the reading of fantasy literature in schools and have called for censorship of certain types of books. In his experiences with such groups, school administrator Rick Traw (1996) found that the presence of magic, witchcraft, and animism caused the most concern. Traw found that even the slightest hint of the supernatural made a book appear on the list of censored materials. For example, a reference to Halloween or a story about a city witch and a country witch might get the work into trouble.

Michael Tunnell (1994) writes about fantasy and censorship as the "double-edged sword." He believes that "fantasy is fundamentally the most important kind of story to share with [children]." He also believes that "children vicariously vent frustrations in healthy ways by subconsciously identifying with . . . heroes." In addition, Tunnell believes that fantasy gives children "a sense of hope about their ultimate abilities to succeed in the world."

What do you think?

In *Tuck Everlasting,* Natalie Babbitt grounds the story in reality by first introducing a setting, a character, and a mood that are perfectly normal in the real world. Winnie Foster, the protagonist, has lost patience with the rules of all the adults in her life and considers running away from home. She is frustrated and wants more adventure. When the plot steps into the realm of the fantastic, Winnie tries to understand how people who drink special water could possibly live forever. As Winnie struggles with the decision she must make, readers are also convinced of the power of the water. They become intrigued with Winnie's dilemma and suspend disbelief in what they rationally know is not possible; they follow Winnie into the fantasy. The author has created a story with internal consistency, and the intertwining of details about characters and plot development leaves no loose threads or contradictions.

MAJOR WRITERS OF FANTASY AND THEIR WORKS

Many writers of fantasy and their works have already been mentioned in this chapter. Here, we highlight a few authors who have made significant contributions to the genre.

Lloyd Alexander

Lloyd Alexander knew that he wanted to write from a young age. He claims that the seeds of his stories were planted by the extensive reading he did as a child, as well as the military assignments that allowed him to travel and live in Wales, Germany, and France. Alexander began his career as a writer for adults, but his fantasy stories for children have been his major literary contribution. The *Chronicles of Prydain* is among the most widely read fantasy series for children and young adults. *The Book of Three* sets the story in the created world of Prydain, in which readers meet Taran, the Assistant Pig-Keeper, who is in search of an oracular pig named Hen Wen. The evil Arawn uses inhumane tactics to fight the nobility in Prydain, and Taran leads the expedition to fight against the evil. The series continues with *The Black Cauldron, The Castle of Llyr, Taran Wanderer,* and *The High King. The Black Cauldron* was named a Newbery Honor Book in 1966, and *The High King* was awarded the Newbery Medal in 1969.

Natalie Babbitt

At age 9, Natalie Babbitt saw the illustrations in *Alice in Wonderland* and decided to become a children's book illustrator. She did so, but she is best known for her writing. Babbitt's book *The Search for Delicious* has elements of mythology and fantasy, as a twelve-year-old is sent out to seek the true meaning of the word "delicious," following a disagreement among members of the court. *Tuck Everlasting* asks whether it would be desirable to have eternal life. The Tuck family drank from a magical spring and will live forever, but they do not want to and are forced to guard the secret from normal humans by living the life of drifters. Babbitt's *The Devil's Storybook* and *The Devil's Other Storybook* are collections of short stories about the devil's efforts to recruit more members for his world.

T. A. Barron

Growing up in the Colorado mountains imbued T. A. Barron with a love of nature, which is apparent in his writing. He has traveled around the world, backpacking and experiencing a variety of lifestyles. Barron's travel experiences and his varied formal studies fuel the imagination from which he writes.

Heartlight is Barron's first book in a series about thirteen-year-old Kate. Kate searches for her grandfather, who has disappeared after inventing the means of traveling faster than light. His mission is to save the sun from extinction, and Kate's mission is to save her grandfather from evil forces that have captured him. In the second book of the series, *The Ancient One,* Kate goes with her grandfather's sister, Aunt Kate, to protest the cutting of redwood trees in Oregon. Barron creates an eerie environment that prepares readers for Kate's falling into a time tunnel that takes her back five centuries, to when the trees were young but still threatened by human greed.

Barron has written several books about Merlin. In *The Merlin Effect,* Kate joins her father on a scientific expedition off the coast of Baja California. One day at dusk, Kate disobeys her father and takes a kayak out too far; her forbidden expedition leads to an encounter with a whale and the discovery of forgotten legends involving Merlin. In *The Lost Years of Merlin,* Merlin is a young boy who has lost his memory and is searching for his identity. His journey to discover his past shows readers how he gained his magical sight and became a wizard.

The story of Merlin continues in *The Seven Songs of Merlin, The Fires of Merlin,* and *The Mirror of Merlin* and concludes with *The Wings of Merlin.*

Grace Chetwin

Grace Chetwin was born in England, lived in New Zealand for a time, and now resides on Long Island. Her works of fantasy often include elements of science fiction and are greatly influenced by European folktales—she incorporates folktale motifs and elaborates on their meaning in the course of the stories.

Chetwin's saga *Tales of Gom in the Legends of Ulm* comprises four of her best fantasies. The saga begins with **Gom on Windy Mountain.** Gom's mother disappears after giving birth to Gom, the youngest of many children. She knows that Gom is the "chosen one" who will carry on the magic for his generation, so she leaves her rune (a charm) with him. When he grows up, Gom goes off to seek his fortune because he is such an outcast—an example of a folktale motif. In the second book, **The Riddle and the Rune,** the rune provides the clue to the riddle of Gom's missing mother. In *The Crystal Stair,* Gom becomes a wizard, and in the final book, **The Starstone,** he seeks and finds a mate.

In **Jason's Seven Magical Night Rides,** Jason longs for a father. A mysterious stranger offers him rides on mythical horses, including Pegasus, Chiron the Centaur, and the Trojan Horse. This stranger serves as a teacher, helping Jason gain the strength to accept his circumstances, overcome his feelings of inadequacy, and become whole by assuming responsibility for himself.

Susan Cooper

Susan Cooper is the author of the acclaimed high fantasy series *The Dark Is Rising.* She was an established writer when she began this series, inspired by a contest. The first book in the series is **Over Sea, Under Stone.** In the second book, **The Dark Is Rising,** a 1974 Newbery Honor Book, eleven-year-old Will Stanton discovers that he is the last of the "Old Ones" and a servant of the Light. In this story, which draws on the legend of King Arthur and other British legends and myths, it is his destiny to fight evil and to protect the Light. The series continues with **Greenwitch, The Grey King,** for which Cooper received the Newbery Medal in 1976, and **Silver on the Tree,** as Will searches for the remaining Things of Power needed to fight the final rising of the Dark. Her more recent book, **King of Shadows,** is a time travel between the present day and the time of Shakespeare, four hundred years earlier. Born and educated in England, Cooper was first married to an American, who brought her to the United States, where she began her writing career. She believes that her imagination was as lonely and homesick as she was and therefore turned to fantasy as a home.

Roald Dahl

Roald Dahl's work is tremendously popular among children. Children who discover his work find themselves compelled to read one book after the other. They are delighted by his stories' irreverent voice and zany events. His portrayals of truly detestable characters—usually adults but sometimes children—powerfully engage children's emotions. For example, Dahl sometimes sets up a character, such as the grandmother in *George's Marvelous Medicine,* or a whole class of characters, such as the witches in *The Witches,* and invites readers to hate them without remorse. Not all teachers and critics are convinced that this is a healthy practice, however.

Some say that Roald Dahl's childhood influenced his writings. Born to Norwegian parents in South Wales, Dahl moved to England with his mother upon the death of his father. He entered boarding school at age 8 and was subjected to disciplinary measures bordering on torture. Dahl's early life is recounted in his book *Boy.* Perhaps his best-known book is *Charlie and the Chocolate Factory,* in which a poor boy finds a lucky golden ticket that allows him to visit Willy Wonka's Chocolate Factory and earn a chance to be Willy Wonka's successor.

Mollie Hunter

Mollie Hunter, whose full name is Maureen Mollie Hunter McIlwraith, received only the legally required minimum of formal education in her native Scotland. But her great-grandmother's songs and stories of Scottish history and Hunter's own informal study of original historical source materials added to her learning. Her love of words and natural storytelling ability, combined with her young sons' requests to create a book out of her stories, initiated her writing career. Her lifetime interest in Celtic folklore and Scottish history fueled her imagination. In Hunter's book of essays about writing for children, *Talent Is Not Enough* (1976), she states her belief that talent is only the beginning of becoming a writer—that it is life's experiences that fully develop the voice behind the story. Hunter's much-acclaimed works of fantasy include *A Stranger Came Ashore* and *The Kelpie's Pearls.*

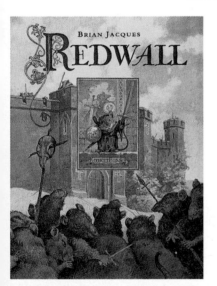

Illustration 10.6
Animals engage in action-packed quests and battles in the *Redwall* high fantasy series. (*Redwall* by Brian Jacques. Illustration copyright © 1996 by Troy Howell. Used by permission of Philomel Books, a division of Penguin Putnam Inc.)

Brian Jacques

Born in Liverpool, England, Brian Jacques became a sailor at age 15. After working as a radio broadcaster, comedian, and truck driver, Jacques wrote his first book to entertain students at a school for the blind. *Redwall,* published in 1987, began a series of fantasies about the animals living at Redwall Abbey. Since then, many other books in the *Redwall* series have been published, and they have a following of readers who are anxious to hear more about the mice, rats, and other field animals engaged in classic fantasy quests and struggles between those who are good and those who are evil. The series includes *Mossflower, Mattimeo, Mariel of Redwall, Salamandastron, Martin the Warrior, The Bellmaker, Outcast of Redwall, The Long Patrol, Marlfox,* and *The Legend of Luke.* Jacques has used his considerable talent in storytelling to create an audiotaped version of *Redwall.* In it, he narrates, and a full cast of characters engagingly tell the story (including his son, who takes on the lead voice of Martin).

Diana Wynne Jones

While studying at Oxford, Diana Wynne Jones attended lectures given by C. S. Lewis and J. R. R. Tolkien, and her classmates included Penelope Lively and Jill Paton Walsh, who also went on to become writers of fantasy literature for children. About her creation of fantasy for children, Diana Wynne Jones observes, "What I am after is an exciting and exacting wisdom, in which contemporary life and potent myth are intricately involved and superimposed" (Olendorf and Telgen, 1993, p. 116). Jones has succeeded in producing not only exciting, diverse, and wise stories but humorous ones as well. She says that, as a child, she "suffered from perpetual book starvation" and began to write. It was not until she had her own children, however, that Jones began writing for children.

Three of Jones's books won Carnegie commendations. ***Dogsbody*** is about Sirius the Dog Star, who is reborn on earth as a puppy and fulfills a mission to find the murder weapon of the stars. ***Power of Three*** is about a curse threatening the English moors and how three children and some strange creatures work together to save them. ***A Charmed Life*** is based on Jones's own unusual childhood and is the first volume in the *Chrestomanci* cycle of linked novels. The protagonist is a young boy magician who is manipulated by his sister. The other titles in the series are ***The Magicians of Caprona,*** in which the children of two feuding families make magical peace; ***Witch Week,*** which takes place in a school where the teacher suspects someone in class is a witch; and ***The Lives of Christopher Chant,*** which recounts the training of the next Chrestomanci, or controller of magic.

Some of Jones's more recent books include ***Dark Lord of Derkholm,*** which tells of a popular tourist destination, where lords and wizards role-play the parts of the dark lord and a wizard while tourists follow their fate as members of Pilgrim Parties. In the sequel, ***Year of the Griffin,*** problems at Wizard's University are destined to be straightened out in response to the havoc created by its students.

C. S. Lewis

As children in Northern Ireland, Clive Staples Lewis and his brother read many books that probably influenced their creation of books about imaginary lands. The animals Lewis made as a child for the created world of Animal-Land proved to be the predecessors to the talking animals in Narnia. At the age of 52, Lewis published the first of the seven Narnia books, ***The Lion, the Witch, and the Wardrobe.*** This book, awarded the Lewis Carroll Shelf Award in 1962, tells the story of four siblings who play in a wardrobe and find that it becomes their entryway into a magical land called Narnia. The children encounter the lion Aslan, whose purpose is to free Narnia from the spell cast by the White Witch. The Narnia stories continue in ***Prince Caspian, The Voyage of the Dawn Treader, The Silver Chair,*** and ***The Horse and His Boy. The Magician's Nephew*** was published as a prequel to the series. The end of Narnia is depicted in ***The Last Battle,*** which won the Carnegie Medal. Lewis's beliefs are embodied throughout his writing in the form of symbolism that reflects Christian allegories.

A. A. Milne

Alan Alexander Milne created personified toy stories based on the stuffed animals of his son, Christopher Robin. Children around the world have come to adore the stories in ***Winnie-the-Pooh*** and ***The House at Pooh Corner,*** which feature Winnie-the-Pooh, Piglet, Eeyore, Tigger, Kanga, Roo, and Owl, who live in the Hundred Acre Wood. Ranging from silly to serious, the interactions among the characters address the events of daily life in the woods from a child's perspective. The illustrations by Ernest H. Shepard in the *Pooh* books contribute to their charm.

Milne credits his own childhood wanderings outdoors with his brother as the source of his inspiration for the adventures these animals have. Interestingly, Milne's son Christopher resented being considered a storybook character; he felt that, contrary to the image of the storytelling father that readers meet in the books, Milne was more of an observer than a participant in his son's growing up.

Philip Pullman

Philip Pullman was born in Norwich, England, but lived in Australia and other parts of the world during his childhood. He had a childhood love of

Illustration 10.7

Lyra is an orphan who embarks on a dangerous journey to save her friends and other children from some kind of terrible experimentation. (Cover illustration by Eric Rohmann, copyright © 1996 by Eric Rohmann, from *The Golden Compass* by Philip Pullman. Used by permission of Alfred A. Knopf Children's Books, a division of Random House, Inc.)

comics, particularly Superman and Batman. He attended Exeter College in Oxford, England, and taught middle school students in Oxford for twelve years. Later, he became a lecturer at Westminster College, Oxford. Although he is now a full-time writer, he still chooses to live in Oxford, where he writes in a shed at the bottom of his garden. Pullman finds the air at Oxford to be inspirational for a writer of fantasy and believes that the ambience of the city has contributed to the fantasy-writing careers of Tolkien, Lewis, and himself. As Silvey (1995) says, "Pullman's greatest strength is his ability to weave complex and riveting plots that wrap the reader in suspense" (p. 544).

His extraordinary fantasy, the *Dark Materials* trilogy, begins with *The Golden Compass,* in which Lyra seeks to save children from scientific experiments that threaten their lives. In the second book, *The Subtle Knife,* Lyra's world extends into the Oxford of a different time; there, she meets Will, who must accept the responsibility for crossing worlds with the aid of the subtle knife. *The Amber Spyglass* closes the story of Lyra and Will, leaving them in the garden.

On his website, Pullman humorously describes two essentials to his writing: Blu-Tack and Post-it Notes. He uses Blu-Tack to stick various pictures, notes, reminders, and whatever else to the wall; and he uses sixty or more of the smallest Post-it Notes to write different scenes and move them around on large sheets of paper until he is satisfied with the order.

J. R. R. Tolkien

John Ronald Reuel Tolkien, a professor of medieval studies at Oxford, is known as one of the foremost creators of fantasy literature. Published in 1937, read by millions of children and adults, and translated into over twenty-five languages, *The Hobbit* is among the most popular of twentieth-century fantasy works written for children. For years, fans clamored for more stories about the hobbits, and in 1954 and 1955, Tolkien produced a trilogy entitled *The Lord of the Rings,* which includes *The Fellowship of the Ring, The Two Towers,* and *The Return of the King.* Based on Tolkien's thorough understanding of mythology, these books allow readers to follow the protagonist, Frodo Baggins, on a quest.

E. B. White

E. B. White wrote extensively all of his life, particularly essays and humorous adult fiction. He was a regular contributor to *The New Yorker* and numerous other magazines. Perhaps his best-known children's book is *Charlotte's Web.* This book has gained such wide popularity over the years that it is considered a classic fantasy of personified animals. Although the tone of the book is lighthearted, the themes of relationships, friendship, death, and legacy are very serious. White wrote two other books for children. *Stuart Little,* published in 1945, was his first. It is the story of a mouse, based on bedtime stories that White told his nieces and nephews. *The Trumpet of the Swan* is about a friendship between a mute swan and a young boy.

Patricia Wrede

Patricia Wrede began writing in the seventh grade and immediately had the support of her family. She would write her stories out by hand, her mother would type them, her father would read them and praise her efforts, and her four younger siblings would listen to them being read aloud. Although she continued writing as she grew older, Wrede believed that her efforts would never amount to more than a hobby. She attributes her early growth as a writer to the Scribblies, a group of friends who formed a critique group.

Wrede's entry into the world of published writers began in 1986 with an invitation to write a short story for an anthology edited by Jane Yolen. Yolen suggested that Wrede expand the story into a novel; it eventually became *Talking to Dragons,* the fourth book in the *Chronicles of the Enchanted Forest* series. In this story, Queen Cimorene sends her sixteen-year-old son to stave off evil magic in the Enchanted Forest. The *Chronicles of the Enchanted Forest* series begins with *Dealing with Dragons,* in which Princess Cimorene, bored with palace life, volunteers to become a dragon's princess to avoid an arranged marriage. She becomes embroiled in a battle with wizards, who are trying to alter the selection of the new dragon king. Next is *Searching for Dragons;* this time, Princess Cimorene teams up with Mendanbar, King of the Enchanted Forest, to try to save the forest. In *Calling on Dragons,* now-Queen Cimorene calls on friends and dragons once again to help her to save the Enchanted Forest from wizards who are soaking up its magic.

Jane Yolen

Jane Yolen is highly regarded as a writer of many genres. Although she is a former president of the Science Fiction Writers of America, she is best known for her work in the world of fantasy. She has written numerous books in the genre and has served as editor of her own imprint of fantasy books, Jane Yolen Books/ Harcourt Brace. Her books have won numerous awards and are frequently on lists of best books. Her professional book *Touch Magic: Fantasy, Faerie and Folklore in the Literature of Childhood* (Yolen, 2000) is now in its second edition and is considered a classic reference. Books in her *Commander Toad* series, such as *Commander Toad and the Voyage Home,* are notable as easy reader science fiction stories. The time-slip book *The Devil's Arithmetic* has been recognized with numerous awards, including finalist for the Nebula Award. Jane Yolen's interests and hobbies span a wide range, from kite flying to folk singing and dancing.

Other Notable Writers of Modern Fantasy

There is no way to include every noteworthy author in a section on major authors and illustrators of modern fantasy. Some noted writers of fantasy are discussed in other chapters. For example, picture book creators Kevin Henkes, Maurice Sendak, William Steig, and Chris Van Allsburg are featured in Chapter 6, and Laurence Yep and Virginia Hamilton are included in Chapter 4. Other writers of fantasy who are very popular among children include Bruce Coville, Lois Duncan, Ursula Le Guin, Tom McGowen, Tamora Pierce, and Meredith Ann Pierce, but much of their work is intended for and read predominantly by young adults.

CRITERIA FOR SELECTING MODERN FANTASY

What makes a good fantasy? The same qualities that make a good story of any kind are necessary. The author has to engage the reader with beautiful language, encourage the reader to continue to the end, and never let the reader down with a broken or unbelievable plot thread. Fantasy writers must try harder to keep a story believable because of the imaginary elements. When eval-

Ask the Author . . . *Jane Yolen*

What do you say to those who criticize your choice to write and publish fantasy books for children?

I think that fantasy books speak to reality heart to heart. They are metaphoric shorthand. No one reading them—children or adults—is fooled into believing them word for word; that is, the reader does not believe in the actuality of dragons, unicorns, flying horses. But these stories are like points on a map, acting as a guide to life as we actually live it by showing us life as it *could* be lived.

For those folks who are afraid of fantasy books, seeing Satan where none exists, I tell them that they do not understand the role of metaphor in literature. But if they persist in seeing devils and the hand of hell in these stories, I cannot change their minds. And I do not try to.

What I look for in fantasy books is a strong storyline, a character who changes and grows, and wonderful chewy prose. I am not interested in generic sword and sorcery, but in invention, imagination, and a prose style that sings. I have read a lot of fantasy novels in my life. So I want to be surprised, delighted, and have the little hairs on the back of my neck stand up with recognition, just as I do when I read a poem by Emily Dickinson. A fantasy book should force me to confront my real world with the imagined world.

Jane Yolen, who has been referred to as "America's Hans Christian Andersen" and the "Twentieth-Century Aesop" because of her many fairytales and fantasy stories, is the author of over 170 books for children and adults. Her fantasy and science fiction imprint, Jane Yolen Books, part of Harcourt Brace & Company, published books by such authors as Bruce Coville (Jeremy Thatcher, Dragon Hatcher, 1991), Patricia C. Wrede (Dealing with Dragons, 1990), Vivian Vande Velde (Companions of the Night, 1995) and Caroline Stevermer (River Rats, 1992).

Favorite Books as a Child

The Andrew Lang Color Fairy Books

The Sword in the Stone by T. H. White

The Jungle Book by Rudyard Kipling

---

uating works of fantasy, teachers and parents should keep the following points in mind:

- Is the story well written, according to generally accepted literary standards?
- How consistent and well developed are the fantasy elements?
- Are the elements that make the story a fantasy convincing? Does the story allow readers to suspend disbelief?
- Does the author maintain a sense of logic and order within the created world?

THE EVOLUTION OF SCIENCE FICTION

The first work of science fiction may have been English author Mary Wollstonecraft Shelley's best-seller **Frankenstein,** published in 1811. It used medical science as the point of departure from reality and anticipated by over a century and a half the possibility of inventing new life forms and of transplanting organs.

In the mid-nineteenth century, the Frenchman Jules Verne was inspired by rapidly advancing technology to publish works of science fiction. Some of his stories anticipated later inventions. The submarine was featured in the 1869 novel *Twenty Thousand Leagues under the Sea,* and rocket travel was part of the 1865 *From the Earth to the Moon.*

At the turn of the century, a biology teacher named H. G. Wells wrote *War of the Worlds,* the first book about an invasion from outer space. Later, on Halloween of 1938, Orson Welles's broadcast of the story as a radio play caused thousands of people to panic. Although the announcer indicated throughout the broadcast that it was a work of science fiction, the genre was so new to American audiences that many believed the earth was under attack from aliens in spaceships.

At about the same time, pulp magazines started publishing stories with science fiction themes. The term "science fiction" was coined by Hugo Gernsback, who began the magazine *Amazing Stories* in 1926; Gernsback later published Science Wonder Stories. Many notable science fiction writers got their start in those pages, including Edgar Rice Burroughs, Isaac Asimov, and Robert A. Heinlein.

Both Heinlein and Asimov owe the early nurturing of their careers to *Amazing Stories* editor John W. Campbell, who later began the magazine *Astounding Science Fiction.* Campbell helped to launch the careers of many science fiction writers of the time. Robert Heinlein is credited with transforming the way science fiction stories are told. Rather than relying on pure fantasy, he researched contemporary scientific discoveries and made careful extrapolations, on which he based the plots of his novels and short stories. Heinlein's 1947 book *Rocket Ship Galileo* and the twelve junior novels that were published in the succeeding years are considered to be the first children's science fiction published in the United States. Isaac Asimov coined the term "robotics" in his prolific writings about robots. He formally outlined the "Three Laws of Robotics" that have guided the way in which robots have been portrayed in science fiction ever since.

In 1957, the Soviet Union launched Sputnik, the first satellite, and spurred not only the U.S. space initiative but also a competition among authors to provide children with imaginative stories set in outer space. Several authors wrote "space fantasies" in the 1950s. Ellen MacGregor wrote the *Miss Pickerell* series. Jay Williams wrote a series of space fantasy stories such as *Danny Dunn and the Anti-Gravity Paint.* Louis Slobodkin's *The Space Ship under the Apple Tree,* published in 1952, was followed ten years later by *The Three-Seated Space Ship: The Latest Model of the Space Ship under the Apple Tree.* Although the limited amount of scientific information in these books is accurate, the premises of the stories are based on imagination.

In the 1960s, the movie *2001: A Space Odyssey* and the television series "Star Trek" enlarged the audience of young devotees of space fiction. In 1969 came the actual landing on the moon by manned spacecraft—a true space adventure; and in the following decade, a few well-made movies, especially *Star Wars* and *E.T.,* continued to enhance the popularity of science fiction.

In 1963, Madeleine L'Engle's *A Wrinkle in Time* was the first science fiction book to be named a winner of the Newbery Medal. Along with the prestige of the award came the recognition that science fiction had a wider readership among children than in years past.

Today, serious themes abound in science fiction for young people. Many authors of science fiction say that they choose to write in this genre because other-world settings help readers to explore serious questions about their own world from a distance and thus with clearer vision. Madeleine L'Engle, for example, explores ethical and theological questions in her books. When, in *Invitation to the Game,* Monica Hughes creates a futuristic society in which educated and talented young people find no employment and are instead invited to play a game that turns out to be a fight for survival in a new world, she is asking her readers to question whether society today is guilty of similarly wasting the talents of young people. In *The Ear, the Eye and the Arm,* Nancy Farmer creates a horrendous community living under the garbage heaps of a city. With a little imagination, a reader can visualize the local landfill producing characters like the vlei people. In the same book, readers enter a controlled, militaristic society in which buildings are hundreds of stories high and no one is safe. Readers are forced to ask themselves how they can prevent this future from becoming reality. Readers of *The Giver,* by Lois Lowry, find a society in which memory of the past is erased and all matters of family, work, and pleasure are determined by an unknown few who control the society. When one child is chosen to receive the memory for the whole society from the Giver of memories, he questions what is important in order to remain human. Good science fiction is entertaining, addictive, and inevitably thought-provoking.

CATEGORIES OF SCIENCE FICTION

Some would prefer the plural term "science fictions" for this genre of literature, for the many works labeled science fiction provide very different reading experiences. Let's look at the most common varieties.

Projecting Scientific Principles

One kind of science fiction takes one or more principles known to science, extrapolates what the principles might lead to, and plays the possibilities out in a narrative, often in an everyday setting not unlike the real world. Peter Dickinson's *Eva* is an example of a book in which a scientific principle is explored in a story about a possible future. After an accident, a young girl's body is destroyed but her brain survives and is transplanted into a chimpanzee's body. The story probes who Eva will be: the human Eva in a chimpanzee's body or the chimpanzee Kelly with a human mind. How will she live: as a human or as a chimpanzee? *Eva* is a gripping work that questions human feelings of superiority to animals.

In *Anna to the Infinite Power* by Mildred Ames, twelve-year-old Anna discovers that she is a clone. In 1981, when the book was published, cloning seemed a science fiction idea; today, it seems less so. The idea of creating a clone has fascinated people for years and is also explored in other books for young readers. William Sleator addresses the idea of multiple clones in *The Duplicate.* At first, sixteen-year-old David thinks that it would be convenient to have a clone, but by the time he realizes the difficulties involved in living with Duplicate A, the experiment has gotten out of hand and Duplicate B arrives.

Utopian and Dystopian Societies

Societies different from the one we live in have been explored in adult literature for thousands of years. The Biblical Eden was one of several detailed versions of an ideal society, or utopia; others were Plato's *Republic* (in the fourth

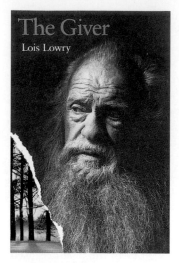

Illustration 10.8
Readers of Lois Lowry's *The Giver* will ponder whether a utopian society can truly exist and whether a controlled society is a desirable goal. (Cover from *The Giver* by Lois Lowry. Copyright © 1999 by Lois Lowry. Reprinted by permission of Clarion Books/Houghton Mifflin Company. All rights reserved.)

century B.C.) and St. Augustine's *The City of God* (in the fourth century A.D.). Dante's *Inferno* (written between 1307 and 1321), a detailed account of what hell is like, provided an early example of a dystopia, a terrible place to live.

The Ear, the Eye and the Arm, by Nancy Farmer, explores a futuristic society in Zimbabwe. What might appear initially to be utopian—a highly efficient, technologically managed society—soon shows its dystopian side as readers are introduced to the vlei people, who live in what was a city dump. Likewise, what appears to be a utopia at the beginning of Lois Lowry's *The Giver* is a supposedly ideal society where people are free from all hardship but also lack freedom of choice. The revealed dystopia highlights the negative implications of social planning. Lowry's book makes readers stop to consider whether an ideal society is possible—or desirable.

Monica Hughes's *Invitation to the Game* introduces a group of teenagers who are told, on the day they graduate from high school, "Congratulations on graduating with honors! Enjoy your leisure years!" Ironically, the educated, eager-to-work protagonists are sent to a community for the unemployed to play "the game"—not a game at all, but a master plan to dispose of excess population. Hughes reports that the situation for the book was suggested by a friend from Liverpool, England, where unemployment has been so entrenched for so long that many teachers see their greatest challenge to be preparing young people for a life without work. Reading about this situation in the genre of science fiction frees readers from making associations with particular social classes and historical moments and helps them to see the larger point of the work: that individual opportunities for a meaningful life may depend on the sort of social and economic system in which a person lives.

Surviving Environmental Catastrophes

Some science fiction deals with survival in the future, following some kind of environmental catastrophe. This catastrophe could be a nuclear holocaust, overpollution, overcrowding, or destruction of other aspects of the earth's environment.

Louise Lawrence's *Children of the Dust* tells of three generations of an English family following a nuclear holocaust. The lives of those who live in a sheltered but restricted bunker are compared with the lives of those who live outside and suffer from mutations.

Initially, *Phoenix Rising,* by Karen Hesse, seems to be a piece of science fiction that deals with the issue of survival following an accident at a nuclear power plant. Nyle's life on a Vermont sheep farm changes as she and others in her family and community attempt to survive the effects of the fallout. She must learn to deal with contamination, illnesses, and death. However, even though something as extreme as what is described in *Phoenix Rising* has not occurred, it *is* possible—and, in fact, was based on the author's response to the Chernobyl incident. Therefore, this book is placed in the genre of realistic fiction.

Science Fantasies

Books that include extrapolations of scientific understandings yet are based predominantly on imagination are classified as science fantasy. What some have previously called space fantasy—books about space travel, interplanetary exploration, alien visitors—are also included in this category. In *Company's Coming,* Arthur Yorinks writes about a spaceship whose alien passengers are invited for dinner (James) Edward Marshall's extraterrestrial creature in *Space*

Case is mistaken for a Halloween trick-or-treater. Pamela Service's **Stinker from Space** and **Stinker's Return** are about an agent from outer space, Tsynq Yr, who, not knowing the nature of the beast, enters the body of an earthly skunk for camouflage.

Paula Danziger's **This Place Has No Atmosphere** is a humorous story about a family's move from the earth to the moon in the twenty-first century. Daniel Pinkwater's science fantasies are based on the foibles of people on earth. In **Fat Men from Space,** invaders attempt to steal all the junk food on earth.

William Sleator's **Interstellar Pig** is another example of science fantasy. Barney, the hero of Sleator's book, gradually discovers that his new neighbors in an isolated Cape Cod beach setting are shape-shifting aliens, involved in a deadly game of keep-away that has been going on for over a century. As the tale of the aliens' game unfolds, readers are led to imagine the many possible consequences of contact between humans and creatures with a far greater variety of body forms, a larger territorial range, and more complex relationships to time.

HOW SCIENCE FICTION WORKS

One of the questions readers ask themselves when they encounter a new book is what genre it belongs to. Some works of science fiction identify their genre right off. For example, because Monica Hughes's **The Keeper of the Isis Light** occurs on a remote planet, readers know from the beginning that they are reading science fiction. Other works plant ambiguous clues. William Sleator's **The Boy Who Reversed Himself** raises readers' curiosity when the protagonist creates mirror writing, but they don't discover until further into the book that, through some scientific process, the boy has reversed himself and can go into the fourth dimension. Like others of Sleator's works, this book gives readers an extra taste of suspense before the genre is made clear, making them wonder not only about the explanations behind events but also about the kind of reality those explanations belong to—the logic of daily life or the more imaginative realm of fantasy or science fiction?

It is easy for an author of science fiction to get caught up in the adventure of the plot or the setting and give insufficient thought to developing the characters. The best works of science fiction, then, are those that draw believable characters—with complex but understandable feelings and perceptions—even when those characters are members of some invented species. Good science fiction makes its premises plausible: There is a logic to the setting, the characters, and the situation that is accessible to young readers so that they can "think their way around" in the work just as they could in any other sort of fiction. Finally, good science fiction does not merely dazzle the reader with bizarre details but plants clues and invites the reader to guess and predict what is happening or what will happen.

Once a work has opened up the possibility of the fantastic—scientific or otherwise—readers interpret events in the work within that realm of possibility and even reconstruct the parts of the work they read earlier in light of fantastic explanations. But even fantasy or science fiction is based on reality. Readers must have some points of identification with a work—something they find familiar and understandable—or they are not likely to be able to comprehend what they read.

Understanding the remote and strange in terms of the familiar is a challenge that readers face not only in science fiction, but also to some degree in all literature. Authors often begin with familiar details and lead readers gradually into the unfamiliar. Pamela Sargent begins *Alien Child* this way:

> Nita's earliest memory was of the day she had nearly drowned in the pool. She was toddling down the wide, lighted hall of her home; but her short legs could not keep pace with her guardian's long strides. Llipel suddenly retracted her claws, picked Nita up as the door to the garden slid open, and carried her outside. (p. 1)

Is Llipel Nita's dog or cat? If so, who is the guardian? Or is Llipel a guardian with claws? The questioning begins after the reader steps into what appears to be a human child's memory. Science fiction plays on the wonderful human capacity to project from real experiences to other-worldly ones. At its best, it allows us to touch the stars from our own living rooms.

MAJOR WRITERS OF SCIENCE FICTION AND THEIR WORKS

Some authors of science fiction and their major works were mentioned earlier in this chapter. Also, many writers who are major contributors to the genre are not listed in this section because their books are read predominantly by young adults rather than by children.

Isaac Asimov

One of the world's most prolific writers until his death in 1992, Isaac Asimov wrote over three hundred books on a wide range of topics, spanning such genres as science fiction, history, hard science, and mysteries. His works of science fiction are carefully researched, and readers—children and adults alike—can gain clear understandings of scientific and technical concepts from them.

Asimov had made his first tries at writing science fiction by the age of 11, and his first published works were short stories that benefited from the guidance of the noted editor of *Astounding Science Fiction,* John W. Campbell. Much of Asimov's work appears in story collections which he himself edited, such as *Fantastic Reading: Stories and Activities for Grades 5–8.* Many of his children's books were coauthored by Janet Asimov, his psychiatrist wife, who also wrote under the pseudonym J. D. Jeppson. Together, they wrote a series about Norby, a robot. In *Norby and the Invaders,* Norby helps to solve a mystery on earth, and in *Norby and the Court Jester,* Norby travels to the planet Izz.

John Christopher

Christopher Samuel Youd is a British author who writes for adults and young people under six pseudonyms. His books for young people written under the name John Christopher are his most successful. Christopher was asked by his publisher to write science fiction for boys, and he now prefers to write for young people. His first book for young readers was *The White Mountains,* which was published in 1967 and became the first volume of the *Tripod* trilogy. *The White Mountains* is about the earth's being conquered by alien Tripods who cap humans' heads, thereby controlling humans by making them docile and enslaved. Henry, Beanpole, and Will embark on a perilous journey to free the humans and rescue the earth from destruction. *The City of Gold and Lead* takes the three boys into the Tripods' secret city to learn more about the Tripods. In *The Pool of Fire,* Will and a group of free people carry out a plan to intercede in the interplanetary war between the Tripods and the Masters. **When the Tripods Came,** about aliens landing on earth, is a prequel to the Tripod trilogy.

As a student in a chemistry lab, Christopher first began experimenting with possibilities that went far beyond his textbooks. He has said that that experience set the stage for his becoming a writer of science fiction. Christopher has written other science fiction in addition to the *Tripod* trilogy. *The Swords of the Spirit* trilogy was published in the 1970s, and a *Fireball* trilogy was published in the 1980s.

Peter Dickinson

Peter Dickinson was born in Zambia and spent his early years there; he eventually moved to England and attended Eton College. After serving in the army and then graduating from Oxford University, he was a crime novel reviewer for a British humor magazine. It was not until he was in his forties that Dickinson turned to writing as a career. He writes for both children and adults.

Dickinson's first book for children, **The Weathermonger,** was published in 1968. It later became part of *The Changes* trilogy, in which Geoffrey and his sister Sally are among those in England who fear the impact of technology and machines that destroy nature; they seek to re-create the culture of the Dark Age. The trilogy was written and published in reverse chronological order. The first book of the trilogy is **The Devil's Children,** in which the siblings are abandoned and homeless; the second book is **Heartsease.** In **The Weathermonger,** Geoffrey controls the weather, but when his power is gone, technology again invades their world.

Robert A. Heinlein

Robert Heinlein began his writing career in 1939 when a need for money prompted him to answer an ad in a science fiction magazine. He wrote so many short stories for *Astounding Science Fiction* magazine that the editor asked him to use a variety of pseudonyms, so Heinlein wrote as Anson MacDonald, Lyle Monroe, John Riverside, Caleb Saunders, and Simon York. Heinlein created highly believable characters as a way of persuading readers to accept what would otherwise be unbelievable actions. His stories appeal to young people as well as to adults because of their fast-paced plots, clear style, and respectful tone that is never condescending. In fact, some of his stories have been published for both audiences.

Heinlein's stories feature characters who use reason to solve problems and escape ills of the earth and other planets or galaxies. In **Farmer in the Sky,** a family settles on another planet to find better resources for living. **Citizen of the Galaxy** is about a slave who is rescued by an unusual beggar so that he can help to fulfill a mission. In **Rocket Ship Galileo,** published in 1948, a scientist and three teenagers build a rocket ship and set off into outer space. **Podkayne of Mars,** published in 1963, had a teenage female protagonist at a time when that was very unusual. Heinlein won the Hugo Award four times and the Locus Award twice and was the first to win the Nebula Grand Master Award, in 1975. Some of Heinlein's books have become the basis of adaptations in other media. For example, his 1948 book **Space Cadet** was transformed into a television series in the 1950s, and **Starship Troopers** became the basis of a movie and a board game. Over forty million copies of Heinlein's books have sold in thirty languages. Robert Heinlein died in 1988.

H. M. Hoover

The topics of Helen Mary Hoover's many books are varied, her vision is original and powerful, and her writing style is impressive. The publication of her first short stories by Scholastic led to her writing of novels. In *Orvis,* two children find an outmoded robot with artificial intelligence in a dump and learn to care about it. In *The Delikon,* an alien race has conquered earth, and Varina, a Delikon, has been assigned to teach two youngsters who revolt against the aliens. The twenty-fourth century is the setting of *Away Is a Strange Place to Be,* in which two children are kidnapped to work in space. A theme in many of Hoover's books is the negative aspects of colonization of one society by another.

Monica Hughes

Although she was born in England and lived in Egypt, Monica Hughes is now known as one of Canada's finest writers for children. Hughes's early interest in science fiction was sparked by her mother and father, who taught her about astronomy and science. In addition, she read all of Jules Verne's science fiction books that had been translated into English, then proceeded to read the rest in French.

Hughes began writing after her own children started school. Her settings are always in the not-too-distant future, so they seem to be logical extensions of contemporary real life. Hughes does not make up the scientific elements of her stories but always bases them on laws of physics.

Her plots, especially in books such as *The Keeper of the Isis Light* in her trilogy about a colony on the planet Isis, combine her interest in the emergence of new cultures and the isolation an individual feels in searching for identity. In *The Dream Catcher,* Ruth feels an isolation and a sense of not belonging in the domed city, so she embarks on a dangerous journey with her companions.

Louise Lawrence

Louise Lawrence's grandfather told stories to her as a child and developed in her a sense of storytelling. It was not until adulthood, when she was living in an isolated farmhouse with her young children, that the fear of mental stagnation compelled Lawrence to begin writing. Her first book, *Andra,* is set two thousand years in the future and is about a girl who receives a brain graft from a boy who died in the 1980s.

In *Star Lord,* Erlich crashes on the mountain Mawrrhyn, not unlike the mountains of Wales, and explains to the children he meets that he comes from eleven light years across space. The brother and sister protect him from the military on earth until he escapes. The story reflects on nature and contrasts the values by which people on earth live with those of people in a future world.

In *The Warriors of Taan,* Khian comes to the planet Taan as a warrior but is intrigued with the nonviolent ways of the Stonewraiths. In this book, Lawrence explores the differences between genders with regard to violence and community.

Madeleine L'Engle

In the 1980s, Madeleine L'Engle was among the top six best-selling authors of children's books (*Dictionary of Literary Biography,* 1986), and her popularity continues today. She won the Newbery Medal in 1963 for *A Wrinkle in Time,* in which three children go to the planet of Camazotz to find Meg and Charles

Wallace's father. Ironically, the story was rejected by twenty-six publishers before being accepted, yet it continues to be L'Engle's most popular novel. In this first book of a trilogy, L'Engle clearly defines the good and evil forces that help and impede the children's search. *A Wind in the Door* expands the story: Meg must save Charles Wallace from the evil in the cosmos as well as from the evil within himself. *A Swiftly Tilting Planet* continues the plot in a fast-moving story involving time shifts and moral dilemmas facing the characters.

In 1981, L'Engle's *A Ring of Endless Light* was a Newbery Honor Book. It explores issues of death, a common theme in L'Engle's books. It also features members of the Austin family, who were first introduced in **Meet the Austins**. Often, characters from one of L'Engle's books appear in others written later.

Madeleine L'Engle says that you can't write science fiction out of your own experience, so you have to search for something deeper. She states that her books are about the clash between good and evil on a cosmic level. L'Engle was the runner-up for the 1964 Hans Christian Andersen Award for the body of her work, and she received the 1984 Catholic Library Association's Regina Award for consistent, sustained quality of work.

Andre Norton

Andre Norton is a pseudonym used by Alice Mary Norton. The name is actually a combination of two other pseudonyms that Norton has also used: Andrew North and Allen Weston. Norton's use of pseudonyms arose from her conviction that masculine names would give her works credibility with male readers. At the start of her writing career in the 1930s, Norton had to convince publishers—who believed that girls would not read science fiction and that boys would not read about female protagonists in a science fiction story—to accept her work.

Often, Norton's stories are based on English folklore, mythology, or history. For example, in **Outside,** a Pied Piper figure leads children living in an enclosed city, where the air has become foul, to the outside, where the formerly hazardous air is now free of nuclear fallout. Norton is also known for her inclusion of various ethnic characters. The heroine of **The Beast Master** is a Navajo. She survives the destruction of the planet and travels to another. Native American culture underpins *The Sioux Spacemen* as well.

Norton most often writes about interplanetary adventures but is also the author of the *Time Travel* series. In **The Time Traders,** the protagonist, Ross Murdock, is rescued from going to jail. Instead, he is sent across several periods of time and finds alien spaceships in the Bronze Age.

Author of over a hundred books, Norton was first published at the age of 20. She was awarded the 1984 Nebula Grand Master Award for lifetime achievement in science fiction.

William Sleator

William Sleator comes from a family of scientists, which may have led to his early interest in science. He believes that his hobbies of playing the piano, reading, and writing allow him to explore his interest in expressing his feelings about the supernatural. After spending many years as an accompanist for ballet companies, he turned to full-time writing. Sleator now lives in Thailand and the United States. He likens his life in an exotic foreign country to being on another planet because he has had to learn a new language and a new lifestyle. *Interstellar Pig* begins with characters playing an unusual board game and then reveals that some of the players are aliens. In *Strange Attractors,* Max finds himself having to protect a time travel device from its inventor and his alter ego from another time warp.

CRITERIA FOR SELECTING SCIENCE FICTION

When evaluating science fiction, teachers and parents should keep the following questions in mind:

- Has the author made clear how the characters (whether invented species or humans) feel about their world and their dilemmas?
- Are there clear plot threads for the reader to follow in the invented world?
- Are there familiar guideposts that serve as jumping-off places from reality to imagination for the reader?
- Does the author allow the reader to feel a sense of delight (even if it is tinged with fear and suspense) that encourages him or her to continue reading about an imaginary place?

AWARDS FOR FANTASY AND SCIENCE FICTION

There are few awards specifically for children's books of fantasy or science fiction, although fantasy and science fiction books qualify for general awards such as the Newbery Medal. There are, however, some general science fiction awards that have categories for juvenile literature. The Hugo Award is named after Hugo Gernsback, the founding editor of *Amazing Stories* magazine and the person who coined the term "science fiction." This award, known officially as the Science Fiction Achievement Award, is given annually for outstanding achievement in the writing of science fiction. Several winners of this award have written science fiction for both adults and children. The Nebula Award is awarded by members of Science Fiction and Fantasy Writers of America. Nebula Awards are given in several categories, one of which is juvenile fiction.

TEACHING IDEAS

Magical Abilities. Select a book that features a character with magical abilities. Would you like to possess such abilities? Why or why not? Explain what your life would be like if you had those magical abilities.

Time Slip. Select a character in a time-slip book, and imagine what it would be like if that person slipped into your present-day life. What would surprise that person about the world you live in? What might seem familiar? What might that person learn?

If *You* Traveled in Time. . . . If you could slip through time, which time period would you select? Explain why you made the choice and what you would hope to learn by slipping into a different time period.

Embellish a Fairy Tale. Select a fairy tale, and write down the essential details of the fairy tale after reading several versions in picture books and collected volumes. What are the unanswered questions? What events make you curious? Using the essential details as the basis, write an expanded version of your own.

EXPERIENCES FOR YOUR LEARNING

1. Fantasy books have often been censored as dangerous and inappropriate reading material for children. Others regard fantasy books as frivolous when there is so much for children to learn through their reading. As the popularity of books such as those in the *Harry Potter* series grows, the objections also increase. Consider these objections, and try to identify through popular media the reasoning behind the objections. If you encountered parents who objected to their children's reading fantasy in school, how might you respond?

2. Identify the purpose of the time-slip device in a time-slip book you have read. Did the character come to a particular understanding that would not have been possible without crossing into another time?

3. Select a book with personified animals. Think about the author's choice of particular animals to represent certain personality traits. Are there animal traits that are carried over to a particular animal character in personified animal stories?

4. A recurring statement made by female authors of fantasy and science fiction is that their publishers have asked them to adopt a male pseudonym to mask their gender. The belief that "boys won't want to read fantasy/science fiction by female writers" prevails even today, as extraordinarily popular author of the *Harry Potter* series was asked to use the initials "J. K." instead of the name under which she submitted her manuscript, Joanne Rowling. How does this belief in the male gender appeal of this genre play out in classrooms filled predominantly with female teachers and school librarians?

RECOMMENDED BOOKS: FANTASY

* indicates a picture book; I indicates interest level (P = preschool, YA = young adult)

Personified Animals

Avi. *Poppy.* Illustrated by Brian Floca. Orchard, 1995. Poppy the deer mouse tries to convince her family to move closer to a large cornfield that could provide plentiful food forever. The frightening king of the forest, a great horned owl named Mr. Ocax, denies them permission to make the move. The story continues in *Poppy and Rye* (1998), *Ragweed* (1999), and *Ereth's Birthday* (2000). (**I:** 9–12)

Bond, Michael. *A Bear Called Paddington.* Illustrated by Peggy Fortnum. Houghton Mifflin, 1960. This is the first of a series of more than twenty books about the adventures of a bear found at Paddington train station and adopted by the Brown family. Other books in the series include *Paddington Helps Out* (1961), *More about Paddington* (1962), *Paddington at Large* (1963), *Paddington Marches On* (1965), *Paddington's Lucky Day* (1974), and *Paddington on Screen* (1982). (**I:** 7–9)

Cleary, Beverly. *The Mouse and the Motorcycle.* Illustrated by Louis Darling. Morrow, 1965. A boy named Keith shows Ralph, a mouse, how to ride a toy motorcycle. Other books in the series include *Runaway Ralph* (1970) and *Ralph S. Mouse* (1982). (**I:** 7–9)

Grahame, Kenneth. *The Wind in the Willows.* Illustrated by E. H. Shepard. Scribner's, 1908/1933. Rat, Mole, Badger, and Toad of Toad Hall, a group of loyal friends with very distinct personalities, enjoy various adventures in the outdoors. (**I:** 7–11)

*Henkes, Kevin. *Chester's Way.* Greenwillow, 1988. Chester and Wilson are very particular about how things are done, and they never vary from their routines. One day, Lilly moves into the neighborhood, and she is full of surprises. (**I:** P–8)

*———. *Lilly's Purple Plastic Purse.* Greenwillow, 1996. When her teacher catches Lilly playing with her new plastic purple purse and confiscates it, Lilly is devastated. (**I:** P–8)

*———. *Sheila Rae, the Brave.* Greenwillow, 1987. Sheila Rae is very brave and quite proud of how

brave she is. One day, she gets lost and finds that she is not as brave and fearless as she thought. (I: P–8)

Howe, James, and Deborah Howe. *Bunnicula*. Illustrated by Leslie Morrill. Atheneum, 1979. This humorous fantasy is about the belief of two family pets that the newest arrival, a rabbit, is actually a vampire bunny. Other books in the series include *Howliday Inn* (1982), *The Celery Stalks at Midnight* (1983), and *Nighty-Nightmare* (1987). (I: 8–10)

*Keller, Holly. *Horace*. Greenwillow, 1991. Horace is a leopard whose dots don't match the stripes of his adoptive tiger family. They constantly reassure him about how much they like his spots and how much they wanted to adopt him when he lost his first family. (I: P–8)

King-Smith, Dick. *Ace: The Very Important Pig*. Illustrated by Mary Rayner. Crown, 1988. Ace is a pig who is born with an ace of clubs mark on his thigh and the exceptional ability to understand human speech. (I: 9–11)

———. *Babe: The Gallant Pig*. Illustrated by Mary Rayner. Crown, 1985. This story is about a barnyard community and how Babe, a pig, learns to be a champion sheepherder. (I: 8–11)

———. *Martin's Mice*. Illustrated by Jez Alborough. Crown, 1989. Martin the cat keeps Drusilla the mouse as his pet. He helps with her babies and protects them from mice-eating cats. (I: 8–11)

———. *Pigs Might Fly*. Illustrated by Mary Rayner. Viking, 1982. Daggie, the runt, rescues his fellow pigs by learning to swim during a flash flood. (I: 9–11)

Lawson, Robert. *Rabbit Hill*. Viking, 1944. The animals on Rabbit Hill anxiously await the arrival of the new folks: Will they bring traps and guns? (I: 7–10)

Lowry, Lois. *Stay! Keeper's Story*. Illustrated by True Kelley. Houghton Mifflin, 1997. Narrated by a dog named Keeper, this humorous account explains a dog's interpretation of life. (I: 8–12)

*Meddaugh, Susan. *Martha Speaks*. Houghton Mifflin, 1992. When Martha, the family dog, eats alphabet soup, she is suddenly able to speak and express her thoughts to her family. Other stories about Martha are *Martha Calling* (1994) and *Martha Blah, Blah* (1996). (I: 7–9)

Oppel, Kenneth. *Silverwing*. Simon & Schuster, 1997. The runt of the Silverwing bat colony, Shade, is separated from the others during a storm and must rejoin them on their dangerous migration South. The sequel is *Sunwing* (2000). (I: 10 and up)

*Potter, Beatrix. *The Tale of Peter Rabbit*. Warne, 1902. This is the classic story of a rabbit who finds himself in trouble when sneaking into Mr. McGregor's garden. It is the first of a number of stories about animals. (I: P–7)

Rylant, Cynthia. *Gooseberry Park*. Illustrated by Arthur Howard. Harcourt, 1995. A Labrador retriever, a hermit crab, and a bat must work together to come to the aid of their friend, a squirrel, who has become separated from her babies during an ice storm. (I: 7–10)

Selden, George. *The Cricket in Times Square*. Illustrated by Garth Williams. Farrar, 1960. Chester the cricket finds himself transported from the country to the city in a picnic basket. With new friends, he finds a home in a newspaper stand in a subway station below Times Square. Other books in the series include *Tucker's Countryside* (1969), *Chester Cricket's Pigeon Ride* (1981), and *The Old Meadow* (1987). (I: 7–11)

Sharp, Margery. *The Rescuers*. Illustrated by Garth Williams. Little, Brown, 1959. Miss Bianca and friends go on a dangerous journey to save a poet from imprisonment. Other books in the series include *Miss Bianca* (1962) and *Bernard the Brave* (1977). (I: 8–11)

Steig, William. *Abel's Island*. Farrar, 1976. A gentrified town mouse named Abel is swept away from his bride, Amanda, in a storm and learns to survive the elements for a year on a deserted island. (I: 8–10)

*———. *The Amazing Bone*. Farrar, 1976. The amazing bone can talk, and this magical ability saves a piglet from being eaten by a fox. (I: P–7)

*———. *Doctor De Soto*. Farrar, 1982. A fox visits a mouse dentist with the hope of having the dentist for dinner after his tooth has been fixed. (I: P–8)

*———. *Sylvester and the Magic Pebble*. Simon & Schuster, 1969. Sylvester, a donkey, comes across a special pebble for his pebble collection—one that grants wishes. The problem arises when Sylvester wishes to turn into a rock temporarily to escape trouble but cannot revert back to being a donkey. (I: P–8)

*Wells, Rosemary. *Max's Breakfast*. Dial, 1985. Ruby tries repeatedly to convince her little brother Max to eat his eggs, but he refuses. (I: P)

*———. *Max's Dragon Shirt*. Dial, 1991. Ruby takes Max on a shopping excursion for new pants, but, as usual, Max's and Ruby's ideas differ—Max wants a dragon shirt instead. (I: P–7)

*White, E. B. *Charlotte's Web*. Illustrated by Garth Williams. Harper & Row, 1952. A runt pig named

Wilbur is saved by Fern, who wants to show him at the fair. Meanwhile, Charlotte the spider enlists the barnyard animals in a campaign to keep Wilbur alive. (I: 7–11)

————. *Stuart Little*. Illustrated by Garth Williams. Harper & Row, 1945. An otherwise normal family has an abnormal experience: Their second son is a mouse. This book describes the humorous adventures of the son, Stuart. (I: 8–11)

————. *The Trumpet of the Swan*. Illustrated by Edward Frascino. Harper & Row, 1970. Louis is a mute swan. Unable to trumpet, he cannot attract the attention of Serena. (I: 9–11)

Personified Toys

Collodi, Carlo. *The Adventures of Pinocchio*. Translated by M. L. Rosenthal. Illustrated by Troy Howell. Lothrop, Lee & Shepard, 1881 /1983. This classic story is about a wooden puppet named Pinocchio whose creator is lonely and longs for company. When Pinocchio comes alive, his naiveté lands him in an adventure that forces him to learn about truthfulness. The story has been published in many other editions. (I: 9–12)

*Conrad, Pam. *The Tub People*. Illustrated by Richard Egielski. HarperCollins, 1989. The wooden tub toy family stays lined up at the edge of the bathtub every day except at bathtime. One day, Tub Child disappears down the drain. In *The Tub Grandfather* (1993), Tub Child finds Tub Grandfather covered in dust under a radiator, where he has been lost for a long time. (I: P–8)

Godden, Rumer. *The Doll's House*. Illustrated by Tasha Tudor. Penguin, 1947/1976. The arrival of a new doll upsets the resident dolls of a Victorian dollhouse. (I: 7–10)

————. *Four Dolls*. Illustrated by Pauline Baynes. Greenwillow, 1984. These four stories about four spirited dolls and their owners were originally published as separate books: *Impunity Jane* (1954), *The Fairy Doll* (1956), *The Story of Holly and Ivy* (1958), and *Candy Floss* (1960). (I: 8–10)

Hoffmann, E. T. A. *The Nutcracker*. Illustrated by Maurice Sendak. Crown, 1816/1984. Clara dreams on Christmas Eve that her toy nutcracker comes to life and takes her to a magical world filled with music and dancing flowers and candy. The story has been published in other editions with various illustrators. (I: 8–11)

Kennedy, Richard. *Amy's Eyes*. Illustrated by Richard Egielski. Harper & Row, 1985. Amy is an orphan who loves her sailor doll. When Captain comes to life, he runs away from the Home for Girls and promises to return for Amy as soon as he has made his fortune. (I: 11 and up)

Martin, Ann M., and Laura Godwin. *The Doll People*. Hyperion, 2000. Anabelle is a doll who is determined to solve the mystery of her Aunt Sarah, who has been missing for nearly fifty years. The arrival of the plastic family next door provides a friend and fellow sleuth, Tiffany. (I: 8–12)

Milne, A. A. *Winnie-the-Pooh*. Illustrated by Ernest H. Shepard. Dutton, 1926. Christopher Robin and his friends Winnie-the-Pooh, Eeyore, Piglet, Owl, Tigger, Kanga, and Roo share many adventures in the Hundred Acre Wood. The sequel is *The House at Pooh Corner* (1928). (I: P–10)

Waugh, Sylvia. *The Mennyms*. Greenwillow, 1994. In England, a family of life-sized rag dolls have continued to live in the house of their deceased creator for forty years, but now the new homeowner intends to come for a visit. See also *Mennyms in the Wilderness* (1996), *Mennyms Alive* (1997), *Mennyms Under Siege* (1997), and *Mennyms Alone* (1998). (I: 10 and up)

*Williams, Margery. *The Velveteen Rabbit*. Illustrated by Michael Hague. Holt, 1922/1983. A well-loved toy rabbit is discarded and then transformed into a real rabbit. Several other editions have been published with various illustrators. (I: 6–9)

Winthrop, Elizabeth. *The Castle in the Attic*. Illustrated by Donna Green. Holiday House, 1985. William receives a wooden model of a castle and discovers that the silver knight comes alive in his hands. Sir Simon leads William on an adventure in which they battle a fiery dragon and an evil wizard. The sequel is *The Battle for the Castle* (1993). (I: 9–11)

Outlandish Characters and Situations

Babbitt, Natalie. *The Devil's Storybook*. Farrar, 1974. This is a collection of short stories about the devil's attempts to recruit more members to his world. The sequel is *The Devil's Other Storybook* (1987). (I: 9–12)

————. *The Search for Delicious*. Farrar, 1969. Twelve-year-old Gaylen is sent out to seek the true meaning of the word "delicious" when there is disagreement among members of the court. What he discovers is a secret plot for the queen's brother to take over the kingdom. (I: 8–11)

Dahl, Roald. *Matilda*. Illustrated by Quentin Blake. Viking, 1988. Matilda uses her intellectual genius and psychic abilities to bestow a childlike interpretation of justice on the good and the bad. (I: 9–11)

Le Guin, Ursula K. *Catwings*. Illustrated by S. D. Schindler. Franklin Watts, 1988. Mrs. Jane Tabby is pleased that her kittens have wings, for they can escape the dangers of the city—only to meet with the dangers of the woods. Sequels are *Catwings Return* (1989) and *Wonderful Alexander and the Catwings* (1994). (I: 7–10)

Lindgren, Astrid. *Pippi Longstocking*. Illustrated by Louis S. Glanzman. Viking, 1945/1950. Pippi Longstocking lives without adult supervision in a town in Sweden. She leads an outrageous lifestyle and keeps the neighborhood children entertained. The sequel is *Pippi in the South Seas* (1959). (I: 7–11)

Travers, Pamela L. *Mary Poppins*. Illustrated by Mary Shepard. Harcourt, 1934/1962. Mary Poppins arrives with the East Wind to care for the Banks children. The nanny's unusual ways surprise and delight the children. Other books in the series include *Mary Poppins Comes Back* (1935) and *Mary Poppins in Cherry Tree Lane* (1982). (I: 7–11)

Magical Powers

Babbitt, Natalie. *Tuck Everlasting*. Farrar, 1975. Winnie discovers that the Tuck family drank from a spring that has given them eternal life. When the Tucks reveal their feelings about having eternal life, an enterprising man overhears the secret and attempts to capitalize on it by selling the water. (I: 8–12)

Barrie, Sir James Matthew. *Peter Pan*. Random House, 1911/1957. Peter Pan teaches three children how to fly to Never Never Land, where they will never have to grow up, but a jealous fairy intervenes and leads them astray into danger on Captain Hook's pirate ship. The story has been published in many editions. (I: 8–12)

Brittain, Bill. *The Wish Giver: Three Tales of Coventry*. Illustrated by Andrew Glass. Harper & Row, 1983. A stranger appears, granting the wishes of a few children who are surprised at the result. Related titles are *The Devil's Donkey* (1981) and *Dr. Dredd's Wagon of Wonders* (1987). (I: 9–12)

Coville, Bruce. *Jennifer Murdley's Toad*. Illustrated by Gary A. Lippincott. Harcourt, 1992. When Jennifer buys a mysterious toad, Bufo, at a discount store, she finds that it leads her into many adventures. (I: 8–10)

———. *Jeremy Thatcher, Dragon Hatcher*. Harcourt, 1991. Jeremy stumbles on Mr. Eilve's Magic Shop, which mysteriously appears. A beautiful ball from the store turns out to be a dragon's egg, and many adventures follow as the dragon grows larger and larger. (I: 9–12)

Duncan, Lois. *Gift of Magic*. Illustrated by Arvis Stewart. Little, Brown, 1971. Grandmother has ESP, and she predicts the gifts that her grandchildren will have: Kirby's is dance, Nancy's is magic, and Brendon's is music. (I: 10–12)

Jones, Diana Wynne. *A Charmed Life*. Greenwillow, 1977. Witchcraft enables Gwen to trade places with a twentieth-century girl in this time travel story. This is the first volume in a series about a young boy magician who is manipulated by his sister. The prequel is *The Lives of Christopher Chant* (1988), about a Chrestomanci-in-training who will become the next controller of magic. The other titles in the *Chrestomanci* series are *The Magicians of Caprona* (1980), in which the children of two feuding families make magical peace, and *Witch Week* (1982), which takes place in a school where the teacher suspects that someone in class is a witch. Short stories about Chrestomanci are found in *Warlock at the Wheel* (1985) and *Dragons and Dreams* (Harper, 1986). (I: 11–YA)

———. *Dark Lord of Derkholm*. Greenwillow, 1998. The story tells of a popular tourist destination, where lords and wizards role-play the parts of the dark lord and a wizard while tourists follow their fate as members of Pilgrim Parties. The sequel is *Year of the Griffin* (2000). (I: 12 and up)

———. *Power of Three*. Greenwillow, 1978. A curse threatens the English moors, and three children and some strange creatures work together to save them. (I: 11 and up)

———. *Stopping for a Spell: Three Fantasies*. Illustrated by Joseph A. Smith. Greenwillow, 1993. Unusual visitors is the theme of three humorous short stories. In one, an Auntie turns up with a conjurer's kit; in another, a little girl gets turned into a teddy bear when four Grannies come to babysit; in the third, pieces of furniture work together to get rid of an unwelcome visitor who has offended them. (I: 8–11)

McGowen, Tom. *The Magician's Apprentice*. Lodestar, 1987. The magician's apprentice is a street urchin chosen by the magician for his courage and intelligence. Together with some talking animal friends, they manage to overcome danger and separation to get to the Wild Lands, where the secrets of magic reside. Other books in the trilogy are *The Magician's Company* (1988) and *The Magician's Challenge* (1989). (I: 10–13)

*Mendez, Phil. *The Black Snowman*. Illustrated by Carole Byard. Scholastic, 1989. Jacob must overcome his anger about being poor and black. A black snowman uses the magical power of an old Ashanti kente cloth to show Jacob why he should be proud of his heritage. (I: 6–9)

O'Shea, Pat. *The Hounds of the Morrigan*. Holiday House, 1985. The forces of good and evil gather to fight over a book of magic that ten-year-old Pidge discovers in an Irish bookstore. (I: 10–YA)

Pierce, Tamora. *Magic Steps*. Scholastic, 2000. In this first book in the *The Circle Opens* quartet, Sandry, a young mage, discovers a boy dancing a spell and becomes his new teacher. The two team up to rid the power of invisible killers. (I: 11–YA)

———. *Sandry's Book*. Scholastic, 1997. In the *Circle of Magic* quartet, four mages-in-training practice the art of magic. The others are *Tris's Book* (1998), *Daja's Book* (1998), and *Briar's Book* (1999). (I: 11–YA)

Pinkwater, Daniel Manus. *Lizard Music*. Dodd, Mead, 1976. Victor finds a mysterious band of lizards playing amazing music late at night on television. The Chicken Man and his hen guide Victor to an invisible island to meet the lizards. (I: 9–12)

*Ringgold, Faith. *Aunt Harriet's Underground Railroad in the Sky*. Crown, 1992. When flying around one day, Cassie and her brother Be Be find a train in the sky. The woman conductor is Harriet Tubman, and she leads Cassie on the Underground Railroad so that Cassie will never forget the experiences of her ancestors. (I: 6–9)

*———. *Dinner at Aunt Connie's House*. Hyperion, 1993. While playing hide-and-go-seek at Aunt Connie's house, Melody and Lonnie find a dozen portraits of African American women. The paintings speak, telling the women's historically significant stories. (I: 7–10)

Rowling, J. K. *Harry Potter and the Sorcerer's Stone*. Scholastic, 1998. An orphaned boy discovers that he is the most famous wizard alive and begins his education at Hogwarts School of Witchcraft and Wizardry. The story continues in *Harry Potter and the Chamber of Secrets* (1999), *Harry Potter and the Prisoner of Azkaban* (1999), and *Harry Potter and the Goblet of Fire* (2000), with three more planned. (I: 9–14)

*Van Allsburg, Chris. *Jumanji*. Houghton Mifflin, 1981. Peter and Judy begin the jungle adventure board game of Jumanji, only to find that with each play, real parts of the jungle appear: Monkeys tear up the kitchen, rhinos stampede through the house, and a monsoon begins in the living room. (I: 6–10)

Vande Velde, Vivian. *Magic Can Be Murder*. Harcourt, 2000. Nola, a witch, tries to hide her magical abilities from authorities, but a scrying spell and a murder threaten to reveal her. (I: 12–YA)

Wrede, Patricia C. *Dealing with Dragons*. Scholastic, 1990. Princess Cimorene, bored with palace life, voluntarily becomes a dragon's princess and fights wizards to keep them from interfering with the dragons as they choose their new king. Other books in the *Enchanted Forest Chronicles* series are *Searching for Dragons* (1991), *Calling on Dragons* (1992), and *Talking to Dragons* (1993). (I: 12–YA)

Yep, Laurence. *Dragon of the Lost Sea*. HarperCollins, 1982. Shimmer is a dragon princess on a quest to find the lost sea that is her home. Although she dismisses the human Thorn as unable to help, she realizes that, being homeless, they have common bonds. Related titles are *Dragon Steel* (1985) and *Dragon Cauldron* (1991). (I: 12–YA)

Embellished Fairy Tales

Levine, Gail Carson. *Ella Enchanted*. HarperCollins, 1997. Ella is given the gift of obedience at the celebration of her birth, and this gift turns out to be more of a curse, as Ella cannot control her obedience. This story has an underlying Cinderella tale but offers readers more depth and richness than in picture book versions. (I: 10 and up)

McKinley, Robin. *Rose Daughter*. Greenwillow, 1997. The author of *Beauty* (1978) once again takes up the story of Beauty and the Beast, expanding it into a full novel of her own creation. (I: 11 and up)

———. *Spindle's End*. Putnam, 2000. In this lengthy expansion of the Sleeping Beauty story, "Rosie" is rescued from the palace and raised by an apprentice fairy who gives her the gift of talking to animals. (I: 12 and up)

Napoli, Donna Jo. *Beast*. Atheneum, 2000. In this story set in ancient Persia, a curse changes Prince Orasmyn into a lion. He struggles to remain true to his human belief in Islamic principles as he travels from India to France, seeking redemption and love. (I: YA)

———. *Crazy Jack*. Delacorte, 1999. In this expansion of the Jack and the Beanstalk story, Jack is tormented by nightmares about his father's absence and called crazy for his behavior, including his sale of a cow for magic beans. (I: 10 and up)

———. *Jimmy, the Pickpocket of the Palace*. Illustrated by Judith Byron Schachner. Dutton, 1995. When a princess kisses a frog with a hurt leg, he turns into a human boy. To revert back into a frog, he must somehow obtain a ring that does not belong to him. A related title is *Prince of the Pond* (1992). (I: 9–12)

———. *Zel*. Dutton, 1996. The story of Rapunzel is explored from three perspectives: the thirteen-year-old peasant girl Zel, the nobleman who falls in love with her, and the mother who loves her daughter too much to let her go. (I: 12–YA)

———, and Richard Tchen. *Spinners*. Dutton, 1999. This story, while remaining true to the details of the traditional tale of Rumpelstiltskin, adds imagined details to better explain the motive of Rumpelstiltskin. (I: 12–YA)

Vande Velde, Vivian. *The Rumpelstiltskin Problem.* Houghton Mifflin, 2000. Six alternative versions explore the "holes" in the traditional Rumpelstiltskin tale: Why did the miller tell the king his daughter could spin straw into gold? Why did Rumpelstiltskin want a baby anyway? (I: 10–YA)

Extraordinary Worlds

Baum, L. Frank. *The Wonderful Wizard of Oz.* Oxford Univ. Press, 1900/1997. Dorothy is transported from her home in Kansas to the Land of Oz by way of a tornado. In her search for a way home, she meets a tin man who wants a heart, a lion who wants courage, and a scarecrow who wants a brain. To get their wishes, they must kill the Wicked Witch of the West. There are forty-seven sequels, of which Baum wrote the first thirteen. (I: 9–12)

Carroll, Lewis. *Alice's Adventures in Wonderland.* Castle Books, 1865/1978. Alice follows a rabbit down a rabbit hole and finds herself in an extraordinary world. (I: 10–YA)

———. *Through the Looking Glass and What Alice Found There.* Macmillan, 1872. When Alice steps through a mirror, she finds herself in a backwards world. (I: 11–YA)

Dahl, Roald. *Charlie and the Chocolate Factory.* Illustrated by John Schindelman. Knopf, 1964. Charlie is one of five lucky winners who find a golden ticket that allows them to tour Willy Wonka's mysterious chocolate factory. Inside the factory are imaginative processes for creating Wonka chocolate. (I: 8–10)

———. *James and the Giant Peach.* Knopf, 1961/1996. James's unhappy life takes a turn when the magical contents of a bag make a peach grow large enough to enter and garden insects grow large enough to be his friends. (I: 7–11)

Ibbotson, Eva. *The Secret of Platform 13.* Dutton, 1998. A doorway at a railway station in London serves as the entrance to a magical island kingdom where fantastical creatures like mermaids and ogres live. This doorway is open for only nine days every nine years, and the infant heir to the kingdom is kidnapped. See also *Island of the Aunts* (2000). (I: 10 and up)

Juster, Norton. *The Phantom Tollbooth.* Illustrated by Jules Feiffer. Random House, 1961. Milo thinks that learning is a waste of time and there's never anything to do. Entering a tollbooth, he finds himself in the Kingdom of Wisdom, where he learns to seek Rhyme and Reason and not to jump to Conclusions; Tock teaches Milo not to waste time. (I: 9–11)

McGraw, Eloise. *The Moorchild.* Simon & Schuster, 1996. Saaski is a child of the "folk," who live in a secret world along the moor but travel invisibly within the human world. When she is traded by the folk for a human child, she grows up realizing that she is not human like her "parents," yet not fully folk either. (I: 10–14)

Norton, Mary. *The Borrowers.* Illustrated by Beth and Joe Krush. Harcourt, 1953. Pod, Homily, and Arietty Clock are a family of little people who "borrow" everyday items from a human family and use them in ways that suit people their size. When Arietty befriends a human boy, the family fears for their safety. There are several more books in the series: *The Borrowers Afield* (1955), *The Borrowers Afloat* (1959), *The Borrowers Aloft* (1961), *Poor Stainless* (1971), and *The Borrowers Avenged* (1982). (I: 8–11)

Supernatural Elements

Almond, David. *Skellig.* Delacorte, 1999. Michael's life is uncertain: His parents are occupied with his baby sister's fight for life, and his family has just moved to a new home. He discovers a "Skellig" in the run-down garage and, with the help of a new friend, must decide how to help the Skellig stay alive. (I: 10–14)

Belden, Wilanne Schneider. *Mind-Hold.* Harcourt, 1987. Carson and his sister, who has ESP, seek new friends in a desert as they try to survive after an earthquake. (I: 11–13)

Bellairs, John. *The House with a Clock in Its Walls.* Illustrated by Edward Gorey. Dial, 1973. Lewis's uncle has magical abilities that Lewis tries to imitate, but when he does, he unexpectedly creates a wicked ghost. The sequels are *The Figure in the Shadows* (1975) and *The Letter, the Witch and the Ring* (1977). (I: 10–12)

Billingsley, Franny. *The Folk Keeper.* Simon & Schuster, 1989. Based on Selkie lore, this is the story of Corrinna, who hides her identity to take the job of the Folk keeper—risking her own safety and well-being to keep the Folk that live underground from doing harm to the world. Her truest identity is revealed through unexpected events, described in journal entry format. (I: 10–14)

Cameron, Eleanor. *The Court of the Stone Children.* Dutton, 1973. The ghost of a French girl from the nineteenth century appears to a contemporary girl. The ghost's father was executed for treason, and now she wants Nina to help prove his innocence. (I: 10–12)

Conrad, Pam. *Stonewords: A Ghost Story.* HarperCollins, 1990. Zoe is visited by the ghost of Zoe Louise, a person from the past. When Zoe realizes that she must prevent Zoe Louise's untimely death, she goes back in time to the 1850s. (**I: 10–12**)

Hahn, Mary Downing. *Wait till Helen Comes.* Clarion, 1986. Helen is a ghost from the nineteenth century who is trying to convince another child to drown in the same lake she did so that they can be playmates. (**I: 8–12**)

Hunter, Mollie. *The Kelpie's Pearls.* Blackie & Son, 1964. An aging loner becomes friendly with a kelpie, whose gift of pearls sets off a series of troublesome events. (**I: 9–12**)

———. *A Stranger Came Ashore: A Story of Suspense.* HarperTrophy, 1975/1994. In a suspenseful story based on Selkie lore, twelve-year-old Robbie suspects that the stranger who came ashore during a terrible storm and was befriended by his family is an evil Selkie. (**I: 9–12**)

Jacques, Brian. *Seven Strange & Ghostly Tales.* Putnam, 1991. This collection of seven scary stories includes humorous as well as frightening elements. (**I: 9–12**)

Lively, Penelope. *The Ghost of Thomas Kempe.* Illustrated by Antony Maitland. Dutton, 1973. James and his family move into an old house in an English village. When the resident ghost begins to act out, James gets blamed. (**I: 10–12**)

Mahy, Margaret. *The Changeover.* Atheneum, 1984. A girl's supernatural abilities save her brother. (**I: 10–13**)

———. *The Haunting.* Macmillan, 1982. Barry, an eight-year-old, begins receiving mental messages from an uncle who was presumed dead. (**I: 10–12**)

Peck, Richard. *The Ghost Belonged to Me.* Viking, 1975. Richard tries to solve the mystery of a missing girl and ends up unwillingly receiving the assistance of Blossom Culp, his nemesis. Sequels are *Ghosts I Have Been* (1977) and *The Dreadful Future of Blossom Culp* (1983). (**I: 10–YA**)

Walsh, Jill Paton. *Birdy and the Ghosties.* Illustrated by Alan Marks. Farrar, 1989. Birdy is able to see ghosties, although her father, who is being pestered by them, cannot. (**I: 6–9**)

Wright, Betty Ren. *Christina's Ghost.* Holiday House, 1985. When Christina finds that she must spend the summer with Uncle Ralph in his old Victorian house, she is unhappy about it. When she discovers that there is a ghost in the house, she is even more distraught. (**I: 9–12**)

———. *The Dollhouse Murders.* Holiday, 1983. The dolls in a dollhouse come to life and try to help

resolve the mysteries of murders that happened long ago. (**I: 9–12**)

Yep, Laurence. *The Ghost Fox.* Illustrated by Jean and Mou-sien Tseng. Scholastic, 1994. While Little Lee's father is away at sea, Little Lee is responsible for taking care of his mother, including getting rid of the ghost that is trying to take over her soul. This is an adaptation of a story taken from the ancient Chinese tradition of ghost storytelling. (**I: 7–10**)

Time Slips

Barron, T. A. *The Ancient One.* Philomel, 1992. Thirteen-year-old Kate goes with her grandfather's sister, Aunt Kate, to protest the cutting of redwood trees in Oregon. Kate falls into a time tunnel that takes her back five centuries, to when the trees were young but still threatened by human greed. (**I: 12–YA**)

Boston, L. M. *The Children of Green Knowe.* Illustrated by Peter Boston. Harcourt, 1989. A lonely boy moves to his grandmother's old English house, only to find that various children who played in the house over the years reappear to be his playmates. There are several sequels: *The Treasure of Green Knowe* (1989), *A Stranger at Green Knowe* (1989), *An Enemy at Green Knowe* (1989), and *The River at Green Knowe* (1989). (**I: 9–11**)

Cooper, Susan. *King of Shadows.* McElderry, 1999. Nat Fielding plays the role of *The Midsummer Night's Dream's* Puck in the newly reconstructed Globe Theatre but finds himself transported four hundred years back to play the same role with Will Shakespeare as Oberon. (**I: 12–YA**)

Fleischman, Sid. *The 13th Floor: A Ghost Story.* Illustrated by Peter Sis. Greenwillow, 1995. Buddy Stebbins steps off an elevator on the thirteenth floor of an old building and follows his sister three hundred years back in time. They end up on a pirate ship captained by one of their own ancestors. (**I: 9–12**)

Hurmence, Belinda. *A Girl Called Boy.* Houghton Mifflin, 1982. Blanche goes back in time to 1853 in North Carolina and experiences slavery when she becomes one of her ancestors. (**I: 10–12**)

Lunn, Janet. *The Root Cellar.* Scribner's, 1983. Rose goes to live with her relatives when she is orphaned. While hiding in a root cellar, she is transported back to 1860 and helps a young woman seek out her loved one, who is missing as a result of the Civil War. (**I: 10–12**)

McKay, Hillary. *The Amber Cat.* Simon & Schuster, 1997. In this time-slip and ghost story, as Robin recovers from chickenpox, he and his friends are fascinated by his mother's stories of a mysterious girl who used to appear in her childhood. (I: 8–11)

Park, Ruth. *Playing Beatie Bow*. Atheneum, 1982. A contemporary Australian girl finds that she has traveled back in time to the nineteenth century. (I: 10–12)

Pearce, Philippa. *Tom's Midnight Garden*. Illustrated by Susan Einzig. Harper, 1984. Tom is bored with his summer until he finds that he can visit a garden that appears only when the grandfather clock strikes thirteen every night. There he develops a special friendship with a mysterious girl named Hatty. (I: 10–12)

Pearson, Kit. *A Handful of Time*. Viking, 1988. A twelve-year-old finds a watch under the floor while visiting her cousins one unhappy summer. The watch takes her back to the time her mother was the same age and allows her to gain insights about her mother. (I: 11–13)

Scieszka, Jon. *Knights of the Kitchen Table*. Illustrated by Lane Smith. Viking, 1991. Joe, Fred, and Sam, the Time Warp Trio, travel back to the days of King Arthur when they open "The Book" that a magician uncle sent Joe for a birthday present. Other *Time Warp Trio* stories include *The Not-So-Jolly Roger* (1991), *The Good, the Bad, and the Goofy* (1992), *Your Mother Was a Neanderthal* (1993), *2095* (1995), *Tut, Tut* (1996), *Summer Reading Will Kill You* (1998), and *See You Later, Gladiator* (2000). (I: 8–11)

Voigt, Cynthia. *Building Blocks*. Atheneum, 1984. A boy's journey back into the time of his father's childhood helps him to understand his father better. (I: 9–11)

Wiseman, David. *Jeremy Visick*. Houghton Mifflin, 1981. A contemporary Cornish boy goes back in time to try to discover the location of a boy named Jeremy, who was lost in a mine accident in 1852. (I: 10–12)

Yolen, Jane. *The Devil's Arithmetic*. Viking, 1988. Hannah finds herself transported as Chaya back to the days of the Holocaust. Through the device of time travel, she grows in her understanding of her Jewish heritage. (I: 9–12)

High Fantasy

Alexander, Lloyd. *The Arkadians*. Dutton, 1995. An unlikely cast of unusual characters each tell a story filled with elements of magic and Greek mythology. Their companionship is based on bravery, loyalty, compassion, and love. (I: 11–13)

———. *The Book of Three*. Holt, 1964/1999. *The Chronicles of Prydain* tells of the struggle between the people of Prydain and the Lord of the Land of Death. Other books in the series are *The Black Cauldron* (1965/1999), *The Castle of Llyr* (1966/1999), *Taran Wanderer* (1967/1999), and *The High King* (1968/1999). (I: 10–13)

———. *The Iron King*. Dutton, 1997. The young king, Tamar, loses his entire kingdom to King Jaya in a dice game and travels to Jaya's kingdom to reclaim his honor. He is joined on his magical and adventurous journey by a diverse group of companions. (I: 11 and up)

———. *The Remarkable Journey of Prince Jen*. Dutton, 1991. In this coming-of-age story, brave Prince Jen embarks on a dangerous journey, bearing six unusual gifts. (I: 10–13)

Barron, T. A. *The Lost Years of Merlin*. Philomel, 1996. Merlin as a young boy searches for his identity. He has lost his memory and doesn't trust that the woman he is with is really his mother. His journey to discover his past introduces the reader to how Merlin gained magical sight and became a wizard. The story continues in *The Seven Songs of Merlin* (1997), *The Fires of Merlin* (1998), and *The Mirror of Merlin* (1999) and concludes with *The Wings of Merlin* (2000). (I: 11–YA)

———. *The Merlin Effect*. Philomel, 1994. Kate joins her father on a scientific expedition off the coast of Baja California. Kate takes a kayak out too far at dusk and finds that her forbidden expedition leads to an encounter with a whale and the discovery of forgotten legends involving Merlin. (I: 11–YA)

Chetwin, Grace. *Gom on Windy Mountain*. Lothrop, Lee & Shepard, 1986. When Gom's father, Stig, sends his strange wife away, Gom's mother leaves him a rune with magical powers. Chetwin's saga *Tales of Gom in the Legends of Ulm* includes *The Riddle and the Rune* (1987), *The Crystal Stair* (Bradbury, 1988), and *The Starstone* (1989). (I: 10–YA)

———. *Jason's Seven Magical Night Rides*. Bradbury, 1994. A mysterious stranger offers Jason rides on mythical horses, including Pegasus, Chiron the Centaur, and the Trojan Horse, and helps Jason to overcome feelings of inadequacy and become whole by accepting responsibility for himself. (I: 11–YA)

Cooper, Susan. *Over Sea, Under Stone*. Illustrated by Alan E. Cover. Atheneum, 1965. A search for King Arthur's grail begins this story of fighting evil and protecting Light. The series continues in *The Dark Is Rising* (1973), *Greenwitch* (1974), *The Grey King* (1975), and *Silver on the Tree* (1977). (I: 10–13)

Jacques, Brian. *Redwall*. Philomel, 1987. Matthias leads the mice in protecting Redwall Abbey from Cluny the Scourge and the rats. The series includes *Mossflower* (1988), *Mattimeo* (1990), *Mariel of Redwall* (1991), *Salamandastron* (1993), *Martin the Warrior* (1994), *The Bellmaker* (1994), *Outcast of Redwall* (1996), *The Long Patrol* (1998), *Marlfox* (1999), and *Legend of Luke* (2000). (I: 11–13)

Jones, Diana Wynne. *The Crown of Dalemark*. Greenwillow, 1993. This final book in a quartet about the mythical kingdom of Dalemark continues the story of Mitt, who is joined by Moril and Maewen in the quest to reunite Dalemark with Adon's gifts: the ring, the sword, and the cup. Earlier books in the quartet are *Cart and Cwidder* (1977), *Drowned Ammet* (1978), and *The Spellcoats* (1979). (I: 12–YA)

————. *Dogsbody*. Morrow, 1988. Sirius, the Dog Star, is reborn on earth as a puppy and fulfills a mission to find the murder weapon of the stars. (I: YA)

Le Guin, Ursula K. *A Wizard of Earthsea*. Illustrated by Ruth Robbins. Parnassus, 1968. This first book in a series describes how Ged studies wizardry, becomes a wizard, and confronts evil. Other books in the series are *Tombs of Atuan* (Atheneum, 1971/ 1985), *The Farthest Shore* (Atheneum, 1972/1985), and *Tehanu: The Last Book of Earthsea* (Atheneum, 1990). (I: 13–YA)

Lewis, C. S. *The Lion, the Witch and the Wardrobe*. Illustrated by Pauline Baynes. Macmillan, 1950. Four children discover that they can go through the back of a wardrobe to enter the magical world of Narnia. There, they meet the lion Aslan, who is trying to free Narnia from the evil spell cast by the White Witch. The Narnia stories continue in *Prince Caspian* (1951), *The Voyage of the Dawn Treader* (1952), *The Silver Chair* (1953), *The Horse and His Boy* (1954), *The Magician's Nephew* (1955), and *The Last Battle* (1956). (I: 9–13)

McKinley, Robin. *The Blue Sword*. Greenwillow, 1982. Princess Aerin's mysterious powers help her to slay dragons as she fights to save her kingdom. The prequel is *The Hero and the Crown* (1984). (I: 12–YA)

Napoli, Donna Jo. *The Magic Circle*. Puffin, 1993/1995. A sorceress draws power from the devil's minions while within the protection of a magic circle, but when the powers are reversed, she is doomed to a life of torment as a witch. The ending of the story explores the witch's perspective on the Hansel and Gretel story. (I: 12 and up)

Pierce, Meredith Ann. *The Darkangel*. Little, Brown, 1982. This is the first book in Pierce's *Darkangel* trilogy. Other titles are *A Gathering of Gargoyles* (1984) and *The Pearl of the Soul of the World* (1990). (I: 13–YA)

————. *Dark Moon*. Joy Street, 1992. In Book 2 of the *Firebringer* trilogy, the protagonist, Jan, is prince of the unicorns, and he journeys to obtain fire from two-footed creatures to save the unicorns from enemies. Book 1 is *Birth of the Firebringer* (1985); Book 3 is *The Son of Summer Stars* (Little, Brown, 1996). (I: 13–YA)

Pierce, Tamora. *Wild Magic*. Atheneum, 1992. In this first book in a series called *The Immortals,* thirteen-year-old Daine faces battle with dreadful immortal creatures. (I: 12–YA)

Pullman, Philip. *The Golden Compass*. Knopf, 1998. In this first book of *His Dark Materials,* Lyra realizes that she must find a way to prevent kidnapped children from being victimized as scientific experiments. The second book is *The Subtle Knife* (1997); the trilogy ends with *The Amber Spyglass* (2000). (I: 11–YA)

Shetterly, Wil. *Elsewhere*. Harcourt, 1991. A runaway teenager finds himself in Bordertown, a magic world peopled by punk elves. The sequel is *Nevernever* (1993). (I: 13–YA)

Smith, Sherwood. *Wren to the Rescue*. Harcourt, 1990. In this second book about Wren, Wren rescues a princess from a wicked king. Other books in the series are *Wren's Quest* (1993) and *Wren's War* (1995). (I: 13–YA)

Sutcliff, Rosemary. *The Sword and the Circle: King Arthur and the Knights of the Round Table*. Dutton, 1981. These stories about King Arthur, Merlin, and Sir Lancelot are mostly drawn from *Le Morte d'Arthur* by Sir Thomas Malory (1485). Sutcliff's rendition of the Arthurian trilogy continues with *The Light beyond the Forest: The Quest for the Holy Grail* (1980) and *The Road to Camlann* (1982). (I: 11–YA)

Tolkien, J. R. R. *The Fellowship of the Ring*. Houghton Mifflin, 1955/1967. This is the first part of the *Lord of the Rings* trilogy, in which Frodo Baggins inherits a magic ring from his Uncle Bilbo (hero of *The Hobbit*) and must eventually take the ring to Mount Doom, where it will be destroyed to help the good forces win against the Dark Lord. Other volumes in the trilogy are *The Two Towers* (1967) and *The Return of the King* (1967). (I: 12–YA)

————. *The Hobbit*. Houghton Mifflin, 1937. Bilbo Baggins, a peaceful Hobbit, is tricked by a wizard into going on a dangerous quest to retrieve stolen dwarf treasure from a dragon. The story of Middle Earth continues in the *Lord of the Rings* trilogy. (**I:** 11–YA)

Yolen, Jane. *Merlin and the Dragons.* Illustrated by Li Ming. Cobblehill/Dutton, 1995. Young King Arthur has troublesome dreams and visits Merlin, from whom he hears stories of Merlin's childhood. On hearing tales of dragons, King Vortigern, and Uther Pendragon, Arthur is reassured of his right to the crown. (**I:** 8–11)

RECOMMENDED BOOKS: SCIENCE FICTION

Projecting Scientific Principles

Ames, Mildred. *Anna to the Infinite Power.* Macmillan, 1981. A twelve-year-old discovers that she is a clone. (**I:** 11–13)

Cross, Gillian. *New World.* Holiday House, 1994. Gillian and Stuart agree to test out a new top-secret virtual reality computer game. The experience turns out to be more frightening than they expected. (**I:** YA)

Dickinson, Peter. *Eva.* Delacorte, 1989. Following an accident, a young girl's body is destroyed, but her brain survives and is transplanted into a chimpanzee's body. As she struggles to establish her identity, will she choose to live with her human family or with the chimps? (**I:** 12–YA)

Etchemendy, Nancy. *The Power of UN.* Front Street/Cricket, 2000. A mysterious old man presents Gib with an "unner"—a device that allows Gib to undo mistakes by going back in time. (**I:** 10–12)

Heinlein, Robert. *Farmer in the Sky.* Ballantine, 1950/1990. Bill and his father leave the overpopulated Earth and settle on Ganymede, the third moon of Jupiter, seeking better resources for living. (**I:** 12 and up)

———. *Red Planet.* Ballantine, 1981. A robot helps earthlings as they make their first exploration of Mars. (**I:** 12–YA)

———. *Rocket Ship Galileo.* Macmillan, 1948. Mystery surrounds efforts to build the first rocket ship. (**I:** 12–YA)

———. *Space Cadet.* Scribner, 1948/1987. The bravest and strongest become Space Cadets, the elite group who work to keep peace in the Solar System, and Matt must prove his worth before being accepted into the ranks. (**I:** 12 and up)

*Pinkney, Brian. *Cosmo and the Robot.* Greenwillow, 2000. In this story set on Mars, Cosmo uses his new "Super Solar System Utility Belt" to locate and repair his damaged robot, Rex. (**I:** 7–10)

Sleator, William. *The Duplicate.* Dutton, 1988. At first, sixteen-year-old David delights in having a clone, Duplicate A. Just when he realizes the complications it causes, Duplicate B arrives. (**I:** 11 and up)

Verne, Jules. *Twenty Thousand Leagues under the Sea.* Washington Square Press, 1976. An eccentric captain successfully makes an electric submarine. (**I:** YA)

Utopian and Dystopian Societies

Auer, Martin. *The Blue Boy.* Illustrated by Simone Klages. Macmillan, 1992. A boy leaves the earth to find a planet safe from violent weapons. (**I:** 8–11)

Butler, Susan. *The Hermit Thrush Sings.* DK Ink, 1999. Leora lives the life of an outcast in her village because her webbed hand marks her as one of the "defectives." When she frees a baby birmba, Leora's life takes a sudden change of course, leading her past the locked gates of her village and into the "outside" forbidden world. (**I:** 12 and up)

Christopher, John. *When the Tripods Came.* Dutton, 1988. The Tripods arrive on earth and brainwash earthlings with hypnotic caps. The *White Mountains* series continues in *The White Mountains* (Macmillan, 1967), *The City of Gold and Lead* (1967), and *The Pool of Fire* (1968). (**I:** 10–13)

———. *Wild Jack.* Macmillan, 1991. In London in the twenty-third century, after being ostracized from society, Clive meets up with a Robin Hood–like character named Wild Jack. (**I:** 10–13)

Farmer, Nancy. *The Ear, the Eye and the Arm.* Orchard, 1994. In Zimbabwe in the year 2194, three mutants—the Ear, the Eye, and the Arm—form a detective agency and are hired to find the kidnapped children of General Matsika. (**I:** 11–YA)

Heinlein, Robert. *Citizen of the Galaxy.* Macmillan, 1957. A young boy is able to leave slavery to fulfill a mission and learns that there is more to the galaxy than he knew. (**I:** 11–13)

Hoover, H. M. *Away Is a Strange Place to Be.* Dutton, 1990. Kidnapped from earth in 2349 to serve as a worker on a construction project, Abby plans her escape. (**I:** 11–13)

———. *The Delikon.* Penguin, 1977. The Delikon is an alien race whose control of the earth is destroyed by two children and their teacher. (**I:** 12–YA)

————. *Only Child*. Dutton, 1992. A young member of a colonizing group, Cody, works to save intelligent insectlike creatures whose lives are threatened by the settlers. (I: 10–13)

————. *Orvis*. Viking, 1987. An outdated robot named Orvis, found in a dump, accompanies twelve-year-old Toby as she runs away from home. (I: 11–13)

Hughes, Monica. *The Dream Catcher*. Macmillan, 1987. Ruth does not fit into life in her domed city and decides to depart on a dangerous journey with her companions. A related title is *Devil on My Back* (1985). (I: 10–YA)

————. *Invitation to the Game*. Simon & Schuster, 1990. Recent high school graduates, unemployed in an overpopulated world, find themselves playing a mysterious game of survival in a different world. (I: 11–YA)

————. *The Keeper of the Isis Light*. Macmillan, 1981. Olwen lives with a robot on a barren planet until another human lands. (I: 12–YA)

Lowry, Lois. *The Giver*. Houghton Mifflin, 1999. Knowledge is controlled in a futuristic society, and Jonah must grapple with the right to make choices when he begins to receive memories. See also *Gathering Blue* (2000). (I: 11–YA)

Norton, Andre. *The Beast Master*. Ballantine, 1987. A Navajo, Hosteem Storm, survives the destruction of her planet and is able to settle on the planet of Arzor. (I: 12–YA)

————. *Outside*. Avon, 1974. When the air in the protected city turns foul, a Pied Piper figure leads the children to the outside, where the air, previously contaminated by nuclear fallout, has regenerated. (I: 11–13)

————. *The Sioux Spacemen*. Gregg, 1978. Kade Whitehawk is a descendent of Sioux warriors and is able to use his knowledge to defend himself and others. (I: 12–YA)

Surviving Environmental Catastrophes

Hughes, Monica. *The Crystal Drop*. Silver Burdett Ginn, 1992. Megan and her younger brother have a harrowing journey to find a semblance of life as it was before a drought. (I: 12–YA)

Karl, Jean. *Strange Tomorrow*. Dell, 1985. This book includes two stories about survival: one about survival on earth when all living things are destroyed and the other about rebuilding a society that has been destroyed. A related title is *The Turning Place* (1976). (I: 10–13)

Lawrence, Louise. *Children of the Dust*. Harper, 1985. Earth is devastated by a nuclear war, and a small group of people in England struggle to survive through three generations in a new world where children are born with mutations. (I: 12–YA)

Macdonald, Caroline. *The Lake at the End of the World*. Dial, 1989. When a boy climbs out of a cave, Diana realizes that someone other than her family has survived the environmental holocaust. (I: 12–YA)

O'Brien, Robert. *Z for Zachariah*. Atheneum, 1975. Ann Burden believes that she is the only person left after a nuclear holocaust, until Mr. Loomis arrives. (I: 12–YA)

Philbrick, Rodman. *The Last Book in the Universe*. Scholastic, 2000. In a postapocalyptic future in which books are only vague memories, an unlikely group—an epileptic youth named Spaz, a courageous old man named Ryter, an orphaned little boy known only as "Little Face," and a genetically perfected "proov" named Lanaya—journey across dangerous gang-controlled "Urbs" in search of a way to keep Spaz's foster sister from dying of leukemia. (I: 11 and up)

Strieber, Whitley. *Wolf of Shadows*. Knopf, 1985. After a nuclear holocaust, a wolf and a woman find a mysterious bond that brings them closer to the spirits of the destroyed earth. (I: 12–YA)

Swinells, Robert. *Brother in the Land*. Holiday House, 1985. England is hit by nuclear war, and Danny and his brother fight for survival in the aftermath. (I: 12–YA)

Walsh, Jill Paton. *The Green Book*. Illustrated by Lloyd Bloom. Farrar, 1982. A group of colonists try to grow food on a hostile new planet called Shine, when the dying planet of earth can no longer sustain life. (I: 9–12)

Science Fantasies

Alcock, Vivien. *The Monster Garden*. Delacorte, 1988. Frankie plays with her father's genetic experiments and creates a monster. (I: 9–12)

Asimov, Janet, and Isaac Asimov. *Norby and the Invaders*. Walker, 1985. Norby is a robot who helps to solve a mystery on earth. See also *Norby and the Oldest Dragon* (1990), in which Jeff faces a mysterious phenomenon on planet Jamyn, and *Norby and the Court Jester* (1991), in which Jeff and robot Norby travel to planet Izz. (I: 10–13)

Barron, T. A. *Heartlight*. Philomel, 1990. Kate travels to a distant star in search of her astrophysicist grandfather, who has disappeared after inventing the means of traveling faster than light. His mission is to save the sun from extinction; Kate's mission is to save her grandfather from evil forces that have captured him. (I: 12–YA)

Bechard, Margaret. *Star Hatchling*. Viking, 1995. Shem witnesses the arrival of a "star" on his planet and views the "hatchling" with fear. He does not know that this is a human girl who has been separated from her family. (I: 8–12)

Chetwin, Grace. *On All Hallows' Eve*. Macmillan, 1992. Characters are transported to a different world on the eve of Halloween. (I: 9–11)

Coville, Bruce. *My Teacher Is an Alien*. Pocket Books, 1991. A teacher comes from outer space to study the human brain, which is believed to be defective, since humans kill one another. This theme is carried on in a series of other titles, such as *Aliens Ate My Homework* (1993). (I: 8–11)

Danziger, Paula. *This Place Has No Atmosphere*. Dell, 1987. Humorous story of a move to the moon by reluctant Aurora and her family. (I: 11–YA)

Dickinson, Peter. *The Devil's Children*. Delacorte, 1986. Abandoned and homeless, Geoffrey and his sister Sally are among those in England who fear the impact of technology and instead re-create the culture of the Dark Age. *The Changes* trilogy continues in *Heartsease* (1969) and *The Weathermonger* (1968). (I: 12–YA)

*Etra, Jonathan, and Stephanie Spinner. *Aliens for Lunch*. Illustrated by Steve Bjorkman. Random House, 1991. Aliens appear out of the microwave, and desserts are at risk in the universe. (I: 7–9)

Gilmore, Kate. *The Exchange Student*. Houghton Mifflin, 1999. Fen is a seven-foot alien exchange student from a planet that is suffering from ecological disasters, including the death of animal life that would have kept the insect life under control. This loss leads to Fen's extraordinary interest in earth's animals. (I: 12 and up)

Gormley, Beatrice. *Wanted: UFO*. Illustrated by Emily Arnold McCully. Dutton, 1990. Elise is surprised at the intention of two aliens that appear in Nick's backyard. (I: 8–11)

Griffin, Peni R. *Otto from Otherwhere*. Macmillan, 1990. A boy from another world lands on earth. (I: 9–11)

Heinlein, Robert A. *Podkayne of Mars: Her Life and Times*. Baen, 1963/1995. Podkayne "Paddy" Fries, a Martian who aspires to be the first female starship captain, jumps at the chance to accompany her uncle on a trip to earth by way of Venus, although she believes that earth isn't fit for habitation. (I: 12 and up)

Howarth, Lesley, *Maphead*. Candlewick, 1994. In this coming-of-age story, a twelve-year-old who has the ability to flash on his head a map of any location returns to earth with his alien father to meet his human mother. The sequel is *Maphead: The Return* (1997). (I: 11 and up)

Klause, Annette. *Alien Secrets*. Delacorte, 1993. Puck befriends a troubled alien while traveling to another planet. (I: 10–YA)

Lawrence, Louise. *Star Lord*. Harper & Row, 1978. Erlich crashes on the mountain Mawrrhyn, not unlike the mountains of Wales, and explains that he comes from eleven light years across space. A brother and sister protect him from the military on earth until he escapes. (I: 12–YA)

———. *The Warriors of Taan*. Harper & Row, 1988. Khian—or Carl Simonson, as he was called on earth—comes to the planet Taan as a warrior but is intrigued with the nonviolent ways of the Stonewraiths. (I: 12–YA)

L'Engle, Madeleine. *A Wrinkle in Time*. Farrar, 1962. Meg and Charles Wallace go to the planet Camazotz to search for their scientist father. The sequels are *A Wind in the Door* (1973) and *A Swiftly Tilting Planet* (1978). (I: 10–YA)

Lively, Penelope. *Uninvited Ghosts and Other Stories*. Dutton, 1985. This book of short stories features both science fiction and fantasy, including "A Martian Comes to Stay," "Uninvited Ghosts," and "A Flock of Gryphons." (I: 9–11)

Mahy, Margaret. *Raging Robots and Unruly Uncles*. Overlook, 1993. Two fathers find that robots behave worse than children. (I: 9–11)

*Marshall, (James) Edward. *Space Case*. Dial, 1980. An extraterrestrial creature is mistaken for a Halloween trick-or-treater. (I: P–8)

Norton, Andre. *The Time Traders*. Baen, 1958/2000. In this book in the *Time Travel* series, the protagonist, Ross Murdock, is saved from going to jail. Instead, he is sent across several periods of time and finds alien spaceships in the Bronze Age. (I: 12 and up)

O'Brien, Robert C. *Mrs. Frisby and the Rats of NIMH*. Illustrated by Zena Bernstein. Atheneum, 1971. Laboratory rats who have been made superintelligent escape and help a field mouse, Mrs. Frisby, who in turn helps them get away. O'Brien's daughter, Jane Leslie Conly, has written two sequels, illustrated by Leonard Lubin: *Racso and the Rats of NIMH* (Harper, 1986) and *R-T, Margaret, and the Rats of NIMH* (Harper, 1990). (I: 10–12)

Peck, Richard. *Lost in Cyberspace*. Dial, 1995. While working on a research paper, two sixth-grade boys discover time travel through a laptop computer. The sequel is *The Great Interactive Dream Machine* (1996). (I: 10–12)

Pinkwater, Daniel. *Alan Mendelsohn, the Boy from Mars*. Dutton, 1979. Alan makes friends with a junior high school boy from earth. (I: 10–12)

———. *Fat Men from Space*. Dodd, Mead, 1977. The men from space are most interested in the earth's junk food. (I: 8–11)

Sargent, Pamela. *Alien Child*. HarperCollins, 1988. Nita and Sven are raised by guardians in an alien society. They discover that they were left as embryos by their parents until a time when earth's inhabitants could overcome the violent and destructive side of their nature. (I: YA)

Service, Pamela. *Stinker from Space*. Scribner's, 1988. Tsynq Yr, a secret agent from space, enters the body of a skunk. The story continues in *Stinker's Return* (1993). (I: 9–12)

Sleator, William. *The Boy Who Reversed Himself*. Puffin, 1998. Laura discovers that Omar has created mirror writing, and that he has reversed himself and can go into the fourth dimension. When Laura, a novice in four-space, tries to go there alone, she realizes that she doesn't know how to get back. (I: 11 and up)

———. *Interstellar Pig*. Dutton, 1984. As Barney plays a strange board game, it becomes real. (I: 11–YA)

———. *Strange Attractors*. Puffin, 1991. In this fictional depiction of chaos theory, "strange attractors" are beings from a parallel universe. Max finds himself having to protect a time travel device from its inventor and his alter ego from another time warp. (I: 11 and up)

Yolen, Jane. *Commander Toad and the Voyage Home*. Illustrated by Bruce Degen. Putnam, 1998. Commander Toad and his homesick crew aboard the Star Warts craft are heading home, but instead land on an uncharted planet. This is another volume in the easy reader series of humorous space travel stories. (I: 7–10)

*Yorinks, Arthur. *Company's Coming*. Crown, 1988. When a space ship lands, Shirley invites two visitors from outer space to dinner, to Moe's chagrin. (I: 6–8)

RESOURCES

Asimov, Isaac. *Asimov on Science Fiction*. Doubleday, 1981.

Barron, Neil, ed. *Anatomy of Wonder 4: A Critical Guide to Science Fiction*. R. R. Bowker, 1995.

———. *What Fantastic Fiction Do I Read Next? A Reader's Guide to Recent Fantasy, Horror, and Science Fiction*. Gale Research, 1997.

Cameron, Eleanor. *The Green and Burning Tree: On the Writing and Enjoyment of Children's Books*. Little, Brown, 1969.

Collier, Laurie, and Joyce Nakamura. *Major Authors and Illustrators for Children and Young Adults: A Selection of Sketches from Something about the Author*. Gale Research, 1993.

Cook, Elizabeth. *The Ordinary and the Fabulous: An Introduction to Myths, Legends, and Fairy Tales*. Cambridge Univ. Press, 1976.

Cooper, Susan. *Dreams and Wishes: Essays on Writing for Children*. McElderry, 1996.

Egoff, Sheila A. *Thursday's Child: Trends and Patterns in Contemporary Children's Literature*. American Library Association, 1981.

Greenlaw, M. Jean. "Fantasy." *Children's Books and Their Creators*. Ed. Anita Silvey. Houghton Mifflin, 1995.

Knight, Damon Francis. *In Search of Wonder: Essays on Modern Science Fiction*. Advent, 1967.

Le Guin, Ursula K. *The Language of the Night: Essays on Fantasy and Science Fiction*, rev. ed. HarperCollins, 1992.

Lynn, Ruth Nadelman. *Fantasy Literature for Children and Young Adults: An Annotated Bibliography*, 3rd ed. R. R. Bowker, 1989.

Sullivan, C. W. III, ed. *Science Fiction for Young Readers*. Greenwood, 1993.

Tymn, Marshall B., Kenneth J. Zahorski, and Robert H. Boyer. *Fantasy Literature: A Core Collection and Reference Guide*. R. R. Bowker, 1979.

REFERENCES

Alexander, Lloyd. "High Fantasy and Heroic Romance." *The Horn Book* 47 (December 1971): 577–94.

———. "Fantasy as Images: A Literary View." *Language Arts* 55 (1978): 440–46.

———. "Future Conditional." *Children's Literature Quarterly* 10.4 (Winter 1986): 164.

Andersen, Hans Christian. *The Princess and the Pea*. Houghton Mifflin, 1840/1979.

Asimov, Isaac, David C. Yeager, and Martin H. Greenberg (eds.). *Fantastic Reading: Stories and Activities for Grades 5–8*. Scott, Foresman, 1984.

Banks, Lynne Reid. *The Indian in the Cupboard*. Doubleday, 1985.

Cooper, Susan. "Escaping into Ourselves." *Celebrating Children's Books: Essays on Children's Literature in Honor of Zena Sutherland*. Ed. Betsy Hearne and Marily Kaye. Lothrop, Lee & Shepard, 1981, pp. 14–23.

Dahl, Roald. *Boy: Tales of a Childhood*. Farrar, 1984.

———. *George's Marvelous Medicine*. Illustrated by Quentin Blake. Knopf, 1982.

———. *The Witches*. Illustrated by Quentin Blake. Farrar, 1983.

de Brunhoff, Jean. *Babar*. Random House, 1937.

Dictionary of Literary Biography, vol. 52. Gale Research, 1986, p. 249.

Egoff, Sheila A. *Worlds Within: Children's Fantasy from the Middle Ages to Today*. American Library Association, 1988.

Elleman, Barbara. "Popular Reading-Time Fantasy Update." *Booklist* 81.19 (1985): 1407–8.

Frye, Northrop. *The Educated Imagination*. Indiana Univ. Press, 1957.

Greenlaw, M. Jean. "Fantasy." *Children's Books and Their Creators*. Ed. Anita Silvey. Houghton Mifflin, 1995a.

———. "Science Fiction." *Children's Books and Their Creators*. Ed. Anita Silvey. Houghton Mifflin, 1995b.

———. "Science Fiction: Images of the Future, Shadows of the Past." *Top of the News* 39 (1982): 64–71.

Heinlein, Robert A. *Starship Troopers*. Putnam, 1959.

Hesse, Karen. *Phoenix Rising*. Holt, 1994.

Hunter, Mollie. *Talent Is Not Enough: Mollie Hunter on Writing for Children*. Harper, 1976.

Jansson, Tove. *Finn Family Moomintroll*. Benn, 1950.

Kipling, Rudyard. *The Jungle Book*. Macmillan, 1894.

Lagerlöf, Selma. *The Wonderful Adventures of Nils*. Dover, 1906–07/1995.

Lawrence, Louise. *Andra*. Collins, 1971.

L'Engle, Madeleine. *Meet the Austins*. Vanguard, 1960.

———. *A Ring of Endless Light*. Farrar Straus, 1980.

Lofting, Hugh. *The Story of Doctor Dolittle*. Stokes, 1920.

Lynn, Ruth Nadelman. *Fantasy Literature for Children and Young Adults: An Annotated Bibliography*, 3rd ed. R. R. Bowker, 1989.

Olendorf, D., and D. Telgen, eds. "Diana Wynne Jones." *Something about the Author*, vol. 70. Gale Research, 1993, pp. 116–17.

MacDonald, George. *At the Back of the North Wind*. Illustrated by Charles Mozley. Penguin, 1871/1985.

Shapiro, Lesley. Unpublished manuscript, 1996.

Shelley, Mary Wollstonecraft. *Frankenstein*. Dutton, 1818/1963.

Silvey, Anita. *Children's Books and Their Creators*. Houghton Mifflin, 1995.

Slobodkin, Louis. *The Space Ship under the Apple Tree*. Macmillan, 1952.

———. *The Three-Seated Space Ship: The Latest Model of the Space Ship under the Apple Tree*. Macmillan, 1962.

Traw, Rick. "Beware! Here There Be Beasties: Responding to Fundamentalist Censors." *The New Advocate* 9.1 (1996): 35–56.

Tunnell, Michael O. "The Double-Edged Sword: Fantasy and Censorship." *Language Arts* 71 (1994): 606–12.

Tymn, Marshall B., Kenneth J. Zahorski, and Robert H. Boyer. *Fantasy Literature: A Core Collection and Reference Guide*. R. R. Bowker, 1979.

Verne, Jules. *From the Earth to the Moon*. Hertzel, 1865.

Wells, H. G. *War of the Worlds*. Random House, 1898/1960.

Williams, Jay. *Danny Dunn and the Anti-Gravity Paint*. McGraw, 1956.

Yolen, Jane. *Tough Magic: Fantasy, Faerie and Folklore in the Literature of Childhood*, 2nd ed. August House, 2000.

11 Informational Books and Biography

Its summit is the highest point on earth, 5½ miles above sea level. For thousands of years, the mountain has been a sacred place for those who live in its shadow. The rest of the world, however, wasn't really aware of the mountain until about 180 years ago. Ever since that time, climbers, scientists, and adventurers have been fascinated by this peak. Many have tried to climb it. Some have succeeded, but many more have failed. Some have died trying.

from The Top of the World: Climbing Mount Everest by Steve Jenkins

Informational books and biographies offer endless possibilities for use in the classroom. Children may select them for independent reading and teachers may choose them for class read-alouds. These books provide material for readers theater and process drama. They support content area and integrated theme study by fostering a spirit of inquiry as well as by supplying facts, concepts, and ideas for children's own investigations and projects. Informational books and biographies also serve as strong models for children's own expository writing.

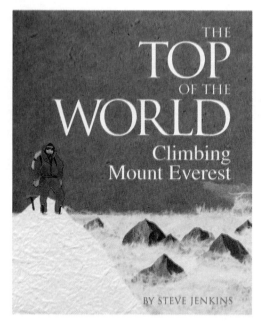

Illustration 11.1
Steve Jenkins guides readers to the summit of Mount Everest in this award-winning book. (Cover from *The Top of The World: Climbing Mount Everest* by Steve Jenkins. Reprinted by permission of Houghton Mifflin Company. All rights reserved.)

INFORMATIONAL BOOKS DEFINED

The Top of the World: Climbing Mount Everest by Steve Jenkins is an example of an informational book, one of a genre created mainly to inform readers about a particular subject, issue, or idea. *Informational books,* sometimes referred to as the *literature of fact,* convey factual information about the world. A good informational book, however, not only informs—it also excites. Russell Freedman has written many wonderful informational books and biographies for children, including the Newbery Medal winner *Lincoln: A Photobiography.* Here is how he describes his mission: "Certainly the basic purpose of nonfiction is to inform, to instruct, hopefully to enlighten. But that's not enough. An effective nonfiction book must animate its subject, infuse it with life. It must create a vivid and believable world that the reader will enter willingly and leave only with reluctance" (Freedman, 1992, p. 3).

Although biographies and informational books are generally classified as nonfiction, many writers of informational books prefer not to refer to their work as "nonfiction." They take exception to the term because it identifies their genre by what it isn't rather than what it is.

Why should informational books be included in a literature program? First, children are naturally curious about their world, and informational books satisfy their desire to know. Books such as *Over the Top of the World: Explorer Will Steger's Trek across the Arctic* by Will Steger and Jon Bowermaster enable children to travel to distant places; books such as *Amistad: A Long Road to Freedom* by Walter Dean Myers allow them to experience the past and reward their curiosity about their ancestors as well as their nation's history. Informational books help children to understand the natural world, explore science topics, learn how things work, play a game, or do a craft.

Even when children are not seeking the answer to a question, a good informational book may hook their attention with a colorful cover or catchy title and then draw them in and deepen their curiosity about a topic while also informing them about science, social studies, mathematics, the arts, or sports.

Both of these reasons lead to a third reason for making informational books readily available: As psychologists since Jean Piaget have pointed out, knowing a little bit about a topic gives a child a basis for learning more about it. When children read an informational book, they establish a framework, or schema, to assist them in reading more complex material about the topic in the future. Therefore, providing interesting informational books has the promise of making children more engaged learners.

It is no small achievement to write a book that will nurture young readers' curiosity at the same time as it informs them. Although people tend to reserve the word "creative" to describe writing that creates fictional worlds, a considerable amount of creativity also goes into producing a successful informational book. Works of fiction can count on plots—narrative structures—to engage their readers' curiosity and pull them into and through a work. Writers of informational books rely on expository structures to do the same thing. The writer of an informational book does not create a fictional world, but he or she must use words (and perhaps illustrations) carefully to create a unique vision of a portion of the actual world and draw readers into wondering about it, observing it, and understanding it. Three expository text structures that are used to do this are asking a question about an effect and then answering it by tracing a cause, following a chronological sequence of events, and comparing and contrasting the members of a group.

Readers benefit in several ways from becoming accustomed to the structure of informational books. In the same way that coming to know story structure enables students to read various stories more successfully, learning to follow expository text enables readers to comprehend informational books more successfully. Wise teachers say, "Children learn to read by reading." It is particularly true that children learn to read informational books by reading informational books.

Another advantage of reading informational books is that they draw children into the patterns of inquiry used by specialists in the fields in which the books are written. Reading James Cross Giblin's ***The Riddle of the Rosetta Stone: Key to Ancient Egypt*** not only informs readers but allows them to think along with a gifted writer doing historical inquiry. Reading ***Volcano: The Eruption and Healing of Mount St. Helens,*** by Patricia Lauber, shows young readers how a person investigates the cause and effect and environmental succession of a volcanic eruption and its aftermath. Studying Walter Wick's magnified stop-action color photographs in ***A Drop of Water*** enables young readers to see the many states of water, such as ice, steam, and dew.

THE EVOLUTION OF INFORMATIONAL BOOKS

Orbis Sensualium Pictus ("The Visible World in Pictures," usually referred to as *Orbis Pictus*), written by Moravian bishop Johannes Amos Comenius, was published in 1657. Considered the first informational book for children, it was a picture dictionary illustrated with woodcuts; the content was in Latin and focused mainly on natural history. It was used as a textbook throughout Europe until the late eighteenth century. In the nineteenth century, travel books emerged as the dominant type of informational books for children. Evelyn L. Wenzel (1982) describes the format of these books: "A family or an adult escorting a group of children takes a series of trips to a foreign land (usually several countries of Europe); the children are instructed by the adult, who, of course, attends to morals as well as to mind" (p. 18).

In 1922, the first Newbery Medal was awarded to an informational book, *The Story of Mankind,* by Hendrik Willem Van Loon. Twenty years later, a book that broke new ground by informing through lavish illustrations was named a Caldecott Honor Book. The author and illustrator was Holling C. Holling. The book, *Paddle-to-the-Sea,* was a fictionalized but geographically accurate account of an expedition through the Great Lakes to the Atlantic Ocean.

Edwin Tunis was a pioneering author/illustrator of informational books whose passion for American history is evident in his books. Tunis's finely detailed black-and-white line drawings present a visual representation of the social history of the United States. *Frontier Living,* one of his many books on colonial life and early American history, was a Newbery Honor Book in 1962.

Informational science books for children have been strongly influenced by the work of Millicent Selsam and Herbert Zim. With a strong background in biology and botany, Selsam published her first book, *Egg to Chick,* in 1946. Herbert Zim, an elementary science teacher, initiated the single-species title, writing focused accounts of individual species in *Snakes, Sharks,* and *Golden Hamsters.*

The photo-essay format made its debut in the world of children's informational books in the 1970s and remains very popular today. In 1976, photographer Jill Krementz published *A Very Young Dancer,* which became the first in a series of photo-essays about individual children engaged in various activities. Also during the 1970s, David Macaulay began crafting informational picture books in which text and illustrations formed a unified whole. Macaulay's specialty is oversized books about architecture illustrated with intricate pen-and-ink drawings. Two books following this format were named Caldecott Honor Books: *Cathedral* in 1974 and *Castle* in 1978.

Even though informational books have a long history, they have often been relegated to second-class status. For much of its history, the genre had the reputation of being boring, best used mainly for report work, and unpleasantly difficult for children to read. In other words, applying the term "nonfiction" to a book was like adding "unsweetened" to chocolate—likely as not, synonymous with "disappointment."

Since the 1980s, however, informational books have gained momentum, establishing a place as a popular and important genre in children's literature. During the 1980s, several nonfiction titles were named Newbery Honor Books: *Sugaring Time* by Kathryn Lasky, *Volcano: The Eruption and Healing of Mount St. Helens* by Patricia Lauber, and *Commodore Perry in the Land of Shogun* by Rhoda Blumberg. *The Glorious Flight: Across the Channel with Louis Blériot, July 25, 1909* by Alice and Martin Provensen received the Caldecott Medal in 1984. This book's carefully researched paintings re-create France in the early twentieth century, the flying machines developed by Blériot, and his dramatic flight across the English Channel in 1909. Informational books did not fare as well in the 1990s in the Newbery and Caldecott categories, with only one honoree. *The Great Fire,* Jim Murphy's carefully researched story of the Chicago fire of 1871, was named a Newbery Honor Book in 1996. Today, informational books abound—they cover a myriad of topics and have exciting, aesthetically appealing formats and strong writing.

Is it acceptable to fictionalize informational books?

A relatively new issue with regard to informational books is the value of a hybrid type often referred to as an *informational storybook.* Although the primary purpose of these books is to inform, they also contain fictionalized elements. The popular *Magic School Bus* books written by Joanna Cole and illustrated by Bruce Degen fit in this category. In these books, Ms. Frizzle and her class experience a fantasy adventure while they learn about the subject of the book, such as the waterworks, dinosaurs, or hurricanes. Because accuracy and authenticity are critical criteria in selecting informational books, this mixing of genres has become a controversial issue. Sayers (1982) stated, "The outstanding tenet of writing for children . . . is the insistence on first-hand authenticity in science, the arts, history, biography, and travel" (p. 97).

The blurring of the lines between fact and fiction is not a new issue. Margery Fisher (1982) has written that "the distinction between fiction and nonfiction is blurred and constantly shifting, but we still use it and need it" (p. 13). Mixed-genre books are the focus of debate because of their popularity with children on the one hand and their potential to mislead and confuse children on the other.

On the positive side, Leal (1993) points out some benefits of informational storybooks. They enable readers to "become involved in an engaging story" (pp. 63–64), identify with a main character, activate prior knowledge about the topic, generate interest for further content study, participate in discussion, and experience a model of process writing. Leal's research has confirmed children's positive responses to informational storybooks. On the other hand, Zarnowski (1995) believes that informational storybooks "introduce irrelevant, distracting, and potentially confusing 'information'" (p. 185). According to this view, students may have difficulty distinguishing fact from fiction in the story and thus may come away confused or with inaccurate information on the subject.

> Supporters and detractors of informational storybooks present compelling arguments. What do you think?

CATEGORIES OF INFORMATIONAL BOOKS

Informational books examine all kinds of topics and appear in many types of formats. Some informational books present a comprehensive view of their subject; others discuss one facet in depth. Let's look at a variety of informational books that are currently available.

Concept Books

Concept books help the youngest readers to know about their physical, natural, and social world. In concept books, information is conveyed through illustrations and text so that concepts are visually represented to young readers. Books about the alphabet, counting, colors, and shapes are popular kinds of concept books; a wide variety of topics are also presented to young readers in concept books. Different feelings and emotions are explained through innovative color photographs of fruit and vegetable sculptures in *How Are You Peeling?*

Foods with Moods by Saxton Freymann and Joost Elffers. Young readers learn about colors and their significance in kente cloth from Ghana and Togo in *Kente Colors* by Debbi Chocolate. John Ward's vivid paintings illustrate the symbolic colors and patterns of the cloth. Frank Asch shares information about the sun in simple text and colorful watercolor illustrations in *The Sun Is My Favorite Star.*

History

Some informational books help readers travel back in time to find out about people, places, and events of long ago. Through such books, children can catch a glimpse of the past.

Children of the Dust Bowl: The True Story of the School at Weedpatch Camp by Jerry Stanley recounts the work of dedicated California educator Leo Hart, who inspired the creation of a school for Okie children in 1940. "Okie" was the term used to describe poor Oklahoma farmers who moved to California during the Depression, when high winds and poor farming practices had made a dustbowl out of once-fertile Midwestern farmland. Stanley, a history professor in California, establishes the reasons for the Okies' mass migration to California and describes the prejudice and discrimination they faced.

Flight by Robert Burleigh takes readers across the Atlantic Ocean with Charles Lindbergh on the *Spirit of St. Louis.* Magnificent, vibrant paintings by Mike Wimmer contribute to the excitement and tension. Every detail of this transatlantic flight is described, including strategies Lindbergh used to stay awake, the critical importance of staying on course, and the means Lindbergh used to lighten the plane. Lindbergh's diary is quoted as a primary source throughout the book.

Two books, *Shipwreck at the Bottom of the World: The Extraordinary True Story of Shackleton and the Endurance* by Jennifer Armstrong and *Ice Story: Shackleton's Lost Expedition* by Elizabeth Cody Kimmel, recount the adventure of Sir Ernest Henry Shackleton, who, in 1914, led an expedition to the Antarctic in the ship *Endurance.* When the ship is crushed, Shackleton must lead his crew across ice and stormy seas to reach inhabited land. Both books are illustrated with maps and archival black-and-white photographs.

Understanding Peoples and Culture

Some informational books introduce young readers to children like themselves who live in other parts of the world or in other areas of the United States. These books help children to understand the concept of culture and appreciate similarities and differences among peoples around the world. A recent trend in photo-essays is to feature one child who lives in another part of the world or in a particular cultural group in the United States. By focusing on the life of one child, these books enable young readers to identify with the child while learning about another culture.

Liam Leathem is 11 years old and lives in Northern Ireland. His daily life is chronicled in *One Belfast Boy* by Patricia McMahon, who takes readers to Liam's school and the Holy Trinity Boxing Club, where Liam is preparing for the county championships. Irish photographer Alan O'Connor visually represents the text with his color photographs.

Award-winning photojournalist Jan Reynolds has traveled the globe to photograph and write books about vanishing cultures. In *Sahara,* readers meet Manda, a young boy from the nomadic Tuareg tribe of the Sahara desert. The text and color photographs allow readers to follow Manda and his father as they

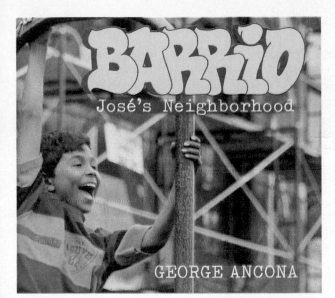

Illustration 11.2
Photographer George Ancona travels to San Francisco to follow the daily life of José, an eight-year-old Mexican American who lives in the Mission District. (Cover illustration from *Barrio, José's Neighborhood* by George Ancona. Photo essay and text copyright © George Ancona. Reprinted by permission.)

travel across the desert to the camel festival. Reynolds has also written *Mongolia,* which features the life of two herder boys, and *The Amazon Basin,* about the Yanomama people.

Author Ann Morris takes primary-aged children on a photographic journey around the globe to share how people celebrate in *Weddings,* work together in *Teamwork,* or live together in *Families.* In her books, Morris communicates the similarities among people of the world while also creating an awareness and appreciation of cultural differences.

Children from various cultures within the United States are the subject of books by Diane Hoyt-Goldsmith, who has teamed with photographer Lawrence Migdale to present portraits of cultures through a child's eyes. Joel introduces the Cajuns of Louisiana and their festivities in *Mardi Gras: A Cajun Country Celebration;* Ryan from San Francisco tells about Chinese traditions in *Celebrating Chinese New Year;* and Clarence Three Irons, Jr., explains the importance of the Buffalo to the Crow Indian Tribe of Montana in *Buffalo Days.* Author and photographer George Ancona shares the life of José Luís, who lives in the Mission District of San Francisco, in *Barrio: José's Neighborhood.*

Nature

Many informational books explore the natural world and lead children to discoveries about animals, plants, geology, geography, and the human body. National Geographic photographer Jim Brandenburg's *To the Top of the World: Adventures with Arctic Wolves* is a firsthand account of the author's experiences on Ellesmere Island, several hundred miles farther north than Alaska in Canada's Northwest Territories, as he carefully observed and photographed the wolves. Or readers can travel with naturalist Robert Bateman in *Safari.* Bateman paints animals of Africa and describes facts about familiar animals such as the leopard, elephant, and giraffe as well as lesser known animals like the wildebeest, cape buffalo, and dik-dik.

For an exciting underwater safari, children can read *Safari beneath the Sea: The Wonder World of the North Pacific Coast* by Diane Swanson, with breathtaking underwater photographs by the Royal British Columbia Museum. Descriptive language entices readers to continue turning the pages and relish the underwater sights. Swanson begins the book by asking readers to "imagine fish that tie themselves in knots, plants that flash lights in the dark, sea stars that turn their stomach inside out and mammals that hammer their food. Life in the sea is bizarre, beautiful, funny, and fabulous" (p. 1).

Informational books even offer adventures inside the human body. In *The Brain: Our Nervous System,* Seymour Simon guides readers inside the human brain to explore its parts and what they do. A photography note explains that the images "were taken by various kinds of scanners, which change X-ray photos in computer code to make clear, colorful graphics."

The Arts

Art, music, drama, and dance enrich people's lives; through the arts, children creatively express thoughts and feelings, tell stories, and celebrate life.

Children are introduced to the art world through books such as *The Sculptor's Eye: Looking at Contemporary American Art* by Jan Greenberg and Sandra Jordan and *Discover Great Paintings* by Lucy Micklethwait. By presenting facts about each painting and posing questions for readers to answer, Micklethwait's book invites readers to investigate famous paintings. Similarly, Greenberg and Jordan connect sculpture to children's personal experiences and involve readers in the text.

Music, opera, and marionettes combine in *The Magic of Mozart: Mozart, the Magic Flute, and the Salzburg Marionettes* by Ellen Switzer. In this three-part book, readers learn about Mozart's life; the story of his opera *The Magic Flute,* as performed by the Salzburg Marionettes; and the Salzburg Marionettes.

The world of theater is brought to children by author and illustrator Aliki in *William Shakespeare & the Globe.* Aliki tells the history of the famous Globe Theatre, describes Shakespeare's life and work, and discusses recent efforts to reconstruct the Globe Theatre in London.

Discovering How Things Work

Children are naturally curious about how things work. David Macaulay's *The New Way Things Work* provides a comprehensive introduction to the mechanics of movement, the elements, waves, electricity, the digital domain, and the invention of machines. The book is heavily illustrated with Macaulay's intricate, detailed drawings, which both convey and clarify information. After reading Macaulay's brief introduction to robots, children might want to pursue the topic in more depth in Gloria Skurzynski's *Robots: Your High-Tech World.* Illustrated with color photographs, this book explains how robots move and are controlled and describes their many uses and their history. In *Super Cool Science: South Pole Stations Past, Present, and Future,* Sandra Markle describes the two research stations at the South Pole and the one that is currently being constructed. She explains how these stations were built and the kinds of investigations that scientists at the stations conduct.

Activity, Craft, and How-to Books

Informational books can help children to develop and pursue hobbies. Children who want to improve their culinary talents might consult *The Little House Cookbook* by Barbara M. Walker, which includes recipes for foods that are mentioned in various *Little House* books and also gives fascinating information about food and cooking during Laura Ingalls Wilder's time. The book has recipes for johnnycake, codfish balls, and salt-rising bread. Another children's cookbook, *To Every Season: A Family Holiday Cookbook,* by Jane Breskin Zalben, instructs children about a wide range of holidays and provides recipes for each one.

To find out how to work with clay and use a potter's wheel, children can consult *The Kids 'N' Clay Ceramics Book* created by Kevin Nierman and written by Elaine Arima. In this book, children will find basic ceramic techniques and detailed instructions for specific projects such as decorating in leather-hard or soft clay. Curtis H. Arima's illustrations help to clarify each step in the directions.

Children can consult informational books for directions on playing a game or enjoying a recreational activity. Mary Lankford provides directions for nineteen variants of the age-old game in *Hopscotch around the World.* A descriptive paragraph tells how each variant is played in the country where it originates, and a diagram accompanies step-by-step directions. In *Lacrosse: The National Game of the Iroquois,* Diane Hoyt-Goldsmith's text instructs children and Lawrence Migdale's color photographs illustrate specific lacrosse skills like cradling the ball and checking with the stick.

Series Books

Series books are developed by publishers to provide groups of works about related topics. The books have a specified format, which means that every book in the series is organized in the same way. A popular series, the *Eyewitness Books,* published by Dorling Kindersley, presents information on many different topics and is extensively illustrated with color photographs. Another series, *Let's Read-and-Find-Out Science,* from HarperCollins, was initiated by Dr. Franklyn M. Branley, an astronomer and former chairperson of the American Museum–Hayden Planetarium. This series introduces primary school children to science by providing them with material for independent reading. Well-known children's authors have contributed—notably Patricia Lauber with *Be a Friend to Trees* and Aliki with *Dinosaurs Are Different.*

HOW INFORMATIONAL BOOKS WORK

What distinguishes informational books from other literary genres? Writers of informational books face the challenging task of compiling all their research on a topic and then selecting facts, concepts, and ideas to include in the book. Further, they must decide how to organize this information in a way that is interesting and accessible to their readers. Authors of informational books employ an expository style of writing to explain, inform, and describe. Expository writing uses various organizational patterns to present information, such as description, chronological sequencing, explanation, comparison/contrast, defining with examples, and problem-solution. For example, Jim Murphy organizes *Across America on an Emigrant Train* sequentially; readers follow Robert Louis Stevenson's travels from Scotland to San Francisco in search of his true love. Vicki Cobb explains and defines terms with examples in *The Secret Life of Cosmetics:* "There has been an almost endless list of *dentifrices,* substances used for cleaning the teeth. These included, at one time or another: ground chalk, ground charcoal, powdered pumice stone, soap, lemon juice, ashes, tobacco mixed with honey, a mixture of cinnamon and cream of tartar (ugh!) to name a few" (p. 25).

Authors of informational books must also generate and maintain readers' interest. The beginning chapters of James Cross Giblin's books pique readers' interest. Note, for example, this first paragraph from *Chimney Sweeps:*

> On a sunny October morning, a van pulls up in front of a ranch-style house in an American suburb. Out jump a young man and woman dressed in black tailcoats and top hats. They are both professional chimney sweeps, and are wearing the costume that has been the trademark of chimney sweeps for almost four hundred years. (p. 1)

An author's enthusiasm for the topic is usually evident in a good informational book. Writers use various literary techniques to engage the reader: posing a question, writing in the first person, addressing the reader directly as "you," and using highly descriptive language and imagery. Informational books need not be serious, and many writers incorporate humor to sustain readers' involvement. A good example is *If You Made a Million* by David M. Schwartz, with its exaggerated, colorful illustrations by Steven Kellogg.

Graphics play an important role in informational books. They can help to clarify abstract concepts that may be unknown to readers or difficult to understand. They can convey specific facts and specialized vocabulary or present a realistic visual rendering of a concept. They can help to provide the background knowledge necessary for readers' understanding. Graphics take many forms, including photographs, paintings, drawings, charts, maps, and copies of documents.

Authors of informational books may provide readers with other aids for locating and understanding material, such as an index, glossary, table of contents, or list of additional facts. A reference list or an acknowledgment regarding the sources or experts consulted is usually included.

Informational books require readers to engage in critical thinking, as they are called on to distinguish fact from opinion and theory. Readers should consider the author's spirit of inquiry and what kind of research and investigation went into the book. Authors have their own points of view and perspectives, and readers must decide whether the author has presented a balanced discussion or biased it in some way. After gleaning all the information in the book, readers draw inferences and reach their own conclusions.

MAJOR WRITERS OF INFORMATIONAL BOOKS AND THEIR WORKS

Many authors write informational books for children. Several who have received recognition for their significant contributions to the genre are discussed in this section.

Aliki

Aliki, a much-loved author and illustrator of informational picture books and biographies for children, wrote her first book, *The Story of William Tell,* in 1960. Since that time, her informational books have spanned a wide range of topics, from dinosaurs to the Middle Ages. Aliki presents complex, detailed subject matter to young children in a clear, accessible manner. Many of her books are appropriate for the early primary grades. Her illustrations make concepts clear and visible to children. Aliki's books often include humorous elements that are complemented by a comic-strip format with dialogue balloons.

In *How a Book Is Made,* selected for the PBS television program "Reading Rainbow," Aliki traces the steps in a book's development and describes the kinds of occupations that are involved in the process. Using cats instead of people as the characters and a comic-strip format, Aliki begins with the author and concludes with the salespeople who sell the book. In *Mummies Made in Egypt,* Aliki leads readers on a fascinating journey to ancient Egypt, presenting a comprehensive view of mummification. Her finely detailed illustrations are accompanied by labels, captions, and longer explanations.

George Ancona

George Ancona, photographer and writer of children's books for thirty years, began his career as an art director in New York City. When he entered the world of children's publishing, he took the photographs for books written by others. He often collaborated with authors Joan Anderson (e.g., *The First Thanksgiving Feast*) and Maxine B. Rosenberg (e.g., *Making a New Home in America*). He also collaborated with Remy Charlip and Mary Beth Miller for the

Handtalk series, four books that introduce children to finger spelling and sign language. The first book he wrote and photographed, ***Monsters on Wheels,*** published in 1974, is an informational book about machines. Several of his recent books, such as ***Mayeros, Pablo Remembers: The Fiesta of the Day of the Dead,*** and ***The Pinata Maker/El Pinatero,*** focus on his Yucatan and Mexican heritage.

Ancona has written and/or photographed more than 75 books for children. Garcia-Johnson (1996) pointed out that Ancona "is renowned for his vivid photo essays that allow children to immerse themselves in new ideas and cultures, to appreciate labor that so often goes unnoticed behind the scenes of daily life, and to accept themselves as well as others" (p. 7). His work has received many honors and consistently appears on the Notable Children's Trade Books in the Field of Social Studies. One of his recent books, ***Carnaval,*** transports readers to Olinda, Brazil, to participate in the five-day Carnaval in February and see the famous giant puppets.

Joanna Cole

Joanna Cole has been writing informational science books for children since the 1971 publication of ***Cockroaches.*** In recent years, she has teamed with Bruce Degen to create the popular *Magic Schoolbus* series, which emphasizes the joy of science and shows that complex information can be conveyed with humor and enthusiasm. ***The Magic School Bus at the Waterworks*** was named a *Boston Globe–Horn Book* Honor Book, and ***The Magic School Bus inside the Earth*** was chosen as a "Reading Rainbow" Feature Selection.

Cole collaborated with photographer Jerome Wexler on several books introducing young children to the anatomy of animals and amphibians: ***A Cat's Body, A Frog's Body,*** and ***A Horse's Body.*** In clear, lucid prose, Cole explains technical vocabulary and presents the animal's anatomy to primary-grade children. Cole's books have been selected as American Library Association Notable Books and as Outstanding Science Trade Books for Children by the National Science Teachers Association. Her contribution to nonfiction literature for children was recognized in 1991 by the *Washington Post*–Children's Book Guild Nonfiction Award.

Gail Gibbons

As an author and illustrator of more than one hundred informational picture books, Gail Gibbons has introduced primary-grade children to a range of topics. After receiving an undergraduate degree in fine arts, she pursued a career as a staff artist for a New York television station. Gibbons has the special ability to explain complicated information lucidly and concisely for young children. Her illustrations help to introduce concepts and show children a visual representation of them.

Through watercolor illustrations and text, ***The Great St. Lawrence Seaway*** gives the seaway's history, explains important vocabulary associated with it (such as "lock" and "canal"), and describes how locks work. The book contains many helpful aids for readers, such as labeled illustrations, maps, and a concluding page of additional information. If young children wish to satisfy their curiosity about spiders, Gibbons's ***Spiders*** will answer their questions. Gibbons explains that spiders are not insects and shows young readers the differences between the two in detailed, labeled diagrams of a spider's body and an insect's body.

Gail Gibbons's work has been widely recognized. Two of her books, ***The Milk Makers*** and ***Sunken Treasure,*** were selected for "Reading Rainbow."

Gibbons received the *Washington Post*–Children's Book Guild Award for her contribution to children's nonfiction.

James Cross Giblin

James Cross Giblin had a successful career as a children's book editor before he began writing nonfiction for children. After majoring in English and dramatic arts at Case Western Reserve University, he earned a master's degree in playwriting from Columbia University. As a writer of children's informational books, he is known for his imaginative and engaging treatment of unusual topics. For example, *From Hand to Mouth or, How We Invented Knives, Forks, Spoons, and Chopsticks and the Table Manners to Go with Them* traces the history of eating utensils in great detail.

Giblin does careful research, not only for his books' text but also for the illustrations, which are carefully selected photographs, prints, and drawings. In *The Riddle of the Rosetta Stone: Key to Ancient Egypt,* Giblin uses illustrations from the British Museum and the Metropolitan Museum of Art. His books have received many honors: *Chimney Sweeps: Yesterday and Today* was awarded the 1983 American Book Award for Children's Nonfiction, and *The Truth about Santa Claus* was named a *Boston Globe–Horn Book* Nonfiction Honor Book in 1986. Giblin's contribution as a writer of nonfiction for children was honored in 1996 when he received the *Washington Post*–Children's Book Guild Award.

James Haskins

As a child living in segregated Demopolis, Alabama, James Haskins (who also writes as Jim Haskins) was prevented from using the public library. His mother purchased an encyclopedia set, volume by volume, from the grocery store, and Jim had read every volume by the time he was 14. He taught special education in New York City and currently is an English professor. Haskins has written over one hundred books on social science topics, many of which have focused on the African American experience. In addition to informational books, Haskins also writes biographies for children. He has developed the popular *Count Your Way* series, which uses a counting format to present information about various cultures.

In *The March on Washington,* Haskins recounts the events of August 28, 1963, when 250,000 people marched on Washington in support of racial equality; the book highlights the courageous individuals who made the march happen and describes the planning that was needed. The history of the Underground Railroad is told in *Get on Board: The Story of the Underground Railroad.* Readers visit the "stations" of the railroad and learn about the remarkable courage of the slaves and those who assisted them.

Kathryn Lasky

A versatile writer who skillfully writes both fiction and nonfiction for children, Kathryn Lasky commented, "People often ask me how and why I do both fiction and nonfiction. I am equally attracted to both kinds of writing because for me the most important thing is if a story is real. Real stories can be either fiction or nonfiction" (Scribner's, 1985). In 1981, Kathryn Lasky received the *Boston Globe–Horn Book* Award for Nonfiction for *The Weaver's Gift,* a collaboration with her husband, photographer Christopher Knight. Another collaboration, *Sugaring Time,* was named a Newbery Honor Book in 1983. Lasky

Ask the Author...

James Cross Giblin

James Cross Giblin

How do you take complex informational material and make it both understandable and appealing to a child audience?

The first thing I do when I begin to research a new nonfiction book is to look for the story line in the material. For every subject—whether it's a biography, or a history of plagues, or the life cycle of the woolly mammoth—has an implicit story line within it, just as every novel has a plot. It's what keeps readers turning the pages, eager to find out what comes next.

A good example of a nonfiction story line can be found in my biography of Charles A. Lindbergh. It embraces the entire sweep of Lindbergh's life, from his historic nonstop flight across the Atlantic in 1927, to the kidnapping and death of his firstborn son, to his determined efforts to keep the United States out of World War II. The story line reaches its climax when Lindbergh became involved late in life with the conservation movement, saying, "I would rather have birds than airplanes."

Young people today are exposed to every facet of a public figure's personality via television and the Internet. In light of this, I believe writers for children have an obligation to present a full and rounded picture of the people and events they explore in their books. That's why I decided to discuss Lindbergh's controversial views in the years before World War II and why I subtitled the biography "A Human Hero." I hoped the phrase would suggest that even a hero like Charles Lindbergh may not always act in a heroic fashion.

When I research a book, I always keep my eye out for details that will flesh out the subject and bring it to life for young readers. Examples of such details are the lavatory facilities (or lack of them) aboard Lindbergh's plane, *The Spirit of St. Louis,* and the way that rats, and the fleas they hosted, spread the deadly Black Death in the Middle Ages. I described the latter in *When Plague Strikes: The Black Death, Smallpox, AIDS.*

Every informational book I research and write is first of all a voyage of discovery for me, the author. And if I shape the material in a lively and dramatic way, I hope it will be just as entertaining and informative a voyage for my readers.

James Cross Giblin is the author of many well-received books for children and young adults. Among his recent titles are The Amazing Life of Benjamin Franklin, The Mystery of the Mammoth Bones, *and* Charles A. Lindbergh: A Human Hero. *When Jim isn't writing, he enjoys reading; going to plays, art exhibits, and movies; and exploring New York City, where he lives.*

Favorite Books as a Child

When I was a child, I loved picture books set in long ago times and far off places. I'd pore over them for hours, virtually memorizing the illustrations. Three of my special favorites were *The Painted Pig,* a story of Mexico by Elizabeth Morrow; *Skippack School,* by Marguerite DeAngeli, about a Mennonite boy in colonial Pennsylvania; and *The Story of Ferdinand,* by Munro Leaf. I identified completely with Ferdinand, the young bull who would rather smell the flowers than fight in the bullring.

---

received the 1986 *Washington Post*–Children's Book Guild Award for her body of work in children's nonfiction.

Lasky and Knight experience firsthand the subjects that they write about and photograph. They traveled to an island south of Iceland to research ***Surtsey: The Newest Place on Earth,*** about the creation of an island by a

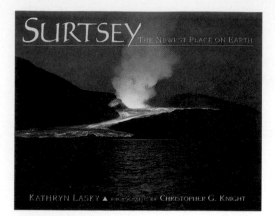

Illustration 11.3
Kathryn Lasky and her husband Christopher Knight received special permission to visit the new island of Surtsey so that they could write all about it. (*Surtsey* by Kathryn Lasky. Text copyright © 1992 Kathryn Lasky. Photographing copyright © 1992 Christopher Knight. Reprinted by permission of Hyperion Books for Children.)

volcanic eruption in the Atlantic Ocean in 1963. Each chapter of the book begins with a selection from the Icelandic creation myth, the *Edda,* as Lasky intertwines Icelandic folklore with a description of the island's creation. Her descriptive language, rich in imagery, engages readers in this amazing event of the natural world.

Patricia Lauber

Patricia Lauber has written more than sixty informational books on science topics for children. She writes, "Overall, my aims are to help children understand how the earth (or its parts) works and to try to imbue them with some of my own sense of wonderment, in the hope that they will grow up to be good stewards, who will take care of the earth, not just use (or abuse) it" (1992, pp. 14–15).

Lauber's books have received much critical acclaim: *Volcano: The Eruption and Healing of Mt. St. Helens* was named a 1987 Newbery Honor Book, and *Seeing Earth from Space* was a 1991 Orbis Pictus Honor Book. Patricia Lauber was recognized for her contribution to children's nonfiction with the 1983 *Washington Post*–Children's Book Guild Award.

In *The News about Dinosaurs,* Lauber promotes the spirit of inquiry as she points out that what were previously considered "facts" about dinosaurs are being altered with new discoveries. She juxtaposes what scientists used to think with "The News Is," which presents the most current scientific knowledge. For example, although "scientists used to think dinosaurs did not take care of their young. . . . The News Is: At least some dinosaurs do seem to have cared for their young" (p. 26).

Milton Meltzer

Milton Meltzer has been writing outstanding informational books and biographies for children for more than forty years. His books focus on history, social issues, and underrepresented groups in society. Meltzer features the authentic voices of people about whom he writes and primary source materials. On writing history for children, Meltzer (1981) says, "The writing of history is as much an art as the writing of poetry or fiction. The writer tries to express his vision of history and to communicate it to the reader. As historian he does not invent that past, but he must give it artistic shape if he is to connect with the reader" (p. 96).

Meltzer's books have received wide recognition and have appeared on various notable book lists. *All Times, All Peoples: A World History of Slavery* was awarded the 1980 Christopher Award; *Never to Forget: The Jews of the Holocaust* was designated a 1976 *Boston Globe–Horn Book* Nonfiction Honor Book; and *The Jewish Americans: A History in Their Own Words, 1650–1950* was named a 1983 *Boston Globe–Horn Book* Honor Book.

In *The Amazing Potato: A Story in Which the Incas, Conquistadors, Marie Antoinette, Thomas Jefferson, Wars, Famines, Immigrants and French Fries All Play a Part,* Meltzer provides a fascinating, thoroughly researched social history of the potato. In the foreword, Meltzer points out that he wanted young readers to see "how such an everyday object, one we scarcely notice except perhaps when we have a hankering for french fries, can be of such vast significance in the history of humankind" (n. pag.).

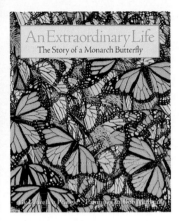

Illustration 11.4

A monarch butterfly's amazing journey from Massachusetts to Mexico and back north again is described by Laurence Pringle and visually represented by Bob Marstall. (*An Extraordinary Life: The Story of a Monarch Butterfly* by Laurence Pringle, paintings by Bob Marstall. Published by Orchard Books, an imprint of Scholastic Inc. Painting copyright © 1997 by Bob Marstall. Reprinted by permission.)

Laurence Pringle

Former editor of *Nature and Society,* published by the American Museum of Natural History, Laurence Pringle has contributed significantly to informational science books for children. Drawing on his degrees in wildlife biology, Pringle has written more than seventy books that focus primarily on nature, wildlife, and ecology and environmental issues. In discussing what it means to "do science," Pringle (1981) wrote, "Doing science means being curious, asking questions. It means having a healthy skepticism toward authority and announced truths. It is both a way of looking at the world and a way of thinking. It values both fantasy and reality, and provides a framework for telling the difference" (p. 110).

In ***Antarctica: The Last Unspoiled Continent,*** Pringle presents an in-depth look at this fascinating continent, including its history, climate, plant and animal life, and political and environmental issues. Pringle selected color photographs from many sources for the book, which includes a glossary of terms and an index. The 1998 Orbis Pictus Award–winning ***An Extraordinary Life: The Story of a Monarch Butterfly*** traces the migratory flight of one monarch butterfly from Massachusetts to its winter home in Mexico and back again. Detailed paintings by Bob Marstell enhance the text, which gives readers information about the life cycle and migration patterns of these beautiful butterflies. Laurence Pringle received the 1999 *Washington Post*–Children's Book Guild Award for Nonfiction.

Seymour Simon

Seymour Simon, a prolific writer of more than 125 informational science books for children, attended the Bronx High School of Science. After receiving a bachelor's degree, he began teaching science in New York City schools. His first children's book, ***Animals in Field and Laboratory: Projects in Animal Behavior,*** was published in 1968. In 1979, after more than twenty years of teaching, Simon stopped to pursue writing full time. He received the Eva L. Gordon Award from the American Nature Society and the *Washington Post*–Children's Book Guild Award for Nonfiction. Many of his books have been named Outstanding Science Trade Books by the National Science Teachers Association.

Simon's conversational, clear, and direct writing style enables children to understand a host of science topics. He immediately creates interest among his readers, as in the beginning of *Sharks* (1995, n. pag.): "It never fails. You're at the ocean, swimming in the surf, and someone pretends to be a shark. They sing ominous music and then lunge at you." Full-page color photographs support the text, which attempts to convey "the truth about sharks" so that readers will "see them as the fascinating creatures they are, instead of the monsters of myth."

CRITERIA FOR SELECTING INFORMATIONAL BOOKS

Informational books have many unique characteristics that distinguish them from other genres of children's literature. Although children's needs and interests should always be foremost in your mind as you choose informational books, there are other specific criteria to consider as well. These are discussed below.

Accuracy and Authenticity

An informational book must be accurate in conveying factual, documented material. To determine accuracy, if you are not knowledgeable about the subject yourself, consider the author's credentials and qualifications. Often authors will credit experts in the field who have assisted them or reviewed the manuscript for accuracy. Has the author provided a reference list or cited sources for the information?

Another indication of accuracy is the copyright date: When was the book published? Is the information outdated? If world events happen so rapidly that an otherwise outstanding book becomes quickly outdated, consider supplementing the inaccurate information with current articles from newspapers and magazines. For example, don't necessarily eliminate all books about the Soviet Union, even though it has been disbanded. On the other hand, if the essence of the book is completely outdated, it's better not to use the book.

Other aspects of accuracy include whether the author makes a clear distinction between known fact and theory or speculation and whether the book offers a balanced presentation of the topic. If there is more than one interpretation or theory about the topic, have they all been fairly presented? Another important consideration is whether the author has avoided stereotypes about race, ethnicity, gender, disabilities, lifestyle, and socioeconomic class.

Organization

A second selection criterion concerns the book's overall organization and the way in which the author has developed ideas and content. Authors have many options regarding how to organize material. One way to organize information is sequentially, or chronologically—that is, in the order in which events or activities occur. Authors may also choose to arrange material by key concepts, main ideas, or distinguishing characteristics. Authors may develop ideas by beginning with generalizations and then becoming more specific. Or authors may begin with a simple aspect of the topic and then gradually add complexity. Often, authors compare a new concept to something already familiar to readers.

If the book is lengthy, has it been divided into chapters? Does the text have headings and subheadings to assist readers in understanding the book's organization? Has the author connected ideas and shown the interrelationships among them? Think about the audience for the book, too. Given the age range of the intended audience, are the scope and organization of content appropriate?

Format and Design

A book's appearance will affect children's interest in it. Is the book visually attractive and appealing? How big is the book? Does it have an unusual format? What size is the type? Can children read it easily? What are the nature and quality of the illustrations—photographs, paintings, drawings, reproductions of realia, graphs, maps, charts? Do illustrations complement, clarify, and extend the text? What kinds of information are they conveying? In thinking about the format, consider whether the placement of illustrations on the page contributes to the overall design.

Writing Style

As you would in evaluating other genres, consider the author's writing style in selecting informational books. How has the author generated interest in and enthusiasm for the topic? Does the author invoke a spirit of wonder and inquiry in the reader? Has technical vocabulary been introduced within a context meaningful to the reader? Does the author's writing include descriptive and figurative language? Is the writing clear and interesting?

BIOGRAPHY DEFINED

Some of the oldest books for children are biographies—works that describe and discuss the lives of real individuals. In earlier periods, it was common to expose children to the (sometimes idealized) lives of national and cultural heroes. The practice still exists but in a somewhat altered form. For one thing, in the United States, there is growing recognition that the society is made up of more than one culture, so the goal of many writers of biography has become promoting a more inclusive view of noteworthy Americans. For another thing, the trend toward exposure-oriented journalism—journalism that delves below the surface—has become steadily stronger since the Vietnam War era. Thus, even children are less likely than they were in previous generations to believe larger-than-life accounts of heroes. Third, the study of history has become less preoccupied with great people and great events and more focused on the common people and the ambience of earlier times. Thus, even though a biography might have a well-known person as its subject, the author is likely to explain that person in the context of his or her time and the concerns, available choices, and social movements of the day.

How does biography differ from historical fiction? Biographies that focus on famous individuals from the past offer insight into historical times just as historical fiction does. However, the information presented in a biography is based on known facts about the individual and her or his time period. Incidents, dialogue, and people are not invented or imagined, as they are in historical fiction. Autobiographies differ from biographies in that their authors are writing about themselves.

Biographies have some unique features that justify their inclusion in a literature program. First, they help children learn from the lives of others. In a biography, children can see how choices a person makes early in life can bear fruit later on or how inauspicious beginnings can lead to a good outcome. Reading biographies can also encourage children to recognize links between people's lives and the social and historical times in which they lived. For instance, in her biography **You Want Women to Vote, Lizzie Stanton?**, Jean Fritz writes, "Yes, Elizabeth Cady Stanton did want women to vote. It was an outlandish idea, but that's what she wanted. Not at first. As a child, she knew that girls didn't count for much, but she didn't expect to change that. First she had to grow up" (p. 1). This biography of Stanton, who dedicated her life to women's suffrage in the United States, describes gender roles during the nineteenth century and reasons for people's beliefs about women's suffrage. Through biographies, children come to understand the people who have shaped history, created inventions, discovered scientific principles, composed music, crafted works of art, and contributed to their local communities. Children realize that they, too, can make a difference in the world.

Illustration 11.5
With humor and insight, Jean Fritz recounts the life of the famous suffragette Elizabeth Cady Stanton. (*You Want Women to Vote, Lizzie Stanton?* by Jean Fritz. Illustration copyright © 1995 by DyAnne DiSalvo-Ryan. Used by permission of G. P. Putnam's Sons, a division of Penguin Putnam Inc.)

THE EVOLUTION OF BIOGRAPHY

In the past, biographies for children were criticized for poor writing, invented details, and exaggeration of the positive side of their subjects. Moreover, in the first half of this century, the subjects of biographies were mostly limited to white males who were political leaders or had made some other historical contribution to society. The prevailing thought—alive and well since ancient times— was that children should hear or read biographies of individuals who displayed admirable virtues and thus could serve as role models for the children to emulate. These individuals were idealized—presented as being morally perfect. Because societal norms dictated that children should not be exposed to the less savory realities of life, such as discrimination, violence, or abuse, early biographies were bland and unrealistic.

Fictionalization was also an accepted practice in earlier children's biographies. For instance, authors routinely invented conversations and scenes for which there was no historic basis. True, authors had good motives for these distortions. In explaining why he fictionalized biography for children, F. M. Monjo (1982) pointed out that he used a child associated with the "great figure" as narrator because it "makes possible a casual intimacy which, I believe, young readers find congenial" (p. 99). Author Robert Lawson included fantastic elements in his fictionalized biographies. His study of Christopher Columbus, *I Discover Columbus,* was narrated by Aurelio, a parrot; Lawson's biography of Benjamin Franklin, *Ben & Me,* was told by a mouse named Amos. Although these books were very popular with children, they raised the question of whether it was necessary to fictionalize biographies to such an extent to make them palatable to young readers. The answer was decades away.

As with informational books in general, critical recognition of biographies for children was slow in coming. The first Newbery Medal for a work of biography was awarded in 1934 to *Invincible Louisa,* a biography of Louisa May Alcott, written by Cornelia Meigs. In 1940, James Daugherty received the Newbery Medal for *Daniel Boone.* (Contemporary readers, though, may be appalled at the book's portrayal of Native Americans.) In the same year, the Caldecott Medal for the best illustrated book of the year went to a biography, *Abraham Lincoln,* by Ingri D'Aulaire and Edgar Parin D'Aulaire. This book is said to have "established the picture-book biography for younger children as a valued staple of library-book collections" (Hoke, 1995, p. 188). Still, biographies for children had a long way to go.

The 1970s were a turning point for children's biographies. With the publication of *And Then What Happened, Paul Revere?* in 1973, author Jean Fritz set a new standard. Fritz created an authentic biography for children without any invented dialogue; she also included "Notes from the Author," containing additional facts keyed to various pages of the book. Fritz did not rely on the fictionalizing of earlier days to make her books congenial to young readers. Her conversational, humorous, and easily accessible writing style—as well as her focus on one or two interesting events—is what drew and still draws readers to her works.

Since the early 1970s, biographies have advanced further, to give children wider representation of noteworthy people. Biographies written in the past three decades have featured men, women, and children of many ethnic and racial backgrounds engaging in a variety of occupations and contributing in many different ways to society. For example, *Sequoyah's Gift,* by Janet Klausner, describes the Cherokee leader who developed the writing system for the Cherokee language; *Cleopatra,* by Diane Stanley and Peter Vennema, highlights the life of the famous Egyptian queen. Contemporary authors handle their subjects with a "new realism," presenting them as human beings with vulnerabilities and weaknesses.

In 1988, Russell Freedman received the Newbery Medal for *Lincoln: A Photobiography,* establishing a new era for the prestige and recognition of authentic biography for children. James Cross Giblin, himself a distinguished author of informational books as well as an editor, explains that the significance of *Lincoln* in the evolution of children's biography is that it offers a "fresh approach to familiar material, demythologizing Lincoln without debunking him," telling "a dramatic true story," emphasizing the visual with its photo-essay format, and providing an "accessible yet literate text" (1992, p. 25).

In 1999, the Caldecott Medal was awarded to *Snowflake Bentley,* written by Jacqueline Briggs Martin and illustrated by Mary Azarian. This picture-book biography describes the life of Wilson Bentley, whose fascination with snowflakes led to his dedicated work photographing snowflakes, documenting the unique features of each one, and becoming an authority on them. Azarian's woodcut illustrations, hand-tinted with watercolors, document Bentley's life and the beauty of snowflakes.

CATEGORIES OF BIOGRAPHIES

Biographies for children feature contemporary people, historical figures, athletes, and entertainers—as well as young people who are similar to those reading the biographies. A current trend in children's biographies is the publication of series biographies. These biographies follow a specified format and include the same types of information for each individual. Carolrhoda Books has several biography series: *Creative Minds,* targeted for children in grades 3–6, includes biographies of Hans Christian Andersen and Milton Hershey; *Trailblazers, Achievers, and Sports Achievers,* for grades 4 and above, features biographies of Zora Neale Hurston, Jackie Kennedy Onassis, and Shaquille O'Neal. Little, Brown and Company touts its *Sports Illustrated for Kids* biographies, which include books about Steffi Graf and Michael Jordan. For primary grades, Random House offers *Step-Up Biographies,* with such titles as **Meet Thomas Jefferson** and **Meet Christopher Columbus;** Holiday House has its *Picture Book Biographies* by David Adler, who has written **A Picture Book of Amelia Earhart** and **A Picture Book of Thurgood Marshall.**

Partial Biographies

Instead of presenting an entire life, a writer may create a more interesting work by selecting one segment from the person's life and exploring it in depth and detail. Jean Fritz's biographies of famous early Americans are good examples of partial biographies. For example, in **Why Don't You Get a Horse, Sam Adams?** Fritz recounts how patriot Samuel Adams walked the streets of pre-Revolutionary Boston promoting independence from England. (Was he earthbound out of fear of horses or because he wanted to stay closer to the people?) Another example of a partial biography is **Coming Home: From the Life of Langston Hughes** by Floyd Cooper, which limits its coverage to the groundbreaking poet's childhood.

Complete Biographies

In a complete biography, the author recounts a person's life from birth to the present or to the person's death if he or she is no longer living. Angela Shelf Medearis chronicles the life of journalist and civil rights activist Ida B. Wells-Barnett in **Princess of the Press: The Story of Ida B. Wells-Barnett.** Readers learn about Wells-Barnett's birth during the Civil War and her accomplishments until her death in 1931. A chronology of Wells-Barnett's life and endnotes are also included. For older readers, Susanna Reich has detailed the life of the German pianist in **Clara Schumann, Piano Virtuoso.** In writing this complete biography illustrated with archival photographs and document reproductions, Reich consulted primary sources such as Clara's diary and letters.

Collective Biographies

A *collective biography* is a book describing the lives of several people who have something in common. In *Indian Chiefs*, Russell Freedman chronicles the lives of six famous Native American leaders: Red Cloud of the Oglala Sioux, Santanta of the Kiowa, Quanah Parker of the Comanche, Washakie of the Shoshoni, Joseph of the Nez Perce, and Sitting Bull of the Hunkpapa Sioux. Freedman points out that "the six chiefs whose stories are told here were called upon to lead their people at a time of crisis" (p. 9).

Another approach to collective biography is seen in the collaborative work of author Kathleen Krull and illustrator Kathryn Hewitt. They have produced many collective biographies, including *Lives of the Musicians: Good Times, Bad Times (and What the Neighbors Thought)*, *Lives of the Artists: Masterpieces, Messes (and What the Neighbors Thought)*, and *Lives of Extraordinary Women: Rulers, Rebels (and What the Neighbors Thought)*. The format of these appealing and humorous books includes biographical sketches of the individuals accompanied by watercolor illustrations. Krull has carefully researched each individual, discovering little-known information that will fascinate readers.

Autobiographies and Memoirs

In an autobiography, a person writes about his or her own life. Many children's authors have written their autobiographies. Children who delight in these authors' books will enjoy reading about their childhoods and how they became writers. Laurence Yep penned *The Lost Garden*, Yoshiko Uchida provided her memoirs in *The Invisible Thread*, and Beverly Clearly wrote *A Girl from Yamhill: A Memoir*. Award-winning children's book illustrator Anita Lobel shares recollections of her childhood as a Polish Jew during the Holocaust in *No Pretty Pictures: A Child of War.*

Ordinary individuals often experience extraordinary events or inspire others with their courage and determination. Ruby Bridges gives readers a glimpse into her childhood in *Through My Eyes.* Ruby was 6 years old in 1960 when federal marshals escorted her to school. Ruby's historic childhood as the young girl who integrated the New Orleans public school is shared in this award-winning book. In another award-winning autobiography, *Leon's Story,* Leon Walter Tillage describes his life as the son of a sharecropper and his experiences living in segregated North Carolina in the years before and during the Civil Rights movement.

Biographies of Explorers of Earth and Space

Discovery and exploration enable civilizations to move forward, as people continue taking risks to tackle the unknown. Maria Mitchell discovered a comet; her life is described in *Maria Mitchell: The Soul of an Astronomer* by Beatrice Gormley. Eratosthenes figured out how to measure the earth's circumference; Kathryn Lasky tells his story in *The Librarian Who Measured the Earth.* Modern-day discoverer Dr. Robert Ballard uncovered the *Titanic*'s sunken remains; his life is described by Rick Archbold in *Deep-Sea Explorer: The Story of Robert Ballard, Discoverer of the Titanic.* Astronaut Dr. Sally Ride was the first woman to fly in space; her life is portrayed in *Sally Ride: Shooting for the Stars* by Jane Hurwitz and Sue Hurwitz.

Biographies of Social and Political Activists

Political leaders have always been a popular subject for biographies. Numerous political biographies of the U.S. presidents, and of many of their

Illustration 11.6

In this award-winning memoir, illustrator Anita Lobel recounts her childhood as a Polish Jew during World War II and its aftermath.

(*No Pretty Pictures: a child of war* by Anita Lobel. Copyright © 1998. Used by permission of Greenwillow, a division of HarperCollins Publishers.)

wives, have been written for children over the years. Authors have also focused on courageous individuals in other parts of the world who have led their people to freedom. For example, Leonard Everett Fisher's *Gandhi* chronicles the life of the man whose nonviolent approach to resistance paved the way for India's independence from Great Britain in 1947. Social reformers are dedicated to the betterment of people's lives. In *Mother Jones: One Woman's Fight for Labor,* Betsy Harvey Kraft provides an insightful look at the story of Mary Harris Jones, an Irish immigrant who helped to organize labor unions, especially among coal miners, in the early twentieth century. Another great woman reformer, Jane Addams, founded the community center called Hull House in an impoverished area of Chicago in 1889. She is featured in *Peace and Bread: The Story of Jane Addams* by Stephanie Sammartino McPherson.

Biographies of Artists and Authors

Many biographies feature individuals who have contributed to the arts through music, art, dance, drama, entertainment, and writing. *Anna Pavlova: Genius of the Dance,* by Ellen Levine, tells the story of the world-famous ballerina. Martha Graham, choreographer and modern dance innovator, is described in Trudy Garfunkel's *Letter to the World: The Life and Dances of Martha Graham.* The life of artist Jacob Lawrence is recounted in *Story Painter: The Life of Jacob Lawrence* by John Duggleby. This acclaimed African American artist grew up during the Harlem Renaissance, and his paintings depict the history of the African American experience. The literary contribution of African American writer Zora Neale Hurston is chronicled in *Sorrow's Kitchen: The Life and Folklore of Zora Neale Hurston* by Mary E. Lyons. Children's authors have been the subject of many biographers. Notable books are *Nothing Is Impossible: The Story of Beatrix Potter* by Dorothy Aldis and *Louisa May: The World and Works of Louisa May Alcott* by Norma Johnston.

Biographies of People Who Persevered

Throughout history, people in cultures and nations throughout the world have faced persecution because of religion or ethnicity or have endured terrible economic or political conditions. The stories of how people have persevered against seemingly insurmountable obstacles provide inspiration and teach valuable lessons.

Religious and ethnic persecution in Europe provided the backdrop for many biographies in this category. In *The Road from Home: The Story of an Armenian Girl,* David Kherdian describes the life of his mother, who, as a child in Turkey, survived the Turkish persecution of Armenians during the early years of the twentieth century. Not all children survived the Holocaust of World War II; in *Hilde and Eli,* David Adler describes the life of two children who perished at the hands of Nazis. Probably the best-known child of the Holocaust, Anne Frank, is remembered in *Anne Frank: A Hidden Life* by Mirjam Pressler.

African Americans' quest for freedom began during slavery; their quest for equal treatment progressed through the civil rights movement and continues today. Those who have been part of this struggle have been featured in many biographies: Martin Luther King, Jr., Harriet Tubman, Frederick Douglass, Sojourner Truth. Rosa Parks became famous for refusing to sit in the back of a Montgomery, Alabama, bus in 1955. Jim Haskins collaborated with Parks to tell her life story in *Rosa Parks: My Story.* An easy-to-read biography for younger readers is *I Am Rosa Parks* by Wil Clay.

HOW BIOGRAPHIES WORK

Biographies are stories about real people. Like the writer of any good story, the biographer must create a main character about whom children care and want to learn more. Biographers develop their subjects' personalities and re-create their lives by describing their actions and interactions with others, what they say, and the ways in which others talk about them. Descriptive language creates visual pictures in readers' minds, which help readers to put themselves in the time and place of the biography's subject. Although biographers present lives of real people based on careful research, they must also interpret facts and events. As Zarnowski (1990) points out:

> While biographers do gather all the information they can, they also filter that information through their minds. Biographers are active decision makers, deciding what to include and what to omit, what to highlight, and what to place in the background, and what to claim as truth and what to suggest as informed speculation. Biographers are interpreters of the information they collect. (p. 9)

Just as biographers interpret information, readers must interpret critically what they are reading. They must decide whether the portrait of the person is balanced, whether any aspects of the person's life have been fictionalized, whether dialogue is authentic, and whether the person is believable.

MAJOR WRITERS OF BIOGRAPHIES AND THEIR WORKS

A number of authors have established themselves as writers of biographies for children. The husband and wife team of Ingri D'Aulaire and Edgar Parin D'Aulaire were pioneers in the field of children's biography; they were both artists known for their oversized picture-book biographies of famous Americans, such as *Abraham Lincoln, Benjamin Franklin,* and *George Washington.* Four contemporary authors who have influenced the nature and evolution of children's biographies are discussed in this section.

David Adler

David Adler, a former math teacher, has written books for children since 1972. A prolific writer of more than one hundred children's books, he pens novels and informational books as well as biographies. Adler is known for his picture-book biographies that primary school children can read independently. He notes, "The picture book biographies must be short, but that makes them very difficult to write" (Olendorf & Telgen, 1993, p. 4). Many of his biographies and informational books focus on Jewish persons or topics.

Our Golda: The Story of Golda Meir, named a Carter G. Woodson Award Honor Book by the National Council for the Social Studies, traces Golda Meir's life from her childhood in Russia through her immigration to Milwaukee in 1906, her marriage and move to Palestine, her participation in the shaping of Israel, and her election in 1969 as Israel's Prime Minister.

In *Jackie Robinson: He Was the First,* Adler follows Robinson's life from his birth in 1919 to his death in 1972. This complete biography is easily accessible to elementary students and includes a table of contents, index, and time line of Robinson's life.

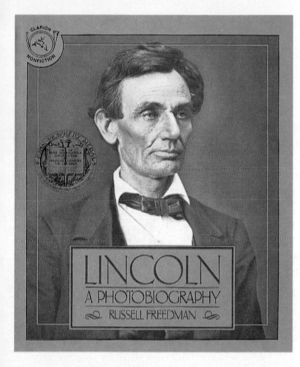

Illustration 11.7

Winner of the Newbery Medal, Russell Freedman's photobiography provides a sympathetic, yet realistic picture of one of the most compelling of the U.S. Presidents. (Cover from *Lincoln: A Photobiography* by Russell Freedman. Jacket copyright © 1987 by Houghton Mifflin Company. Reprinted by permission of Houghton Mifflin Company. All rights reserved.)

Russell Freedman

Russell Freedman graduated from the University of California at Berkeley and worked for the Associated Press and on several television shows before becoming a writer of books for children in 1961. He has distinguished himself as an authentic biographer, conducting meticulous research to craft insightful portraits of real people. His biographies are illustrated with carefully selected photographs and include indexes, references, and lists of places to visit if one wants to learn more about the subjects. Freedman's biographies have received many awards: *Franklin Delano Roosevelt* received the 1991 Orbis Pictus Award; *The Wright Brothers: How They Invented the Airplane* was named a Newbery Honor Book in 1992; and *Eleanor Roosevelt: A Life of Discovery* was a 1994 Newbery Honor Book.

Lincoln: A Photobiography, which received the Newbery Medal in 1988, includes carefully researched illustrations to support and complement the text. In reflecting about this book, Freedman (1992) said, "The more I studied Lincoln, the more I came to appreciate his subtleties and complexities. The man himself turned out to be vastly more interesting than the myth" (p. 9).

Jean Fritz

Jean Fritz has shaped and directed the genre of children's biography for more than twenty-five years. In addition to writing biography, Fritz also writes historical fiction and informational books. Attention to detail, the use of humor, and the ability to present historical figures in an interesting, appealing way are characteristics of her work. Fritz (1995) commented, "I like to think of a historian or a biographer as an artist who has made a compact with the past to be true to it. As an artist, the historian has to use his or her imagination to penetrate the record, to dig deep into the past to the place where life emerges" (p. 257).

Several of Fritz's biographies have received prestigious awards: *Stonewall* and *Will You Sign Here, John Hancock?* were *Boston Globe–Horn Book* Honor Books; *The Great Little Madison* was named both the Orbis Pictus Award winner and the *Boston Globe–Horn Book* Nonfiction Award recipient in 1990; and *Where Do You Think You're Going, Christopher Columbus?* was an American Book Award Honor Book. For her significant contributions to children's literature, Fritz received the Laura Ingalls Wilder Award of the American Library Association in 1986.

Diane Stanley

Diane Stanley has achieved prominence for her picture-book biographies for children in the upper elementary grades. She was born in Texas, grew up in New York City, and began her artistic career as a medical illustrator. She transferred her talent for detailed, realistic drawing and painting to children's books, and her first biography, *Peter the Great,* was published in 1986. Since then, she has collaborated with her husband, Peter Vennema, and her mother, Fay Stanley, to produce more than ten picture-book biographies. Stanley also has self-illustrated several picture books, illustrated books written by others, and written novels. Stanley's work is described in *Something about the Author* (2000):

Acknowledged for clearly identifying what is known and what is speculative about the lives she is outlining, Stanley writes her works in concise prose and illustrates them with elegant, detailed watercolor and gouache illustrations that are done in the artistic style of the periods in which subjects lived. (p. 193)

Her books have been named to the list of *Notable Children's Trade Books in the Field of Social Studies* by the National Council for the Social Studies and have received many awards. She illustrated **The Last Princess: The Story of Princess Ka'iulani of Hawai'i** by Fay Stanley, which received the Carter G. Woodson Award; **Leonardo da Vinci** received the Orbis Pictus Award and the *Boston Globe–Horn Book* Award for Nonfiction. Stanley was named recipient of the 2000 *Washington Post*–Children's Book Guild Award for Nonfiction.

CRITERIA FOR SELECTING BIOGRAPHIES

Like informational books, biographies have many unique characteristics that distinguish them from other genres of children's literature. As when choosing informational books, keep children's needs and interests foremost in your mind as you choose biographies. In addition, consider the following specific selection criteria.

Choice of Subject

The first issue to think about in evaluating a biography is the subject of the work. Is the person someone whose life will be of interest to young readers? Has the individual contributed in a positive way to society? The biography's subject might not be someone famous but rather an ordinary individual whose life inspires and/or interests readers. In some cases, controversial figures and people who have had a negative impact on society are also appropriate subjects for biographies because children's perspectives are broadened by reading about them; children can practice critical thinking by examining the individual's impact on society.

Characterization

In writing a biography, an author must develop the subject so that readers identify with him or her as an authentic, believable human being. Notice how the author handles characterization and what details about the person's life the author includes. Readers learn about characters through their actions and interactions with others, through their thoughts and feelings, and through the things that others say about them. It is important for the author to avoid stereotyping the individual in any way. Another aspect of good characterization is balanced treatment of the subject. Is the individual's life presented honestly? Has the author avoided idealizing the individual and creating a superhuman personality?

Accuracy and Authenticity

A biography needs to reflect careful research about the individual's life to ensure that the information presented is accurate. Generally, authors try to consult primary source material if it is available, such as the subject's personal journal or letters to others. If photographs are used as illustrations, they should be carefully selected to support the biography. In addition, consider what kinds of information the author has selected to include. Has any important information been omitted? The author should include a bibliography that lists the sources of information. An author's note may explain the type of research that was conducted or describe background material.

Writing Style

The author's writing style influences readers' interest and enjoyment of a biography. Has the author written in an engaging style that maintains readers' attention? Has the author created a story line that will involve the reader without sacrificing accuracy? What is the author's tone? It may be serious, humorous, or neutral. From whose point of view is the biography told?

AWARDS FOR INFORMATIONAL BOOKS AND BIOGRAPHIES

Although many awards, such as the Newbery Medal and the Caldecott Medal, may be given to a children's book of any genre, certain awards focus exclusively on nonfiction for children. Many of these awards are indicated on the book in some way—for example, by a seal that appears on the book jacket. The National Council of Teachers of English annually bestows the Orbis Pictus Award for Outstanding Nonfiction for Children, with one book receiving the award and several others being cited as Honor Books. The *Boston Globe–Horn Book* Award, which has a separate category for nonfiction, is given annually to one book, with up to three books being designated as Honor Books. The National Council for the Social Studies sponsors the Carter G. Woodson Book Award to honor children's books that sensitively and accurately deal with ethnic minorities and race relations. The Washington, D.C., Children's Book Guild, in conjunction with the *Washington Post,* annually presents the *Washington Post*–Children's Book Guild Nonfiction Award to an author in recognition of his or her contribution to children's nonfiction. The American Nature Society honors an author for his or her contribution to science writing for children with the Eva L. Gordon Award for Children's Science Literature. The Golden Kite Award of the Society for Children's Book Writers has a nonfiction category, which includes one winner and one Honor Book annually. The Jefferson Cup Award, sponsored by the Virginia Library Association, is presented to a book of fiction and a book of nonfiction dealing with U.S. history or biography. In addition, the Children's Book Council, in cooperation with both the National Council for the Social Studies and the National Science Teachers Association, develops annual lists of outstanding books from all genres: *Notable Children's Trade Books in the Field of Social Studies* and *Outstanding Science Trade Books for Children.*

Bestowed for the first time in 2001, the Robert F. Sibert Informational Book Award is to be presented annually to the author of the most distinguished informational book published during the preceding year. The award honors the long-time president of Bound to Stay Bound Books, Inc. and is sponsored by the company. The American Library Association's Association for Library Services to Children (ALSC) administers the award. In 2001, the Sibert Award went to Marc Aronson for **Sir Walter Ralegh and the Quest for El Dorado.** For the purpose of this award, informational books are defined as "those written and illustrated to present, organize and interpret documentable factual material for children." Poetry and traditional literature are not eligible. Honor books may be named if they are truly distinguished.

TEACHING IDEAS

Writing in a Comparison/Contrast Format. Introduce children to books whose purpose is to compare and contrast two animals or concepts—for example, *Toad or Frog, Swamp or Bog?* by Lynda Graham-Barber, *A Wasp Is Not a Bee* by Marilyn Singer, and *What's the Difference?* by Elizabeth Lacey. After discussing the techniques the author used to make the comparisons, ask children to write their own comparison of two animals, plants, or items.

Studying an Author in Depth. Involve a group of children in an in-depth study of one particular author of informational books or biographies. Have the children read several books by the author and respond to these books in various ways, such as with discussion, writing, art, and drama. Small groups of students can create projects such as murals, mobiles, dioramas, and skits to represent the books and the author.

Critically Reviewing Books on the Same Topic. Ask children to select a topic and read at least two books about it. For example, students can compare *Shipwreck at the Bottom of the World* by Jennifer Armstrong with *Ice Story: Shackleton's Lost Expedition* by Elizabeth Cody Kimmel. Have children develop categories for comparison and chart the similarities and differences in the books. This idea can also be applied to biographies. Ask children to read two or more biographies about an individual and chart their similarities and differences.

Readers Theater. Have groups of three or four children read the same biography (for example, *Kate Shelley: Bound for Legend* by Robert D. San Souci) and create a readers theater script of the biography. After writing the script, the group can present it to the entire class.

EXPERIENCES FOR YOUR LEARNING

1. Review an award-winning informational book such as *The Great Fire* by Jim Murphy and an award-winning biography such as *Eleanor Roosevelt: A Life of Discovery* by Russell Freedman. Critique each book according to the criteria in this chapter. Would you agree that the books are worthy of the awards they received? What do you see as their strengths and weaknesses?

2. Select a topic that interests you—say, wolves. Compare the treatment of the topic in an informational book (such as *To the Top of the World: Adventures with Arctic Wolves* by Jim Brandenburg) to its treatment in other genres such as novels (for example, *Julie of the Wolves* by Jean Craighead George), picture books (*Wolf's Favor* by Fulvio Testa), and folktales (*Peter and the Wolf* retold by Selina Hastings). How do different genres contribute to your understanding of the topic?

3. Select three informational books on the same topic (for example, for the Negro Baseball Leagues, you could use *Black Diamond: The Story of the Negro Baseball Leagues* by Patricia C. McKissack and Fredrick McKissack, Jr., *Shadow Ball: The History of the Negro Leagues* by Geoffrey C. Ward, Ken Burns, and Jim O'Connor, and *Leagues Apart: The Men and Times of the Negro Baseball Leagues* by Lawrence S. Ritter). Review the illustrations in each book. How do the illustrations convey information? What kind of information is presented? What types of illustrations are included—photographs, paintings, drawings, diagrams, charts? Are some illustrations more effective than others? What makes them more effective? Compare the illustrations on a chart, with a column for each book. Share your findings with classmates.

4. Compare the scope, content, and presentation of material about a science topic in an informational book and a textbook. How are the books alike? How are they different? Which type of book do you think is more effective in conveying information? Why? Discuss these issues with your classmates.

RECOMMENDED BOOKS

* indicates a picture book; I indicates interest level (P = preschool, YA = young adult)

History

Anderson, Joan. *The First Thanksgiving Feast.* Photographs by George Ancona. Clarion, 1989. Re-creates the first Thanksgiving with photographs taken at Plimouth Plantation. (I: P–10)

Armstrong, Jennifer. *Shipwreck at the Bottom of the World: The Extraordinary True Story of Shackleton and the Endurance.* Crown, 1998. Chronicles the 1914 expedition to Antarctica led by Ernest Shackleton and the perils he and his crew experienced. (I: 10–YA)

Blumberg, Rhoda. *Commodore Perry in the Land of the Shogun.* Lothrop, Lee & Shepard, 1985. Describes Matthew Perry's important voyage to Japan to open trade and whaling ports to America. (I: 10–YA)

———. *Full Steam Ahead: The Race to Build a Transcontinental Railroad.* National Geographic Society, 1996. A fascinating account of the race between the Central Pacific and the Union Pacific to finish laying the tracks for the transcontinental railroad. (I: 10–YA)

Burleigh, Robert. *Flight.* Philomel, 1991. Chronicles Charles Lindbergh's 1927 solo flight across the Atlantic from New York to Paris. (I: 8–12)

Colman, Penny. *Rosie the Riveter: Women Working on the Home Front during World War II.* Crown, 1995. Details the role of women in the wartime workforce. (I: 9–YA)

*Gibbons, Gail. *Sunken Treasure.* Crowell, 1988. Full-color illustrations help to describe the sinking of an ancient Spanish galleon and the discovery of its treasures. (I: 6–10)

Giblin, James Cross. *The Riddle of the Rosetta Stone: Key to Ancient Egypt.* Crowell, 1990. The story of the discovery of the ancient Rosetta Stone and the deciphering of its hieroglyphics. (I: 8–12)

Haskins, James. *Get on Board: The Story of the Underground Railroad.* Scholastic, 1993. Chronicles the Underground Railroad, which shepherded slaves to freedom in the North. (I: 8–12)

Kimmel, Elizabeth Cody. *Ice Story: Shackleton's Lost Expedition.* Clarion, 1999. When Shackleton's boat, the *Endurance,* is crushed, he and his crew brave a dangerous journey to land. (I: 10–YA)

Lawrence, Jacob. *The Great Migration: An American Story.* HarperCollins, 1993. A narrative sequence of vibrant paintings helps to tell the story of African Americans' migration from the South to the North around World War I. (I: 8–12)

McKissack, Patricia C., and Fredrick L. McKissack. *Christmas in the Big House—Christmas in the Quarters.* Scholastic, 1994. A fascinating and insightful comparison of life in a Virginia plantation house and in the slave quarters around Christmas time in 1859. (I: 8–12)

Murphy, Jim. *Across America on an Emigrant Train.* Clarion, 1993. The story of Robert Louis Stevenson's trip from Scotland to San Francisco in 1879 in search of his true love is combined with a history of the railroad. (I: 10–YA)

———. *The Great Fire.* Scholastic, 1995. Describes the Chicago fire of 1871 and its effects on individual people and the city. (I: 10–YA)

Myers, Walter Dean. *Amistad: A Long Road to Freedom.* Dutton, 1998. The story of the famous rebellion aboard the slave ship *Amistad* and the court cases that followed. (I: 10–YA)

*Provensen, Alice, and Martin Provensen. *The Glorious Flight: Across the Channel with Louis Blériot.* Viking, 1983. In 1909, Blériot flies across the English Channel from France to England in thirty-seven minutes. (I: 7–10)

Stanley, Jerry. *Children of the Dust Bowl: The True Story of the School at Weedpatch Camp.* Crown, 1992. The inspirational story of how educator Leo Hart and Okie children built their own school during the Depression in California. (I: 10–YA)

———. *I Am an American: A True Story of Japanese Internment.* Crown, 1994. Discusses the relocation of Japanese Americans from 1942 to 1945. (I: 10–YA)

Warren, Andrea. *Orphan Train Rider: One Boy's True Story.* Houghton Mifflin, 1996. The story of Lee Nailling, who rode the orphan train in 1926, provides the framework for discussing this train, which transported orphaned and abandoned children from the East Coast to the Midwest from 1854 to 1929. (I: 9–12)

Understanding Peoples and Cultures

*Aliki. *Mummies Made in Egypt*. HarperCollins, 1979. Details the reasons for mummification and explains how it was done. (I: 7–12)

Ancona, George. *Barrio: José's Neighborhood*. Harcourt Brace, 1998. This photo-essay describes the daily life of an eight-year-old Mexican American boy living in the Mission District of San Francisco. (I: 6–10)

———. *Carnaval*. Harcourt Brace, 1999. Travel to Olinda, Brazil, to celebrate the annual Carnaval. (I: 6–10)

———. *Mayeros: A Yucatec Maya Family*. Lothrop, Lee & Shepard, 1997. Photo-essay presents the history and contemporary life of the Mayeros, who live in the Yucatan, Mexico. (I: 6–10)

———. *Pablo Remembers: The Fiesta of the Day of the Dead*. Lothrop, Lee & Shepard, 1993. Pablo remembers his grandmother in the three-day Mexican celebration. (I: 6–10)

———. *The Piñata Maker/El piñatero*. Harcourt Brace, 1994. This bilingual text describes how Don Ricardo crafts piñatas in southern Mexico. (I: 6–10)

Anderson, Joan. *The American Family Farm*. Photographs by George Ancona. Harcourt, 1989. Describes the daily farm life of three families in Georgia, Iowa, and Massachusetts. (I: 8–12)

Cha, Dia. *Dia's Story Cloth: The Hmong People's Journey of Freedom*. Stitched by Chue and Nhia Thao Cha. Lee & Low, 1996. A hand-embroidered story cloth recounts the story of the Hmong people of ancient China and Laos and their emigration to the United States. (I: 8–12)

*Chocolate, Debbi. *Kente Colors*. Illustrated by John Ward. Walker, 1996. Explains the meaning of the colors and patterns of the kente cloth worn by Ashanti and Ewe peoples. (I: P–8)

Giblin, James Cross. *When Plague Strikes: The Black Death, Smallpox, AIDS*. HarperCollins, 1995. Discusses epidemic diseases and their political, social, religious, and cultural consequences. (I: 10–YA)

Hoyt-Goldsmith, Diane. *Celebrating Chinese New Year*. Photographs by Lawrence Migdale. Holiday House, 1998. Ten-year-old Ryan and his family celebrate Chinese New Year. (I: 7–12)

———. *Mardi Gras: A Cajun Country Celebration*. Photographs by Lawrence Migdale. Holiday House, 1995. A Cajun boy introduces readers to his heritage and the holiday of Mardi Gras. (I: 7–12)

———. *Buffalo Days*. Photographs by Lawrence Migdale. Holiday House, 1997. Clarence, a Crow Indian, describes his life on a Montana reservation and the importance of the buffalo. (I: 7–12)

McMahon, Patricia. *One Belfast Boy*. Photographs by Alan O'Connor. Houghton Mifflin, 1999. Share the daily life of eleven-year-old Liam, a Catholic boy in Belfast who enjoys boxing. (I: 8–12)

Meltzer, Milton. *Cheap Raw Material: How Our Youngest Workers Are Exploited and Abused*. Viking, 1994. A compelling account of child labor from long ago to the present. (I: 10–YA)

*Morris, Ann. *Families*. HarperCollins, 2000. Explains how families around the world are alike and different. (I: P–8)

*———. *Teamwork*. Lothrop, Lee & Shepard, 1999. Shows how teams around the world work together to get things done. (I: P–8)

*———. *Weddings*. Lothrop, Lee & Shepard, 1995. Presents marriage customs and rites around the world. (I: P–8)

Onyefulu, I. *Ogbo: Sharing Life in an African Village*. Harcourt, 1996. Six-year-old Obioma explains the Nigerian tradition of ogbo, or age group, in this photo-essay. (I: 7–11)

Osborne, Mary Pope. *One World, Many Religions: The Ways We Worship*. Knopf, 1996. Photographs and text describe the world's major religions: Judaism, Christianity, Islam, Hinduism, Buddhism, Confucianism, and Taoism. (I: 8–YA)

Reynolds, Jan. *The Amazon Basin*. Harcourt, 1993. A photo-essay on the Yanomama people of the Amazon Basin. (I: 7–12)

———. *Mongolia*. Harcourt, 1994. The nomadic way of life in Mongolia is described in this photo-essay. (I: 8–12)

———. *Sahara*. Harcourt, 1991. The Tuareg tribe, who live in the Sahara desert, are featured in this photo-essay. (I: 7–12)

Science and Nature

*Asch, Frank. *The Sun Is My Favorite Star*. Harcourt, 2000. This informational picture book shares ways the sun helps the earth. (I: P–8).

Bash, Barbara. *Ancient Ones: The World of the Old-Growth Douglas Fir*. Sierra Club, 1994. Watercolor paintings enhance this discussion of the life cycle of the Douglas fir and the ecology of the forest. (I: 6–12)

———. *Shadows of Night: The Hidden World of the Little Brown Bat*. Sierra Club, 1993. Describes the life of the brown bat in text and illustrations. (I: 6–12)

Bateman, Robert. *Safari*. Little, Brown, 1998. Animals of Africa are described in text and paintings. (**I: 6–12**)

Brandenburg, Jim. *To the Top of the World: Adventures with Arctic Wolves*. Walker, 1993. Magnificent color photographs enhance this personal account of the author's observations of a wolf pack. (**I: 6–12**)

Brooks, Bruce. *Making Sense: Animal Perception and Communication*. Farrar, 1993. An insightful examination of animals' six senses and how they use them to communicate. (**I: 8–12**)

Cherry, Lynne. *A River Ran Wild*. Harcourt, 1992. This history of the Nashua River in New England explores humans' influence on nature. (**I: 6–12**)

Cole, Joanna. *The Magic School Bus inside the Earth*. Illustrated by Bruce Degen. Scholastic, 1987. Ms. Frizzle and her class investigate geology on a field trip to the center of earth. (**I: 5–8**)

Cone, Molly. *Come Back, Salmon*. Photographs by Sidnee Wheelwright. Sierra Club, 1992. The inspiring story of the students at Jackson Elementary School in Everett, Washington, who adopted the stream by their school and brought it back to life. (**I: 7–12**)

Dewey, Jennifer Owings. *Wildlife Rescue: The Work of Dr. Kathleen Ramsay*. Photographs by Don MacCarter. Boyds Mills, 1994. Describes the wildlife center in rural New Mexico founded by veterinarian Ramsay, who takes care of injured and sick animals. (**I: 7–12**)

*Freymann, Saxton, and Joost Elffers. *How Are You Peeling? Foods with Moods*. Scholastic, 1999. Fruit and vegetable sculptures convey various moods and emotions. (**I: P–8**)

*Gibbons, Gail. *The Milk Makers*. Macmillan, 1985. Describes how dairy cows produce milk and the steps in getting it to the store. (**I: P–8**)

*———. *Spiders*. Holiday House, 1993. A picture-book examination of different kinds of spiders and their characteristics. (**I: P–8**)

Jenkins, Steve. *The Top of the World: Climbing Mount Everest*. Houghton Mifflin, 1999. Discusses attempts to climb Mount Everest and information about mountaineering. (**I: 8–12**)

Lasky, Kathryn. *Sugaring Time*. Photographs by Christopher Knight. Macmillan, 1983. Describes maple sugar time on a Vermont family farm. (**I: 8–12**)

———. *Surtsey: The Newest Place on Earth*. Hyperion, 1992. Describes the creation of Surtsey, a volcanic island off the coast of Iceland. (**I: 8–12**)

Lauber, Patricia. *The News about Dinosaurs*. Bradbury, 1989. Examines new discoveries about dinosaurs that challenge what scientists previously believed. (**I: 6–12**)

———. *Seeing Earth from Space*. Orchard, 1990. NASA photographs complement the text, which provides a unique perspective on the earth. (**I: 10–YA**)

———. *Volcano: The Eruption and Healing of Mount St. Helens*. Bradbury, 1986. Illustrated with color photographs, this book describes the 1980 eruption of Mount St. Helens and its aftermath. (**I: 8–12**)

Markle, Sandra. *Science to the Rescue*. Atheneum, 1994. Describes contemporary problems and discusses ways in which science is solving them. (**I: 8–12**)

McMillan, Bruce. *Summer Ice: Life along the Antarctic Peninsula*. Houghton Mifflin, 1995. A photo-essay about the plants and animals of the Antarctic. (**I: 7–12**)

Pringle, Laurence. *Antarctica: The Last Unspoiled Continent*. Simon & Schuster, 1992. A comprehensive discussion of the continent of Antarctica. (**I: 8–12**)

———. *An Extraordinary Life: The Story of a Monarch Butterfly*. Illustrated by Bob Marstall. Orchard, 1997. Traces migration of the monarch butterfly from Massachusetts to Mexico. (**I: 8–12**)

———. *Fire in the Forest: A Cycle of Growth and Renewal*. Illustrated by Bob Marstall. Atheneum, 1995. An explanation of the fire cycle and its relationship to the forest ecology. (**I: 6–12**)

Simon, Seymour. *Sharks*. HarperCollins, 1995. With full-page photographs, this book dispels many myths about these fascinating creatures. (**I: 7–12**)

———. *Wolves*. HarperCollins, 1993. Color photographs enhance the discussion of the characteristics and habits of wolves. (**I: 5–12**)

Steger, Will, and Jon Bowermaster. *Over the Top of the World: Explorer Will Steger's Trek across the Arctic*. Scholastic, 1997. Follows an expedition by dogsled and canoe across the North Pole from Russia to Canada. (**I: 8–YA**)

Swanson, Diane. *Safari beneath the Sea: The Wonder World of the North Pacific Coast*. Sierra Club, 1994. Underwater color photographs from the Royal British Columbia Museum introduce readers to the plants and animals of the North Pacific coast. (**I: 7–12**)

Wick, Walter. *A Drop of Water*. Scholastic, 1997. Magnificent photographs help explain properties of water and its different forms. (**I: 8–12**)

The Arts

Aliki. *William Shakespeare & the Globe.* HarperCollins, 1999. Discusses Shakespeare's life, the famous Globe Theatre of London, and recent efforts to reconstruct it. (I: 8–12)

Davidson, Rosemary. *Take a Look: An Introduction to the Experience of Art.* Viking, 1993. Experiments and activities introduce children to the history, techniques, and functions of art. (I: 10–YA)

Greenberg, Jan, and Sandra Jordan. *The Sculptor's Eye: Looking at Contemporary American Art.* Delacorte, 1993. Explores modern sculpture—its subject matter and techniques—and important artists. (I: 10–YA)

Micklethwait, Lucy. *Discover Great Paintings.* DK Publishing, 1999. Guides children on how to investigate paintings by famous artists. (I: 6–10)

Sullivan, Charles, ed. *Children of Promise: African-American Literature and Art for Young People.* Abrams, 1991. African American history is chronicled through art, literary excerpts, and poems. (I: 8–YA)

Switzer, Ellen. *The Magic of Mozart: Mozart, the Magic Flute, and the Salzburg Marionettes.* Photos by Costas. Atheneum, 1995. A book with three interrelated sections that describe the life of Mozart, his opera *The Magic Flute,* and the Salzburg Marionettes that perform it. (I: 9–12)

How Things Work

*Aliki. *How a Book Is Made.* Crowell, 1986. Details the steps in book production from the author's idea to when the book is finally in the hands of salespeople in the store. (I: 7–12)

Cobb, Vicki. *The Secret Life of Cosmetics.* Illustrated by Theo Cobb. Lippincott, 1985. Science experiments provide understanding of how shampoo, toothpaste, soap, and nail polish work. (I: 10–YA)

Cole, Joanna. *The Magic School Bus at the Waterworks.* Illustrated by Bruce Degen. Scholastic, 1987. Ms. Frizzle and her class visit a water treatment plant. (I: 5–8)

———. *The Magic School Bus inside the Human Body.* Illustrated by Bruce Degen. Scholastic, 1989. Ms. Frizzle and her class discover how the human body and its systems work. (I: 5–8)

*Gibbons, Gail. *The Great St. Lawrence Seaway.* Morrow, 1992. Explains how this inland waterway system works and permits ships to travel from the ocean to the Great Lakes through canals, locks, and gates. (I: 6–10)

Harris, Robie H. *It's Perfectly Normal: Changing Bodies, Growing Up, Sex, and Sexual Health.* Illustrated by Michael Emberley. Candlewick, 1994. A detailed description of how the reproductive system works, including a section on staying healthy. (I: 10–YA)

Macaulay, David. *Castle.* Houghton Mifflin, 1977. Detailed description of how a thirteenth-century Welsh castle was constructed. (I: 9–YA)

———. *Cathedral: The Story of Its Construction.* Houghton Mifflin, 1973. Explains the intricate process of building a Gothic cathedral. (I: 9–YA)

———. *The New Way Things Work.* Houghton Mifflin, 1998. A tribute to technology, this book explains how all kinds of machines work. (I: 10–YA)

Markle, Sandra. *Super Cool Science: South Pole Stations Past, Present, and Future.* Walker, 1998. Discusses science research stations at the South Pole. (I: 8–12)

Moser, Barry. *Fly: A Brief History of Flight Illustrated.* HarperCollins, 1993. Through illustrations and text, readers learn about various methods of flying that have been tried throughout history. (I: 8–12)

*Schwartz, David M. *If You Made a Million.* Illustrated by Steven Kellogg. Lothrop, Lee & Shepard, 1989. This informational picture book introduces readers to various forms of money and personal finance. (I: 6–12)

Simon, Seymour. *The Brain: Our Nervous System.* Morrow, 1997. Explains how the human brain and nervous system work. (I: 8–12)

Skurzynski, Gloria. *Robots: Your High-Tech World.* Bradbury, 1990. A comprehensive discussion of robots and robotics technology. (I: 8–12)

Activity, Craft, and How-to Books

Hansen-Smith, Bradford. *The Hands-On Marvelous Ball Book.* Scientific American, 1995. Using paper plates, masking tape, and bobby pins, readers follow directions to explore three-dimensional geometry and the unity of shapes and patterns. (I: 8–12)

Hoyt-Goldsmith, Diane. *Lacrosse: The National Game of the Iroquois.* Photographs by Lawrence Migdale. Holiday House, 1998. Information about lacrosse and instructions for playing it. (I: 7–12)

Lankford, Mary D. *Hopscotch around the World.* Illustrated by Karen Milone. Morrow, 1992. Illustrated directions for playing nineteen variants of hopscotch. (I: 5–10)

Nierman, Kevin, and Elaine Arima. *The Kids 'N' Clay Ceramics Book*. Illustrated by Curtis H. Arima. Tricycle Press, 2000. Illustrated step-by-step instructions to create clay ceramics items. (I: 8–12)

Sachar, Louis. *Sideways Arithmetic from Wayside School*. Scholastic, 1989. Logical problem solving is emphasized in this humorous book, which links puzzle-type math to other school subjects. (I: 8–12)

Walker, Barbara M. *The Little House Cookbook: Frontier Food from Laura Ingalls Wilder's Classic Stories*. HarperCollins, 1979. Each of the more than one hundred recipes is accompanied by a short introduction and is featured in one of Wilder's books. (I: 6–12)

Zalben, Jane Breskin. *To Every Season: A Family Holiday Cookbook*. Simon & Schuster, 1999. Explanations of sixteen holidays and recipes to prepare in their celebrations. (I: 6–12)

U.S. Political Leaders

Freedman, Russell. *Eleanor Roosevelt: A Life of Discovery*. Clarion, 1993. The life of a famous first lady, wife of President Franklin Delano Roosevelt, who devoted herself to public service and worked on behalf of human rights. (I: 9–YA)

——. *Franklin Delano Roosevelt*. Clarion, 1990. The life of Franklin Delano Roosevelt, who was president during the Depression and World War II. (I: 10–YA)

——. *Lincoln: A Photobiography*. Clarion, 1987. The biography of Abraham Lincoln, who was president during the Civil War. (I: 9–YA)

Fritz, Jean. *And Then What Happened, Paul Revere?* Illustrated by Margot Tomes. Coward McCann, 1973. A humorous biography of patriot Paul Revere. (I: 7–12)

——. *Bully for You, Teddy Roosevelt!* Illustrated by Mike Wimmer. Putnam, 1991. A biography of the twenty-sixth president, who was also a conservationist. (I: 9–12)

——. *The Great Little Madison*. Putnam, 1989. A biography of James Madison, fourth President of the United States and the father of the Constitution. (I: 9–12)

——. *Why Don't You Get a Horse, Sam Adams?* Illustrated by Trina Schart Hyman. Coward McCann, 1974. Describes the reluctance of Sam Adams to ride a horse while campaigning for independence for the American colonies. (I: 7–12)

——. *Will You Sign Here, John Hancock?* Illustrated by Trina Schart Hyman. Coward McCann, 1974. A biography of the famous signer of the Declaration of Independence. (I: 7–12)

——. *You Want Women to Vote, Lizzie Stanton?* Illustrated by DyAnne DiSalvo-Ryan. Putnam, 1995. A biography of Elizabeth Cady Stanton, a pioneer in the women's suffrage movement. (I: 8–12)

*Marzollo, Jean. *Happy Birthday, Martin Luther King*. Illustrated by Brian Pinkney. Scholastic, 1993. A picture-book biography of the famous civil rights leader. (I: 5–9)

Myers, Walter Dean. *Malcolm X: By Any Means Necessary*. Scholastic, 1993. The life of the black leader who was assassinated in 1965. (I: 10–YA)

U.S. Historical Figures

Freedman, Russell. *Indian Chiefs*. Holiday House, 1987. A collective biography of six famous Native American leaders. (I: 10–YA)

——. *Kids at Work: Lewis Hine and the Crusade against Child Labor*. Clarion, 1994. The biography of photographer and social reformer Lewis Hine, whose photographs helped ensure the passage of child labor laws. (I: 9–YA)

Fritz, Jean. *Stonewall*. Illustrated by Stephen Gammell. Putnam, 1979. A biography of Thomas J. Jackson, the Confederate Civil War general. (I: 10–YA)

——. *Where Do You Think You're Going, Christopher Columbus?* Illustrated by Margot Tomes. Putnam, 1980. A biography of explorer Christopher Columbus. (I: 7–12)

Klausner, Janet. *Sequoyah's Gift: A Portrait of the Cherokee Leader*. HarperCollins, 1993. A biography of the Cherokee leader who developed the system of writing the Cherokee language. (I: 9–12)

Kraft, Betsy Harvey. *Mother Jones: One Woman's Fight for Labor*. Clarion, 1995. A biography of the courageous woman labor leader who worked on behalf of coal miners and child laborers during the nineteenth and early twentieth centuries. (I: 8–12)

Marrin, Albert. *Unconditional Surrender: U. S. Grant and the Civil War*. Atheneum, 1994. This biography describes the role of Ulysses S. Grant as a military leader during the Civil War. (I: 10–YA)

McPherson, Stephanie Sammartino. *Peace and Bread: The Story of Jane Addams*. Carolrhoda, 1993. A biography of the woman who founded Hull House in Chicago and was active in the Women's International League for Peace and Freedom. (I: 9–12)

Medearis, Angela Shelf. *Princess of the Press: The Story of Ida B. Wells-Barnett*. Dutton, 1997. The life of the African American journalist who helped to found the National Association for the Advancement of Colored People. (I: 8–12)

San Souci, Robert D. *Kate Shelley: Bound for Legend.* Illustrated by Max Ginsburg. Dial, 1995. The courage of a fifteen-year-old prevents a train disaster in Iowa in 1881. (I: 8–12)

World Leaders

Adler, David A. *Our Golda: The Story of Golda Meir.* Illustrated by Donna Ruff. Puffin, 1986. Biography of the first female prime minister of Israel. (I: 7–11)

Cooper, Floyd. *Mandela: From the Life of the South African Statesman.* Philomel, 1996. Describes the life of Nelson Mandela from his birth in a tiny South African village in 1918 to his release from prison in 1990. (I: 8–12)

Fisher, Leonard Everett. *Gandhi.* Atheneum, 1995. The biography of Mohandas K. Gandhi, who developed the practice of nonviolent resistance as he led India to independence from England. (I: 9–12)

Krull, Kathleen. *Lives of Extraordinary Women: Ruler, Rebels (and What the Neighbors Thought).* Illustrated by Kathryn Hewitt. Harcourt, 2000. Biographical vignettes of twenty historic women leaders, including Indira Gandhi and Golda Meir. (I: 8–12)

Stanley, Diane. *Peter the Great.* Morrow, 1986. The life of Tsar Peter Alexeevich of Russia. (I: 10–YA)

———, and Peter Vennema. *Cleopatra.* Morrow, 1994. Full-page paintings complement the story of the famous Egyptian queen. (I: 10–YA)

Stanley, Fay. *The Last Princess: The Story of Princess Kaiulanai of Hawaii.* Illustrated by Diane Stanley. Four Winds, 1991. The story of the brave princess who failed to save her country from annexation and died at age 23. (I: 10–YA)

Explorers of Earth and Space

Archbold, Rick. *Deep-Sea Explorer: The Story of Robert Ballard, Discoverer of the Titantic.* Scholastic, 1994. The life of Dr. Robert Ballard, the oceanographer who discovered the wreck of the *Titanic* in 1986. (I: 8–YA)

Aronson, Marc. *Sir Walter Ralegh and the Quest for El Dorado.* Houghton Mifflin, 2000. The life of the English explorer who led voyages to the New World and searched for the legendary city of El Dorado. (I: 10–YA)

Freedman, Russell. *The Wright Brothers: How They Invented the Airplane.* Holiday House, 1991. The lives of Wilbur and Orville Wright. (I: 9–YA)

Gormley, Beatrice. *Maria Mitchell: The Soul of an Astronomer.* Eerdmans, 1995. The story of the first female professional astronomer in the United States, who discovered a comet. (I: 10–YA)

Hurwitz, Jane, and Sue Hurwitz. *Sally Ride: Shooting for the Stars.* Fawcett Columbine, 1989. The biography of America's first woman astronaut to fly in space. (I: 10–YA)

*Lasky, Kathryn. *The Librarian Who Measured the Earth.* Illustrated by Kevin Hawkes. Little, Brown, 1994. A picture-book biography of Eratosthenes, the Greek astronomer who measured the circumference of the earth. (I: 6–12)

*Martin, Jacqueline Briggs. *Snowflake Bentley.* Illustrated by Mary Azarian. Houghton Mifflin, 1998. The life of Wilson Bentley, a self-taught scientist who studied and photographed snowflakes. (I: 6–10)

Provensen, Alice, and Martin Provensen. *The Glorious Flight: Across the Channel with Louis Blériot.* Viking, 1983. A Frenchman builds a flying machine to cross the English Channel in 1909. (I: 6–12)

Sis, Peter. *Starry Messenger.* Farrar, 1996. Exquisite illustrations help recount the life of astronomer Galileo Galilei. (I: 7–11)

Towle, Wendy. *The Real McCoy: The Life of an African-American Inventor.* Illustrated by Wil Clay. Scholastic, 1993. The life of Elijah McCoy, who patented over fifty inventions. (I: 6–12)

Artists and Authors

Ada, Alma Flor. *Where the Flame Trees Bloom.* Illustrated by Antonio Martorell. Atheneum, 1994. A children's author shares stories about her family and growing up in Cuba. (I: 8–12)

*Cooper, Floyd. *Coming Home: From the Life of Langston Hughes.* Philomel, 1994. This picture-book biography focuses on the childhood of the well-known African American poet. (I: 6–12)

Cummings, Pat. *Talking with Artists.* Bradbury, 1992. Biographical interviews with fourteen well-known children's book illustrators. (I: 5–12)

Duggleby, John. *Story Painter: The Life of Jacob Lawrence.* Chronicle, 1998. The biography of the African American painter known for paintings that tell stories about the African American experience. (I: 10–YA)

Garfunkel, Trudy. *Letter to the World: The Life and Dances of Martha Graham.* Little, Brown, 1995. The biography of the dancer and choreographer who pioneered modern dance. (I: 8–12)

Johnston, Norma. *Louisa May: The World and Works of Louisa May Alcott.* Macmillan, 1991. A carefully researched biography of the beloved author of *Little Women.* (I: 10–YA)

Krull, Kathleen. *Lives of the Artists: Masterpieces, Messes (and What the Neighbors Thought)*. Illustrated by Kathryn Hewitt. Harcourt, 1995. Biographical sketches of sixteen artists, including Georgia O'Keefe, Diego Rivera, and Frida Kahlo. (I: 8–12)

———. *Lives of the Musicians: Good Times, Bad Times (and What the Neighbors Thought)*. Illustrated by Kathryn Hewitt. Harcourt, 1993. Biographical sketches of twenty musicians and composers, including Bach and Scott Joplin. (I: 8–12)

Levine, Ellen. *Anna Pavlova: Genius of the Dance*. Scholastic, 1995. A complete biography of the famous Russian ballet dancer. (I: 8–12)

Lewin, Ted. *I Was a Teenage Professional Wrestler*. Orchard, 1993. An autobiography of children's author-illustrator Ted Lewin, who supported himself through art school as a wrestler. (I: 10–YA)

Lobel, Anita. *No Pretty Pictures: A Child of War*. Greenwillow, 1998. The award-winning author and illustrator describes her life as a Polish Jew during World War II and its aftermath. (I: 10–YA)

Lyons, Mary E. *Sorrow's Kitchen: The Life and Folklore of Zora Neale Hurston*. Scribner's, 1990. A biography of the African American folklorist, who lived during the Harlem Renaissance. (I: 10–YA)

Monceaux, Morgan. *Jazz: My Music, My People*. Knopf, 1994. Biographical sketches of jazz musicians from the early years to bebop and modern jazz. (I: 8–12)

Reich, Susanna. *Clara Schumann: Piano Virtuoso*. Clarion, 1999. The life of the German pianist who was the wife of composer Robert Schumann. (I: 10–YA)

Roop, Peter, and Connie Roop. *Capturing Nature: The Writings and Art of John James Audubon*. Illustrated by Rick Farley. Walker, 1993. The life and work of this naturalist and artist are conveyed through his journals. (I: 8–12)

Sills, Leslie. *Visions: Stories about Women Artists*. Whitman, 1993. Biographies of four visionary women artists: Mary Cassatt, Leonora Carrington, Betye Saar, and Mary Frank. (I: 10–YA)

Stanley, Diane. *Leonardo da Vinci*. Morrow, 1996. A picture-book biography of the famous painter and scientist. (I: 10–YA)

Stanley, Diane, and Peter Vennema. *The Bard of Avon: The Story of William Shakespeare*. Morrow, 1992. A picture-book biography of the most famous British playwright. (I: 10–YA)

Uchida, Yoshiko. *The Invisible Thread*. Julian Messner, 1991. An autobiography of a Japanese American children's author whose family spent World War II in an internment camp. (I: 9–12)

Yep, Laurence. *The Lost Garden*. Julian Messner, 1991. A memoir by the award-winning children's author. (I: 8–12)

People Who Persevered

Adler, David A. *Hilde and Eli: Children of the Holocaust*. Illustrated by Karen Ritz. Holiday House, 1994. The story of two Jewish children killed by the Nazis during World War II. (I: 8–12)

———. *Jackie Robinson: He Was the First*. Illustrated by Robert Casilla. Holiday House, 1989. The biography of the first African American to play major league baseball. (I: 5–9)

Bridges, Ruby. *Through My Eyes*. Scholastic, 1999. The life and times of Ruby Bridges, who integrated the New Orleans schools in 1960 when she was 6 years old. (I: 8–12)

Hamilton, Virginia. *Anthony Burns: The Defeat and Triumph of a Fugitive Slave*. Knopf, 1988. In 1854, Anthony Burns escaped from a Virginia plantation and came to Boston, where he was arrested and tried under the Fugitive Slave Act. (I: 10–YA)

Krull, Kathleen. *Wilma Unlimited: How Wilma Rudolph Became the World's Fastest Woman*. Illustrated by David Diaz. Harcourt, 1996. Striking paintings help to tell the story of Wilma Rudolph, who overcame childhood polio to win three gold medals for track at the 1960 Olympics. (I: 6–12)

Littlefield, Bill. *Champions: Stories of Ten Remarkable Athletes*. Illustrated by Bernie Fuchs. Little, Brown, 1993. Ten athletes, including Satchel Paige and Roberto Clemente, are featured in this biographical collection of athletes who persevered to become champions in their sports. (I: 8–YA)

*Parks, Rosa, with Jim Haskins. *I Am Rosa Parks*. Pictures by Wil Clay. Dial, 1997. The first-person account of the life of the courageous woman whose refusal to give up her seat on a Montgomery, Alabama, bus in 1955 led to a boycott. (I: 6–8)

———, with Jim Haskins. *Rosa Parks: My Story*. Dial, 1992. The biography of the courageous woman whose refusal to give up her seat on a Montgomery, Alabama, bus in 1955 led to a boycott. (I: 10–YA)

Pressler, Miriam. *Anne Frank: A Hidden Life*. Translated by Anthea Bell. Dutton, 2000. A description of the life of Anne Frank and the Nazi occupation of the Netherlands during World War II. (I: 10–YA)

Tillage, Leon Walter. *Leon's Story*. Farrar Straus Giroux, 1997. A school custodian recounts his life as a sharecropper's son growing up in the 1940s and 1950s. (I: 8–12).

Toll, Nelly S. *Behind the Secret Window: A Memoir of a Hidden Childhood during World War Two*. Dial, 1993. In this autobiography, Nelly Toll describes her life in hiding with a Polish family during World War II. (**I:** 10–YA)

van der Rol, Ruud, and Rian Verhoeven. *Anne Frank: Beyond the Diary*. Viking, 1993. Heavily illustrated with photographs, this book describes Anne Frank's life before, during, and after her family went into hiding in Holland during World War II. (**I:** 10–YA)

White, Ryan, and Ann Marie Cunningham. *Ryan White: My Own Story*. Dial, 1991. After being infected with AIDS from a blood transfusion, Ryan shared his story about living with the disease that eventually killed him. (**I:** 10–YA)

RESOURCES

Bamford, Rosemary A., and Janice V. Kristo. *Checking Out Nonfiction, K–8: Good Choices for Best Learning*. Christopher-Gordon, 2000.

———, and Janice V. Kristo. *Making Facts Come Alive: Choosing Quality Nonfiction Literature, K–8*. Christopher-Gordon, 1998.

Dunthie, Christine. *True Stories: Nonfiction Literacy in the Primary Classroom*. Stenhouse, 1996.

Freeman, Evelyn B., and Diane Goetz Person. *Connecting Informational Children's Books with Content Area Learning*. Allyn & Bacon, 1998.

———, and Diane Goetz Person, eds. *Using Nonfiction Trade Books in the Elementary Classroom: From Ants to Zeppelins*. National Council of Teachers of English, 1992.

Graves, Donald. *Investigate Nonfiction*. Heinemann, 1989.

Harvey, Stephanie. *Nonfiction Matters: Reading, Writing, and Research in Grades 3–8*. Stenhouse, 1998.

Kobrin, Beverly. *Eyeopeners II*. Scholastic, 1995.

Teale, William H. "Nonfiction, Language Learning, and Language Teaching." *Language Arts* 68.6 (1991).

Tunnell, Michael O., and Richard Ammon, eds. *The Story of Ourselves: Teaching History through Children's Literature*. Heinemann, 1993.

Whitin, David J., and Sandra Wilde. *It's the Story That Counts: More Children's Books for Mathematical Learning, K–6*. Heinemann, 1995.

———, and Sandra Wilde. *Read Any Good Math Lately? Children's Books for Mathematical Learning, K–6*. Heinemann, 1992.

REFERENCES

Adler, David. *A Picture Book of Amelia Earhart*. Holiday House, 1998.

———. *A Picture Book of Thurgood Marshall*. Holiday House, 1997.

Aldis, Dorothy. *Nothing Is Impossible: The Story of Beatrix Potter*. Illustrated by Richard Cuffari. Atheneum, 1980.

Aliki. *Dinosaurs Are Different*. HarperCollins, 1985.

———. *The Story of William Tell*. A. S. Barnes, 1960.

Ancona, George. *Monsters on Wheels*. Dutton, 1974.

Barrett, Marvin. *Meet Thomas Jefferson*. Random House, 1964.

Cleary, Beverly. *A Girl from Yamhill: A Memoir*. Morrow, 1988.

Cole, Joanna. *A Cat's Body*. Photographs by Jerome Wexler. Morrow, 1982.

———. *Cockroaches*. Morrow, 1971.

———. *A Frog's Body*. Photographs by Jerome Wexler. Morrow, 1980.

———. *A Horse's Body*. Photographs by Jerome Wexler. Morrow, 1981.

Daugherty, James. *Daniel Boone*. Viking, 1939.

D'Aulaire, Ingri, and Edgar Parin D'Aulaire. *Abraham Lincoln*. Doubleday, 1939.

———. *Benjamin Franklin*. Doubleday, 1950.

———. *George Washington*. Doubleday, 1936.

de Kay, James T. *Meet Christopher Columbus*. Random House, 1968.

Fisher, Margery. Introduction to *Matters of Fact. Beyond Fact: Nonfiction for Children and Young People*. Ed. J. Carr. American Library Association, 1982, pp. 12–16.

Freedman, Russell. "Fact or Fiction?" *Using Nonfiction Trade Books in the Elementary Classroom: From Ants to Zeppelins*. Ed. E. B. Freeman and D. G. Person. National Council of Teachers of English, 1992, pp. 2–10.

Fritz, Jean. "Voices of the Creators." *Children's Books and Their Creators*. Ed. A. Silvey. Houghton Mifflin, 1995, p. 257.

Garcia-Johnson, R. "Ancona, George." *Something about the Author*, Vol. 85. Ed. K. S. Hile. Gale Research, 1996, pp. 5–13.

George, Jean Craighead. *Julie of the Wolves*. Harper & Row, 1972.

Giblin, James Cross. *Chimney Sweeps: Yesterday and Today*. Illustrated by Margot Tomes. HarperCollins, 1982.

———. *From Hand to Mouth or, How We Invented Knives, Forks, Spoons, and Chopsticks and the Table Manners to Go with Them*. Crowell, 1987.

———. "The Rise and Fall and Rise of Juvenile Nonfiction, 1961–1988." *Using Nonfiction Trade Books in the Elementary Classroom: From Ants to Zeppelins*. Ed. E. B. Freeman and D. G. Person. National Council of Teachers of English, 1992, pp. 17–25.

————. *The Truth about Santa Claus*. Crowell, 1985.

Graham-Barber, Lynda. *Toad or Frog, Swamp or Bog? A Big Book of Nature's Confusables*. Illustrated by Alec Gillman. Simon & Schuster, 1994.

Haskins, James. *The March on Washington*. HarperCollins, 1993.

Hastings, Selina. *Peter and the Wolf*. Illustrated by Reg Cartwright. Henry Holt, 1990.

Hoke, Elizabeth C. "Edgar Parin D'Aulaire and Ingri D'Aulaire." *Children's Books and Their Creators*. Ed. A. Silvey. Houghton Mifflin, 1995, pp. 188–89.

Holling, Holling Clancy. *Paddle-to-the-Sea*. Houghton Mifflin, 1941.

Kherdian, David. *The Road from Home: The Story of an Armenian Girl*. Greenwillow, 1979.

Krementz, Jill. *A Very Young Dancer*. Knopf, 1976.

Lacey, Elizabeth. *What's the Difference? A Young Naturalist's Guide to Some Familiar Animal Look-Alikes*. Clarion Books, 1993.

Lasky, Kathryn. *The Weaver's Gift*. Photographs by Christopher Knight. F. Warne, 1980.

Lauber, Patricia. *Be a Friend to Trees*. Illustrated by Holly Keller. HarperCollins, 1994.

————. "The Evolution of a Science Writer." *Using Nonfiction Trade Books in the Elementary Classroom: From Ants to Zeppelins*. Ed. E. B. Freeman and D. G. Person. National Council of Teachers of English, 1992, pp. 11–16.

Lawson, Robert. *Ben & Me*. Little, Brown, 1939.

————. *I Discover Columbus*. Little, Brown, 1941.

Leal, Dorothy. "Storybooks, Information Books and Informational Storybooks: An Explication of an Ambiguous Grey Genre." *The New Advocate* 6 (1993): 61–70.

McKissack, Patricia C., and Fredrick McKissack, Jr. *Black Diamond: The Story of the Negro Baseball Leagues*. Scholastic, 1998.

Meigs, Cornelia. *Invincible Louisa*. Little, Brown, 1933.

Meltzer, Milton. *All Times, All Peoples: A World History of Slavery*. Illustrated by Leonard Everett Fisher. Harper and Row, 1980.

————. *The Amazing Potato: A Story in Which the Incas, Conquistadors, Marie Antoinette, Thomas Jefferson, Wars, Famines, Immigrants ad French Fries All Play a Part*. HarperCollins, 1992.

————. "Beyond the Span of a Single Life." *Celebrating Children's Books: Essays on Children's Literature in Honor of Zena Sutherland*. Ed. B. Hearne and M. Kaye. Lothrop, Lee & Shepard, 1981, pp. 87–96.

————. *The Jewish Americans: A History in Their Own Words, 1650–1950*. Crowell, 1982.

————. *Never to Forget: The Jews of the Holocaust*. HarperCollins, 1976.

Monjo, F. N. "The Ten Bad Things about History." *Beyond Fact: Nonfiction for Children and Young People*. Ed. J. Carr. American Library Association, 1982, pp. 99–103.

Olendorf, D., and D. Telgen. "David Adler." *Something about the Author*, Vol. 70. Gale Research, 1993, pp. 1–4.

Pringle, L. "Science Done Here." *Celebrating Children's Books: Essays on Children's Literature in Honor of Zena Sutherland*. Ed. B. Hearne and M. Kaye. Lothrop, Lee & Shepard, 1981, pp. 108–15.

Ritter, Lawrence S. *Leagues Apart: The Men and Times of the Negro Baseball Leagues*. Morrow, 1995.

Rosenberg, Maxine. *Making a New Home in America*. Photographs by George Ancona. Lothrop, Lee & Shepard, 1986.

Sayers, F. C. "History Books for Children." *Beyond Fact: Nonfiction for Children and Young People*. Ed. J. Carr. American Library Association, 1982, pp. 95–98.

Selsam, Millicent. *Egg to Chick*. Illustrated by Barbara Wolff. Harper and Row, 1946.

Scribner's. Promotional pamphlet about Kathryn Lasky, 1985.

Simon, Seymour. *Animals in Field and Laboratory: Projects in Animal Behavior*. McGraw, 1968.

Singer, Marilyn. *A Wasp Is Not a Bee*. Illustrated by Patrick O'Brien. Holt, 1995.

Something about the Author, Vol. 115. Ed. S. L. Constantakis. Gail Group, 2000, pp. 191–198.

Testa, Fulvio. *Wolf's Favor*. Dial Books, 1986.

Tunis, Edwin. *Frontier Living*. World, 1961.

van Loon, Hendrik Willem. *The Story of Mankind*. Boni & Liveright, 1921.

Ward, Geoffrey C., Ken Burns, and Jim O'Connor. *Shadow Ball: The History of the Negro Leagues*. Knopf, 1994.

Wenzel, E. L. "Historical Backgrounds." *Beyond Fact: Nonfiction for Children and Young People*. Ed. J. Carr. American Library Association, 1982, pp. 16–26.

Zarnowski, M. *Learning about Biographies: A Reading-and-Writing Approach for Children*. National Council of Teachers of English, 1990.

————. "Learning History with Informational Storybooks: A Social Studies Educator's Perspective." *The New Advocate* 8 (1995): 183–96.

Zim, Herbert. *Golden Hamsters*. Illustrated by Herschel Wartik. Morrow, 1951.

————. *Sharks*. Illustrated by Stephen Howe. Morrow, 1966.

————. *Snakes*. Illustrated by James Gordon Irving. Morrow, 1949.

Three

Creating the Literature-Based Classroom

12 Inviting Children into Literature

Grandpa took Mary Ellen inside away from the crowd. "Now, child I am going to show you what my father showed me, and his father before him," he said quietly.

He spooned the honey onto the cover of one of her books. "Taste," he said, almost in a whisper. Ellen savored the honey on her book. "There is such sweetness inside of that book too!" he said thoughtfully. "Such things . . . adventure, knowledge and wisdom. But these things do not come easily. You have to pursue them. Just like we ran after the bees to find their tree, so you must also chase these things through the pages of a book!"

*from **The Bee Tree**
by Patricia Polacco*

Illustration 12.1
A spirit of joyous adventure marks a romp through the countryside in search of a bee tree. (*The Bee Tree* by Patricia Polacco. Copyright © 1993. Used by permission of Philomel Books, a division of Penguin Putnam Inc.)

Patricia Polacco's wonderful book ***The Bee Tree*** begins when Mary Ellen announces she is tired of reading. So her grandfather invites her to go on an adventure—a hunt for a bee tree. In preparation, Grandpa captures several bees in a jar, and soon Mary Ellen and Grandpa are off and running, following the first bee released from the jar. Before long, the twosome grows into a motley crew as friends and neighbors join the merry chase that ends at the bee tree. Back at Grandpa's, everyone enjoys biscuits, tea, and sweet honey. It is then that Grandpa reminds Mary Ellen that joys as sweet as honey can also be found in books.

Mary Ellen's grandfather knew the importance of motivating children to become readers. As important as it is to teach children how to read, that is not enough to ensure that they will choose to read. The evidence indicates that too many children do not read. Linda Fielding, Paul T. Wilson, and Richard C. Anderson (1986) found that 50 percent of fifth-graders read voluntarily for four minutes a day or less, 30 percent read for two minutes a day or less, and almost 10 percent reported never reading any books during their leisure time. It's little wonder that 45 percent of adult Americans don't read books either (Cole and Gold, 1979).

Mary Ellen's Grandpa was a wonderful teacher, and the lesson he taught Mary Ellen is one that you'll want to pass on to your students: Inside the pages of a book, readers can find adventure, knowledge, and wisdom. You probably won't be able to take your students on romps through the countryside in search of bee trees. How then will you help them discover the joys of reading? We believe that you can best accomplish this by carefully designing your classroom, by reading aloud, by telling stories, by inviting students to dramatize stories, and by demonstrating your enthusiasm for literature.

THE CLASSROOM LIBRARY

A good classroom library is a focal area where children can go to read high-quality children's literature. Is it really necessary to have a library in the classroom, especially if your school has a well-stocked central library? We think it is essential. Children in classrooms containing literature collections read 50 percent more than children in classrooms where literature is not available (Bissett, 1969). What a difference!

Designing the Classroom Library Center

Not all library centers are equally appealing. Children beg to visit some library centers, while others stand unused. Research by Lesley Morrow (1982) has shown how to create classroom libraries that children choose to use. There are a number of design features that make such libraries appealing. These features are summarized in Table 12.1.

The Center Is the Focal Area of the Classroom. Often, when you step into a classroom, your eye is drawn to one area of the room; that eye-catching part is what is meant by "the focal area." It isn't easy to define what makes a library center a focal area; in fact, it may be all the design features taken together that do this. Whatever the explanation, it is important to create an eye-catching center that announces to students "Literature matters in this classroom." In one school, teachers created centers built around themes. One teacher built a seven-foot-high apple tree, using chicken wire covered with paper for the trunk and paper chains for the limbs. Across the tree was hung a banner that read "Don't Sit under the Apple Tree without a Good Book to Read." The apple motif was reflected throughout the center; for example, red beanbag chairs looked just like big apples. Another teacher used a sidewalk café theme and called her center "Café Escape." It was a perfect invitation to escape into a good book. To build ownership of the library center, some teachers invite their students to help come up with the theme of the library center.

The Library Is Partitioned Off. Children prefer to read in areas that are away from lots of hustle and bustle. So it makes sense to use something—for example, bookshelves or old sofas—to partition the library off from the rest of the classroom. One teacher turned the library center into the "O.K. Corral," using mesquite posts to build a fence around it. The possibilities are limited only by your imagination.

The Seating Area Is Large Enough. To make the seating area large enough, you will have to devote a chunk of floor space to the library center. Why not just store the books in a bookcase instead and let students read at

---

Table 12.1   Characteristics of an Appealing Library Center

- The library center is a focal area of the classroom.
- The library center is partitioned off from the rest of the room.
- The library center is large enough to seat five or six children comfortably.
- The library center has two types of bookshelves: some that display the spines of books and others that display the covers of books.
- The library center offers comfortable seating.
- The library center offers a variety of other materials—literature-related displays, stuffed animals, and the like.
- The library center has an organizational system.
- The library center has *books, books, and more books!*

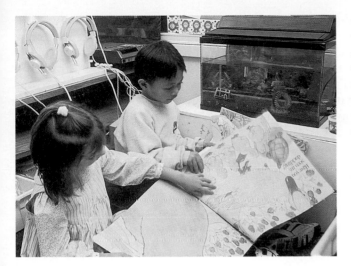

The classroom library center gives children a convenient place to share a book.

their desks? Many children don't find it comfortable to read at their desks, preferring instead to lounge around in a library center. Besides, there are many times when reading becomes a social activity. Children may choose to read with a buddy or to share something they're reading. Imagine reading a riddle book without trying to stump someone! And the optical illusions in Kathleen Westray's *Picture Puzzler* simply must be shared.

The Shelving Displays Both Spines and Covers of Books. Bookshelves that display the spines of books are necessary because they hold a lot of books. But the spines of books don't make for interesting viewing, so it's also necessary to display book covers. This might be the single most important way of enticing children into selecting books, for many have exquisite covers (which is why most booksellers try to display as many book covers as possible).

Bookshelves that are designed to display the covers of books are expensive, and many schools can't stretch their budgets to buy these shelves. So you'll need to use your creativity. Slightly open books can stand alone on standard shelves or on a window ledge. To display paperback picture books, visit a home supply center and buy plastic chain and clothespins. Hang the chain in an accessible spot, and attach the paperbacks to it with the clothespins.

The Seating Is Comfortable. It is obvious why comfortable seating is important in a library center. After all, where do you read for pleasure? Sofas and upholstered chairs are far more appealing than straight-back chairs. Carpeting, beanbag chairs, pillows, and cushions are also comfortable and make the library center cozy.

The Center Uses a Variety of Materials. Materials that highlight literature are assets in the library center. Posters showing the covers of featured books can be obtained from publishers. Displays of book jackets catch children's attention. Children's own artistic responses to literature may be an even better choice of material for decorating the library center. Younger children enjoy cuddling up with stuffed animals when they read or using flannel boards or puppets to act out stories.

The Center Uses an Organizational System. Children like organizational systems in their libraries for the same reason adults do: Organizational systems help them to find books. No one particular system is best. In fact, some teachers nurture ownership of the classroom library by inviting students to create their own system. Systems that classify books on the basis of their difficulty level can be good, especially for beginning readers. Teachers can even set up systems to reinforce the literary language they want students to acquire; for example, books can be grouped by genre. In determining the best system for your classroom, consider the interests and abilities of your students as well as your instructional goals.

The Center Has Books, Books, and More Books! Unless the library center is well stocked with a rich variety of quality books, children will not use it. Jann Fractor, Marjorie Woodruff, Miriam G. Martinez, and William H. Teale

(1993) recommend having four to eight books per child. In fact, the more books you have, the richer the literature context you create in your classroom. Unfortunately, school budgets rarely stretch far enough to allow teachers to buy books for classroom libraries. However, some teachers persuade their administrators to let them order children's literature instead of reading workbooks. Even if your school provides monetary assistance for purchasing books, you'll probably still have to find creative ways of supplementing the collection. Many public libraries allow teachers to check out large numbers of books for extended periods of time. Checking books out of the school library is another alternative. If your students have the financial means to order books from book clubs, the class can earn bonus points that can be cashed in for books. Secondhand book stores can sometimes be a good source of inexpensive copies of worthwhile books.

Stocking the Classroom Library with Books

Which books the classroom library holds is even more important than how many books there are.

High-Quality Literature. You owe it to your students to stock the classroom library with the highest-quality literature. Take care to choose for your center books that have distinctly crafted literary elements. Consider books such as Mary Hoffman's *Amazing Grace* for its wonderful characterization and Jean Craighead George's *My Side of the Mountain* for its distinctive setting. Include books with significant themes, such as Barbara Cooney's *Miss Rumphius,* and don't forget books with exquisite language, such as Cynthia Rylant's *When I Was Young in the Mountains.* But when selecting books to motivate voluntary reading, pay special attention to the story line. A strong story line sells itself. Well-paced, action-oriented stories, such as Kasza Keiko's *The Wolf's Chicken Stew* for younger children and Bruce Coville's *Jeremy Thatcher, Dragon Hatcher* for older children, are especially popular. Children also love books with humorous and unusual story lines, such as Doreen Cronin's *Click, Clack, Moo: Cows That Type* and Judy Blume's *Tales of a Fourth Grade Nothing.* Stories with unusual formats make good additions to the library center—books such as Jon Scieszka's *The Stinky Cheese Man and Other Fairly Stupid Tales* and Sally Grindley's *Shhh!* Finally, children will rush to choose books with distinctive illustrations, such as Audrey and Don Wood's *The Napping House.* A useful resource for identifying books with "kid appeal" is the Children's Choice list that appears annually in the October issue of *The Reading Teacher,* a journal published by the International Reading Association.

A Variety of Genres. Be sure to include as many genres as possible in your library center—fantasy, folktales, contemporary realistic fiction, historical fiction, informational books, and poetry. Also find room for those odds and ends for which there is no apparent genre niche—predictable books, joke books and riddle books, and lift-the-flap and pop-up books. The more choices you provide for students, the more they'll read.

Student Interests. Just as you have particular reading preferences and reading interests, so will your students. Take the time to discover those interests. Talk to students about the books they're reading. Have them keep logs of their voluntary reading, in which they record the author and title of each book they read. Monitor those logs, and fill the classroom library with books related to students' reading interests. Table 12.2 suggests some typical interests of students in different grades.

Illustration 12.2
The barnyard is soon out of control when the cows learn to type and enter into negotiations with the farmer. (*Click, Clack, Moo: Cows That Type* by Doreen Cronin, pictures by Betsy Lewin. Text copyright © 2000 by Doreen Cronin. Illustrations copyright © 2000 by Betsy Lewin. Used by permission of Simon & Schuster Books for Young Readers, an imprint of Simon & Schuster Children's Publishing.)

Table 12.2	Children's Interests at Different Grade Levels
Grades	**Interests**
Grades 1 and 2	Animals, nature, fantasy, child characters, general and science informational materials, history
Grades 3 and 4	Nature, animals, adventure, familiar experiences
Grades 5 and 6	History, science, mystery, adventure, travel, animal stories, fairy tales
Grades 7 and 8	Science fiction, mystery, adventure, biography, history, animals, sports, romance, religion, career stories, comedy

Of course, students' reading interests sometimes include books that are not necessarily recognized as quality literature—for example, series books such as the *Berenstain Bears, Goosebumps, Animorphs, Babysitters Club*, or *Sweet Valley Kids* books. If students' interests are going to be truly honored, then it makes sense to include some titles such as these in the library center. Teachers might want to invite children to talk about the differences they see between series books and other types of books to help them develop their own evaluation criteria.

A Variety of Reading Levels. If a child believes that a book will be too challenging to read, in all likelihood the child won't give it a try. To motivate children to do lots of reading, it's critical that you provide books that they feel comfortable reading. Anticipate a wide range of reading levels in your classroom. A typical second-grade classroom may have some students who are nonreaders and others who are reading at a sixth-grade level. The mythical classroom of "grade-level readers" is just that—a myth. By watching students, you can discover whether they are comfortable with the books in your classroom library.

Kindergartners who have not yet learned to read conventionally need books they can feel comfortable with. Kindergartners are far more likely to "pretend read" predictable books, such as Bill Martin, Jr.'s ***Brown Bear, Brown Bear, What Do You See?*** and Michael Rosen's ***We're Going on a Bear Hunt***.

Beginning readers—whether they are in first grade or higher grades—also respond well to predictable books. In addition, they need picture books with limited text and lots of illustration cues, such as Dick Gackenbach's ***Harry and the Terrible Whatzit*** and Gerald McDermott's ***Anansi the Spider***. Beginning readers soon graduate to very easy-to-read chapter books, such as Cynthia Rylant's *Henry and Mudge* series or James Marshall's comical series about Fox.

More challenging picture books for developing readers include Harry Allard's ***The Stupids Step Out*** and Lois Ehlert's ***Moon Rope: Un lazo a la luna***. When children have made the jump into chapter books, supply them with easier ones—those with fifty to one hundred pages and simple vocabulary. Books that

Illustration 12.3
Who can resist joining in the fun of an exciting bear hunt? (*We're Going on a Bear Hunt* by Michael Rosen, illustrated by Helen Oxenbury. Text copyright © 1989 by Michael Rosen. Illustrations copyright © 1989 by Helen Oxenbury. Used by permission of Margaret K. McElderry Books, an imprint of Simon & Schuster Children's Publishing.)

Illustration 12.4
Vibrant illustrations fill the pages of this folktale featuring the African trickster Anansi. (*Anansi the Spider: A Tale from the Ashanti,* adapted and illustrated by Gerald McDermott. Copyright © 1972 by Landmark Production, Incorporated. Reprinted by permission of Henry Holt and Company, LLC.)

fit this bill include Margaret Sacks's ***Themba*** and Betsy Byars's ***The Seven Treasure Hunts.***

Read-Alouds. Observing in literature-rich classrooms, Janet Hickman (1981) found that children are especially likely to select for independent reading books that have been introduced or read to them. Children are likely to feel more confident picking up a book they have heard read aloud.

Content Units. The library center can be a tool to support and extend children's learning in other areas. For example, if you are doing a unit on slavery, stock the library with books such as Patricia and Fredrick McKissack's ***Christmas in the Big House, Christmas in the Quarters*** and Michael J. Rosen's ***A School for Pompey Walker.*** Just as special collections within the library center support students' learning in the content areas, so too do students' content studies support their voluntary reading, by building background and interest. (See Chapter 14 for a detailed discussion of literature-based content units.)

Multicultural Books. Including multicultural literature in the library is important for all children but especially for those from diverse backgrounds, who need to see themselves in the books they read. A Latino American child once

---

ISSUE TO CONSIDER

Do CD-ROM versions of stories belong in the classroom?

In recent years, as computers have proliferated in classrooms, educational software publishers have brought out increasing numbers of stories on CD-ROM. But do CD-ROM versions of stories belong in classrooms in which teachers are intent on nurturing avid readers of high-quality literature?

Some view CD-ROM stories as just another form of a story, much like a paperback, a hardcover version, or a taped version of a story. These advocates argue that a CD-ROM story has the special advantage of making a story accessible to children who can't yet read it independently. Not only that—because of the audio capabilities of CD-ROM stories, developing readers have access to a model of fluent reading. Further, for reluctant readers of the video and television generation, literature presented via the computer may be the hook that grabs them and turns them into avid readers.

Not everyone agrees that CD-ROM versions of stories belong in the classroom. Although the main presentation of the story might adhere to the basic story line in the print version, the designers of CD-ROM stories typically build animated features into story illustrations. For example, in one story, viewers/readers can click onto a squirrel that appears in an illustration and then watch the squirrel "perform" for the viewer. However, the squirrel in the illustration is merely part of the background and plays no role in the development of the story. Critics argue that such features become distractions that encourage children to play rather than read, and children may even lose the story line owing to an excessive number of distractions.

What do you think?

said to one of us, "They don't have people like us in books." Fortunately, more and more multicultural literature is becoming available, and it is the responsibility of every teacher to ensure that students have ample opportunities to meet characters like themselves in literature.

Some teachers assume that it is not necessary to bring multicultural literature into their classrooms because none of their students are children of ethnic diversity. Nothing could be further from the truth. It is important for children of the mainstream culture to see children different from themselves involved in situations both similar to and different from their own. Schools are preparing children to live in a diverse society, and it is important for them to understand this society. (See Chapter 4 for a complete discussion of these issues.)

READING ALOUD TO CHILDREN

In its report *Becoming a Nation of Readers,* the Commission on Reading declared, "There is no substitute for a teacher who reads children good stories" (Anderson, Hiebert, Scott, and Wilkinson, 1984). That is our sentiment exactly! Research indicates that reading to children has many positive outcomes. First, it whets their appetite for reading. Young children who are read to discover the rewards of reading and are motivated to learn to read. Second, literature nurtures children's language development and comprehension abilities. Through read-alouds, children become acquainted with the cadences of written language and discover how print functions, especially if the adult reader draws attention to print conventions. Finally, through read-alouds, children acquire the real-world knowledge that is so critical for success in school.

Read-alouds support children's literary development: Children are introduced to conventional story openers ("Once upon a time"); they discover literary motifs such as the transformation motif; and they meet stock characters such as the sly fox and the tricky coyote. Read-alouds are the ideal vehicle for encouraging children to think in response to literature, and when discussion is a part of the read-aloud experience, children learn how to participate in literary conversations.

Like the Commission on Reading, we believe that read-alouds are an essential instructional activity for children of all ages. Although older children may have acquired basic understandings of how print functions and how stories are structured, their language, reading, and literary development must continue. Also, there are many books that developing readers do not have the skill to read on their own but will delight in if the books are read aloud to them. In fact, by the time children are able to read some books on their own, the books are no longer age-appropriate.

Research on Read-Aloud Programs

The most recent and comprehensive study on read-aloud programs was done by James V. Hoffman, Nancy L. Roser, and Jennifer Battle (1993). Reports from 537 classrooms across the United States revealed that 74 percent of teachers read to their students on a given day. However, there was a steady decline in the percentage of teachers reading aloud as grade level rose. In kindergarten, 84 percent of the teachers read to their students, but in fifth grade, only 64 percent did so. There is room for improvement. Teachers at every grade level should read aloud at least once a day. All too often, teachers at upper grade levels believe that their students should be reading books on their own—which is true, of course.

However, this is not an either/or situation. We hope teachers will recognize the special value of read-alouds. Another argument made by some intermediate-level teachers is that they have too much content to cover to devote time to reading aloud to students. One way of dealing with this time restriction is "double dipping"—that is, using read-alouds to achieve both literary goals and curricular goals. If students are studying the American Revolution, then read aloud James and Christopher Collier's *My Brother Sam Is Dead.* Patricia Polacco's *Pink and Say* and Karen Ackerman's *The Tin Heart* are perfect read-alouds when a class is studying the Civil War.

Hoffman and his colleagues also looked at the books chosen for read-alouds and at the organization of the read-aloud programs. Well-known authors—Bill Martin, Jr., Maurice Sendak, Roald Dahl, E. B. White, and Judy Blume—were at the top of the list of authors most frequently read. Included among the frequently read titles were *Brown Bear, Brown Bear, What Do You See?, Where the Wild Things Are, Charlotte's Web, James and the Giant Peach,* and *The Indian in the Cupboard.* It is heartening that the quality of these authors and titles is widely recognized, but it is discouraging that not a single multicultural author or title appeared at the top of the list. In fact, one of the titles, *The Indian in the Cupboard* by Lynne Reid Banks, has received criticism for its stereotypical portrayal of Native Americans.

Hoffman, Roser, and Battle found the typical read-aloud session had a number of distinctive characteristics:

- A length of ten to twenty minutes
- A literature selection that was unrelated to a unit of study
- Discussion that took less than five minutes
- No response activity following the read-aloud

A read-aloud becomes a special time for young children when they can gather close to the adult who is sharing the story.

They cautioned that this "typical read-aloud" was not a model, arguing that a daily read-aloud of at least twenty minutes should be scheduled in a specific time slot. Instead of selecting unrelated literature, Hoffman and his colleagues call for organizing read-aloud programs around units. Mature readers often read books related in some way to others that they have read, and literature units encourage students to do this. Hoffman, Roser, and Battle also questioned the adequacy of five minutes of literature discussion. Sustained conversation that can enrich the understanding of all participants does not occur in five minutes.

The Read-Aloud Experience

The read-aloud experience is one of the highlights of the school day for most children. This is especially true when the teacher carefully selects each book and spends time preparing to read it aloud.

When to Read Aloud. Read-alouds shouldn't be used merely to fill time between activities. By scheduling a read-aloud each day, you communicate to students that this is a valued activity. Besides, there is the all-too-real danger that on many days there won't be any extra time between activities.

At lower grade levels, teachers should read aloud several times a day, especially if their students have had only limited experiences with stories before entering school. Some children enter

Illustration 12.5
Many readers are likely to identify with the strong female character in *The Girl Who Loved Caterpillars*. (*The Girl Who Loved Caterpillars* by Jean Merrill, illustrations by Floyd Cooper. Copyright © 1992. Used by permission of Philomel Books, a division of Penguin Putnam Inc.)

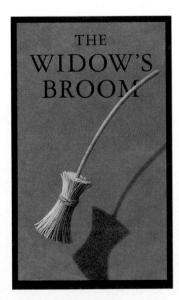

Illustration 12.6
Unexpected twists and turns mark the plot of tale about a broom with special powers. (Cover from *The Widow's Broom* by Chris Van Allsburg. Copyright © 1992 by Chris Van Allsburg. Reprinted by permission of Houghton Mifflin Company. All rights reserved.)

school having listened to thousands of storybook readings; others have not been read to at all. The latter children especially deserve a rich read-aloud program.

Selecting Books for Read-Alouds. Much of what was said about selecting books for the classroom library also applies to selecting read-aloud stories. First and foremost, select high-quality books. Books with strong plots and interesting crafting can make for engaging read-alouds; Louis Sachar's *Holes* is just such a book. We especially encourage you to choose books that deal with significant themes, for these books have the potential to evoke insightful discussions. A book such as Camille Yarbrough's *The Shimmershine Queens* fits this bill, as do Patricia Polacco's *Chicken Sunday* and Jean Merrill's *The Girl Who Loved Caterpillars.*

It is important to read books from a variety of genres, including poetry and informational books. Remember, your preferences might not be the same as those of your students. One first-grade teacher decided to let her students select the daily read-aloud books. The girls selected the same kinds of books their teacher had been selecting—picture storybooks—but much to her surprise, the boys overwhelmingly favored informational books, a genre from which she had never read aloud.

Select age-appropriate books. There are no firm and fast guidelines about which books are appropriate for particular grade levels. In fact, many books appeal to students across grade levels. Nonetheless, as a general rule, simpler, shorter books are more appropriate for younger children and those with limited literature experience. However, this does not mean that picture books are for younger children and chapter books are for older ones. Many picture books, such as Chris Van Allsburg's *The Widow's Broom*, Michael J. Rosen's *Elijah's Angel*, and Barbara Bash's *Tree of Life: The World of the African Baobab*, are wonderful for older children. Conversely, many younger children enjoy listening to chapter books such as Ann Cameron's *The Stories Julian Tells* and E. B. White's *Charlotte's Web.*

Preparing to Read Aloud. To make read-alouds a success, remember one cardinal rule: Never read aloud a book you have not previously read. In fact, you really should read a book out loud to yourself or someone else before reading it to children, because sometimes a book you loved when you read it silently just doesn't flow when it is read aloud. If you plan to read a book with unfamiliar words or language—Gary Soto's *Chato's Kitchen,* for example—it is especially important to practice pronunciations prior to reading aloud.

In preparing for a read-aloud, thoughtfully read the book you select (see Table 12.3). Look for difficulties the story presents that might interfere with comprehension. Be alert to stopping points where you might invite predictions or discussion. Also, be sure to monitor your own responses to the story. The things you notice or wonder about are worth remembering because these spontaneous responses can become conversation starters after the reading.

If you have never read a story aloud before, it makes good sense to practice pacing and expression before reading it to an audience. What feelings and moods can you convey with your voice? Is a character surprised? Does a character become angry? Is a character especially wise or silly or confused? Get to know the characters so that you can bring them to life. Don't be shy. Try out different voices and even facial expressions or gestures. And don't forget to practice holding

Illustration 12.7
Chato's Kitchen is a humorous animal fantasy with a distinctly multicultural flavor. (*Chato's Kitchen* by Gary Soto, illustrated by Susan Guevara. Used by permission of Putnam Publishing Group Juvenile Books, a division of Penguin Putnam Inc.)

the book so that the children can see the illustrations as you read. The result of all this preparation is likely to be an engaging read-aloud experience for your students.

Introducing the Story. Before introducing the story, gather the students together for the read-aloud. If there is room, pull chairs into a circle, and if a picture book is to be read aloud, situate all the children so that they can see the illustrations. Keep your introduction to the book in proper perspective: Time and attention should be devoted primarily to the read-aloud and to subsequent discussion. Nonetheless, an introduction offers you an opportunity to help children expand their store of literary understandings and allows you to "prime" them for the book.

In addition to introducing the story (or poem) by title, remember to mention the name of the author (and, when appropriate, the illustrator). This is an excellent way of helping students begin to develop a sense of author. Also mention other books written by the same author, especially those with which the children are likely to be familiar. Mentioning the book's genre is a way of gently introducing children to some of the language of literature.

Before starting to read the story, you might need to build background. This may be especially important for an informational book. If some concepts needed to understand the book are not adequately explained within the book, pay some attention to these concepts in your introduction. To set expectations for the book, you might want to invite children to make predictions based on the title or the cover illustration. Finally, if the book is being read as part of a literature unit, mention books that you have read previously.

Reading the Story. When you finally read the story, use everything you tried out in preparing for the read-aloud. Vary your reading pace to reflect changes in mood and emotion; read expressively, and use different voices when appropriate.

Some teachers believe that stories should be read straight through without

---

Table 12.3   How to Prepare for a Read-Aloud

- Anticipate difficulties the story may present to students, and prepare to help them through those difficulties.

- Watch for interesting places to stop reading and invite children's predictions or discussion.

- Heed your own responses to the story as one basis for after-reading discussion.

- Practice varying your reading pace to highlight particular portions of the story.

- Become acquainted with the characters and changing moods of the story so that you can read with appropriate expression.

- Try out different voices for different characters.

Pictures are an important source of the support young children need for their first story experiences.

any interruptions so as not to distract from the story line. However, we encourage you to feel free to interrupt the reading of a story to talk with your students, especially younger ones. Older children are able to hold back their responses until the read-aloud is complete, but younger children often forget their observations if they are forced to wait. So if a child interrupts to ask a question or share a response, honor that interruption. Children are also likely to interrupt when you reach a point in the story that begs for predictions. Or there might be times when you need to guide students through a tricky part of the story or briefly fill in information that is important to understanding the story. Finally, when you read predictable books, children enjoy joining in on repeated phrases.

After Reading. The read-aloud experience should not be over as soon as you've read the final page of the story. The literary transaction will continue if you provide ample opportunity after the reading for children to discuss the story. Chapter 13 focuses on literary discussion.

STORIES AND STORYTELLING

Children's literature starts with the telling of stories. For thousands of years before the first story was written down, humans told stories and recited poems. The thousands of years of human experience with stories (compared to a little over a century of mass literacy) surely adapted the human mind to storytelling in a special way and nourished an art of storytelling that still moves hearers deeply. This is why teachers must make storytelling a regular feature in the classroom.

Storytelling: The Tenacious Art

Many cultures have specific storytelling styles and rituals. In Jamaica today, a storyteller still begins a session by asking "Creek?" This means, "Do you want a story?" If the people want one, they answer "Creek," and the storyteller begins. But if they say "Crack," the storyteller passes on to find others willing to hear the tale. Japanese storytellers use *kamishibai,* a large set of pictures with text on the back; these pictures are presented in a box that looks like a traditional theater. Whatever the style, storytelling has never passed out of vogue, even with the proliferation of books. In fact, a number of recent children's books celebrate the power of storytelling—Susan Fletcher's *The Shadow Spinner,* Jane Kurtz's *The Storyteller's Beads,* and Ted Lewin's *The Storytellers.*

Because storytelling is so active—from the point of view of both tellers and listeners—it is an especially appropriate activity to do with younger children. Because it offers a bridge to literature, storytelling is also appropriate with reluctant readers. A wise teacher used to advocate telling stories to students. "Most children," said Edmund Henderson, "will come running when you read a story. But if one does not, tell the story instead. The told story is the older form. Hence it will have more appeal." Telling a story allows you to look your students in the eye and invite them to help you bring the story to life.

Storytelling exercises the often neglected art of using the voice. The teller must provide the excitement, drama, and cadences that pull listeners in and play their emotions like a violin. To tell a story well, the storyteller must decide how the characters sound, where the suspenseful parts are, and what parts should be slow or fast, loud or soft.

Children enjoy telling stories, too, and there are many good reasons why they should. In this section, we will present ways to choose, practice, and tell stories, and most of our advice will apply to both the adult and the child storyteller.

Common Story Types: Personal Tales to Tall Tales

Stories differ in the amount of effort they require to learn or improvise. They also differ in the kind of attention they require of listeners and the sorts of participation they invite. These points will be made clear as we talk about different types of stories.

Story types vary from personal tales, which usually evoke more inventiveness from the teller but offer less form for guidance, to already-heard stories, which offer more form but pose a challenge because they must be learned—they cannot be improvised.

Personal Stories. Personal stories are anecdotes from your own experience—about a camping trip, about being lost, about raising a pet. They can be rambling, especially if you haven't honed them down through practice. That's okay, especially when you're giving an example for children to copy when they do the telling. You can work with personal stories over time to give them more shape.

Family Stories. Family stories are true (well, maybe slightly embellished) stories about someone in your family. Because these stories may have been passed along through several generations, they are usually better formed than personal stories. Family stories often portray what people think is funniest about themselves and their relatives. They can be a lot like stories that are written down—the Ramona Quimby stories come to mind. After all, writers come from families, right?

Friend-of-a-Friend Stories. Friend-of-a-friend stories, or "urban legends," are accounts of bizarre events in a community, told by people who believe that they might have happened. When you try to check them out, though, it always turns out they happened to someone the teller almost knows—"a friend of a friend."

Friend-of-a-friend stories are close to the folktale tradition. In his fascinating collections, the folklorist Jan de Brunvard has compiled urban legends from newspapers, radio, and personal accounts of hundreds of people. Though the tales are generally recounted breathlessly, as if they just happened last week, de Brunvard (1981) is often able to find variations that are hundreds of years old. For example, the story of the vanishing hitchhiker, told in contemporary Georgia, has a song version, "The Phantom 409." Some years ago in West Africa, Frances Temple heard a version of the story from a nervous nun who claimed to have been in the jeep when the hitchhiker disappeared.

Ghost Stories. Ghost stories usually lie somewhere in between friend-of-a-friend stories and folktales. Alvin Schwartz's popular collection *Scary Stories to Tell in the Dark* was collected from folktale sources. Some teachers find ghost stories good fare to tell to middle-grade children or for them to learn and tell. If the children are to do the telling, prepare to screen their choices.

Ask the Author . . . *Jim Aylesworth*

What advice would you offer to novice storytellers?

Know what children like! When using stories with children, you will do well to know what children like about stories.

Once you know, then simply choose to use stories based on that information. It's as simple as that. My best advice to you, the novice teacher/storyteller, is, Know what children like!

It just makes sense, don't you think?

And the best way to learn what children like is to read lots of stories, tell lots of stories, to lots and lots of children. And of course, for you teachers, this will very soon be a part of your daily lives, just as it was for me. You will read or tell stories to your children every school day. Pay attention when you are doing it. Watch their eyes. You will know when they are liking what you are doing. When things are going well, make a note of what they are responding to. Try then to find similar elements in other stories. Over time, you will create a list of things that children especially like. It will be very useful information.

At this point, I know that many of you who are reading these words have not yet had a chance to get started on your lists. You are beginners. Well, don't worry too much. It was the same for me once. No one is born with information, and it will take a while to gather it. In the meantime though, you can lean on me a little, if you want. Use my list as a starter, maybe, and add to it as you see fit. For the sake of your

children, I'd be proud to help you. So get out your yellow highlighter and make some special notations.

Here is my list of things that children especially like about stories:

1. Children like sound, the louder the better. Any old noise will do. Children like onomatopoeia. Children like sound.
2. Even better, children like the more melodic sounds of our language that we call poetry and music. Children like poetry and music. They like rhythm, rhyme, repetitions of sounds. Children like alliteration, assonance. Children like poetry and music.
3. Children like animals.
4. Children like other children.
5. Children like color.
6. Children like pretending, especially silly, ridiculous, absurd pretending. In other words, children like fantasy stories.
7. Children like gross stuff. If it's yucky or gooey or smelly, they will like it. Can't tell you why.

You will find other things to add, I'm sure of it, but these will get you started. Think of me maybe, and give my best to those sweet kids of yours.

Jim Aylesworth taught first grade for twenty-five years and has been writing for children for almost as long. His recent books include The Gingerbread Man, Through the Night, Jim Aylesworth's Book of Bedtime Stories, Aunt Pitty Patty's Piggy, *and* The Full Belly Bowl. *He says, "Writing children's books is my way of being the teacher beyond the walls of my classroom for children that I may never know." He lives in Chicago, Illinois.*

Favorite Books as a Child

Rudolph the Red-Nosed Reindeer
by Robert L. May

The first book that I remember really loving was a Christmas gift in the mid-1940s. I think my mom read it to me every day until June or July.

The Adventures of Jimmy Skunk
by Thornton W. Burgess

Later, I learned to love the animal stories written by Thornton Burgess. I read them all, *Jimmy Skunk* being my favorite because we shared the name. I recently reread some of them and found them great still!

Roy Rogers comic books

I was also a big fan of comic books. They were ten cents apiece back then, and I had a large collection. Roy Rogers was my favorite hero.

Jokes and Riddles. Jokes and riddles aren't stories exactly, but they are so engaging that telling them in front of a group is good practice for children. Also, they are short enough that many children can participate in a single storytelling session.

Folktales and Fables. Folktales, the traditional stories we discussed in Chapter 5, provide excellent fare for storytelling. Because they were passed down orally, folktales have been pared down to their essentials, which makes them well formed and memorable but also leaves room for embellishments by the storyteller. Fables, those brief instructive tales that end with a moral, can also be fun to tell, especially when you stop and ask students to guess the moral.

Myths. Myths range from serious creation stories, such as the Iroquois tale of Da-Ga-Na-We-Da, to the lighter pourquoi tales that explain various natural phenomena, such as the African tale *Why Mosquitoes Buzz in People's Ears* retold by Verna Aardema. Teachers should have no trouble finding collections from many cultures that offer abundant fare suitable for storytelling.

Legends and Tall Tales. Legends are stories about famous cultural heroes that usually have a core of truth to them. The characters may be real; for example, George Washington is the subject of a number of legends. Or the events—like those in the story of John Henry—may portray qualities that people like to claim for themselves. Legends make good fare for oral telling, especially in conjunction with social studies units.

One or two steps removed from legends are tall tales, which tell about exaggerated fictitious characters. These characters also usually have qualities that real people like to claim for themselves. For example, Paul Bunyan didn't exist, but lumberjacks liked to be thought of as tough.

Learning Stories to Tell

As Margaret Read MacDonald (1993) says, it is certainly easiest to learn a story from another teller. A story well told is so much more than the words; it's the voices of the characters, the pauses and dramatic flourishes, the joy and sorrow and excitement and dread, all communicated by the storyteller. If you have a chance to listen to a storyteller who can show you all those things, you're way ahead. If you can't find a live storyteller, you can watch videotapes of live performances.

Learning the story is the first task of the storyteller. Most storytellers agree that the way to prepare a story is not to memorize it. Memorizing will make a story sound flat or set the teller up for a mental block during the telling. Besides, the beauty of a told story is that it is forever invented.

But a story is not random either. A well-told story is crisp, with the beginning, ending, and repeated parts told just so. How does a storyteller achieve this crispness without memorizing the story? Here's one way.

Get some index cards, and read through the story four times, each time with a different purpose:

1. On the first pass, read for the sense of the whole tale.

2. Next time, pay close attention to the different events in the story. Jot down each event in a few words on a separate card.

3. On the third read-through, pay close attention to the characters. On a separate card, name each character and make notes about

the way she or he should sound and move. Note any gestures that you want to associate with each character.

4. Read through the story again and jot down the beginning and ending, as well as any repeated phrases. This is important. If you know exactly how a story begins, you can launch into it confidently. If you know exactly how the story ends, you can wrap it up crisply. So memorize both. In between, pay attention to repeated phrases (such as "Little pig, little pig, let me come in. Not by the hair on my chinny-chin-chin") or repeated patterns of actions.

Practice the Story. Once you have the cards prepared and arranged in the order you find most useful, tell the story repeatedly (to yourself, to a friend, to your cat) until you can tell it confidently without looking at the cards. Later, when you tell the story, keep the cards unobtrusively in your lap—but have them handy in case you begin to forget.

If children are learning stories, have them pair up and tell their stories to each other. Also have them tell the story at home a set number of times as they learn it (say, three times a day).

Refine the Story. Once you have the gist of the story down, the fun part begins. This is when you refine the characterization, the gestures, the pauses, and other dynamics of narration.

Determine the sorts of word choices appropriate to the story you're telling. A story in a traditional setting requires the teller to say "a certain boy" or "There was an old woman who" instead of "this guy" or "this old lady." If your story is an Old English folktale, perhaps you want to sound modest and precise. If it's a Western tale from Texas, your language should be relaxed, expansive, and given to exaggeration.

You don't need to describe the characters fully to the audience, but you should have a clear idea of what they are like so that your voice and gestures will fit. You should decide the following for each main character in your story:

■ How short or tall is she or he? How heavy? How does the character's size make her or him move?

■ Is this character dignified? Sly? Lazy? Vain? How do these traits affect the way he or she talks?

■ What is the character's usual mood?

If you're helping children learn storytelling, ask these questions and follow them up with activities that will give the children practice in developing their characters. Have each child "get into" one of his or her characters as they all parade around the room. Call on several characters to introduce themselves in their own voices—and say what's on their minds.

Visualize the setting. When Jack steps out onto the clouds at the top of the beanstalk, how is his footing? How does he step? When he gets to the giant's castle, how big is the door? How does Jack knock on it? Having thought through such details will enable you to use voices and gestures that will help the audience to visualize—and believe—the setting.

Practice gestures. As a storyteller says the wolf's lines in "The Three Little Pigs," she or he will probably make a fist and pound on an imaginary door. When the storyteller says a pig's lines, she or he may pull at imaginary chin whiskers. A few gestures like these help the story, but too many will distract. Use

Ask the Author . . . W. Nikola-Lisa

What advice would you offer to novice storytellers?

W. Nikola-Lisa

I never planned to be a story-teller; rather, the ability developed within me as an act of self-defense. My first job out of college was teaching in a multi-grade alternative school. Believe me, the ability to tell a good story was essential to maintaining order within the group. But, of course, the value of storytelling far transcends this limited use. Now I tell stories for many reasons: to bring humor to a conversation, to share past personal experiences with friends, to entertain children and teachers. So, what advice might I offer a novice storyteller?

First of all, trust yourself. No matter what your story source, the story is *always* within you. By that I mean a person is drawn to a story because often it speaks to him or her at some deep, unconscious level. Unless I'm staying close to the text of a story, for stylistic reasons, I never worry about "getting lost" in a story. Since it is already a part of me, I have only to let the story lead me along.

Second, don't hide behind props. When I first started telling stories, I looked for all kinds of props to help me tell a story. After a while, I realized that the props just got in the way of the story; rather than an addition, they became a distraction. Now, I look for simple, nondescript props, at most, to embellish a story.

Third, disappear within the story. I try to immerse myself in a story as I'm learning it, but especially as I'm telling it. The irony of this statement is that by losing yourself in the story (i.e., losing your ego) something magical happens: A certain objectivity arises that allows you to keep one eye on the story and one eye on the audience.

And, this leads me to my final piece of advice. When one is telling a story, it's just as important to listen as it is to speak. The "listening" I mean, of course, is to the audience's reaction as the story unfolds. Where I go in a story is often— perhaps even always—predicated upon the audience's reaction.

In the end, the best storytelling experiences are always the ones in which the story, the storyteller, and the audience become an inseparable whole.

W. Nikola-Lisa is the author of numerous picture books including Shake Dem Halloween Bones, The Year with Grandma Moses, *and* Bein' with You This Way. *When he's not writing, or teaching at National-Louis University in Evanston, Illinois, he can be found sharing his writing experiences with elementary school children.*

> ### *Favorite Books as a Child*
>
> My favorite book as a child was Nature. My childhood days were spent in southern Texas riding horses, building forts and tree houses, and hiking to my favorite turtle pond to spend a sunny afternoon. As important as it is to read as a child, it is just as important to play and to daydream. And that is what I did a lot of as a child. Oh, I probably missed out on a lot of good stories, but what I find in my writing is that I am very attuned to rhythm and sound—and that I ascribe to my childhood days outside listening to Mother Nature and her many and varied rhythms.

only such gestures as will give a hint of the setting of a scene, provide the signature of a character, or display a strong emotion.

Also practice facial expressions. Boston storyteller Jay O'Callahan says that storytelling is the theater of the face. Gestures are important, but facial expressions and voices convey most of the story's meaning. Storytellers must learn to make facial expressions that project the way their characters feel: innocent, cunning, frightened, and so on.

If you're working with children, have them stand in a circle. One student decides on a facial expression and, without identifying the expression, "passes" it to the next, who duplicates it and passes it on in turn. This continues until the expression has gone completely around. Take time out to debrief: Were the students understanding the expression correctly? Then another student "passes" a different expression.

The storyteller's voice must be both loud enough to carry to the back of the audience and expressive enough to portray the characters in the tale. For practice, say the line "Twinkle, twinkle, little star" in the voice of each of these characters:

- A pitiful child with a big problem who wants to make an important wish
- A mean giant who is demanding that the star twinkle
- A crafty wizard who is making a magic charm

Many stories are told in the dialect of a region or of an ethnic group, and after watching storytellers on television, you might believe that using dialect is an important part of the storyteller's art. As a general rule, though, if a dialect is not yours, don't use it. It is very easy to insult other people if you appear to make fun of their speech.

Once children have learned stories, they should tell them before audiences that have not heard them practice, such as children in other classes or parents on Parents Night. They will make many friends and bring good cheer if they perform their stories at a Head Start Center or a senior citizens' activity center. You might even arrange a story swap: Senior citizens can tell stories of their own in exchange for the children's stories.

DRAMATIZING STORIES

Dramatization takes many forms, but in any form, it is an especially engaging way of inviting children into literature. In story dramatizations, children become story characters (at least for a little while) and look at the world through their eyes. In this section, we'll look at four different forms of literature-based dramatizations.

Story Theater

Story theater is a form of drama in which participants mime a story as it is read aloud. Because no dialogue is required, it is probably the simplest form of drama and is especially well suited for use with very young children. Also, because groups of participants (or all participants, for that matter) can play the same role in story theater, it is a good introduction to drama for students who feel shy about participating.

Typically, story theater is not performed for an audience. It is the acting out itself that is important for young children. Sometimes children won't be satisfied with playing the story only once and will ask to act the story out again immediately.

What the Player Does in Story Theater. Although the players in story theater don't have to worry about dialogue, they do assume active parts. First, the players must listen to the narrator in order to act out the story line appropriately. Even more important, the players need to attend to characterization, and the teacher might want to encourage discussion about what the characters are like.

Selecting Stories for Story Theater. For story theater, look for stories that rely on extensive narration, have plenty of action, and use minimal dialogue.

Esphyr Slobodkina's *Caps for Sale* works well. The main character is a peddler of hats who carries his wares on his head. One day the peddler goes for a walk in the country. (Imagine how carefully you would have to walk with hats piled high on your head.) When the peddler gets tired, he sits down (very carefully) and leans (very slowly) against a tree to nap; on waking, he reaches up (slowly and carefully) to make sure his hats are still in place. They're gone! (Imagine the peddler's reactions!) After a great deal of looking to the left, right, and all around, the peddler finally looks up into the tree, and on every branch of the tree, there is a monkey wearing a cap. (What a surprise!) The peddler is upset, so he shakes his fist at the monkeys, and what happens? You've heard the saying "Monkey see, monkey do." Well, that is just what happens. The monkeys shake their fists right back at the peddler, and each of the peddler's subsequent expressions of frustration is repeated precisely by the monkeys. Children will insist on playing this story repeatedly.

Readers Theater

In readers theater, students don't act out stories; they read (not memorize) scripted versions of stories and rely on their voices to convey the characters' emotions. Audiences can add to the success of readers theater because students are likely to be motivated to practice and refine their readings in order to do well.

What the Player Does in Readers Theater. Readers theater is more formal than story theater because the aim is for the players to present as polished a reading as possible. Usually, readers need to practice reading a script repeatedly to learn to read their parts fluently and interpret them with sensitivity.

Although the players in a readers theater presentation don't have to worry about how to act out the story, they do have to be concerned with character interpretation. What is the character like? How does he or she react to the events in the story? How (if at all) does the character change over the course of the story? What changes in speaking tone, volume, speed, or pitch might convey particular emotions? Both the teacher and fellow students can offer feedback after each practice reading, sharing what they especially liked about the interpretations and offering suggestions for improvement.

Selecting Stories and Creating Scripts for Readers Theater. Both picture books and chapter books can be used for readers theater. Books containing extensive dialogue are the best choices. Some picture books are perfect for readers theater; these ready-to-use picture books are written in dialogue form without dialogue tags ("he said" or "she replied") and contain no narration. Angela Johnson's *Tell Me a Story, Mama* is a dialogue between a little girl and her mother; Chris Raschka's *Yo! Yes?* is a simple dialogue between two little boys. Picture books that contain some narration and a great deal of dialogue with dialogue tags can be made into readers theater scripts quite easily. A few picture books, such as Richard and Roni Schotter's *There's a Dragon About: A Winter's Revel,* are actually written as scripts. The inside of the dust jacket of Frances Temple's *Tiger Soup* offers a scripted version of this Jamaican folktale. In looking for portions of chapter books to turn into readers theater scripts, look for the same features you would look for in picture books: minimal narration and extensive dialogue.

Older students can help to create scripts. You might want to use teacher-created scripts initially, but once students gain some experience with readers theater, show them how you select text and turn it into scripts. Students will soon be reading stories with an ear toward whether they can be readily made into scripts.

Stories can be brought to life via classroom dramatizations.

Creative Dramatics

In creative dramatics, players act out the story. However, unlike staged productions of plays, creative dramatics involve no sets, few if any props, and usually no audience. And instead of having a script, the players improvise dialogue.

What Is Required of the Player. Creative dramatics can be challenging, especially when students first try their hands at it. Because no one reads the story (unlike story theater), the students must remember the story line. And because there is no script (unlike readers theater), students are on their own in creating dialogue. And, of course, the players in a creative dramatics activity must be as attuned to characterization as the players in story theater and readers theater.

Teacher Support in Creative Dramatics. Teacher support for creative dramatics is important. Geraldine Siks (1958) recommends that teachers support students in creative dramatics in the following ways:

1. Motivate children into a specific mood. Preparing children for a creative dramatics experience begins prior to reading the story aloud, as the teacher sets an appropriate mood for the story.

2. Share the story. The teacher's reading of the story should help the students with their interpretation of it.

3. Guide children in making a plan for playing. The teacher and students need to collaborate to review and list the characters in the story, so as to ensure that all important story roles are filled. They should also review and list the scenes in the story. This will help students to remember the order of story events; if only part of the story is to be reenacted, then the students can use the list of scenes to select the one(s) they want to re-create. The teacher and students should also talk about the staging of the story. What parts of the staging area will be used for which scenes? How will tricky staging problems be handled? And once students have chosen or been assigned parts, the most valuable support a teacher can provide is to help them reflect on characterization.

4. Guide children into creating while they play. Children might need support while reenacting stories, especially if they have had little

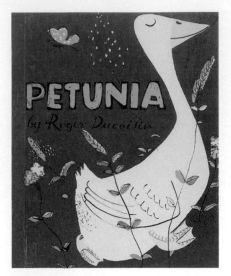

Illustration 12.8
The story of *Petunia,* a silly goose who creates pandemonium in the barnyard, has become a classic. (*Petunia* by Roger Duvoisin, copyright 1950 by Roger Duvoisin. Copyright renewed 1977 by Roger Duvoisin. Used by permission of Alfred A. Knopf Children's Books, a division of Random House, Inc.)

or no experience with creative dramatics. The teacher should lend a helping hand as a coach rather than a director. Teachers can provide support from within the story or from without. They provide support from within by playing the part of one of the characters. As a character, the teacher can create dialogue that signals what happens next in a story or how another character might respond to a situation. For example, a teacher who is playing the part of Petunia in Roger Duvoisin's *Petunia* might signal the upcoming scene (assuming that the students need a signal) by saying "I see Straw the horse, and by the way he's holding his mouth, I bet he has a toothache." With a cue like that, Straw will know what comes next. The teacher can provide support from outside of the story simply by being available to whisper lines to students who get stuck.

5. Praise children and guide them in evaluating the playing. After playing a story, students need to reflect on how the playing went. What did they especially like? What might have been done differently? The teacher shouldn't be the only one giving feedback. Eventually, the students should take over the praising and evaluating.

Selecting Stories for Creative Dramatics. The same sorts of stories that are great for storytelling work well for creative dramatics. In particular, stories with strong action sequences, lots of dialogue, and minimal narration work well—stories such as *Petunia* or "The Three Billy Goats Gruff." Vivian Paley (1981) found that her kindergartners enjoyed playing the longer and more complex fairy tales over and over because the stories had enough depth to challenge the players in their interpretations.

Improvisational Drama

Literature-based improvisational drama is quite different from the other forms of dramatization we have discussed. The players do not re-create a story, but they do become story characters. As the characters, they respond to issues, themes, and situations suggested by the story (Booth, 1985). That is, the teacher creates a situation inspired by the story and students explore it through dramatic improvisation. The situation should be one that helps the students to gain insights into a story theme.

Here is an example to clarify how improvisational drama might work. In Matt Novak's *Mouse TV,* a mouse family loves to watch television. Then one night, the television doesn't work; so the mice turn to other activities: exploring, making things, playing games, singing songs, making scary faces, conducting experiments, reading stories. Stylistically, the story is a lighthearted fantasy, but it has a substantial theme that children can explore further through improvisational drama. After listening to the story, they can become members of the mouse household on the following evening, when the television is working once again. How will the mice choose to spend their time this evening?

What Is Required of the Player. In improvisational drama, players must create their own dialogue and action. Although the dialogue and the action can move in different directions, they must remain within the confines established by the teacher. Further, if the players have taken on the roles of characters from the story, they must act in ways that are consistent with those characters. This might sound like an especially demanding form of drama, and in some ways it is. Yet, in many ways it resembles the way children play when they are on their own: They define the play situation and create action and dialogue within that situation. In fact, educators such as Brian Edmiston (1993) have successfully used improvisational drama even with primary-grade students.

Teacher Support in Improvisational Drama. In improvisational drama, the teacher must carefully structure a context that will enable the children to explore issues raised by a story. For example, in Chapter 18 of Lois Lowry's *The Giver,* Jonas and The Giver talk about the possibility that Jonas could be lost and all the memories he has received could be released on a society that has always been protected from memories. This chapter could easily be used to create a context for improvisational drama, in which the players become members of Jonas's society and receive memories for the first time.

Having introduced the dramatic context to the students, the teacher must help them select the roles they will play. Then, as in creative dramatics, the teacher can support students' playing from within or from outside of the improvisational context. In an improvisation based on *The Giver,* the teacher might become one of the people receiving memories. As a player, she might express joy or pain in response to the memories she receives. If the memories are joyful ones, the teacher might suggest that all the people go to The Giver to demand still more memories. Or the teacher might take a more neutral role that would allow her to question other players in such a way as to suggest directions in which they might move the drama: "I have received none of these memories you speak of. Tell me what they are like!"

Finally, the teacher can join the students in reflecting on the completed improvisation. Participants can talk about why they did and said particular things.

ENGAGING CHILDREN IN POETRY

In this section, we share ideas for engaging children in poetry. There are several ways of doing this: surrounding children with poetry, encouraging children's responses to poetry, encouraging public performances of poems, and helping children write poetry.

Making Songs and Poems a Part of the School Day

Songs and poems fit into the school day in a surprising number of ways, and the more children get used to them, the more they will enjoy them. Poems should be shared often in read-aloud time. They should be read with an expressive voice for pure enjoyment and reflection. Topical poems can be posted around the room as comments on the seasons, on holidays, or on science or social studies. You can find poems appropriate to nearly any occasion in anthologies such as *The Random House Book of Poetry,* edited by Jack Prelutsky, which indexes poems by topic. Children's own poems should be shared and posted along with those of published poets. Poetry can also be included along with other literary works in the readings for a thematic or literary unit (see Chapter 14).

Here are some further ideas for sharing poetry with children and young people.

Songs and Poems in the Reading Circle. Poems and songs make excellent fare for beginning reading instruction. Their catchy rhythms and rhymes give children support and alleviate some of the burden of word recognition. You might introduce kindergartners and first graders to a short poem or song lyric, with the words written on a large chart. Make smaller versions for them to keep in a growing notebook of verses.

Two reliable sources of song lyrics for children are Kathleen Krull's ***Gonna Sing My Head Off!,*** illustrated by Allen Garns, and the collection by Peter Blood and Annie Paterson entitled ***Rise Up Singing.*** Some sources of poems for children are given in the Recommended Books list at the end of Chapter 7.

Poetry and Tell. For older children, we especially like the suggestion that teachers initiate Poetry and Tell sessions (Wolf, 1993). Children are invited to choose a poem (with guidance from the teacher, as necessary) to share with the class.

With younger children, you can extend this idea by inviting them to bring in single words that intrigue them, a particularly vivid description, or a funny or interesting way of saying something—fragments of intriguing language to celebrate with the class. After all, the idea is to encourage—really, to keep alive—the fascination with language that all children were born with.

Poetry Break. Another worthwhile suggestion is having a Poetry Break every day or so (Wolf, 1993). A Poemster of the Day (the principal, a custodian, a parent—or one or more children) is elected to go from class to class reading or reciting a poem—perhaps the same poem in each class. The teacher holds up a big sign that says "Poetry Break!" and the poemster delivers!

Poetry Caravan. When the students have learned poems and interesting ways to present them, the whole class may go from room to room throughout the school, "serenading" the other classes with poetry.

Encouraging Responses to Poetry

For years, teachers believed that the most reasonable way to have children respond to a poem was to have them say what it meant and analyze its parts. But poetry speaks to us on many levels beside the intellectual one, and to assume that it is possible to summarize in so many words what a poem "is really saying" is usually to miss the point. The issue often is not what the poem says or means, but what it does and how it does it.

Often the best way to respond to a poem is not analytically but expressively. Invite children to draw as you read a poem to them. Invite them to invent sound effects or movements to accompany the verses. Invite them to act the poem out. Invite them to shout out the phrases they like best.

Choral Reading and Reciting

Most poetry is anchored in sound and is intended to be read or recited aloud. This section shares suggestions for making an event out of oral reading and reciting. Choral reading and reciting—the reading and reciting of poems by a chorus or "voice choir"—can be great fun, as children explore the dramatic possibilities of poems and of their own voices.

Whole Chorus Presentations. The trick to having a whole chorus of children recite is to keep all the voices animated, not singsongy. Children learn to focus on their sound if they are challenged to make a poem sound a certain way.

Suppose you ask children to recite the traditional poem "The Grand Old Duke of York":

The Grand Old Duke of York
He had ten thousand men.
He always marched them up the hill
Then he marched them down again.
And when they were up they were up
And when they were down they were down.
And when they were only halfway up
They were neither up nor down.

To focus their attention on the sound they want to make, tell children the poem is about a group of soldiers marching along. Ask them, "Are the soldiers wounded and weary, or are they marching snappily in a July 4th parade? Which? OK, then how should they sound? Do they sound one way as they are marching proudly to battle and another way when they're dragging themselves painfully home again?"

Poems in Dialogue. Many poems can be effectively divided between two voices. When children recite A. A. Milne's poem "Happiness" in two voices—one child taking every other line—they can bring out the plodding, two-step gait of a small child in big boots and a raincoat:

John had
    Great Big
Waterproof
    Boots on;
John had a
    Great Big
Waterproof
    Hat;
John had a
    Great Big
Waterproof
    Macintosh—
And that
    (Said John)
Is
    That.

The trick with more than one voice is to keep the poem moving on the beat. Pairs of children can take parts and practice a poem until they can recite it smoothly. You might need to clap out the beat for them the first time through. (You might also have to tell children that in England a raincoat is called a "mackintosh.")

Poems in dialogue can achieve a dramatic effect. Harold Munro's "Overheard in a Salt Marsh" is written for two voices. The performers will need to answer some questions about it: Where is this taking place? Who are the characters and what are they like? How does each one feel? How does each one's voice sound? When does one speak quickly? When slowly and musically?

Nymph, nymph, what are your beads?
    Green glass, goblin. Why do you stare at them?
Give them me.
    No.
Give them me. Give them me.
    No.

Then I will howl all night in the reeds,
Lie in the mud and howl for them.
　　　Goblin, why do you love them so?
They are better than stars or water,
Better than voices of wind that sing,
Better than any man's fair daughter,
Your green glass beads on a silver ring.
　　　Hush, I stole them out of the moon.
Give me your beads, I desire them.
　　　No.
I will howl in a deep lagoon
For your green glass beads. I love them so.
Give them me. Give them.
　　　No.

Poems as Rounds. As children, many of us sang rounds such as "Row, Row, Row Your Boat." Some poems work very well as rounds when they are recited—not sung—by small groups repeating the same verse and starting at staggered intervals.

The traditional poem "Can You Dig That Crazy Music?" can be recited by two or three groups. If you want to use three groups, start by having all the children say the verse through as a single group. Then have Group A read the first line alone. As Group A begins the second line, Group B begins the first. When Group A starts in on the third line, Group C begins the first and Group B begins the second. The third time through, Group A gets to the last line and keeps repeating it until Group B and then Group C reach and recite that line—then the poem is over. The results are amazing! Here is the poem with the accented syllables marked:

Can you dig that crazy music?

Can you dig it? Can you dig it? Can you dig it? Can you dig it?

Can you dig that crazy music?

Can you dig it? Can you dig it? Can you dig it? Can you dig it?

Oh, look. There's a chicken on a barbed wire fence.

Now, now. There's another one, coming down the road.

Ma-ma, ma-ma,

Get that son-of-a-gun off my porch!

You might want to try out other poems as rounds. Many nursery rhymes are well suited to this technique. Try "Diddle, Diddle, Dumpling, My Son John" or "The Grand Old Duke of York."

Inviting Children to Write Poetry

Here's a paradox: Surveys show that children prefer to listen to and read rhymed and rhythmic poetry, yet they have great difficulty writing rhymed and rhythmic poems, at least ones that make good sense. When teachers help children to write poems, they often share techniques that will lead the children to write unrhymed poems. Not only is this the most likely way of ensuring successful poetry-writing sessions, it also broadens children's appreciation for modern poetry, since most poets these days—particularly those writing for adults—do not write rhyming poems. The following are suggestions for writing poems that are expressive but that do not rhyme.

Making Metaphors. Ask students to think of a person they believe has some particular quality—say, a lively personality. (Have them hold off writing the person's name.) They should write the answer to each of these questions on a line by itself:

- If this person were a stage of a fire, what stage (a tiny spark, roaring flames, glowing embers)?
- If this person were a season of the year, what season?
- If this person were weather, what sort of weather?
- If this person were a bird, what kind of bird?
- If this person were landscape, what landscape?
- If this person were music, what kind of music?
- If this person were footwear, what kind of footwear?
- If this person were a car, what kind of car?
- If this person were a time of day, what time of day?

On the line below their last answer, have the children write the person's name. Now they tinker with these lines—move them around, add or take away words, letting the poem speak for itself in the best way it can.

List Poems. Throughout the ages, many fine poems have been developed around lists. Take this medieval prayer, for example:

From Ghoulies
And Ghosties
And long-legged Beasties
And Things that go bump in the night:
Good Lord, deliver us.

You can use the idea of listing by asking students to list all of the things they know that are dark or lonely or round or scary. The effect is heightened when they include both concrete and abstract things in their lists. For example, all of these are round:

- Ripples in a pond when a pebble is thrown in
- A policeman's beat
- The moon's halo
- Subway tokens
- Surprised eyes
- A ghost's mouth
- The world
- Life

It is best if children free-write the lists first, then arrange them for best effect.

Incantations. From oldest times, the power of poetry has been used to summon energy and spirit and marshal concentration to a particular end. (Some call this magic.) In the eighth century, Saint Patrick of Ireland wrote a prayer that is part enchantment (Kennelly, 1981):

St. Patrick's Rune

I bind unto myself today
The virtues of the starlit heaven,
The glorious sun's life-giving ray,
The whiteness of the moon at even;
The flashing of the lightning free,
The howling wind's tempestuous shocks,
The stable earth, the deep salt sea
And all the old eternal rocks.

Ask students to write an incantation to make someone brave, tough, fast, lucky, or smart. Here is a format they can follow:

May the _____ of the _____ ,
The _____ of the _____ ,
The _____ of the _____ , and
The _____ of the _____
Be with me this day.

The Cinquain. A cinquain is a five-line poem tightly focused on one topic. Writing cinquains is a way for children to explore a character in a story they are reading. Here's an example, based on the hero of "Jack and the Beanstalk":

Jack
young, wily
believing, climbing, winning
brave, or just reckless?
Giant-killer

Cinquains are written according to this formula:

1. The first line names the subject in one word.

2. The second line gives two words describing the subject.

3. The third gives three action words related to the subject and ending in -ing.

4. The fourth line has four words, which can be a four-word phrase related to the subject.

5. The fifth line is one word, a synonym for the subject.

In spite of the use of a formula, the results can be striking.

The Diamante. Diamantes are a variation on the cinquain form. Whereas a cinquain describes a character as she or he is now, a diamante describes how a character (or some other aspect of a story) changes over time. Let's look at the character "Jack" again:

Boy
young, simpleton
loafing, goofing, grinning

naive child/plucky hero
"Fetch the axe!"
proven man
Jack

The first half of a diamante relates to the character in the beginning of the story. Then, midway through the poem, the descriptions change and relate to the character at the end of the story. The pattern of a diamante is as follows:

1. The first line is a one-word name for the character as he or she was in the beginning of the story.

2. The second line gives two words describing the character in the beginning.

3. The third line is three action words (-ing words) describing the character in the beginning.

4. In the fourth line, the first two words describe the character in the beginning. Then there is a slash, followed by two words that describe the character at the end of the story.

5. The fifth line has three action words related to the character at the end of the story.

6. The sixth line has two words that describe the character at the end of the story.

7. The seventh line is a one-word name for the character at the end of the story.

Of course, there are many more ways to have children write poems, but space won't permit us to describe them here. Please consult the list of resources at the end of Chapter 7.

OTHER DIMENSIONS OF THE LITERATURE-RICH CLASSROOM

If teachers wish to foster a love of literature, then they must devote ample time to reading, listening, and responding to literature. This is time above and beyond that devoted to teaching reading skills.

DEAR Time

Sometimes teachers tell students they can read "once their work is done." That works fine for the strong students who consistently finish their work early, but many students *never* finish their work early. To ensure that all students get to read every day, many teachers build in a block of time when all the children in the classroom stop what they are doing and choose books, magazines, or newspapers to read. These blocks of reading time are known as DEAR (Drop Everything And Read), SSR (Sustained Silent Reading), or USSR (Uninterrupted Sustained Silent Reading).

Students need to realize that their teacher values DEAR time. Teachers can demonstrate this commitment by scheduling DEAR time daily, beginning with the first day of school, and by spending the DEAR time reading with their students. Students might need to read for shorter blocks of time at the beginning of the year (ten to fifteen minutes) and then work up to longer stretches (thirty to forty-five minutes). DEAR time is for all students; even those not yet reading

Table 12.4   How to Make DEAR a Success

- Make DEAR time a part of students' daily routine.
- Let students choose their own reading materials for DEAR time.
- Ensure that everyone, including the teacher, reads during DEAR time.
- For students who have a difficult time reading for long stretches, begin with a few minutes of reading time (perhaps ten minutes) and build to longer blocks of time (thirty to forty-five minutes).
- For younger readers, don't require that the reading time be silent; beginning readers frequently need to hear themselves read aloud.
- Let kindergartners participate in DEAR time by "pretend reading" stories.

conventionally can engage in pretend reading. There is no reason why beginning readers, for whom silent reading may not be appropriate, can't read their books out loud. (See Table 12.4.)

Author Visits

There is probably no better way to bring both literature and the process of creating literature to life than through a visit by a recognized children's author (or illustrator). Such a visit can usually be arranged by contacting the children's marketing department of the author's publisher.

A visit by an author should be viewed as an opportunity to celebrate literature and literacy. Some schools do this by hosting a Young Authors' Conference in conjunction with the author's visit. Presentations by the visiting author typically get top billing at the conference. Ideally, the author will be able to present to small groups of students. Visiting authors often have wonderful stories to share with students about the inspiration for their work, and illustrators frequently offer fascinating demonstrations of their art. If time permits, it is ideal to organize more informal sessions in which small groups can really talk to the visitor. The author or illustrator is the celebrity of the Young Authors' Conference, but this doesn't mean that other important things aren't happening. Students who attend the conference should be authors or illustrators themselves and should come to the conference prepared to join peer groups in which they share stories and illustrations they have created. A third type of conference event can center on children's literature selections. Students can attend sessions offered by teachers or members of the community, in which they listen to a story read aloud and participate in a response activity based on that story.

Teachers need to prepare students for an upcoming author visit. First, they must ensure that the students know the featured author's work. In the weeks preceding the visit, the teacher should read the visiting author's stories aloud. Children should have the opportunity to respond to the author's work through writing and artwork. Their responses can be displayed throughout the classroom or school. If students will have the opportunity to interview the visiting author, the teacher needs to help them generate questions about some of the author's actual stories as well as questions that will yield insights into how writers (or illustrators) go about their work—where they get ideas, how they budget their time to ensure that their work gets finished, what special techniques they use, and what advice they might offer young writers (or artists).

TEACHING IDEAS

Preparing a Read-Aloud. Prepare to read aloud *The Ghost-Eye Tree* by Bill Martin, Jr. In the story, a mother asks her son and daughter to walk at night to the end of the town to fetch a bucket of milk. The trip to town is uneventful, even though the children must pass the dreaded ghost-eye tree. However, on the walk home, the children, loaded down with a full bucket of milk, are certain that they see the ghost eye. Then, to complicate matters, the children discover that the brother has dropped his much-loved hat by the ghost-eye tree. This story is full of drama, tense moments, and changing emotions. Practice reading it aloud. Because there is so much dialogue between the siblings, you might want to try out different voices for the brother and sister. Vary the pace of your reading. Try reading faster as the children approach the tree. When the siblings see the ghost eye, pick up your pace even more. There are ample opportunities to vary your expression. How might the children sound as they exchange good-natured jibes with each other? How do they feel when they spot the ghost eye? What emotions does the brother experience when his sister announces she will retrieve his hat? Now try reading the story to a group of children.

Setting Up a Student Book Referral Service. You can set up a student book referral service by inviting students to record the books they have read and their responses to those books in a database maintained on the classroom computer. The entry for each book should include title, author/illustrator, genre, summary, and response to book. A computerized database will give students great flexibility in selecting books. If they want to find a good fantasy to read, they simply call up the category "Fantasy." If they want recommendations for books by a particular author, the computer will sort books by authors' names.

Stocking the Classroom Library. Although you will probably want a set of core books to remain in your library center all year, you should rotate additional books through regularly (probably every month or so). When you rotate new books into the library center, don't just place them there without fanfare. Introduce the books one by one, helping students to make connections between the new books and ones they already know: "Here's Sid Hite's latest book; I thought you might enjoy it since we read *It's Nothing to a Mountain*" or "We've been reading and writing a lot of trickster tales, so I've brought in *Tops and Bottoms* by Janet Stevens. I think you'll like the way you read the book from top to bottom—just as the title says."

Inviting Students to Set Up the Organizational System for the Classroom Library. Any library needs to be organized if readers are going to be able to locate books to read with any ease. Although the teacher can always set up the organizational system for the classroom library, there are any number of advantages to inviting the students to help set up the system. First and foremost, student involvement in the process will help ensure that students feel a sense of ownership in the classroom library. Second, as you discuss organizational ideas with your students, you will gain invaluable insights into what they feel are important considerations in selecting books. Although students might not always consider factors that you believe are important, there is no reason the teacher can't bring her own suggestions to the table along with those of the students. It is likely that the end result of this collaborative process will be a classroom library students can use and choose to use.

EXPERIENCES FOR YOUR LEARNING

1. Develop an improvisational drama based on *The Giver*. Often, the ending of a book suggests a situation for improvising. Present the improvisational situation you create for *The Giver* to a group of peers and ask them to join you in the improvisation.

2. Prepare to read aloud a book that will challenge you. If you are not especially proficient in Spanish, then you might want to select *Chato's Kitchen*. For dialect, you might to try your hand at reading a "Brer Rabbit" story. Practice reading the story until you feel confident enough to read it aloud. Then share the story with a group of peers. After reading the story aloud, discuss the challenges the book presented to you and share with your peers recommendations for preparing a challenging read-aloud.

3. Visit a classroom library center. Which of the design features identified by Morrow (on page 432) were evident in the center? Given what you saw, how would you rate the library center: basic, good, or excellent? Why?

4. Interview at least five of your peers to determine how they feel about storytelling. Discuss some of the storytelling activities described in this chapter. Afterwards, talk to the same five people to see whether their attitudes toward storytelling have changed.

RECOMMENDED BOOKS

* indicates a picture book; I indicates interest level (P = preschool, YA = young adult)

Read-Alouds and the Classroom Library Collection

*Aardema, Verna. *Why Mosquitoes Buzz in People's Ears.* Illustrated by Leo and Diane Dillon. Dial, 1975. In this African pourquoi tale, an unexpected chain of events explains why mosquitoes buzz in people's ears. (**I:** P–8)

*Ackerman, Karen. *The Tin Heart.* Illustrated by Michael Hays. Atheneum, 1990. Best friends Mahaley and Flora live on opposite sides of the Ohio River, and when the Civil War breaks out, the ferry stops running. (**I:** 8–12).

*Aliki. *Wild and Woolly Mammoths.* HarperCollins, 1977/1998. This is a fascinating account of the woolly mammoth and its relationship to cave dwellers. (**I:** 6–10)

*Allard, Harry. *Miss Nelson Is Missing!* Illustrated by James Marshall. Houghton Mifflin, 1977. When Viola Swamp becomes the sub in Room 207, the children are desperate to find their missing teacher. (**I:** P–8)

*———. *The Stupids Step Out.* Houghton Mifflin, 1974. An outrageous family is involved in hilarious antics. (**I:** P–8)

*Arnold, Katya. *Duck, Duck, Goose?* Holiday House, 1997. Goose wants to be the most beautiful bird of all, but her quest has unexpected results. (**I:** P–8)

*Aylesworth, Jim. *Aunt Pitty Patty's Piggy.* Illustrated by Barbara McClintock. Scholastic, 1999. Aunt Pitty Patty needs plenty of help to get her new pig through the gate. See also *The Full Belly Bowl,* illustrated by Wendy Anderson Halperin (Atheneum, 1999). (**I:** P–8)

*———. *The Gingerbread Man.* Illustrated by Barbara McClintock. Scholastic, 1998. This is a lively retelling of the tale of the runaway Gingerbread Man. See also *Jim Aylesworth's Book of Bedtime Stories,* illustrated by Jo Ellen McAllister-Stammen, Walter Lyon Krudop, and Eileen Christelow (Atheneum, 1998). (**I:** P–8)

*———. *Through the Night.* Illustrated by Pamela Patrick. Atheneum, 1998. A lonely father has a long drive home to reach his waiting children and wife. (**I:** P–8)

*Barrett, Judi. *Cloudy with a Chance of Meatballs.* Illustrated by Ron Barrett. Atheneum, 1978. Storms of food fall from the sky in the town of Chew-and-Swallow. (**I:** P–8)

*Bash, Barbara. *Tree of Life: The World of the African Baobab.* Little, Brown, 1994. With lyrical language, the author documents the rich ecosystem of the African baobab tree. (**I:** 6–10)

*———. *Urban Roosts.* Little, Brown, 1992. The author explores how birds that live in the city have adapted their nest-building habits to their urban environment. (**I:** 6–11)

*Bauer, Steven. *The Strange and Wonderful Tale of Robert McDoodle: The Boy Who Wanted to Be a Dog.* Illustrated by Brad Sneed. Simon & Schuster, 1999. Determined to be a dog, Robert McDoodle sneaks off to dog school, only to find that a dog's life isn't all he dreamed it was. This humorous story is told in rhythmic, rhyming language. (I: P–8)

*Bloom, Becky. *Mice Make Trouble*. Illustrated by Pascal Biet. Orchard, 2000. Riotous action stems from a little boy's decision to use magic crayons to draw six mice and one hedgehog. (I: P–7)

Blume, Judy. *Tales of a Fourth Grade Nothing*. Dutton, 1972. Peter's little brother causes endless (and funny) complications in his life. (I: 6–10)

Bond, Michael *A Bear Called Paddington*. Illustrated by Peggy Fortnum. Houghton Mifflin, 1958/1998. Paddington Bear becomes a member of the Brown family. (I: P–7)

Byars, Betsy. *The Seven Treasure Hunts*. Illustrated by Jennifer Barrett. HarperCollins, 1991/1998. Two friends design treasure hunts that do not go quite as planned. (I: 6–10)

Cameron, Ann. *The Stories Julian Tells*. Illustrated by Ann Strugnell. Random House, 1981/1996. Julian relates humorous stories about everyday experiences. (I: 5–8)

Cleary, Beverly. *Ramona the Pest*. Morrow, 1968/1992. Ramona makes mischief when she enters kindergarten. (I: 6–10)

*Cole, Brock. *Buttons*. Farrar, 2000. When an old man eats so much his buttons pop off, his three daughters find seemingly foolish ways to replace the buttons. (I: 5–8)

Collier, James Lincoln, and Christopher Collier. *My Brother Sam Is Dead*. Scholastic, 1974. A family is torn apart as father and son take different sides in the American Revolution. (I: 9–12)

*Cooney, Barbara. *Miss Rumphius*. Puffin, 1982. Miss Rumphius finds ways of achieving her three lifelong goals. (I: 6–10)

Cooper, Susan. *King of Shadows*. Simon & Schuster, 1999. Chosen to be part of a group that will perform at the newly reconstructed Globe Theatre, Nat Field finds himself inexplicably transported back in time to Shakespeare's own Globe Theatre. (I: 10 and up)

Coville, Bruce. *Jeremy Thatcher, Dragon Hatcher*. Illustrated by Gary A. Lippincott. Harcourt, 1991. Being selected as a dragon hatcher opens up a world of adventure for Jeremy Thatcher. (I: 8–11)

*Cronin, Doreen. *Click, Clack, Moo: Cows That Type*. Illustrated by Betsy Lewin. Simon & Schuster, 2000. When the cows discover an old typewriter in the barn, Farmer Brown's farm will never be the same again. (I: 5–8)

Dahl, Roald. *James and the Giant Peach*. Illustrated by Nancy Ekholm Burkert. Knopf, 1961. A boy leaves his misery behind when a giant peach, inhabited by magical characters, grows in his backyard. (I: 6–10)

*dePaola, Tomie. *Strega Nona*. Prentice-Hall, 1975. Big Anthony and the townspeople face disaster when Big Anthony can't make the magic pasta pot stop cooking. (I: P–8)

———. *26 Fairmount Avenue*. Putnam, 1999. Memorable moments from a year in Tomie dePaola's boyhood fill the pages of this first chapter book. (I: 6–9)

*Ehlert, Lois. *Moon Rope/Un lazo a la luna*. Harcourt, 1992. In this pourquoi tale, fox convinces mole to climb to the moon on a rope woven of grass. (I: P–8)

Fleming, Denise. *In the Tall, Tall Grass*. Holt, 1995. A caterpillar munches its way through the tall, tall grass in the midst of lively activities. (I: P–7)

Fletcher, Susan. *The Shadow Spinner*. Atheneum, 1998. This novel is built around the story of Scheherazade, the famous storyteller who wins her life each night with cliff hanging stories for the sultan. (I: 10 and up)

*Gackenbach, Dick. *Harry and the Terrible Whatzit*. Houghton Mifflin, 1984. To save his mother, Harry must face the terrible Whatzit that lives in the cellar. (I: P–7)

George, Jean Craighead. *My Side of the Mountain*. Penguin Putnam, 1959/1997. A boy survives alone in the wilds of upper New York State. (I: 10–YA)

*Gibbons, Faye. *Mama and Me and the Model T*. Illustrated by Ted Rand. Morrow, 1999. Because Pa assumes that only the boys need to learn to drive the brand-new motorcar, Ma decides that she needs to take matters into her own hands. (I: 5–9)

*Gray, Libba Moore. *When Uncle Took the Fiddle*. Illustrated by Lloyd Bloom. Orchard, 1999. The whole family feels tired—until uncle starts playing the fiddle. (I: P–7)

*Grindley, Sally. *Shhh!* Illustrated by Peter Utton. Little, Brown, 1992. The reader is invited to join in a trek through the giant's castle and must try all the while to avoid waking the giant. (I: P–8)

Hite, Sid. *It's Nothing to a Mountain*. Holt, 1994. A brother and sister find adventure and friendship in the Blue Ridge Mountains of Virginia. (I: 10–12)

*Hoberman, Mary Ann. *The Two Sillies*. Illustrated by Lynne Cravath. Harcourt, 2000. Acquiring a cat and getting rid of mice aren't simple feats for the two sillies in this easy-to-read story. (I: P–7)

*Hoffman, Mary. *Amazing Grace*. Illustrated by Caroline Binch. Dial, 1991. A little girl's grandmother helps her to realize that she can achieve anything she sets her mind to. (**I:** 6–10)

*Howard, Arthur. *Cosmo Zooms*. Harcourt, 1999. Cosmo believes that he is the only dog without a special talent—until he tries a skateboard for the very first time. (**I:** P–7)

*Howard, Elizabeth Fitzgerald. *Aunt Flossie's Hats (and Crab Cakes Later)*. Illustrated by James Ransome. Clarion, 1991. Stories that accompany the old hats in Aunt Flossie's collection make Sunday visits memorable. (**I:** P–8)

Howe, Deborah, and James Howe. *Bunnicula: A Rabbit Tale of Mystery*. Illustrated by Alan Daniel. Atheneum, 1979. The family pets are certain that the new bunny is a vampire rabbit. (**I:** 6–10)

*Johnson, Angela. *Tell Me a Story, Mama*. Illustrated by David Soman. Orchard, 1989. A little girl ends up being the storyteller when she asks her mother for a story. (**I:** P–8)

*Johnson, Paul Brett. *The Pig Who Ran a Red Light*. Orchard, 1999. When Miss Rosemary's pig starts doing everything the cow does, she is challenged to find a way to make the pig act like a pig. (**I:** P–7)

Karr, Kathleen. *The Great Turkey Walk*. Farrar, 1998. Simon Green never dreams of the adventures he'll encounter when he sets out for Denver in 1860 with a herd of turkeys and a motley crew of companions. (**I:** 9–12)

*Keiko, Kasza. *Don't Laugh, Joe!* Putnam, 1997. Joe is old enough to learn to play dead, something all possums must learn to do, but he gets the giggles every time he tries to do it. (**I:** P–8)

*———. *The Wolf's Chicken Stew*. Putnam, 1987. A chicken outsmarts the wolf who wants her for his dinner. (**I:** P–8)

*Keller, Holly. *Geraldine First*. Greenwillow, 1996. Geraldine's brother copies her every move, and Geraldine is desperate to cure him of his habit. (**I:** P–8)

*Kellogg, Steven. *The Mysterious Tadpole*. Dial, 1972/1997. A boy must find a home for his pet tadpole, which grows to an outrageous size. (**I:** P–8)

*———. *The Three Sillies*. Candlewick, 1999. Convinced that the girl he is courting and her family are outrageously silly, the gentleman declares that he will marry the girl only if he can find three sillier people on his travels. (**I:** P–8)

*Kimmel, Eric A. *Anansi Goes Fishing*. Illustrated by Janet Stevens. Holiday, 1992. The tables are turned when Anansi sets out to trick his friend into doing all the work. (**I:** P–8)

*Kitchen, Bert. *And So They Build*. Candlewick, 1993. Using a distinctive format, the author provides information about the nesting habits of a variety of animals. (**I:** 6–10)

*Koller, Jackie French. *No Such Thing*. Illustrated by Betsy Lewin. Boyds Mill, 1997. A boy is certain that a monster lives under his bed, but his mother won't believe him. Monster is certain that a boy lives above his bed, but his mother won't believe him. (**I:** P–8)

Konigsburg, E. L. *From the Mixed-up Files of Mrs. Basil E. Frankweiler*. Aladdin, 1987/1999. Claudia and her younger brother run away to live in the Metropolitan Museum of Art. (**I:** 9–12)

Kurtz, Jane. *The Storyteller's Beads*. Illustrated by Michael Bryant. Harcourt, 1998. Fleeing their drought- and violence-stricken land, two young Ethiopian strangers overcome their prejudices and find solace in the old stories passed down by one of their grandmothers. (**I:** 9–12)

*Kvasnosky, Laura McGee. *Zelda and Ivy and the Boy Next Door*. Candlewick, 1999. The best-friends relationship of fox sisters Zelda and Ivy takes unexpected twists when a boy moves in next door. (**I:** P–8)

*Lasky, Kathryn. *The Emperor's Old Clothes*. Illustrated by David Catrow. Harcourt, 1999. When Farmer Henry stumbles across new finery cast off (by the emperor who wore no clothes), his new attire causes an uproar in the barnyard. (**I:** 6–10)

*———. *Lunch Bunnies*. Illustrated by Marylin Hafner. Little, Brown, 1996. Clyde was going to start school, and he knew he was ready for everything—except lunch. (**I:** P–6)

Levine, Gail Carson. *The Wish*. HarperCollins, 2000. Given the opportunity to make one wish, Wilma asks to be the most popular person in her school—a wish that she soon realizes was anything but wise. (**I:** 10–12)

*Lewin, Ted. *The Storytellers*. Lothrop, 1998. A boy follows his grandfather through the streets of Fez, Morocco, to the ancient gate of the city where his grandfather will mesmerize the day's audience with magical tales. (**I:** 7–11)

Lindgren, Astrid. *Pippi Longstocking*. Translated by Florence Lamborn. Illustrated by Louis S. Glanzman. Viking, 1950/1997. Living all alone, Pippi—the strongest girl in the world—is free to engage in hilarious antics. (**I:** 5–9)

Lowry, Lois. *The Giver*. Houghton Mifflin, 1993. Living in a controlled society, a boy is given access to the dark secrets that lie beneath the order. The companion book is *Gathering Blue* (2000). (**I:** 11–YA)

*Lyon, George Ella. *One Lucky Girl*. Illustrated by Irene Trivas. Dorling Kindersley, 2000. Even though their trailer is destroyed by a tornado, Hawkeye's family has a great deal for which to be thankful. (I: 5–8)

MacLachlan, Patricia. *Sarah, Plain and Tall*. Harper, 1985. In this story set in pioneer times, two children long for someone to fill the empty place left by the death of their own mother. (I: 8–12)

*Martin, Bill, Jr., and John Archambault. *Barn Dance*. Illustrated by Ted Rand. Holt, 1986/1995. A boy joins in the animals' square dance. (I: P–8)

*———. *The Ghost-Eye Tree*. Illustrated by Ted Rand. Holt, 1985/1995. This story about a brother and sister's scary experience with a haunted tree can easily be adapted for readers theater. (I: P–9)

*Mayer, Mercer. *Liza Lou and the Yeller Belly Swamp*. Aladdin, 1976/1997. Liza Lou proves to be too clever for the witches, haunts, and gobblygooks of the Yeller Belly Swamp. (I: P–8)

*McCloskey, Robert. *Make Way for Ducklings*. Viking, 1941. Mrs. Mallard seeks the perfect home for her ducklings. (I: P–7)

*McDermott, Gerald. *Anansi the Spider*. Holt, 1995. Anansi's sons use their special abilities to rescue their father. (I: P–8)

*McKissack, Patricia. *Flossie and the Fox*. Illustrated by Rachel Isadora. Dial, 1986. Flossie turns the tables on Mr. Fox when he tries to get her basket of eggs. (I: 5–10)

*———. *A Million Fish . . . More or Less*. Illustrated by Dena Schutzer. Knopf, 1992. Visits to the bayou inspire unforgettable yarns. (I: 6–10)

———, and Fredrick L. McKissack. *Christmas in the Big House, Christmas in the Quarters*. Illustrated by John Thompson. Scholastic, 1994. A comparison of Christmas in the big house and in the slave quarters the year before the Civil War breaks out. (I: 9–12)

*McLarey, Kristina Thermaenius, and Myra McLarey. *When You Take a Pig to a Party*. Illustrated by Marjory Wunsch. Orchard, 2000. Havoc breaks out all over when Adelaide takes Sherman the pig to a birthday party. (I: P–7)

*McNaughton, Colin. *Suddenly*. Harcourt, 1995. Oblivious to the danger that looms over him, a little pig saunters through town on his round of errands. (I: P–7)

*Merrill, Jean. *The Girl Who Loved Caterpillars*. Illustrated by Floyd Cooper. Philomel, 1992. A young woman in twelfth-century Japan follows her heart rather than the dictates of her culture. (I: 8–12)

Milne, A. A. *Winnie-the-Pooh*. Illustrated by Ernest H. Shepard. Dutton/Plume, 1924/1999. Winnie-the-Pooh has marvelous adventures in the Hundred Acre Wood with his host of friends—all stuffed animals like him. (I: P–8)

*Miranda, Anne. *To Market, To Market*. Illustrated by Janet Stevens. Harcourt, 1997. A market trip turns into unexpected chaos when the groceries refuse to cooperate. (I: P–8)

Modarressi, Mitra. *Yard Sale!* Dorling Kindersley, 2000. When Mr. Flotsam holds a yard sale, all the items his neighbors purchase do the unexpected: A carpet flies, a typewriter writes by itself, a pasta maker won't turn off. The neighbors are up in arms, until they begin to view their purchases from new perspectives. (I: 5–9)

*Mora, Pat. *A Birthday Basket for Tia*. Illustrated by Cecily Lang. Macmillan, 1992. A little girl puts together the perfect birthday basket for her great-aunt. (I: P–7)

Myers, Walter Dean. *The Righteous Revenge of Artemis Bonner*. HarperCollins, 1992. Artemis Bonner travels west to avenge his uncle's murder in this broadly drawn adventure. (I: 9–12)

Naylor, Phyllis Reynolds. *The Grand Escape*. Illustrated by Alan Daniel. Atheneum, 1993. Two house cats make a grand escape to the outside world, where challenges and opportunities abound. (I: 6–10)

———. *Sang Spell*. Atheneum, 1998. Hitchhiking from Boston to Dallas, Josh finds himself caught in a time warp in which he is forced to face the darkness inside himself. (I: 11 and up)

———. *Shiloh*. Atheneum, 1991. A boy determines to save the dog Shiloh from his abusive owner. (I: 8–12)

Paterson, Katherine. *Bridge to Terabithia*. HarperCollins, 1977. Jesse's friendship with a new girl in his rural neighborhood extends the boundaries of his life. (I: 10–12)

Paulsen, Gary. *Hatchet*. Bradbury, 1987. The survivor of a plane crash, a boy struggles to survive in the wilderness. (I: 10–YA)

———. *Puppies, Dogs, and Blue Northers: Reflections on Being Raised by a Pack of Sled Dogs*. Paintings by Ruth Wright Paulsen. Harcourt, 1996. Paulsen relays his experiences with a litter of pups and their mother, his lead sled dog. (I: 8–12)

Pinkwater, Daniel. *The Hoboken Chicken Emergency*. Atheneum, 1977/1999. The town of Hoboken panics as its residents begin to encounter the 266-pound pet chicken that Arthur has acquired (instead of a Thanksgiving turkey). (I: 6–9)

*Polacco, Patricia. *The Bee Tree*. Philomel, 1993. A little girl and her grandfather are joined by friends in a merry chase through the countryside in search of a bee tree. (I: 5–10)

*———. *Chicken Sunday*. Philomel, 1992. A group of friends extend a hand of friendship across cultural boundaries. (I: 6–10)

*———. *Pink and Say*. Philomel, 1994. During the Civil War, an African American Union soldier befriends a white Union soldier. (I: 8–YA)

Prelutsky, Jack, ed. *The Random House Book of Poetry for Children*. Illustrated by Arnold Lobel. Random House, 1983. An extensive anthology of poems collected by one of America's favorite children's poets. (I: 7–12)

Robinson, Barbara. *The Best Christmas Pageant Ever*. Harper, 1972. Everyone anticipates disaster when the Herdmans participate in the church's Christmas pageant, but much to everyone's surprise, it's the best Christmas pageant ever. (I: 6–10)

*Rosen, Michael J. *Elijah's Angel*. Illustrated by Aminah Brenda Lynn Robinson. Harcourt, 1992. A boy's parents help him to reach across cultural boundaries. (I: 8–YA)

———. *A School for Pompey Walker*. Illustrated by Aminah Brenda Lynn Robinson. Harcourt, 1995. Bought out of slavery, Pompey Walker willingly faces personal dangers to achieve his goal of founding a school for black children. (I: 8–12)

Rowling, J. K. *Harry Potter and the Sorcerer's Stone*. Illustrated by Mary Grandpre. Scholastic, 1997. Harry Potter never dreamed of the adventures awaiting him when he is selected to enter a school for wizards. Sequels include *Harry Potter and the Chamber of Secrets* (1998), *Harry Potter and the Prisoner of Azkanban* (1999), and *Harry Potter and the Goblet of Fire* (2000). (I: 8–12)

Rylant, Cynthia. *The Blue Hill Meadows*. Illustrated by Ellen Beier. Harcourt, 1997. Stories about the Meadow family celebrate family life in a small town. (I: 6–9).

———. *Gooseberry Park*. Illustrated by Arthur Howard. Harcourt, 1995. When disaster strikes Gooseberry Park, Kona, a Labrador retriever, proves himself a hero and true friend of Stumpy the squirrel. (I: 5–9)

*———. *When I Was Young in the Mountains*. Illustrated by Diane Goode. Dutton, 1982. In lyrical language, a girl tells of her life in the mountains. (I: 5–10)

Sachar, Louis. *Holes*. Farrar, 1998. When Stanley Yelnats is sent to a juvenile detention center for a crime he didn't commit, he is sure it is just another instance of the family curse. Little does Stanley dream that his stay at Camp Green Lake will present him with the opportunity to finally break that curse. (I: 10 and up)

Sacks, Margaret. *Themba*. Illustrated by Wil Clay. Puffin, 1994. A South African boy waits for his father to return from the mines. (I: 7–10)

*San Souci, Robert D. *The Talking Eggs*. Illustrated by Jerry Pinkney. Dial, 1989. An African American variant of the Cinderella story. (I: 5–10)

*Say, Allen. *Tree of Cranes*. Houghton Mifflin, 1991. A Japanese boy is introduced to Christmas by his mother. (I: P–8)

*Scieszka, Jon. *The Stinky Cheese Man and Other Fairly Stupid Tales*. Illustrated by Lane Smith. Viking, 1992. A collection of wacky folktale spin-offs. (I: 5–10)

Selden, George. *The Cricket in Times Square*. Illustrated by Garth Williams. Farrar, 1960. Chester the cricket must make a life for himself in the alien world of the Times Square subway station. (I: 6–10)

*Sendak, Maurice. *Chicken Soup with Rice*. Harper, 1962. This is a celebration of the virtues of chicken soup. (I: P–7)

*———. *Where the Wild Things Are*. HarperCollins, 1963/1998. Sent to his room for misbehaving, Max travels to where the Wild Things are and becomes king of all Wild Things. (I: P–8)

Sierra, Judy. *There's a Zoo in Room 22*. Illustrated by Barney Saltzberg. Harcourt, 2000. Miss Darling's class acquires a pet for every letter of the alphabet. A humorous poem introduces each of the pets. (I: P–8)

Soto, Gary. *Baseball in April*. Harcourt, 1990. A collection of short stories about everyday experiences of young Mexican Americans. (I: 11–YA)

*———. *Chato and the Party Animals*. Illustrated by Susan Guevara. Putnam, 2000. Novio Boy, a pound cat, is sad that he doesn't know the date of his birth. So Chato decides to surprise his buddy with a party, but he forgets to invite the guest of honor. (I: P–8)

*———. *Chato's Kitchen*. Illustrated by Susan Guevara. Penguin Putnam, 1995. Chato, the coolest cat in East L.A., can't believe his luck when a family of mice moves in next door. (I: P–8)

*———. *Too Many Tamales*. Illustrated by Ed Martinez. Putnam, 1993. A little girl fears that she has lost her mother's diamond ring in the tamale masa. (I: P–8)

*Stadler, John. *The Cats of Mrs. Calamari*. Orchard, 1997. Mrs. Calamari must use her wits, for she has cats—a lot of cats—and a landlord who hates them. (I: P–7)

*Stanley, Diane. *Raising Sweetness*. Illustrated by G. Brian Karas. Putnam, 1999. Sweetness and the other children know that they are lucky to have been adopted by the sheriff; still, the sheriff's cooking and housekeeping leave something to be desired. So Sweetness sets out to find a solution to their problems. (I: 5–9)

———. *Saving Sweetness*. Illustrated by G. Brian Karas. Putnam, 1996. When the orphan Sweetness runs away from the orphanage, the sheriff sets out to save her, but Sweetness doesn't want to have anything to do with being saved. (I: 5–9)

*Steig, William. *Doctor De Soto*. Farrar, 1982. When a mouse dentist and his wife agree to treat a fox's toothache, only their cleverness saves them from becoming the fox's dinner. (I: P–9)

*Stevens, Janet. *How the Manx Cat Lost Its Tail*. Harcourt, 1992. The Manx cat almost misses the last call to board Noah's ark. (I: P–8)

*———. *Tops and Bottoms*. Harcourt, 1995. Hare tricks lazy Bear by wheeling and dealing in the tops and bottoms of vegetables. (I: P–8)

*Van Allsburg, Chris. *Two Bad Ants*. Houghton Mifflin, 1988. A visit to a kitchen spells near disaster for two bad ants. (I: P–9)

*———. *The Widow's Broom*. Houghton Mifflin, 1992. A broom with special powers brings out the prejudices of the widow's neighbors. (I: 8–12)

*Viorst, Judith. *Alexander and the Terrible, Horrible, No Good, Very Bad Day*. Illustrated by Ray Cruz. Atheneum, 1972. Alexander tells about all the things that have gone wrong in a single day. (I: P–8)

*Wahl, Jan. *Tailypo!* Illustrated by Wil Clay. Holt, 1996. A man cuts off the tail of a night visitor, and it comes back to haunt him. (I: P–8)

*Walsh, Melanie. *Do Donkeys Dances?* Houghton Mifflin, 2000. "Do pigs buzz around flowers? No, bees buzz around flowers." This predictable book is structured around a series of similar questions and answers. Walsh's *Do Pigs Have Stripes?* (1996) is structured in the same way. (I: P–6)

*Westray, Kathleen. *Picture Puzzler*. Ticknor & Fields, 1994. A collection of optical illusions accompanied by explanations. (I: 8 and up)

White, E. B. *Charlotte's Web*. Illustrated by Garth Williams. Harper, 1952. Charlotte the spider proves herself the truest of friends by saving the life of Wilbur the pig. (I: 5–10)

*Wild, Margaret. *Our Granny*. Illustrated by Julie Vivas. Ticknor & Fields, 1994. A celebration of all kinds of grannies. (I: P–8)

*Willard, Nancy. *The High Rise Glorious Skittle Skat Roarious Sky Pie Angel Food Cake*. Illustrated by Richard Jesse Watson. Harcourt, 1990. A girl gets angelic help in making her mother a heavenly birthday cake. (I: 8–12)

*Williams, Shirley Anne. *Working Cotton*. Illustrated by C. Byard. Harcourt, 1992. Readers experience a day in the cotton fields with a migrant family. (I: 6–10)

*Wong, Janet S. *Buzz*. Illustrated by Margaret Chodos-Irvine. Harcourt, 2000. A little boy's morning is filled with buzzes. The book can be done as a read-aloud, with young listeners joining in to produce buzzes at all the right places. (I: P–8)

*Wood, A. J. *Egg!* Little, Brown, 1993. Information about the eggs of different animals is presented in riddles. (I: 5–10)

*Wood, Audrey. *King Bidgood's in the Bathtub*. Illustrated by Don Wood. Harcourt, 1985. Throughout the day and into the night, King Bidgood entertains himself in his tub, much to the distress of the court. (I: P–8)

*———. *The Napping House*. Illustrated by Don Wood. Harcourt, 1984. Animals and humans snooze away a rainy day—until a flea wakes up. (I: P–8)

*———. *Weird Parents*. Dial, 1990. A boy describes his weird parents. (I: 8–12)

Yarbrough, Camille. *The Shimmershine Queens*. Penguin Putnam, 1996. Angie loves to dream about her future, but her dreams begin to fade in the face of peer pressure. (I: 10–YA)

*Yolen, Jane. *Owl Moon*. Illustrated by John Schoenherr. Philomel, 1987. A parent and child share a special time when they go out in search of an owl on a winter's night. (I: P–8)

*Young, Ed. *Lon Po Po*. Philomel, 1989. Sisters outwit the evil wolf in this Chinese variant of "Little Red Riding Hood." (I: 5–9)

Storytelling

Afanasyev, Aleksandr. *Russian Fairy Tales*. Pantheon, 1976. A collection of fine tales, most without illustrations. (I: 7–14)

Briggs, Katherine. *British Folktales*. Dorset, 1989. Some familiar tales are presented in the form in which they were traditionally told. The book also includes new tales. (I: YA)

Courlander, Harold. *The Tiger's Whisker, and Other Tales from Asia and the Pacific*. Holt, 1995. Short, pristine tales, written to be read aloud. (I: 8–11)

Erdoes, Richard, and Alfonso Ortiz. *American Indian Myths and Legends*. Pantheon, 1985. A collection of Native American tales and lore, written for adults but good for read-alouds. (I: 10–YA)

Forest, Heather. *Wonder Tales from Around the World*. August House, 1995. An international collection of fairy tales of enchantment. (I: 8–11)

Hamilton, Virginia. *In the Beginning: Creation Stories from around the World*. Harcourt, 1988. With beautiful illustrations, this collection places the Biblical story of Adam and Eve and the Greek myth of Pandora alongside creation myths from peoples around the world. (I: 8–YA)

————. *Her Stories: African American Folktales, Fairy Tales, and True Tales*. Illustrated by Leo and Diane Dillon. Scholastic, 1995. These stories celebrate African American women. (I: 9–YA)

————. *The People Could Fly: American Black Folktales*. Illustrated by Leo and Diane Dillon. Knopf, 1985. This collection has favorites such as "Brer Rabbit and the Tar Baby" and "Wiley and the Hairy Man." (I: 9–YA)

Haskins, James. *The Headless Haunt, and Other African American Ghost Stories*. HarperCollins, 1994. With lively black-and-white illustrations, this collection was compiled for middle elementary grades and up. (I: 8–13)

Hearne, Betsy. *Beauties and Beasts*. Oryx, 1993. A fascinating collection of stories from around the world, based on the beauty and the beast motif. (I: 9–YA)

MacDonald, Margaret Read. *Twenty Tellable Tales: Audience Participation Folktales for the Beginning Story-Teller*. H. W. Wilson, 1986. These tales have been honed by repeated telling to library groups. (I: 9–YA)

Mayo, Margaret. *Magical Tales from Many Lands*. Dutton, 1993. The tales were collected for adult tellers but are quite suitable for children. (I: 9–YA)

Mourning Dove. *Coyote Stories*. Univ. of Nebraska Press, 1990. Stories of the trickster Coyote, collected in the 1930s by an Okanogan teller. (I: 9–YA)

National Association for the Preservation and Perpetuation of Storytelling. *More Best-Loved Stories Told at the National Storytelling Festival*. National Storytelling Network, 1992. A collection of Native American and African American tales in the voices of their tellers. (I: 9–YA)

National Storytelling Association. *True Tales from America's Past*. National Storytelling Press, 1995. These tales of pioneers, civil rights activists, scientists, and women factory workers bring the social studies curriculum to life. (I: 9–YA)

Perdue, Charles, ed. *Outwitting the Devil: Jack Tales from Wise County, Virginia*. Ancient City Press, 1987. Jack is a trickster in these tales from the Appalachian Mountains, and the devil is his favorite adversary. (I: 9–YA)

Phelps, Ethel Johnston. *Tatterhood and Other Tales*. Feminist Press, 1978. Tales from around the world with strong female protagonists. (I: 9–YA)

Reneaux, J. J. *Cajun Folktales*. August House, 1992. Animal tales, fairy tales, funny folktales, and ghost stories from the Cajun people of the Louisiana bayou country. (I: 9–YA)

Schwartz, Alvin. *Scary Stories to Tell in the Dark*. HarperCollins, 1986. Stories for middle elementary grade students and up, collected by a serious folklore collector. (I: 8–13)

Shannon, George. *A Knock at the Door: An International Collection*. Oryx, 1992. An international collection of intruder tales, such as "The Three Little Pigs" and "Lon Po Po." (I: 9–YA)

Sierra, Judith. *Cinderella: An International Collection*. Oryx, 1992. Two dozen of the 650 variants of the Cinderella tale. (I: 9–YA)

Stoutenburg, Adrien. *American Tall Tales*. Puffin, 1976. This paperback reprint of an older collection includes "Stormalong," "Pecos Bill," "Johnny Appleseed," and others. (I: 8–13)

Van Etten, Teresa Pijoan de. *Spanish American Folktales*. August House, 1990. Twenty-eight tales collected by the author, mostly in New Mexico. (I: 9–YA)

Dramatic Activities

*Brown, Marc. *Arthur's Pet Business*. Little, Brown, 1990. Arthur is in for surprises when he sets up a pet business. This and the many other books about Arthur are easily adapted for readers theater. (I: 6–9)

*Cuyler, Margery. *That's Good! That's Bad!* Illustrated by David Catrow. Holt, 1995. A little boy has some hair-raising adventures on his trip to the zoo. Can be used, as written, as a two-part readers theater script. (I: 5–9)

*Duvoisin, Roger. *Petunia*. Knopf, 1966. The barnyard will never again be the same once the silly goose Petunia finds a book and acquires "wisdom." Excellent for creative dramatics. (I: P–8)

*Fox, Mem. *Hattie and the Fox*. Illustrated by Patricia Mullins. Bradbury, 1987. Hattie spots danger on the farm. Can be easily adapted for readers theater or creative dramatics. (I: P–8)

*Gray, Libba Moore. *Small Green Snake*. Illustrated by Holly Meade. Orchard, 1994. A small green snake has too adventurous a spirit to heed his mother's warnings. (I: P–7)

*Hoose, Phillip and Hannah. *Hey, Little Ant.* Illustrated by Debbie Tilley. Tricycle Press, 1998. This conversation between a boy and an ant explores whether the boy should squish the ant. Can be used, as written, as a two-part readers theater script. (I: 5–9)

*Jorgensen, Gail. *Crocodile Beat.* Illustrated by Patricia Mullins. Macmillan, 1988. The animals' celebration is interrupted when crocodile arrives for dinner. Good for story theater. (I: P–7)

*Kroll, Virginia. *The Seasons and Someone.* Illustrated by Tatsuro Kiuchi. Harcourt, 1994. Through a series of questions and answers, the reader discovers how the seasons change for an Inuit child. Can be used, as written, as a two-part readers theater script. (I: 6–10)

*Lionni, Leo. *Frederick.* Pantheon, 1967. A mouse family discovers how a poet can contribute to their community. Offers interesting opportunities for improvisational drama. (I: 6–10)

*Martin, Bill, Jr. *Brown Bear, Brown Bear, What Do You See?* Illustrated by Eric Carle. Holt, 1967/1998. A series of rhythmical questions and answers reveals what all sorts of animals see. Can be used, as written, for readers theater. (I: P–8)

*———. *White Dynamite and Curly Kidd.* Illustrated by Ted Rand. Holt, 1989/1995. A dialogue between child and father about an upcoming rodeo event. Can be used, as written, for readers theater. (I: 6–10)

*Mazer, Anne. *The Salamander Room.* Illustrated by Steve Johnson. Knopf, 1991. A mother and child discuss the feasibility of bringing a salamander indoors to live. Can be used, as is, as a two-part readers theater script. (I: 5–8)

*Noble, Trinka Hakes. *The Day Jimmy's Boa Ate the Wash.* Illustrated by Steven Kellogg. Dial, 1980. A child recounts her class's out-of-control field trip to a farm. Can be used, as written, as a two-part readers theater script. (I: 5–8)

*Novak, Matt. *Mouse TV.* Orchard, 1994. When their TV set breaks down, a mouse family discovers new ways to pass the evening. Offers opportunities for creative dramatics and improvisational drama. (I: P–8)

*Raschka, Chris. *Yo! Yes?* Orchard, 1993. A simple dialogue between two boys is the beginning of a friendship. Can be used, as written, as a two-part readers theater script. (I: P–8)

*Rosen, Michael. *We're Going on a Bear Hunt.* Illustrated by Helen Oxenbury. Little Simon, 1989/1997. A surprise awaits a family who go on a bear hunt. Perfect for use in story theater. (I: P–8)

*Schotter, Richard, and Roni Schotter. *There's a Dragon About: A Winter's Revel.* Illustrated by R. W. Alley. Orchard, 1994. A group of children set out to perform a play about a fierce dragon, brave damsels and lads, and a gallant knight. Written in script form. (I: 6–10)

*Scieszka, Jon. *The True Story of the 3 Little Pigs!* Illustrated by Lane Smith. Viking, 1989. The wolf tells his side of the story in this spin-off of "The Three Little Pigs." Students will enjoy conducting an improvised trial of the wolf. (I: all ages)

*Slobodkina, Esphyr. *Caps for Sale.* HarperCollins, 1940/1999. A peddler loses his caps to a group of monkeys. Good for story theater or creative dramatics. (I: P–7)

Taylor, Mildred. *Roll of Thunder, Hear My Cry.* Dial, 1976. In the face of racism, an African American family struggles to save the family farm. (I: 10–YA)

*Temple, Frances. *Tiger Soup.* Orchard, 1994. This Jamaican Anansi tale explains why monkeys live high up in trees. A scripted version of the tale appears on the inside of the dust jacket. (I: P–8)

*Voake, Charlotte. *Ginger.* Candlewick, 1997. Ginger the cat is not happy when the little girl brings a new kitten into their home. (I: P–8)

Voigt, Cynthia. *Homecoming.* Atheneum, 1981. When their mother disappears, Dicey and her siblings seek a place to call their home. (I: 10–YA)

*Zarin, Cynthia. *Wallace Hoskins: The Boy Who Grew Down.* Illustrated by Martin Matje. DK Ink, 1999. This is the story of how and why Wallace Hoskins began to grow down (not up) and how the problem was finally solved. (I: 5–8)

*Ziefert, Harriet. *Train Song.* Illustrated by Donald Saaf. Orchard, 2000. A little boy listens and looks as the freight train passes by in this rhythmic and rhyming text. (I: P–6)

RESOURCES

Hamilton, Martha, and Mitch Weiss. *Children Tell Stories: A Teaching Guide.* Katonah, Richard C. Owen, 1990.

Jensen, Julie M., and Nancy L. Roser, eds. *Adventuring with Books: A Booklist for Pre-K–Grade 6,* 10th ed. National Council of Teachers of English, 1993.

Lipson, Eden Ross. *The New York Times Parent's Guide to the Best Books for Children*. Random House, 1991.

Martinez, Miriam, and William H. Teale. "Reading in a Kindergarten Library Center." *The Reading Teacher 41* (l988): 568–72.

Morgan, Norah, and Juliana Saxton. *Teaching Drama: A Mind of Many Wonders*. Heinemann, 1987.

Sawyer, Ruth. *The Way of the Storyteller*. Viking, 1942.

Trelease, Jim. *The Read-Aloud Handbook*, 4th ed. Penguin, 1995.

REFERENCES

Anderson, Richard C., Elfrieda H. Hiebert, Judith A. Scott, and Ian A. G. Wilkinson. *Becoming a Nation of Readers: The Report of the Commission on Reading*. National Institute of Education, 1984.

Banks, Lynne Reid. *The Indian in the Cupboard*. Illustrated by Brock Cole. Doubleday, 1981.

Bissett, D. "The Amount and Effect of Recreational Reading in Selected Fifth Grade Classes." Dissertation, Syracuse University, 1969.

Blood, Peter, and Annie Paterson. *Rise Up Singing*. Sing Out! Publications, 1992.

Booth, David. "Imaginary Gardens with Real Toads: Reading and Drama in Education." *Theory into Practice 24* (1985): 193–98.

Cole, J. Y., and C. S. Gold, eds. *Reading in America 1978: Selected Findings of the Book Industry Study Group's 1978 Study of American Book-Reading and Book-Buying Habits and Discussion of Those Findings at the Library of Congress on October 25 and 26, 1978*. Library of Congress, 1979.

de Brunvard, Jan. *The Vanishing Hitchhiker and Other Urban Legends*. Norton, 1981.

Edmiston, Brian. "Going Up the Beanstalk: Discovering Giant Possibilities for Responding to Literature through Drama." *Journeying: Children Responding to Literature*. Ed. Kathleen E. Holland, Rachael A. Hungerford, and Shirley B. Ernst. Heinemann, 1993, pp. 250–66.

Fielding, Linda G., Paul T. Wilson, and Richard C. Anderson. "A New Focus on Free Reading: The Role of Trade Books in Reading Instruction." *Contexts of Literacy*. Ed. Taffy Raphael and Ralph Reynolds. Longman, 1986.

Fractor, Jann Sorrell, Marjorie Ciruti Woodruff, Miriam G. Martinez, and William H. Teale. "Let's Not Miss Opportunities to Promote Voluntary Reading: Classroom Libraries in the Elementary School." *The Reading Teacher 46* (1993): 476–84.

Hickman, Janet. "A New Perspective on Response to Literature: Research in an Elementary School Setting." *Research in the Teaching of English 15* (1981): 343–54.

Hoffman, James V., Nancy L. Roser, and Jennifer Battle. "Reading Aloud in Classrooms: From the Modal toward a 'Model.'" *The Reading Teacher 46* (1993): 496–503.

Kennelly, Brenda. *The Penguin Book of Irish Verse*, 2nd ed. Penguin, 1981.

Krull, Kathleen. *Gonna Sing My Head Off!* Illustrated by Allen Garns. Knopf, 1992.

MacDonald, Margaret Read. *The Story-Teller's Start-Up Book*. August House, 1993.

Milne, A. A. "Happiness." *When We Were Very Young*. Dutton, 1924.

Morrow, Lesley Mandel. "Relationships between Literature Program, Library Corner Designs, and Children's Use of Literature." *Journal of Educational Research 75* (1982): 339–44.

Munro, Harold. "Overheard in a Saltmarsh." *Collected Poems*. Duckworth, 1953.

Paley, Vivian. *Wally's Stories: Conversations in the Kindergarten*. Harvard Univ. Press, 1981.

Siks, Geraldine Brain. *Creative Dramatics: An Art for Children*. Harper & Row, 1958.

Wolf, Alan. *It's Show Time! Poetry from Page to Stage*. Poetry Alive!, 1993.

13 Encouraging Response to Literature: Literary Discussion

Our two families, the Logans and the Simmses, had never much gotten along. What with the Simmses living less than a mile or so from us on that forty-acre spot of land they tenant-farmed, and we sitting on our own two hundred acres, there was always likely to be trouble, and there was. Now this was back before my papa went and bought that second two hundred acres; but still that two hundred acres we had then, that was a lot, and the Simmses didn't like it—that we had when they didn't. They didn't like it one bit. That was part of the trouble between us. Other part of the trouble was that we were colored and they were white. Fact of the matter was we ain't never had much use for the Simmses, and they ain't never had much use for us either; but seeing that we couldn't hardly afford trouble with them, Papa said best thing to do was try and stay out of their way much as we could. He said it was better to mind our business, let them mind theirs, and just walk away if they tried to start something.

I heeded his words. My brother Hammer didn't.

*from **The Well***
by Mildred D. Taylor

WHAT IS A LITERATURE CIRCLE?

The Well is written in a forthright matter and deals with substantive issues that are not easy for readers of any age to forget once they've read about them. Fortunately, more and more classroom teachers are recognizing the importance of creating opportunities for children to come together to grapple with the issues they encounter in books such as **The Well.** Literature circles or book clubs are one vehicle for organizing literature discussion in classrooms. In fact, educational circles are abuzz with talk about literature circles and creating "interpretive communities" in elementary classrooms. Such talk might be startling to some. It might seem more likely that adults would belong to book clubs and literature majors and scholars would belong to "interpretive communities"; but such is not the case. Many children have been part of interpretive communities, for an interpretive community is simply a group of people (perhaps only two) who get together to talk about a book.

Strategies for engaging students in literature circles are highlighted in this chapter. Some of the examples focus on Phyllis Reynolds Naylor's **Shiloh** and Jerry Spinelli's **Maniac Magee,** books you might want to read if you have not yet done so.

An Interpretive Community

Reading can be an intensely satisfying solitary experience, but it can be even more meaningful when shared with others. Think of times when you've done just that. Perhaps you finished a wonderful book and discovered that a friend had also read it. No doubt you were off and talking. Or perhaps you were in the midst of a story and simply had to stop reading to tell a friend about a hilarious scene. You might even have explored books with peers in more formal settings, such as a book club at your local library. Whatever the context—informal or formal—the odds are that you have been a part of an interpretive community.

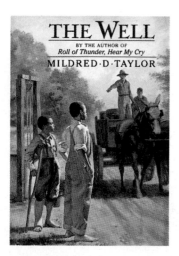

Illustration 13.1
In *The Well,* racial conflict erupts in the midst of a drought in Mississippi in the late nineteenth century.
(*The Well* by Mildred D. Taylor. Copyright © 1995. Used by permission of Dial Books for Young Readers, a division of Penguin Putnam Inc.)

Compare notes with your peers about some of the book discussions you've enjoyed. There are likely to be some common features. These discussions were probably conversational in nature: People have compared book discussions to the kind of stimulating conversations they engage in at a memorable dinner party. You might remember many of these conversations as being lively: Perhaps those involved in the conversations had diverse perspectives on the book that led to some informal debate. These conversations probably moved in different directions: Sometimes, you may have been caught up in the story world—talking about what characters did, why they did those things, and the likely outcomes of their actions. At other times, you may have moved out of the realm of the story world to discuss the ways in which the story related to your own life or to explore the author's craft. Perhaps there have been times when you came away from a book discussion with deeper insights that you gained from others. In short, the members of an interpretive community share impressions, wonder together, challenge ideas, and explore together.

Children in elementary classrooms often form interpretive communities. Sometimes, the entire class talks about a book; at other times, smaller groups of students come together for literature discussion. These interpretive communities are known by various names: literature circles (Harste, Short, and Burke, 1988), book clubs (Raphael, Goatley, McMahon, and Woodman, 1995), literature study groups (Eeds and Wells, 1989), or conversational discussion groups (Wiencek and O'Flahavan, 1994). We have chosen to use the term "literature circle" to describe the interpretive communities at work in classrooms.

An Opportunity for "Grand Conversations"

To get a feel for the type of talk that can occur in literature circles, we'll look in on literature conversations in some classrooms. The following conversation took place in Ms. Gonzalez's second-grade classroom. Not long before this conversation, Ms. Gonzalez had finished reading Elizabeth Winthrop's *Castle in the Attic* aloud. This book is a fantasy in which a young boy named William travels back in time to medieval England, where he confronts a wicked wizard, Alastor, who has taken over the good Sir Simon's kingdom and turned much of the populace to stone. Currently, Ms. Gonzalez is reading *Shiloh,* the Newbery Medal–winning story of Marty, who secretly harbors the dog Shiloh to protect it from abuse by its owner. Ms. Gonzalez has just finished reading the first two chapters, and the class has stopped to talk.

MS. GONZALEZ:	Reread what you wrote in your journals about Chapters 1 and 2. What were your thoughts and wonderings? Matthew?
MATTHEW:	William reminds me of Marty.
ANNA:	Marty is sorta like William because he's so nice to the dog and stuff.
MS. GONZALEZ:	Paul, did you want to bring out somebody else you're reminded of?
PAUL:	William and Marty both found something wonderful. Marty found a dog, and in *Castle in the Attic,* William found the half of the token.
BEN:	He didn't find it.

PAUL:	I mean when the soldier [knight] dropped it. He was looking at William, and he found it.
MS. GONZALEZ:	Albert?
ALBERT:	Judd is like Alastor.
MS GONZALEZ:	How is he like him?
ALBERT:	Because Judd was mean to everybody just like him. And Alastor didn't like anybody either. He froze them. And Judd hurts them.
ADAM:	Judd's like Alastor. The dogs are [like] the people, and get turned to stone. The dogs are sort of like that.
MS. GONZALEZ:	Why do you see them like that?
ADAM:	Cause he [Judd] . . . instead of turning them into stone, he is mean to them.
PAUL:	I disagree. I think Marty is like Tolliver.
MS. GONZALEZ:	You're saying he's more like Tolliver, the young boy in *Castle in the Attic*.
LINDSAY:	I think William and Marty are more alike because they each had to make a choice in the story.
ALEX:	Yeah, because Shiloh has to leave and Mrs. Williams . . .
MS. GONZALEZ:	Excuse me, Alex, I think you mean Mrs. Phillips. Not Mrs. Williams.
ALEX:	Right, Mrs. Phillips. He don't want Mrs. Phillips to go, and Marty don't want Shiloh to go. So, it's kind of like the other.
AMANDA:	When William didn't want Mrs. Phillips to go and Marty didn't want Shiloh to go, because there's two different reasons.

Participants in the next discussion were sixth-graders and their teacher, Ms. Robinson. This literature circle was reading and discussing Jeanette Ingold's **Pictures, 1918,** which begins when a mysteriously set fire destroys the chicken coop of Asia's family. The discussion took place at the point in the book where Asia realizes that her grandmother may have inadvertently set the fire but Boy Blackwell witnessed the event and might have been able to stop it:

SHERRY:	He's crazy.
MS. ROBINSON:	Boy is.
LESLIE:	He is, he's a psycho.
JANA:	That's why he burned down all those places.
MS. ROBINSON:	What did you think of Asia's . . . how she . . . how she said . . .

SHERRY:	She's brave.
JANA:	She's brave.
SHERRY:	I would have never done it.
BECKY:	I would have jumped on his back and hit him.
MS. ROBINSON:	Well, yeah, but I think it's kind of presumptuous for her to blame him for the fire . . .
SHERRY:	It could have been Nick!
MS. ROBINSON:	. . . just because he didn't put it out, I mean she's saying, "You could have prevented it," but how does she know that, and, second, his father just died . . . and they're being so cruel, I think, about his father . . .
LESLIE:	The part about they may have been . . . have stopped it . . . if it was Grandmama, then he could have stopped it. I mean, she's so little and weak . . . and the book . . . how it describes Boy, he could have stopped her . . .
SHERRY:	I know, but I think if Boy had tried to stop her, that Grandma would get all mad at him, or start yelling at him, and then, I . . . don't know what he would have done.
MS. ROBINSON:	Um-hmm. That's a good point.
BECKY:	But then that defeats the whole purpose of . . .
SHERRY:	But then he could have hit her or something . . .
JANA:	Well, that kind of defeats the whole purpose of what Asia saw. Because if Asia saw a shadow . . . and then she saw the picture . . . then . . . . it should have been . . . Boy, right?
MS. ROBINSON:	The shadow?
JANA:	Uh-huh.
MS. ROBINSON:	The picture . . . are you talking about the picture that she took later? That reminded her of the shape of the shadow? Or are you talking about the picture in her mind?
JANA:	Well, the picture in her mind is Boy . . . so . . . and he was the one setting the fire in the shadow, so it had to be Boy, right?
MS. ROBINSON:	He was spying on her. Grandmama set the fire, and Boy did nothing to stop it, so now she's blaming him for his inaction as opposed to his action, which . . .
LESLIE:	Really, I can understand that.

MS. ROBINSON: Well, I think you make a really good point about his size and her size and her frailty and his strength. I didn't think about that before, that he would really have had the strength to stop her. But Sherry's point is good, too—that Grandmother was irrational at that moment, and you can't predict what an irrational person will do.

LESLIE: Yeah, but if . . . yeah, you can't predict it, but if he . . . could understand that you can't predict that, and he . . . well, see first of all, it's not really a relevant point, 'cause he had no idea that she was that irrational at the moment.

MS. ROBINSON: That's a *very* good point.

The children in both of these groups were engaged in the work of interpretive communities. Their lively exchanges were conversational; it was the children, not the teachers, who initiated the topics of discussion. The children did some impressive thinking as they arrived at and defended their own insights and worked together to build meaning. These discussions had all the marks of what Maryann Eeds and Deborah Wells (1989) have called "grand conversations."

Eeds and Wells have contrasted grand conversations with what has been described as "gentle inquisitions," those question-and-answer sessions in which the teacher quizzes students with comprehension questions. Researchers such as Courtney Cazden (1988) and Hugh Mehan (1979) have described the pattern of interaction in these "gentle inquisitions." They found that the teacher initiates a topic by asking a question, the student responds to the question, and the teacher evaluates the student's response—a pattern of interaction called I-R-E (Initiate-Respond-Evaluate). As Taffy E. Raphael, Virginia J. Goatley, Susan I. McMahon, and Deborah A. Woodman (1995) have observed, an overreliance on the I-R-E pattern means "students have little opportunity to raise topics of interest, pursue lines of thinking, or collaborate in critical problem solving" (p. 67).

ORGANIZING LITERATURE CIRCLES

How can teachers ensure that their students have the opportunity to participate in interpretive communities? We believe that five key factors affect the workings of literature circles: the books that are chosen, group size, length and frequency of sessions, who leads discussions, and whether responses are free or guided. There is no single "right" decision with regard to each factor that will ensure that children engage in lively and thoughtful book conversations. However, it is important to understand how each factor affects the workings of a literature circle and to consider thoughtfully the possible decisions you can make.

Selecting Books for Use in Literature Circles

Selecting the books is one of the most important decisions you'll make. Not every book has the same potential to engage children in rich discussion. In their investigation of literature discussion groups, Eeds and Wells (1989) involved groups of fifth- and sixth-graders in reading and discussing one of four books: *Harriet the Spy* by Louise Fitzhugh, *After the Goat Man* by Betsy Byars, *The Darkangel* by Meredith Pierce, and *Tuck Everlasting* by Natalie Babbitt, each of

Ask the Educator... *Pat Scharer*

Patricia L. Scharer

In what ways does book selection affect literary discussion?

One important way in which selection affects discussion depends on who selected the book. Was it assigned or chosen by the reader? Readers approach self-selected texts with an amazing sense of anticipation. I wonder if I'll like this book as much as Robert did? Will I think it is scary like Joanne? Will it be like other books I know by that author? This is a time when the teacher's role can shift from making assignments to sharing book talks about personal favorites and celebrating the opinions of every reader in the room to encourage others to read certain books.

The unique characteristics of each book also affect literary discussion. The sparse, tense prose of *Out of the Dust* by Karen Hesse inspires conversation not only about the relationships within the story, but also about the contribution of the format of the text on every page. Why is the story told with poetic form, a departure from narrative paragraphs, and how does this writing style affect readers' responses to the text? Some readers find the ending of Lois Lowry's *The Giver* unsettling and can't wait to discuss every possibility for what might happen next. Others devour each new *Redwall* or *Harry Potter* fantasy and rush to talk with

Favorite Books as a Child

As a child, I read constantly—under the picnic tables at the park, in a favorite tree, or under the covers quite certain that my parents didn't know I was up past my bedtime. My habit was fed by weekly trips to the public library and my personal collection of nearly every *Bobbsey Twins*, *Nancy Drew*, and *Hardy Boys* book published at that time. But *Charlotte's Web* was the book I loved best and returned to again and again as a child and later as an adult. I'll never forget the new insights I gained several years ago after reading an article describing Charlotte's efforts as a writer—the power of selecting just the right word but also the emotions and pain attached to the writing process. These experiences have inspired my deep appreciation for the talents and perseverance of those who write for children.

a friend about the latest adventure or their favorite part. Picture books invite discussion not only about the text but about the illustrations as well. The elegant gold accents by Leo and Diane Dillon illustrating Virginia Hamilton's *The Girl Who Spun Gold* are important discussion points as readers make connections between the cover art, endpapers, gold-framed art in each two-page spread, and Hamilton's tale of gold-spinning Lit'mahnn and the young girl who must guess his name.

Some books, however, inspire a temporary silence. I read books like Avi's *The Barn* and Janet Hickman's *Jericho: A Novel* in one sitting, lost in the world of the book and unwilling to come out until the final page is turned. Immediately, however, I return to the text to read it one more time—not to find out what happened (I already know that!) but to experience the pleasure of the writing and gain new insights about the author's craft to share with others.

Patricia Scharer is an associate professor at The Ohio State University, where she teaches courses in children's literature and early literacy. Her research on both topics has appeared in many journals such as Reading Research Quarterly, The Reading Teacher, Language Arts, Reading Research and Instruction, *and* Research in the Teaching of English. *She has served as coeditor of the* Journal of Children's Literature *and the* Children's Books *column for* The Reading Teacher. *Patricia is currently coeditor of* Bookbird: A Journal of International Children's Literature.

which is recognized as a high-quality piece of literature. Although the group leaders in all four groups proved to be equally skillful in facilitating discussions, Eeds and Wells found that the students in the group reading *Tuck Everlasting* shared the most insightful responses. They concluded that differences in the books accounted for differences in the quality of talk. Of the four books, only *Tuck Everlasting* had the power to launch the children into discussions of issues touching the very essence of the human experience.

Thematic Discussions. Books that focus on important issues—such as *Tuck Everlasting*—tend to evoke talk at a thematic level. Books likely to engender thematic-level talk include Mildred Taylor's powerful books about the Logan family, which explore racism as well as the sustaining power of family love and unity, and Lois Lowry's *The Giver,* an exploration of a society designed to control the pain and sorrow of life as well its joys.

Discussions about Story Line. Other types of books are likely to move children's talk in other directions (Martinez and Roser, 1995). When children read books with strong story lines, they tend to "step into the story" (Langer, 1992), and their talk reflects their engagement with its characters, conflicts, and events. In particular, books engender lively talk when they center on problems with which the students can easily identify and whose solutions are not readily apparent. Examples of such books are Phyllis Naylor's *Shiloh,* Cynthia Voigt's *Homecoming,* E. L. Konigsburg's *From the Mixed-up Files of Mrs. Basil E. Frankweiler,* and Nancy Farmer's *The Ear, the Eye and the Arm.*

Discussions about Craft. Children are most likely to talk about a book as the creation of a particular author or artist when they read distinctively crafted books such as Chris Van Allsburg's *Jumanji;* David Macaulay's *Black and White,* in which four plot lines are intertwined; Diane Stanley's *Raising Sweetness,* with its rich Texas dialect; or Clifton Taulbert's *Little Cliff and the Porch People,* with its rich use of details. Likewise, children are likely to talk about craft when they read books with distinctive patterns of organization, such as Audrey Wood's predictable book *The Napping House;* Paul Fleischman's *Joyful Noise,* which is a collection of poems for two voices; or Patricia and Fredrick McKissack's *Christmas in the Big House, Christmas in the Quarters,* with its strong comparison/contrast structure. Exquisitely illustrated books, such as Nancy Willard's *Pish, Posh, Said Hieronymus Bosch,* and books with tantalizing language, such as Libba Moore Gray's *Small Green Snake,* also encourage children to examine books as crafted objects.

So to encourage diverse talk during literature circles, it makes sense to use a variety of types of literature: literature with strong story lines, literature that develops significant themes, and distinctly crafted literature.

Discussions across the Curriculum. You will want to consider other factors as well in selecting literature to use in literature circles. Perhaps the class is studying a topic in science or social studies that lends itself to further exploration in a literature circle. A teacher whose students are studying the weather might select Patricia MacLachlan's *Skylark* for use in literature circle. This sequel to the Newbery Medal winner *Sarah, Plain and Tall* is set in the prairie in the nineteenth century and explores the impact on those living there of a devastating

Illustration 13.2
Readers of Chris Van Allsburg's books expect to encounter the fantastic and bizarre. *Jumanji* (winner of the 1982 Caldecott Medal) is no exception. (*Jumanji* by Chris Van Allsburg. Copyright © 1981 by Chris Van Allsburg. Reprinted by permission of Houghton Mifflin Company. All rights reserved.)

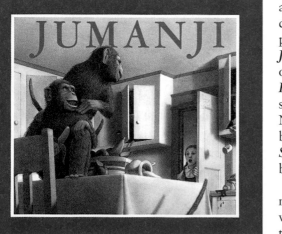

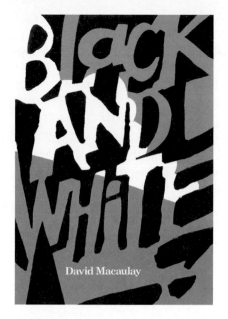

Illustration 13.3
Readers will wonder if they are reading a single story or four different stories in this exquisitely designed Caldecott Medal winner. (Cover from *Black and White* by David Macaulay. Copyright © 1990 by David Macaulay. Reprinted by permission of Houghton Mifflin Company. All rights reserved.)

Illustration 13.4
Set in an earlier era, this story explores the importance of community. (*Little Cliff and the Porch People* by Clifton L. Taulbert, paintings by E. B. Lewis. Copyright © 1999. Used by permission of Dial Books for Young Readers, a division of Penguin Putnam Inc.)

drought. Virginia Hamilton's *Drylongso* also shows the ravaging effects of drought, and the drama of Mildred Taylor's *The Well* unfolds in the context of a drought. Karen Hesse's *Out of the Dust* is set in the Dust Bowl during the Great Depression. Informational books about drought could also be used in the literature circle. Many of the books you choose to support cross-curricular studies are likely to be informational books, and discussions about informational books can be as lively as discussions of fiction.

Genre Considerations. Genre is yet another consideration in choosing books. Joyce Wiencek and John O'Flahavan (1994) note the importance of bringing in books from various genres so that students develop a repertoire of strategies appropriate to different genres. Although variety is important, particular genres do have the potential to offer students especially rich issues and ideas to explore. Many works of realistic and historical fiction, high fantasy, and poetry are especially likely to evoke students' best insights because of the significant themes they explore.

Student Participation in Book Selection. This discussion has implied that the teacher is the one who selects the books for use in literature circles. However, Louise Rosenblatt (1938) reminds us that the ultimate aim is to prepare students to select their own books wisely. Therefore, teachers must ensure that students have some voice in book selection. This can be accomplished by inviting students to suggest themes, authors, or particular titles they would like to read. Or, if a single title is to be used, the teacher can nominate a number of titles as possible candidates and let the students make the final selection. Yet another alternative is to have several small groups, each focusing on a different book, and give students the opportunity to decide which group to join after listening to introductions to the several books and browsing through them.

Forming the Discussion Groups

How many students should participate in a literature circle? How should students be selected for membership in a literature circle? Experienced teachers have found literature circles of widely varying sizes to be successful. Some teachers advocate having the whole class come together to talk about a book (Gonzalez, Fry, Lopez, Jordan, Sloan, and McAdams, 1995); others believe that small groups are ideal (Short and Kauffman, 1995). There is no "best" size. It may, in fact, be a good idea to vary the size of literature circles, depending on the children's previous experience. If you find at the beginning of the school year that most of your students have previously participated in literature discussions, they might be ready to launch immediately into small-group literature circles. However, if you work with very young children or if your students initially appear to be more at ease with traditional "gentle inquisitions," you might want to begin with whole-class literature discussion following read-aloud sessions. Then, once they feel comfortable with this format, students can begin working in small groups of five to seven students.

What factors should teachers take into account before bringing children together in these smaller literature circles? First, consider whether all students in the class will be reading the same book or whether small groups will be reading different books. If each group will be reading a different book, it makes sense to let students listen to book introductions and then choose the group that they want to join. Also, consider group dynamics. Aim for a group that is balanced in terms of the students' leadership, communication, and social skills (Raphael, McMahon, Goatley, Bentley, Boyd, Pardo, and Woodman, 1992).

Length and Frequency of Literature Circles

The length of literature circles will vary. Early in the school year, sessions may be relatively short—ten or fifteen minutes (in addition to the time you may need to read the story to the students). Once children gain experience working in literature circles, they are likely to talk a lot more about engaging books—perhaps thirty or forty minutes, though twenty minutes is a typical length for a session.

The frequency with which literature circles meet will probably depend on other decisions you make. Circles may be part of your read-aloud program, especially if your students do not yet have the reading skills needed to independently read books that have enough "meat" to engender good discussions. If this is the case, then you'll certainly be reading aloud to your students each day, and daily literature discussion will naturally go hand in hand with the read-aloud. Even if your students are able to read meaty books independently, there may still be times when you want to make literature discussion part of the daily read-aloud, especially at the beginning of the year before students are skilled in participating in book conversations. Even after your students have acquired experience as members of an interpretive community, you might sometimes want to make discussion an integral part of the read-aloud experience, especially when reading aloud a challenging chapter book. Some of the most interesting literature conversations occur when students are in the midst of a chapter book rather than at the end—and little wonder, for then students are caught up in a web of events and very naturally have questions and predictions about how that web of events is likely to be sorted out (Martinez and Roser, 1994).

When your students do their own reading in preparation for the literature circle, you'll need to schedule reading time for them. Some teachers give students opportunities to touch base with one another while they are reading the book, even though more focused discussion is scheduled to take place when everyone has finished the book. By meeting briefly every three days or so, students can help one another to clarify any questions they might have about the book they are reading.

Some teachers set up a pacing guide for students' reading (or let students set up their own) and then gather students together for literature circle only after all of them have finished the book. When a schedule guides the literature circle, it's best to have students jot down their thoughts about the book each day, either during or immediately after completing a daily reading assignment. They can bring these notes to the literature circle.

ISSUE TO CONSIDER

Should the teacher participate in children's literature circle conversations?

Many adult readers regularly participate with friends in informal conversations about literature, and those who belong to organized book clubs engage in more formal conversations as well. In recent years, educators have become increasingly aware that they must do more than teach children how to read; they must also take steps to ensure that children become lifelong readers. One way of achieving this goal is by initiating children into the ways of book clubbers. However, there is less agreement on the best way to teach children to actively come together and converse about books rather than answer a teacher's comprehension questions.

Some educators argue that children have become dependent on teachers to ask them questions about the books they read. Educators with this view maintain that the best way to break this dependency is by placing children in literature circles where there is no adult present. In this way, children will have no choice but to take responsibility for their literature conversations. It will be up to them to bring up topics for discussion, pose questions they have about the book, and exchange views on a variety of topics related to the target book.

Those on the opposing side agree that the ultimate goal is for children to learn to carry on literature conversations by themselves. However, they question whether children will learn new roles on their own. They argue that children will best learn these new roles by participating in literature circles with teachers who model new ways of talking about books and even talk with children about the ways in which literature conversations differ from the question-and-answer sessions with which children are probably more familiar.

What do you think?

Once students have finished reading a book, they'll be ready to get together for more focused talk. You might want to devote more than a single day to discussion. The first day could be devoted to sharing responses and even reading journal entries. At the end of the first session, you might ask students to generate a list of ideas for more intensive literature study on subsequent days. As a group, they can choose a topic (or two) from the list and prepare to talk about that topic at their next meeting. Preparation might include rereading relevant portions of the book to find support for their opinions. For example, after reading and sharing impressions about *Maniac Magee,* Mr. Lee's class decided to spend their second literature circle exploring all of the diverse images of home found throughout the book. Such focused explorations of a book are especially likely to lead to in-depth discussion of theme and craft.

THE ROLES OF THE TEACHER IN LITERARY DISCUSSIONS

What roles do teachers play during literature circles? Again, there is no simple answer to this question. The one thing educators agree on is that the teacher should not assume the role of sole leader, whose job is to ask the questions. Beyond that, recommendations vary widely. Opinion is evenly divided on the question of whether the teacher should be present during literature circles. Some educators argue that if teachers want students to learn to participate in literature conversations in much the same way more mature readers do, they must give students the opportunity to do so by bowing out of the picture (Raphael, McMahon, Goatley, Bentley, Boyd, Pardo, and Woodman, 1992). Others argue that students have the best opportunity to learn these skills by talking about books with experienced adult readers who model the appropriate conversational roles (McGee, 1992). Adherents of both positions make valid points, so reducing the question to an either/or proposition (the teacher either is or is not present) might be too simplistic. Perhaps the best question to ask is this: Under what circumstances should the teacher participate in literature circles? We will address this question after taking a closer look at the roles the teacher may choose to play during literature discussions.

As participants in literature circles, teachers may, at various times, want to assume any of four roles: (1) modeling response-based discussion, (2) helping children learn new discussion roles, (3) moving discussion forward, and (4) supporting literary learning as opportunities arise.

Modeling Response-Based Discussion

On arriving in your classroom, many of your students are likely to feel comfortable only when the teacher is in charge of book talk. The typical question-and-answer session that results when students have these expectations is similar to what occurred after Mrs. McDougal read Lillian Hoban's *Arthur's Prize Reader* to her second-graders:

MRS. McDOUGAL:	Okay, Michelle, can you give us our title?
MICHELLE:	*Arthur's Prize Reader.*
MRS. McDOUGAL:	Oh, great. Thank you. Okay, Josh, characters. Give me the major characters first.
JOSH:	Arthur.
MRS. McDOUGAL:	Arthur and who else?

JOSH:	Violet.
MRS. McDOUGAL:	Okay, we should consider them major characters. Were there any other characters in the book that we would consider minor, Josh?

This is *not* literature discussion, and students who have only participated in question-and-answer sessions like this one are reticent when first invited to share their personal thoughts about stories. Yet genuine talk about stories occurs as participants share and reflect on their own responses to them. The best way for students to learn how to do this is by seeing others share their thinking about stories. So it's important for teachers to model response-based meaning making—that is, share their own responses to stories. Students who see their teachers doing this are much more likely to realize that their responses will be valued. As students gain confidence, discussion during literature circles will arise entirely from their responses.

Teachers can also model diverse kinds of thinking about books. Ms. Gonzalez discovered that her students were not asking the questions they had about books. So she decided to model this type of thinking when she and her students were discussing Diane Stanley's **Captain Whiz-Bang,** a story in which a little girl named Annie names her new kitten Captain Whiz-Bang. At first, Annie and Captain Whiz-Bang are inseparable, but as Annie grows up, her interests turn to other things. Finally, she leaves home and marries, leaving Captain Whiz-Bang behind with her parents. But she doesn't forget Captain Whiz-Bang and one day returns with her own child so that the little girl can meet the aged cat.

MS. GONZALEZ:	I wonder what kinds of things Captain Whiz-Bang will do with Annie's little girl. He can't run and jump and play as fast as he did before. So I wonder what kinds of things they did when they played together. Since he wasn't so active.

Ms. Gonzalez found that it wasn't long before her students were sharing their own wonderings about the stories they read.

Helping Children Learn New Roles during Literature Circles

Literature circles are different from traditional book discussions. Unlike a traditional book discussion, in which students typically answer questions posed by the teacher, a literature circle has no one participant who is in charge. Rather, all participants can initiate topics for discussion, and discussion proceeds as a conversation. How do you engage students in such conversations about books if they come to your classroom expecting to answer questions? As Kathy G. Short and Gloria Kauffman (1995) point out, students have plenty of experience participating in conversations in other situations, and they can draw on these experiences during literature circles. Teachers can introduce students to book conversations by inviting them to think about all the times they've talked with their friends about movies or TV shows.

Since no one person is in charge during a literature circle, you might want to establish simple guidelines for group behavior. Lea M. McGee (1995, p. 13) suggests the following:

- Sit in a circle so that everyone can see each other.
- Only one person talks at a time.

■ Listen to each other.

■ Stay on the topic.

One of the most important (and difficult) expectations to establish is that the literature circle is a time for conversation and it is therefore okay for students to talk directly with one another. Many of the teachers with whom we work find it helpful to remind students of this explicitly. By seating students in a circle so that they can talk to each other directly and occasionally reminding them it makes sense to address their thoughts to peers, you will encourage them to engage in real conversations about literature.

Moving Conversation Forward

Teachers make an important contribution to literature circles when they move a flagging conversation forward. Earlier in the chapter, we pointed out that teachers do not direct literature discussion by asking question after question, but that does not mean a teacher should never ask a question. An occasional, well-placed question can get a conversation moving forward. Lea McGee (1995) suggests that, when preparing to meet with a literature circle, a teacher develop one or two interpretive questions that focus on "the significance of the story as a whole" (p. 111). McGee (1992) concluded:

> Although it seemed important for students to explore stories on their own terms, switching from topic to topic in an open-ended conversation prompted by their own responses and questions, it also seemed important to focus the conversation around a teacher-posed interpretive question which called for students to reflect on the work as a whole and to use inferential and critical thinking. (p. 186)

Wendy Saul (1989) calls such questions "literary questions" and observes that they are connected to the story but never have a single correct answer. A teacher might not need to ask these planned questions, depending on the direction in which the students move the conversation. However, if the students do not discuss an aspect of the story that the teacher feels is important, then the teacher may choose to pose a literary question before the literature circle concludes. The preparation of literary questions is discussed later in this chapter.

Louise Rosenblatt reminds us that not all responses are equally valid; rather, their value is determined by the extent to which readers make use of the text to defend and support their ideas (Farrell and Squire, 1990). This point suggests yet another way in which teachers can help to move conversations forward: by encouraging students to reflect on and return to the text to find support for their ideas, as Ms. Gonzalez did when her students discussed *Castle in the Attic:*

CHRIS: I think that [the reason] Calendar didn't want to get the spells that turned the lead people into humans again is because all the guards would probably tell Alastor, and she'd be [turned] into lead.

MS. GONZALEZ: What makes you think that?

CHRIS: Remember the guards wanted to get away. It was against their will to be a guard. They didn't know that anyone was coming and they were obeying Alastor. And if Alastor found out that they didn't tell him, then they would all be turned into lead.

Supporting Literary Learning

Supporting students' literary learning is perhaps the single most important contribution a teacher can make during literature discussions. Literary works are distinctive because of the ways in which writers structure and craft them, and like Ralph L. Peterson and Maryann Eeds (1990), we believe awareness of literary elements and the writer's craft can add a new dimension to students' experiences of stories. But it's important to proceed carefully in helping students learn about literary elements. Teaching about literature in a decontextualized manner—that is, without reference to a particular story—is the surest way to squelch students' love of literature. Lecturing about literature and asking students to memorize the definitions of literary terms have no place in the classroom. Yet we want children to understand how stories work, and the most appropriate way of doing this is by taking advantage of opportunities to foster awareness that arise naturally as students share their observations during literature circles. For example, the student who noticed "all the changes that keep happening in 'Cinderella'" had become aware of the transformation motif that is so prevalent in folklore. This student, who had a concept but not the literary language to name that concept, gave her teacher the perfect opening to introduce the term "transformation." The student's observation provided the teacher with an opportunity to "shoot a literary arrow" (Peterson and Eeds, 1990). Such an opportunity occurs when students, struggling to talk about the author's crafting, indicate that they have grasped a concept even though they do not have the literary language to talk about the element, device, or structure. Observing in elementary classrooms for extended periods of time, both Hickman (1979, 1981) and Kiefer (1983) found that children's talk about stories became more sophisticated when their teachers used the specialized language of art and literature with them during conversations about books.

We began this section with a question: What roles do teachers play during literature circle? The four roles that we have described point toward the answer to that question. At the beginning of the school year, many if not all of your students are likely to have no experience with literature circles and to expect you to pose questions for them to answer. If this happens, you should initially join in as a literature circle participant. Then, as discussions become more conversational, you can let students work independently. However, we do not recommend pulling entirely out of sessions, for opportunities to help students learn about literary crafting can occur at any time.

Preparing to Assume Roles

Preparation is necessary if you are going to successfully assume the roles of modeling response-based discussion, moving discussion forward, and supporting literary learning. How might you best go about such preparation? On a first reading of a story, it makes sense to maintain your own response journal in which you record your initial responses. You will then be able to draw on this record of your first spontaneous responses when modeling response-based discussion during literature circle discussions. To be in the best position to move discussions forward and support literary learning, you might want to return to the story for rereading and reflection. After reading a book that you plan to use with your class, perhaps you can join with other teachers using the same book to share insights and learn from one another. Eeds and Peterson (1990) recommend that teachers prepare to participate in literature discussions by reflecting on literary elements. They recommend that teachers reflect on questions such as the following:

- How has the author set up tension and relieved it?
- What is the central tension?
- How is it that some characters seem fully developed and others flat?
- How do the events in the story bring about the growth and development of characters?
- How does place influence the characters or the mood or the movement of the story?
- Where were you moved by the story, and what did the author do to move you in this way?

RESPONSE STRATEGIES

Teachers often ask whether literature circle conversations should center on the children's free responses or whether instructional strategies should be used to guide the conversation. Once again, this is not an either/or issue. It makes more sense to think about when each approach is appropriate. In this section, we present instructional strategies designed to foster students' free responses as well as strategies for guiding responses.

Invite Students to Share and Reflect

It is critical to begin discussion of a book or poem by inviting students to share and reflect on their own responses to the work. Rosenblatt (1938) has pointed out that problems may emerge when teachers rely too heavily on strategies for guiding students' discussion. Once, she had become totally drawn into a poem she was reading, only to find herself rudely torn away from that web of emotion and reflection when she turned the page to find questions posed by the textbook editor asking her to identify the formal characteristics of the poem. The magic of what Rosenblatt has called the "lived through experience" was destroyed by those questions. By beginning discussions with students' ideas, teachers can avoid trivializing literary works through overinspection (Babbitt, 1990; Cianciolo, 1982).

By responding to a story in their literature journals, children have the opportunity to consider it more thoughtfully.

Although it is ideal for discussions to emerge from students' own responses to stories, this does not mean that the teacher should never guide their talk. There are many times when it may be necessary to move talk in a particular direction in order to reach an instructional goal. For example, assume that one of your goals in a unit entitled "Giants in Stories" is to help students explore the ways in which giants are typically characterized in literature. If students' responses do not focus on characterization, it may be necessary to use an appropriate instructional strategy to ensure that talk eventually moves in that direction.

Have Children Use Journals for Recording Thoughts

How do teachers ensure that literature discussion initially emerges from students' own responses to literature? One especially effective strategy is to have children keep journals and bring them to the literature circle to share. The use of journals announces to participants the legitimacy and value of each individual's independent reaction to stories. Margaret Anzul (1993) suggests that students read with pen in hand so that they can record their immediate thoughts and feelings in their journal entries. Teachers can use a number of different kinds of journals to support literature circle discussions, including free response journals, prompted response journals, literary journals, and dialogue journals.

Free Response Journals. In free response journals, students are encouraged to write about anything they choose in response to a story. The purpose of writing is to record thoughts, feelings, questions, and interpretations. If students are reading a book independently in preparation for literature circle, they can be asked to write in their journals periodically, perhaps after completing each chapter. Wollman-Bonilla and Werchadlo (1995) concluded that the primary value of free response journals was that they encouraged children to "take time to think about what had been read" (p. 566). Children who have engaged in this type of thinking will have far more to contribute when they join their literature circles.

Miriam Martinez, Nancy Roser, James Hoffman, and Jennifer Battle (1992) have found that free response journals can also be used effectively when the teacher reads a story aloud. Students simply spend a few minutes writing in response to the just-completed chapter or story. These few minutes of writing time give students an opportunity to record their thoughts and feelings before they are lost in the midst of discussion. Free response journal entries can serve as wonderful conversation starters. In writing in her journal about the final chapters of *Shiloh,* second-grader Ana recorded her "wonderings" (see Figure 13.1). When shared aloud, questions like Ana's offer rich material for conversation.

Visual response journals can serve a similar purpose. Hubbard, Winterbourne, and Ostrow (1996) invited primary-level children to draw their favorite section of a story or to draw what was going on in their minds as they read or heard a story. They found that responding through drawing led to greater involvement in stories. Further, the children's drawings served as excellent conversation starters when they were shared during literature circles. Even kindergartners can respond with drawings.

When students first start to write in journals, especially free response journals, they might not be very comfortable recording their thoughts and feelings; instead, they might look for an easy way out by writing stock responses such as "I like this book" or "My favorite part was when Maniac McGee runs across the football field." Teachers can keep their own journals so that when students fall into "writing ruts," teachers can share their own entries, thereby modeling new ways of thinking about literature.

Prompted Response Journals. Some teachers use prompted response journals. That is, they give their students

Figure 13.1
The ideas students record in their journals can serve as starters for literature discussion.

April 21–26
Chapters 13–15

I wonder what Marty ment by not carring about the dog??

I wonder if there is a Shiloh Part 2?

a prompt to respond to or they provide a number of prompts and encourage the students to choose one or more to use. The prompts may be generic ones that apply to almost any story:

- Select your favorite character and tell what she or he is like.
- Choose a character you think is changing and growing in this story. Write about the ways in which the character is changing and the reasons for these changes.
- How is the setting important in this story?
- Write about some of the tensest moments in the story. How does the author make those moments tense?

Prompts can also be specific to a story:

- In Chapter 19 of *The Giver,* Jonas learns what "release" means. How do you think this knowledge will affect him?
- Do you think that Marty did the right thing in Chapter 14 of *Shiloh* when he made his bargain with Judd?

Students who initially lack confidence in writing personal responses to a story may benefit from prompts. Specific prompts are also a means of encouraging students to respond to literature in more diverse ways.

Kelly (1990) invited her third-grade students to write in response to three open-ended prompts (What did you notice? How did you feel about the book? How is the book related to your experiences?). She found that, across the school year, her students' responses grew in length and began to move from initial retellings and summaries to more analytic responses and responses that reflected greater emotional involvement with stories. Kelly and Farnan (1991) compared the use of prompts that "emphasized and elicited readers' personal interpretations and interactions with text" (p. 278) to the use of non–reader response prompts ("Tell me about your book"). They found that the reader response prompts elicited more critical and analytic thinking from the fourth-graders in their study.

Literary Journals. Pamela J. Farris (1989) has described the use of literary journals. In this type of journal, students assume the persona of one of the characters in the story and write journal entries as that character. For example, students reading *Shiloh* might become Marty and write in their journals about all their experiences with and feelings for the dog they found. Writing in a literary journal requires the reader to try to step into the shoes of the character and see story events and conflicts as that character might. Therefore, literary journals are more appropriate for older students than for younger ones, who still view the world from a very egocentric perspective.

Dialogue Journals. In a dialogue journal, a student and the teacher or another student maintain a written dialogue about a story. The other types of journals that we have discussed can readily be shared during literature circles to spark group discussion; dialogue journals are more often used to extend discussion beyond literature circles. Cindy Farest and Carolyn Miller (1993) found that fourth-graders' responses deepened as they engaged in written dialogues with adults. Similarly, Marcia Nash (1995) found that dialogue journals allow teachers to gain insights into how their students respond to literature, to model their own responses to literature, and to foster growth in students' responses. For example, through written dialogue with a fifth-grader, one teacher was able to encourage her student to reflect on what constitutes strong plot development (Nash, 1995, p. 222):

STUDENT: *Dolphin Adventure* was a Good Book But it was missing some Good "stuff" I look for. I probably wouldent chose this Bok on my own.

TEACHER: Can you tell me what good stuff you look for in a book that *Dolphin Adventure* didn't have?

STUDENT: I can't relly desribe the "stuff" I look for. [and later] I also read *Mandie and the Cherokee Ledgend.* I thought that was good but it neaded more of that "stuff" I like.

TEACHER: If we could only figure out what that "stuff" is that makes a book good, we would probably become famous. People have been trying to come up with a definition of what makes good literature for centuries. Still, I think it is interesting to think and talk about. For instance, what was it about Joan Carris's style that you liked enough to make you want to read another book by her after you read *Just a Little Ham?*

STUDENT: What a Great Book! [*Aunt Morbelia and the Screaming Skull,* the other Joan Carris book referred to in the previous entry] "stuff" poped out every where! I can define "stuff": comedy mixed in with adventuere and drama = Good Book!

Ask Open-Ended Discussion Questions

Open-ended discussion frameworks can help to ensure that literature discussion is based on students' own thinking. Margaret Anzul recommends beginning discussion with a simple invitation: "Talk about what touched you the most" (Anzul, 1993, p. 190). Miriam Martinez, Nancy Roser, James Hoffman, and Jennifer Battle (1992) have used a three-pronged invitation to encourage children to talk about a piece of literature. This open-ended framework, based on the work of Aidan Chambers (1985), invites students to share their (1) observations, (2) unanswered questions or wonderings, and (3) anything they were reminded of by the story. Frequently, students' observations are so insightful that lively conversations ensue. And students' wonderings, which are legitimate questions, are especially likely to evoke interesting discussions. Such was the case when Eric, a fourth-grader, shared one of his questions about C. S. Lewis's **The Lion, the Witch, and the Wardrobe** with his classmates:

ERIC: I wonder why Edmund wasn't mentioned in the last three chapters?

MS. FRY: Good question. Who wants to respond to that? Why hasn't the author mentioned Edmund in the last three chapters?

CARLO: Probably because they, they could think that Edmund might be like in the special place, like where the witch has them. Except he was a traitor, and they don't want to talk about him. They want to save him, and they talk about the other kids so that . . .

CAROL: And then like they're having the battles, and whoever wins the battle gets Edmund or . . .

JACKIE: 'Cause if they kill the witch, then all the animals . . . she probably created most of her enemies. And then the witch dies; then all of her creatures die, and Edmund isn't a traitor anymore, and they can get him back.

MS. FRY: Boy, you got an answer to the question, I can tell! But the bottom line was that you think the author has some special purpose for holding Edmund aside for these last three chapters. Does anybody else have something to respond about Aslan, I mean keeping Edmund out of it so far?

MICHELLE: Maybe the witch can turn . . . can turn one of those stone beasts into another animal, and then he could be a spy.

MS. FRY: Maybe Edmund . . . that is an excellent idea. Maybe Edmund isn't what Edmund used to be anymore. That is a possibility.

When students are invited to share their own connections to a story, they sometimes offer personal experiences related to the story or connect the story with others they have read. We find that children frequently share some of their most insightful thinking when they compare stories. When her teacher read **Captain Whiz-Bang** aloud, Kim was reminded of E. B. White's **Charlotte's Web:**

KIM: This book reminds me of *Charlotte's Web* because Fern had Wilbur and the little girl had the cat. And as Fern and the little girl got older, they didn't pay much attention to their animals.

An open-ended discussion framework gives students interesting alternatives for responding to a story without rigidly prescribing acceptable ways in which to respond. An added benefit of using this discussion framework is that it also works well as an invitation to journal writing, thereby integrating writing and discussion.

Pose Literary Questions for Discussion

As we noted earlier, there are times during literature discussions when teachers may want to pose questions. For example, if the teacher believes the students have not discussed an important aspect of a story, she or he may try to move discussion forward by asking a literary question. Carefully crafted questions can encourage students to think more insightfully about a story. According to Wendy Saul (1989), literary questions require interpretation and are the "key to literary comprehension, conversation, and enjoyment." She has identified some distinctive features of literary questions, which are listed in Table 13.1. Not every literary question will have all these features, but questions with one or more of them have the potential to "lead children into the story and help them consider the work as a human construction where craft and effect are taken seriously" (p. 297).

Lea McGee (1995) recommends that, in preparing literary questions, teachers read the story thoughtfully, staying in tune with their own responses to the story and noting conclusions they draw from it or noteworthy elements they discover in it. She further notes the importance of focusing on "the significance of the story as a whole" (p. 111). Saul (1989) describes a strategy, called "diagram-

Table 13.1   How to Ask Good Literary Questions

- Ask questions that go beyond what is in the story but that always come back to the story.
- Ask questions that help readers to better understand the story.
- Ask questions that have at least two good answers, either of which can help the reader with the story.
- Ask questions that raise issues which can be argued intelligently in different ways.
- Ask some questions that deal with issues of craft.

ming stories," that helps teachers to "focus on the structural peculiarities of a text, to comment on what in the book or story looms largest to the reader, and to describe, in something close to metaphorical terms, the essence of the book" (p. 297). Figure 13.2 shows a story diagram of Jerry Spinelli's *Maniac*

Figure 13.2
Teachers can prepare to lead literature discussion by creating story diagrams.

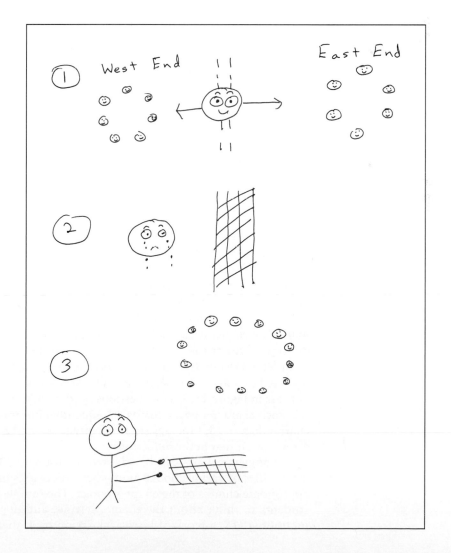

Magee. The teacher who created the diagram explained what she was trying to do in this way:

> At the beginning of the book, there was a "wall" between the West End and the East End that was never supposed to be crossed, and everyone knew there was a wall there—that is, everyone except Maniac. He just went back and forth between the West End and the East End as though there was no wall at all. Then, all of a sudden, on the day everyone was playing in the water from the fire hydrant and the man called Maniac "Whitey," Maniac finally saw the wall, and it almost broke his heart. But finally, Maniac found a way to bring that wall down, and doing that meant he was finally able to have the home and happiness he wanted so much.

Literary questions based on this story diagram might include the following:

- Why wasn't Maniac able to see the "wall" between the East End and the West End?
- Why did it hurt Maniac so much when he finally saw the wall?
- How did Maniac help to bring down the wall?
- What other walls did the author include in the book that had an impact on Maniac?

Each of these questions goes beyond the text, but the answers (and there will be more than one answer to each question) naturally come back to the text. The questions should help readers to understand the story better, and the final question treats the story as a crafted object. Grand conversations may well be sparked when students are invited to respond to the kind of literary questions that Saul advocates.

Prepare Language Charts

Language charts function much as literary questions do: They focus students' thinking about literature. Developed by Nancy Roser, James V. Hoffman, and Cynthia Farest (1990), language charts were originally designed for use with related sets of books. These large charts, intended to be displayed on a classroom wall, are ruled into a matrix. The titles (and perhaps authors and illustrators) of the books in a set are recorded along one axis of the matrix. Questions that are devised to stimulate connections among the books are recorded along the other axis. These questions might focus attention on particular aspects of the story worlds in the featured books, on themes that emerge from the books, or on the crafting of the stories or illustrations. Students' responses to the questions are recorded on the matrix as each book is read and discussed.

A language chart designed for use with a unit entitled "Foxy Figures" appears in Figure 13.3. The questions on this chart encourage students to explore the stock character of the fox as it frequently appears in children's literature. The chart in Figure 13.4 focuses students' attention on the style of Chris Van Allsburg for a unit on that author/illustrator.

Language charts can be adapted for use with chapter books. Rather than listing titles of various books along the vertical axis of the chart, the teacher lists appropriate chunks of the chapter books. The sample chart in Figure 13.5 invites students to think about the theme, setting, and development of characters in *Pictures, 1918,* a work of historical fiction by Jeanette Ingold. Students would

Foxy Figures				
Title	Who were the characters?	How did they meet the fox?	What happened to the fox in the end?	Things that made us laugh
Doctor De Soto				
Wings: A Tale of Two Chickens				
Peeping Beauty				
etc.				

Figure 13.3
The questions on this language chart are designed to help children explore the fox as a stock character in literature.

The Stories of Chris Van Allsburg			
Title	What strange things happened in the story?	What surprise did the ending hold?	What we noticed about Mr. Van Allsburg's illustrations
Jumanji			
The Wreck of the Zephyr			
The Sweetest Fig			
The Polar Express			

Figure 13.4
This chart is designed to help children explore the style of author/illustrator Chris Van Allsburg.

Figure 13.5
The questions on this language chart are designed to help children explore the way in which the author crafted the story's theme, setting, and characters.

Pictures, 1918 How Jeanette Ingold Shows Us			
	. . . how Asia understands pictures	. . . the importance of time in Texas, 1918	. . . characters developing
Chapters 1–3			
Chapters 4–6			
Chapters 7–9			
etc.			

complete a section of this particular chart after reading every three chapters of the book.

Some teachers report that a language chart can become just a "worksheet on the wall" if the class begins to complete the chart too soon after reading. These charts are not meant to displace conversations about books. Rather, teachers and students should turn to the language chart only after having fully discussed a book. Teachers who have used language charts in this way report that they can be effective tools for fostering literary understandings. In fact, many teachers change the design of their language charts throughout the school year to help students continue to explore different aspects of literature. For example, the questions that Ms. Perez, a kindergarten teacher, uses on her language charts at the beginning of the year are designed to help her students learn basic literary language: Who are the characters? What is the setting? What was the problem in the story? Once students have made this terminology their own, she changes the chart questions to focus on other literary understandings.

Develop Story Webs

Story webs are visual displays that show how categories of information are related; the name arose because they often look like the webs spiders build. Teachers use story webs to achieve different purposes, but Karen Bromley (1991) believes that all too often they overlook the potential of webs to foster responses to literature. Story webs, like literary questions, focus students' thinking about

Book webs can support children's thinking about the information or stories they read.

literature. According to Bromley (1995), webs can be used to support and extend students' literary understanding in many ways:

- Webs can help students to identify important issues in stories.
- Webs can be used to focus attention on connections between books.
- Webs can help students to understand how literary and artistic elements work.
- Webs can help students to explore characteristics of different genres.
- Webs can help students to explore the literary devices that authors use (perspective, metaphor, and so on).

Story webs can emerge from children's responses. This happened in Ms. Alducin's class when her students were discussing Barbara Nichol's **Beethoven Lives Upstairs.** Ms. Alducin introduced the web that appears in Figure 13.6 by saying "Someone said earlier that Christoph's feelings about Beethoven changed a lot in the book, and I want us to explore that idea a little more." Just as teachers sometimes create literary questions for possible use during literature circle discussions, they may design webs that will help students to explore a particular aspect of a story. We recommend introducing a story web only after students have engaged in free-ranging discussion about the story.

Barbara Nichol's **Beethoven Lives Upstairs** is told almost exclusively through the correspondence of young Christoph and his Uncle Karl. To make a living after the death of Christoph's father, his mother has rented the upstairs portion of their house to Beethoven. Mistaking the famous composer's eccentric behavior for madness, Christoph is appalled. Over a period of two years, Christoph keeps his uncle updated on the happenings upstairs, and his uncle's letters gently help Christoph to develop compassion for his neighbor. The web in Figure 13.6 chronologically records Christoph's feelings toward Beethoven and

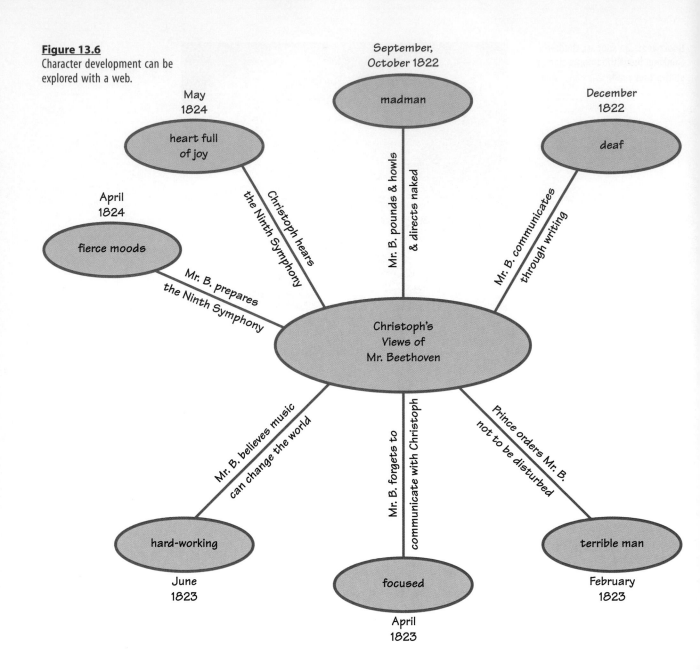

Figure 13.6
Character development can be explored with a web.

September, October 1822

madman

May 1824

heart full of joy

December 1822

deaf

April 1824

fierce moods

Christoph hears the Ninth Symphony

Mr. B. pounds & howls & directs naked

Mr. B. communicates through writing

Mr. B. prepares the Ninth Symphony

Christoph's Views of Mr. Beethoven

Mr. B. believes music can change the world

Mr. B. forgets to communicate with Christoph

Prince orders Mr. B. not to be disturbed

hard-working

June 1823

focused

April 1823

terrible man

February 1823

the story details related to those feelings. Christoph's increasingly mature understanding of Beethoven reveals his own growth as a character.

The story web in Figure 13.7 is based on *Maniac Magee.* In Jerry Spinelli's Newbery Medal–winning book, a boy who began life as Jeffrey Magee becomes a legend nicknamed Maniac. The web shows some of the incidents that led to Maniac's acquiring his nickname.

Figure 13.7
This web reveals how Maniac Magee emerges as a legendary figure in Jerry Spinelli's Newbery Medal–winning book.

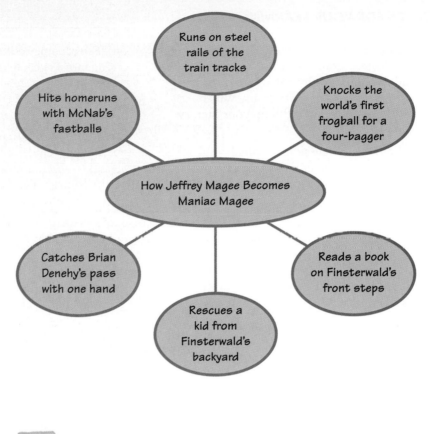

Figure 13.7
This web reveals how Maniac Magee emerges as a legendary figure in Jerry Spinelli's Newbery Medal–winning book.

TEACHING IDEAS

Responses to Books. As you engage children in literature discussions, try modeling a particular type of response. For example, you might repeatedly share the things you wonder about when reading a story or talk about how the book connects to other books you have read. Watch and see whether children begin to share similar responses during literature circle.

Children's Picks versus Teacher's Picks. Both teachers and students can select books for use in literature circle. Try comparing literature conversations about books that you've chosen with those about books that students have chosen. How do the discussions differ? What are the advantages (if any) of involving students in selecting books for literature discussion?

Journal Writing. Try engaging students in literature discussion without having them keep journals. Once they feel comfortable as members of a literature circle, encourage the students to record their responses in journals. You can then use the students' journal entries as conversation starters. How does literature discussion change with the use of journals?

Character Development. Marty's development as a character in *Shiloh* is particularly interesting. To help your students see Marty's growth, create a character web with the students. Make discussion an integral part of the process.

EXPERIENCES FOR YOUR LEARNING

1. Questions can be tools for "gentle inquisitions" or tools that foster "grand conversations." Select a book, and develop questions that you think are likely to promote grand conversations. Which features identified by Saul (1989) do your literary questions have?

2. Reflect on literature discussions in which you've participated. Which were grand conversations? Describe one of these discussions to a fellow student, and explain why you consider it to have been a grand conversation.

3. One way in which teachers can support literary learning is by helping students to become aware of the writer's craft. Distinctively crafted books offer teachers opportunities to talk about different aspects of craft (mood, voice, tension, and so on). Select some well-crafted children's books, and identify in each book the aspects of craft you would like to discuss with students.

4. Create a language chart designed to help children explore the use of the "enchanted journey" motif in modern fantasies. Some books that you might include on the chart include Maurice Sendak's *Where the Wild Things Are,* Chris Van Allsburg's *The Polar Express,* and Arthur Yorinks's *Hey, Al!*

5. Saul's strategy for "diagramming stories" is designed to help teachers focus on the essence of a book (see pp. 488–490 for a discussion of the strategy). Select a book to diagram and then share your diagram with peers who have diagrammed the same story.

RECOMMENDED BOOKS

* indicates a picture book; I indicates interest level (P = preschool, YA = young adult)

Books with Strong Themes

*Ackerman, Karen. *The Tin Heart.* Illustrated by Michael Hays. Atheneum, 1990. Two friends are separated by the American Civil War, but their friendship remains as strong as ever. (I: 8–11)

Almond, David. *Skellig.* Delacorte, 1999. Michael's new sister is desperately ill, and he feels helpless. Then he discovers a strange creature—neither man nor beast—and his world changes forever. (I: 10–YA)

*Aylesworth, Jim. *The Full Belly Bowl.* Illustrated by Wendy Anderson Halperin. Atheneum, 1999. As a result of a good deed, the old man is rewarded with a Full Belly Bowl that will ensure he is never hungry—if the bowl is used wisely. (I: 5–9)

Babbitt, Natalie. *Tuck Everlasting.* Farrar, 1975. A young girl is given the opportunity to drink from a spring that offers eternal life. (I: 10–YA)

*Bercaw, Edna Coe. *Halmoni's Day.* Illustrated by Robert Hunt. Dial, 2000. Jennifer is embarrassed to take her Korean-speaking grandmother to the school's Grandparents' Day until Halmoni shares a story with the class that shows how love can reach over generational and language barriers. (I: 7–10)

*Best, Cari. *Three Cheers for Catherine the Great!* Illustrated by Giselle Potter. DK Ink, 1999. When Sara's Russian-speaking grandmother announces that she wants a birthday party with no presents, Sara's mother explains that there are lots of good "No Presents," as long as they come from deep inside you. The challenge for Sara is to reach deep inside and discover what she can give her grandmother. (I: 6–9)

*Blos, Joan. *Old Henry.* Illustrated by Stephen Gammell. Morrow, 1987. A neighborhood discovers that there is room for all kinds of people. (I: 6–9)

*Brisson, Pat. *The Summer My Father Was Ten.* Illustrated by Andrea Shine. Boyds Mill, 1998. The careless destruction of a neighbor's garden is the beginning of a special friendship for a young boy. (I: 6–10)

*Bunting, Eve. *A Day's Work.* Illustrated by Ronald Himler. Clarion, 1994. Francisco is so anxious to find work for his non-English-speaking grandfather that he lies about the man's qualifications for a gardening job. When the boss discovers that the work has been botched, Francisco's abuelito teaches him a valuable lesson. (I: 6–10)

*———. *The Wednesday Surprise.* Illustrated by Donald Carrick. Clarion, 1989. A little girl surprises her family by teaching her grandmother to read. (I: 6–10)

Clements, Andrew. *Frindle*. Illustrated by Brian Selznick. Simon & Schuster, 1996. Hoping simply to enliven his class, Nick takes an idea that he has learned in school and ends up having a wider impact than he ever imagined when he coins a new word. (I: 9–12)

———. *The Janitor's Boy*. Simon & Schuster, 2000. Ashamed that his father is the school janitor, Jack performs an act of defiance that is intended to hurt his father. Jack's resulting punishment leads him to a deeper understanding of his father and himself. (I: 9–12)

Coerr, Eleanor. *Sadako and the Thousand Paper Cranes*. Penguin Putnam, 1977/1999. A victim of leukemia resulting from the atomic bomb dropped on Hiroshima, Sadako determines to fight for her life by folding a thousand paper cranes. (I: 9–12)

*Cooney, Barbara. *Miss Rumphius*. Puffin, 1982. A woman achieves her life's goals, including the most important one of making the world more beautiful. (I: 6–10)

*Davol, Marguerite. *The Paper Dragon*. Illustrated by Robert Sabuda. Atheneum, 1997. A humble painter must accomplish three tasks to save himself and his village from the fierce dragon. (I: 8–11)

*Demi. *The Donkey and the Rock*. Holt, 1999. When the townspeople attend a trial between a donkey and a rock, they discover the folly of yielding to idle curiosity. (I: 5–8)

DiCamillo, Kate. *Because of Winn-Dixie*. Candlewick, 2000. Ten-year-old Opal adopts a dog that helps her to make an array friends who, in turn, help her to sort out some of the issues that most perplex her. (I: 9–12)

Dorris, Michael. *The Window*. Hyperion, 1997. When her mother is placed in an institution, Rayona discovers an extended family and a world that she never dreamed would exist for her. (I: 10–12)

Fleischman, Paul. *Seedfolks*. HarperCollins, 1997. The transformation of an inner city neighborhood begins when one young Asian girl plants seeds in a vacant, trash-filled lot. (I: 9–12)

Gardella, Tricia. *Blackberry Booties*. Illustrated by Glo Coalson. Orchard, 2000. Mikki Jo uses all her resources to find the perfect gift for her baby cousin. (I: 5–8)

*Garland, Sherry. *The Lotus Seed*. Illustrated by Tatsuro Kiuchi. Harcourt, 1993. When the emperor in Vietnam loses his throne, a young girl sees him cry and takes a lotus seed from the pond to remember that moment. Throughout the war in her country and her relocation to the United States, the girl holds on to the lotus seed as a symbol of life and hope. (I: 6–12)

*Gerstein, Mordicai. *The Wild Boy*. Farrar, 1998. A wild boy is discovered living alone in the forests of France, and through love he is slowly brought into the human community. This book is based on a true story. (I: 8–12)

*Golenbock, Peter. *Teammates*. Illustrated by Paul Bacon. Harcourt, 1990. When Jackie Robinson becomes the first African American to play major league baseball, only one man stands by him—his teammate Pee Wee Reese. (I: 9–12)

*Grimes, Nikki. *My Man Blue*. Illustrated by Jerome Lagarrigue. Dial, 1999. This story of Blue and the boy he is determined to save from the inner-city streets is told through a collection of poems. (I: 8–12)

*Heide, Florence Parry, and Judith Heide Gilliland. *The House of Wisdom*. Illustrated by Mary Grandpre. DK Publishing, 1999. This is the story of the House of Wisdom, a vibrant center of ideas, and the renaissance that flourished in ninth-century Baghdad. (I: 10 and up)

*Hesse, Karen. *Lester's Dog*. Illustrated by Nancy Carpenter. Crown, 1993. A young boy lives on the same street as a vicious and frightening dog that belongs to Lester. The boy is afraid to walk past Lester's dog, but one day he must do so in order to save a kitten. (I: P–8)

———. *Out of the Dust*. Scholastic, 1997. In free-verse poetry, Billie Jo chronicles the seeming hopelessness of her Depression-era life in the Oklahoma panhandle. (I: YA)

Hickman, Janet. *Jericho: A Novel*. Greenwillow, 1994. This story explores the connections among four generations of women as twelve-year-old Angela searches for clues to the woman she will become. (I: 10–14)

*Hobbie, Holly. *Toot & Puddle: You Are My Sunshine*. Little, Brown, 1999. When Toot begins to mope, Puddle does what a real friend would do and sticks with him all the way. (I: 4–8)

*Hoffman, Mary. *Amazing Grace*. Illustrated by Caroline Binch. Dial, 1991. With the support of her grandmother and mother, a young girl discovers that she can be anything she wants to be. (I: 5–10)

Holt, Kimberly Willis. *Mister and Me*. Putnam, 1998. Jolene thinks that her family is complete with just her mother, grandfather, and herself. So she is determined to make her mother see the folly of marrying Mister. (I: 7–9)

*Houston, Gloria. *My Great-Aunt Arizona*. Illustrated by Susan Condie Lamb. HarperCollins, 1992/1997.

Arizona was born in a small community in the Blue Ridge Mountains, where she dreamed of traveling to faraway places. She never left the area but became a teacher who touched the lives of many children by teaching them about the world. (I: 6–10)

Ingold, Jeanette. *Pictures, 1918*. Harcourt, 1998. In the midst of World War I, Asia becomes intrigued with exploring the possibilities of photography and with nurturing her relationship with Nick. (I: 12–YA)

*Johnson, D. B. *Henry Hikes to Fitchburg*. Houghton Mifflin, 2000. Henry and his friend want to travel to Fitchburg. Henry walks the thirty miles while his friend spends the day earning train fare for the trip. (I: 6–10)

*Johnston, Tony. *Amber on the Mountain*. Illustrated by Robert Duncan. Dial, 1994. Amber's lonely mountain life opens up when a friend teaches her to read. (I: 6–10)

*Kajikawa, Kimiko. *Yoshi's Feast*. Illustrated by Yumi Heo. Dorling Kindersley, 2000. Yoshi loves broiled eel, but being a stingy man, he settles on simply smelling the ones his neighbor, the eel broiler, makes. But the eel maker—frustrated at his inability to sell eels—presents Yoshi with a bill for all the eels he has smelled. Only then does Yoshi come up with a plan to work together with his neighbor to achieve mutually beneficial ends. (I: 7–11)

L'Engle, Madeleine. *A Wrinkle in Time*. Farrar, 1962/1990. When Meg's father mysteriously disappears during some experiments with the Fifth Dimension, Meg, her friend, and her brother must face evil forces to rescue him. (I: 10–YA)

*Lester, Helen. *Hooway for Wodney Wat*. Illustrated by Lynn Munsinger. Houghton Mifflin, 1999. Unable to pronounce his r's, Rodney Rat is teased by his classmates—until he single-handedly saves them from the bully who makes their lives miserable. (I: 5–8)

Lewis, C. S. *The Lion, the Witch, and the Wardrobe*. HarperCollins, 1951/1994. Four siblings enter the magical kingdom of Narnia, where they become embroiled in a struggle between good and evil. (I: 8–11)

Lowry, Lois. *The Giver*. Houghton Mifflin, 1993. A boy discovers the secrets behind the controlled society in which he lives. The companion book is *Gathering Blue* (2000). (I: YA)

MacLachlan, Patricia. *Journey*. Delacorte, 1991. Journey spends the summer trying to find out why his mother has abandoned him and his sister. (I: 9–12)

Mazer, Anne. *The Oxboy*. Knopf, 1993. The Oxboy faces prejudice because he is the son of a human and an ox. (I: 9–12)

*McCully, Emily Arnold. *Mirette on the High Wire*. Putnam, 1992. A young girl helps a tightrope walker to rediscover his courage. (I: 5–9)

*Merrill, Jean. *The Girl Who Loved Caterpillars*. Illustrated by Floyd Cooper. Philomel, 1992. A twelfth-century Japanese tale in which a young girl pursues her own dreams rather than those of her parents. (I: 10–YA)

*Mitchell, Margaree King. *Uncle Jed's Barbershop*. Illustrated by James Ransome. Simon & Schuster, 1993. Despite all the adversity he encounters in the segregated South of the 1920s, Uncle Jed never gives up his dream of opening his own barbershop. (I: 9–12)

*Mochizuki, Ken. *Baseball Saved Us*. Illustrated by Dom Lee. Lee & Low, 1993. Living in an internment camp during World War II, a young Japanese American boy finds a way to gain dignity and self-respect. (I: 8–12)

*Nye, Naomi Shihab. *Sitti's Secrets*. Illustrated by Nancy Carpenter. Four Winds, 1994. When Mona visits her grandmother in a Palestinian village on the West Bank, she discovers many connections between her world and her grandmother's, even though their homes are separated by thousands of miles. (I: 6–10)

*Park, Frances, and Ginger Park. *The Royal Bee*. Illustrated by Christopher Zhong-Yuan Zhang. Boyds Mill, 2000. Excluded from school in nineteenth-century Korea because he does not belong to the wealthy class, Song-Ho eavesdrops at the door of the rich children's schoolhouse until a kindly teacher invites him into the schoolroom. (I: 8–12)

Paterson, Katherine. *Lyddie*. Penguin/Lodestar, 1991. Lyddie struggles against injustices in the fabric mills of Massachusetts in the 1840s. (I: 11–YA)

*Polacco, Patricia. *Chicken Sunday*. Philomel, 1992. When three children are falsely accused of throwing eggs at a shopkeeper's window, they discover a way of reaching across a cultural gap to solve a problem. (I: 7–11)

*————. *Pink and Say*. Philomel, 1994. When a young Union soldier of 15 is wounded in the Civil War, a young black soldier reaches out his hand in friendship and takes the white soldier to his home. (I: 8–YA)

*Rylant, Cynthia. *This Year's Garden*. Bradbury, 1984. A descriptive story about planting the family garden. (I: P–8)

*Shannon, George. *Heart to Heart*. Illustrated by Steve Bjorkman. Houghton Mifflin, 1995. Squirrel, desperate to make a Valentine's card for his best friend Mole, discovers the perfect way to express his affection for his friend. (I: P–8)

*Stanley, Diane. *Captain Whiz-Bang*. Morrow, 1987. A little girl grows up and, in the process, seems to forget her beloved cat. (I: P–8)

*Steig, William. *Amos and Boris*. Farrar, 1999. A mouse and a whale form a deep friendship. (I: 6–9)

*———. *Sylvester and the Magic Pebble*. Simon & Schuster, 1989. After making a wish on a magic pebble and being transformed into a rock, Sylvester comes to realize what is important in life. (I: 6–9)

Talbert, Marc. *A Sunburned Prayer*. Simon & Schuster, 1995. Eloy is determined to make the long pilgrimage to Chimayo in hopes of saving his grandmother, who is dying from cancer. (I: 10–YA)

Taylor, Mildred. *Roll of Thunder, Hear My Cry*. Dial, 1976. The Logans stand strong in the face of discrimination when a white man tries to cheat them out of their land. (I: 10–YA)

———. *The Well*. Dial, 1995. Racial tensions escalate between boys when the only available water comes from the Logans' well. (I: 10–12)

*Van Allsburg, Chris. *The Polar Express*. Houghton Mifflin, 1985. A young boy boards a train that takes him to the North Pole, where Santa offers him any gift he would like. (I: P–8)

*———. *The Sweetest Fig*. Houghton Mifflin, 1993. A woman leaves two figs as payment for work on her teeth, telling Monsieur Bibot that the figs make dreams come true. (I: 7–10)

Voigt, Cynthia. *Dicey's Song*. Atheneum, 1982. Dicey and her siblings learn to build a new life with the grandmother they had never known before. (I: 10–YA)

Walter, Virginia. *Making Up Megaboy*. Illustrated by Katrina Roeckelein. DK Publishing, 1998. Robbie Jones won't explain why he shot an old man he didn't even know. So the reader must weave together his story by listening to the voices of people who have been touched by the crime. (I: 11–YA)

Wells, Rosemary. *Mary on Horseback: Three Mountain Stories*. Dial, 1998. Characters in three stories are influenced by Mary Breckinridge, founder of the Frontier Nursing Service. (I: 7–10)

*Wild, Margaret. *Let the Celebrations Begin!* Illustrated by Julie Vivas. Orchard, 1991. Inmates in a Nazi concentration camp maintain their hope by making toys for the children. (I: 10–YA)

*Yolen, Jane. *Encounter*. Illustrated by David Shannon. Harcourt, 1992. Columbus's first landing in America is told through the eyes of a Taino boy. (I: 10–YA)

*Young, Ed. *Mouse Match*. Harcourt, 1997. Mama mouse and Papa mouse set out to find the most powerful one in the world to marry their daughter,

and along the way they learn not just to look but also to see. (I: 6–10)

Books with Strong Story Lines

Avi. *The Barn*. Orchard, 1994. Ben and his two younger siblings must care for their injured father and run the family homestead in 1850's Oregon Territory. (I: 9–12)

*Blake, Robert J. *Akiak: A Tale from the Iditarod*. Philomel, 1997. Akiak, the lead dog, is determined to finish the Iditarod with the team, even though an injury has sidelined her. (I: 7–10)

*Bunting, Eve. *Summer Wheels*. Harcourt, 1992. The Bicycle Man helps two boys learn a lesson about the importance of giving instead of blaming. (I: 7–10)

*dePaola, Tomie. *Helga's Dowry: A Troll Love Story*. Harcourt, 1977. A troll maiden discovers that it is more important to be loved for who she is than for what she has. (I: 7–12)

Dorris, Michael. *Guests*. Hyperion, 1994. Frustrated that white people are to join the village for the harvest meal, Moss leaves for some "away time" in hopes of finding answers to his questions. (I: 9–12)

Farmer, Nancy. *The Ear, the Eye and the Arm*. Orchard, 1994. Set in a futuristic Africa, this imaginative science fiction work explores where the world may be heading. (I: YA)

Fitzhugh, Louise. *Harriet the Spy*. Harper, 1964. Harriet documents her observations of the people around her in her journal. (I: 8–11)

*Fox, Mem. *Wilfrid Gordon McDonald Partridge*. Illustrated by Julie Vivas. Kane/Miller, 1984/1995. Through his gifts, a little boy helps an elderly friend find memories. (I: P–8)

*Gackenbach, Dick. *Harry and the Terrible Whatzit*. Houghton Mifflin, 1977/1984. Sure that his mother has come to harm, a boy dares to confront the Terrible Whatzit living in his basement. (I: P–7)

George, Jean Craighead. *Julie of the Wolves*. Harper, 1972. Lost on the tundra, Julie must depend on a wolf pack for survival. (I: 10–YA)

———. *My Side of the Mountain*. Penguin Putnam, 1959/1997. A young boy relies on his knowledge of nature to survive on his own for a year in the wilderness of upper New York State. (I: 10–YA)

*Goble, Paul. *Iktomi Loses His Eyes*. Orchard, 1999. Iktomi fails to heed a stern warning when a mysterious man shows him how to send his eyes to the top of a fence post and summon them back again. (I: 7–10)

Hamilton, Virginia. *Drylongso*. Illustrated by Jerry Pinkney. Harcourt, 1992. An African American family, victimized by a severe drought, is helped by an unknown boy. (I: 8–11)

Ho, Minfong. *The Clay Marble*. Farrar, 1991. Forced from their war-torn village in Cambodia, Dara and her family are separated in the chaos of war. (I: 10–YA)

Hodge, Merle. *For the Life of Laetitia*. Farrar, 1993. Having grown up with her grandparents in their rural Caribbean home, Laetitia discovers a new and not always happy world when she moves to the city to attend the government secondary school. (I: YA)

Konigsburg, E. L. *From the Mixed-up Files of Mrs. Basil E. Frankweiler*. Atheneum, 1970. Claudia and her brother run away from home and live in the Metropolitan Museum of Art. (I: 9–12)

*Lionni, Leo. *Alexander and the Wind-up Mouse*. Pantheon, 1974. A real mouse longs to be like his friend the wind-up mouse. (I: P–7)

*Luenn, Nancy. *Nessa's Fish*. Illustrated by Neil Waldman. Atheneum, 1990. Nessa and her grandmother walk half a day from their home in the far north to catch fish for the village. When Nessa's grandmother becomes ill, Nessa must take care of her and keep the fish safe. (I: P–8)

MacLachlan, Patricia. *Sarah, Plain and Tall*. Harper, 1985. A brother and sister hope that Sarah will choose to stay on the prairie and become their mother. (I: 9–12)

*McKissack, Patricia. *Flossie and the Fox*. Dial, 1986. Flossie outfoxes the fox who tries to steal her eggs. (I: 5–10)

*Naylor, Phyllis Reynolds. *King of the Playground*. Illustrated by Nola Langner Malone. Atheneum, 1991. When Kevin can't play at the playground because of Sammy's threats, his father helps him learn to handle a difficult situation. (I: P–8)

———. *Shiloh*. Atheneum, 1991. A boy determines to save the dog he loves from further abuse by its owner. (I: 8–11)

———. *Shiloh Season*. Atheneum, 1996. Having saved the dog Shiloh from Judd, the dog's abusive owner, Marty must now deal with Judd's anger. (I: 8–11)

*Novak, Matt. *Mouse TV*. Orchard, 1994. When the TV stops working, a mouse family discovers a host of wonderful alternative activities. (I: P–8)

Paulsen, Gary. *Hatchet*. Bradbury, 1987. A boy stranded in the wilderness has only his hatchet and his wits to help him survive. (I: 10–YA)

*Sabuda, Robert. *The Blizzard's Robe*. Atheneum, 1999. By making amends for burning Blizzard's robe, a young girl gives her people the gift of the northern lights. (I: 6–10)

*Sanderson, Ruth. *Papa Gatto*. Little, Brown, 1995. In this Italian fairy tale, two sisters—one selfish and beautiful and the other plain and kind—each have a turn to care for a litter of motherless kittens. (I: 5–9)

*San Souci, Robert D. *The Talking Eggs*. Illustrated by Jerry Pinkney. Dial, 1989. Adapted from a Creole folktale, this is the story of two sisters: One is lazy and bad-tempered, and the other is sweet and kind. (I: 6–10)

*Sendak, Maurice. *Where the Wild Things Are*. HarperCollins, 1963/1998. Sent to his room, Max travels to where the Wild Things are and becomes king of all Wild Things. (I: P–8)

Speare, Elizabeth. *The Witch of Blackbird Pond*. Dell, 1958. Kit Tyler becomes the focus of a witch hunt when she goes to live in a Puritan community in the Connecticut colony. (I: 10–YA)

Spinelli, Jerry. *Maniac Magee*. Little, Brown, 1990. A homeless boy brings together the segregated sides of his adopted town and, in the process, becomes a legend. (I: 10–YA)

Taylor, Mildred D. *The Gold Cadillac*. Dial, 1987. When an African American family tries to drive their new car into the deep South, they find themselves the victims of racial prejudice. (I: 10–YA)

———. *The Friendship*. Illustrated by Max Ginsburg. Dial, 1987. An old black man is shot when he insists on his right to call a white man by his first name. (I: 10–YA)

———. *Mississippi Bridge*. Illustrated by Max Ginsburg. Dial, 1990. In this story set in Mississippi in the 1930s, African American passengers on a bus are displaced by white passengers. (I: 10–YA)

Taylor, Theodore. *The Cay*. Doubleday, 1969/1987. During World War II, a blind American boy is stranded on an island with a West Indian. (I: YA)

Temple, Frances. *Grab Hands and Run*. HarperCollins, 1995. When his father disappears in El Salvador, Felipe and his family set out on a dangerous trek to Canada. (I: 9–12)

*Van Allsburg, Chris. *Jumanji*. Houghton Mifflin, 1981. A brother and sister find unexpected adventure in a board game they play. (I: 6–10)

*———. *The Stranger*. Houghton Mifflin, 1986. The stranger who stays on the Baileys' farm seems to be accompanied by mysterious changes in the weather. (I: 7–12)

*———. *The Widow's Broom*. Houghton Mifflin, 1992. When a widow comes into possession of a witch's broom, the broom begins to help out around the house, which raises the ire of the neighbors. (I: 8–YA)

*————. *The Wreck of the Zephyr.* Houghton Mifflin, 1983. The wreck of the Zephyr is on a high cliff above the sea. Did a storm with unusually high waves throw the sailboat there, or did a boy sailor use magic sails to sail it through the sky? (I: 8–12)

Voigt, Cynthia. *Homecoming.* Atheneum, 1981. When their mother abandons them, Dicey and her siblings seek out the grandmother they have never met. (I: 10–YA)

*Waber, Bernard. *Ira Sleeps Over.* Houghton Mifflin, 1973. Ira has been invited to sleep over at his best friend's house and must decide whether to risk being laughed at by taking his teddy bear. (I: P–8)

White, E. B. *Charlotte's Web.* Illustrated by Garth Williams. Harper, 1952. Charlotte the spider befriends Wilbur the pig and saves his life. (I: 6–10)

*Willard, Nancy. *The High Rise Glorious Skittle Skat Roarious Sky Pie Angel Food Cake.* Illustrated by Richard Jesse Watson. Harcourt, 1990. A girl discovers her grandmother's secret recipe and, with some heavenly help, makes her mother the birthday present she longs for. (I: 8–11)

Winthrop, Elizabeth. *Castle in the Attic.* Holiday House, 1985. A boy travels back to medieval times and confronts an evil wizard. (I: 7–11)

*Wood, Audrey. *Elbert's Bad Word.* Illustrated by Audrey and Don Wood. Harcourt, 1988. When Elbert blurts out a bad word at an elegant garden party, the wizard gardener helps Elbert discover strong descriptive words to use instead. (I: P–8)

Yolen, Jane. *The Devil's Arithmetic.* Viking, 1988. In this time travel fantasy, Hannah finds herself caught up in the Holocaust. (I: 10–YA)

*Yorinks, Arthur. *Hey, Al!* Illustrated by Richard Egielski. Farrar, 1986. The paradise promised by a bird does not live up to the expectations of Al and his dog. (I: 6–12)

Books with Distinctive Crafting

Avi. *Nothing But the Truth.* Orchard, 1991. A minor incident in which Phillip's teacher asks him to stop humming the national anthem becomes a national scandal in this imaginatively crafted satire of high school politics. (I: YA)

*Banks, Kate. *Baboon.* Illustrated by Georg Hallensleben. Farrar, 1997. On his first trip into the world, Baby Baboon discovers what the world is like in this story filled with repetition and lyrical language. (I: P–8)

*Bradby, Marie. *Momma, Where Are You From?* Illustrated by Chris K. Soentpiet. Orchard, 2000. A little girl asks, "Momma, where are you from?" and her mother answers in poetic detail with a rich description of her own childhood. (I: 5–10)

*Bunting, Eve. *Smoky Night.* Illustrated by David Diaz. Harcourt, 1994. In the midst of the violence of the L.A. riots, Daniel and his mother make a new friend. (I: 6–12)

*Burton, Virginia Lee. *The Little House.* Houghton Mifflin, 1942/1978. As the city grows up around a little house, the house longs to be in the country again. (I: P–8)

*Carle, Eric. *The Very Busy Spider.* Philomel, 1985. In this carefully crafted predictable book, the very busy spider is too busy to take time for the other animals. (I: P–8)

*Cherry, Lynne. *A River Ran Wild.* Harcourt, 1992. Six centuries of change and development are depicted in this story of the Nashua River. (I: 6–12)

*Collier, Bryan. *Uptown.* Holt, 2000. This tour of Harlem is made distinctive through repetitive language and eye-catching illustrations. (I: 8–12)

*Cox, Judy. *Rabbit Pirates: A Tale of the Spinach Main.* Illustrated by Emily Arnold McCully. Harcourt, 1999. Former pirate rabbits, now creatures of peace, must use their wits when their restaurant is threatened by Monsieur Reynard, the fox. (I: 7–11)

Creech, Sharon. *Walk Two Moons.* HarperCollins, 1994. Salamanca Tree Hiddle travels from Ohio to Idaho with her eccentric grandparents in an attempt to understand why her mother left her. (I: 10–YA)

Fleischman, Paul. *Joyful Noise.* Illustrated by E. Beddows. HarperCollins, 1988. This distinctive collection of poems for two voices focuses on insects. (I: 8–YA)

————. *Whirligig.* Holt, 1998. When Brent's car accident results in the death of a young girl, he has an opportunity to redeem himself by building whirligigs and placing them in the four corners of the United States. (I: YA)

*Fleming, Denise. *In the Tall, Tall Grass.* Holt, 1995. From caterpillars and ants to rabbits and bats, a boy explores the world of the animals who live in the tall grass in his backyard. (I: P–7)

*Graham, Bob. *Queenie, One of the Family.* Candlewick, 1997. When Queenie the hen is returned to the farm, the story seems to be over—except for the many surprising twists still to come. (I: P–8)

*Gray, Libba Moore. *Small Green Snake.* Illustrated by Holly Meade. Orchard, 1994. This story of a lively little snake is told in equally lively language. (I: P–7)

*Hamilton, Virginia. *The Girl Who Spun Gold.* Illustrated by Leo and Diane Dillon. Blue Sky Press,

2000. In this West Indian variant of "Rumplestiltskin," a peasant girl's mother tells the King her daughter can spin gold thread. (I: P–8)

*Heide, Florence Parry, and Judith Heide Gilliland. *The Day of Ahmed's Secret.* Illustrated by Ted Lewin. Lothrop, 1990. All day, young Ahmed drives his cart through the streets of Cairo, looking forward to the time when he can share his secret with his family. (I: 7–10)

*Janeczko, Paul B. *Stone Bench in an Empty Park.* Photographs by Henri Silberman. Orchard, 2000. This collection of haiku celebrates the natural beauty found on everyday city streets. (I: 10 and up)

*Johnson, Dinah. *Sunday Week.* Illustrated by Tyrone Geter. Holt, 1999. The author takes readers through the activities and chores of a week in this celebration of an African American community. (I: P–8)

*Kroll, Virginia. *Masai and I.* Illustrated by Nancy Carpenter. Four Winds, 1992. An African American girl discovers the similarities and differences between her life and the life of a Masai girl. (I: 7–10)

*Lowell, Susan. *The Bootmaker and the Elves.* Illustrations by Tom Curry. Orchard, 1997. This "western" retelling of the *Shoemaker and the Elves* is filled with colorful language and hilarious details. (I: 6–10)

*Lyon, George Ella. *Who Came Down That Road?* Illustrated by Peter Catalonotto. Orchard, 1992/1996. While on a walk, a boy asks his mother, "Who came down this path?" She tells the history of the path, tracing it back through his grandparents, Union soldiers, elk, pioneer settlers, Native Americans, and Ice Age animals, to the beginning of time. (I: P–8)

*Macaulay, David. *Black and White.* Houghton Mifflin, 1990. Four stories are intertwined in one in this cleverly crafted book. (I: 6–10)

MacLachlan, Patricia. *Skylark.* HarperCollins, 1994. A sequel to *Sarah, Plain and Tall,* in which a severe drought forces Sarah and the children to journey to Maine. (I: 9–12)

*Mazer, Anne. *The Salamander Room.* Illustrated by Steve Johnson. Knopf, 1991. A little boy tells his mother how he will turn his room into the perfect home for the little orange salamander he wants to keep for a pet. (I: P–8)

McKissack, Patricia C., and Fredrick L. McKissack. *Christmas in the Big House, Christmas in the Quarters.* Scholastic, 1994. Christmas in the big house is compared to Christmas in the slave quarters in the year before the Civil War breaks out. (I: 9–12)

Myers, Walter Dean. *Monster.* Illustrated by Christopher Myers. HarperCollins, 1999. The story of Steve, accused of being an accomplice in a robbery that culminates in a murder, is written in both script and journal format. (I: 11–YA)

*Nichol, Barbara. *Beethoven Lives Upstairs.* Illustrated by Scott Cameron. Orchard, 1994. Through the exchange of letters with his uncle, a young boy comes to see Beethoven, his upstairs neighbor, in a new light. (I: 8–11)

*Polacco, Patricia. *The Keeping Quilt.* Simon & Schuster, 1988. An immigrant family makes a quilt that is used for celebrations in subsequent generations. (I: 6–10)

*Rosen, Michael J. *Elijah's Angel.* Illustrated by Aminah Brenda Lynn Robinson. Harcourt, 1992. Michael's family helps him to understand that the gifts of friendship transcend cultural gaps. (I: 8–12)

*Rylant, Cynthia. *In November.* Illustrated by Jill Kastner. Harcourt, 2000. Using lyrical language, Rylant describes special joys associated with November and the coming of winter. (I: 5–10)

———. *Special Gifts.* Illustrated by Wendy Anderson Halperin. Simon & Schuster, 1999. Lily, Rosie, and Tess live with their Aunt Lucy. Each girl has a distinctive perspective on the world, which helps to make their winter vacation a special one. (I: 6–9)

Sachar, Louis. *Holes.* Farrar, 1998. When Stanley is sent to a work camp for a crime he did not commit, he assumes that he is the victim of the family curse and never dreams that he will have the opportunity to finally break the curse. (I: 10–14)

*Say, Allen. *Grandfather's Journey.* Houghton Mifflin, 1993. A young man recounts the unique cross-cultural experience his family had living in Japan and America. (I: 6–10)

*Scieszka, Jon. *The Stinky Cheese Man and Other Fairly Stupid Tales.* Illustrated by Lane Smith. Viking, 1992. A wacky collection of folktale spin-offs. (I: 6–10)

Sebestyen, Ouida. *Out of Nowhere.* Orchard, 1994. Abandoned by his mother, a boy finds a way to build a new family. (I: 10–YA)

*Seymour, Tres. *Hunting the White Cow.* Illustrated by Wendy Anderson Halperin. Orchard, 1993. A young girl living on a farm in Kentucky tries to catch the white cow that her daddy, her uncles, and their friends have been unable to catch. (I: P–8)

*Shulevitz, Uri. *One Monday Morning.* Scribner, 1974. A little boy in a tenement house imagines the members of a royal court coming to visit him each day in an otherwise dull week. (I: P–8)

*Stanley, Diane. *Raising Sweetness*. Illustrated by G. Brian Karas. Putnam, 1999. After the sheriff adopts Sweetness and seven other orphans, life seems to be going well—except for the sheriff's cooking and housekeeping. This humorous story is filled with rich Texas colloquialisms. This is the sequel to *Saving Sweetness* (1996). (I: 5–8)

*Taulbert, Clifton L. *Little Cliff and the Porch People*. Illustrated by E. B. Lewis. Dial, 1999. When Little Cliff sets out through the neighborhood to get butter for the candied sweet potatoes, he makes an unexpected discovery about community. (I: 6–10)

*Willard, Nancy. *Pish, Posh, Said Hieronymus Bosch*. Illustrated by Leo, Diane, and Lee Dillon. Harcourt, 1991. Strange creatures haunt Hieronymus Bosch's housekeeper. (I: 5–9)

*Wood, Audrey. *King Bidgood's in the Bathtub*. Illustrated by Don Wood. Harcourt, 1984. The members of the royal court try unsuccessfully all day to get the king out of the bathtub. (I: P–8)

*———. *The Napping House*. Illustrated by Don Wood. Harcourt, 1984. A child and her grandmother take a peaceful nap along with the family dog, cat, and a mouse—until a wakeful flea stirs things up. (I: P–8)

RESOURCES

Bromley, Karen D. *Webbing with Literature: Creating Story Maps with Children's Books*. Allyn & Bacon, 1991.

Harste, Jerome C., and Kathy G. Short, with Carolyn Burke. *Creating Classrooms for Authors: The Reading Writing Connection*. Heinemann, 1988.

Hill, Bonnie C., Nancy J. Johnson, and Katherine L. Schlick Noe. *Literature Circles and Response*. Christopher-Gordon, 1995.

Holland, Kathleen E., Rachael A. Hungerford, and Shirley B. Ernst, eds. *Journeying: Children Responding to Literature*. Heinemann, 1993.

Literature Study: Karen Smith's Classroom. Directed by Maryann Eeds, Carole Edelsky, Karen Smith, C. Penka, and B. Love. Center for Establishing Dialogue in Teaching and Learning, 1990.

Peterson, Ralph, and Maryann Eeds. *Grand Conversations: Literature Groups in Action*. Scholastic-TAB, 1990.

Raphael, Taffy E., Susan I. McMahon, Virginia J. Goatley, J. L. Bentley, F. B. Boyd, Laura S. Pardo, and Deborah A. Woodman. "Research Directions: Literature and Discussion in the Reading Program." *Language Arts* 69 (1992): 54–61.

Roser, Nancy L., and Miriam G. Martinez, eds. *Book Talk and Beyond: Children and Teachers Respond to Literature*. International Reading Association, 1995.

Wiencek, Joyce, and John F. O'Flahavan. "From Teacher-Led to Peer Discussions about Literature: Suggestions for Making the Shift." *Language Arts* 71 (1994): 488–98.

REFERENCES

Anzul, Margaret. "Exploring Literature with Children within a Transactional Framework." *Journeying: Children Responding to Literature*. Ed. Kathleen E. Holland, Rachael A. Hungerford, and Shirley B. Ernst. Heinemann, 1993, pp. 187–203.

Babbitt, Natalie. "Protecting Children's Literature." *Horn Book* 66 (1990): 696–703.

Bromley, Karen D. *Webbing with Literature: Creating Story Maps with Children's Books*. Allyn & Bacon, 1991.

———. "Enriching Responses to Literature with Webbing." *Book Talk and Beyond: Children and Teachers Respond to Literature*. Ed. Nancy L. Roser and Miriam G. Martinez. International Reading Association, 1995, pp. 90–101.

Byars, Betsy. *After the Goat Man*. Viking, 1974.

Carris, Joan. *Aunt Morbelia and the Screaming Skull*. Little, Brown, 1990.

———. *Just a Little Ham*. Little, Brown, 1989.

Cazden, Courtney. *Classroom Discourse: The Language of Teaching and Learning*. Heinemann, 1988.

Chambers, Aidan. *Booktalk: Occasional Writing on Literature and Children*. Harper, 1985.

Cianciolo, Patricia J. "Responding to Literature as a Work of Art—An Aesthetic Literary Experience." *Language Arts* 59 (1982): 259–64.

Eeds, Maryann, and Deborah Wells. "Grand Conversations: An Exploration of Meaning Construction in Literature Study Groups." *Research in the Teaching of English* 23 (1989): 4–29.

Farest, Cindy, and Carolyn Miller. "Children's Insights into Literature: Using Dialogue Journals to Invite Literary Response." *Examining Central Issues in Literacy Research, Theory, and Practice*. Ed. Donald J. Leu and Charles K. Kinzer. National Reading Conference, 1993, pp. 271–78.

Farrell, Edmund J., and James R. Squire. *Transactions with Literature: A Fifty-Year Perspective*. National Council of Teachers of English, 1990.

Farris, Pamela J. "Story Time and Story Journals: Linking Literature and Writing." *The New Advocate 2* (1989): 179–85.

Gonzalez, Veronica, Linda Fry, Sylvia Lopez, Julie Jordan, Cindy Sloan, and Diane McAdams. "Our Journey toward Better Conversations about Books." *Book Talk and Beyond: Children and Teachers Respond to Literature.* Ed. Nancy L. Roser and Miriam G. Martinez. International Reading Association, 1995, pp. 168–78.

Grover, W. *Dolphin Adventure.* Greenwillow, 1990.

Harste, Jerome C., and Kathy G. Short, with Carolyn Burke. *Creating Classrooms for Authors: The Reading Writing Connection.* Heinemann, 1988.

Hickman, Janet. "Response to Literature in a School Environment, Grades K through 5." Dissertation, Ohio State University, 1979.

———. "A New Perspective on Response to Literature: Research in an Elementary School Setting." *Research in the Teaching of English 15* (1981): 343–54.

Hoban, Lillian. *Arthur's Prize Reader.* Harper, 1978.

Hubbard, R. S., with N. Winterbourne, and J. Ostrow. "Visual Responses to Literature: Imagination through Images." *The New Advocate 9* (1996): 309–323.

Kelly, P. R. "Guiding Young Students' Response to Literature." *The Reading Teacher 43* (1990): 464–470.

Kelly, P. R., and N. Farnan. "Promoting Critical Thinking through Response Logs: A Reader-Response Approach with Fourth Graders." *Learner Factors/Teacher Factors: Issues in Literacy Research and Instruction.* Ed. Jerry Zutell and Sandra McCormick. National Reading Conference, 1991, pp. 277–84.

Kiefer, Barbara. "The Responses of Children in a Combination First/Second Grade Classroom to Picture Books in a Variety of Artistic Styles." *Journal of Research and Development in Education 16* (1983): 14–20.

Langer, Judith. "Rethinking Literature." *Literature Instruction: A Focus on Students' Response.* Ed. Judith A. Langer. National Council of Teachers of English, 1992, pp. 35–53.

Leppard, L. *Mandie and the Cherokee Legend.* Bethany House, 1983.

Martinez, Miriam, and Nancy L. Roser. "Children's Responses to a Chapter Book across Grade Levels: Implications for Sustained Text." *Multidimensional Aspects of Literacy Research, Theory, and Practice.* Ed. Charles K. Kinzer and Donald J. Leu. National Reading Conference, 1994, pp. 317–24.

———, and Nancy L. Roser. "The Books Make a Difference in Story Talk." *Book Talk and Beyond: Children and Teachers Respond to Literature.* Ed. Nancy L. Roser and Miriam G. Martinez. International Reading Association, 1995, pp. 32–41.

———, Nancy L. Roser, James V. Hoffman, and Jennifer Battle. "Fostering Better Book Discussions through Response Logs and a Response Framework: A Case Description." *Literacy Research, Theory, and Practice:*

Views from Many Perspectives. Ed. Charles K. Kinzer and Donald J. Leu. National Reading Conference, 1992, pp. 303–11.

McGee, Lea M. "An Exploration of Meaning Construction in First Graders' Grand Conversations." *Literacy Research, Theory, and Practice: Views from Many Perspectives.* Ed. Charles K. Kinzer and Donald J. Leu. National Reading Conference, 1992, pp. 177–86.

———. "Talking about Books with Young Children." *Book Talk and Beyond: Children and Teachers Respond to Literature.* Ed. Nancy L. Roser and Miriam G. Martinez. International Reading Association, 1995, pp. 105–16.

Mehan, Hugh. *Learning Lessons: Social Organization in the Classroom.* Harvard Univ. Press, 1979.

Nash, Marcia. "Leading from Behind: Dialogue Response Journals." *Book Talk and Beyond: Children and Teachers Respond to Literature.* Ed. Nancy L. Roser and Miriam G. Martinez. International Reading Association, 1995, pp. 217–25.

Peterson, Ralph, and Maryann Eeds. *Grand Conversations: Literature Groups in Action.* Scholastic-TAB, 1990.

Pierce, Meredith. *The Darkangel.* Atlantic Monthly, 1982.

Raphael, Taffy E., Virginia J. Goatley, Susan I. McMahon, and Deborah A. Woodman. "Teaching Literacy through Student Book Clubs: Promoting Meaningful Conversations about Books." *Book Talk and Beyond: Children and Teachers Respond to Literature.* Ed. Nancy L. Roser and Miriam G. Martinez. International Reading Association, 1995, pp. 66–79.

Raphael, Taffy E., Susan I. McMahon, Virginia J. Goatley, J. L. Bentley, F. B. Boyd, Laura S. Pardo, and Deborah A. Woodman. "Research Directions: Literature and Discussion in the Reading Program." *Language Arts 69* (1992): 54–61.

Rosenblatt, Louise M. *Literature as Exploration,* 3rd ed. Noble & Noble, 1938.

Roser, Nancy L., James V. Hoffman, and Cynthia Farest. "Language, Literature, and At-Risk Children." *The Reading Teacher 43* (1990): 554–59.

Saul, Wendy. "'What Did Leo Feed the Turtle?' and Other Nonliterary Questions." *Language Arts 66* (1989): 295–303.

Short, Kathy G., and Gloria Kauffman. "'So What Do I Do?' The Role of the Teacher in Literature Circles." *Book Talk and Beyond: Children and Teachers Respond to Literature.* Ed. Nancy L. Roser and Miriam G. Martinez. International Reading Association, 1995, pp. 140–49.

Wiencek, Joyce, and John F. O'Flahavan. "From Teacher-Led to Peer Discussions about Literature: Suggestions for Making the Shift." *Language Arts 71* (1994): 488–98.

Wollman-Bonilla, J. E., and B. Werchadlo. "Literature Response Journals in a First-Grade Classroom." *Language Arts 72* (1995): 562–70.

14 Literary and Content Units

Public School No.3

Once upon a time, in a land far away . . .

S o begin many old stories and a few contemporary ones as well. Jane Yolen (1977) once said that "stories lean on stories." Certainly such "leaning" is evident in old tales handed down from past generations. It is also evident in contemporary spin-offs such as *The True Story of the 3 Little Pigs!,* which author Jon Scieszka leaned squarely on the folktale "The Three Little Pigs."

In Chapter 3, we discussed intertextuality, the process of bringing knowledge of one text to make meaning of another. This is something mature readers do, and students can also be encouraged to read one story in light of another. Literature units are especially effective vehicles for encouraging students to make literary connections. In this chapter we explore ways of devising units to achieve this goal, as well as other important literary goals and content area goals.

In the first part of the chapter we discuss the creation of literary units—units designed to achieve literary goals. In the second part of the chapter we explore ways of using literature in content units—units that are concerned primarily with achieving goals related to social studies, science, math, and such. There may be commonalities in the ways that literary units and content units are organized and in some of the instructional activities used in each type of unit. What sets literary units and content units apart is their goals. In developing and implementing literary units, teachers are focused primarily on literary goals. That is, through the study of literature, teachers intend for their students to learn more about literature—about literary elements and devices, characteristics of genres, authors and illustrators, and themes explored through literature. By contrast, teachers organize content units to help students learn more about a particular content area. For example, a fifth-grade teacher might develop a unit incorporating children's literature that is designed to help children understand issues related to slavery. In a unit of this type, children may learn about slavery *through* literature (as well as other resources), but the primary goal is not to learn *about* literature.

Illustration 14.1

To encourage students to make intertextual links, teachers can pair *The True Story of the 3 Little Pigs!* with the story on which it is based—"The Three Little Pigs." (*The True Story of the 3 Little Pigs!* by Jon Scieszka. Text copyright © 1989 by Jon Scieszka. Illustration copyright © 1989 by Lane Smith. Used by permission of Viking Penguin, a division of Penguin Putnam, Inc.)

Although both types of units are important, in this chapter we emphasize literary units because we believe that for too long the literature curriculum has been neglected in the elementary school (Walmsley, 1992). Certainly, in recent years children's books have come to play an increasingly important role in elementary classrooms in the United States (Baumann, Hoffman, Moon, and Duffy-Hester, 1998), but we believe that even today tradebooks are used primarily as tools to teach reading or to achieve content goals. We believe that the time has come to broaden our goals to include literary ones as well.

LITERARY UNITS

In this section, we focus on the goals of literary units and ways of organizing such units. As you read about literary units (and later as you develop your own), you will want to draw on the information you have learned throughout this textbook—information about literary elements, about the ways in which picture books work, about particular children's authors, and about the various genres that have been highlighted.

The Power of Literary Units

Teachers often have students read or listen to individual stories, and at times this may be the best route to follow to achieve particular goals, but we would argue that there are also reasons for sometimes choosing to organize literature into units for literary study. Ralph Peterson and Maryann Eeds (1990) present evidence of the quality of responses that can be evoked when literature is presented in connected sets. They relate the story of a kindergarten teacher who read aloud three of Maurice Sendak's fantasies: *Where the Wild Things Are, In the Night Kitchen,* and *Outside Over There.* In the first book, *Where the Wild Things Are,* Max sails away from his home on a magic boat to "the land where the wild things are," where he proceeds to become the "king of all wild things." Soon, though, Max grows lonesome and chooses to sail back home. Mickey, the protagonist of *In the Night Kitchen,* wakes up one night to the clamorous noise of the night kitchen. Falling out of his bed and into the magical night kitchen, Mickey becomes a hero when he fashions a plane out of bread dough to fly over the Milky Way to procure the milk needed by the bakers in the night kitchen. Mickey's adventure comes to a conclusion as he tumbles back into bed. In the final fantasy, *Outside Over There,* young Ida, having discovered that her baby sister has been stolen by goblins, determines to go "outside over there," where she outwits the goblins to bring her baby sister safely home.

After sharing these three stories with her kindergartners, the teacher invited the children to talk about the commonalities they saw in the stories. This is what they observed (Peterson and Eeds, 1990, p. 26):

- Each book is circular.
- Each book is about a child who makes a trip to an unusual place.
- Each book portrays a powerful child.
- Each book shows a brave child.
- Each book portrays magic moves.
- Each book is scary.

Working with small groups, teachers can present a variety of literary units

Ask the Educator . . . *Nancy Roser*

What are the benefits of engaging children in literature units rather than simply presenting individual books?

Recently, I attended an exhibition in which paintings by Matisse hung next to those by Picasso. The exhibit helped me look more closely at and understand better two artists whose works occupied the same tradition and whose vibrant palettes and similar subjects formed a dialectic—each shaping and being shaped by the other. In a similar way, children understand and respond differently (and more deeply) when related pieces of literature are juxtaposed. When preschoolers or kindergartners, for example, are introduced to Rosemary Wells's *Timothy Goes to School* as well as Kevin Henkes's Wemberly (of *Wemberly Worried*), they are being given opportunity to see patterns and linkages in stories. They may recognize that if two story characters fret about school, maybe others do as well. The discovery that books share ideas or themes (and only a limited set of them!) need not be postponed until high school—or even until first grade.

Older children, too, tend to think, talk, and write differently when related books are pulled together into literature units—and when time is set aside for extended stays within a theme, a genre, or a particular author's works. Some books almost beg to be considered together. For example, children exploring the traits and antics of plucky heroes can connect with and compare Katherine Paterson's *Preacher's Boy* with the "never-say-quit" India Opal Buloni

---

Favorite Books as a Child

Almost every time I read one of these "what were your three favorite books as a child" questions, the answers always sound to me like baby geniuses (as in "I loved *Bridge to Terabithia*, *The Chronicles of Narnia*, and *A Wrinkle in Time*"). Truth is, I met favorite books long before I could read. I loved

■ *The Little Squeegy Bug* (the very first picture book by Bill Martin, Jr.—when Brown Bear wasn't yet a gleam in the author's eye)

■ *Miss Sniff* (who knows who wrote it, but the beautiful black-and-white cat had textured fur, a caretaker named Polly Pinks, and a green and pink room to sleep in)

■ *Pat and Penny*, two sisters with red hair who did everything together— just like Gayle and me.

In my house, we listened to and (at last) read those books until the covers loosened, the pages gave way, and Miss Sniff went bald from touching.

---

of Kate DiCamillo's *Because of Winn-Dixie*. Other units may join pieces of historical fiction with biography and relevant information text. Still others may lead to the discovery of the characteristics of genre, the exploration of story structures, or the appreciation and tracking of tale variants. In any case, good literature units almost guarantee surprising reflections and rich talk.

Further, opportunities to think and talk about books drawn into literature units mean that all learners have entry into the curriculum: When the emphasis is on connecting literature and connecting with literature, no one need be denied access because of reading level. (I know little about art, but I made my own levels of discoveries in the Matisse and Picasso exhibit.)

Finally, when teachers and children share and study related pieces of literature, they seem more likely to give credence to literature in its own right rather than to treat it as an endless source of vocabulary and spelling words, parts of speech, answers to questions, or impetus for "activity." In a study of children and literature units, my colleagues and I found that those who were involved with literature units knew more about books, wrote and talked more insightfully, and read at higher levels than children who did not have literature study in their classrooms. So pull books together. There is strength in unity.

Nancy Roser is not a children's book author. Rather, she teaches teachers at the University of Texas at Austin to rely on children's books in classrooms as fodder for discussion, inspiration for writing, sources of enjoyment, and for learning.

These children did impressive thinking in response to their teacher's invitation to compare Sendak's three stories. Would they have made such perceptive comments if they had listened to only one of the stories? We don't think so; rather, we would argue that it is the power of the literature *unit* that yielded such insightful commentary by kindergartners. Researchers have confirmed that children sometimes read books in light of other books they have read (Farest and Miller, 1993; Short, 1992; Sipe, 1998). Perhaps the best way of encouraging children to make such connections across books is by having them read (or listen to) and talk about books that are linked in one way or another.

Educators have recommended author study, genre study, and thematic study as approaches that encourage students to engage in higher levels of thinking in response to literature (Martinez and Roser, in press), and anecdotal evidence suggests that a unit approach to literature study is indeed effective (e.g., Madura, 1995). For example, Joy Moss (1978) includes in her descriptions of "focus units" rich anecdotal evidence of children's insights, increasing willingness to support their judgments, and "growing store of literary ideas" (p. 485).

Nancy Roser, James Hoffman, and Cindy Farest (1990) moved beyond anecdotal evidence in documenting the effectiveness of their Language to Literacy program, which provided books organized into literature units focusing on author, theme, topic, or genre. Teachers in seventy-eight classrooms read unit books aloud to approximately 2,500 primary-aged children whose first language was Spanish. The teachers modeled and encouraged children's responses and collected those responses on language charts designed to help the children discover the connections among the books. Roser and her colleagues reported significant changes in language arts scores, as well as in the range of literary connections recorded on the language charts (Roser, Hoffman, Farest, and Labbo, 1992).

Developing Different Types of Literary Units

Well-designed literary units provide rich contexts for children's literary learning. In this section, we will discuss four different types of literature units: genre units, author/illustrator units, literary element (or literary device) units, and thematic units. The distinctive goals of each type of literary unit are listed in Table 14.1.

Genre Units. One way of linking books for literary study is on the basis of genre. Through genre study, teachers can help students discover what is

Table 14.1   Goals of Different Types of Literature Units

Type of Unit	Goal of Unit
Genre unit	■ To explore the features of the focus genre that set it apart from other genres
Author/illustrator unit	■ To discover what is distinctive about the work of a particular author and/or illustrator
Literary element (or device) unit	■ To explore how authors develop and use literary elements or devices
Thematic unit	■ To explore a literary theme

Ask the Editor . . . *Judy O'Malley*

Judy O'Malley

What is your theoretical rationale for developing annotated lists of thematically linked books for classroom use?

Using trade books in the classroom can enhance children's understandings of all kinds of information by adding context and excitement to what might otherwise seem dry facts and formulas. However, it's important not to squeeze the juices out of otherwise compelling works of fiction, nonfiction, or poetry by forcing the literature into classroom units or activities. When a choice of genres and styles of literature is offered to children, they will find the titles that bring learning to life for them. Activities, discussion, and the use of other media can all enhance and extend the pleasure of linking stories to children's interests—inside and outside the classroom. But such extensions of the joy of reading and learning need to be integral to the book, not artificial or contrived. Most of the articles that appear in *Book Links* are contributed by teachers and librarians who have "track tested" these books, web sites, and activities in their own classrooms and libraries. We know our readers will use our thematic bibliographies as templates, adapting and fine-tuning them to the needs and interests of their own students and curriculum.

Unlike review journals, *Book Links* is able to connect new books with older titles and to present a mix of genres and approaches to appeal to varying needs, interests, and reading levels. In each issue, several articles present different approaches to a particular curriculum content area—history, science, multiculturalism, nature and the environment, language arts, geography, and the arts. In this way, we hope to offer a menu of approaches and materials to suit a wide range of ages and reading levels, as well as a variety of teaching and learning styles. The eagerness of educators and librarians to contribute their own ideas and book selections is wonderful affirmation of the practicality and flexibility of linking trade books to classroom lessons.

Judy O'Malley is the editor of Book Links: Connecting Books, Classrooms, and Libraries, *a Booklist Publication of the American Library Association. This bimonthly journal assists teachers, school library media specialists, public children's librarians, and parents in their efforts to connect quality children's trade books with the educational curriculum. Before assuming the position of Book Links Editor in November 1996, O'Malley was Associate Editor of General Publications for the H. W. Wilson Company, where she acquired and edited professional books for teachers and children's librarians. She now lives in Chicago, Illinois.*

> ### *Favorite Books as a Child*
>
> I delighted in the classics—or maybe just in adults' surprise that I enjoyed these works—at an early age. Among my favorites were
>
> ■ *Great Expectations* by Charles Dickens (and all his other works)
>
> ■ *Little Women* by Louisa May Alcott (and anything else by or about Alcott)
>
> ■ *Mythology: Timeless Tales of Gods and Heroes* by Edith Hamilton. I was an avid student of Greek mythology, so a well-thumbed copy of these retellings of ancient tales resided on my night table for many years.

distinctive about a particular genre—what sets it apart from other genres. For example, in a traditional literature unit centering on trickster tales, students might discover the following (among other things):

■ Trickster tales have been told around the world.

■ There are often clearly differentiated "good guys" and "bad guys" in trickster tales.

◼ In trickster tales, the character who sets out to do the tricking is all too often the one who is tricked.

◼ Trickster tales are typically filled with unexpected twists and humorous turns of events.

When students develop knowledge of this nature about a particular genre, it affects the way they approach stories. For example, a knowledgeable reader who is told a story is a tall tale will have very different expectations for that story than for a work of contemporary realistic or historical fiction.

In developing genre units, it is first necessary to determine the particular focus of the unit. This is an especially important step in creating a genre unit because of the diversity of books that may fall within a genre. For example, as we discussed in Chapter 5, traditional literature includes myths, legends, a variety of types of folktales, tall tales, and ballads. If you simply selected a story representing each of these subtypes, your unit would contain such a hodgepodge of stories that children would not likely be able to make any discoveries about the genre. Instead, it makes sense to develop units with a more cohesive focus. We will explore what this means by discussing some of the types of units you might build around two different genres.

Because of its diversity, traditional literature lends itself to a variety of engaging ways of organizing literature study. For example, in Chapter 5, you learned about various categories of traditional literature, one of which is the folktale. Within the category of folktale, there are still more types: animal stories, trickster tales, pourquoi tales, tall tales, legends, cumulative tales, fairy tales, hero tales, and numskull tales. Any of these subtypes can provide the underlying link for the study of traditional literature. For example, if they read and compare a variety of fairy tales, students are likely to discover that tales such as "Cinderella," "Snow White and the Seven Dwarfs," and "Rumpelstiltskin" involve magic and that the magic often functions to reward ordinary people for their goodness and steadfastness.

You also learned in Chapter 5 that many works of traditional literature share common plot structures, which have been described by Vladimir Propp and by Joseph Campbell. The work of these scholars could serve as the basis for organizing traditional literature study (though you wouldn't want to actually talk about these scholars with children). For example, you could bring together tales such as Emery Bernhard's *The Girl Who Wanted to Hunt,* Claire Martin's *Boots and the Glass Mountain,* and Vladimir Hulpach's *Ahaiyute and Cloud Eater* and guide your students to discover some of the elements of Campbell's hero cycle (see page 150) in these (and other) hero tales from around the world.

Illustration 14.3
Diane Stanley's *Saving Sweetness* is full of wild exaggeration and memorable colloquialisms. (*Saving Sweetness* by Diane Stanley, illustrated by G. Brian Karas. Copyright © 1996. Used by permission of Putnam Publishing Group Juvenile Books, a division of Penguin Putnam Inc.)

Culture is yet another basis for organizing traditional literature units. As you have learned, the traditional literature from a particular culture frequently shares common features. Through literature study, students can discover some of these distinctive features. For example, in a study of Scandinavian folklore, students could discover the trolls, giants, witches, and hags that frequently appear in tales from Scandinavia. Collections such as Asbjorsen and Moe's *East O' the Sun and West O' the Moon* and Lunge-Larsen's *The Troll with No Heart in His Body and Other Tales of Trolls from Norway* contain a host of Scandinavian tales. Similarly, through a unit devised around African folklore, students could discover that the trickster takes a variety of forms in African folklore; sometimes he is the spider, while in other tales he appears as the turtle or the hare.

Chapter 10 offers useful information for teachers who want to build units designed to help children discover some of the distinctive features of modern fantasy. For example, any of the subcategories of low fantasy can provide an undergirding link for the study of fantasy. For young children, you might devise a literature unit that features personified animals or personified toys. Older students could be invited to delve into a unit structured around Jon Scieszka's time-slip stories. Or by grouping books that feature outlandish characters or situations—books such as Linda White's *Comes a Wind,* Susan Pearson's *Well, I Never!,* Elizabeth Spurr's *The Long, Long Letter,* and Diane Stanley's *Saving Sweetness*—students could explore the use of exaggeration in modern fantasy.

Children need to develop a well-defined sense of how one genre differs from another. This understanding will influence their expectations for particular genres, which in turn will affect the ways in which they read and write these genres. Therefore, it makes sense to sometimes organize literature study on the basis of genres.

Author/Illustrator Units. Mature readers commonly have favorite authors. They are always on the lookout for that writer's next book and might not even wait for the paperback version to be published. Further, readers who are about to begin a new book by a familiar writer have expectations that help them to step into that writer's story world and, when reading, to make connections across the works of the writer. Understanding what sets particular writers apart from others often influences mature readers' book choices and expectations. Children can develop a similar sense of author (or illustrator). Those who discover the humor pervading James Marshall's *George and Martha* books might

---

Books to Include in a Unit on Folktale Spin-Offs

Yours Truly, Goldilocks
by Alma Flor Ada

The Jolly Postman or Other People's Letters
by Janet and Allan Ahlberg

Ruby
by Michael Emberley

Three Cool Kids
by Rebecca Emberley

Bubba, the Cowboy Prince: A Fractured Texas Tale
by Helen Kettleman

The Emperor's Old Clothes by Kathryn Lasky

Cinderella's Rat
by Susan Meddaugh

Once Upon a Time
by John Prater

The Frog Prince Continued by Jon Scieszka

The True Story of the 3 Little Pigs!
by Jon Scieszka

The House That Drac Built by Judy Sierra

Somebody and the Three Blairs
by Marilyn Tolhurst

Illustration 14.4
In *Nana Upstairs & Nana Downstairs*, Tomie dePaola explores the family links that bind generations. (*Nana Upstairs & Nana Downstairs* by Tomie dePaola. Copyright © 1998. Used by permission of Putnam Publishing Group Juvenile Books, a division of Penguin Putnam Inc.)

seek out other books by this author. Those who discover the vivid colors and lively language of Denise Fleming's books know just what to look for in new books created by this author/illustrator.

Patricia Bloem and Anthony Manna (1999) engaged second- and fourth-graders in a study of Patricia Polacco's books to help them discover what Polacco does as a writer and illustrator that gets them to think and feel the way they do. The researchers read Polacco stories aloud, modeled questions they had about Polacco's work, invited the children to share their own questions, and finally had the children conduct an author interview by telephone. Bloem and Manna found that the students responded aesthetically in rich and diverse ways, and over the course of the unit, they found a shift in children's questions from being text-based to revealing connections they were making with Polacco and with her books. The children "delighted in the nuances of the texts, and found great pleasure, at the end of the project, in learning ways that the texts reflected Polacco's history and recorded her family stories" (p. 806).

When a teacher engages students in author or illustrator study, the teacher is helping them to build a store of knowledge about the ways in which particular authors (or illustrators) work. It is through such study that children discover what is distinctive about the work of particular authors and/or illustrators. For example, children who have had the opportunity to explore the story worlds of Steven Kellogg through a literary unit built around this author/illustrator's work are likely to discover that Kellogg usually writes fast-paced and humorous story lines, that he often fills his stories with bigger-than-life characters—be they great Danes, the Loch Ness monster, imaginary Skogs, or legendary characters such as Paul Bunyan—and that he draws illustrations filled with details (which are often hilarious). Students who have explored Steven Kellogg's story worlds through a literature unit are likely to look forward to new books by this author/illustrator.

It is relatively easy to characterize the work of some authors or illustrators because they consistently work in the same genre, repeatedly explore particular types of themes, or write in a relatively consistent style. However, others may have a large and quite diverse body of work. In organizing literature study of a writer whose works vary widely, it may be helpful to narrow the focus of study. For example, a writer such as Tomie dePaola has published many books in widely diverse genres including fantasy, folktales and legends, informational books, realistic fiction, and wordless picture books. Although it would be legitimate to introduce children to the range of this author/illustrator's work in a literature unit, it would make sense to group his works for exploration within the unit. For example, the literature study might start with an investigation of some of dePaola's realistic stories that draw heavily on his own experiences as a child: *Nana Upstairs & Nana Downstairs, Watch Out for the Chicken Feet in Your Soup, Tom, The Art Lesson, The Baby Sitter,* and *26 Fairmount Avenue.* The unit could then move on to explore dePaola's fantasies featuring Strega Nona and Big Anthony, before again moving on to feature some of the folktales and legends retold by this author/illustrator.

Literary Elements and Devices. Teachers can link books in such a way as to help students make discoveries about particular literary elements or literary devices. For example, a teacher might create a unit featuring stories such as Arthur Yorinks's *Hey, Al!,* Chris Van Allsburg's *The Polar Express,* and Maurice Sendak's *Where the Wild Things Are,* in all of which characters take enchanted journeys—a device that is frequently used by fantasy writers. To explore stock characterization, a teacher might link books such as William Steig's *Doctor De*

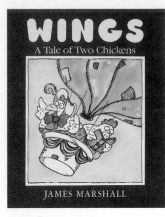

Illustration 14.5

James Marshall's *Wings: A Tale of Two Chickens* can be included in a unit featuring sly foxes or in one featuring humorous stories. (Illustration from *Wings: A Tale of Two Chickens* copyright © 1986 by James Marshall. Published in the U.S. by Viking Penguin. All rights reserved. Used with permission)

Soto, James Marshall's *Wings: A Tale of Two Chickens,* and Mary Jane Auch's *Peeping Beauty,* all of which feature foxes who are sly and untrustworthy. To guide students in exploring plot structure, a teacher might feature books with a cumulative structure such as Jeanette Winter's *The House That Jack Built* and Audrey Wood's *The Napping House.* As students develop a conscious awareness of how writers use such literary devices, they are likely to want to experiment with these same devices in their own writing. The information in Chapter 2 can be used to develop units of this type.

Thematic Units. Because literature is about life, units organized around literary themes have great potential to help students understand what it means to be human. As Joy Moss (1994) has observed, "literary transactions enable readers to enter into the lives of others, to live through their experiences, to see the world through their eyes. In the process, readers have opportunities to gain insights about human experience and to learn about feelings and motivation and relationships" (p. 5). Literary themes such as "Celebrations," "Memories," "Journeys," "Imagination," "Courage," "Making a Difference," and "Hopes and Dreams" offer rich potential for exploring the human experience.

After participating in this type of thematic study, students are likely to emerge with a richer understanding of that theme. For example, in a unit focused on courage, a teacher might choose to include books such as Nancy Luenn's *Nessa's Fish,* in which a girl stranded on the tundra must protect her sick grandmother and safeguard their store of fish; Karen Hesse's *Lester's Dog,* in which a young boy must face the dog he fears in order to save a kitten; and Ann Scott's *Brave as a Mountain Lion,* in which a boy must stand on stage during a spelling bee and face an auditorium full of people. Because the protagonists in the three books display different types of courage under very diverse circumstances, children's understanding of the full range of what it means to have courage is likely to be enriched.

Organizing Literary Units

Once you have decided on the type of unit you wish to create, the next tasks are to select the books for the unit and organize the unit.

Selecting Unit Books. It is legitimate to include picture books, chapter books, or some combination of the two in a unit. What is critical in selecting books for a literature unit is to find the right books—that is, books that are

---

Books to Include in a Unit on Imagination

All the Magic in the World
by Wendy Hartman

The Crooked Apple Tree
by Eric Houghton

Abel's Moon
by Shirley Hughes

Regards to the Man in the Moon
by Ezra Jack Keats

A Mammoth Imagination
by Philip Ross Norman

A Rumbly Tumbly Glittery Gritty Place
by Mary Lyn Ray

The Squiggle
by Carole Lexa Schaefer

Books to Include in a Unit on Celebrations

An Amish Christmas by Richard Ammon	**The Bravest Flute** by Ann Grifalconi	**Moon Festival** by Ching Yeung Russell
Powwow by George Ancona	**Day of the Dead** by Tony Johnston	**On Mardi Gras Day** by Fatima Shaik
Vejigante: Masquerader by Lulu Delacre	**An Island Christmas** by Lynn Joseph	**Celebration!** by Jane Resh Thomas
The World's Birthday: A Rosh Hashanah Story by Barbara Diamond Goldin	**Festivals** by Myra Cohn Livingston	

clearly connected to the undergirding concept of the unit. The lists of recommended books in this text can serve as one source for locating unit books. Colleagues or the school librarian might be able to provide further suggestions. In addition, there will be times when you will need to rely on various book selection aids to locate connected books. These aids include books such as *Adventuring with Books* (Pierce, 2000) and journals such as *Book Links*. Each of these aids is organized by subject, and *Adventuring with Books* is also organized by genre. See Appendix D of this text for a list of other useful book selection aids and Appendix F for a list of helpful web sites.

Unit Structure. Although we will describe various ways of organizing units, there really is no one best way. When you are planning your own literary units, there is no reason not to use variations of the ones we describe or create a new structure that will enable you to pursue the literary goals of your unit.

Nancy Roser, James Hoffman, and Cindy Farest (1990) devised an easy-to-use organizational structure for picture book units in their Language to Literacy Program. Their units revolve around ten related picture books, one of which is read aloud each day over a two-week period, though of course the length of units can vary. This structure works especially well with younger children who might not yet be reading or who might not yet have the reading skills to read more complex books on their own.

Joy Moss (1984) devised a somewhat different format for picture book units that she has termed "focus units." In a focus unit that centers on picture books, a daily read-aloud by the teacher is the central activity. However, children also independently read books related to the focus of the unit.

In Language to Literacy chapter book units, students are engaged simultaneously with two linked books. One book is read aloud daily by the teacher on a chapter-by-chapter basis. Students read the second book independently, pacing their reading through use of a pacing guide provided by the teacher. At the end of the unit, activities such as discussion or the completion of a Venn diagram provide students with the opportunity to make connections across the two books.

In a focus unit centering on chapter books, students are also engaged with more than one book. At the beginning of the unit, the teacher reviews an array of related books that will be available for independent reading, and students select two books each to read on their own. While the teacher reads a chapter book aloud daily on a chapter-by-chapter basis, students read their own two books independently, meeting periodically in small groups to compare the stories they are reading, in preparation for a full class discussion of all the unit books on the final day of the unit.

Unit Activities. In Chapters 12 and 13, we described a variety of activities that can support children's literary learning in the context of literature units. Children can record their personal responses to unit books in literature journals. To give children the opportunity to gather their thoughts in preparation for being active participants in literature discussion, the teacher can invite them to write in their journals immediately following a read-aloud. Journals can also be used with books the students read independently as part of the unit. Because discussion of these books is not likely to occur daily, students will want to draw on the ideas they recorded in the journals when they do meet in small groups or with the entire class to talk about the books.

Literature discussion should be an integral part of literature units. The teacher will want to invite students to join in conversations about unit books that are read aloud, as well as those that students read independently. When teachers participate in these discussions, they can use the tools we discussed in Chapter 13: open-ended questions and literary questions. While writing and discussion are especially widely used as response activities, teachers can also invite children to respond to literature through music, art, and drama.

Literature units are designed to help students make connections across a related set of books, and language charts are tools teachers can use to guide students in making connections across a set of books connected by theme, genre, author, or illustrator. In a picture book unit in which the teacher reads a new book each day, the teacher and students can turn to the language chart following open-ended discussion of the daily read-aloud, to record their thinking regarding how the book relates to the common elements undergirding the unit of study.

LITERATURE ACROSS THE CURRICULUM

For too long, conventional wisdom has held that the textbook is the primary vehicle through which children learn in the content areas. Indeed, textbooks can play an important role in instruction because they often provide a broad view of a topic. Yet textbooks should be just one of the many instructional resources that innovative teachers employ. Children's literature is an alternative resource that holds great potential for nurturing children's learning across the curriculum.

ISSUE TO CONSIDER

Should historical fiction have a place in social studies instruction?

Experts readily agree that well-researched and well-written biographies and informational trade books can enrich social studies instruction by providing a more in-depth and engaging look at various facets of history than textbooks typically do. Yet opinions differ regarding the place of historical fiction in social studies instruction. On one side are those concerned that children too readily believe that the fictional events portrayed in historical fiction actually occurred. In other words, children believe that they are reading history when they read historical fiction. This may be of particular concern with historical novels such as Pam Conrad's *Pedro's Journal* or Esther Forbes's *Johnny Tremain,* in which actual historical figures play a role in the story.

On the opposing side are those who argue that it is through historical fiction that history is most likely to come to life. In historical fiction, dry facts can be infused with the drama that is history. By reading historical fiction, children can begin to understand past events and issues as they may have actually been experienced by the people of earlier times. To help ensure that children understand that historical fiction is indeed fiction and should be read with a critical eye, teachers can invite children to examine the events portrayed in works of historical fiction in light of information they have gathered through informational sources.

What do you think?

Need for Children's Literature in the Content Areas

Textbooks dominate content area teaching and learning at all grade levels (Alvermann and Moore, 1991). Yet increasingly, educators are questioning this reliance on textbooks that critics claim have decreased in difficulty (Chall and Conard, 1991) and offer too much information with little depth (Tyson-Bernstein and Woodward, 1989). Further, the writing in textbooks often lacks clarity and richness in vocabulary and structure (Tomlinson, Tunnell, and Richgels, 1993). Perhaps the greatest indictment of textbooks relates to the superficial manner in which topics are often treated. One way of offsetting some of these limitations is by using trade books in the classroom. Well-written trade books engage children and make them want to keep reading; and when these books open new vistas for children, they encourage young readers to keep learning as well.

Literature can be incorporated into content instruction in different ways. A single book can be used to develop a concept, initiate interest in a topic, launch a project, or generate questions about a subject. For example, a teacher can read *The Doorbell Rang* by Pat Hutchins to introduce the concept of division. The story begins as two children are getting ready to divvy up twelve cookies their mother has just baked. They are pleased to discover that each one will get six cookies—until the doorbell rings and two more children arrive. As more and more friends appear on the doorstep, children will find that each child gets fewer and fewer cookies. Barbara Bash's *Urban Roosts,* which focuses on where city birds build their nests, can launch an investigation of the neighborhood surrounding the school, encouraging children to become careful observers of their own environment. Aliki's *Wild and Woolly Mammoths* can be used to initiate a unit of study on ancient animals. Trade books can also serve as valuable companions to textbooks. For example, in a study of ecosystems, textbooks are likely to offer only a broad overview. Trade books can provide the detailed examples of ecosystems. Barbara Bash has written a series on trees that offers wonderfully fleshed-out examples of ecosystems. Titles in this series include *Tree of Life, Ancient Ones, Desert Giant,* and *In the Heart of the Village.*

Organizing Literature-Based Content Units

Although there are numerous ways in which children's literature can be incorporated into the curriculum, in this section we will highlight the use of trade books in literature-based units. We will illustrate the process of selecting books

---

Books to Use in a Unit on Slavery in America

A Picture Book of Frederick Douglass
by David Adler

A Picture Book of Harriet Tubman
by David Adler

Anthony Burns: The Defeat and Triumph of a Fugitive Slave
by Virginia Hamilton

Sweet Clara and the Freedom Quilt
by Deborah Hopkinson

Christmas in the Big House, Christmas in the Quarters
by Patricia C. McKissack and Fredrick L. McKissack

Jip: His Story
by Katherine Paterson

Pink and Say
by Patricia Polacco

Mine Eyes Have Seen
by Ann Rinaldi

A School for Pompey Walker
by Michael J. Rosen

Minty: A Story of Young Harriet Tubman
by Alan Schroeder

Irene Jennie and the Christmas Masquerade: The Johnkankus
by Irene Smalls

A Strawbeater's Thanksgiving
by Irene Smalls

Follow the Drinking Gourd
by Jeanette Winter

Journey to Freedom: A Story of the Underground Railroad
by Courtni C. Wright

Books to Include in a Unit on Medieval Times

A Medieval Feast by Aliki	*Fourteenth-Century Towns* by John D. Clare	*The Ramsay Scallop* by Frances Temple
The Duke and the Peasant: Life in the Middle Ages by Sister Wendy Beckett	*Catherine, Called Birdy* by Karen Cushman	*Castle Diary: The Journal of Tobias Burgess, Page* by William Platt
Stephen Biesty's Cross-Sections Castle by Stephen Biesty	*The Midwife's Apprentice* by Karen Cushman	*The Executioner's Daughter* by Laura E. Williams
	The Door in the Wall by Marguerite de Angeli	

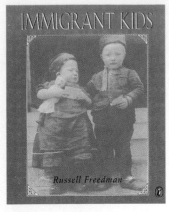

Illustration 14.6
In *Immigrant Kids,* Russell Freedman explores the experience of child immigrants from Europe through photographs and text. (*Immigrant Kids* by Russell Freedman. Copyright © 1995. Used by permission of Puffin Books, a division of Penguin Putnam Inc.)

and structuring a literature-based content unit by describing a social studies unit focused on immigration.

Literature is an especially powerful tool in social studies instruction because students must develop historical or social empathy to develop social studies understandings (Tomlinson, Tunnell, and Richgels, 1993). Children's literature is a logical way of helping students develop such empathy. Linda Levstik (1989) has observed that when literature is used in history instruction, students "encounter the complexities of historical events, where facts from the past become living, breathing drama, significant beyond their own time" (p. 136).

Determining Unit Goals. The first step in planning a literature-based content unit involves outlining the facets of the topic that will be explored. The web in Figure 14.1 identifies some key facets that might be explored through a unit entitled "Coming to America: Immigration across the Years." Students can discover some of the people who have immigrated to the United States across the years and some of the diverse reasons they have come. They can learn about the actual journeys that immigrants have endured. In addition, they can explore what life has been (and is) like for immigrants in the United States, as well as what life has been like for those the immigrants left behind.

Selecting Unit Books. Literature-based content units frequently incorporate literature from diverse genres. An immigration unit would likely include historical fiction, contemporary realistic fiction, biography, informational books, poetry, and oral history. Reading in any of these genres is likely to stimulate children's questions about immigration, yet books from each diverse genre are likely to make their own special contributions to children's learning. For example, works of historical fiction and contemporary realistic fiction provide the drama of human experience. Hence, these particular genres are especially likely to help children develop historical empathy, especially when the book's protagonist is a child. Oral histories allow children to hear the voices of actual immigrants, and informational trade books will provide answers to many of the questions students raise about immigration. Some possible titles from different genres that could be used to explore the various facets of the unit "Coming to America" are listed in Table 14.2.

Figure 14.1
Students can explore various facets of the immigration experience in a literature-based content unit entitled "Coming to America."

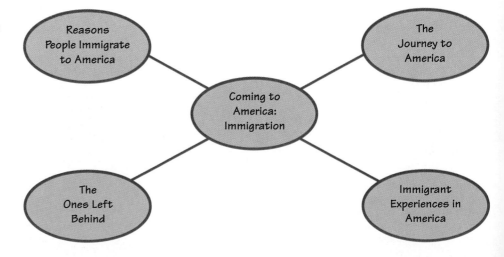

Table 14.2   Trade Books for Possible Use in an Immigration Unit

Genre	Title	Unit Facet
Historical fiction	*Letters from Rifka* (Hesse, 1992)	■ Journey to America ■ Reasons for immigrating
	Goodbye, Walter Malinski (Recorvits, 1999)	■ Immigrant experiences in America
	When Jessie Came across the Sea (Hest, 1997)	■ Journey to America ■ Immigrant experiences in America ■ Reasons for immigrating
Contemporary realistic fiction	*How Many Days to America?* (Bunting, 1988)	■ Journey to America
	Going Home (Bunting, 1996)	■ Immigrant experiences in America ■ Reasons for immigrating
	The Long Road (Garay, 1997)	■ Journey to America ■ Reasons for immigrating
Biography	*Hector Lives in the United States Now* (Hewett, 1990)	■ Immigrant experiences in America
	Lee Ann: The Story of a Vietnamese-American Girl (Brown, 1991)	■ Immigrant experiences in America
	Journey to Ellis Island (Bierman, 1998)	■ Journey to America
Informational books	*Immigrants* (Sandler, 1995)	■ Journey to America ■ Immigrant experiences in America
	Immigrant Kids (Freedman, 1980)	■ Journey to America ■ Immigrant experiences in America
Poetry	*Celebrate America in Poetry and Art* (Panzer, 1994) (selected poems)	■ Immigrant experiences in America
	My Name Is Jorge: On Both Sides of the River (Medina, 1999)	■ Immigrant experiences in America
Oral history	*I Was Dreaming to Come to America* (Lawlor, 1995)	■ Multiple facets

In seeking literature for literature-based content units, you can use the lists of recommended books found in this text. It is likely that you will also need to turn to various book selection aids to locate unit books. *Book Links*, a publication of the American Library Association, is an especially helpful aid for identifying literature for content area units. See Appendix D of this text for a list of other useful book selection aids.

Unit Structure. There is no one best way to organize literature-based content units. But two organizational formats that have been recommended by educators are text sets and literature-based inquiry units.

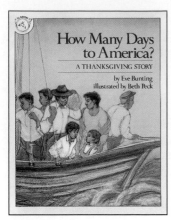

Illustration 14.7

In *How Many Days to America?: A Thanksgiving Story,* Eve Bunting explores the significance of Thanksgiving to a contemporary immigrant family. (*How Many Days to America?* by Eve Bunting, illustrated by Beth Peck. Jacket art copyright © 1988 by Beth Peck. Reprinted by permission of Clarion Books/ Houghton Mifflin Company. All rights reserved.)

Myra Zarnowski (1993) describes the use of text sets to engage students in the study of content area topics. She outlines three steps involved in creating and implementing this organizational plan. Step one is creating and introducing the text set. Text sets are collections of related books that focus on a particular facet of the topic under study. These collections of books are intended to "spark conversation and provide many opportunities for comparison and contrasts" (p. 36). Books in a set can be pulled from different genres and can be written at varied levels of difficulty. Table 14.3 contains possible text sets for our sample unit, "Coming to America." Over the course of the unit of study, text sets can grow as the teacher and students find new material on the topic that they want

Table 14.3   Sample Text Sets for a Unit on Coming to America

Topic of Text Set	Titles in Text Set
Journey to America	*A Journey to the New World: The Diary of Remember Patience Whipple* (Lasky, 1996)
	Across the Wide Dark Sea (Van Leeuwen, 1995)
	The Cat Who Escaped from Steerage (Mayerson, 1990)
	An Ellis Island Christmas (Leighton, 1992)
	Watch the Stars Come Out (Levinson, 1985)
	When Jessie Came across the Sea (Hest, 1997)
	If Your Name Was Changed at Ellis Island (Levine, 1993)
	Hannah's Journal: The Story of an Immigrant Girl (Moss, 2000)
Immigrant Experiences in America	*In the Year of the Boar and Jackie Robinson* (Lord, 1984)
	Klara's New World (Winter, 1992)
	Grandfather's Journey (Say, 1993)
	Together in Pinecone Patch (Yezerski, 1998)
	Immigrant Kids (Freedman, 1980)
	A Day's Work (Bunting, 1994)
	Hoang Anh: A Vietnamese-American Boy (Hoyt-Goldsmith, 1992)
Those Left Behind	*Letters from Rifka* (Hesse, 1992)
	When Jessie Came across the Sea (Hest, 1997)
	Buba Leah and Her Paper Children (Ross, 1991)
	Mama, Across the Sea (Godard, 1998)
	The Trip Back Home (Wong, 2000)

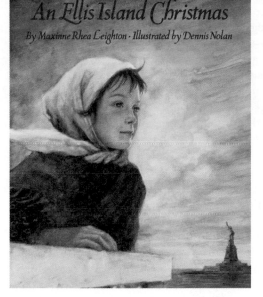

Illustration 14.8
In Maxinne Rhea Leighton's *An Ellis Island Christmas,* an immigrant family faces the threat of not being admitted into the United States. (*An Ellis Island Christmas* by Maxinne Rhea Leighton, illustrated by Dennis Nolan. Copyright © 1994. Used by permission of Puffin Books, a division of Penguin Putnam Inc.)

to add. Zarnowski recommends a brief introduction of each set so that students can choose a study group. These introductions can also help students to decide which books in the text set they want to read.

Study groups meet several times each week. Students prepare for their groups by reading books from their text set and writing journal entries that record ideas, responses, or information that they found interesting and might want to discuss. Group discussions begin with students sharing from their journals.

In the final phase of the investigation, students meet with people from beyond the classroom community to explore their topic in more depth. For example, in a "Coming to America" unit, students might meet with recent immigrants to discuss their experiences with immigration, or they might meet with representatives from the Immigration and Naturalization Service to learn more about the process of immigration. In preparation for these conversations that move beyond the classroom community, students write personal essays related to their topic of study.

Nancy Roser and Susan Strecker (in press) recommend a plan for developing literature-based inquiry units for social studies instruction. The units that they describe are organized into three phases, with each phase lasting approximately two weeks, though these times can be modified to accommodate unit goals and students' interests. In Phase 1, students are involved in a whole-class read-aloud of a chapter book. If the social studies unit is historical in nature, the read-aloud selection is likely to be a piece of historical fiction or a biography. In our "Coming to America" unit, Karen Hesse's **Letters from Rifka** would be a good read-aloud choice to explore the actual experience of getting to America (see Table 14.2).

In Phase 2, Roser and Strecker recommend that students choose to join one of three or four small book clubs to read books that further explore the topic at hand. In a "Coming to America" unit, Phase 2 could be organized in different ways. All the book clubs might read chapter books that explore immigrants' experiences once they arrive in America. The teacher could select books of different difficulty levels to accommodate the different reading abilities that are likely to be represented in a class. Possible book club choices include Laurence Yep's **Dragon's Gate,** Bette Bao Lord's **In the Year of the Boar and Jackie Robinson,** and Helen Recorvits's **Goodbye, Walter Malinski.** As an alternative, instead of having the students explore the same topic in the second phase of the unit, the teacher could form small book clubs that explore different facets of the immigration topic. For example, one small group might choose to continue the exploration of the topic introduced in Phase 1: the experiences immigrants had coming to America. A second book club could explore experiences immigrants had on their arrival in the United States, and a third book club might explore what it was like for those the immigrants left behind. These groups could read and discuss either a chapter book or various picture books. Book clubs could meet either daily or several times a week. Because students read Phase 2 books on their own, they can prepare to participate in their book club discussions by writing in journals while reading. Students can then use journal entries to launch and support their discussions when they meet in small groups.

In the organizational scheme created by Roser and Strecker, the purpose of Phase 3 is to give students an opportunity to explore questions about the topic of study that have emerged during Phases 1 and 2. Phase 3 can be launched by having students once again meet as a whole class, this time to pose their wonderings and questions. An instructional strategy such as Donna Ogle's (1986) K-W-L can be used at this point. In the first phase of K-W-L (what I know), students brainstorm all that they have learned about the topic at hand (for example, immigration) while the teacher records what students know. In the next phase (what I want to know), students pose questions they still have about the topic of exploration, and the teacher records their questions on a chart. The final phase of K-W-L (what I learned) occurs once the students have completed their research.

Inquiry charts can also be used to launch Phase 3 of literature-based inquiry units (Hoffman, 1992). An inquiry chart lists students' questions in columns, with spaces in which they can later record answers they obtain from different sources (see Figure 14.2). Once students have posed questions they want to explore, they can join small inquiry groups to research the questions that are of greatest interest to them.

In this final phase of a literature-based inquiry unit, students turn to a variety of sources to find answers to their questions. Certainly informational trade books are likely to be an especially important resource. However, other sources might include the Internet, old newspapers, experts, and individuals who have personal experience with the topic at hand.

Figure 14.2
Students' questions can be organized in an inquiry chart on which they record the answers they find in the various sources used for research.

	Where do immigrants come from today?	Why do people come to America today?	Where do today's immigrants settle in America?	What work do immigrants do today?	How do immigrants become American citizens?
Immigrants by Martin Sandler					
Immigrant Kids by Russell Freedman					
Quilted Landscapes by Yale Strom					
Still a Nation of Immigrants by Brent K. Ashabranner					
From Exiles to Immigrants by Ronald Takaki					

TEACHING IDEAS

Experimenting with an Illustrator's Artistic Media. Children can gain a greater appreciation of an illustrator's work by trying their own hand at working in an illustrator's signature medium. Select an illustrator whose work your students especially enjoy. For example, young children typically delight in the artwork of Eric Carle, whose books are easily recognized by their unique painted tissue-paper collages. With your students, explore how Eric Carle creates his imaginative illustrations. Useful resources include the video *Eric Carle: Picture Writer* (1993) and the books *The Art of Eric Carle* (Carle, 1996) and *You Can Make a Collage* (Carle, 1998). Once children have studied the illustrator's techniques, they can create their own painted tissue-paper collages.

Connecting Children's Observations. Teachers typically design language charts to help students make important connections among books that the teachers believe are important. This is done by posing particular questions on the chart. For example, in a unit featuring transformation tales, the following questions might be included on a language chart: Who or what is transformed in the tale? Into what are they transformed? How does the transformation occur? Why does the transformation occur? Questions like these will guide students to notice patterns the teacher has previously identified as important. However, students often notice things to which the teacher has paid no attention. One way of inviting children to share their own "noticings" is by adding a final column to the language chart entitled "Other Things We Noticed."

Using Literature Units to Launch Writing. Literature units offer students the opportunity to take an in-depth look at some facet of literature—features associated with a particular genre, literary elements or devices, or themes that emerge from literature. Immersing students in literature in this way also prepares them to try out what they've discovered in their own writing. As a culminating activity in a literature unit, invite students to try out in their own writing what they've discovered writers doing in the just-completed literature unit. If students have been reading fantasies in which characters go on enchanted journeys, they can write their own fantasies using this literary device. Or after listening to and reading trickster tales, students can try their hand at writing a modern-day trickster tale.

EXPERIENCES FOR YOUR LEARNING

1. Author units are designed to help children discover what characterizes the work of a particular author or illustrator. While the primary means of achieving this end is by immersing children in the works of the writer, sometimes it is helpful to also pull certain types of biographical information into the unit. Biographical "facts" such as where or when the author was born are usually less pertinent than information that helps students see how the author's life experiences may have influenced his or her writing. Choose a writer and read a number of that person's books. Then, gather information about the writer's life by turning to a book such as *Children's Books and Their Creators* (Silvey, 1995) or *Something about the Author* (Nakamura, 1998; see Appendix D) or to the author's own web site (see Appendix F). What links (if any) can you discover between the writer's life story and his or her writing?

2. Teachers typically initiate literary study with at least some ideas about the types of links they want children to discover among the books in the unit. However, children are very capable of discovering connections on their own—sometimes connections that their teachers have not seen. Gather together a set of related books and share them with children. For example, you might choose several Cinderella variants such as *Sootface, The Egyptian Cinderella, Cendrillon,* and *Mufaro's Beautiful Daughters.* After reading the books to the children, ask them to brainstorm ways in which the stories are similar and ways in which they are different. In what ways did the children extend your own thinking about the books?

3. Units in which books are only loosely linked are less likely to evoke children's most insightful thinking. One way of helping to ensure that the books you have selected for a unit are linked in meaningful ways is by creating a language chart that might be used with the books. Working with a group of peers, select a theme that could be explored through literature. Themes such as "Celebrations" or "Journeys" offer rich opportunities for thematic study. Gather books that you believe might be appropriate for use in a unit and design a language chart for use with the books. Are the connections that you identified significant ones?

RECOMMENDED BOOKS

* indicates a picture book; I indicates interest level (P = preschool, YA = young adult)

Books about Imagination

*Hartman, Wendy. *All the Magic in the World.* Illustrated by Niki Daly. Dutton, 1993. Joseph the odd-job man shows Lena and her friends how to make magic out of the ordinary objects they find in their neighborhood. (**I:** P–8)

*Houghton, Eric. *The Crooked Apple Tree.* Illustrated by Caroline Gold. Barefoot Books, 1999. When two siblings move to a new home, a crooked apple tree provides the backdrop for their imaginative play. (**I:** P–8)

*Hughes, Shirley. *Abel's Moon.* DK Publishing, 1999. Inspired by the stories their father writes, Adam and Noah create their own adventures in the backyard. (**I:** P–8)

*Keats, Ezra Jack. *Regards to the Man in the Moon.* Macmillan, 1981. Louie shows his friends how, with a little imagination, junk can turn into a great adventure. (**I:** P–8)

*Norman, Philip Ross. *A Mammoth Imagination.* Little, Brown, 1992. Little Bonbon discovers that he can have more fun playing and using his imagination than spending his time eating like the other wild boars. (**I:** P–8)

*Ray, Mary Lyn. *A Rumbly Tumbly Glittery Gritty Place.* Illustrated by Douglas Florian. Harcourt, 1993. Where adults see an ugly old gravel pit, a little girl sees a myriad of possibilities. (**I:** P–8)

*Schaefer, Carole Lexa. *The Squiggle.* Illustrated by Pierr Morgan. Crown, 1996. With a simple string, a little girl transforms her class's walk to the park. (**I:** P–7)

Books about Celebrations

*Ammon, Richard. *An Amish Christmas.* Illustrated by Pamela Patrick. Atheneum, 1996. In this first-person narrative, the reader follows an Amish family through their two-day celebration of Christmas. (**I:** 6–10)

*Ancona, George. *Powwow.* Harcourt, 1993. This informational book highlights the largest Native American powwow in the United States, which is held annually in Crow Agency, Montana. (**I:** 7–11)

*Delacre, Lulu. *Vejigante: Masquerader.* Scholastic, 1993. Ramón has made his own masquerader costume for Carnival. Then, on the very first day of the 28-day celebration, his costume is ripped beyond repair. (**I:** 5–9)

*Goldin, Barbara Diamond. *The World's Birthday: A Rosh Hashanah Story.* Illustrated by Jeanette Winter. Harcourt, 1990. When his sister tells him that Rosh Hashanah is the time to celebrate the world's birthday, Daniel is determined to find a way to throw a birthday party for the whole world. (**I:** P–8)

*Grifalconi, Ann. *The Bravest Flute.* Little, Brown, 1994. The Mayan boy is to lead the New Year's Day parade of farmers into town, but weak from months of hard work, he fears that he will not have the strength to complete the journey. (**I:** 6–10)

*Johnston, Tony. *Day of the Dead.* Illustrated by Jeanette Winter. Harcourt, 1997. A family in a small Mexican town honors their dead loved ones on the Day of the Dead. (**I:** 5–9)

*Joseph, Lynn. *An Island Christmas.* Illustrated by Catherine Stock. Clarion, 1992. Preparations for Christmas on the island of Trinidad include picking red petals for the sorrel drink, mixing up the black currant cake, and singing along with the parang band. (**I:** 6–9)

*Livingston, Myra Cohn. *Festivals.* Illustrated by Leonard Everett Fisher. Holiday House, 1996. This collection of poetry features celebrations around the world. (**I:** 6 and up)

*Russell, Ching Yeung. *Moon Festival.* Illustrated by Christopher Zhong-Yuan Zhang. Boyds Mill, 1997. Ying and her grandmother prepare for their family's autumn celebration of the Moon Festival. (**I:** 6–10)

*Shaik, Fatima. *On Mardi Gras Day.* Illustrated by Floyd Cooper. Dial, 1999. This is a portrait of the Mardi Gras celebration in a close-knit African American community in New Orleans. (**I:** P–8)

*Thomas, Jane Resh. *Celebration!* Illustrated by Raul Colón. Hyperion, 1997. The family gathers for a special Fourth of July celebration. (**I:** 5–9)

Books Featuring Special People in Our Lives

*Bercaw, Edna Coe. *Halmoni's Day.* Illustrated by Robert Hunt. Dial, 2000. Jennifer is embarrassed to take her Korean-speaking grandmother to the school's Grandparents' Day until Halmoni shares a story with the class that shows how love can reach over generational and language barriers. (**I:** 7–10)

*Denslow, Sharon Phillips. *Riding with Aunt Lucy.* Illustrated by Nancy Carpenter. Bradbury, 1991. Walter and Leonard love to accompany Aunt Lucy on her exploring trips because they know they will discover something or someplace or somebody unexpected. (**I:** 5–9)

*Grifalconi, Ann. *Osa's Pride.* Little, Brown, 1990. When Osa becomes a little too proud, her grandmother creates a story cloth that gently teaches Osa a lesson. (**I:** 6–10)

*Grimes, Nikki. *My Man Blue.* Illustrated by Jerome Lagarrigue. Dial, 1999. This story of Blue and the boy he is determined to save from the inner-city streets is told through a collection of poems. (**I:** 8–12)

*Houston, Gloria. *My Great-Aunt Arizona.* Illustrated by Susan Condie Lamb. HarperCollins, 1997. Arizona was born in a small community in the Blue Ridge Mountains, where she dreamed of traveling to faraway places. She never left the area but became a teacher who touched the lives of many children by teaching them about the world. (**I:** 6 and up)

*Lorbiecki, Marybeth. *Sister Anne's Hands.* Illustrated by K. Wendy Popp. Dial, 1998. When Sister Anne,

an African American nun, goes to teach in a small Southern town in the 1960s, she helps her students to discover the joy of learning and the hatefulness of racism. (**I:** 6–10)

*Mitchell, Margaree King. *Uncle Jed's Barbershop.* Illustrated by James Ransome. Simon & Schuster, 1993. Despite all the adversity he encounters in the segregated South of the 1920s, Uncle Jed never gives up his dream of opening his own barbershop. (**I:** 9–12)

*Polacco, Patricia. *Thank You, Mr. Falker.* Philomel, 1998. Trisha's self-esteem plummets as each year of school passes and she fails to learn to read. Then her fifth-grade teacher discovers the secret that Trisha has struggled to hide and helps her become a reader. (**I:** 7–11)

*Rosen, Michael J. *Elijah's Angel.* Illustrated by Aminah Brenda Lynn Robinson. Harcourt, 1992. A boy's parents help him to reach across cultural boundaries when his friend Elijah gives him a special carving. (**I:** 8–YA)

*Wild, Margaret. *Our Granny.* Illustrated by Julie Vivas. Ticknor & Fields, 1994. A celebration of all kinds of grannies. (**I:** P–8)

Books by Lois Ehlert

*Ehlert, Lois. *Color Zoo.* HarperCollins, 1989. As they turn the pages, children see various shapes that unlayer to reveal different animal faces. Shape names and animal names are included. A related title is *Color Farm* (1990). (**I:** P)

*———. *Cuckoo: Cucú.* Harcourt, 1997. Cuckoo may be beautiful, but the other birds believe that she doesn't do her share of the work—until a fire threatens the seed crop. (**I:** P–8)

*———. *Feathers for Lunch.* Harcourt, 1990. A housecat hopes to catch one of the birds in the backyard for lunch, but all get away safely and the cat ends up with only feathers. Bird descriptions are included. (**I:** P–7)

*———. *Fish Eyes: A Book You Can Count On.* Harcourt, 1990. The text is narrated in the voice of a young child who imagines touring the underwater world and seeing brightly colored fish. This counting book includes the concept of "one more," as the guide fish is added to the count on each page. (**I:** P–6)

*———. *Market Day.* Harcourt, 2000. The reader is taken on a tour of the market in this tale told through folk art from Latin America. (**I:** P–7)

*———. *Moon Rope: A Peruvian Folktale/Un lazo a la luna: Una leyenda Peruana.* Harcourt, 1992.

A pourquoi tale in English and Spanish that explains why Mole lives in the ground and why we see Fox's likeness in the moon. (I: 6–10)

*——. *Nuts to You!* Harcourt, 1993. This is the simple story of the antics of school. (I: P–6)

*——. *Snowballs.* Harcourt, 1995. It's snowing and time to create and decorate snow people with all sorts of odds and ends. (I: P–6)

*——. *Top Cat.* Harcourt, 1998. When Top Cat's space is invaded by a new kitten, Top Cat decides to initiate the kitten into all his naughty ways. (I: P–6)

Folktale Spin-Offs

*Ada, Alma Flor. *Yours Truly, Goldilocks.* Illustrated by Leslie Tryon. Atheneum, 1998. The house warming for the three little pigs is threatened when two ferocious wolves show up. This spin-off is told through the exchange of a series of letters written by some familiar characters, including Goldilocks, Peter Rabbit, and Little Red Riding Hood. (I: 6–9)

*Ahlberg, Janet, and Allan Ahlberg. *The Jolly Postman or Other People's Letters.* Little, Brown, 1986. The jolly postman has mail—of all sorts, even junk mail—for some famous characters from folktales. (I: 6–10)

*Emberley, Michael. *Ruby.* Little, Brown, 1990. Ruby, a small mouse in a red cloak, sets out through the city streets to take her granny a batch of pies. Forgetting her mother's advice, Ruby talks to a smooth-talking cat that threatens to turn her grandmother into a meal. (I: 6–9)

*Emberley, Rebecca. *Three Cool Kids.* Little, Brown, 1995. These three goats live in an empty lot in the city. Their lot is overgrazed, and they long to move to the one across the street. But in the sewer under that street lives a fierce rat. (I: 6–9)

*Kettleman, Helen. *Bubba, the Cowboy Prince: A Fractured Texas Tale.* Illustrated by James Warhola. Scholastic, 1997. This modern-day Cinderella variant is set in Texas, where Bubba is the stepson of a wicked rancher. When Miz Lurleen, "the purtiest rancher in Texas," decides to throw a ball to find herself a real cowboy, it takes the help of a fairy godcow and some Texas magic to convert Bubba into the cowboy prince. Humor and western language make for a fun read-aloud. (I: 5–10)

*Lasky, Kathryn. *The Emperor's Old Clothes.* Illustrated by David Catrow. Harcourt Brace, 1999. When Farmer Henry stumbles across new finery cast off (by the emperor who wore no clothes), his new attire causes an uproar in the barnyard. (I: 6–10)

*Meddaugh, Susan. *Cinderella's Rat.* Houghton Mifflin, 1997. Readers learn of the misadventures of the rat that was turned into Cinderella's coachboy and of how the experience changed his life. (I: 6–10)

*Prater, John. *Once Upon a Time.* Candlewick, 1993. A little boy bemoans what promises to be an ordinary day—until a series of folktale characters appear on the landscape. (I: 6–9)

*Scieszka, Jon. *The Frog Prince Continued.* Illustrated by Steve Johnson. Viking, 1991. The Frog Prince isn't too happy in his marriage to the princess. So he sets off to find a witch who will turn him back into a frog. (I: 6–10)

*——. *The True Story of the 3 Little Pigs!* Illustrated by Lane Smith. Viking, 1989. The wolf tells his side of the story in this spin-off of "The Three Little Pigs." (I: All ages)

*Sierra, Judy. *The House That Drac Built.* Illustrated by Will Hillenbrand. Harcourt, 1995. Using the pattern of "The House That Jack Built," the author describes the house that Dracula built. (I: 6–9)

*Tolhurst, Marilyn. *Somebody and the Three Blairs.* Illustrated by Simone Abel. Orchard, 1990. In this upside down spin-off of "The Three Bears," Mr. and Mrs. Blair and Baby Blair go for a walk one morning, only to return home to find their home ransacked by Somebody—a bear, of course. (I: 5–8)

Trickster Tales

*Aardema, Verna. *Borreguita and the Coyote.* Illustrated by Petra Mathers. Knopf, 1991. Coyote is determined to have Borreguita for lunch, but the little lamb proves too clever for Coyote. (I: 5–9)

*Galdone, Paul. *The Monkey and the Crocodile: A Jataka Tale from India.* Houghton Mifflin, 1969/ 1987. Monkey convinces crocodile that he shouldn't eat him until he returns to the tree to get his heart, which is, after all, the tastiest part of him. (I: 5–8)

*Goble, Paul. *Iktomi and the Coyote.* Orchard, 1998. The prairie dogs think that Iktomi is their friend, but Iktomi has a different idea: baked prairie dog for lunch. (I: 5–9)

*Kimmel, Eric A. *Anansi Goes Fishing.* Illustrated by Janet Stevens. Holiday, 1992. The tables are turned when Anansi sets out to trick his friend into doing all the work. (I: P–8)

*McDermott, Gerald. *Coyote: A Trickster Tale from the American Southwest.* Harcourt, 1994. Coyote convinces the crows to teach him how to fly, and the crows agree. But when the crows grow tired of Coyote's boasting, they decide to teach him a lesson. (I: 5–8)

*———. *Zomo the Rabbit: A Trickster Tale from West Africa.* Harcourt, 1992. Zomo the Rabbit is portrayed here wearing an African dashiki. (I: 5–8)

*McKissack, Patricia. *Flossie and the Fox.* Illustrated by Rachel Isadora. Dial, 1986. Flossie turns the tables on Mr. Fox when he tries to get her basket of eggs. (I: 5–10)

*Souhami, Jessica. *The Leopard's Drum: An Asante Tale from West Africa.* Little, Brown, 1995. Humble tortoise outwits the boastful leopard to obtain the leopard's drum for the Sky-God. (I: 5–8)

*Stevens, Janet. *Tops and Bottoms.* Harcourt, 1995. Hare tricks lazy Bear by wheeling and dealing in the tops and bottoms of vegetables. (I: P–8)

Cinderella Variants

*Climo, Shirley. *The Egyptian Cinderella.* Illustrated by Ruth Heller. HarperTrophy, 1989. Rhodopis, a princess snatched from her home in Greece, is sold into slavery in Egypt. There she is befriended by a falcon and chosen by the Pharaoh to be his wife. This is one of the world's oldest Cinderella tales. (I: 8–12)

*Greaves, Margaret. *Tattercoats.* Illustrated by Margaret Chamberlain. Clarkson N. Potter, 1990. In this English version of the Cinderella story, Tattercoats sets out to the king's ball with the goose-boy. (I: 7–10)

*Han, Oki S. *Kongi and Potgi: A Cinderella Story from Korea.* Dial, 1996. Kongi's stepmother doesn't want her to go to the prince's ball, but Kongi's animal friends intervene to make Kongi's dream come true. (I: 8–11)

*Hooks, William. *Moss Gown.* Illustrated by Donald Carrick. Clarion, 1987. A Cinderella story from the author's native eastern North Carolina. (I: 7–10)

*Pollock, Penny. *The Turkey Girl: A Zuni Cinderella Story.* Illustrated by Ed Young. Little, Brown, 1996. This rich pourquoi tale with a moral about keeping one's word is also a valuable take on the Cinderella story, with breathtaking illustrations. (I: 7–9)

*San Souci, Robert D. *Cendrillon: A Caribbean Cinderella.* Illustrated by Brian Pinkney. Simon & Schuster, 1998. When Cendrillon's godmother discovers how much her goddaughter longs to go to the ball, she uses her magic to make the dream come true. (I: 9–12).

*———. *Sootface: An Ojibwa Cinderella Story.* Illustrated by Daniel San Souci. Doubleday, 1994. A mighty warrior with the power to make himself invisible decides to marry the woman who can see

him. Only Sootface, the youngest of three sisters, is able to see the warrior. (I: 8–11)

*———. *The Talking Eggs.* Illustrated by Jerry Pinkney. Dial, 1989. An African American variant of Cinderella. (I: 5–10)

*Steptoe, John. *Mufaro's Beautiful Daughters.* Lothrop, 1987. The humblest and kindest daughter gets the reward in this Caldecott winner. (I: 6–10)

Tomie dePaola Family Stories

*dePaola, Tomie. *The Art Lesson.* Putnam, 1989. Tommy loves to draw and is encouraged by his family to pursue his passion. But at school he encounters frustration until an understanding art teacher lends a helping hand. (I: P–8)

*———. *The Baby Sitter.* Putnam, 1996. Tommy is excited about the new baby sister who is coming, but he is not ready for the stern nana who comes to stay with him when his mother goes to the hospital. (I: P–8)

*———. *Nana Upstairs & Nana Downstairs.* Putnam, 1998. For young Tommy, Sundays were special, for that was when he visited his Nana Upstairs and Nana Downstairs. This is a story about family and remembering family. (I: 5–9)

*———. *Tom.* Putnam, 1993. Tommy is named after his grandfather Tom, and together the two share memorable times. (I: P–8)

———. *26 Fairmount Avenue.* Putnam, 1999. Memorable moments from a year in Tomie dePaola's boyhood fill the pages of this first chapter book. (I: 6–9)

*———. *Watch Out for the Chicken Feet in Your Soup.* Little Simon, 1985. His old-fashioned Italian grandmother embarrasses Joey—until he begins to see her through the eyes of his friend. (I: P–8)

Books about Courage

*Alexander, Sally Hobart. *Maggie's Whopper.* Illustrated by Deborah Kogan Ray. Macmillan, 1992. When Maggie's great uncle is threatened by a black bear, she draws on her quick wits and courage to save the day. (I: 6–9)

*Andrews, Jan. *Very Last First Time.* Illustrated by Ian Wallace. Margaret K. McElderry, 1985. The first time Eva goes under the ocean's ice to find mussels for her family, she must call on reserves of courage she never realized she had. (I: 6–10)

*Hesse, Karen. *Lester's Dog.* Illustrated by Nancy Carpenter. Crown, 1993. A young boy lives on the same street as a vicious and frightening dog that belongs to Lester. The boy is afraid to walk past

Lester's dog, but one day he must do just this to save a kitten. (**I:** P–8)

*Luenn, Nancy. *Nessa's Fish.* Illustrated by Neil Waldman. Atheneum, 1990. A brave Inuit girl defends her ailing grandmother and a cache of fish from marauding animals on the desolate ice. (**I:** 7–10)

Paterson, Katherine. *Preacher's Boy.* Clarion, 1999. Robbie's high-spirited ways often land him in trouble with his preacher father, but when one of his schemes endangers the life of someone else, Robbie finds the courage to face up to the consequences of his actions. (**I:** 9–12)

*Scott, Ann H. *Brave as a Mountain Lion.* Illustrated by Glo Coalson. Clarion, 1996. Frightened at the idea of participating in the school spelling bee, Spider finds courage by seeking advice from his family and listening to his own spirit. (**I:** 6–10)

Books Featuring Exaggeration and Outlandish Situations

*Barrett, Judi. *Cloudy with a Chance of Meatballs.* Illustrated by Ron Barrett. Atheneum, 1978. Storms of food fall from the sky in the town of Chew-and-Swallow. (**I:** P–8)

*Birdseye, Tom. *A Regular Flood of Mishap.* Illustrated by Megan Lloyd. Holiday House, 1994. Ima Bean is only trying to help when she borrows Grandpa's fishing pole, but instead she starts a regular flood of mishap. (**I:** P–8)

*Ehrlich, Amy. *Parents in the Pigpen, Pigs in the Tub.* Illustrated by Steven Kellogg. Dial, 1993. The farm is running smoothly—until the farm animals take over the farmhouse. (**I:** P–8)

*Johnson, Paul Brett. *The Pig Who Ran a Red Light.* Orchard, 1999. When Miss Rosemary's pig starts doing everything the cow does, she is challenged to find a way to make the pig act like a pig. (**I:** P–7)

Lindgren, Astrid. *Pippi Longstocking.* Translated by Florence Lamborn. Illustrated by Louis S. Glanzman. Viking, 1950. Living all alone, Pippi— the strongest girl in the world—is free to engage in hilarious antics. (**I:** 5–9)

*McKissack, Patricia. *A Million Fish . . . More or Less.* Illustrated by Dena Schutzer. Knopf, 1992. Visits to the bayou inspire unforgettable yarns. (**I:** 6–10)

*Pearson, Susan. *Well, I Never!* Illustrated by James Warhola. Simon & Schuster, 1990. This tall tale begins when it rains so hard that the corn grows as tall as trees and continues as Pa bales the sheep and pigs start flying. (**I:** P–8)

*Ray, Mary Lyn. *Alvah and Arvilla.* Illustrated by Barry Root. Harcourt, 1994. Alvah and Arvilla long to see the Pacific, but they must always stay home and tend the farm. To realize their dream, they build a glass wagon, pack up the farm, and head across the country. (**I:** P–8)

*Spurr, Elizabeth. *The Long, Long Letter.* Illustrated by David Catrow. Hyperion, 1996. Aunt Hetta is lonely; so her sister begins writing her a letter—one that takes months and months to write and requires 1,000 stamps to mail. (**I:** P–8)

*Stanley, Diane. *Raising Sweetness.* Illustrated by G. Brian Karas. Putnam, 1999. Sweetness and the other children know that they are lucky to have been adopted by the sheriff; still, the sheriff's cooking and housekeeping leave something to be desired. So Sweetness sets out to find a solution to their problems. (**I:** P–8)

*———. *Saving Sweetness.* Illustrated by G. Brian Karas. Putnam, 1996. When the orphan Sweetness runs away from the orphanage, the sheriff sets out to save her, but Sweetness doesn't want to have anything to do with being saved. (**I:** P–8)

*Wallace, Karen. *Scarlette Beane.* Illustrated by Jon Berkeley. Dial, 2000. Scarlette Beane was born with green fingers, so everyone was certain she would grow amazing gardens. (**I:** P–7)

*White, Linda Arms. *Comes a Wind.* Illustrated by Tom Curry. Dorling Kindersley, 2000. Clement and Clyde's sibling rivalry reaches new heights as they exchange tales about windy days—until a wind they'll never forget blows up on their mother's birthday. (**I:** P–8)

Foxy Books

*Auch, Mary Jane. *Peeping Beauty.* Holiday House, 1993. Poulette, the hen, dreams of becoming a famous ballerina. So when a fox claiming to be a talent scout comes to the farm, Poulette is naively convinced that her dreams are about to come true. (**I:** 5–8)

*French, Vivian. *Red Hen and Sly Fox.* Illustrated by Sally Hobson. Simon & Schuster, 1994. When fox sets out to trick Red Hen, he discovers that she has a few tricks of her own. (**I:** P–7)

*Marshall, James. *Wings: A Tale of Two Chickens.* Viking, 1995. Winnie, a hen who never reads, is lured away by a fox who promises to alleviate her boredom. (**I:** P–8)

*Steig, William. *Doctor De Soto.* Farrar, 1982. A fox visits a mouse dentist with the hope of having the dentist for dinner after his tooth has been fixed. (**I:** P–8)

*Wyllie, Stephen. *Dinner with Fox*. Illustrated by Korky Paul. Dial, 1990. Fox's scheme to eat his neighbors is going just as he planned—until one of his dinner invitations falls into the wrong hands. (I: P–7)

*———. *A Flea in the Ear*. Illustrated by Ken Brown. Dutton, 1995. A big spotted hound, the faithful guardian of the chicken coop, is tricked by a wily fox. (I: P–8)

Books about Medieval Times

*Aliki. *A Medieval Feast*. HarperCollins, 1983. When the lord and lady of the manor learn that the king and his party will soon arrive for a short stay, they begin elaborate preparations for a feast. (I: 6–10)

Beckett, Sister Wendy. *The Duke and the Peasant: Life in the Middle Ages*. Prestel, 1997. In this reproduction of the Duc de Berry's *Book of Hours,* each picture is accompanied by explanations of the scene. (I: 10 and up)

Biesty, Stephen. *Stephen Biesty's Cross-Sections Castle*. Dorling Kindersley, 1994. This book contains various cross sections of a medieval castle. Each cross section is accompanied by text that highlights some facet of life during this period. (I: 10 and up)

Clare, John D. *Fourteenth-Century Towns*. Harcourt, 1993. This informational book covers many facets of life in medieval towns and is accompanied by photographs of reenactments of the period. (I: 10 and up)

Cushman, Karen. *Catherine, Called Birdy*. Clarion, 1994. Through her journal, a young girl chronicles her daily life in medieval England. (I: 11–YA)

———. *The Midwife's Apprentice*. Clarion, 1995. A homeless waif in medieval England is given the opportunity to become a midwife's apprentice. (I: 9–12)

de Angeli, Marguerite. *The Door in the Wall*. Doubleday, 1949/1989. A young boy loses the use of his legs and is still able to save the town and serve the king. (I: 8–12)

Platt, William. *Castle Diary: The Journal of Tobias Burgess, Page*. Illustrated by Chris Riddell. Candlewick, 1999. Sent to be trained as a page in his uncle's castle, Tobias documents in his diary his discoveries about the various facets of castle life. (I: 10 and up)

Temple, Frances. *The Ramsay Scallop*. Orchard, 1994. A young couple's pilgrimage from England to Spain transforms their views of the world and each other. (I: 11–YA)

Williams, Laura E. *The Executioner's Daughter*. Holt, 2000. Born into the family of an executioner, Lily is faced with becoming her father's assistant when her mother dies. Yet Lily is determined to change her fate and instead become a healer. (I: 10–YA)

Books about Slavery in America

*Adler, David. *A Picture Book of Frederick Douglass*. Illustrated by Samuel Byrd. Holiday House, 1993. This is a biography of Frederick Douglass, who escaped from slavery and became a leading abolitionist. (I: 8–11)

*———. *A Picture Book of Harriet Tubman*. Illustrated by Samuel Byrd. Holiday House, 1992. This is a biography of Harriet Tubman, who escaped from slavery and returned to the South to lead more than 300 slaves to freedom. (I: 8–11)

Hamilton, Virginia. *Anthony Burns: The Defeat and Triumph of a Fugitive Slave*. Knopf, 1988. In 1854, Anthony Burns escaped from a Virginia plantation and came to Boston, where he was arrested and tried under the Fugitive Slave Act. (I: 10–YA)

*Hopkinson, Deborah. *Sweet Clara and the Freedom Quilt*. Illustrated by James Ransome. Knopf, 1993. Determined to escape from slavery, Clara sews a quilt that maps the way to freedom. (I: 8–12)

McKissack, Patricia C., and Fredrick L. McKissack. *Christmas in the Big House, Christmas in the Quarters*. Scholastic, 1994. Christmas in the big house is compared to Christmas in the slave quarters in the year before the Civil War breaks out. (I: 9–12)

Paterson, Katherine. *Jip: His Story*. Dutton, 1996. Jip, who has grown up in an orphanage, wonders why no one ever returned for him when he tumbled out of a wagon on West Hill Road. Then he discovers the secret of his ancestry and the horrible consequences it may bring. (I: 10–14)

*Polacco, Patricia. *Pink and Say*. Philomel, 1994. During the Civil War, an African American Union soldier befriends a white one. (I: 8–12)

Rinaldi, Ann. *Mine Eyes Have Seen*. Scholastic, 1998. Annie Brown, the daughter of John Brown, bears witness to the events leading up to her father's attempt to foster a slave insurrection by raiding the federal armory at Harper's Ferry, West Virginia. (I: 11–YA)

Rosen, Michael J. *A School for Pompey Walker*. Illustrated by Aminah Brenda Lynn Robinson. Harcourt, 1995. A former slave remembers how he raised money to build a school for all children. (I: 9–12)

*Schroeder, Alan. *Minty: A Story of Young Harriet Tubman*. Illustrated by Jerry Pinkney. Dial, 1996. This is a fictional account of Harriet Tubman's childhood. (I: 9–12)

*Smalls, Irene. *Irene Jennie and the Christmas Masquerade: The Johnkankus*. Illustrated by Melodye Rosales. Little, Brown, 1996. All the slaves look forward to Christmas Day and the celebration called the Johnkankus. Irene Jennie wants to be joyful, but how can she be when her parents have been loaned to another plantation for Christmas? (I: 8–11)

*———. *A Strawbeater's Thanksgiving*. Illustrated by Melodye Benson Rosales. Little, Brown, 1998. The harvest is in, and the slaves are given one night to celebrate. Jess is determined to be chosen as the special boy who helps the fiddler on this special night. (I: 8–10)

*Winter, Jeanette. *Follow the Drinking Gourd*. Knopf, 1988. This is the story of how one slave family escaped to freedom by following the drinking gourd. (I: 8–11)

*Wright, Courtni C. *Journey to Freedom: A Story of the Underground Railroad*. Illustrated by Gershom Griffith. Holiday House, 1994. This is the story of one slave family's journey to freedom with Harriet Tubman. (I: 9–12)

Books about Immigration

Ashabranner, Brent K. *Still a Nation of Immigrants*. Photographs by Jennifer Ashabranner. Cobblehill, 1993. This book explores immigration in the United States through interviews with immigrants and through personal observations, facts, and statistics. (I: 9–12)

*Bierman, Carol. *Journey to Ellis Island*. Illustrated by Laurie McGaw. Hyperion, 1998. Yehuda has journeyed across the ocean with his family but must now prove to the officials at Ellis Island that they should let a boy with a damaged hand enter America. (I: 8–11)

Brown, Tricia. *Lee Ann: The Story of a Vietnamese-American Girl*. Photographs by Ted Thai. Putnam, 1991. Through text and photographs, this biography describes the life of a young Vietnamese immigrant and her family in the United States. (I: 7–11)

*Bunting, Eve. *A Day's Work*. Illustrated by Ronald Himler. Clarion, 1994. Francisco is supposed to help his grandfather, who speaks no English, get a job as a day laborer. In the long run, it is Francisco who learns important life lessons from his grandfather. (I: 8–11)

*———. *Going Home*. Illustrated by David Diaz. HarperCollins, 1996. Mexico is not home to Carlos and his sisters, but Carlos's parents are excited about their first trip home since they moved to the United States. Carlos and his sisters soon discover the magic of their roots and realize how much their parents left behind so that they might have a better future. (I: 8–12)

*———. *How Many Days to America?* Illustrated by Beth Peck. Clarion, 1988. A Latin American family escapes political persecution and survives the dangerous journey across the sea, arriving in America on Thanksgiving Day. (I: 7–10)

Freedman, Russell. *Immigrant Kids*. Puffin, 1995. Through photographs and text, this book explores the experiences in America of immigrant children from Europe from the late nineteenth century through the early twentieth century. (I: 8–12)

*Garay, Luis. *The Long Road*. Tundra, 1997. When civil war breaks out in their Latin American village, José and his mother undertake an arduous journey to begin a new life in America. (I: 8–11)

*Godard, Alex. *Mama, Across the Sea*. Adapted from the French by George Wen. Holt, 2000. Cecile's mama has gone across the sea to find work, and Cecile's life seems empty without her. Then a letter arrives inviting Cecile to travel across the sea for a visit. (I: 6–9)

Hesse, Karen. *Letters from Rifka*. Holt, 1992/1995. Rifka writes about fleeing Russia and having to stay behind in Belgium when her family travels on to the United States. (I: 9–12)

*Hest, Amy. *When Jessie Came across the Sea*. Illustrated by P. J. Lynch. Candlewick, 1997. Jessie feels that her heart will break when she leaves her grandmother behind in eastern Europe. Her new life in America is complete only when her grandmother finally joins her. (I: 8–12)

*Hewett, Joan. *Hector Lives in the United States Now*. Photographs by Richard Hewett. Lippincott, 1990. Through text and photographs, this biography explores the life of a young Mexican immigrant and his family in the United States. (I: 8–11)

*Hoyt-Goldsmith, Diane. *Hoang Anh: A Vietnamese-American Boy*. Photographs by Lawrence Migdale. Holiday House, 1992. This biography of a young Vietnamese immigrant explores his family's life in the United States and ways in which they maintain their cultural ties to Vietnam. (I: 8–12)

Lasky, Kathryn. *Journey to the New World: The Diary of Remember Patience Whipple*. Scholastic, 1996. Twelve-year-old Mem records in diary format her journey across the Atlantic in the Mayflower and her family's first year in Plimoth. (I: 9–12)

*Lawlor, Veronica. *I Was Dreaming to Come to America*. Puffin, 1995. This is a collection of excerpts from the oral histories of children and young adults that were collected as part of the Ellis Island Oral History Project. (**I:** 8–12)

*Leighton, Maxinne Rhea. *An Ellis Island Christmas*. Illustrated by Dennis Nolan. Viking, 1994. Krysia, her mother, and brothers arrive at Ellis Island on Christmas. Will Krysia's family be allowed to enter the United States? (**I:** 6–10)

Levine, Ellen. *If Your Name Was Changed at Ellis Island*. Illustrated by Wayne Parmenter. Scholastic, 1993. This informational book covers topics ranging from why immigrants came to America to how they came, what happened on their arrival at Ellis Island, and what happened beyond Ellis Island. (**I:** 8–11)

*Levinson, Riki. *Watch the Stars Come Out*. Illustrated by Diane Goode. Puffin, 1985. A brother and sister cross the Atlantic to America, where their parents await them in their new home. (**I:** 5–9)

Lord, Bette Bao. *In the Year of the Boar and Jackie Robinson*. Illustrated by Marc Simont. Harper & Row, 1984. An autobiographical novel about a Chinese girl who learns to love baseball as she adjusts to her new life in the United States. (**I:** 9–12)

Mayerson, Evelyn Wilde. *The Cat Who Escaped from Steerage*. Scribner's, 1990. A Polish girl smuggles a cat on board a ship headed for the United States. (**I:** 9–12)

*Medina, Jane. *My Name Is Jorge: On Both Sides of the River*. Illustrated by Fabricio Vanden Broeck. Boyds Mill, 1999. These bilingual poems are packed with poignant moments in the life of a Mexican immigrant child. (**I:** 9–12)

*Moss, Marissa. *Hannah's Journal: The Story of an Immigrant Girl*. Harcourt, 2000. Told in journal format, this is the story of a young European girl who journeys with her cousin to America. (**I:** 8–11)

Panzer, Nora. *Celebrate America in Poetry and Art*. Hyperion, 1994. Through poetry and art, this collection explores the American experience. (**I:** 10–YA)

Recorvits, Helen. *Goodbye, Walter Malinski*. Illustrated by Lloyd Bloom. Farrar, 1999. It is 1934, and Wanda's immigrant family struggles to make it in America in the midst of the Great Depression. (**I:** 9–12)

*Ross, Lillian Hammer. *Buba Leah and Her Paper Children*. Illustrated by Mary Morgan. Jewish Publication Society, 1991. Buba Leah's children have immigrated to America, and it seems that all that remains for Buba Leah is her sadness and the letters (paper children) her children send. (**I:** 7–11)

Sandler, Martin W. *Immigrants*. HarperCollins, 1995. Through text and photographs, this book explores immigration to the United States in the late nineteenth century and early twentieth century, with a particular focus on European immigrants. (**I:** 9–12)

*Say, Allen. *Grandfather's Journey*. Houghton Mifflin, 1993. A Japanese man emigrates to the United States and learns to love his new home, but he misses his homeland. When he visits Japan, the war keeps him from returning to the United States. (**I:** 6–9)

Strom, Yale. *Quilted Landscapes: Conversation with Young Immigrants*. Simon & Schuster, 1996. This book contains interviews with young immigrants living throughout the United States. (**I:** 9–12)

Takaki, Ronald, Rebecca Stefoff, and Carol Takaki. *From Exiles to Immigrants: The Refugees from Southeast Asia*. Chelsea House, 1995. This book explores Asian immigration to the United States. (**I:** 9–12)

*Van Leeuwen, Jean. *Across the Wide Dark Sea*. Illustrated by Thomas B. Allen. Dial, 1995. A young boy and his family journey on the Mayflower to build a new life in America. (**I:** 6–10)

*Winter, Jeanette. *Klara's New World*. Knopf, 1992. Klara's family leaves their home in Sweden and sails to America, where they build a new home. (**I:** 6–10)

*Wong, Janet S. *The Trip Back Home*. Illustrated by Bo Jia. Harcourt, 2000. A little girl and her mother travel from America to Korea to see the grandparents the girl has never met. (**I:** 6–9)

Yep, Laurence. *Dragon's Gate*. HarperCollins, 1993. In 1837, Chinese men came to the United States and found work digging and dynamiting tunnels through the Sierra Mountains in order for the railroad to cross the nation. (**I:** 11–YA)

*Yezerski, Thomas F. *Together in Pinecone Patch*. Farrar, 1998. In Pinecone Patch, Pennsylvania, Keara's family clings to their Irish roots while Stefan's family clings to their Polish roots. Only as adults do Keara and Stefan dare to reach across ethnic barriers to build a life together. (**I:** 8–11)

Other Books

*Aliki. *Wild and Woolly Mammoths*. HarperCollins, 1977. This is a fascinating account of the woolly mammoth and its relationship to cave dwellers. (**I:** 6–10)

Asbjorsen, Peter Christen, Jorgen Engebretsen Moe, and George Webbe Dasent. *East O' the Sun and West O' the Moon: Fifty-Nine Norwegian Folk Tales from the Collection of Peter Christen*

Asbjorsen and Jorgen Moe. Dover, 1970. This is a collection of Norwegian folktales that were originally published in 1845. (**I:** 8–12)

*Bash, Barbara. *Tree of Life: The World of the African Baobab*. Sierra Club, 1989. With lyrical language, the author documents the rich ecosystem of the African baobab tree. Other titles in this series include *Ancient Ones* (1994), *Desert Giant* (1990), and *In the Heart of the Village* (1996). (**I:** 6 and up)

*———. *Urban Roosts*. Sierra Club, 1990. The author explores how birds that live in the city have adapted their nest-building habits to their urban environment. (**I:** 6–10)

*Bernhard, Emery. *The Girl Who Wanted to Hunt*. Illustrated by Durga Bernhard. Holiday House, 1994. A young girl's courage is tested as she seeks to become a hunter. (**I:** 8–11)

Conrad, Pam. *Pedro's Journal: A Voyage with Christopher Columbus August 3, 1492–February 14, 1493*. Illustrated by Peter Koeppen. Scholastic, 1992. Pedro, the ship's boy on the *Santa Maria*, documents in his journal the trip across the Atlantic on Columbus's ship and the subsequent exploration of the newly discovered islands. (**I:** 9–12)

DiCamillo, Kate. *Because of Winn-Dixie*. Candlewick, 2000. Opal's new dog, Winn-Dixie, helps the 10-year-old come to terms with her mother's abandonment of her seven years before. (**I:** 9–12)

Forbes, Esther. *Johnny Tremain*. Houghton Mifflin, 1943. A silversmith's apprentice becomes part of the Sons of Liberty. (**I:** 10–YA)

*Henkes, Kevin. *Wemberly Worried*. Greenwillow, 2000. Wemberly the mouse worries about everything but especially about her first day at a new nursery school. (**I:** P–8)

*Hulpach, Vladimir. *Ahaiyute and Cloud Eater*. Illustrated by Marek Zawadzk. Harcourt, 1996. To become a warrior, Ahaiyute must accomplish a great deed, so he sets out to slay the giant monster and bring rain back to his people. (**I:** 8–11)

*Hutchins, Pat. *The Doorbell Rang*. Greenwillow, 1986. Two children see their portions of mom's freshly baked cookies dwindle as the doorbell rings and guests continue to arrive. (**I:** 5–8)

Lunge-Larsen, Lise. *The Troll with No Heart in His Body and Other Tales of Trolls from Norway*. Illustrated by Betsy Bowen. Houghton Mifflin, 1999. This is a varied collection of troll tales from Norway. Accompanying illustrations are woodcuts. (**I:** 7–11)

*Martin, Claire. *Boots and the Glass Mountain*. Illustrated by Gennady Spirin. Dial, 1992. Boots, the youngest of three brothers, sets out to be the first to ride his horse to the top of a slippery glass mountain and win the hand of the princess. (**I:** 7–11)

*Sendak, Maurice. *In the Night Kitchen*. Harper, 1970. Mickey awakens to the noise of the night kitchen and embarks on a fantastic trip in which he becomes the hero of the night kitchen. (**I:** P–6)

*———. *Outside Over There*. Harper, 1981. When her baby sister is stolen by the goblins, Ida goes "outside over there" to confront the goblins and rescue her sister. (**I:** P–8)

*———. *Where the Wild Things Are*. HarperCollins, 1963/1989. Sent to his room, Max travels to where the Wild Things are and becomes king of all Wild Things. (**I:** P–8)

*Van Allsburg, Chris. *The Polar Express*. Houghton Mifflin, 1985. A young boy boards a train that takes him to the North Pole, where Santa offers him any gift he would like. (**I:** P–8)

*Wells, Rosemary. *Timothy Goes to School*. Puffin, 2000. Timothy's first day at school is nearly ruined by perfect Claude. (**I:** P–8)

*Winter, Jeanette. *The House That Jack Built*. Dial, 2000. Winter's witty illustrations add action to this familiar cumulative rhyme. (**I:** P–8)

*Wood, Audrey. *The Napping House*. Illustrated by Don Wood. Harcourt, 1984. A child and her grandmother take a peaceful nap along with the family dog and cat and a mouse—until a wakeful flea stirs things up. (**I:** P–8)

*Yorinks, Arthur. *Hey, Al!* Illustrated by Richard Egielski. Farrar, 1986. The paradise promised by a bird does not live up to the expectations of Al and his dog. (**I:** 6–12)

RESOURCES

Cullinan, Bernice E. *Fact and Fiction: Literature across the Curriculum*. International Reading Association, 1993.

Freeman, Evelyn B., and Diane Goetz Person. *Using Nonfiction Trade Books in the Elementary Classroom: From Ants to Zeppelins*. National Council of Teachers of English, 1992.

———. *Connecting Informational Children's Books with Content Area Learning*. Allyn & Bacon, 1998.

Moss, Joy F. *Focus on Literature: A Context for Literacy Learning.* Richard C. Owen, 1990.

———. *Using Literature in the Middle Grades: A Thematic Approach.* Christopher-Gordon, 1994.

Smith, J. Lea, and Holly Johnson. "Models for Implementing Literature in Content Studies." *The Reading Teacher* 48 (1994): 198–208.

Tunnell, Michael O., and Richard Ammon. *The Story of Ourselves: Teaching History through Children's Literature.* Heinemann, 1993.

Zarnowski, Myra, and Arlene F. Gallagher. *Children's Literature and Social Studies: Selecting and Using Notable Books in the Classroom.* Kendall/Hunt, 1993.

REFERENCES

Alvermann, Donna E., and David W. Moore. "Secondary School Reading." Ed. Rebecca Barr, Michael Kamil, Peter Mosenthal, and P. David Pearson. *Handbook of Reading Research,* vol. II. Longman, 1991, pp. 951–83.

Baumann, James F., James V. Hoffman, Jennifer Moon, and Ann M. Duffy-Hester. "Where Are Teachers' Voices in the Phonics/Whole Language Debate? Results from a Survey of U.S. Elementary Classroom Teachers." *The Reading Teacher* 51 (1998): 636–50.

Bloem, Patricia L., and Anthony L. Manna. "A Chorus of Questions: Readers Respond to Patricia Polacco." *The Reading Teacher* 52 (1999): 802–8.

Carle, Eric. *The Art of Eric Carle.* Philomel, 1996.

———. *You Can Make a Collage.* Klutz, 1998.

Chall, J. S., and S. S. Conard. *Should Textbooks Challenge Students?: The Case for Easier or Harder Textbooks.* Teachers College Press, 1991.

Eric Carle: Picture Writer. Directed by Rawn Fulton. Produced by Searchlight Films. Philomel, 1993.

Farest, Cindy, and Carolyn Miller. "Children's Insights into Literature: Using Dialogue Journals to Invite Literary Response." *Examining Central Issues in Literacy Research, Theory, and Practice.* Forty-Second Yearbook of the National Reading Conference. Ed. Donald J. Leu and Charles K. Kinzer. National Reading Conference, 1993, pp. 271–78.

Hoffman, James V. "Critical Reading/Thinking across the Curriculum: Using I-Charts to Support Learning." *Language Arts* 69 (1992): 121–27.

Levstik, Linda. "A Gift of Time: Children's Historical Fiction." *Children's Literature in the Classroom: Weaving Charlotte's Web.* Ed. Janet Hickman and Bernice E. Cullinan. Christopher-Gordon, 1989, pp. 135–45.

Madura, Sandra. "The Line and Texture of Aesthetic Response: Primary Children Study Authors and Illustrators." *The Reading Teacher* 49 (1995): 110–18.

Martinez, Miriam, and Nancy L. Roser. "Children's Responses to Literature." *Handbook of Research on Teaching the English Language Arts,* 2nd ed., in press.

Moss, Joy. "Using the 'Focus Unit' to Enhance Children's Response to Literature." *Language Arts* 55 (1978): 482–88.

———. *Focus Units in Literature: A Handbook for Elementary School Teachers.* National Council of Teachers of English, 1984.

———. *Using Literature in the Middle Grades: A Thematic Approach.* Christopher-Gordon, 1994.

Nakamura, Joyce, ed. *Something about the Author.* Gale Group, 1998.

Ogle, Donna. "K-W-L: A Teaching Model That Develops Active Reading of Expository Text." *The Reading Teacher* 39 (1986): 564–70.

Peterson, Ralph, and Maryann Eeds. *Grand Conversations: Literature Groups in Action.* Scholastic-TAB, 1990.

Pierce, Kathryn Mitchell. *Adventuring with Books: A Booklist for Pre-K–Grade 6.* National Council of Teachers of English, 2000.

Roser, Nancy, James V. Hoffman, and Cindy Farest. "Language, Literature, and At-Risk Children." *The Reading Teacher* 43 (1990): 554–59.

Roser, Nancy L., James V. Hoffman, Cindy Farest, and Linda D. Labbo. "Language Charts: A Record of Story Time Talk." *Language Arts* 69 (1992): 44–52.

Roser, Nancy, and Susan Strecker. "Fostering Thought, Talk, and Inquiry by Linking Literature with Social Studies." *The Reading Teacher,* in press.

Short, Kathy G. "Intertextuality: Searching for Patterns That Connect." *Literacy Research, Theory, and Practice: Views from Many Perspectives: Forty-First Yearbook of the National Reading Conference.* Ed. Charles K. Kinzer and Donald J. Leu. National Reading Conference, 1992, pp. 187–97.

Silvey, Anita, ed. *Children's Books and Their Creators.* Houghton Mifflin, 1995.

Sipe, Lawrence R. "Individual Literary Response Styles of First and Second Graders." *Forty-Seventh Yearbook of the National Reading Conference.* Ed. Timothy Shanahan and Flora V. Rodriguez-Brown. National Reading Conference, 1998, pp. 76–89.

Tomlinson, Carl M., Michael O. Tunnell, and Donald J. Richgels. "The Content and Writing in Textbooks and Trade Books." *The Story of Ourselves: Teaching History through Children's Literature.* Ed. Michael O. Tunnell and Richard Ammon. Heinemann, 1993, pp. 51–62.

Tyson-Bernstein, H., and A. Woodward. "Why Students Aren't Learning Very Much from Textbooks." *Educational Leadership* 47 (1989): 14–17.

Walmsley, Sean A. "Reflections on the State of Elementary Literature Instruction." *Language Arts* 69 (1992): 508–14.

Yolen, Jane. "How Basic Is SHAZAM?" *Language Arts* 54 (1977): 645–51.

Zarnowski, Myra. "Using Literature Sets to Promote Conversation about Social Studies Topics." *Children's Literature and Social Studies.* Ed. Myra Zarnowski and Arlene F. Gallagher. Kendall/Hunt, 1993, pp. 35–41.

Appendix A
Children's Book Awards

There are many more awards and prizes for children's books than are described in this appendix. In some states, children vote for books that are nominated for awards. Information about awards from children can be obtained from various state libraries. Other awards are given in specific genres, such as the Nebula Award for science fiction and the Edgar Allan Poe Award for mystery. Many cultural and ethnic organizations give awards to authors of children's books that contribute to understanding and appreciation of the many cultures within the United States.

JANE ADDAMS BOOK AWARD

The Jane Addams Children's Book Award has been presented annually since 1953 by the Women's International League for Peace and Freedom and the Jane Addams Peace Association to the children's book of the preceding year that most effectively promotes the cause of peace, social justice, and world community.

1953
People Are Important by Eva Knox Evans (Capital)

1954
Stick-in-the-Mud by Jean Ketchum (Cadmus Books, E. M. Hale)

1955
Rainbow Round the World by Elizabeth Yates (Bobbs-Merrill)

1956
Story of the Negro by Arna Bontemps (Knopf)

1957
Blue Mystery by Margot Benary-Isbert (Harcourt Brace)

1958
The Perilous Road by William O. Steele (Harcourt Brace)

1959
No award given

1960
Champions of Peace by Edith Patterson Meyer (Little, Brown)

1961
What Then, Raman? by Shirley L. Arora (Follett)

1962
The Road to Agra by Aimee Sommerfelt (Criterion)

1963
The Monkey and the Wild, Wild Wind by Ryerson Johnson (Abelard-Schuman)

1964
Profiles in Courage: Young Readers Memorial Edition by John F. Kennedy (Harper & Row)

1965
Meeting with a Stranger by Duane Bradley (Lippincott)

1966
Berries Goodman by Emily Cheney Neville (Harper & Row)

1967
Queenie Peavy by Robert Burch (Viking)

1968
The Little Fishes by Erik Christian Haugaard (Houghton Mifflin)

1969
The Endless Steppe: Growing Up in Siberia by Esther Hautzig (Crowell)

1970
The Cay by Theodore Taylor (Doubleday)

1971

Jane Addams: Pioneer of Social Justice by Cornelia Meigs (Little, Brown)

1972

The Tamarack Tree by Betty Underwood (Houghton Mifflin)

1973

The Riddle of Racism by S. Carl Hirsch (Viking)

Honor Book

The Upstairs Room by Johanna Reiss (Crowell)

1974

Nilda by Nicholasa Mohr (Harper & Row)

Honor Books

A Hero Ain't Nothin' but a Sandwich by Alice Childress (Coward, McCann & Geoghegan)

Men Against War by Barbara Habenstreit (Doubleday)

A Pocket Full of Seeds by Marilyn Sachs (Doubleday)

1975

The Princess and the Admiral by Charlotte Pomerantz (Addison-Wesley)

Honor Books

The Eye of Conscience by Milton Meltzer and Bernard Cole (Follett)

My Brother Sam Is Dead by James Lincoln Collier and Christopher Collier (Four Winds)

Viva la Raza! by Elizabeth Sutherland Martinez and Enrigueta Longeaux y Vasquez (Doubleday)

1976

Paul Robeson by Eloise Greenfield (Crowell)

Honor Books

Dragonwings by Laurence Yep (Harper & Row)

Song of the Trees by Mildred D. Taylor (Dial)

Z for Zachariah by Robert C. O'Brian (Atheneum)

1977

Never to Forget: The Jews of the Holocaust by Milton Meltzer (Harper & Row)

Honor Book

Roll of Thunder, Hear My Cry by Mildred D. Taylor (Dial)

1978

Child of the Owl by Laurence Yep (Harper & Row)

Honor Books

Alan and Naomi by Myron Levoy (Harper & Row)

Mischling, Second Degree: My Childhood in Nazi Germany by Ilse Koehn (Greenwillow)

Special Recognition

Amifika by Lucille Clifton (Dutton)

The Wheel of King Asoka by Ashok Davar (Follett)

1979

Many Smokes, Many Moons: A Chronology of American History through Indian Art by Jamake Highwater (Lippincott)

Honor Books

Escape to Freedom by Ossie Davis (Viking)

The Great Gilly Hopkins by Katherine Paterson (Crowell)

1980

The Road from Home: The Story of an Armenian Girl by David Kherdian (Greenwillow)

West Coast Honor Book

Woman from Hiroshima by Toshio Mori (Isthmus)

Special Recognition

Natural History by M. B. Goffstein (Farrar, Straus and Giroux)

1981

First Woman in Congress: Jeannette Rankin by Florence Meiman White (Julian Messner)

Honor Books

Chase Me, Catch Nobody! by Erik Haugaard (Houghton Mifflin)

Doing Time: A Look at Crime and Prisons by Phyllis Clark and Robert Lehrman (Hastings House)

We Are Mesquakie, We Are One by Hadley Irwin (Feminist Press)

1982

A Spirit to Ride the Whirlwind by Athena V. Lord (Macmillan)

Honor Books

Let the Circle Be Unbroken by Mildred D. Taylor (Dial)

Lupita Mañana by Patricia Beatty (Morrow)

1983

Hiroshima no pika by Toshi Maruki, translated from Japanese (Lothrop, Lee & Shepard)

Honor Books

The Bomb by Sidney Lenz (Lodestar/Dutton)

If I Had a Paka: Poems in Eleven Languages by Charlotte Pomerantz (Greenwillow)

West Coast Honor Book

People at the Edge of the World: The Ohlone of Central California by Betty Morrow (Bacon)

Special Recognition

All the Colors of the Race by Arnold Adoff (Lothrop, Lee & Shepard)

Children as Teachers of Peace by Our Children (Celestial Press)

1984

Rain of Fire by Marion Dane Bauer (Clarion/Houghton Mifflin)

1985

The Short Life of Sophie Scholl by Hermann Vinke, with an interview with Ilse Aichinger, translated from German by Hedvig Pachter (Harper & Row)

Honor Books

The Island on Bird Street by Uri Orlev, translated from Hebrew by Hillel Halkin (Houghton Mifflin)

Music, Music for Everyone by Vera B. Williams (Greenwillow)

1986

Ain't Gonna Study War No More: The Story of America's Peace Seekers by Milton Meltzer (Harper & Row)

Honor Book

Journey to the Soviet Union by Samantha Smith (Little, Brown)

1987

Nobody Wants a Nuclear War by Judith Vigna (Albert Whitman)

Honor Books

All in a Day by Mitsumasa Anno (Philomel)

Children of the Maya: A Guatemalan Indian Odyssey by Brent Ashabranner, photographs by Paul Conklin (Dodd, Mead)

1988

Waiting for the Rain: A Novel of South Africa by Sheila Gordon (Orchard/Franklin Watts)

Honor Books

Nicolas, Where Have You Been? by Leo Lionni (Knopf)

Trouble at the Mines by Doreen Rappaport (Crowell)

1989 (tie)

Anthony Burns: The Defeat and Triumph of a Fugitive Slave by Virginia Hamilton (Knopf)

Looking Out by Victoria Boutis (Four Winds Press)

Honor Books

December Stillness by Mary Downing Hahn (Clarion)

The Most Beautiful Place in the World by Ann Cameron (Knopf)

Rescue: The Story of How Gentiles Saved Jews in the Holocaust by Milton Meltzer (Harper & Row)

1990

A Long Hard Journey: The Story of the Pullman Porter by Patricia and Fredrick McKissack (Walker)

Honor Books

Number the Stars by Lois Lowry (Houghton Mifflin)

Shades of Gray by Carolyn Reeder (Macmillan)

The Wednesday Surprise by Eve Bunting (Clarion)

1991

The Big Book for Peace edited by Ann Durell and Marilyn Sachs (Dutton)

Honor Books

The Journey: Japanese Americans, Racism and Renewal by Sheila Hamanaka (Richard Jackson/Orchard)

The Middle of Somewhere: A Story of South Africa by Sheila Gordon (Orchard)

1992

Journey of the Sparrows by Fran Leeper Buss with the assistance of Daisy Cubias (Lodestar)

Honor Book

Now Is Your Time! The African-American Struggle for Freedom by Walter Dean Myers (HarperCollins)

1993

Longer Book: ***A Taste of Salt: A Story of Modern Haiti*** by Frances Temple (Orchard)

Picture Book: ***Aunt Harriet's Underground Railroad in the Sky*** by Faith Ringgold (Crown)

Longer Book: ***Letters from a Slave Girl: The Story of Harriet Jacobs*** by Mary E. Lyons (Scribners)

Honor Book

Picture Book: ***Mrs. Katz and Tush*** by Patricia Polacco (Bantam)

1994

Longer Book: **Freedom's Children: Young Civil Rights Activists Tell Their Stories** by Ellen Levine (Putnam)

Picture Book: **This Land Is My Land** by George Littlechild (Children's Book Press)

Honor Books

Longer Book: **Eleanor Roosevelt: A Life of Discovery** by Russell Freedman (Clarion)

Picture Book: **Soul Looks Back in Wonder** by Tom Feelings (Dial)

1995

Longer Book: **Kids at Work: Lewis Hine and the Crusade against Child Labor** by Russell Freedman (Clarion)

Picture Book: **Sitti's Secrets** by Naomi Shihab Nye, illustrated by Nancy Carpenter (Four Winds Press)

Honor Books

Longer Books: **Cezanne Pinto** by Mary Stolz (Knopf)

I Hadn't Meant to Tell You This by Jacqueline Woodson (Delacorte)

Picture Book: **Bein' with You This Way** by W. Nikola-Lisa, illustrated by Michael Bryant (Lee & Low)

1996

Longer Book: **The Well** by Mildred D. Taylor (Dial)

Picture Book: No award given

Honor Books

Longer Books: **From the Notebooks of Melanin Sun** by Jacqueline Woodson (Blue Sky/Scholastic)

On the Wings of Peace: Writers and Illustrators Speak Out for Peace in Memory of Hiroshima and Nagasaki (Clarion)

The Watsons Go to Birmingham—1963 by Christopher Paul Curtis (Delacorte)

Special Commendation

The Middle Passage by Tom Feelings (Dial)

1997

Longer Book: **Growing Up in Coal Country** by Susan Campbell Bartoletti (Houghton Mifflin)

Picture Book: **Wilma Unlimited** by Kathleen Krull, illustrated by David Diaz (Harcourt Brace)

Honor Books

Longer Books: **Behind the Bedroom Wall** by Laura E. Williams (Milkweed)

Second Daughter: The Story of a Slave Girl by Mildred Pitts Walter (Scholastic)

Picture Book: **The Day Gogo Went to Vote** by Elinor Batezat Sisulu (Little, Brown)

1998

Longer Book: **Habibi** by Naomi Shihab Nye (Simon & Schuster)

Picture Book: **Seven Brave Women** by Betsy Hearne, illustrated by Bethanne Andersen (Greenwillow)

Honor Books

Longer Books: **The Circuit: Stories from the Life of a Migrant Child** by Francisco Jiménez (University of New Mexico Press)

Seedfolks by Paul Fleischman (HarperCollins)

Picture Books: **Celebrating Families** by Rosemarie Hausherr (Scholastic)

Passage to Freedom: The Sugihara Story by Ken Mochizuki, illustrated by Dom Lee (Lee & Low)

1999

Longer Book: **Bat 6** by Virginia Euwer Wolff (Scholastic)

Picture Book: **Painted Words/Spoken Memories: Marianthe's Story** by Aliki (Greenwillow)

Honor Books

Longer Books: **The Heart of a Chief** by Joseph Bruchac (Dial)

No More Strangers Now by Tim McKee, photographs by Anne Blackshaw (A Melanie Kroupa Book/DK Ink)

Restless Spirit: The Life and Work of Dorothea Lange by Elizabeth Partridge (Viking)

Picture Books: **Hey Little Ant** by Phillip and Hannah Hoose, illustrated by Debbie Tilley (Tricycle Press)

i see the rhythm by Toyomi Igus, illustrated by Michele Wood (Children's Book Press)

This Land Is Your Land words and music by Woodie Guthrie, illustrated by Kathy Jakobsen (Little, Brown)

2000

Longer Book: **Through My Eyes** by Ruby Bridges (Scholastic)

Picture Book: **Molly Bannaky** by Alice McGill, illustrated by Chris K. Soentpiet (Houghton Mifflin)

Honor Books
Longer Books: ***The Birchbark House*** by Louise
  Erdrich (Hyperion)
Kids on Strike! by Susan Campbell Bartoletti
  (Houghton Mifflin)

Picture Books
***A Band of Angels: A Story Inspired by the Jubilee
  Singers*** by Deborah Hopkinson, illustrated by
  Raúl Colón (Atheneum)
When Sophie Gets Angry—Really, Really Angry . . .
  by Molly Bang (The Blue Sky Press/Scholastic)

AMÉRICAS AWARD FOR CHILDREN'S AND YOUNG ADULT LITERATURE

The Américas Award is given in recognition of U.S. works of fiction, poetry, folklore, or nonfiction (from picture books to works for young adults) published in the previous year in English or Spanish that authentically and engagingly portray Latin America, the Caribbean, or Latinos in the United States. By combining both languages and linking the Americas, the award reaches beyond geographic borders as well as multicultural boundaries, focusing instead on cultural heritages within the hemisphere. The award is sponsored by the national Consortium of Latin American Studies Programs (CLASP). The commended list is available at http://www.uwm.edu/dept/cla/outreach_americas.

1993
Vejigante Masquerader by Lulu Delacre (Scholastic)

1994
The Mermaid's Twin Sister by Lynn Joseph (Clarion)

1995
Tonight, by Sea by Frances Temple (Orchard)

1996
In My Family/En mi familia by Carmen Lomas
  Garza (Children's Book Press)

Parrot in the Oven by Victor Martínez
  (HarperCollins)

1997
The Circuit by Francisco Jiménez (University of
  New Mexico Press)
The Face at the Window by Regina Hanson, illustrated by Linda Saport (Clarion)

1998
Barrio: José's Neighborhood by George Ancona
  (Harcourt Brace)
Mama and Papa Have a Store by Amelia Lau
  Carling (Dial)

1999
Crashboomlove by Juan Felipe Herrera (University
  of New Mexico Press)

2000
The Composition by Antonio Skármeta, illustrated
  by Alfonso Ruano (Groundwood)
The Color of My Words by Lynn Joseph
  (HarperCollins)

HANS CHRISTIAN ANDERSEN AWARD

The International Board on Books for Young People has given the Hans Christian Andersen Award biennially since 1956 (since 1966 for the illustrator award). It is awarded to one author and one illustrator in recognition of his or her entire body of work.

1956
Eleanor Farjeon, Great Britain

1958
Astrid Lindgren, Sweden

1960
Erich Kästner, Federal Republic of Germany

1962
Meindert DeJong, United States

1964
René Guillot, France

1966
Author: Tove Jansson, Finland
Illustrator: Alois Carigiet, Switzerland

1968
Authors: James Krüss, Federal Republic of Germany
  José Maria Sanchez-Silva, Spain
Illustrator: Jǔrí Trnka, Czechoslovakia

1970
Author: Gianni Rodari, Italy
Illustrator: Maurice Sendak, United States

1972
Author: Scott O'Dell, United States
Illustrator: Ib Spang Olsen, Denmark

1974
Author: Maria Gripe, Sweden
Illustrator: Farshid Mesghali, Iran

1976
Author: Cecil Bødker, Denmark
Illustrator: Tatjana Mawrina, Soviet Union

1978
Author: Paula Fox, United States
Illustrator: Otto S. Svend, Denmark

1980
Author: Bohumil Ríha, Czechoslovakia
Illustrator: Suekichi Akaba, Japan

1982
Author: Lygia Bojunga Nunes, Brazil
Illustrator: Zbigniew Rychlicki, Poland

1984
Author: Christine Nöstlinger, Austria
Illustrator: Mitsumasa Anno, Japan

1986
Author: Patricia Wrightson, Australia
Illustrator: Robert Ingpen, Australia

1988
Author: Annie M. G. Schmidt, Netherlands
Illustrator: Dŭsan Kállay, Czechoslovakia

1990
Author: Tormod Haugen, Norway
Illustrator: Lisbeth Zwerger, Austria

1992
Author: Virginia Hamilton, United States
Illustrator: Květá Pacovska, Czechoslovakia

1994
Author: Michio Mado, Japan
Illustrator: Jorg Müller, Switzerland

1996
Author: Uri Orlev, Israel
Illustrator: Klaus Ensikat, Germany

1998
Author: Katherine Paterson, United States
Illustrator: Tomi Ungerer, France

2000
Author: Ana Maria Machado, Brazil
Illustrator: Anthony Browne, United Kingdom

MILDRED L. BATCHELDER AWARD

This award honors the former executive director of the Association for Library Service to Children (ALSC), a division of the American Library Association (ALA). The citation is given annually to a U.S. publisher for a children's book (defined as any trade book for children from pre-nursery school age through eighth grade) deemed the most outstanding book originally published in a foreign language in a foreign country, and then published in the United States. (From 1968 through 1977, the award was given for a book published in the previous two years; since 1979, the award has been given to a book published in the preceding year.)

1968
The Little Man by Erich Kästner, translated from German by James Krikup (Knopf)

1969
Don't Take Teddy by Babbis Friis-Baastad, translated from Norwegian by Lise Sømme McKinnon (Scribner's)

1970
Wildcat under Glass by Alki Zei, translated from Greek by Edward Fenton (Holt)

1971
In the Land of Ur, the Discovery of Ancient Mesopotamia by Hans Baumann, translated from German by Stella Humphries (Pantheon)

1972
Friedrich by Hans Peter Richter, translated from German by Edite Kroll (Holt)

1973
Pulga by S. R. Van Iterson, translated from Dutch by Alexander and Alison Gode (Morrow)

1974
Petro's War by Alki Zei, translated from Greek by Edward Fenton (Dutton)

1975
An Old Tale Carved Out of Stone by A. Linevski, translated from Russian by Maria Polushkin (Crown)

1976

The Cat and Mouse Who Shared a House by Ruth Hürlimann, translated from German by Anthea Bell (Walck)

1977

The Leopard by Cecil Bødker, translated from Danish by Gunnar Poulsen (Atheneum)

1978

No award given

1979

Konrad by Christine Nöstlinger (published 1977), translated from German by Anthea Bell (Watts)

Rabbit Island by Jörg Steiner (published 1978), translated from German by Ann Conrad Lammers (Harcourt)

1980

The Sound of the Dragon's Feet by Alki Zei, translated from Greek by Edward Fenton (Dutton)

1981

The Winter When Time Was Frozen by Els Pelgrom, translated from Dutch by Maryka and Raphael Rudnik (Morrow)

1982

The Battle Horse by Harry Kullman, translated from Swedish by George Blecher and Lone Thygesen Blecher (Bradbury)

1983

Hiroshima no pika by Toshi Maruki, translated from Japanese through Kurita-Bando Literary Agency (Lothrop)

1984

Ronia, the Robber's Daughter by Astrid Lindgren, translated from Swedish by Patricia Crampton (Viking)

1985

The Island on Bird Street by Uri Orlev, translated from Hebrew by Hillel Halkin (Houghton Mifflin)

1986

Rose Blanche by Christophe Gallaz and Robert Innocenti, translated from Italian by Martha Coventry and Richard Craglia (Creative Education)

1987

No Hero for the Kaiser by Rudolf Frank, translated from German by Patricia Crampton (Lothrop)

1988

If You Didn't Have Me by Ulf Nilsson, translated from Swedish by Lone Thygesen Blecher and George Blecher (McElderry)

1989

Crutches by Peter Härtling, translated from German by Elizabeth D. Crawford (Lothrop)

1990

Buster's World by Bjarne Reuter, translated from Danish by Anthea Bell (Dutton)

1991

A Hand Full of Stars by Rafik Schami, translated from German by Rika Lesser (Dutton)

1992

The Man from the Other Side by Uri Orlev, translated from Hebrew by Hillel Halkin (Houghton Mifflin)

1993

No award given

1994

The Apprentice by Pilar M. Llorente, translated from Spanish by Robin Longshaw (Farrar)

Honor Books

The Princess in the Kitchen Garden by Annemie and Margaret Heymans, translated from Dutch by Johanna H. Prins and Johanna W. Prins (Farrar)

Anne Frank Beyond the Diary: A Photographic Remembrance by Ruud van der Rol and Rian Verhoeven, translated from Dutch by Tony Langham and Plym Peters (Viking)

1995

Boys from St. Petri by Bjarne Reuter, translated from Danish by Anthea Bell (Dutton)

Honor Book

Sister Shako and Kolo the Goat: Memories of My Childhood in Turkey by Vedat Dalokay, translated from Turkish by Güner Ener (Lothrop)

1996

The Lady with the Hat by Uri Orlev, translated from Hebrew by Hillel Halkin (Houghton Mifflin)

Honor Books

Star of Fear, Star of Hope by Jo Hoestlandt, translated from French by Mark Polizzotti (Walker)

Damned Strong Love: The True Story of Willi G. and Stephan K. by Lutz van Dijk, translated from German by Elizabeth D. Crawford (Holt)

1997

The Friends by Kazumi Yumoto, translated from Japanese by Cathy Hirano (Farrar)

1998

The Robber and Me by Josef Holub, translated from German by Elizabeth D. Crawford (Holt)

Honor Books

Hostage to War: A True Story by Tatjana Wassiljewa, translated from German by Anna Trenter (Scholastic)

Nero Corleone: A Cat's Story by Elke Heidenrich, translated from German by Doris Orgel (Viking)

1999

Thanks to My Mother by Schoschana Rabinovici, translated from German by James Skofield (Dial)

Honor Book

Secret Letters from 0 to 10 by Susie Morgenstern, translated from French by Gill Rosner (Viking)

2000

The Baboon King by Anton Quintana, translated from Dutch by John Nieuwenhuizen (Walker and Company)

Honor Books

Collector of Moments by Quint Buchholz, translated from German by Peter F. Neumeyer (Farrar)

Asphalt Angels by Ineke Holtwijk, translated from Dutch by Wanda Boeke (Front Street)

Vendela in Venice by Christina Björk, illustrated by Inga-Karin Eriksson, translated from Swedish by Patricia Crampton (R&S Books)

2001

Samir and Yonatan by Daniella Carmi, translated from Hebrew by Yael Lotan (Arthur A. Levine/Scholastic)

Honor Book

Ultimate Game by Christian Lehmann, translated from French by William Rodarmor (David R. Godine)

THE PURA BELPRÉ AWARD

The Pura Belpré Award, established in 1996, is presented to a Latino/Latina writer and illustrator whose work best portrays, affirms, and celebrates the Latino cultural experience in an outstanding work of literature for children and youth. It is co-sponsored by the Association for Library Service to Children (ALSC), a division of the American Library Association (ALA), and the National Association to Promote Library Services to the Spanish Speaking (REFORMA), an ALA affiliate.

1996

Narrative: An Island like You: Stories of the Barrio by Judith Ortiz Cofer (Melanie Kroupa/Orchard)

Illustration: Chato's Kitchen by Gary Soto, illustrated by Susan Guevara (Putnam)

Honor Books

Narrative: The Bossy Gallito/El gallo de bodas: A Traditional Cuban Folktale by Lucía González, illustrated by Lulu Delacre (Scholastic)

Baseball in April, and Other Stories by Gary Soto (Harcourt)

Illustration: Pablo Remembers: The Fiesta of the Day of the Dead, illustrated by George Ancona (also published in a Spanish language edition: *Pablo recuenta: La fiesta de día de los muertos* (Lothrop)

The Bossy Gallito/El gallo de bodas: A Traditional Cuban Folktale by Lucía González, illustrated by Lulu Delacre (Scholastic)

Family Pictures/Cuadros de familia by Carmen Lomas Garza, Spanish language text by Rosalma Zubizaretta, illustrated by Carmen Lomas Garza (Children's Book Press)

1998

Narrative: Parrot in the Oven: Mi vida by Victor Martinez (Joanna Cotler/HarperCollins)

Illustration: Snapshots from the Wedding by Gary Soto, illustrated by Stephanie Garcia (Putnam)

Honor Books

Narrative: Laughing Tomatoes and Other Spring Poems/Jitomates risueños y otros poemas de primavera by Francisco Alarcón, illustrated by Maya Christina Gonzalez (Children's Book Press)

Spirits of the High Mesa by Floyd Martinez (Arte Público)

Illustration: In My Family/En mi familia by Carmen Lomas Garza (Children's Book Press)

The Golden Flower: A Taino Myth from Puerto Rico by Nina Jaffe, illustrated by Enrique O. Sánchez (Simon & Schuster)

Gathering the Sun: An Alphabet in Spanish and English by Alma Flor Ada, English translation by Rosa Zubizarreta, illustrated by Simón Silva (Lothrop)

2000

Narrative: Under the Royal Palms: A Childhood in Cuba by Alma Flor Ada (Atheneum)

Illustration: Magic Windows by Carmen Lomas Garza (Children's Book Press)

Honor Books

Narrative: From the Bellybutton of the Moon and Other Summer Poems/Del ombligo de la luna y otro poemas de verano by Francisco X. Alarcón, illustrated by Maya Christina Gonzalez (Children's Book Press)

Laughing Out Loud, I Fly: Poems in English and Spanish by Juan Felipe Herrera, illustrated by Karen Barbour (HarperCollins)

Illustration: Barrio: José's Neighborhood by George Ancona (Harcourt Brace)

The Secret Stars by Joseph Slate, illustrated by Felipe Dávalos (Marshall Cavendish)

Mama and Papa Have a Store by Amelia Lau Carling (Dial)

BOSTON GLOBE–HORN BOOK AWARD

This award, which was established in 1967, is cosponsored by the *Boston Globe* and the *Horn Book Magazine*. Originally, the award was given for text and illustration, but in 1976, the categories were changed. Currently, the award goes to one outstanding example of fiction, nonfiction, and illustration each year. The recipients of the awards need not be U.S. citizens; however, the books must have been published in the United States.

1967

Text: The Little Fishes by Erik Christian Haugaard (Houghton Mifflin)

Illustration: London Bridge Is Falling Down by Peter Spier (Doubleday)

1968

Text: The Spring Rider by John Lawson (Crowell)

Illustration: Tikki Tikki Tembo by Arlene Mosel, illustrated by Blair Lent (Holt)

1969

Text: A Wizard of Earthsea by Ursula K. Le Guin (Houghton Mifflin)

Illustration: The Adventures of Paddy Pork by John S. Goodall (Harcourt)

1970

Text: The Intruder by John Rowe Townsend (Lippincott)

Illustration: Hi, Cat! by Erza Jack Keats (Macmillan)

1971

Text: A Room Made of Windows by Eleanor Cameron (Atlantic/Little, Brown)

Illustration: If I Built a Village by Kazue Mizumura (Crowell)

1972

Text: Tristan and Iseult by Rosemary Sutcliff (Dutton)

Illustration: Mr. Gumpy's Outing by John Burningham (Holt)

1973

Text: The Dark Is Rising by Susan Cooper (Atheneum/McElderry)

Illustration: King Stork by Trina Schart Hyman (Little, Brown)

1974

Text: M. C. Higgins, the Great by Virginia Hamilton (Macmillan)

Illustration: Jambo Means Hello by Muriel Feelings, illustrated by Tom Feelings (Dial)

1975

Text: Transport 7-41-R by T. Degens (Viking)

Illustration: Anno's Alphabet by Mitsumasa Anno (Crowell)

1976

Fiction: Unleaving by Jill Paton Walsh (Farrar)

Nonfiction: Voyaging to Cathay: Americans in the China Trade by Alfred Tamarin and Shirley Glubok (Viking)

*Illustration: **Thirteen*** by Remy Charlip and Jerry Joyner (Parents)

1977
*Fiction: **Child of the Owl*** by Laurence Yep (Harper)
*Nonfiction: **Chance, Luck and Density*** by Peter Dickinson (Atlantic/Little, Brown)
*Illustration: **Granfa' Grig Had a Pig and Other Rhymes*** by Wallace Tripp (Little, Brown)

1978
*Fiction: **The Westing Game*** by Ellen Raskin (Dutton)
*Nonfiction: **Mischling, Second Degree: My Childhood in Nazi Germany*** by Ilse Koehn (Greenwillow)
*Illustration: **Anno's Journey*** by Mitsumasa Anno (Philomel)

1979
*Fiction: **Humbug Mountain*** by Sid Fleischman (Atlantic/Little, Brown)
*Nonfiction: **The Road from Home: The Story of an Armenian Girl*** by David Kherdian (Greenwillow)
*Illustration: **The Snowman*** by Raymond Briggs (Random House)

1980
*Fiction: **Conrad's War*** by Andrew Davies (Crown)
*Nonfiction: **Building: The Fight against Gravity*** by Mario Salvadori (Atheneum/McElderry)
*Illustration: **The Garden of Abdul Gasazi*** by Chris Van Allsburg (Houghton Mifflin)

1981
*Fiction: **The Leaving*** by Lynn Hall (Scribner's)
*Nonfiction: **The Weaver's Gift*** by Kathryn Lasky (Warne)
*Illustration: **Outside Over There*** by Maurice Sendak (Harper)

1982
*Fiction: **Playing Beatie Bow*** by Ruth Park (Atheneum)
*Nonfiction: **Upon the Head of the Goat: A Childhood in Hungary, 1939–1944*** by Aranka Siegal (Farrar)
*Illustration: **A Visit to William Blake's Inn: Poems for Innocent and Experienced Travelers*** by Nancy Willard, illustrated by Alice and Martin Provensen (Harcourt)

1983
*Fiction: **Sweet Whispers, Brother Rush*** by Virginia Hamilton (Philomel)

*Nonfiction: **Behind Barbed Wire: The Imprisonment of Japanese Americans During World War II*** by Daniel S. Davis (Dutton)
*Illustration: **A Chair for My Mother*** by Vera B. Williams (Greenwillow)

1984
*Fiction: **A Little Fear*** by Patricia Wrightson (McElderry/Atheneum)
*Nonfiction: **The Double Life of Pocahontas*** by Jean Fritz (Putnam)
*Illustration: **Jonah and the Great Fish***, retold and illustrated by Warwick Hutton (McElderry/Atheneum)

1985
*Fiction: **The Moves Make the Man*** by Bruce Brooks (Harper)
*Nonfiction: **Commodore Perry in the Land of the Shogun*** by Rhoda Blumberg (Lothrop)
*Illustration: **Mama Don't Allow*** by Thatcher Hurd (Harper)

1986
*Fiction: **In Summer Light*** by Zibby O'Neal (Viking)
*Nonfiction: **Auks, Rocks, and the Odd Dinosaur: Inside Stories from the Smithsonian Museum of Natural History*** by Peggy Thomson (Crowell)
*Illustration: **Paper Crane*** by Molly Bang (Greenwillow)

1987
*Fiction: **Rabble Starkey*** by Lois Lowry (Houghton Mifflin)
*Nonfiction: **Pilgrims of Plimoth*** by Marcia Sewall (Atheneum)
*Illustration: **Mufaro's Beautiful Daughters: An African Tale*** by John Steptoe (Lothrop)

1988
*Fiction: **The Friendship*** by Mildred D. Taylor (Dial)
*Nonfiction: **Anthony Burns: The Defeat and Triumph of a Fugitive Slave*** by Virginia Hamilton (Knopf)
*Illustration: **The Boy of the Three-Year Nap*** by Dianne Snyder, illustrated by Allen Say (Houghton Mifflin)

1989
*Fiction: **Village by the Sea*** by Paula Fox (Orchard)
*Nonfiction: **The Way Things Work*** by David Macaulay (Houghton Mifflin)
*Illustration: **Shy Charles*** by Rosemary Wells (Dial)

1990

*Fiction: **Maniac Magee*** by Jerry Spinelli (Little, Brown)

*Nonfiction: **Great Little Madison*** by Jean Fritz (Putnam)

*Picture Book: **Lon Po Po: A Red Riding Hood Story from China*** by Ed Young (Philomel)

Honor Books

*Fiction: **Saturnalia*** by Paul Fleischman (Harper)
Stonewords by Pam Conrad (Harper)

*Nonfiction: **Insect Metamorphosis: From Egg to Adult*** by Ron and Nancy Goor, illustrated with photographs by Ron Goor (Atheneum)

*Picture Book: **Chicka Chicka Boom Boom*** by Bill Martin, Jr. and John Archambault, illustrated by Lois Ehlert (Simon)

1991

*Fiction: **True Confessions of Charlotte Doyle*** by Avi (Orchard)

*Nonfiction: **Appalachia: The Voices of Sleeping Birds*** by Cynthia Rylant (Harcourt)

*Picture Book: **Tale of the Mandarin Ducks*** by Katherine Paterson, illustrated by Leo and Diane Dillon (Lodestar)

Honor Books

*Fiction: **Paradise Cafe and Other Stories*** by Martha Brooks (Joy Street)
Judy Scuppernong by Brenda Seabrooke (Cobblehill)

*Nonfiction: **The Wright Brothers: How They Invented the Airplane*** by Russell Freedman (Holiday House)
Good Queen Bess: The Story of Elizabeth I of England by Diane Stanley and Peter Vennema, illustrated by Diane Stanley (Four Winds)

*Picture Books: **Aardvarks, Disembark!*** by Ann Jonas (Greenwillow)
Sophie and Lou by Petra Mathers (Harper)

1992

*Fiction: **Missing May*** by Cynthia Rylant (Orchard)

*Nonfiction: **Talking with Artists*** by Pat Cummings (Bradbury)

*Picture Book: **Seven Blind Mice*** by Ed Young (Philomel)

Honor Books

*Fiction: **Nothing but the Truth*** by Avi (Jackson/Orchard)
Somewhere in the Darkness by Walter Dean Myers (Scholastic)

*Nonfiction: **Red Leaf, Yellow Leaf*** by Lois Ehlert (Harcourt)
The Handmade Alphabet by Laura Rankin (Dial)

*Picture Book: **In the Tall, Tall Grass*** by Denise Fleming (Holt)

1993

*Fiction: **Ajeemah and His Son*** by James Berry (Harper)

*Nonfiction: **Sojourner Truth: Ain't I a Woman?*** by Patricia and Fredrick McKissack (Scholastic)

*Picture Book: **Fortune Tellers*** by Lloyd Alexander, illustrated by Trina Schart Hyman (Dutton)

Honor Books

*Fiction: **The Giver*** by Lois Lowry (Houghton)

*Nonfiction: **Lives of the Musicians: Good Times, Bad Times (And What the Neighbors Thought)*** by Kathleen Krull, illustrated by Kathryn Hewitt (Harcourt)

*Picture Books: **Komodo!*** by Peter Sís (Greenwillow)
Raven: A Trickster Tale from the Pacific Northwest by Gerald McDermott (Harcourt)

1994

*Fiction: **Scooter*** by Vera Williams (Greenwillow)

*Nonfiction: **Eleanor Roosevelt: A Life of Discovery*** by Russell Freedman (Houghton Mifflin)

*Picture Book: **Grandfather's Journey*** by Allen Say (Houghton Mifflin)

Honor Books

*Fiction: **Flour Babies*** by Anne Fine (Little)
Western Wind by Paula Fox (Orchard)

*Nonfiction: **Unconditional Surrender: U.S. Grant and the Civil War*** by Albert Marrin (Atheneum)
A Tree Place and Other Poems by Constance Levy, illustrated by Robert Sabuda (McElderry)

*Picture Books: **Owen*** by Kevin Henkes (Greenwillow)
A Small Tall Tale from the Far Far North by Peter Sis (Knopf)

1995

*Fiction: **Some of the Kinder Planets*** by Tim Wynne-Jones (Orchard)

*Nonfiction: **Abigail Adams: Witness to a Revolution*** by Natalie S. Bober (Atheneum)

*Picture Book: **John Henry*** by Julius Lester, illustrated by Jerry Pinkney (Dial)

Honor Books

*Fiction: **Jericho*** by Janet Hickman (Greenwillow)
Earthshine by Theresa Nelson (Jackson/Orchard)

Nonfiction: *It's Perfectly Normal: Changing Bodies, Growing Up, Sex, and Sexual Health* by Robie H. Harris, illustrated by Michael Emberley (Candlewick)
The Great Fire by Jim Murphy (Scholastic)
Picture Book: *Swamp Angel* by Anne Isaacs, illustrated by Paul O. Zelinsky (Dutton)

1996

Fiction: *Poppy* by Avi, illustrated by Brian Floca (Jackson/Orchard)
Nonfiction: *Orphan Train Rider: One Boy's True Story* by Andrea Warren (Houghton Mifflin)
Picture Book: *In the Rain with Baby Duck* by Amy Hest, illustrated by Jill Barton (Candlewick)

Honor Books

Fiction: *The Moorchild* by Eloise McGraw (McElderry)
Belle Prater's Boy by Ruth White (Farrar)
Nonfiction: *The Boy Who Lived with the Bears: And Other Iroquois Stories* by Joseph Bruchac, illustrated by Murv Jacob (Harper)
Haystack by Bonnie and Arthur Geisert, illustrated by Arthur Geisert (Houghton)
Picture Books: *Fanny's Dream* by Caralyn Buehner, illustrated by Mark Buehner (Dial)
Home Lovely by Lynne Rae Perkins (Greenwillow)

1997

Fiction and Poetry: *The Friends* by Kazumi Yumoto (Farrar)
Nonfiction: *A Drop of Water: A Book of Science and Wonder* by Walter Wick (Scholastic)
Picture Book: *The Adventures of Sparrowboy* by Brian Pinkney (Simon & Schuster)

Honor Books

Fiction and Poetry: *Lily's Crossing* by Patricia Reilly Giff (Delacorte)
Harlem by Walter Dean Myers, illustrated by Christopher Myers (Scholastic Press)
Nonfiction: *Lou Gehrig: The Luckiest Man* by David A. Adler, illustrated by Terry Widener (Gulliver/Harcourt)
Leonardo da Vinci written and illustrated by Diane Stanley (Morrow)
Picture Books: *Home on the Bayou: A Cowboy's Story* written and illustrated by G. Brian Karas (Simon)
Potato: A Tale from the Great Depression by Kate Lied, illustrated by Lisa Campbell Ernst (National Geographic)

1998

Fiction and Poetry: *The Circuit: Stories from the Life of a Migrant Child* by Francisco Jiménez (University of New Mexico Press)
Nonfiction: *Leon's Story* by Leon Walter Tillage, illustrated by Susan L. Roth (Farrar)
Picture Book: *And If the Moon Could Talk* by Kate Banks, illustrated by Georg Hallensleben (Foster/Farrar)

Honor Books

Fiction and Poetry: *While No One Was Watching* by Jane Leslie Conly (Holt)
My Louisiana Sky by Kimberly Willis Holt (Holt)
Nonfiction: *Martha Graham: A Dancer's Life* by Russell Freedman (Clarion)
Chuck Close Up Close by Jan Greenberg and Sandra Jordan (DK Ink)
Picture Books: *Seven Brave Women* by Betsy Hearne, illustrated by Bethanne Andersen (Greenwillow)
Popcorn: Poems written and illustrated by James Stevenson (Greenwillow)

1999

Fiction: *Holes* by Louis Sachar (Foster/Farrar)
Nonfiction: *The Top of the World: Climbing Mount Everest* written and illustrated by Steve Jenkins (Houghton Mifflin)
Picture Book: *Red-Eyed Tree Frog* by Joy Cowley, illustrated with photographs by Nic Bishop (Scholastic Press)

Honor Books

Fiction: *The Trolls* by Polly Horvath (Farrar, Straus and Giroux)
Monster by Walter Dean Myers, illustrated by Christopher Myers (HarperCollins)
Nonfiction: *Shipwreck at the Bottom of the World: The Extraordinary True Story of Shackleton and the Endurance* by Jennifer Armstrong (Crown)
William Shakespeare & the Globe written and illustrated by Aliki (HarperCollins)
Picture Books: *Dance* by Bill T. Jones and Susan Kuklin, illustrated with photographs by Susan Kuklin (Hyperion)
The Owl and the Pussycat by Edward Lear, illustrated by James Marshall (di Capua/HarperCollins)

Special Citation
Tibet: Through the Red Box written and illustrated by Peter Sís (Foster/Farrar)

2000
Fiction: **The Folk Keeper** by Franny Billingsley (Atheneum)
Nonfiction: **Sir Walter Ralegh and the Quest for El Dorado** by Marc Aronson (Clarion)
Picture Book: **Henry Hikes to Fitchburg** written and illustrated by D. B. Johnson (Houghton)

Honor Books
Fiction: **King of Shadows** by Susan Cooper (McElderry)

145th Street: Short Stories by Walter Dean Myers (Delacorte)
Nonfiction: **Osceola: Memories of a Sharecropper's Daughter** collected and edited by Alan Govenar, illustrated by Shane W. Evans (Jump at the Sun/Hyperion)
Sitting Bull and His World by Albert Marrin (Farrar, Straus and Giroux)
Picture Books: **Buttons** written and illustrated by Brock Cole (Farrar, Straus and Giroux)
a day, a dog illustrated by Gabrielle Vincent (Front Street)

RANDOLPH CALDECOTT MEDAL

The Randolph Caldecott Medal, named in honor of the nineteenth-century illustrator of children's books, is awarded annually under the supervision of the Association for Library Service to Children of the American Library Association. It is awarded to the illustrator of the most distinguished children's book published in the United States in the previous year. Usually, one or more Honor Books are also chosen. The award is limited to residents or citizens of the United States.

1938
Animals of the Bible by Helen Dean Fish, illustrated by Dorothy P. Lathrop (Lippincott)

Honor Books
Four and Twenty Blackbirds by Helen Dean Fish, illustrated by Robert Lawson (Stokes)
Seven Simeons by Boris Artzybasheff (Viking)

1939
Mei Li by Thomas Handforth (Doubleday)

Honor Books
Andy and the Lion by James Daugherty (Viking)
Barkis by Clare Newberry (Harper)
The Forest Pool by Laura Adams Armer (Longman)
Snow White and the Seven Dwarfs by Wanda Gág (Coward)
Wee Gillis by Munro Leaf, illustrated by Robert Lawson (Viking)

1940
Abraham Lincoln by Ingri and Edgar Parin D'Aulaire (Doubleday)

Honor Books
The Ageless Story by Lauren Ford (Dodd)

Cock-a-Doodle Doo by Berta and Elmer Hader (Macmillan)
Madeline by Ludwig Bemelmans (Viking)

1941
They Were Strong and Good by Robert Lawson (Viking)

Honor Book
April's Kittens by Clare Newberry (Harper)

1942
Make Way for Ducklings by Robert McCloskey (Viking)

Honor Books
An American ABC by Maud and Miska Petersham (Macmillan)
In My Mother's House by Ann Nolan Clark, illustrated by Velino Herrera (Viking)
Nothing at All by Wanda Gág (Coward)
Paddle-to-the-Sea by Holling C. Holling (Houghton Mifflin)

1943
The Little House by Virginia Lee Burton (Houghton Mifflin)

Honor Books
Dash and Dart by Mary and Conrad Buff (Viking)
Marshmallow by Clare Newberry (Harper)

1944
Many Moons by James Thurber, illustrated by Louis Slobodkin (Harcourt)

Honor Books
A Child's Good Night Book by Margaret Wise Brown, illustrated by Jean Charlot (Scott)

Good Luck Horse by Chin-Yi Chan, illustrated by Plao Chan (Whittlesey)

The Mighty Hunter by Berta and Elmer Hader (Macmillan)

Pierre Pigeon by Lee Kingman, illustrated by Arnold E. Bare (Houghton Mifflin)

Small Rain: Verses from the Bible selected by Jessie Orton Jones, illustrated by Elizabeth Orton Jones (Viking)

1945

Prayer for a Child by Rachel Field, illustrated by Elizabeth Orton Jones (Macmillan)

Honor Books

The Christmas Anna Angel by Ruth Sawyer, illustrated by Kate Seredy (Viking)

In the Forest by Marie Hall Ets (Viking)

Mother Goose illustrated by Tasha Tudor (Walck)

Yonie Wondernose by Marguerite de Angeli (Doubleday)

1946

The Rooster Crows (traditional Mother Goose) illustrated by Maud and Miska Petersham (Macmillan)

Honor Books

Little Lost Lamb by Golden MacDonald, illustrated by Leonard Weisgard (Doubleday)

My Mother Is the Most Beautiful Woman in the World by Becky Reyher, illustrated by Ruth C. Gannett (Lothrop)

Sing Mother Goose by Opal Wheeler, illustrated by Marjorie Torrey (Dutton)

You Can Write Chinese by Kurt Wiese (Viking)

1947

The Little Island by Golden MacDonald, illustrated by Leonard Weisgard (Doubleday)

Honor Books

Boats on the River by Marjorie Flack, illustrated by Jay Hyde Barnum (Viking)

Pedro, the Angel of Olvera Street by Leo Politi (Scribner's)

Rain Drop Splash by Alvin Tresselt, illustrated by Leonard Weisgard (Lothrop)

Sing in Praise: A Collection of the Best Loved Hymns by Opal Wheeler, illustrated by Marjorie Torrey (Dutton)

Timothy Turtle by Al Graham, illustrated by Tony Palazzo (Welch)

1948

White Snow, Bright Snow by Alvin Tresselt, illustrated by Roger Duvoisin (Lothrop)

Honor Books

Bambino the Clown by George Schreiber (Viking)

McElligot's Pool by Dr. Seuss (Random House)

Roger and the Fox by Lavinia Davis, illustrated by Hildegard Woodward (Doubleday)

Song of Robin Hood edited by Anne Malcolmson, illustrated by Virginia Lee Burton (Houghton Mifflin)

Stone Soup by Marcia Brown (Scribner's)

1949

The Big Snow by Berta and Elmer Hader (Macmillan)

Honor Books

All Around the Town by Phyllis McGinley, illustrated by Helen Stone (Lippincott)

Blueberries for Sal by Robert McCloskey (Viking)

Fish in the Air by Kurt Wiese (Viking)

Juanita by Leo Politi (Scribner's)

1950

Song of the Swallows by Leo Politi (Scribner's)

Honor Books

America's Ethan Allen by Stewart Holbrook, illustrated by Lynd Ward (Houghton Mifflin)

Bartholomew and the Oobleck by Dr. Suess (Random House)

The Happy Day by Ruth Krauss, illustrated by Marc Simont (Harper)

Henry Fisherman by Marcia Brown (Scribner's)

The Wild Birthday Cake by Lavinia Davis, illustrated by Hildegard Woodward (Doubleday)

1951

The Egg Tree by Katherine Milhous (Scribner's)

Honor Books

Dick Whittington and His Cat by Marcia Brown (Scribner's)

If I Ran the Zoo by Dr. Seuss (Random House)

The Most Wonderful Doll in the World by Phyllis McGinley, illustrated by Helen Stone (Lippincott)

T-Bone, the Baby Sitter by Clare Newberry (Harper)

The Two Reds by Will, illustrated by Nicolas (Harcourt)

1952

Finders Keepers by Will, illustrated by Nicolas (Harcourt)

All Falling Down by Gene Zion, illustrated by Margaret Bloy Graham (Harper)

Bear Party by William Pène du Bois (Viking)

Feather Mountain by Elizabeth Olds (Houghton Mifflin)

Mr. T. W. Anthony Woo by Marie Hall Ets (Viking)

Skipper John's Cook by Marcia Brown (Scribner's)

1953

The Biggest Bear by Lynd Ward (Houghton Mifflin)

Honor Books

Ape in a Cape by Fritz Eichenberg (Harcourt)

Five Little Monkeys by Juliet Kepes (Houghton Mifflin)

One Morning in Maine by Robert McCloskey (Viking)

Puss in Boots by Charles Perrault, illustrated by Marcia Brown (Scribner's)

The Storm Book by Charlotte Zolotow, illustrated by Margaret Bloy Graham (Harper)

1954

Madeline's Rescue by Ludwig Bemelmans (Viking)

Honor Books

A Very Special House by Ruth Krauss, illustrated by Maurice Sendak (Harper)

Green Eyes by A. Birnbaum (Capitol)

Journey Cake, Ho! by Ruth Sawyer, illustrated by Robert McCloskey (Viking)

The Steadfast Tin Soldier by Hans Christian Andersen, illustrated by Marcia Brown (Scribner's)

When Will the World Be Mine? by Miriam Schlein, illustrated by Jean Charlot (Scott)

1955

Cinderella, or the Little Glass Slipper by Charles Perrault, illustrated by Marcia Brown (Scribner's)

Honor Books

Book of Nursery and Mother Goose Rhymes illustrated by Marguerite de Angeli (Doubleday)

The Thanksgiving Story by Alice Dalgliesh, illustrated by Helen Sewell (Scribner's)

Wheel on the Chimney by Margaret Wise Brown, illustrated by Tibor Gergely (Lippincott)

1956

Frog Went A-Courtin' retold by John Langstaff, illustrated by Feodor Rojankovsky (Harcourt)

Honor Books

Crow Boy by Taro Yashima (Viking)

Play with Me by Marie Hall Ets (Viking)

1957

A Tree Is Nice by Janice May Udry, illustrated by Marc Simont (Harper)

Honor Books

Anatole by Eve Titus, illustrated by Paul Galdone (McGraw-Hill)

Gillespie and the Guards by Benjamin Elkin, illustrated by James Daugherty (Viking)

Lion by William Pène du Bois (Viking)

Mr. Penny's Race Horse by Marie Hall Ets (Viking)

1 Is One by Tasha Tudor (Walck)

1958

Time of Wonder by Robert McCloskey (Viking)

Honor Books

Anatole and the Cat by Eve Titus, illustrated by Paul Galdone (McGraw-Hill)

Fly High, Fly Low by Don Freeman (Viking)

1959

Chanticleer and the Fox adapted from Chaucer, illustrated by Barbara Cooney (Crowell)

Honor Books

The House That Jack Built by Antonio Frasconi (Harcourt)

Umbrella by Taro Yashima (Viking)

What Do You Say, Dear? by Sesyle Joslin, illustrated by Maurice Sendak (Scott)

1960

Nine Days to Christmas by Marie Hall Ets and Aurora Labastida, illustrated by Marie Hall Ets (Viking)

Honor Books

Houses from the Sea by Alice E. Goudey, illustrated by Adrienne Adams (Scribner's)

The Moon Jumpers by Janice May Udry, illustrated by Maurice Sendak (Harper)

1961

Baboushka and the Three Kings by Ruth Robbins, illustrated by Nicholas Sidjakov (Parnassus)

Honor Book

Inch by Inch by Leo Lionni (Astor-Honor)

1962

Once a Mouse by Marcia Brown (Scribner's)

Honor Books

The Day We Saw the Sun Come Up by Alice E.
Goudey, illustrated by Adrienne Adams
(Scribner's)

The Fox Went Out on a Chilly Night illustrated by
Peter Spier (Doubleday)

Little Bear's Visit by Else Holmelund Minarik, illustrated by Maurice Sendak (Harper)

1963

The Snowy Day by Ezra Jack Keats (Viking)

Honor Books

Mr. Rabbit and the Lovely Present by Charlotte
Zolotow, illustrated by Maurice Sendak
(Harper)

The Sun Is a Golden Earring by Natalia M. Belting,
illustrated by Bernarda Bryson (Holt)

1964

Where the Wild Things Are by Maurice Sendak
(Harper)

Honor Books

All in the Morning Early by Sorche Nic Leodhas,
illustrated by Evaline Ness (Holt)

Mother Goose and Nursery Rhymes illustrated by
Philip Reed (Atheneum)

Swimmy by Leo Lionni (Pantheon)

1965

May I Bring a Friend? by Beatrice Schenk de
Regniers, illustrated by Beni Montresor
(Atheneum)

Honor Books

A Pocketful of Cricket by Rebecca Caudill, illustrated by Evaline Ness (Holt)

Rain Makes Applesauce by Julian Scheer, illustrated
by Marvin Bileck (Holiday House)

The Wave by Margaret Hodges, illustrated by Blair
Lent (Houghton Mifflin)

1966

Always Room for One More by Sorche Nic
Leodhas, illustrated by Nonny Hogrogian
(Holt)

Honor Books

Hide and Seek Fog by Alvin Tresselt, illustrated by
Roger Duvoisin (Lothrop)

Just Me by Marie Hall Ets (Viking)

Tom Tit Tot by Evaline Ness (Scribner's)

1967

Sam, Bangs & Moonshine by Evaline Ness (Holt)

Honor Book

One Wide River to Cross by Barbara Emberley,
illustrated by Ed Emberley (Prentice-Hall)

1968

Drummer Hoff by Barbara Emberley, illustrated by
Ed Emberley (Prentice-Hall)

Honor Books

The Emperor and the Kite by Jane Yolen, illustrated
by Ed Young (World)

Frederick by Leo Lionni (Pantheon)

Seashore Story by Taro Yashima (Viking)

1969

The Fool of the World and the Flying Ship retold by
Arthur Ransome, illustrated by Uri Shulevitz
(Farrar)

Honor Book

Why the Sun and the Moon Live in the Sky by
Elphinstone Dayrell, illustrated by Blair Lent
(Houghton Mifflin)

1970

Sylvester and the Magic Pebble by William Steig
(Windmill/Simon & Schuster)

Honor Books

Alexander and the Wind-Up Mouse by Leo Lionni
(Pantheon)

Goggles! by Ezra Jack Keats (Macmillan)

The Judge by Harve Zemach, illustrated by Margot
Zemach (Farrar)

Pop Corn & Ma Goodness by Edna Mitchell
Preston, illustrated by Robert Andrew Parker
(Viking)

Thy Friend, Obadiah by Brinton Turkle (Viking)

1971

A Story, a Story by Gail E. Haley (Atheneum)

Honor Books

The Angry Moon by William Sleator, illustrated by
Blair Lent (Atlantic/Little, Brown)

Frog and Toad Are Friends by Arnold Lobel
(Harper)

In the Night Kitchen by Maurice Sendak (Harper)

1972

One Fine Day by Nonny Hogrogian (Macmillan)

Honor Books

Hildilid's Night by Cheli Durán Ryan, illustrated by
Arnold Lobel (Macmillan)

If All the Seas Were One Sea by Janina Domanska
(Macmillan)

Moja Means One by Muriel Feelings, illustrated by Tom Feelings (Dial)

1973

The Funny Little Woman retold by Arlene Mosel, illustrated by Blair Lent (Dutton)

Honor Books

Anansi the Spider adapted and illustrated by Gerald McDermott (Holt)

Hosie's Alphabet by Hosea, Tobias, and Lisa Baskin, illustrated by Leonard Baskin (Viking)

Snow White and the Seven Dwarfs illustrated by Nancy Eckholm Burkert (Farrar)

When Clay Sings by Byrd Baylor, illustrated by Tom Bahti (Scribner's)

1974

Duffy and the Devil retold by Harve Zemach, illustrated by Margot Zemach (Farrar)

Honor Books

Cathedral by David Macaulay (Houghton Mifflin)

Three Jovial Huntsmen by Susan Jeffers (Bradbury)

1975

Arrow to the Sun by Gerald McDermott (Viking)

Honor Book

Jambo Means Hello by Muriel Feelings, illustrated by Tom Feelings (Dial)

1976

Why Mosquitoes Buzz in People's Ears by Verna Aardema, illustrated by Leo and Diane Dillon (Dial)

Honor Books

The Desert Is Theirs by Byrd Baylor, illustrated by Peter Parnall (Scribner's)

Strega Nona retold and illustrated by Tomie de Paola (Prentice)

1977

Ashanti to Zulu: African Traditions by Margaret Musgrove, illustrated by Leo and Diane Dillon (Dial)

Honor Books

The Amazing Bone by William Steig (Farrar)

The Contest retold and illustrated by Nonny Hogrogian (Greenwillow)

Fish for Supper by M. B. Goffstein (Dial)

The Golem by Beverly Brodsky McDermott (Lippincott)

Hawk, I'm Your Brother by Byrd Baylor, illustrated by Peter Parnall (Scribner's)

1978

Noah's Ark illustrated by Peter Spier (Doubleday)

Honor Books

Castle by David Macaulay (Houghton Mifflin)

It Could Always Be Worse by Margot Zemach (Farrar)

1979

The Girl Who Loved Wild Horses by Paul Goble (Bradbury)

Honor Books

Freight Train by Donald Crews (Greenwillow)

The Way to Start a Day by Byrd Baylor, illustrated by Peter Parnall (Scribner's)

1980

Ox-Cart Man by Donald Hall, illustrated by Barbara Cooney (Viking)

Honor Books

Ben's Trumpet by Rachel Isadora (Greenwillow)

The Garden of Abdul Gasazi by Chris Van Allsburg (Houghton Mifflin)

The Treasure by Uri Shulevitz (Farrar)

1981

Fables by Arnold Lobel (Harper)

Honor Books

The Bremen Town Musicians retold and illustrated by Ilse Plume (Doubleday)

The Grey Lady and the Strawberry Snatcher by Molly Bang (Four Winds)

Mice Twice by Joseph Low (McElderry)

Truck by Donald Crews (Greenwillow)

1982

Jumanji by Chris Van Allsburg (Houghton Mifflin)

Honor Books

On Market Street by Arnold Lobel, illustrated by Anita Lobel (Greenwillow)

Outside Over There by Maurice Sendak (Harper)

A Visit to William Blake's Inn: Poems for Innocent and Experienced Travelers by Nancy Willard, illustrated by Alice and Martin Provensen (Harcourt)

Where the Buffaloes Begin by Olaf Baker, illustrated by Stephen Gammell (Viking)

1983

Shadow by Blaise Cendrars, illustrated by Marcia Brown (Scribner's)

Honor Books

A Chair for My Mother by Vera B. Williams (Greenwillow)

When I Was Young in the Mountains by Cynthia Rylant, illustrated by Diane Goode (Dutton)

1984

The Glorious Flight: Across the Channel with Louis Blériot by Alice and Martin Provensen (Viking)

Honor Books

Little Red Riding Hood retold and illustrated by Trina Schart Hyman (Holiday House)

Ten, Nine, Eight by Molly Bang (Greenwillow)

1985

Saint George and the Dragon by Margaret Hodges, illustrated by Trina Schart Hyman (Little, Brown)

Honor Books

Hansel and Gretel retold by Rika Lesser, illustrated by Paul O. Zelinsky (Dodd)

Have You Seen My Duckling? by Nancy Tafuri (Greenwillow)

The Story of Jumping Mouse retold and illustrated by John Steptoe (Lothrop)

1986

The Polar Express by Chris Van Allsburg (Houghton Mifflin)

Honor Books

King Bidgood's in the Bathtub by Audrey Wood, illustrated by Don Wood (Harcourt)

The Relatives Came by Cynthia Rylant, illustrated by Stephen Gammell (Bradbury)

1987

Hey, Al! by Arthur Yorinks, illustrated by Richard Egielski (Farrar)

Honor Books

Alphabatics by Suse MacDonald (Bradbury)

Rumpelstiltskin by Paul O. Zelinsky (Dutton)

The Village of Round and Square Houses by Ann Grifalconi (Little, Brown)

1988

Owl Moon by Jane Yolen, illustrated by John Schoenherr (Philomel)

Honor Book

Mufaro's Beautiful Daughters: An African Tale by John Steptoe (Lothrop)

1989

Song and Dance Man by Karen Ackerman, illustrated by Stephen Gammell (Knopf)

Honor Books

The Boy of the Three-Year Nap by Dianne Snyder, illustrated by Allen Say (Houghton Mifflin)

Free-Fall by David Wiesner (Lothrop)

Goldilocks and the Three Bears by James Marshall (Dial)

Mirandy and Brother Wind by Patricia C. McKissack, illustrated by Jerry Pinkney (Knopf)

1990

Lon Po Po: A Red-Riding Hood Story from China by Ed Young (Philomel)

Honor Books

Bill Peet: An Autobiography by Bill Peet (Houghton Mifflin)

Color Zoo by Lois Ehlert (Lippincott)

Hershel and the Hanukkah Goblins by Eric Kimmel, illustrated by Trina Schart Hyman (Holiday House)

The Talking Eggs by Robert D. San Souci, illustrated by Jerry Pinkney (Dial)

1991

Black and White by David Macaulay (Houghton Mifflin)

Honor Books

"More More More," Said the Baby: 3 Love Stories by Vera B. Williams (Greenwillow)

Puss in Boots by Charles Perrault, translated by Malcolm Arthur, illustrated by Fred Marcellino (Farrar)

1992

Tuesday by David Wiesner (Clarion)

Honor Book

Tar Beach by Faith Ringgold (Crown)

1993

Mirette on the High Wire by Emily Arnold McCully (Putnam)

Honor Books

Seven Blind Mice by Ed Young (Philomel)

The Stinky Cheese Man and Other Fairly Stupid Tales by Jon Scieszka, illustrated by Lane Smith (Viking)

Working Cotton by Sherley Anne Williams, illustrated by Carole Byard (Harcourt)

1994

Grandfather's Journey by Allen Say (Houghton Mifflin)

Honor Books

Owen by Kevin Henkes (Greenwillow)

Peppe, the Lamplighter by Elisa Bartone, illustrated by Ted Lewin (Lothrop)

Raven by Gerald McDermott (Harcourt)

In the Small, Small Pond by Denise Fleming (Holt)

Yo! Yes? by Chris Raschka (Orchard)

1995

Smoky Night by Eve Bunting, illustrated by David Diaz (Harcourt)

Honor Books

Swamp Angel by Anne Isaacs, illustrated by Paul O. Zelinksy (Dutton)

John Henry by Julius Lester, illustrated by Jerry Pinkney (Dial)

Time Flies by Eric Rohmann (Crown)

1996

Officer Buckle and Gloria by Peggy Rathmann (Putnam)

Honor Books

Alphabet City by Stephen T. Johnson (Viking)

Zin! Zin! Zin! A Violin by Lloyd Moss, illustrated by Marjorie Priceman (Simon & Schuster)

The Faithful Friend by Robert D. San Souci, illustrated by Brian Pinkney (Simon & Schuster)

Tops & Bottoms by Janet Stevens (Harcourt)

1997

Golem by David Wisniewski (Clarion)

Honor Books

Hush! A Thai Lullaby by Minfong Ho, illustrated by Holly Meade (Kroupa/Orchard)

The Graphic Alphabet by David Pelletier (Orchard)

The Paperboy by Dav Pilkey (Jackson/Orchard)

Starry Messenger by Peter Sís (Foster/Farrar)

1998

Rapunzel by Paul O. Zelinsky (Dutton)

Honor Books

The Gardener by Sarah Stewart, illustrated by David Small (Farrar)

Harlem by Walter Dean Myers, illustrated by Christopher Myers (Scholastic)

There Was an Old Lady Who Swallowed a Fly by Simms Taback (Viking)

1999

Snowflake Bentley by Jacqueline Briggs Martin, illustrated by Mary Azarian (Houghton Mifflin)

Honor Books

Duke Ellington: The Piano Prince and the Orchestra by Andrea Davis Pinkney, illustrated by Brian Pinkney (Hyperion)

No, David! by David Shannon (Scholastic)

Snow by Uri Shulevitz (Farrar)

Tibet: Through the Red Box by Peter Sís (Foster/Farrar)

2000

Joseph Had a Little Overcoat by Simms Taback (Viking)

Honor Books

A Child's Calendar by John Updike, illustrated by Trina Schart Hyman (Holiday House)

Sector 7 by David Wiesner (Clarion)

When Sophie Gets Angry—Really, Really Angry . . . by Molly Bang (Scholastic)

The Ugly Duckling by Hans Christian Andersen, adapted by Jerry Pinkney, illustrated by Jerry Pinkney (Morrow)

2001

So You Want to Be President? by Judith St. George, illustrated by David Small (Philomel)

Honor Books

Casey at the Bat by Ernest Lawrence Thayer, illustrated by Christopher Bing (Handprint)

Click, Clack, Moo: Cows That Type by Doreen Cronin, illustrated by Betsy Lewin (Simon & Schuster)

Olivia by Ian Falconer (Atheneum)

INTERNATIONAL READING ASSOCIATION CHILDREN'S BOOK AWARD

This award is given annually to honor new talent in children's literature. Publishers worldwide are invited to suggest candidates. Since 1987, an award has been given to one author who writes for older readers and one author who writes for younger readers. In 1995, a third award was added for an author of an informational book.

1975

Transport 7-41-R by T. Degens (Viking, United States)

1976

Dragonwings by Laurence Yep (Harper, United States)

1977

A String in the Harp by Nancy Bond (McElderry, United States)

1978

A Summer to Die by Lois Lowry (Houghton Mifflin, United States)

1979

Reserved for Mark Anthony Crowder by Alison Smith (Dutton, United States)

1980

Words by Heart by Ouida Sebestyen (Atlantic/Little, Brown, United States)

1981

My Own Private Sky by Delores Beckman (Dutton, United States)

1982

Goodnight, Mister Tom by Michelle Magorian (Kestrel, Great Britain)

1983

The Darkangel by Meredith Ann Pierce (Atlantic/Little, Brown, United States)

1984

Ratha's Creature by Clare Bell (McElderry, United States)

1985

Badger on the Barge by Janni Howker (Julia MacRae, Great Britain)

1986

Prairie Songs by Pam Conrad (Harper, United States)

1987

Older Readers: After the Dancing Days by Margaret I. Rostkowski (Harper, United States)
Younger Readers: The Line-Up Book by Marisabina Russo (Greenwillow, United States)

1988

Older Readers: The Ruby in the Smoke and *Shadow in the North* by Philip Pullman (Oxford, Great Britain)

Younger Readers: The Third-Story Cat by Leslie Baker (Little, Brown, United States)

1989

Older Readers: Probably Still Nick Swansen by Virginia Euwer Wolff (Holt, United States)
Younger Readers: Rechenka's Eggs by Patricia Polacco (Philomel, United States)

1990

Older Readers: Children of the River by Linda Crew (Delacorte, United States)
Younger Readers: No Star Nights by Anna Egan Smucker, illustrated by Steve Johnson (Knopf, United States)

1991

Older Readers: Under the Hawthorn Tree by Marita Conlon-McKenna (O'Brien Press, Ireland)
Younger Readers: Is This a House for Hermit Crab? by Megan McDonald, illustrated by S. D. Schindler (Orchard, United States)

1992

Older Readers: Rescue Josh McGuire by Ben Mikaelsen (Hyperion, United States)
Younger Readers: Ten Little Rabbits by Virginia Grossman, illustrated by Sylvia Long (Chronicle, United States)

1993

Older Readers: Letters from Rifka by Karen Hesse (Holt, United States)
Younger Readers: Old Turtle by Douglas Wood, illustrated by Cheng-Khee Chee (Pfeifer-Hamilton, United States)

1994

Older Readers: Behind the Secret Window: A Memoir of a Hidden Childhood by Nelly S. Toll (Dutton, United States)
Younger Readers: Sweet Clara and the Freedom Quilt by Deborah Hopkinson, illustrated by James E. Ransome (Knopf, United States)

1995

Older Readers: Spite Fences by Trudy Krisher (Bantam, United States)
Younger Readers: The Ledgerbook of Thomas Blue Eagle by Gay Matthaei and Jewel Grutman, illustrated by Adam Cvijanovic (Thomasson-Grant, United States)
Informational Book: Stranded at Plimouth Plantation 1626 by Gary Bowen (HarperCollins, United States)

1996

Older Readers: **The King's Shadow** by Elizabeth Alder (Farrar, United States)

Younger Readers: **More Than Anything Else** by Marie Bradby, illustrated by Chris K. Soentpiet (Orchard, United States)

Informational Book: **The Case of the Mummified Pigs and Other Mysteries in Nature** by Susan E. Quinlan (Boyds Mills, United States)

1997

Older Readers: **Don't You Dare Read This Mrs. Dunphrey** by Margaret Peterson Haddix (Simon & Schuster, United States)

Younger Readers: **The Fabulous Flying Fandinis** by Ingrid Slyder (Cobblehill, United States)

Informational Book: **Brooklyn Bridge** by Elizabeth Mann (Mikaya Press, United States)

1998

Older Readers: **Moving Mama to Town** by Ronder Thomas Young (Orchard, United States)

Younger Readers: **Nim and the War Effort** by Millie Lee and Yangsook Choi (Farrar, United States)

Informational Book: **Just What the Doctor Ordered: The History of American Medicine** by Brandon Marie Miller (Lerner, United States)

1999

Older Readers: **Choosing Up Sides** by John Ritter (Penguin Putnam, United States)

Younger Readers: **My Freedom Trip: A Child's Escape from North Korea** by Frances and Ginger Park (Boyds Mills, United States)

Informational Book: **First in the Field, Baseball Hero Jackie Robinson** by Derek T. Dingle (Hyperion, United States)

2000

Older Fiction: **Bud, Not Buddy** by Christopher Paul Curtis (Delacorte, United States)

Older Nonfiction: **Eleanor's Story: An American Girl in Hitler's Germany** by Eleanor Ramrath Garner (Peachtree Publishers, United States)

Younger Fiction: **Molly Bannaky** by Alice McGill (Houghton Mifflin, United States)

Younger Nonfiction: **The Snake Scientist** by Sy Montgomery (Houghton Mifflin, United States)

EZRA JACK KEATS NEW WRITERS AWARD

Ezra Jack Keats (1919–1983) was a prolific illustrator of children's picture books who won the Caldecott Medal in 1963 for **The Snowy Day**. The Ezra Jack Keats award is funded by the Ezra Jack Keats Foundation and is given to a promising writer who has had six or fewer children's books published. The writer need not be the illustrator. The books must "reflect the tradition of Ezra Jack Keats," whose books portrayed strong family relationships and universal qualities of childhood; the books must also appeal to children nine years old or younger. The award is presented at two-year intervals and is administered by the Early Childhood Resources and Information Center of the New York Public Library.

1987

The Patchwork Quilt by Valerie Flournoy, illustrated by Jerry Pinkney (Dial)

1989

Jamaica's Find by Juanita Havill, illustrated by Anne Sibley O'Brien (Houghton Mifflin)

1991

Tell Me A Story, Mama by Angela Johnson (Orchard)

1993

Tar Beach by Faith Ringgold (Crown)

1995

Taxi, Taxi by Cari Best, illustrated by Dale Gottlieb (Little, Brown)

1997

Calling the Doves/El canto de las palomas by Juan Felipé Herrera (Children's Book Press)

1999

Elizabeti's Doll by Stephanie Stuve-Bodeen, illustrated by Christy Hale (Lee & Low)

CORETTA SCOTT KING AWARD

The Coretta Scott King Award is presented annually by the Coretta Scott King Task Force of the American Library Association's Social Responsibilities Round Table. It has been awarded to African American authors since 1970 and also to African American illustrators since 1974 for books that encourage understanding and appreciation of people of all cultures and their pursuit of the "American dream." The award celebrates the life of Martin Luther King, Jr., and honors his widow, Coretta Scott King, for her strength and dedication in continuing the fight for racial equity and universal peace. One or more Honor Books may also be chosen each year.

1970

*Author Award: **Dr. Martin Luther King, Jr., Man of Peace*** by Lillie Patterson (Garrard)

1971

*Author Award: **Black Troubadour: Langston Hughes*** by Charlemae Rollins (Rand McNally)

Honor Books

I Know Why the Caged Bird Sings by Maya Angelou (Random House)

Unbought and Unbossed by Shirley Chisholm (Houghton Mifflin)

I Am a Black Woman by Mari Evans (Morrow)

Every Man Heart Lay Down by Lorenz Graham (Crowell)

The Voice of the Children by June Jordan and Terri Bush (Holt)

Black Means by Gladys Groom and Bonnie Grossman (Hill & Wang)

Ebony Book of Black Achievement by Margaret W. Peters (Johnson)

Mary Jo's Grandmother by Janice May Udry (Whitman)

1972

*Author Award: **17 Black Artists*** by Elton C. Fax (Dodd)

1973

*Author Award: **I Never Had It Made: The Autobiography of Jackie Robinson*** by Alfred Duckett (Putnam)

1974

*Author Award: **Ray Charles*** by Sharon Bell Mathis (Crowell)

Honor Books

A Hero Ain't Nothin' but a Sandwich by Alice Childress (Coward-McCann)

Don't You Remember? by Lucille Clifton (Dutton)

Ms. Africa: Profiles of Modern African Women by Louise Crane (Lippincott)

Guest in the Promised Land by Kristin Hunter (Scribner's)

Mukasa by John Nagenda (Macmillan)

*Illustrator Award: **Ray Charles*** by Sharon Bell Mathis, illustrated by George Ford (Crowell)

1975

*Author Award: **The Legend of Africana*** by Dorothy Robinson (Johnson)

1976

*Author Award: **Duey's Tale*** by Pearl Bailey (Harcourt)

Honor Books

Julius K. Nyerere: Teacher of Africa by Shirley Graham (Messner)

Paul Robeson by Eloise Greenfield (Crowell)

Fast Sam, Cool Clyde and Stuff by Walter Dean Myers (Viking)

Song of the Trees by Mildred Taylor (Dial)

1977

*Author Award: **The Story of Stevie Wonder*** by James Haskins (Lothrop)

Honor Books

Everett Anderson's Friend by Lucille Clifton (Holt)

Roll of Thunder, Hear My Cry by Mildred D. Taylor (Dial)

Quiz Book on Black America by Clarence N. Blake and Donald F. Martin (Houghton Mifflin)

1978

*Author Award: **Africa Dreams*** by Eloise Greenfield (Crowell)

Honor Books

The Days When the Animals Talked: Black Folk Tales and How They Came to Be by William J. Faulkner (Follett)

Marvin and Tige by Frankcina Glass (St. Martin's)

Mary McCleod Bethune by Eloise Greenfield (Crowell)

Barbara Jordan by James Haskins (Dial)

Coretta Scott King by Lillie Patterson (Garrard)

Portia: The Life of Portia Washington Pittman, the Daughter of Booker T. Washington by Ruth Ann Stewart (Doubleday)

1979
Author Award: Escape to Freedom: A Play about Young Frederick Douglass by Ossie Davis (Viking)

Honor Books

Skates of Uncle Richard by Carol Fenner (Random House)

Justice and Her Brothers by Virginia Hamilton (Greenwillow)

Benjamin Banneker by Lillie Patterson (Abingdon)

I Have a Sister, My Sister Is Deaf by Jeanne W. Peterson (Harper)

Illustrator Award: Something on My Mind by Nikkie Grimes, illustrated by Tom Feelings (Dial)

1980
Author Award: The Young Landlords by Walter Dean Myers (Viking)

Honor Books

Movin' Up by Berry Gordy (Harper)

Childtimes: A Three-Generation Memoir by Eloise Greenfield and Lessie Jones Little (Harper)

Andrew Young: Young Man with a Mission by James Haskins (Lothrop)

James Van Der Zee: The Picture Takin' Man by James Haskins (Dodd)

Let the Lion Eat Straw by Ellease Southerland (Scribner's)

Illustrator Award: Cornrows by Camille Yarbrough, illustrated by Carole Byard (Coward-McCann)

1981
Author Award: This Life by Sidney Poitier (Knopf)

Honor Books

Don't Explain: A Song of Billie Holiday by Alexis De Veaux (Harper)

Illustrator Award: Beat the Story Drum, Pum-Pum by Ashley Bryan (Atheneum)

Honor Books

Grandmama's Joy by Eloise Greenfield, illustrated by Carole Byard (Philomel)

Count on Your Fingers African Style by Claudia Zaslavsky, illustrated by Jerry Pinkney (Crowell)

1982
Author Award: Let the Circle Be Unbroken by Mildred D. Taylor (Dial)

Honor Books

Rainbow Jordan by Alice Childress (Coward-McCann)

Lou in the Limelight by Kristin Hunter (Scribner's)

Mary: An Autobiography by Mary E. Mebane (Viking)

Illustrator Award: Mother Crocodile: An Uncle Amadou Tale from Senegal translated by Rosa Guy, illustrated by John Steptoe (Delacorte)

Honor Book

Daydreamers by Eloise Greenfield, illustrated by Tom Feelings (Dial)

1983
Author Award: Sweet Whispers, Brother Rush by Virginia Hamilton (Philomel)

Honor Book

This Strange New Feeling by Julius Lester (Dial)

Illustrator Award: Black Child by Peter Magubane (Knopf)

Honor Books

All the Colors of the Race by Arnold Adoff, illustrated by John Steptoe (Lothrop)

Just Us Women by Jeannette Caines, illustrated by Pat Cummings (Harper)

1984
Author Award: Everett Anderson's Goodbye by Lucille Clifton (Holt)

Special Citation

The Words of Martin Luther King, Jr. compiled by Coretta Scott King (Newmarket)

Honor Books

The Magical Adventures of Pretty Pearl by Virginia Hamilton (Harper)

Lena Horne by James Haskins (Coward-McCann)

Bright Shadow by Joyce Carol Thomas (Avon)

Because We Are by Mildred Pitts Walter (Lothrop)

Illustrator Award: My Mama Needs Me by Mildred Pitts Walter, illustrated by Pat Cummings (Lothrop)

1985
Author Award: Motown and Didi by Walter Dean Myers (Viking)

Honor Books

Circle of Gold by Candy Dawson Boyd (Apple/Scholastic)

A Little Love by Virginia Hamilton (Philomel)

1986

Author Award: **The People Could Fly: American Black Folktales** by Virginia Hamilton (Knopf)

Honor Books

Junius Over Far by Virginia Hamilton (Harper)

Trouble's Child by Mildred Pitts Walter (Lothrop)

Illustrator Award: **The Patchword Quilt** by Valerie Flournoy, illustrated by Jerry Pinkney (Dial)

Honor Book

The People Could Fly: American Black Folktales retold by Virginia Hamilton, illustrated by Leo and Diane Dillon (Knopf)

1987

Author Award: **Justin and the Best Biscuits in the World** by Mildred Pitts Walter (Lothrop)

Honor Books

Lion and the Ostrich Chicks and Other African Folk Tales by Ashley Bryan (Atheneum)

Which Way Freedom? by Joyce Hansen (Walker)

Illustrator Award: **Half a Moon and One Whole Star** by Crescent Dragonwagon, illustrated by Jerry Pinkney (Macmillan)

Honor Books

Lion and the Ostrich Chicks and Other African Folk Tales by Ashley Bryan (Atheneum)

C.L.O.U.D.S. by Pat Cummings (Lothrop)

1988

Author Award: **The Friendship** by Mildred D. Taylor (Dial)

Honor Books

An Enchanted Hair Tale by Alexis De Veaux (Harper)

The Tales of Uncle Remus: The Adventures of Brer Rabbit by Julius Lester (Dial)

Illustrator Award: **Mufaro's Beautiful Daughters** by John Steptoe (Lothrop)

Honor Books

What a Morning! The Christmas Story in Black Spirituals selected by John Langstaff, illustrated by Ashley Bryan (Macmillan)

The Invisible Hunters: A Legend from the Miskito Indians of Nicaragua compiled by Harriet Rohmer et al., illustrated by Joe Sam (Children's Book Press)

1989

Author Award: **Fallen Angels** by Walter Dean Myers (Scholastic)

Honor Books

A Thief in the Village and Other Stories by James Berry (Orchard)

Anthony Burns: The Defeat and Triumph of a Fugitive Slave by Virginia Hamilton (Knopf)

Illustrator Award: **Mirandy and Brother Wind** by Patricia C. McKissack, illustrated by Jerry Pinkney (Knopf)

Honor Books

Under the Sunday Tree by Eloise Greenfield, illustrated by Amos Ferguson (Harper)

Storm in the Night by Mary Stolz, illustrated by Pat Cummings (Harper)

1990

Author Award: **A Long Hard Journey: The Story of the Pullman Porter** by Patricia C. McKissack and Fredrick McKissack (Walker)

Honor Books

Nathaniel Talking by Eloise Greenfield (Black Butterfly)

The Bells of Christmas by Virginia Hamilton (Harcourt)

Martin Luther King, Jr. & the Freedom Movement by Lillie Patterson (Facts on File)

Illustrator Award: **Nathaniel Talking** by Eloise Greenfield, illustrated by Jan Spivey Gilchrist (Black Butterfly)

Honor Book

The Talking Eggs by Robert D. San Souci, illustrated by Jerry Pinkney (Dial)

1991

Author Award: **The Road to Memphis** by Mildred D. Taylor (Dial)

Honor Books

Black Dance in America by James Haskins (Crowell)

When I Am Old with You by Angela Johnson (Orchard)

Illustrator Award: **Aida** by Leontyne Price, illustrated by Leo Dillon and Diane Dillon (Harcourt)

1992

Author Award: **Now Is Your Time: The African American Struggle for Freedom** by Walter Dean Myers (HarperCollins)

Honor Book

Night on Neighborhood Street by Eloise Greenfield (Dial)

Illustrator Award: Tar Beach by Faith Ringgold (Crown)

Honor Books

All Night, All Day! A Child's First Book of African American Spirituals selected by Ashley Bryan (Atheneum)

Night on Neighborhood Street by Eloise Greenfield, illustrated by Jan Spivey Gilchrist (Dial)

1993

Author Award: The Dark-Thirty: Southern Tales of the Supernatural by Patricia C. McKissack (Knopf)

Honor Books

Mississippi Challenge by Mildred Pitts Walter (Bradbury)

Sojourner Truth: Ain't I a Woman? by Patricia C. McKissack and Fredrick McKissack (Scholastic)

Somewhere in the Darkness by Walter Dean Myers (Scholastic)

Illustrator Award: The Origin of Life on Earth: An African Creation Myth retold by David A. Anderson, illustrated by Kathleen Atkins Wilson (Sights)

Honor Books

Little Eight John by Jan Wahl, illustrated by Wil Clay (Lodestar)

Sukey and the Mermaid by Robert D. San Souci, illustrated by Brian Pinkney (Four Winds)

Working Cotton by Sherley Anne Williams, illustrated by Carol Byard (Harcourt)

1994

Author Award: Toning the Sweep by Angela Johnson (Orchard)

Honor Books

Brown Honey in Broomwheat Tea by Joyce Carol Thomas (HarperCollins)

Malcolm X: By Any Means Necessary by Walter Dean Myers (Scholastic)

Illustrator Award: Soul Looks Back in Wonder: Collection of African American Poets edited by Phyllis Fogelman, illustrated by Tom Feelings (Dial)

Honor Books

Brown Honey in Broomwheat Tea by Joyce Carol Thomas, illustrated by Floyd Cooper (HarperCollins)

Uncle Jed's Barbershop by Margaree King Mitchell, illustrated by James Ransome (Simon & Schuster)

1995

Author Award: Christmas in the Big House, Christmas in the Quarters by Patricia C. and Fredrick L. McKissack (Scholastic)

Honor Books

Black Diamond: The Story of the Negro Baseball Leagues by Patricia C. and Fredrick L. McKissack (Scholastic)

I Hadn't Meant to Tell You This by Jacqueline Woodson (Delacorte)

The Captive by Joyce Hansen (Scholastic)

Illustrator Award: The Creation by James Weldon Johnson, illustrated by James Ransome (Holiday House)

Honor Books

Meet Danitra Brown by Nikki Grimes, illustrated by Floyd Cooper (Lothrop)

The Singing Man by Angela Shelf, illustrated by Terea Shaffer (Holiday House)

1996

Author Award: Her Stories by Virginia Hamilton (Blue Sky Press)

Honor Books

The Watsons Go to Birmingham—1963 by Christopher Paul Curtis (Delacorte)

Like Sisters on the Homefront by Rita Williams-Garcia (Lodestar)

From the Notebooks of Melanin Sun by Jacqueline Woodson (Blue Sky)

Illustrator Award: The Middle Passage: White Ships, Black Cargo by Tom Feelings (Dial)

Honor Books

Her Stories by Virginia Hamilton, illustrated by Leo and Diane Dillon (Blue Sky)

The Faithful Friend by Robert D. San Souci, illustrated by Brian Pinkney (Simon & Schuster)

1997

Author Award: Slam! by Walter Dean Myers (Scholastic)

Honor Book

Rebels against Slavery: American Slave Revolts by Patricia C. McKissack and Fredrick McKissack (Scholastic)

*Illustrator Award: **Minty: A Story of Young Harriet Tubman*** by Alan Schroeder, illustrated by Jerry Pinkney (Dial)

Honor Books

The Palm of My Heart: Poetry by African American Children by Davida Adedjouma, illustrated by Gregory Christie (Lee & Low)

Running the Road to ABC by Denize Lauture, illustrated by Reynold Ruffins (Simon & Schuster)

Neeny Coming, Neeny Going by Karen English, illustrated by Synthia Saint James (Bridgewater)

1998
*Author Award: **Forged by Fire*** by Sharon M. Draper (Atheneum)

I Thought My Soul Would Rise and Fly: The Diary of Patsy, a Freed Girl by Joyce Hansen (Scholastic)

Honor Book

Bayard Rustin: Behind the Scenes of the Civil Rights Movement by James Haskins (Hyperion)

*Illustrator Award: **In Daddy's Arms I Am Tall: African Americans Celebrating Fathers***, illustrated by Javaka Steptoe (Lee & Low)

Honor Books

Ashley Bryan's ABC of African American Poetry by Ashley Bryan (Jean Karl/Atheneum)

Harlem by Walter Dean Myers, illustrated by Christopher Myers (Scholastic)

The Hunterman and the Crocodile by Baba Wagué Diakité (Scholastic)

1999
*Author Award: **Heaven*** by Angela Johnson (Simon & Schuster)

Honor Books

Jazmin's Notebook by Nikki Grimes (Dial)

Breaking Ground, Breaking Silence: The Story of New York's African Burial Ground by Joyce Hansen and Gary McGowan (Holt)

The Other Side: Shorter Poems by Angela Johnson (Orchard)

*Illustrator Award: **i see the rhythm*** by Toyomi Igus, illustrated by Michele Wood (Children's Book Press)

Honor Books

I Have Heard of a Land by Joyce Carol Thomas, illustrated by Floyd Cooper (Joanna Cotler/HarperCollins)

The Bat Boy and His Violin by Gavin Curtis, illustrated by E. B. Lewis (Simon & Schuster)

Duke Ellington: The Piano Prince and His Orchestra by Andrea Davis, illustrated by Brian Pinkney (Hyperion)

2000
*Author Award: **Bud, Not Buddy*** by Christopher Paul Curtis (Delacorte)

Honor Books

Francie by Karen English (Farrar, Straus and Giroux)

Black Hands, White Sails: The Story of African-American Whalers by Patricia C. and Fredrick McKissack (Scholastic)

Monster by Walter Dean Myers (HarperCollins)

*Illustrator Award: **In the Time of the Drums*** by Kim L. Siegelson, illustrated by Brian Pinkney (Jump at the Sun/Hyperion)

Honor Books

My Rows and Piles of Coins by Tololwa M. Mollel, illustrated by E. B. Lewis (Clarion)

Black Cat by Christopher Myers (Scholastic)

2001
*Author Award: **Miracle's Boys*** by Jacqueline Woodson (Putnam)

Honor Book

Let It Shine! Stories of Black Women Freedom Fighters by Andrea Davis, illustrated by Stephen Alcorn (Gulliver/Harcourt)

*Illustrator Award: **Uptown*** by Bryan Collier (Holt)

Honor Books

Freedom River by Bryan Collier (Jump at the Sun/Hyperion)

Only Passing Through: The Story of Sojourner Truth by Anne Rockwell, illustrated by R. Gregory Christie (Random House)

Virgie Goes to School with Us Boys by Elizabeth Fitzgerald Howard, illustrated by E. B. Lewis (Simon & Schuster)

NATIONAL COUNCIL OF TEACHERS OF ENGLISH (NCTE) AWARD FOR EXCELLENCE IN POETRY FOR CHILDREN

This award was given annually from 1977 to 1982 and every three years after that to a living American poet in recognition of his or her entire body of work for children ages three through thirteen.

1977	David McCord
1978	Aileen Fisher
1979	Karla Kushin
1980	Myra Cohn Livingston
1981	Eve Merriam
1982	John Ciardi
1985	Lilian Moore
1988	Arnold Adoff
1991	Valerie Worth
1994	Barbara Juster Esbensen
1997	Eloise Greenfield
2000	X. J. Kennedy

JOHN NEWBERY MEDAL

The John Newbery Medal has been awarded annually since 1922 under the supervision of the ALA's Association for Library Service to Children. It is presented to the author of the work judged to be the most distinguished contribution to literature for children published in the United States during the previous year. One or more Honor Books are also chosen. Winners must be residents or citizens of the United States.

1922
The Story of Mankind by Hendrik Willem van Loon (Liveright)

Honor Books

Cedric the Forester by Bernard Marshall (Appleton)
The Golden Fleece and the Heroes Who Lived before Achilles by Padraic Colum (Macmillan)
The Great Quest by Charles Hawes (Little, Brown)
The Old Tobacco Shop by William Bowen (Macmillan)
Windy Hill by Cornelia Meigs (Macmillan)

1923
The Voyages of Doctor Dolittle by Hugh Lofting (Lippincott)

Honor Book

No record

1924
The Dark Frigate by Charles Hawes (Atlantic/Little, Brown)

Honor Book

No record

1925
Tales from Silver Lands by Charles Finger (Doubleday)

Honor Books

Dream Coach by Anne Parrish (Macmillan)
Nicholas by Anne Carroll Moore (Putnam)

1926
Shen of the Sea by Arthur Bowie Chrisman (Dutton)

Honor Book

Voyagers by Padraic Colum (Macmillan)

1927
Smoky, the Cowhorse by Will James (Scribner's)

Honor Book

No record

1928
Gayneck, the Story of a Pigeon by Dhan Gopal Mukerji (Dutton)

Honor Books

Downright Dencey by Caroline Snedeker (Doubleday)
The Wonder Smith and His Son by Ella Young (Longmans)

1929
The Trumpeter of Krakow by Eric P. Kelly (Macmillan)

Honor Books

The Boy Who Was by Grace Hallock (Dutton)
Clearing Weather by Cornelia Meigs (Little, Brown)

Millions of Cats by Wanda Gág (Coward)
Pigtail of Ah Lee Ben Loo by John Bennett
 (Longmans)
Runaway Papoose by Grace Moon (Doubleday)
Tod of the Fens by Elinor Whitney (Macmillan)

1930
Hitty, Her First Hundred Years by Rachel Field
 (Macmillan)

Honor Books

Daughter of the Seine by Jeanette Eaton (Harper)
Jumping-Off Place by Marian Hurd McNeely
 (Longmans)
Little Blacknose by Hildegarde Swift (Harcourt)
Pran of Albania by Elizabeth Miller (Doubleday)
Tangle-Coated Horse and Other Tales by Ella
 Young (Longmans)
Vaino by Julia Davis Adams (Dutton)

1931
The Cat Who Went to Heaven by Elizabeth
 Coatsworth (Macmillan)

Honor Books

The Dark Star of Itza by Alida Malkus (Harcourt)
Floating Island by Anne Parrish (Harper)
Garram the Hunter by Herbert Best (Doubleday)
Meggy Macintosh by Elizabeth Janet Gray
 (Doubleday)
Mountains Are Free by Julia Davis Adams (Dutton)
Ood-Le-Uk the Wanderer by Alice Lide and
 Margaret Johansen (Little, Brown)
Queer Person by Ralph Hubbard (Doubleday)
Spice and the Devil's Cake by Agnes Hewes (Knopf)

1932
Waterless Mountain by Laura Adams Armer
 (Longmans)

Honor Books

Boy of the South Seas by Eunice Tietjens (Coward)
Calico Bush by Rachel Field (Macmillan)
The Fairy Circus by Dorothy P. Lathrop
 (Macmillan)
Jane's Island by Marjorie Allee (Houghton Mifflin)
Out of the Flames by Eloise Lownsbery (Longmans)
Truce of the Wolf and Other Tales of Old Italy by
 Mary Gould Davis (Harcourt)

1933
Young Fu of the Upper Yangtze by Elizabeth Lewis
 (Winston)

Honor Books

Children of the Soil by Nora Burglon (Doubleday)

The Railroad to Freedom by Hildegarde Swift
 (Harcourt)
Swift Rivers by Cornelia Meigs (Little, Brown)

1934
Invincible Louisa by Cornelia Meigs (Little, Brown)

Honor Books

ABC Bunny by Wanda Gág (Coward)
Apprentice of Florence by Anne Kyle (Houghton
 Mifflin)
Big Tree of Bunlahy by Padraic Colum (Macmillan)
The Forgotten Daughter by Caroline Snedeker
 (Doubleday)
Glory of the Seas by Agnes Hewes (Knopf)
New Land by Sarah Schmidt (McBride)
Swords of Steel by Elsie Singmaster (Houghton
 Mifflin)
Winged Girl of Knossos by Erik Berry (Appleton)

1935
Dobry by Monica Shannon (Viking)

Honor Books

Davy Crockett by Constance Rourke (Harcourt)
Day on Skates by Hilda Van Stockum (Harper)
Pageant of Chinese History by Elizabeth Seeger
 (Longmans)

1936
Caddie Woodlawn by Carol Ryrie Brink
 (Macmillan)

Honor Books

All Sail Set by Armstrong Sperry (Winston)
The Good Master by Kate Seredy (Viking)
Honk, The Moose by Phil Strong (Dodd)
Young Walter Scott by Elizabeth Janet Gray (Viking)

1937
Roller Skates by Ruth Sawyer (Viking)

Honor Books

Audubon by Constance Rourke (Harcourt)
The Codfish Musket by Agnes Hewes (Doubleday)
Golden Basket by Ludwig Bemelmans (Viking)
Phebe Fairchild: Her Book by Lois Lenski (Stokes)
Whistler's Van by Idwal Jones (Viking)
Winterbound by Margery Bianco (Viking)

1938
The White Stag by Kate Seredy (Viking)

Honor Books

Bright Island by Mabel Robinson (Random House)
On the Banks of Plum Creek by Laura Ingalls
 Wilder (Harper)

Pecos Bill by James Cloyd Bowman (Little, Brown)

1939
Thimble Summer by Elizabeth Enright (Rinehart)

Honor Books

Hello the Boat! by Phyllis Crawford (Holt)
Leader by Destiny: George Washington, Man and Patriot by Jeanette Eaton (Harcourt)
Mr. Popper's Penguins by Richard and Florence Atwater (Little, Brown)
Nino by Valenti Angelo (Viking)
Penn by Elizabeth Janet Gray (Viking)

1940
Daniel Boone by James Daugherty (Viking)

Honor Books

Boy with a Pack by Stephen W. Meader (Harcourt)
By the Shores of Silver Lake by Laura Ingalls Wilder (Harper)
Runner of the Mountain Tops by Mabel Robinson (Random House)
The Singing Tree by Kate Seredy (Viking)

1941
Call It Courage by Armstrong Sperry (Macmillan)

Honor Books

Blue Willow by Doris Gates (Viking)
The Long Winter by Laura Ingalls Wilder (Harper)
Nansen by Anna Gertrude Hall (Viking)
Young Mac of Fort Vancouver by Mary Jane Carr (Crowell)

1942
The Matchlock Gun by Walter D. Edmonds (Dodd)

Honor Books

Down Ryton Water by Eva Roe Gaggin (Viking)
George Washington's World by Genevieve Foster (Scribner's)
Indian Captive: The Story of Mary Jemison by Lois Lenski (Lippincott)
Little Town on the Prairie by Laura Ingalls Wilder (Harper)

1943
Adam of the Road by Elizabeth Janet Gray (Viking)

Honor Books

Have You Seen Tom Thumb? by Mabel Leigh Hunt (Lippincott)
The Middle Moffat by Eleanor Estes (Harcourt)

1944
Johnny Tremain by Esther Forbes (Houghton Mifflin)

Honor Books

Fog Magic by Julia Sauer (Viking)
Mountain Born by Elizabeth Yates (Coward)
Rufus M. by Eleanor Estes (Harcourt)
These Happy Golden Years by Laura Ingalls Wilder (Harper)

1945
Rabbit Hill by Robert Lawson (Viking)

Honor Books

Abraham Lincoln's World by Genevieve Foster (Scribner's)
The Hundred Dresses by Eleanor Estes (Harcourt)
Lone Journey: The Life of Roger Williams by Jeanette Eaton (Harcourt)
The Silver Pencil by Alice Dalgliesh (Scribner's)

1946
Strawberry Girl by Lois Lenski (Lippincott)

Honor Books

Bhimsa, the Dancing Bear by Christine Weston (Scribner's)
Justin Morgan Had a Horse by Marguerite Henry (Rand McNally)
The Moved-Outers by Florence Crannell Means (Houghton Mifflin)
New Found World by Katherine Shippen (Viking)

1947
Miss Hickory by Carolyn Sherwin Bailey (Viking)

Honor Books

The Avion My Uncle Flew by Cyrus Fisher (Appleton)
Big Tree by Mary and Conrad Buff (Viking)
The Heavenly Tenants by William Maxwell (Harper)
The Hidden Treasure of Glaston by Eleanore Jewett (Viking)
Wonderful Year by Nancy Barnes (Messner)

1948
The Twenty-One Balloons by William Pène du Bois (Viking)

Honor Books

The Cow-Tail Switch and Other West African Stories by Harold Courlander (Holt)
Li Lun, Lad of Courage by Carolyn Treffinger (Abingdon)
Misty of Chincoteague by Marguerite Henry (Rand McNally)
Pancakes—Paris by Claire Huchet Bishop (Viking)

The Quaint and Curious Quest of Johnny Longfoot
by Catherine Besterman (Bobbs)

1949
King of the Wind by Marguerite Henry (Rand McNally)

Honor Books
Daughter of the Mountains by Louise Rankin (Viking)
My Father's Dragon by Ruth S. Gannett (Random House)
Seabird by Holling C. Holling (Houghton Mifflin)
Story of the Negro by Arna Bontemps (Knopf)

1950
A Door in the Wall by Marguerite de Angeli (Doubleday)

Honor Books
The Blue Cat of Castle Town by Catherine Coblentz (Longmans)
George Washington by Genevieve Foster (Scribner's)
Kildee House by Rutherford Montgomery (Doubleday)
Song of the Pines by Walter and Marion Havighurst (Winston)
Tree of Freedom by Rebecca Caudill (Viking)

1951
Amos Fortune, Free Man by Elizabeth Yates (Dutton)

Honor Books
Abraham Lincoln, Friend of the People by Clara Ingram Judson (Follett)
Better Known as Johnny Appleseed by Mabel Leigh Hunt (Lippincott)
Gandhi, Fighter without a Sword by Jeanette Eaton (Morrow)
The Story of Appleby Capple by Anne Parrish (Harper)

1952
Ginger Pye by Eleanor Estes (Harcourt)

Honor Books
Americans before Columbus by Elizabeth Baity (Viking)
The Apple and the Arrow by Mary and Conrad Buff (Houghton Mifflin)
The Defender by Nicholas Kalashnikoff (Scribner's)
The Light at Tern Rocks by Julia Sauer (Viking)
Minn of the Mississippi by Holling C. Holling (Houghton Mifflin)

1953
Secret of the Andes by Ann Nolan Clark (Viking)

Honor Books
The Bears of Hemlock Mountain by Alice Dalgliesh (Scribner's)
Birthdays of Freedom, Vol. 1 by Genevieve Foster (Scribner's)
Charlotte's Web by E. B. White (Harper)
Moccasin Trail by Eloise McGraw (Coward)
Red Sails to Capri by Ann Weil (Viking)

1954
. . . And Now Miguel by Joseph Krumgold (Crowell)

Honor Books
All Alone by Claire Huchet Bishop (Viking)
Hurry Home Candy by Meindert DeJong (Harper)
Magic Maize by Mary and Conrad Buff (Houghton Mifflin)
Shadrach by Meindert DeJong (Harper)
Theodore Roosevelt, Fighting Patriot by Clara Ingram Judson (Follett)

1955
The Wheel on the School by Meindert DeJong (Harper)

Honor Books
Banner in the Sky by James Ullman (Lippincott)
Courage of Sarah Noble by Alice Dalgliesh (Scribner's)

1956
Carry On, Mr. Bowditch by Jean Lee Latham (Houghton Mifflin)

Honor Books
The Golden Name Day by Jennie Lindquist (Harper)
Men, Microscopes, and Living Things by Katherine Shippen (Viking)
The Secret River by Marjorie Kinnan Rawlings (Scribner's)

1957
Miracles on Maple Hill by Virginia Sorensen (Harcourt)

Honor Books
Black Fox of Lorne by Marguerite de Angeli (Doubleday)
The Corn Grows Ripe by Dorothy Rhoads (Viking)
The House of Sixty Fathers by Meindert DeJong (Harper)
Mr. Justice Holmes by Clara Ingram Judson (Follett)
Old Yeller by Fred Gipson (Harper)

1958
Rifles for Watie by Harold Keith (Crowell)

Honor Books

Gone-Away Lake by Elizabeth Enright (Harcourt)
The Great Wheel by Robert Lawson (Viking)
The Horse Catcher by Mari Sandoz (Westminster)
Tom Paine, Freedom's Apostle by Leo Gurko
(Crowell)

1959
The Witch of Blackbird Pond by Elizabeth George
Speare (Houghton Mifflin)

Honor Books

Along Came a Dog by Meindert DeJong (Harper)
Chucaro: Wild Pony of the Pampa by Francis
Kalnay (Harcourt)
The Family under the Bridge by Natalie Savage
Carlson (Harper)
The Perilous Road by William O. Steele (Harcourt)

1960
Onion John by Joseph Krumgold (Crowell)

Honor Books

America Is Born by Gerald W. Johnson (Morrow)
The Gammage Cup by Carol Kendall (Harcourt)
My Side of the Mountain by Jean Craighead George
(Dutton)

1961
Island of the Blue Dolphins by Scott O'Dell
(Houghton Mifflin)

Honor Books

America Moves Forward by Gerald W. Johnson
(Morrow)
The Cricket in Times Square by George Selden
(Farrar)
Old Ramon by Jack Schaefer (Houghton Mifflin)

1962
The Bronze Bow by Elizabeth George Speare
(Houghton Mifflin)

Honor Books

Belling the Tiger by Mary Stolz (Harper)
Frontier Living by Edwin Tunis (World)
The Golden Goblet by Eloise McGraw (Coward)

1963
A Wrinkle in Time by Madeleine L'Engle (Farrar)

Honor Books

Men of Athens by Olivia Coolidge (Houghton
Mifflin)
Thistle and Thyme by Sorche Nic Leodhas (Holt)

1964
It's Like This, Cat by Emily Cheney Neville
(Harper)

Honor Books

The Loner by Ester Wier (McKay)
Rascal by Sterling North (Dutton)

1965
Shadow of a Bull by Maia Wojciechowska
(Atheneum)

Honor Books

Across Five Aprils by Irene Hunt (Follett)

1966
I, Juan de Pareja by Elizabeth Borten de Trevino
(Farrar)

Honor Books

The Animal Family by Randall Jarrell (Pantheon)
The Black Cauldron by Lloyd Alexander (Holt)
The Noonday Friends by Mary Stolz (Harper)

1967
Up a Road Slowly by Irene Hunt (Follett)

Honor Books

The Jazz Man by Mary H. Weik (Atheneum)
The King's Fifth by Scott O'Dell (Houghton)
Zlateh the Goat and Other Stories by Isaac Bashevis
Singer (Harper)

1968
*From the Mixed-Up Files of Mrs. Basil E.
Frankweiler* by E. L. Konigsburg (Atheneum)

Honor Books

The Black Pearl by Scott O'Dell (Houghton Mifflin)
The Egypt Game by Zilpha Keatley Snyder
(Atheneum)
The Fearsome Inn by Isaac Bashevis Singer
(Scribner's)
*Jennifer, Hecate, Macbeth, William McKinley, and
Me, Elizabeth* by E. L. Konigsburg
(Atheneum)

1969
The High King by Lloyd Alexander (Holt)

Honor Books

To Be a Slave by Julius Lester (Dial)
When Sheemiel Went to Warsaw and Other Stories
by Isaac Bashevis Singer (Farrar)

1970
Sounder by William H. Armstrong (Harper)

Honor Books

Journey Outside by Mary Q. Steele (Viking)

The Many Ways of Seeing: An Introduction to the Pleasures of Art by Janet Gaylord Moore (World)

Our Eddie by Sulamith Ish-Kishor (Pantheon)

1971

Summer of the Swans by Betsy Byars (Viking)

Honor Books

Enchantress from the Stars by Sylvia Louise Engdahl (Atheneum)

Knee-Knock Rise by Natalie Babbitt (Farrar)

Sing Down the Moon by Scott O'Dell (Houghton Mifflin)

1972

Mrs. Frisby and the Rats of NIMH by Robert C. O'Brien (Atheneum)

Honor Books

Annie and the Old One by Miska Miles (Atlantic/Little, Brown)

The Headless Cupid by Zilpha Keatley Snyder (Atheneum)

Incident at Hawk's Hill by Allan W. Eckert (Little, Brown)

The Planet of Junior Brown by Virginia Hamilton (Macmillan)

The Tombs of Atuan by Ursula K. Le Guin (Atheneum)

1973

Julie of the Wolves by Jean Craighead George (Harper)

Honor Books

Frog and Toad Together by Arnold Lobel (Harper)

The Upstairs Room by Johanna Reiss (Crowell)

The Witches of Worm by Zilpha Keatley Snyder (Atheneum)

1974

The Slave Dancer by Paula Fox (Bradbury)

Honor Book

The Dark Is Rising by Susan Cooper (McElderry)

1975

M. C. Higgins, the Great by Virginia Hamilton (Macmillan)

Honor Books

Figgs and Phantoms by Ellen Raskin (Dutton)

My Brother Sam Is Dead by James Lincoln Collier and Christopher Collier (Four Winds)

The Perilous Gard by Elizabeth Marie Pope (Houghton Mifflin)

Philip Hall Likes Me, I Reckon Maybe by Bette Greene (Dial)

1976

The Grey King by Susan Cooper (McElderry)

Honor Books

Dragonwings by Laurence Yep (Harper)

The Hundred Penny Box by Sharon Bell Mathis (Viking)

1977

Roll of Thunder, Hear My Cry by Mildred D. Taylor (Dial)

Honor Books

Abel's Island by William Steig (Farrar)

A String in the Harp by Nancy Bond (McElderry)

1978

Bridge to Terabithia by Katherine Paterson (Crowell)

Honor Books

Anpao: An American Indian Odyssey by Jamake Highwater (Lippincott)

Ramona and Her Father by Beverly Cleary (Morrow)

1979

The Westing Game by Ellen Raskin (Dutton)

Honor Books

The Great Gilly Hopkins by Katherine Paterson (Crowell)

1980

A Gathering of Days: A New England Girl's Journal, 1830–32 by Joan W. Blos (Scribner's)

Honor Book

The Road from Home: The Story of an Armenian Girl by David Kherdian (Greenwillow)

1981

Jacob Have I Loved by Katherine Paterson (Crowell)

Honor Books

The Fledgling by Jane Langton (Harper)

A Ring of Endless Light by Madeleine L'Engle (Farrar)

1982

A Visit to William Blake's Inn: Poems for Innocent and Experienced Travelers by Nancy Willard, illustrated by Alice and Martin Provensen (Harcourt)

Honor Books

Ramona Quimby, Age 8 by Beverly Cleary (Morrow)

Upon the Head of the Goat: A Childhood in Hungary, 1939–1944 by Aranka Siegal (Farrar)

1983

Dicey's Song by Cynthia Voigt (Atheneum)

Honor Books

The Blue Sword by Robin McKinley (Greenwillow)

Doctor De Soto by William Steig (Farrar)

Graven Images by Paul Fleischman (Harper)

Homesick: My Own Story by Jean Fritz (Putnam)

Sweet Whispers, Brother Rush by Virginia Hamilton (Philomel)

1984

Dear Mr. Henshaw by Beverly Cleary (Morrow)

Honor Books

The Sign of the Beaver by Elizabeth George Speare (Houghton Mifflin)

A Solitary Blue by Cynthia Voigt (Atheneum)

Sugaring Time by Kathryn Lasky (Macmillan)

The Wish Giver by Bill Brittain (Harper)

1985

The Hero and the Crown by Robin McKinley (Greenwillow)

Honor Books

Like Jake and Me by Mavis Jukes (Knopf)

The Moves Make the Man by Bruce Brooks (Harper)

One-Eyed Cat by Paula Fox (Bradbury)

1986

Sarah, Plain and Tall by Patricia MacLachlan (Harper)

Honor Books

Commodore Perry in the Land of the Shogun by Rhoda Blumberg (Lothrop)

Dogsong by Gary Paulsen (Bradbury)

1987

The Whipping Boy by Sid Fleischman (Greenwillow)

Honor Books

A Fine White Dust by Cynthia Rylant (Bradbury)

On My Honor by Marion Dane Bauer (Clarion)

Volcano: The Eruption and Healing of Mount St. Helens by Patricia Lauber (Bradbury)

1988

Lincoln: A Photobiography by Russell Freedman (Clarion)

Honor Books

After the Rain by Norma Fox Mazer (Morrow)

Hatchet by Gary Paulsen (Bradbury)

1989

Joyful Noise: Poems for Two Voices by Paul Fleischman (Harper)

Honor Books

In the Beginning: Creation Stories from Around the World by Virginia Hamilton (Harcourt)

Scorpions by Walter Dean Myers (Harper)

1990

Number the Stars by Lois Lowry (Houghton Mifflin)

Honor Books

Afternoon of the Elves by Janet Taylor Lisle (Orchard)

Shabanu: Daughter of the Wind by Suzanne Fisher Staples (Knopf)

The Winter Room by Gary Paulsen (Orchard)

1991

Maniac Magee by Jerry Spinelli (Little, Brown)

Honor Book

The True Confessions of Charlotte Doyle by Avi (Orchard)

1992

Shiloh by Phyllis Reynolds Naylor (Atheneum)

Honor Books

Nothing but the Truth: A Documentary Novel by Avi (Orchard)

The Wright Brothers: How They Invented the Airplane by Russell Freedman (Holiday House)

1993

Missing May by Cynthia Rylant (Orchard)

Honor Books

The Dark-Thirty: Southern Tales of the Supernatural by Patricia McKissack (Knopf)

Somewhere in the Darkness by Walter Dean Myers (Scholastic)

What Hearts by Bruce Brooks (HarperCollins)

1994

The Giver by Lois Lowry (Houghton Mifflin)

Honor Books

Crazy Lady! by Jane Leslie Conly (HarperCollins)

Dragon's Gate by Laurence Yep (HarperCollins)

Eleanor Roosevelt: A Life of Discovery by Russell Freedman (Clarion)

1995

Walk Two Moons by Sharon Creech (HarperCollins)

Honor Books

Catherine, Called Birdy by Karen Cushman (Clarion)

The Ear, the Eye and the Arm by Nancy Farmer (Richard Jackson/Orchard)

1996

The Midwife's Apprentice by Karen Cushman (Clarion)

Honor Books

What Jamie Saw by Carolyn Coman (Front Street)

The Watsons Go to Birmingham—1963 by Christopher Paul Curtis (Delacorte)

Yolonda's Genius by Carol Fenner (McElderry/Simon & Schuster)

The Great Fire by Jim Murphy (Scholastic)

1997

The View from Saturday by E. L. Konigsburg (Jean Karl/Atheneum)

Honor Books

A Girl Named Disaster by Nancy Farmer (Richard Jackson/Orchard)

Moorchild by Elois McGraw (McElderry)

The Thief by Megan Whalen Turner (Greenwillow)

Belle Prater's Boy by Ruth White (Farrar)

1998

Out of the Dust by Karen Hesse (Scholastic)

Honor Books

Ella Enchanted by Gail Carson Levine (HarperCollins)

Lily's Crossing by Patricia Reilly Giff (Delacorte)

Wringer by Jerry Spinelli (HarperCollins)

1999

Holes by Louis Sachar (Foster/Farrar)

Honor Book

A Long Way from Chicago by Richard Peck (Dial)

2000

Bud, Not Buddy by Christopher Paul Curtis (Delacorte)

Honor Books

Getting Near to Baby by Audrey Couloumbis (Putnam)

Our Only May Amelia by Jennifer L. Holm (HarperCollins)

26 Fairmount Avenue by Tomie dePaola (Putnam)

2001

A Year Down Yonder by Richard Peck (Dial)

Honor Books

Because of Winn-Dixie by Kate DiCamillo (Candlewick Press)

Hope Was Here by Joan Bauer (Putnam)

Joey Pigza Loses Control by Jack Gantos (Farrar, Straus and Giroux)

The Wanderer by Sharon Creech (Joanne Cotler/HarperCollins)

ORBIS PICTUS AWARD FOR OUTSTANDING NONFICTION FOR CHILDREN

The National Council of Teachers of English (NCTE) established the Orbis Pictus Award in 1990 to recognize outstanding nonfiction for children. The annual award is named for *Orbis Pictus (The World in Pictures)*, a 1657 work by John Amos Comenius, believed to be the first book written expressly for children.

1990

The Great Little Madison by Jean Fritz (Putnam)

Honor Books

The Great American Gold Rush by Rhoda Blumberg (Bradbury)

The News about Dinosaurs by Patricia Lauber (Bradbury)

1991

Franklin Delano Roosevelt by Russell Freedman (Clarion)

Honor Books

Arctic Memories by Normee Ekoomiak (Holt)

Seeing Earth from Space by Patricia Lauber (Orchard)

1992

Flight: The Journey of Charles Lindbergh by Robert Burleigh and Mike Wimmer (Philomel)

Honor Books

Now Is Your Time! The African American Struggle for Freedom by Walter Dean Myers (HarperCollins)

Prairie Visions: The Life and Times of Solomon Butcher by Pam Conrad (HarperCollins)

1993

Children of the Dust Bowl: The True Story of the School of Weedpatch Camp by Jerry Stanley (Crown)

Honor Books

Talking with Artists by Pat Cummings (Bradbury)

Come Back, Salmon by Molly Cone (Sierra Club)

1994

Across America on an Emigrant Train by Jim Murphy (Clarion)

Honor Books

To the Top of the World: Adventures with Arctic Wolves by Jim Brandenburg (Walker)

Making Sense: Animal Perception and Communication by Bruce Brooks (Farrar)

1995

Safari Beneath the Sea: The Wonder World of the North Pacific Coast by Diane Swanson (Sierra Club)

Honor Books

Wildlife Rescue: The Work of Dr. Kathleen Ramsay by Jennifer Owings Dewey (Boyds Mills)

Kids at Work: Lewis Hine and the Crusade against Child Labor by Russell Freedman (Clarion)

Christmas in the Big House, Christmas in the Quarters by Patricia and Fredrick McKissack (Scholastic)

1996

The Great Fire by Jim Murphy (Scholastic)

Honor Books

Dolphin Man: Exploring the World of Dolphins by Laurence Pringle, photos by Randall S. Wells (Atheneum)

Rosie the Riveter: Women Working on the Home Front in World War II by Penny Colman (Crown)

1997

Leonardo da Vinci by Diane Stanley (Morrow)

Honor Books

Full Steam Ahead: The Race to Build a Transcontinental Railroad by Rhoda Blumberg (National Geographic)

The Life and Death of Crazy Horse by Russell Freedman (Holiday House)

One World, Many Religions: The Ways We Worship by Mary Pope Osborne (Knopf)

1998

An Extraordinary Life: The Story of a Monarch Butterfly by Laurence Pringle (Orchard Books)

Honor Books

A Drop of Water: A Book of Science and Wonder by Walter Wick (Scholastic)

A Tree Is Growing by Arthur Dorros, illustrated by S. D. Schnidler (Scholastic)

Charles Lindbergh: A Human Hero by James Cross Giblin (Clarion)

Kennedy Assassinated! The World Mourns: A Reporter's Story by Wilborn Hampton (Candlewick)

Digger: The Tragic Fate of the California Indians from the Missions to the Gold Rush by Jerry Stanley (Crown)

1999

Shipwreck at the Bottom of the World: The Extraordinary True Story of Shackleton and the Endurance by Jennifer Armstrong (Crown)

Honor Books

Black Whiteness: Admiral Byrd Alone in the Antarctic by Robert Burleigh, illustrated by Walter Lyon Krudop (Atheneum)

Fossil Feud: The Rivalry of the First American Dinosaur Hunters by Thom Holmes (Messner)

Hottest, Coldest, Highest, Deepest by Steve Jenkins (Houghton)

No Pretty Pictures: A Child of War by Anita Lobel (Greenwillow)

SCOTT O'DELL HISTORICAL FICTION AWARD

The Scott O'Dell Historical Fiction Award was established in 1981 and is administered by the Advisory Committee of the *Bulletin of the Center for Children's Books*. Books must be historical fiction, have unusual literary merit, be written by a citizen of the United States, and be set in the New World. They must have been published in the previous year by a United States publisher and must be written for children or young adults.

1984
The Sign of the Beaver by Elizabeth George Speare (Houghton)

1985
The Fighting Ground by Avi (Harper)

1986
Sarah, Plain and Tall by Patricia MacLachlan (Harper)

1987
Streams to the River, River to the Sea: A Novel of Sacagawea by Scott O'Dell (Houghton)

1988
Charley Skedaddle by Patricia Beatty (Morrow)

1989
The Honorable Prison by Lyll Becerra de Jenkins (Lodestar)

1990
Shades of Gray by Carolyn Reeder (Macmillan)

1991
A Time of Troubles by Pieter VanRaven (Atheneum)

1992
Stepping on the Cracks by Mary Downing Hahn (Clarion)

1993
Morning Girl by Michael A. Dorris (Hyperion)

1994
Bull Run by Paul Fleischman (HarperCollins)

1995
Under the Blood-Red Sun by Graham Salisbury (Harcourt)

1996
The Bomb by Theodore Taylor (Harcourt)

1997
Jip: His Story by Katherine Paterson (Clarion)

1998
Out of the Dust by Karen Hesse (Scholastic)

1999
Forty Acres and Maybe a Mule by Harriette Gillem Robinet (Atheneum)

2000
The Art of Keeping Cool by Janet Taylor Lisle (Simon & Schuster)

MICHAEL L. PRINTZ AWARD FOR EXCELLENCE IN YOUNG ADULT LITERATURE

The Michael L. Printz Award is an award for a book that exemplifies literary excellence in young adult literature. It is named for a Topeka, Kansas, school librarian who was a long-time active member of the Young Adult Library Services Association.

2000
Monster by Walter Dean Myers (Scholastic)

Honor Books
Speak by Laurie Halse Anderson (Farrar, Straus and Giroux)
Skellig by David Almond (Delacorte)

Hard Love by Ellen Wittlinger (Simon & Schuster)

2001
Kit's Wilderness by David Almond (Delacorte)

Honor Books
Many Stones by Carolyn Coman (Front Street)
The Body of Christopher Creed by Carol Plum-Ucci (Harcourt Brace)
Angus, Thongs, and Full Frontal Snogging: Confessions of Georgia Nicolson by Louise Rennison (HarperCollins)
Stuck in Neutral by Terry Trueman (HarperCollins)

ROBERT F. SIBERT INFORMATIONAL BOOK AWARD

Established in 2001, the Robert F. Sibert Informational Book Award is given annually to the author of the most distinguished informational book published during the preceding year. The award is named in honor of Robert F. Sibert, the long-time president of Bound to Stay Bound Books of Jacksonville, Illinois, and is sponsored by the company. The Association for Library Service to Children, a division of the American Library Association, administers the award.

2001
Sir Walter Ralegh and the Quest for El Dorado by Marc Aronson (Clarion)

Honor Books

The Longitude Prize by Joan Dash, illustrated by Dusan Petricic (Frances Foster Books/Farrar, Straus and Giroux)

Blizzard! The Storm That Changed America by Jim Murphy (Scholastic)

My Season with Penguins by Sophie Webb (Houghton Mifflin)

Pedro and Me: Friendship, Loss, and What I Learned by Judd Winick (Holt)

LAURA INGALLS WILDER AWARD

The Laura Ingalls Wilder Award is presented to an author or an illustrator whose books are published in the United States and have made a substantial and lasting contribution to literature for children over a period of years. The award was first presented in 1954 and was given every five years from 1960 to 1980; since then, it has been given every three years.

1954	Laura Ingalls Wilder
1960	Clara Ingram Judson
1965	Ruth Sawyer
1970	E. B. White
1975	Beverly Cleary
1980	Dr. Seuss (Theodor Seuss Geisel)
1983	Maurice B. Sendak
1986	Jean Fritz
1989	Elizabeth George Speare
1992	Marcia Brown
1995	Virginia Hamilton
1998	Russell Freedman
2001	Milton Meltzer

Appendix B
Children's Magazines

American Girl
www.americangirl.com   Girls, ages 7–12
Pleasant Company Publications, Inc. $3.95/issue
8400 Fairway Place $19.95/yr
P.O. Box 620984   6 issues/yr
Middleton, WI 53562-0984
(800)234-1278

This magazine identifies its purpose as "to affirm self-esteem, celebrate achievements, and foster creativity." Each issue includes stories, crafts, games, puzzles, party planning tips, and girl-to-girl advice.

Boomerang!
www.boomkids.com   Ages 6–12
Listen and Learn Home Education, Inc. $5.95/issue
13366 Pescadero Road $39.95/yr
Box 261   12 issues/yr
La Honda, CA 94020
(800)333-7858

This monthly children's audiomagazine comes in the form of cassettes and is designed to entertain and inform. Each issue includes segments on current events, economy, history, geography, music, mystery, and children's book reviews and is accompanied by a seven-fold insert with games, fun facts, and recommended reading.

Boys' Life
www.boyslife.org   Boys, ages 7–17
Boy Scouts of America $15.60/yr
1325 Walnut Hill Lane   12 issues/yr
P.O. Box 152079
Irving, TX 75015-2079
(214)580-2366

Published by the Boy Scouts of America since 1911, *Boys' Life* offers entertaining articles intended for boys. It includes fiction, hobbies, crafts, careers, outdoor activities, sports, history, electronics and general science, food, and dangers of drugs and alcohol. There are separate Cub Scout and Boy Scout editions of *Boys' Life*.

Calliope: Exploring World History
www.cobblestonepub.com/
   pages/callmain.htm   Ages 9–14
30 Grove St., Suite C $29.95/yr
Peterborough, NH 03458   5 issues/yr
(603)924-7209

The goal of this magazine is to inspire in young people an interest in and deep appreciation for people and events of the past. Each issue includes full-length articles, time lines, maps, and historical photos.

Chickadee: The Canadian Magazine for Young Children
www.owlkids.com/chick   Ages 3–9
56 The Esplanade, Suite 306 $22.00/yr
Toronto, ON   10 issues/yr
Canada M5E 1A7
(416)868-6009

This hands-on science and nature publication is designed to entertain and educate. Fiction, easy-to-read stories, puzzles, a science experiment, and a poster are included in each issue.

Children's Digest
www.cbhi.org/magazines/
   childrensdigest/index.shtml   Preteens
Children's Better Health Institute $13.95/yr
P.O. Box 567   8 issues/yr
Indianapolis, IN 46206
(800)558-2376

This magazine features contemporary fiction that encourages preteens to read and think about the problems that they face today. The nonfiction offers a lively depiction of health issues. Columns cover topics such as food and nutrition, the environment, and book reviews.

Children's Playmate
www.cbhi.org/magazines/
   chldrensplaymate/index.shtml   Ages 6–8
Children's Better Health Institute $13.95/yr
P.O. Box 567   8 issues/yr
Indianapolis, IN 46206
(800)558-2376

Beginning readers are offered colorfully illustrated fiction and nonfiction to empower them to make healthy choices. Each issue includes easy recipes, book reviews, and a cartoon.

Click
www.clickmag.com   Ages 3–7
332 S. Michigan Ave., Suite 1100 $27.75/yr
Chicago, IL 60604   10 issues/yr
(312)939-1500

This science and discovery magazine's goal is to encourage young children to explore and discover the world through photographs, illustrations, stories, and articles. Children explore such topics as the human body, building a house, and how animals move.

Cobblestone

www.cobblestonepub.com/
    pages/cobbmain.htm   Ages 9–14
30 Grove St., Suite C $26.95/yr
Peterborough, NH 03458   10 issues/yr
(603)924-7209

Each issue is filled with historic photographs, original illustrations, primary documents, maps, and activities. Historical accuracy and original approaches make the magazine a research tool that offers an imaginative approach to teaching readers about American history.

Creative Kids

www.prufrock.com/mag_ck.html   Ages 8–14
Prufrock Press $19.95/yr
P.O. Box 8813   4 issues/yr
Waco, TX 76714-8813
(800)998-2208

Children's works from all over the world express ideas, questions, fears, concerns, and pleasures. The collection is broad in scope and avoids sexist, racist, or violent expression; it encourages children to strive for a product that merits publication.

Cricket: The Magazine for Children

www.cricketmag.com   Ages 7–14
P.O. Box 300 $35.97/yr
Peru, IL 61354   12 issues/yr
(815)223-1500

Cricket introduces children to fine literature and art through a variety of stories, articles, and activities. It strives to stimulate children's imaginations and their love of reading.

Current Science

www.weeklyreader.com/cs/   Ages 10–14
200 First Stamford Place $35.95/yr
P.O. Box 120023   16 issues/yr
Stamford, CT 06912-0023
(800)446-3355

This news magazine attempts to relate science, health, and technology to middle school students and challenge them to think critically. Features include science projects, mystery photos, questions/answers, trivia, and a way for readers to express their views.

Discover

www.discover.com   Ages 9–12
114 Fifth Ave. $4.99/issue
New York, NY 10011-5690 $19.95/yr
(800)829-9132   12 issues/yr

Discover is a magazine of science and technology, their wondrous uses, and their impact on our lives. There are monthly special reports on the issues of the day that are rooted in science.

Dolphin Log

www.dolphinlog.org   Ages 7–15
The Cousteau Society, Inc. $15/yr
870 Greenbrier Circle, Suite 402   6 issues/yr
Chesapeake, VA 23320
(800)441-4395

This bimonthly magazine highlights science, marine biology, and the environment as they relate to the world's water system. The goal of the magazine is to delight readers, while focusing on an environmental ethic, and to raise understanding of how living organisms are interconnected. Features include news and adventures from Cousteau expeditions, stories about the living creatures of the sea, and appeals to realize how precious oceans are.

Faces

www.cobblestonepub.com/pages/
    facemain.htm   Ages 9–14
Cobblestone Publishing Co. $29.95/yr
30 Grove St., Suite C   9 issues/yr
Peterborough, NH 03458
(603)924-7209

This theme-related magazine seeks to explore human diversity and foster respect for people of other cultures. The editorial staff introduces readers to the many lifestyles, beliefs, and customs found throughout the world.

Highlights for Children

www.Highlights.com   Ages 2–12
803 Church St. $29.64/yr
Honesdale, PA 18431-1895   12 issues/yr
(800)603-0349

With the theme "Fun with a purpose," each issue has crafts, verse, and thinking features interspersed among short stories and factual articles.

Hopscotch: The Magazine for Young Girls

www.hopscotchmagazine.com   Girls, ages 6–12
Bluffton New Publishing and $17.95/yr
    Printing Company   6 issues/yr
P.O. Box 164
Bluffton, OH 45817-0164
(800)358-4732

Hopscotch strives to challenge girls to stretch their imaginations and enjoy more reading. Each issue of *Hopscotch* includes mystery or adventure stories, informational articles, craft projects, science experiments, recipes, jokes and puzzles, poetry, math puzzlers, and contests, as well as columns for readers' letters and pen pal connections.

Jack and Jill

www.jackandjillmag.org	Ages 7–10
Children's Better Health Institute	$21.95/yr
1100 Waterway Blvd.	8 issues/yr
P.O. Box 567	
Indianapolis, IN 46206	
(800)558-2376	

This magazine encourages reading with imaginative fiction, stories about real kids, and informational articles about how our bodies work and how to exercise and eat right. There are mazes, puzzles, hidden picture activities, and more.

Ladybug: The Magazine for Young Children

www.cricketmag.com	Ages 2–6
P.O. Box 300	$5.00/issue
Peru, IL 61354	$35.97/yr
(815)223-1500	12 issues/yr

Ladybug features original stories, poems, learning activities, games, crafts, songs, and finger games for young children, created by highly regarded authors and illustrators from the United States as well as other countries.

Merlyn's Pen: Fiction, Essays, and Poems by America's Teens

www.merlynspen.com	Ages 12–18
98 Main St.	$29.95/yr
P.O. Box 1058	1 issue/yr
East Greenwich, RI 02818	
(800)247-2027	

Merlyn's Pen contains fiction written by teens and is designed for teenagers in search of a "good read." It offers tips for teen writers and encourages their submissions.

Muse

www.musemag.com	Ages 8–14
332 S. Michigan Ave., Suite 1100	$32.97/yr
Chicago, IL 60614	10 issues/yr
(312)939-1500	

Muse is a nonfiction magazine published in conjunction with *Smithsonian* magazine.

National Geographic World

www.nationalgeographic.com/world/	Ages 8–14
1145 17th St. N.W.	$17.95/yr
Washington, DC 20036	12 issues/yr
(202)857-7000	

The goal of *National Geographic World* is to inspire in junior members curiosity about their world and beyond, to encourage geographic awareness, and to provide access to the benefits of membership in and resources of the National Geographic Society. Issues contain projects, games, pull-out posters, and more.

New Moon Magazine

www.newmoon.org	Girls, ages 8–14
P.O. Box 3587	$29.00/yr
Duluth, MN 55803	6 issues/yr
(218)728-5507	

Thematic issues, designed for girls and their parents to read, discuss topics such as eliminating gender inequities.

Odyssey

www.odysseymagazine.com	Ages 8–14
Cobblestone Publishing Co.	$29.95/yr
30 Grove St., Suite C	10 issues/yr
Peterborough, NH 03458	
(603)924-7209	

This theme-related magazine is devoted to space, as well as other scientific disciplines. It also offers a look at professional careers in the sciences.

Owl

www.owlkids.com	Ages 9+
Owl Magazines	$22.00/yr
176 John St., Suite 500	10 issues/yr
Toronto, ON	
Canada M5T 365	
(416)340-2700	

The purpose of *Owl* magazine is to interest kids in science, technology, nature, and the world around them. It challenges readers to see everyday things in new ways through the stories, articles, games, and experiments.

Plays: The Drama Magazine for Young People

www.playsmag.com	Ages 6–17
120 Boylston St.	$30.00/yr
Boston, MA 02116	7 issues/yr
(800)446-5489	

Original, royalty-free plays and programs are provided for school-age actors and audiences.

Ranger Rick

www.rangerrick.org/rangerrick/	Ages 7–12
National Wildlife Foundation	$17.00/yr
8925 Leesburg Pike	12 issues/yr
Vienna, VA 22184-0001	
(703)790-4000	

This nature magazine, published by the National Wildlife Federation, is dedicated to helping children gain a greater understanding and appreciation of nature. Photographs, stories, informational articles, and games and activities foster awareness of the natural environment.

Skipping Stones: A Multicultural Magazine
www.efn.org/~skipping   Ages 7–14
Skipping Stones $25.00/yr (individuals)
P.O. Box 3939   4 issues/yr
Eugene, OR 97403
(541)342-4956

This magazine encourages cooperation and celebration of cultural and linguistic diversity and explores the ecological and social webs of our world. By encouraging student contributions, it offers a unique forum for communication among children from different backgrounds.

Spider: The Magazine for Children
www.spidermag.com   Ages 6–9
P.O. Box 300 $35.97/yr
Peru, IL 61354   12 issues/yr

Spider publishes original stories, poems, informational articles, recipes, crafts, puzzles, games, brainteasers, and math and word activities written by highly regarded authors from throughout the United States and the world.

Sports Illustrated for Kids
www.siforkids.com   Ages 7–13
135 West 50th St. $19.95 or $25.87/yr
New York, NY 10020-1393   10 or 13 issues/yr
(800)528-5000

This magazine includes stories on a large variety of sports, as well as general human interest stories geared for ages 7–13.

Stone Soup: The Magazine by Young Writers and Artists
www.stonesoup.com   Ages 6–13
Children's Art Foundation $33.00/yr
P.O. Box 83   5 issues/yr
Santa Cruz, CA 95063
(800)447-4569

Stone Soup publishes original fiction, poetry, book reviews, and artwork created by children from around the world.

US Kids
www.cbhi.org/magazines/uskids/   Ages 10–12
Children's Better Health Institute $21.95/yr
1100 Waterway Blvd.   8 issues/yr
P.O. Box 567
Indianapolis, IN 46206
(800)558-2376

The purpose of this magazine is to entertain and to inform about good health, fitness, and character development. Each issue includes stories that focus on real kids who do extraordinary things, informational articles, photographs, a poster, and puzzles.

Zoobooks
www.zoobooks.com   Ages 5–12
Wildlife Education Limited $20.95/yr
3590 Kettner Blvd.   12 issues/yr
San Diego, CA 92101
(619)299-5034

Zoobooks is designed to be an entertaining and informative full-color wildlife series, with each issue focusing on a different animal. Photographs, articles, and games are included.

Sources of Information:

Magazines and their web sites.

Stoll, Donald R. (ed.). *Magazines for Kids and Teens: A Resource for Parents, Teachers, Librarians and Kids!* Copublished by the Educational Press Association of America, Rowan College of New Jersey, and the International Reading Association.

Credits

Name/Title Index

Reeder, Carolyn, 536, 569
Regards to the Man in the Moon, 514, 524
Regular Flood of Mishap, A, 528
Reich, Susanna, 411, 425
Reimer, K. M., 87, 88, 133
Reisberg, Mira, 172
Reiss, Johanna, 535, 565
Relatives Came, The, 32, 92, 127, 304, 318, 551
Reluctantly Alice, 303, 310
Remarkable Journey of Prince Jen, The, 386
Remkiewicz, Frank, 311
Reneaux, J. J., 466
Rennison, Louise, 569
Rescue: The Story of How Gentiles Saved Jews in the Holocaust, 536
Rescue Josh McGuire, 553
Rescuers, The, 380
Reserved for Mark Anthony Crowder, 553
Restless Spirit: The Life and Work of Dorothea Lange, 537
Return of the King, The, 367, 387
Reuter, Bjarne, 540
Revolting Rhymes, 273
Rey, H. A., 230
Rey, Margaret, 230
Reyher, Becky, 547
Reynolds, Jan, 398–399, 420
Rezoom, 194, 221
Rhee, Nami, 122
Rhetoric of Fiction, The, 57
Rhoads, Dorothy, 563
Rhodes, Timothy, 124
Rice without Rain, 97, 325, 347
Richgels, Donald J., 322, 323, 324, 348, 517, 518, 533
Richter, Hans Peter, 539
Riddell, Chris, 529
Riddle and the Rune, The, 364, 386
Riddle of Racism, The, 535
Riddle of the Rosetta Stone, The: Key to Ancient Egypt, 395, 404, 419
Riding with Aunt Lucy, 515, 525
Rifles for Watie, 563
Riggio, Anita, 122, 297, 318, 347
Righteous Revenge of Artemis Bonner, The, 463
Ríha, Bohumil, 539
Rinaldi, Ann, 325, 326–327, 333, 341, 342, 343, 348, 517, 529
Ring of Endless Light, A, 377, 392, 565
Ringgold, Faith, 109, 120, 383, 536, 551, 554
Rise Up Singing, 276, 452, 468
Ritter, John H., 345, 554
Ritter, Lawrence S., 418, 427

Ritz, Karen, 425
River, The, 304, 314
River at Green Knowe, The, 385
River Ran Wild, A: An Environmental History, 224, 421, 501
River Rats, 369
Road from Home, The: The Story of an Armenian Girl, 413, 427, 535, 543, 565
Road to Agra, The, 534
Road to Camlann, The, 387
Road to Home, The, 342
Road to Memphis, The, 99, 120, 557
Robber and Me, The, 541
Robbins, Ruth, 387, 548
Robertson, Debra, 131
Robinet, Harriette Gillem, 347, 569
Robinson, Aminah Brenda Lynn, 118, 128, 343, 464, 502, 525, 529
Robinson, Barbara, 317, 464
Robinson, Dorothy, 555
Robinson, Lolly, 130
Robinson, Mabel, 561, 562
Robinson Crusoe, 5, 11, 28, 282, 319
Robison, Deborah, 266, 278
Robots: Your High-Tech World, 400, 422
Rochman, Hazel, 110, 132, 133
Rocket Ship Galileo, 370, 375, 388
Rocklin, Joanne, 290, 309, 312
Rockwell, Anne, 559
Rockwell, Thomas, 317
Rodanas, Kristina, 43, 56, 144, 145
Rodari, Gianni, 539
Roe, Eileen, 125
Roeckelein, Katrina, 499
Roethke, Theodore, 255, 257, 276
Rogasky, Barbara, 167
Rohmann, Eric, 552
Rohmer, Harriet, 172, 557
Rojankovsky, Feodor, 148, 548
Rolie Polie Olie, 204, 227
Roll of Thunder, Hear My Cry, 21, 29, 34, 35, 36, 37, 39, 46–47, 86, 99, 121, 337, 339, 340, 345, 467, 499, 535, 555, 565
Roller Skates, 561
Rollins, Charlemae, 555
Rollock, Barbara, 87, 133
Romeo and Juliet, Together (and Alive) at Last, 299, 314
Ronia, the Robber's Daughter, 540
Room Made of Windows, A, 542
Roop, Connie, 425
Roop, Peter, 425
Rooster Crows, The, 547

Rooster Who Went to His Uncle's Wedding, The, 92, 124, 172
Rooster's Off to See the World, 224
Root, Barry, 528
Root, Kimberly Bulcken, 241, 276
Root, Shelton, 285, 319
Root Cellar, The, 385
Rosa Parks, 95, 118
Rosa Parks: My Story, 413, 425
Rosales, Melodye Benson, 269, 274, 530
Rose Blanche, 110, 128, 227, 540
Rose Daughter, 357, 383
Rose for Pinkerton, A, 227
Rose in My Garden, The, 228
Rosen, Michael J., 128, 230, 277, 343, 435, 436, 439, 464, 467, 502, 515, 517, 525, 529
Rosenberg, Maxine B., 129, 131, 402, 427
Rosenblatt, Louise M., 59, 60, 78, 477, 482, 484, 504
Roser, Nancy L., 63, 67, 77, 78, 437, 438, 467, 468, 476, 479, 485, 487, 490, 503, 504, 509, 515, 521, 533
Rosetti, Christina, 248, 254, 279
Rosie and the Rustlers, 243, 274
Rosie the Riveter: Women Working on the Home Front during World War II, 419, 568
Ross, Gayle, 126, 127, 170
Ross, Lillian Hammer, 531
Ross, Tony, 308
Rostkowski, Margaret, 345, 553
Rosy Cole: She Grows and Graduates, 317
Rosy Cole: She Walks in Beauty, 296, 317
Roth, Susan L., 170, 545
Round Trip, 227
Rounds, Glen, 28, 169
Rourke, Constance, 561
Rowling, J. K., 38, 54, 56, 351, 354, 357, 383, 464
Roxaboxen, 228
Royal Bee, The, 498
R-T, Margaret, and the Rats of NIMH, 390
Ruano, Alfonso, 538
Ruby, 512, 526
Ruby in the Smoke, 553
Rudman, Masha Kabakow, 111, 132, 133, 318
Ruff, Donna, 424
Ruffins, Reynold, 171, 559
Rufus M., 562
Rumbly Tumbly Glittery Gritty Place, A, 514, 524
Rumpelstiltskin, 168, 199, 233, 551

Rumpelstiltskin Problem, The, 384
Runaway Papoose, 561
Runaway Ralph, 379
Runner of the Mountain Tops, 562
Running the Road to ABC, 559
Rush, Ken, 268, 278
Russell, Ching Yeung, 514, 525
Russian Fairy Tales, 465
Russian Folk Tales, 169
Russian Folktales, 169
Russo, Marisabina, 553
Ryan, Cheli Durán, 549
Ryan, Pam Muñoz, 125
Ryan White: My Own Story, 426
Rychlicki, Zbigniew, 539
Rylant, Cynthia, 32, 43, 57, 62, 77, 92, 127, 189, 222, 230, 277, 291, 295, 304, 310, 313, 314, 315, 316, 318, 319, 345, 355, 380, 434, 435, 464, 498, 502, 544, 551, 566

Saaf, Donald, 467
Sable, 313
Sabuda, Robert, 182, 183, 200, 201, 212, 218, 234, 497, 500, 544
Sacajawea, 343
Sachar, Louis, 8, 21, 29, 42, 56, 61, 63, 77, 289, 312, 423, 439, 464, 502, 545, 567
Sachs, Marilyn, 535
Sacks, Margaret, 347, 436, 464
Sadako, 121
Sadako and the Thousand Paper Cranes, 121, 346, 497
Safari, 399, 421
Safari beneath the Sea: The Wonder World of the North Pacific Coast, 399, 421, 568
Sahara, 398, 420
Saint Valentine, 200, 234
Saito, Manabu, 123
Sakade, Florence, 172
Salamandastron, 365
Salamander Room, The, 467, 502
Sale, Roger, 57
Salisbury, Graham, 569
Sally Ride: Shooting for the Stars, 412, 424
Salting the Ocean: 100 Poems by Young Poets, 242, 267, 276
Saltzberg, Barney, 464
Salvadori, Mario, 543
Sam, Joe, 557
Sam, Bangs and Moonshine, 56, 229, 549
Sam and the Lucky Money, 121
Sam and the Tigers, 91, 119
Samir and Yonatan, 541
Sam's Pizza, 218
Sam's Sandwich, 183, 218
Samurai's Daughter, The, 18, 29, 173

Subject Index

Responses to literature, 63–64, 68, 73. *See also* Discussion, literature; Reader response strategies for, 484–487

Rhyme(s)
counting-out, 239
folk, 140
jump-rope, 239
Mother Goose, 148
nursery, 238–239
in poetry, 253–254
vs. poetry, 237
skipping, 148–149

Rhythm
in poetry, 252–253
in prose, 51

Riddles, 149, 444

Rising action, 40

Robert F. Sibert Informational Book Award, 569–570

Roles
of characters, 37
of literature, 83
of schools, 83

Roman myths, 154–155

Romance, 292

Rounds, 454

Russian folktales, 158–159, 169

Scaffolding, 14

Scandinavian folklore, 137–138, 142, 157–158, 168–169

School Library Journal, 26

School life, in realistic fiction, 289–290, 311–312

Science, informational books on, 400

Science fantasies, 372–373, 389–391

Science fiction
authors of, 374–378
awards for, 378
categories of, 371–373
criteria for selecting, 378
defined, 351
dystopian societies in, 371–372, 388–389
environmental catastrophes in, 372
evolution of, 369–371
vs. fantasy, 351–352
theory of, 373

utopian societies in, 371–372, 388–389

Scott O'Dell Historical Fiction Award, 568–569

Scottish folklore, 156

Scratchboard, 202

Second-graders' responses to literature, 64–66

Self-discovery, 286–287, 308–309

Self-reflection, 282

Series books, 284, 296–297
of animal stories, 352–353
of biographies, 411
of high fantasy, 354
of historical fiction, 327–328
informational, 401
of realistic fiction, 296–297

Setting, 31–35
in folktales, 33
in historical fiction, 34, 330–331, 338
in multicultural literature, 34
in realistic fiction, 33–34

Sexism. *See* Gender roles, in literature

Sexuality, in realistic fiction, 285, 292

Shared-text experience, 484

Simile, 50–51

Skipping rhymes, 148–149

Skipping Stones: A Multicultural Magazine, 574

Slavery, literature unit on, 517, 529–530

Social diversity, literature portraying, 112–114, 294

Social order, 45

Social perspective on reader response, 60, 61, 66–70

Songs, in reading circle, 451–452. *See also* Folk songs

Sounds, of language, 5
in alphabet books, 184
in poetry, 252–255, 259
in prose, 51

Special people, literary unit on, 515, 525

Spider: The Magazine for Children, 574

Sports, realistic fiction on, 290–291, 312

Sports Illustrated for Kids, 574

Stances, of reader, 31, 46, 47–48, 62–64

Stereotypes, 87, 90–91, 110–112, 146, 164–165

Stone Soup: The Magazine for Young Writers and Artists, 574

Story diagrams, 489

Story theater, 447–448

Story types, for reading aloud, 442–444

Story webs, 492–495

Storytelling, 441–442
learning stories for, 444–447
selected titles for, 465–466
and story types, 442–444

Structured opposites, 152–153

Style, 49–53
in biographies, 417
in historical fiction, 324

Supernatural elements, in fantasy, 358, 384–385

Survival story, 32
in informational books, 408
in realistic fiction, 291–292, 313–314
in science fiction, 372, 389

Suspense books, 316–317

Sympathetic voice, in poetry, 247–249

Tale type, in folktales, 143

Tall tales, 141, 145, 161, 444

Teachers
and adult literature, 114
in creative dramatics, 449–450
and diverse perspectives, 114–115
in literature circles, 479, 480–484

Textual perspective on reader response, 60, 61, 74–75

Textual theorist, 74

Thematically linked books, 510

Theme, 43–46
discussion of, 476
in historical fiction, 334

Third-graders' responses to literature, 18–19, 64–66

Third-person stories, 48–49

Three-dimensional art, in illustrations, 199

Time slips, in fantasy, 358–359, 385–386

Toy books, 182–183, 218–219

Traditional literature. *See also* Folklore
categories of, 139–140, 144–149
criteria for selecting, 164–165
defined, 137
evolution of, 137–144
psychoanalytic dynamics of, 153–154
stereotypes in, 164–165

Translation, issues concerning, 107–108

Trickster tales, 140, 145
literary unit on, 511, 526–527

Units. *See* Literary units

US Kids, 574

Utopian societies, in science fiction, 371–372, 388–389

Verisimilitude, 32

Visual communication, 190–191

Visual literacy, 190

Voice, in literature, 52–53
urgent, 32

Watercolor, as artistic medium, 199

Welsh folklore, 156

West, books and stories on, 283, 343–344

Women. *See* Gender roles, in literature

Woodcut, 202

Word choice, 49–50

Wordless books, 186, 221
teaching ideas using, 217

World War II, historical fiction about, 346

Writing
journal, 485–487
spare, 50

Zoobooks, 574